Blacker's Boys

9th (Service) Battalion,
Princess Victoria's (Royal Irish Fusiliers) (County Armagh)

&

9th (North Irish Horse) Battalion,
Princess Victoria's (Royal Irish Fusiliers)

1914 –1919

Nick Metcalfe

Blacker's Boys

9th (Service) Battalion, Princess Victoria's (Royal Irish Fusiliers) (County Armagh)

&

9th (North Irish Horse) Battalion, Princess Victoria's (Royal Irish Fusiliers)

1914 –1919

Nick Metcalfe

ISBN: 978-0-9572695-0-7

Published by Nicholas Paul Metcalfe in conjunction with Writersworld, this book is produced entirely in the UK, is available to order from most book shops in the United Kingdom, and is also globally available via UK-based Internet book retailers and www.amazon.com.

Copy edited by Sue Croft

Cover design by Jag Lall

www.writersworld.co.uk

WRITERSWORLD
2 Bear Close Flats
Bear Close
Woodstock
Oxfordshire
OX20 1JX
United Kingdom

The text pages of this book are produced via an independent certification process that ensures the trees from which the paper is produced come from well managed sources that exclude the risk of using illegally logged timber while leaving options to use post-consumer recycled paper as well.

Dedicated to

my great grandfather
Sergeant William Neill DCM

and my father
Darragh Hamilton Stanley Metcalfe

Book Cover

The oil painting reproduced on the front cover was completed in 1919 by Captain W J Menaul MC, one of the 9th Royal Irish Fusiliers' original officers, and is used by permission of Mrs E A Cassidy. It shows Hellfire Corner, an important junction on the routes out of Ypres to the south-east along the Menin Road, that was under constant observation and frequent artillery bombardment.

Also shown on the front cover is an image of a cap badge of Princess Victoria's (Royal Irish Fusiliers) of the First World War era. The two-part badge had been adopted in 1906. It comprised a silver Princess Victoria's coronet over a separate, brass, 'fired' grenade. The body of the grenade was superimposed with a silver 'winged maiden' Irish harp beneath the Prince of Wales' feathers.

The images on the back cover are of two original members of the 9th Royal Irish Fusiliers:

On the left is William Herbert (Herbie) Palmer. Born on 11 November 1894 at Portadown in County Armagh, he worked as a clerk for Hamilton Robb Ltd. He enlisted on 15 September 1914 and served initially in 'D' Company as a signaller. He was promoted to Sergeant on 2 April 1916 and served as the Battalion's Scout Sergeant. He was the first soldier of the 9th Royal Irish Fusiliers to be decorated for gallantry, earning a Military Medal in May 1916. He was commissioned into The Royal Irish Regiment on 26 March 1918 and served with the 7th (South Irish Horse) Battalion in 21st Brigade, 30th Division, for the remainder of the war. After the war he became an accountant in Belfast and during the Second World War he served as Officer Commanding 'C' Company, 4th (Belfast) Battalion, Ulster Home Guard. He died on 18 February 1974, aged 79.

On the right is Captain Thomas Graham (Tom) Shillington. He was born on 9 October 1897, also at Portadown. Considerably underage, he was commissioned into Princess Victoria's (Royal Irish Fusiliers) on 7 January 1915, aged 17, and served as a platoon commander in 'B' Company. During the attack at Hamel on 1 July 1916 he was wounded in both legs by machine-gun fire but rejoined the 9th Royal Irish Fusiliers on 12 December 1916. He was posted back to 'B' Company and then commanded 'A' Company from April 1917. He died of wounds on 18 August 1917, aged 19, in 3rd Australian Casualty Clearing Station, having been shot in the throat during the Battle of Langemarck on 16 August 1917.

Contents

List of Maps

(pages 272 – 292)

Quiet Conquest

A bluebell stood on Kemmel Hill;
It bowed and smiled, as bluebells will.
The cheeky thing! - it didn't care,
Though shells begrudged its presence there.

The tortured earth was gouged and rent
By reeking shells on murder bent -
The bluebell stood on Kemmel Hill,
Dispensing Nature's magic still.

Perhaps it isn't something that
Anyone should wonder at;
When wickedness would evil do,
Virtue doesn't want it to.

So make a stand and hold your ground,
That purity and grace abound,
Truth asserts her sovereign will
And bluebells grow on Kemmel Hill.

Private Charles Honeysett, 6 Platoon, B Company, wrote this after the battle on Kemmel Hill on 18 April 1918 when, after a particularly heavy artillery barrage, he saw a single bluebell standing between two shell-holes. "*It was,*" he said later, "*the only cheerful thing we could see.*"

Foreword

Lieutenant General Sir Philip Trousdell KBE, CB

As this moving account of a Service Battalion goes to print, the United Kingdom, trailing somewhat behind the Republic of Ireland, has announced its plans for the four years of centenary memorial activities from 2014 to 2018. The danger is that the events will only serve to reinforce the legends and myths of that epic struggle rather than explore the history. This exceptional book falls firmly into the telling of history. This is how those soldiers, whose names are inscribed on the Menin Gate and the Thiepval Memorial, who have no known grave, or those who lie in the hundreds of cemeteries, would have told you about what happened. This is the voice of reality impeccably researched.

For me it is rather closer even than that. My grandfather served throughout the war on the western front with the Royal Irish Fusiliers. His diary demonstrates to me how genuinely Nick Metcalfe has touched the sense of the time that my grandfather lived through. He married in 1919 and part of his honeymoon was spent in Ireland with the Stronge family at Tynan Abbey in County Armagh. You will read about Sergeant William Neil DCM and James Stronge in the preface to this volume.

As Colonel of the Royal Irish Regiment I attended a church service in Portadown where we laid up the Colours of a Home Service Battalion of the Regiment. Above me, as I handed over those Colours for safe keeping, hung the Colours of a Royal Irish Fusiliers Service Battalion from County Armagh, laid up just after the end of the First World War. Regimentally we cherish the strong golden thread which stretches from those about whom you will read in this book to those who even now are training to return to the battlefields of Afghanistan.

Nick has written not just a military history of events on a battlefield but also a social history of a particular time in the development of Ireland. It explores much that has perhaps been lost or absorbed by those who have shaped history to their own narrative. This volume will do much to rebalance the context of our understanding of what really happened and how it came to pass.

Sir Philip Trousdell
Colonel, The Royal Irish Regiment

Preface

A few years ago when discussing some now forgotten aspect of military life with my father, he mentioned that his grandfather, William Neill, had served in the Great War and had earned a medal for bravery at Ypres *'for rescuing an officer called James Stronge'*. The Stronge family was once prominent in the life of Ulster and Armagh and, intrigued, I began a search to determine truth from family myth. That search led to a fascination with the men with whom my great-grandfather served, and this book is the result.

My great-grandfather was Sergeant William Neill DCM, an original member of the 9th Royal Irish Fusiliers who left Ireland in 1915 and finally came home in 1919. William Neill was a respected member of the Battalion and his community in Lurgan. He, and Sergeant Herbert Sewell from Portadown, represented the 9th Royal Irish Fusiliers at the dedication ceremony of the Ulster Battlefield Memorial Tower at Thiepval on 19 November 1921.

I like to think that this account would be recognised by my great-grandfather and I hope it is a fitting memorial to all who served, through choice or otherwise, but particularly to those who gave their lives in what everyone hoped would be the war to end all wars.

Acknowledgements

I must acknowledge and thank all of those who kindly gave of their time and contributed extensively to this book. Much of the detail came from the many relatives of the men who served with the 9th Royal Irish Fusiliers, who provided letters, diaries and photographs. They are too numerous to mention individually and I hope that they approve of this record and my use of their family treasures.

I would particularly like to thank Amanda Moreno of the Royal Irish Fusiliers Museum, who made a wealth of material available, and Jonathan Maguire who helped with much research. I cannot thank enough Penny Scott, formerly the Army's senior librarian, and the staff of Prince Consort's Library in Aldershot where I spent many hours immersed in their magnificent collection and where I was treated with great patience. Penny's personal contribution was invaluable. Nigel Henderson researched and produced a huge number of photographs to help ensure that these men are not just a number, rank and name. Phillip Tardiff has researched and collated an impressive amount of information on the North Irish Horse in the First World War and helped keep that part of the record straight. Ralph J Whitehead contributed hugely to my understanding of the German operations prior to and during the attack at Hamel on 1 July 1916. His review of my work is much appreciated. I must also thank Peter Mattock and Mike Whitehead for the use of their photographs.

The material held in the National Archives at Kew has provided the basis for this book and the staff there made my first few forays into the War Office archives totally painless; the details of the source documents are contained in the bibliography. The staff of the Records Section of the Commonwealth War Graves Commission were most helpful—I could not have compiled this record without access to their extensive database. Images from the Imperial War Museum archive appear with the permission of the Imperial War Museum. One piece of detective work with which I was particularly pleased was the identification of the Medical Officer from the United States, Lieutenant H S Morgan MC, who was killed in action in April 1918. In this, the staff of the Modern Military Records Branch, US National Archives, were very keen to help, and the information and photographs provided by Patty Mackey and Patrick Lernout were invaluable. Some of the background material on Captain C B Despard is taken from The Ivan Crossley Story in the F Ivan Crossley File in Lloydminster Regional Archives, Alberta, Canada. This is a fascinating tale of pioneer life in Canada at the beginning of the 20th Century. Finally I must thank the largely anonymous contributors to two superb websites—The British Medals Forum and The Great War Forum. An adjunct to the latter, The Long, Long Trail, is a highly recommended source of detailed information on almost every aspect of the conduct of the war.

Finally, I would like to acknowledge and thank Graham Cook of WRITERSWORLD for his advice and guidance from our very first phone conversation and who made publication achievable, and Sue Croft, my editor, who showed extraordinary patience and consummate professionalism; any remaining errors are mine.

Introduction

In writing about a war fought by an Army made up of regiments that no longer exist, at a time when Ireland was one country, and against a complex political background, I had to decide upon language and terminology that would be understandable and consistent. It is worth explaining some it.

Firstly, regimental and battalion titles. The generic terms 'a battalion', 'a regiment', 'a brigade' and 'a division' become 'the Battalion', 'the Regiment', 'the Brigade' or 'the Division' when referring to a specific unit or formation. In order to avoid confusion, the full titles of British, German and French units have been used throughout. This is with the exception of the units of 36th (Ulster) Division.

The subject of this account is a battalion of Princess Victoria's (Royal Irish Fusiliers); it was not until 1920 that the Regiment became The Royal Irish Fusiliers (Princess Victoria's). There is little consistency in regimental and battalion titles used in documents such as the war diaries. Although the official abbreviation of the 1st Battalion, Princess Victoria's (Royal Irish Fusiliers) was 1 R. Ir. Fus. it appears variously as 1st Royal Irish Fusiliers, 1st Royal Irish Fusrs, 1st Royal Irish Fus, 1st R. Irish Fus. and 1 R.I.F. Consistent with many documents and for clarity and brevity I have shortened the titles of the regiments that made up 36th (Ulster) Division to Royal Irish Rifles, Royal Inniskilling Fusiliers and Royal Irish Fusiliers, appending the battalion number as appropriate. The nickname of Princess Victoria's (Royal Irish Fusiliers)—'Faughs' from the Anglicised Irish language motto *'Faugh a Ballagh'* meaning 'clear the way'—was really only used in relation to the two regular battalions, and, by many, only for the 1st Battalion, the former 87th Regiment of Foot. Consequently, I have used it only in that context.

The battalions of 36th (Ulster) Division were named on 2 October 1914. The County Armagh Battalion in 2nd Brigade was initially titled:

9th (Service) Battalion,
Princess Victoria's (Royal Irish Fusiliers) (County Armagh Volunteers)

The suffix (... Volunteers) was used for all of the battalions of the Ulster Division. The use of this suffix appeared once in the London Gazette—on 27 October 1914; the Gazette that appointed the first officers to the battalions of the Division—and never in the Army List. By November 1914 the word 'Volunteers' had been dropped from all of the battalion titles and this Battalion was now:

9th (Service) Battalion,
Princess Victoria's (Royal Irish Fusiliers) (County Armagh)

The suffix was officially abbreviated as (Co. Armagh). Incorrect variations of the suffix, such as (County Armagh Volunteers), (Armagh Volunteers), or (Armagh, Monaghan and Cavan Volunteers) are seen, particularly in literature in Northern Ireland. The title above was used until the amalgamation with the 2nd North Irish Horse in September 1917 when the Battalion was re-named. The Army Lists of 1918 show the new name as:

9th (North Irish Horse Yeomanry) Battalion (Service),
Princess Victoria's (Royal Irish Fusiliers)

(Officially abbreviated as: 9th (N. Ir. Horse. Yeo.) Battalion (Service))

The Army List is the only source of this title. The North Irish Horse was not a Yeomanry Regiment but a regiment of Special Reserve Cavalry and in every other source, including the London Gazette, the title of the Battalion is given as:

9th (North Irish Horse) Battalion, Princess Victoria's (Royal Irish Fusiliers)

(Officially abbreviated as: 9th (N. I. H.) Battalion)

When required in full I have used the titles in bold above and, for clarity and brevity, when not using the full title I have used 9th Royal Irish Fusiliers throughout.

I have attempted to be consistent with the spelling of towns and villages also. For French place names this has been relatively easy to achieve and most names will be recognised easily; I have corrected some phonetically spelled names used in the war diary. For places in Belgium it is a little more complicated. I have used the spelling of the time (again with some correction to phonetic spelling in the war diaries) and most of the towns and villages are referred to by the French version of their names. Readers should note that today those places in the Flemish Region are spoken of, and seen on maps, with Belgian-Dutch spelling, the best example of which is Ypres/Ieper.

The story told here is pre-Partition and I have tried to use the terminology of the time but in such a way that it does not confuse the reader. Ulster, one of the four provinces that make up Ireland, comprises nine counties, three of which—Cavan, Donegal and Monaghan—are now part of the Republic of Ireland. At that time, however, anyone from the island of Ireland was Irish, and Ulster Protestants had no difficulty in calling Londonderry 'Derry', although the sensitivities over Home Rule were beginning to force changes. Although I have attempted to put the formation of the Ulster Volunteer Force and 36th (Ulster) Division in context, I have not attempted a social history of the time or tried to unravel the complexities of Ulster Unionism, 'Redmondism', and the rise of Sinn Fein. Similarly at the end of the text I have not examined in detail the impact of the conflict in Ireland in the early 1920s on those who survived the war.

ONE

The Formation Of The Battalion

The situation in Ireland has always been complicated, not least in the early part of the last century when self-government, or Home Rule, exercised by an Irish Parliament in Dublin, looked a distinct possibility. John Redmond and his nationalist Irish Parliamentary Party held the balance of power in the House of Commons, and in 1911 Prime Minister H H Asquith secured their support to break the power of the House of Lords in return for the introduction of a Home Rule Bill. The Parliament Act 1911 was duly passed and the House of Lords agreed to restrictions in its powers. Importantly, the House of Lords agreed that its unlimited veto would be replaced by a veto that would last for only two years. A bill passed by the House of Commons in the third year would, therefore, become law without the consent of the House of Lords. The Second Home Rule Bill had been defeated by the House of Lords in 1893 by 419 votes to 41, and with the House of Commons now dominated by pro-Home Rule Liberals and the Irish Parliamentary Party, the Parliament Act 1911 effectively removed the last obstacle to Home Rule.

The Third Home Rule Bill was introduced by Prime Minister Asquith in April 1912. It was passed by the House of Commons by 10 votes, but the House of Lords voted against it by 326 votes to 69. It was only a matter of time, however, before the Bill would receive Royal Assent. As a consequence, there developed considerable opposition in the northern, and largely Protestant, province of Ulster to any measure that would see an end to the Union and a shift in the balance of power and economic priorities away from Belfast.

The stand for the Union was led by Sir Edward Carson MP,[1] a Dublin-born barrister, and Captain James Craig MP, a former Army officer. The most visible representation of the opposition to Home Rule was on 23 September 1911. A parade attended by over 100,000 people from all over Ulster was held at Craig's estate in Craigavon to welcome Carson as the new Unionist leader. As momentum grew through the early part of 1912 when the Home Rule Bill was introduced in Parliament, the Unionist stand became focused on the signing of the Solemn League and Covenant[2] —a pledge to *'defeat the present conspiracy to set up a Home Rule Parliament in Ireland'*.

By August 1912 it had become known that 28 September was to be 'Ulster Day', when the Covenant would be signed across the Province. The programme of meetings to promote the Covenant began in Enniskillen on 18 September when 40,000 members of the Unionist Clubs marched past Sir Edward Carson. This display was repeated across the north of Ireland, culminating in huge rallies in Belfast, and in the towns and villages of Ulster ten days later. At Seagoe, near Portadown, the signing of the Covenant was preceded by a church service, as was the case in many parishes. It was well attended, and as they filed out of church, 569 men and women signed their names. Across Ulster 237,368 men put their names to the Covenant, and 234,046 women signed the accompanying Declaration.

Moves to arm a Unionist militia had begun as early as 1910. It was apparent by late 1912 that the men drilling at their Orange Lodge could provide a focus for the framework of an organisation to signal that Home Rule would be resisted. By January 1913 the Ulster Unionist Council decided that the volunteers for such activities should be united into one body known as the Ulster Volunteer Force. It was determined that recruitment would be limited to 100,000, and all of the volunteers must be signatories of the Covenant and aged between seventeen and sixty-five. The appointed leader of the new force was Lieutenant General Sir George Richardson KCB, a sixty-six year old officer with extensive experience in India, Afghanistan and China. His staff was presided over by another Indian Army officer, Colonel G W Hacket Pain CB,[3] who would be key to the early success of 108th Brigade in the Ulster Division during the forthcoming war.

Men of the 4th (Portadown) Battalion, Armagh Regiment, Ulster Volunteer Force at Carrickblacker House. William Herbert Palmer stands third from the left on the front row.

The organisation of the force progressed quickly. For purposes of organisation Ulster was divided into fourteen divisions: the nine counties, Londonderry, and the four parliamentary constituencies of Belfast. Each of these was organised into a number of regiments and battalions. Fermanagh, for example, comprised three battalions, and Armagh, central to this story, raised five. In addition to these, supporting units were formed to provide communications, transport, and medical facilities. Two units of light cavalry were raised: the Ballymena and Enniskillen Horse.

Men of the 4th (Portadown) Battalion, Armagh Regiment, Ulster Volunteer Force on parade at Carrickblacker House before carrying out rifle practice at Tandragee in the summer of 1914. They are armed with M1904 Mannlicher rifles and each man has a bayonet. According to the original sender of the postcard the rifles were known as Mountjoy Specials, after the *Mountjoy II* (the temporarily renamed *SS Clyde Valley*), which had been used to smuggle them into Ulster in April 1914. Note the high standard of turnout and uniformity.

For the most part, drilling was conducted in the Orange Halls or on the land of supportive landowners. Many of the instructors at this time had served during the South African War and most were ex-British-Army non-commissioned officers. In the early days there were no uniforms and the men wore civilian clothes with leather belts, canvas haversacks and bandoleers. Canvas armbands were worn to distinguish the regiments and battalions. These were khaki (red or blue for officers) printed in black. In the summer of 1913, rifles and ammunition began arriving in Ulster. The training of the Ulster Volunteer Force progressed well, but the small number of weapons that was actually delivered into its hands was insufficient for the force to be declared ready for any significant action. Notwithstanding its successful formation and underpinning organisation, the military power of the Ulster Volunteer Force has been greatly exaggerated. It was short of officers, high quality instructors and equipment.

The Ulster Volunteer Force was a significant influence in Irish politics, however, and the nationalist response was predictable. August 1913 saw the formation of the Irish Volunteers, and although the opposing organisations were not well enough equipped at this stage for open war, the growing militant situation forced a greater effort by Prime Minister Asquith, Sir Edward Carson and John Redmond, the nationalist leader, to find a solution that would avoid armed conflict.

The Orange Order parading through Portadown on 12 July 1914.

Having been twice rejected by the House of Lords, the Home Rule Bill was now approaching its third reading in Parliament, and the Ulster Volunteer Force was readied for any emergency that might occur. The bill was passed on 25 May 1914. Fortunately, the day passed peacefully, as did the following 12 July when the Orange Order held its annual parades. But all was not well. Compromise could not be reached. Although the partition of Ireland was a serious proposal of last resort, neither Carson nor Redmond would accept it. Ireland was tense, and the men of the Ulster Volunteers paraded openly over the north of Ireland. The shooting of Irish nationalists by the British Army in Dublin on 26 July, after guns were landed for the Irish Volunteers at Howth, inflamed the population. To many, war in Ireland seemed certain. Only the outbreak of war in Europe saved the situation. An uneasy and ill-defined political truce developed when the majority of the moderate political leaders in Ireland saw the German invasion of Belgium as a more immediate issue than the Irish question. Ireland's response to the crisis reflected that many were in agreement with this sentiment.

In 1914 Britain's standing Army was a small, well-trained, regular force of just under a quarter of a million men spread between the seven commands that made up the home forces and the overseas commands in India, South Africa and the Mediterranean. The Army Reserve, formed from those who had completed their regular enlistment and those who volunteered for the Special Reserve, had been created to bring units up to full strength on mobilisation. In 1914 it numbered a little over 200,000 men. In addition, the Territorial Force had been formed in 1908 from the Militia and Yeomanry. It comprised fourteen brigades of cavalry and fourteen infantry divisions, although these were all primarily intended for home defence. At the same time it was agreed that the regular Army would field an expeditionary force of six regular infantry divisions and one cavalry division. It was this tiny British Expeditionary Force that landed in France in August 1914.

It was evident after only a few weeks of fighting that the war would not be over quickly and that a much larger force would be required. Lord Kitchener's first move when he was appointed Secretary of State for War on 5 August 1914, was to raise a volunteer army under regular terms of service, rather than using the Territorial Force as the basis for expansion. Kitchener's call for volunteers on 11 August was met by a swift and positive response across the British Isles, including in Ireland. Those on both sides of the political divide flocked to the recruiting offices. They were amongst the immortal 'First Hundred Thousand', the earliest to volunteer across the British Isles for war service, and considered to be amongst the elite of their generation.

The first of Kitchener's New Armies, known as K1, was raised in response to Army Order 324 dated 21 August 1914. It comprised six divisions numbered 9-14 and included the 10th (Irish) Division. This was the first of three divisions raised in Ireland with its men being found from amongst those who were the first to volunteer, including a large number of impatient members of the Ulster Volunteer Force. It reflected the religious and political mix of the country. It was not plain sailing, however, and recruiting was hindered by the number of reservists recalled to the colours, amongst them many men of the Ulster Volunteer Force who were sent to various units across the Army, making them unavailable for the new Irish division. Training also proved problematic, and in its early days it was a less than impressive formation. It sailed for Gallipoli in July 1915 and proved to be a fine fighting division.

The target for K1 was met so swiftly that K2 and K3, another twelve divisions, were raised in early September. Amongst these was the 16th (Irish) Division. Recruiting difficulties meant that it was the last of the three Irish divisions to be fully manned, however, and included in its ranks were men from the Channel Islands. Its first units deployed to France in December 1915. This was predominantly a Catholic division with an Irish Nationalist tradition, but, although many of the men came from Redmond's National Volunteers, there was a significant number of Irish Protestants in its ranks. Like the 10th (Irish) Division, it had two brigades raised largely in the southern counties and one largely from the north. Kitchener's fourth New Army, K4, followed in the autumn of that year, but its battalions were subsequently designated as reserve battalions for the training of recruits and for sending drafts to the battalions raised previously. K5 and K6 soon followed (renamed K4 and K5) and amongst the ranks of the latter would be the men of the Ulster Division.

On the outbreak of war the Ulster Volunteer Force comprised over 80,000 men, many of suitable age for military service. Despite the fact that many of its most experienced men were former soldiers who had already been recalled or who had joined the 10th (Irish) Division, it was evident that it had the potential to become a formidable and powerful fighting force. Soon after his appointment as Secretary of State for War, Lord Kitchener stated his intent to secure the Ulster Volunteer Force as a fighting formation for deployment with the British Expeditionary Force. Carson was placed in a difficult position. Having trumpeted the loyalty of Ulster's Unionists, he could hardly refuse, but he was concerned that Home Rule would be forced on Ulster when the Ulster Volunteer Force was at war in Europe. He could get no firm assurance from the Prime Minister that this would not happen (his fears were realised subsequently when Prime Minister Asquith's government passed the Home Rule Act in September 1915) but the situation in France dictated a swift response. After some discussion with Kitchener, Carson promised a division. The Secretary of State eventually relented to demands for the inclusion of 'Ulster' in its title, a move that reflected similar concessions to lobbying from other areas of the United Kingdom. On 3 September, at a meeting of the Ulster Unionist Council in Belfast, in a long and emotive speech Sir Edward Carson appealed to the men of the Ulster Volunteer Force: *"Go and help to save your country and to save your Empire; go and win honour for Ulster and for Ireland."* Later in the speech he made it clear that: *"If we get enough men to go from the Ulster Volunteer Force they will go under the War Office as a division of their own."*

One man intimately involved with the Ulster Volunteer Force was Major S W W Blacker. Commissioned into the Royal Artillery in 1885, he had served on the North-West Frontier where he was wounded and mentioned in despatches. He had then fought in the South African War before retiring as a major in 1903. The Blacker family had occupied Carrickblacker House near Portadown since 1692 and, being large landlords in the area, were influential in the development of the town. Major Blacker was a well-known and very popular figure amongst the Unionist population of the area, in the Orange Order, and in the Unionist movement. He was a major influence in the Ulster Volunteer Force, in which he commanded the Armagh Regiment and raised and commanded the 4th (Portadown) Battalion. The Unionist people of Portadown held him, and his stand against Home Rule, in extremely high regard. He had been the first in Seagoe to sign the Covenant two years earlier.

Lieutenant Colonel S W W Blacker

Like many reserve officers he was called up in early August 1914 and his orders directed him to Piershill Barracks in Edinburgh. His departure, of sufficient note to gain mention in the Portadown News of 15 August, was cheered by thousands of people from the town who had stopped work to see him off. His volunteers, commanded by Thomas Atkinson, a local solicitor, lined the route to the railway station at Edenderry. When Major Blacker arrived at the station he was obviously overwhelmed by the demonstration of affection. In Edinburgh he remained in touch with developments in Ulster and he knew where his duty lay. Following Carson's announcement that the Ulster Volunteer Force was to be mobilised, he wrote to Canon Archer at Seagoe parish on 4 September expressing his views:

> *'Though convinced in my own mind as to the proper course for every able bodied man to take at this crisis, I have refrained from expressing such opinion until I saw what Sir E Carson's pronouncement on what the duty of the U.V.F. would be. His speech in Belfast on Thursday is absolutely clear, and agrees absolutely with my conception of our duty.*
>
> *"Our Loyalty is not for barter." At this supreme crisis when the fate of the Empire is at stake, it is our solemn duty to sink for the time being our domestic*

differences, and to concentrate all our efforts on defeating the common foe. Every able bodied man that can possibly be spared should come forward for the defence of his country, and volunteer for service anywhere.

I am in hopes that the U.V.F. will form a separate Unit, under a scheme which Sir E Carson says has been approved by Lord Kitchener, under their own Officers.

I expect that this scheme will shortly be promulgated. In the meantime all members of the U.V.F. should work harder than ever to render themselves efficient by constant attendance at drills, and thus be ready when called on to furnish a trained body of men for active service. Those who do not belong to the U.V.F. should at once enlist in the new Regiments of the County Regiment now being formed.

The Empire is in urgent need of every able bodied man. Though confident that in the end we shall be victorious, it will only be by everyone realising what his duty is and doing it, and by a spirit of self-sacrifice and patriotism on the part of all, that we shall win through. May God defend the Right!'

A few days later, James Stronge, the son and heir of the 5th Baronet, Sir James Stronge[4] of Tynan Abbey in County Armagh, wrote a public letter to his men in the Tynan Company of the 1st Armagh Battalion of the Ulster Volunteers, which was published in the Portadown News on 12 September 1914. Believing, as many did, that support for the Crown in the war was sure to help defeat the cause of Home Rule he wrote:

James Stronge

'. . . you have been given an opportunity, such as we scarce dared hope for, of fighting, not among strangers, but side by side with your kindred, your friends and neighbours, for the honour of our country and the safety of our homes against a brutal enemy, as well as for the maintenance of the Union that we all hold so dear.

The country looks to its sons to win for it a glorious place in the Army that Ulster is privileged to put at the orders of our beloved Sovereign. Do not let it look to you in vain, and rest assured that we shall not be allowed to suffer politically for doing our highest duty.'

Following the example of the South Belfast UVF, which marched with Sir Edward Carson and Captain Craig to the new recruiting depot on 4 September, the Ulster Volunteer Force mobilised. Initial recruiting was not, however, without its problems. Concern over the political situation forced many to refuse to serve initially, particularly in the rural areas in the west of the Province. But by no means all of the Ulster Division's recruits were members of the Ulster Volunteer Force. In addition to those who joined from the rest of Ireland and from Great Britain and the Empire, a significant number of local recruits, while all Protestant, were not part of 'Carson's Army', and the level of Ulster Volunteer Force membership varied greatly from unit to unit.

K5 was the largest New Army to be raised. It comprised 142 locally raised battalions across the British Isles, organised into twelve divisions, numbered 30-41, most with regional affiliations. These were the formations amongst which were the 'pals battalions'—locally raised units from towns and villages, workplaces, businesses and professions, which bonded quickly but whose later loss in action had such a detrimental effect on communities across the country. The timing of the formation of the Ulster Division, therefore, secured its number, the 36th, amongst very similar formations.

Thirteen battalions of infantry were raised for the Ulster Division. These were recruited regionally, with the battalions being formed from the larger Ulster Volunteer Force regimental areas, companies from smaller areas within these, and platoons from local districts. In addition, some men transferred from 10th (Irish) Division. All of the battalions were raised in the recruiting areas of the three Irish regiments based in Ulster—The Royal Inniskilling Fusiliers, The Royal Irish Rifles and Princess Victoria's (Royal Irish Fusiliers).

The Ulster Division was formed around three Brigades: the 1st from the City of Belfast; the 2nd from the counties of Antrim, Down, Armagh, Cavan and Monaghan, and the 3rd from Tyrone, Londonderry, Donegal and Fermanagh, and with one battalion from Belfast. In addition, a pioneer battalion was raised in County Down (although it had many County Armagh men in it, mainly from Lurgan), engineers and divisional signals were recruited in Belfast, and a cyclist company was also formed. The cavalry squadron was based upon the Enniskillen Horse, a semi-autonomous, irregular cavalry unit that had joined the Ulster Volunteers in 1913. A large contingent of Royal Army Medical Corps personnel was formed into three field ambulances and an Army Service Corps contingent was raised, mainly from men from rural areas with experience of horses. The only component missing was the divisional artillery because it was considered that raising artillery units in Ulster would delay the departure of the Ulster Division for France. The 36th (Ulster) Division's artillery would be raised in May 1915 in the London boroughs of Croydon, Norbury and Sydenham.

Men of the 4th (Portadown) Battalion, Armagh Regiment, Ulster Volunteer Force.
These were some of the men who enlisted in September 1914.

For those members of the Ulster Volunteer Force responding to Sir Edward Carson's call in Portadown and Lurgan, recruiting began on 15 September, and in Armagh the next day. In Portadown the men of the Ulster Volunteers formed up at their headquarters and, led by their officers including Thomas Atkinson, David Shillington, Charles Johnston and George Lutton, they marched to the parochial hall to await the arrival of the recruiting and medical staff. Shortly after 9.30am the first batch entered the hall. They were all given a card on which was written their name and age and they stripped to the waist for their medical examination. Having been weighed, measured, and checked for poor eyesight and bad teeth, they dressed and presented themselves and their attestation papers to one of three magistrates. Duly sworn in, they were given six shillings. Nearly 220 men paraded that morning, most from Portadown with some from Tandragee and Scarva. Only twenty were rejected, mainly for bad eyesight. Major Blacker was also present. Whilst he was there he received a telegram accepting him for service with the Ulster Division. He left immediately and reported for duty in Belfast.

Sergeant, later Regimental Quartermaster Sergeant, Henry Fox. This photograph was taken in February 1915 in Newtownards; he was eighteen years old.

Although in September 1914 the official recruiting age was between nineteen and thirty-five (raised from thirty in late August), many men over the upper age limit were readily accepted. In contrast, younger men were turned away, but it is clear that some managed to persuade the recruiting staff that they were older than they were. Indeed, some were considerably underage: William John Archer was born in Lurgan in 1901 and enlisted with his father; he did not deploy overseas with 36th (Ulster) Division. David Frederick Bryans enlisted in September 1914, aged 14. After being kept back, he eventually joined the 1st Battalion in France in 1918.

It is impossible to determine how many young men managed to slip through the net, with or without the recruiters noticing, but, in accordance with King's Regulations, there were at least nine discharges from this first draft for *'having made a mis-statement as to age on enlistment'*. Some of them were as a consequence of parents or their representatives writing to the Commanding Officer with an entreaty to release the recruit.

Some of those who enlisted were more successful in concealing their age. Henry Fox, a farmer's son from County Wicklow, had moved to Portadown to seek work, where, being well educated he found employment with the Great Northern Railway as a clerk. When the call came he was amongst the first at the recruiting office and enlisted on 16 September, one day before his eighteenth birthday. Being nearly six feet three inches tall and well built, it is easy to see how he got away with changing his year of birth to 1894. He was not alone; there were at least eighteen soldiers who joined the Battalion in September 1914 and who would be killed in action before they were officially allowed to enlist.

Private, later Corporal, John Sharp.
He was 16 years old when he enlisted.
This photograph was taken in early 1915.

Over the next few days more men from across the county joined up and on 21 September the newly enlisted men of the County Armagh Battalion were mobilised. Their departure for Clandeboye in County Down was typical of the heady atmosphere prevalent across Britain in the early days of the war. In Portadown over 200 men were led by the Salvation Army band to the railway station and were sent on their way by a vast, emotional and excited crowd. In Armagh, led by the band of the Boys' Brigade, the men enjoyed a similar send-off and as the train left the station fog signals were exploded to cheers from the crowd. In Tandragee gifts of pocket bibles, cigarettes, pipes and tobacco were handed out to the sixty or so volunteers. In Lurgan 284 men were led by another Boys' Brigade band and they were joined at the station by the men from Gilford who had travelled there in a convoy of cars and lorries. It is worthy of note that in many areas where Home Rule was supported there was very little overt display of such patriotism; the conflict in Ireland had not been completely over-shadowed. The new battalion arrived in Bangor in County Down later that day. Led by its officers, it marched into camp at Clandeboye where it joined the other battalions of the 2nd Brigade. On arrival it had a strength of twenty officers and 842 other ranks, just short of its full establishment. For more details on this first draft, see Appendix 6.

Like all of those in the Ulster Division, the County Armagh Battalion was essentially Protestant Unionist. Many of the men had deeply-held religious beliefs and their religion was an important part of their lives. This was reflected in the regular organisation of field services and, less constructively, by the intolerance shown to Roman Catholic officers and non-commissioned officers in some quarters. It would not be until late in 1916 that this element of the Battalion's make-up would change. Many of the officers and men were also members of the Orange Order, and lodges met regularly while the battalions were training. Many were friends of long standing who worked together in the linen mills, and there was a significant number of relatives who joined together. The political origins of the Ulster Division, its roots in the Ulster Volunteer Force, its Protestant faith and its links to the Orange Order made it unique, and these are the key factors in understanding the character, *'esprit de corps'* and particular style of its units. The band of brothers from Armagh, Cavan and Monaghan was a battalion with strong bonds. They helped greatly in welding the new unit together and influenced significantly the standards of discipline and behaviour. There were, of course, grave implications for the towns and villages of Armagh, Cavan and Monaghan as the war took its toll.

The hard work and foresight of those organising the recruiting effort, particularly James Craig, and the aid provided by businessmen in Belfast resulted in an immediate issue of 10,000 uniforms, purchased from Moss Bros in London. It also made possible the eventual replacement of tented camps with hutted accommodation at Clandeboye, Ballykinler and Newtownards in the east and at Finner on the Donegal coast. This is in stark contrast to many English New Army battalions that spent weeks in civilian clothes and months in ill-fitting, multi-coloured uniforms, such as 'Kitchener blue'.

Clandeboye camp was shared by the battalions of the 2nd Brigade; those known then as the South Antrim, Central Antrim, 1st County Down and County Armagh Battalions. They quickly established a name for discipline, cleanliness and hard work. The County Armagh Battalion quickly made its mark and soon developed an excellent reputation as one of the best battalions in the Ulster Division. Major Blacker had returned to command the new battalion and everyone held him in great regard. His influence on the early performance of the new unit was striking, and its nickname *Blacker's Boys* reflected the impact and popularity of its Commanding Officer.

Although not the case in every battalion of the Ulster Division, many of the officers in the County Armagh Battalion had served in the Ulster Volunteer Force. In addition to commanding the 1st (Armagh) Battalion of the Ulster Volunteer Force's Armagh Regiment, the new Second-in-Command, Colonel William FitzGerald, was a Militia officer who had commanded the 3rd (Armagh) Battalion of Princess Victoria's (Royal Irish Fusiliers). Captain George Irwin was fifty-eight years old and had served with the Indian Civil Service Political Department. He had retired in 1903, after twenty-five years' service, for which he was made a Companion of the Order of the Star of India, and returned to Ireland. He had served in the Ulster Volunteer Force as Adjutant to Major Blacker. A number of the new officers had commanded an Ulster Volunteer Force company for eighteen months before the outbreak of war. Thomas Atkinson joined the new battalion immediately along with Charles Johnston and David Shillington JP, another well-known figure from a prominent Portadown family. Arthur Allen had served for three years in the Royal North West Mounted Police in the North West Territories and the Yukon, Canada, before he returned to Ireland and joined the Ulster Volunteer Force. Others who had been company commanders for up to a year included Charles Ensor (Annaghmore Company (K Company), 1st (Armagh) Battalion), George Lutton and William Menaul; John Brew, Joseph Johnston and Richard Townsend were also officers. Many of the new warrant officers and non-commissioned officers had also held rank in the Ulster Volunteer Force.

The demands from units at the front for the Reservist and Special Reservists, and the unwillingness of the Ulster Division to take to its heart the Roman Catholic non-commissioned officers of the regular Irish battalions, meant that instructors had to be found from elsewhere. Major F P Crozier was sent to London to recruit instructors and a number of senior non-commissioned officers were found amongst those re-enlisting, although the experience of most was out of date. Nevertheless, the new battalions were joined by a number of regular and reserve non-commissioned officers, many of whom had served in the South Africa war, who would be responsible for training the enthusiastic recruits. Some key personnel in the new County Armagh Battalion were also former regular soldiers. The Quartermaster was a good example; Lieutenant Alexander Ferguson was forty-six years old and had served for twenty-six years with The Royal Scots Fusiliers. He had earned a mention in despatches and the Distinguished Conduct Medal in South Africa before finishing his service in 1911 as a Regimental Quartermaster Sergeant. Regimental Sergeant Major Stilwell had also seen service in the South African War, as had

Regimental Quartermaster Sergeant Thomas Thwaites and Company Sergeant Major Charlie Turner.

Regimental Sergeant Major A Stilwell

Company Sergeant Major C H Turner

The original officers that marched into Clandeboye Camp on 21 September 1914 were:

Commanding Officer:	Lieutenant Colonel S W W Blacker
Second-in-Command:	Colonel W C FitzGerald
Captains:	T J Atkinson, J C Boyle, J G Brew, G R Irwin CSI, C M Johnston, S J Scott, D G Shillington
Lieutenants:	L M Anderson, C H Ensor, J G E FitzGerald, W J Menaul, R S B Townsend
Second Lieutenants:	A D Allen, J A Johnston, G E Lutton, A Small, A B Townsend
Quartermaster:	Honorary Lieutenant A Ferguson DCM

Those from County Armagh were soon joined by officers and men from Counties Cavan and Monaghan, and the regional recruitment of the Battalion was reflected in the organisation of the companies. In general, A Company was formed from those from Armagh city and the south of that county, B Company was made up from men from Portadown, and those from Lurgan joined C Company. D Company had a mix of men from Armagh, Lurgan and Portadown, and they were joined by those recruited from Cavan and Monaghan. On 2 October the new battalions were designated officially as service battalions of the county regiments. This was a source of great pride to the men of the Ulster Volunteer Force. The County Armagh Battalion of 2nd Brigade became the 9th (Service) Battalion, Princess Victoria's (Royal Irish Fusiliers) (County Armagh).[5]

Some of the earliest recruits in 1914. Private Thomas Lyness is standing on the left.

Over the next month the men were issued with their new cap badges. In the case of the men of the 9th Royal Irish Fusiliers this was the two-part badge of Princess Victoria's (Royal Irish Fusiliers) that had been adopted in 1906. It comprised a silver coloured Princess Victoria's coronet over a separate, brass, 'fired' grenade. Superimposed on the body of the grenade was a silver coloured Irish harp beneath the Prince of Wales' feathers. Also issued was shoulder insignia, again in two parts—brass shoulder titles with the initials RIF and small brass grenades that were worn above them. A photograph of the Battalion's senior non-commissioned officers was clearly taken over this period, showing caps being worn with and without the cap-badge.

On 28 October 1914 the new formation was named 36th (Ulster) Division with the Brigades being numbered on 2 November as the 107th, 108th and 109th. The final organisation of the Ulster Division (less the Royal Artillery units) was:

107th Infantry Brigade

8th (Service) Battalion, The Royal Irish Rifles (East Belfast)
9th (Service) Battalion, The Royal Irish Rifles (West Belfast)
10th (Service) Battalion, The Royal Irish Rifles (South Belfast)
15th (Service) Battalion, The Royal Irish Rifles (North Belfast)

108th Infantry Brigade

11th (Service) Battalion, The Royal Irish Rifles (South Antrim)
12th (Service) Battalion, The Royal Irish Rifles (Central Antrim)
13th (Service) Battalion, The Royal Irish Rifles (1st County Down)
9th (Service) Battalion, Princess Victoria's (Royal Irish Fusiliers) (County Armagh)

109th Infantry Brigade

9th (Service) Battalion, The Royal Inniskilling Fusiliers (County Tyrone)

10th (Service) Battalion, The Royal Inniskilling Fusiliers (Derry)
11th (Service) Battalion, The Royal Inniskilling Fusiliers (Donegal and Fermanagh)
14th (Service) Battalion, The Royal Irish Rifles (Young Citizens)

Pioneer Battalion

16th (Service) Battalion, The Royal Irish Rifles (2nd County Down) (Pioneers)

Divisional Troops

1st Service Squadron, 6th (Inniskilling) Dragoons
121st Field Company, Corps of Royal Engineers
122nd Field Company, Corps of Royal Engineers
150th Field Company, Corps of Royal Engineers
36th Divisional Signal Company, Corps of Royal Engineers
36th Divisional Cyclist Company
36th Division Train, Army Service Corps
108th Field Ambulance, Royal Army Medical Corps
109th Field Ambulance, Royal Army Medical Corps
110th Field Ambulance, Royal Army Medical Corps
76th Sanitary Section, Royal Army Medical Corps
48th Mobile Veterinary Section, Army Veterinary Corps

In addition to the units that would make up the fighting component of the Ulster Division, six reserve battalions were formed in 1915, which made up 15th Reserve Brigade. They provided trained drafts of men for the battalions in France and Belgium and were linked to specific service battalions:

12th (Reserve) Battalion, The Royal Inniskilling Fusiliers
9th, 10th and 11th (Service) Battalions, The Royal Inniskilling Fusiliers

17th (Reserve) Battalion, The Royal Irish Rifles
8th, 9th and 10th (Service) Battalions, The Royal Irish Rifles

18th (Reserve) Battalion, The Royal Irish Rifles
11th and 12th (Service) Battalions, The Royal Irish Rifles

19th (Reserve) Battalion, The Royal Irish Rifles
14th and 15th (Service) Battalions, The Royal Irish Rifles

20th (Reserve) Battalion, The Royal Irish Rifles
13th and 16th (Service) Battalions, The Royal Irish Rifles

10th (Reserve) Battalion, Princess Victoria's (Royal Irish Fusiliers)
9th (Service) Battalion, Princess Victoria's (Royal Irish Fusiliers)

The identification badge adopted by 36th (Ulster) Division was a red hand, the heraldic symbol for the province of Ulster. All of the units of the Ulster Division were distinguished by their own 'battle patch', normally worn on the tunic shoulder. These allowed for the identification of like units—in 107th Brigade, for example, it was the only way to tell the battalions of Royal Irish Rifles apart. In 108th Brigade the battle patch was a semi-circle sewn onto the tunic at the top of the arm adjoining the shoulder seam. After 1916 it could also be seen on helmets. Thc patch for the 9th Royal Irish Fusiliers was red.[6]

The training at Clandeboye was typical of that given to the majority of the New Army battalions under a standard War Office syllabus. It consisted primarily of drill, physical training and rifle handling. The day's work began at reveille at 6.00am and in the next half hour the men readied themselves and had a breakfast of coffee and biscuits. A parade followed from 7.00 to 8.00am and then a more substantial meal of bread with tinned meat or jam. In the early days, more drill followed until noon, then lunch and an afternoon of training until 4.30pm. The evenings were relatively free, except for those detailed for pickets. 'Tattoo' was sounded at 9.00pm with lights out an hour later.

Uniform jacket of Second Lieutenant R J Sleator, showing the battle flash of The 9th Royal Irish Fusiliers on the shoulder.

The Division's Commander, Major General C H Powell CB, believed strongly in physical fitness. He ordered that the men must march with alpine-style packs made in Belfast and carried fully loaded. This quickly made everyone tough and fit. Although a lack of rifles caused some difficulties, even when a number of UVF weapons were added to the official stocks, by mid-November each battalion had received 180 service rifles and this allowed a significant improvement in rifle training. The battalion bands were trained alongside everyone else initially, although as time passed their training focused on their use as stretcher bearers and medical orderlies. The training varied greatly, however, as did the standard achieved by the battalions, particularly in the early days. This reflected the quality of the instructors, the very mixed quality of the officers, and the discipline of each unit.

The 'Dixie' badge

The onset of bad weather at the end of October 1914 had led to awful conditions in the tented camp at Clandeboye. An outbreak of meningitis in November, and the fear of it spreading, resulted in A and C Companies moving to barracks in Holywood. The Battalion Headquarters with B and D Companies moved to Victoria Barracks in Belfast. The winter was particularly severe that year and those left in the camps suffered a miserable time. Morale remained high, however, particularly as Christmas leave was granted from 19 December to 3 January. On their return the men resumed training. As the new year progressed, the training of individuals developed into tactical training at platoon, company and battalion level, and the intensive process continued through the spring of 1915.

In late January 1915 it was confirmed that the War Office had authorised a new badge for all units of 36th (Ulster) Division. This rather political development resulted in the 'Dixie Badge', a bronze oval badge made by Sharman D Neill Ltd in Belfast that showed the red hand of Ulster dripping blood from the wrist. Such a badge was unique amongst the newly-raised formations of the New Army. The badge was ordered to be worn on caps and uniform collars for a short period in February 1915 but it quickly fell out of use as regimental tradition prevailed and, in response to protests from across the Division, a return to regimental badges was soon ordered. It can be seen in the photograph of Henry Fox on page 8.

Although the Battalion was well manned, recruits were still required. For two weeks in early February 1915 a large recruiting party of 220 men, led by Colonel FitzGerald, accompanied by Captain Johnston and Lieutenants Ensor, Jackson, Stronge and Townsend, marched through County Armagh where they received a tremendous reception. They would have been joined by their doctor, Lieutenant Berry, but he had fallen victim to flu, so they were accompanied by Lieutenant J L Dunlop.[7] Half of the party, with Captain Johnston at its head, left Armagh at 10.30am and headed for Tynan on Wednesday 10 February. One of the platoons was led by Lieutenant Stronge. Tynan was his home town and was decorated for the occasion with bunting. Arches spanned the streets and Union Flags flew from the houses. A public meeting was held that evening and, setting the tone for the rest of the march, the speeches by local dignitaries were as political and anti-Home Rule as they were anti-German. A common theme was that the Union was not up for negotiation and that service, and therefore sacrifice, in France and Flanders would settle the Home Rule question. A unanimously supported resolution was, however, in keeping with the aim of the recruiting drive:

> *'That we, the men of F Company, 1st Battalion County Armagh Regiment of the U.V.F., hereby extend a hearty welcome to the men of the 9th Battalion R.I.F., our former brothers in arms, now amongst us, and recognising the danger that threatens our country pledge ourselves to her service by enlisting in the Ulster divisions of Lord Kitchener's army.'*

Recruits at Newtownards in early 1915.
The officers in the centre are Second Lieutenant H K Jackson and Captain D G Shillington.
14186 Private (later Corporal) David Frazer is the tallest man in the back row.

This photograph of the senior non-commissioned officers and some of the officers was taken soon after the Battalion's formation and probably soon after it had been named; many of the men have yet to receive their cap badges. Many of the older non-commissioned officers were ex-regulars, as their cap badges and medal ribbons testify.

Top (portraits):
(1) 13968 Sergeant H Anderson, (2) 14611 Sergeant S Porter, (3) 14691 Sergeant R J Sleator, (4) 14202 Sergeant W Gray, (5) 17517 Company Sergeant Major E G Tuck, (6) 15719 Company Sergeant Major F E Cross, (7) Adjutant Captain H W Seton, (8) Second-in-Command Colonel W C Fitzgerald, (9) 17397 Company Sergeant Major C H Turner, (10) Commanding Officer Lieutenant Colonel S W W Blacker, (11) 3324 Regimental Quartermaster Sergeant T Thwaites, (12) 14524 Sergeant J McAlester, (13) 14815 Sergeant E Wilson.

Main group forth row:
(14) 15716 Sergeant J C Woollett, (15) 14011 Sergeant T Boyd, (16) 26534 Sergeant M Banbury.

Third row:
(17) Sergeant Jones (no details known), (18) 23316 Sergeant S G Porter.

Second row:
(19) 14372 Sergeant A Johnston, (20) Sergeant Jarvis (Tailor) (no details known), (21) Canon Watham, (22) Captain G R Irwin CSI, (23) Major A C Pratt, (24) 13527 Regimental Sergeant Major A Stilwell, (25) 12330 Colour Sergeant J Kane, (26) 14701 Sergeant J Sharpe.

First row:
(27) 14694 Sergeant T Stringer, (28) 14210 Sergeant F Girvan, (29) Captain S J Scott, (30) 14666 Sergeant J F Shepherd.

The day after the parade at Tynan, the rest of the recruiting party marched in fine weather with its band from Armagh to Keady, where it was joined by the men from Tynan. They were met by a company of the UVF and, it seemed, most of the town, which had declared an unofficial holiday for the occasion. The recruiting party marched to Newtownhamilton on Friday 12 February and onward to Bessbrook the next day. Bessbrook, the 'model village', established by the Quaker Richardson family to house the workers of Bessbrook Linen Mill, welcomed the men with tea in the Town Hall, which was followed by a concert of music and recitations, including songs by Sergeants David Pollock and Adam Moore, and Corporal George Kirkwood. This was the only occasion where the recruiting march did not become an opportunity for a political rally.

That night the men were billeted with families across the town. In increasingly bad weather the march continued over the next few days to Poyntzpass, Markethill and, finally, to Tandragee. Sadly, this effort resulted in fewer recruits than hoped for. It is noteworthy that recruiting in the rural counties of the north was not significantly higher than in southern counties, almost certainly due to the obvious impact of losing men from farming families. The lack of success resulted in another party of 108 men led by Major Pratt, the new Second-in-Command, conducting a similar scheme through Counties Monaghan and Cavan at the end of the month. By 26 February all of the companies had moved to a new hutted camp at Newtownards where training continued apace and, with the effort of the recruiting teams, the Battalion grew to a strength of twenty-seven officers and 1,073 other ranks.

The support from the people of County Armagh did not wane during this period that the Battalion trained at Newtownards. The newspapers were full of their activities and many people found ways to contribute to the effort. Fund-raising enterprises were widespread. One result of the vast amount of money raised was the ambulances bought for the Ulster Division. On a parade attended by the Brigade Commander, Mrs Shillington and Mrs Blacker, the Battalion was presented with one of the seventeen purchased thus far by Sir James Stronge on behalf of the people of County Armagh. Sir James Stronge's heartfelt speech reiterated how proud the people of Armagh were of their battalion, *'Our Ninth'* as they knew it.

The officers' mess had changed considerably after the first few months with a number of officers having left through illness or to join other units in the Division. Second Lieutenant Alexander Small fell ill with tuberculosis in February 1915 and, unfit for service, he relinquished his commission. At fifty-eight years of age, Captain Irwin was deemed too old for active service and in May he left the Battalion to serve as Assistant Provost Marshal, Marseilles Base, as a staff captain. Colonel FitzGerald and Second Lieutenant Arthur Townsend left on 25 June 1915 to join the newly formed 12th (Reserve) Battalion, The Royal Inniskilling Fusiliers, for a short period, and Captain John Boyle transferred to the Corps of Royal Engineers.

Regular officers, and some of those recalled to the Army, supported all of the newly raised service battalions and the 9th Royal Irish Fusiliers received its share. Major Audley Pratt, the second son of a prominent family from County Cavan and Enniscoe, County Mayo, was a former regular officer who had served with the 1st Battalion, The Royal Scots (Lothian Regiment), in the South African War, where he had been mentioned in despatches. He had retired and transferred to the Regular Army Reserve of Officers in 1913. When he was recalled he joined the Battalion as Second-in-Command. The Adjutant, Lieutenant H W Seton, had arrived in November 1914. He was a regular officer who had been commissioned into 1/9th Battalion, The Gurkha Rifles, in 1908, seeing active service on the north-west frontier the same year.

During this early period, others who had served with the Ulster Volunteer Force and who had enlisted as soldiers on the formation of the Battalion, were commissioned and joined the original officers. Officers were initially appointed on the recommendation of the commanding officer and brigade commander. Some had been trained at an Officer Training Corps but many had little, or no, military experience. From January 1915 a month-long training course catered for non-commissioned officers and soldiers recommended for a commission, and from February 1916 the training for all potential officers was increased to four months and held at one of the officer cadet battalions, or cavalry cadet squadrons, spread around the British Isles.

Junior officers of 36th (Ulster) Division at a course of instruction in bayonet fighting at Victoria Barracks, Belfast, in January 1915.

Officers of the 9th Royal Irish Fusiliers present are Lieutenants J A Johnston & T F Given (top row, second and third from the right), and Lieutenants G E Lutton and L M Anderson (second row, sitting fourth and fifth from the left).

Those appointed to a commission included Lieutenant Thomas Given who was commissioned at the end of September 1914 with Second Lieutenant James Stronge. Second Lieutenant Henry Jackson from Clones, County Monaghan had been commissioned in October and Second Lieutenant John Gibson, formerly a lance sergeant in B Company was commissioned with Second Lieutenant Robert Flood in December. Tom Shillington, the son of Captain David Shillington, was commissioned in January 1915 and Second Lieutenant Ernest Ensor (brother of Charles Ensor) who had also joined as a soldier, was commissioned with Second Lieutenants Marc Lendrum and Samuel O'Neill in March 1915. Second Lieutenants Gilbert Barcroft, George Dickson and William Reid were all appointed in May 1915 along with Second Lieutenant Robert Montgomery, who had been the commandant of the Portadown Ulster Volunteer Force Medical Corps. In the same month Lieutenant Geoffrey Cather, the nephew of Captain David Shillington, joined the Battalion from England. It is worth noting that it was not only the soldiers who joined under age. Tom Shillington had left school early at sixteen and added two years to his age when he filled in his papers to enlist. He was commissioned aged seventeen. It is clear that he followed this path with the blessing of his father, Major Shillington, and the knowledge of Lieutenant Colonel Blacker, a close family friend.

The training of officers in the basics of military life and in their responsibilities was very important in the months after the New Armies were raised. Only a minority had received any significant military instruction and few had any practical experience of leading men in the conditions they would experience in France. Every effort was made in the Ulster Division to train the officers in their duties. Retired officers and officers with experience of the conditions in France and Belgium spoke at the camps where the new battalions were based. Captain Thomas Atkinson kept a diary, and his notes show what was taught. They cover the organisation of divisions, brigades and units and their headquarters, and the role of commanders and their staff. He wrote of how to conduct an 'appreciation' and then how to formulate a plan. The new language of trench warfare runs through the notes as he writes of machine guns, periscopes, loopholes and barbed wire entanglements, and the new technology of war—the aeroplane. He writes extensively about discipline—*'discipline is the thing everyone thought much of at the front'*—and he relates this to the conduct of men on the march, the relief of companies in the trenches, the occupation of billets and, most importantly, sanitation and the prevention of disease. This aspect of military life was one that came naturally to the men of the 9th Royal Irish Fusiliers; it became renowned in France for its cleanliness and the efforts made to improve the lot of the soldiers when out of the line.

Corporals of the 9th Royal Irish Fusiliers, October 1914.
In the centre of the second row is Colour Sergeant (soon to be Company Sergeant Major) F E Cross, and sitting on the front row at the extreme left is Corporal F D R Humphreys who was commissioned in June 1918. Corporal (later Sergeant) W Neill is fourth from the right in the third row.

The officers of the 9th Royal Irish Fusiliers at Newtownards 1915.

Back Row: Second Lieutenant R S Flood, Lieutenant J A Johnston, Lieutenant G E Lutton, Second Lieutenant J E Gibson, Second Lieutenant T G Shillington, Lieutenant A B Townsend.

Middle Row: Second Lieutenant J M Stronge, Lieutenant J G E FitzGerald, Lieutenant W J Menaul, Lieutenant C H Ensor, Second Lieutenant H K Jackson, Lieutenant L M Anderson, Second Lieutenant A D Allen, Second Lieutenant M B Lendrum, Lieutenant R S B Townsend, Second Lieutenant T F Given, Second Lieutenant E N Ensor, Honorary Lieutenant & Quartermaster A Ferguson DCM.

Front Row: Captain J G Brew, Captain D G Shillington, Captain T J Atkinson, Major A C Pratt, Lieutenant Colonel S W W Blacker, Lieutenant H W Seton, Colonel W C FitzGerald, Captain S J Scott, Captain C M Johnston, Lieutenant W S S Berry RAMC.

The 9th Royal Irish Fusiliers on parade at Newtownards in 1915.

The band is on the left of the photograph (with the Second-in-Command Major A C Pratt (white-faced horse) and Quartermaster in front). The companies paraded are 'A' to 'D', their officers in front. Lieutenant Colonel Blacker is on the white horse with the Adjutant, Captain Seton, to his right.

The 9th Royal Irish Fusiliers on parade at Newtownards in 1915.

After seven months of training it was time for the people of Ulster to see their division and a parade was planned for 8 May. The battalions and other divisional units, numbering nearly 17,000 men, marched to Belfast over a period of days. They were inspected at Malone by the well-respected officer and former MP for North Antrim, Major General Sir Hugh McCalmont KCB, CVO. Afterwards the Ulster Division marched through the city. Along the route the streets were decked out with bunting and flags and crowded with local people and the family and friends of those on parade. During the march-past at City Hall, which lasted for over one and a half hours, the salute was taken by the General alongside the Mayor. The parade was attended by Sir Edward Carson, who had travelled from London to see it. Although seen as a farewell, the Ulster Division remained in Ireland for two more months.

The review of 36th (Ulster) Division in Belfast, 8 May 1915.

The training culminated with a divisional deployment in the Antrim hills. It was around this time that Captain Atkinson's training notes record a lecture by the Commanding Officer and amongst the themes was Lieutenant Colonel Blacker's view of the *'Main Things of War'*. Firstly, discipline and the initiative and humour of the privates and junior non-commissioned officers, then, digging, shooting and bayonet work. All of these would be reflected in the training regime of the Battalion when out of the line in France over the next few years.

A Company in early 1915.

B Company in early 1915.

On 1 and 2 July the Ulster Division, waved off by emotional family and friends, embarked on trains at Belfast and travelled to Dublin, arriving at around 5.00pm. The units sailed at 9.00pm from Kingstown (now Dun Laoghaire) for Holyhead in Wales. Only the 9th Royal Inniskilling Fusiliers remained in Ireland, quarantined due to an outbreak of measles. More rail journeys followed through Wales and England to Seaford on the Sussex coast near Brighton, where the Ulster Division would complete its training.

On Seaford Down the men of the Ulster Division were divided between two camps of well-made huts overlooking the sea. South Camp, about one mile from the town, was shared by the men of 9th Royal Irish Fusiliers and 16th Royal Irish Rifles, the pioneer battalion. They soon made an impression on the community of this previously quiet seaside town and were praised for their discipline and faultless behaviour. The people of the town also welcomed into their homes many of the families of the men who travelled from Ireland.

9th Royal Irish Fusiliers Signallers at Seaford. Seated in the centre is the Battalion Signals Officer, Second Lieutenant G E Lutton.

In England the association of the men of the Ulster Division with the Orange Order continued. The 9th Royal Irish Fusiliers renewed a travelling warrant for Loyal Orange Lodge 190 that had previously been used by men of the 3rd (Militia) Battalion in the South African War. For other units of the Ulster Division a number of military warrants were obtained from the Grand Orange Lodge of England, which allowed the establishment of new lodges. Meetings were held in Seaford until the units moved to France, where they continued until the cumulative impact of casualties largely forced their abandonment.[8]

The Ulster Division was inspected in the last week of July and deemed ready for deployment to France. Indeed, the inspecting officer recommended to Lord Kitchener that it was worthy of a higher place on his list of formations ready for the front. In turn, Lord Kitchener inspected the Ulster Division on 27 July. The parade was a grand affair in glorious weather. Alongside Lord Kitchener were a number of Chelsea pensioners and together they watched the Division march past. The cavalry led, followed by the engineers and then the infantry battalions with bayonets fixed and shining in the sun. Sir Edward Carson visited in August.

The Battalion had sustained a number of casualties during its training, and during the final period at Seaford two men died. Private Joseph Topley, a twenty-two-year-old from Tandragee, drowned while swimming in the nearby river on 18 August, and Lieutenant L M Anderson died of cerebral meningitis on 1 September in Seaford hospital. Private Topley was buried in Seaford following an impressive funeral service. It was said that during the Last Post *'you could have heard a pin drop'*. Lieutenant Anderson's family paid for the repatriation of his body and he is buried in Armagh.

Lieutenant L M Anderson

With the completion of musketry training at Martinique Barracks, Borden, in September, and the allocation of some missing equipment, the Ulster Division was now ready for France. However, in the leadership of the 9th Royal Irish Fusiliers, there was to be a major and untimely change. Regimental Sergeant Major Stilwell, who had served as the Battalion's senior soldier since its formation, was charged with drunkenness while the Battalion was training at Borden. He was tried there by a District Court Martial, found guilty and sentenced to be reduced in rank to Warrant Officer Class II. He was replaced as Regimental Sergeant Major by Thomas McKane, an ex-regular soldier from The Royal Warwickshire Regiment, who had joined the 9th Royal Irish Fusiliers in September 1914 and had been quickly appointed as a Company Sergeant Major.

Colonel W G Fitzgerald, Captain A B Townsend and Regimental Sergeant Major E G Tuck, 10th (Reserve) Battalion.

In Ireland, meanwhile, the depot companies had been formed into the 10th (Reserve) Battalion in June 1915. With its headquarters in Brownlow House, Lurgan, its job was to find and train volunteers destined for the 9th Royal Irish Fusiliers, until the spring of 1918 when it moved to England. It was commanded from its formation by Colonel W C FitzGerald and he was joined by Captain A B Townsend who became his Adjutant. Company Sergeant Major Edward Tuck of the 9th Royal Irish Fusiliers was a natural choice for Regimental Sergeant Major. Having been demoted, Albert Stilwell joined the Reserve Battalion as one of its Company Sergeant Majors.

This echoed one last and unexpected change at the top of the Ulster Division. It was under the leadership of Lieutenant General Sir George Richardson that the Ulster Volunteer Force had grown, and he contributed greatly to the successful formation of 36th (Ulster) Division. His age and seniority, however, ruled him out for its command and Major General C H Powell CB, who had a distinguished record in the Indian Army, had been appointed to command the Ulster Division in September 1914. It was through his efforts over most of the year since its formation that it was held in such high regard, and in early September 1915 he and his senior officers went to France to be attached to the 5th and 18th Divisions. It was only on his return that Major General Powell was informed that an officer with experience of France would succeed him. For his efforts he was made a Knight Commander of The Order of the Bath, but his treatment angered many. The new commander was Major General O S W Nugent DSO,[9] an officer who had recently commanded a brigade in France and whose qualities, performance and popularity would link him forever with the name of 36th (Ulster) Division.

The Ulster Division's advance party left England on 26 September and on 30 September the remainder was inspected by the King, who was obviously pleased by the high standard of everything he saw. His message, similar to that delivered to his other new Army Divisions, stated:

> *'Your prompt patriotic answer to the nation's call to arms will never be forgotten. The keen exertions of all ranks during the period of training have brought you to a stage of efficiency not unworthy of my Regular Army. I am confident that in the field you will nobly uphold the traditions of the fine Regiments whose names you bear. Ever since your enrolment I have closely watched the growth and steady progress of all units. I shall continue to follow with interest the fortunes of your Division. In bidding you farewell I pray God may bless you in all of your undertakings.'*

On Sunday 3 October the Battalion left Seaford by train for Southampton. Having spent the remainder of the day in Southampton dock, everyone embarked at 8.30pm onto a ship that was considered too small for the thirty-seven officers and 1,340 men (some of the Ulster Division's artillery was also embarked). Fortunately the sea was calm and the passage uneventful. By 5 October 1915 most of the Ulster Division was in France.

Endnotes, Chapter 1

[1] Sir Edward Carson MP. Born in Dublin 9 February 1854. Studied Law at Trinity College, Dublin. Called to the Bar in 1877. He was appointed Solicitor General of Ireland in 1892. In the same year he was appointed MP for Dublin University, a seat that he held for twenty-six years. He led the prosecution against Oscar Wilde. Knighted 1900. Appointed head of the Ulster Unionist Council at Craigavon on 23 November 1911. During the Great War he served in the coalition Government as Attorney General from May 1915 but resigned in October 1916. Appointed First Lord of the Admiralty by Lloyd George in December 1916. Moved to the War Cabinet July 1917. Elected MP for Duncairn in Belfast in the elections of December 1918. Resigned as MP and as leader of the Ulster Unionists in 1921. In May 1921 he was made Baron Carson Duncairn. Died in Kent 22 October 1935, aged 81. Buried at St Anne's Cathedral, Belfast.

[2] This was a shrewd idea of Carson's that aimed to focus the Unionist people of Ulster, particularly in Belfast, on peaceful protest. It was largely the work of James Craig, and was based on the

Scottish Covenant of 1580/1581 and its successor covenants. Men signed the Covenant while women signed the accompanying Declaration.

The Covenant.

Being convinced in our consciousness that Home Rule would be disastrous to the material well-being of Ulster as well as of the whole of Ireland, subversive of our civil and religious freedom, destructive of our citizenship and perilous to the unity of the Empire; we, whose names are underwritten, men of Ulster, loyal subjects of His Gracious Majesty King George V, humbly relying on the God who our fathers in days of stress and trial confidently trusted, do hereby pledge ourselves in solemn covenant throughout this our time of threatened calamity to stand by one another in defending for ourselves and our children our cherished position of equal citizenship in the United Kingdom and in using all means which may be found necessary to defeat the present conspiracy to set up a Home Rule Parliament in Ireland. And in the event of such a Parliament being forced upon us we further solemnly and mutually pledge ourselves to refuse to recognise its authority. In such confidence that God will defend the right we hereto subscribe our names. And further, we individually declare that we have not already signed this Covenant.

The Declaration.

We, whose names are underwritten, women of Ulster, and loyal subjects of our gracious King, being firmly persuaded that Home Rule would be disastrous to our Country, desire to associate ourselves with the men of Ulster in their uncompromising opposition to the Home Rule Bill now before Parliament, whereby it is proposed to drive Ulster out of her cherished place in the Constitution of the United Kingdom, and to place her under the domination and control of a Parliament in Ireland. Praying that from this calamity God will save Ireland, we hereto subscribe our names.

[3] Brigadier General Sir George William Hacket Pain KBE, CB, MP. Born 5 February 1855. Commissioned from the Militia into the 102nd Foot (Royal Madras Fusiliers) in 1875. Transferred that year to The Royal West Surrey Regiment. Attached to the Egyptian Army 1888-99. Served in Sudan 1888-91 during which time he had a horse shot from under him. Egypt Medal with clasp, Khedive's Star, 3rd Class Medijie. Major in The Worcestershire Regiment in 1894. Appointed to command the 9th Sudanese Battalion and took part in the Expedition to Dongola in 1896; had another horse shot. Mentioned in Despatches, Brevet Lieutenant Colonel, Queen's Sudan Medal, Khedive's Sudan Medal & 2 clasps. Order of Medjidieh 3rd Class, Order of Osmanieh 3rd Class. Nile Expedition 1897-8. Commanded 2nd Battalion, The Worcestershire Regiment in 1900 in the South Africa War. CB, Mentioned in Despatches, Queen's South Africa Medal with 3 clasps, King's South Africa Medal with 2 clasps. Brevet Colonel 1901. On half-pay from 1904-1907. Colonel in charge of infantry records 1907-11, also Commander Number 7 District, Southern Command. Retired in 1912. Temporary Brigadier General 1914 and Commander 108th Brigade until December 1915. 1914-15 Star. Mentioned in Despatches. Commander 15th (Ulster) Reserve Infantry Brigade, 1916. Commander Northern District Irish Command 1916–November 1919. KBE 1919. Divisional Commander Royal Irish Constabulary until the truce in 1921. MP (CU) South Londonderry from 1922. Died 14 February 1924, aged 69.

[4] Sir James Henry Stronge 5th Baronet. Born 8 December 1849. Eton, Oxford, Lincoln's Inn. Served 15 years in the 4th Battalion, The Royal Inniskilling Fusiliers (Tyrone Militia) retiring as an Honorary Major in 1885. High Sheriff of Tyrone (1880) and Armagh (1885), Secretary to the Ulster Defence Union (1894) and Chairman of Armagh District Council 1899-00. Grand Master of the Grand Orange Lodge of Ireland (1914). Died 1928. His son, Lieutenant James Matthew Stronge, was the Battalion's Transport Officer. See footnote Chapter 5 and Appendix 5.

[5] See Introduction for an explanation of the variations of the titles of the battalions of 36th (Ulster) Division.

[6] The battle patches for the other formations may be found in *British Battle Insignia (1) 1914–18* by Michael Chappell, who also produced a comprehensive illustration of the battle patches of 36th (Ulster) Division in *Military Illustrated* in August 1991.

[7] Captain John Leeper Dunlop MC, MB RAMC. Born in 1883 at Keady, County Armagh. MB—Queen's University, Belfast 1906. Practised at the Royal Victoria Infirmary, Belfast. Commissioned into the Royal Army Medical Corps 9 October 1914. To France with 36th (Ulster) Division October 1915 in 108th Field Ambulance. MC awarded for *'fine service rendered since coming to France, but especially by excellent work at Forceville 1 to 5 July 1916'*. Served also with 36th Indian Brigade in Mesopotamia. 1914-15 Star. His brother, Captain William Anketell Leeper Dunlop RAMC, also served during the war.

[8] The Grand Orange Lodge of England issued sixteen military warrants during the First World War; four to the Royal Navy, ten to the Army and two to the Canadian Expeditionary Force. Those issued to units of 36th (Ulster) Division were:

Number 862:	8th (Service) Battalion, The Royal Irish Rifles (East Belfast)
Number 863:	11th (Service) Battalion, The Royal Irish Rifles (South Antrim)
Number 864:	15th (Service) Battalion, The Royal Irish Rifles (North Belfast)
Number 865:	16th (Service) Battalion, The Royal Irish Rifles (2nd County Down) (Pioneers)
Number 868:	9th (Service) Battalion, The Royal Irish Rifles (West Belfast)
Number 869:	10th (Service) Battalion, The Royal Irish Rifles (South Belfast)
Number 870:	11th (Service) Battalion, The Royal Inniskilling Fusiliers (Donegal and Fermanagh)
Number 871:	14th (Service) Battalion, The Royal Irish Rifles (Young Citizens)
Number 882:	110th Field Ambulance

The warrants were returned to the Grand Orange Lodge of England at the end of the war.

[9] Major General Sir Oliver Stewart Wood Nugent KCB, DSO, JP, DL. Born 9 November 1860, educated at Harrow. Commissioned into The Royal Munster Fusiliers on 28 July 1882. Lieutenant King's Royal Rifle Corps 14 April 1883. Captain 15 October 1890. While serving in India he took part in the Hazara Expedition (India General Service Medal with clasp) and the Miranzai expedition in 1891 as Orderly Officer to the GOC. Mentioned in Despatches. Took part in the Isazai expedition in 1892. Served on operations in Chitral in 1895 including storming of Malakand Pun (slightly wounded) and the engagement at Khar. India Medal & clasp. Mentioned in Despatches and DSO *'in recognition of services during the recent operations in Chitral'*. Decorated by Queen Victoria 3 July 1896. Major 21 October 1899. Fought in the South Africa War taking part in operations in Natal 1899 including the action at Talana, where he was dangerously wounded. Mentioned in Despatches, Queen's South Africa Medal & 2 clasps. DAAG HQ Ireland 1901-October 1902. DAQMG 3 Army Corps 19 October 1902-December 1903. Lieutenant Colonel 15 October 1906. Brevet Colonel 23 June 1909. ADC to the King 23 June 1909-31 December 1915. Colonel 15 October 1910. Commander Hampshire Infantry Brigade, Southern Command January 1911-February 1914. Commander 41st Infantry Brigade, 14th (Light) Division 6 May 1915-16 September 1915. Commander 36th (Ulster) Division September 1915. CB 1917. Commander of the Meerut Division in India 3 August 1918, which he led in Afghanistan in 1919. Commander of the Order of St Maurice and St Lazarus (Italy). Retired 1920. KCB 1922. Deputy Lord Lieutenant for County Cavan. Died 31 May 1926, aged 65.

TWO

Arrival in France & Holding the Line at Hamel

While the Ulster Division was being raised and trained it had become evident that the war would not be over as soon as so many had hoped. The trench lines in France and Flanders were being dug deeper and fortified with timber and concrete. The front line trenches, protected by deep swathes of barbed wire and carefully sited machine guns, stretched without break along the whole of the western front from the Channel to the Swiss border. This resulted in a tactical problem that had not been faced by the generals on either side until then; the opportunity for exploiting a weakness and turning an enemy's flank no longer existed. The alternative—frontal attacks, preceded by heavy artillery barrages, across difficult ground and against protected machine guns—proved a costly tactic that rarely made any significant progress. Attempts to break the German line had been repulsed with great loss at Neuve Chappelle in March and at Loos in September.

The stalemate had resulted in the rapid generation of new tactics and equipment, both for attack and defence, in this new era of siege warfare. Trench construction will be dealt with later, but some equipment is worth examining now. Very many of the injuries sustained in the trenches were head wounds. The need to protect those working in the forward trenches or saps led to the issue of steel helmets in small numbers for the first time in the autumn of 1915, but they would not be on general issue until the spring of 1916. Hand grenades, or bombs, were seen by many as the ideal weapon for use in trench fighting. The demand for new bombs resulted in the development of various types of grenade. Many were made locally by the Royal Engineers and were reasonably effective when conditions for their use were perfect, but frequently caused casualties amongst the throwers. The Mills bomb, mass-produced, more efficient and safer, was not issued in large numbers until 1916.

The need to attack the enemy with explosives and shrapnel, particularly prior to an infantry assault or to protect from an enemy attack, led to the development and formulation of shells, fuses and artillery tactics, that were the forerunner of those used in the Second World War and, indeed, today. Throughout the war the Commonwealth gunners excelled in developing innovative tactics. The development of short-range 'artillery' was first seen in the German *minenwerfer* or trench mortar. The early British version, like the bomb, was said to cause more casualties amongst firers than the enemy. Again, it was not until the spring of 1916 that the very effective Stokes mortar made its appearance and revolutionised the indirect fire capability that could be called upon by relatively junior commanders.

All of this equipment and the associated tactics that needed to be taught and practised, resulted in schools being set up at Corps and Army level. They instructed battalion specialists on everything from sanitation and pest control to trench construction and wiring and the use of specialised troops such as snipers, Lewis-gunners and bombers.

One other development required specialised equipment and training—gas warfare. On the evening of 22 April 1915 near Langemarck, north-east of Ypres, the Germans discharged 168 tons of chlorine gas from almost 6,000 cylinders. The target was two French divisions and an adjacent Canadian division along a four-mile front at St Julian. The effect was horrific. The Allied troops were unprepared to face such an attack and one of the French divisions, made up of Algerian and Moroccan troops, fled, leaving an 800 yard gap in the line. Fortunately, the enemy did not exploit this success and the attacks and counter-attacks ground on for three days. By then the Allied troops had been issued with a simple mask of linen soaked in chemicals; and so began the development of gas warfare. Gas masks, or respirators, would continue to develop throughout the war, but the equipment of 1915 was crude at best.

Such was the general situation when the 9th Royal Irish Fusiliers disembarked at Le Havre on the morning of Monday 4 October 1915 with the other elements of 108th Brigade. The war diary reported that it now had a strength of 31 officers and 995 rank and file. This was not, however, the total number of men on the strength of the 9th Royal Irish Fusiliers and it is worth explaining the terminology used.

The strength of a battalion was determined from Army Form B213, the Field Return for Effective Strength of Unit, which was completed weekly. It allowed the make-up of the unit to be described in detail and calculations to be made about its strength. It firstly showed the 'Effective Strength of the Unit'. That was the number of men, animals and vehicles of that unit in the theatre of operations. It then showed the 'Details by Arms attached to Unit as in War Establishment'. These were the officers and men attached to the unit in accordance with its War Establishment to conduct specific functions. A good example is the medical officer and the Army Medical Corps soldiers that formed the regimental aid post and conducted sanitation duties. When added together this gave the 'total' or 'paper' strength. The form also showed the unit's 'War Establishment'—the numbers of men, vehicles and animals that it should have. Subtracting the 'Total' strength from the 'War Establishment' indicated the number of men, animals and vehicles 'Wanting to Complete', which allowed the staff to allocate reinforcements. Also on the form were described those who were attached, attached for rations only, casualties (killed in action, wounded, hospital admissions etc), reinforcements waiting to join, men detached on other duties, and so on. From these could be calculated the 'rationed' strength, which could generally be taken to mean the number of men in the divisional area under the command of the commanding officer. A common term in the Battalion's war diary but not included on Army Form B213 is the 'fighting' or 'trench' strength. This could be defined in a number of ways but was usually the number of men on duty in the trenches, and in support or reserve. It did not include men in the brigade and divisional rear areas, such as the Quartermaster's department or the Battalion Transport. It can be seen that, in general, a battalion's 'total' strength would be greater than its 'effective' strength, which would be greater than its 'ration' strength, which would be greater than its 'fighting' or 'trench' strength. The difference between 'total' strength and 'fighting' strength was often significant and, when calculated across the whole Army, was so large as to result in serious debate in the House of Commons about the appropriate allocation of military manpower. The difference between men 'transferred', 'posted' and 'detached/attached' is explained in Appendix 6.

The officers and principal warrant officers present when the 9th Royal Irish Fusiliers landed are shown below.[1]

Commanding Officer:	Lieutenant Colonel S W W Blacker
Second-in-Command:	Major A C Pratt
Adjutant:	Captain H W Seton

Signalling Officer:	Lieutenant G E Lutton
Machine-gun Officer:	Lieutenant J G E FitzGerald
Quartermaster:	Honorary Lieutenant A Ferguson DCM
Transport Officer:	Lieutenant J M Stronge
Medical Officer:	Lieutenant W S S Berry MB RAMC
Padre:	The Reverend F J Halahan AChD
A Company:	Captain C H Ensor (Officer Commanding), Lieutenant G E Barcroft (Second-in-Command), Second Lieutenant A D Allen (Battalion Range-finding Officer) and Second Lieutenant R T Montgomery
B Company:	Major T J Atkinson (Officer Commanding), Lieutenant W J Menaul (Second-in-Command and Battalion Intelligence & Sniping Officer), Second Lieutenant W F Reid and Second Lieutenant T G Shillington
C Company:	Captain S J Scott (Officer Commanding), Captain C M Johnston (Second-in-Command), Lieutenant J A Johnston and Second Lieutenant G C Dickson (Battalion Scout Officer)
D Company:	Captain D G Shillington (Officer Commanding), Captain J G Brew (Second-in-Command), Lieutenant J E Gibson, Second Lieutenant T F Given and Second Lieutenant H K Jackson
Company unknown:	Second Lieutenant G St G S Cather, Second Lieutenant E N Ensor (Lewis Gun Officer), Lieutenant R S Flood (Battalion Bombing Officer), Second Lieutenant M B Lendrum and Second Lieutenant S O'Neill
Regimental Sergeant Major:	Warrant Officer Class 1 T McKane
Regimental Quartermaster Sergeant:	Warrant Officer Class 2 G W Wilson

Having spent that first day and most of the next in a camp near Flesselles, where the Ulster Division was concentrated, the 9th Royal Irish Fusiliers entrained for the beginning of their move forward to the front. The men were crammed forty or so to a wagon (which were all marked '40 men or 8 horses') in a single train of forty-six wagons and, after an uncomfortable twelve hours, they detrained at 5.30am at Longeau in the southern suburbs of Amiens. Along the way, as the train slowed or stopped, the local people were welcoming and cheerful. Henry Fox, by now a Sergeant, remembered clearly how they sold the local sweet jam to the men as they got off the train at Amiens. The first of many long marches followed with a move of fifteen kilometres through the town to billets in Rainneville. This little village was unable to cope with the demands placed upon it. The majority of the barns, which were shared with 13th Royal Irish Rifles, were dirty and in a state of disrepair, and the water supply was very limited. However, the weather was ideal and for the next three days the 9th Royal Irish Fusiliers trained at company and battalion level, including shooting on an improvised range. This culminated in an inspection on 9 October by General Sir Charles Munro KCB commanding 3rd Army, who thought highly enough of the Battalion to speak of the *'high appreciation which (he) was pleased to express . . . in the appearance, carriage and particularly the steadiness of the men on parade'*.

The next morning, a week after landing, a church service was held, an event that was to be practised as often as possible in the next three years when not engaged in the line. Officiating was the padre, Captain The Reverend F J Halahan, well known to many as the rector of Drumcree parish church, who had joined the Battalion in England at the end of September. Reverend Halahan would contribute much to the Battalion and the Ulster Division over the next few years. That day the Battalion also received its first fresh meat ration and bread. Both (along with potatoes) were considered essential staples. Sunday lunch for the officers included a chicken, given in thanks by a grateful mother whose daughter was operated on by the Medical Officer, Captain Berry.

Training began in earnest the following week with a brigade concentration march on Monday, followed on Tuesday by a battalion field exercise—an attack on an entrenched position—and gas training that afternoon conducted by an officer from GHQ, with everyone passing through a room filled with chlorine gas. The war diary noted that this proved the efficiency of the gas helmets but discoloured the men's tunic buttons. Later that day the 13th Royal Irish Rifles left for St Gratien, and the 9th Royal Irish Fusiliers was billeted over the whole village. Wednesday saw the Battalion engaged in musketry and bombing, with a brigade field exercise the next day, an attack on a position that was unfortunately impeded by fog.

After a final day of company-level training, the Battalion took part in its first divisional field exercise in France when 108th Brigade fought 109th Brigade in an encounter battle—an event that the situation in the line over the next few years would preclude from being conducted for real until 1918. The exercise was not a great success and Major General Nugent was very critical of the standard of training of the men and the conduct of the officers. His stern words had a significant effect, but he remained worried that the Division would not be ready for action when the time came for its committal into the line. 107th Brigade was singled out for particular criticism, and Nugent removed from command the Brigade Commander and, later, the Commanding Officer of 15th Royal Irish Rifles.

On 11 October one of the platoon commanders, Second Lieutenant Geoffrey Cather, the nephew of Major David Shillington and cousin of Second Lieutenant Tom Shillington, celebrated his 25th birthday. The mail service was extremely efficient and many thousands of letters and parcels were delivered every month to men at the front; it took only three days for mail to arrive from Ireland. In reply to his aunts, who had sent some money as a gift, and written to congratulate him, Cather wrote:

> *'My very dear Aunts*
>
> *I can tell you very little of course – practically nothing about myself, except that I am well, busy and comfortable, but I want to thank you as well as I can – which is but poor return for all your kindness.*
>
> *Many thanks for your offers of help. We have done quite well so far – with our boxes from the stores, our rations received here, and the local supplies. There is an institution called the "Expeditionary Forces Canteen" which is useful, as it supplies all kinds of English tinned and other goods. Unfortunately the nearest branch is some distance from our present billets, but we may be nearer one later on.*
>
> *The things I find most difficult in getting at the moment are Quaker Oats, bacon, a good cake and biscuits. I can get all of these from the stores of*

course and am ordering a larger supply in my next consignment, but if you could send us out a little cake I should be glad of it – provided you allow me to pay for it.

We have been manning billets lately – though we have not left the village. There was another battalion in here besides ourselves – and they were moved out as the medical authorities said we were all overcrowded – which we certainly were. Now we have spread out a bit and are more comfortable.

The men of course are in barns and outhouses of all kinds – some of them not too watertight – but the weather has been good so far – they are mostly quite happy and content.

Tom Shillington and I share a room in a farm house, while Madame is most gracious and does all she can for us.

The people are wonderfully friendly and don't seem to resent the wholesale invasion of their homes and control of their lives by a lot of foreigners, at all. When I tell you that no civilian is allowed out of his house after 9 pm without a pass from our Colonel it will give you an idea of the sort of thing they have to put up with.

Lieutenant G St G S Cather

The country round here is very picturesque – great rolling uplands – well cultivated and dotted about with small woods. There are villages every mile or so – consisting of a group of farm houses (there are no farmsteads outside the villages), a few wine shops and a church. Everything is very primitive of course. The villagers draw their water from very deep wells in the villages but there seems to be no springs – only a surface drainage – with the added demand of the soldiers most of the wells are running dry, and the question of water supply is becoming a difficult one. However, the problem is being solved by carting water for the troops.'

On Sunday 17 October the Battalion left Rainneville and marched eight kilometres to new billets at Puchevillers, once more shared with 13th Royal Irish Rifles. The next morning it moved on, this time fifteen kilometres to a tented camp in the park of the chateau at Couin, and reached its final destination, Hebuterne, in glorious weather the following day.

Since the Battle of Loos, when after a long march inexperienced troops had been committed into fierce fighting with terrible results, New Army units underwent training with more experienced formations. The 9th Royal Irish Fusiliers was now attached to 144th Brigade, part of 48th (South Midland) Division—a Territorial Force formation comprising 1/4th and 1/6th Battalions, The Gloucestershire Regiment and 1/7th and 1/8th Battalions, The Worcestershire Regiment. To these battalions were attached A to D Companies respectively, with battalion headquarters attached to 1/4th Gloucesters. The Royal Irish Fusiliers' first experience of the line came quickly. On Thursday 21 October two platoons from each company took over sections of the trenches to receive instruction in the practicalities of trench warfare. The trenches here were particularly well maintained and it was commented that the trenches and dugouts were more comfortable than the billets in Hebuterne. Those in the line in 1/7th Worcesters' area soon had their first experience of shelling, but no casualties were suffered. At 7.00pm that evening the members of the Royal Irish Fusiliers on patrol had their first contact with the enemy.

Patrols were a regular feature of life in the trenches. They were normally commanded by a junior officer and he would normally be accompanied by up to four or six men, although larger, aggressive patrols or patrols by officers alone, or accompanied by only one non-commissioned officer, were common. The most important aim was to dominate no-man's-land, the unoccupied stretch of ground between the opposing trenches. The look and feel of this area changed from sector to sector but it was characterised by the devastation wrought by months, and later years, of artillery bombardment. Pockmarked by craters, littered with the debris of war, often scattered with the bodies of those who had fallen in previous attacks, and cut by thick rows of barbed wire, no-man's-land was not an easy place to patrol. Flares put up in reaction to noise were the signal for machine guns to rake the ground, forcing those on patrol to take cover wherever they could. Although patrolling was a risky business, gathering information on the enemy's defences, identifying units in the line and capturing prisoners to aid in this identification were important tasks, and some took to it readily.

On this first night in the line a joint patrol was sent out. It was led by a subaltern from 1/6th Gloucesters, Second Lieutenant H P Nott,[2] accompanied by Second Lieutenant Tom Shillington, with seven non-commissioned officers and men from the Gloucesters, and seven non-commissioned officers and men from the 9th Royal Irish Fusiliers. The patrol left a forward sap at 7.15pm and moved across no-man's-land to a point about 200 yards out from their own trenches. Here they lay-up in a 'horseshoe' awaiting any German patrols. An hour later at 8.30pm an enemy patrol some thirty men strong was seen advancing towards them in extended line. When they were only ten yards away the enemy patrol copied their opponents and lay down, waiting for a British patrol to show up. Nott decided to attack. Three Number 6 bombs (ignited by pulling a loop at the top of the grenade) failed to light and he ordered rapid fire. The enemy threw two bombs that exploded harmlessly and Nott conducted a fighting withdrawal to a position about thirty yards away, and sent back for more bombs. When the German patrol was reinforced, Nott and Shillington were in danger of being cut off and were ordered to retire. Covering machine guns opened fire and the joint Gloucesters/Royal Irish Fusiliers patrol returned to its lines having taken no casualties and bringing in the body of a soldier from *8. Badisches Infanterie-Regiment Nr. 169.*

Second Lieutenant T G Shillington

The next day the forward platoons were relieved by the other two platoons from each company, and early on the morning of Sunday 23 October the Battalion suffered its first casualty when Private T G Wilson of C Company was wounded in the arm by a machine gun while out with a wiring party. That afternoon the training of the Battalion progressed a stage further when, accompanied by a heavy barrage against the German positions in Gommecourt Wood between 200 and 700 yards away, each company moved into the line to relieve a company of the battalion to which it was attached. After a peaceful twenty-four hours, the 9th Royal Irish Fusiliers moved out of the line and marched back to Couin in bad weather. The only upturn was baths for everyone at Sailly on the way through.

Following this attachment, the commander of 144th Brigade commented favourably on the Royal Irish Fusiliers but noticed that there had been insufficient training with bombs. His criticism was probably a direct result of Second Lieutenant Shillington's patrol, but the use of bombs was an increasingly popular tactic that required good training in order to be effective. In addition, Major General Fanshawe, commanding 48th Division, stated that he had seen the 9th Royal Irish Fusiliers in the trenches and on the march away, and commented that it seemed to be well-trained, well-commanded and disciplined. He obviously had an eye for detail because he criticised the way in which packs were worn by some men and that wagon-men should walk behind the wagons, where they could use the brake, rather than sitting beside the driver. He did comment, however, that the 9th Royal Irish Fusiliers was the best of the New Army battalions that he had seen.

Near the end of that week the Battalion marched sixteen kilometres to billets at Beauval, and the next day marched on to Ribeaucourt. There the Battalion was split between three villages, Ribeaucourt, Domesmont and Lanches, all separated by about 1½ kilometres, and the 9th Royal Irish Fusiliers took over the best billets that they had seen so far in France. The Ulster Division was concentrated in this area with Headquarters 108th Brigade in Ribeaucourt and Headquarters 36th Division in Domart, four kilometres away. Lieutenant Cather wrote home again at the end of October and his letter reflects the general attitude and morale of the Battalion:

> *'My dear Aunt Harriet*
>
> *I am afraid my letter writing has been sadly neglected lately, as it is next door to impossible to find time to write. I have just had another set of duties tacked onto my former ones – as I have been made Assistant Adjutant – which means I am "understudying" the Adjutant. I work in the Battalion's Orderly room in the mornings – when the Battalion is not out in the field – and then carry on with my platoon in the afternoon. With this and running the Mess I am fairly busy! Which is a good thing.*
>
> *Still I want to send you my love and very best wishes for November 5th, which I hope will be a very happy day.*
>
> *I cannot give you much news about our doings of course.*
>
> *We came out of the trenches nearly a week ago – and marched some distance back from the line. We are now settled in billets in a small village where we are resuming our training until required in the firing line again. We are all wonderfully well and the men are in good spirits in spite of the spell of wet weather we have had lately, and which does not add to the comforts of life in the field.*
>
> *Please thank Aunt Miggen for sending on the papers and for shopping for me. I have very little time to read, but get a glance at the papers occasionally. You have asked several times if there is anything the men need so I am giving below a short list of the things they seem to want at the moment. If anyone is asking about sending things out it may be useful:*
>
> *candles* *gloves or mittens*

matches	*socks*
Dubbin for boots	*bootlaces*
chocolate	*knives*
plug tobacco	*forks and spoons*
Woodbine cigarettes	

I must stop now and turn in as I have to be up early in the morning.'

Training continued apace in the first part of November in increasingly wet weather during which the priorities for the companies were bombing, sniping, musketry and bayonet fighting. Early in the month the 9th Royal Irish Fusiliers took part in a divisional exercise which involved a two-brigade attack against a rearguard, the aim being to co-ordinate the attack of the two brigades so that their attacks were simultaneous. The enemy comprised the Service Squadron, 6th (Inniskilling) Dragoons and 36th Divisional Cyclist Company reinforced with one company from the 9th Royal Irish Fusiliers. 107th and 108th Brigades attacked from the south and east respectively and, notwithstanding the awful weather, the exercise was a success. At the end of that week the Battalion was in the field again on a brigade exercise—an attack ending in entrenching on the ground won—and the next day the 9th Royal Irish Fusiliers conducted an attack on a wood. Sunday saw some respite with a church service and an opportunity for everyone to bathe and wash their clothes.

When training began again the battalion field exercises and company training were repeated, including a shooting practice involving each company stopping an attack and using trench fire control procedures, during which each man fired ten rounds with bayonets fixed at head and shoulders targets. After church service the following Sunday, Second Lieutenant W F Reid left for the base depot at Number 19 Camp near Le Havre where he would command and exercise the Battalion's new details. That afternoon new boots arrived for the men and they were issued immediately, an event that was well received. Two hundred pairs of long, trench gum-boots were also delivered; these were put aside to be issued by the quartermaster later in the month with the trench stores. The one item that the men were regularly short of was socks. This (and the need for gloves and mittens) was a common theme in many of Lieutenant Colonel Blacker's letters home, and many pairs were knitted by the women of County Armagh and sent out in bulk as a consequence.

On Monday 15 November the Battalion finally began its move forward to the line. The first march was of twenty-nine kilometres to Puchevillers. Snow had fallen the night before and it made movement for the wagons and mules of the Transport very difficult, particularly where it had frozen hard. The new boots also had a severe effect, making this a tough march. The next day, with the road still heavy with snow, two companies marched to Mailly-Maillet and the remainder to Colincamps, both a distance of twenty kilometres. The 9th Royal Irish Fusiliers was now attached to a regular formation, 10th Brigade of the 4th Division. The Battalion remained in moderately good billets until Thursday evening when it received orders to relieve the 7th (Service) Battalion, Princess Louise's (Argyll and Sutherland Highlanders), a Territorial Force unit on the right of the sector occupied by 10th Brigade. That night it marched to the trenches opposite Beaumont Hamel, north of Albert on the River Ancre. In this stint in the line C and D Companies occupied the first and second line trenches, A Company was the Battalion reserve and B Company was the Brigade reserve, the latter two companies being in Auchonvillers, 800 yards to the west of the second line trenches. On either flank were two regular Irish battalions—the 2nd Battalion, The Royal Irish Regiment on the right and the 2nd Battalion,

The Royal Dublin Fusiliers on the left, the latter of which was hosting a company from 8th Royal Irish Rifles from 107th Brigade.

By now the majority of trenches occupied by the British were dug in a standard pattern. They followed, generally, the best piece of ground from which the enemy could be dominated, or which provided the best cover if the enemy held the high ground. To protect its occupants from shell and machine-gun fire, particularly from a flank, the trenches were dug in short stretches linked by bays, or traverses, which extended forward. To provide sufficient cover it was recommended that they were dug to a depth of over eight feet, although this was not always possible. In the deeper trenches a fire-step was built to allow observation and fire forward in the event of an attack. Strength was given, where possible, by revetting, using corrugated iron sheets, pickets and timber, and the larger dug-outs were reinforced in the same way.

There was little shelter for the men on duty in the line. Some trenches had small dug-outs scraped in the forward wall, that provided a degree of cover from shrapnel, ricochet and the elements. At the top of the front wall of the trench was a parapet, reinforced with sandbags, and to the rear a higher parados. When possible, company headquarters were located in the larger dug-outs, and battalion headquarters was often in the cellars of a farmhouse or building farther back. The front and reserve trenches were linked by communication trenches which were much smaller, both narrower and shallower, but they provided a degree of cover for those moving forward or rearward. In front of the trenches in many sectors were outposts manned by a few men who provided a forward guard in reinforced shell-holes or small trenches. As the war progressed, the trench systems in many sectors became more complex and sophisticated using narrow-gauge railways and extensive telephone communications, but in other areas they comprised little more than deepened ditches or linked shell holes and raised parapets. Enemy snipers and machine guns covered the parapets making movement difficult, and in many areas it was only the coming of darkness that allowed food to be brought up and casualties moved rearward in relative safety.

Where possible, latrines were dug in bays off the communication trenches but in the badly prepared trenches or reinforced shell holes conditions were often squalid. Dirty trenches and filthy men were a breeding ground for pests and disease. Rats infested many areas and no one was immune to lice or 'chats'. Trench fever, virulent colds and flu, scabies, impetigo, pneumonia, bronchitis and a range of other debilitating diseases caused many casualties. Often worse than the German infantry and artillery, the most hated enemy was the weather, which made the life for those at the front a misery. Rain and snow caused many of the trenches to fill with mud and water and broke down the walls that were not reinforced or that had been weakened by shelters scraped under the parapet. Heating was non-existent for all but a few lucky enough to have a brazier and fuel in a dug-out, where there then developed the threat of carbon monoxide poisoning. The heavy frosts and icy storms made rest impossible in the heart of winter when frost bite, chilblains and 'trench foot' were common.

At Beaumont Hamel, the 9th Royal Irish Fusiliers was in the best part of the line. The trenches were wet and muddy, however, and in much need of repair owing to their being badly built, and also due to the combined effect of the winter weather and German artillery. Additionally the dug-outs were in generally poor condition; some were described by Lieutenant Colonel Blacker as *'crowded hovels'*. The first night in the line was freezing cold but the forward companies worked hard to repair their parapets, continuing the next day with work on the fire platforms, traverses and communication trenches. The enemy was very close and generally inactive (German working parties having been dispersed by machine gun fire), but on 20 November the enemy artillery replied to British salvoes with twelve rounds on the Battalion's trenches. No major damage was caused. Later that day the 1st Royal Irish Fusiliers relieved the Royal Dublin Fusiliers. The two battalions welcomed this opportunity to be neighbours in the line for the first time—a partnership that was to be repeated with great effect later in the war after the 1st Battalion joined 108th Brigade.

The repair of the trenches was going well. The barbed wire that provided protection in front of the trenches was replaced at night, and the wiring parties were protected by patrols, although the enemy put up flares and swept the area with machine-gun fire. The poor weather allowed the first German probe against the Battalion's position on 22 November when an enemy patrol under cover of fog attempted to bomb a sap head dug forward from the main trench. Unfortunately for them the fog lifted briefly and the sentries engaged the patrol with rifle fire forcing it to retire and causing at least one casualty. The next evening the Battalion was relieved by 9th Royal Irish Rifles from 107th Brigade and marched back to the billets it had left earlier in the month. No casualties were suffered during this period in the line. The companies managed hot baths at Mailly-Maillet the next day and at 9.30am on 26 November began a long march over three days via Puchevillers and Ribeaucourt to billets at Belancourt, six kilometres east of Abbeville.

The remainder of November and all of December were to be spent here. The weather over the next few weeks was mixed, being generally fine but foggy during the day and freezing cold at night. In response, fur coats were issued, with a second blanket per man arriving two nights later on the last day of the month. Letters home from everyone detailed the bad weather, poor conditions in the trenches and the effect on the men. Those from Lieutenant Colonel Blacker in particular continued to prompt women in parishes across County Armagh to produce mittens, socks and jumpers. Training continued when the weather allowed. Trenches were dug for bombing practice and the Battalion began to be used for the first time for large work parties, primarily on digging tasks and in preparing the billets, horse lines and the general area for the large numbers of troops expected in the spring prior to the next major offensive. Work parties, often numbering the majority of the available men in the Battalion, were a regular feature of life when out of the line. The work was often backbreaking and it was rare that the troops returning to the line were in any way rested.

On Sunday 5 December, after church service, the Battalion was paid a final visit by Brigadier G W Hacket-Pain CB, who had relinquished command of the Brigade to Brigadier C R J Griffith CMG, DSO.[3] The Battalion in turn said farewell to one of its own the next day. Captain H W Seton of the 1/9th Battalion, Gurkha Rifles had been attached since the earliest days as Adjutant. He was ordered back to his battalion and his good work was the subject of a special order of the day by Lieutenant Colonel Blacker. In the event, Captain Seton became the Adjutant of the 20th (Reserve) Battalion, The Royal Irish Rifles, where Lieutenant Colonel Blacker and Major D G Shillington would join him the next year. His replacement as Adjutant was his understudy, Lieutenant Geoffrey Cather. Knowing that the billets at Belancourt would be occupied for some time, much effort was made to ease the lot of the companies. Ablution blocks were built and the Battalion bathing programme was now co-ordinated centrally rather than at company level; by December every man was getting a bath every week. The Commanding Officer and Adjutant attended a meeting at brigade headquarters to gain permission to turn barns into company dining and recreation halls. Reading-material, newspapers and books were sent out from Ireland in large numbers. Sergeants' messes were established at company level and a coffee shop, run by Belgians, was opened. The latter was opposed by the village's café owners but many of the men did not drink alcohol and the cafes offered nothing else. This attempt to increase the standard of accommodation for the soldiers and to maintain the highest standards of cleanliness and hygiene was to be repeated often as the Battalion moved across the front, and it developed a reputation for neatness and cleanliness in billets and in the line. Over this period the weather got steadily worse, and everyone found it difficult to keep dry.

This brass button stick was made out of a shell case and was used to protect uniforms from metal polish when shining buttons. It belonged to Private Sandy Farson.

Training remained a most important aspect of battalion life and much emphasis was placed on effective shooting. The general standard of marksmanship in the New Army units was generally much poorer than that demonstrated by the regular soldiers. The difficulties of shooting wearing gas masks and with bayonets fixed can be illustrated by the results achieved by the companies on two shoots in December. On the first the men fired five rounds at a head and shoulders target at 100 yards while wearing gas masks. The results were consistent but poor—A Company scored 20 hits from 106 firers, B Company scored 27 hits from 107 firers, C Company 39 hits from 125 firers and D Company 35 hits from 147 firers—a hit rate of about five percent on average. Later in the month the companies fired at head and shoulders targets at 200 yards. Five rounds were fired in thirty-five seconds with the firers starting 'at ease', and five more rounds at a deliberate rate but with bayonets fixed. Again the results were consistent—a hit rate of about twelve and a half percent. This was a result that would have shocked the pre-war regular soldier who fired routinely, and accurately, out to 1,000 yards. It was, however, a characteristic of the majority of the New Army soldiers, most of whom had not had the opportunity to fire sufficiently often or receive the level of instruction required to achieve better results.

Each week a company, battalion and brigade class was instructed in bombing, and one officer from each company and one NCO per platoon conducted weekly courses in engineering with the Royal Engineers, who were billeted in Monflieres. However, most training had been cancelled due to the inclement weather and the final exercise before Christmas was a route march to practise a change of station. Left behind were two non-commissioned officers and six men in charge of the surplus baggage and evacuating the sick. During the march the Battalion was inspected by the new Brigade Commander, while the Brigade Staff Captain inspected the billets.

Christmas provided everyone with a welcome break. Much preparation had been made for Christmas Day. Suitable stables and barns were identified in which to have Christmas lunch, and the men foraged far and wide for holly and mistletoe for decoration. The day began with a church service and Holy Communion at 10.30am, and at 1.00pm everyone sat down to a hearty lunch of turkey, goose, ham, plum puddings, plum cakes, oranges, apples, tobacco and cigarettes. The Regimental Institute and the officers provided the meat, with the remainder coming from the Irish Women's Association, the Daily News and the Overseas Club. In the afternoon A and B Companies played C and D companies at football and in the evening there was a battalion 'smoker' and concert. Major Pratt, the Second-in-Command, commented that it was *"a very happy Christmas"*.

Boxing day was spent quietly with a church service in the morning, but on 27 December the Christmas fare was worked off with a route march. The following day the Battalion was inspected by Major General Nugent who expressed his satisfaction at the cleanliness of the billets, the good arrangements for sanitation and for the general comfort provided for the men. He was particularly complimentary of the bathhouse and laundry and the smart turnout of the men, horses, mules and wagons that made up the Transport.

New Year 1916 was heralded by the band led by the Chaplain, the Reverend F J Halahan, playing Auld Lang Syne, Le Marseillaise, Barossa (one of the regimental songs) and God Save The King. However, the New Year provided no opportunity for respite and the companies were employed on fatigues, although A Company managed a turn in the bath house and a football team was put together to play 13th Royal Irish Rifles which resulted in a 1-1 draw. The Battalion football team was to become a force to be reckoned with over the next three years and it would rarely be defeated in the many matches played when the 9th Royal Irish Fusiliers was out of the line: see Appendix 9.

Captain S J Scott

On 2 January the Medical Officer, Captain Berry, went home on leave. His duties were taken on by Captain Samuel Scott. A doctor by profession, Captain Scott was commissioned into Princess Victoria's (Royal Irish Fusiliers) on the formation of the Battalion and he was in command of C Company. His pending transfer to the Royal Army Medical Corps took effect from 11 January and when Captain Berry returned from leave on 19 January he joined 108th Field Ambulance, where he spent the rest of the war.

Training continued with a battalion route march over seventeen kilometres on Monday 3 January. For the rest of the week training was conducted by companies, and the officers attended lectures in the officers' mess, by those who had undertaken classes and demonstrations. By Saturday the Battalion was ready to move and with the rest of 108th Brigade it marched to new billets in Prouville (about halfway between Abbeville and Doulens.

The card sent home by Private John Atwell
at Christmas 1915.
The embroidery clearly shows the symbology used by the men of 36th (Ulster) Division.

The card sent home by Sergeant Henry Fox
at Christmas 1915.
The embroidered flags show the Allies at that time: Great Britain, France, Italy and Serbia.

The next few days were spent in an attempt to recreate the comforts left at Bellancourt, with a bath house, laundry and company ablutions and latrines being prepared and built. The remainder of 108th Brigade was nearby with the brigade headquarters and 12th Royal Irish Rifles in Ribeaucourt, 11th Royal Irish Rifles at Bernaville and 13th Royal Irish Rifles at Beaumetz. It was here that an unusual and amusing treat arrived in the form of 1,000 handkerchiefs from Queen Alexandria's Field Force Fund and, more welcome, 9,600 cigarettes courtesy Messrs Vickers and Sons, and 6,000 cigarettes sent by the Armagh Guardian newspaper. After this break, training began again in earnest on 17 January with trenches being dug for bombing practice and most companies involved in some form of musketry.

Officer training was essential due to the lack of experience of the temporary officers of the New Armies but the quality of such training depended on the quality and style of the brigade and battalion commanders. The ethos emphasised by GHQ was one that focused on offensive tactics; regular training in planning attacks was encouraged. The officers of the Brigade had their opportunity to consider this in an exercise the following week under the eye of the Brigade Commander: a very useful exercise but one that very few of those present that day would practise for real.

That Sunday the Battalion attended a brigade church service at which the Lord Primate of All Ireland preached, although apparently not well. As part of his tour of the Division he visited the Battalion a few days later, accompanied by Sir James Stronge Bt, when they watched the training, including a bombing practice and, according to the war diary, *'addressed some stirring words to the troops'*.

Over the next few days field training again took priority with an interesting exercise aimed at testing the procedures for escorting a convoy. The convoy comprised 12th Royal Irish Rifles, a half squadron of cavalry and half a company of cyclists under the Commanding Officer of 12th Royal Irish Rifles, Lieutenant Colonel G Bull[4]. The attacking force comprised 9th Royal Irish Fusiliers, the other halves of the cavalry squadron and the Cyclists, under the command of Lieutenant Colonel Blacker; the convoy failed to get through. This field training was not popular. As Lieutenant Colonel Blacker put it: *'. . . an awful nuisance. They don't teach us anything that will be useful to us . . .'*

On 26 January the machine gun sections of each battalion in the Brigade were formed into the Brigade Machine Gun Company. To this new unit the 9th Royal Irish Fusiliers provided Lieutenant J G E FitzGerald, Second Lieutenant M B Lendrum, Sergeant W J Brown who became the Company Sergeant Major, Sergeant W Warren and thirty-two other ranks[5]. The other battalions in the Brigade contributed similar numbers. The centralised control of machine guns was felt to be the best way to make maximum use of the firepower that they provided, and the Vickers machine guns in all of the infantry battalions were lost to the brigade companies. They were replaced, however, with four Lewis guns per battalion. The Lewis gun was developed from an American design and fired the standard .303 inch service ammunition. It was handled in a section, which carried the gun's pan magazines and up to 2,000 rounds of ammunition, and was commanded by a junior non-commissioned officer. The weapon was seen by many as an automatic rifle rather than a true replacement for the Vickers, but its mobility and reliability soon convinced the sceptics. A year later the Battalion had four per company. As for those who left the Battalion, Lieutenant FitzGerald served with 108th Brigade Machine Gun Company and then 36th Battalion, Machine Gun Corps, ending the war as a major having earned a Military Cross. Second Lieutenant Lendrum was wounded on

1 July 1916, subsequently joined the Tank Corps, with which he served in North Russia, and ended the war as a captain. Company Sergeant Major Brown, Corporal David Orr, Privates John Courtney and Robert McIlrath were killed in action on 1 July 1916. Private William Uprichard was killed on 14 July 1916 and Lance Corporal Howard Walker and Privates James Christie, James Clow, Richard Fulton and John Woods were killed later in the war. Sergeant James Fitzsimons and Corporal Frank Trueman earned Military Medals, and Sergeant Joseph Murphy was mentioned in despatches.

Lieutenant J G E FitzGerald

With the exception of a divisional tactical exercise near Bernaville, the 9th Royal Irish Fusiliers was engaged in company-level training until the end of the month, when the Battalion was visited by the Corps Commander, The Earl of Cavan. Then, for the first time since its arrival in France, 36th (Ulster) Division was ordered to take over a portion of the line between the area south of the Mailly-Maillet/Serre Road and the River Ancre.

Second Lieutenant M B Lendrum

Sergeant William Warren, who joined 108th Brigade Machine Gun Company in January 1916.

It was usual for inexperienced divisions to be amalgamated with an experienced division and for at least one experienced brigade to move into the line with it on its first deployment. 107th Brigade had been attached temporarily to 4th Division since early November, having exchanged with 12th Brigade, chosen over the others due to its earlier failures. Major

General Nugent requested that his Division was reconstituted as a whole and 107th Brigade soon rejoined it. It is of note that the Ulster Division became the first New Army formation to be committed to the line intact on its first deployment. Now part of XVII Corps, the Ulster Division took over its sector of the line during the first week of February with 107th Brigade on the left, 108th Brigade on the right and 109th Brigade in reserve. The 9th Royal Irish Fusiliers was ordered to move to Longuevillette, a march of about eight kilometres, and on Tuesday 1 February they received orders to move up to the line. This was the first significant deployment for the Battalion; everything had been in preparation for this moment and, unbeknown to everyone, this move would put the Battalion in place for the build-up to the summer offensive along the Somme.

The move forward was assisted by the provision of ten wagons from the Divisional Artillery Column commanded by Lieutenant Pitt. It began on Wednesday morning with a march of fifteen kilometres to good billets at Halloy-les-Pernoise, and the next day everyone marched sixteen kilometres to Puchevillers. From there Lieutenant Colonel Blacker, Lieutenant Cather and two company commanders went by motor vehicle to Martinsart and walked to the trenches at Hamel to make arrangements for the Battalion's move into the line. They returned to Puchevillers that night and the Battalion began its final move to the front the next day. On Friday afternoon D Company marched to Mesnil to relieve a company of The East Lancashire Regiment, and the remainder of the Battalion joined it on Saturday on garrison duties until relieved by the 13th Royal Irish Rifles. This allowed the 9th Royal Irish Fusiliers to take over the trenches near Hamel from the 1st Battalion, The Hampshire Regiment. On the 9th Royal Irish Fusiliers' right was the 16th Battalion, The Lancashire Fusiliers (2nd Salford) of 96th Brigade, 32nd Division, and on the left the 13th Royal Irish Rifles. It is worth describing the ground in this area in some detail as it features greatly in the life of the 9th Royal Irish Fusiliers over the next few months.

B Company, Machine Gun Section.

In the centre is Sergeant W J Brown and on the left is Sergeant W Warren. Some of these men will have been amongst the first to join 108th Brigade Machine Gun Company with them in January 1916.

At this time the area of devastation was confined to a narrow strip encompassing the opposing front lines, with the areas behind mostly undisturbed. Villages were intact and the green fields were still farmed by their owners. Even in the area of the front line, many of the fields around the trenches were still green and with the coming of spring were covered with wild flowers. The River Ancre, a tributary of the River Somme, divided the sector of the front dealt with here into two sub-sectors, known as Hamel and Thiepval Wood, and it is in the former that the 9th Royal Irish Fusiliers spent much of their time. Of the two, Hamel was generally the quieter although artillery and trench mortar barrages were common.

The River Ancre runs from north-east to south-west along a swampy valley scattered with miniature lakes, small islands and scattered copses. The small lakes or ponds had been built to breed fish and were well stocked. The ground rises sharply on either side of the riverbed. Just to the east of the river the small village of St Pierre Divion sits on the side of the Ancre valley, overlooking and dominating it. Well-defended trench lines were dug throughout and around this village and they provided the enemy with clear fields of fire across no-man's-land in front of the British trenches on the left of the Hamel sector. St Pierre Divion marked the western extremity of the Thiepval Wood sub-sector defended by the enemy. Above and east of the village the ground rises 250 feet in 1,000 yards over a convex slope to a plateau that was the site of the Swaben Redoubt. This almost impregnable trench system was heavily fortified and protected by sixteen rows of thick wire. Along the ridge to the south of the redoubt lay Thiepval village, which was also held by the enemy. On the southern slope below Swaben Redoubt was Thiepval Wood, along the northern and eastern sides of which ran the British front line.

The Ancre valley was often flooded and for much of the time the main crossing point in this area was the bridge on the Thiepval/Hamel Road. This was, however, the most northerly crossing point held by the British troops and it was well within range of the enemy's machine guns. Farther south, immediately west of Thiepval Wood, two causeways were built over the river during the preparations for the Somme offensive. During their construction, obstructions in the river were removed, thereby reducing the level of flooding, and the causeways themselves were laid using sandbags filled with chalk. Although wattle screens provided cover from view, the northern causeway remained within range of the enemy and was often swept by machine gun fire. There were also a number of small footbridges that had been built earlier by French troops. The valley was defended by a number of isolated posts such as Castor Post, Stone Bridge and the Mound Keep, the latter being about 400 yards south of the southern causeway. Just east of Hamel was a small mill on the river bank, and another mill farther upriver was east of the German lines near Beaucourt Station.

Along the western bank of the river runs a railway and beyond this the ground rises again. In the north, close to the river, lay Beaucourt-sur-Ancre, which was behind the German front lines. A railway station lay just to the south of the village near a few houses and on the junction with Station Road. The remnants of this road ran in a valley at right angles to the river and railway, west up a shallow valley to Beaumont Hamel. The enemy's trenches lay on the high ground either side of this valley and comprised three rows of trenches also at right angles to the river and railway and about 400 yards from the British lines, although in some cases they were closer. Each of the enemy trench lines was protected by wire and linked to the others by communication trenches. Due to the low, marshy ground near the River Ancre, the enemy constructed a series of trenches running parallel to the river south of Beaucourt. Other positions were constructed in the swampy low ground along the river. One of these was called *Biber Kolonie* (Beaver Colony) due to the way in which it had been built above the high water table. In the Ancre valley, the German front line was extended into the swampy ground by a trench known as *Tal Stellung* (the Valley Position). This was the trench known to the men of 9th Royal Irish Fusiliers as Railway Sap. On the other flank just outside the British left boundary with the Hamel sub-sector, the enemy occupied an area just south of Beaumont Hamel known as Y Ravine. It was opposite here that 107th Brigade had been deployed during its attachment to the 4th Division.

Mill Road Bridge over the River Ancre between Hamel and St Pierre Divion. This photograph was taken after the enemy positions that dominated this area from St Pierre Divion were captured in late 1916. When the 9th Royal Irish Fusiliers was in Hamel, which is off to the right of the picture, this area was dangerous in daylight and swept by machine-gun fire at night. © IWM (Q 4578)

Moving south-west from Beaucourt-sur-Ancre the ground drops steadily in a slight incline from the small ridge immediately in front of the village and the German reserve lines, across the valley sheltering Station Road and down over the German forward trenches towards the British front line. About halfway between the opposing trenches, and parallel to them, was a steep-sided ravine about 300 yards long and between twenty and fifty feet deep running down the hill to the River Ancre valley.[6]

Farther down the slope beyond the ravine, the village of Hamel was incorporated into the British trench system. The village sits in a natural bowl west of the river. This area, including some parts of Hamel, was overlooked by part of the German lines and, across the river, by St Pierre Divion. The trenches in the village and in the open ground to the west were well established when the 9th Royal Irish Fusiliers arrived. Although many were in reasonable condition, the weather was appalling and the trenches and posts were knee deep in water. Poor drainage was the key problem, a difficulty not solved for some months. Most of the main trenches were well protected. At this stage each of the forward brigades had two battalions in the front line and two in reserve with the forward battalions spending about a week in the line. Posts of section strength held the front and support trenches, where sentries were deployed by day and night and the battalions 'stood-to' at dawn.

The ground rises quickly behind Hamel from 80 to 130 feet onto a ridge. Hidden behind it and about one mile from Hamel is the village of Mesnil. Just in front of this village were numerous British artillery observation posts along a trench known as Brock's Benefit, named after the Ulster Division's artillery commander, Brigadier H J Brock. The two villages were linked by road and the infamous communication trench, Jacob's Ladder, which was fully exposed to the enemy. Fortunately, men moving forward by night could use the road with only occasional machine gun fire to contend with, but in daylight troops had to crawl in the thick mud of the trench to avoid artillery, mortar and machine gun fire.

On this first deployment into this part of the front, A and B Companies were in the front line trenches on the slope in front of Hamel village, with D Company in close support and C Company in reserve in the village. C Company also found two detached posts of twelve men each for Castor Post and Stone Bridge, both near the German lines on the River Ancre. The first night in the line was quiet, but most days and nights that followed were characterised by intermittent artillery fire from both sides and the Battalion suffered four men wounded. Work began on improving the trenches, including a new dug-out on the right of the sector where accommodation was very limited. On 9 February a German patrol got within thirty yards of the outpost on the right of the Battalion's position near the old mill. A few grenades were thrown into the mill forcing the enemy to withdraw. That incident undoubtedly contributed to the incident the following night when, as a patrol was returning to the lines, it was fired at by men of the forward company who were not expecting it. Private James Elliott was severely wounded and, evacuated to hospital in England, he was discharged from the Army in June 1916. On 10 February the enemy shelled the trenches and the village but caused no significant damage, and the next day forty 'whizbangs' (a trench mortar known for the peculiar noise it made) were fired into Hamel causing minor damage and slightly wounding one man.

After their first period in the trenches, the 9th Royal Irish Fusiliers was relieved by 12th Royal Irish Rifles. The pairing of these two battalions would continue until early 1918. After the relief the 9th Royal Irish Fusiliers moved back into Mesnil as the Brigade reserve with all but three platoons from D Company, which were sent to hold the Mound Keep. Mesnil, although about a mile from the German front line, was not safe from attack and on its first morning in reserve the Battalion suffered more casualties when twenty 'whizbangs' and twelve large calibre shells landed. It was in this attack that the 9th Royal Irish Fusiliers lost its first man killed in action, Private William Girvan, a cook in C Company. Two others who were carrying rations forward to their friends were wounded and one of them, Private Thomas Nicholson of B Company, died of his wounds the next day. Girvan was buried nearby in Mesnil Ridge Cemetery and Nicholson was buried near the dressing station where he died in Forceville. Another attack that afternoon caused little damage. This was the pattern for the next few days, with enemy artillery searching the valleys for the Division's artillery positions. Many had lucky escapes during these attacks. An officers' billet took a direct hit and Captain Johnston, Lieutenant Johnston and Lieutenant Given narrowly escaped serious injury. Lieutenant Johnston's coat pocket was torn by a shrapnel bullet that also went through a book that was in it, and Lieutenant Given was bruised on the back by part of a spent shell. In another attack six 'whizbangs' landed around Lieutenant Gibson without hitting him.

Large fatigue parties continued to be supplied for trench digging, but some men, notably the snipers, managed some useful training, and on 18 February, after the Battalion had moved back into the line at Hamel, one of the snipers accounted for two of the enemy. During this tour, C and D Companies were now in the front line with B Company in close support and A Company in reserve. The shelling by the enemy was intermittent, but the casualties mounted and a number of men were wounded. The trenches were in poor condition now due to the effect of the incessant and torrential rain; 12th Royal Irish Rifles had lost one man when a falling trench wall smothered him. Repairs were carried out as quickly as possible but the conditions were bad and getting worse. Over this period Lieutenant Colonel Blacker wrote regularly of the terrible weather, the awful state of the trenches, the measures taken to prevent the men getting frostbite (whale oil rubbed into their feet) and the hard work needed to get anything done:

> *'The only possible footwear for the trenches in their present state is the Government long gum boot, which comes up to the thigh. I find it very tiring to walk in but when you come on water over your knees and liquid mud of like depth, no other boots are possible. An awful amount of work there is to be done to keep the existing trenches in order, and then a lot of new necessary work to be undertaken, and few men to do it. Not a man of the 2¼ Coys in front line can be taken from the line. It takes 80 men every night to bring the rations from the Dump 1½ miles away, from which it has to be carried with the greatest difficulty. I can raise 60 men for work at night. There is our main communication trench, 1½ miles long, which has to be cleaned (in parts 2ft deep in solid mud and liquid slush), and each side of it revetted to prevent it falling in. It would take 500 men a fortnight to do it, and the earth removed from the top where it has been piled up from the bottom when cleaning, and keeps tumbling in again. This can only be done at night. There is another communications trench of a mile to the cookers, up which all the men's food is carried for every meal. This keeps falling in, and being on low ground is full of water. The cookers themselves are in a horrible place, liquid mud and impossible to drain or keep clean.'*

As had become usual, the forward companies patrolled no-man's-land and the area of the marsh on the Battalion's right flank. These vital patrols were not always successful or uneventful. On 22 February a small patrol led by Second Lieutenant Arthur Hollywood, and with Second Lieutenant Reginald Wood, two sergeants and four men, went out to the area of the mill on the River Ancre to investigate what a German patrol was up to. They were spotted and engaged with rifle grenades fired from the nearest German trench. Second Lieutenant Wood, who had been with the Battalion for only a month, and Private Samuel Forde were killed. Second Lieutenant Hollywood, wounded along with two others, was praised for his gallantry and coolness in the affair for staying out with the bodies until relief came out to collect them. Wood and Forde were buried in Hamel at 2.00pm the following afternoon during a snowstorm. One of the wounded was Private Charles Bryans who had enlisted in September 1914 aged 18. His wounds left him unfit for further service and he was discharged in September 1916.

With snow and frost deep on the ground, the Battalion was relieved the next evening, again by 12th Royal Irish Rifles, and in biting cold marched back to a reserve position at

Englebelmer. Fifty men went on leave, and for the next three days the companies washed, refitted, provided numerous fatigue parties to clear snow, and got as much rest as possible before moving back to the trenches at Hamel. The relief was complete by 9.10pm on 27 February and a quiet night was spent in deplorable conditions. The rising temperature had caused a thaw, and as a result the trench walls were collapsing under the pressure of water and the trenches themselves were fairly deep in mud and slush. Much work was done over the next day or two to put this damage right, against a background of intermittent artillery and machine-gun fire. During this period Private Harold Binsley was wounded in the leg. Binsley was from County Durham and had enlisted into The Royal Inniskilling Fusiliers aged only sixteen, and was one of the men transferred to Princess Victoria's (Royal Irish Fusiliers) in June 1915. While he was in hospital his mother wrote requesting his discharge. He remained in the Army, however, classified A4 (fit for general service but underage) and transferred to the Labour Corps in April 1918. In July 1918 he was discharged to the Class P Reserve and returned to work as a coalminer in Durham. The action was not all one way. On 2 March one of the forward companies conducted an aggressive attack with Lewis guns and rifle grenades into a German sap near the mill; the outcome of this skirmish is unknown. That evening the Battalion moved out of the line again and by 10.20pm had been relieved by 12th Royal Irish Rifles.

Field kitchens deployed near Hamel in late 1916.
Neither the wagons nor the men are from the Ulster Division but they are typical of the time. The kitchens are deployed along the road leading north out of Hamel towards Beaucourt-sur-Ancre. Over the bank to the left, 'A' Company of 9th Royal Irish Fusiliers attacked from left to right on 1 July 1916. To the right of the picture is the railway and marshy area attacked by the attached platoons from B Company, 12th Royal Irish Rifles. Beyond the final field kitchen and on the left is the ravine that lay in no-man's land on 1 July. © IWM (Q 4566)

In the first week of March the Ulster Division extended its front to the right with 109th Brigade taking over an area south of the River Ancre in Thiepval Wood. This had little immediate impact on the 9th Royal Irish Fusiliers and on the first day out of the line most of the men rested. Unexpectedly, orders were received to deploy two companies to take over a line of trenches held by the 8th Royal Irish Rifles of 107th Brigade one mile north of Mesnil near Auchonvillers and to the left of the positions occupied recently. This new frontage was of about 600 yards and was faced by German trenches on Y Ravine. When B and C Companies took over the line they found the trenches knee-deep in snow and muddy slush, with the water being three feet deep in some places. Although the parapets and the firesteps were in good order, many of the traverses and communication trenches needed considerable work. Thankfully, this dreadful trench-line, 350-500 yards from the enemy, was straight and easy to hold. Throughout this period A and D Companies remained at Mesnil and on 5 March they were relieved by the 11th Royal Inniskilling Fusiliers from 109th Brigade and went into Brigade reserve at Englebelmer. Lieutenant Colonel Blacker, who had been away on a course of instruction for commanding officers at 3rd Army School, arrived back to find that B and C Companies had made their trenches moderately dry and passable, although many communication trenches were still blocked because of the heavy snow.

On 7 March the Division's artillery joined it at last. The four artillery brigades had been raised in London in May 1915. 153rd and 154th Brigades were recruited from Croydon, Norbury and Sydenham in south London, and 172nd and 173rd Brigades were raised in north-east London. The artillery brigades and the Divisional Artillery Column all met for the first time when they moved to Lewes in July 1915. The Ulster Division's artillery now comprised four artillery brigades and, from June 1916, four trench mortar batteries (in addition to the light trench mortar battery in each of the infantry brigades that was manned by soldiers from that brigade). 153rd, 172nd and 173rd Brigades each comprised four batteries, each equipped with four 18-pounder guns. In addition, 154th Brigade comprised three batteries, each equipped with four 4.5-inch howitzers. At this time the Division's artillery was supported by X.36, Y.36 & Z.36 Medium Trench Mortar Batteries, each equipped with four 2-inch Stokes mortars, and V.36 Heavy Trench Mortar Battery, equipped with four 9.45-inch mortars. Having completed their training the artillery brigades took over from those of the 56th (1st London) Division, which had supported the Ulster Division since its arrival in France. They began the registration of targets immediately, naturally causing some retaliation, and on 8 March they successfully attacked their first real target—German transport moving into Beaumont Hamel.

The next relief, in daylight, of B and C Companies by A and D Companies went well, although Private Thomas Stewart was badly wounded when shrapnel from a 'whizbang' hit him in the head; he succumbed to his wounds on 12 March. There was no rest for B Company, which immediately took over 250 yards of trench from 8th Royal Irish Rifles on the left of the trenches already occupied. This was just to the right of the trenches held by the 9th Royal Irish Fusiliers the previous November. Now full of water and slush varying in depth from knee to thigh deep, B Company was forced to work hard all night in freezing weather to dry them with the pumps. The deployment of the Battalion was now A Company on the right of the line, D Company in the centre, B Company on the left and C Company in reserve one mile back.

This was a relatively quiet time, with the Battalion's priority being the clearance and maintenance of the trenches until relieved by 12th Royal Irish Rifles on the evening of 12 March. The relief was complete by 9.30pm and the Battalion marched back into reserve at

Hédauville, with the last company arriving after midnight. Although the billets here left much to be desired, the period of rest was welcome. The weather was now magnificent; there was a real glimpse of spring, and on two consecutive evenings the divisional troupe of follies gave a performance in the recreation hut. Lieutenant Colonel Blacker also managed to get all of the non-commissioned officers together, a rare occurrence, for a talk on their duties and responsibilities as leaders. On 15 March a large working party was provided and the task is indicative of the hard labour often falling to those in reserve. Five hundred men of the Battalion dug a new communication trench five feet deep, four feet wide at the top and two feet wide at the bottom, between Auchonvillers and the forward line, a distance of 300 yards.

There were smaller working parties provided the next night, but on Saint Patrick's day the Royal Irish Fusiliers celebrated. The festivities began at 6.00am with the band and drums marching around the village playing Irish tunes, and then shamrock, sent by Lieutenant General Sir George Richardson, was given to everyone. After a morning spent at company commanders' disposal, the Battalion played football against 14th Royal Irish Rifles (the 'Young Cits' as they were known) from 109th Brigade, which the 9th Royal Irish Fusiliers won 2-1. Major Pratt reported that the evening concert culminated in three cheers for *"Ould Oireland"*.

The festivities provided only a minor respite from the front and the next day the Battalion moved back into the line, again taking over from 12th Royal Irish Rifles in the trenches at Auchonvillers, with A Company on the right, D Company in the centre and C Company on the left. B Company was in reserve at Englebelmer. The relief was completed early at 8.40pm but the night was very bright and clear, which precluded any patrols, although the wire was examined. Stores were brought up to allow the thin areas to be repaired, and good work was done on strengthening the trenches and opening up the main communication trench, known as Broadway.

Captain W J Menaul

Early in this stint in the line Captain W J Menaul led the first of a number of patrols that proved to be of great value to the Battalion in the coming months. On this occasion, on the night of 20 March, he located an enemy sniping post and after a brief skirmish returned to the lines with one wounded corporal. He conducted two similar patrols over the next two nights before being ordered to rest.

In addition to burying telephone cable and continuing the work on Broadway, the Battalion took over a section of the line from 13th Royal Irish Rifles on its right. This now produced a frontage of 1,000 yards and it was the 9th Royal Irish Fusiliers' turn to act as hosts for new units. Eight officers and 40 other ranks from the 10th (Service) Battalion, The East Yorkshire Regiment (1st Hull) from 92nd Brigade, 31st Division, which had just arrived from the Suez Canal defences in Egypt, were attached just before they took over this part of the front. Little occurred for the next few days, which were spent in very cold weather with heavy snow falling, until relieved by the 12th Royal Irish Rifles at 8.45pm on Friday 24 March. The Battalion left this part of the line for the last time and marched five kilometres in bitterly cold conditions back to Hedauville where it became the Brigade reserve, and spent the next four days resting and assimilating the drafts of new men.

On 29 March a readjustment of areas of responsibility took place with the introduction of 31st Division into the line. The 36th (Ulster) Division was now allocated a two-battalion frontage astride the River Ancre holding the line Hamel-Thiepval, with the other two battalions of the forward brigade in reserve. Initially the brigades were deployed with 109th in the line, 108th in reserve and with 107th Brigade an additional reserve farther back. While in reserve the 9th Royal Irish Fusiliers was split, with A and B Companies at Mesnil and the remainder of the Battalion at Hedauville. For the next three weeks everyone worked hard; work parties were provided daily to make battle emplacements, dig new trenches and bury signal cable.

On the last day of March a draft of three officers and thirty other ranks arrived. At the beginning of April the men worked in perfect spring weather but it deteriorated as the month wore on and ended in very wet conditions. To make matters worse, during the intermittent shellfire a single shell hit Mesnil on 3 April and caused twelve casualties in B Company, including Private James Hall, who was killed, and Privates John Vennard and Thomas Houston, both of whom were badly wounded and who later died of their wounds. Private Robert Sturgeon was wounded in the neck and arm. Four men from 11th Royal Inniskilling Fusiliers and the Royal Field Artillery were also wounded by this shell.

It was not only casualties that caused the loss of good men to the Battalion. The evolving tactics of trench warfare resulted in the formation in early 1916 of units in each brigade equipped with the new 3-inch Stokes mortar. In order to establish them with trained men, the battalions of the Ulster Division provided the manpower, and 9th Royal Irish Fusiliers lost Second Lieutenant Samuel O'Neill and some good men to the new 108th Brigade Trench Mortar Battery. For the remainder of the war the Battery would see men from the 9th Royal Irish Fusiliers move in and out of its ranks.

In an attempt to provide some cheer for the men, football matches were organised on Saturday afternoons against the 9th and 10th Royal Inniskilling Fusiliers (both were won 5-1), and Regimental concerts were held afterwards in the evening. A field church service was attended on Sunday by those not on work parties. The concerts were regular events when not in the line and the wealth of talent in the Battalion was harnessed. The style of these, and the preparation involved, can be illustrated by one such event held in a barn decorated for the occasion, and with a stage made from ammunition boxes and heated by trench braziers. A quartet of flautists was followed by Captain Menaul reciting Kipling's 'Drunk and Resisting the Guard'. Company Sergeant Major Sleator gave another recital and a number of men sang songs.

On 20 April the Battalion marched back to the front, taking over from the 14th Royal Irish Rifles in the Hamel sub-sector with 12th Royal Irish Rifles in support at Mesnil. 108th Brigade would retain control of this sector on the left of the divisional front in the months up to the forthcoming offensive. This was the same part of the line occupied throughout February and although muddy, most of the trenches were now open. On the right was the low, marshy ground of the River Ancre, and beyond that the ground leading up to Thiepval Wood occupied by 9th Royal Inniskilling Fusiliers from 109th Brigade. On the left was 4th Battalion, The Worcester Regiment of 29th Division.

The period before Easter was wet and muddy for those in the line, but relatively quiet, although there were a number of casualties, including Private John Atwell who was wounded on 21 April. Easter Sunday was commemorated with Holy Communion at the regimental aid post after stand-down at 4.15am on Sunday 23 April. Unfortunately, there was little time to relax and that night patrols began again. One under the command of Second Lieutenant Montgomery, a quiet and highly-regarded officer, came into contact with an enemy patrol and surprised it by opening fire from about eighty yards; they caused at least one casualty . Second Lieutenant Montgomery and his team withdrew to safety when the Germans put up flares and swept the area with machine-gun fire. Work continued on the trenches with a new sap being started in the area of the orchard near the church in Hamel, and three others were deepened. Predictably, this work attracted the enemy's attention and became the target for mortar fire. Finally, after six days in the line the 9th Royal Irish Fusiliers was relieved by 12th Royal Irish Rifles, and by 1.30am were on their way back to Mesnil. In this short period in the line the Battalion had suffered two serious casualties. Private James Hutchinson, who had just arrived in the last draft, was killed by mortar fire on 25 April, and Private Joseph Bulman was wounded by shellfire; he died of his wounds on 26 April.

As usual there was little rest, and the remainder of the month was spent providing working parties for numerous tasks, mostly assisting 16th Royal Irish Rifles (Pioneers) to improve the trenches at Hamel. The lack of rest for the men was a worry to Lieutenant Colonel Blacker and on one particular night he refused to send forward a working party of 100 men, causing, as he put it, *'excitement and reasons in writing'*. On 1 May the Battalion was ordered to move forward again to support 12th Royal Irish Rifles, who were expecting to be attacked. Nothing materialised and the Battalion suffered only one casualty when Private John Adams was shot in the hand when a rifle was fired accidentally. He wrote of the event in a letter to his mother:

Private, later Sergeant, John Adams

'. . . as my hand is getting alright I will try and explain to you how it happened. It was on Monday night the 1st of May. And we were out of the Trenches at the time. But the Batt that we were doing reserves to was supposed to be attacked. And we got orders to go up to support them. It was about 10 oclock at night and very dark. And when outside our quarters the Order was given to load up our rifles. So I happened to be rather late getting out and when I got out I was standing side ways to where the men were, when one of them by accident let off a round. The bullet passing through my rifle and exploding it in my left hand. The splinters tearing the whole heart out of my hand. I had to go through two operations for to get them out. It did feel sore I may tell you. But you not be uneasy as I am getting alright now, as I have the worse of it over me. And it might have been far worse if I had lost my hand.'

John Adams returned to the 9th Royal Irish Fusiliers in 1917. He earned two Military Medals and was wounded again just before the war ended.

By now news of the rebellion in Dublin had reached the Battalion, although there was no reaction to the news registered in the Battalion's papers. On 2 May Lieutenant Richard Townsend wrote home to his mother, conveying something of life at the front:

'My dear Mother,

I got your letter, no 19, yesterday, it was a good thing you got it posted in England as only a very few letters from Ireland have come through this last week.

Lieutenant R S B Townsend

It is very bad luck the way you are held up and can't get home. They must be having a pretty hot time in Dublin. There is a rumour here that the 10th have gone down but I don't believe it. I wrote to you yesterday but sent it to Armagh, so I don't suppose you will get it, that is why I am writing again today, so as to let you know I am all right.

I sent my stylo pen yesterday to you to get mended.

When you can send a parcel out again you might send me one cake of Wright coal tar soap and a stick of Colgates shaving soap. I won't send you a cheque in this letter as it might never get to you. Could you get me a Twinplex safety razor sharpener (they cost about 15/-) and send me it out and I will send you a cheque for it. It is two rollers with a handle in a metal box, be sure you get the right kind.

The weather is still lovely, we have only had a few showers lately. For every one shell I heard when I first came out – there are about 60 to 100 go now – so it is getting more lively round here night and day.'

After five days out of the line, but hardly rejuvenated, the Battalion moved back to Hamel. For the first few days everything was relatively quiet with those in the front line suffering only desultory shelling and only one casualty. Sergeant David Pollock of B Company, rated by the Commanding Officer as one of the best non-commissioned officers in the Battalion, was hit in the shoulder on 4 May. Captain Menaul conducted patrols nearly every night and on one occasion had to lie low when caught by machine-gun fire. On 7 May at 11.00pm a heavy German barrage started to support a raid against the 1st Battalion, The Dorsetshire Regiment, in 32nd Division, and front line trenches were manned. In preparation for a simultaneous raid by the 9th Royal Inniskilling Fusiliers on the right, the Division's artillery opened up thirty minutes later and both sides were soon hard at it. At 11.50pm the Inniskillings' raiding party entered the enemy trenches and successfully bombed six enemy dugouts. Unfortunately, as the raiding party retired it suffered twenty-two casualties from the curtain fire put down by the enemy artillery. All of the wounded were brought back and, overall, the raid was considered a success. In the 9th Royal Irish Fusiliers' trenches, a German shell had killed Company Sergeant Major Frank Cross, and wounded eight men. Company Sergeant Major Cross was buried nearby. After a quiet day the 9th Royal Irish Fusiliers was relieved again by 12th Royal Irish Rifles and moved back to Mesnil to another week of work parties and fatigues. When the Battalion took its turn in the line again, A Company deployed in the village with the others forward: B Company on the right, C Company in the centre and D Company on the left.

Company Sergeant Major
F E Cross

The ability to communicate an emergency quickly to battalion headquarters and thence to the guns was an important safety measure for those in the line, and towards the end of the week, during very thick mist, communications were tested successfully on 18 May using rocket, visual signals (lights) and runners. That night another officer was lost when Second Lieutenant George Dickson, a platoon commander in C Company, was wounded by machine-gun fire while with a wiring party in Number 14 Sap at Hamel when a bullet lodged under his right arm. He took five months to recover and did not serve with the Battalion again. Like many who recovered after a period of service at home he was transferred to the Labour Corps. Captain Menaul led out another patrol on the same night, this time to explore the ravine which lay to the front of the 9th Royal Irish Fusiliers' position and which, unbeknown at the time, would feature greatly in the Battalion's action in just over a month. Three nights later he was out again with six men along the eastern side of the railway, an area to which he returned the next night accompanied by one man, crawling until he got close to a German listening post. They were seen by a German covering patrol about five yards away, and were shot at but managed to get away pursued by rifle and grenade fire. This courageous officer's final escapade that month was two nights later when he took out a patrol of eight men who lay up on their side of the ravine and waited for enemy activity. Soon a patrol was seen, and as it passed under Menaul and his men, it was engaged with sixteen bombs, killing at least two of the enemy. Enemy fire caused Menaul to retire, and by 10.15pm all of the patrol was safely back in the lines.

Second Lieutenant
G C Dickson

Captain E A Godson MC,
pictured later in the war

Not all of the action was against the enemy. Lieutenant Edwin Godson, a platoon commander in A Company, was a Special Reserve officer who had been mobilised on the outbreak of the war and had served with the 4th (Queen's Own) Hussars in France before being wounded in November 1914. Having transferred to Princess Victoria's (Royal Irish Fusiliers) he joined the 9th (Service) Battalion in March 1916. He had noticed that the man-made ponds in the Ancre valley were full of fish, and wrote later of a fishing expedition:

'The weather was fine and on a sunny afternoon, after scanning the German lines with binoculars to look for any activity, the eye was attracted by the glint of the sun on a school of these fishes in a pond about 40 yards in front of our wattle, on the enemy side. It occurred to mind that I was forgetting what fish tasted like, the spell in the line was a long one, but not over-exhausting. Would a Mills Bomb serve as a substitute for line and fly? Decided to make the experiment. After crawling out on belly, drew the pin and threw the bomb out on a school of fish.

Lo and behold about 40 fish lay on their sides on the top of the water! Threw off uniform, jumped in, swam about, throwing out the fish to the number of 40 or 50, round about 1/2 lb. apiece. The fish in water soon began to `come-to' and swam away, collected the 'bag' which were distributed to the Platoons in the Front Line and all had a taste of fresh fish.'

He had been spotted, however, by an officer in the front line running up from the Ancre towards Thiepval Wood who considered this an *'unsporting affair'*. The Commanding Officer was more appreciative and told Godson to *'have another go tomorrow'*. Godson continued his tale:

'I ruminated over the proposal and was of opinion that our enemy were very methodical and watchful people and it might not be quite so comfortable next time. The event had been at 5 minutes past 4. I decided not to repeat the experiment. At 4 p.m. next day I watched the pond from a distance. Sure enough at 4.5 p.m. four guns of a German close-up 77mm battery burst four shrapnel over the pond, threshing up the water hugely and perhaps the fish.'

The next few days were characterised by artillery fire both ways, with some success on both sides. Sweeping machine-gun fire was directed against the parapet of the enemy trenches and a sniper pair out forward near the ravine accounted for a German soldier who was foolishly standing on the parados of the enemy front line. After being relieved again on 24 May, A and B Companies enjoyed a rare bath, but the rest period was short-lived. For the remainder of the month large working parties went out every day digging and repairing Jacob's Ladder and the trenches at Hamel and Thiepval Wood, and carrying mortar bombs forward, until orders were received to march the eight kilometres back to billets at Varennes. Unfortunately, just before the move at 6.30pm on the evening of 31 May, the village was shelled, killing Private Thomas James McKeown and wounding fifteen others. Lieutenant John Gibson was wounded and Private Hugh Fulton died of his wounds the next day. Private Joseph Vennard was also one of those wounded. He remained in hospital for over a year and was finally discharged from the Army in 1918. He never recovered from his injuries and died at home in Portadown on 14 June 1918. Private Isaac Hayes was wounded in the foot and returned to the Battalion in August 1916. Private James Pierson was wounded in the arm and chest and did not serve with the Battalion again. Like many recovered wounded he transferred to the Labour Corps. Over this period a number of drafts and recovered sick and wounded joined the Battalion. They included Private Ephraim McFarland from Tandragee, who had been evacuated sick to the base depot in April. While in hospital he was commended for his gallantry by the commandant of the base depot for rousing his comrades and evacuating the tents during a fire.

The Allied offensive along the Somme was imminent, and throughout June the men of the Ulster Division completed their preparations for their part in the attack.

Endnotes, Chapter 2

[1] The biographical details for these officers and warrant officers are contained at Appendices 5 and 6. Only Regimental Quartermaster Sergeant G W Wilson served with the 9th Royal Irish Fusiliers throughout the war after becoming Quartermaster on 15 September 1916. In summary: twelve were killed in action or died of wounds or illness; two relinquished their commissions on account of ill-health caused by wounds; four were wounded and served elsewhere for the remainder of the

war; twelve were posted or transferred to other units or the staff; one was wounded, served on the staff and returned in 1918, and one was was released from service, aged 50.

[2] Lieutenant Henry Paton Nott. One of three brothers from Stoke Bishop, Bristol, who served with the 1/6th Battalion, The Gloucestershire Regiment. Mentioned in Dispatches. Killed in action by shellfire on 27 April 1916, aged 21, and was buried in Hebuterne Military Cemetery. His brothers, Lieutenant Colonel T W Nott DSO and Captain L C Nott MC (Commanding Officer and Adjutant), were killed in action on 17 April 1917 by a mine with a delayed fuse in the cellar occupied as battalion headquarters.

[3] Brigadier Charles Richard Jebb Griffith CB, CMG, DSO. Born 4 October 1867. Commissioned into The Bedfordshire Regiment 14 September 1887. Served in South Africa. DSO (LG 27 September 1901) *'in recognition of services during the operations in South Africa'*, Mentioned in Despatches, Queen's South Africa Medal & 4 clasps, King's South Africa Medal. Major 2 April 1906, Lieutenant Colonel 16 October 1913. Battalion Commander 1914-15. Commander 108th Brigade 1915-18. Commander 20th Training Reserve Brigade, 1st Machine Gun Corps 6 January – 31 December 1918. Member of the standing committee of enquiry on Prisoners of War from 1 January 1919. Brevet Colonel (1 January 1916), CMG (1915), CB (1918), Mentioned in Despatches eight times, Officer of the Legion d'Honneur (France). Died 4 August 1948, aged 80.

[4] Lieutenant Colonel (later Brigadier General) Gerald Bull DSO. Born 10 May 1877. Served in South Africa (Queen's Medal with 4 clasps, King's Medal with 2 clasps). Second Lieutenant The Royal Garrison Regiment 9 December 1903. Second Lieutenant The Prince of Wales's Leinster Regiment (Royal Canadians) 7 June 1905. Lieutenant Princess Victoria's (Royal Irish Fusiliers) 3 February 1907. In France he was four times Mentioned in Despatches and was made Brevet Major. Wounded in 1915. Commanded 12th (Service) Battalion, The Royal Irish Rifles (Central Antrim) in 108th Brigade. Commanded 8th Infantry Brigade, 3rd Division. DSO – King's Birthday Honours 1916, no citation. Wounded on 3 July 1916 and died of these wounds on 11 December 1916.

[5] All but two have been identified—see Appendix 6.

[6] This ravine is now the site of the Ancre British Cemetery.

THREE

The Battle of Albert: 1 July 1916

Discussions on the timing and location of the Allied offensive in 1916 began at the Chantilly conference in December 1915. General Joffre, Chief of the French General Staff, favoured a simultaneous attack by the allies on the Western, Eastern and Italian Fronts. On the Western Front he desired an attack in Picardy. His request to General Sir Douglas Haig, newly appointed Commander-in-Chief of the British Expeditionary Force, was for a simultaneous offensive with the British attacking in the north between Arras on the River Scarpe, and the River Somme, and the French attacking south of the River Somme. After considerable discussion about the role of the British it was agreed that a simultaneous attack would be mounted by the two Allied armies sometime about the beginning of July 1916. With planning underway, the march was stolen in February 1916 by Falkenhayn, Chief of the German General Staff, who launched his offensive against Verdun. He knew France would defend Verdun to the last, and on cue Joffre threw his infantry into the defence there in huge numbers. To allow the French to move troops to the beleaguered fortifications, Haig took over more of the line in the north and, as casualties mounted at Verdun, the planned French participation in the Somme offensive was reduced.

The original plan was for forty French and twenty-five British divisions to attack on a forty-nine-mile-long front, but in the event thirteen British and five French divisions were allocated on a shortened front and with more limited objectives. Joffre continued to press for an early attack and discussions about where and when it would take place continued throughout the spring. On 26 May Haig finally agreed that the attack would begin on 1 July, with the major effort being made by the British. The plan for the attack was the subject of much discussion and disagreement between Haig and General Sir Henry Rawlinson, commanding the Fourth Army, who would lead the main thrust. After a number of revisions, the British plan called for an attack along a 25,000-yard front to secure objectives to a depth of one and a half miles. In the north, VII Corps of Third Army would attack the Gommecourt salient; in the centre, Rawlinson's Fourth Army, comprising III, XIII and XV Corps and reinforced by VIII and X Corps of the Third Army, would make the major effort in an attack from Serre to Montauban. Finally, in the south, three corps of the French *6e Armée* would attack on the right of the British.

In the X Corps area, 36th (Ulster) Division would attack on the left with 32nd Division on the right and 49th (West Riding) Division in reserve. Advancing on the left of the Ulster Division would be 29th Division of VIII Corps. To 36th (Ulster) Division fell the responsibility for the Thiepval plateau.

Notwithstanding the reduction in the forces that would be engaged, the scale of the proposed attack was enormous and meant a vast amount of planning and logistic preparations. Contrary to popular belief, the staff work and planning for this complex offensive were thorough and detailed. The logistic support was extensive. Accommodation, food and water was required for 400,000 men and 100,000 horses; light railways and roads needed to be laid or re-laid; bridges were rebuilt and strengthened; communications were improved with many miles of cable laid and new telephone exchanges established; medical services had to be identified and sited and, importantly, artillery ammunition had to be moved forward, dumped and protected. Although much of this work was carried out by specialist troops, the labour for the more menial tasks, particularly moving stores and digging, fell to the infantry battalions in reserve.

At the end of May the Thiepval Wood and Hamel sub-sectors were manned by 107th Brigade, with 108th Brigade in support in Martinsart and 109th Brigade training farther to the rear. It was in this area that 36th (Ulster) Division would attack on the left flank of X Corps. In order to allow the latter brigades to train together, 147th Brigade from 49th (West Riding) Division, which would be the X Corps reserve, took over 108th Brigade's work parties, allowing it to move out of the line and back to a hutted camp at Varennes on Thursday 1 June. Billets were shared between the 9th Royal Irish Fusiliers and the brigade headquarters, with 11th and 13th Royal Irish Rifles based at Harponville and 12th Royal Irish Rifles at Lealvillers. Lieutenant Colonel Blacker commented that the billets here were crowded, cooking conditions primitive and water scarce.

The first week out of the line began with medical inoculations and equipment inspections, but comprehensive training started within days, conducted over an elaborate series of dummy trenches marked to represent the trenches to be attacked. Initially the effort concentrated on exercises against representations of the trenches north of Thiepval, and after a week of this a simultaneous attack by 108th and 109th Brigade was mounted, watched by Major General Nugent, Lieutenant General Sir Thomas Moreland commanding X Corps, and General Sir Henry Rawlinson commanding Fourth Army.

The plan for the forthcoming attack changed in the second week of June. On 11 June General Joffre requested that the attack be brought forward, and it was agreed that the preparatory artillery bombardment would begin on 24 June with the attack proper on the morning of 29 June. The following day, Monday 12 June, the men of the 9th Royal Irish Fusiliers were informed that they would be attacking over the familiar ground north of Hamel alongside 12th Royal Irish Rifles, and they now found themselves practising over an area marked to represent the German trenches between Hamel and Beaucourt-sur-Ancre. Over six days all of the phases of the attack were practised, including the rapid wiring required by the support troops responsible for consolidation to protect the newly secured strong-points from counter attack.

By this time the efforts of the Quartermaster had improved the billets considerably. The huts now had waterproof sheets for roofs, rather than sacking, that were much appreciated in the mixed, wet weather. Ablution places had been built with brick floors and pathways, and the laundry, baths and incinerators were in action. The weather now took a turn for the worse with heavy rain turning the ground to mud, making cross-country tracks impassable. Consequently, the carriage of ammunition was extremely difficult and the conditions for work parties very uncomfortable. On 18 June Captain Berry, the Medical Officer, who was based with the 108th Field Ambulance and the Battalion's details in Mesnil, experienced the difficulties in moving in these conditions for himself as he made a foray forward through Mesnil, down Jacob's Ladder to join a battalion in the trenches at Hamel, and he recognised the problems that would be experienced in moving casualties rearward by this route.

Unfortunately, the demands of training did not negate the need for work parties. That night almost all of the Battalion—twelve officers, fifty-four non-commissioned officers and 600 men—worked throughout the dark hours moving gas cylinders into the trenches at Thiepval Wood. The next few days were relatively quiet with time for training to be conducted at company level. A final practice attack took place on Thursday 22 June. The 9th Royal Irish Fusiliers moved back into the line at Hamel the next day in preparation for the assault, scheduled to take place six days later. Lieutenant Godson commented that, *'we were in high fettle looking forward to accomplishing something - maybe even the end of the war'.*

The front for which 36th (Ulster) Division was responsible was divided into four sectors, to be attacked by 108th and 109th Brigades, with 107th Brigade in reserve. The right and right-centre sectors ran north and north-east from Thiepval Wood and were the responsibility of 109th Brigade. For this it was reinforced by 11th and 13th Royal Irish Rifles from 108th Brigade and 15th Royal Irish Rifles from 107th Brigade. The left-centre sector, immediately east of the River Ancre and including the area around St Pierre Divion, was not to be attacked directly. The left sector (previously the Hamel sub-sector) would be attacked by the remaining two battalions of 108th Brigade—12th Royal Irish Rifles and 9th Royal Irish Fusiliers. The attacking Brigades were tasked with clearing the enemy's first, second and third lines before 107th Brigade captured the enemy's fourth line, the Division's final objective. All of the strong-points to be captured by the Division were named after well-known towns in Ulster. In the German 'A Line' there was Kilrea, Lisburn, Cavan and Moy. In the 'B Line' were Gobbins, Larne, Bushmills, Lurgan, Clones and Dungannon. Farther back in the 'C Line' were Coleraine, Portadown, Enniskillen, Strabane, Omagh and Lisnaskea. Finally in the D Line, and the final objectives, were Portrush, Bundoran and Derry City.[1]

The German *26. Reserve-Division* held the line from Pozieres to Serre. This first-class and experienced formation comprised two brigades; *52. Reserve-Infanterie-Brigade* held the line south of the River Ancre with *51. Reserve-Infanterie-Brigade* to the north. Opposing the Ulster Division in front of Thiepval Wood were the men of *Reserve-Infanterie-Regiment Nr 99* (RIR 99). North of the River Ancre the 9th Royal Irish Fusiliers faced the men of a battalion from *Württembergisches Reserve-Infanterie-Regiment Nr 119* (RIR 119). Facing Hamel, Sectors B5, B6 and B7 were each manned by a company. The enemy reserve here was based on the 2nd Recruit Company, men who were not yet fully trained, positioned in *Feste Alt Württemberg,* a strong-point on the outskirts of Beaucourt (called Beaucourt Redoubt by the 9th Royal Irish Fusiliers). Across these three sectors the 9th Royal Irish Fusiliers faced three Maxim MG 08 machine guns from the 2nd Machine Gun Company. Its two other guns were on the high ground near Beaumont Hamel. Two machine guns were located east of the River Ancre near St Pierre-Divion.[2]

The artillery provided for the Division's action was enormous. In addition to its own batteries, a brigade of four batteries was attached from 49th Division and a regiment from the French. The preliminary bombardment was to last for five days from 24 to 28 June, designated 'U Day' to 'Y Day', and was aimed at cutting the enemy wire and destroying the front line trenches. The barrage during the attack itself on 'Z Day' would not be a true creeping barrage, but after a final intensive bombardment of sixty-five minutes it would fire upon each German line in succession. The plan called for it to lift from the A to the A1 line at Zero, from the A1 line at Zero plus three minutes and from the B line at Zero plus eighteen minutes to a line 400 yards east of this objective.

It was assumed that the infantry would move rapidly over no-man's-land and would be in the second line trenches with little difficulty, still covered by the artillery barrage falling on the German depth positions. Mortars would also take part in the final bombardment.

Medical support was thoroughly planned. Basic life-saving treatment would be carried out at the Regimental Aid Post and Advanced Dressing Stations. Casualties would be assessed further at Main Dressing Stations and then moved back to an Advanced Operating Centre or to Casualty Clearing Stations. After basic surgery there, and when stabilised, casualties would be moved rearward by train to the hospitals near the coast. For the men of the Ulster Division an Advanced Dressing Station was established at Aveluy Wood south of Hamel to give immediate treatment to the most seriously wounded. To relieve pressure on this dressing station, casualties from the 9th Royal Irish Fusiliers and 12th Royal Irish Rifles attacking on the west of the River Ancre would be moved via a specially dug trench from Hamel to a point where the Hamel/Albert Road was screened from observation, and walking wounded would then move around Aveluy Wood to a collecting post just west of Martinsart. The Field Ambulances' motor vehicles were parked near here but many of the wounded would move by lorries and horse-drawn wagons to the Main Dressing Stations at Bouzincourt, Forceville and Warloy. Alternatively some of the more seriously wounded would be moved to the Advanced Operating Centre at Warloy. Casualty Clearing Stations were established at Puchevillers (3rd and 44th), Beauval (4th) and Doullens (19th, 20th, 41st and 43rd).

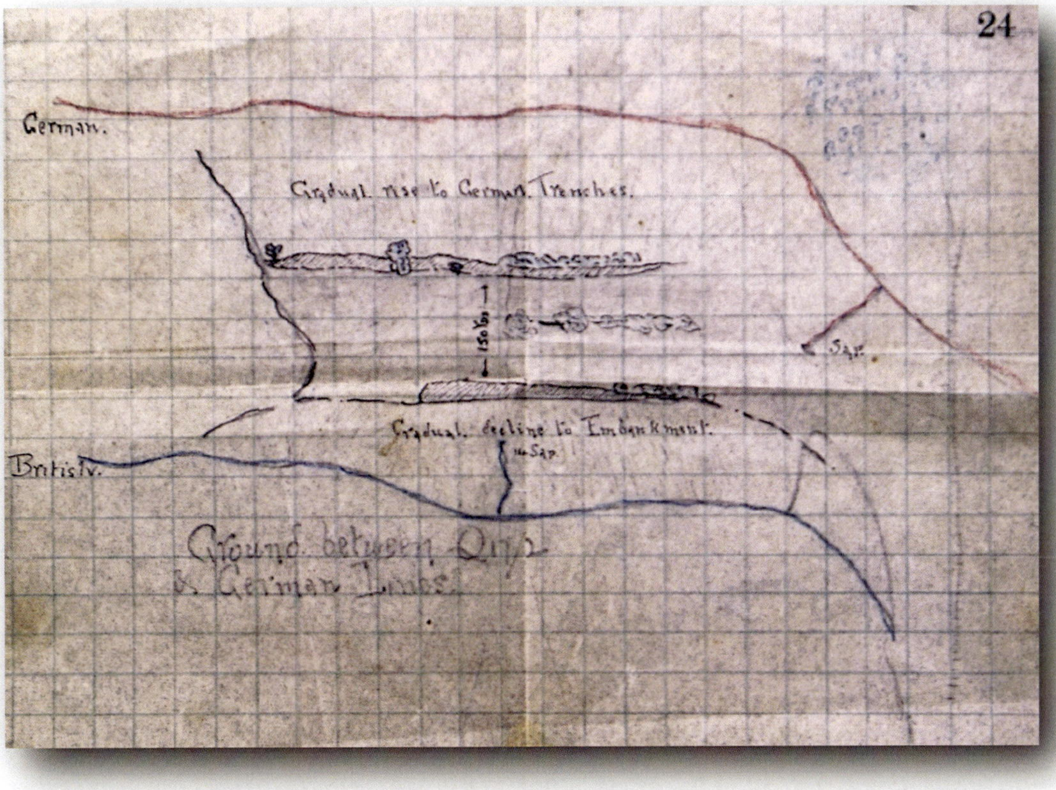

This simple but accurate map was drawn in a notebook by CQMS H Fox, C Company. It shows the area at Hamel attacked on 1 July 1916.

The plan for the attack in the Hamel sub-sector required the 9th Royal Irish Fusiliers to attack on the right and 12th Royal Irish Rifles on the left. The British and German front line trenches were about 400 yards apart, with the ravine, reconnoitred previously by Captain Menaul, about half way between them. The ravine was known to be steep in places with sides twenty to thirty feet deep, which would provide cover from machine-gun fire but not artillery. Both battalions were extremely familiar with the ground they had to cover, and the training in Varennes allowed detailed planning of the actions required at company and platoon level when the objectives were reached.

The 9th Royal Irish Fusiliers was to attack up the western bank of the River Ancre from Hamel village to Beaucourt Station against a frontage of the German line a little over 500 yards wide. The Battalion's left boundary was a line from A25, a point in the German front line trenches, to one of the houses behind Beaucourt Station and then south-east to the River Ancre. The first objective was the forward trench from A25 on the left to Railway Sap on the right. Then A Company would clear Railway Sap from the junction with the German front line trench and send a Lewis gun out as right flank guard. B Company was ordered to clear the easternmost communication trench that ran back to the German second and third lines, and C Company was ordered to clear the communication trench that ran from A24 to B24 (Larne). Then B, C and D Companies were to attack and consolidate the trenches and strong-points B21 (Bushmills), B22 and B23; each strong-point would be reinforced by a Vickers gun from 108th Brigade Machine Gun Company. Finally, A and B Companies (the latter minus one platoon to be left at Bushmills) were to attack the final objective—the system of trenches behind Beaucourt Station, and '*rush out small patrols*' to occupy the mill and the house to its north-west. This final part of the attack would be covered by C and D Companies (less consolidating platoons at B22 and B23). Meanwhile, 12th Royal Irish Rifles would establish strong-points at B26 (Gobbins) and B24 (Larne). B Company, 12th Royal Irish Rifles was under command 9th Royal Irish Fusiliers to provide a platoon to attack Railway Sap, a platoon to patrol the marsh on the right of the 9th Royal Irish Fusiliers' attack, and to provide a reserve of two platoons.

As was customary, a number of officers and men were to be left out of the attack. The operation order produced by 108th Brigade stipulated that a maximum of twenty officers was to attack, and detailed those others that would be left out in order that the Battalion could be reconstituted quickly in the event of large casualties. The 9th Royal Irish Fusiliers officers left out for this attack were Captains H W F M Vanston (OC D Company), A D Allen (Second-in-Command A Company) and J A Johnston (Second-in-Command C Company), Lieutenants T F Given, R S Flood, E N Ensor, E A Godson and C P Wingfield, and Second Lieutenants G D Craig, H T Ozzard, W F Reid, G H Richardson and T W Boyd. Most difficult of all for Lieutenant Colonel Blacker was the order that he and his battalion headquarters must not advance with his men. Lieutenant Godson related how he was chosen to be left out. He and his fellow subalterns referred to the forthcoming attack as '*Der Tag*', German for 'The Day'. It was ordered that all training courses for officers would carry on as arranged, but this order was, he noted, counter-ordered two or three times. Of the four platoon commanders in A Company only three would take part in the attack and they drew lots to decide who was 'in' and who was 'out'.

> '*Meanwhile the Bn. C.O., Col. S.B. Blacker* (sic) *received orders to nominate one of his subalterns for a Transport Course at Havre. He said to me that as I had been in the Cavalry I was obviously the one to go to it. The main Order became subject to counter-order and re-order more than once. Lots were thus drawn and I was 'in for Der Tag'. Ozanne was 'out' of us four. Forty eight hours before Zero final order came that Courses were all 'on', so off I went to Havre, and Deus Vult, my inglorious part in 'July 1st' was to listen to the distant bombardments from that place.*'

(Ozanne was not an officer of this Battalion; it is believed that he refers to Lieutenant A C Hollywood.)

The officers that played a part were:

Commanding Officer:	Lieutenant Colonel S W W Blacker
Second-in-Command:	Major A C Pratt
Adjutant:	Lieutenant G Cather
Intelligence Officer:	Captain W J Menaul
Signalling Officer:	Lieutenant G E Lutton
A Company:	Captain C H Ensor, Lieutenant A C Hollywood, Second Lieutenant G E Barcroft and Second Lieutenant R T Montgomery
B Company:	Major T J Atkinson, Lieutenant T G Shillington, Second Lieutenant A Seggie and Second Lieutenant W J Stewart
C Company:	Captain C M Johnston, Lieutenant R S B Townsend, Second Lieutenant A A Andrews and Second Lieutenant E M Smith
D Company:	Captain J G Brew, Captain J E Gibson, Lieutenant H K Jackson
Forward in the Line:	Lieutenant R S Flood and Second Lieutenants A D Allen and E N Ensor
Regimental Sergeant Major:	Warrant Officer Class 1 T McKane

Attached:

B Company, **12th Royal Irish Rifles**:

Captain C S Murray and Lieutenant A D Lemon

108th Brigade Machine Gun Company:

Lieutenant J G E FitzGerald and Second Lieutenant M B Lendrum (both formerly 9th Royal Irish Fusiliers)

B Section, **108th Brigade Trench Mortar Battery**:

Lieutenant S O'Neill (formerly 9th Royal Irish Fusiliers, transferred to the General List in March 1916 for service with a trench mortar battery.)

As well as those in battalion headquarters, including signallers, runners and stretcher-bearers, the operation order specified all those to be left with Lieutenant Stronge at the transport lines a mile behind the front line on the Englebelmer/Bouzincourt Road. They included the drivers, grooms and shoeing smiths of the Transport, the Quartermaster, Captain A Ferguson, with his men, and the cooks, sanitation squads, train loaders, tailors and shoe makers, and some of the regimental police.

In addition, each company left out a number of key men including the Company Sergeant Majors, Company Quartermaster Sergeants, Lewis gun teams of two non-commissioned officers and two men, a signalling instructor, a bombing instructor and the very new and inexperienced men. Henry Fox, the Company Quartermaster Sergeant of C Company, produced a detailed roll just prior to the attack that allocated tasks to men of the company. The paper strength of his company was 249 men. Of these, nine were struck off strength having been evacuated to hospital in England, four more were sick in hospital and two had recently returned to duty and would not take part in the attack. Six men were at the Base Depot, two were 'On Command' and two others on unspecified details. Seven men were on detached duty; one each to headquarters 36th (Ulster) Division, 36th Division Signal Company, 36th (Ulster) Division Reserve Company and 108th Brigade Trench Mortar Battery, and three men were at headquarters 108th Brigade. Nine men were on duty with the Quartermaster's Stores or as company storemen, and nine men were with the Transport, including the company groom. One man was on duty with the battalion orderly room, two at the regimental command post, and Company Sergeant Major Turner, Henry Fox and a clerk were at company headquarters. Seven men were signallers at the headquarters' visual transmitting station, the forward transmitting station or as linemen. Only one man was specifically designated as battle surplus; Lance Corporal Magowan, a Lewis gunner. Private Clay, the servant for Captain J A Johnston, would also not take part in the attack. The other companies had similar detachments.

The remainder of C Company, 184 men, were available for duty. Henry Fox specified the duties of these men; all would play a part in the attack, although some would not advance with the main body of the company:

Battalion runner	2
Company runner	8
Bombing team	20
Company bomb carrier	6
Battalion bomb carrier	7
Lewis gunner	12
Lewis gun ammunition carrier	8
Vickers gun ammunition carrier	3
Bangalore torpedo men	5
Company signaller	3
Stretcher bearer	3
Company NCOs & riflemen	107

The 108th Brigade operation order also specified the equipment to be carried by each man: a waterproof sheet, wool waistcoat, rifle and equipment (less pack), 170 rounds of ammunition, two Mills bombs, two sandbags, one iron ration and two smoke helmets and goggles. Regimental officers were ordered to wear trousers and puttees rather than breeches and boots and were to carry the same equipment as the men in order to reduce the chance of being identified by a sniper. Those responsible for carrying the extra bombs for the bombing teams, for the final consolidation of the captured positions or for supporting the mortars and machine-guns, were also laden with all of their necessary stores. The load was heavy, but those in the leading waves of the Ulster Division were equipped as lightly as possible and the heavier loads in the later waves were shared between sections. In order to indicate progress in the attack, yellow flags were to be carried by each platoon and bombing parties were to carry yellow metal discs. Flares were distributed amongst the officers and NCOs for use when objectives were reached. Orders detailed that they were to be fired in a row at three or four paces apart, 15 seconds between the firing of each flare. Officers were to carry designated maps. For the officers of the Ulster Division these were a 1:20,000 scale map sheet (57D South East) and a special Corps map. They were instructed to refer to the maps in all reports and messages. The quantity of spare ammunition and grenades to be held in reserve was also detailed in orders: 150,000 rounds of ammunition in the front trenches, 200,000 rounds in the 'old Battalion store' with 3,000 grenades in the front line and 2,000 more also in the 'old Battalion store'.

The bombardment of the German trenches began at 5.00am on 'U Day', Saturday 24 June. The British artillery concentrated on cutting the wire in front of the German line faced by the 9th Royal Irish Fusiliers, while the German response was to shell the front and support lines with 77mm shells. Added to the miserable weather, this made for a most uncomfortable period for the men who had returned to their trenches the previous day in preparation for the assault. A number of men were wounded, including Privates William Harry Guy, John Simons, Alexander Weatherall and Robert Willis. Privates William Sands and William Wylie were evacuated with shell-shock. Private Weatherall died of his wounds the next day. On 'V Day', 25 June, the process continued and German artillery killed seventeen-year-old Private Harry Molloy and wounded eleven other men. Three men were killed on 'W Day', 26 June: Sergeant John McCappin, Private William James Cordy who was hit in the side by shell fragments as he carried rations forward to his Company, and Private Matthew Ogle. Sergeants Frank Girvan and Abraham Vennard and Private Thomas Henry Boyce were wounded; the latter was erroneously reported as killed in action. On the fourth day of the bombardment, 'X day', 27 June, Private John Thomas Quinn was killed and sixteen men were wounded. On 'Y Day', Wednesday 28 June, the rain began to fall even more heavily and the British bombardment increased. The German reply killed Lance Corporal John Hutchinson (whose brother had been killed at Hamel in April) and wounded four men. One of the worst incidents in the day preceding the attack involved 11 Platoon and the battalion headquarters of 13th Royal Irish Rifles in Martinsart, which were moving out of the village to relieve a battalion at Thiepval Wood on the night of 28 June. A shell fell amongst the men, killing fourteen and wounding many others, of whom ten died later. One of those killed was Rifleman David Frame, whose brother James was serving with the 9th Royal Irish Fusiliers.

Captain C M Johnston

In the five days of the preparatory bombardment seven men had been killed and at least forty were wounded, some most severely, but the appalling weather forced a postponement of the attack for forty-eight hours. The 9th Royal Irish Fusiliers was relieved in the line by 12th Royal Irish Rifles, and moved back to Mesnil for a rest. Typically this was disrupted; the British howitzers located nearby allowed little sleep and in the evening the enemy sent over a number of shells that wounded seven men, including Sergeant George Thompson. The relief for the 9th Royal Irish Fusiliers, if it could be called that, was short lived, and the Battalion moved back into the line up routes marked with red and green lanterns at midnight on Friday 30 June in preparation for the assault the following morning. More casualties were suffered as the men moved into the line, including Sergeant Frederick Foster who was killed by shellfire and Private Thomas Cuthbertson, who was wounded. Sergeant Frederick Foster would be awarded the Military Medal for his gallantry in May and June 1916. Sergeant Foster, and Sergeant W H Palmer who also earned the Military Medal for his gallantry over the same period for his work with the Battalion Scouts, were the first men of the 9th Royal Irish Fusiliers to be decorated.

Sergeant W H Palmer MM

By about 3.00am the men of the 9th Royal Irish Fusiliers were complete in their positions, with twenty officers and a little over 600 men ready for the assault. Over 100 men from B Company, 12th Royal Irish Rifles were also in place. The Battalion was organised on a four-company front. On the right was A Company, in the right-centre B Company, in the left-centre C Company and on the left D Company. The leading wave comprised a platoon from each company along with the Battalion's twelve Lewis guns. Each leading platoon also had four lengths of Bangalore torpedo, a long tube filled with explosive and used for cutting lanes in the enemy wire. The second wave also comprised a platoon from each company, and these two waves, along with two Stokes mortars from the 108th Brigade Trench Mortar Battery, were assembled in the front line trenches. The third wave comprised the supporting platoons and they assembled in the communication trenches with three Vickers machine guns from the 108th Brigade Machine Gun Company. Two more guns were kept in reserve with Lieutenant J G E FitzGerald who was now the Second-in-Command of the Machine Gun Company. The consolidating platoons were in the fourth and final wave and were assembled in the second line trenches. Also in the last wave were a bombing squad from each company that was to be responsible for clearing the bypassed enemy dugouts.

B Company of 12th Royal Irish Rifles, commanded by Captain C S Murray, comprised 5, 6, 7 and 8 Platoons. Two were responsible for the right flank: 6 Platoon, assembled at Lancashire Post, was responsible for Railway Sap and subsequent clearance along the railway, and 8 Platoon, at Crow's Nest, was responsible for the marsh between the River Ancre and the railway. The other two platoons were in support to the 9th Royal Irish Fusiliers; 5 Platoon was to act as a carrying platoon in the rear of the 9th Royal Irish Fusiliers' advance, while 7 Platoon was an uncommitted reserve. Both were assembled at Hedgerow Trench on the northern edge of Hamel.

Zero Hour was planned for 7.30am on Saturday 1 July. Much has been made of this auspicious date, the original anniversary of the Battle of the Boyne, and, although seen as a good omen by many, it can have given little comfort during the last hours under the enemy guns. Intermittent shellfire had continued throughout the night, and in the few hours remaining before the attack began the enemy shelling intensified, killing or wounding a further fifty men. There were also some narrow escapes; before dawn, Sergeant J Whitsitt, who was in the third wave, was talking to Lieutenant Hollywood, one of A Company's platoon commanders in the second wave, who showed him the holes in his helmet where it had been hit without injuring him.

By the end of the preliminary bombardment, the positions occupied by the Württembergers of the forward three companies of *1. Battalion, RIR 119* were severely damaged. The dugouts had proved effective, however, and the enemy had lost fewer than twenty men killed and ninety men wounded. Much of the wire had been cut and the road rearward from the front line to Beaucourt was littered with dead animals and wagons from the Transport that had attempted to bring rations and supplies forward and evacuate the injured. Of the three machine guns of 2nd Machine Gun Company, Gun Number 8, commanded by *Schütze* (Private) Manz, had been forced to move due to the destruction of its position during the preliminary bombardment. Its new position and the effect of artillery fire meant that it could only fire into the left flank of the Ulstermen attacking from Thiepval Wood and this, therefore, left only two machine guns from 2nd Machine Gun Company to face the attack by the two battalions of 108th Brigade north of the Ancre.

The ravine at Hamel showing the area over which C and D Companies attacked on 1 July 1916. The flat area on the left beyond the ravine is where 12th Royal Irish Rifles attacked.

The weather on the morning of the attack was glorious; the air was still and the sun, which had risen hours earlier, quickly warmed the ground. The plan called for the leading waves to be within 150 yards of the German trenches at Zero, and the first wave crossed the parapet of Elgin Avenue at 7.10am and moved into no-man's-land, much of which was still green and covered in high weeds. Much has been made of the Ulster Protestant history of the Division and the links with the Orange Order. Many writers have commented on the use of *"No Surrender"* being used as a battle-cry by the men attacking out of Thiepval Wood. It is clear, however, that the traditions of the Regiment were strong in the 9th Royal Irish Fusiliers and it is reported that their battle-cry, as the attack began from Hamel, was the Regimental battle-cry of *"Faugh a Ballagh!"*.

The first wave was followed at five-minute intervals by the second and third waves and finally at 7.30am by the fourth wave. The final bombardment was still falling on the German first line trenches and 4.5-inch trench mortars were filling the Ancre valley with smoke as the leading waves quickly made for the ravine. The first platoons suffered few casualties getting through the marked routes in their own wire, which had been cut in preparation for the attack. During the advance on the ravine, however, casualties mounted at a considerable rate as they were engaged by the machine guns of 2nd Machine Gun Company and by the German artillery summoned by the enemy firing red flares.

The men of the German machine-gun companies had been carefully selected for their task and were well trained. Each Maxim machine-gun had a crew of six men, and the time that had been spent by these men in this sector ensured that they were very familiar with the terrain over which they would fire. In addition, each gun had detailed range cards on which were registered every target and feature within range of their gun. The accuracy of the machine gunners was increased by the use of the Goerz prismatic gun-sight. The first of the Maxim machine guns firing upon the 9th Royal Irish Fusiliers was Gun Number 7 located in Sector B5 opposite Mary Redan in the strong-point known to the Ulstermen as A27. It was commanded by *Unteroffizier* (Corporal) Kaeser. One man of this gun-crew, *Schütze* Baptist Vogt, was killed by shellfire before the attack began. This gun engaged the left flank of the 9th Royal Irish Fusiliers as the men advanced towards the ravine. It had a clear field of fire with only the ravine itself being in dead ground. Gun Number 7 was briefly put out of action due to artillery fire, but its crew returned it to action and during the course of the attack they fired over 2,500 rounds. Gun Number 9, commanded by *Unteroffizier* Huss, was located in the German second line between the strong-points designated by the Ulstermen as A24 and B23. After the attack began, its crew brought the gun up out of their dugout and quickly brought it into action against the advancing Ulstermen. One of its crew, *Schütze* Gustav Bäzner, was mortally wounded by a shell splinter, but this gun remained in operation throughout the attack. It too fired over 2,500 rounds. Enfilade fire was also brought to bear from machine guns firing from the right flank in St Pierre-Divion. Casualties were particularly heavy on the left where the nature of the ground meant that the troops were very exposed. The second wave in particular suffered terribly.

The ravine at Hamel. In the low ground in the centre lies the railway and the River Ancre. A Company attacked on a line from right to left through the site of the Ancre British Cemetery. The high ground in the distance was the limit of the attack by the remainder of 36th (Ulster Division).

The scene of the attack by the 9th Royal Irish Fusiliers.

On the left of the attack Captain Brew was wounded in the head soon after the attack began and the majority of the other officers of the two left companies were killed or wounded before reaching the ravine. The men of the leading waves of the two left companies who reached the ravine were within 150 yards of the German trenches. They were reorganised into one line and the advance continued under sustained machine-gun fire. Unsupported, the attack on the left faltered, although small groups of men reached the enemy first line. Captain Johnston was held up about thirty yards short of the ravine. The runner he sent back, the only one to get through from any of the companies that day, carried the message *'cannot advance without support'*. The two reserve platoons, 5 Platoon and 7 Platoon from B Company, 12th Royal Irish Rifles under Captain Murray (who was wounded as the attack began) were ready to advance. When Captain Johnston's message was received, Lieutenant Colonel Blacker ordered forward 7 Platoon but it was almost wiped out as it crossed the wire. About 8.45am Captain Johnston was shot and badly wounded in both legs but he managed to crawl into a shell hole. Private Richard Pantlin of 108th Trench Mortar Battery, who was also badly wounded, joined him there. Sergeant John Keith and Private James Henry of B Company saw both men in the shell hole and the latter left his water bottle with them. Captain Johnston eventually succumbed to his wounds there some time in the afternoon.

In the right-centre, B Company pushed forward without its Company Commander. Sergeant Keith later wrote, *'we were going over the parapet and I saw Major Atkinson hit, it seemed badly. He dropped on our own wire'*. Sergeant Keith was later shot in the face but survived that attack and was able to rejoin the Battalion when he recovered. He survived the war and earned a Meritorious Service Medal. Private Thomas McCrory passed where Major Atkinson had fallen, and as he withdrew a few hours later saw his body still lying over the wire. There were many other casualties early in the attack including Second Lieutenant William Stewart leading 8 Platoon in B Company, who was killed at about 8.00am by a shell that landed beside him. His Platoon Sergeant, Sergeant Hugh William Courtney, was wounded later.

Captain C H Ensor

Meanwhile, the third and fourth waves had climbed out of Elgin Avenue and were caught in severe machine-gun fire from the trenches around St Pierre Divion on the east bank of the River Ancre. Coupled with the artillery barrage falling between the 9th Royal Irish Fusiliers' lines and the ravine, this practically annihilated these eight platoons. The men of the Machine Gun Company, gallantly moving their guns forward, were also hit badly. Corporal David Orr was one of those wounded. He was hit in the arm, but he continued to move his gun forward until he was finally shot again, this time in the stomach. He died where he fell.

The attack progressed most strongly on the right, where A and B Companies had penetrated the German first line. Although the enemy appeared to surrender at first, they realised that these small groups were unsupported and continued fighting, supported by men from the second line. Two Lewis guns were captured here and few of the 9th Royal Irish Fusiliers survived. One of these Lewis guns was probably that of Lance Corporal William Stringer of A Company. One of the officers wrote later, *'There seems fairly conclusive evidence that Stringer behaved most magnificently. He got as far as the German wire, and got his gun into action, but the Boches apparently concentrated machine guns on him, and he could hardly have survived many minutes. Considering the terrific fire of the Boches machine guns and artillery, which so few of our men survived, his performance was absolutely magnificent. He must have known it meant certain death and yet he evidently never hesitated a moment.'* Lance Corporal Stringer was eighteen years old. On the extreme right others of Captain Ensor's company reached the German wire. Before he was wounded, Sergeant Whitsitt saw Lieutenant Hollywood jump into the German trench there but no more progress was made. Captain Ensor was wounded in the right leg near the ravine and could proceed no farther, and nearby Second Lieutenant Montgomery was wounded in the foot.

On the right flank of the 9th Royal Irish Fusiliers, the other two platoons from 12th Royal Irish Rifles were equally shot up. 6 Platoon, under the command of forty-one year old Lieutenant Archie Lemon, was responsible for the Railway Sap (*Tal Stellung*). He left the trenches with his men (and six men attached from 8 Platoon) just before zero, with A Company immediately on his left. Before reaching the ravine all but Lieutenant Lemon and twelve men were casualties, including his attached Lewis gun team. Unsupported, he advanced with his remaining men over the railway line to the sap. Only nine of them got there and they fought their way in. Lance Sergeant Miller moved to the right with three men to bomb down the sap, but they were all killed or wounded. Lieutenant Lemon and the other five men advanced up the main sap but their way was blocked by thick wire and they faced machine-gun fire from a small tunnel. Rifleman Gamble cut the wire while Lieutenant Lemon climbed above the sap with some bombs, sending the men on along the trench. Soon after, Gamble was killed and Lieutenant Lemon was shot and killed by two German officers who fired on him from a dug-out leading into the tunnel containing the machine-gun.[3] A bomb thrown by one of the Riflemen immediately killed them.[4] Of the men who made it to the sap only Corporal Burgess and Rifleman McNeilly escaped. McNeilly lost Corporal Burgess on the way back and he alone reported to two non-commissioned officers of the 9th Royal Irish Fusiliers. They were the only two men of their platoon to escape alive and unwounded.

Meanwhile, 8 Platoon under Sergeant Hoare had left Crow's Nest and lay outside the wire in preparation for the advance through the marsh. The Platoon was divided into three; Sergeant Herbert Hamilton commanded a section on the left, Sergeant James Benison on the right with Sergeant Hoare in the centre. Attached was a Lewis gun under the command of Second Lieutenant M Neill. The platoon suffered heavy shelling and machine-gun and rifle fire from the bottom end of Railway Sap on the left, and from the enemy positions south of St Pierre Divion on the right, the latter of which had not been silenced despite the efforts of a battery of 172nd Brigade firing into St Pierre Divion from Hamel. Sergeant Hoare's party was soon all killed or wounded and, on the left, a small party of only three or four men made it into the first sap, but the enemy fire made their position untenable. On the right, Sergeant Benison was killed and the survivors of his section with the platoon's Lewis gun sustained heavy fire until Sergeant Hoare sent back for orders and Lieutenant Colonel Blacker ordered that they retire.

The indomitable Intelligence Officer, Captain Menaul, reported on the Battalion's progress. Prior to the attack he and five scouts proceeded to Shooters Hill, about 400 yards from the German lines close to the centre of 12th Royal Irish Rifles' front line. From here he could view all of the ground over which the 9th Royal Irish Fusiliers would attack, except on the extreme right. The scouts acted as runners over the 1,000 yards of trenches to the battalion headquarters, and from 7.30am to 4.00pm he kept the Commanding Officer informed of the progress of events. This information was, in turn, passed by telephone to brigade headquarters. For his courageous work over the previous days and during the attack he was awarded the Military Cross, the first awarded to an officer of the Battalion. Sergeant Robert Lucas, the senior scout, received the Military Medal.

Lieutenant
A C Hollywood

Company Sergeant
Major R Lucas

By 10.00am many of the survivors were back in the trenches at Hamel with hundreds of dead and wounded left in no-man's-land. When the extent of the casualties was realised, every available man was sent to hold the front line under the command of Major Pratt. Following a request for reinforcements, two companies of the 1/5th Battalion, The York and Lancaster Regiment, were sent up to assist and Lieutenant FitzGerald moved forward a machine-gun team reformed from the survivors of his section.

Second Lieutenant Montgomery had found shelter in a shell-hole near the German first line trench. Hearing a wounded man cry out for some water he left his shelter but was hit in the head immediately and killed. During the day survivors attempted to consolidate small strong-points in no-man's-land or to move back to the 9th Royal Irish Fusiliers' lines. Many were unsuccessful; at about midday Private Charles Stewart of A Company was close to the enemy line and saw Lieutenant Hollywood killed by a machine-gun bullet as he left the German first line trench. Some took an age to return to safety; Private James Nelson eventually managed to crawl back, having lain wounded beside the dead Lieutenant Hollywood for two days and a night near the German wire. Many of those who were unable to make it back died of their wounds in the shell-holes of no-man's-land. A few days after the attack one man wrote of the death of Private Andy Rowan:

> *'Poor Andy Rowan is dead. Of that there can be little doubt. He was wounded at first and was assisted to a shell hole by John Kerr (of Chapman's Ltd). Kerr was wounded himself and was unable to get Andy further so had to go the rest of the way himself. He reported Andy's whereabouts as soon as he got in. There was another wounded man in the same shell hole as Andy and he came in after Kerr and reported that Andy was dead. W J Lynn who is a stretcher bearer went out under fire as soon as he had finished bandaging the man he was at. Only a few minutes had elapsed from the time Kerr reported Andy first*

until Lynn was with him and he was dead. He had been hit again I believe.'

Private Andrew Rowan (Loughgilly), B Company, killed in action.

On the 9th Royal Irish Fusiliers' left, 12th Royal Irish Rifles had fought bravely but had also been unable to take their objectives. The initial attack was met by withering machine-gun fire that covered the largely undamaged and partially concealed German wire on the right of the attack. Advancing alongside D Company of the 9th Royal Irish Fusiliers, C Company of 12th Royal Irish Rifles suffered huge losses. A and D Companies on the left made some progress but those that managed to reach the German trenches were outnumbered and could not hold their positions. A second push by about 100 men of 12th Royal Irish Rifles in the mid-morning also failed and at 12.30pm the remnants of the Battalion, numbering forty-six men, were gathered together and prepared for yet another attempt on the German first line in support of an attack by the men of 29th Division on their left. This attack did not take place and the men were ordered to hold their own line. By 2.00pm the Royal Irish Rifles' line had been secured and they were relieved at 3.30pm by a battalion of The York and Lancaster Regiment from 148th Brigade.

Sergeant David McCullough

On the right, the remainder of the Ulster Division had moved forward at Zero against the formidable defences on the Thiepval plateau. Beyond the first line trenches was the strongly built Swaben Redoubt, overlooked by Thiepval Village on the right and by the villages west and north of the River Ancre on the left. Having swept through the first line trenches there was bitter fighting for the Redoubt that involved most of the attacking battalions. The Redoubt was entered at 8.00am and, despite heavy losses, was taken by 8.30am. At 9.15am 107th Brigade passed through the forward units of the two leading Brigades and advanced on the next objective in front of Grandcourt. Many casualties were taken but the position was entered and captured. Sadly, the effort and courage of the attacking troops was in vain; with no protection on the flanks, where the attacks by 29th and 32nd Divisions had failed, the leading troops were forced back to the Swaben Redoubt that afternoon. Delays in sending up reinforcements, the domination of the ground by German machine gunners, and repeated counter-attacks eventually forced the decision that the remnants of the Ulster Division must retire to the German front line. This was carried out in good order at 10.00pm after nearly fourteen hours of fighting, and during the night most of the survivors were withdrawn farther to Thiepval Wood, although small groups remained within the German lines.

This photograph was taken in 1921 near the site of Shooter's Hill from which Captain Menaul reported the progress of the attack. On the horizon on the right can be seen the remnants of Thiepval Wood, and just to the right of centre is the Ulster Tower.

That evening, on the other side of the Ancre, the remnants of the 9th Royal Irish Fusiliers and 12th Royal Irish Rifles were withdrawn back into Hamel village, leaving the line held by companies of The York and Lancaster Regiment. Several parties were organised to search an area of about 450 yards by 500 yards of no-man's-land where the casualties lay. This continued over the next four nights although the Battalion had withdrawn to Martinsart at noon on 2 July. Lieutenant Colonel Blacker's orders were to *'concentrate all energies on getting in the wounded',* consequently relatively few bodies were recovered. Men of 16th Royal Irish Rifles, the Division's pioneer battalion, assisted with this work.

It was with these search parties that the Adjutant, Lieutenant Geoffrey Cather, was killed. From 7.00pm until midnight on the day of the attack, Lieutenant Cather searched no-man's-land and brought in three wounded men. At 8.00am in the light of the morning he continued his search and, against the odds, in full view of the enemy and under direct machine-gun and intermittent artillery fire, he brought in another wounded man from within 150 yards of the German wire and managed to give water to some others for whom he arranged rescue. At 10.30am he took out water to another man, and having seen to him, called out to see if there were any more wounded nearby. He was answered by a wave and in moving towards this unknown Royal Irish Fusilier he was killed by machine-gun fire just out of sight of the Battalion's front line. The two men who went out to find him that night found that he had been shot in the head. They recovered his body and brought back the wounded man that he had been going to help. Lieutenant Cather was buried near Hamel, but his grave was lost subsequently and he is commemorated on the Thiepval Memorial. For his bravery and sacrifice he was awarded the Victoria Cross, one of nine awarded on those two days, of which the Ulster Division earned four. After the award of the Victoria Cross was made known, his mother offered through her brother, Major Shillington, to provide photographs of her son to any officers or men who wanted one. These were duly sent to France and given out by Major Shillington. A letter to the War Office from his mother indicates that his personal effects were inadvertently sent to

Dublin to the relatives of Lieutenant William Turner Richardson of 108th Brigade Machine Gun Company (and formerly The Royal Irish Rifles), who had been killed on the other side of the Ancre the previous day.

Cather VC
This print, by Alfred Pearse, shows Lieutenant and Adjutant Geoffrey Cather in that act that earned him the Victoria Cross.

Many others, including the rest of the officers who did not take part in the attack, worked hard in these terrible conditions to rescue relations and friends. Some, like Captain Menaul, were wounded themselves. Sergeants Jack Robinson and David McCullough were commended for bringing in wounded men, as was Private James Elliott. One of those severely injured in the fighting was his brother Lance Corporal Henry Elliott, who died of his wounds on 4 July. Some men lay for days before they were found and brought back. Captain Ensor was one of four men brought back on the fourth night after the attack. He had managed to crawl into a shell hole where he was to remain until he was found by a search party led by Major Pratt, spending his last ten hours there in water up to his armpits. Private Thomas Burnett was also brought in that night severely wounded, having crawled some of the way back from the German wire. Privates Edward Lynas and John Gillespie, who had been wounded by the same shell, crawled back 700 yards; both men had also been trapped in a water-filled shell-hole.

The wounded were evacuated quickly thanks to the immense effort given to the organisation of the medical services in support of the Ulster Division, and the good weather. Indeed, it worked so well that the Casualty Clearing Stations became congested. 29th Casualty Clearing Station at Gezaincourt received 5,346 men in one day alone. 108th Field Ambulance saw over 300 stretcher cases during daylight on 1 July and received a total of 1,725 lying and over 3,000 sitting wounded in the period up to 5 July. Farther back, however, the scale of the casualties overwhelmed the transport system evacuating the wounded to the hospitals on the coast and to England.

On the evening after the attack, the Company Sergeant Majors and Quartermaster Sergeants had the terrible task of facing the few men left, and as they called the roll the awful extent of the Battalion's destruction hit them. Company Quartermaster Sergeant Henry Fox kept the rolls compiled before and after the attack and they show starkly how C Company was devastated. Prior to the attack, Privates William Guy, William Sands, John Simons, Alexander Weatherall, Robert Willis and William Wylie were wounded on 24 June (Weatherall died on 25 June), Private Matthew Ogle was killed on 26 June and Private Thomas Cuthbertson was wounded on 30 June. One hundred and seventy-six men of C Company took part in the attack; 136 became casualties:

	Took Part	Killed in Action	Died of Wounds	Wounded	Unwounded
Battalion runner	2	-	-	-	2
Company runner	8	1	-	5	2
Bombing team	18	5	-	8	5
Company bomb carrier	6	2	-	3	1
Battalion bomb carrier	7	-	-	1	6
Lewis gunner	12	6	1	5	-
Lewis gun ammunition carrier	7	1	-	4	2
Vickers gun ammunition carrier	3	1	-	1	1
Bangalore torpedo men	5	3	-	-	2
Company signaller	3	1	-	2	-
Stretcher bearer	3	-	-	1	2
Company NCOs & riflemen	102	37	2	46	17
Total	176	57	3	76	40

Although later battles would claim casualties of a similar magnitude, the first day of the Somme offensive remains the most costly in British military history. The statistics are almost meaningless and impossible to imagine: 21,392 men were killed and 35,493 were wounded. The Ulster Division suffered over 5,100 casualties and the 9th Royal Irish Fusiliers had been almost destroyed. In total 535 all ranks were reported as killed, wounded and missing. This was the third-highest casualty total in the Ulster Division. Only 13th Royal Irish Rifles and 11th Royal Inniskilling Fusiliers suffered more casualties (595 and 589 respectively) and these three Irish battalions were amongst thirty-two battalions that suffered over 500 casualties that day.

The total casualty figures in the war diary of the 9th Royal Irish Fusiliers have proven to be accurate, although the breakdown of casualties was adjusted as the facts became known. The war diary shows:

	Officers	Other Ranks
Killed in action	2	56
Wounded	9	303
Missing	6	159
Total	17	518

Major T J Atkinson, killed in action leading A Company.

The officer casualties recorded in the war diary were two officers killed (including Lieutenant Cather who died on 2 July), five missing believed killed, one missing, eight wounded and one a casualty from shell shock. In fact, those declared missing had been killed. In total, eight of the fifteen officers who crossed the parapet at Zero were dead: Major Atkinson, Captain Johnston, Lieutenants Townsend and Hollywood (whose brother James was killed while attacking with the 12th Royal Irish Rifles) and Second Lieutenants Montgomery, Seggie and Stewart. In addition, Lieutenant Lemon from 12th Royal Irish Rifles was killed in Railway Sap; Captain Murray commanding B Company, 12th Royal Irish Rifles, died of his wounds on 2 July;[5] Lieutenant O'Neill, who had been attached to 108th Trench Mortar Battery, was missing in action; he was later declared killed in action.

The other eight officers who took part in the attack were wounded. From A Company, Captain Ensor, who had been mistakenly reported as killed in action on the casualty lists at home, spent five months in hospital undergoing major operations, and the remainder of the war with the 10th (Reserve) Battalion. Second Lieutenant Barcroft, who was severely wounded, did not return until the summer of 1917. The only surviving officer from B Company, Lieutenant Tom Shillington had been wounded in both legs by machine-gun fire but he managed to rejoin the Battalion after more than three months' convalescence. The two platoon commanders in C Company who survived had both been with the Battalion for only three months. Second Lieutenant Arthur Andrews was shot in the right thigh; he relinquished his commission as a result, and Second Lieutenant E M Smith also did not serve with the Battalion again. All three of the officers in D Company survived.

Sergeant John Bryans (Lurgan), C Company, killed in action.

Captain Brew, who had been wounded in the head, returned to the 9th Royal Irish Fusiliers after six months and Captain Gibson, who had been shot in the shoulder as he lay in no-man's-land, was able to rejoin in early 1917. Lieutenant Henry Jackson had been shot in the right arm and suffered severe nerve damage, forcing him to relinquish his commission. In addition, one officer waiting in the trenches behind the attack, Second Lieutenant George Craig, was deafened by a shell and spent the rest of the war serving at home. Second Lieutenant Marc Lendrum, who had joined 108th Brigade Machine Gun Company in January, was wounded; when recovered he joined the Tank Corps.

Private William Culley (Tullyallen), C Company, killed in action

The war diary recorded that fifty-six other ranks were known to have been killed and 159 other ranks were missing. In fact, all but one of the missing men were killed; 214 men of the 9th Royal Irish Fusiliers are now known to have been killed in action on 1 July 1916. One of the missing men was Private Thomas Warren. Across the Ulster Division only 165 men were captured and Warren was the only man of the 9th Royal Irish Fusiliers known to have been taken prisoner. He succumbed to his wounds on 4 July. In addition, seven men had been killed in action or died of wounds received during the preparatory bombardment between 'U Day' and the morning of the attack.

The platoon sergeants, amongst the best men in the Battalion, suffered particularly badly and the loss of twenty-four sergeants was a critical blow. In A Company Sergeants Moore and Wilson were killed and Hegan, Kirkwood, McCourt and Whitsitt were wounded. In B Company Sergeants Jackson and Magee were killed and Sergeants Barr, Caulfield, Courtney, Johnston and Keith were wounded. In C Company Sergeants Bryans, Brown and Hobbs were killed (two of Hobbs' three brothers were also killed). In D Company Sergeants Bunting, Gordon, Mullen and Thornbury were killed and Balmer, Hare, Hughes and Sewell were wounded. Sergeant Hughes died of his wounds on 11 July and Sergeants McCourt, Whitsitt, Caulfield and Sewell were badly injured; all were discharged as no longer physically fit for war service due to wounds. In B Company, 12th Royal Irish Rifles Sergeants Benison and McIlwaine were killed.[6]

14419 Private Thomas Lyness, C Company, wounded.

Only seven of forty-eight Lewis-gunners survived. The men who had left in January to join the Brigade Machine Gun Company also fared badly. Company Sergeant Major W J Brown was waiting in a dugout with a reserve gun. He and the men with him were killed when the dugout took a direct hit from a shell. Corporal Orr's death has been described, and Privates J Courtney, R A McIlrath and J Rountree were also killed.

The war diary records that a total of 303 men were wounded. Many of these men have been identified, but incomplete records make it impossible to confirm the number of wounded or the extent of their injuries. The accuracy of the war diary is such, however, that this figure should be accepted. Some men were only slightly wounded and were able to return to duty a few days after the attack. Others were severely injured, such as Privates Edward Atwell and Thomas Burnett who both had a leg amputated. Before the end of July, twenty-four men would die of their wounds. Private Robert Bulman died of his wounds on 12 October 1920 and Private Thomas Best died after 31 August 1921. Consequently, he was commemorated on the Portadown War Memorial but not by the Commonwealth War Graves Commission.

The revised casualty tally for the attack on 1 July 1916 is:

	Final Officers' Tally	Final Other Ranks Tally	Final Casualty Tally*
Killed in action	8	214	222
Died of wounds	-	25	25
Wounded	9	278	287
Captured & died of wounds	-	1	1
Total	17	518	535

* These figures do not include the seven men killed and over forty men wounded in the period between 'U Day' and the morning of the attack. The total casualty figure for the period beginning 24 June 1916 is, therefore, no less than 582 casualties of whom 254 were killed in action or died of wounds.

Company Sergeant Major W J Brown (Portadown), Machine Gun Corps, killed in action.

It is impossible to know how many of the bodies of those killed were never found. Lieutenant Colonel Blacker had given orders to concentrate on the wounded. With no-man's-land swept by machine-gun fire, and with time limited, he did not wish to risk unnecessary loss of life. As a consequence, only those who lay near the 9th Royal Irish Fusiliers' line were recovered and buried near Hamel. It is known that amongst these were Second Lieutenant Hollywood and Corporal David Orr from the Machine Gun Company. Many others, however, lay in no-man's-land until later in the year when that area was captured. It was only then that many families knew for certain the fate of their loved ones. Only seventy-four all ranks are buried in named graves in the Hamel area. Forty-seven men of the Battalion are known to be buried in un-named graves. The bodies of some men were destroyed in later fighting before they could be buried. Others were not identified when they were finally found. Most of the smaller cemeteries in the Hamel area were concentrated after the war and many men were not identified positively during the re-interment. As a consequence, four officers and 151 men of the 9th Royal Irish Fusiliers who were killed during the attack have no known graves and are commemorated on the Thiepval Memorial. Amongst the other men commemorated there are Lieutenant Lemon and Sergeant Benison of 12th Royal Irish Rifles, and four men of the 9th Royal Irish Fusiliers who joined 108th Brigade Machine Gun Company—Company Sergeant Major W J Brown, Corporal D Orr and Privates J Courtney and R A McIlrath.[7]

The tight-knit Battalion had been recruited from very close communities and the impact at home in the days and weeks that followed was immense. Initially, there was celebration as word of the scale of the offensive and the success of the Ulster Division was reported in the local press. Then came the telegrams and casualty notification letters, the casualty reports and the stories from the returning wounded. The families of the missing endured a long wait of months, or years in some cases, before it was confirmed that their men-folk had been killed. Some heard the worst news unofficially. The mother of Private William

Patterson received documents sent to her by a soldier from another regiment who wrote that he had found Patterson lying dead.

Private Moore Hill, died of illness on 10 May 1916. His brother, Robert, died of wounds on 17 July 1916.

Although only a handful of the 9th Royal Irish Fusiliers' casualties came from Belfast city and Counties Antrim, Down, Londonderry, Fermanagh, Tyrone and Donegal, every county in Ulster was represented. However, the bulk of the Battalion had been recruited from County Armagh, with a sizeable number from Counties Monaghan and Cavan, and this was reflected in the casualty lists. County Cavan suffered least of the three, but half of the casualties from this small, rural county came from Cootehill. County Monaghan had twice as many killed, an indication of its relative size, and most were from the larger towns. Five men from Clones were killed, including brothers John and Joseph Burke. Over three-quarters of the casualties, however, were from County Armagh. Most were from the area around Portadown and Lurgan and each of these towns was particularly badly hit.

Most of the men from Portadown who were killed in mid-1916 were Royal Irish Fusiliers and almost all were from the 9th (Service) Battalion. At least sixty-six of those killed at Hamel at the end of June and on 1 July were from Portadown and its surrounding villages. Park Road claimed three, in West Street there were four, and the three men of the Battalion from Seagoe who were killed in the war fell at Hamel. The four Stothers brothers from Bright Street had joined the 9th Royal Irish Fusiliers together in September 1914. The first, Joseph, died at Hamel and within six months two of his brothers would be dead also. Three of the six men from Charles Street who were killed in the war died that day, including Absolom and James Abraham; their brother Thomas would be killed at Vimy Ridge in 1917 serving with the Canadian Infantry. The Hill family from Carelton Street had lost a son, Moore, in May who died after becoming seriously ill in France. His brother Robert had been seriously wounded in the attack and died on 17 July. They share a grave at Drumcree. In the Jones family, Private Edward Jones was killed and his brother, Corporal Henry Jones, was wounded. Two other brothers were wounded later, Private David Jones and Private Joseph Jones, the latter having transferred to the Machine Gun Corps. Another brother, James Jones, served with 44th (Manitoba) Battalion, Canadian Infantry. A number of other families lost pairs of brothers or close relatives, such as those of Private James and Sergeant William Gordon, Privates James and Thomas Hewitt and Private James and Sergeant Robert Magee. Private Richard Sherman was wounded, and a few days later his brother, Private Ephraim Sherman, was killed by shellfire while serving with the 1st Battalion.

Private Richard Stewart (Armagh), killed in action.

In Lurgan the story was much the same. At least forty-seven men from Lurgan were killed at Hamel. Included were at least four sets of brothers or close relatives, including Privates Alexander and James Hamilton, Private George and Sergeant Joseph Thornbury, and Privates Frederick and James Watson. The worst tragedy was to befall Mrs Hobbs of 143 Union Street who was told on 8 July that three of her four sons were dead. The fourth, Private Herbert Hobbs, was wounded and reported missing but he had been evacuated to England. He returned home in August and was discharged in 1917.

The Hobbs Brothers from Lurgan.
From left: Sergeant Robert Hobbs, Private Andrew Hobbs & Private David Hobbs were killed in action & Private Herbert Hobbs was wounded.

More than twenty men from Armagh were killed, including Privates John and Thomas Neville, Richard and William Stewart and Matthew and Robert Wilson. Before the impact of the Somme battle, the small town of Richhill had already had to face the loss of James and John Hutchinson who were killed by shellfire at Hamel in April and June 1916. A further seven men from the town died on 1 July. It should be reiterated that these figures are for the 9th Royal Irish Fusiliers alone.

Whole streets and towns were in mourning across Ulster. On Sunday 9 July a special service was held at St Annes' Cathedral in Belfast. It was reported in the Irish Times that, '*Dean Grierson, who preached, exhorted the people in their sorrow that day to be strong and calm and trustful*'. During the service the organ was played by Captain C J Brennan who would later briefly join the 9th Royal Irish Fusiliers. The Orange Order cancelled its celebrations on 12 July for the first time since its founding. In the days after the attack Lieutenant Colonel Blacker had written daily to his wife and described the horror and sadness at losing so many friends. Two weeks after the battle he wrote to Colonel FitzGerald, now commanding the 10th (Reserve) Battalion, to describe the actions and death of the Battalion. His anguish is evident:

Private Robert Douglas Meredith (Tandragee), wounded.

> *'The Battalion in the hour of trial was splendid as I knew it would be, but I am heartbroken. The gallant friends and comrades we shall see no more. So few have come back unwounded it is hard to get any information as to individuals...*
> *I am still dazed at the blow and the prospect in front of us all...'*

The Sloan Brothers, Lurgan.
From left: AB David Sloan, HMS Impregnable, Sergeant Alexander Sloan Royal Field Artillery, Sergeant William John Sloan Princess Victoria's (Royal Irish Fusiliers), Sergeant James Henry Sloan 5th (Service) Battalion, The Royal Irish Rifles.
Far right: Private Joshua Sloan 9th Royal Irish Fusiliers, died of wounds 2 July 1916, aged 19.

Top row, from left: Private George Ferris (Tandragee), Private James Gregg (Portadown) & Lance Corporal Herbert Calvert (Keady).
Middle row, from left: Private James Joyce (Portadown), Private William McCallum (Lurgan) & Corporal Johnston McCullough (Bessbrook).
Bottom row, from left: Private Thomas Troughton (Richhill) & Private John Samuel McKnight (Newry). All were killed in action on 1 July 1916.

Wounded soldiers at a hospital in England.
Private David Watson (seated far right), C Company, was wounded on 1 July 1916. Like many men unfit for duty as infantry, when he recovered he transferred to a support corps, in his case to the Army Service Corps. His wounds forced his discharge, however, in August 1918.

Private William Sands (centre) (Clare, County Down) in hospital. He was wounded (shell-shock) on 24 June 1916.

Back in France, the relief of the Ulster Division by 49th (West Riding) Division was not complete across the front until 10.00am on 3 July when the last troops moved out of the line and began the journey to the well-known training area near St Omer, far to the north. Only eighty-two men of the 9th Royal Irish Fusiliers were left unwounded and, with those who had been left out of the attack or who were part of the Quartermaster's department and the Transport, the ration strength of the 9th Royal Irish Fusiliers was only 281 all ranks when it left Mesnil on 2 July. On the afternoon of 3 July the 9th Royal Irish Fusiliers marched on the first leg to Forceville and it was here the next day that 108th Brigade was addressed by Major General Nugent. He congratulated everyone on the manner in which the attack had been carried out, sympathised with them on the very heavy casualties that they had suffered and exhorted them to maintain the fair name of the Division.

The withdrawal of the Battalion continued over the next ten days. Five days were spent resting in Puchevillers before marching to the railhead at Frevent, and having detrained in the Pas de Calais, the 9th Royal Irish Fusiliers ended up in Eperlecques, five miles north-west of St Omer, and settled into billets. Reinforcements were to arrive in the Ulster Division in great numbers (193 officers and 2,182 other ranks in July alone) and on 15 July the first draft of fifty-three men arrived from the 10th (Reserve) Battalion. Some of those who had been only slightly wounded also rejoined, bringing the ration strength of the 9th Royal Irish Fusiliers up to 351 all ranks by 16 July.

For the next four days low-level training took place until orders were received to move again to the front, this time to Flanders. Having marched six miles to the railhead, the 9th Royal Irish Fusiliers entrained at 9.15am on Thursday 20 July and set off for Belgium and the Second Army area. The Battalion camped initially two miles west of Poperinghe and the war diary notes that it had *'the honour of being conducted (there) by HRH The Prince of Wales who was DAQMG XIV* Corps'.[8] Over the next two days the Battalion marched and bussed south, ending up in the hutted camp known as Red Lodge in the north-west corner of Ploegsteert Wood, known by everyone as Plugstreet Wood.

Since leaving the Somme the Ulster Division had been under command of XIV Corps, but with this Corps moving south, the Division was incorporated into V Corps. It was to have responsibility for an area of the front north of Ploegsteert Wood previously occupied by 20th (Light) Division. Only three weeks after its near destruction at Hamel, the Ulster Division took over a portion of the line opposite Messines.

Endnotes, Chapter 3

1 The original plan developed by Major General Nugent was to attack from the Ancre valley on the left flank through St Pierre Divion and up onto the ridge. This would allow the Swaben Redoubt to be taken from a flank. This was opposed by GOC 32nd Division who believed, probably correctly, that it would leave his left flank open to machine-gun fire and counter-attack from the Swaben Redoubt.

2 The information on the German dispositions and the actions of 2nd Machine Gun Company are summarised from the detailed research conducted by Ralph J Whitehead - see bibliography.

3 Second Lieutenant Archibald Dunlap Lemon (some records show his name spelled in error as Dunlop). Born 2 April 1875. From Strandtown, Belfast, he was a flax mill manager in Carrickfergus. Served as a company officer in the UVF. Joined the 12th (Service) Battalion, The Royal Irish Rifles (Central Antrim) in September 1914 and was commissioned. Killed in action 1 July 1916, aged 41. Commemorated on the Thiepval Memorial. Pier and Face 15A and 15B.

4 Probably Leutnant Otto Frech and Leutnant Karl Sütterlin of *3. Company 1. Battalion Württembergisches Reserve-Infanterie-Regiment Nr 119.*

5 Captain Charles Stephenson Murray. Born on 17 July 1870. Served pre-war as a Captain in the 4th (Militia) Battalion, The Royal Irish Rifles. Also served in the Military Mounted Police and the British South Africa Police. Commissioned into 12th (Service) Battalion, The Royal Irish Rifles (Central Antrim) as a Captain in September 1914. Officer Commanding B Company. Wounded on 1 July 1916 and died of wounds on 2 July 1916, aged 44, in 92nd Field Ambulance. Buried in Warloy-Baillon Communal Cemetery Extension I. A. 13.

6 Sergeant James Benison. From Monkstown, County Antrim. 8 Platoon, B Company, 12th (Service) Battalion, The Royal Irish Rifles (Central Antrim). Killed in action 1 July 1916, aged 22. Thiepval Memorial Pier and Face 15A and 15B.

Sergeant John McIlwaine. From Carrickfergus, County Antrim. B Company, 12th (Service) Battalion, The Royal Irish Rifles (Central Antrim). Killed in action 1 July 1916, aged 22. Thiepval Memorial Pier and Face 15A and 15B.

7 The men who died as a result of the attack at Hamel (from 24 June 1916) provide an excellent example of the difficulty in accounting for the bodies of those killed in such an action. The location of the named burials also provide a guide as to the route taken by the wounded from the front line back to Ireland.

	Named Graves	
Buried in the immediate vicinity of Hamel:		
Ancre British Cemetery	39	+ 42 unknown
Hamel Military Cemetery	23	
Buried in concentration cemeteries in the Thiepval/Hamel area:		
AIF Burial Ground	2	
Connaught Cemetery	1	
Martinsart British Cemetery	1	
Mesnil Communal Cemetery Extension	2	+ 2 unknown
Mesnil Ridge Cemetery	1	
Mill Road Cemetery	2	
Serre Road Cemetery	3	+ 3 unknown
Buried in cemeteries close to casualty clearing stations and hospitals:		
Abbeville Communal Cemetery	1	
Boulogne Eastern Cemetery	1	
Bouzincourt Ridge Cemetery	1	
Doullens Communal Cemetery Extension Number 1	2	
Etaples Military Cemetery	1	
Forceville Communal Cemetery and Extension	4	
Portsdown (Christ Church) Military Cemetery	1	
Puchevillers British Cemetery	5	
St Marie Cemetery, Le Havre	1	
St Sever Cemetery	3	
Warloy-Baillon Communal Cemetery Extension	1	
Buried in a former German cemetery having been captured:		
Favreuil British Cemetery	1	
Buried in Ireland or England having succumbed to wounds:		
Cladymore Presbyterian Churchyard	1	
Drumcree Church of Ireland Churchyard	1	
Newcastle-upon-Tyne (St John's Westgate and Elswick) Cemetery	1	
No known grave and commemorated on a memorial to the missing:		
Thiepval Memorial	155	
Total	254	

[8] A logistic staff appointment - Deputy Assistant Quartermaster General.

FOUR

Holding the Line at Messines

The Ypres salient had its origins in the fighting of 1914 when the German Army was fought to a standstill around the town and began to consolidate on the high ground. There is little space here to discuss the political and military strategic reasons for the effort in men and material put into maintaining the salient. Suffice to say its unique position, en route to the channel ports, and its survival as the last substantial Belgian town not held by the German Army, were both key justifications. A semi-circle of ridges formed the salient, stretching from Bixschoote six miles north of the town, in a line running generally south-east through Pilckem and St Julien, south through Hooge and south-west along the wooded feature to St Eloi. From there the German line ran generally south along the Wytschaete/Messines ridge before sweeping east around the north of Ploegsteert Wood.

This high ground was not much higher than the low ground held by the British. The ridges lie between thirty metres above sea-level in the north and seventy metres above sea-level in the south, with the line held by the British between twenty and forty metres lower. By the summer of 1916, however, the advantage of this high ground was significant. With the vegetation having been cut away by shellfire, the views from the ridges were unimpaired, providing excellent fields of view and fire. Conditions on the ridges were much better than in the low ground where the millions of shells had destroyed the drainage system built by farmers over hundreds of years and where the water table was high.

On 23 July, 108th Brigade moved on foot into the line at the southern end of the Wytschaete/Messines ridge about one and a half miles north of Ploegsteert Wood. 12th Royal Irish Rifles was in the front line trenches. The 9th Royal Irish Fusiliers was in support as the brigade reserve, having taken over from the 10th Battalion, The Rifle Brigade (The Prince Consort's Own) of 59th Brigade, 20th (Light) Division.

The German line here followed the high ground south-west from St Eloi to Wytschaete, south to a point about 2,000 yards west of Messines, then east towards the town before dropping south again along the ridge to the Messines-Ploegsteert Road, which it joined at La Petite Douve Farm. The line then lay generally south-east towards Warneton. This meant that the area of high ground of most interest to the Ulster Division over the next few months was itself a small salient jutting into the British-held area.

To the west the ground falls away rapidly from the ridge to a narrow north-south stream, the Steenbeck. Beyond this river runs a wide open plain dominated by the German-held ridge in the east and the lonely Kemmel Hill in the west. Kemmel Hill was one of the few dominating features held by the Allies along the line of the salient and it was a focus for logistic dumps, transport lines, bivouac accommodation and, most importantly, for observation and the direction of artillery. In the south the low ground is characterised by the River Douve valley, a wide flood plain running west to east, littered with isolated farmhouses turned into strong-points. South of the River Douve the ground rises again and Hill 63, about 3,000 yards south-west of Messines, provided a vantage-point for the

Allies and some cover for Ploegsteert Wood to its south. At this time much of the north-west corner of the wood was still standing, but it was criss-crossed by tracks, communication trenches and the detritus of over a year of shell and mortar fire.

The British positions lay in the low ground in front of the ridge along the River Douve valley with the front line between 150 and 400 yards from the German positions. The 1st Battalion had been here in November 1914 and the general geography had changed little, but there were now fewer man-made landmarks intact. The trenches, ruins and landmarks shown on the trench maps, bore many names linked to the Royal Irish Fusiliers.

A firing trench on the Messines-Wulverghem Road.
The 'breastwork' position can be clearly seen. A sandbag wall with wire and wood revetting affords protection. The depth to which men were able to dig due to the high water table can be seen in the foreground. The implications, given the dominating position held by the enemy, are evident.
© IWM (Q 380)

Although the 1st Battalion had managed to dig trenches in the thick soil of the Douve valley, the fire trenches across much of the area were very often now sandbag breastworks built above ground. Where possible they were built over shallow trenches. Many of the defence works in and around the salient were built in this fashion because of the very high water table. The problems with standing water were exacerbated by the frequency with which the River Douve burst its banks, the techniques developed by the Germans on the high ground to drain their trenches down the slopes into the British lines, and the destruction of the old drainage systems wrought by two years of artillery fire. The German positions were much better, characterised by concrete blockhouses, and farms reinforced into strong-points and surrounded by trenches and thick belts of wire. They were sited to provide good fields of fire over the British line. The most visible of these were La Petite Douve Farm and Ontario Farm to its north-west. Hidden from view in folds in the ground were reinforced concrete dugouts that provided protection for the German infantry that were off duty when in the line.

The Ulster Division had taken over a sector of a single brigade frontage. 108th Brigade was deployed forward on a two-battalion front with the left battalion sub-sector astride and north of the Wulverghem-Messines Road and the right battalion sub-sector south of the road and astride the River Douve. The brigade headquarters was in Neuve Eglise. At this stage, 109th Brigade was in reserve and 107th Brigade still making its way from France. Within two days the Ulster Division had been joined by its artillery, which quickly began to register targets on the ridge opposite. The 9th Royal Irish Fusiliers soon moved forward to take over an additional stretch of the line from 1/7th Battalion, The Northumberland Fusiliers, who had been on the right of the Brigade and who, in turn, took over a stretch of the line further to their right.

The Battalion now held the trenches and breast-works C1, C2, Barrier Redoubt, the Loop, 141 and 142, also shown on the trench maps as U.1.7 to U.1.11 and T.6.1 to T.6.3. These lay along the northern edge of the Messines/Wulverghem Road facing north to the southern edge of the small German salient. This position was not good. The reinforced blockhouses of Ontario Farm and the German trenches were only 150 to 450 yards away and they completely overlooked the 9th Royal Irish Fusiliers' position. The raised breastworks in the British line offered the enemy an easy target. In addition, there was little trace of protective wire in front of them, and at the second line wire was non-existent. The normal routine in this area appeared to be heavy machine-gun and rifle fire during darkness with little happening during the day. For the next week the 9th Royal Irish Fusiliers manned these positions in extreme heat while attempting to improve the fortifications and wiring. Lewis gunners and snipers were used to engage opportune targets, such as the German soldier, working to the rear of the enemy parapet early one morning, who was shot by Corporal James Bratton.

Reinforcements continued to arrive and these were integrated to the best that was possible. Five men wounded in the Somme attack on 1 July returned to the Battalion, but twenty-two other men who had recovered were posted to the 2nd Battalion, The Royal Irish Rifles in 74th Brigade, 25th Division; they protested by letter at their treatment.

Just before the 9th Royal Irish Fusiliers left the line at the end of the month, a most unfortunate incident occurred. A Company, now commanded by Captain A D Allen, occupied trenches 141 and 142 on the extreme right of the sub-sector. The company was responsible for a bombing post seventy yards in front and to the right of trench 141 protecting the British line where it turned south. Twelve men were detailed to this task with six of the men in the main post, four more in two groups to the right of the post about ten yards apart, and two men on patrol. At night an officer of the company was always on duty in this part of the line and was ordered to visit all of the posts.

Second Lieutenant
H H Dunwoody

In the early hours of 31 July, Second Lieutenant Hugh Henderson Dunwoody was on trench duty from 12.30am to 2.30am. He was new to the Battalion, having joined on 20 June, and was inexperienced. His training in the 10th (Reserve) Battalion had been cut short and he and five others had been sent out early. Although he had been in the trenches under instruction once, this was his first tour of duty alone. Privates Robert Rowntree and Robert Seaton manned one of the sentry positions to the right of the bombing post and at about 2.00am Second Lieutenant Dunwoody visited their position. He had been there for about ten minutes when he thought he heard something in front, and Private Rowntree was given permission to investigate. Having crawled out twenty yards, nearly to the wire, Rowntree suddenly heard a noise to his left and saw a man with a revolver raised in his hand. He fired once, the man dropped, and Private Rowntree returned to the post claiming to have *"shot a Boche"*. Unfortunately, he had shot Second Lieutenant Dunwoody who, according to Private Seaton, had followed Private Rowntree out of the post. Private Seaton saw him shot, and when the body was recovered soon afterwards, it was confirmed that the twenty-seven-year-old officer had been shot through the head and had died instantly. Both soldiers claimed that Second Lieutenant Dunwoody had not said that he was going to go out and no blame was attached to Private Rowntree.

Just after midnight on 1 August the 9th Royal Irish Fusiliers moved into Brigade reserve billets at Red Lodge, a collection of dirty dugouts and wooden huts located at the north-west corner of Ploegsteert Wood, and the closest billets to the front line. During the relief, Captain P C Radbourne and one soldier were wounded, the latter accidentally. Captain Radbourne had served with the Natal Mounted Police. He was commissioned into Durban Light Infantry and had served in the campaign in German East Africa. He had been with the 9th Royal Irish Fusiliers for less than a week and when he recovered from his wounds he served the remainder of the war with the Labour Corps. The billets at Red Lodge were shared with 12th Royal Irish Rifles. The poor state of these grubby and poorly equipped huts and dugouts were pointed out to Major General Nugent when he visited Lieutenant Colonel Blacker. The response was quick and the Ulster Division's 'Q' branch and Royal Engineers officers arrived to find out what they could do. Lieutenant Colonel Blacker told them: *"Well, for two years you've been strafing us, now you're getting your own back"*. In a letter home he wrote: *'It's delicious and a grand strafe; men fairly roused; the whole staff boiling; and I will be horribly disliked, but it's the order . . . Same story, the fighting officers and men living in squalor, no one behind caring a damn as long as they are comfortable themselves.'*

For the next eight days the 9th Royal Irish Fusiliers trained at company level to bring the reinforcements up to the standard set before the Somme battle. This was conducted without A Company, which had been ordered to reinforce 13th Royal Irish Rifles in the reserve positions of the line recently vacated. Drafts and recovered wounded continued to arrive, mostly from Ireland, but for the first time, the 9th Royal Irish Fusiliers now received a draft of English soldiers, the first of five such drafts that the Battalion would receive during the course of the war. The war diary reported that ninety men of The Sherwood Foresters (Nottinghamshire and Derbyshire Regiment) arrived on 8 August. More detail on these drafts can be found at Appendix 6.

By midnight on Wednesday 9 August the 9th Royal Irish Fusiliers had moved forward to the right sub-sector to trenches 134 to 137 (also referred to on maps as U.8.4 to U.2.3) in the River Douve valley immediately north of the river and due west of La Petite Douve Farm. La Petite Douve Farm was a reinforced strong-point situated on the road to Ploegsteert, about 1,500 yards down the hill from Messines on the forward slope of the ridge. Dominating the low ground to its west and south, it comprised a number of concrete blockhouses, and a formidable belt of wire surrounded it.

Berkshire Corner Cemetery Extension, Ploegsteert Wood.

Located at 'Hyde Park Corner', this cemetery was sheltered by Hill 63 behind it to the north-west. Nearby was the billet area known as Red Lodge. The cemetery was expanded after the war when graves were brought in from other cemeteries in the area. © IWM (Q 17867)

Opposite it in the British line, two companies were in the forward line with two in reserve. The battalion headquarters was in Stinking Farm, so named in 1915 because of a large store of rotting potatoes in its cellar. Again, most of the firing line comprised raised sandbag breastworks, but on the right it was almost derelict, being held by a small bombing and listening post and one Lewis gun; this badly-protected trench was also enfiladed from Messines. The general activity experienced on the last tour in the line was repeated with enemy machine-gun, mortar and artillery attacks taking place nightly. All of this caused little damage, but the machine-gun fire was hard to predict and on Friday 11 August two Portadown men from B Company, Lance Corporal Samuel Joseph Corkin and Private Samuel John McCommick were wounded as they carried rations forward. Lance Corporal Corkin was severely wounded in the right leg by an explosive bullet and never fully recovered; he died soon after the war. McCommick transferred to the Labour Corps but was discharged in May 1918 as no longer physically fit for war service due to his wounds. Enemy activity lessened, however, after good work by the 18-pounders and 4.5-inch howitzers of A and D Batteries of 153rd Brigade of the Ulster Division's artillery, which were in support in this sector. As the days passed the trenches and breastworks were improved gradually and the protective wire strengthened.

On 12 August the Quartermaster, Lieutenant Alex Ferguson, was formally gazetted as Adjutant, and on Monday 14 August the King visited Bailleul. Here the Chaplain, Reverend Halahan and Sergeant Robert Lucas had the honour of being presented to him, along with others from the Ulster Division who had distinguished themselves in July. Lieutenant Colonel Blacker wrote that:

'The Gen. is immensely proud of the Div. He ran that show for the King the other day very well. There were men there from 2 other Divs, whose C'drs did nothing. When the King came to our Div Gen N. took hold of him, and as he came to each man he read out what gallant action he was there for, and the King chatted and shook hands with each. The padre was quite pleased really, and greatly impressed with the way the Gen. did it. When he got to the Padre he said "This, your Majesty, is the finest type of parson".'

Alex Ferguson was replaced as Quartermaster by George Wilson, the Regimental Quartermaster Sergeant, who was commissioned as an Honorary Lieutenant. He remained in this post until the 9th Royal Irish Fusiliers was disbanded in 1919. He was replaced as Regimental Quartermaster Sergeant by Charles Milne, one of the Company Quartermaster Sergeants.

Lieutenant and Quartermaster G W Wilson

That afternoon a most successful ruse was initiated by the Adjutant and Lieutenant Godson, acting as the Intelligence Officer as well as being a platoon commander in A Company. It had been known for some time that the enemy could pick up telephone conversations and, to test the theory, Godson and the Adjutant openly discussed the planned movement of an officer and three men from the right of the Le Rossignol-Messines Road to reconnoitre a clump of willows in no-man's-land at midnight that night. At 9.30pm Lieutenant Godson led out a patrol comprising Lieutenant Wingfield and fourteen men (Godson's account records that he was accompanied by Second Lieutenant Henahan and sixteen men; Henahan did not arrive in the Battalion until October 1916). They left A Company's position and moved to a point near that mentioned; by 10.00pm they were in place. Godson recounted:

'I reckoned that any German patrol, they were usually somewhat larger than ours, would be 8 to 10 men, that it would take us 1/2 hour to 1 hour to crawl the 300 yards, and that if the Germans were to lie for us about the Willows they should get into position well before the midnight hour, say about 11.30pm. A night had been chosen when the moon at that time of night would be about ¾ of full moon, rising at 9.30pm, so that we could see a bit of what we were doing. Setting 3 men and myself facing E, the German wire, 5 men facing S, with 4 men W, and 4 N, feet all pointing inwards, outside length of the square would be 16 feet and my subordinate officer 2nd Lieut Henehan (sic spelling) (actually Wingfield) *in centre, to attend to any man who, by signing, might need him or required admonition from him. It was now clear in the dusk that there was an exit gap in the German wire at this point where Willows met it.*

Captain E A Godson MC

At 11.00pm I see, I see - what do I see? A little black mark in the grass forty yards in front that was not there when I looked before. Yes it was. I look about. The moon is very full out now on our right front. What a nice night, and so quiet! Not a sound from the German lines. I look to the front again. I am getting fed up with this. I am wet from head to foot crawling through this wet grass. This is not a job for one man to be at day after day. Everyone ought to take his turn at this. The discomfort is beastly. It is all right till I move, then I have to warm a new place in the dank grass. Hullo! By Jove, I've forgotten that black spot, the only thing in sight I had made a mental note to look at again......It's growing bigger. What the devil is it? There's another behind, and another. They're coming! I have heard of hearts leaping into the mouth. It meant nothing to me, but by Jove that's what mine did. It nearly made me dizzy just for two seconds. I collect myself. Twenty-five yards off and coming, oh, so slowly and cautiously, moving down a little ditch in the open that I had not noticed......I sign to the sick scout to stop his noise and lie close to the ground. I level my revolver. They're coming. And one of the other men is sure to make a noise or cough.....I see the first distinctly now, ten yards off, - nine, eight, seven, six, five. He sees something, he whips round, all turn behind him; as far as I can see, three, four, five, six, seven how many? Bang, bang, bang, ring out the rifles! I let off five with my revolver, and they have disappeared as if by magic. 'Come on boys!' I'm up and out. I see a figure on his back. I leap at his throat. 'Kamerad, Kamerad!' he shouts, and waves his hands (he had a revolver with dagger attached in one). Clements whips by me then Ervin and Breen.'

The end result was two of the enemy killed and four captured, including the patrol commander, an Unteroffizier. Godson's patrol suffered three men lightly wounded. At Stinking Farm the four prisoners were questioned but gave the impression that they did not speak English. Lieutenant Colonel Blacker decided to test them and phoned the Brigade Major and asked loudly if he should shoot them. There was no reaction from the prisoners but the Brigade Major, thinking that Lieutenant Colonel Blacker was serious, said *"For God's sake don't!"*. The prisoners, described by Lieutenant Colonel Blacker as *"Prussians, fine well set up, in good condition, one obviously pleased, others sullen"*, were sent to brigade headquarters.

For this courageous exploit Lieutenant Godson was awarded the first of his two Military Crosses. It was presented to him by The Duke of Connaught and Field Marshal Lord Plumer, the Commander of 2nd Army. Corporal Thomas Clements, having been recommended for a Distinguished Conduct Medal, was awarded the Military Medal. Clements was subsequently promoted to Sergeant and killed in action on 22 November 1917 near Moeuvres. Private John Breen was subsequently promoted to Sergeant and declared missing (probably captured) during the retreat in March 1918. Private Ervin has not been identified; it is likely that his name was misspelt in Godson's account.

The impact of the attack on 1 July was never far from the minds of many in the Battalion, and when news was received that more bodies had been recovered at Hamel by a battalion of The Durham Light Infantry, Lieutenant Colonel Blacker wrote to his wife:

'Have just had a letter from O.C. Durhams saying that they have found Atkinson's body and buried it, and about 40 bodies of men, all of whom they have buried. Will you go and see Mrs Atkinson and I will not write until tomorrow. I suppose at the back of my mind there was a feeling of hope about 'At' for all the news of his having been found came as a shock. As I have said before, he and Charlie Johnston I feel more than any of them. I have been so closely associated with them for so long, and both were such splendid types of Ulster at its very best. The Battalion will never see their like again.'

Officers in a dugout near Ypres. These are officers of an Australian unit, but the shelter is similar to those near Red Lodge. © IWM E(AUS)661

The next night the 9th Royal Irish Fusiliers was relieved and moved back to Red Lodge where training continued and work parties were provided for the forward battalions. More drafts were received, including on 16 August fifteen Second Lieutenants.[1] Three were Roman Catholics (Eyre, Kiely and O'Flaherty-Johnston) a point of sufficient importance to be mentioned in a letter home by Lieutenant Colonel Blacker, and a sign that the make-up of the 9th Royal Irish Fusiliers was slowly changing. On 20 August Major Pratt, the Second-in-Command, left to assume temporary command of the 11th Royal Inniskilling Fusiliers in 109th Brigade. After an all too brief respite, the 9th Royal Irish Fusiliers went back to the trenches on 22 August, 386 all ranks strong, and the activity of the previous tours was repeated. The men worked hard; wiring parties went out on most nights, duck boards were re-laid, traverses repaired, trenches deepened, drains dug, corduroy tracks lifted, strengthened and re-laid, and a washing place was made at the River Douve. This activity was not without risk; during one of the wiring party details on 23 August Lieutenant C P Wingfield was severely wounded in the stomach. He was shot through the back as he stooped to help a man in the party who had been wounded. One of the new officers, Second Lieutenant C M Black, was also slightly wounded. Lieutenant Wingfield, who was only 18 years old and very well thought of by Lieutenant Colonel Blacker, did not serve again with the 9th Royal Irish Fusiliers. When he recovered from his wounds he transferred to the Royal Flying Corps where he spent the rest of the war. He subsequently joined the Royal Air Force and served until 1948, retiring as a Group Captain.

Mining operations had been a feature of life in the south of the salient along the Wytschaete/Messines ridge, and indeed along the whole of the western front, since the stalemate of 1914. The British and Commonwealth miners were recognised as experts in this most dangerous form of warfare. The engineering task was complex, but the idea was simple. Mine galleries were dug from the Allies' trenches under the German line in critical areas, ending in an explosive chamber that was filled with waterproof containers of explosives, normally Ammonal. The gallery was then blocked or 'tamped' to ensure that the force of the explosion was directed upwards. When exploded, the power of tens of thousands of pounds of explosive shattered the defences above and allowed ground to be seized relatively easily. Although not all the offensive operations involving mines had been successful, the impact of large mines exploded on the Somme, such as that at the Hawthorne Redoubt in July 1916, had confirmed the value of this tactic before a major offensive.

The idea to mount a large mining operation under the ridge was developed in July 1915 and begun in December of that year. With confirmation that General Plumer's Second Army would conduct an offensive in Flanders, the material and manpower to complete twenty-four mines were made available. These mines, aimed at dislodging the German infantry from their fortified towns and pillboxes on the ridge, were dug from Hill 60 in the north to the Birdcage, an area east of Ploegsteert containing four mines, in the south. By mid-August 1916 nineteen of the twenty-four mines were in place under the ridge. The mine under La Petite Douve Farm was begun in March 1916 in the area between trenches 134 and 135. The gallery ran east-south-east along the slope of the ridge just north of the River Douve. The 9th Royal Irish Fusiliers and their predecessors had worked with the tunnellers to clear away the distinctive blue clay. It had to be removed some distance from the tunnel head in order to conceal the number and whereabouts of the mines. It was the Royal Engineer tunnelling companies that deserve all the credit, however, for their Herculean task in awful conditions. By 16 August they had excavated a gallery 875 feet long, and a charge of 50,000 pounds of Ammonal had been placed below the fortified ruins of the farm. A second gallery had been dug north-east from the main gallery and by 23 August it was 390 feet long and ended in a chamber under the German defences 150 yards north of the farm. The German miners had spent considerable effort on countermining against the Allied engineers and it was clear that they were close to discovering the main charge. This forced a decision to blow a camouflet, or countermine, to frustrate their efforts and to protect the mine. On Friday 25 August the camouflet was blown successfully about 100 feet along the branch gallery, killing a number of German miners. The smoke and debris rising from the German tunnel was seen clearly from the 9th Royal Irish Fusiliers' lines.

Lieutenant Godson had recently returned from his sniper course, and in the last few days of this tour in the line, the snipers were active. On 26 August an enemy soldier deliberately exposed himself to draw sniper fire. The enemy retaliated against the sniper's position with three rifle grenades. They later used a dummy head to draw more fire but the 9th Royal Irish Fusiliers' sniper did not react. The following night Lieutenant Godson took a out patrol of eight snipers without result. He later recounted his trial of a camouflage sniper suit:

> *'High-up decision had been that casualties would be saved if patrols and snipers wore camouflaged suits instead of uniform when on their active duty. Travelling down the chain of command there arrived a canvas multicoloured garment. C.O. Bn presented it to me as Bn. Intelligence Officer saying "do something about this, I have got to send back a report on it in active use". It occurred to me that if one put it on and went into no-man's land, however good our new camouflage school were, it would be asking for trouble. However, at*

the extreme of our line the scene had been blotted-out by trench mortars and our trench evacuated. A row of trees, 10 feet apart, ran from our line to the German, the trunks were demolished to varying stubs from 3 to 10 feet each in height, and the enemy not so likely to be very alert in these circumstances. The trenches were 70 yards apart. Naturally each side used periscopes, with sentries thus peering over the area. It occurred to me that, if I masqueraded as a tree trunk one afternoon when the heavy eating and drinking Germans (for they were reputed to have beer!) might be having a snooze, it would be a pretty good test. So after crawling out along the tree line I gradually stood up and remained for 20 minutes standing as a tree trunk, a new use for soldiery. Nothing happened, so I duly made my way back and sent in a very favourable report, probably not by any means minimized by gratitude at a safe return.'

View across the River Douve from Hill 63.
The line of the river can be seen along the course of trees and low bushes. Ruined farm buildings, typical of those that dotted the area, can be seen in the centre of the photograph just below the skyline. © IWM (E(AUS) 1316)

On 28 August the underground war continued when the enemy blew a camouflet of their own at 8.30am some way into no-man's-land, blowing in 400 feet of the British main gallery. This cut the firing leads and entombed four miners from 171st Tunnelling Company.[2] To prevent further compromise of the extensive operation under the ridge, the mine under La Petite Douve Farm was abandoned, where it remains to this day. To confound German efforts at opening up the mine, the tunnellers later succeeded in pumping water from the River Douve into the German shafts, and this eventually forced the enemy to abandon their efforts. After the explosion a German soldier was seen looking at the site of the blast through binoculars. He was shot at by one of Godson's snipers and seen to fall back into the German trench.

That night, the 9th Royal Irish Fusiliers was relieved and moved back to Red Lodge. Out of the line large work parties continued to be provided every day and night. A number of casualties were sustained due to the periodic shelling of the area, although this did not halt work or training. On the night of 31 August/1 September, as one of the wiring parties was returning along Spring Street Trench, Second Lieutenant Harold Lyness was shot. He was evacuated but succumbed to his wounds early the next morning in Number 2 Casualty Clearing Station at Bailleul. Lieutenant Colonel Blacker wrote to his parents:

> *'He had gone out in charge of a party wiring in front of our line, and was bringing his men back at the conclusion of a night's good work when he was hit by a chance shot, while in the communication trench. The bullet entered his left side and passed through his body. I sympathize most deeply with you in your sorrow. He had only been a few months with us, and had already made his mark in the battalion. Keen, always ready for any job, absolutely reliable and cheery. I knew that any work given to your son would be well and thoroughly carried out. The battalion can ill afford to lose such an officer. I realised that in your son I had he very stamp of officer I wanted; now he has gone and we are left to mourn the loss of another gallant comrade.'*

The River Douve flooded by winter rain.
It can be seen how nearby positions would suffer if the river broke its banks, which it did regularly in winter. © IWM (E(AUS) 1292)

Notwithstanding the hard work improving the drainage in the trenches, the terrible weather allowed everyone to see for the first time the effect of the poor drainage in this area when the River Douve rose five feet, flooding nearby trenches and fortifications and making the bridges at Spring Street and Douve Dugouts impassable.

The changing face of the Battalion, which had now absorbed a large number of men from English units and from other battalions of the Royal Irish Fusiliers, was reflected in the first Mass held for Roman Catholics on Sunday 3 September. For the rest of the war, up to four Sunday services would be held whenever possible to cater for the various denominations that now made up the unit: Presbyterians, Wesleyans, Anglicans and Roman Catholics.

The period in and out of the line over the next few weeks was characterised by worsening weather. The worst of it precluded many of the planned work details, but foggy days, which covered the men from view, allowed some progress to be made. A recruiting party under Lieutenant Ensor had a most welcome trip home to bolster the recruiting effort in Ireland, and drafts of both fresh troops and those recovered from wounds continued to arrive. On 11 September one of the drafts that reported to the 9th Royal Irish Fusiliers included sixteen of those posted to 2nd Royal Irish Rifles at the end of July. Their welcome return meant that by the middle of the month the trench strength had risen to 419 all ranks.

Throughout these tours minor skirmishes with the enemy, routine patrols and work parties continued, as did trench mortar, machine-gun and artillery duels. There were a few casualties, however, the most serious being Corporal G Robinson MM of the Transport who was hit by a machine-gun bullet as he brought rations forward; he died of his wounds on 12 September. Out of the line, work parties provided the main, and most unwelcome, activity, and everyone worked hard to improve the quality of their accommodation in the huts in Ploegsteert Wood. Training with new gas helmets was an interesting diversion. On 17 September the 9th Royal Irish Fusiliers returned to the line. The next six days were characterised by regular artillery and machine-gun fights and extensive patrolling by both sides before the Battalion returned to Red Lodge (with the exception of A Company that was at La Plus Douve Farm in support of 13th Royal Irish Rifles).

Earlier in September notification had arrived of the award of the MC to Captain Menaul. On 12 September it was announced that Lieutenant Cather had been awarded a posthumous Victoria Cross, and on 23 September the Corps Commander presented Lieutenant Godson with his Military Cross, and Sergeant Lucas with his Military Medal, but unfortunately, Corporal Clements was in hospital and could not attend the ceremony to receive his award.

In mid-September Lieutenant Godson had begun training for another scheme. Over forty men prepared for a raid scheduled for the beginning of October against the strongly-wired and fortified position at La Petite Douve Farm. The raid was extremely well planned and rehearsed by Lieutenant Godson, and the men trained almost daily for it when out of the line. On 21 September Godson, accompanied by Second Lieutenants Richard Miles and Patrick Kiely, and a Sergeant, conducted a reconnaissance patrol to inspect the wire protecting the farm. Godson recorded:

> *'It was a still dark night, and we issued out at 11.00pm to crawl there. Trenches there, 75 yards apart. I had to alter the direction a bit to avoid an enemy wiring party who would have a 'covering' party between the workers and our line; finally got into a large 16ft crater, 15 yards from enemy wire, which was prepared for holding a machine gun post at their end, being about 10 yards from the proposed points of entry for the raid. A sap, cut through the crater lip, as I saw when we crawled into it (crawling on elbows*

and inside of knees) I signed to the others to stop, and crawled to the sap putting my head, from eyes upwards, into the 6-inch curve of sap gap. In the adjoining crater I saw it contained a wired-over saphead in which, I presume, there was a sentry: although only 5ft away it was impossible to see in the dusky darkness through the ball of wire. He must have pulled his cord, running back to his trench for signal purposes, for a flare was immediately sent up from the trench. In the glare I saw a Hun bending in the wire ball. I could have touched him with a walking stick; and then I heard men coming quietly into the saphead, one made a 'hiss', as if he suspected something. So I sheared off the gap and we crawled back to our trench with quite a few flares going up, but the enemy could not detect us crawling (in patchy grass about 5 inches high). The B'de Commander came down for my report on the patrol. I told him that unless we were allowed to choose our own night, for it must be wet and windy, my scheme for a silent raid there would be hopeless. He said we could not choose our own night, probably for some perfectly good reason, so a scheme for the usual pattern of raid, with artillery preparation, was substituted and when soon put into operation was, also unfortunately 'as usual', a failure. It may be noticed that the reconnoitring patrol was composed, rather unusually, of 3 Officers, a S'gt and no ORs. This was for two reasons: (a) In order that each of the leaders of the silent raid should be conversant with every yard to be later covered in that raid. (b) Because at that time with mainly 'newly out' ORs to fill the losses of July 1st on the Somme, the new men were not yet practiced in crawling. It may be hazarded that if proper crawling had not been used, but just a movement on hands and knees, the party would certainly not have come back without casualty, indeed it would not have reached the sap.'

On 25 September Godson briefed the men on the detail of their task. Many senior officers considered that long spells in the trenches without such activity reduced the fighting ability of a unit. Raids were seen as an opportunity for fostering the offensive spirit of a battalion. Many others felt, however, that such attacks achieved very little and resulted in the loss of too many of a battalion's best men, who were naturally the ones chosen for such a venture. The Ulster Division mounted nine raids across its front in September and October, with another later in November. Two on 11 September had been relatively successful, but another was foiled by the depth of wire confronting the raiders on Saturday 30 September. 11th Royal Irish Rifles, immediately on the right of the 9th Royal Irish Fusiliers, cancelled their attack on the same night when a bomb exploded accidentally as the raiders were forming up, killing Lance Corporal Joseph Webb and wounding fifteen other men.

Captain T F Given MC

On 29 September the 9th Royal Irish Fusiliers moved forward again, this time with C Company (Captain J A Johnston) and D Company (Lieutenant T F Given) in the front line, B Company commanded by Lieutenant E N Ensor at Winter Trench, and A Company commanded by Captain A D Allen at La Plus Douve Farm. This period in the line, which lasted until the night of 4 October, was more eventful. On the first evening Stinking Farm was shelled and elsewhere three men suffered bullet wounds. As has been mentioned, one man of 11th Royal Irish Rifles was killed, and fifteen wounded while forming up for a raid on 30 September. On most nights patrols went out. On three occasions the patrols engaged in the grizzly task of securing items for identification from the remains of German soldiers in no-man's-land.

At about 11.30pm on the night of 3 October men were seen in front of a forward listening post commanded by Lance Sergeant Dick Wolfe. They began to cut the wire and the sentry on duty reported this to Lance Sergeant Wolfe who crawled out to verify the report. He confirmed that enemy were cutting the wire, returned to the listening post and sent his men back to the main trench. He threw bombs at the enemy, who retaliated in the same fashion, and then returned to the trench for more bombs. With these he returned to the listening post and threw them at the enemy, then returned to the main trench and directed the fire of a Lewis gun. The following morning at 'stand to' he went out to search for identification. He was praised on a special order by the Commanding Officer for '*complete disregard of danger and great coolness*'.

The next period out of the line at Red Lodge involved fewer work parties and the 9th Royal Irish Fusiliers managed to hold preliminary matches in the inter-company tug-of-war and boxing competitions. The next day, 7 October, saw the morning occupied by a regimental sports competition, and in the afternoon, the finals of the boxing competition. That evening there was a concert, at which the Ulster Division's band played. During the night the weather turned for the worse and a storm raged overhead. In the strong wind a branch overhanging the guard tent broke off. It crashed through the tent, injuring a number of men including Private Maxwell Stothers who suffered a fractured skull and died. He was buried by his friends in Nieppe Communal Cemetery. On 9 October D Company beat C Company 2-1 in the inter-company football final.

On 11 October the Battalion deployed forward with two companies in the front line—A Company commanded by Captain A D Allen, and B Company commanded by Lieutenant E N Ensor, with C Company (Captain G E Lutton) at La Plus Douve Farm, and D Company (Lieutenant T F Given) at Winter Trench. Lieutenant Godson's raiding party, a mix of experienced and new men, remained at Red Lodge until just before their attack, when they moved forward into the trenches. Lieutenant Godson did not take part in the attack himself and the fifty-two raiders were led by Second Lieutenant Miles, accompanied by Second Lieutenants Kiely and Matthew Buchanan, all three of whom had joined the 9th Royal Irish Fusiliers less than two months before.

Captain A D Allen

At 2.00am on Wednesday 12 October the 18-pounders, 4.5-inch howitzers and 2-inch trench mortars of the Ulster Division's artillery, assisted by 3-inch Stokes mortars of 108th Brigade Trench Mortar Battery, fired a preparatory barrage. Four guns from the Brigade Machine Gun Company fired on the enemy positions immediately to the north of the farm. Moving quickly out of the forward trenches and through their own wire in the light of a full moon, the raiders then dashed across the 200 yards of no-man's-land along the slope of the hill to the enemy wire. Here the raiders were bombed heavily and, although they fought hard, they could not penetrate to the enemy trenches. All of the officers were wounded. Second Lieutenant Buchanan was severely injured in one eye and in his arm early in the attack, but he reached the German parapet and bombed the enemy until he was forced to retire, and he remained with his party until they were all back in their trenches. Second Lieutenant Kiely was also severely wounded in the arms and legs but he also continued to lead his party until they were back in the lines. Second Lieutenant Miles remained out until the last moment, under fire, helping to extricate the wounded from the German wire. He was aided by Lance Sergeant Dick Wolfe who, having got close to the enemy's position, hurled bombs at very short range until it became necessary to help the wounded back. Sergeant Albert Grundle, Lance Corporals Harrison and Lockhart, and Privates Joseph Craven, Davidson, John Hamilton and William Heathfield also assisted in this work.[3] As the wounded were brought in, the enemy quickly put up a heavy artillery barrage on the 9th Royal Irish Fusiliers' front line trenches. The flying shrapnel greatly hindered the evacuation of the wounded by the unwounded raiders and the stretcher-bearers from A, B and D Companies under the command of the medical officer, Lieutenant Burrows, and Company Quarter Master Sergeant James Shepherd. Privates John Raynor and Edmund Gray were particularly commended for their work.

Sergeant R J Wolfe MM

Private Edmund Gray

The final casualty list included the three officers and twenty-seven other men, of whom Privates Robert Lockhart, Robert McGivern and Robert Reaney died later in the day from the wounds they received. Private Alexander Hollywood died of wounds on 18 October. Men known to be wounded included Lance Corporal Thomas Morrison and Privates James Andrews and John Raynor. The courage of Second Lieutenant Miles was rewarded with the Military Cross, and Lance Sergeant Wolfe and Private Craven (who was also promoted) received the Military Medal. The other two raids that night, mounted by 107th and 109th Brigades, were more successful with a number of prisoners taken.

Wolfe's award was noted elsewhere. Lieutenant Colonel Pratt, now serving with 11th Royal Inniskilling Fusiliers in 109th Brigade, wrote to Wolfe's father:

Nov 5, 1916

Wolfe,

Please accept my heartiest congratulations on Dick being awarded the Military Medal. It is a medal which takes a deal of getting. Dick has brought credit to himself, to his family and to his regiment. How pleased you and Mrs Wolfe will be, I am proud of him too.

What about the boys now who spend their existence staying at home and who eventually die having done nothing to really mark their existence in this world.

I must go over and see Dick as soon as I can. I hear George is wounded and at home but I'll hear all details when I see Dick.

Yours very truly
AC Pratt Lt Col
11th Bn R Innis'g Fusrs

(His brother, Lance Corporal George Hendren Wolfe, had injured his back serving with another battalion of the Royal Irish Fusiliers.)

The enemy artillery barrage continued on and off for the next four days, in one attack wounding two of the Battalion's cooks. The 9th Royal Irish Fusiliers was relieved on Monday 15 October. Reinforcing drafts continued to trickle in, although a draft of fifty-four men sent from the 10th (Reserve) Battalion was diverted to 16th (Irish) Division. Following a protest by the Commanding Officer this decision was overturned and forty-nine men arrived on 28 October. The end of the month was characterised by almost constant rain, and the onset of this bad weather prompted a conference attended by all the commanding officers to discuss the best way of holding the front during the winter. During the final tour in the line that month there were sporadic contacts with enemy patrols and the predictable intermittent artillery fire, but luckily, there were no casualties.

On this tour Company Sergeant Major Bob Sleator wrote to his brother from B Company's position at La Plus Douve Farm:

Dear George,

Your letter of 28th August received and I fully intend answering same sooner than this but always put it off from time to time, but as our Company are at present finding a support to the Companies in the front line, this means a decent rest for me (but not much for the men, they are still on the go), so I thought I would get out of your debt. It's not often it comes round our turn to get into this place as two Battalions have to get their turn and only one Company at a time, but nearly two weeks of this is alright and a very nice place it has been at one time although now greatly dilapidated. It has once been a gentleman's residence and a very fine cellar underneath the dwelling house, which is my home and habitation during my stay here. I have a fine fire which my man keeps burning day and night, two chairs - one an armchair which I occupy and my Qr. Mas. Sgt. occupies the other. I have also got 3 very good beds and plenty of blankets so I'm pretty comfortable. In fact I could stay here for any length of time.

It seems a long way off now the 1st July but it's a day I will never forget. The scenes of that morning will hardly ever fade from my eyes. A lot of brave men fell that day and a lot more have fallen since but it's grand to think it was not all in vain. Things seem to be going well in that part now. Strange something told me when I was writing those postcards and trying to get them through during that trying time that the home people would just look at things the way they did. Oh I know them well, and to tell you the truth very often years ago I felt rather inclined to lose my temper over the manner in which they used to take things and worry themselves over matters that had no foundation whatever. When you wrote your letter you were in Portadown. I note your remarks as to what the people of that place think of Mr Shillington. Words could hardly express his goodness. He is one of the finest gentlemen I ever met. At present he is 2nd in Command. Possibly you have seen his promotion in the papers. No position in the Army could be too good for him. It was a pleasure to work in the Company when he was in it. Our late Adjutant whose photo you will have seen in the papers as having won the VC was a nephew of his and he was a young man everyone in the Battalion would have done anything for. Yes I knew Brown very well, he was a Sergt. in 'B' Coy. when I came to it. The officer who went on the recruiting party to Ireland from our Battalion is now my Coy. Officer and he and I get along very well together. Forbes has not got the job of Qr. Mas. Sgt. yet. I am informed someone from another Battalion has been appointed and he is working in the office. I had a day with Jack McKennell before he left this part. He came along to where our Battalion was lying. It was a beautiful day and we had a great time together. Tom McKennell was not long out before he was back in England again. Very unfortunate for him, but he says he is not very badly wounded, this time he got it in the back. I was almost sure he would have been at the base for a good while after coming out. The frost set in for a few days but has gone and we are having the weather pretty mild at present. Trusting this will find you well, as for myself I'm still in good form.

Your fond brother
Bob

Those referred to were: Sergeant W J Brown who left to become Company Sergeant Major of the Brigade Machine Gun Company and was killed on 1 July; the Company Commander was Captain E N Ensor, and the McKennells were Sleators's cousins. Private Thomas McKennell served with Princess Patricia's Canadian Light Infantry (Eastern Ontario Regiment). He was killed in March 1918 and is buried at Thélus, near Vimy. Private John (Jack) McKennell served with the North Irish Horse. Bob Sleator was commissioned into the Battalion on 1 November and became a platoon commander in C Company.

Large work parties continued to be provided when out of the line, with many dedicated to the movement of gas containers, codenamed 'ROGER', into trenches U.2.1 and U.2.2 just south of the Messines Road. Large groups of men also made improvements to the trenches and to the encampment at Red Lodge. In November, as enemy artillery activity increased, the weather worsened steadily and the water level rose quickly. By 3.30am on 8 November Stinking Farm was flooded to a depth of three to four feet and the trenches at Currie Avenue, Nugent, Spring Street, Douve Dugouts and Little Winter alongside the river were all flooded. Movement to the front line was possible only across the open. The front line, however, remained dry and the water receded from the support lines after a day. After a short respite in mid-November, during which the 9th Royal Irish Fusiliers acted as divisional reserve at Bulford Camp at Kortepyp (now Korte Pijp) and which included a day in Bailleul, the 9th Royal Irish Fusiliers returned to trench duty to find the weather even worse and the first snow falling. There was little unusual activity over this period, but from C Company's position on the left of the forward line Sergeant Lucas managed to shoot a pigeon that was flying towards the German trenches. When it was recovered it was found to contain a message in German cipher.

The time out of the line was spent training, playing sport when possible, mainly football (although the officers played rugby), and providing work parties. Officers and men

Regimental Sergeant Major C H Turner. The effect of the war may be seen by comparing this photograph with that in Chapter 1, page 11, taken in 1915.

continued to be posted in and out. Late in October six officers had been posted to the 1st Battalion: Lieutenants Best and Caiger-Watson and Second Lieutenants Eyre, Lee, Locke, and Sloan. In early November Company Sergeant Major Charles Turner had been promoted to replace Regimental Sergeant Major McKane. Charles Turner was born in Warwickshire in 1879 and had enlisted into The Royal Warwickshire Regiment in October 1896. Like many soldiers of his era he served in the South Africa War. The final three years of his service were with The Cheshire Regiment before he was discharged to the Army Reserve in December 1911. He settled in Ballynafeigh, Belfast, and was employed as a pottery worker. On 2 November 1914 he had joined the 9th Royal Irish Fusiliers and was soon made Company Sergeant Major of C Company. He would prove to be a most effective, popular and respected Regimental Sergeant Major and would serve the Battalion well for nearly two years. He was replaced as Company Sergeant Major in C Company by Sergeant Lucas MM.

Drafts continued to swell the Battalion's numbers and on 23 November a large draft arrived comprising thirty-four Irishmen from the 10th (Reserve) Battalion, 102 Englishmen and one Russian. This was the second draft of English soldiers to arrive and comprised men of The London Regiment. The war diary recorded the Russian as 6816 Private M T Pwyanefsky. This is believed to be 43314 Private M J Pyanowski; more details on this draft and on Pyanowski may be found at Appendix 6. They arrived on 26 November at Aldershot Camp for training, which was conducted by an experienced team comprising Lieutenant Flood, Second Lieutenants Bennett and Boyd, Company Sergeant Major Girvan, Sergeants L Nicholson and R Lucas, and Corporals M Simpson and Brown. This draft brought the 9th Royal Irish Fusiliers' ration strength to forty-two officers and 762 NCOs and men. With so many men away on courses, leave, or working with the Battalion details in the rear, the trench strength when the 9th Royal Irish Fusiliers returned to the line the next day was only thirty officers and 381 other ranks.

By now the weather had made the conditions in the trenches and fortifications deplorable and no sooner were they repaired and drained than the weather would worsen and they would flood again. On the last day of the month the enemy line was subjected to a major barrage, which caused considerable damage. In the retaliatory attack the 9th Royal Irish Fusiliers suffered one casualty when Private Robert Robinson, from B Company attached to 108th Trench Mortar Battery, had three fingers blown off. After he recovered he returned to serve with 108th Trench Mortar Battery and earned a Military Medal. It was at this time that the Battalion heard that its Chaplain, Reverend Francis Halahan, was to be appointed the Senior Chaplain to the Ulster Division.

Officers of the 10th (Reserve) Battalion, Newtownards 1916.

Front row (left to right): Two unknown officers of The Royal Irish Regiment, Captain D G Shillington, Captain C J Brennan, Major F M Beddington, Colonel W C FitzGerald, Unknown, Unknown, Lieutenant A B Townsend, Lieutenant and Quartermaster R McFarland, Unknown.

Most of the Second Lieutenants shown here would join the 9th Royal Irish Fusiliers and most would become casualties. Only two can be identified: Second Lieutenants R I McCrum (second row, third from left) and F C Hartness (third row, second from left).

The enemy on the long ridge opposite now comprised men from three very different divisions of the German Army. In the north was *2. Infanterie-Division*, an experienced East Prussian formation that had arrived from the Russian front in February. Farther south holding Messines was *40. Division*, a formation recruited from the west of the Kingdom of Saxony, also experienced; it was estimated to have suffered losses of seventy percent on the Somme. *40. Division* was considered to be very good in defence but with a passive attitude. It was this formation that the 9th Royal Irish Fusiliers was up against. Also in this area was *3. Bayerisches Infanterie-Division* (translated as the 3rd Royal Bavarian Division).

December brought fog and frost. Artillery duels continued, as did the routine work on the line. Patrols were out on most nights and the majority were uneventful, but on occasion contact was made with the enemy. Just before midnight on 1 December a patrol of two officers and twelve other ranks moved out from the 9th Royal Irish Fusiliers' lines to an area where an enemy work party had been seen the night before. The night was cold and misty and the patrol got into position without being noticed, about thirty yards from the enemy's wire, where they set up the two Lewis guns and two ammonal tubes, the latter to blow up and cut the protective wire. At about 2.00am, a German wiring party was seen coming out. It was allowed to continue with its work for some time and, when it was well bunched together, the order was given to fire. Both Lewis guns fired into the middle of the group and the remainder of the patrol threw bombs into their midst. Of the dozen or so Germans in the party few escaped being hit. The wire was too thick to fight through so no prisoners were taken, but the 9th Royal Irish Fusiliers' patrol returned to its lines without a single casualty.

Generally, the routine throughout the rest of December was unchanged, with training interspersed with work parties, the occasional visit to Bailleul, leave for a lucky few and relatively uneventful periods in the line. The weather got steadily worse as snow fell and the trenches flooded. Coupled with the damage caused by the intermittent shelling, there was continuous and much needed work required to keep the trenches and fortifications in an acceptable state of repair.

Officers and men continued to arrive throughout the month, including Captain Brew and Lieutenant Shillington, both of whom had recovered from the wounds they had received on 1 July. The largest reinforcement for some time, one officer and 106 other ranks, was taken on strength on 12 December and a further draft of fifty-two men arrived five days later. Eighty-nine of these men were English recruits from The Prince of Wales's Own (West Yorkshire Regiment). This was the third draft of English recruits to the Battalion; more details on this draft can be found at Appendix 6. Two officers and eighteen men arrived on 27 December.

Not everyone left the Battalion due to wounds or sickness. Private Henry Waring was born in Belfast on 21 June 1900. He enlisted, aged 15, in January 1916 and was one of the reinforcements who had joined the 9th Royal Irish Fusiliers in France in July 1916. In October 1916 his mother requested his return due to his age and he was ordered home. He left for England on 26 December 1916 and joined the 10th (Reserve) Battalion pending discharge. Before he could be discharged he deserted on 4 March 1917.

Although the 9th Royal Irish Fusiliers had suffered heavy shelling and machine-gun fire almost every day in the line, there had been surprisingly few serious casualties, but this changed when, on 22 December, the sector was bombarded heavily and considerable damage was done to the trenches immediately south of the road. During this attack Second Lieutenant Walter Peacock was killed, one soldier was wounded and a shrapnel bullet from a shrapnel shell hit Second Lieutenant John Crymble in the right leg. Peacock was buried the next day and Crymble died in Number 2 Casualty Clearing Station six days later. Peacock was twenty years old, Crymble was nineteen, and both had been with the Battalion only since October.

As Christmas approached, the weather worsened further. On 23 December a gale blew all day, severely damaging screening and blowing down several large trees, and the River Douve rose again, flooding Currie Avenue so that it became impassable. At 5.00pm that evening, with a strong breeze blowing towards the enemy lines, the engineers released gas, and six minutes later the enemy reacted by putting up warning lights. A brief retaliation caused little damage and two patrols, each comprising an officer, eight men and a sapper from K Company, 3rd Battalion, Special Brigade, Royal Engineers, moved forward either side of the Messines Road up to the enemy trenches to determine the effect of the gas. They returned at 8.30pm having heard nothing and seen no movement in the German first line positions, which had probably been evacuated.

Enemy retaliation the next day was heavier causing severe damage to Currie Avenue and Well Lane (also, as patrols later determined, to the protective wire) and burying a Royal Engineer who, although not injured, was very shaken by his experience. Christmas Day was very quiet, but the artillery duels began again on Boxing Day and continued on and off causing some damage but no casualties. The 9th Royal Irish Fusiliers was relieved on 29 December and moved back into divisional reserve at Bulford Camp.

The next day was devoted to inspections and bathing, and the delayed Christmas festivities began in the evening with a concert given by the Ulster Division's band. On New Year's day everyone attended a church service and at 1.00pm had Christmas lunch. The fare was superb with turkey, goose, boiled ham, roast beef, vegetables, plum pudding and fruit and nuts. As was tradition, the platoon officers carved. The warrant officers and sergeants dined at 7.00pm.

1917 began with good news as the Battalion began a month out of the line, refitting and training. In the New Year's Honours List Lieutenant Colonel Blacker was awarded the Distinguished Service Order; it was a popular award and well deserved.

The training began again at company level with work on the ranges. Sport played an important part in the activities with football and cross-country running being the key events. 16th Royal Irish Rifles, the Ulster Division's pioneer battalion, had been ordered to work on the light railways being laid to support the forthcoming summer offensive in the Ypres area, which left the Ulster Division without the capability to continue large construction projects. A 'works battalion' was formed with a nucleus of pioneers and with one company from each brigade. The 9th Royal Irish Fusiliers provided Second Lieutenants Turner and Malone and forty men for this unpopular task, which was rotated through the Battalion every week or so. The month also provided the opportunity for many of the officers to attend courses of instruction and they, in turn, were able to pass on their new-found expertise to their platoons and companies. In the inter-platoon football competition, the semi-final was played on 9 January; 10 Platoon beat 16 Platoon and 13 Platoon beat 7 Platoon. The final was held on 12 January and 13 Platoon emerged as the victors.

It was during this period that one of the relatively few men of the Battalion to appear before a court-martial was tried and convicted. 17903 Private W J Edgar from A Company had been charged with desertion in December. Lieutenant Godson had been appointed the 'soldier's friend'. He wrote in December:

> *'Busy looking into the defence of Private Edgar who is charged with 'desertion' and looks as if he will suffer the extreme penalty. This is a stigma for the Batt'n & if possible to be avoided. On looking into the case it strikes one as being very pathetic as he gave a false age on enlistment in order to be able to join up and is now only 18½ & has been in the Army 2 years. He got a dose of gonorrhoea in Ireland and it has weakened him physically & morally. On the night before he fell out of the ranks on the way up to the trenches he undoubtedly was done up & did not realise what his action would bring him in for. If he were 12 years older his action would be unpardonable but I think it will be hard for the youngster to be shot.'*

At his Field General Court Martial on 5 January, considered fair by Lieutenant Godson, he was found not guilty of desertion but found guilty of being absent without leave. He was sentenced to six months' imprisonment with hard labour. Godson wrote that *'. . . this is too light, not good for the Bn, but it is something of a personal triumph'.* It is not known if his sentence was suspended but that is likely; Edgar was captured in August 1917. Details of the other officers and men tried by court martial may be found at Appendix 8.

On 13 January the 9th Royal Irish Fusiliers marched seven miles in heavy rain, aided by extra transport provided by the Army Service Corps of the Divisional Train, to new billets at Meteren. The march was completed quickly and before snow began to fall. At Meteren, besides the usual training, an inter-company competition was held where C Company won the boxing and D Company the cross-country running, but B Company, having won the football and bayonet fighting, was judged the best to represent the 9th Royal Irish Fusiliers in the Brigade competition. In the latter part of the month, B Company won the competition. Although beaten at football by A Company, 12th Royal Irish Rifles, it won the bayonet fighting (Sergeant Pentland won the prize for the best individual performance) and tied for first place in the 3-mile cross-country run with an 11th Royal Irish Rifles company. Its prize was a silver bugle.

This period out of the line also allowed the officers the opportunity to hold a dinner in the *'Canon d'Or'* in Bailleul. The guests for the evening were Lieutenant Colonel Blacker, who was temporarily in command of the Brigade, Major G F Cavendish-Clarke, Lieutenant Campbell and Lieutenant Godson, who were on the staff of 108th Brigade (Godson temporarily attached), the 108th Brigade staff interpreter Brey Lazart, Captain J G E FitzGerald MC who had left the 9th Royal Irish Fusiliers in January 1916 to join the Machine Gun Corps, Captain W H Barry RAMC, the medical officer, and Lieutenant J Butler MC, an officer of the 1st Battalion attached to the Royal Flying Corps. It was a relaxed affair with toasts and speeches following dinner.

Over this period officers and men continued to join the Battalion but one or two were posted out. They included Second Lieutenant F W D Grundy, who had already served for some time with the 7th (Service) Battalion in 16th (Irish) Division and who was posted to the 1st Battalion on 22 January. Unfortunately, he suffered multiple gunshot wounds on 19 February and subsequently caught tetanus and died in Number 8 General Hospital at Rouen a week later.

The poor weather had forced the postponement of the Battalion's final field exercise but it eventually took place and involved the attack and defence of a convoy. The 9th Royal Irish Fusiliers then moved forward to Kortepyp at the end of the month, taking three hours in a dangerous wind. The village lay about one mile south-west of Neuve Eglise (now Nieuwkerke) and three miles west of Ploegsteert Wood. Soon after the 9th Royal Irish Fusiliers' arrival there the defence plan for the portion of the line to be held was explained to the officers, who then conducted a detailed reconnaissance. The men who had been attached to the Works Battalion returned, which somewhat made up for the number of men still attached to schools of instruction.

The area to be held by 108th Brigade was the left sub-sector, slightly to the north of that held previously. On 2 February the 9th Royal Irish Fusiliers, under the temporary command of Captain Brew, relieved 12th Royal Irish Rifles. The line to be held was opposite Ontario Farm, a large German strong-point on the lower ground west of Messines. A Company was at Forbes Terrace, and B Company had two platoons on the right of the line and two at Agnes Street and at Forbes Terrace. C Company was at Ugbrooke Farm, and D Company had two platoons on the left of the line and two at Agnes Street and at Marine Terrace. The battalion headquarters was at St Quinten Cabaret, about 1,500 yards from the front line trenches and just south of the nearly ruined village of Wulverghem. The roads and tramways (notably the Durham Line) were in quite good condition here and allowed stores to be brought forward by the transport to battalion headquarters where rations were dumped and then brought forward on the tramway. The weather was cold but relatively dry. Clear nights made for a heavy frost and the white landscape was marred only by trench lines and new shell craters.

The 9th Royal Irish Fusiliers quickly settled into a routine similar to that experienced farther south, suffering intermittent machine-gun fire and working hard on improving the trenches and fortifications. The Lewis gunners had their share of action early in this tour. During the early hours of 4 February an enemy patrol was seen about forty yards out from the 9th Royal Irish Fusiliers' wire and engaged by the Lewis gunners in the forward posts. Daylight showed two dead and two wounded Germans. At 10.45am a large notice was put up in the enemy lines: *'Let save two wounded kamerads. Answer'*. A message was signalled back that two men could go out and bring the wounded bodies to the 9th Royal Irish Fusiliers' wire. Immediately a junior officer and nine men left the German line and took one body into their trenches; the proceedings were then halted. The next morning at 1.15am an officer and one man went out from the 9th Royal Irish Fusiliers' lines to search for the remaining bodies but could not find them in the snow and ice. Later, at about 5.00am, Tom Shillington and another officer, wearing white shirts for camouflage in the very bright moonlight, went out and were successful in finding a body. It was frozen to the ground, and although it could not be moved in the time available, his pistol, shoulder straps and identification papers were taken back. He was a young man, twenty years old, who had recently been transferred from *Infanterie-Regiment Nr 133* to *Infanterie-Regiment Nr 181*, both Saxon regiments from Chemnitz, part of *40. Division.* Shillington's act was described by Lieutenant Colonel Blacker as *'a very gallant deed'*.

The 9th Royal Irish Fusiliers also suffered some casualties. Most occurred while on wiring parties, but on 3 February Corporal Charles Graham was killed in a grenade accident while at bombing school. Lieutenant A E Nicholl of 13th Royal Irish Rifles, the instructor in charge, was also killed and five men were wounded. On 7 February Private William Hickey was seriously wounded by a sniper as he looked over the parapet and he died of his injuries later the same day.

Even against this background of harsh routine in the line, sport continued. The Brigade boxing competition was held while the 9th Royal Irish Fusiliers was in the line, but Corporal Johnston and Privates William Marriner and Kenzer Gumble, a Romany from London, took part in the final. Private Marriner won the featherweight but Corporal Johnston lost in the heavyweight category to Corporal Grogan of the 13th Royal Irish Rifles. Private Gumble's result was not recorded. On Thursday 8 February, the Battalion was relieved by 12th Royal Irish Rifles and was complete in its support positions by 5.30pm. A Company remained forward in Forbes Terrace and Fisher's Place in support to the left and right sub-sectors, B and D Companies were at Shankhill Huts, and C Company remained at Ugbrooke Farm. Over the next five days the usual round of inspections and work parties took place, with the latter mainly in support of 171st Tunnelling Company. Before it moved back into the line the available members of the Battalion twice marched with the band to watch the football team enhance its reputation with victories over 2nd Royal Irish Rifles (2-0) and 10th Royal Inniskilling Fusiliers (8-0).

Captain J A Johnston

The relief of 12th Royal Irish Rifles on Wednesday 14 February was complete by 5.15pm. This tour began quietly and, although a few casualties were suffered due to intermittent mortar fire, none were serious and the enemy's guns were silenced quickly by the Ulster Division's howitzers. Enemy snipers were also active and on the following Sunday the Battalion lost another officer who had been with it since its formation. Having served as an officer in the UVF for 18 months, Captain Joseph Allen Johnston had joined the 9th Royal Irish Fusiliers in September 1914 and had commanded C Company from July 1916. The morning of 18 February was misty and Captain Johnston took the chance to examine the wire at about 7.00 am. Although warned not to by Sergeant William Mitchell, who worked for Johnston's father, he stood on the fire step to look out at the wire and was shot and killed. He was buried late that afternoon at a service at St Quinten Cabaret. His successor was Second Lieutenant Michael Henahan, a former soldier in the Irish Guards, who was soon promoted to Acting Captain and who would prove to be a most able officer. Lieutenant Colonel Blacker wrote of the loss of Captain Johnston:

> *'He is a fearful loss to the Battalion. Always cheerful, with a thorough knowledge of his duties, keen and splendid at handling men. I am very low at the thought I shall not see his cheery face again, and at the serious loss the Battalion has sustained....We laid Joseph to rest this afternoon, and as accustomed as one is to death out here, there were not many dry eyes amongst those of us who stood by his grave. His loss takes me back to the July days. He was a man one could absolutely rely on; when he was in the front line I was quite happy.'*

During this week Regimental Quartermaster Sergeant Charles Milne left for Ireland and the 7th Officer Cadet Battalion. He was subsequently commissioned into The Royal Inniskilling Fusiliers and distinguished himself by earning the Military Cross and Belgian *Croix de Guerre*. He was replaced by Company Quartermaster Sergeant Henry Fox. Henry Fox was a day short of his eighteenth birthday when he enlisted and he was now a Warrant Officer with considerable responsibility at the age of twenty.

The weather warmed and the frost and snow thawed with initially little adverse effect on the trenches and fortifications. As the warmer weather continued, however, the water level rose, making it necessary to clear Spring Walk, Agnes Street and Day Street. On the left flank, the 6th (Service) Battalion, The Connaught Rangers, of 47th Infantry Brigade, attempted a daylight raid and the 9th Royal Irish Fusiliers' line was evacuated except for the Lewis gunners and those operating smoke bombs in support. Unfortunately, the enemy, who seemed to be ready, repulsed the raid and the Connaughts suffered a number of casualties. It was arranged with the enemy that unarmed stretcher-bearers would be allowed out into no-man's-land to bring in the killed and wounded, and the 9th Royal Irish Fusiliers assisted in this task. Accompanying the stretcher-bearers was Second Lieutenant J R Dobson. Originally a soldier with 1/9th (Highlanders) Battalion, The Royal Scots (Lothian Regiment) in 81st Brigade, 27th Division, he was commissioned in January 1916 and had been with the 9th Royal Irish Fusiliers since November that year. When he went out into no-man's-land he was wearing his pistol, and the enemy, seeing this, called upon him to surrender. He refused and was promptly shot and critically wounded; he died a few hours later in Number 2 Casualty Clearing Station. Also wounded was Company Sergeant Major Charlie Turner, who was hit over the right eye. For his gallantry in bringing in the wounded that morning, Private John Hamilton was awarded the Military Medal.

Having been relieved again by 12th Royal Irish Rifles and moved into support, the officers attended Second Lieutenant Dobson's funeral at Bailleul Military Cemetery and the companies began the usual round of work details and training. The football team managed two more matches, losing to 8th Royal Irish Rifles 5-4 and beating 153 Brigade RFA 6-0. After a relatively uneventful week in support, the next tour in the line was very quiet also. The snipers and the artillery kept the enemy quiet, although the enemy artillery did its fair share of work. The only action of real note occurred when a wiring party was heard in front of the German line. A small patrol went out to pinpoint it and, having been successful, the enemy party was dispersed by fire from the Lewis guns. After the next relief 12th Royal Irish Rifles were not so lucky and suffered a very severe artillery bombardment on 8 March lasting over two hours. It killed five men, caused a number of other casualties and did considerable damage to the front line. The 9th Royal Irish Fusiliers helped by sending work parties forward to rebuild the line in most unpleasant weather with falling snow, and later, heavy rain. The remainder of the Battalion continued to train, and thirty-six men of the draft from The London Regiment, who had enlisted as Territorial Force, were re-enlisted into the Regular Army and into Princess Victoria's (Royal Irish Fusiliers).

Back in the line from 10 March the priority was to continue the work to repair the trenches but this was hampered by very heavy rain. The River Douve again rose rapidly and the area around battalion headquarters flooded, as did some of the trenches, although they were drained during the day. It was common practice for officers of battalions new to a sector to be attached to a unit in the line in order to conduct a reconnaissance and to familiarise themselves with the activity and routine. During this tour the 9th Royal Irish Fusiliers hosted a number of officers and NCOs from 2nd New Zealand Brigade.

It was in this period that another officer who had been with the Battalion since its early days was wounded: Captain A D Allen had served for three years in the Royal North West Mounted Police in Canada and had also commanded a company in the UVF for eighteen months. He had commanded A Company since July 1916 and was badly injured in the foot and leg by enemy shellfire on 15 March and was sent to hospital. He subsequently relinquished his commission due to his injuries.

Just before the 9th Royal Irish Fusiliers moved back into reserve, the line held was extended when B Company took over trenches from Durham Road to the Wulverghem/Wytschaete Road from 1st Battalion, The Royal Munster Fusiliers. The 9th Royal Irish Fusiliers did not have to hold this extended sector for long because the next day the Battalion was relieved by the 1st Ottago Battalion, 2nd New Zealand Brigade, and moved to billets in Neuve Eglise. After a night's rest, everyone moved to Caestre, far to the west of Bailleul, where the good billets were most welcome.

The strengths of the 9th Royal Irish Fusiliers reflected the devotion and hard work of its first Commanding Officer, but Lieutenant Colonel Blacker, at the age of fifty-two, was now ordered to hand over command and return to Ireland. On the evening of 15 March a farewell dinner was held for him at the Café Francais in Caestre, and at 8.30am the next morning the Battalion assembled in full marching order for his final parade. After he had addressed everyone, the men lined the streets and the band led his car through the village. The new Commanding Officer arrived that afternoon. Lieutenant Colonel Stafford James Somerville was a forty-five year-old regular officer of The Royal Inniskilling Fusiliers with twenty-seven years service. He had served with the 1st Battalion, The Royal Inniskilling Fusiliers in 87th Brigade, 29th Division, and had taken command at Gallipoli on 2 May 1915 until he was wounded.

The River Douve today.
The British line ran across the picture just beyond the hedge. Across this field the raiders led by Second Lieutenant Miles attacked La Petite Douve Farm (out of shot to the right) in the early hours of 12 October 1916.

The 9th Royal Irish Fusiliers was to spend just over two months out of the line, refitting, training, and towards the end providing work parties at the front. This period began in very crowded billets at Le Quatre Fils Aymon, which the Battalion attempted to improve in the snow and sleet, although A and B Companies finally moved to a camp under canvas. The emphasis, however, was on training at platoon level and in absorbing the drafts of officers and men arriving from other battalions and from Ireland. These included fifty-nine men who arrived on 19 March, most of whom were recovered wounded returning to the Battalion. On 23 March the 9th Royal Irish Fusiliers had thirty-four officers and 580 men on parade. By early April all of the companies were in Keersbroom Camp, cold and muddy in the April rain, with battalion headquarters remaining in Le Quatre Fils Aymon. Working parties increased in size and, with much of the work concentrating on railway construction, it was evident that a major offensive was in the offing. Across the rear areas of the Ypres salient, camps, railways, storage areas and ammunition dumps were seen to be growing.

Over 5 and 6 April the Battalion moved to new billets scattered over the Mount des Cats/Le Rossignol area in preparation for twelve days of concentrated training. Tactics had evolved somewhat since July 1916 and the platoons worked hard for four days before having well-deserved baths, followed by two days of company training and inter-platoon and inter-company competition, in preparation for the Brigade competition. The inter-platoon competition involved drill, the use of Lewis guns, bombs, rifle grenades and the box respirator, which were won by 15 Platoon followed by 12, 8 and 4 Platoons. The inter-company competition involved stretcher bearing, revolver shooting, tug-of-war and running; it was won by A Company, D Company, C Company and, again, A Company respectively. On 14 April, the first battalion-level exercise was held and General Plumer, commanding Second Army, accompanied by the Divisional Commander, watched the practice attack. The next day the new Chaplain, Reverend S Mayes, officiated at the weekly church service. The Rector of Kilmore in County Armagh, Reverend Mayes had volunteered for service late the previous year and had served in Flanders since January 1917 with 110th Field Ambulance. Over these two days the 9th Royal Irish Fusiliers had participated in 108th Brigade's inter-battalion competition; in the revolver shooting the 9th Royal Irish Fusiliers was fourth but came second in the sniping. The running race was won convincingly, and joint honours were shared with 12th Royal Irish Rifles in the stretcher-bearing. The Transport was second in its part of the competition and the Scouts were third in theirs.

A second battalion attack took place on the following Monday in conjunction with 11th Royal Irish Rifles, and the pilot and observer of the contact aircraft visited in the afternoon to discuss the morning's work. These aircraft were used to provide information as to the progress of battalions and where major problems were encountered. Although another attack on a two-battalion front took place the next day, the poor weather put an end to the training earlier than planned. On Thursday 19 April the 9th Royal Irish Fusiliers marched in drizzling rain to a new camp, Wakefield Huts on the Dranouter/Loker Road west of Mount Kemmel, which was rather cramped but in good condition.

Here, in the last two weeks of the month the number of work parties increased, mainly in support of the 150th Field Company, Royal Engineers and the Ulster Division Signal Company, in the case of the latter burying signal cable up to six feet deep. However, there was still time for a few football matches against teams from the neighbouring 16th (Irish) Division, which would spend nearly four months in the line fighting alongside the Ulster

Division in the Ypres Sector. The Battalion maintained its fine record with victories over 2nd Royal Dublin Fusiliers (7-0) and 6th Connaught Rangers (2-0). The latter match was watched by a huge crowd, estimated at nearly 3,000 men from 36th (Ulster) and 16th (Irish) Divisions. By the end of April the 9th Royal Irish Fusiliers' ration strength had increased to fifty-eight officers (including forty-four Second Lieutenants) and 967 other ranks, although the trench strength was only forty-four officers and 773 other ranks.

This period, from the end of July 1916 to the end of April 1917, was the longest period that the 9th Royal Irish Fusiliers would spend between major attacks or engagements in the course of the war. The routine of life in the trenches, the endless work parties when in support, and the time farther back spent training, although broken by a harsh winter, were all relatively easy by comparison to that which had been faced on 1 July 1916 and that which was to come. Nevertheless, the constant artillery and machine-gun fire, the ever-present risk and the conditions in the trenches were wearing on mind and body. The Battalion had lost a steady stream of experienced officers and men who became casualties over the nine months. The casualties included five officers and thirteen other ranks who had been killed, died of wounds, illness or accident in France and Belgium, and five men who had died of illness or by accident at home. A considerable number were wounded, many severely, and many had been rendered unfit through sickness over the winter. This was the lowest casualty rate that the 9th Royal Irish Fusiliers would record.

The Battalion was much changed from that which had arrived in France eighteen months previously, but the majority of its men were still from Ireland and there were enough of the originals to preserve its style and ethos. It would be sorely tested, and irrevocably changed, however, in the offensive to come.

The 9th Royal Irish Fusiliers Transport.
Seated in the centre (fifth from left) is Lieutenant J M Stronge.
On his left is Sergeant W Neill.

Endnotes, Chapter 4

[1] This draft of fifteen Second Lieutenants was:

C M Black - Wounded and later joined the 1st Battalion. Died of gastro-enteritis on 9 July 1917

J Brown - Evacuated to England sick in September 1916 and did not rejoin the Battalion.

M S Buchanan - Wounded on 12 October 1916 and relinquished his commission as a result of his wounds.

B J Eyre - Posted to the 1st Battalion. Captured 27 March 1918.

F W D Grundy - Posted to the 1st Battalion. Died of wounds 26 February 1917

E M Hutson - Evacuated to England sick in September 1916 and then served with The London Regiment.

R W Johnston - Wounded on 16 August 1917 and relinquished his commission as a result of his wounds.

F P Kiely - Wounded and then joined the 1st Battalion where he was killed in action on 24 June 1917.

S Lee - Posted to the 1st Battalion. Ordered to resign his commission.

R D Miles - Died of wounds on 17 August 1917.

A S Nolan - Wounded and then served with the Egyptian Labour Corps.

G I O'Flaherty-Johnston - Captured 21 March 1918.

F G B Pascoe - Posted to the 1st Battalion. Killed in action on 2 July 1917 serving with the Royal Flying Corps.

N E W Sloan - Posted to the 1st Battalion. Wounded then transferred to the Machine Gun Corps.

A Caiger-Watson - Posted to the 1st Battalion.

[2] The miners were from 171st Tunnelling Company, Corps of Royal Engineers, which had worked alongside 36th (Ulster) Division in the Spanbroekmolen/Douve sector since April 1917. 171st Tunnelling Company was formed from specially enlisted miners and men selected from the 1st and 3rd Battalions, Royal Monmouthshire Royal Engineers (Militia). Its strength was supplemented by attached infantrymen. The Company was first employed in March 1915 south of Ypres at the Hill 60/Bluff sector before moving to Ploegsteert in July 1915, where it commenced mining operations in the St Yves (St Yvon) sector north-east of Ploegsteert Wood (the Birdcage mines). It was engaged in mining operations at Spanbroekmolen, Kruisstraat (four mines), La Petite Douve Farm and Ontario Farm.

The men entombed on 28 August 1916 were:

Corporal Robert Woodward 86607 Corps of Royal Engineers. Born at Nottingham. From New Higham, Alfreton, Derbyshire. A coal miner/hewer at Alfreton colliery. Enlisted into The Sherwood Foresters (Nottinghamshire and Derbyshire Regiment) (16008). To France 19 March 1915. Transferred to the Corps of Royal Engineers and posted to 171st Tunnelling Company. Killed in action 28 August 1916. Ploegsteert Memorial, Panel 1.

Sapper Alexander Irvine 136495 Corps of Royal Engineers renumbered 86607. From Gorebridge, Edinburgh. 171st Tunnelling Company. Killed in action 28 August 1916. Ploegsteert Memorial, Panel 1.

Sapper Ernest John Jones 137596 Corps of Royal Engineers. From Ebbw Vale, Monmouthshire. Enlisted into the Royal Monmouthshire Royal Engineers (Militia) (1755). Transferred to the Corps of Royal Engineers (renumbered 137596) and posted to 171st Tunnelling Company. Killed in action 28 August 1916. Ploegsteert Memorial, Panel 1.

Private Charles Noble 351612 The Royal Scots (Lothian Regiment). Born at South Shields, County Durham. From Edinburgh. Attached to 171st Tunnelling Company. Killed in action 28 August 1916. Ploegsteert Memorial, Panel 1.

[3] Lance Corporals Harrison and Lockhart and Private Davidson cannot be identified positively.

FIVE

The Battle of Messines, 7 June 1917 & The Battle of Langemarck, 16 August 1917

For some time Field Marshal Haig had desired an attack in Flanders. He saw the enemy railway centre at Roulers as a critical target, and pressure from the Admiralty to capture the German naval bases on the Belgian coast reinforced his perception that this was where the main effort should be. Early in 1917 Haig had attacked at Arras in support of General Nivelle's French offensive along the Chemin des Dames in Champagne. The former was a success but the latter was a costly stalemate, and the heavy casualties imposed on the French contributed directly to the mutinies that broke out across the French Army on 3 May. Nivelle's successor, Petain, needed room to manoeuvre in order to rebuild the morale of the French Army, and an offensive by the British in the summer of 1917 would serve him well. Haig managed to persuade the War Cabinet to back his plans for an attack in Flanders—a limited offensive, supported by the French and in two parts, which he described to his Army commanders on 7 May.

The first phase, to be launched by the Second Army commanded by General Sir Herbert Plumer, aimed at straightening the Ypres salient by the capture of the Wytschaete/Messines Ridge. The second aimed to break through the German line at Ypres to out-flank the German right using General Sir Hubert Gough's Fifth Army. The first part of the attack was scheduled for early June. The second was likely to take place some weeks later due to the need for more 'holding attacks' at Arras, where British troops remained committed. Preparations for the first phase were extensive. Plumer had long planned on taking the ridge and, in addition to the twenty-four mines being dug under the German line, the logistic effort to support nine assaulting divisions with three more in support was vast. In May 1917 36th (Ulster) Division was part of IX Corps and still in the line in the area of the River Douve north of Ploegsteert Wood.

Life in the line here was quiet, but the conditions in which the men lived resulted in rheumatism, bronchitis, pneumonia, influenza and 'trench fever'. The latter was caused by the faeces of body lice, which infected everyone, and resulted in symptoms similar to flu. The rising number of illnesses required mass inoculations and the 9th Royal Irish Fusiliers was treated at the beginning of May while billeted at Wakefield Huts, one of many camps to the rear of Kemmel Hill. Those not recovering from their inoculations provided work parties in support of the Ulster Division's Royal Engineers field companies.

In contrast with life at the front, the conditions experienced by those lucky enough to attend a course of instruction at 2nd Army Central School were somewhat better, as this extract from a letter by Tom Shillington to his sister Mollie in May 1917, while he was attending an adjutant's course, shows:

> *'We are having a great time down here. The school is in a very large convent and we have rooms in very comfortable huts in the grounds. The country round here is very fine and the course is very good. There are just a few of us here and we have our own work, not mixing with the ordinary course. I am going out this afternoon to a town near here. In fact we are enjoying life and all very glad we have got here.'*

Sport continued to feature when out of the line, particularly for the gladiatorial football team, which had won more matches than it had lost and which beat 9th Royal Inniskilling Fusiliers 5-0 on 5 May. A horse show on Monday 7 May attracted a large attendance. The horses in the Ulster Division had always been well looked after and the prizes were evenly distributed. The white pony, formerly belonging to Lieutenant Colonel Blacker and now ridden by Captain Henahan, took 3rd prize in the officers' cob class, being ridden in the show by Second Lieutenant Miles. Later in the month a sports competition was held against a sister battalion in 16th (Irish) Division, the 7th/8th Royal Irish Fusiliers (the 7th and 8th (Service) Battalions had been amalgamated in October 1916). The competition was held on the football field at Brulooze Corner and on this occasion teams competed in football, tug-of-war, bombing and the use of the Lewis Gun, all won by the 9th Royal Irish Fusiliers, and wrestling on horseback, won by the 7th/8th Battalion. In the evening the officers of the battalions dined together and at 9.00pm everyone attended an open air concert by the performance troupes of both battalions. The next day after church services for the various denominations, the two battalions competed in cross-country running, won by the 7th/8th Battalion. It was not all play, however, and work parties were provided every day while the resting platoons conducted low-level training.

Sergeant J Barbour, later Regimental Quartermaster Sergeant

This period out of the line was marred by a sad incident on the evening of the day after the horse show. Bob Sleator had joined the Battalion on the outbreak of war, became the Company Sergeant Major of B Company and was commissioned in November 1916. He was known as a cheerful and capable officer, as his letter home just before he was commissioned showed, but he was sent to hospital on 15 February suffering from severe depression. This was almost certainly due to the cumulative effects of eighteen months in the trenches, in particular the impact of seeing so many of his friends killed during the attack at Hamel. There are indications that thc death of his friend and the Officer Commanding C Company, Captain J A Johnston, who was killed by a sniper on 18 February, a few days after Sleator moved to hospital, added to his depression. After a month in hospital and at the Ulster Division Depot he rejoined the 9th Royal Irish Fusiliers on 19 March and was made Assistant Quartermaster, an appointment aimed at allowing him longer to recover. It is evident, however, that he continued to suffer from depression, and at about 7.20pm on the evening of 8 May, Sergeant Jack Barbour ran into the Quartermaster's store having heard a shot and found Second Lieutenant Sleator sitting on his bed. He did not appear hurt and denied hearing a shot being fired. Sergeant Barbour left the room only to hear another shot five minutes later, and when he returned to the Quartermaster's store he found Sleator dead on his bed.

Second Lieutenant R J Sleator, taken when he was Company Sergeant Major, B Company.

Sergeant John Crozier ran into the Quartermaster's store soon afterwards and Sergeant John Keith was called in by Sergeant Barbour. Sleator's revolver was on the office table at the foot of his bed; when it was unloaded by Sergeant Keith he confirmed that two rounds had been discharged. When examined by Captain Burrows, the new Medical Officer, it was found that Sleator had two wounds, *'one bullet wound in the region of his heart and another in the region of his genital organs'*. Later that day the facts of the incident were examined by a Board of Inquiry, comprising Major Brew, Captain Given and Captain Henahan. The Medical Officer, and Sergeants Barbour, Crozier and Keith gave evidence and the Adjutant described Sleator's depression and attendance at hospital. The board of inquiry concluded that Second Lieutenant Sleator *"died from two gunshot wounds, self-inflicted"*. He was buried in Dranoutre Military Cemetery at Bailleul the next afternoon.

A few weeks later in a letter from Major Shillington, by then serving with the 10th (Reserve) Battalion, to a gentleman acting on behalf of Sleator's family, there was some indication of the effect that the manner of his death must have had:

> *'I need not say how shocked I was to hear of Lt. Sleator's death, as already stated I was in charge of the Coy for some months of which he was Sgt. Major, and a more satisfactory Sgt. Major in every way I could never have. I was also with the 9th for some months after he got his commission and the good opinions I had already formed as to his capabilities were confirmed more and more the longer that I knew him. His Coy. Commander, Capt. Johnston of Lurgan, who unfortunately was killed a few weeks previously, had I know a very high opinion of him, and I know that Sleator was devoted to him, I think that Capt. Johnston's death was a very great shock to him.'*

Tragic though this sort of incident was, nothing interfered with the routine in and out of the line. The daily work parties continued until the Battalion moved on from Wakefield Huts when 108th Brigade took over the Spanbroekmolen Sector. The 9th Royal Irish Fusiliers became the Brigade reserve, taking over from 14th Royal Irish Rifles in a camp of tents and bivouacs in the lee of the south-west slope of Kemmel Hill. The weather was fine and warm and the provision of working parties was the main source of activity and effort for the next few days. Only one serious casualty was suffered in this period when Private John Murphy of A Company was badly wounded on the night of 16/17 May while on a work party. He died the next day.

The 9th Royal Irish Fusiliers continued to receive drafts of officers and men, but some of the officers moved on, including some of the most experienced. Captain E N Ensor had been with the Battalion since its arrival in France and had commanded B Company since September 1916. However, having spent four years in China with the Imperial Chinese Maritime Customs Service, he was an ideal candidate for service with the Chinese Labour Corps and he left on 18 May. Lieutenant D H Wright replaced him as OC B Company.

On the evening of 21 May the 9th Royal Irish Fusiliers moved forward in bright weather and took over the right sub-sector of the Brigade front from 12th Royal Irish Rifles. This was in an area just to the north of that occupied during the previous month. This sector was about 800 yards wide with the right boundary along the remains of the Wytschaete/Wulverghem Road. The left boundary ran along Piccadilly, the long communication trench due west of Spanbroekmolen. The front line ran a ragged course on the lower ground south from Spanbroekmolen, cut east towards the German line for 200 yards and then south again to the Wytschaete/Wulverghem Road. Opposite, on the high ground at the top of a moderate slope, were the German front line positions known as Narrow Trench and Nathan Trench. They were very close to the British lines along most of this sector. Here they were manned by the Saxons of *Infanterie-Regiment Kronprinz Nr 104*.

The first few days and nights were warm and very quiet; the intermittent artillery fire caused no real damage and there was little activity on either side. Second Lieutenant Miles led a patrol out to examine the ruins which lay almost in the middle of no-man's-land south of Spanbroekmolen, and aircraft were very active overhead with three falling within sight of the Battalion's positions in as many days. The only casualties were the result of negligence. At 4.00am on the morning of 23 May just after stand-down, the men of Sentry Post 6 started to clean their rifles. At the subsequent inquiry, presided over by Major Brew, Private Thomas Colclough stated that: *"I took out the magazine first and started to oil my rifle. I omitted to remove the bolt and . . . accidentally pulled the trigger discharging a round which was in the chamber."* The shot hit Private William Limbert in the head. He was killed instantly. It also wounded Private Edward Linzey in the neck. Colclough was tried at court martial, found guilty, and sentenced to 56 days Field Punishment Number 1. He would be killed in action on 16 August. Lance Corporal English, who was in command of the sentry post, was tried by the same court martial for failing to ensure that his men followed the rules for rifle discipline in the trenches. He was also found guilty and sentenced to 28 days Field Punishment Number 2 and reduced in rank.

On the right of the 9th Royal Irish Fusiliers' position was 15th Royal Irish Rifles of 107th Brigade, and on 24 May this battalion raided the German line opposite which the 9th Royal Irish Fusiliers had previously been deployed. Unfortunately the efforts of the raiders, two officers and thirty-eight men, were futile because the enemy had evacuated its front line positions. The German artillery retaliated immediately across the Brigade front and in the 9th Royal Irish Fusiliers' lines it mortally wounded three men, Privates W A N Boyd, George Honey and Harry Parker, who are recorded as having died of wounds on 25 May. Nine others were wounded, including Second Lieutenant D J Fullerton who was hit in the neck, although he was able to return to duty. The burials were conducted by Reverend Mayes, and his return (Army Form W3314) for Honey and Parker shows a burial date of 24 May 1917.

Over the next few days the weather got hotter and hotter and the activity at the front returned to normal with only intermittent shelling by the Ulster Division's artillery on the German rear area. In response, just before the Battalion was relieved on 28 May, the German artillery began a major barrage on the British rear areas that caused significant damage. When the 9th Royal Irish Fusiliers left the line, handing over to 12th Royal Irish Rifles, they moved back to the bivouacs near Kemmel Hill. Just after midnight, the enemy began shelling the rear area again, concentrating on Danoutre and the Danoutre/Lindenhoek Road. Some of these shells fell short and landed amongst the lines occupied by A and B Companies, but luckily only one man was wounded. This shelling of the rear area allowed little rest, and it was not helped by the predictable provision of large work parties of up to 350 men, until the 9th Royal Irish Fusiliers moved into the line again on 2 June. By now the strength of the 9th Royal Irish Fusiliers had increased significantly. The Battalion had a paper strength of fifty-eight officers and 985 other ranks, an effective strength of fifty-four officers and 908 other ranks and a ration strength of forty-six officers and 740 other ranks. The number of junior officers in the Battalion allowed for many to be sent to the various Corps and Army schools of instruction, which was a welcome break.

After a short church service for those going back to the trenches, the 9th Royal Irish Fusiliers moved into the same portion of the line recently vacated. Battalion headquarters was, however, much reduced, with only the Adjutant, Captain Alex Ferguson, and one clerk in the line, in a corner of a barn at Locrehof Farm being used as the Quartermaster's store. The remainder of the orderly room staff was moved back to the Transport lines. By the evening of 3 June the battalion headquarters and B and C Companies had moved back to bivouacs on Kemmel Hill, being replaced by two companies of 13th Royal Irish Rifles. Their Commanding Officer, Lieutenant Colonel A P Maxwell, took over command of the sub-sector.

The need to determine the condition of the German positions and the extent of the protective wire to their rear, before the forthcoming attack, prompted raids by both the 9th Royal Irish Fusiliers and the 13th Royal Irish Rifles. The 9th Royal Irish Fusiliers' raid was planned for 4 June against a section of the Spanbroekmolen salient, and throughout that day the Ulster Division's artillery had been shelling the enemy rear areas. Led by Captain Henahan and Second Lieutenants J I Hamilton, A S Nolan, S P Colquhoun and H T Ozzard, eighty men waited in Piccadilly, the long communication trench that ran forward along the left boundary of the Irish Fusilier's position. Lieutenant Godson had been attached to Headquarters 108th Brigade since January. He recorded his memory of the planning for the raid:

> *'The customary night attempt was decided upon by Div'l and B'de. H.Qs. As B'de Intelligence Officer I had, the week before, watched, as it was a new departure, a daylight raid by 16th Div. on our left and seen a very easy and successful entry of and return from the German lines, with prisoners. I decided that the artillery and other preparations for the Messines Battle had so weakened and cowed the Germans that a daylight raid might be repeated with promise of better things than the usual perchances of a night raid. I so reported to Gen Griffith, B'de. Commander, 108 B'de. He said he was not adverse to the change, but the consent of the Div'l Commander Major-Gen Sir Oliver Nugent would have to be obtained.*
>
> *Time was short. The latter was reckoned a 'straffer' and feared by his subordinates. As befits a Regular, Griffith shared in this fear, they have to watch their careers, and fearful of crossing Nugent, Griffith said to me he would prefer me to go and see Nugent rather than himself. So I went to Div'l H.Q. and after a short discussion with him he gave his consent to the change. Plans were changed and the daylight raid duly took place.'*

At 2.00pm in the sunshine of early summer, the raiders emerged into no-man's-land from the head of the trench. A particularly heavy barrage from the Ulster Division's artillery and that of II ANZAC Corps covered them; 9,000 artillery rounds, 1,800 mortar rounds and 96,000 machine-gun rounds would be fired during this short attack. The raiders rushed 200 yards up the gentle slope before entering the German positions on the south-west corner of the Spanbroekmolen complex of trenches. There was no wire left to protect the front or support line trenches and the raiders had to rely on their own barrage to keep direction. Just behind the front line trenches the enemy occupied a number of dugouts which were not very deep but which had strong concrete providing over-head cover about four feet thick. Although they had been partially revealed by the shelling, the dugouts were mostly passed over early in the raid without being noticed, but they were spotted and attacked as the raiding party returned from the barrage limit. In many cases the occupants refused to come out, but after being attacked by bombs and phosphorus grenades the survivors surrendered reluctantly. Some German soldiers fought on, however, and one who attempted to get a machine gun into action was bayoneted and the gun captured.

The raiders were in the German positions for twenty minutes, during which time they killed about twenty of the enemy and captured one German officer and thirty-one soldiers. Importantly, details of the wire about 500 yards to the rear of the German front line positions, thought to be protecting parts of the line out of view of the British observation posts, were also obtained successfully. Sergeant Campbell McConkey was one of the last two men back into the Irish Fusiliers' lines, bringing with him two of the wounded. Lieutenant Godson recorded his view of the raid:

> *'During it I observed from the extreme right of our sector line in question. As there was little enemy response while our men were 'over' I showed my body over the parapet. A German sniper, away from the front directly affected, put a bullet very close to my head. 30 to 40 prisoners were taken with very few casualties. One of our casualties I saw happening. A man pulled out the pin of a Mills bomb, looked over the rim of the steps of a deep dug-out and dropped the bomb down them and watched it go off! No wonder he was a casualty.'*

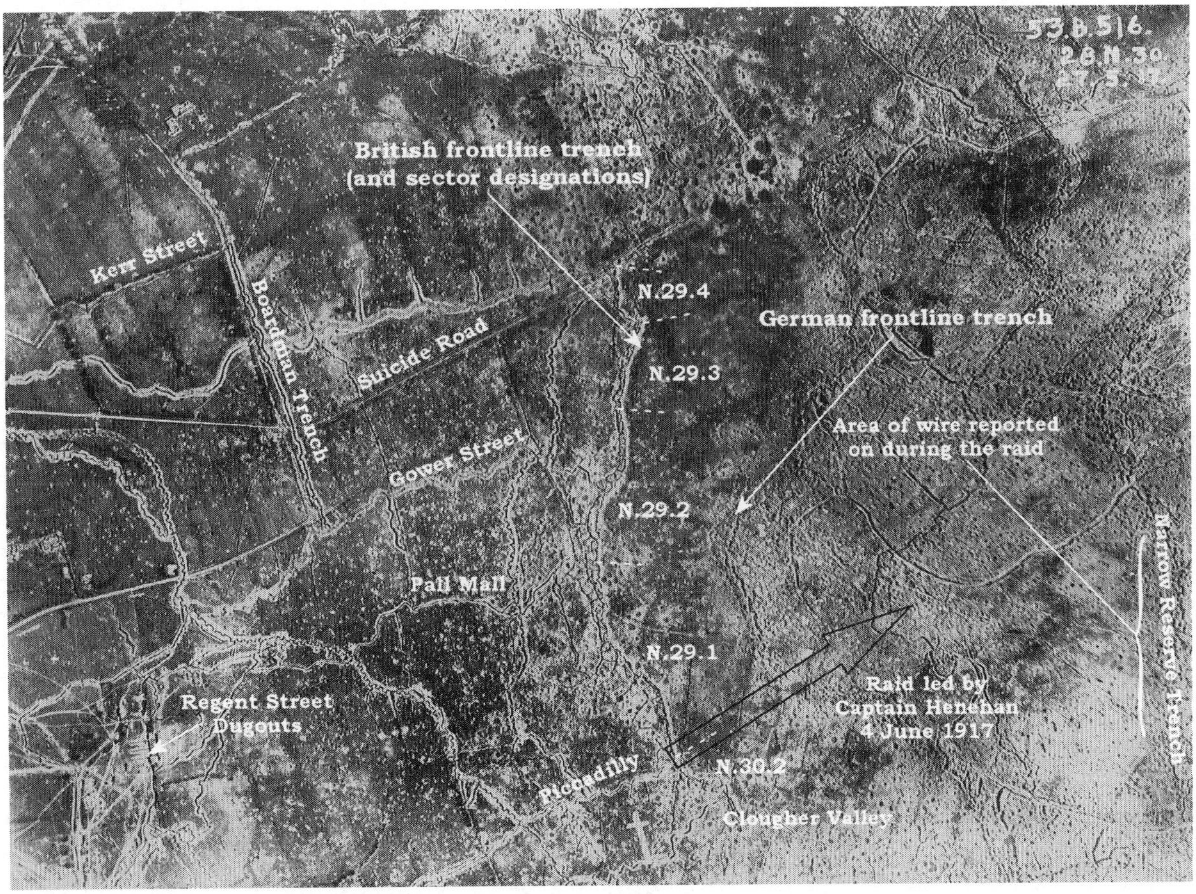

Spanbroekmolen.

This air photograph, taken on 27 May 1917, was used by the Intelligence Officer, Lieutenant J H Partridge, to plan the raid at Spanbroekmolen on 4 June 1917. The photograph is orientated with north to the top. Overlaid text by the author.

Sergeant J C H McConkey MM

In the course of the operation only two men were killed, Lance Corporal John Scott of D Company and Private George William Cave (formerly of The Sherwood Foresters (Nottinghamshire and Derbyshire Regiment)) from A Company. Those wounded were Privates James Frame, Hugh McCleary, Robert McGeown and David Patterson of C Company, Private James Sloane of D Company, Sergeant Benjamin Stringer and Private John Richardson. Frame and Sloane later returned to duty only to be killed in August during the Battle of Langemarck. For their bravery during this raid Captain Henahan and Second Lieutenant Ozzard were awarded the Military Cross, and Sergeant McConkey and Privates Sloane, Andrew Magowan and David McGrann earned the Military Medal. McGrann was slightly wounded a few days later and he too was killed in action at the Battle of Langemarck.

The attack by Second Army that would herald the push out from the Ypres salient was now imminent. For the assault upon the ridge, Plumer's plan required II ANZAC Corps to advance on the right, with IX Corps in the centre and X Corps on the left in the north. The IX Corps front extended from the Wytschaete/Wulverghem Road in the south for over 6,000 yards to the Diependaal Beek, a small river just south of St Eloi. Across this frontage would attack 36th (Ulster) Division on the right, 16th (Irish) Division in the centre and 19th (Western) Division on the left. It is often stated that this was the first time that the two divisions from Ireland would fight side by side, but they had, of course, spent time together in the line since the end of April, and this pairing would be repeated in the later offensive at Ypres. The attack by the Ulster Division was to be made by 107th Brigade on the right and 109th Brigade on the left, each with a battalion from 108th Brigade attached, and the remainder of that brigade in support.

The preparations for the attack were meticulous. Artillery was targeted using air photographs taken every day to ensure that maximum destruction was done to the German positions. Plans were devised for the supporting barrage that would use trench mortars and machine-guns. To ensure the maximum co-operation between the attacking troops and their artillery, communication methods were worked out to the smallest detail. Detailed instructions were written for the evacuation and treatment of the wounded, and much attention was paid to how food, water and ammunition would be supplied. These preparations required considerable work, including the building or rebuilding of roads and railways to allow the movement of the vast quantity of resources to the front line over small streams and numerous ditches. The attack itself was planned and rehearsed using a scale model built by the engineers of IX Corps and which could be viewed by a company of troops at any one time.

Although there had been regular artillery bombardment of the ridge, the intensity of the attacks increased five days before the day of the infantry assault—'Z' Day. All of the available Field and Garrison Artillery batteries were brought to bear to cut the wire, demolish the concrete blockhouses and to flatten the fortified towns on the ridge. The co-ordination of this artillery and machine-gun fire before and during the attack was a key aspect of the preparatory work. It was an excellent example of what could be achieved by careful planning. During the preliminary bombardment 108th Brigade held the line allowing the assaulting brigades to prepare fully. In the few days remaining before the Ulster Division attacked the ridge, the 9th Royal Irish Fusiliers and 13th Royal Irish Rifles alternated in the front line. There was generally little enemy retaliation against the continuous British barrage. Some enemy fire was effective, however, and Private William McIlroy was killed. Six men were wounded: Second Lieutenant G Robinson, who was shot in the chest, Sergeants William McClean and Joseph Smyth, Corporal Joseph Gray and Privates William Goodfellow and David McGrann.

View across the River Douve with shells falling on Messines in June 1916.
A few days later the Ulster Division attacked farther along the ridge to the left. © IWM (Q 2295)

By the evening of 6 June the 9th Royal Irish Fusiliers was in reserve in trenches in an area known as Fort Victoria, about 1,500 yards behind the front line on the Wytschaete/Lindenhoek Road. The dugouts here had been built by the Battalion during its many work details in early May. Here, men were issued extra bombs and ammunition; Private Laurence Gordon Ranger recalled that he received fourteen bombs and *'anything to clear the QM-Stores'*.

At 3.10am on 7 June, as the final preparatory barrage opened up, the mines that had taken so long to prepare were exploded along the front. Of the twenty-four mines one (at La Petite Douve Farm, described earlier) was lost to the enemy in August 1916. It had been decided in May 1917 that four other mines that had been placed in the 'Birdcage' on the eastern side of Ploegsteert Wood would not be used in the forthcoming attack. Most of the remaining nineteen detonated simultaneously and all within minutes of each other. The noise caused by over 400 tons of explosive was indescribable; it was reported to have been heard in London. Under the large German position around Spanbroekmolen in front of the Ulster Division a mine shaft nearly 500 yards long had been dug and a charge of 91,000lbs of explosive had been laid. It was late going off and the leading troops had moved out of their trenches when it exploded suddenly. The

German position was completely destroyed, which contributed directly to the complete success of the attack, and the leading battalions took their portion of the ridge with little difficulty. At 3.45am the men of the 9th Royal Irish Fusiliers in the reserve position saw the first prisoners, described as *'a hell-stricken lot'*.

The crater left by the mine that exploded at Spanbroekmolen on 7 June 1917, which devastated the German position, was 40 feet deep, 230 feet in diameter with a rim 90 feet across. The extent of the crater, known now as the 'Pool of Peace', is partially concealed by new trees.

At 8.00pm the 9th Royal Irish Fusiliers received orders to move forward and relieve 10th and 15th Royal Irish Rifles of 107th Brigade on the Black Line, where the heaviest fighting had been. This was the fourth, and final, planned objective of the first attack. The new front line lay more than 2,500 yards from the original British positions and the relief was eventually completed at 1.30am on 8 June. The march forward was made uncomfortable by the shower of rain that fell just as the Battalion moved off. Under the command of Major Brew, the 9th Royal Irish Fusiliers had three companies forward with one in support. The new line ran for about 750 yards from Ochre Trench, just south of Wytschaete, to Lumm Farm, a complex about 150 yards east of and halfway along the Wytschaete/Messines Road on the Division's right boundary with 25th Division of II ANZAC Corps. The support company position was in the centre of this area along the road at Pick House with battalion headquarters at L'Enfer Wood to the west of the road. The new positions were consolidated throughout the night in the numerous shell-holes that covered this area. Platoon strong-points were made at Lumm Farm, Moat Point (a large semi-circular lake in the centre of the line) and Pick House. Private Laurence Gordon Ranger recalled:

> *'By the time we got dug in it had got quite quiet so we thought it was time to go souvenir hunting and to see any sights about our new ground. We found a few souvenirs including a bayonet, cap & field glasses. We found a lot of soda water in a German dugout and as there was no water where we were it came in very useful.'*

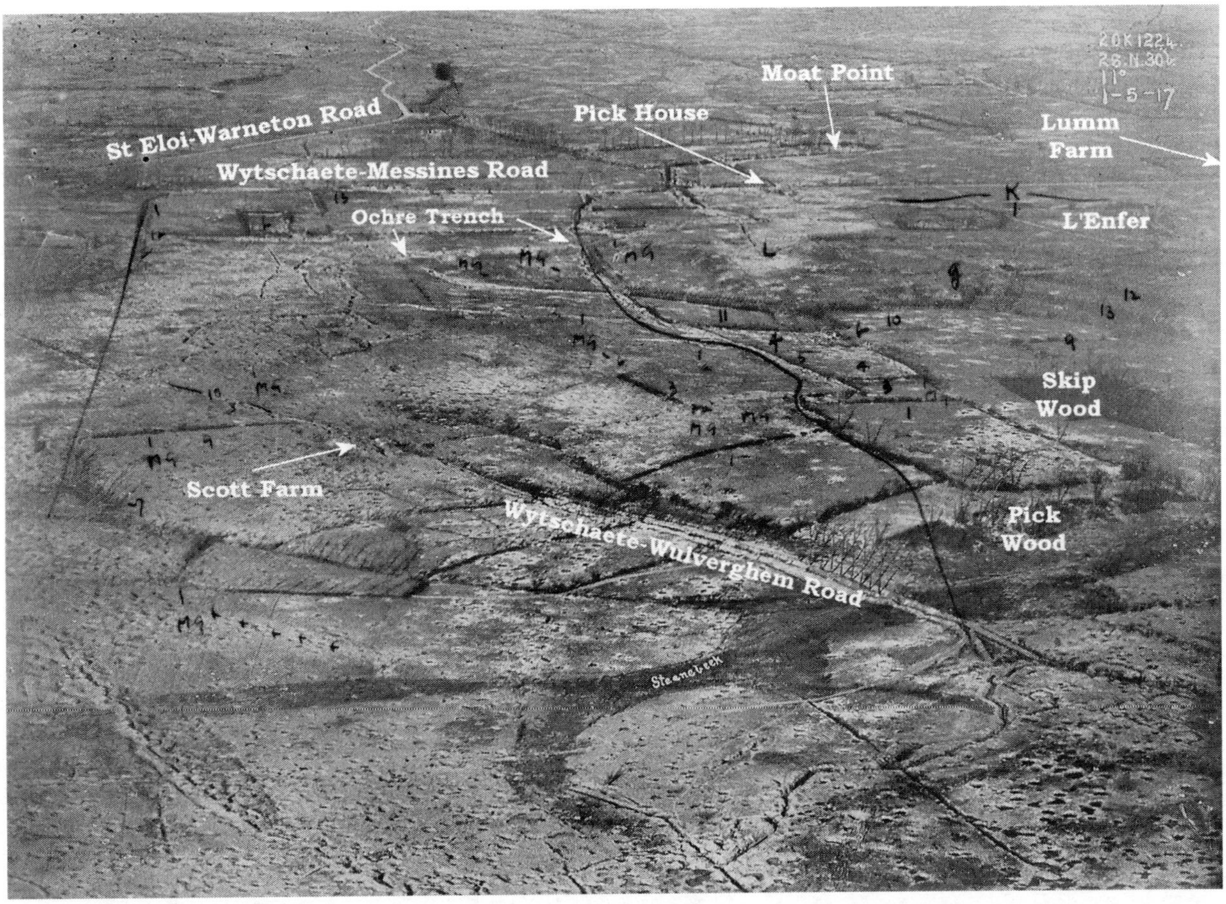

Messines Ridge.

This oblique air photograph, taken on 1 May 1917, shows the area secured by 9th Royal Irish Fusiliers when it relieved 15th Royal Irish Rifles on the night of 7 June 1917. The marks in blue of German positions and machine gun posts were made by the Intelligence Officer, Captain J H Partridge. The photograph is orientated with north to the left. Overlaid text by the author.

At 3.30pm the next afternoon the Battalion was ordered to move forward again to take over the Mauve Line from 11th Royal Irish Rifles. This was about 1,200 yards forward of thc Black Line generally along the St Eloi/Warneton Road and was the final limit of the advance. The 9th Royal Irish Fusiliers moved forward that evening, completing the relief by 10.30pm and again had three companies in the front line with one in support. The men worked throughout the night consolidating the position and wiring under continuous shellfire, mainly from 150mm high explosive shells. The right and centre companies suffered most but, luckily, no casualties were sustained. Although the trenches were deepened, other work was almost impossible during the next day as the line was under enemy observation and any movement drew fire. Nonetheless, the 9th Royal Irish Fusiliers was well supplied by the Transport, which had no difficulty in getting up supplies of ammunition, rations and water. Finally, after dark on 9 June the 9th Royal Irish Fusiliers was relieved by a battalion of The Duke of Wellington's (West Riding Regiment) from 49th (West Riding) Division.

Having been in reserve throughout this most successful attack, casualties for the 9th Royal Irish Fusiliers over its forty-eight hours in the line had been remarkably light. Three men from C Company were killed by shell-fire: Privates Charles Batterbee, William Rountree and Alfred Wainwright. The war diary records that twenty-three men were wounded. One man, Private Thomas Randerson, also of C Company, succumbed to his wounds on 12 June. The rest were Company Quartermaster Sergeant James Shepherd, Sergeants Harold Barton and John Redpath, Lance Sergeant Robert Johnston, Corporals Jacob Brown and Thomas Wilson, Lance Corporals Albert Baxter, Hugh Morton and Samuel Page and Privates Maurice Andrews, Robert Blackburn, John Cahal, Samuel Copeland, William Herron, Robert Jackson, Robert Morrison, David Morton, Joseph Patterson, Joseph Rogers, Alfred Simpson, James Toomay, John Wilson and Thomas Winn.

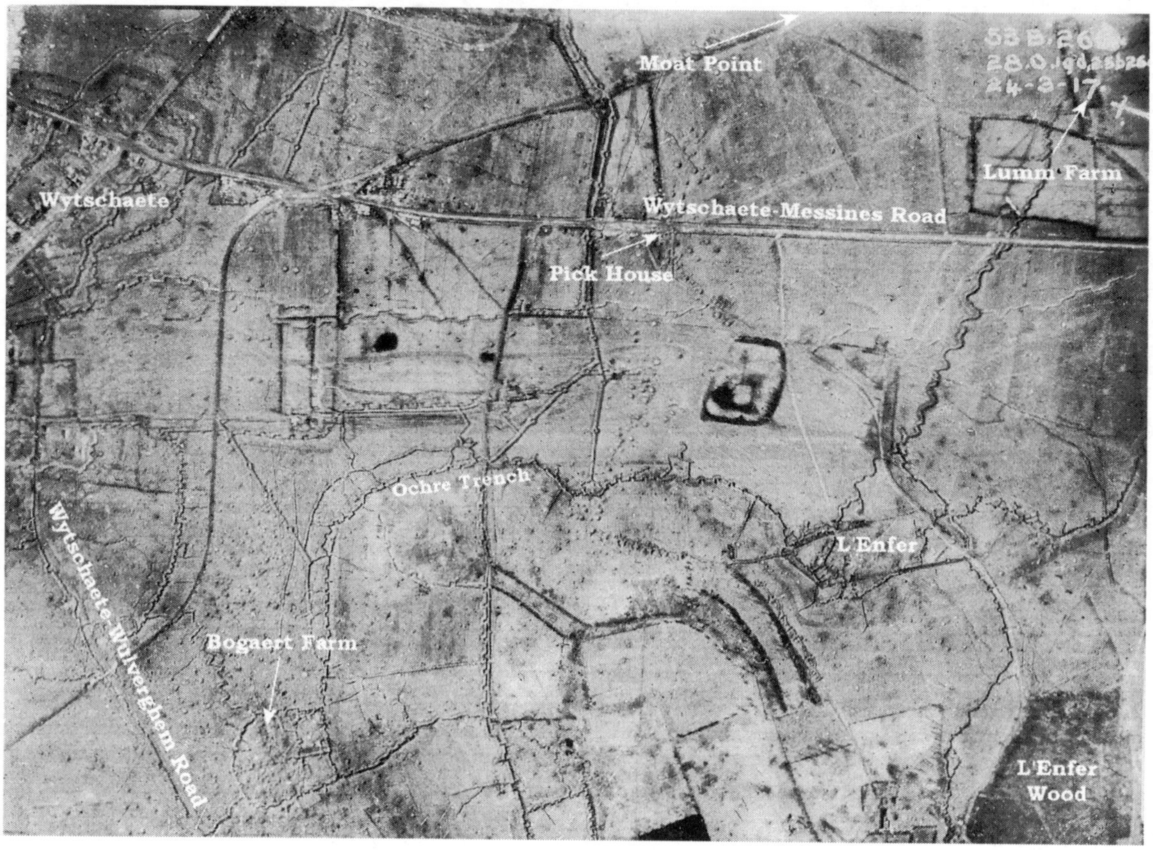

Messines Ridge.
This overhead air photograph, taken on 24 March 1917, shows the area south of Wytschaete secured by the 9th Royal Irish Fusiliers when it relieved 15th Royal Irish Rifles on the night of 7 June 1917. The photograph is orientated with north to the left. Overlaid text by the author.

During the fighting the Reverend Halahan, now the Ulster Division's Senior Chaplain, worked hard to help the wounded. His work as a stretcher-bearer was commented on by the Commanding Officer of 110th Field Ambulance, Lieutenant Colonel Fawcett, who wrote to the Deputy Chaplain General:

> *'Major F J Halahan performed most valuable service not only as a stretcher bearer but as a dresser; also during the days previous to the action when the village of Dranoutre and its neighbourhood was frequently shelled this officer set a fine example of coolness and courage.'*

After moving back to the bivouacs on the side of Kemmel Hill there was little time for rest, and for the next few days the 9th Royal Irish Fusiliers provided large work parties conducting salvage tasks and moving artillery ammunition in the areas newly captured.

The planned move of the 9th Royal Irish Fusiliers due to take place on the evening of 13 June was cancelled and more work parties were ordered. At 7.00pm the next evening the remainder of the Battalion finally left the Kemmel area and marched to a new camp farther in the rear near Westoutre. The camp was shared with two companies of 13th Royal Irish Rifles, and the men slept in tents in fields around the farmhouse that held the battalion headquarters. For three days the 9th Royal Irish Fusiliers provided more work parties, mainly moving artillery ammunition, until on Sunday 17 June it was ordered to move to Merris, a few miles south-west of Bailleul. This order was cancelled later that evening, however, and the Ulster Division was moved into the line again, farther north than previously, to take over the Corps front from 11th (Northern) Division. 107th and 109th Brigade were ordered to take over the front and support lines with 108th Brigade in reserve.

A German concrete strongpoint near Messines.

This was typical of the German strong-points built on the higher ground at Wytschaete and Messines that overlooked the Allies' positions. This type of structure would be faced by the 9th Royal Irish Fusiliers during the attack to come in August. © IWM (E(AUS) 1285)

The 9th Royal Irish Fusiliers led the Brigade column back past Kemmel Hill and then north-east for one and a half miles to a field south of Vierstraat. The tents and bivouacs arrived about three hours after the men, at about 11.00pm, and that night and the next morning were spent settling in. The weather was generally warm, but there were a few thundershowers over the next few days as the men formed work parties to carry out salvage between the camp and the old front line. On 21 June, for the first time in many weeks, no work parties were required and the Battalion conducted low-level training with Lewis guns, bombs and rifle grenades in the morning, and many of the men were also able to bathe. That night the area of the camp was shelled by a long-range gun but only minor casualties were suffered. The band was particularly lucky not to have anyone hurt when their tent was blown up. Work parties resumed the next day, with two platoons working in the morning and two in the afternoon under Second Lieutenant Cowdy, the acting Brigade Salvage Officer. This was the format for the next week. A few casualties, caused mainly by shellfire were sustained over this period, but the 9th Royal Irish Fusiliers had suffered much less than the men in the forward brigades who took the brunt of the enemy artillery fire. On 26 June those officers not on duty undertook their own training. In the morning they had musketry practice and communications drills, led by Lieutenant Mitchel, riding exercise before lunch with Lieutenant Stronge, and physical drill and bayonet fighting in the afternoon led by Company Sergeant Major Instructor R G Lean of the Army Gymnastic Staff.[1] The next day the Battalion football team added to its honours by beating the Divisional Artillery 7-2. The 9th Royal Irish Fusiliers was relieved on 29 June by the 10th (Service) Battalion, The Loyal North Lancashire Regiment, recently arrived in the Ypres Sector after a period out of the line resting and training with the rest of 37th Division, and proceeded as originally planned to billets in Merris.

Casualties in other battalions in the Ulster Division resulted in eleven junior officers leaving at the end of the month to join The Royal Irish Rifles. Second Lieutenants J W Campbell, A Davidson and J I Smith were all attached to the 11th (Service) Battalion; Second Lieutenants J F Ashe, H K Brady, H P Connar, W F Irvine, R G McCall, E M Montgomery and J A Stokes joined the 12th (Service) Battalion, and Second Lieutenant J H Dougan joined the 16th (Service) Battalion (Pioneers).[2]

July 1917 was largely uneventful. The month began with training at Merris in individual skills with bayonet, bomb and rifle and general fitness training on route marches. After five days the 9th Royal Irish Fusiliers moved farther west to Borre, followed the next day by a march of fifteen miles to Corbonne. Finally on 7 July the men marched fourteen miles to Boisdinghem, about six miles west of St Omer, where the Battalion was to remain for most of the month. The Ulster Division found itself in the southern portion of the training area used after the Somme attack the previous summer, but the facilities were not as good. The weather was glorious, however, and more than made up for the cramped billets. Life here was very pleasant, particularly for those battalions relatively unscathed by the recent fighting. The 9th Royal Irish Fusiliers began a round of training at all levels and in every skill required for trench warfare, including battalion and brigade-level field exercises with tanks. This was the first time that the men of the 9th Royal Irish Fusiliers had trained with these new machines.

Naturally, 12 July was a holiday. Nowhere is it recorded what the reaction by the Irish Catholic or English soldiers of the Battalion was to this celebration of Protestantism. There are no records of any tensions in the 9th Royal Irish Fusiliers over politics or religion in the war diary or anywhere else, on this day or any other. Captain McCarthy-O'Leary, himself the son of a landed Catholic family from County Cork, and a regular officer who had recently arrived having recovered from wounds received in Salonika while with the 2nd Battalion, directed a sports competition in fine weather. It was followed in the evening by a concert.

Towards the end of the month the 9th Royal Irish Fusiliers moved north-east towards Ypres to billets at Winnezeele, where the Battalion remained for four days until, on 30 July, it moved into billets and tents at Watou, about six miles west of Poperinge. At Winnezeele the tents were taken over from the 6th (Service) Battalion, The Connaught Rangers. This had been a relaxing month for the Battalion, which was now trained, fit and ready for its commitment into the line. It was to be the last time for a year that the 9th Royal Irish Fusiliers would have such a protracted period to train, accept drafts, and develop the spirit of the original volunteers. The drafts had provided significant numbers of reinforcements, including a large number of Second Lieutenants, and by the end of the month the Battalion's total strength was 66 officers and 1068 other ranks, an effective strength of 65 officers and 960 other ranks, and, with the Battalion concentrated in one place, a fighting strength of 65 officers and 958 other ranks.

William Moore, the son of a surgeon from Belfast, was one of the Second Lieutenants to join over this period. His brother Archie joined a battalion of The Royal Irish Rifles about the same time. William Moore's letters home give a feel for the events of late-June and July from a junior officer's perspective, as these extracts show:

> *20 June*
>
> *We are living in tents here and although there was a heavy thunderstorm accompanied by torrential rains last night, we were proof against it all.*
>
> *24 June*
>
> *The food here is excellent and the mess is cheaper than at Newtownards, which is surprising in view of the fact that N'Ards was well known for its cheap mess.*
>
> *1 July*
>
> *I am in very good form and my only complaint is a little stiffness after some horse-riding and a strenuous football match. By the way, would it be too much trouble to ask you to look for 2 little books which would be very useful to me out here? The names of the books are:*
>
> *'Maps and Map-reading', by Courtney Terrell, Inns of Court O.T.C. It is a long-shaped white paper-backed pamphlet (hardly a book).*
>
> *'French-English Technical Military Terms', by Marius D. Eshumbert. It is a red paperbound volume with about 50 pages.*
>
> *10 July*
>
> *It is quite interesting to march about the country and stay at so many different billets and try my hand at speaking French. I have at least the satisfaction of knowing that I am about the only officer in the company who can make himself understood at all times. Some can speak a few words but the majority are usually at a loss. I am living here in a tent and could not be better off even in the little bungalow in Donaghadee.*
>
> *Preparations for the 12th go on apace and we have the usual band-playing and drum-beating. There is to be a holiday on that famous day, so that we are looking forward to a joyous celebration. Just at present we are having rather damp and cool weather here, but it is not disagreeable. The training here is not hard and is interesting.*
>
> *18 July*
>
> *Mitchell (sic)* (Lieutenant F D Mitchel) *arrived here about a week after I joined, and, owing to his second star, is second in command of a company. We have had quite an influx of officers lately, and the result is that a number have been transferred to the Rifles, as we are well over-strength. One chap who was transferred is now second on the list for leave, so that he considers that, taking all things into consideration, he is not so unlucky after all. I am afraid that my seniority as regards date of commission has all gone by the board, as it appears that seniority here is practically reckoned from length of service in France. I recognise the justice of this, but of course just a shade of*

disappointment mingles with this.

I saw by the paper that Charles Black (Lieutenant C M Black) *was dead. You will no doubt remember him; I think you met him one day at N'Ards, a Scottish fellow, very dark and wiry-looking. He came from Queen's at the same time that I went to N'Ards, and was a great favourite with us all. He died suddenly at Portrush after a successful operation for ptomaine poisoning. It was curious that he got a nice blighty just a couple of months ago, and was congratulating himself and being congratulated all round for his luck.*

This afternoon there is to be another break in the training, for a Divisional gymkhana is to be held in a neighbouring village. It is to be composed of events such as tug-of-war on horseback, wrestling on horseback, V-C race, costume race etc. It ought to be interesting if the weather keeps up, but the prospects are not too good at present. I expect to see Archie over there; I have not seen him very lately, although he passes through this village regularly on his way out of the training ground.

I am at present 'hors de combat' owing to an unfortunate little accident which took place on the 13th July. I was playing football and came into contact with another officer's head. My left eyebrow got a fairly severe bash and I had to have 3 stitches put in it. I had to wear a bandage across my face for a couple of days, but am now fixed up with a plaster.'

Still sceptical about the chance of success at Ypres, the War Cabinet withheld permission for Haig to launch the second part of his offensive, but authorised that he could continue with his preparations. The delay lasted for seven weeks and it was not until 25 July that Haig was allowed to proceed. Notwithstanding Plumer's success at Messines, command of the operation was vested in General Sir Hubert Gough. His plan was for an offensive on a twenty-mile front stretching from Warneton, a village just east of Ploegsteert Wood in the south, to Dixmude on the east bank of the Yser Canal twelve miles north of Ypres. The principal part of the attack was to be conducted by Gough's Fifth Army with a corps from Second Army on its right and the French *1re Armée* on its left.

The weather during the Third Battle of Ypres, as this battle would become known, has been the subject of much discussion. An analysis of rainfall in previous years, and the forecast and predictions by Haig's meteorological staff, pointed to mixed weather, but the region suffered an early, abnormally heavy and continuous downpour of rain in early August just after the offensive began. Since the formation of the salient in late-1914 it had been subject to artillery bombardment from both sides. For this attack there would be a preliminary barrage lasting ten days, considered by many of the enemy to be the worst barrage suffered in the course of the war. The high water table and composition of the ground in the Ypres area had forced farmers to develop a complex drainage system over hundreds of years. This was utterly destroyed by shellfire, and with the onset of the heavy rain, the consequence was a battlefield of almost indescribably difficult conditions. The small rivers or 'beeks' that crossed the salient turned into areas of wide and deep marshland. Everywhere else shell craters filled with water, and the ground turned to a thick mud which trapped men and animals and slowed any advance to a pace that made the German machine-gunners' task much easier.

Following the preliminary barrage, twelve divisions attacked on 31 July. In the XIX Corps area north-east of Ypres, 55th (West Lancashire) Division and 15th (Scottish) Division attacked on a line between the old Ypres/Passchendaele railway and a point just north of

Wieltje, with 55th Division on the left and 15th Division on the right. The attack was a relative success but the devastation wrought by the German machine-gunners so weakened the leading battalions that they were not able to withstand the enemy counter-attack. They were driven back to the line of their second objective between 2,000 and 2,500 yards from their start line and this was the line consolidated over the next two weeks.

Across the front the new line comprised consolidated, muddy craters that afforded no shelter to their occupants and, consequently, sapped the energy of the troops. This was in contrast to conditions for the German machine-gunners who, although suffering from the effects of the weather, were sheltered in pillboxes spread across the front in the new German tactic of defence in depth, with the arcs of fire of each gun interlocking with others. These pillboxes were almost impervious to artillery fire and required destruction in detail. The scale of the casualties and the crop of animal and human corpses that littered the battlefield added to the horror of the conditions; the stench and sight of which would not be forgotten by anyone who fought there.

Stretcher bearers at Ypres.

This photograph was taken near and to the north of Boesinghe, a few days before the 9th Royal Irish Fusiliers' attack. It illustrates the worst of the conditions faced by the Ulster Division in mid-August 1917. Not everywhere was as bad as this, but even in the areas with less standing water, the thick clay made movement difficult. © IWM (Q 5935)

It had been planned that the troops that had conducted the first assault would remain in the line until the eve of the next attack, but the number of casualties and the worsening conditions made this impossible. In consequence, 36th (Ulster) and 16th (Irish) Divisions were committed to the line early. This decision had a major impact on the fitness of both Divisions to conduct an aggressive attack in such awful circumstances.

On 2 August 107th Brigade, reinforced by two battalions from each of the other two brigades in the Ulster Division, was allocated to 55th (West Lancashire) Division as a reserve and it moved forward to relieve 165th and 166th Brigades in the captured German positions. 9th Royal Irish Fusiliers and 13th Royal Irish Rifles reinforced from 108th Brigade. The 9th Royal Irish Fusiliers had been based at Watou since the end of July. From here the initial reconnaissance of the forward area had been conducted by Lieutenant Colonel Somerville and some of the company officers before the Battalion received notification on the night of 2 August that it would take over part of the original front line. The following afternoon 9th Royal Irish Fusiliers and 13th Royal Irish Rifles moved on foot and by train to their new positions near Wieltje, that had previously been the forward positions from which 55th (West Lancashire) Division attacked. The two reinforcing battalions from 109th Brigade took over the other half of the support line. The relief was conducted in continuous rain, deep mud and heavy artillery fire, and the confusion and difficulty cost the Brigade dear. In the 9th Royal Irish Fusilier's area A Company was deployed forward to the old front line trench just east of Wieltje in particularly bad conditions. Little was left of the original trenches, which had been destroyed by shellfire and the awful weather.

About 800 yards farther back B, C and D Companies were in the trenches known as Congreve Walk, which were also in poor condition being very crowded and deep in mud. Battalion headquarters was also in this area in a wet, narrow mineshaft at the Vinery which afforded some protection but was not big enough. The trench strength of the 9th Royal Irish Fusiliers was about 700 men with the remainder, those not taking part in the attack, located with the Battalion Transport. The night was quiet but very wet, and the next morning four officers and 300 men were detailed as a work party to bury signal cable. For five hours they laboured in appalling conditions, suffering five men wounded, before they returned to the trenches and spent the rest of the day attempting to improve their lot in marginally better weather. Little was accomplished before the exhausted men moved out before dawn on the morning of 5 August, under attack from gas shells, to Query Camp, a muddy collection of tents near Brandhoek, about four miles west of Ypres.

In this area was focused much of the activity required to support the units at the front. Tented camps, transport lines, dumps of every kind, casualty clearing stations and ambulance parks were littered along the road and railways which led east to Ypres and west to Poperinge. After twenty-four hours refitting, cleaning equipment and bathing, the Battalion was tasked to provide work parties. Most of the officers and many of the NCOs were, however, able to reconnoitre the front areas or visit the scale model of the XIX Corps front. The next phase of the battle was scheduled to begin on 16 August. Over the next few days, in addition to providing ever-larger work parties in gradually improving weather, the 9th Royal Irish Fusiliers re-organised and prepared to move forward. The letters of William Moore provide a typically understated view of events in early August:

> *1 August*
>
> *Today the rain is coming down in bucketfulls, but we manage to keep up our spirits wonderfully. My little wound has healed up again.*

6 August

We are lying slightly behind the lines at present and expect to be in the thick of it before long again. If you do not hear from me for a few days, attribute it to the fact that we will be doing what we have come out to do, which is our plain and simple duty.

11 August

We are having much better weather now, and our hope is that it will continue. This country where we are now in bivouacs would be extremely pretty to our eyes if the attentions of our old friend Mr. Bosch did not render it rather too exciting to enjoy it. After a muddy stint in the trenches, I was glad to get a good hot bath to-day in well-appointed bath-houses.

12 August

With regard to the late advances, nearly everybody says it would have been an overwhelming success, if the terribly wet weather had not interfered with the progress of the operations. As it was, we did as well as could be expected and the Hun has again proved himself to be inferior to our men in every respect. As you probably know, the area of the British push was for a long time the most uncomfortable part of the line, so it behoves us to get rid of the Hun in this district, and we mean to do so.

The weather at present is beautiful, and if it keeps up, it should be a great to help to us.

14 August

I write these few lines to tell you that the Ulster Division will shortly be in action again, and that we all hope that there will be a successful upshot to our 'little bit' of the attack. The weather has taken up a good deal lately and it will be necessary to push home the advantage which this gives us. We are all in good form and it will not be our fault if the attack is not a success.

I am sure you will not expect me to write much, as you can understand we are very busy. Whatever happens don't worry.

Although every effort was made to spare the six battalions of the Ulster Division that would attack on the next phase of the offensive, everyone took a turn in the line. Finally, thc 9th Royal Irish Fusiliers moved up to the trenches again on 14 August as the weather broke. That day saw one of the heaviest deluges of rain experienced during the battle and the Battalion moved to the front in very difficult, tiring conditions that left the men soaked through and ill-prepared for the action to come. In his understated diary entry for 14 August 1917 Private Laurence Gordon Ranger reported: *'Nothing special in the morning. Played house in the afternoon. Got three days rations and moved to front line. Started 7.00pm. Got lost going to the line but arrived there at 4.00am.'*

Just before the attack the paper strength of the 9th Royal Irish Fusiliers was sixty-six officers and 1070 other ranks. With twenty-four officers and 286 other ranks detached, the ration strength of the Battalion was forty-two officers and 784 other ranks. Only twenty-three officers and 640 other ranks would take part in the attack, the remainder being with the Battalion's Transport and rear details or designated as 'battle surplus'.

The lack of detailed records or first-hand accounts make it difficult to show accurately how the 9th Royal Irish Fusiliers was organised for any particular attack and who commanded at company and platoon level. This difficulty is compounded by the knowledge that some were left out as battle surplus and some officers would be detached temporarily, or were ill. For the attack on 16 August 1917 the organisation of the battalion was three platoons in each of the four companies. It is clear that three out of the four company commanders took part, but there is no record of Captain M Henahan leading C Company that day. Given the need for twelve platoon commanders it is not clear why fourteen junior officers took part in the attack, although one may have commanded C Company and some may have helped lead forward the reinforcements as the battle stalled, but they are not mentioned specifically in any of the notes written at the time. It is also not clear why the Transport Officer, Lieutenant Stronge, took part in the attack given that the Transport was some miles to the rear near Ypres.

As far as can be determined the order of battle for the attack on 16 August was:

Commanding Officer:	Lieutenant Colonel S J Somerville
Second-in-Command:	Captain T F Given
Adjutant:	Captain A Ferguson DCM
Transport Officer:	Lieutenant J M Stronge
Quartermaster:	Honorary Lieutenant G W Wilson
Medical Officer:	Captain O V Burrows MB RAMC
Padre:	Captain S Mayes AChD
A Company:	Captain T G Shillington, Lieutenant S P Colquhoun and Second Lieutenants H Hamill, R W Johnston and B M Malone
B Company:	Lieutenant D H Wright, Lieutenant A S Nolan and Second Lieutenants W M Seymour and S L Trinder
C Company:	Lieutenant W G Boyd and Second Lieutenants F Baker, R D Miles MC and W Moore
D Company:	Captain R S Flood, Lieutenant C W S Magill and Second Lieutenants H E Cowdy, D J Fullerton and J I Hamilton
Regimental Sergeant Major:	Warrant Officer Class 1 C H Turner

Attached:
Number 3 Section, 108th Brigade Machine Gun Company:
Lieutenant J G S Thomas[3]

For the second time 36th (Ulster) Division would be fighting alongside 16th (Irish) Division, which would advance on its right. On its left was 48th (South Midland) Division of XVIII Corps. Within the Ulster Division, 109th Brigade was deployed forward on the left with 108th Brigade on the right and 107th Brigade in reserve. In 108th Brigade, the 9th Royal Irish Fusiliers was to attack on the right with 13th Royal Irish Rifles on their left. During the preparatory phase before the attack, the 9th Royal Irish Fusiliers was deployed on a frontage of 400 yards. A and B Companies were on the right and left respectively in the front line captured by 55th (West Lancashire) Division centred on the old German strong-point known as Pommern Redoubt. C Company was in support and D Company positioned about 2,300 yards to the rear along the old British front line near Warwick Farm. Battalion headquarters was at Plum Farm about 1,000 yards back from the forward companies. The left boundary with 13th Royal Irish Rifles ran from an old gun position north of Pommern Redoubt north-east to a road junction known as Kansas Cross. The right boundary with 16th (Irish) Division rested on an old trench line that ran from the right of Pommern Redoubt to Iberian Farm, and north-east to Gallipoli Copse. Beyond this boundary would advance 7th Royal Inniskilling Fusiliers, supported by 7th/8th Royal Irish Fusiliers.

The 9th Royal Irish Fusiliers' objectives were, firstly, the Green Line, the original objective of 55th (West Lancashire) Division, 600 yards east of Pommern Redoubt and running along the line of an old lane through the strong-point at Gallipoli Farm. Another 400 yards farther on was the Dotted Green Line, an intermediate objective, and the final objective, the Red Line, lay 1,500 yards from the start line. In the area to be attacked by the 9th Royal Irish Fusiliers the ground was dominated on the right by a formidable strong-point on Hill 35 which lay about 400 yards forward of the start line. Slightly farther away on the left was Gallipoli Farm, a well-built strong-point, heavily protected by a double belt of wire that ran obliquely across the line of advance south and east of the Farm. This wire was a significant obstacle and it could not be seen fully from the 9th Royal Irish Fusiliers' start point. In contrast, the enemy had an excellent view and fields of fire from their fortified positions in Somme Farm and Aisne House over the area to be attacked on the left by 13th Royal Irish Rifles. Iberian Farm and the strong-points on Hill 37 over the right boundary (the objectives for 7th Royal Inniskilling Fusiliers) dominated the area over which the 9th Royal Irish Fusiliers would have to advance to reach its final objective. The ground to be covered by the 9th Royal Irish Fusiliers was as bad as anywhere along the front. It was very muddy, torn up by shellfire and in some areas deep in quagmire. The implications of the enemy's dispositions, and the conditions, must have been evident to the men as they waited during the day before the attack, and the feelings amongst those who had attacked at Hamel cannot be imagined.

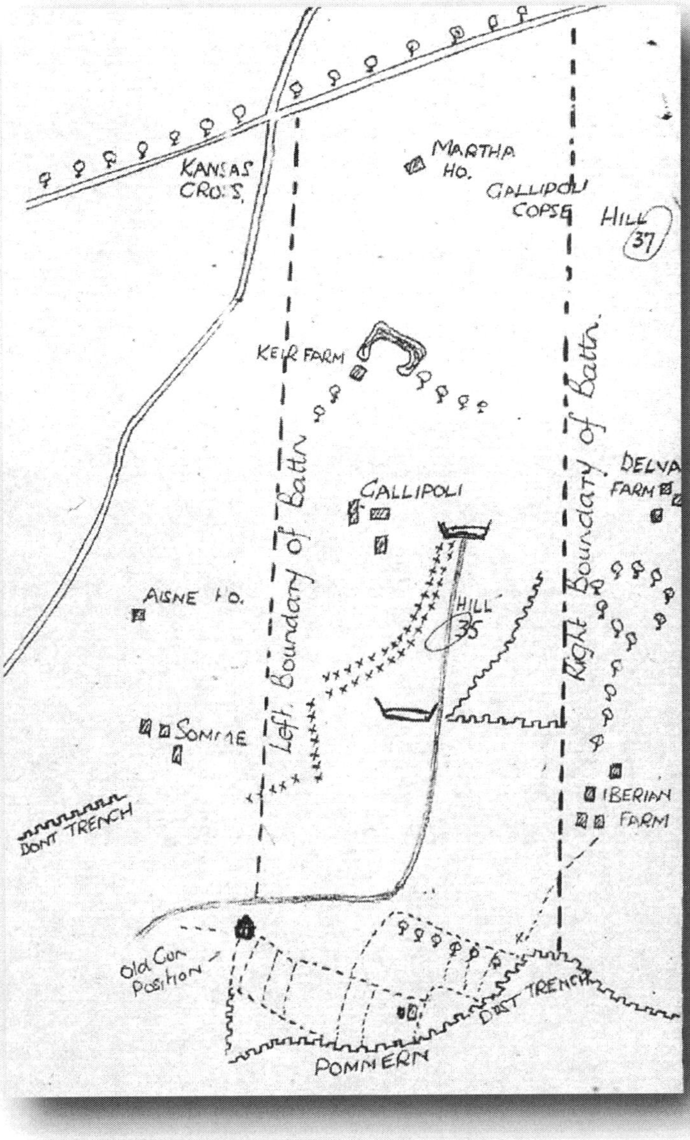

This sketch was drawn in the days after the attack on 16 August 1917 to illustrate the 9th Royal Irish Fusiliers' war diary.

The rifle companies spent a night and a day in their positions during which time the forward trenches were shelled at regular intervals. Evacuation of the wounded was carried out under appalling conditions. On the night before the attack, battalion headquarters and the two reserve companies moved forward to the assembly trenches either side of Pommern Redoubt, hindered by the waning moon and the difficult, muddy ground. The Transport moved to lines just east of Ypres. Captain Godson, recently promoted and still serving as 108th Brigade Intelligence Officer, visited the line:

> *'At 6.00pm went by car to Wieltje dugout, the 9th R.Ir.Fus., and 13th R.Ir.R., moving to the front line for the big attack. I then went down to the line to give Zero time to the COs and then to look at the ground along the Steenbecque* (sic) *Valley, the actual front line, in order to report to Brigadier, Gen Griffith, upon the ground round Pommern 'Castle' (so called) and farmstead. The objective is to be Hill 35 and 'Gallipoli Farm', uphill from the Steenbecque Stream, about 300 yards. At Plum Farm I found Col Somerville, Lt Shillington, 2nd Lt Miles, Capt Given and Burroughs* (sic)*, all quite cheerful. How little did I think that was the last time I should see them.'*

Casualties at a Regimental Aid Post near Ypres. © IWM (Q 5732)

The two brigades of the Ulster Division were to attack with two battalions forward, each of which would advance with two companies forward. The 9th Royal Irish Fusiliers now had

A and B Companies on the right and left respectively and each responsible for half of the Battalion's frontage. C and D Companies were in support, each covering one of the forward companies. Each company would attack in two waves, each 100 yards apart, and each wave in two lines ten yards apart. This meant that the 9th Royal Irish Fusiliers would attack in four waves over a depth of over 300 yards, with the second and forth waves being weaker due to C and D companies having been temporarily reduced to three platoons due to the battle surplus detached to the rear. Throughout the night of 15 August, during a sustained German barrage across the front, Lieutenant Colonel Somerville and Captain T F Given, acting as Second-in-Command, visited the assembly trenches and shell holes to check everything was in order. In the two days during this preliminary period the 9th Royal Irish Fusiliers suffered one man killed, Lance Corporal Isaac Hague, and an unknown number wounded. The wounded were moved back through the deep mud with as many as six or eight men carrying each stretcher. The constant shelling, lack of sleep, and the conditions in the trenches meant that no-one was rested.

At Zero, 4.45am on Thursday 16 August 1917, about an hour before dawn, the leading companies left their trenches to follow the creeping barrage. The barrage moved at a steady one hundred yards in five minutes and it was planned that this would continue until it reached the Green Line where it would pause for thirty-five minutes. Also providing support were ten machine-guns from the Brigade Machine Gun Company. As the lead companies left the trenches and shell holes where they had been sheltering the enemy artillery shortened its range. In his diary entry Private Laurence Gordon Ranger reported: *'I am got into no-man's-land and stopped till attack started. Attack started 4.00am, went ten yards and stopped a shell. Got into a shell hole.'*

The leading companies were not hit too badly but the enemy artillery caught the support companies in the third and forth waves. In front, A and B Companies were met by very heavy machine-gun fire, particularly from Hill 35. Amongst those killed early in the attack was Second Lieutenant Bristow Malone, commanding 4 Platoon, whose Platoon Sergeant, William Foster, saw him shot and killed instantly.

On the right, A Company with C Company in support, maintained its formation until, having advanced to within fifty yards of the first enemy positions, fire was opened and the leading platoons began their assault with riflemen attempting to move forward covered by rifle-bombs and Lewis guns. As A Company reached a hastily entrenched position south of the strong-point on Hill 35, the German machine-gun fire increased, and on account of the number of casualties, each company was formed into one wave. The German infantry fought hard, unwilling to allow themselves to become prisoners. As a result of more casualties and before this trench and strong-point were taken, A Company and C Company had combined. Having captured the trench, even heavier opposition was met at the strong-point on Hill 35. The original plans to by-pass these positions and allow them to be 'mopped up' proved impossible, and Hill 35 had to be taken. Lieutenant Colonel Somerville went forward to lead the attack on this feature but the enemy fought until practically every man was killed and it took twenty minutes of hard fighting before Hill 35 was finally captured. A platoon was detached to consolidate the position, joined by Lieutenant Thomas and his two machine-guns from the Brigade Machine Gun Company, and the remainder of A and C Companies pushed on.

Over the Battalion's right boundary, 7th Royal Inniskilling Fusiliers had moved forward quickly and had taken most of their initial objectives. By 5.55am B Company of that battalion was consolidating its position just to the north of Delva Farm. The supporting barrage now moved away from the attacking infantry and as it did so more enemy posts along the front were able to open fire.

The remnants of A and C Companies of 9th Royal Irish Fusiliers were unable to progress until Gallipoli on their left was captured and on the right 7th Royal Inniskilling Fusiliers, reinforced by the leading companies from 7th/8th Royal Irish Fusiliers, was also unable to advance much farther. The machine-gun post on Hill 37 now dominated the ground over which all of these battalions would have to advance.

Pommern Redoubt and the start line for the 9th Royal Irish Fusiliers' attack on Hill 35 on 16 August 1917 lay on a line running across the photograph in the low ground just beyond the farm. The forward strong-point on Hill 35 is marked by the posts on the left. B Company advanced directly towards the photographer.

On the left, B and D Companies had also taken heavy casualties. With some of those who had taken Hill 35, they eventually reached the thick, newly laid, double row of wire lying across the line of advance and protecting Gallipoli Farm. It was during this push that Lieutenant William Boyd was killed and a number of men wounded when a shell burst above their heads. Sergeant J Pentland (Boyd's platoon sergeant), Sergeant T Venard and Corporal C B O'Neill, a section commander in 5 Platoon, all saw him lying in a shell hole soon after the shell burst, mortally wounded in the head and stomach. He died soon after being found. Corporal O'Neill was also wounded but eventually found his way back to his own lines.

The wire in front of Gallipoli Farm was cut only in one or two places with these gaps covered by machine-guns. The attacking men were halted by the heavy fire brought to bear on them from dug-outs and strong-points and by long range machine-gun fire from Aisne House on the left, Martha House farther forward and Hill 37 far to their right. In A Company all of the officers had been killed or wounded and command devolved to Sergeant S Carvell. After they were forced to withdraw he reorganised the men around him and led them forward again under heavy machine-gun fire.

Casualties were very heavy now and it was found impossible for any of the platoons to push on or even to stay in the untenable position outside Gallipoli Farm. At around 8.00am those still able to fight were forced to retire and take up a position in and around the strong-point on Hill 35, and in a trench running east/west just to the south of the hill. The two Vickers machine-guns were now protecting the left flank of the 7th Royal Inniskilling Fusiliers and 7th/8th Royal Irish Fusiliers at Delva Farm. On the extremity of the ground held at Hill 35 Lieutenant Wright and some men of B Company had moved forward to attack an enemy concrete strong-point from which a machine-gun was in action. Seeing that a move rearward on his left meant that his only support was the troops of the 16th (Irish) Division on his right, Wright sent a runner to their company commander explaining the position asking him to hold the ground gained. The weight of fire was too heavy, however, and Lieutenant Wright was forced to withdraw to a more favourable position. He found himself in company with some isolated groups of men from 16th (Irish) Division.

In the main battalion position on Hill 35, during the desperate attempt to consolidate the ground taken, Lieutenant Colonel Somerville was mortally wounded. Although more help had arrived from the battalion headquarters led by Captain Given, who was also soon wounded, there were too few officers and men to hold the position against a concerted counter-attack. In addition, machine-guns firing at long range from Hill 37 were raking the trench, which was not traversed, causing more casualties. Captain Flood was now in command of the remnants of the Battalion and he was forced to conduct a further withdrawal of 100 yards west to the trench lying across the original line of advance short of the strong-point on Hill 35. This was consolidated, but being so close to the Battalion's right boundary its security was reliant on the units on the right holding the ground that they had taken.

This captured German concrete strong-point is typical of those faced by the 9th Royal Irish Fusiliers on 16 August. © IWM (Q 6045)

Lieutenant W G Boyd

At about 9.00am Bavarian troops of *5. Bayerische Infanterie-Division* launched a well-planned counter-attack, known by the enemy as Scheme F, from the north against Hill 35 and Delva Farm. Lines of infantry, well equipped with bombs, advanced over the ridge between Hill 35 and Hill 37. With an unprotected left flank, the men of the 7th Royal Inniskilling Fusiliers and the 7th/8th Royal Irish Fusiliers were pushed back from Delva Farm by these strong enemy attacks.

The small group led by Lieutenant Wright was attacked and completely cut off. They held out for two hours in the hope that the ground would be retaken, but were finally overpowered by a well-organised bombing attack and, as their ammunition had run out, they were forced to surrender; Wright and nine men were captured. Despite the efforts of Lieutenant Thomas and his Vickers guns, the withdrawal on the right allowed German machine-gunners to move into Iberian Farm on that flank and again fire down the line of the trench held by the 9th Royal Irish Fusiliers. This position was now untenable and Captain Flood co-ordinated a well-ordered move back to the start-line. Here the scale of the casualties became apparent for the first time, and with the majority of the officers killed or wounded it was left to Regimental Sergeant Major Turner to supervise the defence of the line and organise arrangements for the evacuation of those wounded that had managed to crawl back, or who had been carried by their friends. Similar actions were repeated across the Ulster Division's front, and although small parties of men made it as far as the Green Line, they could not be reinforced and had to fall back. It was clear that a second attempt to reach the Green Line would not be possible and the reserve battalions were ordered forward to hold the line. That night Major General Nugent ordered 107th Brigade to relieve the two attacking Brigades and this was eventually accomplished with great difficulty in terrible conditions.

Captain Godson had moved forward at first light to watch the attack and report on its progress to Brigadier General Griffiths. His account is worth adding:

> *' 'Der Tag' again. Hopes ran high. Zero hour, 4.45am, too dark to see. First messages were not too hopeful. As soon as it seemed light enough I went out to near Jasper Farm for observation, saw many men moving on Hill 35, but could not make much of the situation for dimness and smoke. At 6.45am flares lighted on the right near Gallipoli Copse and I reported this by runner to B'de. About 8.30am saw many of our men coming back, and then Germans in the Battery gun pits on Hill 35. Things looked bad, so I moved up to the front line at Bank Farm. There I found chaos. Col Maxwell a casualty. B'ns all mixed up after coming back. Also Major Workman (2nd in command of 13th R. Ir. R.) in his HQ wounded, Capt Cahill killed, and, of the 9th R. Ir. Fus. Col Somerville badly wounded (died soon afterwards), Capt Shillington badly wounded (died of*

wounds), 2nd Lt Miles badly hit (died of wounds afterwards), likewise Lt Trinder, a gallant Irishman. The Boche had beaten us, and the slaughter terrific. I went along the line, trying to cheer up the men, and telling any Officers I met that the 'Black' line must be held, there must be no question of going back from it. The Div on our right coming back had over-passed it. Sent a message back to B'de as to all this, but it never got there, and seeing nothing more to do moved across from the ground in front of Pommern Castle to Track 4, there I had the narrowest shave I ever had. Close range shells were shrieking overhead so I got no warning. A 77mm HE ('whizz bang') suddenly burst in mud 2 yards away and blew me clean over. It was very soft ground, so the metal did not spread, to that I owed escape. Plumped myself in a shell hole 5 yards from the new plank bridge over the Steenbecque and whizz bang—whizz bang—whizz bang—bang-bang-whizz—followed in quick succession all round me. I realized they were shooting for the bridge which was 5 yards away, determined it was necessary to 'dash for it'. This I did as fast as I could for 100 yards, and luckily escaped the target. Back at Wieltje Dugout excitements seemed to be over, but the Div'l Commander telephoned saying he wanted to have another attack made at 7.30pm. This I did my best to help oppose. The men were in a state to do nothing but a dud show. It did not take place.'

Wounded being treated in a dressing station prior to be evacuated to a Casualty Clearing Station. Only the most basic first aid was carried out here to stabilise the casualties for onward movement. © IWM (E(AUS) 672)

Sergeant William Neill DCM, Transport Sergeant.

During the course of the relief, search parties went out in the most difficult of circumstances under heavy fire to find wounded men in the water-filled shell holes and trenches. Many were found badly wounded and they owed their chance of survival to the courage of those who worked through the night in the mud and under constant shell and machine-gun fire. One example of this was the effort of Sergeant William Neill, the Transport Sergeant, who called for volunteers to help him find Lieutenant James Stronge, the Transport Officer, who he knew to be badly wounded somewhere near Hill 35. He chose four men and they succeeded in finding him; it is not known whether he was dead or mortally wounded when he was found, but he did not survive.[4] The mud made the work of the stretcher-bearers difficult and they were often easy targets. Private Edward Jones, one of five brothers from Portadown who served during the war, was a stretcher-bearer in C Company. He was shot in the back while carrying a wounded man back from the line. Private Laurence Gordon Ranger, whose shrapnel wound in his thigh had prevented him moving out of the shell hole in which he had taken cover, was one of a number of men found on the night of 17 August. Stretcher bearers pulled him out and he arrived at Poperinghe in the early hours of 18 August. Most of the wounded were dealt with by Captain Burrows, the Medical Officer, assisted by the Chaplain, Samuel Mayes, in Plum Farm. The Medical Officer treated over 300 men in forty hours in appalling conditions under shell and machine-gun fire before they were evacuated to the three Casualty Clearing Stations near Brandhoek west of Ypres. Unfortunately, many did not make it through the night and they were buried in the cemeteries nearby. Many more were never found and their bodies lay where they fell in the mud, destroyed and buried by shellfire.

This is the photograph of Lieutenant J M Stronge sent by his mother to Sergeant William Neill. (See endnote[4])

Captain Burrows and Padre Mayes were finally relieved at 5.00am on 17 August. Not all of the men reported as 'missing' and later declared 'killed in action' were left in no-man's-land and the fate of Private Albert Henry Clark provides a most poignant example of how sterile records conceal the true events. Clark was a 20-year-old dock labourer from Shadwell in London who had enlisted under the Derby scheme in November 1915 and had been mobilised in July 1916. Having joined The London Regiment, he made up one of the draft of men from The London Regiment that joined the 9th Royal Irish Fusiliers in November 1916. He had attacked with the men of 4 Platoon in A Company and was wounded by machine-gun fire in the arm and leg. Carried to the dressing station by another man of the 9th Royal Irish Fusiliers, who waited with him until his wounds were dressed, he was placed in an ambulance of 48th Field Ambulance. On its way to the Casualty Clearing Station the ambulance was destroyed by shellfire. Clark was subsequently listed as 'missing' and in January 1919 was declared as having been killed in action on 16 August 1917. It is almost certain that other men of the 9th Royal Irish Fusiliers were aboard that ambulance.

Reverend S Mayes

Criticism was levelled at the Ulster and Irish Divisions for not achieving more but it is hard to know how they could have done so. The effect on the battalions of the Ulster Division that day was on a par with the impact of the Somme attack. Having seen his Division decimated a second time and in contrast to the language used after the Somme attack, Major General Nugent wrote some time later: *'The two Irish Divisions were broken to bits, and their Brigadiers called it murder. They were violent in their denunciation of 5th Army for having put their men into the attack after 13 days of shelling'.* The new German tactic of defence in depth and the reinforced concrete dugouts that withstood the reliminary and creeping barrages contributed significantly to the failure of the attack. Captain Godson wrote: *'These strong points were our undoing'.* However, the combination of the weather, its effect on the ground conditions and, most importantly, the state of the attacking troops all played a great part in the outcome of the battle.

The brigade commanders were right to be angry; the casualties were indeed severe. Between 2 and 18 August the Ulster Division suffered 144 officers and 3,441 other ranks killed in action, wounded and missing. The 9th Royal Irish Fusiliers' casualty total was the highest in 108th Brigade. The initial casualty report, which included those killed and wounded in the period that the battalion was waiting to advance, showed 456 casualties:

	Officers	Other Ranks	Total
Killed in action	4	32	36
Died of wounds	4	-	-
Wounded	9	310	323
Shellshock		12	12
Missing (believed killed)	2	-	2
Missing	1	82	83
Total	20	436	456

These figures would be adjusted as the detail became clear. The 7th/8th Royal Irish Fusiliers was equally badly cut up, losing seventeen officers and two thirds of its men killed and wounded. Much has been made of the near destruction of the 9th Royal Irish Fusiliers, at Hamel in July 1916, but the scale of the casualties on 16 August 1917 was nearly as severe, and the conditions in which the men fought were much worse. The final report would make grim reading.

Reverend Mayes compiled a list for the 9th Royal Irish Fusiliers that recorded casualties by company. This is the only major action where the records are sufficiently complete to allow a detailed analysis of the casualties as reported at the time, and in reality after the event. The figures below are based on the list of officer casualties in the war diary and the list of other rank casualties compiled by Reverend Mayes. The final tally reflects the Commonwealth War Graves Commission records and is supported by an analysis of available service records. Predictably, many of those noted as 'missing' had been killed in action, and the wounded who died on 16 August were to be declared killed in action on that date.

Officer Casualties

	War Diary Record	Final Tally
Killed in action	4	6
Died of wounds	4	4
Wounded/Injured	9	9
Missing	3	-
Captured	0	1
Total	20	20

A Company

	Mayes' Record	Final Tally
Killed in action	16	34
Died of wounds	1	2
Wounded/Injured	78	65
Missing	9	-
Captured	-	3
Total	104	104

B Company

	Mayes' Record	Final Tally
Killed in action	4	34
Died of wounds	1	2
Wounded/Injured	84	77
Missing	26	-
Captured	-	1
Total	115	114*

*One man reported missing rejoined.

C Company

	Mayes' Record	Final Tally
Killed in action	7	37
Died of wounds	1	2
Wounded/Injured	73	66
Missing	29	-
Captured	-	5
Total	110	110

D Company

	Mayes' Record	Final Tally
Killed in action	7	28
Died of wounds	-	2
Wounded/Injured	66	63
Missing	20	-
Captured	-	-
Total	93	93

The revised casualty tally for the attack on 16 August 1917:

	Final Officers' Tally	Final Other Ranks' Tally*	Final Casualty Tally*	
Killed in action	6	133	139	
Died of wounds	4	8	12	
Wounded & Injured	9	271	280	
Missing	-	-	-	
Captured	1	9	10	
Missing & Rejoined	-	1	1	
Total	20	422	442	**

*Not included in these totals is Lance Corporal Isaac Hague, who was wounded by shellfire near Wieltje and died of wounds in 114th Casualty Clearing Station on 13 August 1917, nor men wounded on 14/15 August.

**The discrepancy with the war diary figure of 456 casualties is probably due to men wounded in the two days prior to the attack on 16 August being included in the war diary total, but not by Reverend Mayes.

The Hamilton Brothers (Lurgan)

From left: 14283 Private Joseph Hamilton - Wounded at Hamel 1 July 1916.
17950 Private Albert Hamilton.
14288 Corporal James Hamilton - Killed in action Hamel 1 July 1916.
14282 Private John Hamilton MM - Killed in action 16 August 1917.

Captain T G Shillington. Commissioned in 1915, aged 17. Died of wounds on 18 August 1917, aged 19.

Captain Flood was the only officer who took part in the attack who did not become a casualty. The six officers killed in action were: Lieutenants Stronge and Boyd and Second Lieutenants Cowdy, Malone, Moore and Seymour (Malone and Seymour had been reported as missing and were later confirmed as having been killed). Lieutenant Colonel Somerville died of wounds later in the day, Second Lieutenants Miles MC and Trinder died of wounds the next day and Captain Shillington died of wounds on 18 August. Lieutenant Wright was captured. Most of the nine wounded officers were injured severely and few rejoined the Battalion. Captain Given's injuries rendered both arms useless. Lieutenant Colquhoun, who had been with the 9th Royal Irish Fusiliers for only three months, recovered to serve with the 10th (Reserve) Battalion at home until he transferred to the Indian Army in 1918. Second Lieutenant Hamill had been in France for five months and he too joined the Indian Army when he had recovered later that year.

Second Lieutenant H E Cowdy

Second Lieutenant Hamilton was badly wounded in the right thigh and left shoulder and his wounds precluded further service. Second Lieutenant Johnston was severely wounded by machine gun bullets in the chest and left arm and he remained in hospital until late 1918. Lieutenant Magill suffered a severe wound to his left leg, which shortened it by over an inch, and he remained in hospital until September 1918 and saw no further service. Lieutenant Nolan was shot in the throat while leading his platoon against the strong-points on Hill 35 and lay for ten hours in a shell hole full of water and mustard gas before he was found and evacuated; his recovery took until mid-1918 and he served the remainder of the war with the Egyptian Labour Corps. Second Lieutenants Fullerton and Baker were also wounded and neither served with the Battalion again. In his efforts to support the 9th Royal Irish Fusiliers, Lieutenant Thomas of the Machine Gun Company was wounded twice before he finally withdrew his guns from the front line at 9.00pm that night.

Second Lieutenant F Baker MM

Lieutenant Colonel A C Pratt DSO

Also killed that day was Lieutenant Colonel A C Pratt, the 9th Royal Irish Fusiliers' popular Second-in-Command until earlier that summer, who had taken command of 11th Royal Inniskilling Fusiliers in 109th Brigade. He was killed at the Wieltje dug-outs as his battalion's advance began. In addition, four of the seven platoon commanders who had been attached to the 12th Royal Irish Rifles earlier in the summer also became casualties during their attack: Second Lieutenant Stokes was killed, Lieutenant Brady was wounded when blown up by a shell but was able to return to duty, Second Lieutenant McCall was hit by shrapnel in the thigh and took until mid-1918 to recover, and Second Lieutenant Ashe was also wounded.

The non-commissioned officers and men also suffered terribly. Of the 640 men who took part in the attack, 421 were killed, wounded or captured. One hundred and fifty-one men were killed in action or would die of wounds. In addition to Company Sergeant Major William Medland of C Company, who was killed in action, the twenty-one other casualties amongst the experienced sergeants were a great blow. Four were killed in action, seventeen were wounded and one was wounded and captured. Those killed were Sergeant Samuel Culbert and Lance Sergeants James Joseph McEvoy and Dick Wolfe MM from C Company, and Acting Sergeant Joseph Balmer from D Company. The wounded included Sergeants Herbert Anderson, David Henry Bethel, Thomas Clements MM, William Cowan, George Hennesey, Arthur Johnson, Robert Johnston, Patrick Mackle, Campbell McConkey MM, Thomas Philpott, Samuel George Porter, John Reid, William John Stevenson, James Wilson, James William Yeman, Acting Sergeant John McMahon and Lance Sergeant Alan Brooke Wimpey. Sergeant William John Maxwell was wounded and captured.

Lance Corporal William James Graham, from Crann, Middletown. Killed in action 16 August 1917.

The death of Sergeant R J Wolfe MM was widely remarked upon and his father received letters from, amongst others, Lieutenant Colonel Blacker and the Baron Inchiquin:

Sunday, Sept 2, 1917

Dear Mr Wolfe

In the list of casualties in my old Battalion sent me today by the Adjt, I grieved to see that your boy Dick is among the killed. Though no longer with them myself, I must write to tell you what a very high opinion I had of your son during the time he was with me. He was a splendid type of lad, brave as a lion, always ready for any job, no matter how dangerous, cheery, and no matter what the hardships, always with a smile, and sticking it to the end. I made him Scout Sergt and he did splendid work with the scouts, his old training at home stood to him. He took part in numerous raids and was a tower of strength. I always knew that when Dick was out all would go well and it did. I am sure he was doing more than his duty when he met his death and setting an example of coolness and bravery to all. We can ill spare such lads and I grieve with you in loss. He has gone over in excellent company with Lt Col Audley Pratt, to whom he was devoted and who as you know was killed the same day. He died a gallant soldier's death and in gallant company one cannot ask for better when it comes to our own time. I am sure he would so have wished it, but his loss is hard to bear, I and all well know. My deepest sympathy goes out to you.

Yours faithfully
SW Blacker
Lieutenant Colonel

Dromoland Castle
Newmarket on Fergus
Co Clare

Sept 7th 1917

Dear Sir,

Both Her Ladyship and I are very much distressed to hear that your son Dick has been killed and indeed everybody on the place was very sorry to hear it as he was most popular here.

He certainly was a very nice boy, and did his work most conscientiously and hard, and you have the deepest sympathy from both Lady Inchiquin and myself in your very sad loss.

I am sorry to hear about your other boy who has hurt his spine, but I do trust he will gradually recover from this, and be a comfort to you.

I will certainly let my Keeper Andrew know that your boy has been killed.

My boy is out at the front and we hear from him once a week or ten days but it is very anxious times for us all.

With my deepest sympathy in your sad loss.

Yours faithfully
Inchiquin

Two hundred and seventy-one men were wounded. Some were hurt only slightly and others were able to rejoin the Battalion in the days and weeks after the attack. Many were injured severely, however, and would never recover fully. It is known that seventy-seven of these men were discharged as no longer physically fit for war service due to wounds.

The make-up of the battalion was reflected in the casualty figures. Most of the casualties were from Ireland but ninety-five men were from the English regiments that had reinforced the 9th Royal Irish Fusiliers at the end of 1916. Many of the counties of Ireland were represented, notably Counties Cavan, Down, Monaghan and Tyrone, as was Belfast, Londonderry and Dublin, reflecting the widespread posting of men between battalions as required by the demand for manpower.

The largest proportion of the casualties (169 men), however, were from County Armagh, and the vast majority of those from the north of the county from Lurgan and Portadown and the surrounding villages and farm lands: forty-one from Lurgan, forty-six from Portadown, seven from Tandragee, five from Richhill and three from Loughgall. Armagh city and the surrounding villages were also hit: twenty-five casualties from the city, five from Milford and four from Hamiltonsbawn. From the south-east of the county nine casualties were from Bessbrook, two each from the tiny villages of Glenanne and Mountnorris, and seven from Newry.

Although many acts of bravery and self sacrifice would go unrecognised, a number of well-deserved awards were made. Sergeant Carvell was awarded the Distinguished Conduct Medal for taking command of A Company, and the Military Cross would be awarded to Captains Flood and Given, RSM Turner, and the Medical Officer, Captain

Private Leonard Fox, from Redbourn, Hertfordshire. Wounded on 16 August 1917.

Private Thomas Binns (standing right), from Keighley, Yorkshire. Initially reported missing, he was wounded on 16 August 1917. His brother served with The Prince of Wales's Own (West Yorkshire Regiment) and was captured in 1918.

Private Isaac Hanna, from Ballynarry. Wounded on 16 August 1917.

Sergeant John Adams MM, seen here earlier in the war with Private Robert Crozier (D Company) (left) and Lance Corporal Thomas Moffett (The Royal Irish Rifles). All were from Kingsmills, Whitecross, County Armagh.

Sergeant Samuel Culbert, from Lurgan. Killed in action 16 August 1917.
Private Joseph Allen, from Portadown. Killed in action 16 August 1917.
Private William James Johnston, from Belfast. Killed in action 16 August 1917.
Private George Ostick, from Retford, Nottinghamshire. Killed in action 16 August 1917.
Private Joseph Woolf, from London. Died of wounds 21 August 1917.

Burrows, for the exploits recounted earlier. Lieutenant Thomas of 108th Brigade Machine Gun Company was also awarded an MC for the way he handled his guns on Hill 35. Major Halahan was awarded a bar to his MC for organising and assisting in the evacuation of large numbers of wounded under heavy shell-fire, and Captain E S Sowerby RAMC, who had been attached as Medical Officer throughout December 1916, was awarded an MC for similar actions with 108th Field Ambulance. The Military Medal went to Sergeants Adams, McCullough and Turkington, Corporal Knaggs, Lance Corporals Jackson and Whiteside, and Privates Elliott, Lynn, McCormick, Morton, Rogers, Shanks and Steele.

The 9th Royal Irish Fusiliers, with the other remnants of 108th and 109th Brigades, moved back to camps west of Ypres on the morning of 17 August and that night they were followed by 107th Brigade. The next day the Ulster Division moved by bus to tented camps at Winnezeele, where they began the process of refitting and recovering from their ordeal. It was here that the 9th Royal Irish Fusiliers welcomed their new Commanding Officer, Lieutenant Colonel P E Kelly, a regular officer who had been wounded whilst Adjutant of the 5th Royal Irish Fusiliers during the Gallipoli campaign. He had served with the 1st Battalion until his new appointment, at the age of twenty-eight. For four days the Battalion rested but there was to be little respite. By the end of the month the Ulster Division would be in the line again farther to the south at Havrincourt near Cambrai.

Endnotes, Chapter 5

[1] 787 Acting Company Sergeant Major Instructor Robert Graham Lean. Born on 21 June 1890 at Wall, Cornwall. He studied in London and became a school teacher. Enlisted into The Northamptonshire Regiment (50930) 30 November 1915. Trained as a Physical and Bayonet Training Instructor and transferred to the Army Gymnastic Staff. To France 16 June 1916. Posted first to 3rd Army School, he was almost immediately attached to 36th (Ulster) Division as a Physical and Bayonet Training Instructor on 29 June 1916. Throughout his time in France and Belgium he was attached to 108th Brigade as a Physical and Bayonet Training Instructor. MSM, *'In recognition of valuable services rendered with the forces in France'*. Appointed Acting Warrant Officer Class II 22 June 1918. To hospital injured (synovitis knee) 28 October 1918 and was evacuated to hospital in England on 7 December 1918. Treated at Northampton War Hospital. Transferred to the Class Z Reserve 4 February 1919. He returned to teaching physical training in schools and was appointed to His Majesty's Inspectors of Schools as HM Staff Inspector of Physical Training. Died in 1976, aged 86, at Hertfordshire.

[2] Only Second Lieutenant A Davidson and Second Lieutenant J I Smith rejoined the 9th Royal Irish Fusiliers. Second Lieutenant J A Stokes was killed in action on 16 August 1917. Second Lieutenants J F Ashe, H K Brady and R G McCall were wounded that day. Brady and McCall later joined the Indian Army, the latter serving with 7th Duke of Connaught's Rajputs. Second Lieutenants E M Montgomery and J W Campbell also joined the Indian Army, the latter serving with 3/1st Battalion, King George's Own Gurkha Rifles (The Malaun Regiment). Second Lieutenant W F Irvine was captured on 21 March 1918. Second Lieutenant H P Connar transferred to the Tank Corps. Second Lieutenant J H Dougan remained with The Royal Irish Rifles.

[3] Captain John Glyne Sanby Thomas MC. Born in 1896 at Merthyr Tydfil, Glamorganshire. Educated at King's School, Worcester. Commissioned into The Worcestershire Regiment 1 January 1916. To France 24 June 1916. Transferred to the Machine Gun Corps. MC—*For conspicuous gallantry and devotion to duty in charge of two guns with the attacking infantry. He was wounded in the advance and most of his men became casualties, but he got his guns into action and successfully withdrew them after the infantry had retired, though in doing so he was again wounded in the wrist.* Relinquished his commission in September 1921. After the war he became a doctor. His brother, Lieutenant David Cecil Sanby Thomas The Welsh Regiment attached Royal Flying Corps, was killed in a flying accident on 16 February 1918.

[4] Sergeant Neill subsequently wrote to the Stronge family and outlined the events of that day. He was sent a gift by the family and invited to visit after the war, which he did on a number of occasions. Lieutenant Stronge's death meant that the title was inherited by Sir Walter Lockhart Stronge (6th Baronet), his father's cousin, in 1928. The title passed then to the brother of the 6th Baronet in 1933 and in 1939 to the 8th Baronet, the Rt Hon Sir Charles Norman Lockhart Stronge. The 8th Baronet was born on 23 July 1884. A former officer in the Ulster Volunteer Force, Sir Norman Stronge had served as an officer in the 10th (Service) Battalion, The Royal Inniskilling Fusiliers (Derry), with which he earned an MC and Croix de Guerre (Belgium) and was twice Mentioned in Despatches. By February 1918 he was Adjutant of that battalion and subsequently of the 15th (Service) Battalion, The Royal Irish Rifles (North Belfast). He was wounded during the crossing of the Lys on 20 October 1918. He joined the Ulster Special Constabulary in 1921 as the Commandant of Coleraine District. He married in 1921 and moved to Tynan Abbey in 1939 when he succeeded to the Baronetcy. Elected MP for mid-Armagh from 1938 he became Speaker at Stormont in 1945 and served in that position until 1969. He became a Privy Councillor (Northern Ireland) 1946. He also served as HM Lieutenant County Armagh (1939), as a JP in County Londonderry and County Armagh, as High Sheriff of County Londonderry and as Honorary Colonel of the 5th Battalion, The Royal Irish Fusiliers (Princess Victoria's) from 1949-63. He was also President of the Northern Ireland Council of the Royal British Legion and Sovereign Grand Master of the Black Institution. He was made a Knight of the Order of St John of Jerusalem and a Commander of the Order of Leopold (Belgium), the latter in 1946. His son and heir was James Matthew Stronge. Born 21 June 1932, he was commissioned into the Grenadier Guards. On the resignation of his father, he was elected MP for mid-Armagh in 1969 and served until 1973. He was also a JP for County Armagh and a Reserve Constable in the Royal Ulster Constabulary. At 9.45pm on 21 January 1981 the family home, Tynan Abbey, was attacked by the Provisional IRA. 86 year-old Sir Norman Stronge and his 48 year-old son were both murdered in the library of the grand house, and the building, which had stood for 230 years, was destroyed by fire-bombs. Although fired upon by a patrol of the Royal Ulster Constabulary, the gunmen escaped. At the joint funeral Sir Norman's coffin was borne by men of the 5th Battalion, The Royal Irish Rangers, and that of James Stronge by men of the RUC Reserve. They were buried in the family plot where Sir Norman's wife had been laid to rest the previous year. The shell of Tynan Abbey stood empty until it was finally demolished in early 1999.

SIX

The Battle of Cambrai: November 1917

The sector in which the 36th (Ulster) Division found itself at the end of August 1917 was known as the 'devastated area'. Unlike the battlefields recently fought over, continuous shellfire had not destroyed this wide swath of land. The ground was unbroken, crops ran wild in the fields and woods and copses were still standing. However, this was the area left behind when the enemy moved back to the Hindenburg Line in February 1917, and everything of use to the advancing allies had been destroyed—houses and hamlets had been razed to the ground, bridges and roads smashed and cratered, and orchards ruined. It was here, near Cambrai, that the Ulster Division would take part in an attack alongside the first massed deployment of tanks. This attack, considered in outline since June and authorised in October, was originally envisaged as a large raid, but it grew to become a major offensive.

The severely reduced Ulster Division, now part of General Sir Julian Byng's Third Army, took over a sector of the line from 9th (Scottish) Division about eight miles south-west of Cambrai. A sub-sector was allocated to each of the brigades and they deployed in line along a frontage of about 6,000 yards with 107th Brigade on the right, 108th Brigade in the centre and 109th Brigade on the left. 108th Brigade had responsibility for the Havrincourt Sector, in which lay Havrincourt Wood. The wood was nearly four square miles in area. Although many of the trees on the northern edge had been cut down by the Germans to assist in building the fortifications and dugouts in the Hindenburg Line, it still provided good cover. North of the wood the ground fell away into a shallow valley and then rose again to the town of Havrincourt, which lay within the German front line trenches. On the left of the sector lay the Canal du Nord. It was an important feature in the area, and north of Havrincourt it was incorporated into the German defensive system. The canal had been about half completed when the war broke out and the section here varied in depth from 15 to 100 feet, but it only had a few feet of water in it.

The sub-sector to be occupied by the 9th Royal Irish Fusiliers lay on the left of the Brigade area. The trenches were generally along the northern edge of Havrincourt Wood, centred on the feature known as Cheetham Hill. The left of the sub-sector was bounded by the canal, beyond which lay 109th Brigade. The left company position, however, was also just over the canal at the site of the demolished bridge on the Havrincourt-Hermies Road where a small redoubt, known as R3, had been built, separated from the German line immediately to its east by the width of the canal.[1] This company also provided a platoon to the mine dugout on the canal bank due south of the shattered village of Hermies.

Five hundred yards south of R3 on the eastern side of the canal, where it turned to the west along Grand Ravine, was a large spoil heap made from the chalk excavated during the canal's construction. On top was the centre company position in a small trench system known as Yorkshire Bank. This position also included an outpost line of four small posts: Wigan Post to the west just over the canal, Yorkshire Post on the north edge of the spoil heap, Antrim Post on its eastern side and Hubert Post 150 yards to the south at the end of a trench called Hubert Avenue. The right company position was in the front line trenches south of Yorkshire Bank facing north-east towards Havrincourt. Hubert

Avenue formed the Battalion's right boundary. Battalion headquarters and the reserve company were located at Broken House Dump at the north-west corner of Havrincourt Wood, about 1,000 yards back from the front line trenches. Very often reserve platoons would be deployed farther forward to the reserve trenches within the wood, about 500 yards south of the right company's position. The Battalion Transport was located at another spoil heap south-west of Hermies. For the first time the 9th Royal Irish Fusiliers were on good ground, a great improvement on the low ground at Hamel and Messines and incomparable to the awful conditions at Ypres.

The site of the Havrincourt-Hermies Road bridge in March 1917. The company position known as R3 was on the higher ground on the left of the picture. © IWM (Q 56827)

Russian prisoners had been forced to build the enemy trenches of the Hindenburg Line in 1915 and 1916. It consisted of two well-prepared lines between 500 and 2,000 yards apart, each with front and support trenches. They had been well sited, enhanced by man-made and natural features such as the canal. The dugouts were deep and well constructed and extensive belts of wire protected the whole system. It was the most formidable system encountered by the Allies during the war. The German line opposite 36th (Ulster) Division ran south from Moeuvres, crossed the canal at Havrincourt and then east to Ribecourt. Besides the main position, the Germans had established a number of outposts in an arc around the north and eastern edges of Yorkshire Bank. North of Yorkshire Bank, almost halfway between the opposing lines, lay a large post in a small wood called Wigan Copse. Farther east in no-man's-land lay Etna, one of three large craters in the area, also reinforced as a post. The other craters were Vesuvius, on the Havrincourt-Hermies Road just west of the village, which contained a trench mortar, and Snowdon, just south of the village and beyond the 9th Royal Irish Fusiliers' right boundary, which was also occupied as a post. Another reinforced post, Boggart Hole, had a *minenwerfer* 'run into and out of a cave in a quarry shaft on railway rails', and a machine-gun post. Due south of Etna another small stand of trees, Dean Copse, harboured a smaller and rather exposed post. The enemy position between Havrincourt and R3 was split by a regimental boundary that ran north-east from Wigan Copse. The 9th Royal Irish Fusiliers faced two enemy companies from two different regiments that sat astride this boundary. Enemy activity in this sector comprised a constant round of short artillery and mortar barrages and the occasional bombing raid.

The Canal du Nord near Havrincourt today, taken from the bridge on the Havrincourt-Hermies Road. The enemy occupied a position on the left. Opposite, behind the photographer, was the British position known as R3. Yorkshire Bank, now covered in trees, can be seen in the distance on the right.

Having arrived at Havrincourt Wood at the end of August, the first week of September was spent in support, providing work parties for 12th Royal Irish Rifles in the front line and for tunnelling and camouflaging. The move forward into the line soon came, however, and on Wednesday 5 September the 9th Royal Irish Fusiliers relieved 12th Royal Irish Rifles. C Company deployed onto Yorkshire Bank and occupied the four forward posts; B Company deployed on the right with two platoons in the front trench and a platoon farther left on Yorkshire Bank; A Company was the battalion reserve at Broken House Dump, with two platoons in the reserve trench. D Company was at R3. The relief went smoothly and for the next five days the 9th Royal Irish Fusiliers had a rather uneventful time with little activity. The enemy were heard to call *"Jock, have you been here before?"* but patrols saw nothing. The few *minenwerfer* fired at Yorkshire Bank did not cause any casualties. As a consequence, every effort was made to improve the trenches, particularly on Yorkshire Bank, the most exposed part of the sector, and in strengthening the wire along the front.

The last few days of this tour were a different matter. On 11 September a small enemy patrol of seven men probing south of Yorkshire Bank was driven off, and in retaliation the enemy later shelled D Company's position at R3, severely wounding Lieutenant J A L Johnston in the jaw, leg and foot. He was an experienced officer who had been with the Battalion for eleven months. His wounds were severe enough to keep him in hospital until early 1919. That night a patrol under Lieutenant Partridge went out at 10.00pm to the area south of Dean Copse near where the German patrol had approached the previous night. It worked in conjunction with a patrol from 13th Royal Irish Rifles on the 9th Royal Irish Fusiliers' right flank and both patrols hoped to ambush any more enemy forays into no-man's-land. They lay out close to the enemy wire until 4.00am the next morning but saw nothing. On 12 September shelling again caused damage to the trenches in this sector, completely blocking the communication trenches and badly wounding a man in B Company in the left eye. This was to be the last day in the line and 108th Brigade moved into reserve, with the 9th Royal Irish Fusiliers moving back to billets in Nissen huts and tents in Ruyaulcourt, a village about three miles to the south-west of Havrincourt.

Second Lieutenant F C Hartness (left) with Second Lieutenant J H Partridge, the 9th Royal Irish Fusilier's Intelligence Officer.

As usual, work parties were provided on all of the six days out of the line, but they involved relatively small numbers of men, and most of the Battalion worked to improve the accommodation. Huts were erected for one of the companies and transport lines were constructed under the eye of Second Lieutenant Bennett, appointed temporarily as the Battalion Works Officer. Life here was generally better than it had been since the 9th Royal Irish Fusiliers' arrival in France; trips to Amiens were organised, the divisional canteens were well stocked with fresh food, and the cinema, concert party and band regularly entertained everyone.

In the period out of the line an event occurred that had a most demoralising effect upon the enemy. On 14 September Havrincourt was attacked using the Livens projector. This was an eight-inch-diameter, simple mortar with an electrically initiated propellant charge. It was used to fire a projectile containing various chemical or flammable contents. It was cheap and effective and, because each could be fired only once during an attack, hundreds were deployed to create a barrage effect. On this occasion, six hundred were dug into the area near the bend in the canal and loaded with gas canisters. They were fired into the village in a single salvo causing considerable casualties and forcing the relief of at least one German infantry battalion.

In preparation for a visit by the Corps Commander, the Brigade Commander, Brigadier Griffith, carried out a pre-inspection on Saturday 15 September. The next day after church parade, at which the combined bands of the 1st and 9th Royal Irish Fusiliers played, the football team was again in action, predictably victorious 6-0 over 13th Royal Irish Rifles. The Corps Commander inspected the following day and he seemed satisfied with what he saw. After more work parties, relieved by another football match (another victory, this time 2-0 against the 108th Brigade team) and a cross-country run, the 9th Royal Irish Fusiliers returned to the line and took over the same sector that they had recently vacated. The gas attack had undoubtedly had an effect on the enemy's morale, and as a result the 9th Royal Irish Fusiliers' tour began quietly. D Company was again at R3, C Company garrisoned Yorkshire Bank, A Company was deployed on the right and B Company was in reserve. Patrols sent out in front of Yorkshire Bank, to the vicinity of Wigan Copse and Dean Copse led by Second Lieutenants Richardson and Gilliard, did not encounter the enemy.

The eastern edge of Yorkshire bank is on the left. The line of trees leads to Dean Copse on the right. The enemy occupied a line along the ridge in the distance.

Although The Military Service Act 1916, which introduced conscription, had increased the flow of recruits, there remained a general shortage of infantry, largely due to the casualty rate. The Military Service Act applied only in Great Britain, and in Ireland recruiting continued to drop off. The Ulster Division had not been reinforced in any numbers since May, and in the autumn of 1917 it saw considerable change to its make-up. Two regular battalions arrived: 1st Battalion, Princess Victoria's (Royal Irish Fusiliers) joined 107th Brigade from 4th Division, and 2nd Battalion, The Royal Irish Rifles joined 108th Brigade from 25th Division. Both were replacements for the loss of two service battalions of the Royal Irish Rifles resulting from the amalgamation of the 8th with the 9th in 107th Brigade in August, and the 11th with the 13th in 108th Brigade in November.

The 9th Royal Irish Fusiliers was also to enjoy reinforcement as part of the reorganisation over this period when it was amalgamated with the 2nd North Irish Horse. The North Irish Horse and the South Irish Horse were Special Reserve Regiments of Cavalry. They were raised originally for service in the South African War as the 60th (North Irish) and 61st (South Irish) Companies of the 17th Battalion, Imperial Yeomanry. In 1902 the formation of the North of Ireland Imperial Yeomanry was approved and four squadrons were raised: A Squadron in Belfast, B Squadron in Londonderry, C Squadron in Enniskillen and D Squadron in Dundalk, alongside the Regimental Headquarters. On the reorganisation of the Territorial and Reserve Forces in 1908, the Regiment was reformed as a Special Reserve Regiment of Cavalry and renamed the North Irish Horse. The South Irish Horse was similarly formed from the South of Ireland Imperial Yeomanry.

When the war began, A Squadron, North Irish Horse, was the high readiness squadron, and it was mobilised on 4 August 1914. Less than two weeks later it sailed from Dublin to France with a squadron of the South Irish Horse aboard the SS Architect, arriving on 17 August as General Headquarters Troops. These were the first non-regular troops to be deployed to the British Expeditionary Force. C Squadron of the North Irish Horse followed on 22 August as the cavalry squadron of 5th Division. All had been in action in late-August/early-September 1914 acting as rearguards in the retreat from Mons.

Trooper William Lipsett,
North Irish Horse

Thereafter, the squadrons of the North Irish Horse served independently as divisional cavalry squadrons until May 1916. In the late spring of 1916 General Headquarters issued an order to form corps cavalry regiments:

'In consequence of the growth of the Army and the development of the Corps organization, much of the independence of action & movement formerly belonging to the Division has now passed to the Corps. It has been found necessary, therefore to reconsider the organization & distribution of the Mounted Troops hitherto allotted to Divisions. The allotment of these troops was originally made with a view to providing the Divisional Commander with a small mobile force under his immediate control for reconnaissance; protective & escort duties; & on the assumption (originally correct) that the Division would be moving either independently or with one or more roads allotted for its exclusive use.

These conditions are unlikely to recur; any future movement will be by Corps, marching & fighting in depth on a comparatively narrow front. The mounted troops belonging to the Corps must therefore be assembled under the direct control of the Corps Commander, and organized as Corps units. The C in C has accordingly decided:

(a) To convert the Squadrons of Divisional Cavalry into Corps Cavalry Regiments composed of Headquarters & 3 Squadrons each; one Regiment being allotted to each Corps.

(b) To withdraw the Cyclist Companies from Divisions to reconstitute them into battalions of 3 companies each, & to allot one battalion to each Corps.

(c) To allot one Motor Machine Gun Battery to each Corps. This battery will normally be attached to the Cyclist Battalion.

In most cases this brought together again the squadrons of the Territorial Force Yeomanry Regiments and the Special Reserve Regiments of Horse. The squadrons of the North Irish Horse formed two corps cavalry regiments and were brought together as follows:

D Squadron had landed in France in May 1915 as the cavalry squadron of 51st (Highland) Division. E Squadron was the last of the squadrons of the North Irish Horse to land in France, which it did as part of 34th Division in January 1916. Also in January 1916, A Squadron left General Headquarters and became the cavalry squadron of 55th (West Lancashire) Division. These three squadrons were amalgamated on 10 May 1916, retitled the 1st North Irish Horse and formed VII Corps Cavalry Regiment. The 1st North Irish

Horse transferred to XIX Corps in July 1917 and V Corps in September 1917 before becoming V Corps Cyclist Battalion (North Irish Horse) in March 1918.

Meanwhile, C Squadron, which had left 5th Division in October 1914 and joined A Squadron as General Headquarters Troops, became the cavalry squadron of 3rd Division from April 1915. On 11 May 1916 it was attached to 49th (West Riding) Division and on 1 June 1916 it was attached to 36th (Ulster) Division. F Squadron arrived in France on 17 November 1915 as the cavalry squadron of 33rd Division. It served with 33rd Division until 1 May 1916 when it was attached to 1st Cavalry Division for training. It joined 49th (West Riding) Division on 16 May and, four days later, it became the cavalry squadron of 32nd Division. It was re-designated as B Squadron on 25 May 1916[2]. 2nd North Irish Horse was formed at Toutencourt on 21 June 1916 by the amalgamation of B (formerly F) Squadron, C Squadron and the Service Squadron of 6th (Inniskilling) Dragoons.

Officers and Senior Non-commissioned Officers of the Service Squadron, 6th (Inniskilling) Dragoons in January 1915.
The men who are numbered joined the 9th (North Irish Horse) Battalion in 1917.
Top row: Sergeants W T Moffitt (1), J O'Neill (2) and W J McKeown
Seated: Lieutenant C B Despard (4) and Captain A Hulse (5).

The latter was a unique unit. Like much of the rest of the Ulster Division, the core of the manpower of its cavalry squadron came from the Ulster Volunteer Force, in this case from one of its two irregular cavalry units, the Enniskillen Horse. When the infantry battalions of the Ulster Division became service battalions of the county regiments, its cavalry squadron became the service squadron of 6th (Inniskilling) Dragoons. It landed in France with the Ulster Division in October 1915.

Immediately upon its formation, 2nd North Irish Horse was designated as X Corps Cavalry Regiment. All of the squadrons of the new regiment comprised well-trained and experienced horsemen. When it was formed, however, they were largely untested in action. The first tasks for 2nd North Irish Horse were in the aftermath of the attacks on 1 July 1916. In addition to the routine of escorts for senior officers, observation patrols and road control, the regiment was tasked in support of 32nd Division to conduct battlefield clearance and to form burial parties. From the end of the month the regiment returned to more routine cavalry duties and training. During the attack at Messines in June, the squadrons of the regiment were in support of the divisions of X Corps but were not committed. At the beginning of the Battle of Ypres, X Corps was in support and the regiment was again uncommitted, although some men spent time in the line with their supported divisions.

In mid-July 1917 the regiment was informed that it was to transfer for infantry service. This was in accordance with Army Order 204 of 1916, which allowed for the compulsory transfer of men *'in the interests of the Service'*. They would retain cavalry rates of pay in accordance with Army Council Instruction 2084 of 1916. On 23 July the horses were tested for glanders, an infectious equine disease, in preparation for their transfer to Egypt; sixty-seven horses were dispatched as unsuitable for service overseas. In early August all of the horses were inspected by Deputy Director Remounts, resulting in 131 horses classed as R1 (suitable for cavalry) exchanged for horses classed as R2 (suitable for yeomanry). On 14 August Lieutenant T H M Leader led a party of about eighty men and 265 horses classed as R2 to the railway station at Beaurainville. Men and horses were loaded into railway wagons and set off for Marseilles. On 25 August 1917 they sailed on the horse transport SS Bohemian for Egypt, where the horses would be handed over to the Australian Light Horse. Corporal Francis MacMahon wrote of the experience:

Trooper Thomas Bratty,
North Irish Horse

> *'We entrained the horses for Marseilles, although we didn't know our destination at that time. With an officer and some men we were put in charge of the horses and ultimately arrived in Marseilles where an Indian regiment officered by English officers took the horses from us. We hung around Marseilles for 2 weeks and then joined a ship with 850 horses, as usual, destination unknown. We set sail on an overcrowded ship with indentured Indians returning home. There were 2 Japanese destroyers acting as escort for the ship. Conditions on board were really tough, with bad food, the constant grooming of horses and cleaning out the manure at night. It had to be done at night because the manure floated on the sea and was a real give away for German submarines. We arrived at Malta but were not allowed ashore. After taking on stores and water we sailed again and finally arrived in Alexandria where the Australians took over the horses. After a short time in Alexandria we boarded a ship (destination unknown). Arriving at some Greek islands we lay up by day and sailed on at night due to a submarine scare. We arrived at Salonika, Greece, then Taranto, Italy. We entrained here and crossed Italy, being held up at Firenze whilst the "brass" discussed using us as reinforcements on the Italian front, where there was an Irish Division already reinforcing the Italians. Then back through France to Le Havre...'*

Meanwhile, on 15 August the remainder of 2nd North Irish Horse handed their saddlery in to the stores. The next day the Regimental Transport departed, leaving the Regiment with no horses for the first time in its existence. Routine training was undertaken until 23 August when the Regiment marched to Beaurainville and moved by train to Le Havre and then to Harfleur. There it joined 36 Infantry Base Depot. Two days were spent exchanging cavalry equipment for infantry equipment and then began a short period of infantry training.

Corporal, later Company Quartermaster Sergeant, Francis MacMahon, North Irish Horse. This photograph was taken during his trip to Egypt with the Regiment's horses. Inset is a photograph of his sister, Josie.

Trooper Charles Magill (right). These three Troopers of the North Irish Horse were amongst the party of men from the North Irish Horse that delivered the Regiment's horses to Egypt in September 1917. The other two men are unidentified but almost certainly joined the 9th Royal Irish Fusiliers.

With their training complete by mid-September, the men of the North Irish Horse moved by train to join the 9th Royal Irish Fusiliers. They arrived at Ruyaulcourt on Monday 25 September where the band and the men not in the line welcomed them. No event like this would be complete without a football match, which the residents won 2-1. In this first draft there were 304 men. Those who took the Regiment's horses to Egypt, with the exception of a few sick men who were evacuated to hospital in England, returned to France via Italy in late September 1917. On 12 October 1917 these seventy-two men joined the retitled 9th (North Irish Horse) Battalion, Princess Victoria's (Royal Irish Fusiliers).[3] A total of 569 men of the North Irish Horse are known to have joined the 9th Royal Irish Fusiliers in September and October 1917.

Trooper George Adams Henry, later promoted Lance Sergeant, earned a Military Medal with the 9th Royal Irish Fusiliers.

Meanwhile, the men of the 9th Royal Irish Fusiliers in the line on the morning of 25 September saw the Ulster Division's artillery begin a heavy bombardment of the enemy trenches. In retaliation the German artillery opened up at 10.00am, shelling Yorkshire Bank heavily. A direct hit on the front line killed Lance Corporals John Black and John Stratton, and

Private John Campbell, and severely wounded Private William James McDowell, who died later in the day. After another few days of desultory shelling along the canal bank, which did not cause any further casualties, the 9th Royal Irish Fusiliers moved back to Ruyaulcourt in fine weather. One man was wounded during the relief by 13th Royal Irish Rifles.

The first week of October was spent at sport, training, and providing the obligatory work parties. Training was afforded a higher priority than usual in order to weld together the new drafts and the old hands. On the sports field a competition was held against the 1st Royal Irish Fusiliers, which saw the 9th as victors. By the end of September the paper strength of the Battalion had increased to fifty-one officers and 970 other ranks with a rationed strength of thirty-four officers and 731 other ranks. Major J G Brew, who had left in December 1916 to attend the Senior Officers' Course, returned as the Second-in-Command.

One of the men who had joined from the North Irish Horse was Private Johnnie King. The son of a farming family from Whitecross in County Armagh, he had joined the North Irish Horse in 1913 and deployed to France in 1914. Just after the amalgamation he wrote home:

> *Dear Mother,*
>
> *Just a few lines to let you know that we have joined our Battalion nearly a week ago but I had not much time to write but we are all settled now and I think we will get on all right. I was speaking to Harry Hadden and John Adams. They are in the same Battalion. Our new address is C Company 9th Royal Irish Fusiliers and my number is changed to 41302. The only thing we can complain of is rations - they have been very low these last few days but they are beginning to improve again but it is a queer change from our own Regiment. I hope you will excuse this short note. I will write again as soon as possible. Hoping all is well and give all my best wishes.*
>
> *I remain your affectionate son,*
> *J King*

Lance Corporal Robert Henry Knowles (Harry) Hadden & Sergeant John Adams MM were both original members of the 9th Royal Irish Fusiliers.

A holiday was declared for 5 October and the 9th Royal Irish Fusiliers spent the day competing in the Divisional sports competition. In its rivalry against the 1st Battalion, the final tally of results shows fifteen 'firsts' and seven 'seconds' to the 9th, and seven 'firsts' and five 'seconds' to the 1st. After church parade on Sunday 7 October the 9th Royal Irish Fusiliers moved back to the front line in heavy rain to relieve 12th Royal Irish Rifles. A Corps Order had directed all battalions in the line to be continually on the offensive, and the 9th Royal Irish Fusiliers had a number of patrols planned, most as reconnaissance for a raid early in November. At 2.10am on the morning of 9 October a patrol of one officer and twenty-two men moved across no-man's-land in extended line, through Wigan Copse and up to the enemy wire. No enemy were found in the copse or the rifle pits dug just north of it, but movement heard from the enemy wire was subjected to bombing; the patrol was back in by 4.35am. A similar patrol the next night was uneventful and a smaller patrol of one officer and three men left R3 to patrol up the canal. Having covered 350 yards without incident they found only an abandoned post. On 14 October attention switched to Dean Copse. A small patrol carried out a reconnaissance in the early hours, and that evening, just after dark, one subaltern and sixteen men moved across no-man's-land and probed the trees. The enemy fought this group off and it retired with two casualties.

During this tour shellfire caused three minor casualties. Farther back the Commanding Officer and Second-in-Command led work to reinforce the sandbag protection of battalion headquarters, but the efforts of others caused some amusement and were less appreciated. The war diary states: *'The Padre and Doctor claimed they did the lion's share of the work, but evidently they never worked before'.*

The Battalion was relieved by 12th Royal Irish Rifles on 15 October and moved back to the accommodation at Ruyaulcourt, which was by now all huts, and everyone worked in the better weather to further improve the conditions at this camp. The quiet period in the line was reflected in the comments written by Johnnie King when he wrote home for the last time on 19 October:

> *Dear Mother*
>
> *Just a few lines in answer to your very welcome letter and cigs which I received a few days ago. It is a pity the other two parcels, Meta's and yours, did not turn up, but they may come yet. We are having very nice weather now and a fairly good time. We got our first turn in the trenches over very soft, but this is a very quiet part of the line and to tell you the truth I am far more content here than in the cavalry and I never felt in better health and you need not be afraid of me going into danger except I can't help it, and as for putting in for my commission I won't do it. I will just finish it the way I started. I am not afraid to soldier it out as a private as some of the boys were. It was easy in the North Irish Horse but it is not so easy in the infantry.*

In the first two weeks of October more drafts had arrived, totalling over one hundred and twenty-three men. They included the seventy-two men of the North Irish Horse who had returned from Egypt, and eighteen old hands rejoining the Battalion. Amongst the officers who joined was Captain G W N Barefoot MC, a regular officer from the 1st Royal Irish Fusiliers, who arrived to take up the post of Adjutant. Apart from some new second lieutenants, most of the officers were from the North Irish Horse. Captain C B Despard[4] and Lieutenant G W Vesey (the brother of Lieutenant M B Lendrum who had left the 9th Royal Irish Fusiliers in 1916) were noteworthy arrivals who would distinguish themselves over the coming months. The officers' mess gained little stability from this reinforcement, however. Of the nineteen officers from the North Irish Horse that joined the 9th Royal Irish Fusiliers one would be severely wounded within weeks, by December twelve would have moved to other units (with most going to the Tank Corps), and only six others would remain longer, all of whom would become casualties.

Amidst the work parties and training with the reinforcements, the football team finally lost a match, 2-0 against 8th/9th Royal Irish Rifles, but made up for it with an 8-0 win over the 108th Brigade team. The gallantry awards earned on the attack on 16 August had been announced on 4 October but were not promulgated in the Battalion until 21 October; they were published in the London Gazette on 18 October (MC), 19 October (DCM) and on 19 November (MM) (one award of the MM was gazetted on 1 April 1920).

By 24 October the weather was better and the 9th Royal Irish Fusiliers was back in the line. This tour was very active. On the night of 25/26 October two patrols went out. The first was a small reconnaissance patrol of two officers and eight men that moved north-west of Wigan Copse. The second was a fighting patrol that also aimed to conduct reconnaissance for the forthcoming raid. Two officers and forty men set out at 1.30am and managed to get through the enemy wire at Wigan Copse. Although engaged with rifles and bombs, the 9th Royal Irish Fusiliers returned fire and drove the enemy back from the copse and the rifle pits to the north of it. That evening three officers led fifty-four men out on a fighting patrol back to the area of Wigan Copse. When two parties of the enemy, numbering about forty-six men, entered the copse just before 9.00pm they were ambushed with rifle fire and bombs. The surprise of the attack, the weight of fire and a charge by the 9th Royal Irish Fusiliers drove the Germans back to their main trench again, at the cost of one man killed and another wounded. The enemy artillery in response was heavy on the right of the 9th Royal Irish Fusiliers' line and a direct hit on a Lewis gun post killed all three men. These four fatal casualties on 26 October were the first of many from the North Irish Horse reinforcements—Sergeant George Reid and Privates Victor Bell, Thomas Dickinson and John Dunn.

A typical studio portrait postcard of three unknown men of the 9th Royal Irish Fusiliers.

Machine-gun fire from Etna and Boggart Hole and artillery fire continued to harass the forward trenches the next night but the enemy did not try to re-enter Wigan Copse. Attention shifted, therefore, to the enemy using Dean Copse and Etna, which were the subject of increasingly heavy Lewis gun and rifle fire, occasionally supported by artillery that caused an unknown number of enemy casualties. Although machine-gun and sniper fire were returned, there were no more 9th Royal Irish Fusiliers casualties, and on 1 November the Battalion moved out of the line again to the refurbished billets at Ruyaulcourt. The effective strength of the 9th Royal Irish Fusiliers had now risen to seventy-four officers and 1,291 other ranks with a rationed strength of thirty-five officers and 713 other ranks.

The raid for which the 9th Royal Irish Fusiliers had been preparing was to be conducted by C Company led by Captain Henehan, whose performance at Messines made him an ideal choice to command the operation. It aimed to demoralise the enemy and to gain information that might be of use in the forthcoming offensive. Most of the sixty-seven men that were to take part were found from the ranks of the newly-arrived draft from the North Irish Horse. Also included were four men of the Royal Engineers and six stretcher-bearers.

At 4.30pm on the afternoon of Wednesday 3 November, while A and B Companies provided work parties and D Company remained in Ruyaulcourt, C Company marched up to the line at dusk. Captain Henehan was to be assisted in this scheme by three officers: Lieutenant T E C Crosbie, a twenty-year-old platoon commander who had been with the Battalion since March; Second Lieutenant J J Murphy, a strong-willed ex-Sergeant who had earned the Distinguished Conduct Medal on a tough raid in July 1916 while with the 8th Royal Irish Fusiliers and, having been commissioned, had been with the 9th Royal Irish Fusiliers for little over a month, and Lieutenant W H Hutchinson, formerly of thc North Irish Horse, who had joined the Battalion at the beginning of October.

For this raid, for which there was to be no preliminary bombardment, the raiders were organised into four groups. Number One party, led by Second Lieutenant Murphy, was the advance party and at 7.30pm it moved out from Yorkshire Bank and crawled silently down into the empty canal. Covered by its steep walls this party moved north and, just short of the fallen bridge near R3, the men climbed the canal wall. They attacked through the gap in the enemy's wire that had been cut to allow the German outposts forward to their positions. Enemy resistance was such that half of Murphy's men were engaged with these outposts, but he pushed on into the front trench, which he and his remaining men cleared, killing a number of the enemy in the process. The men were led in this initial push by Sergeant W R Pamenter who, having got past the enemy outposts and up to the wire, was confronted by a large party of Germans coming through a gap. He immediately charged, shot and bayoneted six of them, cleared the gap and then led his men into the trench. Having sent them in the right direction he then established blocks farther down the trench to help protect the raiders from counter-attack.

Yorkshire Bank

Yorkshire Bank (now covered in trees) is on the left. In the distance on the right is Havrincourt Wood. On 3 November 1917 the raiders, led by Captain Murphy, used the cover of the canal (then empty of water) as Numbers 1 and 3 parties crawled over no-man's land from Yorkshire Bank.

Number Three party, led by Captain Henehan, now joined the advance party and both then penetrated the German line from the canal to about 150 yards east of it. When the initial contact was made, a red flare brought down heavy artillery, trench mortar and machine-gun protective barrages on all the trenches and strong-points, including the posts at Vesuvius, Etna, Dean Copse, Boggart Hole and Canal Copse, preventing enemy reinforcement.

While One and Three parties were gaining entry to the trenches and just before the artillery barrage began, Number Four party successfully crawled across no-man's-land. This group of seven men, led by Lieutenant Crosbie, had been detailed to blow a gap in the enemy wire in the centre of the area to be attacked. A Bangalore torpedo, a metal tube filled with explosive, was placed under the first belt of wire which Lieutenant Crosbie then blew successfully, cutting the wire. Although under heavy attack by bombs that wounded three of his seven men, he cut his way through the second belt by hand and then drove the enemy out of some nearby posts.

Meanwhile, on the right of the attack, Number Two party, led by Lieutenant Hutchinson and which had also crawled across the open ground, found that the wire that had been cut previously by artillery had been repaired and they met unexpected resistance from German bombers. It was here that most of the casualties occurred amongst the raiders—Lieutenant Hutchinson was wounded and eight of his party were killed or wounded.

Throughout the engagement the fighting was very severe. Many of the enemy refused to surrender. For over twenty minutes the 9th Royal Irish Fusiliers remained in the German trenches, killing over forty of the enemy. As each dugout or bunker was cleared the four Sappers placed explosive charges and blew them up. At about 9.00pm when C Company finally withdrew back down the canal to Yorkshire Bank, it brought all but a few of its number back. After getting back to Ruyaulcourt, it was clear that some of the missing were dead but there was a chance that men were lying wounded near the enemy wire. Lieutenant Crosbie and Second Lieutenant Murphy returned again to the trenches and penetrated far into no-man's-land in search of them. They succeeded in bringing in a number of wounded men, in one case from close to the enemy wire over a distance of 400 yards under heavy fire. Second Lieutenant Murphy went out four times and did not return to the billets until twelve hours after the raid started; he was unable to find the last three missing men, Privates Ford, Heathwood and King.

Although the raiders were criticised by some for not returning with more prisoners (Major General Nugent wrote later: *'they got excited and killed everyone instead of taking some prisoners as proof of success'*), the raid was generally considered a success. The final casualty toll was not particularly high for an attack of this type; Captain Henehan was wounded by a bomb but was able to return to duty, and Lieutenant W H Hutchinson had been injured in the chest (a piece of shell had sliced through his lung) and legs. As a result of the severity of his wounds he remained in Ireland with the North Irish Horse Reserve Regiment after he recovered. Sergeant Richard Irwin had been Hutchinson's troop sergeant since 1916 and was killed during the attack; he was buried in Neuville-Bourjonval cemetery with those others of the 9th Royal Irish Fusiliers who had died over the previous few weeks. Privates John Ford and Johnnie King were killed in action and they were buried by the Germans near Cambrai. Also reported missing believed killed in action was Private Robert Heathwood. The enemy may have found his body but the location of his grave is unknown. All four of these men had come from the North Irish Horse. Fourteen men were wounded. They included Sergeant Thomas Hare, Lance Corporal Thomas Alexander Murphy, Private Thomas Charles Hawthorne and a Royal Engineers NCO who was severely hurt. For their gallant conduct Lieutenant T E C Crosbie and Second Lieutenant J J Murphy were awarded the Military Cross. Sergeant W R Pamenter earned a Distinguished Conduct Medal and was later commissioned into the Machine Gun Corps. Military Medals went to Corporals G Craig and H Mackinson and Privates R Averell, M Chambers and J Morrison. The day following the raid, whilst the rest of the Battalion was engaged on work parties, Major General Nugent inspected the raiders and expressed his satisfaction at their efforts.

Private Robert Averell MM

The offensive at Cambrai was now imminent and, not unnoticed by the troops in the front line, the preparations for the attack were extensive. It had been decided to keep 51st (Highland) and 62nd (2nd West Riding) Divisions, who would attack on the principal front allocated to IV Corps, in the rear areas for as long as possible. As a consequence, much of the preparatory work on this, the main front of IV Corps, fell to 36th (Ulster) Division. The work parties continued until the 9th Royal Irish Fusiliers moved back to the front line in heavy rain on 8 November. This was back-breaking work: laying roads south and east of the Canal du Nord, making bridges for trenches, enlarging dugouts, and building shacks and shelters in the villages and in Havrincourt Wood for the assembly of troops. This was also the first time that many of the men had seen tanks, which were moving forward to be concealed in the woods and copses behind the front.

Back in the line there was no chance of any respite. The awful weather was causing the trenches on Yorkshire Bank to flood and A Company, assisted by men from across the Battalion, worked hard on clearing and draining them. Other than this, the first few days of this tour were uneventful. This relative peace was shattered on 14 November, however, when enemy trench mortars fired on Yorkshire Bank in retaliation for the work done by the Ulster Division's artillery. The war diary records that three men were killed and that one man was severely wounded. It has not been possible to identify these men; there are no records of men of Princess Victoria's (Royal Irish Fusiliers) being killed in this area over this period. It is possible that one of those killed was Private Daniel Sturgeon, who is listed as killed in action on 16 November 1917.

The attack at Cambrai was to be conducted by Third Army, reinforced by the five divisions of the Cavalry Corps. III Corps would attack on the right and IV Corps on the left leaving V Corps in reserve. The initial breakthrough would involve seven divisions of infantry drawn from III and IV Corps and three brigades of tanks that would attack north between the Canal du Nord on the left and the Canal de l'Escaut on the right—a frontage of about 10,000 yards. During the initial stage of the attack, planned for 20 November, 56th (1st London) Division, under command of IV Corps for this attack, was to fight on IV Corps' left flank with 36th (Ulster) Division on its right. Both divisions would attack along the west bank of the Canal du Nord. On the opposite bank, 62nd (2nd West Riding) and 51st (Highland) Divisions would attack onto the Flesquires Ridge.

The Ulster Division was to attack along the German front line of the Hindenburg system from south to north as far as the Bapaume-Cambrai Road. This task fell to 109th Brigade with the other two brigades in support. It made necessary the move of the Ulster Division out of the line at Havrincourt. Consequently, 51st (Highland) and 62nd (2nd West Riding) Divisions, whose attacks would begin from the British line south and south-east of the village, relieved 107th and 108th Brigades on Wednesday 17 November. In order to deceive the enemy that no reinforcement had taken place, the front-line battalions of these two brigades left their men in the outposts.

The 9th Royal Irish Fusiliers was relieved by 2/5th Battalion, The King's Own (Yorkshire Light Infantry) and moved out of the line at Havrincourt Wood for the last time, leaving a platoon from C Company on Yorkshire Bank to man the outposts. The remainder marched three miles to Bertincourt and the next day moved the short distance to Barastre for a very short rest in comfortable billets in Nissen huts and tents. After an inspection by the Commanding Officer, they moved forward the following afternoon to Velu Wood in preparation for the attack. At 6.20am on 20 November the attack was launched. West of the canal 109th Brigade advanced quickly, bombing along the enemy trench lines behind the fleeing troops of *20. Landwehr-Division*, soldiers of poor quality who had been in the line for only two days. This fact should not detract, however, from a superb action conducted with great courage by 109th Brigade. At 8.20am those of the 9th Royal Irish Fusiliers who were to take part moved forward to a position 500 yards to the north-east. The remainder of the Battalion's details remained in Velu Wood under the command of Major Brew. The Battalion Transport was positioned farther to the east just south of Hermies. For 109th Brigade the attack went well and by the end of the first day it had penetrated to a line 500 yards north of the Bapaume-Cambrai Road. As 109th Brigade advanced north, the 9th Royal Irish Fusiliers had moved over familiar ground in the rear of the attacking troops and stayed in dugouts at R3 for the night. Throughout the next day 109th Brigade again fought hard but, having sustained heavy casualties, gained only another 1,000 yards before being held up by heavy machine-gun fire on the outskirts of the village of Moeuvres. For the 9th Royal Irish Fusiliers the day was very quiet. The Battalion did not move until 3.00pm when it was called forward in heavy rain to the newly captured enemy positions at Lock 7 on the Canal du Nord north of Havrincourt. Here it again spent the night in dugouts.

Royal Inniskilling Fusiliers of 109th Brigade with German prisoners 20 November 1917.
© IWM (Q 3186)

Across the front the gains had been considerable but they were not exploited and the attack, which had promised so much during the early stages, was beginning to founder. On 22 November 62nd (2nd West Riding) Division and 51st (Highland) Division were to improve and consolidate their positions on the right. Meanwhile, the Ulster Division and 56th (1st London) Division on the left were ordered to make more ground. The Ulster Division was to continue its attack, astride the canal now, with 107th Brigade on the east and 108th Brigade on the west.

In 108th Brigade's area 12th Royal Irish Rifles was ordered to capture Moeuvres and, when it was secure, the 9th Royal Irish Fusiliers was to take Inchy, 1,500 yards to its north. Moeuvres was a large village sitting in a shallow natural bowl, embedded in the German front line and surrounded by trenches. Particularly dangerous were the trenches to the west around the cemetery and on higher ground, which could not be attacked easily and which allowed heavy machine-gun fire to be directed at the attacking troops. They were ideal also for the assembly and launch of a German counter-attack.

Men of 16th Royal Irish Rifles (Pioneers) moving forward during the actions near Moeuvres, November 1917. © IWM (Q 6291)

At 6.30am on 22 November the 9th Royal Irish Fusiliers moved off to take up a position north of the Bapaume-Cambrai Road. They arrived two hours later and waited in the rain for 12th Royal Irish Rifles to seize Moeuvres and for the order to begin their own attack. Attached in support were two guns from 108th Brigade Machine Gun Company under the command of Lieutenant H M Kitchen[5]. These were laid on the German reserve positions in Hobart Trench. In reserve behind the 9th Royal Irish Fusiliers were 2nd and 11th/13th Royal Irish Rifles. By 11.45am, after a hard fight, 12th Royal Irish Rifles had captured much of the town along with two officers and eighty German soldiers, but the Royal Irish Rifles was unable to clear the trenches east of the village.

On the east of the canal 107th Brigade was held up by a series of strong-points. Here the 1st Royal Irish Fusiliers had a hard fight against the enemy in Round Trench and at Lock Number 5. At 4.00pm the enemy was seen moving out of Inchy towards Moeuvres preparing to counter-attack. One company of 9th Royal Irish Fusiliers moved up in support but, being slowed by enemy artillery and flanking machine gun fire, it was unable to help before the German counter-attack, estimated at two battalions in strength, drove the Royal Irish Rifles from the village. In response to a call for support, the two machine guns attached to the 9th Royal Irish Fusiliers fired 10,000 rounds between 6.45 and 7.30pm. 9th Royal Irish Fusiliers was given the order to retake the village and at 8.30pm A, B and C Companies attacked in darkness and rain. This attack was unsuccessful and the attacking companies, held up by thick wire, were finally driven back to the trenches immediately south of the village. Here a defensive position was established with 12th Royal Irish Rifles. Everyone spent an uncomfortable night as the bad weather added to the misery of the situation. Two men had been killed during this attack: twenty year old Sergeant Thomas Clements MM and Lance Corporal Hugh Flanagan. Private William Petty was missing; he would later be declared killed in action. A number of men were wounded.

On 23 November IV Corps was to press on across the front. 51st (Highland) Division and 40th Division were to secure Fontaine and Bourlon Village in the east while 36th (Ulster) Division and 56th (1st London) Division were to continue the advance up the canal on the west. The Ulster Division again aimed to advance with 107th Brigade on the east of the canal, this time supported by tanks, with 108th Brigade on the west where Moeuvres remained the key obstacle. 169th Brigade of 56th (1st London) Division would advance on Ulster Division's left. The requirement for a co-ordinated attack across the Corps front delayed the delivery of orders and the earliest possible time for Zero Hour was 10.30am. Realising that a single battalion attack would fail, it was decided that 108th Brigade would attack in force with three battalions. In the hours of darkness before dawn, the assaulting battalions assembled in the trenches a little over 500 yards south of the village. 12th Royal Irish Rifles was on the left with 9th Royal Irish Fusiliers on the right and 2nd Royal Irish Rifles in support behind its sister battalion. The need for quick and reliable communications resulted in command of the attack being exercised from an advanced battalion headquarters about 200 yards farther back on the Havrincourt Road. Here were based Captain Godson, the 108th Brigade Intelligence Officer who had arrived the previous night, and the Adjutants and Intelligence Officers of 12th Royal Irish Rifles and the 9th Royal Irish Fusiliers (in the case of the latter, Captain M Henahan MC and Captain J H Partridge). The commanding officers of the two leading battalions were also together 1,000 yards back, just north of the Bapaume-Cambrai Road, and these headquarters were linked by telephone to each other and to brigade headquarters. Captain Godson recorded that he had had a *'devil of a day'*.

The morning of the attack was cold and windy. At 9.00am the preparatory artillery barrage began and after ninety minutes 12th Royal Irish Rifles and the 9th Royal Irish Fusiliers attacked. On the right the assault began with a feint launched by C Company over open ground against the strongly wired trench running east from the village to the canal. This attack was successful. C Company penetrated and cleared the trench as far as the canal and held out there until dusk. Meanwhile A and D Companies, with B Company in support, attacked over the small ridge that bordered the south-east of the village. 12th Royal Irish Rifles attacked on the left of the main assault beyond the main road running into and through the village; 2nd Royal Irish Rifles followed to deal with the trenches to the north-west. The enemy had brought forward more machine guns and the weight of fire on the left was such that 12th Royal Irish Rifles could make no headway.

On the right the 9th Royal Irish Fusiliers was in the villageby 11.00am. In A Company, on the left of the attack, all of the officers were wounded before they reached the village. Company Quartermaster Sergeant J Robinson, who was acting as Company Sergeant Major, took command and led the advance and then the clearance of the enemy from

Captain F D Mitchel

houses and cellars when the village was reached. On the right flank D Company, commanded by Captain Despard, was successful in clearing a portion of the village but Captain Mitchel, the Company Second-in-Command, was severely wounded when he was shot in the face. The predictable enemy counter-attack swept in at 11.45am from the trenches to the west. In A Company's area, Corporal H Roe had taken command of the flank when his platoon commander was wounded and he held up the enemy's advance with great determination. The enemy was finally driven off after thirty minutes of hard fighting. Casualties and pressure from the enemy forced the committal of a reserve platoon from B Company, which was taken forward by Company Sergeant Major Vennard, who also reorganised a group of other men and led them forward as well.

Captain Godson's impression of the attack was somewhat critical:

> *'I went to advanced B'n. H.Q. and found Capt Hall, Adjutant of the 12th in command, but unwilling to take any responsibility without reference to Col Goodwin who was out of touch through shelling at the B'n. H.Q. until 3.00pm. As I was representing the Brigadier difficulties were obvious. At 10.30 am the 12th, after yesterday's attack and present shelling, were not in much form and dispirited, and soon fell back to their assembly points. The 9th R. Ir. Fus. had not made much, if any, better progress. So I took the responsibility of ordering 2 Coy's of the 12th to organize another attack.'*

By early afternoon the three companies of the 9th Royal Irish Fusiliers had cleared the south-east of the village. At 2.00pm, as they attempted to consolidate their position, the two companies from 12th Royal Irish Rifles and three from 2nd Royal Irish Rifles attacked again and this time penetrated into the village on the west. Prompted by this success, two companies of 9th Royal Irish Fusiliers pushed forward again on the right at 2.30pm but their progress was impeded by machine-gun fire from the high ground to the north-west. Communications throughout the day had been very difficult; the line between the advanced battalion headquarters and brigade headquarters had been cut repeatedly and the companies relied on runners and pigeons. Trapped by the heavy machine-gun fire inside the village, the 9th Royal Irish Fusiliers sent off a pigeon requesting an artillery bombardment of the German trenches. The artillery fire successfully relieved the pressure, allowing the companies of the 2nd and 12th Royal Irish Rifles to make a little more progress.

Out to the right of the attacking companies heavy fire was coming from a strong-point south-west of Bourlon Wood. This post was attacked repeatedly by the pilot of an Allied aircraft, who was finally shot down nearby.[6] Meanwhile, the 9th Royal Irish Fusiliers was unable to make contact with the troops on their left and it was soon apparent that the hard fighting and courage of all three battalions was for naught. Unsupported, unable to consolidate the portion of the town that they had captured, and in danger of being cut off, the 9th Royal Irish Fusiliers was forced to withdraw at about 4.30pm that evening as dusk fell. The withdrawal and the evacuation of all of the wounded were successfully co-ordinated by Captain Despard. His company then held a line with C Company on the sunken road south of the village, while A and B Companies, which had borne the brunt of the fighting, moved back to the trenches north of the Bapaume-Cambrai Road. The Royal Irish Rifles consolidated in the shattered houses on the south-western edge of the village.

In the hard fighting of 22 and 23 November the 9th Royal Irish Fusiliers had suffered eighty-nine all ranks killed and wounded:

	Officers	Other Ranks
Killed in Action	1	13
Died of Wounds	1	2
Wounded	5	67
Total	7	82

Private James Sleator, killed in action on 23 November 1917.

Given the scale of the fighting, relatively few had been killed in the attacks. Seventeen officers and men were killed in action or died of wounds. Second Lieutenant L H Martin, who had joined only two months previously, was killed, and Captain Mitchel died of his wounds on 24 November. In addition to the three men killed on 22 November, ten men were killed in action on 23 November: Sergeant Thomas Ballantine, Lance Corporal Fred Scanlon and Privates David Bryans, Samuel Malcolmson, Christopher McWilliams, Henry Orr, Samuel Price, James Sleator, William James Turkington and William Williamson. Private George Galbraith was severely wounded and died the next day. Private John Smyth was badly wounded and succumbed to his wounds on 1 December. Five officers were wounded. Two were platoon commanders in A Company—Second Lieutenant T A Gilliard, who was shot in the face but recovered and transferred to the Tank Corps, and Second Lieutenant J B A Young who was shot in the left arm. He also recovered and rejoined the 9th Royal Irish Fusiliers in mid-1918. Second Lieutenant J C Bennet from D Company was slightly wounded and he soon rejoined. Second Lieutenant St C E J Barrett, a former soldier in the Battalion, was also wounded but his wounds precluded further service with infantry. The name of the fifth wounded officer is not known. Sixty-seven other ranks were wounded including Lance Sergeant Hubert Roe and Privates Alexander Armstrong, James Faulkner, James Norman Fulton, James Henry Forde, George Edmund Clugston Geary, Henry Hutchinson, Robert John Kennedy, and John Edward Riddell.

The gallantry of the officers and men during this hard fight was rewarded with Military Crosses for Captain Despard and Captain J C Partridge, the Intelligence Officer who had gone out under heavy shell and machine-gun fire to keep in touch with the situation. The Distinguished Conduct Medal was awarded to Company Sergeant Major Vennard, Company Quartermaster Sergeant Robinson and Corporal Roe, and the Military Medal was awarded to Privates R Buckley, J W Marshall and C A Thompson. A former officer of the 9th Royal Irish Fusiliers also earned a Military Cross during the Cambrai attack. Lieutenant E T Owles had left the Battalion in May 1916 to join the Royal Flying Corps. On 22 September, while serving with 12 Squadron, he made a successful wire reconnaissance along the Corps front, concentrating on the area over Bourlon Village farther to the east of the 9th Royal Irish Fusiliers' attack. He did this at a height of 300 to 800 feet and under heavy machine-gun and rifle fire.[7]

The fighting that day was the last faced by the 9th Royal Irish Fusiliers before being relieved before dawn on 24 November by 11th Royal Inniskilling Fusiliers of 109th Brigade. The fighting at Cambrai continued, however, with a German counter-attack and two days of heavy shelling. The Ulster Division was finally relieved by 2nd Division on 26 November. This relief and the march that followed were conducted in terrible weather. Exhausted

Corporal, later Lance Sergeant Hubert Roe DCM (centre). Also here are his brothers, Private William Arthur Roe (left), who was wounded (lost his right eye) serving with The King's Royal Rifle Corps and who later served with the Labour Corps, and Private George C Roe (right), who served with The Hertfordshire Regiment and the Corps of Royal Engineers.

after the fighting and with their strength sapped by the poor weather over the last three days, the men battled through driving, freezing snow and high winds to the area around Hermies. There was little shelter available and they spent an uncomfortable night. The next day the Ulster Division moved to billets about ten miles to the south-west, where everyone was able to clean up. On 29 November the Division was transferred to XVII Corps and moved by foot and train to the area north-west of Bapaume, arriving at Gomincourt at 7.30pm on 30 November.

It was hoped that the Ulster Division would be allowed a few weeks out of the line, but this was not to be. That day the Germans launched a counter-offensive, the biggest attack by the enemy since Verdun, and on the southern flank the enemy broke through the British lines. The Ulster Division was ordered to move back to the front. Trains were not available for the return journey and the Ulster Division marched for two days back to the area it had recently vacated. The 9th Royal Irish Fusiliers ended up at Metz-en-Couture near Havrincourt Wood where the men rested briefly before moving up to the front. On 3 December 36th (Ulster) Division came under command of III Corps, and amidst confusing orders and counter-orders, 108th Brigade was finally instructed to relieve 88th Brigade of 29th Division south of Marcoing.

A salient had been formed here and due to the risk that it might fall, a withdrawal was conducted to the support trenches of the Hindenburg Line that left the town of Marcoing in enemy hands. It was into this area that the Ulster Division was deployed, to the south of the village along the Couillet Valley. On either side of this heavily-wooded valley were two ridges—Welsh Ridge on the south-east and Highland Ridge on the north-west. The old enemy trenches of the Hindenburg Support Line crossed these ridges at right angles just south of Marcoing.

At 8.00pm on 3 December the 9th Royal Irish Fusiliers marched from Metz-en-Couture to the support trenches in the valley south of the town between the ridges, being in place by 5.30am. Then, early on the morning of 5 December, it relieved 2nd Battalion, The Hampshire Regiment, and 1st Battalion, The Essex Regiment, in the front line trenches. 109th Brigade meanwhile deployed onto Welsh Ridge and, as it did so, encountered an enemy attack coming over the ridge from the east along the Hindenburg Support Systems. Although tired, unsupported by artillery and short of bombs, the men of the 9th Royal Inniskilling Fusiliers fought backwards and forwards over this ridge. During this fearsome action Second Lieutenant J S Emerson earned a posthumous Victoria Cross. After twenty-four hours they were relieved by 11th Royal Inniskilling Fusiliers who threw the enemy off the high ground and consolidated the position.

There was little action on the front of 108th Brigade in the valley where the 9th Royal Irish Fusiliers was deployed with two companies in the front line, one in support and one in reserve as the counter-attack company. However, the intermittent shelling began to cause casualties soon after the Battalion moved into the line. A most serious loss was Captain R S Flood MC, one of the 9th Royal Irish Fusiliers' few remaining original officers, who was killed by shrapnel at 9.00am on 5 December. Corporal Joseph Clarke and Private William Moore were also wounded by shrapnel. The shelling increased the next day, wounding five men, including Private William Thompson who died of wounds. Second Lieutenant S F Moran was also wounded; he remained in hospital until March 1918. In addition to the discomfort caused by the enemy artillery, the trenches were in poor condition and the men worked hard to improve them, making latrines, strengthening the wire and salving several *'articles of war'*. The heavy shelling continued unabated for the four days the 9th Royal Irish Fusiliers was in the line. Eight more men were wounded on 7 December and five men were wounded the following day. A very experienced officer was lost when Captain Godson was hit in the thigh; he did not rejoin the 9th Royal Irish Fusiliers until mid-1918.

While D Company manned a communication trench running south from the front line, the remainder of the 9th Royal Irish Fusiliers was relieved by 12th Royal Irish Rifles on 8 December and moved into Brigade support for four days. Here the tired and wet troops had no opportunity to recover as large work parties, often two companies strong, were required to carry stores and wire to the front. After being relieved in this role by 2nd Royal Irish Rifles on 12 December, the 9th Royal Irish Fusiliers moved forward and took over from 12th Royal Irish Rifles again, this time with B Company in the outpost line, A and C Companies in the front line trenches and D Company in support. This tour started relatively quietly, although a German soldier from *Reserve-Infanterie-Regiment Nr 6* was captured in the early hours of 13 December and there was every indication that a large attack was to take place later that morning. In reaction to this rumour a general 'stand-to' was ordered along the front, but dawn arrived without an accompanying artillery barrage and the attack did not materialise. Shelling over this period had caused another six casualties including, on 15 December, Second Lieutenant H E Bray who was wounded severely in the shoulder and foot, and Privates Thomas McMurray who was wounded in the thigh, and William Edwin Warke who was shot in the head.

Having suffered over 3,200 men killed, wounded and missing since 20 November, it was clear now that the men of the Ulster Division were on their last legs and would be unable to withstand another concerted attack by the enemy. The troops were physically exhausted having undertaken a major action in mid-August from which there had been little time to recover. September, October and much of November had been spent in the line at Havrincourt, and working hard even when in reserve, and they had been in constant action with the enemy for three weeks during the Battle of Cambrai. The winter weather over this period had also taken its toll. The men were dirty and many were ill and it was this latter aspect, the subject of representation by the medical services, which forced the relief of the Ulster Division. The relief began on 14 December with 107th Brigade, now on Welsh Ridge, being replaced by 189th Brigade of 63rd (Royal Navy) Division.

The final scheme, mounted by the 9th Royal Irish Fusiliers before leaving the line, took place just after dark on 16 December when a fighting patrol took on a German post in a trench running out from the 9th Royal Irish Fusiliers' lines. Captain G W Vesey led the patrol and he was successful in rushing the post. A German machine-gunner was bayoneted, a number of others killed, and before they withdrew with the captured machine gun, the patrol established a block in this trench increasing the security of the Battalion's own posts. Everyone returned safely and for their efforts Captain Vesey was awarded the Military Cross, and Sergeant G A Henry and Lance Corporal A G H Clarke were awarded the Military Medal.

The final casualties in this sector were Privates Patrick Sheridan and Samuel Shiels. Sheridan was shot in the chest, which left him paraplegic; he died of his wounds on 9 December 1918 aged 22. Shiels was wounded in the back and evacuated to hospital in England. He recovered from his wounds and rejoined the Battalion in June 1918. He was subsequently sent to hospital with a hernia, and having been posted back to the Battalion he sailed from Kingstown on 10 October 1918 on RMS Leinster. He was one of 529 casualties who drowned when the ship was torpedoed by the German submarine U123.

Finally, before the 9th Royal Irish Fusiliers was relieved later that night, the body of Second Lieutenant Gordon Caulfield was buried. An officer of the 7th (Service) Battalion, Prince Albert's (Somerset Light Infantry), he was killed in the defence mounted here by 61st Brigade, 20th Division on 30 November. The circumstances behind the recovery of his body are unknown, and unfortunately his grave was lost subsequently. Second Lieutenant Caulfield is commemorated on the Cambrai Memorial. During this period in the line a great deal of material had been 'salved' or collected from the area captured, including fifty rifles, several thousand rounds of ammunition and boxes of grenades. All of this was secured before the relief was completed at 9.00pm by the 7th (Service) Battalion, The Royal Fusiliers (City of London Regiment) of 190th Brigade, 63rd (Royal Navy) Division.

The 9th Royal Irish Fusiliers then left this sector for the last time. The weather was now very cold with snow falling thickly. The dirty and exhausted companies marched six miles in this awful weather to Metz-en-Couture where they billeted overnight before a march of five miles to Etricourt. After a cold night in tents there, 108th Brigade moved by train to Mondicourt, twenty-five miles to the north-west near Doullens, followed by a final march of three miles through deep snow to their billets at Coullemont where they were to remain for ten days. The Transport, meanwhile, was delayed by the snow and did not arrive until much later. Forty men and an officer from each company worked all of the next day clearing snow from the roads, many of which had completely disappeared under the deep drifts, but everyone else spent their time cleaning up.

By Christmas Day the 9th Royal Irish Fusiliers was well rested, and after a church service the companies had a Christmas lunch. The snow continued to fall heavily but the Battalion was not greatly affected until 27 December when men of A and D Companies were detailed to sandbag a nearby aerodrome. The next day the 9th Royal Irish Fusiliers left Coullemont and by the early afternoon was in Boves, just to the south-east of Amiens. The Transport again arrived much later due to the weather. It was here the 9th Royal Irish Fusiliers saw in the New Year and spent the first week of January. By now the Battalion, reinforced somewhat, had a ration strength of 39 officers, 868 men, 39 horses and 16 mules. On 7 January, three weeks after leaving Marcoing, it moved out of its billets and headed for a new area of the front. By 17 January the 9th Royal Irish Fusiliers had moved by train another forty miles east, staging through hamlets in shell-shattered countryside, thickly covered with snow, to reserve billets at Grand Seraucourt, three miles behind the front line at St Quinten. Here the 9th Royal Irish Fusiliers would remain until the German offensive in March 1918.

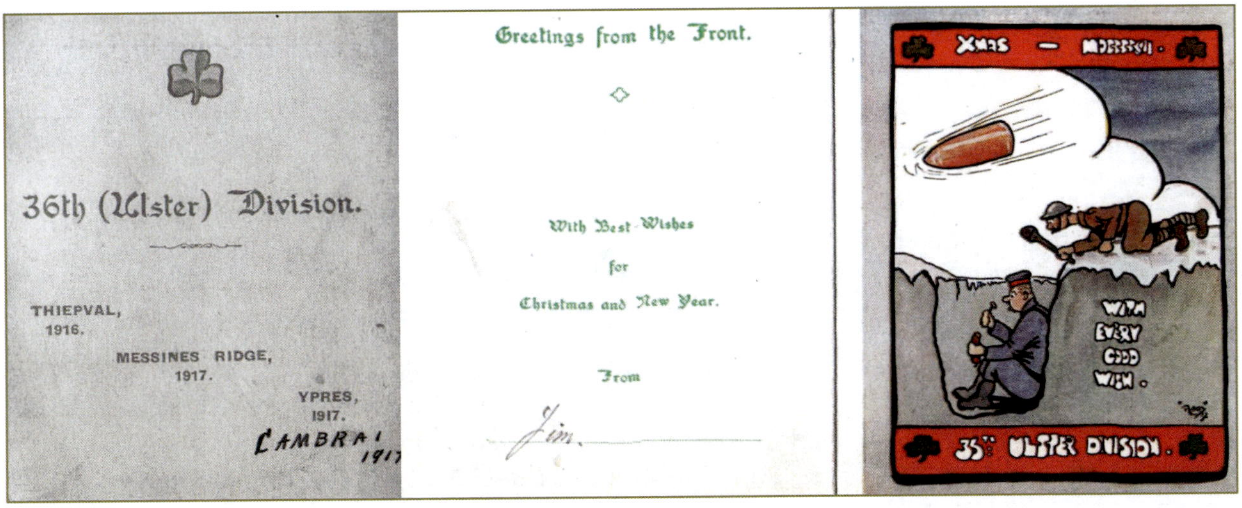

The Christmas card sent home by Captain J H Partridge.
Note the addition of *'Cambrai 1917'* to the front of the card.

Endnotes, Chapter 6

1 When Havrincourt was captured during the Cambrai offensive the area was visited by Captain E A Godson MC, the 108th Brigade Intelligence Officer. In the German line opposite R3 he found a *'German mine shaft down and under the 70ft East bank of the Canal du Nord which had reached the middle of the canal bed and was to come on up and under our 70ft bank and blow up our defence point'*.

2 The history of the original B Squadron was more complicated. It was based at Antrim until it was attached to 59th (2nd North Midland) Division in August 1915. It may not have actually joined 59th (2nd North Midland) Division in Hertfordshire before being re-designated as F Squadron and forming part of the Reserve Regiment at Antrim.

3 The North Irish Horse was disbanded in 1919 but remained in 'suspended animation'. It was reconstituted in September 1939 as an armoured car regiment and from late-1941 was employed as an anti-invasion force equipped with Churchill tanks in England. It sailed for Algeria in January 1943, where it fought with the First Army, and then with the Eighth Army in Italy from April 1944. The North Irish Horse was disbanded in 1946, but in 1947 it was reconstituted as an armoured car regiment in the Territorial Army. A number of reorganisations followed and after November 1998 the North Irish Horse comprised B (North Irish Horse) Squadron, Queen's Own Yeomanry and 69 (North Irish Horse) Signal Squadron, 40th (Ulster) Signal Regiment, based in Belfast and Limavady, County Londonderry respectively. As a consequence of the Strategic Review of Reserves in 2010, 40th (Ulster) Signal Regiment was reduced to a squadron titled 40 Signal Squadron, and 69 (North Irish Horse) Signal Squadron ceased to exist.

4 Ivan Crossley was an Irish emigrant and a founding member of a community named Lloydminster in Saskatchewan. In his memoirs he recounted his meeting with Charles Despard in Canada in 1910.

> *'I had always liked the job of handling horses and stock of all kinds so I was soon up to my neck in the business of buying and selling and doing very well. I had five livery teams and used to drive the police and doctors all over the country. I started a cartage business in town, hauling stores and produce from the railroad depot to the different stores.*
>
> *Business grew with the town and I soon found myself almost snowed under looking after everything. One evening during the winter I was doing my books at the office when a team drove up and needed stabling for the night. It was about 40 degrees*

below and the driver was very cold and hungry, having driven down from Edmonton, some 200 miles to the west.

I got him into the warm office after stabling and feeding his horses. We started talking and I soon detected that he was an Irishman like myself. Very soon it developed that he too had come from Belfast and had been out in the woods near Edmonton working at a lumber camp. He had previously been in the Lloydminster district and had taken up a homestead but could not afford to stay at that time. He had come back to "put in his time" as required by the government.

I asked his name and was told it was "Despard". "Not Charlie Despard, surely," I said. "Yes," he said and who was I? I soon told him and we found that we had attended the same school and church many years ago and we knew one another's families.

I took Charlie into partnership with me in the business and we worked together many years and made money for us both. He was a born soldier and had fought in the Boer War. When the First World War broke out he was a reservist in the Enniskillen Dragoons so nothing could stop him from leaving at once to join his old regiment. He said he would go and that I should remain at home and look after his share of the business while he was away.

Charlie had no wife at that time, so was free to go if he thought it his duty. In Charlie's death I lost the best friend I ever had. My wife and children also loved him and we all felt the loss terribly.

He had married his old sweetheart in the south of Ireland during one of his leaves. Years later when I took my family to Ireland we visited his wife at Killkenny. She was proud to show us his war mementoes and medals. I eventually bought out his share in our business at a satisfactory price to his wife and myself.'

[5] Lieutenant Colonel Hugh Melville Kitchen MC*. Born on 13 December 1894 at Allahabad, West Bengal, India. Commissioned into The Highland Light Infantry 10 September 1915. Transferred to the Machine Gun Corps 27 March 1916. To France 1 July 1916. Lieutenant 1 January 1917. Posted to 108th Brigade Machine Gun Company. MC - *For conspicuous gallantry and devotion to duty. He kept his guns in action throughout the day against repeated enemy attacks, holding his position to the last. Some days later he organised a party of machine gunners acting as infantry, and charged the enemy, inflicting heavy casualties and driving them back. He showed fine courage and dash.* Captain 24 March 1918. Bar to MC - *For most conspicuous gallantry, dash and initiative during offensive operations near Moorseele on October 15th 1918. When the advance was being checked by an enemy machine-gun he rushed forward alone across an open field to within twenty yards of the gun, lay down in the open, and shot at the enemy gun team with his rifle. He hit two, and the remainder got up and ran. He then turned the enemy machine-gun on to the retreating party, killing all except the officer, whom he ran after and took prisoner. He did splendid work, and his action saved the attacking troops many casualties and enabled them to continue the advance.* Reverted to Lieutenant 2 February 1919. Transferred to the Regular Army Reserve of Officers. Captain 20 August 1920. Relinquished his commission on completion of service 16 October 1920. After the war worked for the Eastern Bengal Railway, India. He served in the Second World War with the Corps of Royal Engineers.

[6] The aircraft was a DH5 flown by 30-year-old Lieutenant Albert Griggs of 68 (Australian) Squadron, Royal Flying Corps (also known as 2 Squadron, Australian Flying Corps). He was born in Meridian, Mississippi, USA and was one of a number of Americans flying with the Australian Flying Corps. Griggs was fatally wounded when he was shot down and died of his wounds. Two weeks later a note appeared in The Times: *'To an unknown airman, shot down on November 23rd, 1917, whilst attacking a German strong-point south west of Bourlon Wood, in an effort to help out a company of Royal Irish Fusiliers when other help had failed.'* He is commemorated on the Arras Flying Services Memorial.

[7] Lieutenant E T Owles' action over Bourlon was not the only time that his exploits came to notice. A communiqué written in late-1917 described how Owles, accompanied by another pilot from 12

Squadron, Lieutenant Black, flew five flights on 12 December on reconnaissance along the Corps front at 300 feet. In four contact patrols they fired 2,200 rounds and dropped ten bombs. One of the bombing runs was against an enemy incursion into the British line, which they drove back with machine-gun fire and bombs from forty feet.

SEVEN

The German Offensive: March & April 1918

January 1918 began quietly for the 9th Royal Irish Fusiliers in rest billets at Boves just outside Amiens. After a week of relative inactivity, the Battalion marched for three days east to St Quentin with the rest of 108th Brigade in cold but dry weather over roads thickly covered with snow. The dry weather had given way to thick sleet just before most of 108th Brigade finally arrived in reserve billets two miles behind the line in villages on the Ham/St Quentin Road. The 9th Royal Irish Fusiliers was billeted at Villeselve. On 14 January, after a short rest, the Ulster Division relieved the French *6e Division d'Infanterie* and 107th and 109th Brigades deployed into the line, with 108th Brigade in reserve. The 9th Royal Irish Fusiliers moved to Grand Seraucourt.

After weeks of snow and frost the relief took place in milder weather. Consequently, the defences suffered from the effects of the thaw and were in much need of repair. The next few weeks were hard work for everyone, rebuilding the existing trenches and digging new ones. The front was generally quiet, although the enemy mounted a few raids to identify who was facing them. By now the rationed strength of the 9th Royal Irish Fusiliers had risen to forty officers and 846 other ranks. As usual, only about two thirds of this number was with the Battalion in the line.

The 9th Royal Irish Fusiliers continued to add to its share of decorations when earlier in the month the Divisional Commander had presented ribbons to those decorated after the actions at Moeuvres and Marcoing. Three members of the Battalion also received Belgian awards: Captain E A Godson and Corporal W Knaggs received the *Croix de Guerre*, and Private T Stewart of B Company received the *Decoration Militaire*. On 26 January Reverend H S Bally relieved the Reverend Mayes as Chaplain. Mayes returned to Ireland to Diamond Grange Parish Church, where he was the minister until his retirement in 1946. Howard Bally was from Lancashire and was the first, and only, Chaplain to serve with the 9th Royal Irish Fusiliers who was not from Ireland; he would serve the Battalion with great distinction.

At the end of the month 108th Brigade moved forward and took its turn in the trenches, relieving 9th Royal Inniskilling Fusiliers as brigade support on 28 January, and then relieving 14th Royal Irish Rifles on 29 January. The sector occupied by the 9th Royal Irish Fusiliers was on the right of the brigade front around Sphinx Wood, south of St Quentin and about 1,200 yards west of the village of Itancourt. Here the ground was generally open and gently undulating. The enemy held a line about 1,000 yards away in the outskirts of St Quentin along a line that ran east to Neuville-St Amand and then south-east through Itancourt, generally along the line of the railway. This tour for the 9th Royal Irish Fusiliers was relatively quiet. Patrols went unchallenged, seeing little of the enemy, and short artillery and machine-gun duels wounded only three men. The enemy opposite comprised Prussians of *Grenadier-Regiment König Friedrich I (4. Ostpreußisches) Nr 5*, one of whom was shot in front of A Company's position on 31 January. On 4 February the 9th Royal Irish Fusiliers was relieved by 12th Royal Irish Rifles and moved into brigade support. The trenches occupied by three of the companies were 2,000 yards north of Essigny-le-Grand on the road to St Quentin, and one company deployed forward to the trenches 1,000 yards north-east of the main battalion position. The days that followed were uneventful, and although occasional shelling left two men wounded, the routine of unit life occupied everyone.

On 9 February the 9th Royal Irish Fusiliers was relieved by its sister 1st Battalion and moved forward to take over the left sub-sector of the brigade front from 11th/13th Royal Irish Rifles. This area was just to the west of the St Quentin/Laon Road and near the area previously occupied. It was again quiet, with only occasional artillery fire and sniper fire that wounded five men including Private John Johnston, who subsequently died of his wounds. For most this tour, the control of the companies in the line was left to the acting Second-in-Command, Captain Henahan, after Major Brew who was acting as Commanding Officer, and the battalion headquarters with the orderly room staff and the Chaplain, moved back to the area occupied the previous week.

A major change occurred in the Ulster Division over this period. With the offensive on the Eastern Front all but over, thirty-five German divisions were released to reinforce those in France and Flanders. There has been much discussion of the position taken by the Prime Minister, Lloyd George, and the War Cabinet over this period but, regardless of the grand strategic manoeuvrings, the result was that nearly half a million men were kept back in England. The British Expeditionary Force had experienced an increasing shortage of trained soldiers, and reorganisation was the only solution available to Field Marshal Haig. He ordered the reduction in strength of each division from twelve to nine infantry battalions in three brigades—a loss of nearly 150 battalions. Regular and first line Territorial Force battalions were preserved, and, consequently, the Service battalions bore the brunt of the cuts.

In 36th (Ulster) Division, six Service battalions were disbanded—8th/9th, 10th, 11th/13th and 14th Royal Irish Rifles and 10th and 11th Royal Inniskilling Fusiliers. Additionally, however, three Regular Irish battalions joined the Ulster Division—1st Royal Irish Rifles from 8th Division and 1st and 2nd Royal Inniskilling Fusiliers from 29th and 32nd Divisions respectively. To allow like units to serve together, some battalions were transferred between brigades. In common with the pioneer battalions of the other divisions, 16th Royal Irish Rifles (Pioneers) was reduced by one company. In addition, the 21st, 22nd and 23rd Entrenching Battalions were formed from the surplus manpower after the reorganisation.[1] 36th Battalion, Machine Gun Corps, was formed from the three brigade machine gun companies along with a fourth company, the 266th, which had joined the Ulster Division in January.

The result was that by the end of the month 36th (Ulster) Division comprised five Regular and five Service battalions, including the Pioneer battalion. Over the last year the Ulster Division had lost eight of its original battalions and this latest round of amalgamations radically changed its make-up. Although the Service battalions still had strong links to their home recruiting areas, the numbers coming from Ireland were not large enough to sustain them without additional English reinforcement drafts. The battalions were now a real mix of Irish and English, Protestant and Roman Catholic, regular soldiers, special reservists, volunteers and conscripts. Nevertheless the Ulster Division remained very much an Irish division, and it was in this guise that it would see out the rest of the war, as shown here:

107th Infantry Brigade:

1st Battalion, The Royal Irish Rifles
2nd Battalion, The Royal Irish Rifles
15th (Service) Battalion, The Royal Irish Rifles (North Belfast)
107th Trench Mortar Battery

108th Infantry Brigade:

12th (Service) Battalion, The Royal Irish Rifles (Central Antrim)
1st Battalion, Princess Victoria's (Royal Irish Fusiliers)
9th (North Irish Horse) Battalion, Princess Victoria's (Royal Irish Fusiliers)
108th Trench Mortar Battery

109th Infantry Brigade:

1st Battalion, The Royal Inniskilling Fusiliers
2nd Battalion, The Royal Inniskilling Fusiliers
9th (Service) Battalion, The Royal Inniskilling Fusiliers (County Tyrone)
109th Trench Mortar Battery

Pioneer Battalion:

16th (Service) Battalion, The Royal Irish Rifles (2nd County Down) (Pioneers)

Divisional Artillery:

153rd Artillery Brigade, Royal Field Artillery
173rd Artillery Brigade, Royal Field Artillery
X.36 Medium Trench Mortar Battery, Royal Field Artillery
Y.36 Medium Trench Mortar Battery, Royal Field Artillery

Divisional Troops:

121st Field Company, Corps of Royal Engineers
122nd Field Company, Corps of Royal Engineers
150th Field Company, Corps of Royal Engineers
36th Divisional Signal Company, Corps of Royal Engineers
36th Battalion, Machine Gun Corps
233rd Divisional Employment Company, Labour Corps
36th Division Train, Army Service Corps
108th Field Ambulance, Royal Army Medical Corps
109th Field Ambulance, Royal Army Medical Corps
110th Field Ambulance, Royal Army Medical Corps
48th Mobile Veterinary Section, Army Veterinary Corps

The 9th Royal Irish Fusiliers was reinforced early in the month by a large draft of eleven officers and 213 other ranks from 7th/8th Royal Irish Fusiliers, which was disbanded when 16th (Irish) Division underwent a similar reorganisation. About the same number of men from the 7th/8th moved to the 1st Battalion.[2] With this reinforcement the 9th Royal Irish Fusiliers' effective strength was 47 officers and 1,071 other ranks by the end February.

All but one of the eleven recently arrived officers were platoon commanders and most brought with them the added experience of having been soldiers: Lieutenant W F Reid was a former soldier of the 9th Royal Irish Fusiliers, who was commissioned in May 1915 and rejoined the 9th Royal Irish Fusiliers; after being evacuated sick, he joined the 7th/8th Battalion. Second Lieutenant W H Roche was a former soldier who had been forced to resign his first commission for inefficiency; he was commissioned again in July 1917. Lieutenant A Wilding MC and Second Lieutenants T Bremner, W G Greenaway and T Slatter were also former soldiers who had been commissioned in August 1917, as had Second Lieutenant G Hardy who, at eighteen years of age was one of the youngest officers to serve with the 9th Royal Irish Fusiliers. Lieutenant J Benson and Second Lieutenant J Darling were former soldiers who had been commissioned in September 1917, and Second Lieutenants J F Caldwell and D J Miller had been commissioned in October 1917. By the end of April seven would be casualties.

Officers of the 10th (Reserve) Battalion in early 1918.

Many of these officers are recovering from wounds; almost all of the other second lieutenants will join the 9th Royal Irish Fusiliers in the first half of 1918.

Front Row (left to right): Unknown, Unknown, Captain C H Ensor, Captain A B Townsend (Adjutant), Unknown, Colonel W C Fitzgerald (Commanding Officer), Major A Ferguson MC, DCM, Captain T F Given MC, Unknown, Unknown, Unknown.

The tallest officer of the left of the photograph is Second Lieutenant A L Dobbyn MC. Standing between Ferguson and Given is Second Lieutenant F Baker MM. Note the number of officers with wound stripes.

In addition to this major reorganisation, the British Expeditionary Force was ordered to take over nearly thirty miles of front held by the French Army, and the manner in which defence was to be conducted was changed radically. Based on the German concept of 'defence in depth', the front was organised into three zones. The Forward Zone was essentially an outpost line in front of a line of supporting redoubts that would be held in enough strength to delay the enemy but from which its defenders would move back to the main line of defence—the Battle Zone—when attacked in strength. The Battle Zone, about two to three thousand yards back, comprised a series of well-built defence systems and redoubts that dominated the ground over which the enemy would attack. Reserves would also be available here to conduct local counter-attacks or to reinforce areas of particular threat. The third zone, the Corps Line, was to be set up in rear of the Battle Zone, but this was never achieved. The plan was a good one but, as would be proved, the troops were too thinly spread and insufficiently trained in it to make it effective.

In 36th (Ulster) Division's area the ground was crossed by a series of ridges and valleys parallel to the front line. In the north, the outpost line lay on the same feature occupied by the enemy, and behind it lay the Grugies valley. This gave good cover from view and direct fire but provided a natural corridor along which the enemy could outflank the forward battalions. In addition, the front line of 14th (Light) Division on the right ran almost north-south, and the right flank was therefore weak and unlikely to hold if the villages of Urvillers and Essigny were captured. To the rear, the redoubts of the Forward Zone were on the next ridge, and farther back the redoubts of the Battle Zone lay on the low ridge along which ran the Essigny/Contescourt Road. The Ulster Division's frontage was divided into three sectors, each allocated to a brigade. 108th Brigade was on the right, 107th Brigade held the centre and 109th Brigade was on the left.

In the 108th Brigade sector the outpost trenches of the Forward Zone ran for 1,000 yards north-west from Sphinx Wood on the right of the sector. These outposts covered an area 800 yards deep, with the reserve line, 1,000 yards in the rear, centred on Jeanne d'Arc Redoubt. The battalion in the Forward Zone manned both lines and it was from here that the 9th Royal Irish Fusiliers was relieved on the evening of 22 February and moved into brigade reserve at Grand Seraucourt. The latter part of the tour had cost the Battalion one man killed, Private William Hilton, and Second Lieutenant J E Scott and one man were wounded. The last week of the month was spent training and providing work parties to reinforce the new defences in the Battle Zone. Just before the 9th Royal Irish Fusiliers moved up again, Major Alex Ferguson left to attend a medical board in England, which resulted in an end to his service with the 9th Royal Irish Fusiliers. Having been Quartermaster since its formation, and then Adjutant since Lieutenant Cather was killed at Hamel, his experience would be sorely missed.

On the evening of 1 March the 9th Royal Irish Fusiliers marched forward to relieve the 1st Royal Irish Fusiliers at Essigny Station. The men spent the next week working hard on improving the defences of Station Redoubt, the main redoubt of the Battle Zone, which lay 700 yards to the west of Essigny. It was a formidable position—heavily wired and covering an area of about 500 yards across by 400 yards deep. After this period of intensive labour there was no rest for the tired men and on 7 March they marched forward into the front line trenches, again relieving the 1st Royal Irish Fusiliers. On the 9th Royal Irish Fusiliers' right was the inter-division boundary over which lay the 8th (Service) Battalion, The King's Royal Rifle Corps of 41st Brigade, 14th (Light) Division, and on the left was the 2nd Royal Irish Rifles from 107th Brigade.

The first two days in the line were characterised by short artillery bombardments and harassing machine-gun fire. One of these machine guns was identified by Second Lieutenant W G Greenaway at a point where the German trenches were closest to the 9th Royal Irish Fusiliers' line, some 300 yards away across no-man's-land. With three men he crawled out in daylight to attack it. Having got as far as the German wire he was spotted but he managed to rush the post, drive off the enemy and capture the machine gun before he and his men returned safely to their trenches. For this daring exploit he was rewarded with a Military Cross. He left the 9th Royal Irish Fusiliers on 13 March 1918 to join the RFC as an observer, where he spent the remainder of the war.

Due to the activity heard behind the German lines, analysis of air photographs and the word of deserters, it was well known that the enemy planned to attack soon and the Battalion's activities in the line reflected this. Patrols went out nightly for the next week and wiring parties strengthened the wire in front of the 9th Royal Irish Fusiliers' positions. Meanwhile, the Ulster Division's artillery was very active cutting the enemy's wire and sweeping likely enemy assembly areas. The German artillery, however, was uncharacteristically quiet. Notwithstanding the early morning fog, the otherwise fine weather and good visibility meant that there was also a great deal of aerial activity over the line. At 8.00pm on 14 March the 9th Royal Irish Fusiliers moved out of its positions and back into reserve at Grand Seraucourt, having been relieved by 12th Royal Irish Rifles. On 17 March everyone enjoyed the last day of peace for some time when they celebrated St Patrick's day with a church parade conducted by the new Chaplain, the Reverend Bally. The sports matches in the afternoon were the last enjoyable event in the war for many in the Battalion, and for the next three days extensive training was conducted. The American Medical Officer, Lieutenant Syd Morgan, wrote on 19 March to another American Medical Officer with whom he had served before joining the 9th Royal Irish Fusiliers:

Lieutenant H S Morgan,
US Army Medical Corps

> *'As it happens, I am still with the worthy 9th, in reserve right now at Grand Seracourt* (sic). *Our tours in the line have been simple enough lately and casualties rare. It has been good sport, however, for the weather recently has been absolutely perfect, giving wonderful observation. I've seen plenty of Boche and have missed his machine-gun bullets successfully. One night the C.O. and I went all around the line about twelve o'clock, going out into the saps and wandering about in No-man's Land. Incidentally a machine-gun turned near us and d___ near cut the grass between our legs. The Boche is quiet these days, however, and he hardly replies at all to the rather heavy strafing he gets night and day. One thing certain now is our guns are not afraid to speak. The best sight I have seen recently was watching the tremendous shell of a 12-inch howitzer flying off into space. It is very remarkable how one can see the shell for fully a minute or two from the moment it leaves the muzzle until it goes out of view.'*

On 21 March the storm broke. The long-awaited German offensive, *Operation Michael*, was launched by Ludendorff against the junction of the French and British Armies on the Somme. It aimed to break through the Allied lines and turn north to trap the British Expeditionary Force. The divisions of the Fifth Army had not had sufficient time to prepare their defences fully, nor was training in the new defensive doctrine complete, particularly for the staff charged with controlling the brigades and battalions in a mobile defence. As a consequence, the gaps in the forward defences would prove too great to hold back the fresh German divisions. When the assault began, the 12th Royal Irish Rifles was in the trenches of the Forward Zone, 1st Royal Irish Fusiliers was in the Battle Zone, centred on Station Redoubt, and 9th Royal Irish Fusiliers was in billets in Grand Seraucourt. The 9th Royal Irish Fusiliers' strength here, including the Transport, was about 700 all ranks. The officers of 9th Royal Irish Fusiliers' officers over this period were:

Commanding Officer:	Lieutenant Colonel P E Kelly
Commanding Officer: (On 26 Mar 18)	Major J G Brew
Second-in-Command:	Major J G Brew
Second-in-Command: (From 26 Mar 18)	Captain C B Despard MC
Adjutant:	Captain M Henahan MC
Adjutant: (From 22 March)	Second Lieutenant J E Scott
Transport Officer:	Lieutenant E J L Turner
Quartermaster:	Honorary Lieutenant G W Wilson
Medical Officer:	Lieutenant H S Morgan US Army Medical Corps
Padre:	The Reverend H S Bally AChD
A Company:	Captain W Vesey MC (Officer Commanding), Second Lieutenant A W Henry (Officer Commanding from 25 March), Lieutenants T Bremner & A Davidson and Second Lieutenant R L Smith
B Company:	Captain J H Partridge MC (Officer Commanding), Lieutenants E Hamilton & W F Reid & Second Lieutenants D J Miller and D Prenter
C Company:	Captain T E C Crosbie MC (Officer Commanding), Lieutenant F L H Donaldson & Second Lieutenants J Benson, J H Connor, J Darling & G Hardy
D Company:	Captain H S Dean (Officer Commanding), Lieutenants J A Cooke (Assistant Adjutant), A F Maxwell, G I O'Flaherty Johnson & C J T Perkins & Second Lieutenants N Clarke and W H Roche
Company Unknown:	Lieutenant R I McCrum & Second Lieutenants J F Caldwell, H L Davies, V A Davies, T C Leahy, R A Orr & T Slatter
Detached:	Captain C J Brennan (Staff), Captain W J Menaul MC (Headquarters 108th Brigade), Lieutenant E H Gilmer (Headquarters 108th Brigade), Lieutenant F C Hartness (Leave), Lieutenant G H Richardson (England, sick), Lieutenant J I Smith (12th Royal Irish Rifles), Lieutenant J Woods (England, sick), Second Lieutenant W G Graham (Instructor at First Army Infantry School), Second Lieutenant W F Irvine (12th Royal Irish Rifles), Second Lieutenant C H Kerr (Leave), Second Lieutenant J J Murphy (Leave) & Second Lieutenant J J McE Pollock (108th Trench Mortar Battery)
Regimental Sergeant Major:	Warrant Officer Class 1 C H Turner MC

Although there were some anticipatory British artillery barrages in the early hours, the night of 20/21 March was generally quiet. At 4.35am, however, the German offensive began with an intensive artillery barrage across the entire front. Employing guns and mortars firing high explosive, shrapnel and gas, it struck anything of importance, particularly communications, to a depth of two to four miles over a period of five hours. Between 6.00am and 9.40am the German infantry began its infiltration and advance. Forty-three divisions of the German 2nd and 18th Armies faced the British 5th Army (comprising eleven infantry divisions in the line, one in support and most of three cavalry divisions) and, farther north, nineteen divisions of the German 17th Army faced the British 3rd Army, which comprised ten infantry divisions in the line and seven infantry divisions in support. All of the British formations were under strength.

At St Quentin, the leading troops of the German 18th Army (*18. Armee)* attacked 36th (Ulster) Division just after dawn. On the 108th Brigade front, the enemy troops advanced in strength through the thick dawn mist from the right flank near Grugies. The attack came along the shallow valley that ran westward along the front line and which provided excellent cover for the German infantry. The heavy and well-planned barrage destroyed communications cable and telephone exchanges with the result that communications between the forward battalions and their supporting artillery were quickly lost.

The attack resulted in the immediate encirclement of 12th Royal Irish Rifles in the Forward Zone. They fought hard and held out for most of the day but were forced to surrender after heavy casualties were sustained.[3] Meanwhile, by 6.00am the 9th Royal Irish Fusiliers had taken up a position south-east of Grand Seraucourt. 108th Brigade Headquarters moved forward at 6.30am and Captain Sowerby followed it into Grand Seraucourt with nineteen stretcher-bearers. He was a familiar face in the Brigade and had been the 9th Royal Irish Fusiliers' Medical Officer in late 1916.

As the morning mist lifted around midday it was evident that the troops of the battalion from 14th (Light) Division on the right flank had been pushed back, and the enemy was in Essigny. Just after noon, D Company, commanded by Captain H S Dean, was ordered to move forward to support the 1st Royal Irish Fusiliers in Station Redoubt just west of Essigny Station. The remainder of the 9th Royal Irish Fusiliers had been ordered to take up a line behind Essigny Station facing north-east to prevent the enemy encroaching farther into the Ulster Division's right flank. Lieutenant Colonel Kelly deployed A Company forward, B Company in support and detailed C Company as the battalion reserve. Second Lieutenant Perkins, commanding 16 Platoon in D Company, was ordered to establish an outpost between Station Redoubt and A Company.

The 1st Royal Irish Fusiliers and D Company were attacked in strength just after 1.00pm but managed to hold Station Redoubt until dusk, and at 8.45pm orders were received to withdraw west of the St Quentin canal. The survivors were forced to leave behind nearly 300 officers and men killed, wounded and captured. Amongst them was D Company's Quartermaster Sergeant Francis MacMahon who narrowly evaded capture and made his way to safety with a wounded arm. It had been planned that Second Lieutenant Perkins' platoon should come in from the outpost position before dawn, but he did not receive the order to retire when the rest of his Company withdrew with the 1st Royal Irish Fusiliers. At first light he saw a small party of Germans through the fog who he called upon to surrender, but they ran off having been fired at. It was then that he saw that Station Redoubt had been captured. Perkins made off with his twelve men into open country and after half a mile he saw some men and made towards them. When he got close he realised that it was a group of British prisoners with a guard of six Germans. Covering the guard with his revolver he ascertained that the 9th Royal Irish Fusiliers had retired and that the enemy was now up to four miles in his rear. This curious scene ended with Perkins and his platoon making off again in the hope of finding the 9th Royal Irish Fusiliers, but he soon ran into another German unit and was captured.

The remainder of D Company, having held their position against strong attacks and under heavy artillery and machine-gun fire, and having earlier fallen back, now protected the left flank of the 9th Royal Irish Fusiliers, which had also withdrawn. In its new position the 9th Royal Irish Fusiliers managed to hold the enemy back, and between 10.00pm and midnight orders were received to withdraw to a line near Happencourt as soon as possible. By now the enemy was in Grand Seraucourt, threatening the 9th Royal Irish Fusiliers' rear and right. The Adjutant, Captain Henahan, sent out orders to the Company Commanders to pull back, but the runner he sent to A Company returned an hour later saying that he had got lost in the fog and had not found it. Major Brew, unwilling to lose a company to the enemy, ordered Captain Henahan to go with the runner and find Captain Vesey. He managed to do so at about 1.00am and conveyed the order to withdraw. Severely depleted by the fighting, A Company pulled back, but as it was doing so an enemy force over 200 strong attacked it and a brutal fight ensued. Although about half of the surviving members of A Company, including its officers, fought hard and managed to withdraw, the remainder was nearly wiped out. Captain Henahan and thirty men were captured. During the withdrawal west across the Canal de St Quentin on the night of 21 March, more men were lost when two more platoons from the 9th Royal Irish Fusiliers, led by Second Lieutenants Connor and O'Flaherty-Johnston, and a platoon from the 1st Royal Irish Fusiliers, were cut off and captured when the bridges were blown before they could cross.

Second Lieutenant J H Connor

The remainder of 108th Brigade spent all day on 22 March fighting at Happencourt. As the scale of the enemy offensive became clear, 5th Army was ordered to hold a line roughly east/west along the Canal de la Somme and the Canal de St Quentin. The 9th Royal Irish Fusiliers, with the remainder of 108th Brigade, conducted a rapid withdrawal across the canal at Pithon that night. 108th Brigade now held the centre of the Ulster Division's line with 61st Brigade—from 20th (Light) Division and now under command 36th (Ulster) Division—on its right and 21st Entrenching Battalion on the left. In the 108th Brigade area a small, composite battalion, commanded by Major J G Brew, was made up of details and men returning from courses. It was deployed in an outpost line along the canal with the two Royal Irish Fusilier battalions slightly farther back, with the 9th on the right near Ollezy and the 1st on the left. The remainder of the Ulster Division comprised three small battalions; 16th Royal Irish Rifles (Pioneers) were in Sommette-Eaucourt on the left, 9th Royal Inniskilling Fusiliers, all that remained of 109th Brigade, was in reserve in Brouchy, and 2nd Royal Irish Rifles, the last of 107th Brigade, was in Cugny.

The depleted 9th Royal Irish Fusiliers was now reduced to fewer than 400 all ranks having suffered about a third of its number killed and captured, and the survivors had lost all but their fighting equipment. At Ollezy, alongside the remnants of the 1st Royal Irish Fusiliers on its left, the Battalion found itself in a salient facing north towards the canal with troops of the 61st Brigade to their rear. In the rearguard action here on 23 March the fighting was hard and fierce and many acts of gallantry were seen as the two battalions refused to be pushed back. It was here that Sergeant J Hughes (who had won a Military Medal while with the 1st Royal Irish Fusiliers in 1917) succeeded in knocking out with a Lewis gun an enemy machine gun that was firing on the Battalion's right flank. Although his team was disabled and he was wounded, he kept the gun in action until his position was reinforced. Sergeant Hughes was killed in action later in the withdrawal. On 23 March the remnants of 36th (Ulster) Division had been reorganised and 108th Brigade now comprised the few men left from 12th Royal Irish Rifles, 1st and 9th Royal Irish Fusiliers, 21st Entrenching Battalion and the composite unit of 'details'. Later in the day 16th Royal Irish Rifles (Pioneers) was placed under command of the 9th Royal Irish Fusiliers and the remnants of the two units fought hard until darkness fell, when there was some relief as the German attack slowed. The enemy attacked again mid-morning on 24 March, but the greatly reduced 1st and 9th Royal Irish Fusiliers held their line until noon when the enemy attacked in strength. Outflanked, the two Royal Irish Fusiliers battalions were then forced back to Villeselve where the 9th Royal Irish Fusiliers' defence was centred on a farmhouse in front of the village.

Captain J H Partridge MC

Here the fighting was chaotic and at about 3.00pm the French and British troops in the area were ordered to fall back. Pressure was relieved briefly when a detachment of about 150 cavalrymen of 6th Brigade, 3rd Cavalry Division, the only available reserve, charged the enemy that had succeeded in pushing to the edge of Villeselve. The 9th Royal Irish Fusiliers, tired as they were, followed up, and the combined force drove the enemy out of the village, taking about 150 prisoners. The pressure was unrelenting, however, forcing a further withdrawal. The evening of 24 March saw 1st Royal Irish Fusiliers firm in Berlancourt with 9th Royal Irish Fusiliers farther south in Guiscard. During the night the villages were shelled heavily and there was severe fighting before the reserve French divisions were finally deployed either side of Guiscard. As the French formations held the line, the Ulster Division withdrew through the French *62e Division d'Infanterie* leaving behind the 9th Royal Irish Fusiliers to fight a rearguard action that allowed the remainder to retire. This action was successful. The 9th Royal Irish Fusiliers fought hard but suffered grievously as a consequence. Amongst those that the Battalion could ill afford to lose were two of the Company Commanders, Captain J H Partridge MC, who was killed, and Captain G W Vesey MC who was severely wounded and died two days later in a French dressing station. It was here that Company Sergeant Major Lucas took control and rallied the men. His actions were instrumental in saving the situation and ensuring the success of this vital action; he would be recommended for the Victoria Cross for his bravery here. Second Lieutenant Darling also distinguished himself, refusing to leave his men although he was wounded twice in the course of the day during his platoon's successful coverage of much of the withdrawal.

On the morning of 25 March the much depleted 108th Brigade began a long march of over twenty miles west through Bussy, Avricourt, Tilloloy, Popincourt, Grivillers, Marquivillers and Guerbigny, finally arriving at Erches at 11.00am on the morning of 26 March. Duc to the action at Guiscard, the 9th Royal Irish Fusiliers was the last unit to arrive at the village, completely worn out by the lack of food and sleep and the continuous fighting over four days. After only a couple of hours' rest, they were stood-to again. The enemy had broken through at Roye and only the remnants of the 30th and 36th (Ulster) Divisions stood between the enemy and Amiens.

By now the surviving battalions of the Ulster Division were little more than companies, having lost most of their officers and men killed, wounded and captured. There was no relief in sight, however, and the Ulster Division was ordered to hold a narrow line from the River Avre at Guerbigny to the Amiens/Roye Road at Bouchoir. The Ulster Division deployed forward of Erches with 109th Brigade on the right, 108th Brigade on the left and with 107th Brigade in reserve in Guerbigny. A quick reconnaissance of the area identified an old French trench line, still protected by some wire and with a number of concrete machine-gun posts. It was here that the remnants of 108th Brigade would make their stand.

108th Brigade now comprised the few men left in the 1st Royal Irish Fusiliers, the 9th Royal Irish Fusiliers—the latter reduced to about 200 strong after the last four days' fighting—and 122nd Field Company, Royal Engineers. The Royal Engineers were placed behind the line of the forward troops out on the left flank with what was left of 36th Battalion, Machine Gun Corps. The 9th Royal Irish Fusiliers, meanwhile, was divided into two groups. Lieutenant Colonel Kelly had been wounded slightly and, with his departure to a dressing station set up by 108th Field Ambulance, command of the first group fell to Major Brew. It deployed forward of Erches into the old French trenches. The second group, under Captain Despard, formed the brigade reserve, west of the village.

Second Lieutenant
J E Scott

The half of the 9th Royal Irish Fusiliers deployed in front of Erches was based loosely on A and C Companies. On its right was the handful of men that made up the 1st Royal Irish Fusiliers, but the left flank was open. The Royal Irish Fusiliers were ordered to hold at all cost. Second Lieutenant Scott was now the acting Adjutant and Second Lieutenant R L Smith was ordered to remain in battalion headquarters in case either Scott or Major Brew became casualties. The remnants of 108th and 109th Brigades now faced two German divisions whose infantry, supported by artillery and machine guns firing at close range, attacked soon after Major Brew and his men had taken up their position.

In Erches the men of the 108th Field Ambulance had been ordered to get some sleep but at 9.00am were prompted into action by the arrival of the now wounded Lieutenant Colonel Kelly with information that the enemy was only a few miles away. Captain Sowerby took two other officers, two ambulance cars and eight men forward towards Andechy. On the way there they were fired upon by a German machine gun, which riddled one of the cars and wounded two men. Skilful driving allowed both cars to be extracted back to Erches without further casualties. Meanwhile, Second Lieutenant J J McE Pollock, who had been attached to 108th Trench Mortar Battery, was ordered by the Brigade Commander to take command of the remnants of 12th Royal Irish Rifles, about seventy men. This group was the last to leave the village because Pollock had to organise ammunition for the men, and as they advanced on the area held by the Royal Irish Fusiliers they were engaged by enemy machine-gun fire. Forced into an old trench, Pollock and his new command moved down the trench line and joined the men of the 9th Royal Irish Fusiliers in their position.

Sergeant David McCullough, captured during the retreat from St Quentin.

Major Brew ordered patrols to be sent out to the right to establish contact with the 1st Royal Irish Fusiliers. In addition, Second Lieutenant Bremner sent out some men to the left, but although elements of 30th Division and the mixed force of Royal Engineers and machine-gunners were meant to be there, his two patrols found no one. A Company on the left, now commanded by Lieutenant Henry and only fifty men strong, was therefore turned to defend that flank. Also with this company was Second Lieutenant Slatter who had been in the rear with the battalion details until 25 March. He had been unable to walk due to suffering badly on long marches in ill-fitting field boots and had been ordered to remain behind with the field ambulance. However, knowing the pressure the 9th Royal Irish Fusiliers was under, he asked to go forward and took with him fifteen men of the Royal Irish Rifles to assist in forming the left flank. The first enemy attack was in strength at 1.00pm from the north-west against this flank, and during the initial assault the enemy bombed Slatter's position but did not break through.

Private George Johnston, wounded during the retreat from St Quentin. He died on 13 October 1918 in a French medical unit at the Chateau de Perreuse. There is no recorded explanation for his death and burial so far from where the 9th Royal Irish Fusiliers was located throughout 1918.

Both battalions repulsed several attacks that day. When ammunition ran low Second Lieutenant Smith was sent to Erches to bring more back in a pause between attacks, which he succeeded in doing. In this lull Major Brew went across to the 1st Royal Irish Fusiliers to consult the Commanding Officer, Lieutenant Colonel M J Furnell[4]. Both Commanding Officers went back to Erches to find the brigade headquarters to determine what was happening. In their absence command devolved to Major Clements of the 1st Royal Irish Fusiliers, and Second Lieutenant Scott, who had been with the 9th Royal Irish Fusiliers for a little over six months.

The enemy made more unsuccessful attempts to break through early that night before the front quietened down. More patrols were sent out to the left, but again they found nothing, and those sent out to get water and ammunition did not return. Two platoons were turned to face Erches with the result that the 9th Royal Irish Fusiliers was now defending three sides of a square with the 1st Royal Irish Fusiliers along the fourth side. Machine-gun fire was heard in Erches in the early morning and Second Lieutenant Scott went to find Major Clements to discuss the situation. It was decided to hold the position. Knowing that the position was surrounded, Second Lieutenant Bremner and his men played havoc with the German

Private Harry Frazer, wounded during the retreat from St Quentin.

troops, particularly their transport, which was attempting to follow up the advance on the left flank.

While the infantry of the German *28. Division* attacked the small force of Royal Irish Fusiliers in front of Erches, cutting them off and preventing orders or ammunition getting forward, they also attacked the village. Throughout the action the brigade headquarters was in a small wood next to the Guerbigny/Andechey Road just over one mile from the Royal Irish Fusiliers' positions. On the evening of 26 March, without warning, rifle and machine-gun fire rang out behind it. Lieutenant Colonel Furnell, Major Brew and Lieutenant Colonel C O Place, the GSO1 of 36th (Ulster) Division, had just left the headquarters on their way back to the battalion positions in Lieutenant Colonel Place's car to prepare for the withdrawal of the battalions, when they drove into a German patrol. In the ensuing melee Lieutenant Colonel Place was wounded and all three men were captured. As the prisoners were being escorted away from the area another group of German infantry fired on them thinking that they were all British, and in this encounter Major Brew was shot in the chest and severely wounded. Lieutenant Colonel Furnell and Lieutenant Colonel Place moved him to the side of the road and made him as comfortable as possible, but he was unable to move and the enemy refused to help. He was left where he fell. His fate immediately afterwards is not known, but the German Red Cross notified the British authorities that he had died in captivity eleven days later on 6 April.

Soon after this incident the brigade headquarters came under heavy fire. Second Lieutenant Gilmer, attached from the 9th Royal Irish Fusiliers as Assistant Signalling Officer, was separated with a corporal and some men from the Brigade Commander and the rest of the staff. They took cover in a ploughed field and saw some troops nearby but they could not identify them as friend or foe; some French cavalry had already reinforced the area and more were expected. After a wide detour he met up with the Brigade Commander again four miles farther back on the outskirts of Davenescourt, briefed him on what he had seen and volunteered to try and find out who the unidentified troops were. With a private of the wireless section who volunteered immediately to accompany him, he walked along the road out of the village. After he had gone about 250 yards a party of eighty Germans appeared and opened fire. Having fired one round back at the enemy the soldier with him was hit in the chest and killed and Gilmer was hit in the knee. He did not have his revolver with him because he had left it with a casualty the previous day. The Brigade Commander's party fired on the enemy but Gilmer was captured and it transpired that this was the same party of German infantry that had captured Lieutenant Colonels Furnell and Place and Major Brew about fifteen minutes beforehand. The brigade headquarters was now in danger of being rounded up and it withdrew quickly, suffering only Brigadier Griffiths slightly wounded.

On the afternoon of 27 March the Germans launched a heavy attack against the French on the right of 36th (Ulster) Division. When the French gave way the remnants of 109th Brigade were forced to follow. What was left of 108th Brigade was now exposed on both flanks and bore the brunt of the attacks by the German *28. Division*. Finally, at 2.00pm the 1st Royal Irish Fusiliers sent a message to the 9th on their left that they had to give way soon as there was no ammunition left (100 rounds had been sent over from the 9th Royal Irish Fusiliers earlier); only one officer and nineteen men got away. It was during this attack that Second Lieutenant Roche, standing near Second Lieutenant W H Grey of the 1st Royal Irish Fusiliers, was shot in the throat and killed. By now there was a heavy barrage of trench mortar and artillery fire falling between the battalions. Second Lieutenant Henry, with Second Lieutenants Smith, Bremner and Slatter moved A Company to take up a position to reinforce the rear of the 1st Royal Irish Fusiliers. During this manoeuvre, conducted under a heavy barrage, they suffered considerable casualties, and at dusk the Germans brought up field guns and blew the remaining men out of their positions. They retired a little and held on. Eventually, with no ammunition left and with many wounded and out of action, those left in A Company were overwhelmed and forced to surrender.

Second Lieutenant
J F Caldwell

Just to the north the remainder of the 9th Royal Irish Fusiliers was in a similar position. Second Lieutenant Donaldson in C Company suffered the enemy firing into his men at point-blank range with a battery of 5.9 inch guns and a barrage of machine-gun fire. It was impossible to fight it out and he, with Second Lieutenants Caldwell and Clarke (commanding 13 Platoon from D Company) and Second Lieutenant Pollock and the remnant of 12th Royal Irish Rifles, having run out of water and ammunition, destroyed as much as possible before surrendering.

Captain C B Despard

With the destruction or capture of the Royal Irish Fusiliers deployed forward of Erches, the brigade reserve, uncommitted to the earlier fighting, was forced to fall back late on 27 March. Led by Captain Despard, Captain Crosbie and Captain Dean, this small group of 9th Royal Irish Fusiliers, numbered under 200 all ranks. Nevertheless, it was commanded by three of the most senior surviving officers of 108th Brigade and was its largest surviving component. Reluctantly leaving behind their comrades, this small band moved back to Arvillers where it spent the night. The next day they moved on foot and by transport via Hangest-en-Santerre, Plessier, Moreuil and Mailly-Raineval to Sourdon, spending another night at last out of sight, if not the sound, of the battle following them. The last three days of the month saw the remnants of the Ulster Division march farther west in wet weather to Amiens where it entrained for Gamaches, a small town south-west of Abbeville on the Norman coast, and the 9th Royal Irish Fusiliers moved into billets in St Quentin-le-Motte just inland from the former holiday resort of Ault.

Wounded during the retreat from St Quentin: Sergeant James Bratton, Sergeant William McKeown, Private Robert William Jamison and Corporal Ernest Hugh Ramsey.

In the vital and courageous actions fought by 36th (Ulster) Division during the retreat it had suffered an estimated 7,310 casualties of which over 5,700 were missing—many more than had been lost at Hamel and Thiepval. This was the highest casualty rate of any division facing the German attack. The 16th (Irish) Division and the 66th (2nd East Lancashire) Division also suffered over 7,000 casualties, and six other divisions lost over 5,000 men. Some of the missing men were later found or made their way back to their units, and in the case of 36th (Ulster) Division the casualty total was revised at 6,109 all ranks. 108th Brigade had been reduced to a fighting strength of fourteen officers and 321 other ranks, most of them men of the 9th Royal Irish Fusiliers.

Nevertheless, the 9th Royal Irish Fusiliers had been badly mauled. The war diary recorded the casualties as:

	Officers	Other Ranks
Killed in action	2	15
Wounded	6	75
Missing (believed wounded)	1	1
Missing	14	406
Total	23	497

The casualty totals for both the officers and the other ranks require study and revision. The officers' list did not include Lieutenant Colonel Kelly, who was wounded, nor Second Lieutenant J F Caldwell, who had joined the 9th Royal Irish Fusiliers on 21 March and was missing in action. The other ranks' casualty list was produced after 7 April 1918. It records 497 men as killed in action, wounded or missing, and also twenty-four men who had been considered missing who rejoined the 9th Royal Irish Fusiliers between 2 and 7 April. It also records Sergeant John Palmer of A Company who had been evacuated to hospital sick some time during the course of the retreat. It is now clear that some of the men listed as missing were actually killed in action or wounded. The summary of casualties below is based on the casualty lists of officers and other ranks in the war diary. The final tally reflects the Commonwealth War Graves Commission records and is supported by an analysis of available service records and other sources. The tally does not include the men who rejoined between 2 and 7 April. Those men identified as 'missing' but known to have transferred to other units later in the war are assumed to have been wounded or injured and are listed here as 'believed wounded'. Those men identified as 'missing' and for whom no other information exists are assumed to have been captured and are listed here as 'believed captured'.

From left to right:
Private William Biggart from Ballymoney, County Antrim. Wounded and captured. Died of wounds 3 April 1918.
Private George Gilroy from Ballymacarrett, County Down. Killed in action 27 March 1918.
Private Thomas Maloney from Belfast. Died of wounds 28 March 1918.
Private George McBride from Belfast. Missing during the retreat from St Quentin. Like many, his death was recorded as being on 29 March 1918.

Officer Casualties

	Casualty Record	Final Tally
Killed in action	2	3
Died of Wounds	-	1
Died of Wounds in Captivity	-	1
Missing	15	-
Identified Wounded	6	5
Believed Wounded	-	-
Identified Captured	-	15
Believed Captured	-	-
Total	23	25

A Company

	Original Casualty Record	Final Tally
Killed in action	3	8
Died of Wounds	-	2
Died of Wounds in Captivity	-	2
Missing	111	-
Identified Wounded	22	21
Believed Wounded	-	4
Identified Captured	-	26
Believed Captured	-	73
Total	136	136

B Company

	Original Casualty Record	Final Tally
Killed in action	1	3
Died of Wounds	-	-
Died of Wounds in Captivity	-	-
Missing	87	-
Identified Wounded	11	19
Believed Wounded	-	11
Identified Captured	-	14
Believed Captured	-	52
Total	99	99

C Company

	Original Casualty Record	Final Tally
Killed in action	8	9
Died of Wounds	-	2
Died of Wounds in Captivity	-	2
Missing	98	-
Identified Wounded	21	30
Believed Wounded	-	14
Identified Captured	-	21
Believed Captured	-	49
Total	127	127

D Company

	Original Casualty Record	Final Tally
Killed in action	3	10
Died of Wounds	-	1
Died of Wounds in Captivity	-	2
Missing	111	-
Identified Wounded	21	26
Believed Wounded	-	12
Identified Captured	-	24
Believed Captured	-	60
Total	135	135

The revised casualty tally for the period 21-28 March 1918 is:

		Officers	Other Ranks
Killed in action		3	30
Died of Wounds		1	5
Died of Wounds in Captivity		1	6
Missing		-	-
Identified Wounded		5	96
Believed Wounded		-	41
Identified Captured		15	85
Believed Captured		-	234
	Total	25	497

Captured during the retreat from St Quentin:
Top Row (left to right): Sergeant William Moffitt, Privates Thomas Angus, John Conway, Henry Emerson & Joseph Gibson.
Middle Row: Privates Robert Hanley, Hugh Higgins, James Lenaghan, Alexander McLellan & Robert Neill.
Bottom Row: Privates Thomas Owens, Hugh Reid, Frederick Ryan, Henry Simms & William Tighe.

Major J G Brew

Private Thomas Bratty. Captured during the retreat from St Quentin, he was forced to work in a Silesian salt mine.

The three officers killed in action were Captain J H Partridge MC and Second Lieutenants D Prenter and W H Roche. Major J G Brew and Captain Vesey died of their wounds. The five officers wounded were: Lieutenant Colonel Kelly, who was only lightly wounded and rejoined the 9th Royal Irish Fusiliers on 5 April; Lieutenant W F Reid, who was shot in the left arm and joined the Indian Army when he recovered; Second Lieutenant J Darling, who spent the next five months in hospital but was able to return to the 9th Royal Irish Fusiliers; Lieutenant A F Maxwell, who was wounded in the back and arm and saw no further service, and Second Lieutenant H L Davies, who was wounded by shell splinters in the legs but quickly rejoined.

In addition to Major Brew, fifteen officers were captured—Captain M Henahan MC, Lieutenants F L H Donaldson, E H Gilmer (attached to Headquarters 108th Brigade), G I O'Flaherty Johnson and C J T Perkins, and Second Lieutenants T Bremner, J F Caldwell, N Clarke, J H Connor, A W Henry, W F Irvine (attached to 12th Royal Irish Rifles), J J McE Pollock, J E Scott, T Slatter and R L Smith, who was also wounded. Second Lieutenant B J Eyre, who had served with the 9th Royal Irish Fusiliers in 1916, was captured while serving as a platoon commander in the 1st Battalion.

The non-commissioned officers and men suffered grievously. Given the scale of the fighting, fatal casualties were relatively light, primarily because the 9th Royal Irish Fusiliers had not borne the brunt of the enemy's initial assault; thirty men were killed in action. The number of men wounded or captured is based on available evidence and, due to incomplete records, may not be exact, but it is believed that 137 men were wounded, of whom five men would die of their wounds and 319 men were captured, including six men who would die of their wounds. The deprivations of those held as prisoners of war (discussed in the final chapter) resulted in the death of a further ten men due to sickness before their repatriation at the end of the war.

For the third time since its formation, the 9th Royal Irish Fusiliers had been almost destroyed. The ration strength had been reduced to just over 200 all ranks including those with the Transport and Quartermaster. Exhausted by the fighting and the long move to the rear, the 9th Royal Irish Fusiliers spent the first week of April refitting and conducting low-level training to assist in the assimilation of the few reinforcements that were available. 108th Brigade absorbed men from the Entrenching Battalions, mainly into 12th Royal Irish Rifles, a few volunteers from Ulster that joined from the 10th (Reserve) Battalion, and a larger number of English conscripts. The English soldiers that joined the 9th Royal Irish Fusiliers were a second draft from The London Regiment numbering 122 men who arrived on 4 April, previously destined for the 22nd or 24th (County of London) Battalions, The London Regiment (The Queen's). These reinforcements were very young, most having been called up on their eighteenth birthday, but they were reportedly of good quality. The 9th Royal Irish Fusiliers also received fourteen men, recovered wounded and new recruits, destined for The Royal Irish Rifles, who were also transferred at the Base Depot.

Private Charles Honeysett

One of the men to join the 9th Royal Irish Fusiliers on 4 April was Charles Honeysett, a Londoner from Thornton Heath, and his background will give an indication of the standard of training of some of these new arrivals. He enlisted on 26 January 1917 on his 18th birthday and had begun his training with 110th Training Reserve Battalion in Wimbledon in April 1917. This was followed by nearly five months of more advanced training at the 22nd (Reserve) Battalion, The London Regiment in 2nd London Reserve Brigade at Chiseldon Camp, Wiltshire. He went home on leave on the day the remnants of the Ulster Division fought at Erches. The next day he received a telegram ordering him to return to duty. He sailed to France a few days later destined for the

1/22nd (County of London) Battalion, The London Regiment (The Queen's), whose cap badge can be seen in his photograph. At the Infantry Base Depot he and his friends were rebadged as Royal Irish Fusiliers and they joined the 9th (North Irish Horse) Battalion on 4 April. He became a Lewis gunner in 6 Platoon, B Company. Another man to join at this time was Private Frank Homersham. Five days younger than Charlie Honeysett, he went through the same process but also trained as an Assistant Instructor, Physical and Bayonet Training at the Headquarters Gymnasium, Aldershot, on course number eighteen in December 1917. He was tough and fit and would represent the 9th Royal Irish Fusiliers at football as well as demonstrating the greatest gallantry in action.

There was little time, however, to do much training with these new men because Ludendorff's second offensive, *Operation Georgette*, against the British First and Second Armies south of Ypres, began on 7 April. In the southern sector two Portuguese divisions holding a long front retired under the force of the assault and considerable pressure was exerted against the British line. Within two days Armentieres and Estaires had fallen. Then, as Charlie Honeysett put it: *'The Battalion, what there was left of it, was located some distance from the front when we heard something about a "wall".'* Haig had issued his famous 'backs to the wall' order. This Special Order was to have been briefed to all ranks in order to explain the severity of the situation and what was required. It is hard to know what the reaction was amongst the men of the 9th Royal Irish Fusiliers, but it is likely that few cared about the detail and the response was probably sarcastic, humorous and dismissive.[5]

Soldiers on a Physical and Bayonet Training Course at Aldershot in 1918.
Second from the left in the rear row is Private Francis Homersham. This photograph is a counter to the common view that recruits arriving in units in early 1918 were undernourished youngsters.

Soldiers of the 22nd (Reserve) Battalion, The London Regiment at Chiseldon Camp, Swindon, Christmas 1917. These men were destined for the 1/22nd or 1/24th (County of London) Battalions, The London Regiment (The Queen's). How many joined the 9th Royal Irish Fusiliers is not known. Private John Wakefield is sitting on the ground on the far left.

The 9th Royal Irish Fusiliers now had an effective strength of twenty-two officers and 728 other ranks but a ration strength of sixteen officers and 547 other ranks. The officers known to be with the 9th Royal Irish Fusiliers in early April 1918 were:

Commanding Officer:	Lieutenant Colonel P E Kelly
Second-in-Command:	Captain C B Despard MC
Transport Officer:	Lieutenant E J L Turner
Quartermaster:	Honorary Lieutenant G W Wilson
Medical Officer:	Lieutenant H S Morgan US Army Medical Corps
Padre:	The Reverend H S Bally AChD
Officers Commanding	
A Company:	Lieutenant A Davidson
B Company:	Lieutenant E Hamilton
C Company:	Captain T E C Crosbie MC
D Company:	Captain H S Dean
Platoon Commanders:	Lieutenants J A Cooke (D Company) and R I McCrum Second Lieutenants J Benson (C Company), V A Davies, G Hardy (C Company), T C Leahy (B Company), D J Miller (B Company) & R A Orr.
Regimental Sergeant Major:	Warrant Officer Class 1 C H Turner MC
Regimental Quartermaster Sergeant:	Warrant Officer Class II J Barbour MC

Just south of Ypres the British Second Army held the line. It was to here that 108th Brigade was ordered forward to act as the reserve for II Corps. The reinforced 9th Royal Irish Fusiliers and the reformed but still weak 1st Royal Irish Fusiliers and 12th Royal Irish Rifles were placed at the disposal of 19th (Western) Division and moved to the defences near Kemmel Hill as part of the Corps reserve.

Private Dominick Livingstone

Having moved forward by narrow gauge railway on 9 April, the 9th Royal Irish Fusiliers detrained at Poperinghe Station west of Ypres, which was shelled heavily as everyone was getting off the train. Privates Patrick Behan and Dominick Livingstone were killed and a number of others were seriously wounded. They included Lance Sergeant Harry Makinson MM and Private William John McAuley, who both died of their wounds two days later.

The 9th Royal Irish Fusiliers' initial destination was Siege Camp, one of the large billet areas in the rear area, south-east of Elverdinghe. On 10 April the 9th Royal Irish Fusiliers was deployed farther south into the line at the Kemmel defences at Lindenhoek Corner just east of the hill on the Kemmel/Neuve Eglise Road. There was no time to settle here due to the pressure on the line from the renewed German offensive and 108th Brigade was hurried farther forward. By 7.00am on 11 April 108th Brigade was in position on the Wulverghem/Messines Road on familiar ground to those who had been with the 9th Royal Irish Fusiliers in July the previous year. 12th Royal Irish Rifles had deployed onto the Wulverghem-Spanbroekmolen Ridge with 1st Royal Irish Fusiliers to the north of the Wulverghem-Messines Road and on the right of the South African Brigade (actually little more than a South African battalion reinforced with a battalion from each of 108th Brigade and 56th Brigade). The 9th Royal Irish Fusiliers was in support farther south between the road and the River Douve. Lieutenant Colonel Kelly now returned and took command of this sub-sector from the battalion headquarters sited in Stinking Farm.

In his diary Charlie Honeysett recorded that the trench was open and the dugouts flooded. As they waited for the enemy to attack he and his friends discussed their future:

> *'One chap I remember, Jones, a promising young scientist by all accounts with his future in front of him, was saying what a criminal thing war was and an insult to the mind of man. Then somebody else said that anybody who got out of this lot should speak up for anybody who didn't. Then Bill Fowler, who was a barrow boy from Lambeth, said that after this it was up to all the straight-up nations to stand shoulder to shoulder.'*

Both Irish Fusilier battalions suffered intensive shelling throughout that night and it was particularly heavy on the ridge itself. At 3.30pm the enemy moved north from Ploegsteert and attacked in strength. The fighting was fierce and the men in the forward trenches were pressed back, but a spirited counter-attack by the 1st Royal Irish Fusiliers and the South Africans restored the line. That evening the bombardment began again. Charlie Honeysett was in the thick of it:

> *'My first indication that the barrage had started was having my tin hat suddenly whisked off me 'ead, and the shells that had done it, the wind from them, exploded immediately after, luckily just over the parapet of the trench.....for the next five or six hours we were punch drunk with what came over. It seemed that the intention was to blot us off the face of the earth.'*

Second Lieutenant
D J Miller

The troops on the left of the South Africans were pushed back and Hill 63 to the south was captured, opening the flanks of 108th Brigade to heavy machine-gun fire. The situation was grave, and to avoid losing more men, 108th Brigade was pulled back and the front pivoted around 9th Division which was firm in Wytschaete in the north of the sector. 12th Royal Irish Rifles remained on the Wulverghem/Spanbroekmolen Ridge and 9th Royal Irish Fusiliers moved back towards Wulverghem with the much depleted 1st Royal Irish Fusiliers farther to the rear in support. This was not an entirely orderly withdrawal. When Charlie Honeysett and his friends looked round as the barrage died away, they could not see any officers or NCOs to report to: *'So we did what they had done and 'opped it.'* The men from a number of units walked back to Kemmel and were fed and rested before being taken to a marshalling point near Locre. There they were re-formed and returned to their units, arriving back on 13 April.

The new troops had fought well, but the casualties were again severe, and on 12 April the 1st Royal Irish Fusiliers was formed into a composite company and attached to the 9th Royal Irish Fusiliers under the command of Lieutenant Colonel Kelly. At 6.40pm as dusk fell on another day spent under heavy shellfire, the 9th Royal Irish Fusiliers was attacked from La Petite Douve Farm where they had seen the enemy massing. The fierce German assault drove in the left flank but the Commanding Officer ordered an immediate counter-attack by the reserve company. Lieutenant Hamilton and the men of B Company rose from their trenches and attacked with a small party from 12th Royal Irish Rifles. The enemy were sweeping the road with machine-gun fire and there were casualties immediately, including Private John McFetridge, who was wounded, and Lieutenant Hamilton. Lance Corporal Sidney Scott, the Company runner, saw Lieutenant Hamilton shot in the head and killed as he crossed the road. Second Lieutenants D J Miller and G Hardy fell soon afterwards. Hardy was seen to be hit in the head by grenade fragments and was presumed killed. In fact, he was captured, but, badly wounded, died of his wounds on 30 April. Lieutenant Syd Morgan, the American Medical Officer was also killed and Second Lieutenant Orr was wounded. Lieutenant Morgan was tending to the wounded with two stretcher-bearers when he was hit on the leg. As he was being placed on a stretcher, a shell killed him and buried one of the stretcher-bearers. Morgan, a graduate of Johns Hopkins University, had joined the US Army in September 1917 and, like a number of his contemporaries, had been seconded to the British Army to gain experience and to help reduce the shortage of battalion medical officers. He had distinguished himself working with the wounded in harsh conditions during the long retreat in March and his presence right at the front seems typical of the man.

Lieutenant H S Morgan MC

When it was clear that there were no officers left, Sergeant Robert McBride rallied the remaining men and led them forward. The speed of the 9th Royal Irish Fusiliers' counter-attack beat back the enemy and restored the line. While the survivors of this gallant action consolidated the position, Sergeant McBride went out from a trench three times under very heavy fire and rescued three wounded men. The enemy attacks continued as darkness fell, and at 10.12pm Lieutenant Colonel Kelly reported that his right flank had now moved back north of Wulverghem. With the withdrawal of 25th Division on that side, the enemy was able to fire into the 9th Royal Irish Fusiliers' flank again.

Throughout 13 April the 9th Royal Irish Fusiliers repulsed a series of minor attacks but the enemy managed to push into Neuve Eglise to their south until the gap was filled by a battalion of 178th Brigade. These fierce actions had drained the depleted 9th Royal Irish Fusiliers still further and the companies were now the size of large platoons. Fit for little else, they were relieved in the early hours of 14 April by 1/7th Battalion, The Sherwood Foresters (Nottinghamshire and Derbyshire Regiment) and moved back to the Kemmel defences, remaining under command of 19th (Western) Division.

Pond Farm Cemetery.
The 9th Royal Irish Fusiliers withdrew over this area in April 1918 towards Kemmel Hill, seen in the distance. The cemetery contains the graves of six soldiers of the 9th Royal Irish Fusiliers who died in the area in previous actions in May and June 1917.

There was little opportunity to rest at Kemmel and shellfire continued to take its toll, causing more casualties and allowing no decent sleep as the enemy shelled the front heavily throughout 14 April. Before dawn on 15 April the line was pulled back west of Wulverghem and, due to the pressure on the forward troops, the 9th Royal Irish Fusiliers was committed forward again. That morning they occupied trenches and dugouts about one mile north of Wulverghem in the old British reserve line. Not long afterwards a strong enemy attack pushed hard on the 9th Royal Irish Fusiliers left and broke through in the gap between 178th Brigade and 12th Royal Irish Rifles. An aggressive counter-attack by the 1st Royal Irish Fusiliers company and some men from the 12th Royal Irish Rifles, led by Major Holt Waring, checked the enemy advance. It allowed the 9th Royal Irish Fusiliers to consolidate a position in Kingsway, an old communication trench running east-west up to the old British front line positions near the Spanbroekmolen salient. This brave action was not without loss, and Major Waring, formerly of the North Irish Horse, was one of a number killed.

Captain T E C Crosbie MC

Two platoons from C Company, led by Captain Crosbie, were sent forward to Regent Street Dugouts to plug the gap on the left of the Battalion. This was, in effect, an outpost position and at dusk it was heavily attacked and surrounded. Few got back unscathed. Among the casualties was Captain Crosbie, who was severely wounded and died later that night at a dressing station on Kemmel Hill. He had been with the 9th Royal Irish Fusiliers for a little over a year and, although only twenty years old, had earned the Military Cross during a raid at Havrincourt in November 1917 and would be awarded a bar for his actions at St Quentin a few weeks before he was killed. In the course of this action the rescue of the wounded under shell and machine-gun fire was led by the 9th Royal Irish Fusiliers' Chaplain, Captain Bally, who went out time and again with stretcher bearers and volunteers to find the wounded and recover them to safety.

Finally, at 2.15am on 16 April the 9th Royal Irish Fusiliers was relieved and moved back to Clydesdale Camp in the lee of Kemmel Hill to rest, but predictably there was little chance to recover. This area, previously relatively safe, was now within range of the German artillery and the 9th Royal Irish Fusiliers suffered more casualties from shellfire in the next forty-eight hours. 108th brigade now existed in name only. On 17 April, when ordered to form a two-company battalion of no less than 400 men, the remnants of the 1st and 9th Royal Irish Fusiliers with a Lewis gun detachment from 12th Royal Irish Rifles were amalgamated as a composite battalion under the command of Lieutenant Colonel Kelly.

Private Robert Park (Magherafelt), killed in action in the period 11-18 April 1918.

By now the enemy had captured much of the ground west of the Messines Ridge that had always been in Allied hands, including the town of Bailleul, and it was evident that Kemmel Hill must be held. This small and exhausted body of men was committed to a reserve position in support of 2/5th Battalion, The Sherwood Foresters (Nottinghamshire and Derbyshire Regiment) on the rear slope of Kemmel Hill in the early hours of 18 April. This area was poorly protected and the 9th Royal Irish Fusiliers suffered in an intense artillery barrage as they approached their position and then sat in shallow trenches and half-collapsed dugouts and holes scraped with their bayonets. It was here that Charlie Honeysett wrote his poem *'Quiet Conquest'* and recorded in his diary, *'Lost 125 men in ½ hour'*. In fact, there were many fewer killed and wounded, but they included Captain Despard, whose performance in action since he joined the 9th Royal Irish Fusiliers had marked him out as one of the Battalion's best officers. When going forward to organise a relief a shell landed beside him wounding him severely in the thigh. He was taken to an aid post but he died soon after he arrived. He was the last surviving captain in 108th Brigade.

It was here at Kemmel Hill that the ordeal finally ended for what was left of 108th Brigade fighting under the name of the Royal Irish Fusiliers. At 8.00pm on 18 April, as French troops took over the Kemmel defences, this spent force was relieved and marched back to Siege Camp. Even here there was danger and Lieutenant Colonel Kelly was one of a number wounded by shell splinters, and evacuated.

There is no formal record of the casualties sustained over these few harsh days. From the available records it is known that there were at least eighty-nine all ranks killed, wounded or captured between the shellfire at Poperinghe Station on 9 April and the relief at Kemmel Hill on 18 April:

	Officers	Other Ranks	
Killed in Action	4	35	
Died of Wounds	1	11	
Died of Wounds in Captivity	1	-	
Wounded	3	25	*
Captured	-	9	*
Total	9	80	

*These are known casualties. The total for other ranks wounded and captured over this period may be higher.

Casualties from April 1918:
Private William Thomas Elliott from Letterbreen, County Fermanagh. Missing in the period 11-18 April 1918, like many he was recorded as killed in action on 19 April 1918.
Private John McFetridge. Wounded on 12 April 1918.
Private James Smiton from Belfast. Captured in the period 11-18 April 1918.
Private William Joseph Matchett from Tandragee, County Armagh. Wounded on 12 April 1918.

Casualties amongst the officers robbed the 9th Royal Irish Fusiliers of much of its residual expertise. In summary, those killed were Captain Despard, Captain Crosbie, Lieutenant Hamilton, Second Lieutenant Miller, who had been with the 9th Royal Irish Fusiliers for less than two months, and the American Medical Officer, Lieutenant Morgan. Four officers were wounded: Lieutenant Colonel P E Kelly, who recovered and returned to the 9th Royal Irish Fusiliers in August as commanding officer; Captain H S Dean (D Company) and Second Lieutenant R A Orr, neither of whom served with the 9th Royal Irish Fusiliers again, and Lieutenant E J L Turner, the Transport Officer. The severity of Turner's wound forced him to relinquish his commission in early 1919. Second Lieutenant Hardy was the only officer captured and he died of wounds on 30 April. Of the nine other ranks captured, three would die of sickness and not see home again.

On 20 April the 9th Royal Irish Fusiliers' ration strength was eleven officers and 489 other ranks, which included the Transport, Quartermaster's men and other Battalion details. Reinforcements soon arrived; the first draft of four officers and thirty men joined on 23 April and the 9th Royal Irish Fusiliers spent the last days of April assimilating and training the drafts in preparation for the next period in the line, which was not long away. This process was not an easy one. Having lost so many officers, warrant officers and sergeants in less than a month, most of the experience generated by two and a half years at the front was gone. With the best will in the world the Battalion could not be judged wholly ready for operations when it was committed to the line again at the end of April.

Having related the details of the fighting in March and April and the severe casualties suffered, it would be remiss not to detail the decorations earned by the officers and men of the 9th Royal Irish Fusiliers during these hard-fought actions. Over the eight days of the withdrawal from St Quentin the Battalion earned fifteen decorations: Captain Despard was awarded a DSO for his handling of the rearguard, Company Sergeant Major R Lucas MM earned a DCM (recommended for a Victoria Cross) as did Sergeant J Hughes MM, the latter for his gallantry at Guiscard. Captain Crosbie and Captain Dean were awarded an MC for the manner in which they commanded their companies in the early period of the withdrawal from Grand Seraucourt. An MC was also earned by Lieutenant Turner for his handling of the Transport during the heavy fighting, and by Second Lieutenant Darling for his conduct covering the withdrawal at Guiscard. Lieutenant Morgan, the Medical Officer, was also awarded the MC. All of these officers were killed or wounded in April. The MM was awarded to Sergeants A Venard and G Nesbitt and Privates W Adamson, R J Ferguson, R Ingram, T A McClelland and F C Rogers (a Bar to the MM he earned with the 7th/8th Royal Irish Fusiliers). The gallantry of the remnants of the Ulster Division in the fighting at Erches was also recorded publicly by the Commander-in-Chief who, in his despatch published in the London Gazette on 21 October 1918, stated:

> *'Though the enemy had penetrated behind them and had taken Erches, troops of the 36th Division at Andechy maintained a most gallant resistance until the afternoon of the 27th March, thereby playing no small part in preventing the enemy from breaking through between the Allied Armies.'*

For the action at Wulverghem in early April the Chaplain, Captain Bally, was awarded the MC and Sergeant R J McBride earned a DCM for his bravery during the counter-attack on 12 April. The MM was awarded to Sergeant W S Mitchell and Privates W Kelly, W McCarley, G F Miller and B Wasson.

Private William McCarley MM

Thus began 1918 for the men of the 9th Royal Irish Fusiliers. Their committal into the line at Kemmel in April so soon after the fighting retreat from St Quentin meant that they, and those in the 1st Royal Irish Fusiliers and 12th Royal Irish Rifles, were in much worse condition than those in the other brigades of the Ulster Division. There was much to be done to bring the Battalion up to strength and to prepare it for the challenges ahead.

Endnotes, Chapter 7

1 21st Entrenching Battalion was made up of men from 8/9th and 10th Royal Irish Rifles and 10th Royal Inniskilling Fusiliers. 22nd Entrenching Battalion was made up of men from 11/13th Royal Irish Rifles. 23rd Entrenching Battalion was made up of men from 14th Royal Irish Rifles and 11th Royal Inniskilling Fusiliers.

2 The war diaries differ slightly in the number of men in these drafts. The war diary of the 9th Royal Irish Fusiliers records receiving eleven officers and 213 other ranks (but see Appendix 6). The war

diary of the 1st Royal Irish Fusiliers records receiving nine officers and 241 other ranks. The war diary of the 7th/8th Royal Irish Fusiliers records the following postings/transfers:

	Officers	Other Ranks
1st Battalion, Princess Victoria's (Royal Irish Fusiliers)	12	240
9th (North Irish Horse) Battalion, Princess Victoria's (Royal Irish Fusiliers)	11	220
6th (Service) Battalion, The Connaught Rangers	2	34
7th/8th (Service) Battalion, The Royal Inniskilling Fusiliers	1	34
1st Battalion, The Royal Munster Fusiliers	1	44
Royal Guernsey Light Infantry	-	18

3 12th Royal Irish Rifles' War Diary records five officers and 107 men left at the end of the week's fighting and twenty-two officers and 566 men missing. There is an excellent description of this action and the courage of the 12th Royal Irish Rifles in Cyril Falls' *History of the 36th (Ulster) Division.*

4 Lieutenant Colonel Michael John Furnell. Born on 27 May 1877. Commissioned into Princess Victoria's (Royal Irish Fusiliers) on 7 May 1898 (from Local Militia Forces, Canada). Lieutenant 24 February 1900. Fought in South Africa War 1899 - 1902. Wounded 17 September 1901. Mentioned in Despatches. Queen's South Africa Medal and 5 clasps, King's South Africa Medal and clasps 'South Africa 1901' and 'South Africa 1902'. Captain 19 September 1906. Brevet Major 3 June 1915. Mentioned in Despatches. Major 1 September 1915. Acting Lieutenant Colonel and commanding officer of 5th (Service) Battalion 3 December 1915 to 5 November 1916 in the Balkans and Aegean. Commanding officer of the 9th (Service) Battalion, The Prince of Wales's Volunteers (South Lancashire Regiment) 6 November 1916 - 9 February 1917 in the Balkans and Aegean. Temporary Lieutenant Colonel 10 February 1917. Brevet Lieutenant Colonel 3 June 1917. Mentioned in Despatches. Commanding officer of the 1st Battalion, Princess Victoria's (Royal Irish Fusiliers) November 1917. Captured 27 March 1918. Released from service 3 April 1919. Order of the White Eagle 4th Class (Serbia). Commanding officer of the Depot, Armagh January 1921. Retired 1923. Lived in England until 1927 then returned to Ballysheedy, County Limerick. Died 10 March 1958, aged 80.

5 The Special Order was issued by Field Marshal Sir Douglas Haig to all ranks of the British Armies in France on 11 April 1918. It read:

> *'Three weeks ago today the enemy began his terrific attacks against us on a fifty mile front. His objects are to separate us from the French, to take the channel ports and destroy the British Army.*
>
> *In spite of throwing already 106 Divisions into the battle and enduring the most reckless sacrifice of human life, he has as yet made little progress towards his goals.*
>
> *We owe this to the determined fighting and self sacrifice of our troops. Words fail me to express the admiration which I feel for the splendid resistance offered by all ranks of our Army under the most trying of circumstances.*
>
> *Many amongst us are now tired. To those I would say that Victory will belong to the side that holds the longest. The French Army is moving rapidly and in great force to our support.*
>
> *There is no other course open to us but to fight it out. Every position must be held to the last man: there must be no retirement. With our backs to the wall and believing in the justice of our cause each one of us must fight on to the end. The safety of our homes and Freedom of Mankind alike depend on the conduct of each one of us at this critical moment.'*

EIGHT

Bailleul: Summer 1918

In early May 108th Brigade moved to rejoin the Ulster Division. It had been deployed since the end of March in a sector along the Ypres Canal, north of the town and with its forward right positions in the Wieltje area. 108th Brigade was initially allocated a reserve role. The three reconstituted battalions spent their first week at the front engaged in work parties reinforcing the trenches of the outpost line (the Green Line) and the line of resistance (the Yellow Line). The men managed to complete some specialist training, however, and, notwithstanding the losses of the previous months, there was still some spark in the 9th Royal Irish Fusiliers and the football team was active once again, beating the Belgian Cyclist Battalion in the sector to its left, 4 goals to nil. Charlie Honeysett remembered:

> *'It was at a farm where there was a canal and flax growing in the field. I can still see the Irish boys sitting round supping buttermilk from their mess tins while the red headed Corporal performed some sort of a dance to a tune which the Irish boys chanted out. It went on and on, it could have been at least twenty verses to it. It was a bit of old Ireland really and I've never heard the tune since.'*

This period, a mix of recuperation, training and hard physical work, ended on the evening of 4 May when the 9th Royal Irish Fusiliers relieved 12th Royal Irish Rifles farther forward. All four companies were deployed in the line near Wieltje between Middlesex and Belgian battalions. This was just to the north of the area occupied before the attack from Pommern Redoubt the previous August. After a rather uneventful four days the 9th Royal Irish Fusiliers was relieved by the 1st Royal Irish Fusiliers. Twenty men per company were posted from the 1st to the 9th Royal Irish Fusiliers to balance numbers in the reconstituting battalions, and every effort was made to continue the training of the new drafts in a period characterised by brilliant sunshine and intense heat. Work parties were an unpleasant and tiring interruption to this week out of the line and the demand for labourers did not reduce when the 9th Royal Irish Fusiliers took over from 2nd Royal Irish Rifles on 17 May as brigade reserve when 108th Brigade relieved 107th Brigade in excellent weather. The Battalion was deployed with B and C Companies on the east of the canal near Zouave Villa and battalion headquarters, and A and D Companies on the west of the canal near Essex Farm. For six nights the Battalion worked hard on improving the defences, and endured occasional shelling. The war diary records that one man was killed on 17 May but he has not been identified.

On 23 May the Battalion began its last tour in the line here when it relieved 12th Royal Irish Rifles in the right sub-sector. A Company was deployed at Wieltje[1], B Company was in reserve at Irish Farm, C Company with a platoon from D Company was in Caliban Trench and D Company, the counter-attack company, was at Wieltje Farm. The battalion headquarters was at Hill Top Camp. Activity during this tour was moderate with intermittent shelling during the day. A series of fighting patrols were mounted at night to reconnoitre the ruined farms (Von Hugel Farm, Cheddar Villa, Jasper Farm and Rat Farm) forward of the Royal Irish Fusiliers' position and harry the enemy, but little was seen. The German artillery and machine-gun fire was sporadic and not particularly effective. In this tour in the line Private Francis James Morrison was killed on 25 May,

Private William John Withers died of wounds on 27 May and three men were wounded (one self inflicted). The 9th Royal Irish Fusiliers left the line for the last time on 29 May, having been relieved by 2nd Royal Irish Rifles. The entraining point at Zouave Siding was shelled during the relief but no casualties were suffered and the Battalion moved by train to Hospital Farm Camp, north of Vlamertinghe. Having had a day cleaning up, the last day of May saw two companies on work parties and the other two training, but everyone managed to get a bath.

In June the Ulster Division was transferred to II Corps and became the Corps reserve located in the wooded area, north-west of Poperinghe near Proven. In safe and pleasant surroundings and with good weather, the focus for the next month was on assimilating the new drafts and training. By 10 June the effective strength of the 9th Royal Irish Fusiliers had increased to thirty-four officers and 974 other ranks with a ration strength of twenty-three officers and 781 other ranks. Some of the drafts that had made up the numbers comprised the last men to come from the 10th (Reserve) Battalion in Ireland. In April the 10th (Reserve) Battalion and the 4th (Extra Reserve) Battalion had been absorbed by the 3rd (Reserve) Battalion and moved to Rugeley near Cannock Chase in England, where it became part of the West Riding Reserve Brigade. A similar fate befell all of the reserve battalions that had served the Ulster Division so well. The 4th (Extra Reserve) and 12th (Reserve) Battalions of The Royal Inniskilling Fusiliers were absorbed by that regiment's 3rd (Reserve) Battalion, which joined the West Lancashire Reserve Brigade at Oswestry. The 17th (Reserve), 18th (Reserve), 19th (Reserve) and 20th (Reserve) Battalions of The Royal Irish Rifles were absorbed by the 3rd (Reserve) Battalion, and with the 4th (Extra Reserve) and 5th (Extra Reserve) Battalions made up the Irish Reserve Brigade at Larkhill. The majority of reinforcements over this period, however, were English soldiers. As has been described, men of The London Regiment had joined in early April, and on 8 and 9 June another large draft, recorded in the war diary as 127-men strong, arrived from the Base Depot. This reinforcing draft comprised men who had been compulsorily transferred from the Army Service Corps and Army Veterinary Corps. In fact, 105 men of the Army Service Corps and sixty-eight men of the Army Veterinary Corps joined in early May. Most were experienced soldiers, some being pre-war regulars, and many had served in France with the Mediterranean Expeditionary Force, or in Egypt. Twenty-three of these men were bakers by profession.

The 9th Royal Irish Fusiliers had by now changed irrevocably from the battalion that landed on the shores of France in October 1915 but every effort was made to develop pride in the Battalion and the standards previously met by the original volunteers. As a consequence, the new men were put through a comprehensive training package, although until 15 June it was interrupted regularly by the need to provide large work parties to the railway line east of Poperinghe, and the only real benefit of these activities was the toughening effect on the young men new to the front. During this period one of the few officers to face a Field General Court Martial was tried in Proven. Second Lieutenant Albert Davidson was tried on 21 June on charges of desertion and leaving his post. What prompted the charges is not known. He was found not guilty. In the middle of the month the 9th Royal Irish Fusiliers moved with the rest of the Brigade to the Bois St Acaire training area for an extensive period of shooting practice, exercises at company and battalion level, and training for the scouts, snipers, Lewis gunners and other specialists and those in positions of responsibility, such as the section commanders. The importance of this training cannot be underestimated. From 25 June shooting and battalion-level training was conducted in the large training area at St Omer, thirty miles farther west, in a process that was now well developed.

Lieutenant Colonel G M Forde MC

None of the Battalion's original officers were left now and few had been present through the fighting of the last few months, but the new officers were an experienced group and would soon become an effective team. With Lieutenant Colonel Kelly still in hospital, Lieutenant Colonel G M Forde MC had been acting as the Commanding Officer since 22 April. He was a schoolmaster from Ballykelly who had served with the 11th Royal Inniskilling Fusiliers since 1914, earned the MC twice and had been wounded at Messines Ridge in June 1917. Major R G Kerr MC had joined on 31 May as Second-in-Command. He also was an officer of The Royal Inniskilling Fusiliers and, aged only twenty-eight, had commanded the 7th/8th Royal Inniskilling Fusiliers before joining the 9th Royal Irish Fusiliers. The new Adjutant also arrived in May; Captain W Sparks MC had served with the 7th/8th Royal Irish Fusiliers and had distinguished himself at the Battle of Langemarck in August 1917. Two subalterns were attached to battalion headquarters—Lieutenant G H Richardson had served with the 9th Royal Irish Fusiliers for some time but had just returned from sick leave, and he was made Assistant Adjutant; newly arrived Second Lieutenant C A Ross was made the Intelligence Officer. Lieutenant G W Wilson provided much needed continuity as the Quartermaster. The new Transport Officer was Lieutenant J B K Morrow, from the disbanded 11th/13th Royal Irish Rifles. Lieutenant F G McGuinness RAMC had been acting as the Medical Officer since May, and Reverend W B Allman AChD replaced the gallant Reverend Bally in June.

Captain W Sparks MC

The lack of senior company officers resulted in acting rank of Captain being granted to the four Company Commanders: Lieutenant C H Kerr commanding A Company and Second Lieutenant J J Murphy MC, DCM commanding B Company, had returned to the 9th Royal Irish Fusiliers in April. Second Lieutenant J Benson had joined in February from the disbanded 7th/8th Royal Irish Fusiliers and now commanded C Company. Command of D Company had been vested in Lieutenant J A Cooke until he injured his foot in May, and then in Lieutenant J I Smith, who was also promoted. He commanded the company until the arrival of Lieutenant R H Lindsay in July. Lieutenant Lindsay had recently recovered from enteric fever, caught in December 1916 while serving with the 6th Royal Irish Fusiliers in Salonica. When replaced in D Company, Lieutenant Smith was posted to the 1st Royal Irish Fusiliers.

Of the platoon commanders, Lieutenants A L Dobbyn MC, R I McCrum and G Robinson, and Second Lieutenants W G Graham, H L Davies (who had recently rejoined having been wounded at Guiscard in March), T C Leahy and S F Moran (who had recently rejoined having been wounded in December 1917) had served with the 9th Royal Irish Fusiliers for some time. Most of the other junior officers were new, although some had considerable experience to offer: Lieutenant F S Bale transferred to the infantry after serving with the Army Service Corps; Lieutenant J D Baker had served with the 7th/8th Royal Irish Fusiliers and joined in April; Second Lieutenant A Davidson had recently rejoined the Battalion, as had Second Lieutenants A J Galloway and E W Reynolds after a period of illness; Second Lieutenant F J E McFarland MC had returned to duty having been severely wounded while serving with the 5th Royal Irish Fusiliers in Egypt; Second Lieutenants N C Mateer, C F W Greenwood, H C Burrows, T W White, C S Ratcliffe, J

Boyd, and J Bryson were newly commissioned; only White had not seen active service as a soldier, and Mateer, Boyd and Bryson had been senior non-commissioned officers with the latter having earned a mention in despatches and a Belgian Croix de Guerre. In the companies and platoons the warrant officers and sergeants that were lost in March and April were replaced by promotions from amongst the most able junior ranks.

Lieutenants A L Dobbyn MC, R I McCrum and G Robinson.

In addition, two key changes were made in the Ulster Division's command structure over this period. On 6 May Major General Nugent, who had commanded the Ulster Division since its arrival in France, left to take up command of a division in India. He was replaced by Major General C Coffin VC, DSO [2], an officer of the Corps of Royal Engineers, who had earned his VC at Ypres as a Brigade Commander. A few days later Brigadier General Griffith relinquished his command of 108th Brigade to Brigadier General E Vaughn DSO[3].

By July 1918 the 9th Royal Irish Fusiliers was as fit and as well trained as this period out of the line would allow. It was billeted for the first two days of July at Road Camp near St Jan-ter-Biezen in fine weather, and the final day of relaxation for many was spent at the Divisional horse-show held in the grounds of the nearby aerodrome on 1 July. It was followed by a hard day at East Poperinghe when all of the companies worked on the railway line. 36th (Ulster) Division, part of Second Army, was ordered then to relieve the French *41e Division d'Infanterie* north-west of Bailleul. The 9th Royal Irish Fusiliers moved south to Steenvoorde on 3 July, taking over from the *3e Battalion* of the *79e Regiment d'Infanterie* in the Divisional rear area. More training was managed at company level before moving farther forward to Piebrouck, just inside the French border, on the evening of 6 July to relieve the reserve battalion of the French *42e Regiment d'Infanterie.*

In mid-1918 the British Army was a sophisticated machine that had developed its organisation and tactics over nearly four years of continuous fighting. For most of this period the establishment of an infantry battalion had been thirty-four officers and 966 other ranks, although actual strengths had fluctuated widely. As a result of the casualties sustained in March and April 1918 the established strength of an infantry battalion was reduced to 900. This establishment total was eventually increased to 932, but the intensity of the fighting in the latter months of the war precluded manning any battalion to full strength. Platoons now comprised the platoon commander, platoon sergeant, runner, batman (who acted as a runner) and scout, two rifle sections, each of an NCO and six men, and a Lewis gun section of an NCO and ten men with two Lewis guns. Each of the four companies retained four platoons, and a battalion comprised, therefore, thirty-two rifle sections and sixteen Lewis gun sections organised into sixteen platoons. In addition to the officers, battalion headquarters numbered over 130 men split into fighting and administrative elements and included scouts, regimental police, pioneers, clerks, signallers, cooks, those trained in sanitary and water duties, transport, grooms, shoemakers, tailors, batmen and orderlies.

The need to reconstitute a battalion quickly in the event of large casualties dictated that a number of officers and men were left behind when a battalion went into battle. In 1918 this 'battle surplus' was laid down as sixty-four other ranks. It was recommended that, chosen from across a battalion were, two company sergeant majors, four signallers, one runner, one musketry instructor, two Lewis gun instructors, one bombing instructor and one gas instructor. From each company came one sergeant, one corporal, one lance corporal, one signaller and two runners, and from each platoon one rifle bomber, one scout/sniper, and two Lewis gunners. In addition, it was estimated that the average number of sick and those engaged in brigade or divisional details numbered about fifty, and those on leave, classes and courses numbered about ninety. A commanding officer could expect, therefore, a maximum of about 600 men to be available for duty in the line, but this figure was almost always reduced further.

In July 1918 the strength of the 9th Royal Irish Fusiliers fell well short of this with nineteen officers and 592 other ranks in the line, and a further eight officers and ninety-seven other ranks with the Battalion details at Eecke, collocated with those of the 1st Royal Irish Fusiliers and 12th Royal Irish Rifles. A further eleven officers were detached. The Battalion officers in July 1918 were:

Commanding Officer:	Lieutenant Colonel G M Forde MC
Second-in-Command:	Major R G Kerr MC
Adjutant:	Captain W Sparks MC
Assistant Adjutant:	Lieutenant G H Richardson
Intelligence Officer:	Second Lieutenant C A Ross
Transport Officer:	Captain J B K Morrow
Quartermaster:	Honorary Lieutenant G W Wilson
Padre:	Reverend W S Allman AChD
Medical Officer:	Captain C R Brown RAMC
Officers Commanding	
A Company:	Captain C H Kerr
B Company:	Captain J J Murphy MC, DCM
C Company:	Captain J Benson
D Company:	Captain R H Lindsay
Platoon Commanders:	Lieutenants F S Bale, A L Dobbyn MC, R I McCrum, J E McFarland & G H Robinson
	Second Lieutenants J Boyd, H C Burrows, A J Galloway, W G Graham, C F W Greenwood, T C Leahy, N C Mateer, C S Ratcliffe & E W Reynolds

Detached:	Lieutenant Colonel P E Kelly (hospital), Captain C J Brennan (Staff), Captain E A Godson MC (Staff), Captain W J Menaul MC (Staff), Lieutenant A Davidson (leave) and Lieutenant E S L Tees and Second Lieutenant J Bryson (training course), Second Lieutenant H L Davies (sick leave), Second Lieutenant S F Moran (training course), Second Lieutenant T W White (hospital, sick) and Second Lieutenant C R Wilson (training course)
Regimental Sergeant Major:	Warrant Officer Class 1 C H Turner MC
Regimental Quartermaster Sergeant:	Warrant Officer Class II J Barbour MC

The sector finally occupied by the Ulster Division in July 1918 was at the north-west edge of the salient formed by the German infantry during their attack on Bailleul. There was little happening here, although across the front the Allies were beginning the push to the east. The high ground occupied by the Ulster Division near Mont Noir, and by the formations on either flank, gave a distinct advantage to the Allies. As preparations were made for the forthcoming advance, the battalions in the front line conducted raids and generally harried the enemy.

After twenty-four hours in reserve the 9th Royal Irish Fusiliers moved forward on the evening of 7 July into the Brigade left sub-sector, known as *Croix de Poperinghe,* on the lower slopes between Mont Noir and Bailleul. The relief of a battalion of the French *23e Regiment d'Infanterie* was complete by 2.00am on 8 July. The line here was a series of outposts dug into the boggy ground without any regular trenches, that ran for about 1,100 yards east-north-east from a point on the Bailleul/Mont Noir Road. The enemy were in a similar position farther down the slope, generally along the Bailleul/Loker Road. To the east lay Kemmel Hill. This imposing feature and Bailleul were both still held by the enemy. This was familiar ground to those in the Ulster Division who had fought near Messines in late 1916 and early 1917 when this was the rear area, and also familiar to those who fought at Kemmel with their *'backs to the wall'* in April. Although fighting had all but destroyed the towns and villages here (Bailleul was now in ruins), many of the farmhouses had been fortified by both sides. Crops grew everywhere and the high wheat was cut down to provide fields of fire for the outposts on both sides of the line.

The relief went well and for three days the tour was quiet with little activity during the day and intermittent machine-gun and trench mortar fire at night. The very few casualties suffered by the 9th Royal Irish Fusiliers seemed too good to be true. Just after midnight on the last night of the tour the Commanding Officer, Lieutenant Colonel Forde, and the Second-in-Command, Major Kerr, were in the front line trenches when Major Kerr was killed; he had been with the Battalion for only six weeks. Eight men were wounded. With three battalions in 108th Brigade there was now a three-way rotation around the forward two sub-sectors and the reserve trenches. Having been relieved by 1st Royal Irish Fusiliers on 12 July, the 9th Royal Irish Fusiliers moved back to Mont Noir into brigade reserve and the usual round of work parties. Charlie Honeysett described the rudimentary shelter here as *'...some little shelters dug in the side of the sand hill called Mont Noir - horrible little place.'* This area was not safe, however, being within range of the enemy artillery, and the sporadic shellfire caused two casualties on 15 July. Private Arthur James Stanley was killed and Private Henry John Lake was wounded by shrapnel. Lieutenant

N C Mateer, a new officer who had been with the 9th Royal Irish Fusiliers since April, was hospitalised with shell-shock; he did not serve at the front again.

The ruins of Bailleul, 1 September 1918. This was once the scene of regular visits by men of the 9th Royal Irish Fusiliers when off duty in early 1917. There was nothing familiar left.
© IWM (Q 7024)

The British line in the right sub-sector lay about 1,800 yards north of Bailleul. It ran almost west-east along the south-facing slope of a spur known as Meulenhouck to the Bailleul/Mont Noir Road, the boundary between the two sectors. The enemy occupied a series of trenches and strong-points only 500 yards away to the south-east. One of the key enemy strong-points in this sub-sector was the fortified position known as Shoddy Farm. It dominated the line here opposite the right company sitting 750 yards away on higher ground on the northern edge of a spur that rose gradually out of the shallow valley that was no-man's-land. A farther 400 yards to the south-east of the farm was a reinforced position in the ruins of the Asylum on the northern outskirts of Bailleul, the site of an important hospital until it was occupied by the enemy in April 1918.

On 16 July 12th Royal Irish Rifles launched an unsuccessful raid against Shoddy Farm. At midnight on the night of 17/18 July an artillery barrage prompted a stand-to in expectation of an attack. In fact, the enemy sealed off the left sub-sector with a box barrage and raided the 1st Royal Irish Fusiliers, causing twenty-eight casualties killed, wounded and missing. The postponed relief of 12th Royal Irish Rifles by the 9th Royal Irish Fusiliers took place that night. It was over this period that the new Second-in-Command arrived. Commissioned into the 6th (Service) Battalion, The Connaught Rangers, on the outbreak of war, Major R J A Tamplin DSO had been Adjutant and a Company Commander in his own battalion before taking up this post.

Across the Western Front the tide was turning and the first Allied counter-offensive was launched by the French on 18 July. The next day 9th (Scottish) Division on the Royal Irish Fusiliers' right flank, one of four British divisions to participate in this attack, captured Meteren, just to the west of Bailleul. With the line straightened, the next few days were relatively quiet.

Raids remained a feature of life for battalions in the line, calculated by commanders to give these newly reconstituted units some experience of aggressive action against the enemy and to maintain pressure on the exhausted German infantry. On 20 July the Commanding Officer, Lieutenant Colonel Forde, and Captain Murphy, the Officer Commanding B Company, conducted a reconnaissance of the enemy's position in Shoddy Farm at close quarters, in preparation for a raid that Murphy's company was to mount two nights later. The reconnaissance, which took nearly seven hours, was successful. The enemy garrison was estimated at fifty to seventy men with up to five machine guns. Routes in and out of the position were identified and the details of the plan were developed over the next day. The aim of the raid had three parts: to gain identification (the enemy were believed to be from *Infanterie Regiment Nr 186*), to inflict loss on the enemy and to definitively locate enemy positions opposite the right company front. The targets for the raid were three enemy strong-points. The first was a small post on the lane 100 yards north of Shoddy Farm; the second was the strong-point built in the ruins of the farm and its cellars, and the third was a post established in Soot Farm, 100 yards south east of Shoddy Farm. The raid was to be conducted by three platoons of B Company under Second Lieutenants Reynolds, Leahy and Ratcliffe, and 15 Platoon from D Company. Second Lieutenant J E McFarland MC also volunteered to go out with the raiders. He had joined the 9th Royal Irish Fusiliers only three weeks before the raid having just recovered from wounds he received while with the 5th (Service) Battalion in Palestine.

Second Lieutenant
J E McFarland MC

Major R J A Tamplin DSO

Before midnight on the night of 21/22 July, the first platoon left A Company's trenches and moved south to secure the assembly point, 200 yards due west of the farm in no-man's-land, and to act as the covering party. Just after midnight the remainder of the raiding platoons crawled out from A Company's trenches and moved to the assembly point. Everyone waited for the artillery barrage on the ruins of the asylum on the northern outskirts of Bailleul from which German infantry could have interfered with the raid.

Artillery support was provided by A, B, C and D Batteries of 153rd Brigade Royal Field Artillery, a mix of eighteen 18-pounders and six 4.5-inch howitzers, commanded by Lieutenant Colonel C F Potter DSO. The fire plan targeted a single 18 pounder at a house known to contain an enemy post that was 650 yards due south of Shoddy Farm, with the other guns of that battery and two other batteries targeting a 500-yard line along the Bailleul/Loker road to seal off the asylum. The fourth battery, meanwhile, would 'search' within the area of the asylum itself. The guns of the 18-pounder batteries would fire high-explosive shells at a rate of three rounds per gun per minute for the first five minutes. This would then reduce to two rounds per gun per minute for the next ten minutes and then one round per minute until the order to stop firing (two green flares) was received. The 4.5-inch howitzers would fire three rounds per gun every two minutes into the asylum throughout the barrage. This meant a healthy 765 rounds in the first fifteen minutes.

At 1.00am, as the barrage began, the raiders, led by Captain Murphy and Second Lieutenant Leahy's platoon, moved quickly over the open ground towards the enemy wire. The party was seen and Leahy rushed forward alone, under heavy machine-gun fire to cut a gap in the enemy wire for his platoon to get through. Covered by the fire of the Lewis gunners, the three raiding platoons then pushed through the gap. Working south and up the steeper slope near the farm, they successfully cleared the outpost positions and then the farm buildings and cellars with rifles and grenades, seizing two light machine guns in the process. One of these was captured by Captain Murphy who charged it single-handed and shot two of the section manning it.

The enemy had managed to get off a flare to signal their difficulty and, with a barrage expected, the raiders prepared to move back to their own lines. The raid had taken less than an hour. It accounted for one German soldier captured and about thirty others killed. Having achieved their aim, the raiders moved quickly north-east across no-man's-land to the area in front of C Company. As they left the German trenches the enemy laid down machine-gun fire from the south-west. An artillery barrage in no-man's-land soon followed. Both caused a number of casualties including the carrier of one of the captured machine guns, which was lost. In front of C Company's position at Miller Trench, lanes had been cut in the wire and members of that company were waiting to guide the raiders back into the safety of the trenches.

At this stage it was noticed that Second Lieutenants McFarland and Ratcliffe and four or five of the men had not returned (unusually, the war diary is not clear; both numbers are reported in different places). A party was sent back to look for them but they were not found and it was presumed that they had been killed or taken prisoner. A patrol went out the following night to try and locate these men but none was found. Some days later it was rumoured that Second Lieutenant McFarland's body had been found and buried by the 9th Royal Inniskilling Fusiliers. A later, contradictory report from Lance Corporal D Clarke MM indicated that McFarland was named on a German document as having been captured during the raid. This snapshot indicates the difficulty in determining the fate of those missing in such operations. In fact five of the six (or seven) missing men were killed in the attack: Second Lieutenants McFarland and Ratcliffe, Corporal Charles James Threadgold and Privates William Frederick Christy Arthur and William Herbert Lawrence. Eleven men were slightly wounded, including Private William Francey. The operation was

Sergeant John Adams MM, who earned a Bar to his Military Medal during the Shoddy Farm raid.

a success, however, and the bravery of the raiders was rewarded with an MC for Captain J J Murphy (his second), and Second Lieutenant T C Leahy. Sergeant J Lockhart was awarded a DCM for his gallantry in leading a bombing party. MMs were awarded to Sergeant J Adams (his second), Sergeant R Johnston and Private E Pye.

The days following the attack were relatively quiet. Platoon-sized patrols went out on two successive nights to try and find the missing officers and men but they were unsuccessful. On the second night after the patrol returned, the 9th Royal Irish Fusiliers completed its relief with 9th Royal Inniskilling Fusiliers, and 108th Brigade went into divisional reserve at Spotterke, west of Mont Noir. The camp into which it now moved was under enemy observation and no movement was allowed in daylight, which, given the time of year, left about six hours during which the whole battalion was engaged in work parties on the Berthen defences. Charlie Honeysett, who had returned to the 9th Royal Irish Fusiliers after a period in hospital, described one of these work parties in some detail:

'Working parties from 8.30pm to 3.30am. There is a march up to 1½ km behind line. Needless to say there is much swinging of lead in order to avoid this little caper. We are at Mont des Cats each night at 8.30. We fall in just when the dugout looks cozy. Guns in the next field barrage away and plug shells into Armentieres. We move in artillery formation passing over Mont des Cats. From there to Berthen the road is dangerous as Gerry plugs shells along and around it. It makes one sad as one passes through deserted village squares where once everyone was busy farmers with their vegetables, gossiping over the local scandal... We drop into the separate trench - a shallow ditch with stinking water at the bottom - like a sewer animal, and crouch down. What a life. Corporal Campbell later on called my name along with two other fellows... He took us to a stinking little dugout and put us on our turns, two hours on and four hours off. There was one flare to send for cloud gas and another to send if gas shells came over. We found we were on a better thing than our mates. For one thing we could have four hours sleep during the night or burn a candle and smoke. Things the others couldn't do.'

Over the next few days enemy artillery activity increased; in one attack the medical tent was hit causing a number of casualties, including Private John William Marshall MM, who was killed, and Private Thomas Spence, who was wounded. On 27 July the men were finally moved in small groups to a new billeting area farther west on Mont des Cats out of view of the enemy. Here everyone was accommodated in various dugouts, houses and tents. This interval at Mont des Cats lasted until the end of the first week in August. Most days were taken up by training at company level in the morning and range-work, kit inspections and specialist training in the afternoon. At night, however, the obligatory work parties continued and most of these involved company groups working in deteriorating weather on the defences at Berthen. As Charlie Honeysett described, these activities were never without risk. In the period from the raid at Shody Farm until the end of July twenty men were wounded. Two more were wounded on 1 August and on the night of 2 August Corporal J R Seymour and Private J E Riddell were killed by shellfire and four men were wounded, of whom Private Samuel Speers died of his wounds the next day.

Regimental Sergeant Major G A Williams MM, later in life

At the end of July the strength of the 9th Royal Irish Fusiliers had increased to thirty-five officers and 973 other ranks. This was a critical time for the Battalion that required continuity, but a lynch pin of the 9th Royal Irish Fusiliers since its earliest days was lost with the departure of the Regimental Sergeant Major, Charles Turner. He was posted to the depot as Regimental Sergeant Major before moving on to the 3rd (Reserve) Battalion in October where he remained until discharged at the end of 1919. He was replaced briefly by Henry Hickie, formerly a regular soldier with 2nd Battalion, The Lancashire Fusiliers, who had been Regimental Sergeant Major of 8th (Service) Battalion, The Royal Irish Rifles. Later in August Company Sergeant Major George Williams joined the 9th Royal Irish Fusiliers from the 1st Battalion on the request of the Commanding Officer. George Williams was born in Newport in September 1884. He had enlisted into Princess Victoria's (Royal Irish Fusiliers) in 1906 and joined the 1st Battalion. By trade he was a saddler and he became the Battalion Saddler Sergeant. Having requested to serve in a rifle company and after a period as an instructor with the 3rd (Reserve) Battalion and at Portobello Barracks, Dublin, he rejoined the 1st Battalion in late 1917. During the retreat from St Quentin he acted as Company Sergeant Major and earned a Military Medal. He became the last Regimental Sergeant Major of the 9th Royal Irish Fusiliers on 18 September 1918.

On 8 August, as the British Fourth Army and the French *1re Armée* advanced far to the south at Amiens, 108th Brigade moved into the line again and the 9th Royal Irish Fusiliers relieved 2nd Royal Inniskilling Fusiliers of 109th Brigade in the sub-sector at Meulenhouck. Although one casualty was incurred due to enemy shelling, the relief went well and the rest of the night was quiet. The next forty-eight hours in the trenches were very active and began with an enemy aircraft attacking one of the trenches with machine-gun fire. The fine weather meant that there was much aerial activity during the day and aircraft from both sides were seen regularly over the line, spotting for artillery or attempting to down the enemy machines involved in similar activity.

Enemy machine-gunners were very busy at night and the area was regularly swept with fire, which succeeded in making patrolling very difficult. Two patrols managed to get out in the early hours of 9 August, however, but both were detected by the enemy. The first, from the front right company, was fired upon when just forward of the Royal Irish Fusiliers' wire and forced to withdraw. The second, led by Second Lieutenant J Boyd, was about 700 yards forward of the left-hand company when it was bombed from a house held by the enemy and two men were wounded, one of whom was Lance Corporal Percival Henry Reid. On the following night an enemy patrol at the Royal Irish Fusiliers' wire was driven off and thc 9th Royal Irish Fusiliers sent out four patrols of its own. Those led by Captain Benson and Second Lieutenant Behannah, the latter having just joined the

Battalion, conducted a reconnaissance of Shoddy Farm, which had been re-occupied by the enemy after the raid a few weeks before and which was to be attacked again. Both patrols successfully avoided contact with the enemy and Second Lieutenant Behannah estimated that the farm's garrison was about forty men. On the left of the sector a patrol led by Lieutenant A L Dobbyn managed to get into the German line, but the enemy had moved out leaving behind only a greatcoat and a pack. The fourth patrol, led by Second Lieutenant Burrowes, got to a series of shell holes that had been occupied and consolidated by the enemy near to the farm from where Second Lieutenant Boyd's patrol had been bombed. The Royal Irish Fusiliers mounted a short and aggressive attack on this post and after a short fight withdrew safely to its own trenches.

Working on the information gained on the reconnaissance of Shoddy Farm and with a plan based on the experience of the previous attack, thirty-two men from C Company, led by Captain Benson and Second Lieutenant Behannah, attempted to raid the farm again on the night of Sunday 11/Monday 12 August. This time it was unsuccessful. The raiders crawled to within thirty yards of the ruined farmhouse and saw several of the enemy close by. The position was very strongly held and Captain Benson realised that an attack would be folly. He ordered the men to pass the word to retire by the same route that they had used previously but suddenly an enemy patrol attacked the rear of the party. After throwing a volley of hand grenades, the German infantry charged. Captain Benson rushed to the rear but he received a blow on the head that knocked him out. A desperate hand-to-hand struggle ensued and casualties were inflicted on both sides, but the raiders managed to withdraw eventually to their trenches. Two men were killed, Privates William Brown and Andrew Pepper, and Lance Corporal James Taggart and one other man were wounded. Meanwhile, out in no-man's-land Captain Benson lay stunned throughout the night. When he regained consciousness after daybreak he crawled to a shell hole to await night-fall and the opportunity to return to his own line. His war ended when a German machine-gunner sprang up, threatened him with a revolver and took him prisoner.

The actions of the aircraft overhead were of great interest to the men in the trenches. Everyone witnessed a fascinating spectacle on the evening of 14 August when two enemy aircraft crossed the line and were attacked by four British machines. One German aircraft fled for home and the other surrendered, indicating this by firing a red flare, after which he was escorted to the local aerodrome.

Meanwhile in the forty-eight hours after the aborted raid on Shoddy Farm everything had been very quiet; patrols mounted during the short nights had returned without result. The two patrols that went out on 14 August proved more eventful. At dawn that morning a deserter had come over to the 1st Royal Irish Fusiliers, which had moved into the line on the left of the 9th Royal Irish Fusiliers on 12 August, and provided valuable information as to the dispositions of the enemy. In order to confirm this, a joint patrol was mounted by both battalions. This small patrol comprised Lieutenant J I Smith (who had been posted from the 9th to the 1st Battalion in June) Sergeant J Downey, also of the 1st Battalion, and Lieutenant Dobbyn of the 9th Royal Irish Fusiliers. In broad daylight they crawled out across no-man's-land on the boundary between the two units and at 5.15pm got to a point in the enemy line near that entered by Lieutenant Dobbyn a few nights before. Lieutenant Dobbyn showed the other two the gap in the wire and they entered the enemy trenches where they killed one German soldier, wounded a second and forced six others to flee. Forced to retire by heavy machine-gun fire, the small party withdrew and kept up a running fight until the gun had ceased firing. They then quickly re-entered the German trench and captured the wounded man. This provided confirmation that the enemy facing the Battalion were from *Infanterie-Regiment Nr 118* of *58. Infanterie-Division.* For this escapade Lieutenants Dobbyn and Smith were awarded the MC, and Sergeant Downey the DCM.

A second patrol, led by Second Lieutenant C A Ross, was less successful. It was seen by the enemy and engaged with accurate machine-gun fire and bombs that wounded three men before the patrol was able to withdraw. That night was spent under a heavy artillery duel and in the morning part of the 9th Royal Irish Fusiliers' line suffered forty-three shells in half an hour. After this the next thirty-six hours were quiet and the relief by 2nd Royal Irish Rifles was without incident. The 9th Royal Irish Fusiliers moved back to brigade reserve at Mont Noir. As usual, work parties began immediately conducting salvage over the ground recently captured near Berthen. Although enemy artillery was active around Mont Noir, the 9th Royal Irish Fusiliers was not involved in any significant activity over the next week.

On the right flank 9th (Scottish) Division advanced again on 18 August and was successful in capturing the ridge south-east of Meteren. It was now up to the Ulster Division to improve upon its position. Orders for a series of attacks were finally received on 21 August and the next day 107th Brigade, led by 15th Royal Irish Rifles, advanced on Mural and Wirral Farms on the right of the Ulster Division's line. The second phase was an attack by 108th Brigade between Bailleul and Mont Noir, south-east from Meulenhouck. The preparations were a manpower-intensive process. The 9th Royal Irish Fusiliers was lucky not to suffer heavy casualties when its work was interrupted by a heavy barrage of shells of various calibres, including gas, at 11.30pm on 22 August when the enemy attempted a counter-attack against Mural Farm. The attack was successfully repulsed. The only injury recorded was to Private Thomas Zebedee, who fell and broke his leg while moving into the line.

On 23 August everyone was given his final instructions for the attack to come, and final preparations were made. At 8.30pm the Royal Irish Fusiliers moved into the line in the left sub-sector at Meulenhouck. The plan called for the 9th Royal Irish Fusiliers to attack on the right with 1st Royal Irish Fusiliers providing B Company (Captain H Haughey) and two platoons from A Company (Captain R W Kingham MC) on the left. During the night parties went forward to cut gaps in the wire to ease the forward passage of the attacking companies. Those who were to attack waited expectantly throughout a quiet night until 2.30am when the enemy opened the shelling for an hour against the area to the left of the Royal Irish Fusiliers. By 3.00am the attacking troops were in their assembly areas concealed from enemy air reconnaissance by coconut matting. The waiting companies in the forward trenches were organised with A Company (Captain G H Robinson) on the left, B Company (Captain J J Murphy MC DCM) in the centre, D Company (Captain R H Lindsay) on the right and C Company (temporarily commanded by Lieutenant E W Reynolds) in reserve. The men from the two companies of the 1st Battalion were astride the Bailleul/Mont Noir Road. The operation was commanded by Lieutenant Colonel Forde. The morning of 24 August was dull and wet. At 6.45am the Royal Irish Fusiliers left their trenches and crawled through the gaps cut in the wire into the corn field that was no-man's-land. The British barrage opened at 7.00am with machine guns and trench mortars, and a minute later the artillery joined in. When the artillery barrage began, the companies attacked, charging forward in two waves into the German line. The wire here was weak and the Royal Irish Fusiliers had no difficulty in entering the rudimentary German defences, where all those showing resistance were shot and bayoneted. After a few minutes the enemy signalled for support and the German guns fired. The fire fell first upon the 1st Battalion and then swept across the 9th, the effect of which was added to by a number of shells from the Ulster Division's own guns that fell short. Damp signal rockets prevented the Royal Irish Fusiliers calling for an adjustment in range.

This envelope was addressed in cartoon style by Private (later Corporal) Bertie Dunseith. The incident to which it refers is unidentified.

The enemy, however, was taken by surprise and seemed more inclined to run than fight, allowing A and D Companies to overrun their objectives. In the centre B Company had a harder fight. Here Sergeant W J McClean, having recovered from the wound he received in March, was now acting as Company Sergeant Major. During the attack he got round the flank of a machine gun that was causing casualties and put the gun out of action, killing four of the enemy in the process. This was one of eleven machine guns captured by the Royal Irish Fusiliers that day. Meanwhile, A Company had secured its objective by 7.20am, and by 8.00am all of the objectives had been taken. C Company, following behind the lead companies, mopped up then helped with the consolidation before three platoons went back to the old front line to act as a reserve, with the fourth remaining forward with B Company.

The trenches were well sited for the attacking troops to defend and consolidation was quick. By 8.30am wire had been put up in front of the position and Lewis gun sections were pushed forward to disrupt local counter-attacks. Captain Robinson, commanding A Company, had been wounded during the attack, but remained forward until the whole company had dug in on the objective; he was finally ordered to have his wound dressed. Although many of the enemy retired quickly, forty-eight were captured and about seventy killed in this short action. At 10.00am the supporting artillery stopped firing, as did the enemy artillery. This lull allowed a contact aircraft to observe the progress along the front and another aircraft dropped boxes of ammunition onto the Royal Irish Fusiliers' new position—a new and imaginative, if somewhat limited, method of re-supply.

Corporal Bertie Dunseith

In the afternoon the enemy prepared to counter-attack and were shelled by the Ulster Division's artillery. In response, enemy aircraft flew over the line and signalled their artillery, which resulted in an increase in the enemy fire. At 6.30pm the enemy laid down a smoke barrage but were seen massing for a counter-attack. The signal rockets calling for artillery support and fired by the Royal Irish Fusiliers' forward companies were not seen. All was not lost, however, as one of the British aircraft managed to signal the guns, and Private W Simons ran through a severe artillery barrage to the battalion headquarters, which then also called for fire. The artillery responded, and with the support of two Lewis guns sited by Acting Company Sergeant Major McClean, the attack was broken. For the relatively inexperienced men of the 9th Battalion this was a successful and courageous action. Later that night 108th Brigade was relieved by 109th Brigade and 9th Royal Irish Fusiliers handed over the new line at 11.00pm to 2nd Royal Inniskilling Fusiliers and moved back into divisional reserve at Mont des Cats.

The surprise achieved by the attack and the close proximity of the two battalions' aid posts contributed to relatively low casualties:

	Officers	Other Ranks*
Killed in Action	-	9
Died of Wounds	-	2
Wounded	4	47
Total	4	58

*The war diary records five other ranks killed and fifty-three wounded.

In addition to Captain Robinson, three officers were wounded: Second Lieutenant Behennah was hit by a shrapnel bullet behind the right shoulder; Second Lieutenant Davies, having just recovered from the wounds he received in March, was buried by a shell in a dug-out causing injury to his back and head, and Lieutenant Tees, who had just joined the Battalion, was wounded by shell fragments. None of these three subalterns saw service with the 9th Royal Irish Fusiliers again. Eleven men were killed in action or died of wounds: Sergeant W G W Irwin, Corporals W Smyth and A G Bailey, Lance Corporal A Camlin and Privates F E Browning, W Clifton, J Kelly, W W Russell, P Schwenk, F Webb and G Wilson. Forty-seven men were wounded, including Corporals W J Hunter and William Irving and Private T S Holt. The background of those killed during this attack indicates the mix of soldiers now serving in the 9th Royal Irish Fusiliers. With the exception of Lance Corporal Camlin, all of the fatal casualties had joined from other units and only Lance Corporal Camlin and Sergeant Irwin were Irish. The 1st Battalion also suffered relatively few casualties with two officers and seven men killed, one man missing and thirty-seven wounded. For their gallantry during the attack, Captain Robinson was awarded the MC and Company Sergeant Major McClean and Private Simons earned the DCM. Lance Corporals D Clarke and J Sharp and Privates J Coulter, D Crichton, J Crilly, J Paul, A Peers and T Scott earned the MM.

Sunday 25 August was spent cleaning up. Church services were held in the afternoon and Lieutenant Colonel Kelly returned to the 9th Royal Irish Fusiliers and resumed command. Life over the next week was for many a round of training during the day and relaxing in the evening, although company-sized work parties were provided most nights. Most involved hard labour, digging and deepening the communication trench running forward from Meulenhouck and, as usual, such work carried a degree of risk. One particularly unpleasant enemy attack involved the use of gas shells that injured several men.

Finally, on 29 August the 9th Royal Irish Fusiliers was relieved by 15th (Service) Battalion, The Sherwood Foresters (Nottinghamshire and Derbyshire Regiment) (Nottingham) and moved into Corps Reserve at St Sylvestre Capelle, five miles to the rear. It had been planned that the Brigade would spend a fortnight out of the line resting and training. The detail of this had been planned and briefed to everyone. It was not to be the case. The 9th (Scottish) Division on the right flank had already been relieved by 31st Division and its patrols found that the enemy had withdrawn. The Ulster Division was ordered to move back to the front immediately and at 7.00pm on 30 August the 9th Royal Irish Fusiliers moved by light railway to a station near Mont des Cats and then on foot to their billets, relieving the battalion which had so recently replaced them. The next day the Royal Irish Fusiliers was back in the line at Meulenhouck, the battalion headquarters at Sammy Farm, in support as 109th Brigade resumed the advance.

Company Sergeant Major W J McClean DCM. He is pictured in the uniform of the Royal Ulster Constabulary, with which he served for six years before being forced to retire due to the impact of his wounds.

The first day of the new month was spent making shelters, and at dusk the 9th Royal Irish Fusiliers relieved the 1st Battalion at Cyprian Farm, nearly 4,000 yards forward of the old front line. The battalion headquarters was nearby on the railway. For the next two days the 9th Royal Irish Fusiliers would be in support to the other two battalions of 108th Brigade. Kemmel Hill had been recaptured and in the Ulster Division's area 109th Brigade had followed the withdrawing enemy to a line about 500 yards from the western edge of Neuve Eglise. 108th Brigade received orders to pass through and continue the attack, and advanced to the outskirts of the ruined village with little interference.

At dawn on 2 September an attack was launched by the Ulster Division on a front of just over one mile, aiming to secure a line between Red Lodge, in Ploegsteert Wood, and South Midland Farm on the Wulverghem/Messines Road. 108th Brigade attacked Neuve Eglise. This was a tough task against the old British front line, but by nightfall 12th Royal Irish Rifles had captured Neuve Eglise, and Wulverghem had fallen to 30th Division. The front line now extended south past the eastern edge of Neuve Eglise, and the leading battalions had advanced to the old GHQ Line east of the village, which was secured by 6.40am the following morning.

After very little rest the leading battalions pushed on along the River Douve valley. The tough fighting against isolated machine-gun posts continued until dusk on 3 September when the two battalions had secured a line from L'Alouette, a mile east of Neuve Eglise, to La Plus Douve Farm. This area was well known to the few originals of 108th Brigade who were now left and who had spent many months here in late 1916 and early 1917.

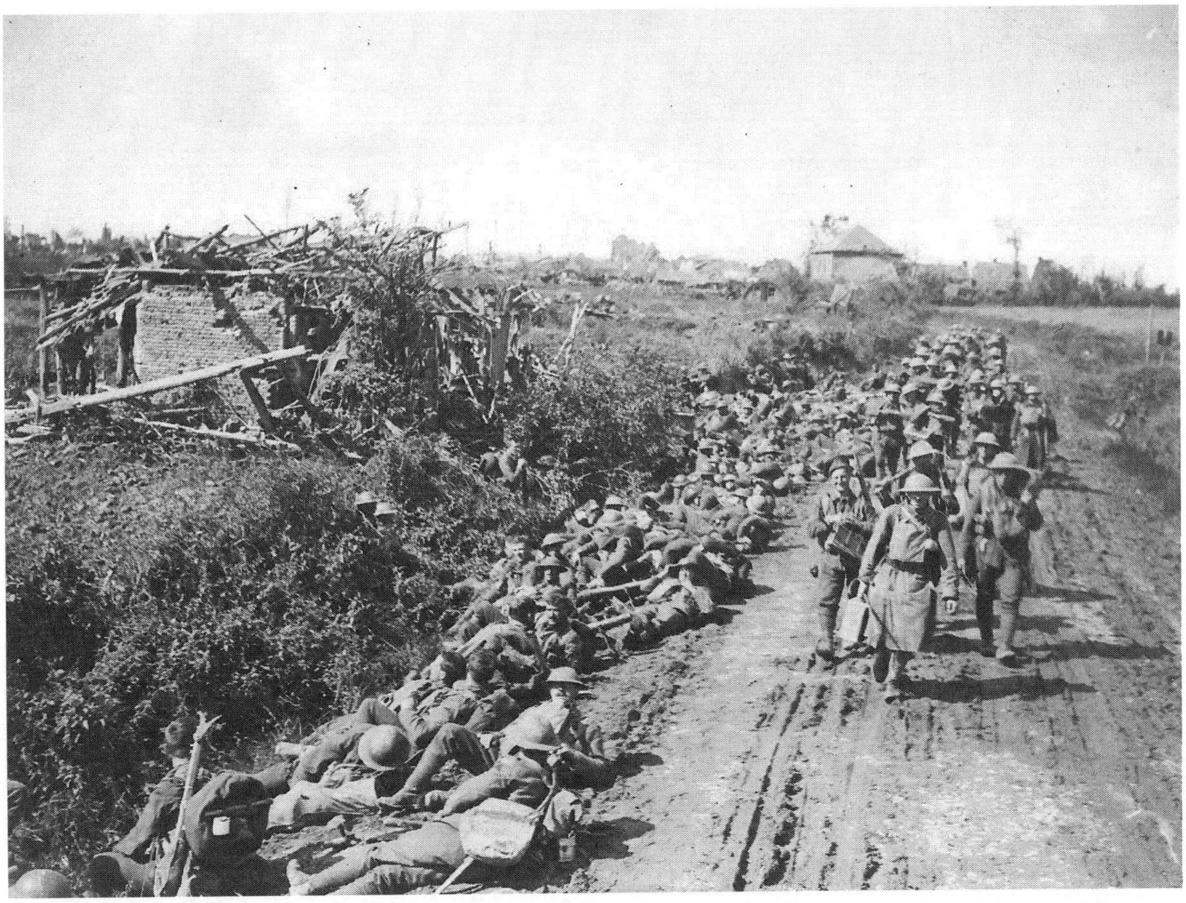

Royal Inniskilling Fusiliers of 109th Brigade advancing along the road from Bailleul to Neuve Eglise, 1 September 1918. © IWM (Q 7023)

Heavy machine-gun fire from the vital high ground at Hill 63 north of Ploegsteert Wood had hindered the advance of 108th Brigade. It was clear that it had to be captured to secure the right flank of any advance over the Ploegsteert/Messines Road. This task fell to the 29th Division with 9th Royal Irish Fusiliers in support on the left. 29th Division's plan was received by 108th Brigade as 9th Royal Irish Fusiliers had begun its move forward to relieve the other two battalions of 108th Brigade. By 11.30pm the brigade headquarters had passed on its orders by telephone for 9th Royal Irish Fusiliers to attack the following morning. The relief of 1st Royal Irish Fusiliers and 12th Royal Irish Rifles was complete by 12.40am and the forward positions were occupied by all four companies in line, with A on the right to D on the left.

The plan required the 9th Royal Irish Fusiliers to attack between the River Douve and the Wulverghem/Messines Road as 29th Division advanced on Hill 63. On the left of the Royal Irish Fusiliers, the brigade from 30th Division north of the road would send patrols forward onto the Messines Ridge. During the night Lieutenant Colonel Kelly and his officers planned the attack. A preparatory artillery barrage was arranged for 8.30am that would suppress the enemy positions north-east of La Plus Douve Farm as far forward as Hanbury Support South. First, A Company was ordered to provide protection on the right flank by achieving a line between White Gates and La Plus Douve Farm in conjunction with 88th Brigade of 29th Division on its right. On completion of the attack, the company was then to move forward to the southern portion of King Edward Trench at Stinking Farm. In the centre, C and D Companies (the left-centre and left companies respectively) were to attack between the river and the road, with Calgary Avenue as the boundary between them. B Company, in a support role, was to occupy the trenches to the south of South Midland Farm. Once the attack began, battalion headquarters would move forward to a position on the road at St Quentin Cabaret.

Royal Inniskilling Fusiliers of 109th Brigade west of Neuve Eglise, 1 September 1918.
© IWM (Q 7022)

At about 8.00am on the morning of 4 September D Company moved off, followed a few minutes later by C Company. Initially, 29th Division was successful in its attack which made the job of the Royal Irish Fusiliers easier. The enemy line was relatively thinly held, comprising some thick wire and a number of well-sited, mutually-supporting, machine-gun positions. The attack went well, allowing the 9th Royal Irish Fusiliers to make ground quickly on a wide front. Two of the machine-gun positions were put out of action by Lance Corporal Gracey who, having taken command after his section commander was wounded, led a charge on the two enemy positions. Although wounded himself, he later assisted the stretcher-bearers in bringing in the wounded under heavy machine-gun fire.

Due to the very wide frontage, D Company's platoons were split—one remained on the road but the other three lost direction and moved to their right. Having passed between

Stinking Farm and Gooseberry Farm, they eventually ended up behind C Company in Winter Trench. Seeing the gap on the left, Lieutenant Colonel Kelly ordered the two supporting platoons of C Company to move into this gap, and just before noon the 9th Royal Irish Fusiliers' objectives had been captured. Before the Battalion could be reorganised into a stronger position, however, 88th Brigade on the right was forced to retire. This left the 9th Royal Irish Fusiliers in an awkward situation. As the enemy advanced its machine guns on both flanks, the Battalion was forced to withdraw. Some men on the right were cut off and captured.

To the rear the 1st Battalion had been ordered farther forward, and at 4.00pm its D Company had been moved to fill the gap on the right flank between White Gates and La Plus Douve Farm. The left of the Royal Irish Fusiliers' new line was established from the Wulverghem/Messines Road (the boundary with 30th Division) south behind Bristol Castle to the river, the portion held by C and B Companies. A Company, meanwhile, held the line along a breastwork trench from La Plus Douve Farm south to the position held by D Company of the 1st Battalion forward of White Gates. This left a gap between B and A Companies just south of the river. D Company, 9th Royal Irish Fusiliers was moved into support slightly farther west along the road running north from La Plus Douve Farm. The gap along the river provided the enemy with an obvious route for a counter-attack.

At 4.15pm, after a preliminary artillery barrage, a German counter-attack was launched along Well Lane, an old British light railway line, but the Lewis-gunners and heavy rifle fire drove the enemy back with heavy casualties. With the enemy attack halted, the 9th Royal Irish Fusiliers consolidated as best it could and waited for darkness under machine gun and sniper fire. Both had been heavy all day, as had been the artillery fire, although the latter was confined to the area around St Quentin Cabaret. The position was strengthened further when, at 7.00pm, C Company of the 1st Battalion commanded by Lieutenant J J Mitchie, was ordered forward to fill the gap between A and B Companies near La Plus Douve Farm. On the right, D Company from the 1st Battalion was ordered to remain forward and 9th Royal Irish Fusiliers was reinforced with two sections from the Division's Machine Gun Battalion. At dusk strong patrols were sent out on the left to advance the line behind Bristol Castle, but they were unable to make headway against the intense machine-gun fire. The enemy also sent out a number of patrols and the men in the forward positions heard work being carried out on the German trenches and breastworks. The old and damaged trenches occupied by the Royal Irish Fusiliers did not provide much shelter for the tired men as they waited for their next attack in heavy rain that fell throughout the night.

Private John Wakefield, from London. Wounded 4 September 1918.

Orders for the next phase of the attack were received at 2.00am. There were only three hours to prepare before the attack began at 5.00am on 5 September. The plan called for two platoons from each of B and C Companies and two companies (B and D) from the 1st Battalion to attack towards Hanbury Support North and Stinking Farm and on a line down to Irish Farm. The 1st Royal Irish Fusiliers' companies were held up by booby-trapped wire near La Plus Douve Farm and heavy machine-gun fire. They did not get to the start line and were unable to attack. For the 9th Royal Irish Fusiliers' companies the fighting was hard and confused, not helped by the dismal weather. On the right the platoons from B Company did not make any significant progress due to being held up by wire, and they were forced to retire. C Company, meanwhile, got into King Edward Trench but, being unsupported on both flanks, was only able to hold out for an hour before being forced to move back to the jumping-off trench just after 9.30am. The enemy had used artillery only against the area around St Quentin Cabaret but the machine-gun fire, active due to the light British supporting barrage, was very heavy.

The remainder of the day, which was relatively quiet, was spent mainly watching and waiting in the steadily falling rain, although a strong patrol got to within 100 yards of Stinking Farm. It was engaged by machine-gun fire and forced to withdraw. That night, after another patrol against Stinking Farm had met the same fate, the 9th Royal Irish Fusiliers and the supporting company from the 1st Battalion in the centre of the position were relieved by 2nd Royal Irish Rifles and D Company of 1st Royal Irish Rifles from 107th Brigade. This was a torturous process inhibited by a very heavy barrage of German gas shells that caused even more casualties before 108th Brigade finally moved back over bad roads into the divisional support line at Cyprian Farm. The exhausted, wet and hungry men of the 9th Royal Irish Fusiliers eventually reached their new billets at 4.30am. Notwithstanding the minor reverses, the attack had gone well and the three brigades had been well supported by the Ulster Division's artillery, machine guns, engineers and dressing stations.

In forty-eight hours the 9th Royal Irish Fusiliers had made good gains in ground and had captured a number of prisoners, an anti-tank rifle, a trench mortar and three machine guns (including a British Vickers being used by the enemy), but at a cost. The casualties sustained on 4 and 5 September were recorded in the 9th Royal Irish Fusiliers' war diary and, again, demand re-examination. The war diary records four officers wounded, twenty other ranks killed in action, 103 wounded and twenty missing. The officer casualties are known: four were wounded. It is now known that thirty other ranks were killed in action or died of wounds in the days after the action. Fifteen men have been identified as having been wounded. Only one prisoner of war from this period has been identified: Corporal Edward Gear. Two assumptions may be made about the other casualties. The first is that the 9th Royal Irish Fusiliers' war diary is accurate (given previous analysis of casualties, this is a fair assumption) and the second is that, due to the nature of the fighting and the ability to recover the bodies of the dead and wounded, those recorded as missing may be assumed to have been captured. The final casualty figures for the actions on 4 and 5 September are:

	Officers	Other Ranks	
Killed in Action	-	25	
Died of Wounds	-	5	
Identified Wounded	4	15	
Believed Wounded		78	*
Identified Captured	-	1	
Believed Captured		19	*
Total	4	143	

*Estimated casualties based on war diary totals.

The four officers wounded were: Captain Murphy, who was slightly injured; Lieutenants A G F Bell and S Lyons (both attached from The Royal Inniskilling Fusiliers), who were shot and badly wounded. Bell, the brother of Captain E N F Bell VC, was unfortunate to be wounded very near to where he had been wounded in 1916, again being hit in the right forearm. Second Lieutenant W Laird MM, commissioned into Princess Victoria's (Royal Irish Fusiliers) from The Royal Inniskilling Fusiliers, was also injured. These latter three officers had only been with the 9th Royal Irish Fusiliers for a few weeks and did not serve with the Battalion again. The senior non-commissioned officers killed in this action were: Company Quartermaster Sergeant Charles Ingledew and Sergeants Robert John Morton, Dennis Roddy and Thomas Scott MM.

Private James Kelly, from Belfast. Died of wounds 5 September 1918.

Sergeant Thomas Scott MM, from Tynan. Killed in action 4 September 1918.

Colour Sergeant Charles Ingledew, from Belfast. Killed in action 5 September 1918.

Private Samuel Chambers, from Darkley, County Armagh. Killed in action 5 September 1918.

Sergeant Dennis Roddy, from Londonderry. Killed in action 4 September 1918.

Lance Corporal Ingram Dick MM. He also earned the Belgian *Croix de Guerre*. Unemployed after the war, he drowned in an accident while looking for work aboard ships at Queen's Quay, Belfast, in 1919.

The gallantry of the officers and men in this hard-fought battle was recognised subsequently with a number of awards. Second Lieutenants J Bryson and H C Burrowes were both awarded the MC for the manner in which they handled their platoons during the attack, and Lance Corporal J Gracey earned a DCM for his actions. The MM was awarded to Corporals B Atkins, J E Long and H G Williams, Lance Corporals R Gillanders and L Leburn.

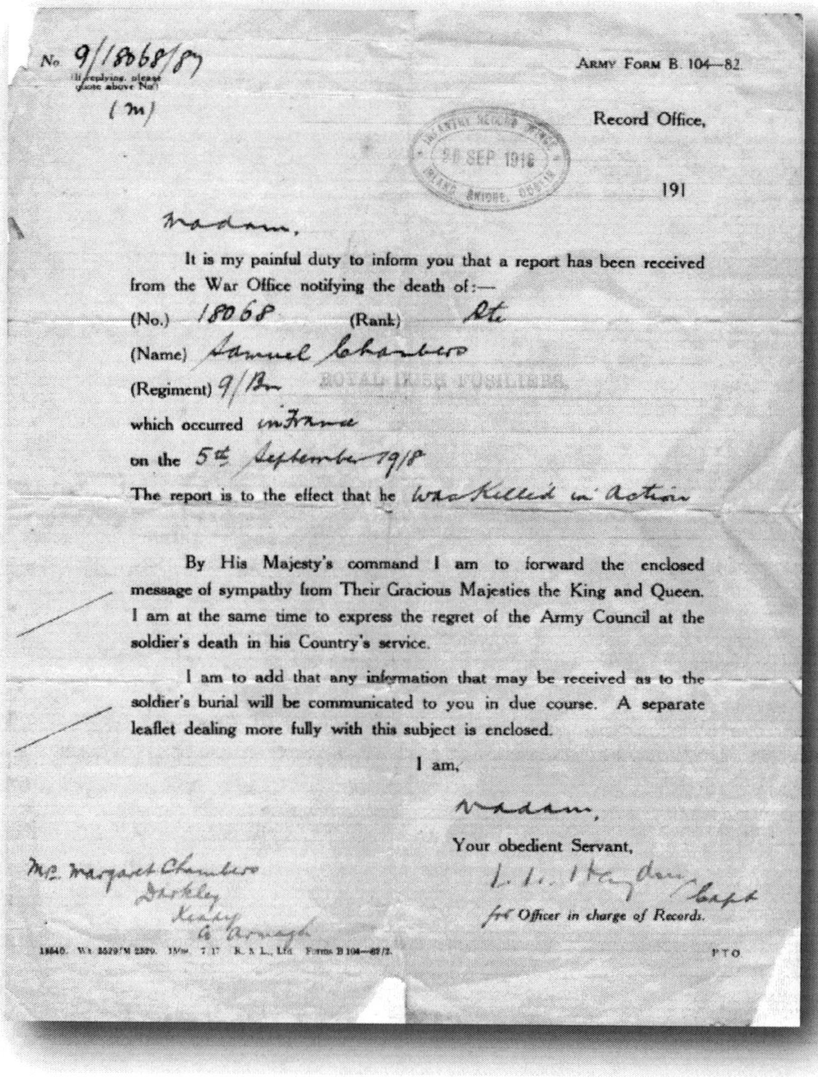

No 9/18068/87
(If replying, please quote above No.)
(m)

ARMY FORM B. 104—82.

Record Office,

191

Madam,

It is my painful duty to inform you that a report has been received from the War Office notifying the death of:—

(No.) 18068 (Rank) Pte

(Name) Samuel Chambers

(Regiment) 9/Bn ROYAL IRISH FUSILIERS.

which occurred in France

on the 5th September 1918

The report is to the effect that he was Killed in Action

By His Majesty's command I am to forward the enclosed message of sympathy from Their Gracious Majesties the King and Queen. I am at the same time to express the regret of the Army Council at the soldier's death in his Country's service.

I am to add that any information that may be received as to the soldier's burial will be communicated to you in due course. A separate leaflet dealing more fully with this subject is enclosed.

I am,

Madam,

Your obedient Servant,

L. L. Hayden Capt

for Officer in charge of Records.

Mrs. Margaret Chambers
Darkley
Keady
Co. Armagh

PTO

Army Form B104-82.

The death of an officer was notified to his next of kin by telegram. The next of kin of other ranks was informed by post. The letter contained Army Form B104-82. In this case it informs the mother of Private Samuel Chambers that he was killed in action on 5 September 1918.

Throughout the next two days, in the continuing cold and wet weather, the Ulster Division's advance was continued by 107th Brigade. In the rear, the 9th Royal Irish Fusiliers made the poor billets habitable and generally cleaned up after their period in the line, with most men managing to get a complete change of clothing. On Saturday 8 September the 9th Royal Irish Fusiliers marched forward again into a reserve position near Berthen. After a church parade on Sunday the Battalion was visited by the Corps Commander. During the following week, as the troops of 109th Brigade consolidated the new positions in the lee of the Messines ridge, 108th Brigade conducted unit level training until everyone was moved forward on 16 September, when the 9th Royal Irish Fusiliers took over the recently captured Asylum at Bailleul. During this period Lieutenant Colonel Forde was wounded by shellfire and evacuated. He had reverted to Second-in-Command when Lieutenant Colonel Kelly returned and now Major Tamplin took over as Second-in-Command again. This period of rest and training continued at Terdegem and Watou to the west of Poperinghe and every effort was made to prepare the 9th Royal Irish Fusiliers for the demands of the imminent push to the east.

Endnotes, Chapter 8

1 In his history of the Ulster Division, Cyril Falls describes the terrible conditions at Wieltje:

> *'Wieltje dugouts! Who that saw it will forget that abominable mine with its 'town major', its thirteen entrances, the water that flowed down its passages and poured down its walls, its smells, its sickly atmosphere, its huge population of men – and of rats? From behind sack-curtained doorways the coughing and groaning of men in uneasy slumber mingled with the click of typewriters.'*

The dugouts were also described by Captain E A Godson MC when he was 108th Brigade Intelligence Officer:

> *'A word about this dugout, one of the prides of the RE mining, originally initiated by the Germans. It ran for about 300 yards underground, all told, under the demolished village. It had 13 entrances and 40 feet of headcover, dirty black drops of water dripping everywhere, no room to stand upright and on the whole an abominable den. Further, the enemy, from the rim of hills and observation posts, watched every entrance, and spasmodically took appropriate action.'*

2 Major General Clifford Coffin VC, CB, DSO*. Born on 10 February 1870 at Blackheath. Commissioned into The Corps of Royal Engineers from RMA Woolwich on 17 February 1888. Served in South Africa at the Relief of Kimberley, Operations in the Orange Free State February - May 1900, Operations in the Transvaal May - June 1900 and July - 29 November 1900, Operations in Cape Colony, north of Orange River, Operations in the Transvaal December 1900, March - July 1901 & October 1901 - May 1902, Operations in Orange River Colony September 1901, Operations in Cape Colony January - February 1901 and August 1901. Mentioned in Despatches. Queen's South Africa Medal with 4 clasps, King's South Africa Medal with clasps 'South Africa 1901' and 'South Africa 1902'. Served as a Lieutenant Colonel RE in 1914 and then as a Brigade Commander. DSO. Mentioned in Despatches three times, Brevet Colonel. As a Brigade Commander he earned a VC for his actions at Ypres on 31 July 1917: '*For most conspicuous bravery and devotion to duty. When his command was held up in an attack owing to heavy machine gun and rifle fire from front and right flank, and was establishing itself in a forward shell-hole line, he went forward and made an inspection of his front posts. Though under the heaviest fire from both machine guns and rifles, and in full view of the enemy, he showed an utter disregard of personal danger, walking quietly from shell-hole to shell-hole, giving advice generally and cheering the men by his presence. His very gallant conduct had the greatest effect on all ranks, and it was largely owing to his personal courage and example that the shell hole line was held in spite of the very heaviest fire. Throughout the day his calm courage and cheerfulness exercised the greatest influence over all with whom he came into contact, and it was generally agreed that Brigadier-General Coffin's splendid example saved the situation, and had it not been for his action the line would certainly have been driven back.*' Awarded a bar to the DSO during the events of March 1918: '*For his work as a Brigade Commander in covering the withdrawal of the remainder of the division, and on one occasion commanding the infantry of the division with marked success, and on all occasions inspiring all ranks with his own courage and example.*' Took command of 36th (Ulster) Division on 6 May 1918. Mentioned in Despatches, CB, Order of St Stanislas 3rd Class with Swords (Russia), Commander of the Ordre de La Couronne (Belgium), Officer of the Legion d'Honneur (France). ADC to the King 1920-24. Retired 1924. Colonel Commandant The Corps of Royal Engineers 1936-40. Died 4 February 1959, aged 88.

3 Brigadier General Edward Vaughn CMG, DSO, DL, JP. Born on 20 October 1866. Commissioned into The Manchester Regiment on 10 November 1888. Lieutenant 10 September 1890. Captain 1 November 1897. Served in the South Africa War 1899 to 1902. Mentioned in Despatches twice. Queen's South Africa Medal and five clasps, King's South Africa Medal with clasps 'South Africa 1901' and 'South Africa 1902'. Brevet Major 22 August 1902. Major 17 February 04. Lieutenant Colonel 1 September 1916. DSO – King's Birthday Honours 1917, no citation. Temporary Brigadier

General 20 April 1918 and Commander 108th Brigade. CMG. Knight of the Legion d'Honneur (France). Croix de Guerre (France). Colonel 1 September 1920. Retired 1923. Died 12 February 1956, aged 89.

NINE

The Final Advance: 20 September to 26 October 1918

In September 1918, II Corps, part of the British Second Army and comprising the 9th (Scottish), 29th and 36th (Ulster) Divisions, was ordered north to prepare for the next offensive. During this final push to the east the Allied armies would be attacking across a broad front for the first time in the war. Four major attacks were launched in successive days. In the south the French Fourth Army and the American First Army attacked between the River Meuse and Reims on 26 September. The next day the British Third Army struck near Cambrai, and on 28 September the British Second Army attacked alongside the Belgian Army in Flanders. Finally, on 29 September the British Fourth Army and the French First army attacked the Hindenburg Line at St Quentin.

In preparation for their part in the attack by the British Second Army, the leading elements of the Ulster Division moved north by train. The 9th Royal Irish Fusiliers had spent twelve days training at Berthen and Bailleul and on 20 September began their move via Terdeghem to Watou where a further five days was spent training. On 26 September the Battalion left Watou and marched to Road Camp at St Jan ter Biezen and on 28 September arrived at Siege Camp near Vlamertinghe, west of Ypres. That day the attack began with the 9th (Scottish) and 29th Divisions attacking to the east of Ypres. The accommodation at Siege Camp was very poor but, due to the speed and success of the attacking divisions, the 9th Royal Irish Fusiliers had to endure only one night there before they were moved forward to Rifle Farm on the Menin Road and then to Glencourse Wood and Reutel, six miles east of Ypres and a mile west of Beselare. After a night subjected to continuous rain and biting cold, 109th Brigade attacked in fine weather on 29 September and captured Terhand, halting on the outskirts of Dadizeele, which was then captured by the 9th (Scottish) Division.

The success of the 9th (Scottish) Division had taken the attack close to the Menin/Roulers (Roeselare) road on the north of the Corps front, but in the south 29th Division was held up south of Beselare. The 9th Royal Irish Fusiliers, with the rest of 108th Brigade, was in support to 109th Brigade and had taken up a position closer to Beselare with 12th Royal Irish Rifles on its left.

It was now the turn of 108th Brigade to lead the Ulster Division forward. At the brigade headquarters Lieutenant Colonel Kelly received verbal orders for an attack to begin at dawn on 30 September. Advancing with the leading battalions either side of the Terhand/Vijfwegen road, 108th Brigade aimed to seize three objectives: firstly, a line running north-south through Vijfwegen; secondly, the line of the railway half a mile beyond the Menin/Roulers road, and finally Moorseele.

The enemy defences in this area centred on an area of rising ground known as Hill 41, between Vijfwegen, the limit of 109th Brigade's advance, and the Menin/Roulers road. On the hill were three farms that had been reinforced with concrete, and the hedges that covered the hill concealed smaller strong-points; it presented a formidable position. At the southern end of the feature was Goldflake Farm which had strong pillboxes positioned nearby providing support. This strong-point dominated the ground to the west and south of Hill 41. In the centre and near the crest of the hill was Mansard Farm. To the north, on the left of the Battalion's axis, and nearer the advancing troops, was Twigg Farm, close to the remains of a minor road that ran south down to Cheviot Corner.

Preparations for this attack were not quite what they should have been and the 9th Royal Irish Fusiliers spent an uncomfortable night with neither shelter from the heavy rain nor food before they moved forward at 5.30am, covered by an advance guard. Lieutenant Colonel Kelly was told that 109th Brigade now held Terhand and Dadizeele with 1st and 9th Royal Inniskilling Fusiliers. From 7.00am 108th Brigade passed through their forward lines with 12th Royal Irish Rifles on the left, the 9th Royal Irish Fusiliers on the right and the 1st Royal Irish Fusiliers eight hundred yards back in support.

As he passed through the 1st Royal Inniskilling Fusiliers, Lieutenant Colonel Kelly realised that there was no contact with 29th Division on the right. He dispatched an officer's patrol to find its forward elements. This patrol was successful but reported the nearest troops, men of the 1st Battalion, The Lancashire Fusiliers, as being 2,000 yards to the rear. This dictated how Lieutenant Colonel Kelly must advance and he deployed the companies to maintain contact with the units on both flanks. On the left A Company was to advance due east on a line just south of the road into Vijfwegen and on to Kezelberg, with D Company moving along the road in support. On the right B Company was ordered to push forward on a line about 800 yards south of the road towards the lower, south-western slopes of Hill 41. To its right rear C Company advanced to protect the 9th Royal Irish Fusiliers' flank and to maintain contact with the forward elements of the 29th Division. The ground in this area was generally good, although it was marshy in places and the heavy and continuous rain that fell throughout the day did not help. The rain also made observation difficult, but the companies were able to see and respond to the signals flashed to them by Lucas lamp.

Lieutenant Colonel P E Kelly

As the 9th Royal Irish Fusiliers advanced, B and C Companies on the right flank ran into trouble soon after they had passed through the forward elements of 109th Brigade. On the left flank, meanwhile, 12th Royal Irish Rifles advanced quickly and unopposed to the outskirts of Dadizeele, and A Company of the 9th Royal Irish Fusiliers made swift progress until it reached the east of Methuen Wood. Here it was checked by machine-gun fire from some houses south-west of Vijfwegen. Hearing that the 9th Royal Inniskilling Fusiliers was holding the Terhand/Vijfwegen Road and that its line ran east of Vijfwegen, Lieutenant Colonel Kelly decided to send D Company into Vijfwegen and then south to cut off the positions that were holding up A Company's advance. At about 9.30am, as D Company approached the village, it too was halted by machine-gun fire from Leadhall Copse and from the same houses that were holding up A Company. An officer of the Royal Inniskilling Fusiliers belatedly reported that his battalion had pulled back from the hamlet earlier and that the enemy now held it. At about 10.00am A and D Companies were ordered to attack and clear the ground south-west of Vijfwegen. Their objective was a 700-yard section of the light railway beside the road running south-west from the hamlet. As the companies advanced, the Germans conducted a fighting withdrawal moving from house to house, and A and D Companies reached their objectives with only a few casualties.

Lieutenant E W Reynolds

On the right flank B and C Companies had advanced more cautiously in the face of heavy machine-gun fire. The platoons of B Company attacked to clear the enemy from Walpole Copse, Turnbull Farm, Goldsmith Farm, Pawn Farm and the outposts in front of them. The German infantry were of no inclination to withdraw from the farms, which were strongly held with wire thickly laid to protect all of the strong-points. During an attack on one of these farms C Company was halted by machine-gun fire from a formidable position. One of the platoon commanders, Second Lieutenant Reynolds, crawled to the enemy wire, cut a gap and then led his platoon round the enemy's position. Outflanked and surrounded, the garrison surrendered. During the fighting on this flank Captain Cross was mortally wounded and, although Second Lieutenant Logan brought him back under heavy machine-gun fire, he died later that day. By 10.30am B Company had cleared a number of farms but were again held up by heavy fire from the south-east and south. From C Company's position to the right rear it could be seen that the leading elements of 29th Division, with which a number of patrols made contact, were also held up farther back and could offer no help.

On the left the advance continued until about 11.00am when A and D Companies were again halted by a strong-point, a pillbox and two fortified farms. To assist 12th Royal Irish Rifles, about to attack farther left, these positions had to be taken. The strong-point near Dime House was attacked successfully by D Company, and by 12.30pm twelve prisoners and two machine guns had been captured and an enemy officer and twenty of his men were killed. The remainder of its garrison, numbering nearly 100 men, was pursued for about 300 yards up the hill before heavy machine-gun fire from the flanks forced the 9th Royal Irish Fusiliers back to the captured position. Dime House was also occupied and this was now the extreme left flank of the Battalion. The attack farther south on Stansfield Farm was, however, unsuccessful. As the men from A Company reached it they were surprised by the enemy who had crawled down the hedgerows and attacked from a flank. A second attempt at 1.30pm also failed due to heavy crossfire from the south and from farther forward at Cheviot Corner.

As the day progressed the enemy machine-gun, artillery and mortar fire had increased steadily, particularly around Leadenhall Copse. This was without a corresponding response by the Ulster Division's artillery, and support from the Stokes mortar attached to the 9th Royal Irish Fusiliers was not possible due to the effect of the rain on the propellant cartridges. By 4.00pm any movement was very difficult. With a frontage of 2,500 yards, and having lost five officers and about 100 men, Lieutenant Colonel Kelly decided to hold firm until the 29th Division made progress on his right flank. On the left, meanwhile, 12th Royal Irish Rifles launched an attack from the north-west onto Hill 41 and after a stiff fight reached a line just short of the crest. Their victory was short-lived as a counter-attack from two directions drove them back down the slope to Dime House.

At 6.00pm 2nd Royal Irish Rifles from 107th Brigade moved up to and then through the positions held by B and C Companies and took up a line across the front of the 9th Royal Irish Fusiliers. At 10.00pm Lieutenant Colonel Kelly was ordered to withdraw his two companies and move them into reserve, leaving A and D Companies forward on the left in support of 2nd Royal Irish Rifles. That night a patrol commanded by Second Lieutenant Reynolds went out to maintain contact with 2nd Royal Irish Rifles and he managed to send back vital information on the state of the front before patrolling into the enemy lines. Although his patrol was cut off before he could withdraw, he kept low and brought his patrol back safely the next night. By now all of the men of the 9th Royal Irish Fusiliers were tired and hungry having not eaten for over a day, and a concerted effort was made to get rations forward that night to all of the companies.

After a reconnaissance by moonlight, two companies of the 1st Royal Irish Fusiliers moved forward in the early hours of 1 October in preparation for an attack on Hill 41 from the west. The assault began at 6.15am through a wet mist, this time with effective artillery support, but progress was painfully slow due to heavy machine-gun fire from the farms that had previously held up B Company's advance. At 9.30am after the Faughs succeeded in capturing Twigg Farm, along with twenty-eight prisoners, the supporting company was committed to the attack. Casualties mounted quickly, however, and at 9.30am the 9th Royal Irish Fusiliers was ordered to attack Sandsfield Farm from which machine-gun fire was interfering with the 1st Battalion's attack. At 11.00am, just before the attack could be launched, the enemy counter-attacked onto Hill 41. The 1st Royal Irish Fusiliers held out and the 9th Royal Irish Fusiliers was ordered to remain in support in case the enemy attempted to break through again.

The 9th Royal Irish Fusiliers now occupied a line around the western end of Hill 41 and had troops as far forward as Kezelberg in the south. At 9.15pm 2nd Royal Irish Rifles from 107th Brigade moved through this line and all of the companies were gradually withdrawn. At 5.00am on 1 October the 9th Royal Irish Fusiliers moved to an area west of Terhand. The 9th Royal Irish Fusiliers was not spared during this move and the relief cost them another officer and fifteen other casualties.

During these two days of intense and fluid fighting the 9th Royal Irish Fusiliers had lost 147 all ranks killed, wounded and missing. The final casualty figures for this action were:

	Officers*	Other Ranks**
Killed in Action	2	27
Died of Wounds***	2	5
Identified Wounded	3	11
Identified Captured	1	1
Believed Wounded or Captured	-	95
Total	8	139

*The war diary records three officers killed, one died of wounds and four wounded.
**The war diary records 139 other ranks killed, wounded and missing.
***Identified as wounded during the attack at Vijfwegen.

The two officers who were killed in action were: Captain G H Cross, who had been with the 9th Royal Irish Fusiliers for just over a month having served since November 1914 with the Army Service Corps, and Second Lieutenant F H Hall, who had been on strength for two weeks. Second Lieutenants J Kernaghan, who had served with 11th Royal Irish

Rifles before being commissioned in June 1918 and had been with the 9th Royal Irish Fusiliers for a little over a week died of his wounds on 1 October 1918, as did Second Lieutenant S F Moran, who had served with the South Irish Horse before being commissioned. He had rejoined the 9th Royal Irish Fusiliers in June, having recovered from wounds he received in December 1917 at Marcoing. An officer who had served previously with the 9th Royal Irish Fusiliers, Lieutenant W R Graham, was killed while fighting with the 1st Battalion. Second Lieutenant R A Richey was captured (having been presumed killed in action) and three other officers were wounded: Lieutenant R H Lindsey, OC D Company, was only lightly wounded and rejoined a few days later; Lieutenant C R Wilson was evacuated to hospital in England and spent the rest of the war with the 3rd (Reserve) Battalion; Second Lieutenant J B A Young was wounded serving with 108th Trench Mortar Battery. He too was evacuated to hospital in England and saw no further service.

Private Samuel Meeke. From Ahoghill, County Antrim. Meeke was barely 16 years old when he enlisted in 1915 and was soon discharged. He enlisted again in May 1916 into The Royal Irish Rifles, still aged 16. Repeatedly absent without leave in Ireland, he was punished by periods of detention. He was released from his final period of detention on 30 May 1918 and sent to France. He joined the 9th Royal Irish Fusiliers on 22 September 1918. Wounded during the attack at Vijfwegen on 30 September or 1 October 1918, he died of wounds on 6 October 1918, aged 19.

Second Lieutenant R A Richey

Lieutenant W R Graham

Thirty-two men were killed or subsequently died of their wounds. Most of those killed and wounded were the victims of the heavy and sustained machine-gun fire. They included Lance Corporal William Gregg, a regular soldier who had joined the 9th Royal Irish Fusiliers after serving with the 1st Battalion. He had led his section in hand-to-hand fighting on 30 September and successfully deployed his Lewis gun against an enemy machine gun killing seven of its team; he was killed on 1 October and earned a DCM for his conduct the previous day. The 9th Royal Irish Fusiliers had fought hard in difficult conditions and the other officers and men rewarded for their gallantry were: Lieutenant E W Reynolds and Second Lieutenants S Logan and C H Steele, who earned the MC for the way in which they handled their platoons; Second Lieutenant J B A Young who earned an MC for his actions while attached to 108th Trench Mortar Battery, and Company Quartermaster Sergeant H Selby, who had personally carried bags of rations through heavy fire to his company and earned a DCM. The Military Medals earned cannot be differentiated from those earned later in October.

The officers and principle warrant officers with the 9th Royal Irish Fusiliers after the initial action on Hill 41 were:

Commanding Officer:	Lieutenant Colonel P E Kelly
Second-in-Command:	Major R J A Tamplin DSO
Adjutant:	Captain W Sparks MC
Intelligence Officer:	Second Lieutenant C A Ross
Transport Officer:	Captain J B K Morrow
Quartermaster:	Honorary Lieutenant G W Wilson
Padre:	Reverend W S Allman AChD
Medical Officer:	Captain C R Brown RAMC
Captains:	G H Gibson, C H Kerr, R H Lindsay & P E MacLean
Lieutenants:	J B Barnett, R I McCrum & J J Murphy MC, DCM
Second Lieutenants:	J Boyd, J Bryson, H C Burrows, J Darling, R S Duncan, W G Graham, F D R Humphreys, J M Inglis, T C Leahy, S Logan, E W Reynolds, C H Steele & F W Vint
Regimental Sergeant Major:	Warrant Officer Class 1 G A Williams MM
Regimental Quartermaster Sergeant:	Warrant Officer Class 2 J Barbour MC

Reverend W S Allman AChD

The harsh conditions experienced over the last few days due to the bad weather, lack of sleep and food and the efforts involved inthe recent fighting on Hill 41, had a considerable effect on men of the 9th Royal Irish Fusiliers. Many of them had also experienced action for the first time. A welcome, albeit short, period was spent resting, refitting and preparing for the next phase of the advance. Although a great deal of experience had been lost in the spring of 1918, the 9th Royal Irish Fusiliers had now been successful in action throughout August and September and it was ready for the final effort. When the 9th Royal Irish Fusiliers relieved 9th Royal Inniskilling Fusiliers on Hill 41 on 4 October, it did so with thirteen officers and 390 other ranks.

For three days 109th Brigade had held most of Hill 41 and along the front the line was stable, but a further advance was impossible without a concerted attack. Both 107th Brigade, which had been relieved by troops of the 35th Division, and 109th Brigade moved back for some rest. The first two days at Hill 41 were relatively quiet for 108th Brigade with only harassing shell and machine-gun fire behind the 9th Royal

Irish Fusiliers' positions. On 6 October a relatively quiet day was spent preparing to move forward, and that night the 9th Royal Irish Fusiliers moved onto Hill 41 and occupied a small copse on the western slope and Mansard Farm close to the crest of the hill. During this operation a few casualties were caused by machine-gun fire. Goldflake Farm was still occupied by the enemy and a patrol went out to determine the strength of the garrison. It was led by Second Lieutenant Bryson, a pre-war, regular cavalry Sergeant who had been commissioned directly into Princess Victoria's (Royal Irish Fusiliers) in June and who had joined the 9th Royal Irish Fusiliers a few days later. This experienced and gallant officer was lost during the patrol, killed by shellfire, but his party returned and reported that the farm was held in force. Second Lieutenant Bryson's body was recovered seven days later. In the period up to 9 October a little over twenty casualties were suffered through machine-gun fire. They included Corporal Richard Hathaway who died of his wounds on 7 October, and Private David Currie who was wounded in the chest and died of his wounds on 8 October. Second Lieutenant F D R Humphreys, who had been with the 9th Royal Irish Fusiliers for only three weeks, was shot in the head and badly wounded on 7 October, and Lance Corporal T A Murphy was wounded on 9 October. The lack of artillery support had been keenly felt. The poor roads, bad weather and the volume of traffic behind the line all conspired to delay the arrival of the Ulster Division's artillery but by 7 October it was in place and able to reply to the heavy barrage that fell continuously on those in the line.

Pioneer Sergeant A L W Steele and his three sons, all serving in the 1st Battalion before the war. Standing from left to right (and with final ranks): Captain C H Steele MC*, Colour Sergeant D W J Steele & Private P G Steele.

Over this period an incident occurred that resulted in the loss of one of the 9th Royal Irish Fusiliers' toughest officers, although not to enemy action. B Company had been under regular artillery attack for two or three days and Dime House, where the company headquarters had been set up in the cellar, was hit frequently. In the middle of the afternoon of 7 October the Company Commander, Captain Murphy, went over to A Company headquarters before walking with Captain Kerr to battalion headquarters for a conference. It was evident that Murphy had been drinking. This was not an unusual occurrence in the line for those who managed to hoard some alcohol, and was relatively common in the officers' shelters. At the conference he *'expressed himself plainly'* to Lieutenant Colonel Kelly. Murphy was known as a brusque man who spoke his mind, but on this occasion his behaviour annoyed the Commanding Officer sufficiently for him to later report Captain Murphy as drunk and relieve him of command of B Company. His decision was undoubtedly influenced by the situation as seen by the Adjutant that night. Just after 9.00pm Captain Sparks visited B Company and found Captain Murphy asleep in his company headquarters. He awoke briefly but Captain Sparks completed his rounds with Second Lieutenant Reynolds, who was on duty. Lieutenant Colonel Kelly's remarks after the event are revealing; he stated that Captain Murphy was a brave man, conducting himself well in action, but that he was worried about his drinking, about which he had warned him previously, and that his '*lack of education and his want of self control renders him unsuitable to command a company as he is incapable of setting his subalterns an example of how to behave*'. In addition, it was felt that he could not be kept in the Battalion as a platoon commander because there was no-one strong enough or senior enough to command him.

The statements on the incident were passed quickly to Brigadier General Vaughan, commanding 108th Brigade, who did not support a plea for leniency from Lieutenant Colonel Kelly and who passed the case up the chain of command. Major General Coffin passed the matter to II Corps and recommended Captain Murphy's removal. GOC II Corps, Lieutenant General Mack, supported the recommendation, and at Second Army, General Plumer concurred. However, at II Corps the staff insisted that any action must be lawful and felt that if there was enough evidence to support Lieutenant Colonel Kelly's allegations then there should be enough for a court martial. Major General Coffin ordered that further evidence should be gathered. Awaiting the result of an enquiry and the deliberations of the generals, Captain Murphy left his men and joined the 9th Royal Irish Fusiliers' details at the Base Depot. A number of officers and men wrote statements in relation to this incident supporting Captain Murphy. Captain Kerr was clear that, although he had been drinking, Captain Murphy was able to do his job. A number of others, including Captain MacLean, Second Lieutenant Steele, Sergeant Lockhart, who was acting as Company Sergeant Major of B Company, Corporal Robinson and Lance Corporal Scott, later testified that he was not drunk. The investigation ground on, and by the time the matter got to the staff of the Commander-in-Chief, Lieutenant Colonel Kelly would be dead and it would be decided that no court martial action could be taken.

Sergeants John Scott (left) and Robert Slator. Slator was killed in action at Hill 41 on 30 September or 1 October. Like many, his recorded date of death is 3 October 1918.

Captain J J Murphy was an interesting and complex character and an able soldier. He was born in 1886 in County Limerick and at the age of 15 enlisted into the Royal Marine Artillery. By the end of his period of regular service in January 1914 he had been promoted to Corporal. In May 1915 he re-enlisted and joined the 8th (Service) Battalion, Princess Victoria's (Royal Irish Fusiliers) in 49th Brigade, 16th (Irish) Division. He was quickly promoted to Sergeant. In 1916 he was wounded and earned a DCM during a difficult raid when he and an officer (Captain G W Eaton) forced their way through thick, partially destroyed wire into a strongly-held trench. Commissioned into Princess Victoria's (Royal Irish Fusiliers) in June 1917, he joined the 9th (North Irish Horse) Battalion in September that year. Awarded an MC for his part in the raid at Havrincourt on 3 November 1917, he was made Officer Commanding B Company in April 1918, earned a bar to his MC for leading the raid at Meulenhouck on 22 July and was promoted to acting Captain. He had two brothers in the Army, one of whom was killed at Loos.

Captain Murphy left the Base Depot for England in December 1918 and was finally ordered to resign his commission in April 1919. He re-enlisted into the 45th (Service) Battalion, The Royal Fusiliers (City of London Regiment) on its formation in June 1919 as a Company Sergeant Major for the duration of its deployment to north Russia. He was reportedly commended again for his bravery in action. He was discharged to the Class Z Reserve but re-enlisted in January 1920 into The Prince of Wales's Leinster Regiment (Royal Canadians) and joined the 2nd Battalion in January 1920 as a Private. He was discharged as a Corporal when the Regiment was disbanded in July 1922. Having given over twenty years' service in four regiments and having been decorated for gallantry three times, Murphy went to work in a quarry. In 1929 he was refused a war gratuity for his commissioned service due to having been ordered to resign his commission—a sad end to a full and colourful military career. He was killed in an explosion at the cement works at Mungret, Limerick in April 1938.

The shellfire that had been given as an excuse by some for Captain Murphy's behaviour increased in the period up to 10 October as the enemy, expecting another attack, fired on likely assembly areas at dawn and dusk. This caused about twenty more casualties. Plans were now being laid to capture Goldflake Farm, and as a prelude the post at Mansard Farm was recaptured. This post had been abandoned on 10 October due to the British artillery wire-cutting operations in preparation for the next advance and Mansard Farm had been re-occupied quickly by the enemy. At dusk on 10 October, under cover of a smoke barrage, a small party of 9th Royal Irish Fusiliers rushed the post forcing the enemy to flee back to their own lines, leaving behind a machine gun.

At dawn on 11 October Second Lieutenant J Darling MC and two platoons from C Company, numbering thirty men, were in position at Twigg Farm. One platoon from B Company was in a copse on the lower slope of the hill ready to assist by pushing in on Goldflake Farm from the west if the attack faltered. The 9th Royal Irish Fusiliers waited through the damp, cold morning for the artillery and mortar barrage that would precede their assault. Throughout the night salvoes had been fired every half hour and a final, heavy bombardment fell from 5.15 to 5.30am. After that there was silence from the Ulster Division's artillery and the trench mortars until the barrage for the attack, including smoke, fell on the farm at 10.00am. It totally suppressed the enemy and Second Lieutenant Darling and the small party of 9th Royal Irish Fusiliers moved forward quickly along the eastern side of the road running from Twigg Farm to Cheviot Corner on the Vijfwegen/Kezelberg road.

At 10.05am the artillery fire lifted from the farm and the two platoons rushed in, with a section taking on a pillbox just west of the main objective. The attack was a success and after a hard fight, during which about ten of the enemy were killed and fourteen prisoners and three machine guns captured, the attackers began consolidation. An immediate counter-attack was prevented by friendly artillery and mortar fire to the east and south of the farm. Casualties amongst the Royal Irish Fusiliers during the attack were light, with one killed and two wounded. During the course of the afternoon the enemy artillery fire was heavy but the farm was held. At about 5.50pm it was evident that the enemy was about to counter-attack all three strong-points on Hill 41. A fierce barrage preceded the attack but the small garrison at Goldflake Farm managed to inflict heavy casualties on the assembling German infantry before conducting a fighting withdrawal, firing into the enemy at point-blank range.

The garrison in Mansard Farm on the crest of the hill was surrounded, but the 9th Royal Irish Fusiliers managed to fight their way back to the main position. A small party in front of Twigg Farm, meanwhile, held the enemy back and a counter-attack from the 9th Royal Irish Fusiliers' lines drove the enemy back to Mansard and Goldflake farms, which the enemy managed to hold onto throughout the night. During the day the enemy shellfire had taken its toll and Lieutenant Colonel Kelly was killed while at one of the company headquarters. That night the Royal Irish Fusiliers was relieved by 12th Royal Irish Rifles and went into brigade reserve near Terhand where the first day out of the line was again spent reorganising and checking equipment. The casualties from the attack on Goldflake Farm and the subsequent German counter-attack were recorded in the war diary as two officers and 25 other ranks killed and wounded. The finally tally of casualties was:

	Officers	Other Ranks
Killed in Action	1	6
Died of Wounds	-	1
Identified Wounded	1	4
Believed Wounded	-	14
Total	2	25

In addition to Lieutenant Colonel Kelly, those killed were Corporal R J Hull, Lance Corporals J Deery and E Mellor, and Privates L E W Blake, W Mattock, and F Streather. Private J Stevenson was severely injured and later succumbed to his wounds.

For this courageous and important attack Second Lieutenant Darling was awarded a bar to his MC. Those who earned the MM for this action cannot be positively identified, but those decorated for their bravery since 30 September/1 October were Sergeants R Edin and F Homersham, who earned bars to their MMs, and Sergeant W Moorehead and Private R Norris.

On 12 October Major R A Tamplin DSO took over command of the 9th Royal Irish Fusiliers and the next day was spent in preparation for the resumption of the advance. Arranged between 35th Division on the right and 29th Division on the left, 36th (Ulster) Division was to attack and secure the Courtrai/Ingelmunster railway between the River Lys and the northern outskirts of Heule six miles to the east. The plan required 107th and 109th Brigades to attack, with 108th Brigade in support. At 5.35am, in heavy fog and under a very heavy artillery and mortar barrage, the British Second Army advanced, and the forward brigades of the Ulster Division attacked on a front of 1,000 yards. By the end of the day the Allied armies had advanced four miles, captured 10,000 prisoners and had suffered only light casualties. The 9th Royal Irish Fusiliers had followed up the swift advance, spending most of that day in Kezelberg and the next day just west of Moorseele. The Ulster Division had seized its objective by the evening of 15 October and at 2.00am the next morning 108th Brigade moved forward towards the River Lys. Patrols from 9th Royal Inniskilling Fusiliers indicated that there were no enemy troops up to the river.

The town of Courtrai sits astride the River Lys connected by four road bridges and a railway bridge. The enemy had evacuated its north-west portion and had withdrawn over the river, blowing the five bridges to deny crossing points to the advancing Allies. At 5.35am, under a poor artillery barrage that fell short causing three casualties, the 9th Royal Irish Fusiliers moved forward on the right of the 108th Brigade advance alongside 12th Royal Irish Rifles. A Company advanced on the right, B Company on the left, C Company in support and D Company in reserve. The barrage was stopped when it was realised that the enemy was concentrated on the far bank. With the exception of one machine gun on the railway on the 9th Royal Irish Fusiliers' right flank that was dealt with successfully, no opposition was met. Just after 8.30am, as 12th Royal Irish Rifles entered Courtrai, to the obvious pleasure of the town's inhabitants, the 9th Royal Irish Fusiliers reached the river, with A and B Companies taking up a position commanding the opposite bank in the western outskirts of the town. The bridge over the river here had been destroyed and the nearby railway bridge was partially destroyed at the opposite bank. Unable to cross, C Company formed a defensive flank along the railway with D Company remaining to the north-west in support. The 9th Royal Irish Fusiliers was in touch with 12th Royal Irish Rifles on the left and during the morning both battalions made preparations to cross the river.

The destroyed railway bridge over the River Lys at Courtrai.
When the 9th Royal Irish Fusiliers' attack was halted on 16 October 1918, C Company formed a defensive flank here. The men on the bridge abutments on the left give an indication of scale. The houses in the distance mark the site of the assault river crossing by 9th Royal Irish Fusiliers. IWM (Q 46674)

Brigadier Vaughan had decided to force a crossing in daylight and the task was given to the 9th Royal Irish Fusiliers, supported by a bridging party from 122nd Field Company, Royal Engineers. The initial crossing and bridgehead were to be made and established by fifty-four men of D Company led by Second Lieutenants C H Steele and S Logan, who had

Second Lieutenant C G Steele MC*

both distinguished themselves during the first attacks on Hill 41 two weeks earlier.

At 12.30pm the Royal Engineers brought the pontoons forward to thirty yards from the river bank and concealed them behind some houses. At 2.00pm artillery and mortars fired smoke to conceal the initial crossing.[1] While A and B Companies held the near bank, the first boat, commanded by Second Lieutenant J J A Fagan from 122nd Field Company, and with Sergeant F Homersham commanding the small group of 9th Royal Irish Fusiliers, moved down to the river and began to cross. Under heavy machine-gun fire the boat grounded short of the bank. Sapper James Neill dived overboard and took the boat's rope ashore so that it could be pulled to the bank. When it landed, Sergeant Homersham led his men forward onto the main road into Courtrai and onto the river bank from where they could cover the bridging site. In command of the Lewis-gun section was Lance Corporal Robert Armstrong. Sergeant Homersham established the Lewis gun in a position from which Lance Corporal Armstrong was able to fire to great effect, neutralising two enemy machine guns. Second Lieutenant Fagan's team landed more men until he was wounded.

A Lewis gun in action. © IWM (Q 10609)

Meanwhile a second section from 122nd Field Company led by Second Lieutenant A J Towlson MM began to bridge the river and Second Lieutenant Steele led his platoon across. The artillery support was not wholly effective, however, and the smoke screen did not last long enough. As Second Lieutenant Logan's platoon followed, the smoke cleared, giving the German infantry on the railway to the south-west a clear view of the bridge, which they then swept with machine-gun and artillery fire. This partially destroyed the bridge, killing Second Lieutenant Towlson, wounding Captain E A Wheatley, who was in charge of the bridging operation, and killing and wounding fifteen men from 122nd Field Company. By 2.45pm the toll had risen to twenty four Royal Engineers killed and wounded and the sixty men of the 9th Royal Irish Fusiliers who had crossed were now stranded on the opposite bank.

For four hours this small party held out and made every attempt to strengthen their position. During the fight Second Lieutenant Logan led a rush on an enemy machine-gun post in a house commanding the bridge, capturing it and its team of six men. The German infantry fought hard to regain the initiative, and when they were massing for a counter-attack Lance Corporal Armstrong moved his gun across the main street to a position from which he could attempt to break up the attack, which he managed successfully. The plan for 36th (Ulster) Division to attack through Courtrai proved unnecessary; 108th Brigade was ordered to retire from the town and, with the rest of the Ulster Division, move north-east along the river in preparation for an attack four miles upstream. With the bridgehead redundant, the order to retire was given as darkness fell. Sergeant Homersham volunteered to swim across the canal with a rope to pull the pontoon boat across. This brave action succeeded and the 9th Royal Irish Fusiliers was ferried back successfully with six prisoners from *Reserve-Infanterie-Regiment Nr 15.*

C Company, meanwhile, moved up and relieved B Company. That evening, having recovered the elements of D Company from the enemy bank, the 9th Royal Irish Fusiliers was relieved by the 23rd (Service) Battalion, The Duke of Cambridge's Own (Middlesex Regiment) (2nd Football). Given the intensity of the fighting during this difficult operation, serious casualties had been surprisingly light: Lance Corporal C E Ditton, a Londoner, was killed; Second Lieutenant J M Inglis (whose role during the attack is unknown) was badly wounded and he would succumb to his wounds ten days later. Just nineteen years old, he had been a platoon commander for just over three weeks and was the youngest officer to be killed serving with the Battalion. Twenty-four men of the 9th Royal Irish Fusiliers were wounded, including Sergeant Atkins MM and Privates G E C Geary, J F Keenan and A G Phillips. In addition to Second Lieutenant Towlson, three men from 122nd Field Company were killed and a considerable number were wounded.[2]

The gallantry of those who made the river crossing was well rewarded. Second Lieutenants Logan and Steel earned a bar to the MC they had earned at the beginning of the month, and the DCM was awarded to Sergeant Homersham MM and Lance Corporal Armstrong. In 122nd Field Company, Captain Wheatley and Second Lieutenant Fagan earned the MC and four men, including Sapper Neill, earned a DCM for their most courageous work on the river.[3]

Having marched four miles back to Drie Masten, the 9th Royal Irish Fusiliers rested for the next three days before moving north to Landelede on Monday 20 October where everyone managed to bathe in the captured German baths. The depleted and tired Ulster Division was not allowed to rest long. The Allied attack across the Lys was to be led by II Corps, and on the left flank of the advancing British Army the initial crossing would be made by

The 108th Brigade Staff that efficiently co-ordinated the actions of its three battalions, trench mortar battery and attached elements throughout the Advance to Victory.

Back Row: Captain A A Lazard, Brigade Interpreter; Captain S S McDowell The Royal Irish Rifles, Brigade Signals Officer; Second Lieutenant Perkins Corps of Royal Engineers Signal Service; Captain W J Menaul MC Princess Victoria's (Royal Irish Fusiliers), Assistant Staff Captain.

Front Row: Captain C F Wilkins DSO, MC The Royal Irish Rifles, Brigade Major; Brigadier General E Vaughan DSO; Captain V B Rogers MC; General List, Staff Captain.

When the Brigade Interpreter first arrived and introduced himself by his full name, André Armand Lazard, the previous Brigade Commander, Brigadier General Griffiths, replied, *"That's much too long-you're Percy."* According to Captain Rogers, *''Percy' he remained until he left us at Mouscron.'*

36th (Ulster) Division, a significant honour and testament to the Division's ability, ably demonstrated over the fighting during the last month. On the Division's left was the advancing French Army and on the right was 9th (Scottish) Division, which would cross after the bridgehead had been secured by 109th Brigade. 29th Division was in support.

The initial crossing and attack by 109th Brigade was conducted superbly by the 9th Royal Inniskilling Fusiliers leading the 1st Royal Inniskilling Fusiliers over the river and, after heavy fighting at close quarters, the villages on the southern bank were secured. 107th Brigade crossed in the early hours of 20 October and fought all day to secure Dries. On their right, troops of the 9th (Scottish) Division had also crossed and made good progress. That night 108th Brigade crossed to relieve 109th Brigade. At 7.30am on 21 October the Ulster Division attacked again, now south of the river, with 108th Brigade on the left and 107th Brigade on the right. 108th Brigade used a company of 12th Royal Irish Rifles to finally secure Dries in a very successful attack at 7.00am before the main attack began, led by 1st Royal Irish Fusiliers with the 9th Royal Irish Fusiliers in support. Although unsupported by artillery, which had not yet made the crossing, the 1st Royal Irish Rifles in

107th Brigade made good progress on the right, advancing to a point just north of Vichte, but 108th Brigade was held back due to the difficulties experienced by the French 133rd Infantry Regiment on its left, held up by machine-gun fire. On 22 October 107th Brigade conducted an aggressive fight for the crest of high ground north of Vichte while 108th Brigade advanced under heavy machine-gun fire to the Deerlyk/Waereghem road. In the early hours of 23 October a German runner was captured and the information he carried indicated that the enemy was about to withdraw. 108th Brigade, led by 1st Royal Irish Fusiliers, pushed on later that morning and found the enemy in Heirweg.

Throughout this period the weather was fine, although dull, and the 9th Royal Irish Fusiliers was not over-taxed for the first few days of the advance, having been in reserve throughout. A few casualties were suffered, however, including Lance Corporal G D Broggi, who was wounded on 20 October, and Private W J Wallace, who was killed in action on 23 October. On 24 October 12th Royal Irish Rifles relieved 1st Royal Irish Fusiliers as the leading battalion of 108th Brigade. The 9th Royal Irish Fusiliers was now in support and in this role advanced behind 12th Royal Irish Rifles towards Anseghem on the morning of 25 October. On this, its final attack, the 9th Royal Irish Fusiliers went into action with thirteen officers and 276 other ranks in the line. This attack was bravely conducted by 12th Royal Irish Rifles, which managed to advance 1,000 yards in the face of heavy fire from machine guns in every house (ten were captured during the day's fighting) and gas shells fired across the whole front. Although in support, the 9th Royal Irish Fusiliers sustained forty-six casualties from the heavy machine-gun fire.

The weather improved greatly overnight and on 26 October the Ulster Division paused. That evening artillery fire increased significantly, with many of the shells carrying gas, and the 9th Royal Irish Fusiliers suffered its final casualties in action. Amongst them were Private H B Worth, a Londoner, who was killed, and Sergeant R E Matthews, a fellow Londoner, and Corporal S G Young from Dorset who were severely wounded; they died of their wounds on 1 November and 8 November respectively. Exhausted, depleted, and with the French attack held back on its left, 36th (Ulster) Division made its final short advance on 27 October against the retiring enemy moving off the Klineberg Ridge. On the left 109th Brigade secured its final objectives without a shot being fired. There was some resistance against 108th Brigade but by dusk the 9th Royal Irish Fusiliers had secured the railway halt just west of Anseghem without incurring any further casualties. Here the captured positions were consolidated.

Orders were received on the afternoon of 27 October that 36th (Ulster) Division, which had suffered over 3,100 casualties since 27 September, would be withdrawn to rest and reorganise. At dusk, the 9th Royal Irish Fusiliers was relieved in the line for the last time, on this occasion by 1/4th Battalion, The Royal Sussex Regiment of 34th Division, and the tired men marched back to Hulste, north-east of Courtrai, to good billets where the civilian population, pleased to see the Allies, treated the men kindly and cooked their food. After a night there the 9th Royal Irish Fusiliers moved to new billets in Lauwe, four miles to the south-west of Courtrai.

The war diary entry for 25 October reported two officers wounded, seven other ranks killed in action and thirty-seven men wounded. The absence of any further reference to casualties indicates that this total probably includes the men killed and wounded on 26 October. With adjustments for those who succumbed to their wounds, the final casualty figures for 25 and 26 October were:

	Officers	Other Ranks
Killed in Action	-	12
Died of Wounds	1	7
Identified Wounded	1	6
Believed Wounded	-	19
Total	2	44

On 25 October Lieutenant F W Vint, who had joined in September, had been shot in the leg and the courageous Second Lieutenant J Darling MC had been critically wounded. Second Lieutenant Darling died of his wounds on 26 October, as did Second Lieutenant Inglis, who had been wounded on 16 October. They were the last officers to die serving with the 9th Royal Irish Fusiliers.[4]

Twelve men are now known to have been killed in action on 25/26 October. Seven others died of wounds suffered on those two days and twenty-five men were wounded. The 9th Royal Irish Fusiliers had been in almost constant action since the end of September and had suffered a little under 300 casualties, of whom sixty-six were killed in action or would die of wounds. In this last period of intense fighting and rapid movement it had acquitted itself extremely well, notwithstanding the youth and limited battle experience of many of its men. It is clear that the final actions of 36th (Ulster) Division and the 9th Royal Irish Fusiliers have not been reported upon to the same degree as the earlier battles, particularly those at Hamel, Messines and Ypres. The make-up of the battalions of 36th (Ulster) Division at this stage of the war had much to do with this. It may have been that to the people of Ulster the Division was not really theirs anymore. There were so few originals, and indeed Ulstermen, left in the 9th Royal Irish Fusiliers by then that the 'Final Hundred Days' may not have been reported through letters and newspapers in Ireland in the same way as the earlier battles. After the war, most of the talk of this period in the 9th Royal Irish Fusiliers' history took place in the pubs of northern England and London. Nevertheless, those who served with the 9th Royal Irish Fusiliers had every right to be as proud of their achievements as were the original volunteers.[5]

Some of the 9th Royal Irish Fusiliers' final casualties:
Private William McCormick, from Belfast. Wounded on 25/26 October 1918 and died of wounds 3 November 1918.
Private George Pennell, from Belfast. Killed in action 25 October 1918.
Private George Moorhead Shannon from Belfast. Killed in action 25 October 1918.

Few reinforcements had been received since the beginning of the offensive operations. It is not known what the total strength of the 9th Royal Irish Fusiliers was when it was relieved on 27 October (the last time the strength of the Battalion was recorded was on 25 October) but it is estimated at less than 300 all ranks. Some reinforcements would arrive over the next month, but for the men of the 9th Royal Irish Fusiliers the war was all but over.

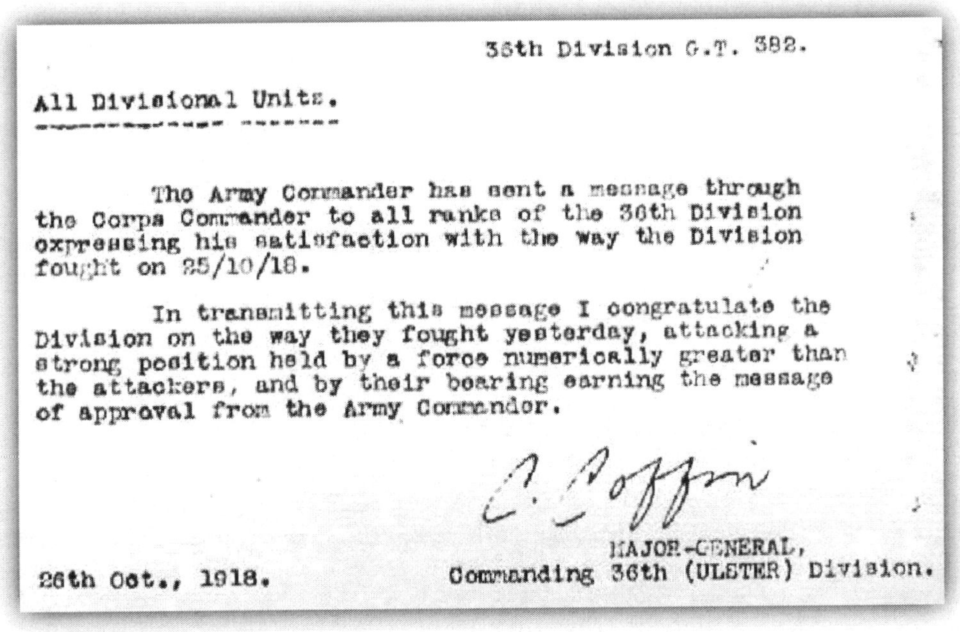

36th Division G.T. 382.

All Divisional Units.

The Army Commander has sent a message through the Corps Commander to all ranks of the 36th Division expressing his satisfaction with the way the Division fought on 25/10/18.

In transmitting this message I congratulate the Division on the way they fought yesterday, attacking a strong position held by a force numerically greater than the attackers, and by their bearing earning the message of approval from the Army Commander.

C. Coffin

MAJOR-GENERAL,
Commanding 36th (ULSTER) Division.

26th Oct., 1918.

This congratulatory order praised the conduct of the Battalion on its last day in action, 25 October 1918.

Endnotes, Chapter 9

1 The officers of 122nd Field Company, Corps of Royal Engineers who took part in this operation were:

Captain Edward Augustus Wheatley MC Corps of Royal Engineers. Enlisted into King Edward's Horse (The King's Overseas Dominions Regiment) (898 Private). To France 22 April 1915 with 'B' or 'C' Squadron. Commissioned into the Corps of Royal Engineers 24 February 1917. Acting Captain 12 September 1918. MC – Courtrai, 16 October 1918, where he was wounded. *'On October 16th, 1918, at Courtrai he was in charge of bridging stores by the canal bank, and was detailed to control the infantry landing parties and sapper carrying parties under heavy fire. When the officer in charge of the bridge was wounded, he took up a position in the open at the highest point and directed everything in the most orderly manner, under the cross-fire of several machine guns. His coolness and ability until seriously wounded ensured the success of the whole operation.'* He was moved to safety by Sapper Ernest Lake. Relinquished his commission on account of ill-health caused by wounds 6 December 1920. 1914-15 Star.

Lieutenant John Joseph Aloysius Fagan MC Corps of Royal Engineers. Commissioned into the Corps of Royal Engineers 21 April 1917. To France 14 August 1917. MC – Courtrai, 16 October 1918, where he was wounded. *'For conspicuous gallantry and devotion to duty, under withering machine-gun fire from a close range, on the morning of October 16th, 1918, at Courtrai. He carried out his work of bridging the Lys with exceptional coolness, until severely wounded in the left leg later in the day, and was an inspiring example to both the infantry and his own men.'* Relinquished his commission on account of ill-health caused by wounds. Silver War Badge (number 210095). Served with the Corps of Royal Engineers in the Second World War (Second Lieutenant 11 May 1942).

Promoted to Major. Served in the Italian campaign and was Mentioned in Despatches and awarded the United States Bronze Star Medal.

Second Lieutenant Albert John Towlson MM Corps of Royal Engineers. Born in 1893 at Norwich, Norfolk. Worked as a draughtsman at the India Rubber, Gutta-Percha and Telegraph Cable Company at Silvertown, London. Enlisted 13 August 1914 and joined 1st London Field Company, Royal Engineers (Territorial Force) (T/1099 Sapper). Employed as a draughtsman. To France 12 December 1914 and served with 1st London Field Company in 6th Division. Promoted to Corporal. Awarded the 6th Division Good Service Card. MM – 1916. Renumbered 546214 in February 1917. Commissioned into the Corps of Royal Engineers 29 June 1917. Killed in action at Courtrai 16 October 1918. Dadizeele New British Cemetery, I.A.5. 1914 Star.

[2] The other ranks from 122nd Field Company, Corps of Royal Engineers who were killed in action were:

Lance Corporal Walter Augustus Hollington 546283. Born 6 February 1883 at Mile End Old Town, London. Enlisted into the 12th (Prince of Wales's Royal) Lancers in August 1899. Served in the South Africa War. Queen's South Africa Medal with clasps 'Cape Colony' & 'South Africa 1902'. Discharged to the Army Reserve January 1903. Worked as a cabinet maker. Enlisted in August 1914 and joined 1st London Field Company, Royal Engineers (Territorial Force) (T/1288 Sapper). To France 12 December 1914 with 1st London Field Company in 6th Division. Wounded or injured in late 1915 and evacuated to hospital in England. Renumbered 546283 in February 1917. Posted to 122nd Field Company, 36th (Ulster) Division. Killed in action 16 October 1918 at Courtrai. Re-interred in Dadizeele New British Cemetery in 1920, III.A.7.

Sapper William Richard Chesher 546397. Born 15 February 1883 at Kensington, London. Served for seven years with 18th Middlesex Volunteer Rifle Corps. Enlisted 7 April 1915 and joined the 2/1st London Field Company, Royal Engineers (Territorial Force) (T/2068 Sapper). To France 21 February 1916 and joined 1st London Field Company in 6th Division. Employed as a carpenter and joiner. Injured his finger with a chisel in January 1917 and evacuated to hospital in England 28 January 1917. Renumbered 546397 in February 1917. To France 2 April 1918 and joined the Royal Engineers Base Depot. Joined 122nd Field Company, 36th (Ulster) Division 10 April 1918. Killed in action 16 October 1918 at Courtrai. Re-interred in Dadizeele New British Cemetery in 1920, III.A.6.

Sapper Thomas Goodwin 476850. Born in 1896 at Brightside Bierlow, Sheffield, Yorkshire. Enlisted and joined 2/1st West Riding Field Company, Royal Engineers (Territorial Force) (T/2931). To France and served with 1st West Riding Field Company in 29th Division. Renumbered 476850 in February 1917. Posted to 122nd Field Company, 36th (Ulster) Division. Died of wounds sustained on 16 October 1918 at Courtrai. Re-interred in Dadizeele New British Cemetery in 1920, I.A.6.

[3] The four men from 122nd Field Company, Corps of Royal Engineers who earned the DCM for this action were:

Lance Corporal Joseph Bloom 471702. From Upton-on-Severn. Enlisted and joined 2/1st West Riding Field Company, Royal Engineers (Territorial Force) (T/2306). To France and served with 1st West Riding Field Company in 29th Division. Renumbered 471702 in February 1917. Posted to 122nd Field Company, 36th (Ulster) Division. DCM – Courtrai, October 1918. *'On the 16th October, 1918, during the bridging operations at Courtrai, he was one of the volunteers to get the rope across for the first pontoon, and displayed marked gallantry and coolness. He made several crossings of the River Lys with the first pontoon, and when the pontoons were destroyed by artillery fire and his officers and senior NCOs killed or wounded by machine-gun fire, he superintended the landing, and personally pulled two successive boatloads of infantry across the canal.*

Sapper Ernest Lake 131210. Born in 1889 at Trimdon Colliery, West Wingate, County Durham. Posted to 122nd Field Company, 36th (Ulster) Division. DCM – Courtrai, October 1918. *'For conspicuous gallantry and devotion to duty under heavy fire during the bridging operations at Courtrai, on the 16th October, 1918. Although wounded early in the operations, he carried on for eight hours. When the bridging party was withdrawn, he returned through heavy machine-gun fire, and brought in his officer, who was lying out wounded in a most exposed position. He remained at duty, and acted as a guide and runner under heavy shelling, until the far side of the river was evacuated.'*

Sapper James Neill 64121. Born in 1895 at Belfast. A fitter at an engineering works. Enlisted 27 January 1915 into the Corps of Royal Engineers and joined 122nd Field Company in 36th (Ulster) Division. To France with 36th (Ulster) Division 5 October 1915. Injured on 2 September 1918 when the wheel of a water cart ran over his foot as he adjusted a loose hay net. DCM – Courtrai, October 1918. *'For conspicuous gallantry on the 16th October, 1918, during the bridging operations at Courtrai. When the first pontoon across the River Lys was grounded near the enemy side, he, under heavy machine-gun fire, dived overboard, and brought the rope ashore, thus saving any delay. Later, he volunteered to swim across the canal to deliver a message, and after two attempts succeeded, thus rendering valuable service.'* Tried by Field General Court Martial on 13 December 1918 charged with stealing; found guilty and sentenced to four months' imprisonment with hard labour. The sentence was suspended by GOC Fifth Army. Posted to England 24 March 1919 and transferred to the Class Z Reserve 4 June 1919. 1914-15 Star. His suspended sentence was subsequently remitted. Emigrated to the United States and lived at Springfield, Missouri.

Sapper Baldwin Richard Wright 25322. Born 5 October 1898 at Malta, the son of a regular soldier (then a Corporal) of the Corps of Royal Engineers. The family settled at Crosshaven, County Cork. Enlisted into the Corps of Royal Engineers. Posted to 122nd Field Company in 36th (Ulster) Division. *'During the bridging operations at Courtrai on 16th October, 1918, he helped to ferry the infantry across the canal in the first boat, standing all the time under direct machine-gun fire. Whilst so employed he was hit by one of our 'P' Grenades, which fell short, and though severely burned he jumped into the river and remained on the enemy side, and later took part in the fighting with the infantry. Throughout his gallantry and devotion to duty were most marked.'* Awarded the Medaille Militaire (France). Re-enlisted for Regular Army service with the Corps of Royal Engineers and served with 41st Field Company.

4 Captain S J Scott RAMC, a former company commander with the 9th Royal Irish Fusiliers, died of wounds in Ireland on 27 May 1920. Second Lieutenant T F Espie (formerly 14155 Corporal T F Espie) was commissioned into Princess Victoria's (Royal Irish Fusiliers) and served with the 5th/6th (Service) Battalion. He died on 6 February 1919 as a result of illness aggravated by war service.

5 The congratulatory message sent by GOC II Corps, Lieutenant General C N Jacob, to General Coffin praises the performance of 36th (Ulster) Division and confirms its standing as one of the better New Army divisions:

> *'The 36th (Ulster) Division has been fighting continuously since 28th Septr in the operations in FLANDERS. The spirit, dash and initiative shewn by all ranks have been splendid and beyond all praise. The leadership displayed by yourself and your Brigade and other Commanders could not have been better. The conditions under which the men have had to fight have been and are still very trying, but nothing seems to stop your gallant Division.*
>
> *I have also been much struck with the good staff work of the Division and it is very creditable to all concerned.*
>
> *Will you kindly express to the Commanders, Staffs and all ranks of the Division my heartiest congratulations and thanks for their work.*
>
> *When the history is written of what the Division has done in Flanders during the past month, it will prove to be a record of magnificent fighting and wonderful progress, for during this period an advance has been made of about 25 miles over the worst of country and under the heaviest machine-gun fire ever experienced in this war. The advance has entailed constant fighting but the 36th (Ulster) Division has overcome every obstacle and has proven itself one of the best fighting divisions in the Army, well commanded and well staffed.'*

TEN

'Finis'

In order to recount the events of the final months of the life of the 9th Royal Irish Fusiliers more clearly, this chapter is sub-divided into subject areas rather than presenting a purely chronological narrative.

The Final Days in Belgium

While the 9th Royal Irish Fusiliers recovered in Lauwe from its recent efforts, it became clear that the war was finally coming to a close. There were still uncertainties, but the feeling in the air was that the Germans were beaten. Although there was little need for work parties, the usual round of inspections and low-level training continued in fine weather. As always, sport featured, but the success of the football team was not reflected in the performance of the rugby team, which was soundly beaten by 12th Royal Irish Rifles on Friday 1 November. That night after everyone had bathed they were entertained at a dance held by the civilian population at the town school. Meanwhile, the Battalion's officers held a dinner and hosted guests from headquarters and the other units of 108th Brigade. The following day the 9th Royal Irish Fusiliers moved to new billets in Luingne, south-east of Mouscron. That afternoon a concert was given by the recently liberated inhabitants of the town followed by a display by the massed drums of the 1st and 9th Royal Irish Fusiliers. This drew a large crowd and a rousing reception.

D Company, Mouscron, 23 November 1918.
Seated in the centre in the lighter cap is Captain H C Burrows. On his left is Second Lieutenant C H Steele MC*. On his right is Second Lieutenant M T Sheehan and Company Sergeant Major Jack Robinson DCM.

During the next week the weather changed for the worse and it rained almost every day. On the afternoon of Wednesday 6 November the 9th Royal Irish Fusiliers moved into billets in Mouscron. Here Major R L Emerson MC, a regular officer of Princess Victoria's (Royal

Irish Fusiliers), joined the Battalion as Second-in-Command. At last, during the night of 10 November news was received that the Armistice had been signed and would take effect from 11.00am the following morning. The night was lit by flares and rockets with the fifes and drums adding to the celebrations in the streets of the town. When the news was confirmed the next morning there was widespread rejoicing that it was all over. There was not to be an immediate return home, however, and the battalions of the Ulster Division, which had now transferred to XV Corps, continued training. This was greatly scaled down from that normally carried out when preparing for another tour in the line, and the emphasis was firmly on keeping the men fit, occupied and in good spirits.

B Company, Mouscron, 23 November 1918.

A small number of reinforcements arrived from the Base Depot and, in addition to Major Emerson, the officers who joined were Captain A P Faris, another regular officer who joined from the 1st Battalion and was posted to D Company, Lieutenant A L Dobbyn MC, who rejoined from hospital having recovered from the wounds he received at Hill 41 while serving with the 1st Battalion, and Lieutenant K C Coombs-Jones, who joined from The Duke of Cambridge's Own (Middlesex Regiment) as Signalling Officer.

Although there was growing frustration at not getting home, there was no trouble in the 9th Royal Irish Fusiliers, unlike in some other battalions. As the weather turned frosty the men trained in the morning and played sport in the afternoon. Sport played an increasing part in the life of the 9th Royal Irish Fusiliers; it was an ideal way to keep men fit and occupied without the sense of unnecessary training. Numerous events were organised including boxing, running, riding classes for the officers, and even an introduction to basketball, courtesy of two American unit teams. Concerts were given by the Battalion's natural entertainers—the 'Sandbags Troupe'.

To assist everyone in returning to civilian life a battalion education committee was formed and it was decided to establish a battalion school. It was duly opened in St Charles Convent, Mouscron (a school for girls and today the *Institute St. Charles*). The first day was less than successful when no-one turned up, but the next day forty-three men attended. By January the lectures and education classes were compulsory and well attended. The classes were run by Second Lieutenant Kemp, who taught reading, writing, arithmetic, history and geography, and Second Lieutenant Lees, who taught book-keeping, shorthand and commercial subjects.

Company Sergeant Major Jack Robinson DCM (seated left) and Sergeants of D Company on 23 November 1918. Standing at the far right is Sergeant F S Homersham DCM MM*.

Private Billy Baxter (far left) and friends, Mouscron, 23 November 1918.

On 23 November the Battalion paraded for photographs. Photographs were taken of each company and of other groups, such as the band and the Sandbags Troupe. It is evident that the company officers and groups of friends also had their photographs taken together. Unfortunately, the camera broke before the officers' photograph could be taken. The highlight at the end of the month was the Battalion sports day. Led by the bands of the 1st and 9th Royal Irish Fusiliers, everyone marched to the football ground at Turcoing on 26 November and had an entertaining day competing in a range of sports and activities and watching the Divisional brass band and the antics of two clowns. A concert was held back at the billets that evening when the prizes were presented. Just before the end of the month the 9th Royal Irish Fusiliers moved into new billets in Luingne, on the outskirts of Mouscron.

9th Royal Irish Fusiliers Band, Mouscron, 23 November 1918.
The officer in the centre is the Adjutant, Captain W Sparks MC.

'Sandbags Troupe', the Battalion players, Mouscron 23 November 1918.
The uncomfortable-looking officer in the centre, front row, who was responsible, presumably, for their activities, is Lieutenant R I McCrum.

The officers finally had their photographs taken on 1 December outside the chateau that was battalion headquarters, as did the football team which went on to beat the 1st Royal Irish Fusiliers team 6-0. Training and sport continued on most days and on 6 December the 9th Royal Irish Fusiliers marched to the airfield at Halluin and took part in a Divisional Review and March Past. The following day six officers and 150 other ranks went to Roubaix, where King George V was visiting. On 10 December the 108th Brigade cross-country running competion was held, for which the 9th Royal Irish Fusiliers team had been training hard. The 9th Royal Irish Fusiliers was beaten by the 1st Battalion, with 12th Royal Irish Rifles in third place. On 12 December Private Leslie Edwards, a coal miner from

Merthyr Tydfil in Wales, was the first man sent home for demobilisation. On 16 December another parade was held at Halluin, this time in front of the Corps Commander. Low-level training, including ceremonial drill under the direction of Regimental Sergeant Major Williams, education and sport continued up to Christmas, by which time the 9th Royal Irish Fusiliers was fitter than it had been since the early days after its arrival in France. On Christmas Day church services were held for all denominations. The efficient organisation of the 9th Royal Irish Fusiliers, which had characterised its performance throughout the war, ensured that a good dinner was had by all that evening. Lieutenant Colonel Tamplin visited the men at their meal and called in on the Warrant Officers and Sergeants Mess, where the men were evidently having a thoroughly good time, before dining with the officers at 8.00pm—*'The proceedings being of a merry nature'*.

The officers of the 9th Royal Irish Fusiliers, Mouscron, 1 December 1918.

Back Row: Lieutenant J B Barnett, Captain H C Burrows MC (OC D Company), Lieutenant K Coombs-Jones, Unknown Second Lieutenant, Lieutenant T F H Graves, Unknown, Unknown, Unknown, Unknown MC*, Second Lieutenant A H Warren.

Third Row: Unknown MC*, Lieutenant A Carr, Lieutenant A L Dobbyn MC*, Unknown Second Lieutenant MC, Lieutenant G Robinson MC, Captain W H Sutcliffe MC RAMC (Medical Officer), Lieutenant E W Reynolds MC, Second Lieutenant W Elliott MM, Second Lieutenant R L Lees, Second Lieutenant A Wightman.

Seated Row: Captain C H Kerr (OC A Company), Reverend W B Allman AChD (Chaplain), Captain W Sparks MC (Adjutant), Lieutenant Colonel R J A Tamplin DSO, Captain R L Emerson (Second-in-Command), Captain W G Graham (OC B Company), Captain J E Gibson (OC C Company).

Front Row: Lieutenant & Quartermaster G W Wilson, Second Lieutenant W Mahoney, Second Lieutenant M T Sheehan, Second Lieutenant C H Steele MC*, Captain J B K Morrow (Transport Officer), Lieutenant R I McCrum, Lieutenant F C Hartness, Lieutenant A Valin (Interpreter).

Present and Unidentified: Second Lieutenants J Boyd, R S Duncan, J R Gregory, T C Leahy MC, S Logan MC*, J J Murphy MC*, DCM & C A Ross (Intelligence Officer).

Officers of C Company, Mouscron, 23 November 1918.
Back row (left to right): Second Lieutenant H Kemp MM, Unknown (possibly Second Lieutenant T C Leahy MC), Lieutenant R L Lees (attached from 12th Royal Irish Rifles), Second Lieutenant A Wightman.
Front Row: Lieutenant R I McCrum (Second-in-Command), Captain J E Gibson (Officer Commanding).

This must have been a frustrating period for everyone, however, knowing that the war was over yet having to spend another Christmas away from home. Towards the end of the month it was announced that four awards of the French *Croix de Guerre* were to be made to Lieutenant Colonel Tamplin DSO, Captain C H Kerr, Sergeant J Campbell MM and Private J Moran MM. Twenty-three awards were made by other nations to men of the 9th Royal Irish Fusiliers; the details may be found at Appendix 4. The period up to and over New Year was equally quiet, and confirmation that hostilities had truly ended was seen in subtle changes such as the end to mail censoring on 3 January.

Demobilisation

In January 1919 demobilisation began in earnest. The plan for demobilisation was a complicated one and it was evident that it would not be popular with everyone. It was well planned, however, and rehearsals had even been carried out in early 1918 when it was recognised that such a plan would have to be put into place as soon as the war ended. Those to whom the rules for demobilisation did not apply were the men of the Regular Army who remained in the Army until their period of engagement was completed. Those vital to industry, or who would be most easily absorbed back into society, were the first to go home, regardless of length of service. Understandably this caused some grumbles and the process was modified to allow those with long service to demobilise quickly. The last to go were those who volunteered or were conscripted in 1918. Those who wished to re-enlist into the post-war Regular Army were asked to come forward, and about forty men from the 9th Royal Irish Fusiliers attended the initial medical examination (more details on this process and a list of those men who re-enlisted for Regular Army service may be found at Appendix 6). Lieutenant Graves and second Lieutenant Steele were posted to the 1st Battalion; both would continue to serve in the Regular Army.

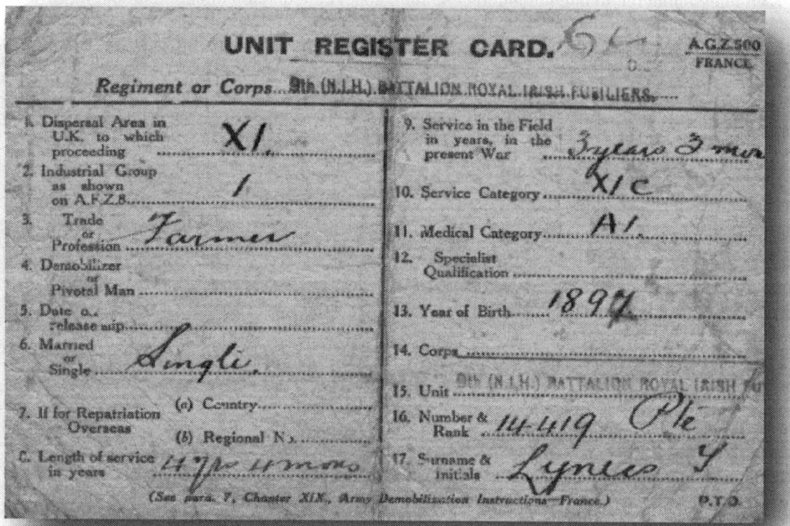
UNIT REGISTER CARD. A.G.Z.500 FRANCE.

Regiment or Corps... 9th (N.I.H.) BATTALION ROYAL IRISH FUSILIERS.

1. Dispersal Area in U.K. to which proceeding ... XI.
2. Industrial Group as shown on A.F.Z.8 ... 1
3. Trade or Profession ... Farmer
4. Demobilizer or Pivotal Man ...
5. Date of release slip ...
6. Married or Single ... Single
7. If for Repatriation Overseas (a) Country ... (b) Regional No. ...
8. Length of service in years ... 4 yrs 4 mos
9. Service in the Field in years, in the present War ... 3 years 3 mos
10. Service Category ... X/C
11. Medical Category ... A1
12. Specialist Qualification ...
13. Year of Birth ... 1897
14. Corps ...
15. Unit ... 9th (N.I.H.) BATTALION ROYAL IRISH FU
16. Number & Rank ... 14419 Pte
17. Surname & Initials ... Lyness T

(See para. 7, Chapter XIX, Army Demobilisation Instructions—France.) P.T.O.

This form (Form AGZ 500 - Unit Register Card) was used by those moving back to Great Britain for demobilisation. This card belonged to Private Thomas Lyness.

On 7 January six more men were sent for early demobilisation and the careful organisation required for the imminent demobilisation of the rest of the Battalion resulted in Captain MacLean being appointed Demobilisation Officer on 18 January, in addition to his new duties as Adjutant. That day the officers said farewell to the interpreter, Lieutenant A Valin. The next day Captain Morrow became the first officer of the 9th Royal Irish Fusiliers to leave. He was replaced as Transport Officer by Lieutenant Abram Carr. Fifty-one years old, Lieutenant Carr had been commissioned into Princess Victoria's (Royal Irish Fusiliers) in 1916 and had served as Transport Officer in a number of regiments and with the Army Service Corps. He remained with the 9th Royal Irish Fusiliers until early March when he was evacuated after an accident with a horse, which broke his leg.

Lieutenant A Valin, Battalion Interpreter.

By the end of January the 9th Royal Irish Fusiliers had been reduced in strength by one officer and 104 other ranks, most leaving in the last few days of the month. In addition, Lieutenant F C Hartness had been evacuated sick on 9 January. February began with a visit to the billets by The Prince of Wales but the general routine changed little. Captain W Sparks MC left for demobilisation and was replaced as Adjutant by Captain P E MacLean. By 10 February the Battalion had reorganised into two companies with the Battalion Transport and the Quartermaster's department remaining separate. Number 1 Company comprised those men destined for the Army of Occupation, and Number 2 Company the remainder. On 22 February the spare horses of the Transport were sent for dispersal. By the end of the month another 7 officers and 298 other ranks had left for demobilisation and the battalion school was closed. The final twenty men of the 9th Royal Irish Fusiliers destined for demobilisation left on 8 March. A total of eight officers and 423 other ranks had now departed.

The 9th Royal Irish Fusiliers now comprised the men that were to join the Army of Occupation and a small cadre to manage the Battalion's equipment. On 19 March the cadre of the 1st Battalion, seven officers and fifty-one other ranks, left for Ireland. They left behind those to be demobilised or transferred to the Army of Occupation, and these men joined the 9th Royal Irish Fusiliers and were split between the two companies. The demobilisation of the forty-nine men of the 1st Battalion trickled on until the last man left on 19 May.

The demobilisation of the 9th Royal Irish Fusiliers and of the 1st Battalion men who joined in March is summarised here:

	9th Battalion		1st Battalion	
	Officers	Other Ranks	Officers	Other Ranks
December 1918	-	1	-	
January 1919	1	104	-	
February 1919	7	298	-	
March 1919	-	20	1	31
April 1919	-	-	3	7
May 1919	-	-	1	11
Total	8	423	5	49

The last six men had left for the Army of Occupation by 7 June and, on 9 June, with only the cadre of three officers and twenty-three other ranks left, Lieutenant Colonel Tamplin signed off his last entry in the war diary: *'Finis'*, with a flourish. On 29 June 1919 the 9th (Service) Battalion, Princess Victoria's (Royal Irish Fusiliers) (County Armagh), lately the 9th (North Irish Horse) Battalion, Princess Victoria's (Royal Irish Fusiliers) formally ceased to exist four years and nine months after it had been raised.

Transfer of Men to the British Army of the Rhine

The occupation of the Rhineland took place after the Armistice and involved troops from Britain, France, Belgium and the United States. The first British troops entered Germany in December 1918 and by March 1919 the British Army of the Rhine had been formed. It comprised a cavalry division and five corps, each of two infantry divisions. All of its battalions, including 12th Royal Irish Rifles, the only battalion of 36th (Ulster) Division to join the British Army of the Rhine, required reinforcement. The men of the Royal Irish Fusiliers were to transfer to The Royal Irish Regiment for service with 5th (Service) Battalion, The Royal Irish Regiment (Pioneers). The men of the units posted to the Army of Occupation (as it was initially known) were all compulsorily retained in the Army and awarded the 'War Bonus', based on their substantive rank (many with acting rank lost it). Those who volunteered to join the Army of Occupation signed a declaration agreeing to voluntary retention in the Army (Army Form W5084), which stated that:

> *'(I).....do hereby declare my willingness to surrender all claims to be now demobilised and express my desire to continue serving under the same conditions as soldiers retained for service with the Armies of Occupation.'*

The 5th Royal Irish Regiment had been raised at Clonmel, County Tipperary, in September 1914, part of 29th Brigade, 10th (Irish) Division. In June 1915 it became 10th (Irish) Division's Pioneer Battalion and landed at Suvla Bay on 7 August that year. After withdrawal from the Dardanelles, 5th Royal Irish Regiment spent nearly two years in Salonica before moving to Egypt in September 1917. On 1 April 1918 it was transferred to 52nd (Lowland) Division and sailed for France ten days later but was transferred out of 52nd (Lowland) Division in May 1918 for Line of Communication duties. In July 1918 it transferred to the 50th (Northumbrian) Division as its Pioneer Battalion. In March 1919 it was transferred again, this time to the 2nd Division, which became the Light Division in II Corps in the British Army of the Rhine. It was based at Nettersheim, south of Cologne. Over the next month it was brought up to strength by officers and men from other Irish regiments.

At Mouscron, those men from the 9th Royal Irish Fusiliers who were to join the Army of Occupation were organised into Number 1 Company on 11 February. On 20 March the first to join 5th Royal Irish Regiment departed—two officers and twenty-seven men. The total departures from the 1st and 9th Royal Irish Fusiliers that were recorded in the war diary are summarised here:

	Officers	Other Ranks
March 1919	7	106
April 1919	2	43
May 1919	-	5
June 1919	-	1
Total	9	155

Nine officers and sixty-nine of these men were from the 9th Royal Irish Fusiliers (the other ranks are listed at the end of Appendix 6) and the remainder were from the 1st Battalion. In addition, on 27 March eleven officers and thirty-nine other ranks were attached to the 7th/8th Royal Inniskilling Fusiliers from the 5th/6th Royal Irish Fusiliers pending transfer to the 5th Royal Irish Regiment. The 5th/6th Royal Irish Fusiliers subsequently dispatched another nine men to the 5th Royal Irish Regiment. The total number from Princess Victoria's (Royal Irish Fusiliers) known to have joined the 5th Royal Irish Regiment, therefore, is twenty officers and 203 other ranks.[1]

Sergeant F S Homersham DCM, MM. This picture was taken on a Rhine cruise while he was serving with the 5th Royal Irish Regiment in the British Army of the Rhine.

Not all of the men posted to the 5th Royal Irish Regiment actually made it. Private Brownlow Thompson had left the 9th Royal Irish Fusiliers on 10 November 1918 for a period of leave in Ireland. He did not return and was listed as absent without leave. Assuming that he would eventually turn up or be apprehended, he was posted to the 5th Royal Irish Regiment in his absence. Sadly, Private Thompson had contracted influenza, then developed pneumonia and died in Queen Alexandria Military Hospital in London on 7 December.

On arrival at Nettersheim the men from the 9th Royal Irish Fusiliers were posted to C Company and the men from the 1st Battalion were posted to D Company. The officers that joined, now using their substantive ranks, were Lieutenants J E Gibson, C H Kerr, N C Mateer, R I McCrum and G Robinson

MC, and Second Lieutenants W Elliott MM, W G Graham, J R Gregory and M J Sheehan, who was immediately made Assistant Adjutant.

The 5th Royal Irish Regiment soon moved to Longerich on the outskirts of Cologne where it was joined by 12th Royal Irish Rifles. Both battalions were soon fully engaged in a round of training and sport, very similar to the life left behind in France. The singular difference was the need for dress and turn-out to be close to pre-war, Regular Army standards. Demobilisation began in the late-summer of 1919 and by the end of September 1919 5th Royal Irish Regiment had been reduced to two companies in strength, with most of the remainder having left that month. The final task for the 5th Royal Irish Regiment was as guard to a logistic dump where the 2nd Battalion Machine Gun Corps was relieved just before being broken up. Finally, on 4 November 1919 the 5th Royal Irish Regiment was disbanded and its cadre was sent home.

The King's Colour and its Laying Up at Armagh Cathedral

Soon after the war ended, in recognition of the service during the war of the battalions under his command, Field Marshall Haig had proposed the presentation of Colours to each battalion that did not already possess them. The proposal secured the consent of King George V and the Army Council directed that the proposal would apply to the whole Army.[2] Many of the Regular Army and 1st Line Territorial Force battalions sent for their Colours; two officers and a colour guard, who had been sent to Armagh in December 1918, brought out the Colours of the 1st Royal Irish Fusiliers on 4 January 1919.

Battalion Colours were impressive totems. All Regular Army and 1st Line Territorial Force infantry battalions (with the exception of rifle battalions) had a 'stand' of Colours comprising a King's Colour and a Regimental Colour. The King's Colour was a hand-stitched, silk, Union Flag, trimmed with a two-inch, gold, fabric fringe and emblazoned in the centre with the regiment's crest or insignia. The Regimental Colour was of hand-stitched, coloured silk (usually in the colour of the regiment's uniform facings), trimmed with a two-inch, gold, fabric fringe and emblazoned with the regiment's crest or insignia and its battle honours. Originally designed to allow troops to rally on the battalion's position, by the First World War a battalion's colours were the representation of its spirit and a focus for pride in its history, traditions and achievements.

The new Colours were to be presented to the service battalions, young soldiers battalions, graduated battalions and garrison battalions of the Regular Army, the 2nd and 3rd Line Territorial Force battalions and the battalions of overseas troops that had served as infantry. To receive Colours a battalion had to have served abroad during the war. The cost of providing a full stand of hand-made Colours was quickly identified as prohibitively expensive and would take too long. It was authorised, therefore, that a machine-stitched King's Colour would be presented to each battalion.

Although described in Parliament as '*merely silk Union Flags given to Service Battalions now serving with the British Armies in France for ceremonial purposes*', this was a proud moment, particularly for the few remaining original members of the 9th Royal Irish Fusiliers. The Battalion had been practising since December and the final rehearsal for the parade was held on the airfield at Herseaux on 25 January. Three days later, on the morning of 28 January, the King's Colours of the battalions of 36th (Ulster) Division were consecrated on an altar of drums and the 9th Royal Irish Fusiliers was presented in its turn with its consecrated King's Colour by the Corps Commander, Lieutenant General Sir Beauvoir de Lisle KCB, DSO.

On 9 June the cadre of the 9th Royal Irish Fusiliers, comprising Lieutenant Colonel Tamplin, Captain H C Burrows MC, Lieutenant T C Leahy MC, twenty-three other ranks and the Medical Officer, Captain W H Sutcliffe MC, left Mouscron for Ireland. The colour guard was made up of the few men who had deployed with the 9th Royal Irish Fusiliers to France in October 1915 and who were still serving in its ranks. Company Quartermaster Sergeant Thomas McConville and Sergeant John Keith had both been awarded the Meritorious Service Medal in January 1919 and they were accompanied by Sergeant Samuel Cummins, Lance Corporal Herbert Cole, Privates Albert Moore, Joseph Powell and William Vance. The Battalion's cadre arrived in Armagh on Saturday 14 June to a warm welcome, and the King's Colour was laid up in the Cathedral Church of St Patrick during a special service on Sunday 15 June. Present at the ceremony were the Comrades of the Great War,[3] including many original members of the 9th Royal Irish Fusiliers commanded by Captain C H Ensor, and a detachment of thirty men from Princess Victoria's (Royal Irish Fusiliers) Depot commanded by Lieutenant Colonel R J Shuter DSO and accompanied by Major G M Forde DSO, MC, Lieutenant and Adjutant D A Davison, and Lieutenant T F Graves. The new Commanding Officer of the reformed 2nd Battalion, Brevet Colonel H L Knight, also attended. The King's Colour was borne by Captain Burrows MC. During the service he handed it over to the Primate of All Ireland, Archbishop John Crozier, who then addressed the congregation. Predictably, his address focused on the events of 1 July 1916 and nothing was said of the actions of the 9th Royal Irish Fusiliers since then. This reinforces the perception that the history of 36th (Ulster) Division and the 9th Royal Irish Fusiliers was limited in the minds of many to the actions at Thiepval and Hamel.

The King's Colour.
This photograph was taken after it had been emblazoned with the Regiment's First World War battle honours.

All of the King's Colours of the war service battalions of Princess Victoria's (Royal Irish Fusiliers) were laid up after the war. The details of the location and dates for the other ceremonies may be found at Appendix 1.

When first issued the Colours had no embellishments, but later the use of the embellishments authorised for the King's Colour of the regular battalion was approved. The added embellishments were to be at regimental expense. After the Battles Nomenclature Committee (which named each of the battles fought during the war, often using names that were wholly unfamiliar to the men who had fought there) completed its report in July 1920, it fell to regimental committees to determine the battle honours to which each battalion of the regiment was entitled (see Appendix 4). In September 1922 regimental committees were instructed to select ten of the regiment's First World War battle honours to be emblazoned on the Kings Colour. The regimental committee of Princess Victoria's (Royal Irish Fusiliers) ordered that they be sewn onto each of the King's Colours of the war service battalions. The King's Colour of the 9th Royal Irish Fusiliers was temporarily removed from the church for the addition of embellishments and battle honours, and then returned. Shamefully, it was stolen from the Cathedral in 1976.

Prisoners of War

One group of men that returned home relatively early in the process of demobilisation was the prisoners of war. The majority of prisoners from the 9th Royal Irish Fusiliers had fallen into enemy hands in March 1918 but there were a few men who had been in captivity since August 1917. It is difficult to determine exactly how many men were taken prisoner, but an analysis of casualties indicates that at least 366 all ranks were captured:

	Officers	Other Ranks		Total	
1 July 1916	-	1	*	1	
16 August 1917	1	9		10	
21-28 March 1919	16	325		341	
11-18 April 1919	1	9		10	
11/12 August 1918	1	-		1	
4 September 1918	-	1	**	1	
30 September/1 October 1918	1	1	**	2	
Total	20	346		366	***

*Private Thomas Warren died of wounds in captivity on 4 July 1916.
**This is the *known* figure for these actions.
***This figure does not include the officers or others ranks captured while serving elsewhere.

Many of the men of Princess Victoria's (Royal Irish Fusiliers) who had been captured owed much to the efforts of Mr Delmage Trimble of the Armagh Guardian who organised a 'Comfort Fund' to ensure a food supply and the provision of some other small amenities. His records were maintained on a card index and they recorded the man's size, for clothing, hats and boots, whether or not he was a smoker and, if so, whether he preferred pipe or cigarette tobacco. For his good work he was appointed an OBE and was presented with a silver cup by the 2nd Battalion. The Ulster Women's Gift Fund also produced a considerable amount to make life a little easier for the men at the front and those held prisoner. Notwithstanding the efforts of the Red Cross and those like Delmage Trimble, the death rate of the Allied troops in captivity was a little under 4%. Two officers of the 9th Royal Irish Fusiliers died of wounds after being captured (one of whom was Major Brew who, as has been recounted, was shot after he was captured) as did eight other ranks. Thirteen men died of illness, including Private R W Kerr who died of heart disease in December 1918 before he could be repatriated. One prisoner of war, Private J Magill, was killed by aircraft bombs dropped by French aircraft on 6 June 1918.

British prisoners of war.
Sergeant David McCullough is holding the axe.

Many of the British prisoners who were held close to the front line were simply released just after the war ended and groups varying in size from a few tens to hundreds made their way back to the Allied lines, surviving on what was given to them by civilians. In Germany and East Prussia (now Poland) most prisoners were moved quickly to the coast and began arriving in England at the beginning of December 1918. The prisoners had received mixed standards of treatment; most were undernourished, many were very ill. The majority had been employed in one way or another on the German economy. The lucky ones had worked on farms in the rural areas, but less lucky were those that worked in the factories and mines alongside prisoners from all over Europe. Some had worked just behind the front line where the threat of violent death remained. For the men too ill to return to duty, a spell in hospital followed their repatriation and the fit were sent to reserve battalions before being transferred to the Class Z Reserve in the first few months of 1919. Those rendered unfit for further service as a result of wounds received before being captured, or due to illness, were discharged as no longer physically fit for war service. Repatriated officers were required to produce a report laying out the circumstances of their capture. If no blame was to be attached to them for the circumstances of their capture, their names appeared on an 'Exonerated Officers List'.

The experiences of Private Henry Emerson were typical of many. Emerson enlisted into the Service Squadron, 6th (Inniskilling) Dragoons and joined the 9th Royal Irish Fusiliers on the amalgamation with the 2nd North Irish Horse in September 1917. He was captured in the action at Erches on 28 March 1918. After his capture, he and the others of the 9th Royal Irish Fusiliers taken that day were held at Nesle for a day before being moved to Ham. He reported:

> *'We were kept one day at Ham. I was never searched or interrogated at all. We stayed in cages during the nights before we got to St. Quentin in old buildings. During the three days we were simply marched about. There was no ill-treatment during that three days. There were some wounded, and men were told off to look after them. The wounded got very little medical attention, and there were plenty of bad cases among them. We were given water to drink, and we were not interfered with. I was taken to St. Quentin on the 30th*

March. I remained for three weeks. At St. Quentin we were put in what had been a cottage or cow-house. There were French prisoners there as well. There were no beds or blankets given us, and our clothes were never off us. It was very cold weather, and there was no heating apparatus, not even a roof on the buildings. The food here was a small loaf of black bread to four men per day (1,400 grammes of bread to each four men); soup, very thin, once a day, preserved turnips seemed to be in it; coffee made of burnt barley; tea in the evenings, only it was not tea; no meat, no fats. There was only a small quantity of each kind of food, and all them men got very low on this diet. No clothes were taken away from us, I was captured with just the clothes I stood up in. The work I had to do here was burying the dead. I spent the whole of the three weeks at this. The guard indulged in plenty of abuse and knocked us about, but I do not know any case of any man being badly injured. The place we were accommodated in was called Martin-Henri. We were in big rooms with the roofs all shattered, and not wired round. The latrines were old places dug out in the yard. It was very filthy and dirty, and there was no payment for work. It was not until my last week at St. Quentin that I was allowed to write home. I was then given a field card and I addressed it to my home. I don't know when it reached there. I received no clothing from the Germans. I did not ask for any, but I do not think I should have received any if I had done so. The German soldiers were short themselves and offered to buy clothes from us. I never received any letters from home there or anywhere else while a prisoner. I never received any parcels, and nobody with me did. The German guards at St. Quentin had better rations than we did. No persons died at St. Quentin while I was there. There were only Portuguese and French and a few Russians there; I think the French had the best treatment. Our men cooked for the whole of the prisoners; they would also get better jobs.

From St. Quentin I was taken with 40 others, all British, to Esmery-Hallon, 6 kilometres south of Ham. This was about the 21st April, and I remained there until about the 30th June. At Esmery-Hallon we lived in an old building, no roofs, no beds, no blankets, no protection from the weather. I remained all the time I was there in this building. I had just the clothes I stood up in and nothing else. The food here was just the same as at St. Quentin. We worked here as engineers, cutting timber, digging holes, and erecting an electric cable. We worked eight hours a day; no night work, no payment received. Worked the eight hours straight through without a spell. The latrines here were very bad, filthy and dirty, and a very bad stench. There was plenty of ill-treatment from the guards, abuse and beating with rifles, and kicking. This the guard did to anyone, not only when there was a refusal to work. I do not know of anyone who had bones broken. The guards, both at St. Quentin and here, were old men who had never been in the line. Only once was I allowed to write home from here. This was about the middle of May, and I do not know whether this got home. The other men there, at this time, were only allowed to write home this once. No mails or parcels were received, and we received no clothes here. We worked seven days a week here also. There were very few smokes. A German corporal was in charge of the camp; there was a camp commandant, but he never came near it. There were two British sergeants there, and they were made to work also. There was a hospital there for those who went sick, but they had to be very bad before they were sent there. There was no doctor at the camp, and if a man reported sick, he went to the hospital and it was decided there. I think the treatment in the hospital was not so bad. The guards at Esmery-Hallon had better rations than we had. There was no canteen here, and there was no time allowed us for recreation. There was plenty of sickness, dysentery, and some disease like dropsy. When at Esmery-Hallon we used to be taken down the line to work at a place called Ognolles, near Roye, and were shelled there. There were no casualties, but shells used to fall all round us. We worked most of our time there, and we had to walk here, a distance of about eight kilometres. That means we had to walk 10 miles a day, besides doing our day's work. No prisoners died at Esmery-Hallon while I was there.

About the 30th June I was moved to Fresnoy-le-Grand with my party. I remained here six days, while waiting to go to Hautmont. We did no work here, and were given only half rations. We lived in a cow-shed without any conveniences, no bed, or blanket, or covering. I was then taken to Hautmont, near Maubeuge, where I remained until the 9th September. At Hautmont we were accommodated in an old building which had a roof. We had no beds or blankets. We worked at a salvage dump, eight hours a day, seven days a week, pretty heavy work. We received pay here, 1s. 2d. per hour. The food here was just the same as at Esmery-Hallon, but the treatment here was bad. We were beaten and kicked by the guard. This was the usual thing. The guards constantly ill-treated us like this. There was no one to complain to; if we complained to an officer, he would give us the same. I wrote home from here, but I do not know whether it reached home. In this letter we were told to give an address for our letters to be addressed to. No parcels were received in my time. There was no canteen and no means of buying anything. I saw Italian prisoners at Hautmont; they were getting good treatment.

On the 9th September I was taken back to Fresnoy, and escaped from there on the 15th September. At Fresnoy there were 1,500 Portuguese prisoners when I escaped. All these men had been captured since March, and were to go to Germany on the 16th. The brigade had been split up, and some had been kept to work behind the lines, and some had been sent to Germany. My treatment behind the lines was just the same all the time; no improvement. I escaped from Fresnoy on the 15th September. One other man escaped with me, Lance-Corporal Bennett, 1st Royal Irish Rifles.'

The officer who questioned him about his experiences commented that he thought that Emerson had '*received worse treatment than he had been able to express clearly*'.

Arrival Back in Ireland

Those arriving home were warmly welcomed. Towns across the region had functions to fete the returning men, such as that on Thursday 30 January 1919 when the 9th Royal Irish Fusiliers' Prisoners of War Fund held a Welcome Home Banquet in Portadown Town Hall. Throughout the spring and early summer of 1919 the Irishmen of the 9th Royal Irish Fusiliers arrived home from Mouscron. They were given a hero's welcome by their communities and formal functions were held across County Armagh, such as the function held at Bessbrook Town Hall on Friday 11 April 1919. Attendance for 'Tea' at 6.30pm was by invitation and each man received three tickets to the 'Smoking Concert' afterwards. More generally, these men returned to an uncertain future. Many encountered problems with employment. Young men who were not old enough or had not volunteered to fight

were now employed in the factories, small businesses and farms across the country. Some businesses had closed due to the impact of the war and many had not been able to hold jobs open. Many men were not re-engaged in the same position that they had left or were paid lower wages. Others were so affected by their experiences, mentally and physically, that they were not able to hold down a job. Rural Ulster was hit badly and, although the population grew rapidly in the 1920s, it would be many years before the children of those injured and killed were able to take on work to keep their families. The English men who had served with the Ulster Division arrived home to broadly the same problems, but the unique nature of Irish politics added another dimension.

As if those who had suffered on the Western front had not had enough to contend with, they returned to an Ireland at the dawn of a new era in Irish politics and conflict. In 1918 Ireland was represented in Parliament by 105 MPs in 103 constituencies. The majority of Irish MPs were nationalists and members of the Irish Parliamentary Party, formed in 1882 by Charles Stewart Parnell. The minority parties were the Irish Unionist Party, which opposed Home Rule and was largely confined to the northern counties of Ulster, and Sinn Féin, founded in 1905 by Arthur Griffith, *'to establish in Ireland's capital a national legislature endowed with the moral authority of the Irish nation'*. Voting in the 1918 general election began on 14 December and the result was a shock to many. Sinn Féin candidates were elected in seventy-three constituencies (although four candidates were elected for two constituencies resulting in the total number of Sinn Féin MPs being sixty-nine). The Irish Unionist Party secured twenty-two seats, largely limited to Ulster, and the Southern Unionists were elected only in the constituencies of the University of Dublin and Rathmines. Three Labour Unionist and one Independent Unionist MPs were also elected. The Irish Parliamentary Party won only six seats.

After the election the elected Sinn Féin MPs chose to boycott the Westminster Parliament and formed the revolutionary parliament—*Dáil Éireann* (Assembly of Ireland). On the same day two members of the Royal Irish Constabulary guarding quarry explosives were ambushed and killed at Soloheadbeg in Tipperary by members of the Irish Volunteers. The *Dáil* chose to recognise the Irish Volunteers as the army of the Irish Republic, and the ambush as an act of war against Great Britain. Thus began the Anglo-Irish War that would ultimately result in the formation of the Irish Free State in 1922 and the partition of

Ireland. In this climate of civil war, brutal sectarian attacks and political extremism, former soldiers in many areas of the southern counties found it more difficult to get work when their war service became known. In the northern counties Catholic ex-servicemen had similar experiences.

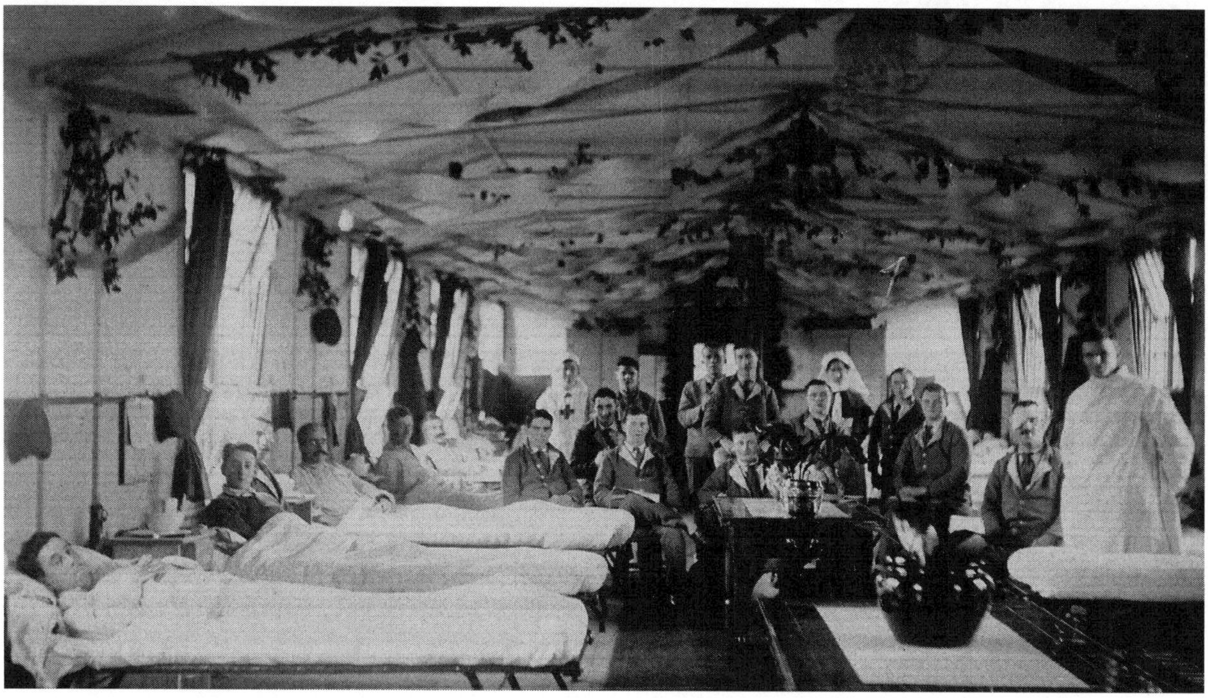

Ward 2, Cannock Chase Military Hospital, Christmas 1918.
Not everyone was able to return home when the war ended. Thousands of men remained in hospital. This 594-bed hospital was established for general surgical cases at Cannock Chase Camp near Rugeley in Staffordshire. The clean, tidy and well-aired ward was a far cry from the conditions in Flanders in 1917 that resulted in RQMS Henry Fox (seated in the centre at the table) being wounded. The men are wearing the blue uniforms with red facings that identified them as in-patients.

The response by Protestant Unionists to the attacks of the Irish Republican Army in 1920 and 1921 was to form local militias across Ulster, based loosely on the pre-war UVF and manned by many former soldiers. In an effort to regulate these and to bolster the efforts of the police, the government agreed to the creation of the Ulster Special Constabulary as a reserve element of the Royal Irish Constabulary. This was achieved using existing legislation: the Special Constables (Ireland) Act, 1832. The Ulster Special Constabulary was divided into several categories. The first was a uniformed, regular cadre, the 'A' category. The second and largest was the part-time 'B' category, who served in their home districts. Finally, there was the 'C' category, who served only occasionally and in static guard duties near their homes, and the 'C1' category, who formed the strategic reserve. The 'A' and 'B' categories were further divided. About half of the 'A Specials' were assigned to duty in police barracks and acted as uniformed police, with the other half being formed into motorized platoons, each with 67 officers and men, who functioned as soldiers. The 'B Specials' in Belfast were trained and operated as police reservists, while those in the rest of the country served as territorial defence troops.

Some of the men who served with the Irish and Ulster Divisions sought out the militias and joined their ranks again. The attraction of the Specials to men of the Ulster Division,

39th Platoon, Ulster Special Constabulary, Armagh, 1923.
The Platoon commander, former Lieutenant A D Allen, is on the right of the County Commandant, Captain C H Ensor.

Ulster Special Constabulary, Armagh, B Platoon, 1925.
Seated on the front row are Captain G C Dickson (third from left), Captain C H Ensor OBE (fifth left) and Sergeant (formerly Private 14086) A Cust (second right). Sitting on the left on the ground is Constable (formerly Private 13999) J Burden.

particularly to those who had joined the UVF before the war, is obvious. Those who joined the Specials included Sergeant William Neill DCM, who became an A Special, Charles Ensor who was appointed County Commandant for County Armagh, a post that he held until he retired in 1952, aged seventy-four, and John Adams, who served with the Ulster Special Constabulary for twenty years, also retiring in 1952. Some men served with the Royal Irish Constabulary and later the Royal Ulster Constabulary, such as Corporal David Frazer, Private Henry Downey, Private William Scott, who retired in 1948, and Privates Sampson Trotter and William Lipsett, both of whom retired in 1954.

John Adams MM (left) and CH Ensor, Ulster Special Constabulary County Commandant.

Others gravitated back into uniform as regular soldiers. One hundred and four men who served at some time with the 9th Royal Irish Fusiliers are known to have re-enlisted into (or remained in) the Regular Army with Princess Victoria's (Royal Irish Fusiliers) and twenty-four men re-enlisted into other regiments. Some, such as J J Murphy and Lieutenant E H Gilmer, volunteered to fight in north Russia (see Appendices 5 and 6). The longest serving, original member of the 9th Royal Irish Fusiliers was Warrant Officer Class II Alfred Moore MBE who enlisted in September 1914. He was discharged to the Army Reserve in April 1949 after nearly thirty-five years' service, and joined the Territorial Army in which he served until 1952.

Sergeant Francis Homersham DCM, MM had a very different second military career. He returned to the technical education that he had left when conscripted and in 1925 was commissioned into the Royal Air Force. He served as a pilot in the Middle East before transferring to the Reserve of Air Force Officers in 1930. During the Second World War he commanded a flying training school, took part in a number of bombing raids and was awarded the Air Force Cross.

Two former member of the 9th Royal Irish Fusiliers died while serving during the Second World War: Lieutenant P C Radbourne (formerly Captain P C Radbourne) died in 1944 while serving with the South African Internment Corps, and Warrant Officer Class 2 C H Turner MC (formerly 17397 Warrant Officer Class 1 C H Turner MC) died in 1940 while serving with 6th (Home Defence) Battalion, The Royal Ulster Rifles. The most senior officer of the 9th Royal Irish Fusiliers was Brigadier T F Given DSO, OBE, MC. He served with The Royal Munster Fusiliers until it was disbanded and then transferred to The East Yorkshire Regiment. In the Second World War he earned a DSO and after the war joined the Colonial Service. In 1952 he was killed while trying to stop tribesmen looting on the border between British Somaliland and south-eastern Ethiopia. The record of many of the others who served in the Second World War can be seen at Appendices 5 and 6 and in the section on Awards For Previous or Subsequent Service in Appendix 4. The death in that second great war of the sons of so many who served with the 9th Royal Irish Fusiliers is a tragic footnote to the entries in those appendices.

The sectarian violence of the 1920s could not be compared with the ferocity of trench warfare in France and Flanders, but it must have been an unpleasant and wholly unwelcome time for those who had seen enough of violent death. It must have contributed to the decision by many to seek a new life abroad and emigrate to Australia, New Zealand, Canada and South Africa. It is striking that so many officers of the 9th Royal Irish Fusiliers went on to become doctors: St C E J Barrett TD, MRCS served as a Lieutenant Colonel with the RAMC during the Second World War and was mentioned in despatches for his gallantry as a doctor in a Japanese prisoner of war camp; A L Dobbyn MC*, MB was a general practitioner in England; J R Gregory OBE, MD was awarded the OBE for his service as Director of the British Red Cross Society in the East African Territories; J A L Johnston OBE, MD was awarded the OBE for his service as Consultant Physician, North-west Hospitals Group in Londonderry; C H Kerr DSO, MD served as a Colonel with the RAMC during the Second World War and was awarded the DSO for his gallant service at El Alamein, and F W Vint OStJ, MD was appointed to the Venerable Order of the Hospital of St. John of Jerusalem for his service with the East African Medical Service.

The impact of war injuries foreshortened the lives of a number of the men of the 9th Royal Irish Fusiliers but many went on to lead full and very long lives. Private Clarence Oswald served with the Army Veterinary Corps before joining the 9th Royal Irish Fusiliers in May 1918; he died at Wolverhampton in 1992, aged 100. Seven former soldiers of the Battalion are known to have lived into their nineties, as did eight former officers including Henry Vivian Day, an officer of 6th (Inniskilling) Dragoons who served briefly with the 9th Royal Irish Fusiliers in October 1917 before transferring to the Royal Flying Corps. He founded a family haulage company (H V Day and Sons) at Glenfield in Leicestershire and died in 1992, aged 98. As far as can be ascertained, the last surviving soldier of the 9th Royal Irish Fusiliers was Private Billy Baxter who enlisted in November 1915, a month before his sixteenth birthday and who died in 1993, aged 94.

Wing Commander F S Homersham AFC, DCM, MM* RAF.

William Lipsett. His medals testify to a lifetime of service: 1914 Star, British War Medal 1914-20, Victory Medal, Defence Medal 1945, and the Police Long Service & Good Conduct Medal.

C Company, 4th Belfast Battalion, Ulster Home Guard, led by Lieutenant W H Palmer MM. The black uniform of the Ulster Special Constabulary, upon which the Ulster Home Guard was based, was worn until the issue of Army uniforms.

Commemoration

Eventually, as was the case throughout the British Isles, the attention of those who had survived and the families of those who had died turned to commemoration. In March 1921 the War Office published the 'final and corrected' casualty figures for the war. In the period of active operations from 4 August 1914 to 30 September 1919, the British army had suffered 673,375 all ranks killed in action, died of wounds, died of other causes and missing and 1,643,469 wounded. The casualties of 36th (Ulster) Division numbered 32,186 killed in action, died of wounds, died of other causes and missing. The casualty figures for the 10th (Irish) and 16th (Irish) Divisions were 9,363 and 28,398 men respectively. Although by 1918 all of these divisions were manned by men from all over the British Isles, the Irish casualties were substantial. The figures do not include the men who died of their wounds, or through illness aggravated by war service, after September 1919. In 1926 the Registrar General recorded the number of Irish deaths in the British Army as 27,405. It is hard to say how casualties on this scale contributed to the course of Irish history, but the loss of so many men must have had an effect in the immediate post-war years. The loss of wounded men from the workforce and the care required for the badly-wounded also had a significant impact on society.

The exact number of casualties of the 9th Royal Irish Fusiliers cannot be determined exactly, but it is now known that 774 all ranks were killed in action, died of wounds or died of other causes serving with the Battalion, and a further fifty-two former members of the Battalion were killed in action, died of wounds or died serving elsewhere. About two-thirds of these men were from Ireland and most of those were from Ulster. These figures are for the period up to 31 August 1921, after which war-related deaths were not commemorated officially. The number of men wounded or evacuated due to illness is estimated at between three and four times the number killed. Although many soldiers recovered and were passed fit for general service later, many more were sufficiently debilitated by their wounds or illness to allow only service at home, or to necessitate discharge. Over 630 all ranks have been identified as being entitled to the Silver War Badge as a consequence of having to relinquish their commission or having been discharged. Some of these men were discharged prior to service overseas or having been wounded or fallen ill while serving elsewhere, but the majority were awarded to officers and men serving with the 9th Royal Irish Fusiliers. This number includes those who were categorised as *'no longer physically fit for war service due to wounds or sickness'*, those who were *'discharged after service overseas in the armed forces of the Crown, on account of disablement or ill-health caused otherwise than by misconduct'*, and those who were discharged as *'surplus to military requirements having suffered impairment since entry into the service'*.

The men who succumbed to wounds or illness in Ulster were buried there, as were some men who died in Great Britain. Most of the remainder had been buried in graves in France and Flanders. In the years immediately after the war, bodies were collected from the battlefields and smaller cemeteries and concentrated in larger burial grounds maintained by the new Imperial War Graves Commission. The men who had served at some time with the 9th Royal Irish Fusiliers and whose remains could be identified, are interred in a total of 121 cemeteries in Belgium, France, England, Ireland, Egypt and Germany. It is worth noting, however, that over a third of the officers and more than half of the other ranks have no known grave. For many their bodies were never recovered. For others their graves were lost or destroyed in the fighting, and for others the graves and remains that were found during the concentration process bore no marks of identification. These men are commemorated on nineteen of the many memorials to the missing in France and Belgium, and as far afield as Burma, Italy, Germany and Poland. The decision to leave the dead in battlefield graveyards meant that nearly every community at home felt the need for a memorial of some sort as a focus for their grief, and in respect for the fallen.

The commemoration of war-dead in the Irish Free State caused much heated debate after partition, resulting in many fewer traditional memorials being built there than in Northern Ireland. Across Northern Ireland, however, nearly every town and many villages and parish churches planned memorials of various sizes and designs, from simple obelisks to ornate statues, memorial halls and gardens. These memorials did not only commemorate the dead. There are many memorials, particularly in parish churches, that commemorate those who served and returned home. Many had been badly wounded and recognition of their sacrifice was deemed important.

The greatest debate was always over the form of the memorial, with those in favour of practical buildings such as halls and schools evenly balanced against those in favour of something more decorative and ornamental. The erection of these memorials was hindered almost always, however, by a lack of money and many projects were completed on a much smaller scale than planned, or not at all. The lack of money, or consensus, delayed the unveiling of many memorials until the late 1920s and some were not completed until the eve of the Second World War. In Lurgan, the Urban Council discussed the building of a memorial as early as July 1917, but original plans were abandoned in 1921 and a decorative memorial was finally unveiled in May 1928. Conversely, in Portadown a number of memorials were erected quickly. At Seagoe parish church impressive memorial gate pillars were built of Portland stone and dedicated on 19 June 1921. Built into each was a tablet of red granite inscribed with the names of fifty-two men connected with the church and parish, fourteen of whom were 9th Royal Irish Fusiliers. A larger memorial dedicated to all of the men of Portadown was erected in the town centre in 1925 and the church tower of St Mark's Church of Ireland was replaced in memory of those killed. It is noteworthy that some men not commemorated officially were commemorated after 31 August 1921 on local memorials, having succumbed to their war injuries or to illness aggravated by war service.

Edenderry Presbyterian Church Memorial, Portadown.
Of the thirteen men listed here who gave their lives, six were amongst the first to enlist into the 9th Royal Irish Fusiliers.

Large collective acts of remembrance began in 1919. One such act took place on Sunday 22 June 1919 at St Mark's Church, Portadown, in memory of the soldiers of the parish who fell in the war. Over 200 former soldiers paraded at the Parochial Hall under the command of Lieutenant Colonel S W W Blacker DSO, accompanied by Major D G Shillington. They marched to the parish church headed by Parkmount Flute Band, whose members had suffered ten killed and thirteen captured. The pulpit was draped in a Union Flag, and laid over the altar was the King's Colour of the 9th Royal Irish Fusiliers, brought from the Cathedral in Armagh for the occasion. Lieutenant Colonel Blacker read the lesson. At the end of the service buglers from the 9th Royal Irish Fusiliers played the last post. Such services were repeated in parishes across the United Kingdom until after the unveiling of the stone Cenotaph in London on 11 November 1920, after which 11 November became the primary focus for acts of remembrance.

Notwithstanding the suffering that accrued over the course of the First World War, it was the first day of the Somme battle that had the greatest impact on the people of Ulster. The heady feeling of euphoria that the Ulster Division had acquitted itself with honour was replaced within a few days with the awful realisation of what it had all cost. This was seen by many as the blood sacrifice of Ulster for the Union, and its commemoration took on special significance. The focus for the homage to the dead of Ulster was to be a memorial on the site of the Ulster Division's attack at Thiepval. After much discussion, the idea of a replica of Helen's Tower on Clandeboye Estate near Newtownards in County Down was proposed in November 1919 by Sir James Craig. The original tower would have been familiar to all of the original members of the Ulster Division who trained there in 1914 and 1915. It was the first official memorial raised on the Western Front when it was opened and dedicated on Saturday 19 November 1921. More details on all of these memorials may be found at Appendix 3.

The memorial gate pillars at Seagoe parish church. The upper panels commemorate those who died in the First World War. The lower panels were added to commemorate those who died in the Second World War.

The dedication of the Ulster Battlefield Memorial Tower was the start of an increasingly Protestant, Unionist celebration of the history of 36th (Ulster) Division and commemoration of the First World War in Northern Ireland. This politicisation of the dead may be seen in the public comments of some of those commemorating the war in the decade after its end, such as those by Sir James Craig at the dedication of the war memorial at Coleraine on 11 November 1922, who stated, *"Those who passed away have left behind a great message to stand firm, and to give away none of Ulster's soil"*. The political and religious divisions across Northern Ireland saw the almost total dominance of public life by Protestant Unionists and the consequent reduction in participation in public ceremonial by Roman Catholics. In turn, the First World War and the rituals of commemoration were used until recently by militant Nationalists as an example of British imperialism. Today the attack at Thiepval is part of the mythology of the Orange Order and a rallying cry for those who, echoing the men of the Ulster Volunteers, oppose a united Ireland. This can be seen in some of the disgracefully sectarian language written in the memorial books in the cemeteries around Thiepval.

I hope that this history of the 9th Royal Irish Fusiliers reaffirms a more accurate view of the actions of 36th (Ulster) Division and of those who fought in its ranks. The last word must be left to Major General Sir Oliver Nugent who, at the dedication of the war memorial in Virginia, County Cavan, in August 1923, stated:

> *'The day is not, I hope, far distant when the memory of all those of our country who gave their lives for civilisation as we interpret it and in obedience to what they believed to be their duty will be honoured and perpetuated in every town and village in Ireland'.*

The Ulster Tower from Mill Road Cemetery before the renovation of the cemetery by the Imperial War Graves Commission.

Endnotes, Chapter 10

1 The officers from 5th/6th Royal Irish Fusiliers who joined the 5th Royal Irish Regiment were Captains W A Beattie MC & D T Figgis, Lieutenant H B Reynell and Second Lieutenants T J Gallagher, J Thornton, L Ward DCM, J Carroll MC, P J T Cater, P L Davis, G E Chiplin & J C G Nicolls.

2 The official order for the presentation of Colours was laid out in Army Council Instruction 444 dated 21 July 1919.

3 The Comrades of The Great War was one of the original four ex-service associations that amalgamated on 15 May 1921 to form The British Legion.

Maps

&

Appendices

Maps

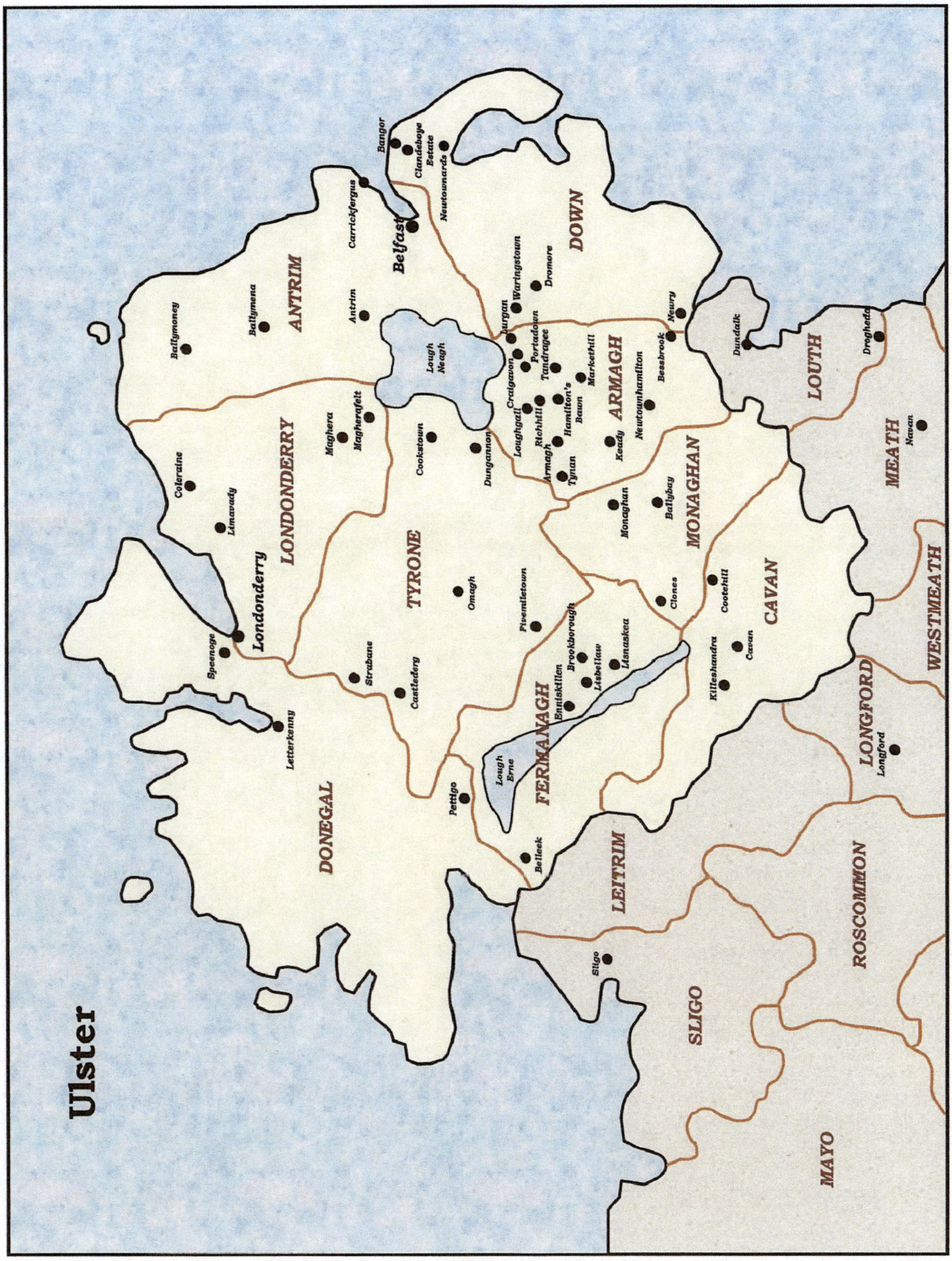
Ulster
ANTRIM
Ballymoney
Ballymena
Antrim
Carrickfergus
Belfast
Bangor
Clandeboye Estate
Newtownards
DOWN
Waringstown
Dromore
Lurgan
Craigavon
Portadown
Tandragee
Markethill
Lough Neagh
Newry
Bessbrook
Newtownhamilton
ARMAGH
Hamilton's Bawn
Richhill
Loughgall
Armagh
Tynan
Keady
Dundalk
Drogheda
LOUTH
MEATH
Navan
LONDONDERRY
Coleraine
Limavady
Londonderry
Maghera
Magherafelt
Cookstown
Dungannon
TYRONE
Omagh
Fivemiletown
MONAGHAN
Monaghan
Ballybay
Clones
Cootehill
CAVAN
Cavan
Killeshandra
WESTMEATH
LONGFORD
Longford
Speenoge
Strabane
Castlederg
Brookborough
Lisnaskea
Lisbellaw
Enniskillen
FERMANAGH
Lough Erne
Letterkenny
DONEGAL
Pettigo
Belleek
LEITRIM
ROSCOMMON
Sligo
SLIGO
MAYO

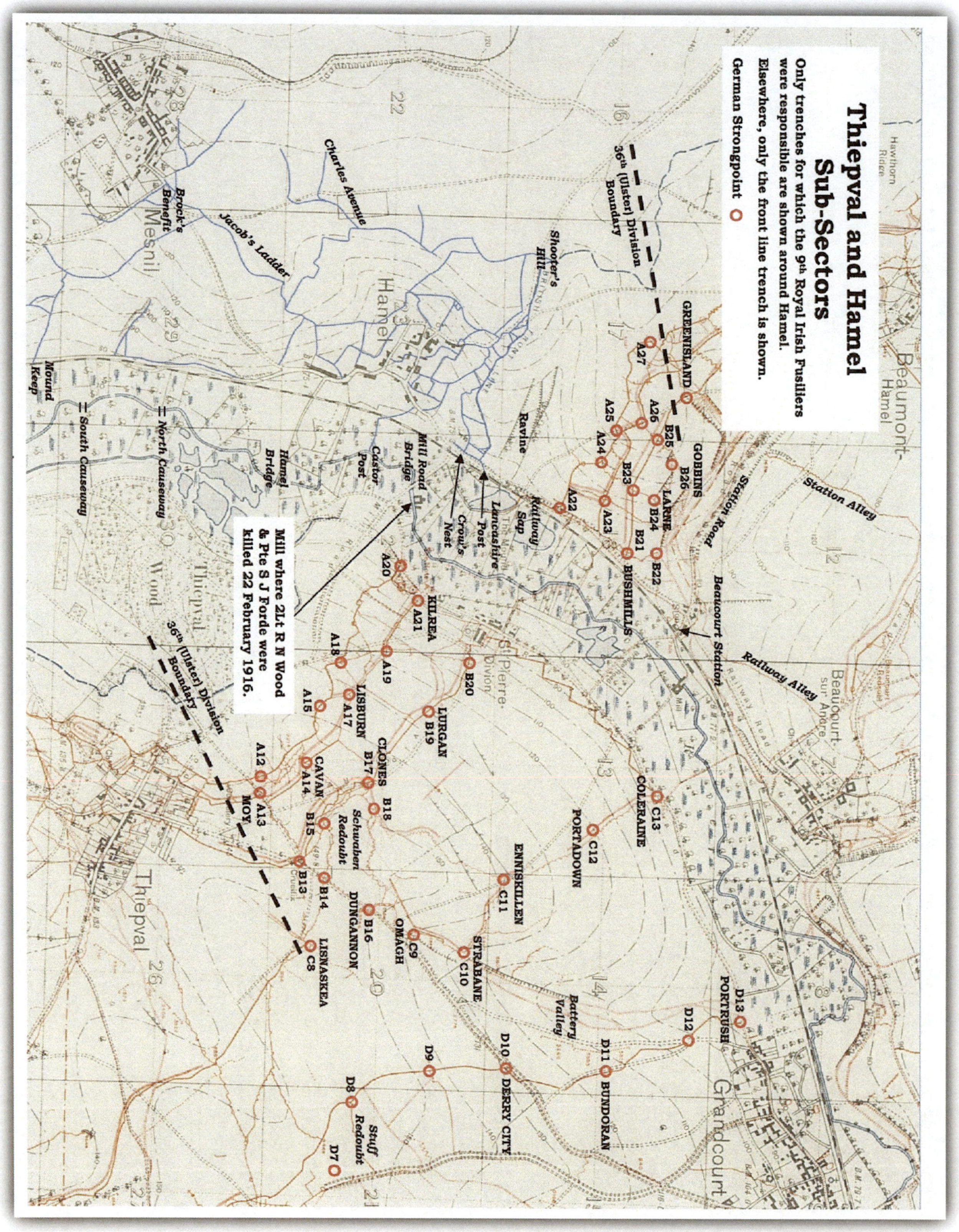
Thiepval and Hamel Sub-Sectors
Only trenches for which the 9th Royal Irish Fusiliers were responsible are shown around Hamel.
Elsewhere, only the front line trench is shown.
German Strongpoint
36th (Ulster) Division Boundary
Charles Avenue
Brock's Benefit
Jacob's Ladder
Mesnil
Shooter's Hill
Hamel
Mound Keep
South Causeway
North Causeway
Hamel Bridge
Castor Post
Mill Road Bridge
Ravine
Crow's Nest
Lancashire Post
Railway Sap
GREENISLAND
A27
A26
A25
A24
B25
GOBHINS
B26
B23
LARNE
B24
A22
A23
B21
B22
BUSHMILLS
Station Road
Station Alley
Beaucourt Station
Railway Alley
Beaumont Hamel
Beaucourt sur Ancre
Mill where 2Lt R N Wood & Pte S J Forde were killed 22 February 1916.
A20
KILREA
A21
A18
A19
B20
St Pierre Divion
LISBURN
A17
A15
LURGAN
B19
CLONES
B17
B18
CAVAN
A14
A12
A13
MOY
B15
Schwaben Redoubt
COLERAINE
C13
PORTADOWN
C12
ENNISKILLEN
C11
B13
B14
DUNGANNON
B16
OMAGH
C9
STRABANE
C10
LISNASKEA
C8
Thiepval
Thiepval Wood
PORTRUSH
D13
D12
Battery Valley
D11
BUNDORAN
D10
DERRY CITY
D9
D8
Stuff Redoubt
D7
Grandcourt

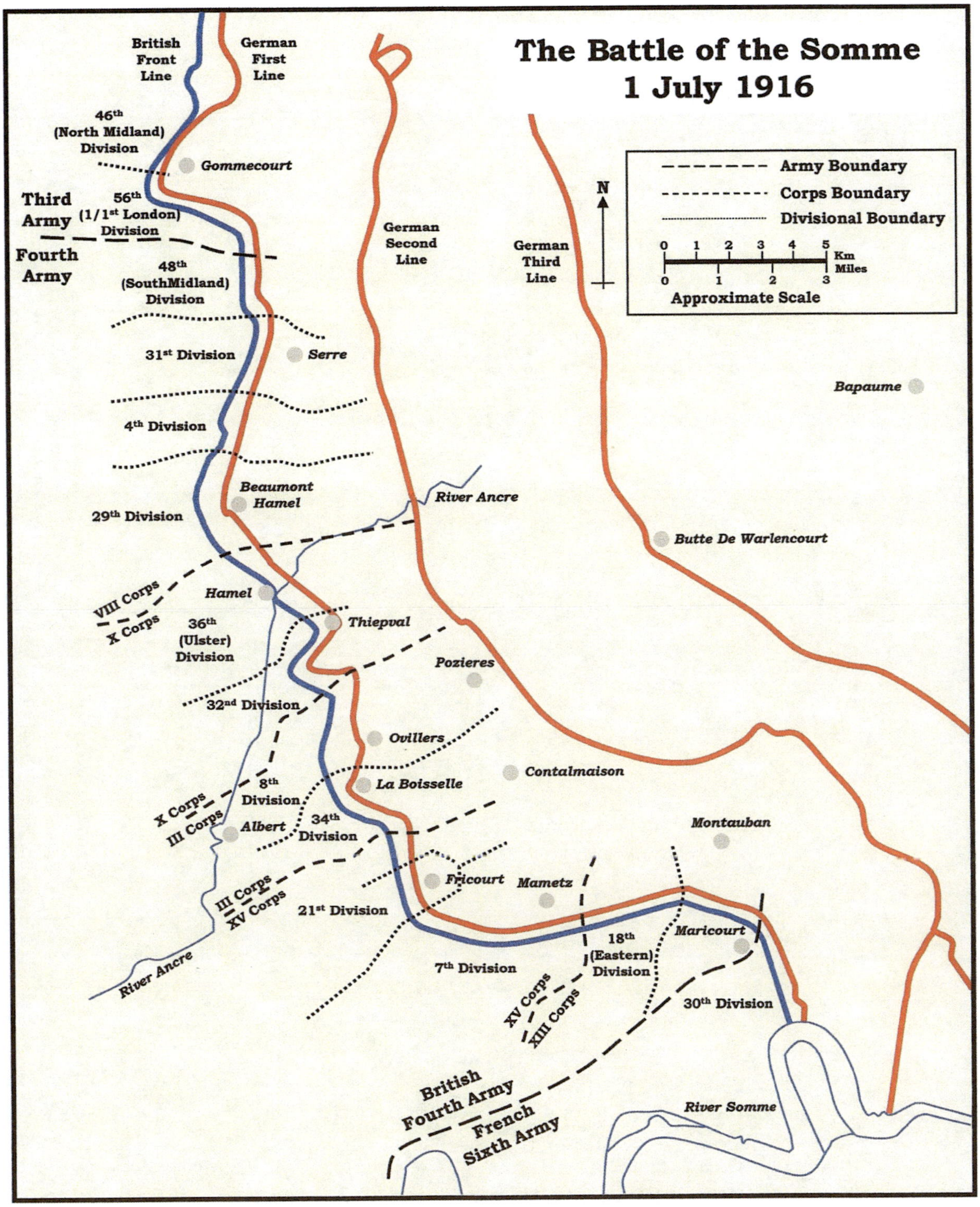

The Battle of the Somme
1 July 1916
British Front Line
German First Line
German Second Line
German Third Line
Army Boundary
Corps Boundary
Divisional Boundary
N
0 1 2 3 4 5 Km
0 1 2 3 Miles
Approximate Scale
46th (North Midland) Division
Gommecourt
Third Army
56th (1/1st London) Division
Fourth Army
48th (SouthMidland) Division
31st Division
Serre
4th Division
Bapaume
Beaumont Hamel
River Ancre
29th Division
Butte De Warlencourt
VIII Corps
X Corps
Hamel
36th (Ulster) Division
Thiepval
Pozieres
32nd Division
Ovillers
Contalmaison
X Corps
III Corps
8th Division
La Boisselle
Albert
34th Division
Montauban
III Corps
XV Corps
Fricourt
Mametz
21st Division
18th (Eastern) Division
Maricourt
River Ancre
7th Division
XV Corps
XIII Corps
30th Division
British Fourth Army
French Sixth Army
River Somme

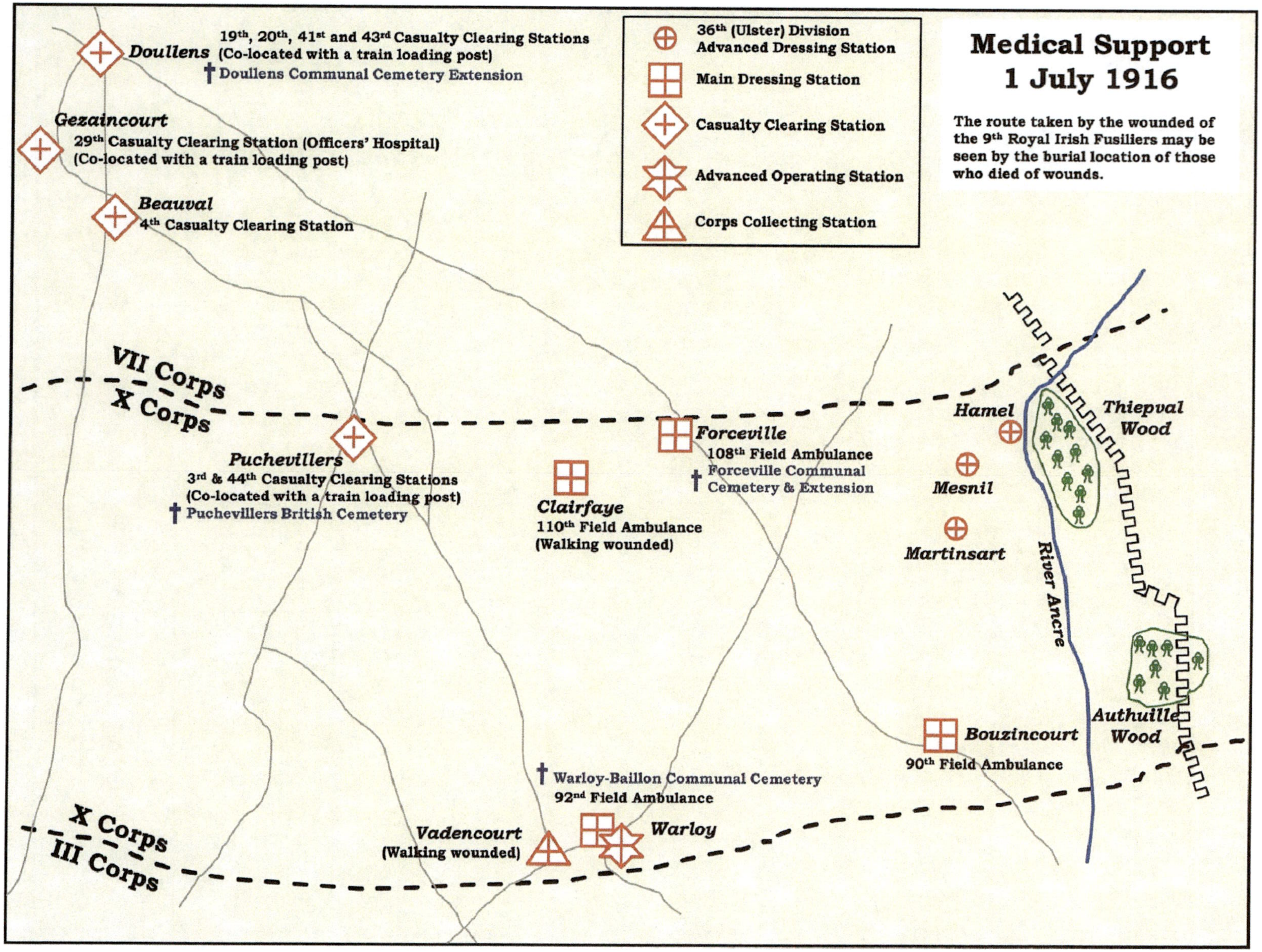

Medical Support
1 July 1916
The route taken by the wounded of the 9th Royal Irish Fusiliers may be seen by the burial location of those who died of wounds.
36th (Ulster) Division Advanced Dressing Station
Main Dressing Station
Casualty Clearing Station
Advanced Operating Station
Corps Collecting Station
Doullens
19th, 20th, 41st and 43rd Casualty Clearing Stations (Co-located with a train loading post)
Doullens Communal Cemetery Extension
Gezaincourt
29th Casualty Clearing Station (Officers' Hospital) (Co-located with a train loading post)
Beauval
4th Casualty Clearing Station
VII Corps
X Corps
Puchevillers
3rd & 44th Casualty Clearing Stations (Co-located with a train loading post)
Puchevillers British Cemetery
Clairfaye
110th Field Ambulance (Walking wounded)
Forceville
108th Field Ambulance
Forceville Communal Cemetery & Extension
Hamel
Mesnil
Martinsart
Thiepval Wood
River Ancre
Authuille Wood
Bouzincourt
90th Field Ambulance
Warloy-Baillon Communal Cemetery
92nd Field Ambulance
Warloy
Vadencourt
(Walking wounded)
X Corps
III Corps

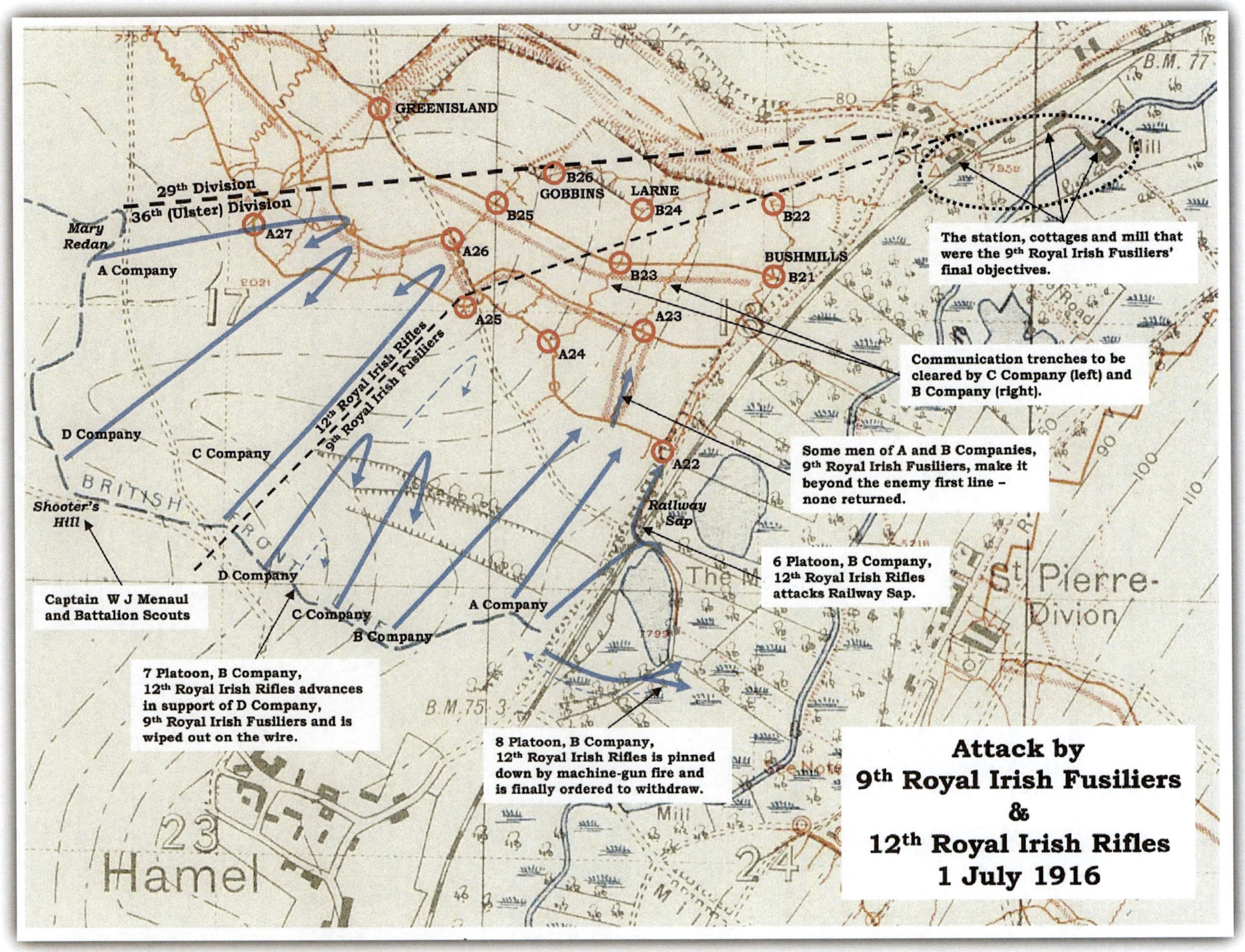

Attack by
9th Royal Irish Fusiliers
&
12th Royal Irish Rifles
1 July 1916
GREENISLAND
GOBBINS
LARNE
BUSHMILLS
B26
B25
B24
B23
B22
B21
A27
A26
A25
A24
A23
A22
29th Division
36th (Ulster) Division
Mary Redan
A Company
D Company
C Company
12th Royal Irish Rifles
9th Royal Irish Fusiliers
BRITISH FRONT LINE
Shooter's Hill
D Company
C Company
B Company
A Company
Railway Sap
Captain W J Menaul and Battalion Scouts
7 Platoon, B Company, 12th Royal Irish Rifles advances in support of D Company, 9th Royal Irish Fusiliers and is wiped out on the wire.
8 Platoon, B Company, 12th Royal Irish Rifles is pinned down by machine-gun fire and is finally ordered to withdraw.
6 Platoon, B Company, 12th Royal Irish Rifles attacks Railway Sap.
Some men of A and B Companies, 9th Royal Irish Fusiliers, make it beyond the enemy first line – none returned.
Communication trenches to be cleared by C Company (left) and B Company (right).
The station, cottages and mill that were the 9th Royal Irish Fusiliers' final objectives.
St Pierre-Divion
Hamel
Mill
B.M. 77
B.M. 75 3

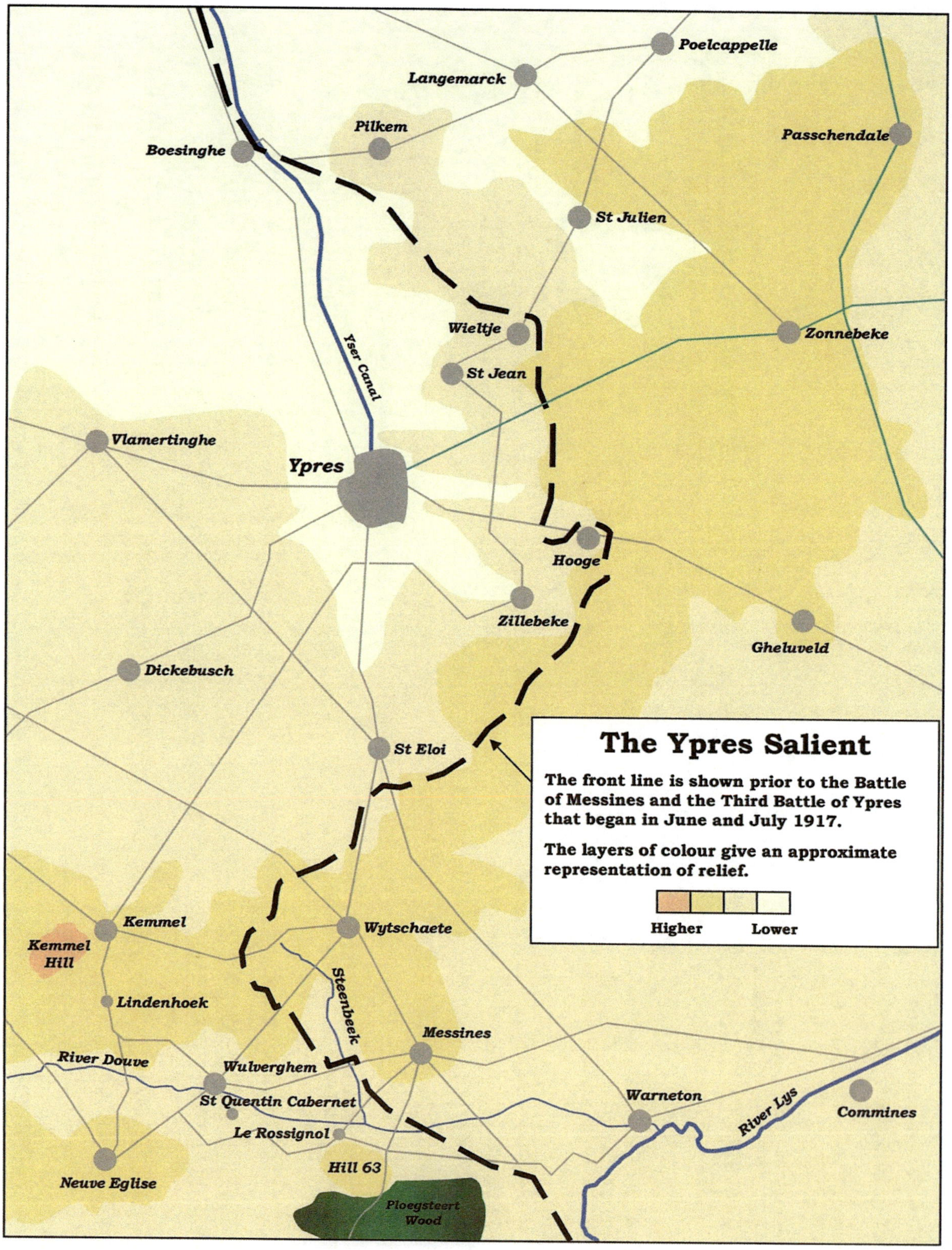
Poelcappelle
Langemarck
Pilkem
Boesinghe
Passchendale
St Julien
Wieltje
St Jean
Zonnebeke
Yser Canal
Vlamertinghe
Ypres
Hooge
Zillebeke
Gheluveld
Dickebusch
St Eloi
The Ypres Salient
The front line is shown prior to the Battle of Messines and the Third Battle of Ypres that began in June and July 1917.
The layers of colour give an approximate representation of relief.
Higher
Lower
Kemmel
Kemmel Hill
Wytschaete
Lindenhoek
Steenbeek
Messines
River Douve
Wulverghem
St Quentin Cabernet
Le Rossignol
Warneton
River Lys
Commines
Hill 63
Neuve Eglise
Ploegsteert Wood

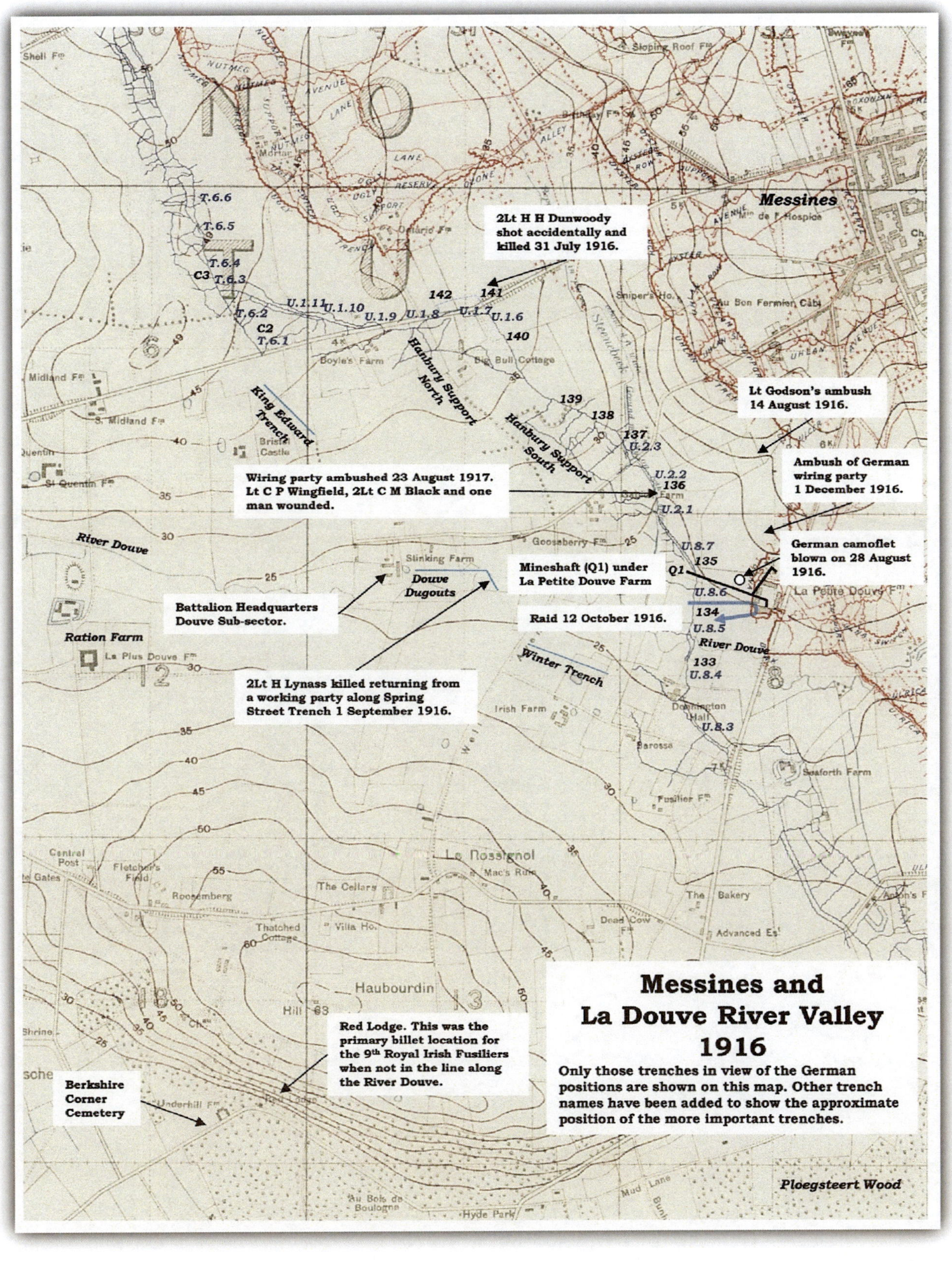

Messines and La Douve River Valley 1916

Only those trenches in view of the German positions are shown on this map. Other trench names have been added to show the approximate position of the more important trenches.

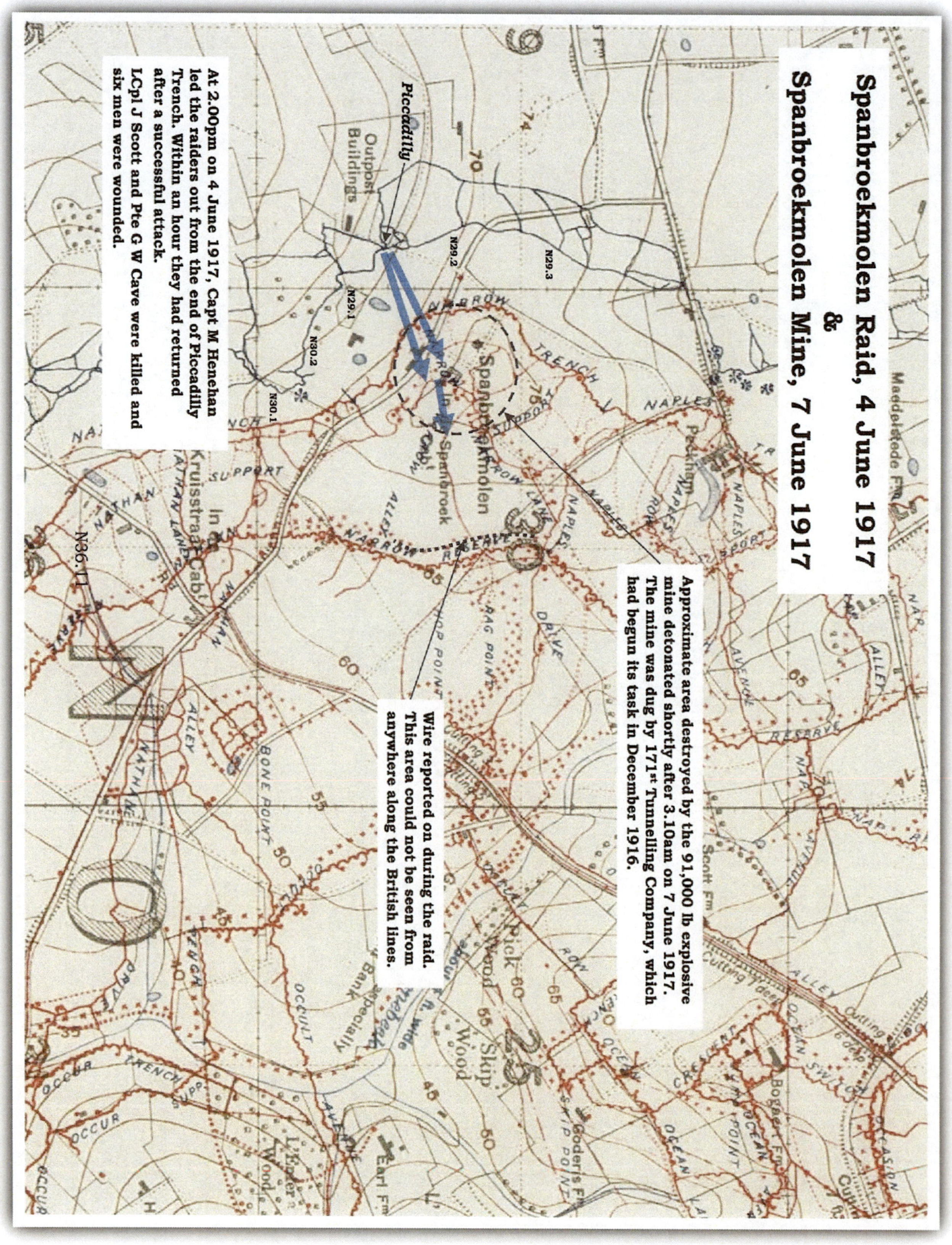
Spanbroekmolen Raid, 4 June 1917
&
Spanbroekmolen Mine, 7 June 1917
Approximate area destroyed by the 91,000 lb explosive mine detonated shortly after 3.10am on 7 June 1917. The mine was dug by 171st Tunnelling Company, which had begun its task in December 1916.
Wire reported on during the raid. This area could not be seen from anywhere along the British lines.
At 2.00pm on 4 June 1917, Capt M Henehan led the raiders out from the end of Piccadilly Trench. Within an hour they had returned after a successful attack.
LCpl J Scott and Pte G W Cave were killed and six men were wounded.
Piccadilly
Outpost Buildings
Spanbroekmolen
Spanbroek
N29.1
N29.2
N29.3
N30.1
N30.2
N36.T1
Maedelstede Fm
Peckham
Scott Fm
Skip Wood
Kruisstraat Cab
Earl Fm
L'Enfer Wood
Goderis Fm
Bogaert Fm
NARROW TRENCH
NAPLES
NAPLES ROW
NAPLES SUPPORT
NARROW RESERVE
NARROW LANE
RAG POINT
HOP POINT
BONE POINT
OCCULT
OCCUR TRENCH
OCEAN
CRESCENT
NATHAN
NATHAN SUPPORT
ALLEY
DRIVE
AVENUE
RESERVE

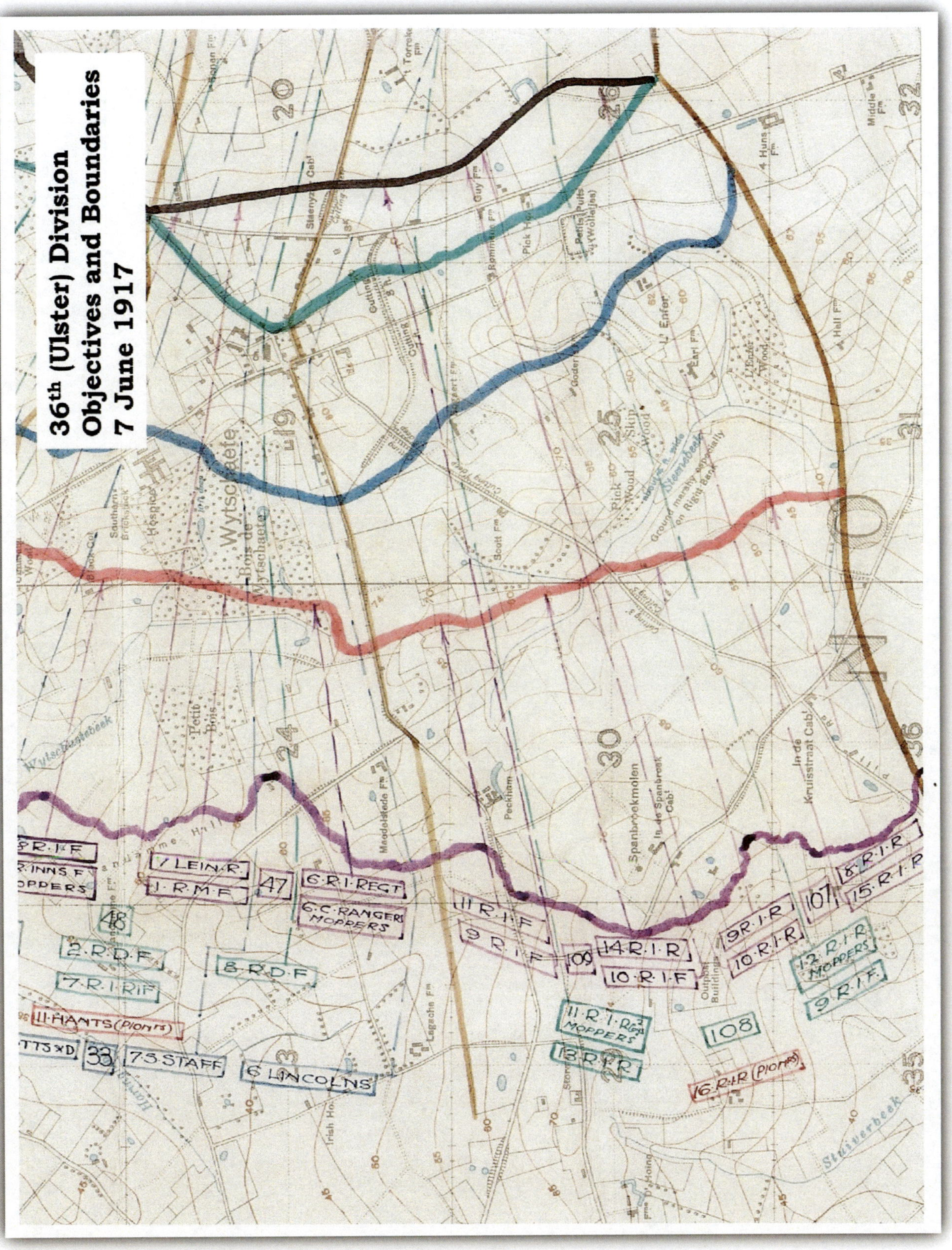

36th (Ulster) Division Objectives and Boundaries 7 June 1917

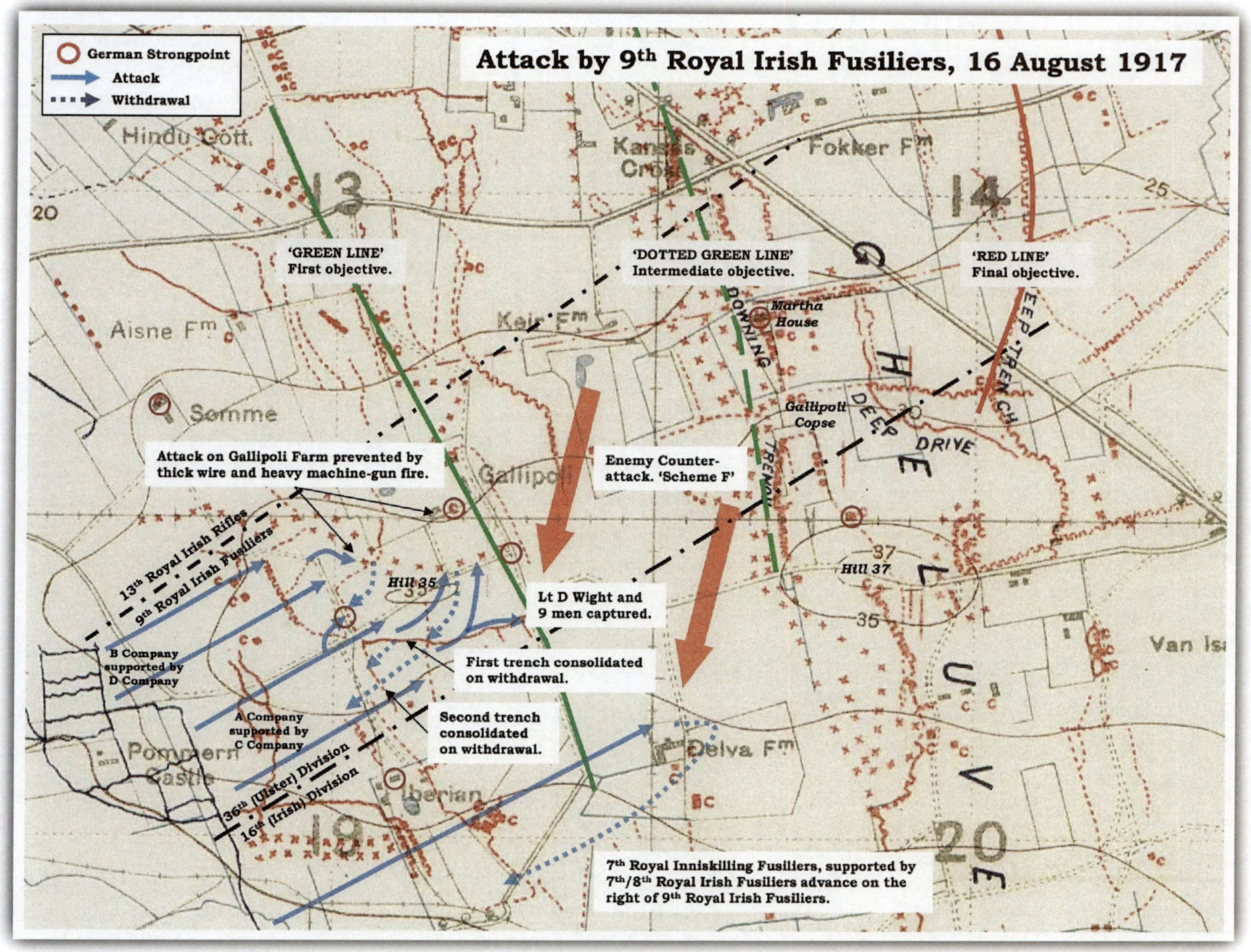

Attack by 9th Royal Irish Fusiliers, 16 August 1917
German Strongpoint
Attack
Withdrawal
Hindu Cott.
Kansas Cross
Fokker Fm
Aisne Fm
Kei Fm
Somme
Gallipoli
Martha House
Gallipoli Copse
DOWNING TRENCH
DEEP DRIVE
DEEP TRENCH
Hill 35
Hill 37
Van Is
Delva Fm
Pommern Castle
Iberian
'GREEN LINE' First objective.
'DOTTED GREEN LINE' Intermediate objective.
'RED LINE' Final objective.
Attack on Gallipoli Farm prevented by thick wire and heavy machine-gun fire.
Enemy Counter-attack. 'Scheme F'
13th Royal Irish Rifles
9th Royal Irish Fusiliers
Lt D Wight and 9 men captured.
B Company supported by D Company
First trench consolidated on withdrawal.
A Company supported by C Company
Second trench consolidated on withdrawal.
36th (Ulster) Division
16th (Irish) Division
7th Royal Inniskilling Fusiliers, supported by 7th/8th Royal Irish Fusiliers advance on the right of 9th Royal Irish Fusiliers.

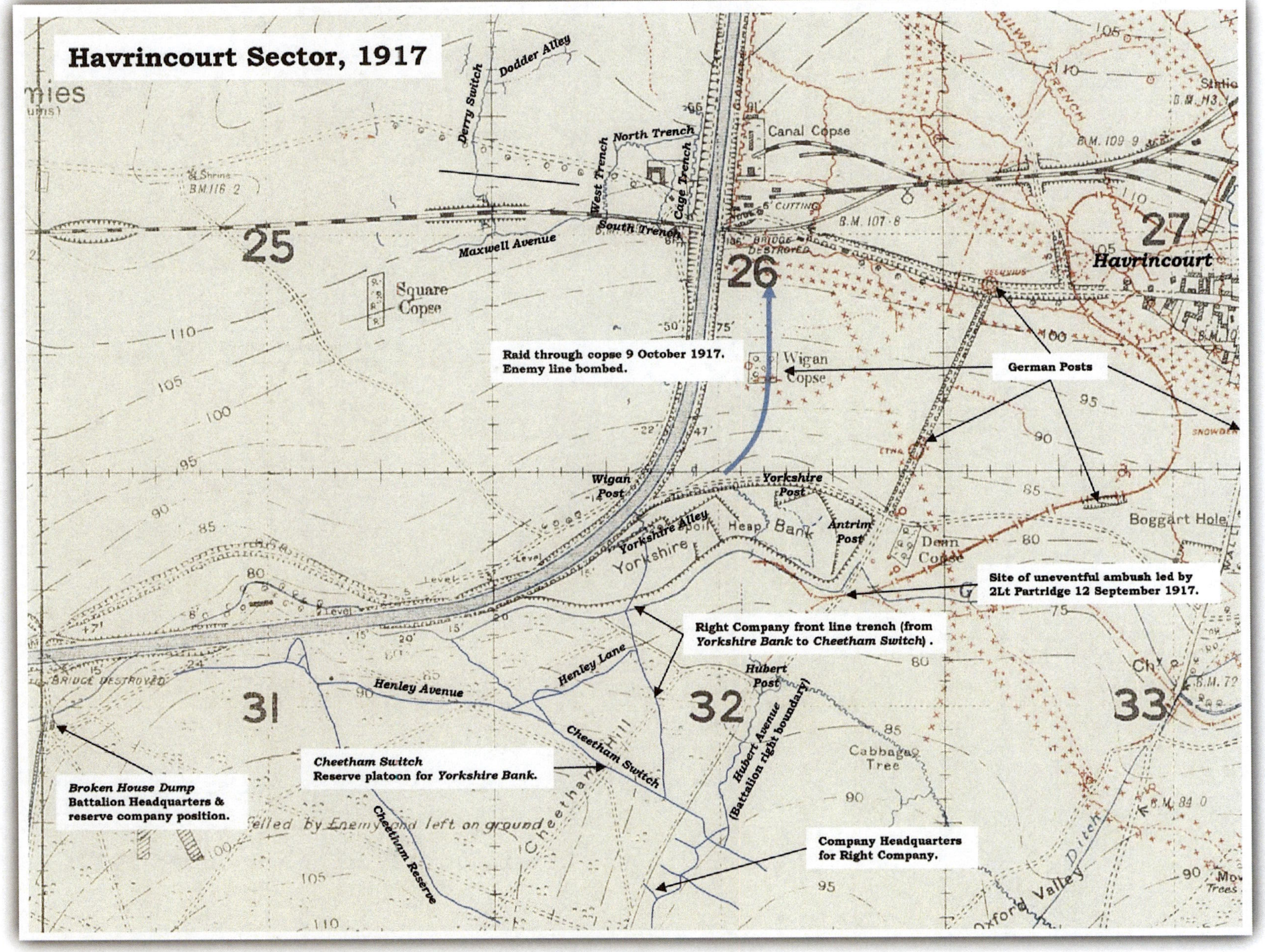
Havrincourt Sector, 1917
Dodder Alley
Derry Switch
North Trench
West Trench
Cage Trench
South Trench
Maxwell Avenue
Canal Copse
Square Copse
Havrincourt
Raid through copse 9 October 1917.
Enemy line bombed.
Wigan Copse
German Posts
Wigan Post
Yorkshire Post
Yorkshire Alley
Antrim Post
Boggart Hole
Site of uneventful ambush led by 2Lt Partridge 12 September 1917.
Right Company front line trench (from Yorkshire Bank to Cheetham Switch).
Henley Lane
Henley Avenue
Hubert Post
Hubert Avenue
(Battalion right boundary)
Cabbage Tree
Cheetham Switch
Cheetham Switch
Reserve platoon for Yorkshire Bank.
Broken House Dump
Battalion Headquarters & reserve company position.
Cheetham Reserve
Company Headquarters for Right Company.
Oxford Valley Ditch

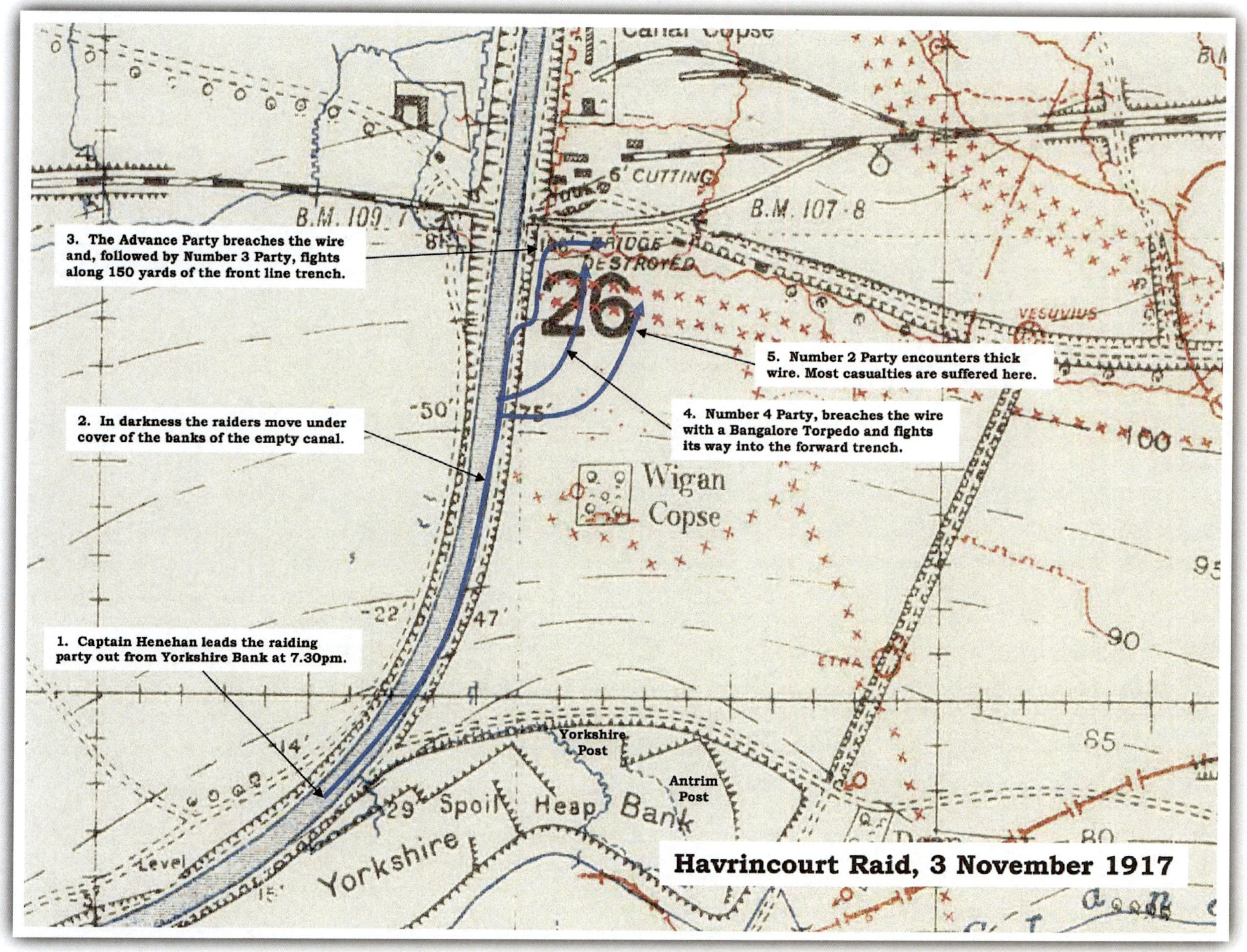

Havrincourt Raid, 3 November 1917

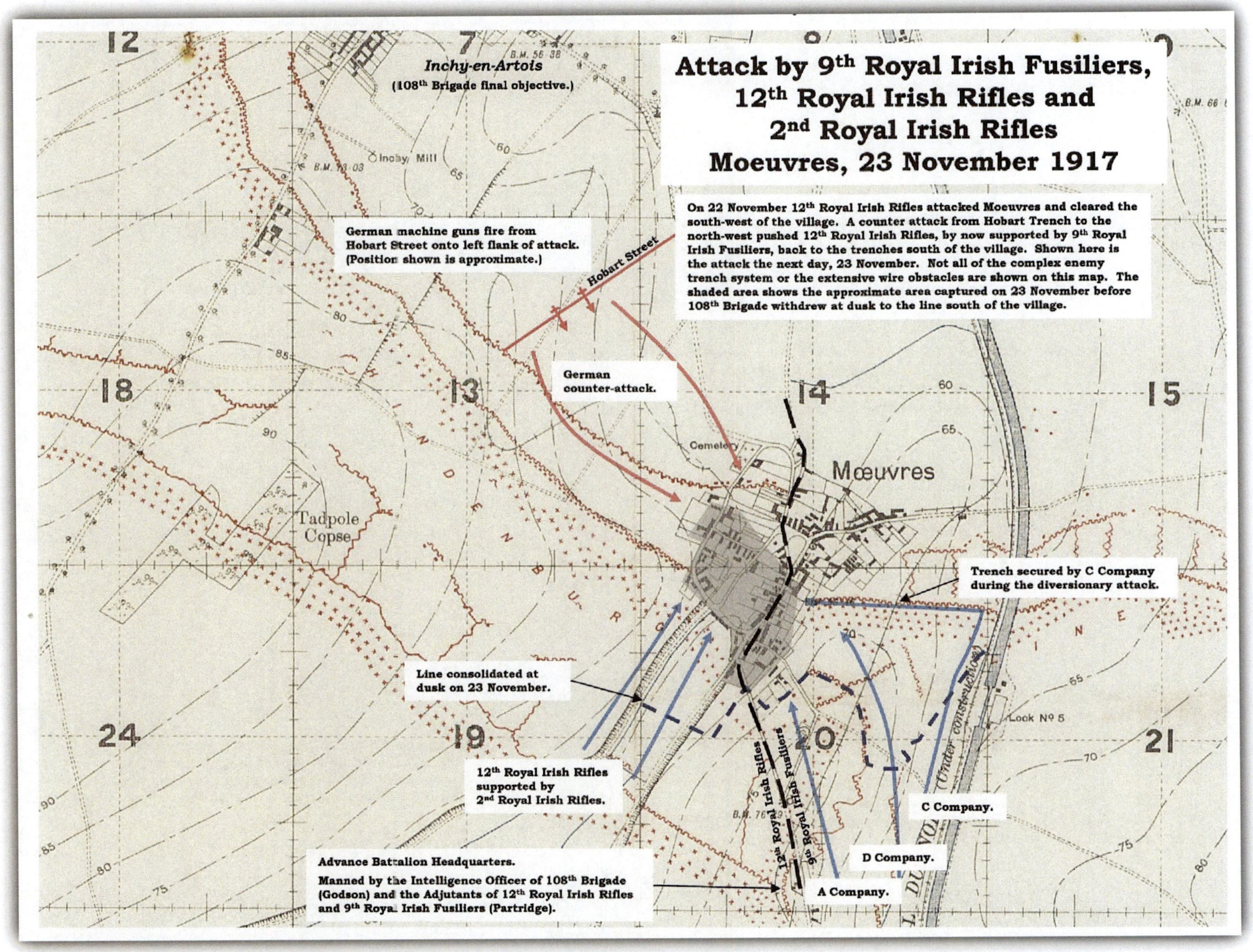
Attack by 9th Royal Irish Fusiliers,
12th Royal Irish Rifles and
2nd Royal Irish Rifles
Moeuvres, 23 November 1917
On 22 November 12th Royal Irish Rifles attacked Moeuvres and cleared the south-west of the village. A counter attack from Hobart Trench to the north-west pushed 12th Royal Irish Rifles, by now supported by 9th Royal Irish Fusiliers, back to the trenches south of the village. Shown here is the attack the next day, 23 November. Not all of the complex enemy trench system or the extensive wire obstacles are shown on this map. The shaded area shows the approximate area captured on 23 November before 108th Brigade withdrew at dusk to the line south of the village.
Inchy-en-Artois
(108th Brigade final objective.)
Inchy Mill
German machine guns fire from Hobart Street onto left flank of attack. (Position shown is approximate.)
Hobart Street
German counter-attack.
Cemetery
Mœuvres
Tadpole Copse
Trench secured by C Company during the diversionary attack.
Line consolidated at dusk on 23 November.
12th Royal Irish Rifles supported by 2nd Royal Irish Rifles.
12th Royal Irish Rifles
9th Royal Irish Fusiliers
Lock Nº 5
(Under construction)
C Company.
D Company.
A Company.
Advance Battalion Headquarters.
Manned by the Intelligence Officer of 108th Brigade (Godson) and the Adjutants of 12th Royal Irish Rifles and 9th Royal Irish Fusiliers (Partridge).

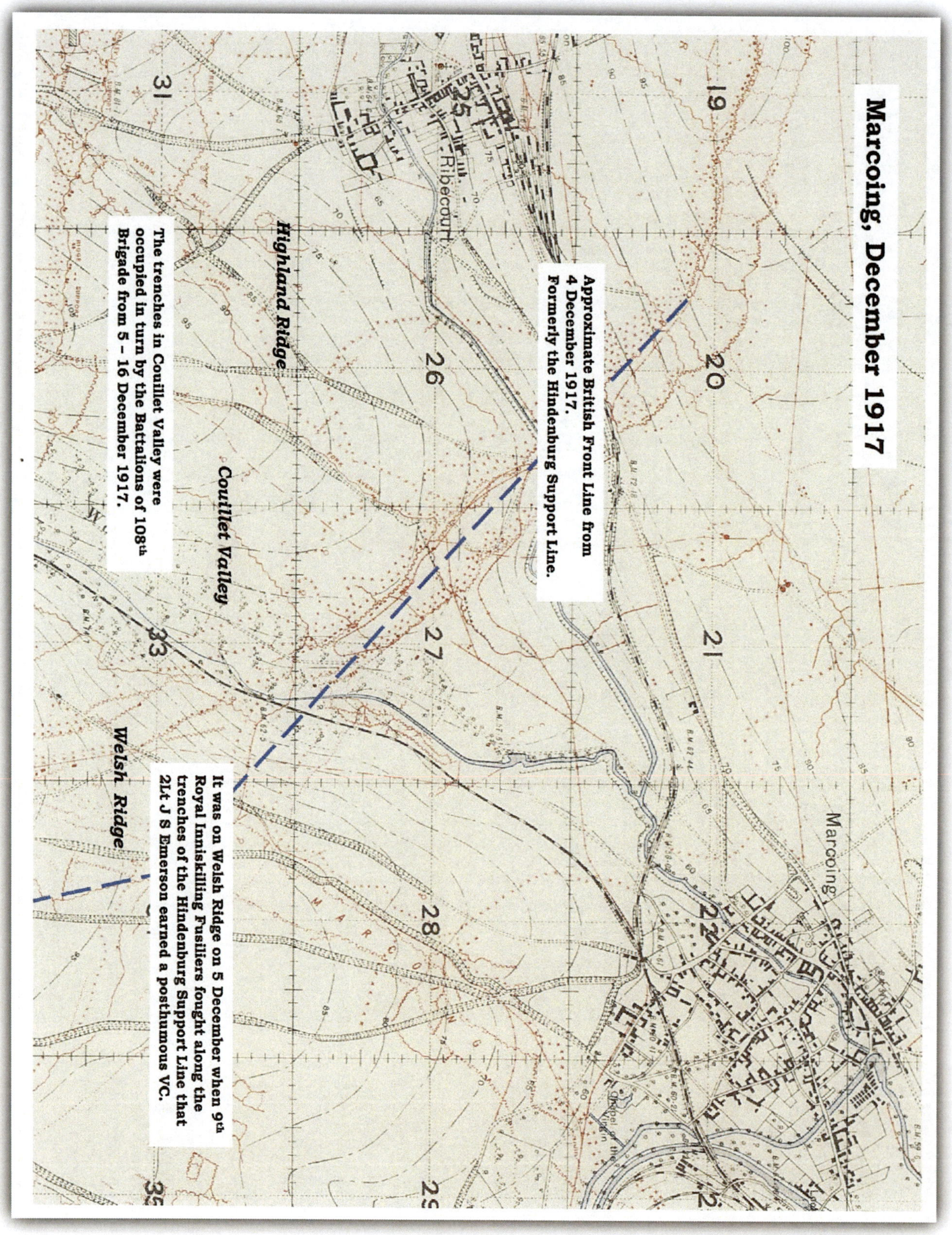
Marcoing, December 1917
Approximate British Front Line from
4 December 1917.
Formerly the Hindenburg Support Line.
Ribecourt
Highland Ridge
The trenches in Couillet Valley were
occupied in turn by the Battalions of 108th
Brigade from 5 – 16 December 1917.
Couillet Valley
Welsh Ridge
It was on Welsh Ridge on 5 December when 9th
Royal Inniskilling Fusiliers fought along the
trenches of the Hindenburg Support Line that
2Lt J S Emerson earned a posthumous VC.
Marcoing
19
20
21
22
25
26
27
28
31
33

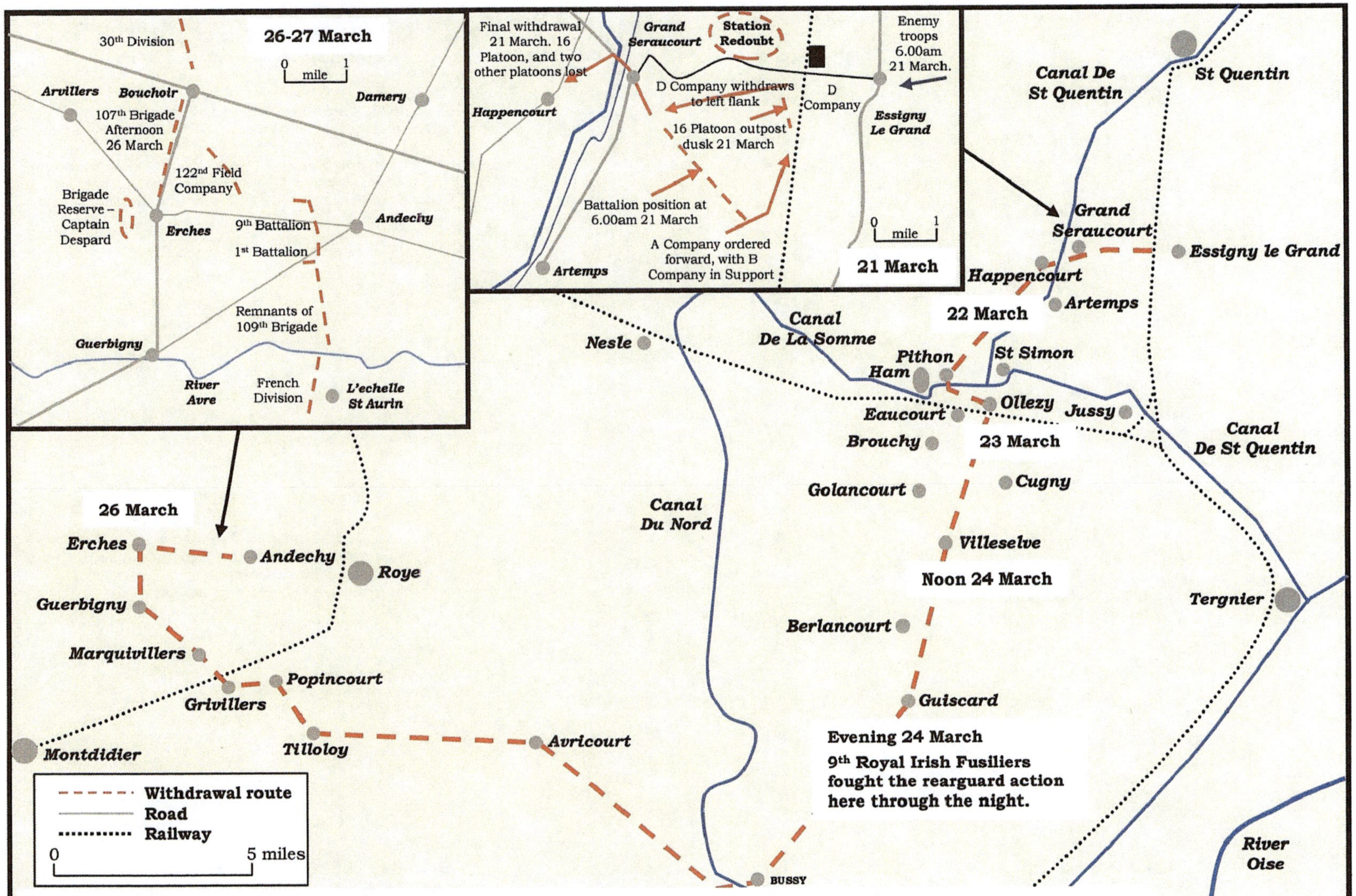

The Withdrawal from St Quentin to Erches – 21-27 March 1918

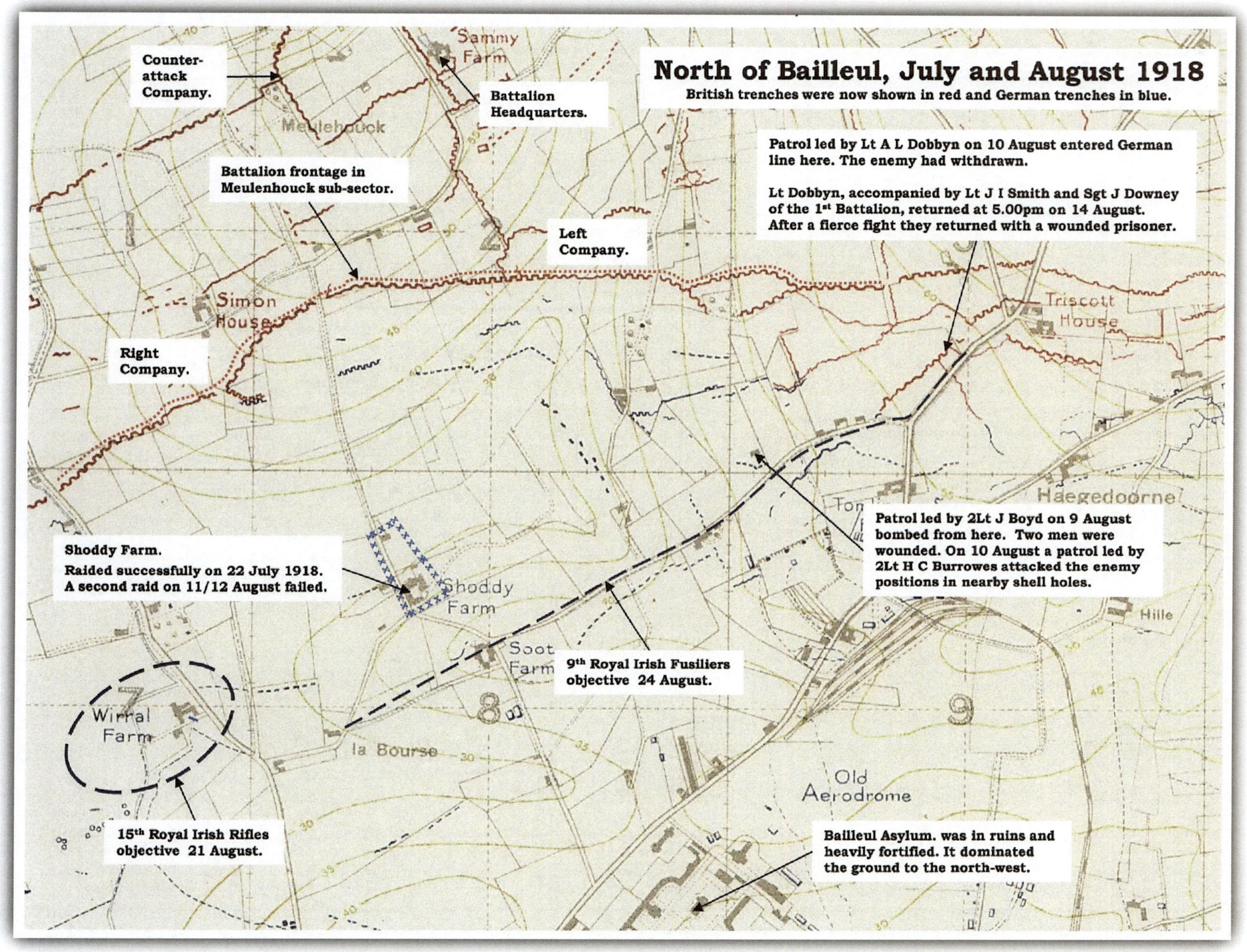
North of Bailleul, July and August 1918
British trenches were now shown in red and German trenches in blue.
Counter-attack Company.
Battalion Headquarters.
Battalion frontage in Meulenhouck sub-sector.
Left Company.
Right Company.
Patrol led by Lt A L Dobbyn on 10 August entered German line here. The enemy had withdrawn.
Lt Dobbyn, accompanied by Lt J I Smith and Sgt J Downey of the 1st Battalion, returned at 5.00pm on 14 August. After a fierce fight they returned with a wounded prisoner.
Patrol led by 2Lt J Boyd on 9 August bombed from here. Two men were wounded. On 10 August a patrol led by 2Lt H C Burrowes attacked the enemy positions in nearby shell holes.
Shoddy Farm.
Raided successfully on 22 July 1918. A second raid on 11/12 August failed.
9th Royal Irish Fusiliers objective 24 August.
15th Royal Irish Rifles objective 21 August.
Bailleul Asylum. was in ruins and heavily fortified. It dominated the ground to the north-west.
Sammy Farm
Meulehouck
Simon House
Triscott House
Haegedoorne
Shoddy Farm
Soot Farm
Wirral Farm
la Bourse
Old Aerodrome
Hille

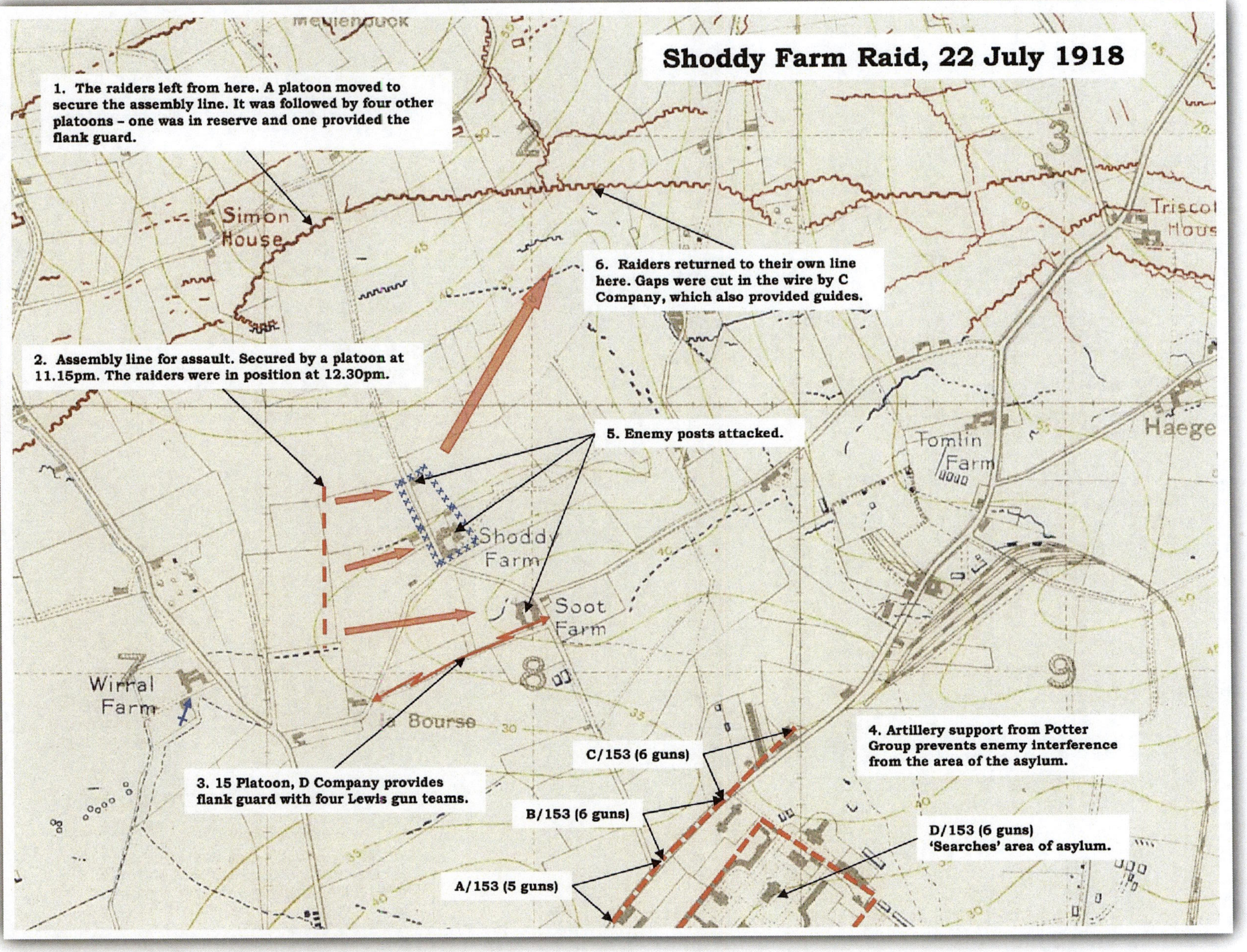
Shoddy Farm Raid, 22 July 1918
1. The raiders left from here. A platoon moved to secure the assembly line. It was followed by four other platoons – one was in reserve and one provided the flank guard.
2. Assembly line for assault. Secured by a platoon at 11.15pm. The raiders were in position at 12.30pm.
3. 15 Platoon, D Company provides flank guard with four Lewis gun teams.
4. Artillery support from Potter Group prevents enemy interference from the area of the asylum.
5. Enemy posts attacked.
6. Raiders returned to their own line here. Gaps were cut in the wire by C Company, which also provided guides.
C/153 (6 guns)
B/153 (6 guns)
A/153 (5 guns)
D/153 (6 guns)
'Searches' area of asylum.
Simon House
Shoddy Farm
Soot Farm
Tomlin Farm
Wirral Farm
Triscot House
Haege
Bourse

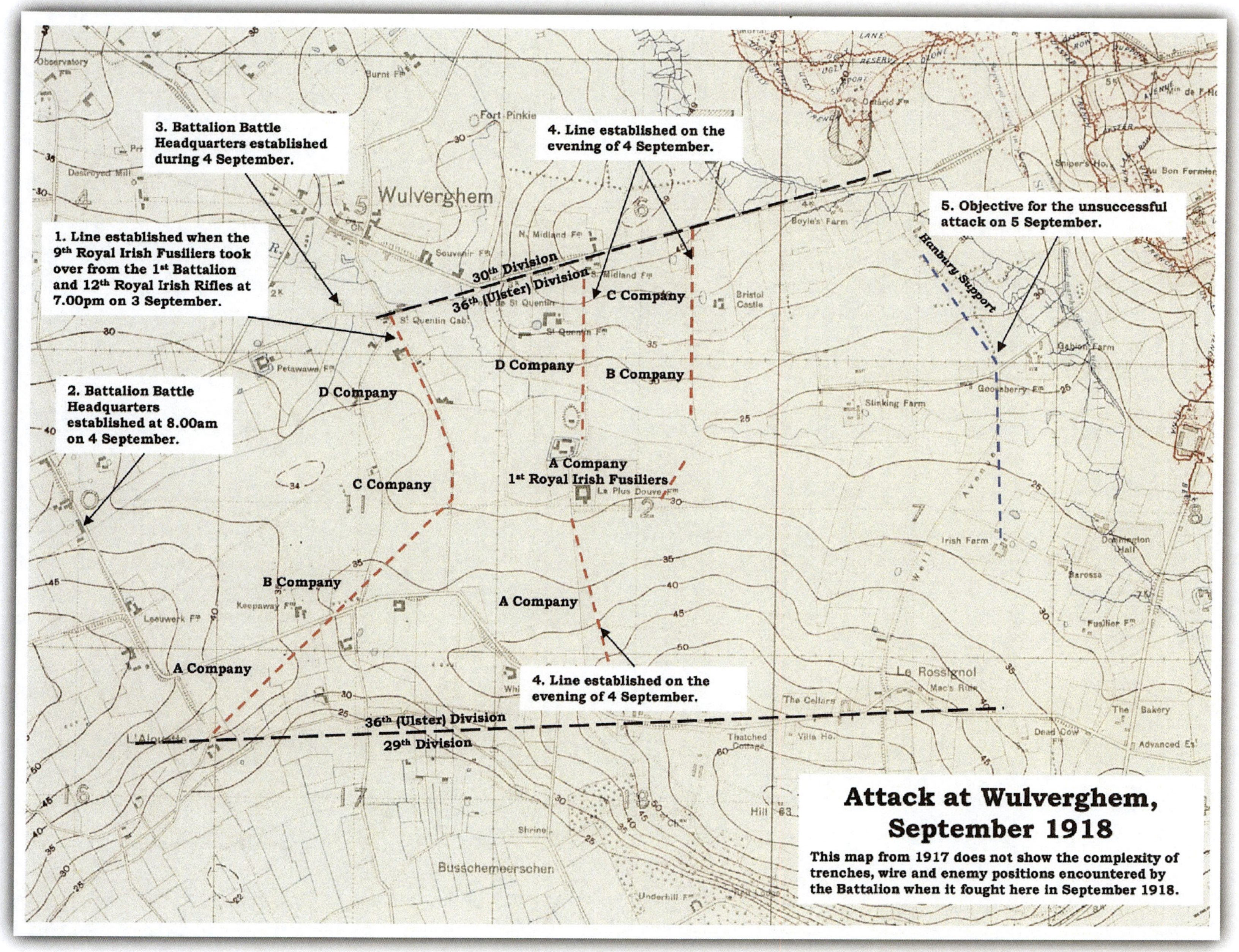

Attack at Wulverghem, September 1918

This map from 1917 does not show the complexity of trenches, wire and enemy positions encountered by the Battalion when it fought here in September 1918.

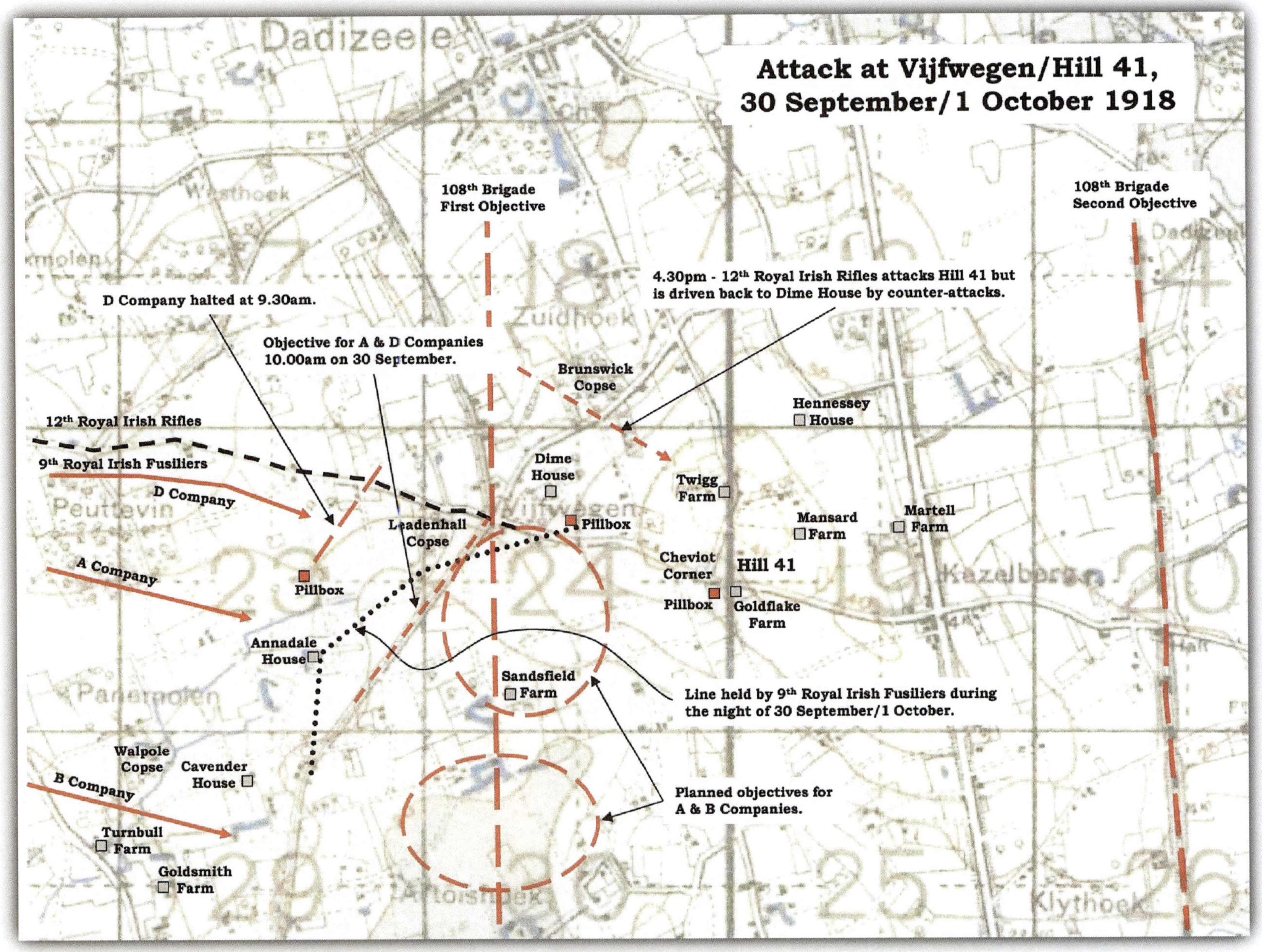
Attack at Vijfwegen/Hill 41,
30 September/1 October 1918
108th Brigade First Objective
108th Brigade Second Objective
D Company halted at 9.30am.
Objective for A & D Companies 10.00am on 30 September.
4.30pm - 12th Royal Irish Rifles attacks Hill 41 but is driven back to Dime House by counter-attacks.
12th Royal Irish Rifles
9th Royal Irish Fusiliers
D Company
A Company
B Company
Brunswick Copse
Hennessey House
Dime House
Twigg Farm
Leadenhall Copse
Pillbox
Mansard Farm
Martell Farm
Cheviot Corner
Hill 41
Goldflake Farm
Annadale House
Sandsfield Farm
Line held by 9th Royal Irish Fusiliers during the night of 30 September/1 October.
Walpole Copse
Cavender House
Turnbull Farm
Goldsmith Farm
Planned objectives for A & B Companies.
Dadizeele
Zuidhoek
Vijfwegen
Kazelberg
Klythoek

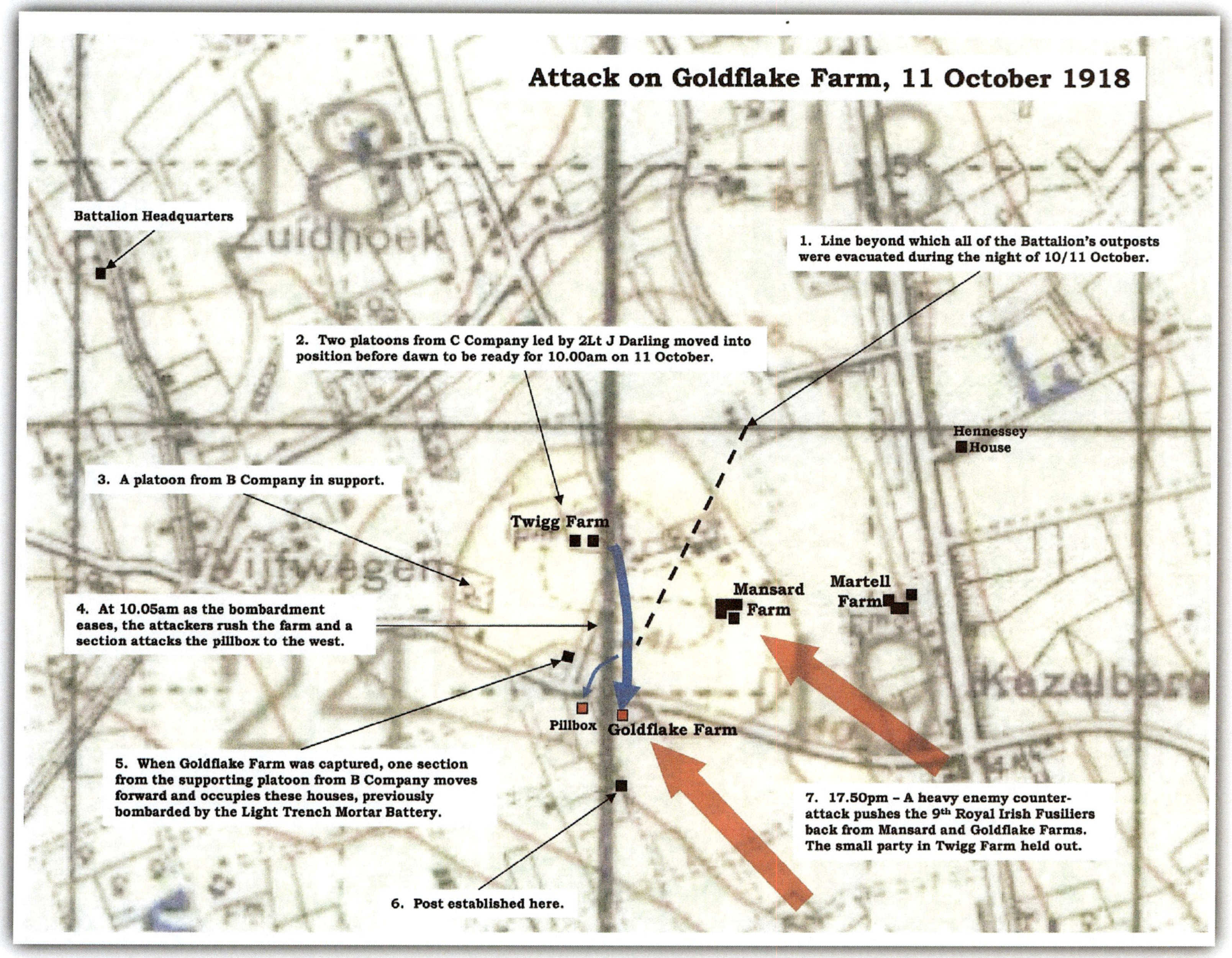
Attack on Goldflake Farm, 11 October 1918
Battalion Headquarters
Zuidhoek
1. Line beyond which all of the Battalion's outposts were evacuated during the night of 10/11 October.
2. Two platoons from C Company led by 2Lt J Darling moved into position before dawn to be ready for 10.00am on 11 October.
Hennessey House
3. A platoon from B Company in support.
Twigg Farm
Wijfwegen
Mansard Farm
Martell Farm
4. At 10.05am as the bombardment eases, the attackers rush the farm and a section attacks the pillbox to the west.
Kazelberg
Pillbox
Goldflake Farm
5. When Goldflake Farm was captured, one section from the supporting platoon from B Company moves forward and occupies these houses, previously bombarded by the Light Trench Mortar Battery.
7. 17.50pm – A heavy enemy counter-attack pushes the 9th Royal Irish Fusiliers back from Mansard and Goldflake Farms. The small party in Twigg Farm held out.
6. Post established here.

APPENDIX 1

History of Princess Victoria's (Royal Irish Fusiliers) & the Battalions Raised in the First World War

The Regiment has a proud and distinguished history that began just after the declaration of war between Britain and France in February 1793. At this time the British Army was augmented by many new regiments including the 87th and 89th Regiments of Foot. Both were raised in Ireland in September and December of that year. Early in 1794 both regiments underwent rudimentary training in England before embarking for Holland. They were part of a force of over seven thousand men under the Earl of Moira that was sent to reinforce the Army of the Duke of York; they saw action against the French for the first time at Alost. By April 1795, however, the 87th was in captivity and the 89th had been decimated through action and illness. So began a long and eventful record of service across the globe.

In 1796 the reformed 87th sailed for the West Indies, returning after eight years having lost 790 officers and men, mainly to disease. The 89th, meanwhile, was engaged in Ireland against the rebellious United Irishmen and in 1799 it sailed for Sicily. Thereafter, it served at the siege of Malta and in Egypt against the French, returning to Ireland in 1802. In 1804 both regiments were authorised to raise a second battalion, initially for home service. In late 1806 the 1st/87th was dispatched to South America where it fought at Montevideo in February 1807. Then, reinforced with drafts from regiments returning to England, it sailed for the Cape of Good Hope. Both the 1st/87th and 1st/89th served in the Far East in 1810 in the islands of the South Indian Ocean before the 1st/89th was sent to Java as part of a force that would capture the Dutch East Indies, then allied to France.

It was the 2nd/87th that joined Wellington's Army in the Peninsula War, winning battle honours at Talavera and Barrosa. At the latter the Regiment charged, crying *"Faugh-a-Ballagh!" ("Clear the way!")* and Sergeant Patrick Masterson famously captured the gilded silver French Imperial Eagle of the *8e Régiment d'Infanterie de Ligne*, the first to be captured in the Napoleonic wars. The 2nd/87th fought also at Tarifa and Vittoria before moving into France with the invading armies and securing honours at Nivelle in 1813 and Orthes and Toulouse in 1814. Peace with France brought about a reduction in the Army and the 2nd/87th was disbanded in 1817 although many men volunteered to join the 1st Battalion in India. The 2nd/89th, meanwhile, fought briefly in a minor engagement in Spain in 1810 and then in North America in 1813-14, before it too was disbanded. In North America it was instrumental in foiling the American attempt at conquering Canada. The 1st Battalions of both Regiments had remained in India, where the 1st/87th had spent 1816 fighting in the north, and the 1st/89th had a relatively uneventful time. Both regiments found themselves in Burma in 1825-26, where they suffered terribly through disease. After this short campaign, the 89th returned to India and the 87th returned home, having spent thirty-one of its thirty-three years overseas.

With the agreement of King George IV, the 87th was named The Royal Irish Fusiliers in 1827. After absorbing recruits from Ireland to bring it up to strength, it moved to Mauritius, where it remained until 1843. After a brief period at home dealing with civil disturbances it sailed for India in April 1849. The 89th had left India in 1831, having spent twenty-five years away from home, but after only three years moved again, this time to the West Indies. The hot, wet climate and disease again claimed many before it moved north to Canada in 1841. The 89th returned home again in 1847 and was engaged initially in police duties in England before moving to Ireland, although it was not involved in the skirmishes of 1848.

This symbology of Princess Victoria's (Royal Irish Fusiliers) combines the coronet of Princess Victoria, the *aigle de drapeau* (Flag Eagle) of the *8e Régiment d'Infanterie de Ligne,* and the Anglicised Irish language motto *'Faugh-a-Ballagh'.*

This later symbology of Princess Victoria's (Royal Irish Fusiliers) combines the 1870 crown of Queen Victoria, the winged maiden Irish harp, and the Prince of Wales' feathers. These sit over a 'fired' grenade emblazoned with a French Imperial Eagle. Surrounding the grenade is a wreath of shamrock and beneath is the motto *'Faugh-a-Ballagh'.*

The crest of the Regiment shown on a printed silk cigarette card and as a jewelled and enamelled broach.

During the Crimean War the 89th reinforced the troops forming the besieging forces in the horrors at Sevastopol in 1856 where it suffered grievously through cholera. Ravaged by the same disease and sunstroke, the fate of the 87th in India over this period was no less tragic. In 1860 the 87th was sent to China and the next twenty-one years saw a spread of short postings in Dublin, Malta, Canada, back to Ireland and then to the Channel Islands, and finally Aldershot in 1881. The 89th had a similar round of postings: Gibraltar, South Africa and India, from the mutiny in 1857 to 1865, when the Regiment moved to England. It was here that the 89th received new Colours and was named Princess Victoria's Regiment. The growth of the Fenian Movement and the threat of a rising in 1865 forced extra troops to Ireland, so the 89th moved to Dublin where it remained until 1869. Relatively quiet and comparatively healthy tours in India and Burma followed.

Under the reforms instigated by Lord Cardwell in 1881, the Regiments of Foot were linked in order to maintain a balance between the number deployed at home and abroad. From 1 July of that year they were organised into territorial regiments of four or more battalions of which the 1st and 2nd were regular and the remainder militia. The 87th and 89th became, respectively, the 1st and 2nd Battalions, Princess Victoria's (Royal Irish Fusiliers). The associated Armagh, Cavan and Monaghan militia battalions became the 3rd, 4th and 5th Battalions. Armagh became the depot, with recruits found from Counties Armagh, Cavan, Louth and Monaghan.

The 1st Battalion deployed the next year to Egypt, fighting at Tel-el-Kebir in September 1882 before sailing to India. It served in Burma in 1896 and returned to Egypt in 1898. The 2nd Battalion, meanwhile, left India in 1882 and moved to the Sudan, where it earned the battle honour 'Egypt 1884'. It finally left Egypt in 1886 and served in England until October 1899. Both battalions served with distinction in South Africa during the South African War, and in 1902 the 1st Battalion returned to Britain for the first time since 1883, initially to Palace Barracks at Holywood just outside Belfast, followed by moves to Dublin (1906), Aldershot (1908), Borden (1910) and finally Shorncliffe in 1911. The 2nd Battalion, meanwhile, moved to India where it was stationed in Quetta at the outbreak of the First World War. The 1st Battalion landed in France on 23 August 1914 as part of 10th Brigade, 4th Division. The 2nd Battalion arrived in England from India in November 1914 and joined 82nd Brigade in 27th Division. It landed in France on 19 December 1914.

Irish Infantry Regiments in the First World War

A little over 206,000 Irishmen served in the armed forces of the United Kingdom during the First World War. This figure does not include the Irish emigrants who joined units raised in England and Scotland or those who joined the Dominion armies. Irishmen served in many of the regiments and corps of the British Army and also joined the Royal Navy, Royal Naval Air Service, Royal Marines and, later, the fledgling Royal Air Force. Irish women also served, mainly in Voluntary Aid Detachments and with other medical units. But most of the wartime volunteers joined the three New Army divisions raised in Ireland.

In the massive reorganisation demanded by the First World War, infantry battalions were designated as Regular, Territorial Force, Service, Reserve, Garrison or Reserve Garrison. The role and place of the regular battalions is evident, and the Territorial Force battalions were the result of the reorganisation of the volunteer and part-time Militia and Yeomanry regiments to form the Territorial Force in 1908. The service battalions were those formed after Lord Kitchener's call for volunteers in August 1914. Reserve battalions provided trained men for the regular and service battalions. The garrison battalions served in security duties in rear areas across the globe, and their men, often recovered wounded or those too old for general service, came from the reserve garrison battalions, some of which were used for security duties around the British Isles also.

In addition to eighteen regular battalions, by the end of the war forty-two service battalions, twenty-eight reserve battalions and eight garrison or reserve garrison battalions had been raised in Ireland (for completeness these totals include the Irish Guards, which also recruited in English cities). There were no Irish Territorial Force battalions.

	Regular Battalions	Service Battalions	Reserve Battalions	Garrison Battalions	Reserve Garrison Battalions	Total
Irish Guards	2	-	1	-	-	3
The Royal Irish Regiment	2	4	2	1	1	10
The Royal Inniskilling Fusiliers	2	8	3	-	-	13
The Royal Irish Rifles	2	11	7	1	-	21
Princess Victoria's (Royal Irish Fusiliers)	2	6	3	2	1	14
The Connaught Rangers	2	2	2	-	-	6
The Prince of Wales's Leinster Regiment (Royal Canadians)	2	2	3	-	-	7
The Royal Munster Fusiliers	2	4	3	1	1	11
The Royal Dublin Fusiliers	2	5	4	-	-	11
Total	18	42	28	5	3	96

In addition, three English regiments raised four service battalions and four Territorial Force battalions that, initially, were manned largely with Irish migrants or men of Irish descent:

24th (Service) Battalion, The Northumberland Fusiliers (1st Tyneside Irish)
25th (Service) Battalion, The Northumberland Fusiliers (2nd Tyneside Irish)
26th (Service) Battalion, The Northumberland Fusiliers (3rd Tyneside Irish)
27th (Service) Battalion, The Northumberland Fusiliers (4th Tyneside Irish)
1/8th (Irish) Battalion, The King's (Liverpool Regiment)
2/8th (Irish) Battalion, The King's (Liverpool Regiment)
1/18th (County of London) Battalion, The London Regiment (London Irish Rifles)
2/18th (County of London) Battalion, The London Regiment (London Irish Rifles)

Helped by the economic situation that had resulted in many job losses in mid and late 1914, recruitment in Ireland was at its height in the first six months of the war but it reduced steadily as the war progressed. Although Ulster compared well with the rest of Britain, the recruiting figures for Ireland as a whole were generally lower than for England and Scotland. The impact of casualties, the absence of conscription and, to a lesser degree, the increasing influence of the Irish separatist movement, meant that insufficient volunteers were available to sustain all of the Irish infantry battalions as the war progressed. This resulted in an influx of English soldiers that began towards the end of 1916 and the amalgamation of Irish battalions in late 1917 and early 1918.

Princess Victoria's (Royal Irish Fusiliers) in the First World War

In addition to its two regular battalions, Princess Victoria's (Royal Irish Fusiliers) raised six service battalions, three reserve battalions, two garrison battalions and one reserve garrison battalion during the First World War. All of the battalions of Princess Victoria's (Royal Irish Fusiliers) served with distinction, at an official total of 3,524 men killed in action, died of wounds or died of other causes.

1st Battalion. The 1st Battalion deployed to France with 10th Brigade, 4th Division of the British Expeditionary Force on 23 August 1914. It transferred to 107th Brigade in 36th (Ulster) Division on 3 August 1917. It transferred to 108th Brigade, 36th (Ulster) Division on 8 February 1918 where it remained until March 1919 when the cadre moved to Gosport in England.

2nd Battalion. The 2nd Battalion returned from India in November 1914 and deployed to France with 82nd Brigade, 27th Division on 19 December 1914. It landed in Salonika in November 1915 and transferred to 31st Brigade in 10th (Irish) Division on 2 November 1916. It served in Egypt and Palestine until the end of the war. Disembodied at Cairo in Egypt in June 1919, its cadre joined the newly disembodied 3rd (Reserve) Battalion, which reformed as the 2nd Battalion.

3rd (Reserve) Battalion. Formerly the 3rd (Armagh) Battalion, manned by men of the militia and Special Reserve, it was employed in home defence and draft finding in Ireland, initially in Armagh, then Buncrana from April 1915 and Clonmany, County Donegal from November 1916. In April 1918 it moved to Rugeley, Cannock Chase in England where it absorbed the 4th (Extra Reserve) and 10th (Reserve) Battalions. It was part of the West Riding Reserve Brigade at Bawdsey, Suffolk from July 1918, and from October 1918 was based at Southend. Disembodied on 25 July 1919, it was reconstituted as the 2nd Battalion. Its King's Colour was laid up in the Cathedral Church of St Patrick, Armagh, on 23 November 1924.

4th (Extra Reserve) Battalion. Formerly the 4th (Cavan) Battalion, manned by men of the militia and Special Reserve, it was also employed in home defence and draft finding in Ireland. It was first in Belfast and Carrickfergus and from April 1916 at Portobello Barracks, Dublin, and then in Ballincollig, County Cork from November 1917. In April 1918 it moved to England and was absorbed by the 3rd (Reserve) Battalion. Its King's Colour was laid up in the Cathedral Church of St Patrick, Armagh, on 16 November 1924.

5th (Service) Battalion. The 5th (Monaghan) Battalion had been disbanded in 1908. The 5th (Service) Battalion was raised in August 1914 in Armagh as part of K1. It deployed in July 1915 as part of the Mediterranean Expeditionary Force in 31st Brigade, 10th (Irish) Division. It landed at Suvla Bay on 7 August 1915. It moved to Salonika in October 1915 and absorbed the 6th (Service) Battalion on 2 November 1916. In September 1917 the 5th/6th Battalion moved to Egypt and then Palestine. It was transferred from 10th (Irish) Division in April 1918 and joined 66th (2nd East Lancashire) Division in France on 23 July 1918. On 24 August 1918 it transferred to 48th Brigade, 16th (Irish) Division. It absorbed the 11th (Service) Battalion on 29 August 1918. It was disbanded in June 1919. Its King's Colour was laid up in the Cathedral Church of St Patrick, Armagh, in 1920.

6th (Service) Battalion. Raised in August 1914 in Armagh as part of K1. History as for the 5th (Service) Battalion. Its King's Colour was laid up in the Cathedral Church of St Patrick, Armagh, on 13 February 1921 (at this ceremony the Colours of the 1st Battalion were also laid up).

7th (Service) Battalion. Raised in September 1914 in Armagh as part of K2. In September 1915 it moved to Pirbright, Hampshire, as part of 49th Brigade, 16th (Irish) Division, where it finished its training. It deployed to France in February 1916. It absorbed the 8th (Service) Battalion on 15 October 1916. The 7th/8th (Service) Battalion was disbanded in France on 10 February 1918. Its King's Colour was laid up in the First Presbyterian Church, Armagh, on 31 October 1920.

8th (Service) Battalion. Raised in September 1914 in Armagh as part of K2. History as for the 7th (Service) Battalion. Its King's Colour was laid up in the First Presbyterian Church, Armagh, on 31 October 1920.

9th (Service) Battalion (County Armagh)/9th (North Irish Horse) Battalion. Raised in September 1914 as part of 108th Brigade, 36th (Ulster) Division. It was disbanded in June 1919. Its King's Colour was laid up in the Cathedral Church of St Patrick, Armagh, on 15 June 1919. The Colour was stolen from the Cathedral in 1976.

10th (Reserve) Battalion. Raised in Lurgan in September 1915 from the depot companies of the 9th (Service) Battalion as one of the six reserve battalions of 15th (Ulster) Reserve Brigade, which found and trained drafts for 36th (Ulster) Division. It moved to Newtownards in January 1916 and Armagh in August 1917. In April 1918 it moved to Rugeley, Cannock Chase, and was absorbed by the 3rd (Reserve) Battalion. The 10th (Reserve) Battalion was not presented with a King's Colour, but the Union Flag that was used on ceremonial occasions, was laid up in St Mark's Church, Portadown, date not known. In addition, in 1937 Colonel W C FitzGerald, the former Commanding Officer, donated a banner that had belonged to the 10th (Reserve) Battalion to Armagh County Museum.

11th (Service) Battalion. Raised at Greatham, West Hartlepool on 1 June 1918 from a cadre from the 3rd (Reserve) Garrison Battalion. It absorbed the 7th (Service) Battalion, The Royal Dublin Fusiliers on 18 June 1918. On 28 June 1918 it transferred to 48th Brigade, 16th (Irish) Division at Aldershot. It deployed to France in July 1918 and was absorbed by the 5th/6th (Service) Battalion on 29 August 1918. Its King's Colour was laid up in St Mark's Church, Portadown, on 5 December 1920.

1st Garrison Battalion. Raised in Dublin in September 1915 and made up mainly of over-age, former soldiers for service in India. It served with the 6th Poona Divisional Area from February 1916 and the Burma Division from May 1917. It sailed for England in November 1919 and was disbanded. Its King's Colour was laid up in St Mark's Church, Portadown, on 5 December 1920.

2nd Garrison Battalion. Raised in Dublin in March 1916, also mainly from over-age, former soldiers, for service in Salonika. It moved to Salonika in August 1916 on garrison security duties. Transferred to 228th Brigade (attached to 28th Division) from 1 March 1917 to 6 August 1917. It moved to Macedonia in September 1918 on line of communication security duties. It was disbanded in 1919. Its King's Colour was laid up in Shankill Parish Church, Lurgan, on 8 May 1921.

3rd (Reserve) Garrison Battalion. Raised in Dublin in December 1916 as the reserve battalion for the 1st and 2nd Garrison Battalions. It moved to Bere Island, Bantry Bay, in April 1917. It then joined the Tees Garrison in County Durham, firstly at Seaton Carew, south of Hartlepool, in May 1918, then at Greatham, south of Hartlepool, in June 1918 and finally at Castle Eden, north of Hartlepool, in October 1918. Like the 10th (Reserve) Battalion, the 3rd (Reserve) Garrison Battalion was not presented with a consecrated King's Colour. The Union Flag that it used is in the custody of the Territorial Army Centre, Portadown.

The cap badge of Princess Victoria's (Royal Irish Fusiliers) as worn during the First World War.

The battle patch of the 9th Royal Irish Fusiliers, worn on both shoulders.

APPENDIX 2

Roll of Honour

This Roll of Honour commemorates 826 men who served at some time with the 9th Royal Irish Fusiliers and who were killed in action, died of wounds, or died of other causes before 31 August 1921.

774 all ranks were killed in action, died of wounds or died of other causes serving with the 9th Royal Irish Fusiliers.

52 all ranks were killed in action, died of wounds or died of other causes serving elsewhere.

The Roll of Honour is laid out in five parts:

- Commonwealth War Graves Commission Non-Commemorations.
- Commonwealth War Graves Commission Incorrect Commemorations.
- Commemorated as Killed in Action, Died of Wounds or Died Serving with the 9th Royal Irish Fusiliers.
- Commemorated as Killed in Action, Died of Wounds or Died Serving Elsewhere.
- Post War Commemorations.

The information has been gleaned from a number of sources and, while every attempt has been made to check the detail, there may be some inaccuracies. In particular, there are three actions where the dates of death were not always accurately recorded. The first was during the withdrawal in March 1918 and the subsequent fighting in April 1918. Due to the pace of events, the registration of the deaths of many of those killed or reported missing only occurred afterwards. As a consequence, many of those killed over the period 21-28 March 1918 are shown as having died on 29 March 1918 and many of those killed between 11 and 18 April 1918 were given a date of death of 19 April 1918. Both of these dates were the first on which the battalion headquarters was able to consolidate records. This occurred also during the fighting at Vijfwegen on 30 September and 1 October 1918; some men are shown as having been killed in action over the period 30 September to 3 October or specifically on either 2 October or 3 October.

For those who are buried in a known grave the details of the cemetery are provided, followed by the plot, row and grave number. These are usually a Roman numeral, a letter and an Arabic numeral respectively, although there are one or two variations and the smaller cemeteries show just a row and grave number. For those without a known grave, details are shown of the memorial on which they are commemorated.

In October 1916 a committee was established to oversee the design and production of a commemorative memorial plaque for the next of kin of men and women whose deaths were attributable to the war. A competition to select the design was won by Edward Carter Preston in March 1918.

The plaque was accompanied by a short letter:

> *'Buckingham Palace*
> *I join my grateful people in sending you this memorial of a brave life given for others in the Great War.*
> *George R.I.'*

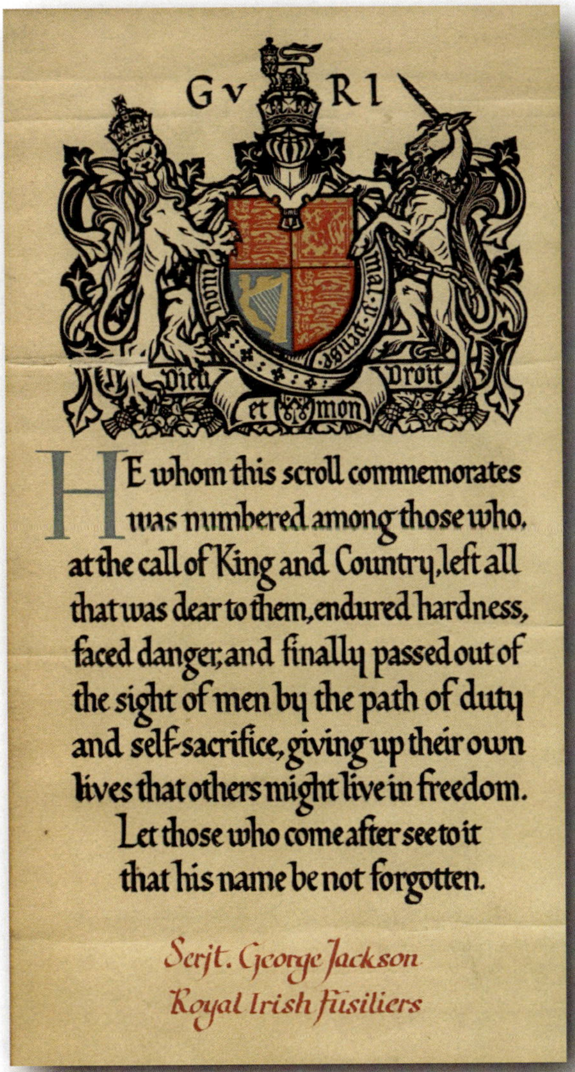

GvRI

Dieu et mon Droit

HE whom this scroll commemorates was numbered among those who, at the call of King and Country, left all that was dear to them, endured hardness, faced danger, and finally passed out of the sight of men by the path of duty and self-sacrifice, giving up their own lives that others might live in freedom.
Let those who come after see to it that his name be not forgotten.

Serjt. George Jackson
Royal Irish Fusiliers

In October 1917 it was decided that next of kin would also receive a commemorative scroll. The wording was drafted by Dr Montague Rhodes James, Provost of King's College Cambridge, with minor changes being made at the suggestion of the King, and the novelist Charles Keary.

Commonwealth War Graves Commission Non-Commemorations

Those who died as a consequence of the war were officially commemorated if they died before 31 August 1921. In the course of research for this book, six soldiers were identified as having been killed in action or died as a result of wounds or of illness contracted on active service or aggravated by war service but, by omission, were not commemorated by the Commonwealth War Graves Commission.

CHAMBERS Private S 18068 was killed in action on 5 September 1918. He has no known grave. He is now commemorated by the Commonwealth War Graves Commission and his name has been included on the addenda panel on the Tyne Cot Memorial.

GUMBLE Private Kenzer 43321 died on 9 June 1920 of pulmonary tuberculosis and haemoptysis after gassing. He is now commemorated by the Commonwealth War Graves Commission. He is buried in Plumstead Cemetery, London.

JACKSON Private W A 22983 died of pulmonary tuberculosis on 7 April 1919. He is buried at Belfast City Cemetery and is now commemorated by a Commonwealth War Graves Commission headstone.

MAXWELL Private A 14434 died of pulmonary tuberculosis on 3 July 1918. He is believed to be buried at Friends Burial Ground, Lurgan and is commemorated by the Commonwealth War Graves Commission in the United Kingdom Book of Remembrance.

McGAHEY Private S 14521 was killed in action on 1 July 1916. He has no known grave. He is now commemorated by the Commonwealth War Graves Commission and his name has been included on the addenda panel on the Thiepval Memorial.

REID Lance Corporal P H A 41548 died of pulmonary tuberculosis on 24 May 1921. He is now commemorated by the Commonwealth War Graves Commission and his name has been included on Brookwood (United Kingdom 1914-1918) Memorial.

The deaths of two men are under investigation:

MULDOON Private Samuel 24703. Died in 1921.

WARKE Private William Edwin 41457. Died on 12 July 1921. He is buried in Londonderry City Cemetery.

Commonwealth War Graves Commission Incorrect Commemorations

Two men have been identified as being incorrectly commemorated by the Commonwealth War Graves Commission:

LOUGHEED Private J 17409. Killed in action on 1 July 1916. Commemorated as Longheed on Thiepval Memorial, Pier and Face 15A.

WILSON Sergeant T 41876. Died as a prisoner of war on 3 October 1918. He is commemorated as serving with the 12th (Service) Battalion, The Royal Irish Rifles (Central Antrim). The error is compounded by his regimental number being shown as 19826; his correct Royal Irish Rifles number prior to transferring to Princess Victoria's (Royal Irish Fusiliers) was 19326.

Commemorated as Killed in Action, Died of Wounds or Died Serving with the 9th Royal Irish Fusiliers

ABERCROMBIE Private W J 41507. Killed in action 30 September 1918. Re-interred in Dadizeele New British Cemetery in 1920. IV. F. 24.

ABRAHAM Private A 13974. Killed in action 1 July 1916. Thiepval Memorial, Pier and Face 15A.

ABRAHAM Private J W 20292. Killed in action 1 July 1916. Thiepval Memorial, Pier and Face 15A.

ADAMS Private T 20035. Died as a prisoner of war 15 July 1918. St Souplet British Cemetery. II. D. 6.

ADDIS Private R 13972. Killed in action 1 July 1916. Thiepval Memorial, Pier and Face 15A.

ALLEN Private G 41982. Killed in action 3 October 1918. Tyne Cot Memorial, Panels 140 to 141.

ALLEN Private J 24847. Killed in action 16 August 1917. Tyne Cot Memorial, Panels 140 to 141.

ALLEN Private W J 20531. Killed in action 1 July 1916. Thiepval Memorial, Pier and Face 15A.

ALLISON Private T W 40050. Killed in action 16 August 1917. Tyne Cot Memorial, Panels 140 to 141.

ANDERSON Private F 17340. Died of wounds 3 July 1916. Puchevillers British Cemetery. I. B. 50.

ANDERSON Lance Corporal G A 13970. Died 8 January 1916. Armagh (St Mark) Church of Ireland Churchyard. 2. 52.

ANDERSON Lieutenant L M. Died 1 September 1915. Armagh (St Mark) Church of Ireland Churchyard. 3. 14.

ANDREWS Private F 24735. Killed in action 16 August 1917. Tyne Cot Memorial, Panels 140 to 141.

ARNELL Private J T 45797. Killed in action 25 October 1918. Harlebeke New British Cemetery. VI. B. 14.

ARTHUR Private W F C 41366. Killed in action 22 July 1918. Bailleul Communal Cemetery Extension. III. F. 108.

ATKINSON Private R 20338. Killed in action 1 July 1916. Thiepval Memorial, Pier and Face 15A.

ATKINSON Major T J. Killed in action 1 July 1916. Ancre British Cemetery, Hamel. VIII. A. 5.

BAILEY Lance Corporal A G 25250. Killed in action 24 August 1918. Mont Noir Military Cemetery. III. C. 8.

BAILEY Corporal H J 40037. Killed in action 16 August 1917. Tyne Cot Memorial, Panels 140 to 141.

BAIRD Private J 17937. Killed in action 1 July 1916. Thiepval Memorial, Pier and Face 15A.

BAIRD Private R 13998. Killed in action 1 July 1916. Ancre British Cemetery. VIII. A. 33.

BAIRD Private W 21577. Killed in action 16 August 1917. Tyne Cot Memorial, Panels 140 to 141.

BAKER Private W H 43312. Killed in action 16 August 1917. Tyne Cot Memorial, Panels 140 to 141.

BALES Private J 43229. Died of wounds 18 April 1918. Haringhe (Bandaghem) Military Cemetery. II. F. 23.

BALLAM Lance Corporal R C 22977. Died 5 December 1918. Tourcoing (Pont-Neuville) Communal Cemetery. H. 1.

BALLANTINE Sergeant T 18322. Killed in action 23 November 1917. Cambrai Memorial, Panel 10.

BALMER Acting Sergeant J 13986. Killed in action 16 August 1917. Tyne Cot Memorial, Panels 140 to 141.

BARK Private H R 43431. Killed in action 19 April 1918. Tyne Cot Memorial, Panels 140 to 141.

BARNES Private J 11454. Killed in action 16 August 1917. Tyne Cot Memorial, Panels 140 to 141.

BATTERBEE Private C 43374. Killed in action 9 June 1917. Menin Gate Memorial, Panel 42.

BEATTIE Private A 19763. Died of wounds 9 July 1916. Doullens Communal Cemetery Extension Number 1. IV. D. 7.

BEHAN Private P 27637. Killed in action 9 April 1918. Tyne Cot Memorial, Panels 140 to 141.

BELL Private J 14027. Killed in action 1 July 1916. Thiepval Memorial, Pier and Face 15A.

BELL Private J A 41333. Killed in action 19 April 1918. Wulverghem-Lindenhoek Road Military Cemetery. V. C. 23.

BELL Private R 14035. Killed in action 1 July 1916. Thiepval Memorial, Pier and Face 15A.

BELL Private V N 41254. Killed in action 26 October 1917. Neuville-Bourjonval British Cemetery. E. 19.

BERRY Private F W 42491. Killed in action 30 September to 3 October 1918. Re-interred in Dadizeele New British Cemetery in 1920. IV. B. 21.

BEST Private J 41396. Died of wounds 3 October 1918. Re-interred in Dadizeele New British Cemetery in 1920. II. D. 4.

BEST Private W H 13977. Killed in action 1 July 1916. Thiepval Memorial, Pier and Face 15A.

BIGGART Private W 41388. Died of wounds as a prisoner of war 3 April 1918. Pozieres Memorial, Panels 76 and 77.

BLACK Second Lieutenant C M. Died 9 July 1917. Knockbreda Church of Ireland Churchyard. A 146.

BLACK Private D 16094. Killed in action 1 July 1916. Thiepval Memorial, Pier and Face 15A.

BLACK Lance Corporal J E 18862. Killed in action 25 September 1917. Bourjonval British Cemetery. E. 24.

BLACK Private T H 14002. Killed in action 1 July 1916. Ancre British Cemetery. VIII. A. 85.

BLAKE Private L E W 42500. Killed in action 11 October 1918. Re-interred in Dadizeele New British Cemetery in 1920. IV. D. 25.

BLAKELY Private J 14039. Killed in action 1 July 1916. Thiepval Memorial, Pier and Face 15A.

BLOOMFIELD Private M 42451. Killed in action between 30 September and 3 October 1918. Re-interred in Dadizeele New British Cemetery in 1920. IV. B. 14.

BOWDEN Private J A 41287. Killed in action 19 April 1918. Tyne Cot Memorial, Panels 140 to 141.

BOWLES Private W 13976. Killed in action 1 July 1916. Thiepval Memorial, Pier and Face 15A.

BOYD Private R 14000. Killed in action 16 August 1917. Tyne Cot Memorial, Panels 140 to 141.

BOYD Private W A N 23897. Died of wounds 25 May 1917. Pond Farm Cemetery. N. 9.

BOYD Lieutenant W G. Killed in action 16 August 1917. Tyne Cot Memorial, Panels 140 to 141.

BOYLES Private W J 22644. Killed in action 1 July 1916. Thiepval Memorial, Pier and Face 15A.

BREW Major J G. Died of wounds as a prisoner of war 6 April 1918. Originally buried in Hattencourt French and German Cemetery. Reinterred in 1920 in Roye New British Cemetery. IV. D. 9.

BRIEN Private J 42455. Killed in action 3 October 1918. Re-interred in Dadizeele New British Cemetery in 1920. IV. F. 26.

BRIGGS Private T H 42092. Killed in action 25 October 1918. Harlebeke New British Cemetery. VI. A. 9.

BROLLY Private T P 40118. Killed in action 16 August 1917. Tyne Cot Memorial, Panels 140 to 141.

BROOKS Private D 14005. Killed in action 1 July 1916. Thiepval Memorial, Pier and Face 15A.

BROOMFIELD Private S 28687. Killed in action 4 September 1918. Ploegsteert Memorial, Panel 9.

BROWN Lance Corporal J 14013. Killed in action 16 August 1917. Tyne Cot Memorial, Panels 140 to 141.

BROWN Lance Corporal J 18560. Killed in action 1 July 1916. Thiepval Memorial, Pier and Face 15A.

BROWN Private J S 18121. Killed in action 16 August 1917. Tyne Cot Memorial, Panels 140 to 141.

BROWN Sergeant J 14033. Killed in action 1 July 1916. Ancre British Cemetery. VIII. A. 71.

BROWN Private W 41451. Died of wounds 12 August 1918. Originally buried in Wolfhoek British Cemetery. Reinterred in 1919 at Mont Noir Military Cemetery. II. E. 3.

BROWN Private W H 40053. Died as a prisoner of war 5 September 1918. Cologne Southern Cemetery. XIII. B. 1.

BROWNING Private F E 42127. Died of wounds 25 August 1918. Arneke British Cemetery III. E. 24.

BROWNLEE Private J 14019. Killed in action 1 July 1916. Thiepval Memorial, Pier and Face 15A.

BRYANS Private D 14043. Killed in action 23 November 1917. Cambrai Memorial, Panel 10.

BRYANS Sergeant J 13987. Killed in action 1 July 1916. Thiepval Memorial, Pier and Face 15A.

BRYSON MC Second Lieutenant J. Killed in action 6 October 1918. After seven days his body was recovered and buried but his grave was not identified during the concentration of cemeteries in the Dadizeele area. Tyne Cot Memorial, Panels 140 to 141.

BULMAN Private J 20319. Died of wounds 26 April 1916. Forceville Communal Cemetery and Extension. I. B. 9.

BULMAN Private R 20308. Died of wounds 12 October 1920. Newcastle-upon-Tyne (St John's Westgate and Elswick) Cemetery. X. U. 648.

BUNTING Lance Sergeant T 13997. Killed in action 1 July 1916. Thiepval Memorial, Pier and Face 15A.

BURKE Private J 17543. Killed in action 1 July 1916. A.I.F. Burial Ground. XVI. J. 1.

BURKE Private J 17817. Killed in action 1 July 1916. Puchevillers British Cemetery. I. B. 19.

BURNS Lance Corporal J 13981. Killed in action 1 July 1916. Thiepval Memorial, Pier and Face 15A.

BURNS Private R 14030. Killed in action 29 March 1918. Pozieres Memorial, Panels 76 and 77.

BURROWS Private D J 14028. Killed in action 1 July 1916. Ancre British Cemetery. II. D. 2.

BURROWS Private F 23724. Killed in action 16 August 1917. Tyne Cot Cemetery. V. C. 19.

BUTTERS Lance Corporal A 43275. Killed in action 29 March 1918. Pozieres Memorial, Panels 76 and 77.

BUTTON Private A F 43206. Killed in action 16 August 1917. Tyne Cot Memorial, Panels 140 to 141.

CABLE Private J 40058. Killed in action 16 August 1917. Tyne Cot Memorial, Panels 140 to 141.

CALLAGHAN Private G 14117. Killed in action 16 August 1917. Tyne Cot Memorial, Panels 140 to 141.

CALVERT Lance Corporal H J 17147. Killed in action 1 July 1916. Thiepval Memorial, Pier and Face 15A.

CAMLIN Lance Corporal A 14091. Killed in action 24 August 1918. Bailleul Communal Cemetery Extension. III. G. 13.

CAMPBELL Corporal D O 18238. Killed in action 16 August 1917. Tyne Cot Memorial, Panels 140 to 141.

CAMPBELL Private H 20333. Killed in action 16 August 1917. Tyne Cot Cemetery. VI. H. 19.

CAMPBELL Private J 14097. Killed in action 25 September 1917. Neuville-Bourjonval British Cemetery. E. 22.

CAMPBELL Private J 20024. Killed in action 1 July 1916. Ancre British Cemetery. VIII. A. 10.

CAMPBELL Private W J 24952. Killed in action 16 August 1917. Bedford House Cemetery. Enclosure 4, XIII. F. 9.

CAMPKIN Private E S 43362. Killed in action 21 March 1918. St Souplet British Cemetery. I. G. 27.

CARROLL Private G F 23230. Died of wounds 3 July 1917. Wimereux Communal Cemetery. II. N. 11A.

CARSON Private R 24849. Killed in action 16 August 1917. Tyne Cot Memorial, Panels 140 to 141.

CARSON Private R 14061. Killed in action 1 July 1916. Thiepval Memorial, Pier and Face 15A.

CARTMILL Private T 41523. Killed in action 29 March 1918. Pozieres Memorial, Panels 76 and 77.

CATHER VC Lieutenant G St G S. Killed in action 2 July 1916. Thiepval Memorial, Pier and Face 15A.

CATLIN Private F W 43383. Killed in action 16 August 1917. Tyne Cot Memorial, Panels 140 to 141.

CAVE Private G W 43209. Killed in action 4 June 1917. Menin Gate Memorial, Panel 42.

CHAMBERS Lance Corporal G 14065. Killed in action 1 July 1916. Ancre British Cemetery. VIII. A. 37.

CHAMBERS Private J 14074. Killed in action 16 August 1917. Tyne Cot Memorial, Panels 140 to 141.

CHAMBERS Private J 14089. Killed in action 1 July 1916. Hamel Military Cemetery. I. E. 12.

CHAMBERS Lance Corporal J H 14052. Died of wounds 29 July 1920. Knockamuckley (St Matthias) Church of Ireland Churchyard, County Armagh.

CHAMBERS Private S 18068. Killed in action 5 September 1918. Addenda Panel, Tyne Cot Memorial.

CHAMBERS Private T 21676. Killed in action 1 July 1916. Hamel Military Cemetery. I. B. 7.

CHAPMAN Private S H 17934. Killed in action 1 July 1916. Thiepval Memorial, Pier and Face 15A.

CLARK Private A H 43338. Killed in action 16 August 1917. Tyne Cot Cemetery. XV. F. 3.

CLARK Private G W 40009. Killed in action 16 August 1917. Tyne Cot Memorial, Panels 140 to 141.

CLARK Private J R 40010. Killed in action 16 August 1917. Tyne Cot Memorial, Panels 140 to 141.

CLARKE Private W 17928. Killed in action 1 July 1916. Thiepval Memorial, Pier and Face 15A.

CLARKSON Private J 20321. Died 28 September 1916. Gateshead Fell (St John) Churchyard. 56.

CLEMENTS MM Sergeant T 17151. Killed in action 22 November 1917. Cambrai Memorial, Panel 10.

CLIFTON Private W G 42280. Killed in action 24 August 1918. Ploegsteert Memorial, Panel 9.

CLULOW Private J 26914. Killed in action 16 August 1917. Tyne Cot Memorial, Panels 140 to 141.

COCHRANE Private R 24397. Killed in action 29 March 1918. Pozieres Memorial, Panels 76 and 77.

COLCLOUGH Private T L 43334. Killed in action 16 August 1917. New Irish Farm Cemetery. XV. D. 17.

COLE Private J 18467. Killed in action 1 July 1916. Thiepval Memorial, Pier and Face 15A.

COLLINS Corporal R P 10054. Killed in action 30 September 1918. Duhallow ADS Cemetery. IX. E. 10.

CONLON Private T 43041. Killed in action 21 March 1918. Pozieres Memorial, Panels 76 and 77.

COOKE Private C W E 45795. Killed in action 3 October 1918. Re-interred in Dadizeele New British Cemetery in 1920. IV. B. 23.

COOKE Private F St G 41694. Killed in action 19 April 1918. Tyne Cot Memorial, Panels 140 to 141.

COOLE Private T J 16098. Killed in action 1 July 1916. Thiepval Memorial, Pier and Face 15A.

CORDNER Private S 22809. Killed in action 16 August 1917. Tyne Cot Memorial, Panels 140 to 141.

CORDNER Private W 14111. Killed in action 1 July 1916. Thiepval Memorial, Pier and Face 15A.

CORDY Private W J 14048. Died of wounds 26 June 1916. Hamel Military Cemetery. I. C. 9.

CORKIN Private J 14106. Killed in action 1 July 1916. Thiepval Memorial, Pier and Face 15A.

COULTER MM Private J 41530. Killed in action 1 October 1918. Re-interred in Dadizeele New British Cemetery in 1920. IV. B. 12.

COUPLAND Private L 43247. Killed in action 16 August 1917. Tyne Cot Memorial, Panels 140 to 141.

COUSINS Private I 22641. Killed in action 1 July 1916. Thiepval Memorial, Pier and Face 15A.

COWDY Second Lieutenant H E. Killed in action 16 August 1917. Tyne Cot Memorial, Panels 140 to 141.

CRAIG MM Lance Sergeant G 23438. Killed in action 29 March 1918. Pozieres Memorial, Panels 76 and 77.

CRAMPTON Private T 24927. Killed in action 16 August 1917. Tyne Cot Memorial, Panels 140 to 141.

CRAWFORD Private A S 41485. Killed in action 29 March 1918. Pozieres Memorial, Panels 76 and 77.

CROSBIE MC Second Lieutenant (Acting Captain) T E C. Died of wounds 15 April 1918. Buried in Lindenhoek Cemetery, but his grave was not identified during the concentration of cemeteries. Tyne Cot Memorial, Panels 140 to 141.

CREANEY Private J 14113. Killed in action 1 July 1916. Thiepval Memorial, Pier and Face 15A.

CROOK Private L W 45754. Killed in action 19 April 1918. Tyne Cot Memorial, Panels 140 to 141.

CROSS Warrant Officer Class II, Company Sergeant Major F E 15719. Killed in action 8 May 1916. Hamel Military Cemetery. I. E. 25.

CROSS Captain G H. Killed in action 30 September 1918. Re-interred in Dadizeele New British Cemetery in 1920. IV. F. 27.

CROZIER Corporal W 24004. Killed in action 24 July 1918. Bertenacre Military Cemetery. I. B. 5. (See Appendix 6.)

CRYMBLE Second Lieutenant J G. Died of wounds 28 December 1916. Bailleul Communal Cemetery Extension. III. A. 203.

CULBERT Sergeant S 14098. Killed in action 16 August 1917. Tyne Cot Memorial, Panels 140 to 141.

CULLEN Lance Corporal C 23694. Killed in action 16 August 1917. Dochy Farm New British Cemetery. VI. E. 26.

CULLEY Private W 17816. Killed in action 1 July 1916. Ancre British Cemetery. VIII. A. 57.

CUNNINGHAM Private W F 19093. Killed in action 4 September 1918. Originally buried at Bristol Castle Cemetery. Reinterred at Messines Ridge British Cemetery in 1920. I. E. 10.

CURRIE Private D 42513. Died of wounds 8 October 1918. Lijssenthoek Military Cemetery. XXX. C. 1.

CURRY Private A 20316. Killed in action 1 July 1916. Thiepval Memorial, Pier and Face 15A.

CURTIS Private W 16099. Killed in action 1 July 1916. Thiepval Memorial, Pier and Face 15A.

DALZELL Private H 24114. Killed in action 16 August 1917. Tyne Cot Memorial, Panels 140 to 141.

DARLING MC Second Lieutenant J. Died of wounds 26 October 1918. Kezelberg Military Cemetery. I. A. 13.

DAVEY Private A 41589. Killed in action 19 April 1918. Tyne Cot Memorial, Panels 140 to 141.

DAVIS Private J 19735. Killed in action 1 July 1916. Thiepval Memorial, Pier and Face 15A.

DAVIS Private T H 16100. Killed in action 1 July 1916. Thiepval Memorial, Pier and Face 15A.

DAWSON Private A 20344. Died as a prisoner of war 8 July 1918. Berlin South-Western Cemetery. I. B. 3.

DAWSON Sergeant E 13389. Died 1 January 1917. Grange Church of Ireland Churchyard, County Armagh.

DAWSON Private T W 22176. Killed in action 16 August 1917. Tyne Cot Memorial, Panels 140 to 141.

DEERY Lance Corporal J 41244. Killed in action 11 October 1918. Re-interred in Dadizeele New British Cemetery in 1920. IV. B. 16.

DESPARD DSO, MC Captain C B 6th (Inniskilling) Dragoons. Killed in action 18 April 1918. Buried in Kemmel Cemetery but his grave was not identified during the concentration of cemeteries. Tyne Cot Memorial, Panel 3.

DEVINE Private R 43285. Killed in action 30 September 1918. Reinterred in Dadizeele New British Cemetery in 1920. IV. F. 29.

DEVINE Private S 41156. Died 24 February 1918. Gloucester Old Cemetery. NG 249.

DICK MM Lance Corporal I 20441. Drowned 30 December 1919. Belfast City Cemetery. C. 434.

DICKINSON Private T 41078. Killed in action 26 October 1917. Neuville-Bourjonval British Cemetery. E. 21.

DICKSON Lance Corporal T J I 23697. Died of wounds 18 April 1918. Haringhe (Bandaghem) Military Cemetery. I. F. 10.

DILLON Private S G 14130. Died 7 January 1916. Seagoe Cemetery.

DILLON Private V S 14135. Killed in action 1 July 1916. Thiepval Memorial, Pier and Face 15A.

DITTON Lance Corporal C E 43387. Killed in action 16 October 1918. Re-interred in Dadizeele New British Cemetery in 1920. III. A. 8.

DIXON Private D 18654. Killed in action 1 July 1916. Thiepval Memorial, Pier and Face 15A.

DIXON Lance Corporal T G 24019. Killed in action 30 September 1918. Duhallow ADS Cemetery. IX. E. 9.

DOBSON Second Lieutenant J R. Died of wounds 19 February 1917. Bailleul Communal Cemetery Extension. III. B. 55.

DONNELL Private W 18091. Killed in action 16 August 1917. Tyne Cot Memorial, Panels 140 to 141.

DONNERY Corporal F 18976. Killed in action 16 August 1917. Tyne Cot Cemetery. IV. F. 1.

DORRIAN Private H 8065. Killed in action 16 August 1917. Tyne Cot Cemetery. III. G. 15.

DRAFFIN Private S 24947. Killed in action 16 August 1917. New Irish Farm Cemetery. XV. C. 16.

DRURY Private G 20240. Killed in action 1 July 1916. Thiepval Memorial, Pier and Face 15A.

DUFF Private T E 20332. Killed in action 16 August 1917. Tyne Cot Cemetery. XI. G. 10.

DUFFY Private F 18393. Killed in action 29 March 1918. Noyon New British Cemetery. III. B. 6.

DUNN Private J 41077. Killed in action 26 October 1917. Neuville-Bourjonval British Cemetery. E. 20.

DUNNE Lance Corporal J 9210. Killed in action 14 March 1918. Thiepval Memorial, Pier and Face 15A.

DUNWOODY Second Lieutenant H H. Killed in action 31 July 1916. Buried in St Quentin Cabaret Military Cemetery, Wulverghem. He was reinterred in Ration Farm (La Plus Douve) Cemetery. III. B. 3.

EDEN Private W 43335. Killed in action 16 August 1917. Tyne Cot Memorial, Panels 140 to 141.

ELLIOTT Lance Corporal H 14158. Died of wounds 4 July 1916. Puchevillers British Cemetery. I. B. 34.

ELLIOTT Private W T 41159. Killed in action 19 April 1918. Tyne Cot Memorial, Panels 140 to 141.

ELLISON Private W H K 49736. Killed in action 2 October 1918. Tyne Cot Memorial, Panels 140 to 141.

ERSKINE Lance Corporal A 41235. Died of wounds 10 October 1918. Lijssenthoek Military Cemetery. XXX. B. 10.

EYTON Private C G 43359. Died of wounds 30 May 1917. Dranoutre Military Cemetery. I. J. 19.

FARR Private T 23790. Killed in action 1 July 1916. Connaught Cemetery. XIII. E. 2.

FARRELL Private W 18261. Killed in action 1 July 1916. Thiepval Memorial, Pier and Face 15A.

FERGUSON Private E 27534. Killed in action 14 October 1918. Re-interred in Dadizeele New British Cemetery in 1920. III. D. 5.

FERGUSON Private J 18258. Killed in action 16 August 1917. Tyne Cot Memorial, Panels 140 to 141.

FERGUSON Private J 18607. Killed in action 29 March 1918. Pozieres Memorial, Panels 76 and 77.

FERGUSON Private W 14197. Killed in action 1 July 1916. Serre Road Cemetery Number 1. X. E. 17.

FERRIS Private G 14174. Killed in action 1 July 1916. Mill Road Cemetery. I. E. 8.

FIRTH Sergeant H 43469. Killed in action 19 April 1918. Tyne Cot Memorial, Panels 140 to 141.

FISHER Private E C 43503. Killed in action 4 September 1918. Originally buried at Bristol Castle Cemetery. Reinterred at Messines Ridge British Cemetery in 1920. I. D. 1.

FITZSIMMONS Private W J 42551. Killed in action 25 October 1918. Harlebeke New British Cemetery. VI. B. 10.

FITZSIMONS Private R 14177. Died 20 February 1916. St Sever Cemetery. A. 17. 26.

FLANAGAN Lance Corporal H 41229. Killed in action 22 November 1917. Cambrai Memorial, Panel 10.

FLEMING Private W 16154. Killed in action 1 July 1916. Thiepval Memorial, Pier and Face 15A.

FLOOD MC Captain R S. Killed in action 5 December 1917. Ribecourt British Cemetery. I. E. 1.

FORBES Private J 41453. Killed in action 29 March 1918. Pozieres Memorial, Panels 76 and 77.

FORD Private J 41535. Killed in action 3 November 1917. Cambrai East Military Cemetery. VII. B. 3.

FORDE Private S J 17671. Killed in action 22 February 1916. Hamel Military Cemetery. I. B. 18.

FORREST Private R H 42271. Died 27 June 1918. Bleue-Maison Military Cemetery. A. 5.

FOSTER MM Sergeant F 14175. Killed in action 1 July 1916. Hamel Military Cemetery. I. B. 7.

FOSTER Private R 15450. Killed in action 29 March 1918. Pozieres Memorial, Panels 76 and 77.

FOX Lance Sergeant G R 14173. Killed in action 1 July 1916. Ancre British Cemetery. VIII. A. 28.

FRAME Private J 24907. Killed in action 16 August 1917. Tyne Cot Memorial, Panels 140 to 141.

FRAZER Private W 9852. Died of wounds 16 August 1918. Arneke British Cemetery. III. C. 13.

FREEMAN Private S W 43241. Killed in action 21 March 1918. Buried initially in Essigny-Le-Grand German Cemetery. His grave was not identified during the concentration of cemeteries into Grand-Seraucourt British Cemetery. Commemorated there on Essigny-Le-Grand German Cemetery Memorial 4.

FULTON Private H 14178. Died of wounds 1 June 1916. Forceville Communal Cemetery and Extension. I. D. 10.

FULTON Private J 14170. Killed in action 1 July 1916. Thiepval Memorial, Pier and Face 15A.

GALBRAITH Private G 41188. Died of wounds 24 November 1917. Grevillers British Cemetery. VIII. B. 2.

GALBRAITH Private P 24581. Killed in action 16 August 1917. Tyne Cot Memorial, Panels 140 to 141.

GASKIN Private J 6391. Killed in action 16 August 1917. Tyne Cot Memorial, Panels 140 to 141.

GASTON Private G F 50016. Killed in action 4 September 1918. Ploegsteert Memorial, Panel 9.

GIBSON Private H 14239. Killed in action 1 July 1916. Thiepval Memorial, Pier and Face 15A.

GIBSON Lance Corporal W J 14225. Killed in action 1 July 1916. Thiepval Memorial, Pier and Face 15A.

GIBSON Private W J 18254. Killed in action 16 August 1917. Tyne Cot Memorial, Panels 140 to 141.

GIFFEN Private D 17297. Killed in action 16 August 1917. Tyne Cot Memorial, Panels 140 to 141.

GILKINSON Private J 14235. Killed in action 29 March 1918. Pozieres Memorial, Panels 76 and 77.

GILLESPIE Private J 14242. Killed in action 19 April 1918. Tyne Cot Memorial, Panels 140 to 141.

GILMANEY Private J 20343. Killed in action 1 July 1916. Thiepval Memorial, Pier and Face 15A.

GILMORE Private J 3017. Died as a prisoner of war 18 October 1918. Originally interred in the cemetery at Merseburg Prisoner of War Camp, Saxony. Reinterred at Berlin South-Western Cemetery in 1925. XVI. D. 6.

GILMORE Private McC 18633. Died of wounds 28 July 1916. Cladymore Presbyterian Churchyard.

GILROY Private G 15258. Killed in action 27 March 1918. Pozieres Memorial, Panels 76 and 77.

GIRVAN Private J 19796. Died 18 March 1917. Armagh (St Mark) Church of Ireland Churchyard. 4. 30.

GIRVAN Lance Sergeant J 14241. Died of wounds 4 July 1916. St Sever Cemetery. A. 22. 7.

GIRVIN Private W 14206. Killed in action 12 February 1916. Mesnil Ridge Cemetery. I. 7.

GLASS Private J 22982. Killed in action 1 July 1916. Thiepval Memorial, Pier and Face 15A.

GLASS Private P J 3428. Killed in action 19 April 1918. Tyne Cot Memorial, Panels 140 to 141.

GLENN Private W 14209. Killed in action 1 July 1916. Hamel Military Cemetery. I. D. 7.

GORDON Private J 14217. Killed in action 1 July 1916. Thiepval Memorial, Pier and Face 15A.

GORDON Sergeant W 14221. Died of wounds 2 July 1916. Hamel Military Cemetery. I. B. 7.

GOUCHER Sergeant T 19318. Killed in action 22 January 1918. Grand-Seraucourt British Cemetery. I. G. 14.

GRACEY Corporal T 23378. Killed in action 16 August 1917. Tyne Cot Cemetery. VII. B. 2.

GRAHAM Private A 14204. Died of wounds 22 March 1917. Kemmel Chateau Military Cemetery. M. 85.

GRAHAM Private A 14208. Killed in action 1 July 1916. Thiepval Memorial, Pier and Face 15A.

GRAHAM Private C 17406. Died 3 February 1917. Bailleul Communal Cemetery Extension. III. A. 76.

GRAHAM Corporal R W 23321. Died 5 August 1917. St Marie Cemetery, Le Havre. Division 62. I. G. 6.

GRAHAM Lance Corporal W 23215. Killed in action 16 August 1917. Tyne Cot Memorial, Panels 140 to 141.

GRAHAM Private W G 20336. Killed in action 1 July 1916. Thiepval Memorial, Pier and Face 15A.

GRANT Private T J 17153. Killed in action 1 July 1916. Thiepval Memorial, Pier and Face 15A.

GRAY Private E 14201. Killed in action 16 August 1917. Tyne Cot Memorial, Panels 140 to 141.

GREER Private C 49744. Died of wounds 4 October 1918. Haringhe (Bandaghem) Military Cemetery. III. A. 2.

GREER Private J 23783. Died of wounds 4 August 1917. Brandhoek New Military Cemetery. III. B 3.

GREER Private W 21405. Killed in action 16 August 1917. Tyne Cot Memorial, Panels 140 to 141.

GREGG Private J 17556. Killed in action 1 July 1916. Thiepval Memorial, Pier and Face 15A.

GREGG DCM Lance Corporal W 11216. Killed in action 1 October 1918. Re-interred in Dadizeele New British Cemetery in 1920. II. D. 21.

GRIBBEN Private W 20986. Killed in action 19 April 1918. Tyne Cot Memorial, Panels 140 to 141.

GRIBBIN Private A 23011. Killed in action 19 April 1918. Tyne Cot Memorial, Panels 140 to 141.

GRIMASON Private R 14238. Killed in action 1 July 1916. Thiepval Memorial, Pier and Face 15A.

GROVES Private J 27746. Died as a prisoner of war 3 August 1918. Hautmont Communal Cemetery. V. B. 17.

GUMBLE Private Kenzer 43321. Died of pulmonary tuberculosis and haemoptysis after gassing 9 June 1920. Plumstead Cemetery, London.

HAGUE Lance Corporal I 43265. Died of wounds 13 August 1917. Brandhoek New Military Cemetery. VI. D. 3.

HAIRE Private T J G 21645. Killed in action 27 March 1918. Pozieres Memorial, Panels 76 and 77.

HALES Private C J 17399. Killed in action 1 July 1916. Thiepval Memorial, Pier and Face 15A.

HALL Private A J 45745. Killed in action 19 April 1918. Tyne Cot Memorial, Panels 140 to 141.

HALL Second Lieutenant F H The Royal Irish Rifles. Killed in action 30 September 1918. Buried initially 1¾ miles north of Gheleuwe but was reinterred in Dadizeele New British Cemetery in 1920. IV. F. 21.

HALL Private J 14260. Killed in action 3 April 1916. Mesnil Ridge Cemetery. B. 10.

HALL Private J 20092. Killed in action 1 July 1916. Thiepval Memorial, Pier and Face 15A.

HALL Private J 17386. Killed in action 1 July 1916. Thiepval Memorial, Pier and Face 15A.

HALL Private R 22770. Killed in action 16 August 1917. Tyne Cot Memorial, Panels 140 to 141.

HALL Private W 14332. Killed in action 1 July 1916. Ancre British Cemetery. I. F. 34.

HALLIDAY Private R 18226. Killed in action 1 July 1916. Ancre British Cemetery. II. D. 35.

HALLIGAN Private R 14326. Died 10 December 1916. Boulogne Eastern Cemetery. VIII. C. 198.

HALLIGAN Private T W H 14335. Died of wounds 25 October 1918. Duhallow ADS Cemetery. IV. I. 27.

HAMILTON Private A 14287. Killed in action 1 July 1916. Hamel Military Cemetery, Special Memorial B2.

HAMILTON Lieutenant E. Killed in action 14 April 1918. Tyne Cot Memorial, Panels 140 to 141.

HAMILTON Corporal J 14288. Killed in action 1 July 1916. Hamel Military Cemetery. I. B. 7.

HAMILTON MM Private J 14282. Killed in action 16 August 1917. Tyne Cot Memorial, Panels 140 to 141.

HAMILTON Warrant Officer Class II, Company Sergeant Major J 14271. Killed in action 25 October 1918. Harlebeke New British Cemetery. VI. B. 3.

HAMILTON Private R 18259. Killed in action 19 April 1918. Tyne Cot Memorial, Panels 140 to 141.

HAMILTON Lance Corporal S 14264. Killed in action 1 July 1916. Thiepval Memorial, Pier and Face 15A.

HAMMOND Private H W 45740. Died as a prisoner of war 27 September 1918. Le Cateau Military Cemetery. I. B. 133.

HANNA Private W 14281. Died of wounds 10 September 1917. Boulogne Eastern Cemetery. VIII. I. 13.

HARDINGTON Lance Corporal J J 43363. Died as a prisoner of war 14 August 1918. Hautmont Communal Cemetery. V. C. 4.

HARDY Second Lieutenant G. Died of wounds as a prisoner of war 30 April 1918. Kortrijk (St Jean) Communal Cemetery. C. 23.

HARPER Private H 21119. Killed in action 19 April 1918. Tyne Cot Memorial, Panels 140 to 141.

HARPER Private W J 14247. Killed in action 1 July 1916. Thiepval Memorial, Pier and Face 15A.

HARPUR Private T 41433. Died of wounds as a prisoner of war 18 May 1918. Avesnes-sur-Helpe Communal Cemetery. D. 12.

HARRIS Private P J 45766. Died of wounds 15 April 1918. Haringhe (Bandaghem) Military Cemetery. II. D. 12.

HART Private J 25181. Killed in action 16 August 1917. Tyne Cot Memorial, Panels 140 to 141.

HATHAWAY Corporal R 43436. Died of wounds 7 October 1918. Haringhe (Bandaghem) Military Cemetery. III. A. 34.

HAWTHORNE Private J 18065. Killed in action 16 August 1917. Tyne Cot Memorial, Panels 140 to 141.

HAYES Private J 14303. Killed in action 1 July 1916. Ancre British Cemetery. VIII. A. 20.

HAYES Private W 18558. Killed in action 1 July 1916. Ancre British Cemetery. VIII. A. 14.

HAYWOOD Private H E 43233. Killed in action 16 August 1917. Tyne Cot Cemetery. IV. E. 3.

HAZLETT Private J A 16108. Killed in action 1 July 1916. Thiepval Memorial, Pier and Face 15A.

HEATHWOOD Private R 41285. Killed in action 3 November 1917. Thiepval Memorial, Pier and Face 15A.

HEFFERNAN Private A F 43316. Died of wounds 31 August 1917. St Sever Cemetery Extension. II. B. 2A.

HENRY MM Lance Sergeant G A 41401. Died of wounds 26 March 1918. St Sever Cemetery Extension. VI. H. 125.

HENRY Private J 14312. Killed in action 16 August 1917. Tyne Cot Memorial, Panels 140 to 141.

HENRY Private W G 14276. Killed in action 1 July 1916. Ancre British Cemetery. VIII. A. 11.

HERRING Private J W 43215. Killed in action 16 August 1917. Tyne Cot Memorial, Panels 140 to 141.

HEWITT Private J 14309. Killed in action 1 July 1916. Thiepval Memorial, Pier and Face 15A.

HEWITT Lance Corporal J 16423. Killed in action 1 July 1916. Thiepval Memorial, Pier and Face 15A.

HEWITT Private T 14315. Killed in action 1 July 1916. Thiepval Memorial, Pier and Face 15A.

HEWITT Private T 22755. Killed in action 1 July 1916. Thiepval Memorial, Pier and Face 15A.

HICKEY Private W 20018. Died of wounds 7 February 1917. Hazebrouck Communal Cemetery. I. D. 1.

HICKS Private F H 23854. Killed in action 16 August 1917. Tyne Cot Memorial, Panels 140 to 141.

HILL Private J 14311. Killed in action 16 August 1917. Tyne Cot Memorial, Panels 140 to 141.

HILL Private M 14299. Died 10 May 1916. Drumcree Church of Ireland Churchyard. Grave 235.

HILL Private R 16431. Died of wounds 17 July 1916. Drumcree Church of Ireland Churchyard. Grave 235.

HILTON Private W 23491. Killed in action 19 February 1918. Grand-Seraucourt British Cemetery. I. A. 4.

HOBBS Private A 14259. Killed in action 1 July 1916. Thiepval Memorial, Pier and Face 15A.

HOBBS Private D 14305. Killed in action 1 July 1916. Thiepval Memorial, Pier and Face 15A.

HOBBS Sergeant R 14302. Killed in action 1 July 1916. Thiepval Memorial, Pier and Face 15A.

HOLLAND Private A 14310. Killed in action 1 July 1916. Thiepval Memorial, Pier and Face 15A.

HOLLAND Private T 18062. Killed in action 1 July 1916. Thiepval Memorial, Pier and Face 15A.

HOLLYWOOD Private A 22749. Died of wounds 18 October 1916. Bailleul Communal Cemetery Extension. III. A. 257.

HOLLYWOOD Lieutenant A C. Killed in action 1 July 1916. Although it was reported that his body was brought back and buried behind Hamel Village, his grave was not identified during the concentration of cemeteries. Thiepval Memorial, Pier and Face 15A and 15B.

HOLMES Private T H 14250. Killed in action 1 July 1916. Thiepval Memorial, Pier and Face 15A.

HONEY Private G 43230. Died of wounds 25 May 1917. The burial return (Army Form W3314) shows a burial date of 24 May 1917. Pond Farm Cemetery. N. 8.

HOOKER Sergeant G H 43390. Killed in action 3 October 1918. Re-interred in Dadizeele New British Cemetery in 1920. IV. F. 22.

HOUSTON Private F 20342. Killed in action 1 July 1916. Mesnil Communal Cemetery Extension. III. A. 6.

HOUSTON Private J F 17150. Died of wounds 22 June 1918. Esquelbecq Military Cemetery. III. B. 32.

HOUSTON Private S 22154. Killed in action 1 July 1916. Thiepval Memorial, Pier and Face 15A.

HOUSTON Private T 20305. Died of wounds 10 April 1916. Doullens Communal Cemetery Extension Number 1. I. E. 12.

HUGHES DCM, MM Colour Sergeant J 4517. Killed in action 29 March 1918. Roye New British Cemetery. IV. B. 1.

HUGHES Sergeant W 14321. Died of wounds 11 July 1916. Boulogne Eastern Cemetery. VIII. D. 104.

HULL Corporal R J 41576. Killed in action 11 October 1918. Re-interred in Dadizeele New British Cemetery in 1920. I. D. 10.

HULL Corporal W 14268. Killed in action 1 July 1916. Thiepval Memorial, Pier and Face 15A.

HUMMERSTONE Private C S 42188. Killed in action 4 September 1918. Originally buried at Bristol Castle Cemetery. Reinterred at Messines Ridge British Cemetery in 1920. I. D. 11.

HUNTER Private W 14253. Killed in action 1 July 1916. Thiepval Memorial, Pier and Face 15A.

HUTCHINSON Private J A 22151. Killed in action 25 April 1916. Hamel Military Cemetery. I. E. 24.

HUTCHINSON Lance Corporal J 14272. Died of wounds 28 June 1916. Forceville Communal Cemetery and Extension. I. E. 6.

HUTCHINSON Private W 18044. Killed in action 16 August 1917. Tyne Cot Memorial, Panels 140 to 141.

HYNES Private H 14329. Killed in action 1 July 1916. Thiepval Memorial, Pier and Face 15A.

INGLEDEW Sergeant C 13080. Killed in action 5 September 1918. Wulverghem-Lindenhoek Road Military Cemetery. IV. B. 26.

INGLIS Second Lieutenant J M. Died of wounds 26 October 1918. Terlincthun British Cemetery. VI. D. 2.

IRWIN Private R 41080. Killed in action 14 April 1918. Tyne Cot Memorial, Panels 140 to 141.

IRWIN Sergeant R 41268. Killed in action 3 November 1917. Neuville-Bourjonval British Cemetery. E. 17.

IRWIN Sergeant W G Wolsey 41146. Died of wounds 26 August 1918. Arneke British Cemetery. III. D.

IRWIN Private W T 29440. Died 16 May 1919. Shankill Cemetery, County Armagh. Grave 324.

JACKSON Sergeant G W 14361. Killed in action 1 July 1916. Thiepval Memorial, Pier and Face 15A.

JACKSON Private T H 17932. Killed in action 1 July 1916. Thiepval Memorial, Pier and Face 15A.

JACKSON Private W A 22983. Died 7 April 1919. Belfast City Cemetery. K2. 400.

JENNINGS Lance Corporal A R 43435. Died of wounds 14 October 1918. Haringhe (Bandaghem) Military Cemetery. III. A. 50.

JOHNSTON Private A 14349. Killed in action 1 July 1916. Thiepval Memorial, Pier and Face 15A.

JOHNSTON Private A 14371. Died of wounds 16 July 1916. St Sever Cemetery. A. 31. 14.

JOHNSTON Captain C M. Killed in action 1 July 1916. Mesnil Communal Cemetery Extension. III. B. 17.

JOHNSTON Private G 41169. Died 13 October 1918. Perreuse Chateau Franco British National Cemetery. I. C. 9.

JOHNSTON Corporal H C 22761. Killed in action 16 August 1917. Tyne Cot Memorial, Panels 140 to 141.

JOHNSTON Captain J A. Killed in action 18 February 1917. St Quentin Cabaret Military Cemetery. II. B. 2.

JOHNSTON Private J F 41126. Died of wounds 25 March 1918. Roye New British Cemetery. IV. B. 3.

JOHNSTON Private J 41107. Died of wounds 11 February 1918. Grand-Seraucourt British Cemetery. V. G. 4.

JOHNSTON Private R 14365. Killed in action 1 July 1916. Thiepval Memorial, Pier and Face 15A.

JOHNSTON Private W 14373. Killed in action 1 July 1916. Thiepval Memorial, Pier and Face 15A.

JOHNSTON Lance Corporal W 18061. Died of wounds 9 September 1918. Arneke British Cemetery. VII. A. 6.

JOHNSTON Private W J 22152. Killed in action 16 August 1917. Tyne Cot Memorial, Panels 140 to 141.

JONES Private E 14363. Killed in action 16 August 1917. Tyne Cot Memorial, Panels 140 to 141.

JONES Private J 14353. Died of wounds 2 July 1916. Puchevillers British Cemetery. I. C. 51.

JONES Private S 14368. Killed in action 1 July 1916. Thiepval Memorial, Pier and Face 15A.

JOYCE Private J 14355. Killed in action 1 July 1916. Ancre British Cemetery. IV. 4. 17.

JOYCE Private T J 16114. Killed in action 1 July 1916. Thiepval Memorial, Pier and Face 15A.

JUDGE Private C 43360. Killed in action 16 August 1917. Tyne Cot Memorial, Panels 140 to 141.

KANE Private W J 14382. Killed in action 1 July 1916. Ancre British Cemetery. VIII. A. 21.

KEARNEY Private P 12354. Killed in action 16 August 1917. Tyne Cot Cemetery. XV. F. 4.

KELLER Private A G 25103. Killed in action 14 April 1918. Tyne Cot Memorial, Panels 140 to 141.

KELLS Private J J 16115. Killed in action 1 July 1916. Martinsart British Cemetery. I. A. 6.

KELLY Private C 18398. Killed in action 1 July 1916. His body was recovered in September 1916 and buried in Hamel Military Cemetery. II. C. 33.

KELLY Private J 41577. Died of wounds 5 September 1918. Arneke British Cemetery. III. D. 28.

KELLY Private J 27583. Killed in action 24 August 1918. Mont Noir Military Cemetery. II. C. 14.

KELLY Lieutenant Colonel P E. Killed in action 11 October 1918. Buried in Meulenhouck Military Cemetery, near Beselare. Re-interred in Dadizeele New British Cemetery in 1920. II. D. 8.

KELLY Private W 14378. Killed in action 1 July 1916. Ancre British Cemetery. VIII. A.

KENNEDY Private J W 17931. Killed in action 1 July 1916. Hamel Military Cemetery. I. A. 19.

KERNAGHAN Second Lieutenant J. Died of wounds 1 October 1918. Ypres Reservoir Cemetery. II. E. 15.

KERR Lance Sergeant B 20949. Killed in action 12 April 1918. Tyne Cot Memorial, Panels 140 to 141.

KERR MC Major (Acting Lieutenant Colonel) R G The Royal Inniskilling Fusiliers. Killed in action 11 July 1918. Buried in Bertenacre Military Cemetery. II. F. 8.

KERR Private R W 41696. Died as a prisoner of war 4 December 1918. Hamburg Cemetery. XVI. D. 8.

KIERANS Private J 16344. Killed in action 16 August 1917. Tyne Cot Cemetery. VII. G. 7.

KILPATRICK Private T 14379. Died of wounds 11 July 1916. Abbeville Communal Cemetery. V. E. 13.

KING Private J D 41302. Killed in action 3 November 1917. Cambrai East Military Cemetery. VII. B. 2.

KINSELLA Private P 42506. Killed in action 2 October 1918. Tyne Cot Memorial, Panels 140 to 141.

KIRK Private J A 40014. Died of wounds 18 August 1917. Brandhoek New Military Cemetery Number 3. II. E. 21.

LALLY Private G 42509. Killed in action 30 September 1918. Originally buried at a point south-east of Dadizeele. In the process of concentrating isolated graves, two unidentified soldiers of Princess Victoria's (Royal Irish Fusiliers) were found near that point and buried as unknown soldiers in Dadizeele New British Cemetery. It was presumed that Lally was one of them (the other was believed to be Private W Wakelam of the 1st Battalion) and he is commemorated there on Special Memorial 7 as 'believed to be buried in this cemetery'.

LANDLES Private J 21763. Killed in action 1 July 1916. Thiepval Memorial, Pier and Face 15A.

LARKIN Private J 20580. Died in Ireland 26 March 1917. Lurgan New Cemetery. D. 280.

LAVERY Private H 26841. Killed in action 19 April 1918. Tyne Cot Memorial, Panels 140 to 141.

LAWLEY Private E 40016. Killed in action 19 April 1918. Tyne Cot Memorial, Panels 140 to 141.

LAWRENCE Private W H 42155. Killed in action 22 July 1918. Ploegsteert Memorial, Panel 9.

LEARY Lance Corporal F 16119. Killed in action 1 July 1916. Thiepval Memorial, Pier and Face 15A.

LEARY Private J 18253. Died of wounds 4 December 1916. Bailleul Communal Cemetery Extension. III. A. 181.

LEE Private M 41642. Killed in action 29 March 1918. Pozieres Memorial, Panels 76 and 77.

LEINSTER Private W G 41266. Killed in action 19 April 1918. Tyne Cot Memorial, Panels 140 to 141.

LENNON Private A 18362. Killed in action 16 August 1917. Tyne Cot Memorial, Panels 140 to 141.

LENNON Private A 14424. Killed in action 1 July 1916. Thiepval Memorial, Pier and Face 15A

LESLIE Private W 24954. Killed in action 16 August 1917. Tyne Cot Memorial, Panels 140 to 141.

LIMBERT Private W 40046. Accidentally killed 23 May 1917. Pond Farm Cemetery. N. 11.

LINDSAY Private W 41084. Killed in action 19 April 1918. Tyne Cot Memorial, Panels 140 to 141.

LINNELL Private F W 43210. Killed in action 16 August 1917. New Irish Farm Cemetery. XVI. D. 20.

LIVINGSTONE Private D 24692. Killed in action 9 April 1918. Tyne Cot Memorial, Panels 140 to 141.

LLOYD Private T 14404. Killed in action 1 July 1916. Thiepval Memorial, Pier and Face 15A.

LONEY Private A 20027. Killed in action 1 July 1916. Thiepval Memorial, Pier and Face 15A.

LONG Private J 19888. Killed in action 1 July 1916. Hamel Military Cemetery. I. B. 7.

LONGHEED Private J 17409. See Private J Lougheed below.

LOUGHEED Private J 17409. Killed in action 1 July 1916. Incorrectly commemorated as Longheed on Thiepval Memorial, Pier and Face 15A.

LUNN Private W 14405. Killed in action 1 July 1916. Hamel Military Cemetery. I. B. 7.

LYNCH Private M 20592. Killed in action 29 March 1918. Pozieres Memorial, Panels 76 and 77.

LYNCH Private R 18713. Died of wounds 2 July 1916. St Marie Cemetery, Le Havre. Division 19. H. 2.

LYNESS Second Lieutenant H. Died of wounds 2 September 1916. Bailleul Communal Cemetery Extension. II. F. 66.

LYNESS Private J 14421. Killed in action 1 July 1916. Serre Road Cemetery Number 1. VII. A. 4.

LYONS Private T 41325. Killed in action 29 March 1918. Pozieres Memorial, Panels 76 and 77.

LYTTLE Private J 19948. Killed in action 1 July 1916. Ancre British Cemetery. VIII. A. 88.

LYTTLE Lance Corporal J S 14398. Killed in action 1 July 1916. Thiepval Memorial, Pier and Face 15A.

MACK Private R J 42493. Killed in action 25 October 1918. Ingoyghem Military Cemetery. B. 6.

MAGEE Private J 14460. Killed in action 1 July 1916. Thiepval Memorial, Pier and Face 15A.

MAGEE Private J 14459. Killed in action 16 August 1917. Tyne Cot Memorial, Panels 140 to 141.

MAGEE Sergeant R 14466. Killed in action 1 July 1916. Ancre British Cemetery. VIII. A. 36.

MAGILL Private J 41435. Killed by aircraft bombs while a prisoner of war 6 June 1918. Ham British Cemetery. II. E. 27.

MAGOWAN MM Lance Corporal A 18058. Killed in action 16 August 1917. Tyne Cot Cemetery. VIII. D. 13.

MAGOWAN Private J 22142. Died of wounds 2 July 1916. Forceville Communal Cemetery and Extension. II. B. 11.

MAKINSON MM Lance Sergeant H 18869. Died of wounds 11 April 1918. Locre Hospice Cemetery. II. C. 21.

MALAM Lance Corporal W 17095. Killed in action 16 August 1917. Tyne Cot Memorial, Panels 140 to 141.

MALCOLMSON Private S 14454. Killed in action 23 November 1917. Cambrai Memorial, Panel 10.

MALONE Second Lieutenant B M. Killed in action 16 August 1917. Tyne Cot Memorial, Panels 140 to 141.

MALONE Private J J 16122. Died of wounds 20 July 1916. St Sever Cemetery. A. 33. 13.

MALONE Lance Corporal T 14437. Killed in action 1 July 1916. Thiepval Memorial, Pier and Face 15A.

MALONEY Private T 22734. Died of wounds 28 March 1918. St Sever Cemetery Extension. VII. H. 25.

MARK Private G 41562. Killed in action 4 September 1918. Ploegsteert Memorial, Panel 9.

MARSHALL MM Private J W 18252. Killed in action 25 July 1918. Bertenacre Military Cemetery. I. B. 6.

MARTIN Private J 12951. Died of wounds 27 December 1918. Les Baraques Military Cemetery. VII. D. 5.

MARTIN Second Lieutenant L H. Killed in action 23 November 1917. Moeuvres Communal Cemetery Extension. III. A. 9.

MARTIN Private L W 45062. Died of wounds 1 November 1918. Kezelberg Military Cemetery. I. C. 21.

MATHER Private J 15542. Killed in action 29 March 1918. Pozieres Memorial, Panels 76 and 77.

MATTHEWS Sergeant R E 43342. Died of wounds 1 November 1918. Kezelberg Military Cemetery. I. C. 20.

MATTOCK Private W A 42194. Killed in action 11 October 1918. Tyne Cot Memorial, Panels 140 to 141.

MAXWELL Private A 14434. Died 3 July 1918. Friends Burial Ground, Lurgan. Commemorated by the Commonwealth War Graves Commission in the United Kingdom Book of Remembrance.

McALEER Private A 42433. Killed in action 1 October 1918. Tyne Cot Memorial, Panels 140 to 141.

McALLISTER Private J 27558. Killed in action 25 October 1918. Tyne Cot Memorial, Panels 140 to 141.

McAULEY Private J 42466. Killed in action 25 October 1918. Harlebeke New British Cemetery. IV. C. 4.

McARTHUR Private J 20324. Killed in action 16 August 1917. Tyne Cot Memorial, Panels 140 to 141.

McAULEY Lance Corporal W J 41556. Died of wounds 11 April 1918. Lijssenthoek Military Cemetery. XXVI. H. 11.

McBRIDE Private G 22029. Killed in action 29 March 1918. Pozieres Memorial, Panels 74 and 75.

McCABE Private A 14573. Killed in action 1 July 1916. Thiepval Memorial, Pier and Face 15A.

McCAFFERY Private J 22851. Killed in action 29 March 1918. Pozieres Memorial, Panels 76 and 77.

McCAFFERY Private V 3556. Killed in action 24 March 1918. Pozieres Memorial, Panels 76 and 77.

McCALLUM Private W 17951. Killed in action 1 July 1916. Ancre British Cemetery. VIII. A. 9.

McCAMBLEY Corporal J 14492. Killed in action 1 July 1916. Ancre British Cemetery. VIII. A. 3.

McCAMMOND Corporal A 14539. Killed in action 16 August 1917. Tyne Cot Memorial, Panels 140 to 141.

McCANN Private A 22780. Killed in action 16 August 1917. Tyne Cot Memorial, Panels 140 to 141.

McCANN Private R 14507. Killed in action 1 July 1916. Serre Road Cemetery Number 1. IX. C. 5.

McCAPPIN Sergeant J 14576. Killed in action 26 June 1916. Hamel Military Cemetery. I. D. 7.

McCLEAN Private J H 29536. Died of wounds 13 September 1918. Arneke British Cemetery. VII. A. 13.

McCLEARY Private J 14548. Died of wounds 10 May 1918. Donaghcloney (Holy Trinity) Church of Ireland Churchyard. Grave 156.

McCONNELL Private R 41445. Killed in action 19 April 1918. Tyne Cot Memorial, Panels 140 to 141.

McCONVILLE Private J 14570. Killed in action 1 July 1916. Thiepval Memorial, Pier and Face 15A.

McCORMICK Private T H 23364. Killed in action 16 August 1917. Tyne Cot Memorial, Panels 140 to 141.

McCORMICK Private W 41607. Died of wounds 3 November 1918. Kezelberg Military Cemetery. II. A. 14.

McCULLOUGH Corporal J 14502. Killed in action 1 July 1916. Thiepval Memorial, Pier and Face 15A.

McCULLOUGH Private W J 23299. Died of wounds 21 November 1916. St Marie Cemetery, Le Havre. Division 3. P. 6.

McDADE Private J 23284. Died of wounds 20 July 1916. Portsdown (Christ Church) Military Cemetery. C. 63.

McDONALD Private A 14506. Killed in action 1 July 1916. Thiepval Memorial, Pier and Face 15A.

McDOWELL Private J 14527. Died of wounds 25 September 1917. Neuville-Bourjonval British Cemetery. E. 27.

McEVOY Lance Sergeant J J 20673. Killed in action 16 August 1917. Tyne Cot Memorial, Panels 140 to 141.

McFALLS Private P 24852. See Privatc B Vance below.

McFARLAND MC Second Lieutenant F J E. Killed in action 22 July 1918. Tyne Cot Memorial, Panels 140 to 141.

McFARLAND Private G 14574. Killed in action 1 July 1916. Thiepval Memorial, Pier and Face 15A.

McGAFFIN Private W J 24734. Killed in action 16 August 1917. Tyne Cot Cemetery, Zonnebeke VI. H. 24.

McGAHEY Private S 14521. Killed in action 1 July 1916. Addenda Panel, Thiepval Memorial.

McGAHEY Private W 41609. Killed in action 19 April 1918. Tyne Cot Memorial, Panels 140 to 141.

McGAUGHEY Private J 24606. Killed in action 25 October 1918. Harlebeke New British Cemetery. VI. B. 7.

McGEOWN Private R 14551. Killed in action 16 August 1917. Tyne Cot Cemetery. V. H. 21.

McGIFFIN Private S 3501. Killed in action 16 August 1917. Tyne Cot Memorial, Panels 140 to 141.

McGILL Private B 20348. Killed in action 1 July 1916. Ancre British Cemetery. VIII. A. 42.

McGINTY Private G 23062. Killed in action 1 July 1916. Thiepval Memorial, Pier and Face 15A.

McGIVERN Private R W 23947. Died of wounds 12 October 1916. Bailleul Communal Cemetery Extension. II. F. 253.

McGIVERN Private W 18457. Killed in action 1 July 1916. Thiepval Memorial, Pier and Face 15A.

McGRANE Private W 10752. Killed in action 19 April 1918. Tyne Cot Memorial, Panels 140 to 141.

McGRANN MM Private D 7963. Killed in action 16 August 1917. Tyne Cot Memorial, Panels 140 to 141.

McHUGH Private P 20993. Died of wounds as a prisoner of war 21 October 1918. His date of death has also been recorded as 18 January 1919; this is likely to be the date on which his death was notified. Anor Communal Cemetery; South end, near entrance.

McILROY Private W 22984. Killed in action 4 June 1917. Pond Farm Cemetery. P. 10.

McILROY Lance Corporal W J 20357. Killed in action 16 August 1917. New Irish Farm Cemetery. XVI. E. 18.

McINTYRE Private R 21639. Killed in action 1 July 1916. Ancre British Cemetery. VIII. A. 58.

McKEOWN Private T J 23917. Killed in action 31 May 1916. Mesnil Ridge Cemetery. I. 12.

McKERR Private F 14542. Killed in action 1 July 1916. Thiepval Memorial, Pier and Face 15A.

McKINLEY Private A 23318. Died of wounds 9 September 1917. Mendinghem Military Cemetery. VII. F. 32.

McKNIGHT Private J S 14546. Killed in action 1 July 1916. Thiepval Memorial, Pier and Face 15A.

McLEAN Private S 18652. Killed in action 1 July 1916. Thiepval Memorial, Pier and Face 15A.

McMANUS Private J 14504. Died of wounds 28 April 1918. St Sever Cemetery Extension. XI. H. 12A.

McMANUS Lance Corporal R E 41505. Killed in action 19 April 1918. Tyne Cot Memorial, Panels 140 to 141.

McMULLAN Private A 14569. Killed in action 16 August 1917. Tyne Cot Memorial, Panels 140 to 141.

McMULLAN Private W 42464. Died of wounds 5 October 1918. Re-interred in Dadizeele New British Cemetery in 1920. II. D. 29.

McMULLAN Private W J 14545. Killed in action 1 July 1916. Ancre British Cemetery. VII. C. 48.

McMURRAY Private W H 18274. Killed in action 1 July 1916. Thiepval Memorial, Pier and Face 15A.

McNALLY Private F 14515. Killed in action 1 July 1916. Thiepval Memorial, Pier and Face 15A.

McNALLY Private J 21654. Killed in action 1 July 1916. Thiepval Memorial, Pier and Face 15A.

McNALLY Private W J 21521. Killed in action 1 July 1916. Thiepval Memorial, Pier and Face 15A.

McNAYE Private J 27798. Killed in action 4 September 1918. Originally buried at Bristol Castle Cemetery. Commemorated on Bristol Castle Cemetery Memorial, Messines Ridge British Cemetery.

McSTAY Private J 24699. Killed in action 16 August 1917. Tyne Cot Memorial, Panels 140 to 141.

McTEAGUE Private J 24329. Killed in action 16 August 1917. Tyne Cot Memorial, Panels 140 to 141.

McVEIGH Private M 41456. Killed in action 25 October 1918. Harlebeke New British Cemetery. VI. B. 12.

McWHIRTER Private S 14543. Died of wounds 1 July 1916. Hamel Military Cemetery. I. B. 7.

McWILLIAMS Private C 41085. Killed in action 23 November 1917. Cambrai Memorial, Panel 10.

McWILLIAMS Private R J 19764. Killed in action 1 July 1916. Thiepval Memorial, Pier and Face 15A.

MEDLAND Warrant Officer Class II, Company Sergeant Major W H 9259. Killed in action 16 August 1917. Tyne Cot Cemetery. IV. H. 16.

MEEKE Private S 42492. Died of wounds 6 October 1918. Haringhe (Bandaghem) Military Cemetery. III. A. 27.

MELLOR Lance Corporal E 43278. Killed in action 11 October 1918. Re-interred in Dadizeele New British Cemetery in 1920. II. C. 6.

MELLOR Lance Corporal S H 27820. Killed in action 30 September 1918. Duhallow ADS Cemetery. VIII. D. 30.

MELVIN Private J T 40019. Killed in action 16 August 1917. Tyne Cot Memorial, Panels 140 to 141.

MILES Sergeant E C 43440. Killed in action 19 April 1918. Tyne Cot Memorial, Panels 140 to 141.

MILES MC Second Lieutenant R D. Died of wounds 17 August 1917. Brandhoek New Military Cemetery Number 3. II. F. 18.

MILLER Second Lieutenant D J. Killed in action 12 April 1918. Tyne Cot Memorial, Panels 140 to 141.

MILLER Private W 29555. Killed in action 4 September 1918. Ploegsteert Memorial, Panel 9.

MILLIGAN Private F W 42218. Killed in action 30 September 1918. Tyne Cot Memorial, Panels 140 to 141.

MILLNS Lance Corporal J 43267. Killed in action 16 August 1917. Tyne Cot Memorial, Panels 140 to 141.

MILLS Private R 41087. Died 26 October 1919. Fivemiletown Church of Ireland Churchyard. South-East part.

MITCHEL Lieutenant (Acting Captain) F D. Died of wounds 24 November 1917. Grevillers British Cemetery. VIII. E. 4.

MITCHELL Corporal J S 16127. Killed in action 29 March 1918. Pozieres Memorial, Panels 76 and 77.

MOFFAT Private J 20307. Killed in action 1 July 1916. Thiepval Memorial, Pier and Face 15A.

MOLLOY Private H 17929. Died of wounds 25 June 1916. Hamel Military Cemetery. I. E. 13.

MONAGHAN Private W 23300. Killed in action 16 August 1917. Tyne Cot Memorial, Panels 140 to 141.

MONTGOMERY Second Lieutenant R T. Killed in action 1 July 1916. Thiepval Memorial, France. Pier and Face 15A.

MOON Private J 41412. Killed in action 29 March 1918. Pozieres Memorial, Panels 76 and 77.

MOORE Sergeant A D 14438. Killed in action 1 July 1916. Thiepval Memorial, Pier and Face 15A.

MOORE Private J 18256. Killed in action 1 July 1916. Ancre British Cemetery. II. D. 13.

MOORE Second Lieutenant W. Killed in action 16 August 1917. Tyne Cot Memorial, Panels 140 to 141.

MOOREHEAD Lance Corporal A 16121. Killed in action 1 July 1916. Thiepval Memorial, Pier and Face 15A.

MORAN Second Lieutenant S F. Died of wounds 30 September 1918. Haringhe (Bandaghem) Military Cemetery. III. B. 12.

MORGAN MC Lieutenant H S United States Army Medical Corps. Killed in action 12 April 1918. Flanders Field American Cemetery Memorial Chapel.

MORRISH Private F G 43253. Killed in action 16 August 1917. Tyne Cot Memorial, Panels 140 to 141.

MORRISON Private F J 41112. Killed in action 25 May 1918. Gwalia Cemetery. II. C. 29.

MORRISON Private G 41610. Died of wounds as a prisoner of war 22 April 1918. Hautmont Communal Cemetery. I. A. 20.

MORRISON Private N R 20350. Killed in action 1 July 1916. Ancre British Cemetery. VIII. A. 29.

MORRISON Private W 22849. Killed in action 16 August 1917. Tyne Cot Memorial, Panels 140 to 141.

MORROW Private G 23606. Killed in action 16 August 1917. Tyne Cot Memorial, Panels 140 to 141.

MORROW Corporal W 14457. Killed in action 1 July 1916. Thiepval Memorial, Pier and Face 15A.

MORTIMER Private H 24909. Killed in action 16 August 1917. Tyne Cot Memorial, Panels 140 to 141.

MORTON Private E 17407. Killed in action 1 July 1916. Thiepval Memorial, Pier and Face 15A.

MORTON Private E 28773. Died of wounds 18 April 1918. Haringhe (Bandaghem) Military Cemetery. II. F. 19.

MORTON Private H 42151. Killed in action 4 September 1918. Mont Noir Military Cemetery. I. E. 14.

MORTON Sergeant R 18064. Killed in action 4 September 1918. Ploegsteert Memorial, Panel 9.

MORTON Private W 14468. Died 24 December 1915. Armagh (St Mark) Church of Ireland Churchyard. 2. 62.

MORTON Private W 22619. Died as a prisoner of war 17 October 1918. Buried in Dietkirchen Prisoner of War Cemetery. His grave was not identified and remained there when Commonwealth graves were concentrated into Niederzwehren Cemetery in 1923. Commemorated on Dietkirchen Prisoner of War Cemetery Memorial 1.

MOSES Private H 40065. Killed in action 16 August 1917. Tyne Cot Cemetery. V. B. 15.

MOWBRAY Private T 20301. Killed in action 4 September 1918. Ploegsteert Memorial, Panel 9.

MURDOCK MM Private A M W 24053. Killed in action 16 August 1917. Tyne Cot Memorial, Panels 140 to 141.

MURPHY Private F 11737. Killed in action 30 September 1918. Tyne Cot Memorial, Panels 140 to 141.

MURPHY Private J 14444. Died of wounds 18 May 1917. Bailleul Communal Cemetery Extension. III. B. 152.

MURRAY Private W McC 22891. Killed in action 30 September 1918. Hooge Crater Cemetery. VI. J. 1.

NELSON Private G 19824. Killed in action 1 July 1916. Bouzincourt Ridge Cemetery, Albert. E. 2.

NESBITT Private R 14585. Killed in action 1 July 1916. Thiepval Memorial, Pier and Face 15A.

NEVILLE Lance Corporal J 14591. Killed in action 1 July 1916. A.I.F. Burial Ground. XV. A. 10.

NEVILLE Private T 14584. Killed in action 1 July 1916. Thiepval Memorial, Pier and Face 15A.

NICHOLL Private J 41611. Died as a prisoner of war 22 July 1918. Hautmont Communal Cemetery. V. B. 10.

NICHOLSON Private H 40069. Died of wounds 21 June 1918. Esquelbecq Military Cemetery. III. B. 30.

NICHOLSON Private T 16425. Died of wounds 13 February 1916. Forceville Communal Cemetery and Extension. I. D. 11.

NORTH Private W 20842. Killed in action 16 August 1917. Tyne Cot Memorial, Panels 140 to 141.

NOWELL Private W 45746. Killed in action 19 April 1918. Tyne Cot Memorial, Panels 140 to 141.

O'BRIEN Private D 11108. Killed in action 14 August 1917. Tyne Cot Memorial, Panels 140 to 141.

O'CALLAGHAN Private B 13231. Killed in action 16 August 1917. Tyne Cot Memorial, Panels 140 to 141.

O'DONNELL Private M 29667. Killed in action 2 October 1918. Tyne Cot Memorial, Panels 140 to 141.

OGDEN Private R 15518. Killed in action 21 March 1918. Noyon New British Cemetery. II. B. 6.

OGLE Private M 14594. Killed in action 26 June 1916. Hamel Military Cemetery. I. D. 16.

OGLESBY Private A 42448. Killed in action 30 September 1918. Re-interred in Dadizeele New British Cemetery in 1920. IV. F. 18.

O'REILLY Private A E 27874. Died of wounds 29 March 1918. St Sever Cemetery Extension. VII. L. 1A.

ORR Private H 41091. Killed in action 23 November 1917. Cambrai Memorial, Panel 10.

OSTICK Private G 43268. Killed in action 16 August 1917. Buried originally in a battlefield grave near St Julien. Reinterred in 1921 in New Irish Farm Cemetery. XVI. C. 11.

PAINE Private S A 45775. Died of wounds 6 September 1918. Longuenesse (St Omer) Souvenir Cemetery. V. E. 16.

PARK Private R 41353. Killed in action 19 April 1918. Tyne Cot Memorial, Panels 140 to 141.

PARKER Private H 40022. Died of wounds 25 May 1917. The burial return (Army Form W3314) shows a burial date of 24 May 1917. Pond Farm Cemetery. N. 7.

PARKS Private J 14599. Killed in action 1 July 1916. Ancre British Cemetery. VIII. A. 90/93.

PARTRIDGE Private J E 45788. Died as a prisoner of war 27 October 1918. Buried in Heilsberg Prisoner of War Cemetery. Commemorated on Malbork Memorial, Poland.

PARTRIDGE MC Captain J H. Killed in action 24 March 1918. Pozieres Memorial, Panels 76 and 77.

PATTERSON Private R G 14596. Killed in action 16 August 1917. Tyne Cot Memorial, Panels 140 to 141.

PATTERSON Private W 18610. Killed in action 1 July 1916. Thiepval Memorial, Pier and Face 15A.

PATTISON Private J 6313. Killed in action 16 August 1917. Tyne Cot Memorial, Panels 140 to 141.

PATTON Private G 14618. Killed in action 1 July 1916. Thiepval Memorial, Pier and Face 15A.

PEACOCK Second Lieutenant W. Killed in action 22 December 1916. Ration Farm (La Plus Douve) Cemetery. III. D. 1.

PENNELL Private G 42531. Killed in action 25 October 1918. Tyne Cot Memorial, Panels 140 to 141.

PENTLAND Private W H 17842. Killed in action 1 July 1916. Ancre British Cemetery. VIII. A. 7.

PEPPER Private A 41427. Killed in action 12 August 1918. Ploegsteert Memorial, Panel 9.

PETTY Private W J 41406. Killed in action 22 November 1917. Cambrai Memorial, Panel 10.

PHILLIPS Private E G 43364. Died of wounds 25 April 1918. Etaples Military Cemetery. XXXII. C. 9.

PHILLIPS Private J 18246. Killed in action 1 July 1916. Thiepval Memorial, Pier and Face 15A.

PILKINGTON Private W 45817. Killed in action 19 April 1918. Tyne Cot Memorial, Panels 140 to 141.

PINKERTON Private S 41133. Killed in action 4 September 1918. Ploegsteert Memorial, Panel 9.

POLLOCK Private J 42467. Died of wounds 7 December 1918. Tourcoing (Pont-Neuville) Communal Cemetery. H. 6.

POOLMAN Private P C 42263. Killed in action 3 October 1918. Re-interred in Dadizeele New British Cemetery in 1920. IV. F. 23.

POYNTZ Private W 18675. Killed in action 1 July 1916. Thiepval Memorial, Pier and Face 15A.

PRENTER Second Lieutenant D. Killed in action 21 March 1918. Pozieres Memorial, Panels 76 and 77.

PRICE Private S 41167. Killed in action 23 November 1917. Cambrai Memorial, Panel 10.

PROCTOR Private W 23071. Killed in action 16 August 1917. Tyne Cot Cemetery. XXV. F. 4.

PUSHMAN Private A 43324. Killed in action 16 August 1917. Tyne Cot Memorial, Panels 140 to 141.

QUINN Private J 14625. Killed in action 16 August 1917. Tyne Cot Cemetery. VI. D. 12.

QUINN Private J T 14622. Killed in action 27 June 1916. Hamel Military Cemetery. I. C. 10.

RANDERSON Private T H 40026. Died of wounds 12 June 1917. Menin Gate Memorial, Panel 42.

RATCLIFFE Second Lieutenant C S. Killed in action 22 July 1918. Ploegsteert Memorial, Panel 9.

RAYNOR Private J J 43273. Killed in action 19 April 1918. Tyne Cot Memorial, Panels 140 to 141.

REANEY Private R 18070. Killed in action 12 October 1916. Ration Farm (La Plus Douve) Cemetery. III. C. 7.

REECE Private H 42261. Died of wounds 4 September 1918. Ploegsteert Memorial, Panel 9.

REID Sergeant G C 41529. Killed in action 26 October 1917. Neuville-Bourjonval British Cemetery. E. 18.

REID Corporal N H 14657. Died of wounds 17 August 1917. Brandhoek New Military Cemetery Number 3. II. F. 28.

RICHARDS Private W 40139. Killed in action 16 August 1917. Tyne Cot Memorial, Panels 140 to 141.

RICHARDSON Lance Corporal G 14664. Killed in action 1 July 1916. Thiepval Memorial, Pier and Face 15A.

RIDDELL Private J E 41403. Killed in action 3 August 1918. Bertenacre Military Cemetery. I. C. 7.

RINGROSE Private A 40024. Killed in action 29 March 1918. Pozieres Memorial, Panels 76 and 77.

ROBB Private H 22804. Died of wounds 20 April 1918. Mendinghem Military Cemetery. X. B. 23.

ROBB Corporal W 14626. Killed in action 1 July 1916. Hamel Military Cemetery. I. B. 7.

ROBERTS Private H J 45769. Killed in action 4 September 1918. Mont Noir Military Cemetery. I. F. 2.

ROBERTS Private R 17449. Killed in action 16 August 1917. Tyne Cot Cemetery. VI. D. 15.

ROBERTS Corporal T J 43428. Killed in action 29 March 1918. Pozieres Memorial, Panels 76 and 77.

ROBINSON MM Corporal G 17944. Died of wounds 12 September 1916. Bailleul Communal Cemetery Extension. II. F. 214.

ROBINSON Private S 18243. Killed in action 1 July 1916. Hamel Military Cemetery. I. A. 11.

ROCHE Second Lieutenant W H. Killed in action 27 March 1918. Found by German infantry and buried at Hattencourt. Reinterred in Roye New British Cemetery. IV. D. 19.

RODDY Sergeant D 29590. Killed in action 4 September 1918. Originally buried at Bristol Castle Cemetery. Reinterred at Messines Ridge British Cemetery in 1920. II. B. 13.

RODGERS Private W K 43280. Died of wounds as a prisoner of war 14 April 1918. Avesnes-sur-Helpe Communal Cemetery. D. 2.

ROONEY Private T 18332. Killed in action 4 September 1918. Ploegsteert Memorial, Panel 9.

ROSE Lance Corporal E C 43380. Died of wounds 10 September 1917. Wimereux Communal Cemetery. VI. A. 23.

ROSENBERG Private B 40025. Killed in action 16 August 1917. Ypres Reservoir Cemetery. XI. B. 4.

ROUNTREE Private W 23880. Killed in action 9 June 1917. Menin Gate Memorial, Panel 42.

ROWAN Private A 14655. Killed in action 1 July 1916. Ancre British Cemetery. VIII. A. 8.

RUSK Private J 17553. Killed in action 1 July 1916. Thiepval Memorial, Pier and Face 15A.

RUSSELL Lance Corporal T J 14630. Killed in action 1 July 1916. Thiepval Memorial, Pier and Face 15A.

RUSSELL Private W 14659. Died of wounds 3 July 1916. Forceville Communal Cemetery and Extension. II. B. 13.

RUSSELL Private W W 22447. Killed in action 24 August 1918. Bailleul Communal Cemetery Extension. III. G. 14.

SALLIS Private S H 19103. Killed in action 16 August 1917. Tyne Cot Memorial, Panels 140 to 141.

SCANLON Lance Corporal F 41482. Killed in action 23 November 1917. Cambrai Memorial, Panel 10.

SCARCE Lance Corporal W F 43308. Killed in action 16 August 1917. Tyne Cot Memorial, Panels 140 to 141.

SCHWENK Private P 45756. Killed in action 24 August 1918. Ploegsteert Memorial, Panel 9.

SCOTT Lance Corporal J 16134. Killed in action 4 June 1917. Pond Farm Cemetery. P. 9.

SCOTT MM Sergeant T 22556. Killed in action 4 September 1918. Ploegsteert Memorial, Panel 9.

SEELEY Private J 5978. Died of wounds 19 April 1918. Tyne Cot Memorial, Panels 140 to 141.

SEGGIE Second Lieutenant A. Killed in action 1 July 1916. Ancre British Cemetery. VIII. A. 86.

SELBY Private J 15855. Killed in action 1 July 1916. Thiepval Memorial, Pier and Face 15A.

SEMPLE Private J 17935. Killed in action 1 July 1916. Thiepval Memorial, Pier and Face 15A.

SEYMOUR Corporal J R 43262. Killed in action 3 August 1918. Bertenacre Military Cemetery. I. C. 6.

SEYMOUR Second Lieutenant W M. Killed in action 16 August 1917. Tyne Cot Memorial, Panels 140 to 141.

SHANNON Private G M 41428. Killed in action 25 October 1918. Harlebeke New British Cemetery. VI. B. 13.

SHARPE Private J W 5851. Killed in action 4 September 1918. Ploegsteert Memorial, Panel 9.

SHEEHAN Private D 16199. Killed in action 16 August 1917. New Irish Farm Cemetery. IV. C. 6.

SHERMAN Corporal R 14673. Died of wounds 1 April 1918. St Sever Cemetery Extension. VII. E. 9A.

SHERIDAN Private P 41581. Died of wounds 9 December 1918. Drumcor Catholic Churchyard.

SHERRIFF Private E P 17914. Killed in action 1 July 1916. Thiepval Memorial, Pier and Face 15A.

SHIELS Private R J 16133. Killed in action 1 July 1916. Thiepval Memorial, Pier and Face 15A.

SHIELS Private S 41622. Died 10 October 1918. Ballybay First Presbyterian Churchyard.

SHILLINGTON Lieutenant (Acting Captain) T G. Died of wounds 18 August 1917. Brandhoek New Military Cemetery Number 3. II. E. 31.

SHORTT Private S 23589. Killed in action 16 August 1917. Tyne Cot Memorial, Panels 140 to 141.

SIMPSON Private A 43204. Died of wounds as a prisoner of war 28 April 1918. Hautmont Communal Cemetery. I. A. 11.

SIMPSON Private W J 18053. Killed in action 1 July 1916. Thiepval Memorial, Pier and Face 15A.

SITTLINGTON Private T 41627. Killed in action 21 March 1918. Pozieres Memorial, Panels 76 and 77.

SKEE Private C 40082. Killed in action 19 April 1918. Tyne Cot Memorial, Panels 140 to 141.

SKELTON Private F T 16146. Died of wounds 8 June 1916. Clones (St Tighernach) Church of Ireland Cemetery.

SLADE Private W 20740. Killed in action 16 August 1917. Tyne Cot Memorial, Panels 140 to 141.

SLATOR Sergeant R 18345. Killed in action 3 October 1918. Tyne Cot Memorial, Panels 140 to 141.

SLEATOR Private J 41418. Killed in action 23 November 1917. Cambrai Memorial, Panel 10.

SLEATOR Second Lieutenant R J. Died 8 May 1917. Dranoutre Military Cemetery. II. H. 8.

SLOAN Private J 14698. Died of wounds 2 July 1916. Warloy-Baillon Communal Cemetery Extension. A. 4.

SLOANE MM Private J 22726. Killed in action 16 August 1917. Tyne Cot Memorial, Panels 140 to 141.

SMYLIE Private W J 23209. Killed in action 1 July 1916. Thiepval Memorial, Pier and Face 15A.

SMYTH Lance Corporal H 14696. Killed in action 4 September 1918. Ploegsteert Memorial, Panel 9.

SMYTH Private J 16149. Killed in action 1 July 1916. Ancre British Cemetery. I. F. 39.

SMYTH Private J 41205. Died of wounds 1 December 1917. St Sever Cemetery Extension. V. C. 6B.

SMYTH Private Robert 14684. Killed in action 1 July 1916. Thiepval Memorial, Pier and Face 15A.

SMYTH Private W H 23793. Died of wounds 18 April 1918. Mendinghem Military Cemetery. X. A. 41.

SMYTH Corporal W 42167. Killed in action 25 August 1918. Mont Noir Military Cemetery. I. A. 13.

SNOWDEN Private A 43270. Killed in action 16 August 1917. Tyne Cot Memorial, Panels 140 to 141.

SOMERVILLE Lieutenant Colonel S J The Royal Inniskilling Fusiliers. Killed in action 16 August 1917. Brandhoek New Military Cemetery Number 3. II. F. 17.

SOPER Private G 45739. Killed in action 19 April 1918. Tyne Cot Memorial, Panels 140 to 141.

SPEERS Private S 41579. Died of wounds 3 August 1918. Bertenacre Military Cemetery. I. C. 5.

SPENCE Private W 19749. Killed in action 1 July 1916. Thiepval Memorial, Pier and Face 15A.

SPROULE Private A L A 16129. Died of wounds 31 July 1916. Etaples Military Cemetery. IX. B. 10A.

STANLEY Private A J 42247. Killed in action 15 July 1918. Bertenacre Military Cemetery. II. F. 7.

STARRETT Corporal W 23656. Died of wounds 24 March 1917. Bailleul Communal Cemetery Extension. III. B. 25.

STEPHENSON Private R 43309. Killed in action 16 August 1917. Tyne Cot Memorial, Panels 140 to 141.

STERRETT Private H 14700. Killed in action 1 July 1916. Thiepval Memorial, Pier and Face 15A.

STEVENSON Private J 31417. Died of wounds 13 October 1918. Etaples Military Cemetery. XVII. J. 25.

STEVENSON Private W R 14674. Killed in action 16 August 1917. Tyne Cot Memorial, Panels 140 to 141.

STEWART Private R 14687. Killed in action 1 July 1916. Thiepval Memorial, Pier and Face 15A.

STEWART Private T 18066. Died of wounds 12 March 1916. St Marie Cemetery, Le Havre. Division 19. T. 4.

STEWART Second Lieutenant W J. Killed in action 1 July 1916. Thiepval Memorial, Pier and Face 15A.

STEWART Private W J 14692. Killed in action 1 July 1916. Thiepval Memorial, Pier and Face 15A.

STOTHERS Private J 14683. Killed in action 1 July 1916. Thiepval Memorial, Pier and Face 15A.

STOTHERS Private M 14680. Died 7 October 1916. Nieppe Communal Cemetery. III. B. 6.

STOVES Private J 20347. Killed in action 1 July 1916. Thiepval Memorial, Pier and Face 15A.

STRATTON Lance Corporal J 20351. Killed in action 25 September 1917. Neuville-Bourjonval British Cemetery. E. 23.

STRATTON Private W J 16132. Killed in action 1 July 1916. Thiepval Memorial, Pier and Face 15A.

STREATHER Private F 43501. Killed in action 11 October 1918. Re-interred in Dadizeele New British Cemetery in 1920. II. C. 18.

STRINGER Lance Corporal W 14704. Killed in action 1 July 1916. Thiepval Memorial, Pier and Face 15A.

STRONGE Private G W 41561. Died as a prisoner of war 8 July 1918. Hautmont Communal Cemetery. V. B. 5.

STRONGE Lieutenant J M. Killed in action 16 August 1917. Brandhoek New Military Cemetery Number 3. II. F. 22.

STUART Private W P 41598. Died of wounds as a prisoner of war 30 March 1918. Buried originally in Villers St Christophe Churchyard, his grave was not identified during the concentration of cemeteries into Ham British Cemetery. Commemorated on Villers St Christophe Churchyard Memorial 29.

STURGEON Private D 23207. Killed in action 16 November 1917. Neuville-Bourjonval British Cemetery. E. 15.

TANNER Private G F 43394. Killed in action 16 August 1917. Tyne Cot Memorial, Panels 140 to 141.

TATE Private F 41195. Killed in action 21 March 1918. Noyon New British Cemetery. II. B. 5.

TAYLOR Private J 20365. Died of wounds 4 July 1916. Thiepval Memorial, Pier and Face 15A.

TAYLOR Private P C 43396. Killed in action 16 August 1917. Tyne Cot Memorial, Panels 140 to 141.

TAYLOR Lance Corporal T 17661. Died of wounds 6 July 1916. Puchevillers British Cemetery. I. C. 32.

TEGGART Private M 14712. Killed in action 1 July 1916. Thiepval Memorial, Pier and Face 15A.

TERRY Private E 49840. Killed in action 4 September 1918. Kandahar Farm Cemetery. I. A. 10.

THOMPSON Private R 19729. Killed in action 1 July 1916. Thiepval Memorial, Pier and Face 15A.

THOMPSON Private W 41407. Died of wounds 6 December 1917. Rocquigny-Equancourt Road British Cemetery. VI. D. 13.

THOMPSON Private W J 14737. Killed in action 1 July 1916. Thiepval Memorial, Pier and Face 15A.

THORNBURY Private G 14731. Killed in action 1 July 1916. Ancre British Cemetery. VIII. A. 54.

THORNBURY Sergeant J 11947. Killed in action 1 July 1916. Ancre British Cemetery. VIII. A. 26.

TIERNEY Private J 23995. Killed in action 16 August 1917. Tyne Cot Memorial, Panels 140 to 141.

TIMBEY Private W F 41232. Killed in action 4 September 1918. Ploegsteert Memorial, Panel 9.

TIMM Private J 43213. Killed in action 16 August 1917. Tyne Cot Memorial, Panels 140 to 141.

TODD Private T 20315. Killed in action 1 July 1916. Thiepval Memorial, Pier and Face 15A.

TOPLEY Private J 14714. Drowned 18 August 1915. Seaford Cemetery. Grave 2663.

TOPLEY Lance Corporal T 14729. Killed in action 16 August 1917. Tyne Cot Memorial, Panels 140 to 141.

TOTTON Private R 17554. Killed in action 1 July 1916. Ancre British Cemetery. VIII. A. 4.

TOWNSEND Lieutenant R S B. Killed in action 1 July 1916. Ancre British Cemetery. VIII. A. 18.

TRAVIS Private J 43282. Died as a prisoner of war 5 July 1918. Chauny Communal Cemetery British Extension. I. B. 13.

TRINDER Second Lieutenant S L. Died of wounds 17 August 1917. Brandhoek New Military Cemetery Number 3. II. F. 21.

TROUGHTON Private T 14196. Killed in action 1 July 1916. Thiepval Memorial, Pier and Face 15A.

TUDOR Private A 43327. Killed in action 16 August 1917. Tyne Cot Memorial, Panels 140 to 141.

TURKINGTON Corporal E 14725. Killed in action 1 July 1916. Ancre British Cemetery. VIII. A. 6.

TURKINGTON Private W J 41173. Killed in action 23 November 1917. Cambrai Memorial, Panel 10.

VALLELY Private J 16428. Killed in action 1 July 1916. Thiepval Memorial, Pier and Face 15A.

VANCE Private B 24852. Served as Private P McFalls. Killed in action 16 August 1917. Tyne Cot Memorial, Panels 140 to 141.

VANCE Private J 14741. Killed in action 1 July 1916. Thiepval Memorial, Pier and Face 15A.

VANCE Private T 14744. Killed in action 1 July 1916. Thiepval Memorial, Pier and Face 15A.

VENNARD Private J 19750. Died of wounds 9 April 1916. Beauval Communal Cemetery. D. 30.

VENNARD Private J 18564. Died of wounds 14 June 1918. Milltown Church of Ireland Churchyard. Grave 225.

VESEY MC Captain G W. Died of wounds 26 March 1918. Buried initially in Ressons-sur-Matz French Military Cemetery near Roye. Reinterred in Vignemont French National Cemetery. F. 3.

WAINWRIGHT Private A 20029. Killed in action 9 June 1917. Menin Gate Memorial, Panel 42.

WALKER Private C O 40077. Killed in action 16 August 1917. Tyne Cot Memorial, Panels 140 to 141.

WALKER Private J 43200. Killed in action 16 August 1917. Tyne Cot Memorial, Panels 140 to 141.

WALLACE Lance Corporal M 16141. Killed in action 1 July 1916. Thiepval Memorial, Pier and Face 15A.

WALLACE Private W J 41096. Killed in action 23 October 1918. Harlebeke New British Cemetery. VI. B. 18.

WALSH Private J 17912. Killed in action 1 July 1916. Thiepval Memorial, Pier and Face 15A.

WARDEN Private R 19798. Killed in action 1 July 1916. Ancre British Cemetery. V. A. 29.

WARREN Private T 20500. Died of wounds as a prisoner of war 4 July 1916. Favreuil British Cemetery. I. D. 7.

WATSON Private D 14755. Died of wounds 5 July 1916. Doullens Communal Cemetery Extension Number 1. IV. C. 17.

WATSON Private F 14771. Killed in action 1 July 1916. Thiepval Memorial, Pier and Face 15A.

WATSON Private J 14770. Killed in action 1 July 1916. Hamel Military Cemetery. I. D. 6.

WATSON Private J 21403. Killed in action 1 July 1916. Hamel Military Cemetery. I. B. 7.

WATSON Private V C 22988. Died of wounds 15 January 1918. Etretat Churchyard Extension. II. A. 9.

WATSON Lance Corporal W J 14759. Killed in action 16 August 1917. Dochy Farm New British Cemetery. V. E. 22.

WATTERS Private W 14775. Killed in action 16 August 1917. Tyne Cot Cemetery. VIII. C. 11.

WEBB Private F 42108. Killed in action 24 August 1918. Mont Noir Military Cemetery. II. E. 1.

WELSH Private F J 17933. Killed in action 27 March 1918. Pozieres Memorial, Panels 76 and 77.

WETHERALL Private A 14773. Died of wounds 25 June 1916. Hamel Military Cemetery. I. E. 11.

WHITE Private B 20341. Died 22 February 1917. Bailleul Communal Cemetery Extension. III. A. 22.

WHITE Private J H 43320. Killed in action 16 August 1917. Tyne Cot Memorial, Panels 140 to 141.

WHITE Private L F 45789. Died of wounds 12 April 1918. Lijssenthoek Military Cemetery. XXVI. H. 19.

WHITESIDE Private T 18465. Killed in action 1 July 1916. Thiepval Memorial, Pier and Face 15A.

WICKES Private E 42252. Killed in action 4 September 1918. Ploegsteert Memorial, Panel 9.

WILCE Private R 40076. Killed in action 16 August 1917. Tyne Cot Memorial, Panels 140 to 141.

WILKINSON Private A 24910. Killed in action 16 August 1917. Tyne Cot Memorial, Panels 140 to 141.

WILKINSON Private J 14747. Killed in action 1 July 1916. Ancre British Cemetery. IV. D. 52.

WILKINSON Private W 40079. Killed in action 16 August 1917. Tyne Cot Memorial, Panels 140 to 141.

WILLIAMS MM Lance Sergeant H G 42157. Killed in action 3 October 1918. Tyne Cot Memorial, Panels 140 to 141.

WILLIAMSON Private W 14766. Killed in action 23 November 1917. Cambrai Memorial, Panel 10.

WILLIAMSON Corporal W G 14764. Died 17 May 1917. Mullabrack (St John) Church of Ireland Churchyard, County Armagh.

WILSON Private A 16151. Killed in action 1 July 1916. Ancre British Cemetery. VIII. A. 34.

WILSON Sergeant E 14815. Killed in action 1 July 1916. Thiepval Memorial, Pier and Face 15A.

WILSON Corporal F O 17657. Died of wounds 19 August 1917. Etaples Military Cemetery. XXII. Q. 21A.

WILSON Private G 42124. Killed in action 24 August 1918. Bailleul Communal Cemetery Extension. III. F. 107.

WILSON Private I 18371. Killed in action 1 July 1916. Thiepval Memorial, Pier and Face 15A.

WILSON Private J 14803. Died 23 May 1919. Tandragee (Meeting House) Presbyterian Churchyard, County Armagh.

WILSON Private J W C 24255. Died of wounds 20 August 1917. Wimereux Communal Cemetery. II. Q. 15A.

WILSON Private M 14758. Killed in action 1 July 1916. Thiepval Memorial, Pier and Face 15A.

WILSON Lance Corporal R 14778. Killed in action 1 July 1916. Hamel Military Cemetery. I. B. 7.

WILSON Private R 20639. Killed in action 16 August 1917. Tyne Cot Memorial, Panels 140 to 141.

WILSON Private S 16144. Killed in action 1 July 1916. Thiepval Memorial, Pier and Face 15A.

WILSON Sergeant T 41876. Died as a prisoner of war 3 October 1918. Niederzwehren Cemetery. I. E. 8. He is commemorated as The Royal Irish Rifles, incorrectly numbered as 19826; his previous regimental number being 19326.

WILSON Corporal W J 14767. Killed in action 1 July 1916. Thiepval Memorial, Pier and Face 15A.

WILSON Private W J 17070. Killed in action 1 July 1916. Mill Road Cemetery. VI. C. 3.

WITHERS Private W J 28900. Died of wounds 27 May 1918. Gwalia Cemetery. II. C. 31.

WOLFE MM Sergeant R J 18609. Killed in action 16 August 1917. Tyne Cot Memorial, Panels 140 to 141.

WOOD Second Lieutenant R N. Killed in action 22 February 1916. Hamel Military Cemetery. I. A. 23.

WOODHEAD Private F 40035. Killed in action 16 August 1917. Tyne Cot Memorial, Panels 140 to 141.

WOODS Lance Corporal D 17662. Died of wounds 1 July 1916. Forceville Communal Cemetery and Extension. II. A. 12.

WOODS Lance Corporal F J 14796. Killed in action 1 July 1916. Thiepval Memorial, Pier and Face 15A.

WOODS Private J 19809. Killed in action 1 July 1916. Thiepval Memorial, Pier and Face 15A.

WOOLF Private J 43389. Died of wounds 21 August 1917. Brandhoek New Military Cemetery Number 3. II. A. 1.

WOOLFORD Private H E 42250. Killed in action 4 September 1918. Originally buried at Bristol Castle Cemetery. Commemorated on Bristol Castle Cemetery Memorial, Messines Ridge British Cemetery.

WORTH Private H B 45800. Killed in action 26 October 1918. Harlebeke New British Cemetery. VI. B. 6.

WRIGHT Private J 24071. Killed in action 16 August 1917. Dochy Farm New British Cemetery. IX. A. 23.

WRIGHT Lance Corporal M 22990. Killed in action 3 October 1918. Re-interred in Dadizeele New British Cemetery in 1920. IV. B. 26.

WRIGHT Private N 42216. Killed in action 4 September 1918. Ploegsteert Memorial, Panel 9.

WRIGHT Private R 18059. Killed in action 1 July 1916. Thiepval Memorial, Pier and Face 15A.

WRIGHT Private S G 43361. Killed in action 29 March 1918. Pozieres Memorial, Panels 76 and 77.

WYLIE Private W S 18104. Killed in action 1 July 1916. Thiepval Memorial, Pier and Face 15A.

YOUNG Corporal S G 43439. Died of wounds 8 November 1918. Terlincthun British Cemetery. VII. D. 27.

Commemorated as Killed in Action, Died of Wounds or Died Serving Elsewhere

(Men who served at some time with the 9th Royal Irish Fusiliers.)

BERRY Corporal J 48656 The Royal Inniskilling Fusiliers (formerly 42161 Princess Victoria's (Royal Irish Fusiliers)). Killed in action 8 September 1918 while serving with the 2nd Battalion, The Royal Inniskilling Fusiliers. Ploegsteert Memorial, Panel 5.

BROWN Second Lieutenant W The Royal Munster Fusiliers (formerly 19947 Corporal W Brown). Killed in action 1 March 1918 while attached to the 2nd Battalion, The Royal Inniskilling Fusiliers in 109th Brigade. Grand-Seraucourt British Cemetery. II. B. 2.

BROWN Company Sergeant Major W J 17775 Machine Gun Corps (formerly 15859 Princess Victoria's (Royal Irish Fusiliers)). Killed in action 1 July 1916 while serving with 108th Brigade Machine Gun Company. Thiepval Memorial, Pier and Face 5C and 12C.

BURNS Private A 26109. Killed in action 27 September 1917 while serving with the 1st Battalion. Metz-en-Coutre Communal Cemetery British Extension. II. C. 15.

CAIRNS Private H 19484 Machine Gun Corps (formerly 14196 Princess Victoria's (Royal Irish Fusiliers)). Killed in action 23 March 1918 while serving with 36th Battalion, Machine Gun Corps. Villers-Faucon Communal Cemetery Extension, Somme, France. III. C. 25.

CHRISTIE Private J 17785 Machine Gun Corps (formerly 14124 Princess Victoria's (Royal Irish Fusiliers)). Killed in action 28 May 1918 while serving with 47th Battalion, Machine Gun Corps. Franvillers Communal Cemetery Extension. I. C.17.

CLOW Private J M 17781 Machine Gun Corps (formerly 14085 Princess Victoria's (Royal Irish Fusiliers)). Killed in action 29 September 1918 while serving with 18th Battalion, Machine Gun Corps. Templeux-le-Guerard British Cemetery. II. F. 21.

COURTNEY Private J 17783 Machine Gun Corps (formerly 14123 Princess Victoria's (Royal Irish Fusiliers)). Killed in action 1 July 1916 while serving with 108th Brigade Machine Gun Company. Thiepval Memorial, Pier and Face 5C and 12C.

DAVIS Second Lieutenant V A The Prince of Wales's Leinster Regiment (Royal Canadians). Killed in action 4 September 1918 while serving with the 2nd Battalion, The Prince of Wales's Leinster Regiment (Royal Canadians). Wulverghem-Lindenhoek Road Military Cemetery. V. F. 6.

DUNDAS Private W H 41399. Killed in action 1 October 1918 while serving with the 1st Battalion. Tyne Cot Memorial, Panels 140 to 141.

DUNWOODY Second Lieutenant J M The Royal Dublin Fusiliers (formerly 14181 Private J M Dunwoody). Died 4 May 1917 when the troopship "Transylvania," was sunk off Cape Vado, Italy. Savona Memorial.

ESPIE Second Lieutenant T F (formerly 14155 Corporal T F Espie). Served with the 5th/6th (Service) Battalion. Died 6 February 1919. Seagoe Cemetery.

FULTON Private R 17788 Machine Gun Corps (formerly 14269 Princess Victoria's (Royal Irish Fusiliers)). Killed in action 21 March 1918 while serving with 36th Battalion, Machine Gun Corps. Pozieres Memorial, Panels 90 to 93.

GLENVILLE Private A 43328. Died as a prisoner of war 29 May 1918 after being captured while serving with the 1st Battalion. Avesnes-sur-Helpe Communal Cemetery. D. 1.

GRAHAM Lieutenant W R. Killed in action 1 October 1918 while serving with the 1st Battalion. Buried at Mansard Farm Cemetery, Dadizeele. Reinterred in Dadizeele New British Cemetery in 1920. II. C. 10.

GRUNDY Second Lieutenant F W D. Died of wounds 26 February 1917 while serving with the 1st Battalion. St Sever Cemetery. B. 4. 8.

HAYES Corporal R 43335 The Royal Inniskilling Fusiliers (formerly 42183 Princess Victoria's (Royal Irish Fusiliers)). Died of wounds 2 October 1918 while serving with the 1st Battalion, The Royal Inniskilling Fusiliers. Tyne Cot Memorial, Panels 70 to 72.

HENRY Private W R 364647 Labour Corps (formerly 24645 Private W R Henry). Died 10 February 1919. Carnmoney Cemetery.

HEWITT Private J 14306. Killed in action 4 September 1918 while serving with the 1st Battalion. Ploegsteert Memorial, Panel 9.

HUSTWAYTE Private F 4848898 The Leicestershire Regiment (formerly 43263 Princess Victoria's (Royal Irish Fusiliers)). Died 15 September 1920 while serving in Ireland with the 1st Battalion, The Leicestershire Regiment. Nottingham Northern Cemetery. M. 23. 44.

JEANS Sergeant J C 45852 The Royal Irish Rifles (formerly 42079 Princess Victoria's (Royal Irish Fusiliers)). Killed in action 2 October 1918 while serving with 1st Battalion, The Royal Irish Rifles. Dadizeele New British Cemetery. IV. D. 39.

KENNEDY Private W 7042139 (formerly 41442 Private W Kennedy). Died 30 August 1921 while serving with the 1st Battalion in Egypt. Cairo War Memorial Cemetery. P. 134.

KIELY Second Lieutenant F P. Killed in action 24 June 1917 while serving with the 1st Battalion. Menin Gate Memorial, Panel 42.

McCREADY Private W 18093. Died 23 September 1918 while serving with the 5th/6th (Service) Battalion. Houchin British Cemetery. III. D. 19.

McILRATH Private R A 17798 Machine Gun Corps (formerly 16126 Princess Victoria's (Royal Irish Fusiliers)). Killed in action 1 July 1916 while serving with 108th Brigade Machine Gun Company. Thiepval Memorial, Pier and Face 5C and 12C.

McILROY Private A 14512. Killed in action 30 September 1918 while serving with the 1st Battalion. Re-interred in Dadizeele New British Cemetery in 1920. IV. F. 25.

MILLER Private R 27574. Killed in action 23 November 1917 while serving with the 1st Battalion. Cambrai Memorial, Panel 10.

MILLIGAN Private W 14481. Died in Burma 10 February 1918 while serving with the 1st Garrison Battalion. Buried at an unknown location and commemorated on Taukkyan Memorial.

MONTGOMERY Private J 333801 Labour Corps (formerly 20313 Princess Victoria's (Royal Irish Fusiliers)). Died 1 May 1920 while serving with the Labour Corps. Tullylish (All Saints) Church of Ireland Churchyard.

O'NEILL Lieutenant S General List. Killed in action 1 July 1916 while attached to 108th Trench Mortar Battery. Thiepval Memorial, Pier and Face 4C.

ORR Corporal D 17778 Machine Gun Corps (formerly 14592 Princess Victoria's (Royal Irish Fusiliers)). Killed in action 1 July 1916 while serving with 108th Brigade Machine Gun Company. Thiepval Memorial, Pier and Face 5C and 12C.

PASCOE Lieutenant F G B. Killed in action 2 July 1917 while serving with 53 Squadron, Royal Flying Corps. Arras Flying Services Memorial.

PRATT DSO Lieutenant Colonel A C. Killed in action 16 August 1917 while commanding the 11th (Service) Battalion, The Royal Inniskilling Fusiliers (Donegal and Fermanagh). Ypres Reservoir Cemetery. IV. E. 23.

REID Lance Corporal P H A T/453128 Royal Army Service Corps (formerly 41548 Princess Victoria's (Royal Irish Fusiliers)). Died 24 May 1921. His place of burial is unknown and he is commemorated on Brookwood (United Kingdom 1914-1918) Memorial.

ROE DCM Lance Sergeant H 41147. Died of wounds 8 April 1918 while serving with the 1st Battalion. Wimereux Communal Cemetery. X. B. 3.

SADLER Corporal J W 45847 The Royal Irish Rifles (formerly 42134 Princess Victoria's (Royal Irish Fusiliers)). Killed in action 3 September 1918 while serving with 12th (Service) Battalion, The Royal Irish Rifles (Central Antrim). Nieuwkerke (Neuve-Eglise) Churchyard. Z. 1.

SCOTT Captain S J Royal Army Medical Corps. Died of wounds in Ireland 27 May 1920. Bessbrook Church of Ireland Churchyard Extension.

SHEEKEY Lance Corporal W 17887. Died as a prisoner of war 29 September 1918 after being captured while serving with the 1st Battalion. Hautmont Communal Cemetery. IV. A. 30.

SHERIDAN Private P 23754. Killed in action 2 September 1918 while serving with the 1st Battalion. Wulverghem-Lindenhoek Road Military Cemetery. IV. G. 21.

STOKES Second Lieutenant J A. Killed in action 16 August 1917 while attached to the 12th (Service) Battalion, The Royal Irish Rifles (Central Antrim). Tyne Cot Memorial, Panels 140 to 141.

STOTHERS Private J 14706. Died 7 January 1917 while held on the strength of the 10th (Reserve) Battalion. Grangegorman Military Cemetery. CE 657.

THOMPSON Private B 41372. Died 7 December 1918 while attached to 108th Brigade Trench Mortar Battery. Eglish (Drumsallen) Church Of Ireland Churchyard.

THREADGOLD Corporal C J 42137. Killed in action 22 July 1918 while serving with the 1st Battalion. Memorial in Bertenacre Military Cemetery.

TEMPLETON Private R 16138. Died of wounds 25 October 1918 while attached to 108th Trench Mortar Battery. Duhallow ADS Cemetery. IV. I. 31.

TREASURE Corporal B H G 45855 The Royal Irish Rifles (formerly 43136 Princess Victoria's (Royal Irish Fusiliers)). Died of wounds 19 July 1918 while serving with 2nd Battalion, The Royal Irish Rifles. Esquelbecq Military Cemetery. III. E. 25.

UPRICHARD Private W H 17806 Machine Gun Corps (formerly 14738 Princess Victoria's (Royal Irish Fusiliers)). Killed in action 14 July 1916 while serving with 108th Brigade Machine Gun Company. Menin Gate Memorial, Panel 56.

WALKER Lance Corporal H P T 17807 Machine Gun Corps (formerly 14785 Princess Victoria's (Royal Irish Fusiliers)). Killed in action 26 October 1918 while serving with 36th Battalion, Machine Gun Corps. Ingoyghem Military Cemetery. C. 10.

WATT Private R 24853. Killed in action 24 March 1918 while serving with the 1st Battalion. Pozieres Memorial, Panels 76 and 77.

WILLIAMSON Lieutenant H A The Manchester Regiment (formerly 14780 Private H A Williamson). Attached to the Royal Flying Corps. Killed in action 2 July 1916 while serving with 34 Squadron. Arras Flying Services Memorial.

WOODRUFF Corporal R 45853 The Royal Irish Rifles (formerly 43138 Princess Victoria's (Royal Irish Fusiliers)). Died of wounds 21 October 1918 while serving with 1st Battalion, The Royal Irish Rifles. Harlebeke New British Cemetery. VIII. A. 2.

WOODS Private J R 17808 Machine Gun Corps (formerly 16145 Princess Victoria's (Royal Irish Fusiliers)). Killed in action 31 May 1918 while serving with 36th Battalion, Machine Gun Corps. Gwalia Cemetery. I. F. 34.

VANSTON Captain H W F M. Died 1 September 1917 while attached to 1/4th Battalion, The Essex Regiment in Egypt. Cairo War Memorial Cemetery. F. 300.

Post-War Commemorations

Other men are known to have died after 31 August 1921 due to the injuries they sustained, or were deemed by their communities to have died as a result of their war service. They are commemorated on local memorials but not by the Commonwealth War Graves Commission. Three men are known to be commemorated in this way:

BEST Private T H 13980. Portadown War Memorial.

CORKIN Lance Corporal S J 23876. Portadown War Memorial.

PENTLAND Private R J 14615. Portadown War Memorial.

One former member of the 9th Royal Irish Fusiliers died while serving with The Royal Irish Fusiliers (Princess Victoria's) after the First World War:

GRAY Warrant Officer Class II W 7040580 (formerly 14202 Warrant Officer Class II W Gray). Died 19 October 1931 while serving at the Army Training School, Chepstow.

Two former member of the Battalion died while serving during the Second World War:

RADBOURNE Lieutenant P C (formerly Captain P C Radbourne). Died on 9 April 1944 while serving with the South African Internment Corps. Durban (Stellawood) Cremation Memorial.

TURNER MC Warrant Officer Class 2 C H (formerly 17397 Warrant Officer Class 1 C H Turner MC). Died 16 April 1940 while serving with 6th (Home Defence) Battalion, The Royal Ulster Rifles. Carnmoney Cemetery. H. 135.

APPENDIX 3

Cemeteries & Memorials

The known graves of those who served at some time with the 9th Royal Irish Fusiliers and who died in the First World War lie in 121 cemeteries. These 'silent cities' are scattered close to the front line in France and Flanders, near the sites of Casualty Clearing Stations and Field Hospitals, along the lines of communication back to the Channel, in England and Ireland, and as far afield as Egypt and Germany.

Four hundred and five men have no known graves, or are known to be interred in a particular cemetery but in an unidentified grave. Some bodies were never recovered from the battlefields or were buried in graves that were lost or destroyed in subsequent fighting. Most, however, were not identified positively when battlefield burials were concentrated after the war. In addition, some remote graves were abandoned and others were destroyed in the Second World War. These men are commemorated on nineteen memorials in Belgium, Burma, France, Italy, Germany, Great Britain and Poland. The principal memorials to the missing are eloquently dedicated to those *'whom the fortune of war denied the known and honoured burial given to their comrades in death'*. In addition, the United Kingdom Book of Remembrance commemorates one casualty who was not formerly recorded by the Commonwealth War Graves Commission and whose place of burial has not yet been located or confirmed.

This appendix describes briefly the cemeteries and memorials that commemorate the men who served with the 9th Royal Irish Fusiliers. It is laid out in four parts:

- Commonwealth War Graves Commission Cemeteries
- Commonwealth War Graves Commission Memorials to the Missing
- Ulster Battlefield Memorial Tower
- Other Memorials

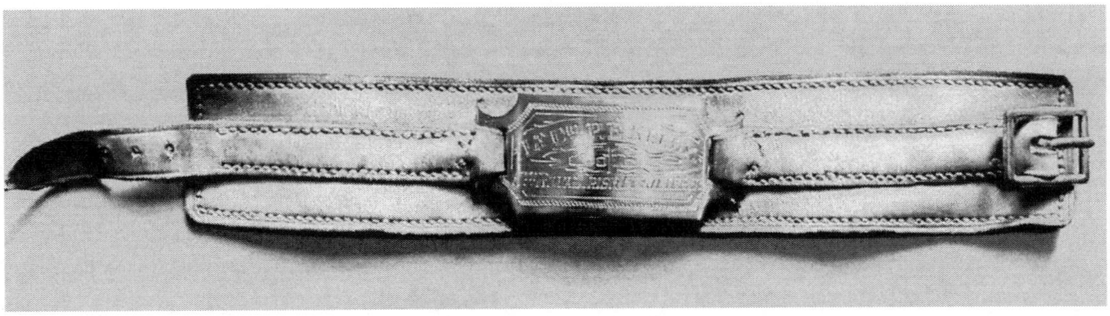

Additional forms of identification, such as this one belonging to Lieutenant Colonel P E Kelly, were commonly worn in addition to identity discs. A single aluminium disc had been worn by British soldiers since 1907. This was replaced by a single, red, vulcanised, asbestos fibre disc in late 1914. This single disc was removed from the body for administrative purposes, making subsequent post mortem identification extremely difficult. From late 1916 two discs were worn: a green octagonal disc that remained on the body and the red disc that was removed for administrative purposes.

The King visiting a cemetery at Thiepval in July 1917, a year after the near destruction of the Ulster Division. Most of the cemeteries in the Thiepval area were concentrated into larger cemeteries after the war and it is unlikely that this one still exists. © IWM Q5641

Commonwealth War Graves Commission Cemeteries

Abbeville Communal Cemetery, France. Established near the site of a number of hospitals, this cemetery contains 774 First World War graves and thirty from the Second World War. Buried here is Private T Kilpatrick who was wounded on 1 July 1916 and who died ten days later.

AIF Burial Ground, France. Begun by the Australian Imperial Force in 1916, the cemetery became a large concentration cemetery after the war and now contains 3,475 graves. Amongst them are those of Private J Burke and Lance Corporal J Neville, which were moved here in 1927 from the Ancre/Thiepval area.

Ancre British Cemetery, France. Set in the ravine that lay in no-man's-land across which the 9th Royal Irish Fusiliers attacked on 1 July 1916, this cemetery contains the graves of 2,497 Commonwealth casualties, memorials to forty-three others believed to be buried here, and memorials to sixteen men who were buried elsewhere but whose graves were destroyed. Almost all of the graves are of those killed in the three attacks here in 1916. Most of them were moved from seven nearby battlefield cemeteries after the war. Four officers and seventy-eight other ranks of the 9th Royal Irish Fusiliers are known to have been buried here and many of the graves are of multiple burials. All were killed on 1 July 1916. Of these only three officers and thirty-six other ranks were identified by name. In addition to the other forty-two graves known to belong to men of the 9th Royal Irish Fusiliers, it is likely that other men of the Battalion lie in some of the wholly unidentified graves.

Ancre British Cemetery - the ravine at Hamel in 1921.

Ancre British Cemetery today - the majority of the graves of men of the 9th Royal Irish Fusiliers lie on the right near the Cross of Sacrifice.

Anor Communal Cemetery, France. This cemetery was established by the German Army and amongst the three Commonwealth graves here is that of Private P McHugh who died while a prisoner of war on 21 October 1918.

Armagh (St Mark) Church of Ireland Churchyard, Northern Ireland. There are five Commonwealth graves here, including those of Lieutenant L M Anderson, Lance Corporal G A Anderson and Privates J Girvan and W Morton, all of whom died of wounds or illness.

Arneke British Cemetery, France. Arneke was a major railway centre surrounded by training depots and its cemetery contains many who died having been wounded in the

Ancre British Cemetery.
A visitor in November 1921 standing by the grave of Major T J Atkinson.

Ypres area. Six soldiers of the 9th Royal Irish Fusiliers are buried here: Private W Frazer who died of wounds on 16 August 1918, Private F E Browning and Sergeant W G W Irwin who were wounded during the attack north of Bailleul on 24 August 1918 and died of wounds on 25 and 26 August respectively, and Lance Corporal W Johnston and Privates J Kelly and J H McClean who were all wounded during the attack near Hill 63 on 4 September 1918 and died of wounds over the next few days.

Avesnes-sur-Helpe Communal Cemetery, France. Established by the Germans and used until November 1918, this cemetery contains the graves of Privates T Harpur and W K Rodgers who were wounded and captured in the fighting near St Quentin in March 1918 and died of wounds subsequently. Also here is the grave of Private Alfred Glenville who died while a POW, having been captured when serving with the 1st Battalion.

Bailleul Communal Cemetery Extension, France. This large cemetery on the eastern outskirts of Bailleul contains 4,003 Commonwealth graves. Here are buried three officers and eight soldiers killed in the line at Messines during the period from late 1916 to mid-1917 and four men killed in July and August 1918.

Ballybay First Presbyterian Churchyard, County Monaghan, Ireland. Buried here, in one of the two Commonwealth war graves, is Private S Shiels. He was drowned at sea off the Irish coast when RMS Leinster was torpedoed by UB123 on 10 October 1918.

Beauval Communal Cemetery, France. This beautiful small cemetery contains 248 graves, mainly of those who died of wounds in the nearby Casualty Clearing Station, including Private J Vennard who was mortally wounded by shellfire in April 1916.

Bedford House Cemetery, Belgium. Located south of Ypres, this is an unusual and beautiful cemetery partially surrounded by a moat. This concentration cemetery contains 5,139 Commonwealth graves. Buried here is Private W Campbell who was killed on 16 August 1917. His grave was moved here from a battlefield cemetery after the war.

The original headstone erected for Private J Murphy in Bailleul Communal Cemetery Extension.

Belfast City Cemetery, Northern Ireland. Private W A Jackson, who died of pulmonary tuberculosis on 7 April 1919, and Lance Corporal I Dick MM who drowned on 30 December 1919, are buried here amongst 296 Commonwealth burials from the First World War.

Berlin South-Western Cemetery, Germany. In 1922 it was decided that the graves of Commonwealth soldiers who were buried in Germany should be concentrated in four cemeteries. This is one of the chosen cemeteries. There are 1,176 Commonwealth soldiers commemorated here including Privates A Dawson and J Gilmore, the latter captured in March 1918, who both died while prisoners of war. Gilmore was originally interred in **Merseburg Prisoner of War Camp Cemetery**, Saxony.

Bertenacre Military Cemetery, France. Many of the graves in this cemetery are of men of 36th (Ulster) Division killed in the Meulenhouck area in mid-1918. Major R G Kerr MC and six soldiers were killed there in July and August 1918 and are buried on this site. Also commemorated here is Corporal C J Threadgold who was posted to the 1st Battalion and was also killed in July 1918. He is commemorated on a special memorial as a result of his grave being destroyed by shellfire in the Second World War.

Bessbrook Church of Ireland Churchyard Extension, County Armagh, Northern Ireland. The cemetery contains only one grave from the First World War, that of Captain S J Scott RAMC, who died on 27 May 1920 as a result of injuries sustained during war service.

Bleue-Maison Military Cemetery, France. This small cemetery of sixty Commonwealth graves served four Casualty Clearing Stations in the area in 1918. Buried here is Private R H Forrest who died of pneumonia in June 1918.

Boulogne Eastern Cemetery, France. Serving hospitals in the Boulogne area, this civilian cemetery contains 5,577 Commonwealth graves from the First World War. Like most of the cemeteries in the Boulogne area the gravestones are laid flat because of the sandy soil. Buried here are Sergeant W Hughes and Private W Hanna, who died of wounds on 11 July 1916 and 10 September 1917, and Private R Halligan, who succumbed to pneumonia in December 1916.

Bouzincourt Ridge Cemetery, France. This was the site of a Dressing Station on 1 July 1916 and on the route for the motor ambulances of 108th and 110th Field Ambulances from Martinsart to the Ulster Division's two Main Dressing Stations. The cemetery contains 709 Commonwealth graves, most of which were brought in from nearby cemeteries after the war. Private G Nelson, who was wounded on 1 July 1916, is known to be buried here.

Brandhoek New Military Cemetery, Belgium. Located at the site of the 32nd, 44th and 3rd Australian Casualty Clearing Stations during the Third Battle of Ypres, the cemetery contains 530 Commonwealth graves. Included are those of Lance Corporal I Hague and Private J Greer, mortally wounded by shellfire near Wieltje in the days before the attack on 16 August 1917. Interesting to note, also buried in this cemetery is Captain N G Chavasse VC and bar, MC, RAMC.

The grave of Captain T G Shillington in Brandhoek New Military Cemetery Number 3.

Brandhoek New Military Cemetery Number 3, Belgium. Begun when Brandhoek New Military Cemetery became full, this cemetery contains 975 graves. The five officers and three soldiers buried here were wounded or killed on 16 August 1917. They include Lieutenant Colonel S J Somerville whose grave shows the badge of The Royal Inniskilling Fusiliers, the Regiment into which he was commissioned. Also buried here is Private H V Barr who was killed in action with 36th Signal Company, Royal Engineers, also on 16 August 1917.

Bristol Castle Cemetery, Belgium - see **Messines Ridge British Cemetery**, Belgium.

Cairo War Memorial Cemetery, Egypt. Here is buried Captain H W F M Vanston, who died of dysentery on 1 September 1917 in Narieh Schools Military Hospital while serving with 1/4th Battalion, The Essex Regiment, and Private W Kennedy, who died of heart disease on 30 August 1921 while serving with the 1st Battalion.

Cambrai East Military Cemetery, France. Formerly a German graveyard, the British section contains the graves of Private J Ford and J D King, both formerly North Irish Horse, both from C Company and both killed on 3 November 1917 during the raid at Havrincourt. It is most likely that their remains were moved from the Havrincourt area and buried soon after the action by German troops.

Carnmoney Cemetery, County Antrim, Northern Ireland. Amongst forty-six Commonwealth burials here of the First World War lies Private W R Henry, who died on 10 February 1919.

Chauny Communal Cemetery British Extension, France. This concentration cemetery of over 1,000 graves contains many who were buried previously in German cemeteries, including Private J Travis who was captured in March 1918 and died while a prisoner of war in July 1918.

Cladymore Presbyterian Churchyard, County Armagh, Northern Ireland. Buried here is Private M Gilmore who died of wounds on 28 July 1916.

Clones (St Tighernach) Church of Ireland, County Monaghan, Ireland. Buried here is Private F T Skelton who died of wounds in June 1916.

Cologne Southern Cemetery, Germany. This is one of the four concentration cemeteries in Germany and it contains 2,482 graves or memorials to Commonwealth soldiers, most of which were gathered from 183 other cemeteries across Germany. Here is buried Private W H Brown who was captured in March 1918 and died while a prisoner of war in September 1918. Of interest, also buried here is Private D Gamble of the 1st Battalion who was shot with two others while trying to escape. He was originally buried in Crefeld New Cemetery.

Connaught Cemetery, France. Close to the start line for the Ulster Division attack on Thiepval and near the Ulster Tower, this cemetery contains 1,268 graves. All but 228 graves were collected from the cemeteries in the surrounding area after the war and they reflect the range of units that fought here in the summer and autumn of 1916. Buried here is Private T Farr who was killed on 1 July 1916.

Dadizeele New British Cemetery, Belgium. Amongst over 1,029 Commonwealth graves and commemorations, this cemetery contains those of three officers and nineteen other ranks killed in the area of Vijfwegen/Hill 41 between 30 September and 11 October 1918, and two men, Lance Corporal C E Ditton and Private E Ferguson, killed near Courtrai in mid-October 1918. All had been buried in smaller cemeteries nearby and were relocated here in 1920. Notably, the graves here include those of Lieutenant Colonel P E Kelly and Lance Corporal W Gregg DCM. The grave of Private G Lally, who was killed on 30 September 1918 and who was buried nearby, was not positively identified after the war and he is commemorated on a memorial here. Three former members of the Battalion are also buried here: Lieutenant W R Graham and Private Alfred McIlroy, both killed while serving with the 1st Battalion, and Sergeant J C Jeans who was killed serving with 1st Battalion, The Royal Irish Rifles.

The Special Memorial gravestone of Private G Lally indicating that he is buried somewhere in Dadizeele New British Cemetery. He was originally buried at a point south-east of Dadizeele. In the process of concentrating isolated graves, two unidentified soldiers of Princess Victoria's (Royal Irish Fusiliers) were found near that point and buried as unknown soldiers in Dadizeele New British Cemetery. They were believed to be Lally and Private W Wakelam of the 1st Battalion.

Dietkirchen Cemetery, Germany. See **Niederzwehren Cemetery**, Germany.

Dochy Farm New British Cemetery, Belgium. This concentration cemetery is located on the Zonnebeke/Langemarck Road, one of the 9th Royal Irish Fusiliers' objectives during the attack on 16 August 1917. It contains the graves of nearly 1,439 soldiers who died in this area during the Third Battle of Ypres. Three soldiers of the Battalion are known to be buried here alongside men of the 7th/8th (Service) Battalion: Lance Corporals C Cullen and W J Watson and Private J Wright. It is likely that others lie in some of the many unidentified graves.

Donaghcloney (Holy Trinity) Church of Ireland Churchyard, County Down, Northern Ireland. Here is buried Private J McCleary who was wounded in March 1918 and died of wounds in May 1918.

Doullens Communal Cemetery Extension Number 1, France. This cemetery contains the graves of 1,335 men, most of whom died of wounds in the nearby hospitals. Buried here are Private T Houston, who died of wounds on 10 April 1916, and Privates A Beattie and D Watson, who were wounded on 1 July 1916 and died a few days later.

Dranoutre Military Cemetery, Belgium. Located at the rear of the area held by the Ulster Division in early 1917, this cemetery contains 458 Commonwealth graves. Here are buried Second Lieutenant R J Sleator, who took his own life in May 1917, and Private C G Eyton, who was mortally wounded near Spanbroekmolen at the end of that month.

Drumcor Catholic Churchyard, County Cavan, Ireland. Here is buried Private P Sheridan who was left paraplegic after being wounded in December 1917 and died of wounds almost exactly a year later.

Drumcree Church of Ireland Churchyard, County Armagh, Northern Ireland. Amongst the six burials from the First World War, here lie two brothers, Privates M and R Hill. The former died on 10 May 1916 and the latter on 17 July 1916, having been wounded on 1 July 1916. Also buried here is the Rector of Drumcree and the 9th Royal Irish Fusiliers' first Chaplain, Reverend F J Halahan, who died in 1951.

Duhallow ADS Cemetery, Belgium. Opened to serve an Advanced Dressing Station at the beginning of the Third Battle of Ypres in July 1917, this cemetery contains 1,544 Commonwealth graves. Buried here are four soldiers killed in the final attacks in 1918: Corporal R P Collins (August), Lance Corporal S H Mellor and Private T G Dixon (September) and Private T W H Halligan (October). Private R Templeton, who was killed while serving with 108th Trench Mortar Battery in October 1918, is also buried here.

Eglish (Drumsallen) Church Of Ireland Churchyard, County Armagh, Northern Ireland. There is one Commonwealth burial here - Private B Thompson who died of pneumonia in December 1918 while on leave.

Esquelbecq Military Cemetery, France. South of Dunkirk, this cemetery was used between April and September 1918 to serve the 2nd Canadian and 3rd Australian Casualty Clearing Stations. It contains the graves of Privates J F Houston and H Nicholson who died of wounds there in June 1918, and of Corporal B H G Treasure who died of wounds on 19 July 1918 while serving with 2nd Battalion, The Royal Irish Rifles.

Essigny-Le-Grand German Cemetery, France - see **Grand-Seraucourt British Cemetery**, France.

Etaples Military Cemetery, France. The site of training camps, hospitals and depots, Etaples was on the route into and out of France for the BEF from 1914. This is the largest British cemetery in France and contains over 10,771 Commonwealth graves. Buried here are Corporal F O Wilson, and Privates E G Phillips, A L A Sproule and J Stevenson, who died of wounds in hospitals nearby.

Etretat Churchyard Extension, France. Situated on the coast near Le Havre, this cemetery served Number 1 General Hospital from December 1914 and Number 2 (Presbyterian USA) Base Hospital Unit from July 1917. Buried here is Private V C Watson, who died of wounds in the latter hospital on 15 January 1 918.

Favreuil British Cemetery, France. Originally held by the Germans, this cemetery changed hands three times and was a mix of German and British graves. The German graves were removed after the war and the cemetery was added to by the remains of British soldiers brought from three German cemeteries nearby. Reinterred here was Private T Warren, who was wounded and captured on 1 July 1916 and died a few days later.

Fivemiletown Church of Ireland Churchyard, County Tyrone, Northern Ireland. There are three burials of the First World War here, including Private R Mills who died on 26 October 1919.

Forceville Communal Cemetery and Extension, France. One of a few experimental architectural designs developed in the early years of the Imperial War Graves

Commission, this cemetery contains 304 Commonwealth graves in four plots. Here are buried four soldiers wounded near Hamel between February and June 1916 (Plot 1) and three who were wounded on 1 July 1916 (Plot 2). All died of their wounds in the nearby Main Dressing Station.

Franvillers Communal Cemetery Extension, France. This cemetery was used from April to August 1918 by units and Field Ambulances engaged in the defence of Amiens. Amongst the 248 men commemorated here lies Private J Christie, who was killed in action on 28 May 1918 while serving with 47th Battalion, Machine Gun Corps.

Gateshead Fell (St John) Churchyard, England. Buried here amongst ten Commonwealth graves of the First World War is Private J Clarkson who died on 28 September 1916.

Gloucester Old Cemetery, England. This cemetery contains 158 First World War graves, including that of Private S Devine, who died on 24 February 1918.

Grand-Seraucourt British Cemetery, France. Located near St Quentin and close to the front line that was held until March 1918, this concentration cemetery contains over 2,000 graves that were moved here from smaller cemeteries between 1920 and 1926. Most are unidentified. Buried here are three men who died in February and March 1918 – Sergeant T Goucher and Privates J Johnston and W Hilton. Also buried here is Second Lieutenant W Brown of The Royal Munster Fusiliers who had served as a Corporal before being commissioned. He was killed in action on 1 March 1918 while attached to 2nd Battalion, The Royal Inniskilling Fusiliers. Commemorated here on **Essigny-Le-Grand German Cemetery Memorial 4** is Private S W Freeman who was killed on 21 March 1918. Ninety-nine graves, mostly of men of the Ulster Division, were moved from that cemetery.

Grange Church of Ireland Churchyard, County Armagh, Northern Ireland. Here is buried Sergeant E Dawson who died on 1 January 1917.

Grangegorman Military Cemetery, Ireland. Opened in 1876 for British military personnel and their families, this cemetery contains 613 graves from the First World War including that of Private J Stothers, who died in Dublin on 17 January 1917.

Grevillers British Cemetery, France. This cemetery was the site of the 3rd, 29th and 3rd Australian Casualty Clearing Stations during the Cambrai battle. It contains 2,106 graves, including those of Captain F D Mitchel and Private G Galbraith who were wounded on 23 November 1917 during the attack on Moeuvres and who died the next day.

Gwalia Cemetery, Belgium. Located in the centre of the camps, stores and hospitals around Poperinghe, this cemetery now contains 467 Commonwealth graves, including those of Privates F J Morrison and W J Withers who were killed near Bailleul in May 1918 and Private J R Woods, who was killed in action with 36th Battalion, Machine Gun Corps the same month.

Ham British Cemetery, France. Just south of Ham, this concentration cemetery of 485 graves sits alongside Muille-Villette German cemetery. Many of the British graves are from the retreat of March 1918. Buried here is Private J Magill and on **Villers St Christophe Churchyard Memorial 29** is commemorated Private W P Stuart whose original grave has not been found. Both men were captured in March 1918.

Hamburg Cemetery, Germany. This is one of the four cemeteries in which British graves previously scattered throughout Germany are now concentrated. Amongst 708 Commonwealth graves lies Private R W Kerr who was captured in March 1918 and died of heart disease in December 1918 before he could be repatriated.

Hamel Military Cemetery, France. This cemetery was opened in July 1915 and was also known as 'Brook Street Trench' and 'White City'. It was enlarged after the war when 48 graves were concentrated there. It now contains 492 graves. Here is buried one officer, Second Lieutenant R N Wood, and three soldiers killed in Hamel in early 1916, and twenty-three soldiers killed in the few days before the attack on 1 July 1916 or on that fateful day itself. Ten of the men who died on 1 July 1916 are buried together (Plot I, Row B, Grave 7) alongside Rifleman W Brown of 16th Royal Irish Rifles (Pioneers). Private Alexander Hamilton is known to be buried in the cemetery but his grave cannot be identified positively. He is commemorated on **Special Memorial B. 2.**

Hamel Military Cemetery by Private Harry Frazer.
This sketch was made in 1916. On the left can be seen the grave of Second Lieutenant R N Wood who was killed in action on 22 February 1916. The grave on the right is probably that of Lance Corporal Samuel Beattie, 12th Royal Irish Rifles who was killed on 7 March 1916.

Haringhe (Bandaghem) Military Cemetery, Belgium. Bandaghem, Dozinghem and Mendinghem were nick-names given to the Casualty Clearing Stations in this area. This cemetery was opened to serve the Casualty Clearing Stations supporting the initial attacks at Ypres in July 1917. 36th Casualty Clearing Station was set up here from April to October 1918 and the cemetery contains the graves of four soldiers who died of wounds in April 1918. Also buried here are Second Lieutenant S F Moran, who died in Number 3 Australian Casualty Clearing Station, and four soldiers who were fatally wounded at Vijfwegen/Hill 41 in early October 1918.

Harlebeke New British Cemetery, Belgium. Located south of the River Lys, this concentration cemetery contains 1,116 Commonwealth commemorations. Buried here is Private W J Wallace, who was killed on 23 October 1918, eight men killed on 25 October 1918, and Private H B Worth who was killed on 26 October 1918 - the last soldier to be killed in action. All are in Plot VI, Row B. One of these men is twenty-six-year-old Company Sergeant Major J Hamilton who was the last of the 9th Royal Irish Fusiliers' original volunteers to be killed in action - three years and three weeks after landing in France. Also buried here is Corporal R Woodruff, who died of wounds on 21 October 1918 while serving with 1st Battalion, The Royal Irish Rifles.

Hamel Military Cemetery.

This was located on the southern side of the village held by the 9th Royal Irish Fusiliers throughout early-1916. Twenty-eight men of the Battalion are buried here. Ten of the men who died on 1 July 1916 are buried together in the central grave marked by the row of touching gravestones, alongside Rifleman W Brown of 16th Royal Irish Rifles (Pioneers). The notorious communication trench, Jacobs Ladder, followed a line up the hill to Mesnil behind the Cross of Sacrifice.

Hautmont Communal Cemetery, France. This cemetery was used by German troops for prisoners who died in local hospitals. Amongst the 246 Commonwealth graves are those of six soldiers captured in March 1918 and who died in captivity. Also buried here is Lance Corporal W Sheekey who was posted to the 1st Battalion, captured and died in captivity.

Hazebrouck Communal Cemetery, France. Located at an important railway junction, the site of a busy headquarters and a number of Casualty Clearing Stations, this cemetery contains the grave of Private W Hickey, who died of wounds on 7 February 1917.

Heilsberg Prisoner of War Cemetery, Lidzbark Warmiński, Poland - see **Malbork Memorial**.

Hooge Crater Cemetery, Belgium. This large concentration cemetery contains 5,923 Commonwealth graves, most of which were brought here after the war. Buried here is Private W McC Murray who was killed during the attack near Dadizeele on 30 September 1918.

Houchin British Cemetery, France. Buried here is Private W McCready who died nearby in 6th Casualty Clearing Station on 23 September 1918 while serving with the 5th/6th (Service) Battalion.

Ingoyghem Military Cemetery, Belgium. Located south of the River Lys near the scene of the 9th Royal Irish Fusiliers' final action, this small cemetery contains 88 Commonwealth and 54 German graves. Buried here is Private R J Mack killed on 25

October 1918. Also buried here is Private H P T Walker, who was killed in action with 36th Battalion, Machine Gun Corps on 26 October 1918.

Kandahar Farm Cemetery, Belgium. Recaptured from the Germans in early September 1918, the cemetery contains 443 graves including that of Private E Terry who was killed in the attack on Hill 63 on 4 September 1918.

Kemmel Chateau Military Cemetery, Belgium. The cemetery contains 1,135 Commonwealth graves, mostly of soldiers killed in the southern part of the Flanders front. Here is buried Private A Graham who died of wounds on 22 March 1917.

Kezelberg Military Cemetery, Belgium. This very small cemetery contains 147 Commonwealth graves. It was opened in October 1918 after the area was captured by 15th Royal Irish Rifles. Buried here are Second Lieutenant J Darling MC, who died of wounds on 26 October 1918 and three soldiers who were wounded at Anseghem on 25/26 October 1918 and died of wounds in the first few days of November 1918 - Sergeant R E Matthews and Privates L W Martin and W McCormick.

Kezelberg Military Cemetery near Dadizeele.
Buried in this small cemetery are some of the men who were severely wounded in the final action of the 9th Royal Irish Fusiliers.

Knockbreda Church of Ireland Churchyard, Northern Ireland. There are two First World War graves here including that of Second Lieutenant C M Black, who died of gastro-enteritis in Belfast on 9 July 1917 while recovering from a wound sustained in Flanders.

Knocknamuckley (St Matthias) Church of Ireland Churchyard, County Armagh, Northern Ireland. Amongst three Commonwealth graves of the First World War lies that of Lance Corporal J H Chambers, who died of wounds on 29 July 1920.

Kortrijk (St Jan) Communal Cemetery, Belgium. Until its capture by 12th Royal Irish Rifles, this was a German cemetery. Here is buried Second Lieutenant G Hardy who was wounded and captured near Wulverghem on 12 April 1918 and died while a prisoner of war on 30 April 1918.

Le Cateau Military Cemetery, France. After its capture in 1914 Le Cateau became an important German railhead and hospital centre. There are over 5,000 German and 698 Commonwealth commemorations here, including Private H W Hammond who died as a prisoner of war in September 1918.

Les Baraques Military Cemetery, France. Situated on the coast near Calais, this was one of two cemeteries that served five large hospitals. It contains 1,303 Commonwealth graves including that of Private J Martin who died of wounds on 27 December 1918.

Lijssenthoek Military Cemetery, Belgium. Situated at the site of a number of Casualty Clearing Stations fed by a light railway, this is the second largest war cemetery in the area after Tyne Cot, containing 9,901 Commonwealth graves. Buried here are Privates W J McAuley and L F White, who died of wounds in April 1918, and Lance Corporal A Erskine and Private D Currie who died of wounds in October 1918.

Locre Hospice Cemetery, Belgium. Opened in 1917, the cemetery contains 244 Commonwealth graves including that of Lance Sergeant H Makinson MM who died of wounds on 11 April 1918, just before the site was captured in the German advance.

Longuenesse (St Omer) Souvenir Cemetery, France. Located on the route to the channel ports and the site of a number of hospitals, the cemetery contains 2,874 Commonwealth graves from the First World War including that of Private S A Paine who died of wounds in hospital at St Omer on 6 September 1918.

Lurgan New Cemetery, County Armagh, Northern Ireland. Here is buried Private J Larkin who died on 26 March 1917, aged only seventeen.

Martinsart British Cemetery, France. This concentration cemetery contains 488 Commonwealth graves. Unusually the gravestones are all of red sandstone. Amongst them is that of Private J J Kells, who was killed on 1 July 1916. The fourteen men of the 13th Royal Irish Rifles killed in Martinsart by a single shell blast on 28 June 1916 are buried here in Plot 1, Row A.

Mendinghem Military Cemetery, Belgium. Opened at the site of a group of Casualty Clearing Stations, the cemetery contains 2,391 Commonwealth graves including those of Private A McKinlay, who died of wounds in September 1917, and Privates H Robb and W H Smyth, both of whom died of wounds in April 1918.

Merseburg Prisoner of War Camp Cemetery, Germany - see **Berlin South-Western Cemetery**.

Mesnil Communal Cemetery Extension, France. This concentration cemetery contains 333 Commonwealth graves, mainly from the battles here in 1916 and the German advance in 1918. They include those of Captain C M Johnston and Private F Houston, both killed on 1 July 1916, and two other unknown soldiers of the 9th Royal Irish Fusiliers. It is likely that others members of the 9th Royal Irish Fusiliers are buried here in unnamed graves.

Mesnil Ridge Cemetery, France. This small cemetery contains ninety-eight graves of soldiers from units that manned the trenches on the forward slope of the ridge near Hamel from August 1915 to July 1916. It is situated near the site of the supporting Field Ambulances. Amongst a row of 36th (Ulster) Division graves lie Private W Girvan, the first soldier killed in action (12 February 1916), and Private T J McKeown, who was killed on 31 May 1916. Private J Hall, who was killed on 3 April 1916, is also buried in this cemetery. All three men were killed by shell fire.

Messines Ridge British Cemetery, Belgium. In addition to the memorial to the New Zealanders killed in the salient, this concentration cemetery contains 1532 Commonwealth graves or commemorations. Four soldiers who were killed in action during the attack on Hill 63 on 4 September 1918, and who, originally buried in Bristol Castle Cemetery near Wulverghem, are interred in identified graves here. Privates J McNaye and H E Woolford, who were known to be buried in Bristol Castle Cemetery, are commemorated on the **Bristol Castle Cemetery Memorial**, which also commemorates those from Bousbeque East German Cemetery and Lumm Farm Cemetery.

Mesnil Communal Cemetery Extension, 1921.
The grave of Captain C M Johnston is in the centre foreground with the hat and cane lying on it. The white cross in front of and to the right of the visitor sits over the double grave of Privates J Ingham and A J Selby of 2nd Battalion, The Royal Welsh Fusiliers. The diamond-shaped markers are those of Bombardier E E Mackenzie and Sergeant N J Paxton of the Canadian Field Artillery.

Mesnil Communal Cemetery Extension, 1921.

Metz-en-Coutre Communal Cemetery British Extension, France. This cemetery served a number of Field Ambulances located nearby from April 1917 until the enemy captured the area in March 1918. Nearly five hundred Commonwealth casualties are buried or commemorated in the original plot including Private A Burns, killed in action while serving with the 1st Battalion on 27 September 1917.

Mill Road Cemetery, France. This concentration cemetery, which lies between the Ulster Tower and the site of the Swaben Redoubt, is the biggest in the Thiepval area with 1,304 graves. Here are buried Privates G Ferris and W J Wilson, who were killed on 1 July 1916 and originally buried elsewhere. Other members of the 9th Royal Irish Fusiliers may be buried amongst the 815 unidentified graves.

Milltown Church of Ireland Churchyard, County Armagh, Northern Ireland. Buried here is Private J Vennard, who died of wounds on 14 June 1918.

Mullabrack (St John) Church of Ireland Churchyard, County Armagh, Northern Ireland. Here is buried Corporal W G Williamson who died on 17 May 1917.

Moeuvres Communal Cemetery Extension, France. This cemetery lay within the Hindenburg Line defences and was largely maintained by the Germans. It was added to after the war and now contains 565 Commonwealth graves. The Germans buried Second Lieutenant L H Martin here after he was killed in action at Moeuvres on 23 November 1917.

Mont Noir Military Cemetery, France. Opened in April 1918, this small cemetery contains 149 Commonwealth graves. About half of the graves were relocated here after the war, including those from Wolfhoek British Cemetery. Here lie seven soldiers who were killed in action in August and September 1918.

Neuville-Bourjonval British Cemetery, France. Located south-west of Havrincourt, this cemetery contains the graves of ten soldiers killed in the Havrincourt sector. Four were killed by a single shell on 25 September 1917, four were killed on the night of 26 October 1917, Sergeant R Irwin was killed on a raid on 3 November 1917, and Private D Sturgeon was killed by an enemy mortar on 16 November 1917.

New Irish Farm Cemetery, Belgium. Located north-east of Ypres in the area of the reserve lines during the Ulster Division's attack on 16 August 1917, this concentration cemetery now contains 4,715 graves of which nearly three-quarters are unidentified. There are six named graves of soldiers killed during the attack on 16 August 1917. It is likely that there are many more men of the 9th Royal Irish Fusiliers buried here whose graves remain unidentified.

Newcastle-upon-Tyne (St John's Westgate and Elswick) Cemetery, England. This civilian cemetery, the largest in Newcastle, contains 284 graves from the First and Second World Wars. They include that of Private R Bulman, who died of wounds on 12 October 1920.

Niederzwehren Cemetery, Germany. Located ten kilometres south of Kassel, the cemetery is one of four containing the graves of British prisoners of war who died in Germany. Buried or commemorated here are 1,796 Commonwealth soldiers. Twenty-eight graves of soldiers from Irish regiments were moved here from Dietkirchen Prisoner of War Cemetery. Buried here is Sergeant T Wilson, who died in captivity on 3 October 1918. Private W Morton, who was captured on 27 March 1918 and died on 17 October 1918, was buried in Dietkirchen Prisoner of War Cemetery, but his grave was not identified and he is commemorated on **Dietkirchen Prisoner of War Cemetery Memorial 1**.

Nieppe Communal Cemetery, France. North-west of Armentieres, this small cemetery contains sixty-two graves, mainly of those who died in nearby Dressing Stations. They include that of Private M Stothers, who died on 7 October 1917.

Nieuwkerke (Neuve-Eglise) Churchyard, Belgium. This churchyard was used by field ambulances and fighting units when the area was in Allied hands. Buried here are ninety-two Commonwealth soldiers including Corporal J W Sadler, who was killed in action on 3 September 1918 while serving with the 12th Royal Irish Rifles.

Nottingham Northern Cemetery, England. Amongst 158 Commonwealth war graves, mainly from the Second World War, is buried Private F Hustwayte. He re-enlisted for Regular Army service in 1919 and died of a fractured spine on 15 September 1920 while serving with the 1st Battalion, The Leicestershire Regiment, during the Irish War of Independence.

Noyon New British Cemetery, France. This is a small concentration cemetery containing the graves of over 250 Commonwealth soldiers who were killed in 1918. Many are unidentified but the known graves include those of three soldiers killed during the retreat from St Quentin in March 1918 – Privates F Duffy, R Ogden, and F Tate. It is likely that others of the 9th Royal Irish Fusiliers are buried here.

Perreuse Chateau Franco British National Cemetery, France. Located sixty kilometres east of Paris, this small cemetery contains 150 Commonwealth graves moved here after the war. Buried here is Private G Johnston who died on 13 October 1918, probably in a French medical unit. There is no recorded explanation for his death and burial so far from where the 9th Royal Irish Fusiliers was located throughout 1918.

Pond Farm Cemetery, Belgium. Amongst the 296 Commonwealth burials in this cemetery are those of six soldiers who died in the area west of the Messines ridge in May and June 1917. They include Private W Limbert who was killed accidentally by another soldier who fired his rifle while cleaning it.

Portsdown (Christ Church) Military Cemetery, England. Many of those buried here died in the Queen Alexandra Hospital, Cosham. Here is buried Private J McDade who was wounded on 1 July and died on 20 July 1916.

Puchevillers British Cemetery, France. Two Casualty Clearing Stations were located here during the Somme battle of July 1916. Buried here are five soldiers who died of wounds between 1 and 6 July 1916.

Ration Farm (La Plus Douve) Annexe, Belgium. The 9th Royal Irish Fusiliers occupied La Plus Douve Farm regularly in late 1916 and early 1917. This cemetery of 202 Commonwealth burials includes the graves of Second Lieutenants H H Dunwoody and W Peacock, and Private R Reaney, who were killed in the Douve Valley in 1916.

Ribecourt British Cemetery, France. This area was captured during the Cambrai battle on 20 November 1917 and lost again in March 1918 during the German offensive. The cemetery contains 295 graves. Here is buried Captain R S Flood MC who was killed by shellfire near Marcoing on 5 December 1917.

Rocquigny-Equancourt Road British Cemetery, France. The cemetery contains 1,838 Commonwealth graves. Most of them are of men who had been wounded in the fighting on the Hindenburg Line and in the Battle of Cambrai, and who died in nearby Casualty Clearing Stations. Buried here is Private W Thompson who was mortally wounded by shellfire near Marcoing and who died on 6 December 1917.

Roye New British Cemetery, France. This concentration cemetery was developed after the war and contains 565 Commonwealth burials and commemorations. Memorial headstones commemorate 117 men whose graves in four other cemeteries were lost. Here lie Sergeant J Hughes DCM, MM, killed on 21 March 1918, Private J F Johnston who was wounded during the retreat and died on 25 March 1918, Second Lieutenant W H Roche who was killed in action on 27 March 1918, and Major J G Brew, who was mortally wounded on 26 March 1918 and died while in captivity.

Ribecourt British Cemetery.
This is a very good example of a battlefield cemetery. The graves of eighty-one men were destroyed by shellfire; they are commemorated on the Special Memorials around the edge of the cemetery.

Seaford Cemetery, England. This cemetery contains 253 graves from the First World War, mainly of men of the 36th (Ulster) Division, British West Indies Regiment or the Canadian Forces based at the training centre; most of the latter group died during the influenza pandemic in 1918/19. Amongst four members of 36th (Ulster) Division who are buried here lies Private J Topley who drowned in a river nearby on 18 August 1915.

Seagoe Cemetery, County Armagh, Northern Ireland. Buried here are Private S G Dillon who died on 7 January 1916, and Lieutenant T F Espie who had served as a Corporal in the Battalion before being commissioned into The Royal Inniskilling Fusiliers. He died on 6 February 1919.

Serre Road Cemetery Number 1, France. Located north of Beaumont-Hamel, this cemetery was begun in May 1917 for bodies from the Somme attacks of 1916. It was expanded after the war and now contains 2,426 graves of which 1,728 are unidentified. Included here are the graves of six soldiers killed on 1 July 1916 – Privates W Ferguson, who was only seventeen, J Lyness, R McCann and three unknown. It is probable that other men of the 9th Royal Irish Fusiliers lie in some of the many unidentified graves.

Shankill Cemetery, County Armagh, Northern Ireland. Here is buried Lance Corporal W T Irwin who died on 16 May 1919.

Shwebo Cantonment Cemetery, Burma - see **Taukkyan Memorial**, Burma.

St Marie Cemetery, Le Havre, France. Situated near the hospitals of Le Havre, this cemetery contains the graves of four soldiers who died of wounds and illness between March 1916 and August 1917 – Corporal R W Graham and Privates R Lynch, W J McCullough and T Stewart.

St Quentin Cabaret Military Cemetery, Belgium. North of the River Douve, this small cemetery sits near the site regularly used as a Battalion Headquarters. Amongst the graves here is that of Captain J A Johnston, killed by a sniper on 18 February 1917.

St Sever Cemetery, France. Rouen was the site of a number of hospitals throughout the war. The original cemetery contains 3,082 Commonwealth graves. Amongst them are

Private R Fitzsimons, who died in February 1916, and three men wounded on 1 July 1916 who died later - Lance Sergeant J Girvan and Privates A Johnstone and J J Malone. Also buried here is Second Lieutenant F W D Grundy who died of wounds in February 1917.

St Sever Cemetery Extension, France. Seven soldiers are buried amongst 8,346 Commonwealth graves in the cemetery extension; two died of wounds in 1917 and five died of wounds in March and April 1918.

St Souplet British Cemetery, France. This is a concentration cemetery and many of those buried were found and buried by the enemy or died as prisoners of war following the battles of March 1918. They include Private E S Campkin who was killed in action on 21 March 1918, and Private T Adams who died while a prisoner of war on 15 July 1918.

Tandragee (Meeting House) Presbyterian Churchyard, County Armagh, Northern Ireland. Buried here is Private J Wilson, who died on 23 May 1919.

Templeux-le-Guerard British Cemetery, France. This cemetery was begun in April 1917, used until August 1917 and then again in September and October 1918. It was added to after the war by the concentration of graves from the surrounding battlefields and it now commemorates over 750 First World War casualties. Buried here is Private J M Clow who was killed in action on 29 September 1918 while serving with 18th Battalion, Machine Gun Corps.

Terlincthun British Cemetery, France. This large cemetery was opened in June 1918 to serve a number of hospitals in the Boulogne area when other local cemeteries became full. Buried here are Second Lieutenant J M Inglis and Corporal S G Young, both of whom were severely wounded in October 1918.

Tourcoing (Pont-Neuville) Communal Cemetery, France. A hospital and two Casualty Clearing Stations were based here from November 1918, and buried in this cemetery are two soldiers who were wounded in the last action in October 1918 and who died of wounds in December 1918 – Lance Corporal R C Ballam and Private J Pollock.

Tullylish (All Saints) Church of Ireland Churchyard, County Down, Northern Ireland. Here is buried Private J Montgomery who died on 1 May 1920 while serving with the Labour Corps.

Tyne Cot Cemetery, Belgium. This is the biggest Commonwealth war cemetery in the world, containing 11,956 graves; over two thirds are unidentified. It is also the site of the Tyne Cot Memorial. Nineteen soldiers are buried here. All were killed on 16 August 1917, and it is likely that others lie in some of the unidentified graves.

Vignemont French National Cemetery, France. This cemetery was begun by a French Military Ambulance in April 1918, and Captain G W Vesey MC is one of ten British casualties buried here. He died of wounds on 26 March 1918 and was originally buried in Ressons-sur-Matz French Military Cemetery, near Roye.

Villers-Faucon Communal Cemetery Extension, France. The cemetery extension was begun in April 1917 and used until the area was captured in March 1918 after which it was used by the Germans. British burials resumed in September and October 1918 and after the war it became a concentration cemetery. There are now 459 Commonwealth burials and commemorations here. Here lies Private H Cairns who was killed in action on 23 March 1918 while serving with 36th Battalion, Machine Gun Corps.

Villers St Christophe Churchyard, France - see **Ham British Cemetery**, France.

Warloy-Baillon Communal Cemetery Extension, France. A Medical Services Advanced Operating Centre was set up here for the battle on 1 July 1916. There is a total of 1,331 Commonwealth graves here, including that of Private J Sloan who enlisted in September 1914 aged only seventeen. He died of wounds on 2 July 1916 and was one of five soldiers of the 9th Royal Irish Fusiliers who died aged seventeen. Also buried here is Captain C S Murray who was wounded commanding B Company, 12th Royal Irish Rifles on 1 July 1916.

The grave of Private Joshua Sloan

Wimereux Communal Cemetery, France. Located near a hospital centre on the coast north of Boulogne, this cemetery contains 2,847 Commonwealth graves including those of Lance Corporal E C Rose and Privates G F Carroll and J W C Wilson, all of whom died of wounds between July and September 1917, and Lance Sergeant H Roe DCM who died of wounds on 8 April 1918. Also buried here is Lieutenant Colonel J McCrae, the Canadian doctor and author of 'In Flanders Fields'.

Wolfhoek British Cemetery, Belgium - see **Mont Noir Military Cemetery**, Belgium.

Wulverghem-Lindenhoek Road Military Cemetery, Belgium. Originally called Wulverghem Dressing Station Cemetery, this became a concentration cemetery after the war. Moved here were the remains of Private J A Bell (killed on 19 April 1918), Second Lieutenant V A Davis (killed serving with the 2nd Battalion, The Prince of Wales's Leinster Regiment (Royal Canadians) on 4 September 1918) and Sergeant C Ingledew (killed on 5 September 1918 near Hill 63). Sixteen men of the 1st Battalion killed on 2 and 3 September 1918 were also moved here.

Ypres Reservoir Cemetery, Belgium. One of three cemeteries started to the north-west of the town, this is the only one that remains and it became a concentration cemetery after the war. There are 2,613 Commonwealth burials and commemorations on this site. They include that of Private B Rosenberg, killed on 16 August 1917, and Second Lieutenant J Kernaghan who was wounded near Dadizeele on 30 September 1918 and died the next day. Also buried here is Lieutenant Colonel A C Pratt DSO, the former Second-in-Command, who was killed in action on 16 August 1917 while commanding the 11th Royal Inniskilling Fusiliers.

Commonwealth War Graves Commission Memorials to the Missing

Arras Flying Services Memorial, France. Situated in the British Military Cemetery on the Faubourg d'Amiens, the memorial commemorates the missing of the Royal Flying Corps, Royal Naval Air Service and the Royal Air Force. On it are commemorated Lieutenants F G B Pascoe and H A Williamson. Also commemorated here is the pilot killed while supporting the 9th Royal Irish Fusiliers at Moeuvres – Lieutenant A Griggs, Australian Flying Corps.

Brookwood (United Kingdom 1914-1918) Memorial, England. Brookwood Military Cemetery is the largest Commonwealth war cemetery in the United Kingdom and contains 1,601 Commonwealth burials of the First World War. The Brookwood (United Kingdom 1914-18) Memorial was created in 2004 to commemorate those Commonwealth casualties who died in the United Kingdom during the First World War but for whom no graves could be found. Many of these casualties have been recently identified by projects such as *In From The Cold,* or private researchers. Where the burial place has since been discovered the commemoration details are now recorded under the appropriate Cemetery Register.

Commemorated here is Lance Corporal P H A Reid who died of pulmonary tuberculosis at Lisburn on 24 May 1921.

Cambrai Memorial, France. The memorial commemorates 7,048 men who fell in the Battle of Cambrai and who have no known grave. Thirteen soldiers who died during the attacks on Moeuvres are commemorated here as is Private R Miller, killed in action while serving with the 1st Battalion. All were killed on 22/23 November 1917.

Detail from one of the accurate and detailed stone carvings on the Cambrai Memorial.

Flanders Field American Cemetery Chapel Memorial, Belgium. The cemetery contains the graves of 368 American officers and soldiers who were killed or died in 1918. The Memorial Chapel lists the names of forty-three Americans missing in Flanders and who have no known graves. Here is commemorated Lieutenant H S Morgan MC, US Army Medical Corps, the Medical Officer who was killed near Wulverghem in April 1918.

Flanders Field American Cemetery Chapel Memorial.

Malbork Memorial, Poland. Malbork (formerly Marienburg) lies south-east of Gdansk (Danzig). The Malbork Memorial forms the entrance to the Commonwealth War Cemetery and it commemorates thirty-nine British soldiers and one Royal Marine who were buried in **Heilsberg Prisoner of War Cemetery** (Heilsberg, then a small town in East Prussia, is now Lidzbark Warmiński, Poland). The graves of these men could not be maintained and were abandoned in 1960. The bodies of twelve other British soldiers originally buried there were removed to **Berlin South-Western Cemetery**. Commemorated on this memorial is Private J E Partridge, who died while a prisoner of war on 27 October 1918.

Menin Gate Memorial, Belgium. Situated on the Menin Road on the eastern outskirts of Ypres, the Menin Gate Memorial commemorates the 54,896 British troops who died in the Ypres salient between 1914 and 15 August 1917 and who have no known graves. Those of Australia, Canada, India and South Africa who were killed up to the end of the war and who have no known graves, are also commemorated here. The New Zealanders missing in the salient are commemorated in Messines Ridge British Cemetery and on the Tyne Cot Memorial. Five soldiers are commemorated on the memorial; all were killed in June 1917. Also commemorated here are Private W H Uprichard who was killed in action on 14 July 1916 while serving with 108th Brigade Machine Gun Company, and Second Lieutenant F P Kiely, who was killed in June 1917 on a bombing raid while with the 1st Battalion.

Berkshire Corner Cemetery Extension, Ploegsteert Wood.

Ploegsteert Memorial, Belgium. Located at the north-west corner of Ploegsteert Wood, the Ploegsteert Memorial to the Missing, and Berkshire Corner Cemetery Extension, lie on a point known during the war as Hyde Park Corner. The memorial commemorates those with no known grave from the battles in this southern part of the Ypres salient. Originally planned to be built in Lille, it also commemorates those with no known grave from the battles of Armentieres and Aubers Ridge in 1914, Loos and Fromelles in 1915, Estaires in 1916 and Hazebrouck, Scherpenberg and Outtersteene Ridge in 1918. There are 11,447 names on the memorial and in the concentration cemetery lie 876 men. Commemorated here are one officer, Second Lieutenant C S Ratcliffe, nineteen soldiers and two former members of the Battalion. All were killed in July, August and September 1918.

Pozieres Memorial, France. Situated in Pozieres Military Cemetery, the Memorial to the Missing commemorates 14,644 men killed on the Somme between 21 March and 7 August 1918 and who have no known grave. Included are the names of 12,741 men who died during the period of heaviest fighting between 21 March and 5 April 1918. Two officers and twenty-nine soldiers are commemorated here, as is Private R Fulton, who was killed serving with 36th Battalion, Machine Gun Corps.

Savona Memorial, Italy. This memorial commemorates 275 casualties who have no known grave. All were on board the troopship 'Transylvania', which was sunk by U63 while it was under way to Salonika on 4 May 1917. Some of the bodies recovered are buried nearby. Commemorated here is a former soldier of the Battalion, Second Lieutenant J M Dunwoody of The Royal Dublin Fusiliers. Of interest, also listed on the memorial is a former officer of Princess Victoria's (Royal Irish Fusiliers) - Lt A H Sturrock of the Machine Gun Corps.

Taukkyan Memorial, Burma. Located near Yangon (formerly Rangoon) this memorial commemorates nineteen British soldiers who died in the First World War and twenty-six who died in the Second World War and who are buried in cemeteries throughout Burma that could not bc maintained. Commemorated here is Private W Milligan who died in February 1918 while serving with the 1st Garrison Battalion.

Berkshire Corner Cemetery Extension and the Ploegsteert Memorial.

Thiepval Memorial, France. Designed by Sir Edward Lutyens and located near the site of the Thiepval Chateau and on part of the Leipzig Redoubt, the Thiepval Memorial is dedicated to the British and French who died on the Somme up to 20 March 1918. It was dedicated in 1932. Recorded on slabs of Portland stone are the names of over 72,000 British and South African troops who have no known grave. Nearly 300 of those named on its walls have been found since its completion and buried in named graves. An addenda panel records the names of those men omitted when it was built. This panel now includes Private S McGahey who was identified as having been killed on 1 July 1916. In total four officers and 154 soldiers are commemorated on the memorial. All but two were killed on 1 July 1916 or died of wounds soon after. The two other men are Private R Heathwood, killed in a raid at Havrincourt on 3 November 1917, and Lance Corporal J Dunne, killed in action on 14 March 1918 near St Quentin. Also commemorated here are Second Lieutenant S O'Neill who was killed while serving with 108th Brigade Trench Mortar Battery and Company Sergeant Major W J Brown, Corporal D Orr and Privates J Courtney and R A McIlrath, who joined the Brigade

The dedication of the Thiepval Memorial in 1932.

Machine Gun Company and were killed on 1 July 1916. Lieutenant W T Richardson of 108th Brigade Trench Mortar Battery and Lieutenant A D Lemon and Sergeant J Benison of B Company 12th Royal Irish Rifles were killed fighting with the 9th Royal Irish Fusiliers on 1 July 1916 and they are also commemorated here. The concentration cemetery behind contains 300 British and 300 French soldiers from across the Somme battlefield; most are unknown. They include one soldier of the Ulster Division – Private J Ritchie, 14th Royal Irish Rifles, who was killed on 1 July 1916.

Tyne Cot Memorial, Belgium. Located on the eastern wall of Tyne Cot Cemetery, this memorial commemorates the 34,857 British, New Zealand and Newfoundland troops who died in the Ypres salient between 16 August 1917 and the end of the war and who have no known grave. Other Commonwealth countries are commemorated on the Menin Gate. Twelve officers and 155 soldiers are commemorated here (compare with the Thiepval Memorial). Of these, five officers and 105 soldiers were killed in action or died of wounds on or just after 16 August 1917; four officers and thirty-five men were killed in the fighting in April 1918; one officer, Second Lieutenant F J E McFarland MC was killed in action on the raid at Shoddy Farm on 22 July 1918, and Second Lieutenant J Bryson and ten men were killed in action between 30 September and 11 October 1918 near Vijfwegen/Hill 41. Two men were killed on 25 October 1918. An addenda panel records the names of those men omitted when it was built; it now includes Private S Chambers who was killed in action on 5 September 1918. Also commemorated here is Second Lieutenant J A Stokes, killed on 16 August 1917 while serving with the 12th Royal Irish Rifles, Private W H Dundas, killed on 1 October 1918 while serving with the 1st Battalion, and Corporal R Hayes, who died of wounds on 2 October 1918 while serving with the 1st Royal Inniskilling Fusiliers.

United Kingdom Book of Remembrance. The Book of Remembrance commemorates the death of Private A Maxwell, who died in July 1918, was not formerly recorded by the Commonwealth War Graves Commission, and whose place of burial in Lurgan has not yet been located or confirmed.

Ulster Battlefield Memorial Tower

The Ulster Battlefield Memorial Tower was proposed in November 1919 by Sir James Craig. It was designed by Bowden and Abbott Ltd of London and built quickly by Fenning & Co Ltd, specialists in granite memorials, and the *Société de Construction et Travaux Publics d'Arras*. The land had been purchased from three families that farmed the area around Thiepval. It was the first official memorial raised on the Western Front.

The Ulster Tower, as it has become known, was opened and dedicated on Saturday 19 November 1921 and the level of planned national representation indicates the importance of the event. The original plan was for the Prime Minister of Northern Ireland, Sir James Craig, to welcome the visitors and for Lord Carson to unveil the commemorative tablet in the memorial chamber. Both were ill and unable to attend, nonetheless it is Lord Carson's name that is inscribed on the memorial tablet. The party that travelled to the ceremony numbered about 100 people, including Field Marshal Sir Henry Wilson Bt, GCB, DSO, Chief of the Imperial General Staff, representatives of all of the battalions of the Ulster Division and some widows of the fallen. They travelled by train to Dover and then sailed to Calais on Friday 18 November. On arrival at Amiens they were greeted by the mayor and senior French Army officers, a guard of honour and a large crowd. A military band played the national anthem of both countries. The visitors stayed overnight in Amiens. It was originally planned that Major General Nugent would give an account of the Thiepval attack during the ceremony but, due to constraints on time, it was decided that he would speak at a meeting at the Hotel du Rhin the evening before. His overview was very well received, as were the additional comments by Captain C C Craig MP, the brother of Sir James Craig. He was a Company Commander during the attack and had been wounded and captured. Field Marshal Sir Henry Wilson spoke about the war generally. It is unlikely that many of the audience who had been at Thiepval or Hamel on 1 July would otherwise have heard about the attack from the perspective of senior commanders.

The next morning, which was frosty but clear, the visitors departed from Amiens in a convoy of motor cars and *charabancs*. The journey, about thirty miles, was at first uneventful and no obvious signs of war were seen. As the convoy approached Albert, however, that changed. Albert was still in ruins; not a single stone or brick building was standing, and beyond the town the roads were badly cut up. As the convoy approached the memorial along a narrow road (now the D73) the devastation of Thiepval Wood and the British and German trenches could be seen, altered little since the end of the war. The ceremony was due to begin at 11.00am but was delayed by about an hour because a car bringing some of the visitors from Amiens had broken down. This gave the visitors the opportunity to look at the trenches nearby. The area was littered with rusting rifles, helmets, pieces of shell and even items of clothing. The barbed wire that still protected the trenches caught and ripped the coats of the unwary.

Those who attended the ceremony included:

From France:

> The mayors of Albert, Aveluy, Auchonvillers, Authuile, Beaucourt sur l'Ancre, Beaumont Hamel, Englebelmer, Grandcourt, Mesnil, Martinsart, Mailly-Mailly & Thiepval.
>
> Préfet & Sous Préfet de la Somme.
>
> Sous Préfet de Peronne.
>
> Minister of Devastated Areas.
>
> General M Weygand.

From the United Kingdom (ranks, titles and decorations are as at November 1921):

> Lord Primate of All Ireland
>
> Moderator of the General Assembly of the Presbyterian Church in Ireland
>
> President of the Methodist Church in Ireland
>
> Field Marshal Sir Henry Wilson Bt, GCB, DSO, Chief of the Imperial General Staff, and his wife Lady Cecile Wilson.
>
> Duchess of Abercorn.
>
> Marquess and Marchioness of Londonderry.
>
> Marquess and Marchioness of Dufferin and Ava.
>
> Sir Robert Liddell DL.
>
> Major General Sir Charles Powell KCB.
>
> Major General Sir Charles Sackville-West KBE, CB, CMG.
>
> Major General O S W Nugent CB, DSO.

Right Reverend Dr J M Simms CB, CMG (formerly Principal Chaplain to the Forces).

Brigadier General A St Q Ricardo CMG, CBE, DSO.

Lieutenant Colonel Sir William Allen DSO MP (formerly The Royal Irish Rifles).

Lieutenant Colonel W B Spender DSO, MC (formerly Royal Regiment of Artillery).

Lieutenant Colonel R G Shuter DSO, The Royal Irish Fusiliers (Princess Victoria's).

Major J C Boyle (formerly 9th (Service) Battalion, Princess Victoria's (Royal Irish Fusiliers (County Armagh) and Corps of Royal Engineers).

Major J D M McCallum DSO.

Major J A Mulholland MC (formerly The Royal Irish Rifles).

Captain C C Craig MP (formerly The Royal Irish Rifles).

Captain J A L Johnston (formerly 9th (Service) Battalion, Princess Victoria's (Royal Irish Fusiliers (County Armagh)).

Captain R M Pryde (formerly The Royal Irish Rifles).

Captain S W Knox (formerly The Royal Irish Rifles).

Reverend J A Carey Precenter of Down and Rector of Bangor.

Reverend C C Manning MC (formerly Army Chaplains Department).

Honourable Lady Kennedy (wife of Sir Robert Kennedy KCMG) and her daughters.

Right Honourable R G Glendinning PC (formerly MP for North Antrim) & Mrs Glendinning.

Mr T E McConnell MP, Councillor H McKeag (Belfast), Mr T S Wilson JP (Bangor Urban Council), Mr F G Maguire (Ulster Volunteer Force Hospital Committee) & Mr A Wilson-Hungerford (Secretary to the Ulster Unionist Council).

Participants in the dedication ceremony for the Ulster Battlefield Memorial Tower examining the trenches nearby before the ceremony.

A newspaper appeal had been published on Friday 28 October 1921 to raise the funds required to send representatives of the units of 36th (Ulster) Division to the ceremony. Note the use of the new regimental abbreviation '*RUR*' (Royal Ulster Rifles). This was used also in subsequent news reports about the dedication of the Ulster Division battlefield memorial. Those who signed are identified in full:

Dear Sir,

The feeling has been expressed that representatives from each of the battalions of the Ulster Division should be present at the dedication ceremony of the Ulster Division battlefield memorial at Thiepval. Arrangements are being made to send representatives of the rank and file from each battalion. The cost of sending out a representative will be £25. We appeal to officers and friends to help us in this endeavour, and shall be glad to receive subscriptions, which may be sent to any of us at the Old Town Hall, Belfast.

Signed

J D McCallum 8th Batt RUR	(Major J D M McCallum DSO)
H R Haslett 9th Batt RUR	(Major H R Haslett)
E H R May 10th Batt RUR	(Major E H R May DSO)
H A Pakenham 11th Batt RUR	(Colonel H A Pakenham CMG)
W R Goodwin 12th Batt RUR	(Lieutenant Colonel W R Goodwin CMG, DSO)
R D P Maxwell 13th Batt RUR	(Lieutenant Colonel R D P Maxwell DSO)
Alan Mulholland 14th Batt RUR	(Major J A Mulholland MC)
G Ford Hutchinson 15th Batt RUR	(Lieutenant Colonel G H Ford Hutchinson DSO)
W J Allen 16th Batt RUR	(Lieutenant Colonel Sir William Allen DSO MP)
S W Blacker 9th Batt R Irish Fus	(Lieutenant Colonel S W W Blacker DSO)
A St Q Ricardo 9th Batt R Innis Fus	(Brigadier General A St Q Ricardo CMG, CBE, DSO)
R S Knox 10th Batt R Innis Fus	(Lieutenant Colonel R S Knox DSO)
C B Falls 11th Batt R Innis Fus	(Captain C B Falls)

As a result, the following men were sent to represent the units of 36th (Ulster Division) that fought on 1 July 1916 (original unit titles are used):

Corps of Royal Engineers:
Warrant Officer Class II J Gamble, Sergeant W L Doggart

9th (Service) Battalion, The Royal Inniskilling Fusiliers (County Tyrone):
Lieutenant T McClay DCM, MM, Sergeant W Barker DCM

10th (Service) Battalion, The Royal Inniskilling Fusiliers (Derry):
Lieutenant J Douglas, Sergeant J Given

11th (Service) Battalion, The Royal Inniskilling Fusiliers (Donegal and Fermanagh):
Sergeant T McClintock MM

8th (Service) Battalion, The Royal Irish Rifles (East Belfast)
Sergeant W B Blythe, Rifleman R Patterson

9th (Service) Battalion, The Royal Irish Rifles (West Belfast):
Sergeant R Silvey, Rifleman J Brady

10th (Service) Battalion, The Royal Irish Rifles (South Belfast):
Sergeant J Patterson DCM, MM, Rifleman R Carson MM

11th (Service) Battalion, The Royal Irish Rifles (South Antrim):
Sergeant A Leach DCM, Sergeant T Ward

12th (Service) Battalion, The Royal Irish Rifles (Central Antrim):

Warrant Officer Class II J Johnston, Lance Corporal W Geary

13th (Service) Battalion, The Royal Irish Rifles (1st County Down):
Sergeant J Edgar, Corporal W Greer

14th (Service) Battalion, The Royal Irish Rifles (Young Citizens):
Sergeant J Kenning, Sergeant J Shields MM

15th (Service) Battalion, The Royal Irish Rifles (North Belfast):
Sergeant S Jordan

16th (Service) Battalion, The Royal Irish Rifles (2nd County Down) (Pioneers)
Sergeant R J Martin, Sergeant W J Taylor

9th (Service) Battalion, Princess Victoria's (Royal Irish Fusiliers) (County Armagh):
Sergeant H Sewell, Sergeant W Neill DCM

Thc Frcnch guard of honour
before the ceremony.

At the tower, a French guard of honour was in place and Field Marshal Sir Henry Wilson inspected the troops as he walked to the tower, accompanied by General Maxime Weygand, the former chief of staff to Marshall Foch. The event was filmed for Pathe News. Major J C Boyle, who had been commissioned into the 9th Royal Irish Fusiliers on its formation and transferred to the Corps of Royal Engineers in 1915, was an original member of the memorial committee and stood in for Sir James Craig. He formally asked Field Marshal Sir Henry Wilson to open the tower. The key was made of silver and presented to the Field Marshal in a casket. The casket was inscribed:

> *Presented to Field-Marshal Sir Henry M. Wilson, Bart., G.C.B., D.S.O., Chief of the Imperial General Staff, first Colonel Commandant of the Royal Ulster Rifles, on the occasion of the opening by him of the Ulster Battlefield Memorial Tower at Thiepval, 19th November, 1921, on behalf of the subscribers.*

The Field Marshall then addressed the crowd in French, after which the memorial committee and senior visitors went into the memorial chamber. The memorial chamber, sixteen feet along each side, has a lintel around the room inscribed with words written by Lord Tennyson of Helen's Tower:

Helen's Tower here I stand,
Dominant over sea and land.
Son's love built me, and I hold
Ulster's love in lettered gold.

Here General Weygand unveiled the commemorative tablet, made of white marble.

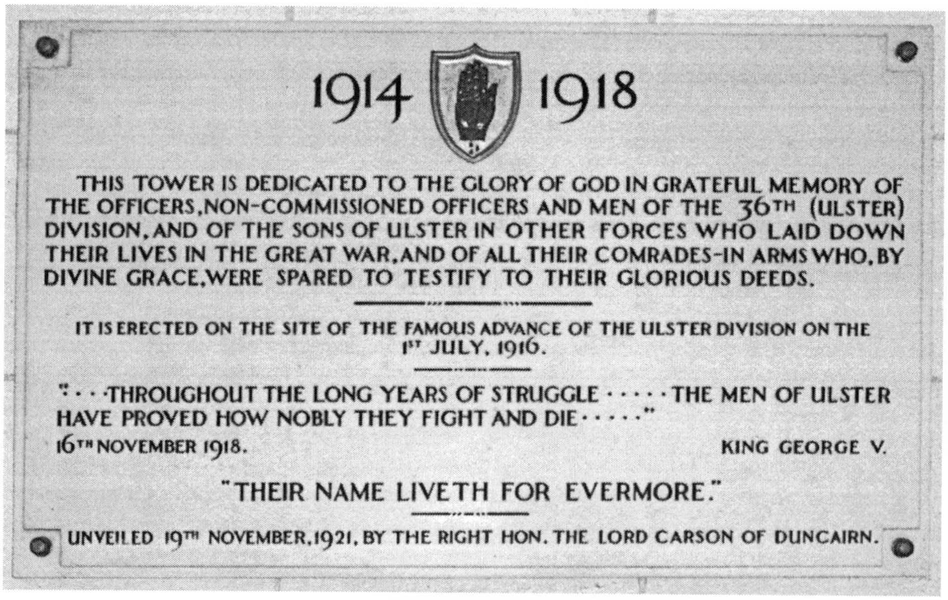

Thereafter followed a service of dedication led by the Primate of All Ireland, the Most Reverend Dr C D'Arcy, the Moderator of the Presbyterian Church, the Right Reverend Dr W J Lowe, and the President of the Methodist Church in Ireland, the Reverend W H Smyth. All spoke at length about the men of the Ulster Division and their achievements and also of the *'cause of Ulster'*. At the end of the service of dedication Lieutenant Colonel Sir William Allen MP formally handed over the custody of the tower to the committee of the Ulster Volunteer Force Patriotic Fund, represented by Sir Robert Liddell. Both men spoke and then, following a final benediction, the national anthem was sung.

To cheers from the crowd, the Duchess of Abercorn appeared on the tower roof and proceeded to unfurl a Union Flag and a French flag; both were then raised together. The final act was conducted by the representatives of the units and organisations associated with 36th (Ulster) Division, who planted trees brought from Ireland to form an avenue leading to the tower from the road. Sergeant William Neill DCM and Sergeant Herbert Sewell planted the tree on behalf of the 9th Royal Irish Fusiliers.

Trees were planted by:

Field Marshal Sir Henry Wilson Bt, GCB, DSO

Major General Sir Charles Powell KCB & Major General O S W Nugent CB, DSO
Together representing 36th (Ulster) Division.4

Guardsman Gill (not identified) — *For the men of Ulster in other units.*

Mr T E McConnell MP — *Representing Lord Carson.*

Lieutenant Colonel W B Spender DSO, MC
Representing the Prime Minister of Northern Ireland.

General M Weygand — *For 'Our Allies'.*

Duchess of Abercorn — *For the women of Ulster.*

Préfet de la Somme — *For the French civil population.*

Lieutenant Colonel R G Shuter DSO
For the 2nd Battalion, The Royal Irish Fusiliers (Princess Victoria's).

Warrant Officer Class II Sims (not identified)
For the 1st Battalion, The Royal Ulster Rifles.

Brigadier General A St Q Ricardo CMG, CBE, DSO
For 9th (Service) Battalion, The Royal Inniskilling Fusiliers (County Tyrone).

Lieutenant J Douglas
For 10th (Service) Battalion, The Royal Inniskilling Fusiliers (Derry).

Sergeant T McClintock MM
For 11th (Service) Battalion,
The Royal Inniskilling Fusiliers (Donegal and Fermanagh)

Major J D M McCallum DSO
For 8th (Service) Battalion, The Royal Irish Rifles (East Belfast).

Sergeant R Silvey
For 9th (Service) Battalion, The Royal Irish Rifles (West Belfast).

Sergeant J Patterson DCM, MM
For 10th (Service) Battalion, The Royal Irish Rifles (South Belfast).

Mrs Blair Oliphant & Sergeant A Leach DCM
For 11th (Service) Battalion, The Royal Irish Rifles (South Antrim).

Warrant Officer Class II J Johnston
For 12th (Service) Battalion, The Royal Irish Rifles (Central Antrim).

Sergeant J Edgar
For 13th (Service) Battalion, The Royal Irish Rifles (1st County Down).

Sergeant J Kenning
For 14th (Service) Battalion, The Royal Irish Rifles (Young Citizens).

Sergeant S Jordan
For 15th (Service) Battalion, The Royal Irish Rifles (North Belfast).

Lieutenant Colonel Sir William Allen DSO MP & a Sergeant
For 16th (Service) Battalion,
The Royal Irish Rifles (2nd County Down) (Pioneers).

Sergeant H Sewell & Sergeant W Neill DCM
For 9th (Service) Battalion,
Princess Victoria's (Royal Irish Fusiliers) (County Armagh).

Right Reverend Dr J M Simms CB, CMG & Reverend C C Manning MC
For the 36th (Ulster) Division Chaplains.

Mrs Thompson (wife of Lieutenant Colonel R G Thompson CMG)
For the 36th (Ulster) Division Artillery.

Major J C Boyle
For the 36th (Ulster) Division Engineers & Signallers.

Captain J B Stewart
For the 36th (Ulster) Division Army Service Corps.

Dr (formerly Captain) S P Rea MB
For the 36th (Ulster) Division Royal Army Medical Corps.

Mr T S Wilson JP *For Ulstermen in the Royal Navy.*

Marquess of Londonderry *For Ulstermen in the Royal Flying Corps.*

Major General Sir Charles Powell KCB
Representing Lieutenant Colonel F H Crawford: For the Ulster Volunteer Force.

Honourable Lady Kennedy *For the War Pensions Committee.*

Mrs L Ainsworth Barr *For the Ulster Woman's Gift Fund.*

Miss Cunningham (not identified) *For the Soldiers and Sailors Work Committee.*

Mrs C C Craig *For Lady Carson's fund.*

Mr F G Maguire *For the Ulster Volunteer Force Hospital Committee.*

Marquess of Dufferin and Ava & Mrs R Boyd
For the ex-Service Men's Association.

Mr A Wilson-Hungerford *For the Ulster Unionist Labour Association.*

Marquess of Londonderry, Captain CC Craig MP, & Mrs Wilson-Hungerford
For the Ulster Unionist Council.

Lieutenant Colonel Sir William Allen DSO MP, Lieutenant J Johnston, Sergeant W J Taylor & Rifleman R Johnston *For the Grand Orange Lodge of Ireland.*

Sir Robert Liddell DL *For the Ulster Patriotic Fund.*

Captain S W Knox *For the British Legion.*

Mrs Corscadden (not identified) *For Derry city.*

The service of dedication at Ulster Battlefield Memorial Tower

Sergeant William Neill DCM (in overcoat on the left). In front is the first caretaker of the tower, former Sergeant Joseph Savage, 9th (Service) Battalion, The Royal Irish Rifles (West Belfast) and his French wife.

Some of the visitors attending the dedication of the Ulster Tower in November 1921. Nearest the camera to the left of centre are the Duchess of Abercorn and General Weygand. In the background can be seen the remnants of Thiepval Wood.

During the Second World War, the original trees were unable to be properly tended and suffered from disease. They have been replanted since 1945. The plaques giving the details of those who planted the original trees were removed. Today, inside the tower is a framed list of the units and organisations on behalf of which the original trees were planted, and the names of those who planted them.

Those who had brought wreaths took time at the end of the ceremony to lay them at the foot of the tower. Twenty-two flower wreaths were noted including one inscribed:

> *'In memory of officers, warrant officers, non-commissioned officers and men of the 9th Battalion Royal Irish Fusiliers who fell on 1st July, 1916 – From Portadown.'*

Although this is a poor photograph, it gives a good indication of the size and beauty of the wreaths laid at the tower. The large white wreath in the centre is in the shape of a crown. It was laid by the Ulster Ex-Servicemen's Association.

The Ulster Tower from the area of Mill Road Cemetery, November 1921.

In the early afternoon, later than planned, the visitors drove to Albert where the visitors had lunch, presided over by Captain Craig. The lunch was accompanied by speeches and toasts. The notable speakers were Captain Craig, the Marquis of Londonderry, Field Marshal Sir Henry Wilson, General Weygand, Lord Dufferin and Major General Nugent.

The Ulster Tower is currently owned and managed by the Somme Association, based at the Somme Heritage Centre at Newtownards.

Other Memorials

In addition to the numerous memorials erected in cities, towns and villages across the United Kingdom and Ireland, and those commemorating members of specific churches, workplaces, fraternal lodges and so on, there are a number of other memorials that commemorate the men of 36th (Ulster) Division:

Belfast City Hall, Northern Ireland. Amongst the many memorials in and around Belfast City Hall there are two stained glass windows. The first, in the entrance hall, is dedicated to the men of the North Irish Horse who were killed in both World Wars, and the other, at the top of the grand staircase, commemorates the men of 36th (Ulster) Division.

Island of Ireland Peace Park, Belgium. To promote peace across the island of Ireland by commemorating those who died in the First World War, the Island of Ireland Peace Park near Messines was opened on 11 November 1998. The park is divided into four sections representing the Provinces of Ireland and on the site stands an imposing Irish round tower of pre-reformation design.

Ireland's Memorial Records, Ireland. In July 1919, a National War Memorial Trust was established in Dublin to commemorate Ireland's war dead. In 1923 eight volumes were published that list the Irish men and women killed during the war, and those of other nationalities who died while serving with Irish regiments. The records may be viewed at the Irish National War Memorial.

Irish National War Memorial, Ireland. Following the partition of Ireland, the commemoration of the men and women from Ireland who had died in the First World War caused much heated debate. The establishment of a national memorial was finally agreed and a site in the western part of Dublin at Islandbridge was chosen. Sir Edwin Lutyens, who was so intimately involved in the creation of the Imperial War Graves Commission sites, was appointed as architect. The project took until 1938 to complete. Neglected after the Second World War, the park was restored in the mid-1980s and in 1988 it was formally dedicated to Ireland's war dead by the representatives of the four main churches.

Memorial Orange Lodges. After the war, moves were made by former members of The Royal Irish Rifles, particularly those who had belonged to the war-time LOL 862, to form a Memorial Orange Lodge in Ulster. Warrant 977 was granted to the 36th (Ulster) Division Memorial LOL on 5 May 1919. Colours were made by the Royal School of Needlework in 1937 and dedicated to the memory of the men of the Ulster Division. A number of other Orange Lodges commemorate individuals or units of 36th (Ulster) Division in some way, such as 36th (Ulster) Division Memorial LOL 1914, City of Leicester, Thiepval Memorial LOL 1916, and The Somme Memorial LOL 842, Bristol.

National Memorial Arboretum, England. Amongst the many memorial stands of trees is that of 'The Irish Infantry Grove'. It was dedicated in May 2000 and commemorates all of the Irish infantry soldiers who have fallen in battle since the formation of The Royal Irish Regiment in 1684. At its centre lies a plinth of Irish granite bearing the names of the Irish infantry regiments, and an Irish oak tree of a variety unique to Ireland, brought from the slopes of Slieve Donard in Tollymore Forest.

The Royal Irish Fusiliers (Princess Victoria's) Memorial Chapel, Northern Ireland. The memorial in the Cathedral Church of St Patrick in Armagh commemorates all of those who died while serving with the County Regiment from its formation until its amalgamation in 1967.

Royal Military Academy Sandhurst Memorial Chapel, England. Built to commemorate those gentlemen cadets from The Royal Military College who died in the First World War, the chapel displays their names by regiment on its marble pillars and walls. Commemorated here are two Commanding Officers – Lieutenant Colonel P E Kelly and Lieutenant Colonel S J Somerville.

St George's Memorial Church, Belgium. Designed by Sir Reginald Blomfield, the church was built near the town's cathedral to cater for the large number of British living in the Ypres area after the war, and for the many visitors to the battlefields and cemeteries. It was dedicated in 1929. Nearly everything in the church is a memorial to an individual or a unit. The dead of Princess Victoria's (Royal Irish Fusiliers) are commemorated on a brass plaque on an interior wall.

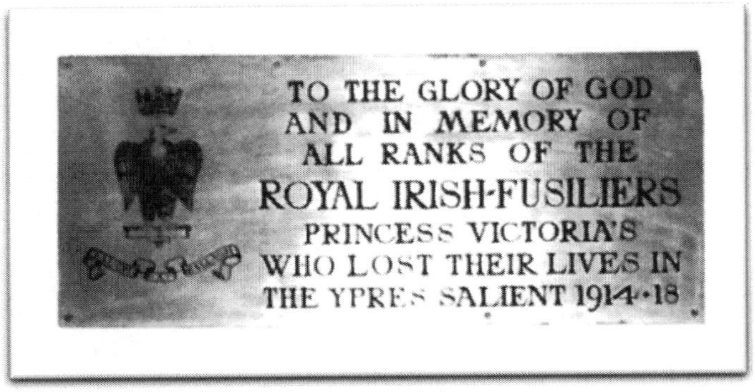

St George's Memorial Church.

APPENDIX 4

Honours & Awards

The award of decorations for gallantry has always been an emotive subject. During the First World War only the Victoria Cross and a Mention in Despatches could be awarded posthumously and there were very many deserving officers and soldiers who demonstrated great bravery but who were killed in the act and received no formal recognition of their heroism. Many other courageous acts were unseen and went unreported. Nevertheless, 293 awards for war service were made to men who served at some time with the 9th Royal Irish Fusiliers.

	First Award	Bar/ Additional Awards	Total	Earned with this Battalion	Earned Elsewhere
Victoria Cross	1	-	1	1	-
The Most Excellent Order of the British Empire	4	-	4	-	4
Distinguished Service Order	6	1	7	4	3
Distinguished Conduct Medal	21	-	21	19	2
Military Cross	47	9	56	36	20
Military Medal	105	5	110	87	23
Meritorious Service Medal	4	-	4	3	1
Mention in Despatches	42	14	56	25	31
Foreign Awards	34	-	34	23	11
Total	264	29	293	198	95

This appendix is unlikely to be complete due to the difficulty in tracking records, particularly for the men who moved between units. The ranks and regimental details shown are those held at the time of the award (with the exception of the thirty-three awards granted prior to the war, or for later service, or in other conflicts and not included in the table above. Where ranks and regimental details are shown, they are those held at the end of the careers of those listed). Citations are as published in the London Gazette (LG) and the date of publication is shown. An asterisk indicates a bar. Parent regiments and corps are shown for those not gazetted as Princess Victoria's (Royal Irish Fusiliers). Awards of the 1914 Star, 1914-15 Star, and other campaign medals such as those for the South Africa war, the India General Service Medal and the General Service Medal 1918-1962, and Long Service and Good Conduct medals, are annotated in Appendices 5 and 6.

Battle Honours

After the Battles Nomenclature Committee completed its report in July 1920 it fell to regimental committees to determine the battle honours to which each battalion of the regiment were entitled. To qualify for a battle honour a unit had to have been deployed with its headquarters and fifty percent of its strength within the geographical boundaries and dates set by the nomenclature committee. The results were forwarded to the War

Office for approval. A full list of the battle honours for the war was published in Army Order 55 in February 1925. Forty-four battle honours were granted to The Royal Irish Fusiliers (Princess Victoria's). Sixteen of those were awarded to the 9th Battalion and were shared variously with the 1st, 2nd, 7th, 8th and 7th/8th Battalions.

Battle Honour:	Dates:	Also Awarded To:
Ypres, 1917	June - November 1917	1st and 7th/8th Battalions.
Ypres, 1918	March - April 1918	1st Battalion.
Somme, 1916	July - November 1916	1st, 7th and 8th Battalions.
Somme, 1918	March 1918	1st Battalion.
Albert, 1916	1-16 July 1916	1st Battalion.
Messines, 1917	June 1917	7th/8th Battalion.
Messines, 1918	April 1918	1st Battalion.
Langemarck, 1917	August 1917	7th/8th Battalion.
Cambrai, 1917	November 1917	1st and 7th/8th Battalions.
St Quentin	March 1918	1st Battalion.
Rosieres	March 1918	1st Battalion.
Lys	April 1918	1st Battalion.
Bailleul	15-30 April 1918	1st Battalion.
Kemmel	25 April 1918	1st Battalion.
Courtrai	October 1918	1st Battalion.
France and Flanders, 1914-1918		1st, 2nd 7th and 8th Battalions.

A maximum of ten of the battle honours awarded could be selected to be borne on the King's Colour of each Regiment. It is evident that the Regimental Council decided to combine seven individual battle honours to form three battle honours (for Ypres, Somme and Messines) and, therefore, fourteen Battle honours are actually borne on the King's Colour. They are 'Le Cateau', 'Marne, 1914', 'Ypres, 1915, 17, 18', 'Somme, 1916,18', 'Arras 1917', 'Messines, 1917, 18', 'Lys', 'Macedonia, 1915-17', 'Suvla' and 'Palestine, 1917-18'. Seven of these were awarded to the 9th Battalion.

British Awards

Victoria Cross

Instituted in 1856, the Victoria Cross was the foremost decoration for gallantry awarded to British and Commonwealth troops during the course of the war. Six hundred and thirty-three awards were made between 1914 and 1919 with nine being earned by officers and men serving with 36th (Ulster) Division. There were two awards of the Victoria Cross to Princess Victoria's (Royal Irish Fusiliers), one of which was to an officer of the 9th Royal Irish Fusiliers. In addition, there was at least one other recommendation (see Company Sergeant Major R Lucas DCM, MM below):

CATHER Lieutenant and Adjutant G St G S - Posthumously after the attack at Hamel on 1/2 July 1916 (LG 9 September 1916).

> *For most conspicuous bravery near Hamel, France, on 1st July 1916. From 7pm till midnight he searched 'No-Man's Land,' and brought in three wounded men.*

Next morning, at 8am, he continued his search, and brought in another wounded man, and gave water to others, arranging for their rescue later. Finally at 10.30 am, he took out water to another man, and was proceeding further on when he was himself killed. All this was carried out in full view of the enemy, and under direct machine-gun fire and intermittent artillery fire. He set a splendid example of courage and self-sacrifice.

King George V presented the Victoria Cross to his mother at Buckingham Palace on 31 March 1917. His brother, Captain Dermot Cather RN, presented the Victoria Cross to the Regiment's Museum in Armagh in 1979.

The Most Excellent Order of the British Empire

Until 1917 existing awards for valuable service were restricted almost entirely to those in public service or who held public office at a senior level. The demand for an award for officers for services not in action was complicated by a similar need to reward civilians for meritorious service. The solution was a new order, The Most Excellent Order of the British Empire, which was instituted in June 1917. The majority of the awards made were to civilians and, although members of the Navy and Army had been admitted to the order since its creation, it was not until December 1918 that a Military Division was created and backdated to June 1917. As far as can be ascertained, four officers who served with the 9th Royal Irish Fusiliers were made Officers of the Order (OBE) for meritorious service having moved on to other appointments:

BERRY MB Major W S S Royal Army Medical Corps - For services as Deputy Assistant Director of Medical Services on the Staff of X Corps and then at Headquarters Army of the Rhine (LG 3 June 1919).

FITZGERALD Colonel W C - For services as Commanding Officer of the 10th (Reserve) Battalion, Princess Victoria's (Royal Irish Fusiliers).

IRWIN CSI Captain G R - For his war service as Head of Section of the Contraband Department, Foreign Office (LG 30 March 1920).

WHITLA Major V G 3rd (King's Own) Hussars - For service as an Aide-de-Camp (LG 3 June 1919).

The Distinguished Service Order

The Distinguished Service Order was instituted by Royal Warrant in 1886 for meritorious or distinguished service in war. Bars for subsequent acts of gallantry were permitted as a result of a Royal Warrant in August 1916. Due to the wording of the original Warrant, between 1914 and 1916 some awards were made for circumstances not under fire. It was felt by many that the Distinguished Service Order should be restricted to services performed in action, and this was the subject of an order issued in January 1917. In the period from August 1914 to May 1920, 9,767 War Office awards were made, including bars, with 882 Admiralty awards and 61 Air Ministry awards.

Four officers were made Companions of the Distinguished Service Order for gallantry while serving with the 9th Royal Irish Fusiliers:

BLACKER Lieutenant Colonel S W W - For gallantry as Commanding Officer. King's New Year Honours Gazette - no citation (LG 1 January 1917).

DESPARD MC Captain C B 6th (Inniskilling) Dragoons - The withdrawal from St Quentin 22 - 27 March 1918 (LG 16 September 1918).

For conspicuous gallantry and devotion to duty. During five days of retirement, while as second-in-command of the battalion, he throughout displayed very high qualities as a leader. While in command of the rearguard the gallantry and determination with which he disputed the ground was largely responsible for the safe withdrawal of the rest of the main body.

FORDE MC* Lieutenant Colonel G M The Royal Inniskilling Fusiliers - Commanding Officer, 20 July 1918, north of Bailleul (LG 15 October 1918).

For conspicuous gallantry and devotion to duty. In company with another officer he crawled out about 400 yards from the front line under full observation from the enemy lines, and remained out about seven hours, making a most daring reconnaissance of the enemy's position, and gaining most valuable information from which he organised a successful raid on the enemy's position. By his personal courage and coolness he set a splendid example to his battalion.

PRATT Major A C - For gallant service as Second-in-Command up to August 1916. King's New Year Honours Gazette - no citation (LG 1 January 1917).

Two officers who had served with the 9th Royal Irish Fusiliers were made Companions of the Distinguished Service Order for gallantry while serving elsewhere; one was awarded a bar:

McCARTHY-O'LEARY MC Major (Acting Lieutenant Colonel) H W D - Commanding Officer, 1st Battalion, The Royal Irish Rifles, Zonnebeek Redoubt, Battle of Langemarck, 16 August 1917 (LG 26 September 1917).

For conspicuous gallantry and devotion to duty. During a heavy hostile counter-attack, which had driven in his advance post and recaptured part of the position, he went forward with one runner, rallied his men and led them forward again, driving the enemy back and restoring the situation. He remained encouraging his men until he was himself severely wounded half an hour later, but he did not leave the field until he had reported the situation to his Brigadier.

Bar - Commanding Officer, 1st Battalion, The Royal Irish Rifles, Erches, 27 March 1918 (LG 16 September 1918).

For conspicuous gallantry and devotion to duty. He was wounded, but refused to be evacuated, and during the severe fighting which ensued he remained in action in command of his battalion until again severely wounded. He displayed marked ability in encouraging and handling his troops, and showed great cheerfulness and disregard for his own safety.

TAMPLIN Captain R J A The Connaught Rangers - Company Commander, 6th (Service) Battalion, The Connaught Rangers, 16th (Irish) Division at Guillemont, 3 September 1916 (LG 14 November 1916).

For conspicuous gallantry in action. He led his company with the greatest courage and determination, and was instrumental in capturing the position. He was wounded.

Distinguished Conduct Medal

After its institution by Royal Warrant in December 1854, the early years of the Distinguished Conduct Medal were complicated by various changes to the Warrant but, in essence, it was awarded to soldiers for individual acts of distinguished conduct in the field. During the period from August 1914 to May 1920, 25,072 awards were made, including 472 bars and nine second bars. While there were fewer cases of the Distinguished Conduct Medal being awarded for valuable conduct behind the lines, an order was issued in January 1917, like that for the Distinguished Service Order, restricting the award of the Distinguished Conduct Medal as far as possible to the 'Fighting Services'. The medal was highly prized and many awards were made for acts that fell just short of the level of gallantry required of the Victoria Cross.

Of the seventy-eight awards made to men of Princess Victoria's (Royal Irish Fusiliers), nineteen were awarded to men serving with the 9th Royal Irish Fusiliers:

ARMSTRONG Lance Corporal R 41695 - Courtrai, 16 October 1918 (LG 2 December 1919).

> *On 16th October, 1918, at the crossing of the Lys Canal at Courtrai, he was in command of a Lewis gun section which he took across in the first boat under machine-gun barrage, having volunteered for the job. By getting his gun into position on the other side of the canal he was able to cover the remainder of the party. He personally fired the gun and put out of action two enemy machine-guns. When the enemy were massing for a counter-attack he crossed a main street to get into a position from which he could fire and disperse the enemy, inflicting many casualties. Throughout the day he showed a splendid fighting spirit.*

BARTON Sergeant H 14040 (LG 1 January 1918).

> *For conspicuous gallantry and devotion to duty over a long period. He has taken part in many important engagements, and has always shown courage and leadership of a high order and great coolness under fire. On one occasion he took command during an action with great success when all his officers became casualties.*

CARVELL Sergeant S 17545 - The first award of the Distinguished Conduct Medal to a soldier of the Battalion. Battle of Langemarck, 16 August 1917 (LG 19 November 1917).

> *For conspicuous gallantry and devotion to duty when left in command of his company owing to casualties. He led the men forward, and after being forced to withdraw, reorganised them and led them forward again under heavy machine-gun fire.*

GRACEY Acting Lance Corporal J 41572 - Attack at Wulverghem, 4 September 1918 (LG 5 December 1918).

> *For conspicuous gallantry and devotion to duty. After his section commander had been wounded he took command and led a charge on two enemy machine-gun positions, inflicting heavy casualties on the enemy. Subsequently, though wounded himself, he assisted the stretcher-bearers in bringing in the wounded under heavy machine-gun fire.*

GREGG Lance Corporal W 11216 - Attack at Vijfwegen, 30 September 1918. Lance Corporal Gregg was killed in action the next day (LG 10 January 1920).

> *Near Dadizeele, on 30th September, 1918, this non-commissioned officer led*

his section with remarkable courage. During hand-to-hand fighting, he saved his officer's life by killing one of the enemy who was about to shoot him. When a hostile machine-gun got into action on the flank, he brought his Lewis gun across, killed seven of the team and silenced the gun.

HOMERSHAM MM* Sergeant F S 45807 - Courtrai, 16 October 1918 (LG 2 December 1919).

For conspicuous gallantry and good work. At Courtrai on the 16th October, 1918, during the crossing of the River Lys, which was made under heavy machine-gun fire, he was one of the first to land from a small boat and skilfully led his men to the attack. He established a post in such a position as to minimise the effect of an enemy machine-gun and eventually put it out of action. When our force was ordered to retire he volunteered to swim across the canal, carrying a rope to pull the pontoon boat across.

HUGHES MM Sergeant J 4517 - Guiscard during the withdrawal from St Quentin, 23 March 1918. Sergeant Hughes was killed in action a few days later (LG 3 September 1918).

For conspicuous gallantry and devotion to duty. He went forward with a Lewis gun and knocked out an enemy machine-gun which was firing on our right flank. When the team was disabled, although wounded himself, he kept the gun in action until reinforcements came up.

LOCKHART Acting Sergeant J 41148 - Earned in 1918, including for a raid at Shoddy Farm north of Bailleul, 22 July 1918 (LG 3 September 1919).

For conspicuous gallantry and good work in the line during the past year, including the following engagements: St Quentin, March, 1918; Kemmel, April, 1918. He has at all times shown great keenness in carrying out minor enterprises and showed great gallantry in leading a bombing party, when his company carried out a raid in July, 1918.

LUCAS MM Company Sergeant Major R 14414 - Withdrawal from St Quentin, March 1918 (LG 3 September 1918). Recommended for the Victoria Cross.

For conspicuous gallantry and devotion to duty. Displayed great coolness and courage in rallying the line round a village and by his fine example was instrumental in saving a critical situation.

McBRIDE Sergeant R J 23566 - Wulverghem, 12 April 1918 (LG 3 October 1918).

For conspicuous gallantry and devotion to duty. When all the officers of his company had become casualties he rallied his men, whom he led with great gallantry and ability in a successful counter attack. During the consolidation of the new position he used the Lewis gun with great effect, forcing the enemy machine-gunners to vacate their positions. On three separate occasions, he left the cover of one trench to go out into the open, under heavy rifle fire at close range, to bring in three wounded men, which he succeeded in doing. His courage in facing what looked like certain death was a wonderful example to all around him.

McCLEAN Acting Company Sergeant Major W J 14556 - Attack at Meulenhouck north of Bailleul, 24 August 1918 (LG 15 November 1918).

During an attack he got round the flank of a machine-gun that was causing casualties to our men, and killed four of the team and put the gun out of action. When the enemy counter attacked, he skilfully disposed two Lewis guns, and opening fire on the enemy at point blank range he broke up the counter attack on his front with very heavy losses. He displayed great gallantry and very high qualities of leadership and initiative.

McCULLOUGH Sergeant J 14555 - For gallantry as the Battalion Signals Sergeant (LG 3 September 1919).

As signalling sergeant to the battalion he has always shown great gallantry and devotion to duty in the field. During heavy fighting in March and April, and again later, the battalion was without a signalling officer. He never failed to perform all the duties which fell upon his shoulders with the most conspicuous efficiency and success. His cheerfulness and total disregard of fatigue and danger under the most trying of circumstances proved a splendid example to all who have come in contact with him.

NEILL Sergeant W 14577 - For gallantry as the Battalion Transport Sergeant (LG 21 October 1918). (The notifications of his death in the local (Lurgan) press by his family indicate that he had a Bar to the DCM. His gravestone also reflects this. No record of a Bar has been found. His medals, which are held by the family, show a rosette sown on the DCM ribbon.)

For conspicuous gallantry and devotion to duty. He has been with the battalion since its formation, and has rendered very valuable service as transport sergeant. His unfailing cheerfulness, coolness under fire and zealousness have been most marked.

PAMENTER Sergeant W R 43351 - Raid at Havrincourt, 3 November 1917 (LG 28 March 1918).

For conspicuous gallantry and devotion to duty in leading the advance party during a raid having skilfully got past the enemy outposts and up to the gap in his wire. Seeing a large party coming through the gap he immediately charged and himself shot and bayoneted no less than six of the enemy who offered a fierce resistance. Having cleared the gap, he led his men into the trench, saw the party started in the right direction, and then established blocks.

ROBINSON Company Quarter Master Sergeant J 14642 - Attack on Moeuvres, 23 November 1917 (LG 28 March 1918).

For conspicuous gallantry and devotion to duty when acting as company sergeant major in an attack on a village. He took command when his officers were wounded and displayed initiative and boldness in leading the advance and in clearing the enemy from houses and cellars when the village was reached. He rendered valuable assistance in repelling an enemy counter attack.

ROE Corporal H 41147 - Attack on Moeuvres, 23 November 1917 (LG 28 March 1918).

For conspicuous gallantry and devotion to duty. When his platoon commander was wounded he took command of the left flank and secured it against counter attacks. He held up the enemy's advance with great determination, and was responsible for bringing into our lines several wounded men.

SELBY Company Quarter Master Sergeant H 18240 - Attack at Vijfwegen, 30 September 1918 (LG 10 January 1920).

For conspicuous gallantry and devotion to duty near Dadizeele, 30th September, 1918. Owing to the exposed position of his company he got the mules as close as possible, and personally carried bags of rations through the heaviest fire to his company. His self-sacrifice on behalf of the welfare of his company was beyond praise.

SIMONS Private W 14689 - Attack at Meulenhouck north of Bailleul, 24 August 1918 (LG 11 March 1920).

He has served in France since 4th October, 1915, and continuous engagements from 28th September to November 1918. On August 24th, during an enemy counter attack, he went through severe hostile barrage with valuable information to battalion, enabling them to bring down artillery support which broke the counter attack.

VENNARD Company Sergeant Major T 14746 - Attack on Moeuvres, 23 November 1917 (LG 28 March 1918).

For conspicuous gallantry and devotion to duty. He took command of a reserve platoon and led it into action under intense fire. He collected and reorganised men of several units and led them forward, setting a splendid example of initiative and leadership throughout the action.

Two awards of the Distinguished Conduct Medal were made to men before they joined the 9th Royal Irish Fusiliers:

MERVYN Corporal M 5631 - At Armentieres in 1915 serving with the 2nd Battalion in 82nd Brigade, 27th Division (LG 14 January 1916).

For conspicuous gallantry. When the flank of his company had become exposed, on his own initiative, he crawled, under fire, to a neighbouring trench, whence by firing his rifle and using flares during the night, he led the enemy to believe the trench was still occupied.

MURPHY Sergeant J J 20071 - On a raid with 8th (Service) Battalion, 49th Brigade, 16th (Irish) Division on 11 July 1916. (LG 22 September 1916). He was one of only two men (the other being Captain G W Eaton) from his party of thirty men to enter the enemy line. Subsequently Second Lieutenant J J Murphy MC*, DCM.

For conspicuous bravery during a raid on a hostile trench, when he forced his way through the enemy's entanglement in spite of being wounded and partially stunned. He stuck to his work and protected the flank by throwing bombs, although severely wounded again.

Military Cross

The lack of a suitable award for gallantry for junior officers and warrant officers of the Army resulted in a Royal Warrant in December 1914 instituting the Military Cross for distinguished and meritorious service. As was the case with the Distinguished Service Order and Distinguished Conduct Medal, this was restricted to acts of gallantry in the field from January 1917. During the period from August 1914 to May 1920, 40,236 awards were made including 2,983 first bars, 168 second bars and four third bars.

A total of fifty-six awards was made to men who served with the 9th Royal Irish Fusiliers, which includes two awards made to Warrant Officers and nine bars. Of these, thirty-six awards were made for acts of gallantry by men while serving with the 9th Royal Irish Fusiliers:

BALLY Captain The Reverend H S Army Chaplains' Department - Wulverghem, 13 April 1918 (LG 16 September 1918).

For conspicuous gallantry and devotion to duty in action, when he constantly went out, under heavy shell and machine-gun fire, to find and collect wounded who were lying in the open and to bring them in. Throughout the night he set a splendid example of devotion to duty.

BARBOUR Regimental Quartermaster Sergeant J 13994 - For distinguished and gallant service with 36th (Ulster) Division in France since October 1915. King's Birthday Honours Gazette - no citation (LG 3 June 1918).

BRYSON Second Lieutenant J - Wulverghem, 4 September 1918 (LG 2 December 1918).

This officer led his platoon with great dash and gallantry over open ground, subjected to heavy machine-gun fire, capturing one gun and its crew. He then formed a defensive flank with his platoon, maintaining his position, under withering machine-gun fire, both frontal and enfilade, until it became necessary to withdraw.

BURROWS Second Lieutenant H C - Wulverghem, 4 September 1918 (LG 2 December 1918).

This officer led and commanded his platoon with great courage, and displayed considerable initiative in working round enemy machine-guns. He maintained his position on the objective till both his flanks were turned, and then extracted his men from a difficult situation with much coolness.

BURROWS Captain O V Royal Army Medical Corps - Battle of Langemarck, 16 August 1917 (LG 18 October 1917).

For conspicuous gallantry and devotion to duty. For 40 hours he worked unceasingly succouring the wounded, about 300 of whom passed through his hands during that period.

CROSBIE Second Lieutenant T E C - Raid at Havrincourt, 3 November 1917 (LG 18 January 1918).

For conspicuous gallantry and devotion to duty when in charge of a party detailed to blow a gap in the enemy wire. He successfully fired his ammonal tube, cutting the first belt, and though heavily bombed and having three of his seven men wounded, cut his way through the second belt by hand, and drove the enemy out of some shell holes. After returning to our lines he went out with a search party and brought in a wounded man a distance of 400 yards under heavy fire. After going back three miles to billets, and finding that there were more men missing he returned and searched "No Man's Land" again.

Bar - (Captain) Withdrawal from St Quentin, 21 March 1918 (LG 16 September 1918).

For conspicuous gallantry and devotion to duty during a retirement. He handled his company with great coolness, and by his fine disregard of personal danger encouraged them to successfully cover the retirement of the battalion. He saw to the evacuation of all wounded under heavy artillery and machine-gun fire, and throughout set a splendid example of courage and determination.

DARLING Second Lieutenant J - Withdrawal on 24 March 1918 (LG 16 September 1918).

For conspicuous gallantry and devotion to duty. Although twice wounded in the course of the day, this officer refused to leave his men, and with his platoon rendered great service in covering a retirement and re-establishing the line.

Bar - Goldflake Farm, Hill 41 near Dadizeele, 11 October 1918 (LG 15 February 1919).

At Hill 41 near Dadizeele on October 11th, 1918, he was in charge of two platoons which attacked a strongly held farm. With great skill and courage he led the party, captured the farm with fourteen prisoners, three machine-guns and killed about ten of the enemy. He rushed a post that was giving trouble, thus averting many casualties. His cheerfulness and coolness throughout the day inspired all ranks. When the enemy counter attacked he kept the garrison under complete control firing point blank into the enemy who attacked in mass. He held on until nearly surrounded and then skilfully withdrew his party still fighting.

DEAN Captain H S - Withdrawal from St Quentin over the period 21-23 March 1918 (LG 16 September 1918).

For conspicuous gallantry and devotion to duty. When all the troops on his left had retired, this officer held his position with great determination, subsequently falling back and protecting the left flank.

DESPARD Captain C B 6th (Inniskilling) Dragoons - Moeuvres, 23 November 1917 (LG 4 February 1918).

For conspicuous gallantry and devotion to duty. During the attack he commanded his company with the greatest skill and gallantry, clearing a portion of the village on the flank of the battalion. At dusk, seeing that he was in danger of being cut off, he withdrew his own and two other companies, evacuated all the wounded, and held a line south of the village. During all this time he moved about under very heavy machine-gun fire, regardless of personal danger, and displayed the greatest coolness and courage.

DOBBYN Lieutenant A L - Raid at Meulenhouck near Bailleul, 14 August 1918. Accompanied by Sergeant J Downey of the 1st Battalion who was awarded a DCM and Second Lieutenant J I Smith, who had been attached to the 1st Battalion since June 1918 (LG 7 November 1918). This award is a **Bar**, see first award below, page 381.

For conspicuous gallantry in entering the enemy's lines in daylight to obtain an identification. He showed the officer and NCO who accompanied him a gap in the wire, and they entered the lines, where a sharp hand-to-hand fight ensued, and several of the enemy were killed or wounded. He displayed the greatest gallantry and disregard of danger, and obtained the identification.

FERGUSON DCM Major A - For his service as Adjutant. New Year's Honours Gazette - no citation (LG 1 January 1918).

FLOOD Captain R S - Battle of Langemarck, 16 August 1917 (LG 18 October 1917).

For conspicuous gallantry and devotion to duty when in command of his company during an attack. He secured the objective after stubborn resistance. When compelled to retire owing to the troops on his flanks falling back, he conducted the withdrawal with great coolness, and held a position further back.

GIVEN Captain T F - Battle of Langemarck, 16 August 1917 (LG 16 October 1917).

For conspicuous gallantry and devotion to duty as second-in-command of his battalion. Before the attack he visited every wave and saw that everything was in order. He took forward a party of details from battalion headquarters to reinforce the centre which had suffered heavy casualties and was being very hard pressed. He remained in command at this point, although twice wounded, and was only persuaded to leave his post after receiving a third wound, which rendered both arms useless.

GODSON Lieutenant E A - Patrol near Messines, 14 August 1916. This was the first Military Cross awarded to an officer of the Battalion (LG 26 September 1916). This is a first award, see **Bar** below, page 381.

> *For conspicuous gallantry and good work. He organised and led a patrol which took four enemy prisoners and killed two without any loss to our side.*

GREENAWAY Second Lieutenant W G - South-west of St Quentin, 9 March 1918 (LG 13 May 1918).

> *For conspicuous gallantry and devotion to duty. He located an enemy machine-gun some 300 yards in front of our lines, and crawled out in daylight with three men to attack it. Though he was observed by the enemy while crawling through their wire he rushed the post, drove off the enemy and captured the machine-gun. He set a splendid example of daring and initiative.*

HALAHAN Captain The Reverend F J Army Chaplains' Department - For his gallantry as Chaplain to the 9th Royal Irish Fusiliers. King's Birthday Honours Gazette - no citation (LG 4 June 1917). This is a first award, see **Bar** below, page 381.

HENAHAN Captain M - Raid at Spanbroekmolen, 4 June 1917 (LG 16 August 1917).

> *For conspicuous gallantry and devotion to duty. When in command of a strong raiding party, he led them with great skill and complete success, inflicting heavy casualties upon the enemy and capturing many prisoners. He has previously displayed leadership of a very high standard.*

LEAHY Second Lieutenant T C - Raid at Shoddy Farm north of Bailleul, 22 July 1918 (LG 15 October 1918).

> *For conspicuous gallantry and devotion to duty during a raid. When his party was discovered by the enemy before the raid was due to start he rushed forward alone, under heavy machine-gun fire, and cut a gap in the enemy wire to enable his platoon to get through. By his fine example of personal courage he kept his platoon together, captured two machine-guns, and enabled the rest of the party to withdraw.*

LOGAN Second Lieutenant S - Attack at Vijfwegen, 30 September 1918 (LG 1 February 1919).

> *For conspicuous gallantry near Dadizeele on the 30th September, 1918, while leading his platoon in the attack on an enemy strong-point, which was captured and a number of the enemy killed or taken prisoner. Later, when his company commander was mortally wounded and lying in the open, he went out under withering fire and brought him in.*

Bar - Crossing of the Lys Canal at Courtrai, 16 October 1918 (LG 8 March 1919).

> *At Courtrai, on 16th October, 1918, he was ordered to take his platoon, under very heavy machine-gun fire, across a pontoon bridge thrown across the Lys Canal to reinforce a party who had already crossed. While crossing, the bridge was destroyed but he crossed on a pontoon boat, and for 4 hours maintained his position on the enemy side of the canal and was of the greatest assistance to the bridgehead party. He showed cool courage and able leadership.*

MENAUL Captain W J - The attack at Hamel, 1 July 1916 (LG 14 November 1916).

> *For conspicuous gallantry during operations. With five scouts he observed the operations from an exposed position only 400 yards from the enemy lines. He was under heavy shell and machine-gun fire throughout the day, but sent in twenty-one clear messages to his CO. He has also done fine work on patrol.*

MILES Second Lieutenant R D - For service in the field including a raid on 12 October 1916. King's Birthday Honours Gazette - no citation (LG 4 June 1917).

MORGAN Lieutenant H S United States Army Medical Corps - Withdrawal from St Quentin, March 1918. (LG 24 October 1918).

> *For conspicuous gallantry and devotion to duty during the retirement from Grand Seraucourt on the morning of March 22nd. This officer was retiring behind the rearguard, and on approaching Artemps was told that some wounded were still lying in Grand Seraucourt. Although he knew that the enemy was already on the outskirts of the village he returned at once with some stretcher bearers and succeeded in bringing out the wounded. He thus at the commencement of the operations set a splendid example to his stretcher bearers of devotion and courage.*

MURPHY DCM Second Lieutenant J J - Raid at Havrincourt, 3 November 1917 (LG 18 January 1918).

> *For conspicuous gallantry and devotion to duty when in charge of the advance party of a raid. Though half the party were engaged with the outposts, he pushed on and cleared the front trench, killing many of the enemy, and then withdrew all his men successfully. He went back twice with search parties looking for missing men, and brought in one under heavy fire. After getting to billets three miles behind the line, finding some men missing, he returned again to the trenches and penetrated 400 yards beyond. In all he went out four times, and did not finally return till twelve hours after the raid.*

Bar - Raid at Shoddy Farm north of Bailleul, 22 July 1918 (LG 15 October 1918).

> *For conspicuous gallantry and devotion to duty. He made a most daring reconnaissance of the enemy's position from close quarters and gained valuable information. Two nights later, while leading a raiding party, he single-handed rushed a machine-gun and shot two of the team, making the rest run. He has continuously shown great courage and ability in every operation he has undertaken.*

OZZARD Second Lieutenant H T - Raid at Spanbroekmolen, 4 June 1917 (LG 16 August 1917).

> *For conspicuous gallantry and devotion to duty while taking part in a successful raid upon enemy trenches. He showed great courage and firm leadership, and has on previous occasions distinguished himself in a similar manner.*

PARTRIDGE Captain J H - Attack on Moeuvres, 23 December 1917 (LG 1 January 1918).

> *For conspicuous gallantry and devotion to duty. During an attack and the subsequent withdrawal he went out under very heavy shell and machine-gun fire and attempted to keep touch with the situation, which was very involved. He sent back frequent messages, which were of the utmost assistance to his commanding officer. He displayed untiring energy and a total disregard of personal danger.*

REYNOLDS Second Lieutenant E W - Attack at Vijfwegen, 30 September and 1 October 1918 (LG 1 February 1919).

> *For conspicuous gallantry near Dadizeele on 30th September and 1st October, 1918. When the advance of his company was held up by the enemy in a farm, he went forward and cut a gap in the strong enemy wire, under close machine-gun fire, and then led his platoon round the enemy's position, and so*

enabled his company to capture it. That night he did excellent work in command of a patrol, sending back much useful information and patrolling deep into the enemy lines. Being unable to get back before dawn, he remained out all day, and successfully brought his men back next night. His courage and successful handling of his platoon were a great asset to his company.

ROBINSON Captain G - Attack at Meulenhouck north of Bailleul, 24 August 1918 (LG 7 November 1918).

For conspicuous gallantry in action. He led the company of which he was in command with much determination and skill during an attack. He was wounded, but remained with his men until he had seen the whole company dug in on the objective, and then left the line to have his wound dressed only when ordered to do so. He set a fine example of courage and endurance.

STEELE Second Lieutenant C H - Attack at Vijfwegen, 30 September and 1 October 1918 (LG 1 February 1919).

For conspicuous gallantry near Dadizeele on the 30th September and 1st October, 1918, while commanding his platoon. His leadership was largely instrumental in the capture of an important strong-point, when many of the enemy were killed and captured. For 36 hours he held an exposed position under heavy trench mortar and machine-gun fire.

Bar - Crossing of the Lys Canal at Courtrai, 16 October 1918 (LG 8 March 1919).

At Courtrai on 16th October, 1918, he was in charge of a party of about fifty-four men who were to form a bridgehead to a pontoon bridge being thrown across the Lys Canal. When the bridge was constructed, he led his party across under heavy machine-gun fire. The bridge was destroyed by shell fire immediately afterwards. He rushed an enemy machine-gun post in a house commanding the bridge, and captured it with a team of six men. By his great courage and dash he rendered valuable service.

TURNER Regimental Sergeant Major C H 17397 - Battle of Langemarck, 16 August 1917 (LG 18 October 1917).

For conspicuous gallantry and devotion to duty in going forward with reinforcements to the front line, where they were being heavily pressed and had suffered heavy casualties. After the majority of the officers had been killed or wounded he supervised the defence of the line and organised arrangements for the evacuation of the wounded.

TURNER Lieutenant E J L - Withdrawal from St Quentin, 21 to 26 March 1918 (LG 16 September 1918).

For conspicuous gallantry and devotion to duty. This officer, in charge of the transport, never failed to bring rations to the battalion during a weeks fighting. One day he brought up ammunition when it was urgently required, bringing it through a heavy barrage, and through villages which were being shelled, and getting his limbers safely back. His courage and judgement resulted in him keeping his transport intact.

VESEY Captain G W - Fighting patrol at Marcoing, 15 December 1917 (LG 4 March 1918).

For conspicuous gallantry and devotion to duty. He led a patrol and rushed and captured an enemy machine-gun which was in action in a trench running out from our lines and killed several of the crew. He then established a block in the trench and so improved the position. His initiative and resource were a splendid example to his men.

Twenty awards of the Military Cross were made for acts of gallantry by men while serving elsewhere:

BAREFOOT Captain G W N - Company Commander, 1st Battalion, 10th Brigade, 4th Division. South of Serre, 1 July 1916 (LG 22 September 1916).

For conspicuous gallantry in action. He held on to the position gained until ordered to withdraw 18 hours later, having successfully repulsed three enemy attacks. When he withdrew he brought back a trench gun, a machine-gun, three prisoners and all his wounded.

DOBBYN Second Lieutenant A L - 8th (Service) Battalion, 49th Brigade, 16th (Irish) Division, Leuze Wood near Ginchy, 6 September 1916 (LG 14 November 1916). This is a first award, see **Bar** above, page 377.

For conspicuous gallantry in action. When the enemy made a counter attack on a wood, he showed great pluck and initiative under heavy shell fire. It was partly due to his fine example that the enemy was driven off.

FITZGERALD Captain J G E Machine Gun Corps - For service with 108th Brigade Machine Gun Company. New Year's Honours Gazette - no citation (LG 1 January 1917).

FITZSIMON Second Lieutenant C R D M O'C The Prince of Wales's Leinster Regiment (Royal Canadians) - Platoon Commander, 2nd Battalion, The Prince of Wales's Leinster Regiment (Royal Canadians) at Gheleuwe, 30 September 1918 (LG 15 February 1919).

For conspicuous gallantry and able leadership at Gheleuwe on September 30th, 1918. When his company in the attack was held up by very severe machine-gun fire he most skilfully continued to get his platoon forward to a position 400 yards in advance of the remainder of the line, thus enabling the company to move forward and capture the position. His fine leadership and gallant behaviour were responsible for the success of the operation.

FORDE Captain G M The Royal Inniskilling Fusiliers - Company Commander, 11th (Service) Battalion, The Royal Inniskilling Fusiliers (Donegal and Fermanagh), 109th Brigade. King's birthday Honours Gazette - no citation (LG 4 June 1917).

Bar - Company Commander, 11th (Service) Battalion, The Royal Inniskilling Fusiliers (Donegal and Fermanagh), 109th Brigade. Attack at Wytschaete, 7 June 1917 (LG 17 September 1917).

For conspicuous gallantry and devotion to duty in leading his company in the attack. He sent back valuable information, and although severely wounded as he reached the final objective, he issued full instructions for the consolidation before being carried back.

GODSON Captain E A - Brigade Major of 107th Brigade in October 1918 (LG 8 March 1919). This is a **Bar**, see first award above, page 378.

For conspicuous gallantry and devotion to duty from 9th to 23rd October, 1918, whilst acting as Brigade Major, 107th Infantry Brigade. On the 19th October, in the neighbourhood of Oyghem Wood, and on the 22nd October, in the neighbourhood of the Klitzberg, he made two reconnaissances bringing back important information. He set a fine example to all ranks. His work during the whole period of active operations was excellent.

HALAHAN Captain The Reverend F J Army Chaplains' Department - For his gallantry as 36th (Ulster) Division Chaplain at the Battle of Langemarck, 16 August 1917 (LG 18 October 1917). This is a **Bar**, see first award above, page 378.

For conspicuous gallantry and devotion to duty. Under heavy shell fire he organised and assisted personally in the evacuation of large numbers of wounded.

KERR Major R G The Royal Inniskilling Fusiliers - 7th (Service) Battalion, The Royal Inniskilling Fusiliers, 49th Brigade, 16th (Irish) Division. New Year's Honours Gazette - no citation (LG 1 January 1917).

McCARTHY-O'LEARY Captain H W D - Adjutant of the 2nd Battalion in France in 82nd Brigade, 27th Division. New Year's Honours Gazette - no citation (LG 14 January 1916).

McFARLAND Second Lieutenant F J E - 5th/6th (Service) Battalion, 31st Brigade, 10th (Irish) Division during General Allenby's advance in Palestine (LG 26 July 1918).

For conspicuous gallantry and devotion to duty. Though wounded early while in a difficult position under heavy machine-gun fire, he continued to encourage his platoon. Wounded again, he stayed till the situation was cleared.

MILNE Captain C W The Royal Inniskilling Fusiliers - Formerly Regimental Quartermaster Sergeant. For service with 109th Brigade Trench Mortar Battery. King's Birthday Honours Gazette - no citation (LG 3 June 1919).

OWLES Lieutenant E T - Earned as a pilot with the Royal Flying Corps during a reconnaissance patrol over Bourlon Village, 22 November 1917 during the Battle of Cambrai (LG 18 January 1918).

For conspicuous gallantry and devotion to duty. He made a successful wire reconnaissance along a corps front at a height of 300 to 800 feet under heavy machine-gun and rifle fire. On another occasion when on a reconnoitring patrol he had four encounters with enemy aeroplanes, in one of which he was attacked at 800 feet by five enemy scouts. By his clever manoeuvring the enemy machines were driven off, and he completed a valuable reconnaissance. He showed the greatest keenness and determination at his work.

SAUNDERSON Second Lieutenant W R - 108th Trench Mortar Battery (LG 11 January 1919).

Whilst in command of a section of mortars in operation, he went forward with the infantry and with great courage and skill engaged several hostile machine-guns which were holding them up, thus enabling them to advance. Later, during severe fighting, he located two enemy snipers who were firing at our men, and going forward, killed one and took the other prisoner.

SMITH Second Lieutenant J I - 1st Battalion. Raid at Meulenhouck, Bailleul, 14 August 1918. Accompanied by Sergeant J Downey, also of the 1st Battalion, who was awarded a DCM, and Second Lieutenant A L Dobbyn of the 9th Royal Irish Fusiliers (LG 7 November 1918).

For conspicuous gallantry and devotion to duty. Accompanied by another officer and an NCO he entered the enemy's trenches in daylight. He killed and wounded some of the enemy, and was then forced to retire by a machine-gun. After the gun had ceased firing he re-entered the enemy's lines and brought back one of the enemy, who had been wounded, thus obtaining an identification. He displayed great courage and determination throughout.

SOWERBY Captain E S Royal Army Medical Corps - Medical Officer, 108th Field Ambulance. Battle of Langemarck, 16 August 1917 (LG 18 October 1917).

> *For conspicuous gallantry and devotion to duty in guiding parties of bearers and bringing back wounded in the open over most difficult ground and under heavy fire. On one occasion he led a party through a heavy barrage and succeeded in collecting many wounded from close to the enemy's lines.*

SPARKS Lieutenant W - 7th/8th (Service) Battalion, 49th Brigade, 16th (Irish) Division) at the Battle of Langemarck, 16 August 1917 (LG 18 October 1917).

> *For conspicuous gallantry and devotion to duty. When a heavy counter-attack on our positions led to a certain amount of confusion, he went forward through a heavy barrage of shells and machine-gun fire and reorganised the battalion and established a sound line of defence, so averting what would have been a most critical situation.*

SUTCLIFFE Captain W H Royal Army Medical Corps - 103rd Field Ambulance, 34th Division, 27/28 July 1918 during an attack by the French XXX Corps at the Marne (LG 7 November 1918).

> *For conspicuous gallantry when acting as ambulance bearer officer. He superintended the clearing of wounded under heavy fire, and successfully evacuated all casualties from the posts under very trying conditions. Though several of his stretcher bearers were wounded he kept in constant touch with the units in the line. His untiring devotion was a splendid example to the men.*

WILDING Lieutenant A - 7th/8th (Service) Battalion, 49th Brigade, 16th (Irish) Division. Fontaine Les Croisilles, west of Cambrai, 20 November 1917 (LG 18 February 1918).

> *For conspicuous gallantry and devotion to duty. He led forward a party and captured an enemy machine-gun emplacement which was causing heavy casualties, taking twenty-three prisoners and two machine-guns. He showed splendid gallantry and fearlessness.*

YOUNG Second Lieutenant J B A - 108th Trench Mortar Battery. Attack at Vijfwegen, 30 September 1918 (LG 1 February 1919).

> *For conspicuous gallantry and devotion to duty south-east of Dadizeele on 30th September, 1918. He brought his trench mortar into action in the open under heavy machine-gun fire 250 yards from a farm. When his base plate broke, he stood up and held the mortar until all his ammunition was fired, putting a machine-gun out of action. He then used his team as infantry and joined in the attack protecting a flank. He was eventually wounded, after much good work.*

Military Medal

In line with the creation of the Military Cross, the Military Medal was instituted by Royal Warrant in March 1916 for non-commissioned officers and men of the Army for acts of bravery in the field. A number of awards were made retrospectively but the majority were granted after May 1916. In total, 121,554 awards were made up to May 1920, including 5,796 first bars, 180 second bars and one third bar. Very few citations were produced for the Military Medal but it has been possible to identify where the majority that are listed here were earned.

Eighty-seven awards of the Military Medal for acts of gallantry were made to men serving with the 9th Royal Irish Fusiliers. This includes three bars to first awards earned with this Battalion and one bar to a first award that had been earned elsewhere:

ADAMS Sergeant J 13971 - Battle of Langemarck, 16 August 1917 (LG 19 November 1917).

Bar - Raid at Shoddy Farm north of Bailleul, 22 July 1918 (LG 13 November 1918). Recommended for the Distinguished Conduct Medal.

ADAMSON Private W 41271 - Withdrawal from St Quentin, 21-27 March 1918 (LG 29 August 1918).

ANDERSON Private J 49974 - Crossing of the River Lys, mid-October 1918 (LG 17 June 1919).

ATKINS Corporal B 43461 - Attack at Wulverghem, 4 September 1918 (LG 13 March 1919).

AVERELL Private R 41534 - Raid at Havrincourt, 3 November 1917 (LG 23 February 1918).

BAIRD Sergeant T H 5581 - Wulverghem, April 1918 (LG 7 October 1918).

BUCKLEY Private R 14021 - Attack at Moeuvres, 23 November 1917 (LG 25 April 1918).

CAMPBELL Sergeant J 13501 - Crossing of the River Lys, mid-October 1918 (LG 17 June 1919).

CHAMBERS Private T C 41256 - Raid at Havrincourt, 3 November 1917 (LG 23 February 1918).

CLARKE Lance Corporal A G H 41483 - Fighting patrol at Marcoing, 15 December 1917 (LG 19 March 1918).

CLARKE Lance Corporal D 14077 - Attack north of Bailleul, 24 August 1918 (LG 24 January 1919).

CLEMENTS Corporal T 17151 - Ambush near Messines, 14 August 1916 (recommended for Distinguished Conduct Medal) (LG 21 September 1916).

COULTER Private J 41530 - Attack north of Bailleul, 24 August 1918 (LG 24 January 1919).

CRAIG Corporal G 23438 - Raid at Havrincourt, 3 November 1917 (LG 23 February 1918).

CRAVEN Lance Corporal J 43276 - Raid on La Petite Douve Farm, 12 October 1916 (LG 19 February 1917).

CRICHTON Private D 11864 - Attack north of Bailleul, 24 August 1918 (LG 24 January 1919).

CRILLY Private J 14090 - Attack north of Bailleul, 24 August 1918 (LG 24 January 1919).

DICK Lance Corporal I 20441 - Attack at Wulverghem, 4 September 1918 (LG 13 March 1919).

EDEN Lance Corporal R H 43346 - Attack at Wulverghem, 4 September 1918 (LG 13 March 1919).

Bar - (Sergeant) Attacks at Vijfwegen/Hill 41 near Dadizeele between 30 September and 14 October 1918 (LG 17 June 1919).

ELLIOTT Private J 14154 - Battle of Langemarck, 16 August 1917 (LG 19 November 1917).

FEGAN Corporal J 21059 - Crossing of the River Lys, mid-October 1918 (LG 17 June 1919).

FERGUSON Sergeant R 14188 - North of Bailleul, August 1918 (LG 11 February 1919).

FERGUSON Private R J 22994 - Withdrawal from St Quentin, 21-27 March 1918 (LG 29 August 1918).

FOSTER Sergeant F 14175 - Hamel, May/June 1916 (LG 14 December 1916).

For gallantry in carrying in wounded under shellfire while himself wounded.

GILLANDERS Private R 16105 - Attack at Wulverghem, 4 September 1918 (LG 13 March 1919).

GORMAN Private M 20938 - The attack at Hamel, 1 July 1916 (LG 9 December 1916).

HAMILTON Private J 14282 - In the line near the River Douve, 19 February 1917 (LG 26 April 1917).

For conspicuous gallantry and devotion to duty in securing and rescuing wounded men for a neighbouring division from 'No Man's Land' on the morning of February 19th, 1917.

HENRY Sergeant G A 41401 - Fighting patrol at Marcoing, 15 December 1917 (LG 19 March 1918).

HOMERSHAM Lance Corporal F S 45807 - Attack at Wulverghem, 4 September 1918 (LG 13 March 1919).

Bar - (Sergeant) Attacks at Vijfwegen/Hill 41 near Dadizeele between 30 September and 14 October 1918 (LG 17 June 1919).

JACKSON Lance Corporal E 24174 - Battle of Langemarck, 16 August 1917 (LG 19 November 1917).

JENNINGS Lance Corporal F 41338 - (LG 20 August 1919).

JOHNSTON Sergeant R 14358 - Raid at Shoddy Farm north of Bailleul, 22 July 1918 (LG 3 November 1918).

KELLY Private W 14393 - Wulverghem in April 1918 (LG 7 October 1918).

KENNEDY Lance Corporal J 20947 - Crossing of the River Lys, mid-October 1918 (LG 17 June 1919).

KNAGGS Acting Corporal R W 16117 - Battle of Langemarck, 16 August 1917 (LG 19 November 1917).

LEBURN Private L E 42447 - Attack at Wulverghem, 4 September 1918 (LG 13 March 1919).

LONG Corporal J E 43464 - Attack at Wulverghem, 4 September 1918 (LG 13 March 1919).

LUCAS Sergeant R 14414 - The attack at Hamel, 1 July 1916 (LG 21 October 1916).

LYNN Private W J 15864 - Battle of Langemarck, 16 August 1917 (LG 19 November 1917).

MAGOWAN Lance Corporal A 18058 - Raid at Spanbroekmolen, 4 June 1917 (LG 28 July 1917).

MAKINSON Corporal H 18869 - Raid at Havrincourt, 3 November 1917 (LG 23 February 1918).

MARSHALL Private J W 18252 - Attack at Moeuvres, 23 November 1917 (LG 25 April 1918).

McBRIDE Lance Corporal W 22935 - (LG 13 March 1918).

McCARLEY Private W 41329 - Wulverghem, April 1918 (LG 17 October 1918).

McCLELLAND Private G 49741 - North of Bailleul, August 1918 (LG 11 February 1919).

McCLELLAND Private T A 41307 - Withdrawal from St Quentin, 21-27 March 1918 (LG 29 August 1918).

McCONKEY Sergeant C 20444 - Raid at Spanbroekmolen, 4 June 1917 (LG 28 July 1917).

McCORMICK Private R J 14566 - Battle of Langemarck, 16 August 1917 (LG 19 November 1917).

McCULLOUGH Sergeant J 14555 - Battle of Langemarck, 16 August 1917 (LG 1 April 1920).

> *During the operations at Wieltje on the 14th/17th August, 1917, he showed conspicuous gallantry by going forward under intense artillery and machine-gun fire and collecting valuable information, which he sent to battalion headquarters.*

McGRANN Private D 7963 - Raid at Spanbroekmolen, 4 June 1917 (LG 28 July 1917).

MILLER Private G F 43201 - Wulverghem, April 1918 (LG 7 October 1918).

MITCHELL Sergeant W J 14474 - Wulverghem, April 1918 (LG 7 October 1918).

MOOREHEAD Sergeant W 14482 - Attacks at Vijfwegen/Hill 41 near Dadizeele between 30 September and 14 October 1918 (LG 14 May 1919).

MORAN Private D 41064 - (LG 19 March 1918).

MORAN Private J 8895 - Crossing of the River Lys, mid-October 1918 (LG 17 June 1919).

MORRISON Private J 41327 - Raid at Havrincourt, 3 November 1917 (LG 23 February 1918).

MORTON Private J 14447 - Battle of Langemarck, 16 August 1917 (LG 19 November 1917).

NEESON Private J 22735 - Crossing of the River Lys, mid-October 1918 (LG 17 June 1919).

NESBITT Sergeant G 41198 - Withdrawal from St Quentin, 21-27 March 1918 (LG 29 August 1918).

NORRIS Private R 13447 - Attacks at Vijfwegen/Hill 41 near Dadizeele between 30 September and 14 October 1918 (LG 14 May 1919).

O'HANLON Private J 13314 - (LG 14 May 1919).

PALMER Sergeant W H 14601 - Hamel, May 1916 (LG 14 December 16. Shown as The Royal Irish Regiment. Corrected LG 19 February 1917).

> *For coolness and good leading when in charge of a patrol in the Hamel Sector in May 1916. He encountered an Enemy Patrol, killing four and wounding two without sustaining any loss to his own party. And for continuous good work, as Scout Sergeant of the Battalion, on numerous patrols from January to July, 1916.*

PAUL Private J 41355 - Attack north of Bailleul, 24 August 1918 (LG 24 January 1919).

PEERS Private A 42244 - Attack north of Bailleul, 24 August 1918 (LG 24 January 1919).

PYE Private E 43447 - Raid at Shoddy Farm north of Bailleul, 22 July 1918 (LG 13 November 1918).

RODGERS Private J 20353 - Battle of Langemarck, 16 August 1917 (LG 19 November 1917).

ROGERS Private F C 23504 - Withdrawal from St Quentin, 21-27 March 1918 (LG 29 August 1918) **Bar** - see first award below, page 388.

SCOTT Private T 22556 - Attack north of Bailleul, 24 August 1918 (LG 24 January 1919).

SHANKS Private C 23826 - Battle of Langemarck, 16 August 1917 (LG 19 November 1917).

SHARP Lance Corporal J 14708 - Attack north of Bailleul, 24 August 1918 (LG 24 January 1919).

SLOANE Private J 22726 - Raid at Spanbroekmolen, 4 June 1917 (LG 28 July 1917).

SMALLWOOD Lance Corporal J 40085 - (LG 26 April 1917).

STEELE Private G 22562 - Battle of Langemarck, 16 August 1917 (LG 19 November 1917).

STEVENSON Sergeant (Acting Company Sergeant Major) W 14667 - (LG 20 August 1919).

THOMPSON Private C A 40073 - Attack at Moeuvres, 23 November 1917 (LG 25 April 1918).

TUGHAN Private R 41280 - Withdrawal from St Quentin, 21-27 March 1918 (LG 29 August 1918).

TURKINGTON Sergeant A 14720 - Battle of Langemarck, 16 August 1917 (LG 19 November 1917).

VENNARD Sergeant A 14740 - Withdrawal from St Quentin, 21-27 March 1918 (LG 29 August 1918).

WALKER Private G 40034 - (LG 13 March 1918).

WARE Private F S 49929 - North of Bailleul, August 1918 (LG 11 February 1919).

WASSON Private S 41414 - Wulverghem, April 1918 (LG 7 October 1918).

WHITESIDE Corporal S 14748 - Battle of Langemarck, 16 August 1917 (LG 19 November 1917).

WILLIAMS Lance Sergeant H G 42057 - Attack at Wulverghem, 4 September 1918 (LG 13 March 1919).

WOLFE Sergeant R J 18609 - Raid on La Petite Douve Farm, 12 October 1916 (LG 21 December 1916).

Twenty-three awards of the Military Medal for acts of gallantry, including one bar, were made to men while serving elsewhere. The numbers and ranks shown are as at the time of award:

BAKER Sergeant F 13845 - Earned with the 1st Battalion on a daylight raid near Berles au Bois, 17 April 1916 (LG 3 June 1916). Subsequently Second Lieutenant F Baker MM.

BURKE Private T 23108 - Earned with the 8th (Service) Battalion in defence against a German attack on 27 April 1916 (LG 8 August 1916).

ELLIOTT Lance Corporal W 17308 - Earned with the 11th (Service) Battalion, The Royal Inniskilling Fusiliers (Donegal and Fermanagh) at the Battle of Langemarck, 16 August 1917 (LG 8 November 1917). Subsequently Second Lieutenant W Elliott MM.

FITZSIMONS Sergeant J 17787 - Earned with the Machine Gun Corps (LG 29 August 1918). Formerly 14176 Private Princess Victoria's (Royal Irish Fusiliers).

FLYNN Sergeant B 6328 - Earned with the 7th/8th (Service) Battalion in late-1917 (LG 19 March 1918).

GILLAN Sergeant T F 9458 - Earned with the 2nd Battalion in Salonika in 1916 (LG 22 January 1917).

GRAHAM Lance Corporal J 14233 - Earned with 108th Trench Mortar Battery (LG 19 February 1917).

GRAHAM Lance Corporal W 18926 - Earned with the 1st Battalion (LG 9 July 1917).

HOAR Private W 43341 - Earned with the 1st Battalion in its latter battles in 1918 (LG 13 March 1919).

HUGHES Sergeant J 4517 - Earned with the 1st Battalion during the attacks near the Chemical Works at Roeux, April and May 1917 (LG 9 July 1917).

KEMP Company Quartermaster Sergeant H 42517 - Earned with the 1st Battalion, The Royal Inniskilling Fusiliers, 109th Brigade during the withdrawal from St Quentin, March 1918 (LG 29 August 1918). Subsequently Second Lieutenant H Kemp MM.

LAIRD Sergeant W 14695 - Earned with the 11th (Service) Battalion, The Royal Inniskilling Fusiliers (Donegal and Fermanagh) (LG 9 December 1916). Subsequently Second Lieutenant W LAIRD MM*.

Bar - Also earned with the 11th (Service) Battalion, The Royal Inniskilling Fusiliers (Donegal and Fermanagh) (LG 22 January 1917).

McCREADY Private E 21411 - Earned with the 7th/8th (Service) Battalion at Messines on 7 June 1917 (LG 17 September 1917).

MOORHEAD Private R A 304862 - Earned with 17th Armoured Car Battalion, Tank Corps. (LG 20 October 1919). Formerly 14442 Private Princess Victoria's (Royal Irish Fusiliers).

> *For gallantry and devotion to duty during the advance from Catillon to Liessies, and particularly on November 9 at Haut Lieu, when his car was ditched within 150 yards of the enemy's position and was fired upon by both machine-gun and shell fire. Although the car was under direct observation, this soldier, knowing that the armoured car was urgently wanted to protect our infantry, set a fine example and showed great gallantry in working under fire to get the car back into action.*

MOYLES Private T 16024 - Earned with the 7th/8th (Service) Battalion in late-1917 (LG 19 March 1918).

ROBERTS Corporal T J 5121 - Earned with 74th Trench Mortar Battery while detached from 2nd Battalion, The Royal Irish Rifles (LG 18 October 1916). Subsequently 43428 Corporal T J Roberts MM Princess Victoria's (Royal Irish Fusiliers).

ROBINSON Corporal R E 20086 - Earned with 108th Trench Mortar Battery (LG 19 February 1917). Reportedly for '*continuing to operate a trench mortar when all his companions were killed*'.

ROGERS Private F C 23504 - Earned with the 7th/8th (Service) Battalion (LG 19 March 1918). This is a first award, see **Bar** above, page 387.

ROONEY Sergeant T 23829 - Earned with the 7th/8th (Service) Battalion in late-1917 (LG 19 March 1918).

TRUEMAN Corporal F 17805 - Earned while serving with the Machine Gun Corps (LG 28 February 1918). Formerly 14736 Private Princess Victoria's (Royal Irish Fusiliers).

TWEEDIE Corporal R 13751 - Earned with the 9th (Service) Battalion, The Royal Irish Rifles (West Belfast) (LG 14 November 1916). Subsequently Second Lieutenant R Tweedie MM.

WILLIAMS Colour Sergeant G A 9428 - Earned with the 1st Battalion during the withdrawal from St Quentin, 21-27 March 1918 (LG 25 April 1918).

Meritorious Service Medal

Instituted in 1845, the Meritorious Service Medal was awarded until 1916 to non-commissioned officers above the rank of Corporal for valuable and meritorious service, in which length of service was a factor. There was a need, however, to recognise those acts of gallantry not in the face of the enemy that fell short of the standard required for an award of the Albert Medal. As a consequence, the Meritorious Service Medal was also awarded for '*gallant conduct in the performance of military duty otherwise in action against the enemy, or in attempting to save the life of an officer or soldier, or for devotion to duty in a theatre of war*'. Awards were specified as being for gallantry in the performance of military duty, devotion to duty or valuable services. Between 1916 and 1920, 25,235 awards were made for valuable services. These awards were all earned by four men who had enlisted into the 9th Royal Irish Fusiliers in September 1914:

KEITH Sergeant J 14391 - (LG 18 January 1919).

LESTER Sergeant R 17794 Machine Gun Corps (formerly 14415 Private R Lester) - Earned for his service with the Machine Gun Corps (LG 17 June 1918).

McCONVILLE Company Quartermaster Sergeant T 14516 - (LG 18 January 1919).

McLOUGHLIN Lance Corporal H 14534 - (LG 3 June 1919).

Mention in Despatches

The use of despatches by Commanders in the Field to bring deserving formations, units and officers to the attention of higher authority, was well established in the campaigns of the nineteenth century. In the despatches of Sir Douglas Haig, the Commander-in-Chief, 36th (Ulster) Division was mentioned briefly for the success of its actions at Messines, during the early stages of the Cambrai battle, and during the attacks in September 1918. But it was during the German offensive of March 1918 that the Ulster Division received its greatest accolades. Amongst the more general commentary on the Division's actions, 1st Royal Inniskilling Fusiliers was specifically mentioned for its performance on 22 March 1918. The spirited defence at Andechy a few days later caused Sir Douglas Haig to write:

> *'Though the enemy had penetrated behind them and had taken Erches, the troops of the 36th Division at Andechy maintained a most gallant resistance until the afternoon of the 27th March, thereby playing no small part in preventing the enemy from breaking through between the Allied Armies.'*

Despatches also detailed those whose '*distinguished and gallant service and devotion to duty*' deserved special recognition. Official statistics show that there were 141,082 mentions in despatches between 1914 and 1920. In 1919 approval was given for a certificate to be issued to commemorate a mention in despatches, and from 1920 the award was indicated by a multiple-leaved, bronze oak leaf for wear on the Victory Medal. The list below shows forty-two officers and men who were mentioned in despatches on a total of fifty-six occasions. Included are thirty-one awards earned by men serving elsewhere. If multiple mentions were made, the ranks and other awards shown are those held at the time of the first award:

BARBOUR Sergeant J 13994 - For gallant service during the attack at Hamel on 1 July 1916 (LG 4 January 1917).

BAREFOOT MC Captain G W N - Mentioned twice; firstly for gallant service with the 1st Battalion (LG 22 September 1916) and then for his service on the Staff in 1918 (LG 5 July 1919).

BERRY MB Captain W S S Royal Army Medical Corps - Mentioned twice; for gallant service as the Medical Officer in 1916/17 (LG 24 December 1917) and on the Staff (LG 5 July 1919).

BEST Captain W J - For gallantry in July 1916 while serving with the 1st Battalion.

BIRD Sergeant H A 43343 - (LG 9 July 1919).

BLACKER Lieutenant Colonel S W W - Mentioned three times for gallant service as the Commanding Officer (LG 15 June 16, 4 January 1917 & 25 May 1917).

BRATTON Sergeant J 14017 - (LG 28 December 1918).

BRENNAN Captain C J - For service on the Staff of HQ 36th (Ulster) Division (LG 9 July 1919).

BREW Major J G - For his gallant service during the retreat from St Quentin to Erches in March 1918 (LG 24 May 1918).

BROWN Private W 14022 - (LG 9 July 1919).

BRYSON Sergeant J 820 - For gallant service in 8th (King's Royal Irish) Hussars before being commissioned into Princess Victoria's (Royal Irish Fusiliers) (LG 11 December 1917).

BUCKLEY MM Private R 14021 - (LG 24 May 1918).

CLARK Lieutenant St G H L - For gallant service in command of a Trench Mortar Battery (LG 21 December 1917).

CROSS Captain G H - For service with the Army Service Corps before joining the 9th Royal Irish Fusiliers (LG 24 December 1917).

ELLIOTT MM Sergeant W 17308 - For gallant service with 11th (Service) Battalion, The Royal Inniskilling Fusiliers (Donegal and Fermanagh) before being commissioned into Princess Victoria's (Royal Irish Fusiliers) (LG 24 May 1918).

ENSOR Captain E N - For gallant service as Officer Commanding B Company (LG 4 January 1917).

FERGUSON DCM Captain A - For gallant service as Adjutant (LG 25 May 1917).

FORDE DSO, MC* Lieutenant Colonel G M The Royal Inniskilling Fusiliers - For gallant service as Commanding Officer of the 9th Royal Irish Fusiliers (LG 27 December 1918).

GIVEN MC Captain T F - For gallant service as Officer Commanding D Company (LG 25 May 1917).

GODSON MC Captain E A - For gallant service as Officer Commanding A Company in the latter half of 1917 (LG 21 December 1917).

GRANT Captain J - Probably for gallant service with the North Irish Horse (shown on his medal index card - no London Gazette entry found).

HARVEY Private P 21120 - Earned while serving with the 8th (Service) Battalion in 49th Brigade, 16th (Irish) Division (LG 19 March 1918).

HALAHAN Captain F J Army Chaplains' Department - Mentioned twice; firstly for his gallant service as Chaplain, particularly during and immediately after the attack on 1 July 1916 (LG 4 January 1917) and then for his services as 36th (Ulster) Division Chaplain (LG 30 December 1918).

HENAHAN Captain M - For gallant service as Officer Commanding C Company (LG 25 May 1917).

KELLY Captain P E - Mentioned twice; firstly for gallant service as Adjutant of the 5th (Service) Battalion in 31st Brigade, 16th (Irish) Division at Gallipoli (LG 28 January 1916) and secondly as Commanding Officer of the 9th Royal Irish Fusiliers in March and April 1918 (LG 24 May 1918).

KERR Captain C H - Mentioned twice; firstly for gallant service in late-1917 or early-1918 (LG 24 May 1918) and secondly for gallant service as Officer Commanding A Company (LG 28 December 1918).

MacLEAN Captain P E - For gallant service as the Adjutant of the 10th (Service) Battalion, The Royal Irish Rifles (South Belfast) before joining the 9th Royal Irish Fusiliers (LG 18 December 1917).

MAHONEY Lieutenant W - Earned as 15789 Acting Sergeant W MAHONEY Corps of Royal Engineers (LG 18 May 1917).

McCARTHY-O'LEARY Captain H W D - Mentioned five times. These include two awards for gallant service with the 2nd Battalion as Adjutant in France (LG 22 June 15) and Salonica (LG 1 January 1916) and three for gallant service as Commanding Officer of the 1st Battalion, The Royal Irish Rifles (LG 21 December 17, 28 December 18 and 9 July 1919).

MENAUL Captain W J - Mentioned twice. Firstly for gallantry as the Intelligence Officer (LG 14 November 1916) and secondly for service on the Staff (LG 5 July 1919).

MILNE Captain C W The Royal Inniskilling Fusiliers - For gallantry while serving with 109th Brigade Trench Mortar Battery (LG 30 December 1918). Formerly 15865 Warrant Officer Class II Regimental Quartermaster Sergeant C W Milne.

MURPHY Sergeant J 17796 - For gallantry while serving with 108th Brigade Machine Gun Company (LG 2 January 1917). Formerly 17402 Corporal J Murphy Princess Victoria's (Royal Irish Fusiliers).

NAPIER Sergeant R 14578 - (LG 9 July 1919).

PRATT DSO Lieutenant Colonel A C - Mentioned twice, both for gallant service as Commanding Officer of the 11th (Service) Battalion, The Royal Inniskilling Fusiliers (Donegal and Fermanagh) in 109th Brigade (LG 4 January 1917 & 18 December 1917).

PRICE Trooper H 1254 - Earned with the North Irish Horse (LG 15 May 1917). Subsequently 41409 Private H Price Princess Victoria's (Royal Irish Fusiliers).

SAUNDERSON Lieutenant W R - For gallant service with 108th Trench Mortar Battery during the action at Cambrai in November 1917 (LG 21 December 1917).

STRINGER Sergeant B 23653 - (LG 9 July 1919).

TAMPLIN Captain R J A The Connaught Rangers - Mentioned twice, both for gallant service with the 6th (Service) Battalion, The Connaught Rangers in 47th Brigade, 16th (Irish) Division (LG 28 January 1916 & 4 January 1917).

WHITLA Major V G 3rd (King's Own) Hussars - For gallant service with 2nd North Irish Horse, X Corps Cavalry Regiment (from Medal index Card; no London Gazette entry found).

WILLIAMSON Lieutenant H A - For gallant service with the Royal Flying Corps.

WILSON Honorary Lieutenant and Quartermaster G W - For gallant service as Quartermaster (LG 28 December 1918).

YOUNG Second Lieutenant J B A - Probably awarded for gallantry at Moeuvres, 23 November 1917 (LG 24 May 1918).

'B' List Press Mentions

'B' List Press Mentions were used to recognise the valuable service of both military personnel and civilians, both in the United Kingdom and in the Dominions and Colonies, who had been *'brought to the notice of the Secretary for War for valuable services rendered in connection with the War'*. This award did not equate to a Mention in Despatches and recipients were not entitled to wear the oak leaf emblem. Lists of these awards were published in The Times rather than in the London Gazette. One former member of the 9th Royal Irish Fusiliers was so mentioned:

FITZGERALD Colonel W C - For service as Commanding Officer of the 10th (Reserve) Battalion, Princess Victoria's (Royal Irish Fusiliers).

Certificate for Gallantry

In April 1917 a Certificate for Gallantry was instigated for men of 36th (Ulster) Division who had distinguished themselves during the attack on 1 July 1916. The certificate detailed the act of gallantry for which the recipient was commended. The first awards of the certificates were published in May 1917. It is not known how many were awarded. The certificates continued to be awarded throughout the war. Six examples are cited here:

BARBOUR Sergeant J 13994 - Earned during the attack at Hamel, 1 July 1916.

ELLIOTT Private J 14154 - Earned during the attack at Hamel, 1 July 1916 (Private Elliott's brother, 14158 Lance Corporal H Elliott, was one of those wounded on 1 July 1916; he succumbed to his wounds a few days later). Private Elliott later earned the Military Medal.

> *...., for gallantry and devotion to duty in rescuing wounded under fire at Hamel, on July 1st 1916. He carried wounded to the dressing station, a distance of a mile, only desisting when completely exhausted.*

LESTER Sergeant R 17794 Machine Gun Corps (formerly 14415 Private R Lester) - Earned for his service with 108th Brigade Machine Gun Company.

McCLEAN Lance Sergeant W J 14556 - Earned during the attack at Hamel, 1 July 1916.

> *...., for gallantry and devotion to duty when in charge of a Bombing Team at Hamel, on July 1st 1916. He led his men courageously until all were killed or wounded.*

McCULLOUGH Sergeant D 14554 - Earned during the attack at Hamel, 1 July 1916.

> *...., for gallantry in bringing in wounded at Hamel under machine gun fire on July 1st 1916 though himself wounded.*

ROBINSON Sergeant J 14642 - Earned during the attack at Hamel, 1 July 1916. Sergeant Robinson later earned the Distinguished Conduct Medal.

> *...., for gallantry on the attack at Hamel, on July 1st 1916, he dressed wounded men in "No Man's Land" and helped them back to our trenches under heavy machine gun fire.*

Similar certificates were awarded in other divisions. Eight men who earned such an award later joined the 9th Royal Irish Fusiliers:

AUSTIN Corporal L D 25133 - Earned the 16th (Irish) Division Parchment Certificate for Gallantry and Devotion to Duty for his actions during the Battle of Langemarck on 16 August 1917 while serving with the 7th/8th (Service) Battalion.

BOSWELL Lance Corporal B J 44084 - Earned the 8th Division Parchment Certificate for Gallant Conduct and Devotion to Duty for his actions at Passchendaele between 1 and 3 January 1918 while serving with the 1st Battalion, The Royal Irish Rifles. Subsequently 42501 Lance Corporal B J Boswell Princess Victoria's (Royal Irish Fusiliers).

CAMPBELL Sergeant J 13501 - Earned the 16th (Irish) Division Parchment Certificate for Gallantry and Devotion to Duty for his actions during the Battle of Cambrai in November 1917.

McCREADY Private E 21411 - Earned the 16th (Irish) Division Parchment Certificate for Gallantry and Devotion to Duty for his actions at Messines on 7 June 1917, for which he was awarded the Military Medal, while serving with the 7th/8th (Service) Battalion.

McMORROW Sergeant O J 16192 - Earned the 16th (Irish) Division Parchment Certificate for Gallantry and Devotion to Duty for his actions at Ginchy in September 1916 while serving with the 7th/8th (Service) Battalion.

MURPHY Sergeant J J 20071 - Earned the 16th (Irish) Division Parchment Certificate for Gallantry and Devotion to Duty for his actions on a raid on 11 July 1916, for which he was awarded the Distinguished Conduct Medal, while serving with the 8th (Service) Battalion. Subsequently Second Lieutenant J J Murphy Princess Victoria's (Royal Irish Fusiliers).

MURRAY Private W J 20958 - Earned the 16th (Irish) Division Parchment Certificate for Gallantry and Devotion to Duty for his actions at Messines on 7 June 1917 while serving with the 7th/8th (Service) Battalion.

ROGERS Private F C 23504 - Earned the 16th (Irish) Division Parchment Certificate for Gallantry and Devotion to Duty for his actions during the Battle of Langemarck on 16 August 1917, for which he earned the Military Medal, while serving with the 7th/8th (Service) Battalion.

Commendations

From time to time soldiers were commended on Divisional, Brigade or Base Depot orders for acts of gallantry or meritorious service that did not attract a formal award. One example is shown here:

McFARLAND Private E 14567 - at 36 Infantry Base Depot.

> *While a patient in hospital on 25th April, the marquee in which Private McFarland was sleeping was completely destroyed by fire. He, while the tent was one mass of flames, gallantly woke all his comrades and when he saw them in safety ran round the other tents and cleared them out, and it was by his presence of mind that no patient received the slightest injury in what might otherwise have resulted in serious burns if not loss of life.*

Silver War Badge & King's Certificate

Also known, incorrectly, as the Discharge Badge, Silver Wound Badge, Services Rendered Badge or the King's Silver Badge, this one-and-a-quarter-inch-diameter, circular, sterling silver brooch badge was worn on the right lapel of civilian clothes. It was inscribed FOR KING AND EMPIRE - SERVICES RENDERED. Instituted on 12 September 1916, it was awarded to those who had been honourably discharged. Most recipients had sustained a wound or injury or had suffered illness that precluded further service and which resulted in discharge under Paragraph 392 (xvi) or (xvia) of King's Regulations, i.e. *'no longer physically fit for war service'* or *'surplus to military requirements (having suffered impairment since entry into the service)'*. Other reasons for discharge included having reached the upper age for service, but those who came to the end of a normal term of engagement were not eligible. About 1,150,000 badges were issued. Each was uniquely numbered on the reverse and was accompanied by an official certificate of entitlement. Those that have been identified are annotated at the relevant entries in Appendices 5 and 6.

In May 1918 King's Certificate on Discharge was authorised for award to officers who relinquished their commissions and to other ranks who had been discharged under Paragraph 392 (xvi) or (xvia) of King's Regulations, i.e. *'no longer physically fit for war service'* or *'surplus to military requirements (having suffered impairment since entry into the service)'*. The disabilities must have been contracted following service overseas in a theatre of operations with an Expeditionary Force, and caused or aggravated by military service or, if not overseas with an Expeditionary Force, directly attributable to the action of the enemy, such as air or naval raids. Additionally, officers and other ranks were eligible for the King's Second Certificate on Discharge, which was awarded to those who, after having become eligible for the award of the King's Certificate, voluntarily served again, and again relinquished their commissions or were discharged under the same conditions as for the King's Certificate. Due to the many honourable reasons for discharge under King's Regulations Paragraphs 392, the award of a Silver War Badge did not necessarily result in the award of a certificate. Those entitled to a certificate, however, would have been entitled to a Silver War Badge also.

Foreign Awards

Twenty-three Belgian and French decorations were awarded to officers and men serving with the 9th Royal Irish Fusiliers, and a further eleven awards were made to officers and men serving elsewhere. One Chinese award was made to an officer serving with the Chinese Labour Corps.

Ordre de La Couronne (Belgium)

King Leopold II instituted the *Ordre de La Couronne* in 1897 in order to reward distinguished service in the Congo. It was incorporated into the Belgian honours system in 1908 and was awarded in five classes: Grand Cross, Grand Officer, Commander, Officer, and Knight. An award of the order for gallantry also attracted the award of the *Croix de Guerre*. Two awards were made:

McCARTHY-O'LEARY DSO*, MC Lieutenant Colonel H W D - Made an *Officier* (Officer) of the Order and awarded the *Croix de Guerre* for service as the Commanding Officer of the 1st Battalion, The Royal Irish Rifles (LG 24 October 1919).

WILSON Honorary Lieutenant and Quartermaster G W - Made a *Chevalier* (Knight) of the Order and awarded the *Croix de Guerre* for service as the Quartermaster (LG 24 October 1919).

Ordre de Leopold II

King Leopold II instituted the *Ordre de Leopold II* on 24 August 1900 as an order also for service in the Congo. It was incorporated into the Belgian honours system in 1908 and was awarded in five classes: Grand Cross, Grand Officer, Commander, Officer, and Knight. Military personnel who were mentioned in despatches were awarded a gold or silver palm to be worn on the ribbon. An award of the order for gallantry also attracted the award of the *Croix de Guerre*. One award was made:

WILLIAMS MM Regimental Sergeant Major G A 9428 - Made a *Chevalier* (Knight) of the Order and awarded the *Croix de Guerre* for his war service (LG 24 October 1919).

Croix de Guerre (Belgium)

This award was instituted in October 1915 and awarded for acts of courage on the battlefield or for continuous and exceptional service against the enemy. Ten awards were made to officers and men serving with the 9th Royal Irish Fusiliers and seven awards were earned elsewhere:

BERRY MB Major W S S Royal Army Medical Corps - For services as Deputy Assistant Director of Medical Services on the Staff of X Corps (LG 4 September 1919).

BRYSON Sergeant J 820 - For gallant service with 8th (King's Royal Irish) Hussars before being commissioned into Princess Victoria's (Royal Irish Fusiliers) (LG 11 December 1917).

DICK MM Lance Corporal I 20441 - (LG 4 September 1919).

EDWARDS Corporal C G 14153 - (LG 4 September 1919).

GODSON MC* Captain E A - Probably awarded for gallant service as Officer Commanding A Company (LG 12 July 1918).

GRAHAM Second Lieutenant W G - (LG 4 September 1919).

HULSE Major A - For gallant service as Second-in-Command of 9th (Service) Battalion, The Royal Inniskilling Fusiliers (County Tyrone) in 109th Brigade in 1918 (LG 4 September 1919).

JONES Corporal A 42078 - For gallant service with the 1st Battalion (LG 4 September 1919).

KNAGGS MM Acting Corporal R W 16117 - (LG 12 July 1918).

LOCKHART DCM Acting Sergeant J 41148 - (LG 4 September 1919).

McCARTHY-O'LEARY DSO*, MC Lieutenant Colonel H W D - Awarded when he was made an Officer of the *Ordre de La Couronne* for service as the Commanding Officer of the 1st Battalion, The Royal Irish Rifles (LG 24 October 1919).

MENAUL MC Captain W J - For service on the Staff of Headquarters 108th Brigade in 1918 (LG 4 September 1919).

MILNE MC Captain C W - For service with The Royal Inniskilling Fusiliers (LG 4 September 1919).

MOOREY Lance Sergeant A 45046 - (LG 12 July 1918).

SPARKS MC Captain W - (LG 4 September 1919).

WILLIAMS MM Regimental Sergeant Major G A 9428 - Awarded when he was made a Knight of the *Ordre de Leopold II* for service as the Regimental Sergeant Major (LG 24 October 1919).

WILSON Honorary Lieutenant and Quartermaster G W - Awarded when he was made a Knight of the *Ordre de La Couronne* for service as the Quartermaster (LG 24 October 1919).

Decoration Militaire (Belgium)

The *Decoration Militaire* was instituted in 1900 and was awarded to soldiers of the Allied armies for courage, self-sacrifice and personal achievement. Two awards were made to soldiers of the 9th Royal Irish Fusiliers:

SIMONS DCM Private W 14689 - (LG 7 October 1919).

STEWART Private T 14688 - (LG 15 April 1917).

Legion D'Honneur (France)

Instituted in 1802, the *Legion d'Honneur* was expanded to five classes of award in 1805. It is the premier award of France and may be conferred for courage, honour and services to France. When awarded for bravery in action the recipient also receives the *Croix de Guerre*. The five classes are: Grand Cross, Grand Officer, Commander, Officer, and Knight. One award was made:

BLACKER DSO Lieutenant Colonel S W W - Made an Officer of the Order for gallant service as the Commanding Officer (LG 14 July 1917).

Croix de Guerre (France)

The *Croix de Guerre* was instituted in 1915 and awarded to all ranks of the armed services who were mentioned in despatches. It was also awarded to personnel of Allied armies for courage in action. Six awards were made to officers and men of the 9th Royal Irish Fusiliers. One award was made to a former soldier of the Battalion:

BLACKER DSO Lieutenant Colonel S W W - Awarded when he was made an Officer of the *Legion d'Honneur* for gallant service as the Commanding Officer (LG 14 July 1917).

CAMPBELL MM Sergeant J 13501 - (*Avec étoile en bronze*) (LG 19 June 1919).

KERR Captain C H - (*Avec étoile en bronze*) (LG 19 June 1919).

LESTER Sergeant R 17794 Machine Gun Corps (formerly 14415 Private R Lester) - Earned for his service with 31st Battalion, Machine Gun Corps (LG 19 June 1919).

MORAN MM Private J 8895 - (*Avec étoile en bronze*) (LG 19 June 1919).

O'HANLON Private J 13314 - (LG 17 June 1919).

TAMPLIN DSO Lieutenant Colonel R J A - (*Avec étoile en argent*) For gallant service as the Commanding Officer in 1918 (LG 19 June 1919).

Medaille Militaire (France)

The *Medaille Militaire* was instituted in 1852 and awarded to non-commissioned officers and other ranks for bravery and courage in action. Two awards were made to men of the 9th Royal Irish Fusiliers and one was earned elsewhere.

LAIRD MM* Sergeant W 14695 - For gallant service with 11th (Service) Battalion, The Royal Inniskilling Fusiliers (Donegal and Fermanagh) in 1917 before being commissioned into Princess Victoria's (Royal Irish Fusiliers) (LG 14 July 1917).

McBRIDE DCM Sergeant R J 23566 - (LG 29 January 1919).

SCOTT Private W J 20068 - (LG 14 July 1917).

Order of *Wen-Hu* (Order of the Striped Tiger - China)

Awarded in five classes by the Republic of China for military or naval service. It was issued to British officers who served with the Chinese Labour Corps, or in command of Chinese auxiliaries serving with the Royal Army Medical Corps. One award was made:

ENSOR Captain E N - For service with the Chinese Labour Corps (LG 13 February 1920).

Awards for Previous or Subsequent Service

At least thirty-three awards were made in previous and subsequent conflicts or in the wider careers of some of those who served with the Battalion. This list is likely to be incomplete.

The Most Honourable Order of the Bath

CALDWELL KC, CB, LLM J F (formerly Lieutenant J F Caldwell) - Appointed an Ordinary Member of the Civil Division of the Third Class, or Companion (CB), for service as the First Parliamentary Draftsman, Ministry of Finance, Northern Ireland. (LG 1 January 1952).

The Most Exalted Order of the Star of India

IRWIN CSI G R (subsequently Captain G R Irwin CSI, OBE) - Made a Companion of the Order (CSI) on his retirement from the Indian Civil Service after twenty-five years' service (LG 1 January 1901).

The Most Excellent Order of the British Empire

ADAMS MBE, MM* J (formerly 13971 Sergeant J Adams MM*) - Made a Member of the Order (MBE) (Civil) for his service as Adjutant of the Ulster Special Constabulary (LG 1 June 1953).

BRENNAN C J OBE (formerly Captain C J Brennan) - Made an Officer of the Order (OBE) (Civil) for services to musical education in Northern Ireland (LG 9 June 1949).

DEAN OBE, MC Lieutenant Colonel H S The Royal Ulster Rifles - Made an Officer of the Order (OBE) (Military) for military service (LG 1 January 1947).

DYNES MBE Captain R A (formerly 14142 Private R A Dynes) - Made a Member of the Order (MBE) (Military) for his war service as Warrant Officer Class 1, Regimental Sergeant Major, Canadian Infantry Corps, serving with The Black Watch (Royal Highland Regiment) of Canada (LG 1 January 1946).

ENSOR OBE, DL Colonel C H Late The Royal Irish Fusiliers (Princess Victoria's) - Made an Officer of the Order (OBE) (Civil) for his service as a County Commandant in the Ulster Special Constabulary (LG 3 June 1924).

FULTON OBE Lieutenant Colonel J N The Royal Inniskilling Fusiliers - Made an Officer of the Order (OBE) (Military) in recognition of meritorious service commanding the 4th Belfast Battalion in the Ulster Home Guard (LG 29 December 1944).

GIVEN DSO, OBE, MC Brigadier T F Late The East Yorkshire Regiment - Made an Officer of the Order (OBE) (Civil) for his service as Political Secretary, British Administration, Somalia (LG 8 June 1950).

GREGORY OBE, MD J R (formerly Lieutenant J R Gregory) - Made an Officer of the Order (OBE) (Civil) for his service as Director of the British Red Cross Society in the East African Territories during the Second World War (LG 1 January 1944).

IRVINE MBE Major W F The Royal Ulster Rifles - Made a Member of the Order (MBE) (Civil) for service as the treasurer of the Northern Ireland Area of the British Legion (LG 14 June 1969).

JOHNSTON OBE, MD J A L (formerly Lieutenant J A L Johnston) - Made an Officer of the Order (OBE) (Civil) for his service as Consultant Physician, North-west Hospitals Group, Londonderry (LG 1 January 1962).

MOORE MBE Regimental Quartermaster Sergeant A - Made a Member of the Order (MBE) (Military) for his service as Regimental Quartermaster Sergeant of the 5th Battalion, The Royal Irish Fusiliers (Princess Victoria's) (Territorial Army) (LG 1 January 1957).

The Distinguished Service Order

GIVEN DSO, OBE, MC Brigadier T F Late The East Yorkshire Regiment - For gallant and distinguished service as a Lieutenant Colonel on operations in the Second World War (LG 11 July 40).

KERR DSO, MD Colonel C H Royal Army Medical Corps (formerly Captain C H Kerr Princess Victoria's (Royal Irish Fusiliers)) - For gallant and distinguished service as a Major, Acting Lieutenant Colonel, commanding 176th Field Ambulance, 51st Highland Division at the Second Battle of El Alamein in 1942 (LG 8 July 1943).

Air Force Cross

HOMERSHAM AFC, DCM, MM* Wing Commander F S Royal Air Force (formerly 45807 Sergeant F S Homersham DCM, MM*) - For gallantry as an Acting Wing Commander while serving with the Royal Air Force in the Second World War (LG 1 April 1941).

The Venerable Order of the Hospital of St John of Jerusalem

VINT OStJ, MD F W (formerly Lieutenant F W Vint) - Appointed a Serving Brother in the Order (LG 3 January 1939). Promoted to Officer (Brother) of the Order (LG 4 January 1944).

Distinguished Conduct Medal

FERGUSON Colour Sergeant A 1481 (subsequently Major A Ferguson MC, DCM) - For gallantry while serving as a Colour Sergeant in the 2nd Battalion, The Royal Scots Fusiliers in the South African War (LG 27 September 1901).

The Medal of the Order of the British Empire for Meritorious Service (British Empire Medal)

McCLELLAND MM, BEM T A (formerly 41307 Private T A McClelland MM) - Awarded The Medal of the Order of the British Empire for Meritorious Service (Civil) for his service as the Assistant Superintendent, Travelling Post Offices Section, General Post Office (LG 9 June 1949).

ORR BEM R A (formerly Major R A Orr) - Awarded The Medal of the Order of the British Empire for Meritorious Service (Civil) for his service as the sub-postmaster at Newtownstewart, County Tyrone (LG 1 January 1965).

Polar Medal

MATEER N C (formerly Lieutenant N C Mateer) - Awarded the Polar Medal (Bronze) with clasp 'Antarctic 1930-31' for participation in the British Australian and New Zealand Antarctic Research Expedition (LG 1 May 1934).

Meritorious Service Medal

HAMMERSLEY Sergeant H W 131713 (formerly 27840 Sergeant H W Hammersley) - Awarded for service with the 46th (Service) Battalion, The Royal Fusiliers (City of London Regiment) in the North Russia Relief Force in 1919 (LG 3 January 1920).

MOORE MBE Regimental Quartermaster Sergeant A - Awarded in 1952 after 38 years' service.

Territorial Efficiency Decoration

BARRETT TD Lieutenant Colonel St C E J Royal Army Medical Corps (formerly Lieutenant St C E J Barrett Princess Victoria's (Royal Irish Fusiliers)) - Medal and first clasp awarded for 15 years' service (LG 19 October 1951).

Mention In Despatches

BLACKER Captain S W W Royal Regiment of Artillery (subsequently Lieutenant Colonel S W W Blacker DSO) - For gallantry while serving as Captain commanding the guns of 51st Field Battery of the Royal Regiment of Artillery at Shabkadr on the North West Frontier in 1897 (LG 4 January 1898).

BARRETT TD Lieutenant Colonel St C E J Royal Army Medical Corps (formerly Lieutenant St C E J Barrett Princess Victoria's (Royal Irish Fusiliers)) - For gallant and distinguished service while serving as the senior Medical Officer in Chungkai prison (labour) camp during the Second World War (LG 12 September 1946).

DEAN OBE, MC Lieutenant Colonel H S The Royal Ulster Rifles - For distinguished service while serving as a Major with the 2nd Battalion, The Royal Ulster Rifles in Palestine in 1938 (LG 25 April 1939).

DESPARD Lieutenant C B Imperial Yeomanry (subsequently Captain C B Despard DSO, MC 6th (Inniskilling) Dragoons) - For gallantry while serving as a Subaltern with the 74th Imperial Yeomanry during the extraction of a convoy from a difficult situation near Griquatown, Cape Colony on 24 August 1901 during the South African War (LG 3 December 1901).

FERGUSON Colour Sergeant A 1481 (subsequently Major A Ferguson MC, DCM) - For gallantry while serving as a Colour Sergeant in the 2nd Battalion, The Royal Scots Fusiliers in the South African War (LG 4 September 1901).

GILMER Lieutenant E H The Royal Fusiliers (formerly Lieutenant E H Gilmer Princess Victoria's (Royal Irish Fusiliers)) - For gallantry while serving with 46th (Service) Battalion, The Royal Fusiliers (City of London Regiment) in North Russia in 1919 (LG 3 February 1920).

KERR DSO, MD Lieutenant Colonel C H Royal Army Medical Corps (formerly Captain C H Kerr Princess Victoria's (Royal Irish Fusiliers)) - For gallant and distinguished service with the medical services of 51st Highland Division in Sicily in 1943 (LG 21 March 1944).

PRATT Lieutenant A C The Royal Scots (Lothian Regiment) (subsequently Lieutenant Colonel A C Pratt DSO The Royal Inniskilling Fusiliers) - For gallantry while serving as a Subaltern in The Royal Scots (Lothian Regiment) in the South African War (LG 10 September 1901).

WHITLA Captain V G 2nd Dragoon Guards (Queen's Bays) (subsequently Major V G Whitla 3rd (King's Own) Hussars) - For gallantry while a Captain in the 2nd Dragoon Guards (Queen's Bays) serving with the expeditionary force during the Expedition to Dongola in the Sudan in 1896 (LG 3 November 1896).

The reverse of the Victoria Cross awarded posthumously to Lieutenant and Adjutant G St G S Cather for his actions on 1/2 July 1916.

The medals of Lieutenant G St G S Cather VC.
From left: Victoria Cross, 1914-15 Star, British War Medal 1914-20, Victory Medal.

The medals of Warrant Officer Class II R Lucas DCM, MM.
From left: Distinguished Conduct Medal, Military Medal, 1914-15 Star, British War Medal 1914-20 (reverse), Victory Medal (reverse).

The medals of J Adams MBE, MM*.
From left: Badge of a Member of the Most Excellent Order of the British Empire, Military Medal and Bar, 1914-15 Star, British War Medal 1914-20, Victory Medal, Defence Medal, Jubilee Medal 1935, Special Constabulary Long Service Medal with first 'Long Service' clasp.

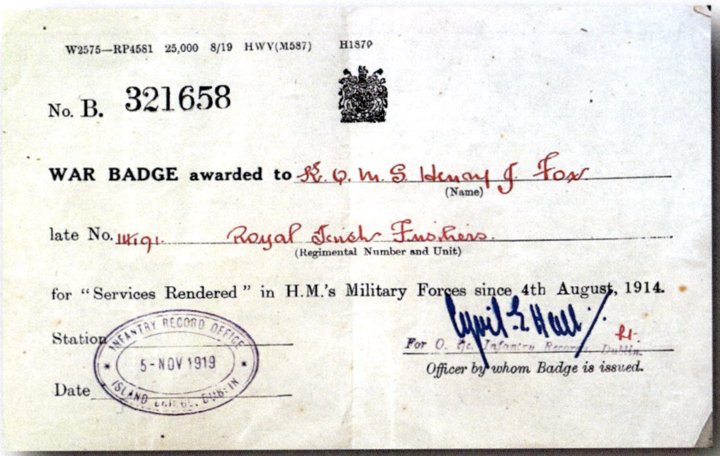
W2575—RP4581 25,000 8/19 HWV(M587) H1879

No. B. 321658

WAR BADGE awarded to R. Q. M. S. Henry J. Fox
(Name)

late No. 14191 Royal Irish Fusiliers
(Regimental Number and Unit)

for "Services Rendered" in H.M.'s Military Forces since 4th August, 1914.

Station INFANTRY RECORD OFFICE 5-NOV 1919 ISLAND BRIDGE DUBLIN

Date

Cyril E. Hall Lt.
For O. C. Infantry Records, Dublin.
Officer by whom Badge is issued.

This certificate accompanied each of the individually numbered Silver War Badges.

Silver War Badge

22228 Pte. Moses Simpson
Royal Irish Fusiliers
Served with honour and was disabled in the Great War.
Honourably discharged on 9th August 1918
George R.I.

The King's Certificate on Discharge.

This certificate was awarded to Private Moses Simpson, a Special Reservist who served with the 1st Royal Irish Fusiliers in France from 22 August 1914. He was discharged at the end of his period of service on 29 October 1915, re-enlisted and was posted to the 9th Royal Irish Fusiliers. He was wounded at the Battle of Langemarck on 16 August 1917 and discharged as no longer physically fit for war service due to wounds, on 9 August 1918.
Certificates issued to officers replaced '*Honourably discharged...* ' with '*Invalided from the service...* '.

Headquarters, Second Army,

No. 14556 C.S.M., W.J. McCLEAN,

To Royal Irish Fusiliers.

I congratulate you on the gallant act by which you have won the

DISTINGUISHED CONDUCT MEDAL.

19th Sept. 1918. *Commanding Second Army*

PRINTED IN FRANCE BY ARMY PRINTING AND STATIONERY SERVICES. PRESS A—

Certificates such as this were presented to recipients of gallantry medals, often when they were presented with their medal ribbons. The presentation of the actual medal would often take place some time later.

The medals of Captain C H Steele MC*.
From left: Military Cross and Bar, 1914 Star with clasp '5th Aug-22nd Nov 1914', British War Medal 1914-20, Victory Medal, General Service Medal 1918-62 with clasps 'Iraq' & 'NW Persia'.

Military Medal awarded to Corporal J Fegan.

36th (Ulster) Division Certificate for Gallantry.

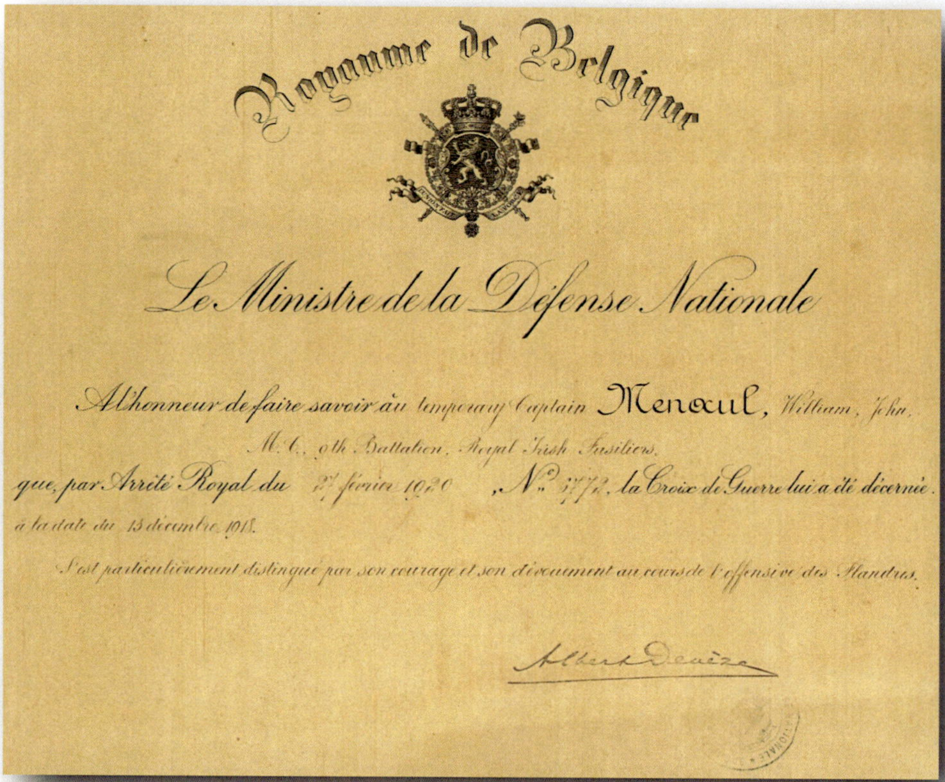
Royaume de Belgique

Le Ministre de la Défense Nationale

A l'honneur de faire savoir au temporary Captain Menaul, William, John, M.C., 9th Battalion, Royal Irish Fusiliers,
que, par Arrêté Royal du 27 février 1920, N° 3772, la Croix de Guerre lui a été décernée.
à la date du 15 décembre 1918.

S'est particulièrement distingué par son courage et son dévouement au cours de l'offensive des Flandres.

Albert Devèze

Certificate awarded to Captain W J Menaul MC, which accompanied the award of the *Croix de Guerre* (Belgium).

The miniature medals of Warrant Officer Class 1 G A Williams MM. From left: Military Medal, 1914 Star with clasp '5th Aug-22nd Nov 1914', British War Medal 1914-20, Victory Medal, Medal of a *Chevalier de L'Ordre de Leopold II* (Belgium) and the *Croix de Guerre* (Belgium).

APPENDIX 5

Roll of Officers

Two hundred and forty-nine officers (including eight Medical Officers and four Chaplains) served with the 9th Royal Irish Fusiliers at some time from its formation in September 1914 to its final demise in 1919. They came from every walk of life, from all over Ireland, from the rest of the British Isles, and from Canada, South Africa and Australia. Although English soldiers made up a large proportion of its soldiers from late-1916, the 9th Royal Irish Fusiliers was led largely by Irish officers throughout the war.

Although a handful of Regular, Special Reserve and Territorial Force officers served with the 9th Royal Irish Fusiliers, most held temporary commissions for the duration of the war. Initially in the New Armies, commissions were granted to those who had undergone training at one of the various Officer Training Corps, and over 20,000 such young men had their temporary commissions granted in the period up to March 1915. From January 1915 those men who were recommended for a commission by their commanding officers were given a training course of four weeks before commissions were confirmed for those deemed suitable. In February 1916 it was directed that all of those recommended for a commission were to attend an officer training unit, an officer cadet battalion, cavalry cadet squadron or similar unit for the other arms. The training lasted for four months.

Twenty-one of the original officers who joined soon after the formation of the 9th Royal Irish Fusiliers had been members of the Ulster Volunteer Force, as was its first Medical Officer. About one third of those who were commissioned into the 9th Royal Irish Fusiliers after it had sailed for France came by way of the 7th Officer Cadet Battalion at Fermoy in County Cork. This was formerly the Cadet Company of the 7th (Service) Battalion, The Prince of Wales's Leinster Regiment (Royal Canadians), which had been formed prior to that Battalion's move to England with 47th Brigade, 16th (Irish) Division. The majority of the remaining officers were trained at other Officer Cadet Battalions in England and Scotland. A few of the officers of the 9th Royal Irish Fusiliers who had been commissioned from the ranks, were regular soldiers, but the majority of the soldiers commissioned were war-time volunteers. Most were from infantry regiments, although only a small proportion, a fifth, was from battalions in the Ulster Division. In some cases, exceptional and experienced non-commissioned officers were commissioned directly without undergoing further training. After completing their initial training the newly-commissioned officers were posted to one of the reserve battalions.

Although some arrived as individual reinforcements, many of the newly-commissioned officers were held in the reserve battalions for some time until required at the front. There were a number of occasions when large groups of second lieutenants were dispatched to France or Flanders. The big changes occurred after the attacks at Hamel in July 1916, at Ypres in August 1917, and after the retreat in March and April 1918 when large drafts replaced those killed and wounded. The largest single such draft was of fifteen Second Lieutenants who arrived on 15 August 1916. By the end of the year, six had been posted to the 1st Battalion and, within a year, seven of those who remained had been evacuated, wounded or sick, to hospital in England, and one had died of wounds.

A proportion of the officers transferred from other regiments and corps, both individually and in larger groups. The first large draft from another unit arrived after the amalgamation with the 2nd North Irish Horse in September 1917. Thirty officers are known to have been posted to the newly-named 9th (North Irish Horse) Battalion but eleven officers did not join; five were found unfit for service with the infantry, four sought transfer to the Indian Army Reserve of Officers, one transferred to the Tank Corps and one was injured before he could join. Few of the nineteen officers who did join remained for any length of time. By December 1917, eleven had transferred to other regiments—six to the Tank Corps, which was recruiting heavily in preparation for the formation of its fourth brigade, four to other infantry regiments and one to the Royal Flying Corps. Of the remaining eight officers, three were wounded or injured by December 1917 and the other five became casualties in March or April 1918; two were killed in action, two were captured and one was wounded.

The second draft from another unit arrived in 1918 when the 7th/8th (Service) Battalion was disbanded. Ten officers joined the 9th Royal Irish Fusiliers on 16 February 1918, with one joining in March 1918 and two in May 1918. They were even less fortunate than those from the North Irish Horse. Although one officer transferred to the Royal Flying Corps (after earning an MC) and one was sent home to rest after nearly three years at the front, the remainder were committed immediately into the battles fought in March and April 1918. In less than two months after their arrival eight officers were casualties; two were killed in action, four were captured (one of whom died of wounds in captivity) and two were wounded (one of whom returned to the 9th Royal Irish Fusiliers and was killed in action in October 1918). Two officers were captured later in the war. Only one, Captain W Sparks MC, ended the war with the 9th Royal Irish Fusiliers.

A smaller draft of five officers arrived from the disbanded 11th (Service) Battalion on 28/29 August 1918. Three were wounded in the first week of September and one was killed in action at the end of that month.

The turnover of officers was rapid. Half of the officers who served with the 9th Royal Irish Fusiliers did so for less than three months, with half of those becoming casualties of one kind or another. Those who moved on to other units were posted to other battalions of Princess Victoria's (Royal Irish Fusiliers), transferred to other infantry regiments or were posted back to their own regiment after an attachment to the 9th Royal Irish Fusiliers. Some were attached or transferred to the new Machine Gun Corps (three officers), the Tank Corps (eleven officers) or the Royal Flying Corps (five officers). Seventeen officers transferred to the Indian Army or the Indian Army Reserve of Officers. A few experienced officers were transferred to the General List for service on the Staff. These moves, coupled with the high casualty rate, resulted in a new generation of officers about every six months.

The vast majority of the officers of the 9th Royal Irish Fusiliers held temporary commissions, i.e. for the duration of the war and, unlike other ranks, the officers of the 9th Royal Irish Fusiliers were not discharged either under King's Regulations Paragraph 392 during the course of the war or to the Army Reserve at the end of the war. Those who, through wounds, injury or sickness, were unable to continue to serve, relinquished their commissions. Those who were serving at the end of the war were released from service in accordance with Army Order 10 of 1919 and had no liability for reserve service; they subsequently relinquished their commissions, most in 1921.

Commanding Officer		
S W W BLACKER	September 1914 – March 1917	Appointed Commanding Officer of 20th (Reserve) Battalion, The Royal Irish Rifles.
S J SOMERVILLE	March – August 1917	Killed in action 16 August 1917.
J G BREW	June 1917	Acting Commanding Officer for the Messines attack. Appointed Second-in-Command on the arrival of Kelly.
P E KELLY	August 1917 – April 1918	Wounded 26 March and 18 April 1918.
J G BREW	March 1918	Acting Commanding Officer at Erches. Died of wounds as a prisoner of war 6 April 1918.
G M FORDE	April – August 1918	Acting Commanding Officer. Reverted to Second-in-Command on the return of Kelly.
P E KELLY	August – October 1918	Killed in action 11 October 1918.
R J A TAMPLIN	October 1918 – 1919	Released from service.
Second-In-Command		
W C FITZGERALD	September 1914 – early 1915	Appointed Commanding Officer of the 10th (Reserve) Battalion.
A C PRATT	Early 1915 – August 1916	Appointed Commanding Officer of the 11th (Service) Battalion, The Royal Inniskilling Fusiliers (Donegal and Fermanagh).
D G SHILLINGTON	August 1916 – April 1917	To hospital then appointed Second-in-Command of the 10th (Reserve) Battalion.
T F GIVEN	August 1917	Wounded 16 August 1917.
J G BREW	September 1917 – March 1918	Appointed acting Commanding Officer.
C B DESPARD	March – April 1918	Killed in action 18 April 1918.
R G KERR	May – July 1918	Killed in action 11 July 1918.
R J A TAMPLIN	July – August 1918	Replaced by Forde.
G M FORDE	August – September 1918	Wounded 16 September 1918.
P E MacLEAN	October 1918	Replaced by Emerson.
R L EMERSON	November 1918 – 1919	Released from service.
Adjutant		
H W SETON	November 1914 – December 1915	Appointed Adjutant of 20th (Reserve) Battalion, The Royal Irish Rifles.

G St G S CATHER	December 1915 – July 1916	Killed in action 1 July 1916.
A FERGUSON	July 1916 – September 1917	Replaced by Barefoot.
G W N BAREFOOT	September – October 1917	Posted back to the 1st Battalion.
M HENAHAN	November 1917 – March 1918	Captured 21 March 1918.
W SPARKS	May 1918 – February 1919	Released from service.
P E MacLEAN	February – May 1919	Released from service.

Officer Commanding A Company

C H ENSOR	October 1915 – July 1916	Wounded 1 July 1916.
A D ALLEN	July 1916 – March 1917	Injured 15 March 1917.
E A GODSON	September 1916 & November 1916	Temporary.
R W JOHNSTON	December 1916	Temporary.
R S FLOOD	March 1917	Temporary.
T G SHILLINGTON	April – August 1917	Died of wounds 18 August 1917.
E A GODSON	August – December 1917	Wounded 5 December 1917.
G W VESEY	December 1917 – March 1918	Died of wounds 26 March 1918.
A W HENRY	March 1918	Captured 27 March 1918.
A DAVIDSON	April 1918	Temporary.
G H RICHARDSON	May 1918	Temporary.
C H KERR	June 1918 – 1919	Released from service.

Officer Commanding B Company

T J ATKINSON	October 1915 – July 1916	Killed in action 1 July 1916.
D G SHILLINGTON	July – August 1916	Appointed Second-in-Command.
E N ENSOR	September 1916 – March 1917	Transferred to the Labour Corps.
T G SHILLINGTON	December 1916	Temporary.
R S FLOOD	February 1917	Temporary.
D H WRIGHT	March – August 1917	Captured 16 August 1917.
I E McCAUSLAND	August – December 1917	Replaced by Partridge.
J H PARTRIDGE	December 1917 – March 1918	Killed in action 24 March 1918.
E HAMILTON	March – April 1918	Killed in action 12 April 1918.
J J MURPHY	April – October 1918	Relieved of command in October 1918.
W G GRAHAM	October 1918 – 1919	Released from service.

Officer Commanding C Company

S J SCOTT	October 1915 – January 1916	Transferred to the Royal Army Medical Corps.
C M JOHNSTON	January – July 1916	Killed in action 1 July 1916.
J A JOHNSTON	July 1916 – February 1917	Killed in action 18 February 1917.
G E LUTTON	October 1916	Temporary.
S W WALLACE	December 1916	Temporary.
M HENAHAN	February – November 1917	Wounded 3 November 1917.
T E C CROSBIE	November 1917 – April 1918	Killed in action 15 April 1918.
J BENSON	April – August 1918	Captured 12 August 1918.

J E GIBSON	August 1918 – March 1919	Attached to the 5th (Service) Battalion, The Royal Irish Regiment (Pioneers).
E W REYNOLDS	September 1918	Temporary.
G H CROSS	September 1918	Temporary. Killed in action 30 September 1918.
H C BURROWS	March – June 1919	Released from service.
Officer Commanding D Company		
D G SHILLINGTON	October 1915 – April 1916	Appointed Officer Commanding B Company.
H W F M VANSTON	April 1916 – March 1917	Attached to the 1/4th Battalion, The Essex Regiment.
T F GIVEN	September 1916	Temporary.
J G BREW	July 1916	Officer commanding for the Somme attack. Wounded 1 July 1916.
R S FLOOD	November 1916	Temporary.
T F GIVEN	March – May 1917	Replaced by Flood.
G H GIBSON	March 1917	Temporary.
R S FLOOD	June – October 1917	Replaced by Despard.
C B DESPARD	October 1917 – February 1918	Appointed Second-in-Command.
H S DEAN	February – April 1918	Wounded 12 April 1918.
J A COOKE	April – May 1918	Injured May 1918.
J I SMITH	May – June 1918	Posted to the 1st Battalion.
R H LINDSAY	July – October 1918	Wounded 18 October 1918.
G H GIBSON	October 1918 – 1919	Released from service.
Quartermaster		
A FERGUSON	September 1914 – July 1916	Appointed Adjutant.
G W WILSON	September 1916 – 1919	Released from service.
Transport Officer		
J M STRONGE	1915 – August 1917	Killed in action 16 August 1917.
E J L TURNER	August 1917 – April 1918	Wounded 12 April 1918.
J B K MORROW	April – December 1918	Released from service.
A CARR	December 1918 – March 1919	Injured 3 March 1919.
Chaplain		
F J HALAHAN	September 1915 – March 1917	Appointed Divisional Chaplain.
S MAYES	March 1917 – January 1918	Released from service.
H S BALLY	January – June 1918	Appointed Chaplain to 110th Field Ambulance.
W B ALLMAN	June 1918 – 1919	Released from service.
Medical Officer		
W S S BERRY	1915 – June 1917	Posted to the Staff.
E S SOWERBY	December 1916	Temporary.
O V BURROWS	June 1917 – January 1918	Posted.

S H RICHMAN	September 1917	Temporary.
H S MORGAN	January – April 1918	Killed in action 12 April 1918.
F G McGUINNESS	May & June 1918	Temporary.
C R BROWN	July 1918	Temporary.
W H SUTCLIFFE	August 1918 – 1919	Released from service.

Biographies

These short biographies are based on information gleaned from a number of sources, including a list of officers prepared for Headquarters 3rd Echelon British Expeditionary Force in March 1919, nominal rolls attached to the War Diary, records in the Regimental Museum, the officers' personal records held in the National Archives, the Army List, and the reference books and histories detailed in the bibliography. It is difficult, however, to determine the career of many of the officers as their movements were not always recorded and, while every effort has been made to check the detail, there may be some inaccuracies.

In describing the movement of officers between units the terminology used is that of the time. Officers could be *'detached from'* the 9th Royal Irish Fusiliers and *'attached to'* another unit, and vice versa, e.g. 'attached for service with 108th Brigade Trench Mortar Battery'. When attached to another unit he remained part of his parent corps. *'Posted'* meant that an officer was moved to another battalion or unit of his corps. For officers of the 9th Royal Irish Fusiliers this meant joining another battalion of Princess Victoria's (Royal Irish Fusiliers). *'Transferred'* meant that an officer was permanently moved to another corps. The officers from other regiments who joined as reinforcement drafts were usually transferred from their regiments to Princess Victoria's (Royal Irish Fusiliers) and posted to the 9th Royal Irish Fusiliers.

The Commanding Officers are shown first, in the order that they commanded. They are followed, in alphabetical order, by the other officers, the Medical Officers and the Chaplains. Finally, those soldiers of the 9th Royal Irish Fusiliers who were commissioned and served elsewhere are listed, as are those officers who were posted in but who did not join. In an attempt to avoid confusion, battalion and regimental titles are shown in full, with the exception of 9th Royal Irish Fusiliers and the other battalions of Princess Victoria's (Royal Irish Fusiliers). Again to avoid confusion, the Battalion is referred to throughout as 9th Royal Irish Fusiliers, regardless of whether the event being described is before the Battalion was formally named, or after the amalgamation with the North Irish Horse. Service numbers are shown also for those who served at some time in the ranks. Where known, the National Archives' reference to the officer's personal file is included at the end of each entry. Some files are not held or have not been found.

Commanding Officers

The Commanding Officers are listed in chronological order of holding command. They include Major J G Brew who twice acted in the absence of the Commanding Officer, and was captured and killed on the second occasion.

BLACKER DSO, JP, DL. Lieutenant Colonel Stewart Ward William Born on 4 July 1865 at Carrickblacker, County Armagh. Commissioned into the Royal Regiment of Artillery from the Royal Military Academy, Woolwich in 1885. Captain 1895. Served on the North West Frontier 1897 where he commanded the guns of 51st Field Battery at Shabkadr in August 1897 and where he was severely wounded in the thigh. **Mention in Despatches**. India Medal with clasp 'Punjab Frontier 1897-98'. Fought in the South African War 1899-1900. Adjutant 3rd Division Royal Artillery. Major 1900. Queen's South Africa Medal. Retired 3 May 1905 and married (Eva St John Fitzroy). JP Armagh. Signed the Ulster Covenant 28 September 1912. Raised and commanded the 4th (Portadown) Battalion, Armagh Regiment, Ulster Volunteer Force in 1912. Recalled for service in August 1914 and posted initially to Edinburgh. Transferred to Princess Victoria's (Royal Irish Fusiliers) and promoted Temporary Lieutenant Colonel, 15 September 1914 and appointed to command the 9th Royal Irish Fusiliers. To France with 36th (Ulster) Division in October 1915. 1914-15 Star. Commanding officer on 1 July 1916. Awarded the **DSO**, **Mentioned in Despatches** three times and was made **Officer of the *Legion d'Honneur*** and ***Croix de Guerre* (France)**. He left the 9th Royal Irish Fusiliers on 9 March 1917 and relinquished command on 15 March 1917. He transferred to The Royal Irish Rifles and assumed command of 20th (Reserve) Battalion, The Royal Irish Rifles at Newtownards from 18 April 1917 until 16 May 1918. Relinquished the rank of Temporary Lieutenant Colonel 16 May 1918 and transferred to the Reserve of Officers. Brevet Lieutenant Colonel 31 May 1918. After the war he settled in Bridport, Devon and died after an early morning swim on 6 September 1935, aged 70. His eldest son, Lieutenant Colonel William Desmond Blacker DSO, was killed in action by mortar fire on 11 July 1944 in Normandy while commanding 179th Field Regiment, Royal Regiment of Artillery, having taken command on3 July.

SOMERVILLE. Lieutenant Colonel Stafford James Born on 18 February 1871, the son of the Reverend D Somerville, Chaplain to the Forces. Commissioned from the Royal Military College, Sandhurst into The Royal Inniskilling Fusiliers on 29 November 1890. Lieutenant 21 September 1892. Served with the Peshawar Column and 5th Brigade, Tirah Expeditionary Force on the North West Frontier 1897-98. India Medal with clasps 'Punjab Frontier 1897-98' and 'Tirah 1897-98'. Captain 1 July 1898. Major 3 November 1910. Served with 1st Battalion, The Royal Inniskilling Fusiliers in 87th Brigade, 29th Division from March 1915. 1914-15 Star. Assumed command at Gallipoli on 2 May 1915 until **wounded** in the shoulder and evacuated to hospital in England on 6 May 1915. Deployed to France in December 1916 and was attached to and assumed command of the 9th Royal Irish Fusiliers on 16 March 1917. **Killed in action** on 16 August 1917 on Hill 35 during the Battle of Langemarck, aged 46. He is commemorated in the Memorial Chapel at the Royal Military Academy Sandhurst. The eldest of his two sons, Captain Stafford Dudley Somerville, 5th (Service) Battalion, King's Own (Yorkshire Light Infantry), was killed in action at Hamel on 5 July 1916, fighting in the trenches recently vacated by the 9th Royal Irish Fusiliers.

BREW. Major John George Born in Gateshead, County Durham on 14 December 1876. Went to sea in 1893. Worked for the Ulster Steamship Company in Belfast. Awarded the Silver Medal of the German Red Cross Society for saving life at sea in 1902 while serving as 3rd Officer on the SS Torr Head. Obtained his Master's Certificate. Member of the 4th (Portadown) Battalion, Armagh Regiment, Ulster Volunteer Force. Joined the 9th Royal Irish Fusiliers on its formation and was commissioned on 15 September 1914. Captain 1 December 1914. To France with 36th (Ulster) Division in October 1915. 1914-15 Star. **Wounded** in the head on 1 July 1916 at the Ancre when Officer Commanding 'D' Company and admitted to 8th General Hospital, Rouen. Evacuated to hospital in England 6 July 1916. To France 6 December 1916 and rejoined the 9th Royal Irish Fusiliers on 11 December 1916. Major 27 January 1917. Acting Commanding Officer during the Messines operations in early June 1917. Left to attend the Senior Officers' Course and was appointed Second-in-Command on 3 September 1917. On 26 March 1918, when acting Commanding Officer, he was **captured** in Erches with the GSO1 of 108th Brigade and the Commanding Officer of the 1st Battalion. Soon after his capture he was shot in the chest. He **died of wounds** in captivity on 6 April 1918, aged 41. **Mention in Despatches**. His brother-in-law, *Conducteur* (Ambulance Driver) Malcolm Percy Clow, served with the *Croix Rouge Francaise* attached to French forces in Serbia in 1917. He died of dysentery in Macedonia on 10 July 1917 and is commemorated on the Portadown War Memorial and in Edenderry Parish Church. (WO 339/14255)

KELLY. Lieutenant Colonel Philip Edward Born on 5 April 1889 in Newport, County Mayo. Commissioned from the Royal Military College, Sandhurst into Princess Victoria's (Royal Irish Fusiliers) on 14 October 1908 and served with the 1st Battalion. Posted as Adjutant to the 5th (Service) Battalion in 31st Brigade, 10th (Irish) Division. He landed at Sulva Bay, Gallipoli in August 1915. 1914-15 Star. **Wounded** on 10 August while hunting for snipers near battalion headquarters. **Mention in Despatches**. He was evacuated to hospital in England from Egypt on 14 October 1915. When fully recovered he served with the 1st Battalion from 27 June 1917, was briefly Commanding Officer of the Divisional Troops then assumed command of the 9th Royal Irish Fusiliers on 19 August 1917. Brevet Major 31 August 1917. **Wounded** slightly during the withdrawal to Erches on 25/26 March 1918. Commanding officer of a composite battalion comprising the 9th Royal Irish Fusiliers and one company of the 1st Battalion in April 1918 and then of the composite battalion formed from the remnants of 108th Brigade on 17 April 1918. **Wounded** by shrapnel in the right leg on 18 April 1918 near Kemmel and admitted to hospital at Boulogne. Evacuated to hospital in England 8 May 1918. **Mention in Despatches**. Took command of the 9th Royal Irish Fusiliers again from 26 August 1918. **Killed in action** by shellfire at a company HQ on 11 October 1918 at Hill 41 near Dadizeele, aged 29. Commemorated in the Memorial Chapel, Royal Military Academy Sandhurst. (WO 339/7190)

FORDE DSO, MC*. Lieutenant Colonel Gordon Miller Born on 16 April 1886. From Portrush, County Antrim. Attended Durham University, serving in the Officer Training Corps from 1909-11 and then became a schoolmaster in Ballykelly. Commissioned into The Royal Inniskilling Fusiliers on 10 November 1914 and served with the 11th (Service) Battalion, The Royal Inniskilling Fusiliers (Donegal and Fermanagh) in 109th Brigade. To France with the advance party from 36th (Ulster) Division 16 September 1915. 1914-15 Star. **MC**. Major 1 May 1917. **Wounded** when hit by a shrapnel bullet in the left knee on 7 June 1917 when in command of a company during the attack at Messines; earned a Bar to the **MC**. Evacuated to hospital in England via 7th General Hospital at St Omer. Transferred to Princess Victoria's (Royal Irish Fusiliers) 15 March 1918. Posted to the 9th Royal Irish Fusiliers as Second-in-Command on 21 April 1918. Acting Lieutenant Colonel and Commanding Officer from his arrival until 25 August 1918 when Lieutenant Colonel Kelly returned. Reverted to Major 27 August 1918. **Mention in Despatches**. **Wounded** on 16 September 1918 by shell fragments in the head, face and hand and was evacuated to hospital in England. **DSO**. After his recovery he rejoined the 3rd (Reserve) Garrison Battalion, Princess Victoria's (Royal Irish Fusiliers) in England and then was attached to the 11th (Service) Battalion, The Leicestershire Regiment (Midland Pioneers) in 6th Division. Relinquished his commission 31 March 1920. Reported missing on 6 December 1934, aged 48, and was declared dead in May 1944. His brother, Lieutenant Kenneth Rowley Forde, was killed in action on 23 July 1915 serving with the 2nd Battalion, The Buffs (Royal East Kent Regiment), and is buried in Dranoutre Churchyard. (WO 339/13245)

TAMPLIN DSO. Lieutenant Colonel Robert James Abbott Born on 24 November 1881. Educated at King's College, London. Joined the civil service in Dublin as a clerk in 1901 and worked as a civil servant with the Inland Revenue Service in Belfast. Enlisted into the 6th (Service) Battalion, The Connaught Rangers on the outbreak of war. Lieutenant 9 October 1914. To France 15 December 1915 in 47th Brigade, 16th (Irish) Division. 1914-15 Star. Appointed Adjutant until 30 June 1916 when he was appointed Second-in-Command. Major 21 June 1916. **Mention in Despatches** (twice), earned the **DSO** at Guillemont on 3 September 1916, where he was **wounded**. ***Croix de Guerre (étoile en argent) (France)***. After the 6th (Service) Battalion, The Connaught Rangers was reduced to a cadre he was attached to the 9th Royal Irish Fusiliers as Second-in-Command on 17 July 1918. Replaced in that appointment by Lieutenant Colonel G M Forde. Transferred to Princess Victoria's (Royal Irish Fusiliers), Temporary Lieutenant Colonel and appointed Commanding Officer 15 October 1918. Commanding officer at Mouscron where the 9th Royal Irish Fusiliers was based until it was disbanded in 1919. Served with the Ulster Special Constabulary as an Area Commandant and during the Second World War he commanded the 4th Armagh (Armagh) Battalion of the Ulster Home Guard. Died 18 September 1974, aged 92 and was buried at Whitechurch Parish Church, Dublin.

Officers

Ranks shown are the highest attained by the officer during the course of the war, including acting rank if held for a protracted period, or the highest rank attained by those who served post-war.

ALLEN. Captain Arthur Dawson Born on 6 May 1883 in Keady, County Armagh. Educated at The Royal School, Armagh and at Trinity College, Dublin. In Canada he served in the Royal North West Mounted Police in the North West Territories and the Yukon from 1902-06. On returning to Ireland he joined the Ulster Volunteer Force and commanded 'M' Company (Richhill), 1st (Armagh) Battalion, Armagh Regiment, Ulster Volunteer Force for eighteen months. Signed the Ulster Covenant 28 September 1912. He joined the 9th Royal Irish Fusiliers on its formation and was commissioned as a Second Lieutenant on 15 September 1914. To France with 36th (Ulster) Division in October 1915 as a platoon commander in 'A' Company and also range-finding officer. 1914-15 Star. Commanded 'A' Company July 1916 to March 1917. **Wounded** slightly 13 February 1917 in the line near the River Douve. **Wounded** in the foot and leg in the line near the River Douve on 24 February 1917 and was evacuated to hospital in England on 15 March 1917. He subsequently relinquished his commission on grounds of ill health caused by wounds on 11 July 1917. Silver War Badge, number 341336. Served with the Ulster Special Constabulary (39th Platoon, 'A' Specials). High Sheriff of County Armagh 1934. He turned the family home, 'The Retreat' in Armagh, into a hospice for the mentally ill. During the Second World War he commanded an Ulster Home Guard unit in Rostrevor. Died at Rostrevor on 9 April 1963, aged 79. (WO 339/14252)

ANDERSON. Lieutenant Leigh Maxwell (Max) Born on 22 June 1875 at Armagh, County Armagh. He played both rugby and cricket for Armagh. Member of Armagh County Council. Commanded 'B' Company, 1st (Armagh) Battalion, Armagh Regiment, Ulster Volunteer Force. A stock broker and businessman, he closed his businesses in order to enlist. Enlisted into the 9th

Royal Irish Fusiliers on its formation and was immediately commissioned on 15 September 1914. Lieutenant 1 December 1914. Admitted to Seaford Hospital, Sussex on 30 August 1915 with cerebral meningitis and **died** on 1 September 1915, aged 40. (WO 339/14253)

L M Anderson

ANDREWS. Second Lieutenant Arthur Alexander Born on 27 August 1894 at Dungannon, County Tyrone. Signed the Ulster Covenant 28 September 1912. A bank clerk in Bangor, he was commissioned into Princess Victoria's (Royal Irish Fusiliers) on 23 August 1915, joined the 9th Royal Irish Fusiliers on 2 April 1916 and was posted to 'C' Company. **Wounded** in the right thigh during the attack at Hamel 1 July 1916 and evacuated to hospital in England on 14 July 1916. Lieutenant 1 July 1917. He relinquished his commission on account of ill-health caused by wounds (which left his leg over an inch shorter) on 13 January 1918. Silver War Badge, number 233447. He lived in Dungannon after the war. He died in 1978, aged 84. (WO 339/44469)

ASHE. Lieutenant John Francis Born in 1899 at Tuam, County Galway, the son of Constable Charles Ashe, Royal Irish Constabulary. Commissioned into Princess Victoria's (Royal Irish Fusiliers) on 1 March 1917. Joined the 9th Royal Irish Fusiliers on 13 May 1917 and was posted to 'C' Company. Attached to 12th (Service) Battalion, The Royal Irish Rifles (Central Antrim) in 108th Brigade on 30 June 1917 and was **wounded** at the Battle of Langemarck on 16 August 1917. Evacuated to hospital in England 20 August 1917. Lieutenant 1 September 1918. When recovered he served with the Indian Army until released from service. He relinquished his commission on 29 October 1920. After the war he became an architect. Commissioned from the Officers' Emergency Reserve as a Captain 24 August 1939 into The Royal Irish Fusiliers (Princess Victoria's). Dismissed the Service by sentence of General Court Martial 10 May 1941.

ATKINSON. Major Thomas Joyce Born on 30 January 1878. Educated at Trinity College, Dublin, graduating MA and LLB. Intimately involved with the activities of Seagoe Parish Church. A barrister before becoming a solicitor in Portadown with the firm Carleton, Atkinson and Sloan. He was a company commander in the 4th (Portadown) Battalion, Armagh Regiment, Ulster Volunteer Force for eighteen months. Signed the Ulster Covenant 28 September 1912. Enlisted into the 9th Royal Irish Fusiliers on its formation on 16 September 1914 and was immediately commissioned in the rank of Captain. Major 2 July 1915. To France with 36th (Ulster) Division in October 1915 as Officer Commanding 'B' Company. 1914-15 Star. **Killed in action** during the attack at Hamel 1 July 1916, aged 38. His body was found and buried by men of The Durham Light Infantry in mid-August 1916. (WO 339/14254)

AUBER. Lieutenant Joseph Born on 12 August 1892 at Burton-on-Trent, Staffordshire. A jeweller, he enlisted into 1/6th Battalion, The Prince of Wales's (North Staffordshire Regiment), a Territorial Force battalion, at Burton-on-Trent on 24 September 1914. Posted to the 2/6th Battalion when it was formed in November 1914 (2960 - Sergeant) and served in England. Commissioned into The King's (Liverpool Regiment) on 24 September 1915 and joined the 16th (Reserve) Battalion, The King's (Liverpool Regiment) at Prees Heath. Transferred to the 1st Reserve Regiment of Cavalry and then served with the Service Squadron of 6th (Inniskilling) Dragoons in 36th (Ulster) Division until June 1916 when it became part of the 2nd North Irish Horse, X Corps Cavalry Regiment. Lieutenant 27 August 1917. Transferred to Princess Victoria's (Royal Irish Fusiliers) and joined the 9th Royal Irish Fusiliers on 8 November 1917. Left on 16 November 1917 to transfer to the Tank Corps but returned to France on 19 December 1917. Returned to England on 7 February 1918 and transferred to the General List for service on probation with the Indian Army 8 March 1918. Appointed as Lieutenant Indian Army 14 April 1918 (to rank from 24 June 1917). He served with the 5th Cavalry. Lieutenant Indian Army Reserve of Officers 25 October 1920 (with seniority from 24 September 1916). Captain Indian Army Reserve of Officers 5 November 1920. He relinquished his commission in the Indian Army Reserve of Officers 21 December 1921. He took on his father's business as a jeweller and was made bankrupt in 1938. (WO 339/43557)

F Baker

BAKER MM. Lieutenant Frederick Enlisted into Princess Victoria's (Royal Irish Fusiliers) (13845) in September 1914. To France on 14 June 1915 and joined the 1st Battalion. 1914-15 Star. Promoted Lance Sergeant. **MM**. Commissioned into Princess Victoria's (Royal Irish Fusiliers) on 26 April 1917 and joined the 9th Royal Irish Fusiliers on 5 July 1917. Served with 'C' Company. **Wounded** at the Battle of Langemarck on 16 August 1917. Evacuated to hospital in England 18 August 1917. His wounds precluded further service. Lieutenant 26 October 1918. He relinquished his commission on 30 May 1919 on account of ill-health contracted on active service. Silver War Badge, number B230565. Lived in Hastings, Sussex after the war.

BAKER. Lieutenant John Dudley Born on 6 November 1897 in London. Joined the Inns of Court Officer Training Corps on 8 July 1915 and was commissioned into Princess Victoria's (Royal Irish Fusiliers) on 20 November 1915. Served with the 4th (Extra Reserve) Battalion and then the 7th/8th (Service) Battalion in 49th Brigade, 16th (Irish) Division. Lieutenant 1 July 1917. Joined the 9th Royal Irish Fusiliers on 25 May 1918. Attached in July 1918 to 108th Trench Mortar Battery, where he was **wounded** at Courtrai on the morning of 30 October 1918 by a gas shell. He saw no further service and relinquished his commission on 16 January 1919. (WO 339/48136)

BALE. Lieutenant Frank Stewart Born on 8 May 1888 in Australia. He served as a regular soldier in the 1st Battalion, The Cheshire Regiment from 1906-08. A shipping traveller, he enlisted into 3/28th Battalion, The London Regiment (3164) on 14 January 1915 and joined 'D' Company. To France and joined 1/28th (County of London) Battalion, The London Regiment (Artist's Rifles), which was now an Officer Training Corps at St Omer, on 11 August 1915. 1914-15 Star. Sergeant 16 October 1915. Commissioned into the Army Service Corps on 6 November 1915. After attending Supply School at Boulogne in November 1915, he served in Abancourt from December 1915. Lieutenant 1 July 1917. Transferred for infantry service to Princess Victoria's (Royal Irish Fusiliers), he joined the 9th Royal Irish Fusiliers on 26 June 1918 as a platoon commander. To hospital suffering from a major gastric illness 14 September 1918 and was evacuated to hospital in Liverpool on 7 November 1918. He saw no further service and relinquished his commission on 16 October 1919. He died in Yorkshire in 1961, aged 73. (WO 339/46396)

BARCROFT. Captain Gilbert Evelyn Born on 14 June 1883 at Stangmore House, Dungannon, County Tyrone. A mill manager in Dungannon, he also worked as a civil engineer in Honduras; he returned to Ireland in February 1915. Commissioned into Princess Victoria's (Royal Irish Fusiliers) on 22 May 1915 and joined the 9th Royal Irish Fusiliers. To France with 36th (Ulster) Division in October 1915 in 'A' Company. 1914-15 Star. **Wounded** severely in the head during the attack at Hamel 1 July 1916 and evacuated to hospital in England on 3 July 1916. Rejoined the 9th Royal Irish Fusiliers on 4 March 1917, where he served until 18 October 1917. Captain 12 July 1917. He attended a medical board while on leave and subsequently served with The Royal Inniskilling Fusiliers and on the Staff. Employed as a Railway Transport Officer in late 1919. Relinquished his commission 15 October 1920. After the war he joined the Ulster Special Constabulary. Lived at Ennismore House, The Birches, near Portadown. High Sheriff of County Armagh 1932. Gazetted as a Second Lieutenant (298558) for service with the Army Cadet Force in Northern Ireland Command 1 November 1943. He died on 21 February 1945, aged 61.

BAREFOOT MC. Lieutenant Colonel George William Norman Born on 5 March 1894. Educated at Epsom College. Commissioned from the Royal Military College, Sandhurst into Princess Victoria's (Royal Irish Fusiliers) on 3 September 1913. Joined 'D' Company of the 1st Battalion as a platoon commander. To France 22 August 1914. 1914 Star. Lieutenant 18 October 1914. Appointed Officer Commanding 'D' Company. For his actions on 1 July 1916 he was awarded the **MC** and **Mentioned in Despatches**. **Wounded** 7 July 1916. When recovered he served briefly as a Town Major and was attached to a brigade in preparation for posting as a Staff Captain. Joined 11th Infantry Brigade on 21 January 1917. Joined the 9th Royal Irish Fusiliers on 16 October 1917 as Adjutant but was transferred to the General List for duty on the Staff 31 October 1917. Staff Captain Quartermaster General's Branch General Headquarters, February to May 1918; Staff Captain 148th Brigade, May 1918 to March 1919; Staff Captain 71st Brigade, March to May 1919 and Staff Captain 3rd Brigade in the British Army of the Rhine, May to November 1919. **Mention in Despatches**. Rejoined the 1st Battalion 13 February 1920. 'B' Company. Adjutant after the amalgamation of the 1st and 2nd Battalions from 11 August 1922 to 10 August 1925. Instructor at the Small Arms School, India 30 January 1930 to 29 January 1934. Major 4 April 1935. Retired 9 May 1936. Recalled from the Regular Army Reserve of Officers in 1939. Lieutenant Colonel 27 September 1945. Served with the Allied Control Commission in Germany. Died in Chelmsford, Essex 30 January 1960, aged 65. His son, Captain George Charles Richard Barefoot, served during the Second World War with The Royal Irish Fusiliers (Princess Victoria's) and the Glider Pilot Regiment.

BARNES. Lieutenant Reginald Victor Born on 23 June 1896 in Dublin. He attended Dublin University and joined the Officer Training Corps. Enlisted into The Prince of Wales's Leinster Regiment (Royal Canadians) (4416 - Private). Joined the 2nd Battalion, The Prince of Wales's Leinster Regiment (Royal Canadians) in 73rd Brigade, 24th Division near Wulverghem on 10 April 1916. Served at Delville Wood and Guillemont in August and September 1916 and Vimy Ridge in April 1917 before joining the 7th Officer Cadet Battalion. Commissioned into The Prince of Wales's Leinster Regiment (Royal Canadians) on 31 October 1917. Attached to the 9th Royal Irish Fusiliers on 17 April 1918 but fell ill with appendicitis on 23 April 1918 and was evacuated to hospital in England on 17 May 1918. On his recovery he was attached to the 7th then 2nd Labour Companies, The Duke of Cambridge's Own (Middlesex Regiment) and 41st Prisoner of War Company. Relinquished his commission 9 January 1920. After the war he worked in Australia as a tally clerk. Died in Merseyside in early 1975, aged 78. (WO 339/114717)

BARNETT. Lieutenant John Bolton Born on 20 August 1889 at West Derby, Liverpool, Lancashire. Worked as a commercial clerk in Limerick. Commissioned into The Royal Inniskilling Fusiliers on 29 April 1915 and served with the 10th (Service) Battalion, The Royal Inniskilling Fusiliers (Derry) in 109th Brigade until it was disbanded on 19 February 1918. Lieutenant 1 July 1917. Attached to the 9th Royal Irish Fusiliers on 25 August 1918, where he spent the rest of the war. Attached briefly to the 23rd (Service) Battalion, The Royal Fusiliers (City of London Regiment) (1st Sportsman's) 16 November 1918. Later served on the Staff in the British Army of the Rhine as an Assistant Camp Commandant. Relinquished his commission 21 August 1922. Owned a car dealership in Kensington, London. Died 5 January 1940 in Hove, Sussex, aged 50.

BARRETT TD MRCS. Lieutenant Colonel St Clair Edward John Born in 1898 at Belfast. Enlisted into Princess Victoria's (Royal Irish Fusiliers) (23761 - Private) in 1916 and joined the 9th Royal Irish Fusiliers. Promoted Lance Corporal. Commissioned into Princess Victoria's (Royal Irish Fusiliers) 27 June 1917 and rejoined the 9th Royal Irish Fusiliers on 30 September 1917. Left on 26 October 1917, ordered to England (probably for medical reasons). Spent the remainder of the war employed with the Ministry of Labour. Lieutenant 27 December 1918. Relinquished his commission 8 December 1921. He subsequently qualified as a doctor in 1925 and practiced in London. Member of the Royal College of Surgeons. Commissioned as Lieutenant in the Royal Army Medical Corps (74454) 29 March 1938. Captain 29 March 1939. **Captured** in 1943 and was held in Chungkai prison (labour) camp where he was the senior doctor. **Mention in Despatches**. Major 1 May 1947 (seniority 9 April 1941). Acting Lieutenant Colonel 1 May 1947. Served with the Territorial Army. **Territorial Efficiency Decoration** and **1st Clasp**. Retired from the Territorial Army Reserve of Officers as Honorary Lieutenant Colonel 5 September 1953. He emigrated to Australia and practiced medicine in New South Wales. He died there in 1984. His brother, Lieutenant Knox Gordon Barrett Royal Field Artillery, was killed in action on 20 September 1917 on the first day of the Battle of the Menin Road Ridge serving with Z20th Medium Mortar Battery in 20th (Light) Division. His brother, Captain Ernest William Barrett Royal Flying Corps, was killed in action on 29 May 1916 flying a DH2 of 29 Squadron. Having achieved a confirmed victory that morning, he was engaged by two enemy aircraft at 8.45am and crashed near Voormezeele. His brother, Sub-Lieutenant Norman James Barrett Royal Navy Reserve, is also commemorated on the First World War memorial in Saint Comgall's Parish Church, Bangor; the details of his death are unknown.

BAYLIFF. Second Lieutenant Gabriel Thomas Lane (Gay) Born on 8 March 1898 at Alexis Creek, British Columbia, Canada. The son of a rancher, he attended Officer Training Corps at Charterhouse and joined the University of London Officer Training Corps on 26 June 1916. Commissioned into the 6th (Inniskilling) Dragoons on 17 February 1917. Served with the 2nd North Irish Horse, X Corps Cavalry Regiment. Transferred to Princess Victoria's (Royal Irish Fusiliers) and joined the 9th Royal Irish Fusiliers on 20 October 1917. Transferred to the Tank Corps in December 1917 and joined the Tank Corps Depot, Wareham, Dorset for training. Posted to the 10th Battalion, Tank Corps. On 21 August 1918 when his tank was knocked out he was **wounded** by a bullet in the right wrist and **captured**. Repatriated on 13 December 1918. Attached to the 6th (Inniskilling) Dragoons 21 December 1919. Relinquished his commission 12 November 1920. He returned to Canada and farmed cattle on Chilancoh Ranch, Chilcotin in British Columbia. He died on 4 November 1977, aged 79 and was buried on the ranch. His son, Timothy Bayliff, served in the Royal Canadian Navy. (WO 339/73879)

BEHENNAH. Second Lieutenant William Born on 3 May 1894 at Dublin. A clerk, he enlisted into the 7th (Service) Battalion, The Royal Irish Rifles (6087 - Private) in 47th Brigade, 16th (Irish) Division on 2 May 1915. To France on 19 December 1915. Sergeant 30 March 1916. Company Quartermaster Sergeant 8 July 1916. Joined 9th Officer Cadet Battalion at Gailes, Ayrshire on 16 February 1917. Commissioned into The Royal Irish Rifles on 30 May 1917 and joined the 13th (Service) Battalion, The Royal Irish Rifles (1st County Down) in 108th Brigade. Attached to 9th Royal Irish Fusiliers on 6 August 1918 and was posted to 'C' Company. **Wounded** near Bailleul on 24 August 1918 when he was hit by a shrapnel bullet behind the right shoulder. He was evacuated to hospital in England on 10 September 1918. Lieutenant 30 November 1918. He saw no further service and was released from service on 25 July 1919. Relinquished his commission 16 November 1920. (WO 339/88895)

BELL. Lieutenant Alan George Frankland Born on 13 September 1887 at Liverpool. Commissioned into The Royal Inniskilling Fusiliers on 22 February 1915 and served with the 11th (Service) Battalion, The Royal Inniskilling Fusiliers (Donegal and Fermanagh) in 109th Brigade. **Wounded** by a gunshot to the right forearm on 12 August 1916 near Hill 63 at Ploegsteert and was evacuated to hospital in Liverpool. Lieutenant 1 July 1917. Briefly attached to the 11th (Service) Battalion, Princess Victoria's (Royal Irish Fusiliers). Posted to the 9th Royal Irish Fusiliers in August 1918 when the 11th (Service) Battalion was disbanded and joined on 28 August 1918. **Wounded** on 4 September 1918 at Neuve Eglise when shot in the left chest and, again, in the right forearm. Evacuated to hospital in England 15 September 1918. After he recovered he was attached to 348th Motor Transport Company, Army Service Corps. He relinquished his commission on 25 November 1919. His father, Captain Edward

Henry Bell, formerly retired Lieutenant and Quartermaster The Royal Irish Regiment, served as Adjutant of a garrison battalion of Princess Victoria's (Royal Irish Fusiliers). He relinquished his commission in 1918 on account of ill-health contracted on active service. His brother Captain Eric Norman Frankland Bell VC, The Royal Inniskilling Fusiliers attached to 109th Brigade Trench Mortar Battery, was killed in action at Thiepval on 1 July 1916. His brother Lieutenant Haldane Frankland Bell also served with The Royal Inniskilling Fusiliers and relinquished his commission in 1918 on account of ill-health caused by wounds. (WO 339/24224)

BENNET. Lieutenant James Cecil Born on 17 July 1891 at Belfast. An engineer, he enlisted into the 21st (Service) Battalion, The Royal Fusiliers (City of London Regiment) (4th Public Schools) on 17 September 1914 (2421 - Private) in 98th Brigade, 33rd Division. Appointed Lance Corporal and deployed to France on 14 November 1915. 1914-15 Star. Joined 6th Officer Cadet Battalion at Balliol College, Oxford on 12 March 1916 and was commissioned into Princess Victoria's (Royal Irish Fusiliers) on 5 August 1916. Served with the 10th (Reserve) Battalion until October 1916. Joined the 9th Royal Irish Fusiliers on 31 October 1916 and was posted to 'D' Company as a platoon commander. **Wounded** at Moeuvres on 23 November 1917. He returned to duty quickly but left the 9th Royal Irish Fusiliers on 16 December 1917 to transfer to the Tank Corps. Joined the Tank Corps Depot, Wareham, Dorset. Lieutenant 5 February 1918. Served for the remainder of the war with the Tank Corps and the Ministry of Munitions until released from service on 18 February 1919. Relinquished his commission on 1 September 1921. After the war he lived at Coventry, Warwickshire, where he died on 11 March 1960, aged 68. His brother, Lieutenant Trevor Moutray Bennet MC, served with the 10th (Service) Battalion, The Royal Irish Rifles (South Belfast) and was killed serving as a Flying Officer (Observer) with the Royal Flying Corps on 10 November 1916. (WO 339/60058)

BENSON. Captain John Born on 2 May 1884 near Huddersfield, Yorkshire. A cabinet-maker, he enlisted into Princess Victoria's (Royal Irish Fusiliers) (9913 - Private) on 2 May 1908 and transferred to the Royal Army Medical Corps on 20 October 1909 (renumbered 4481 - Private). He was transferred to the Army Reserve on 1 May 1911. Mobilised from the Army Reserve on 6 August 1914. To France 27 August 1914 with 6th Stationary Hospital. 1914 Star. Corporal 1 August 1916. Acting Sergeant 7 January 1916. Commissioned into Princess Victoria's (Royal Irish Fusiliers) on 26 September 1917 and was posted to the 7th/8th (Service) Battalion in 49th Brigade, 16th (Irish) Division. Joined the 9th Royal Irish Fusiliers on 16 February 1918 from 7th/8th (Service) Battalion on its disbandment, and was posted to 'C' Company. Acting Captain 30 April 1918 to 25 March 1919. Commanded 'C' Company April 1918 to August 1918. He led a raid on Shoddy Farm, Meulenhouck on the night of 11/12 August 1918 where he was **captured**. Repatriated on 13 December 1918. Lieutenant 26 March 1919. Posted to the 2nd Battalion, he subsequently transferred to the Machine Gun Corps on 4 May 1920. He resigned his commission on 11 May 1921. (WO 374/5901)

BEST. Captain William James Born in 1893 at Dungannon, County Tyrone. Educated at Dungannon Royal School. Worked at Tate's Medical Hall, Belfast. Enlisted into the 18th or 19th (Service) Battalion, The Royal Fusiliers (City of London Regiment) (1st or 2nd Public Schools). Commissioned into Princess Victoria's (Royal Irish Fusiliers) on 15 June 1916 and joined the 4th (Extra Reserve) Battalion. Served in France with the 1st Battalion from July 1916. **Mention in Despatches**. Joined the 9th Royal Irish Fusiliers on 1 September 1916 and was posted to 'D' Company. Posted back to the 1st Battalion 21 October 1916 and joined on 27 October 1916. Lieutenant 1 January 1917. **Wounded**. Transferred to the General List for service on probation with the Indian Army. Appointed Lieutenant Indian Army on probation 13 May 1918 (to rank from 15 March 1917). Relinquished his commission in the British Army on appointment to the Indian Army 13 May 1919. Served with 2/55th Coke's Rifles (Frontier Force), where he was promoted to Captain. Retired from the Indian Army 1 April 1923.

BLACK. Second Lieutenant Charles Morrison Born on 28 April 1898 at Belfast. From Edinburgh. Educated at George Heriot's School, Edinburgh. Worked as a manager with Marcus Ward & Company Ltd, Belfast. He enlisted into the 2/9th (Highlanders) Battalion, The Royal Scots (Lothian Regiment) on 17 March 1914 (1666 - Private). Commissioned into Princess Victoria's (Royal Irish Fusiliers) on 24 December 1915 and served with the 10th (Reserve) Battalion before he joined the 9th Royal Irish Fusiliers on 17 August 1916. **Wounded** by shell fragments in the thigh while with a wiring party on 23 August 1916. When he recovered he rejoined the 10th (Reserve) Battalion. Joined 36 Infantry Base Depot on 28 February 1917 and then joined the 1st Battalion on 24 March 1917. **Wounded** in the wrist on 9 April 1917 and was evacuated to 6th British Red Cross Hospital at Etaples on 10 April 1917. While recovering from his wound in Belfast in July 1917 he contracted gastro-enteritis and **died** on 9 July 1917, aged 19. His brother, Lance Corporal Walter Cairns Black, was killed in action on 23 December 1914 serving with 1/14th (County of London) Battalion, The London Regiment (London Scottish). His brother, Gunner Edward Gilchrist Black, served with the Royal Garrison Artillery. (WO 339/51131)

BOYD. Second Lieutenant John Born on 11 June 1893 in Londonderry. Enlisted into The Royal Inniskilling Fusiliers (15337 - Private) on 15 September 1914 and joined the 10th (Service) Battalion, The Royal Inniskilling Fusiliers (Derry) in 109th Brigade. Sergeant 29 May 1915. To France with 36th (Ulster) Division October 1915. Evacuated to hospital in England with an injured ankle 21 June 1916. Released from hospital in August 1916 he joined the 12th (Reserve) Battalion, The Royal Inniskilling Fusiliers at Finner Camp. Joined 11th Officer Cadet Battalion in Pirbright on 7 September 1917. Commissioned into Princess Victoria's (Royal Irish Fusiliers) on 18 December 1917. Joined the 9th Royal Irish Fusiliers on 27 April 1918 where he served for the remainder of the war. Released from service 26 April 1919. (WO 339/108654)

BOYD. Lieutenant Thomas Wallace Born on 3 March 1897 in Carrickfergus, County Antrim. Joined the 10th (Reserve) Battalion, Princess Victoria's (Royal Irish Fusiliers) on 17 August 1915 from Queen's University, Belfast Officer Training Corps and was commissioned on 23 August 1915. Joined the 9th Royal Irish Fusiliers on 2 April 1916 and was posted to 'A' Company. Fractured his left tibia when he fell from his horse while being taught to ride at 2nd Army Central School on 16 August 1916. Evacuated to hospital in England 22 August 1916. Joined the 10th (Reserve) Battalion on 15 December 1916. He was passed fit for General Service in March 1917 but remained with the 10th (Reserve) Battalion until he joined the 1st Battalion on 23 April 1918. Lieutenant 1 July 1917. Released from service 15 February 1919. Relinquished his commission on 1 September 1921. Brother of Lieutenant William Graham Boyd. His brother, Cadet Robert Heaney Boyd, also served with Princess Victoria's (Royal Irish Fusiliers). (WO 339/44472)

BOYD. Lieutenant William Graham Born on 8 March 1896 in Carrickfergus, County Antrim. Educated at the Royal Belfast Academical Institution. Enlisted into the 17th (Reserve) Battalion, The Royal Irish Rifles on 6 April 1915. Lance Corporal 20 August 1915. Commissioned into Princess Victoria's (Royal Irish Fusiliers) on 23 August 1915. Served with the 10th (Reserve) Battalion before he joined the 9th Royal Irish Fusiliers on 25 July 1916. Served with 'C' Company. Lieutenant 23 February 1917. **Killed in action** at the Battle of Langemarck on 16 August 1917 by shellfire, aged 21. Brother of Lieutenant Thomas Wallace Boyd. His brother, Cadet Robert Heaney Boyd, served with Princess Victoria's (Royal Irish Fusiliers). (WO 339/44470)

W G Boyd

BOYLE JP, DL. Major John Charters Born on 5 August 1869. From Desart, County Armagh. Educated at Cheltenham College and the Royal Indian Engineering College, Cooper's Hill, Surrey, England. Assistant Engineer on the construction of the Assam Bengal Railway 1892 and 1897. Town surveyor for Armagh 1897. Member of the Armagh Regiment, Ulster Volunteer Force. Joined the 9th Royal Irish Fusiliers on its formation and was immediately commissioned as a Second Lieutenant 15 September 1914. Captain 26 October 1914. Transferred to the Corps of Royal Engineers in early 1915. Major 1 May 1915. Served continuously in France and Flanders throughout the war in 36th (Ulster) Division with 122nd Field Company and then as Officer Commanding 150th Field Company. Evacuated to hospital sick in April 1919. He relinquished his commission on 26 June 1919. Returned to his post as town surveyor for Armagh. JP for County Tyrone and County Armagh. Deputy Lieutenant of County Armagh. High Sheriff of County Armagh 1926. Senator (Northern Ireland) 1937 to 1950. Died 10 May 1950, aged 80. (WO 339/15298)

BRADY. Lieutenant Hugh Kiernan (Harry) Born on 19 May 1882 in County Cavan. A journalist with 'The Daily Mail', he enlisted into the Army Pay Corps (1982 - Private) on 28 September 1914. He served in France from 14 April to 24 November 1915 when he joined the Mediterranean Expeditionary Force. Served with the Field Cashier, 22nd Division in Salonika until his return home on 16 July 1916. Joined 7th Officer Cadet Battalion on 4 November 1916 and was commissioned into Princess Victoria's (Royal Irish Fusiliers) on 27 March 1917. Joined the 9th Royal Irish Fusiliers on 26 June 1917 and was posted to 'B' Company. Attached to the 12th (Service) Battalion, The Royal Irish Rifles (Central Antrim) in 108th Brigade on 3 July 1917, where he was **wounded** slightly when blown up by a shell during the attack at the Battle of Langemarck on 16 August 1917 and **wounded** in the right arm by shrapnel from a bomb during a raid near Cambrai on 6 October 1917. Evacuated to hospital in England 18 October 1917. After he recovered he worked for the Ministry of Munitions. He applied unsuccessfully to transfer to the Indian Army Reserve of Officers. He saw no further service and relinquished his commission on account of ill-health caused by wounds on 24 June 1919. Silver War Badge, number B275077. He returned to work at 'The Daily Mail' and lived at Brixton, London. (WO 339/76191)

BRAY. Lieutenant Harold Edwin Born on 28 August 1892 at Salisbury, Wiltshire. A school teacher, he enlisted into 3/1st Royal Wiltshire Yeomanry on 13 April 1915 and served at Tidworth. Corporal 1 December 1915. Sergeant 22 September 1916. Joined 1st Cadet Cavalry Squadron on 6 December 1916. Commissioned into the 1st Reserve Cavalry Regiment on 17 February 1917 and deployed to France on 8 May 1917 to serve with the 2nd North Irish Horse, X Corps Cavalry Regiment. Transferred to Princess Victoria's (Royal Irish Fusiliers) and joined the 9th Royal Irish Fusiliers on 4 November 1917. **Wounded** severely at Marcoing on 15 December 1917 in the shoulder and foot. Evacuated to hospital in England 30 January 1918, where he remained until July 1918 when he joined the Officers' Command Depot for rehabilitation training. On his recovery he rejoined 1st Reserve Cavalry Regiment at the Curragh and he saw no further service with the 9th Royal Irish Fusiliers. Lieutenant 17 August 1918. Relinquished his commission 26 March 1919. Died at Weymouth, Dorset in 1967, aged 74. (WO 339/80304)

BREENE. Lieutenant Harold Born on 22 July 1889 at Belfast. He attended Queen's University, Belfast Officer Training Corps. Commissioned into Princess Victoria's (Royal Irish Fusiliers) on 8 January 1916. Joined the 9th Royal Irish Fusiliers on 9 September 1916 and was posted to 'C' Company. Evacuated to hospital in England on 28 March 1917 after he contracted chronic bronchitis. His illness caused permanent disability and he relinquished his commission on account of ill-health contracted on active service 10 July 1918. Silver War Badge, number 383215. Lived in Belfast. (WO 339/51989) Three brothers served during the First World War: Lieutenant Thomas Frederick Breene The Royal Warwickshire Regiment was killed in action on 1 July 1917 while attached to the Machine Gun Corps; Lieutenant Nicholas Breene served with the 13th (Service) Battalion, The Royal Warwickshire Regiment and Chaplain to the Forces 4th Class Richard Simmons Breene served with the Army Chaplains Department.

BREMNER. Second Lieutenant Thomas Born on 28 December 1892 at Edinburgh. Joined 7th (Service) Battalion, Seaforth Highlanders (Ross-shire Buffs, The Duke of Albany's) in 26th Brigade, 9th (Scottish) Division at Fort George on 1 September 1914 (2840 - Private). Served in France 10 May 1915 to 9 April 1917. Fought at Loos in September 1915. **Wounded** 14 July 1916 at Longueval. Sergeant 19 July 1916. Company Sergeant Major 13 October 1916 in 'D' Company. Joined 16th Officer Cadet Battalion at Rhyl on 5 May 1917. Commissioned into Princess Victoria's (Royal Irish Fusiliers) on 29 August 1917 and served with the 7th/8th (Service) Battalion in 49th Brigade, 16th (Irish) Division until its disbandment. Joined the 9th Royal Irish Fusiliers on 16 February 1918 and was posted to 'A' Company. **Captured** on 27 March 1918 at Erches. Repatriated 18 December 1918. Lieutenant 1 March 1919. Relinquished his commission 4 April 1919. (WO 339/103014)

BRENNAN OBE, MA, BMus. Captain Charles John Born on 25 October 1876 at Gosport, Hampshire. Organist and choirmaster Clifton, Bedfordshire, 1892. Graduated in music from Durham University. Organist and choirmaster Strabane Parish Church 1897. Organist and choirmaster Elmwood Presbyterian Church, Belfast, 1901. Organist and choirmaster at St Anne's Cathedral, Belfast 1904-1964. Belfast City Organist 1908. He served for seven years as an instructor with Queen's University Belfast Officer Training Corps. He was requested by the Commanding Officer of 10th (Reserve) Battalion, Princess Victoria's (Royal Irish Fusiliers) to become an instructor and he joined the 10th (Reserve) Battalion in early 1916. His commission was confirmed on 20 March 1916. Promoted Captain, he served as an instructor in the 10th (Reserve) Battalion until he joined the 9th Royal Irish Fusiliers on 23 February 1918. Attached soon after to the Staff of HQ 36th (Ulster) Division. Later served on the Staff of the Military Secretary to the Commander in Chief France where he remained until 7 January 1919. **Mention in Despatches**. Relinquished his commission on 3 April 1919. Post-war he returned as organist and choirmaster at St Anne's Cathedral, Belfast, was conductor of the Ulster Male Choir and presided over the Ulster Society of Organists and Choirmasters into the 1940s. He was also a lecturer in music at Queen's University, Belfast, from which he was awarded an honorary MA. **OBE (Civil)** for services to music. Died 8 May 1972, aged 95. (WO 339/59117)

BROWN. Lieutenant Colonel John Born in 1896. Enlisted into the South Irish Horse. Commissioned into Princess Victoria's (Royal Irish Fusiliers) on 5 October 1915. Joined the 9th Royal Irish Fusiliers on 16 August 1916 where he served until 25 September 1916 when he was evacuated to hospital in England sick. Returned to France 22 April 1917 and was posted to the 9th Royal Irish Fusiliers but was evacuated to England sick on 12 May 1917 before he could rejoin. Posted to the 7th/8th (Service) Battalion in 49th Brigade, 16th (Irish) Division where he was **wounded**. Lieutenant 1 July 1917. Relinquished his commission 4 February 1920. Commissioned from the Officers' Emergency Reserve as Lieutenant 26 August 1939 (seniority 20 January 1937) and rejoined The Royal Irish Fusiliers (Princess Victoria's). Served in Europe July 1944 – August 1946. Lieutenant Colonel November 1944. Relinquished his commission in 1946. Chairman of the Dublin branch, Old Comrades Association 1957-59. Moved to England in 1959 where he ran a hotel.

BRYSON MC. Second Lieutenant Joseph Born in June 1888 in County Leitrim. Enlisted into the 8th (King's Royal Irish) Hussars on 15 August 1907 (820 - Trooper). Served in India. Corporal 29 September 1909. Sergeant 22 October 1912. Served in France with the Indian Army Expeditionary Force from 15 October 1914 in the Ambala Cavalry Brigade, 1st Indian Cavalry Division. **Wounded** in the groin on 21 June 1917. **Mention in Despatches**. ***Croix de Guerre* (Belgium)**. Posted to Number 2 Cavalry Depot on 9 July 1917 and joined 2nd Reserve Cavalry Regiment at the Curragh 28 July 1917. Rejoined the 8th (King's Royal Irish) Hussars on 7 April 1918. Commissioned directly for service in the field into Princess Victoria's (Royal Irish Fusiliers) on 26 June 1918 and joined the 9th Royal Irish Fusiliers a few days later. Awarded an **MC** for his actions during the attack at Wulverghem on 4 September 1918. **Killed in action** by shellfire while patrolling in the area of Goldflake Farm on Hill 41 west of the Menin-Roulers Road on 6 October 1918, aged 30. (WO 374/10425)

BUCHANAN. Second Lieutenant Matthew Scott Born on 23 June 1894 in Londonderry. A student teacher, he joined the Customs and Excise Service on 22 August 1914 before joining Queen's University, Belfast Officer Training Corps on 19 July 1915. He was commissioned into Princess Victoria's (Royal Irish Fusiliers) on 8 October 1915 and served with the 10th (Reserve) Battalion before he joined the 9th Royal Irish Fusiliers on 17 August 1916. **Wounded** severely by a bomb during a raid on La Petite Douve Farm on 12 October 1916 and lost his right eye. He was evacuated to hospital in England on 29 October 1916. Fit for home service only he rejoined the 10th (Reserve) Battalion but he relinquished his commission on account of ill-health caused by wounds 9 November 1917. (WO 339/44952)

BURROWS MC. Captain Henry Charles Born on 7 September 1890 in Cahir, County Tipperary. A gas engineer, he enlisted into the 3rd (Reserve) Battalion, The Duke of Wellington's (West Riding Regiment) at North Shields on 10 December 1915. Transferred to the 11th (Reserve) Battalion, The Royal Dublin Fusiliers on 2 March 1917. Lance Corporal 19 May 1917. Joined 4th Officer Cadet Battalion at Oxford on 10 August 1917 and was commissioned into Princess Victoria's (Royal Irish Fusiliers) on 28 November 1917. To France in March 1918 and joined the 9th Royal Irish Fusiliers on 27 April 1918. Awarded an **MC** for his actions during the attack at Wulverghem on 4 September 1918. Acting Captain and commanded 'C' Company temporarily in October 1918, then joined 'D' Company and then commanded 'C' Company again from March 1919 to 17 June 1919, after which he was released from service. Lieutenant 28 May 1919. Relinquished his commission 1 September 1921. (WO 339/109829)

CAIGER-WATSON. Captain Aubrey Born on 25 January 1894 at Hassock, Sussex. Commissioned into Princess Victoria's (Royal Irish Fusiliers) on 27 April 1915. Joined the 1st Battalion on 24 November 1915. 1914-15 Star. To the field ambulance in December 1915 and again in January 1916 sick (influenza). Lieutenant 17 March 1916. To hospital with tonsillitis 13 February 1916 and evacuated to hospital in England. Posted to the 9th Royal Irish Fusiliers on 16 August 1916. Posted back to the 1st Battalion on 21 October 1916. Transferred to the Indian Army on probation 25 November 1917 (seniority as Lieutenant 27 January 1917). Relinquished his commission on appointment to the Indian Army 25 November 1918. Served with 94th Russell's Infantry, Hyderabad Rifles during the Mesopotamian Campaign and in the post-war Iraq Occupation Force. General Service Medal 1918-1962 with clasps 'Iraq' and 'NW Persia'. Served with the renamed 1st (Russell's) Battalion, 19th Hyderabad Regiment from 1922. Retired from the Indian Army 12 January 1923. Lived in India and worked as a broker. Returned to the United Kingdom with his family on 4 July 1929 and lived in Dublin. Died at Ilsington near Newton Abbot, Devon on 27 September 1964, aged 70. His brother, Major Geoffrey Caiger-Watson MC, served with Princess Victoria's (Royal Irish Fusiliers) and the Royal Flying Corps.

CALDWELL CB, KC. Lieutenant John Foster Born on 3 May 1892 at Londonderry. After attending Trinity College, Dublin he joined the Hudson Bay Company in 1913, initially at the post at Fort Chimo before taking charge of the post at George River in Northern Quebec until 1916. He joined 7th Officer Cadet Battalion on 5 July 1917 and was commissioned into Princess Victoria's (Royal Irish Fusiliers) on 30 October 1917. Served initially with the 7th/8th (Service) Battalion in 49th Brigade, 16th (Irish) Division. Joined the 9th Royal Irish Fusiliers on 21 March 1918 and was **captured** on 27 March 1918 at Erches. Repatriated on 18 December 1918 and released from service on 6 September 1919. He became a barrister in Belfast and served in the Civil Service as First Parliamentary Draftsman, Ministry of Finance. Statute Law Committee 1945. King's Counsel 25 October 1946. President Civil Service Rugby Club 1951-52. **CB** for services as First Parliamentary Draftsman. Died at Chippenham, Wiltshire in 1981, aged 89. (WO 339/104488)

CAMPBELL. Captain James Whittaker Born on 2 April 1895 at Portadown, County Armagh. Member of the 4th (Portadown) Battalion, Armagh Regiment, Ulster Volunteer Force. Enlisted into the 9th Royal Irish Fusiliers on its formation (14050 - Private). To France with 36th (Ulster) Division in October 1915. 1914-15 Star. He spent some time in hospital in early 1916. Lance Sergeant 24 August 1916 (vice W Neill – promoted). Joined 2nd Officer Cadet Battalion at Pembroke College, Cambridge on 16 December 1916. Commissioned into Princess Victoria's (Royal Irish Fusiliers) on 1 March 1917, rejoined the 9th Royal Irish Fusiliers on 24 April 1917 and was posted to 'A' Company. Briefly attached to the 11th (Service) Battalion, The Royal Irish Rifles (South Antrim) in 108th Brigade from 30 June 1917. He left the 9th Royal Irish Fusiliers on 4 July 1917 and transferred to the Indian Army Reserve of Officers. He sailed for India on 12 August 1917 and served with the 3/1st Battalion, King George's Own Gurkha Rifles (The

Malaun Regiment). Captain and company commander 27 May 1919. Retired from the Indian Army 1 May 1922. (WO 339/83281)

CARR. Lieutenant Abram Born in 1868. Commissioned into Princess Victoria's (Royal Irish Fusiliers) as a Lieutenant on 10 May 1916 and joined the 7th (Service) Battalion in 49th Brigade, 16th (Irish) Division as Transport Officer on 5 July 1916. He remained in this post after the amalgamation with the 8th (Service) Battalion in September 1916. Was also Brigade Transport Officer for some time. Applied for a transfer home on account of his age (49 years) and became the messing officer of the 3rd (Reserve) Battalion in August 1917. Served as the Military Cattle Shipping Officer at Drogheda from 24 September 1917. Subsequently attached to the 2/1st Battalion, The Cambridgeshire Regiment in Canterbury and, having applied to transfer to the Army Service Corps, he left on 15 January 1918 to become Military Cattle Shipping Officer at Drogheda again. After a short time, he was attached to the Army Service Corps on supply duties in Belfast. He was attached to 52nd (Graduated) Battalion, The South Wales Borderers near Ipswich, part of 67th (2nd Home Counties) Division, as the Transport Officer. To France 1 August 1918. Joined the 9th Royal Irish Fusiliers on 16 November 1918 at Mouscron and appointed Transport Officer on the departure of Captain J B K Morrow. Fractured his leg as a result of an accident with a horse on 6 February 1919 and was evacuated to hospital in England on 4 March 1919. He was released from service on 1 September 1921, aged 53. (WO 339/64659)

CATHER VC. Lieutenant and Adjutant Geoffrey St George Shillington Born on 11 October 1890 at Streatham Hill, London. His parents were both originally from Ireland; his mother was the sister of Major D G Shillington. Educated at Hazelwood, Limpsfield and Rugby schools. Employed in the tea trade by Tetley's in London. Served in the Territorial Force in 1/28th Battalion, The London Regiment (Artist's Rifles) from 1909-11. Worked in Canada and America 1912-14. Enlisted into the 19th (Service) Battalion, The Royal Fusiliers (City of London Regiment) (2nd Public Schools) in September 1914. Commissioned into Princess Victoria's (Royal Irish Fusiliers) on 22 May 1915 and joined the 9th Royal Irish Fusiliers. To France with 36th (Ulster) Division in October 1915 as a platoon commander. 1914-15 Star. Appointed Assistant Adjutant in addition in mid-October 1915 and appointed Lieutenant and Adjutant on 7 December 1915. He was **killed in action** at Hamel on 2 July 1916, aged 25 and was awarded a posthumous **Victoria Cross** for his actions there. His body was recovered by officers of the 9th Royal Irish Fusiliers and buried nearby but his grave was not identified during the concentration of graves after the war. Nephew of Major D G Shillington. Cousin of Captain T G Shillington. (WO 339/273)

CLARK. Captain St George Henry Lismore Born on 18 May 1889. From Blackrock, County Dublin. A mercantile clerk. Commissioned into Princess Victoria's (Royal Irish Fusiliers) on 28 August 1915. To France 9 March 1916 and joined the 1st or 2nd Battalion. Acting Lieutenant 24 October 1916. Served with a Trench Mortar Battery through 1917 and much of 1918. Lieutenant 1 July 1917. **Mention in Dispatches**. Acting Captain and appointed to command a Trench Mortar Battery from 28 April to 22 May 1918. Transferred to the General List and promoted Captain on appointment as Chief Instructor at a school of instruction from 22 May 1918. Joined the 9th Royal Irish Fusiliers on 4 January 1919. Lived in Dublin and West Acton, Middlesex. Appointed Lieutenant in the Auxiliary Military Pioneer Corps 14 June 1940. Died at London in 1972, aged 83. His son, Flying Officer Ronald Belmore Gower Edward Clark, was killed in action on 11 June 1940 while serving with 15 Squadron, Royal Air Force when his Blenheim was involved in a mid-air collision over France with another Blenheim. Flying Officer Clark retained control to enable his crew to bale out but he was unable to leave the aircraft before it crashed. He is buried at Bayeux War Cemetery.

CLARKE. Lieutenant Newcombe Born on 11 August 1896 at Dublin. A clerk, he enlisted into the South Irish Horse on 12 August 1914 (957 - Private) and served in 'B' Squadron. Served in France from 23 November 1915 to 11 January 1917. 1914-15 Star. Joined 7th Officer Cadet Battalion on 9 March 1917. Commissioned into Princess Victoria's (Royal Irish Fusiliers) on 27 June 1917. Joined the 9th Royal Irish Fusiliers on 12 October 1917 and was posted to 'D' Company as Officer Commanding 13 Platoon. **Captured** on 27 March 1918 near Erches. Lieutenant 27 December 1918. After his repatriation on 18 December 1918 he served with the Chinese Labour Corps. Relinquished his commission 11 June 1920. After the war he joined the Colonial Service and served in Nigeria, where his only son died in infancy. Died in Tavistock, Devon in 1977, aged 81. (WO 339/98819)

COLQUHOUN. Captain Samuel Paul Born on 28 October 1897 at Omagh, County Tyrone. Enlisted into the 12th (Reserve) Battalion, The Royal Inniskilling Fusiliers on 31 August 1915. Joined 7th Officer Cadet Battalion on 3 July 1916 and was commissioned into Princess Victoria's (Royal Irish Fusiliers) on 25 October 1916. Joined the 9th Royal Irish Fusiliers in January 1917 and was posted to 'A' Company. **Wounded** at the Battle of Langemarck on 16 August 1917. After he recovered he served with the 10th (Reserve) Battalion until he transferred to The Royal Irish Regiment on 26 March 1918. Transferred to the General List for service on probation with the Indian Army as a Lieutenant 29 July 1918. Served with 2/7th Duke of Connaught's Rajputs and then as a Captain with 47th (Sikh) Regiment of Bengal Infantry. Captain 25 July 1921. India General Service Medal. General Service Medal 1918-1962 with clasp 'Iraq'. He returned to England on 10 May 1922 and retired from the Indian Army on 25 August 1922. He subsequently emigrated to Kenya where he farmed at Ukunda near Mombasa. He narrowly avoided death when hunting cape buffalo. Served with the African Colonial Forces in the Second World War (Captain); he resigned on account of disability on 1 August 1944. He died at Mombasa on 15 May 1973, aged 75. (WO 339/64694)

CONNAR. Lieutenant Henry Percy Born on 14 September 1891 at Belfast. Enlisted into the North Irish Horse (1091 - Trooper) on 3 September 1914. Served in 'D' Squadron in France from 26 April 1915 to May 1916 in 51st (Highland) Division. 1914-15 Star. Joined 7th Officer Cadet Battalion on 29 May 1916 and was commissioned on 26 September 1916 and held on the General List for duty with the Royal Flying Corps until 27 April 1917 when he transferred to Princess Victoria's (Royal Irish Fusiliers). He was married the next day. He joined the 9th Royal Irish Fusiliers on 30 May 1917 and was posted to 'C' Company. Attached to 12th (Service) Battalion, The Royal Irish Rifles (Central Antrim) in 108th Brigade on 30 June 1917 where he remained until 15 December 1917. He transferred to the Tank Corps on 27 December 1917 and joined the Tank Corps Depot, Wareham, Dorset for training. Posted to the 16th Battalion, Tank Corps. Lieutenant 26 March 1918. He broke his leg in an accident at the Tank Corps Depot on 29 July 1918 and saw no further service. Released from service on 25 February 1919. Lived in Greenisland, County Antrim and north Belfast. (WO 339/55047)

CONNOR. Lieutenant James Herbert Born on 22 April 1892 at Belfast. He worked in his father's grocery shop. He enlisted into the Machine Gun Corps (1550 - Private) on 27 May 1915 and served in France with 14th Medium Machine Gun Battery from 17 July 1915. 1914-15 Star. Joined 5th Officer Cadet Battalion at Trinity College, Cambridge on 4 November 1916 and was commissioned into Princess Victoria's (Royal Irish Fusiliers) on 28 March 1917. Joined the 9th Royal Irish Fusiliers in June 1917 and was posted to 'C' Company. **Captured** on the night of 21 March 1918 crossing the River Somme on the withdrawal from St Quentin. Lieutenant 28 September 1918. Repatriated on 25 December 1918. Released from service on 4 March 1919. Relinquished his commission 1 September 1921. (WO 339/66168)

COOKE. Captain John Anthony Born on 27 August 1878 at Clontay, Dublin. Enlisted into the 18th (Reserve) Battalion, The Royal Irish Rifles on 2 December 1915. Commissioned into Princess Victoria's (Royal Irish Fusiliers) on 7 July 1916. To France 27 February 1917 and joined the 9th Royal Irish Fusiliers on 19 March 1917. Posted to 'D' Company. Assistant Adjutant August 1917. Lieutenant 7 January 1918. Commanded 'D' Company April 1918 until he suffered an injury to his left foot in late May 1918 and was evacuated. He joined the 1st Battalion on 19 October 1918 and was released from service on 4 February 1919. Relinquished his commission on 1 September 1921. (WO 339/57703)

COOMBS-JONES. Captain Kenneth Charles Born on 17 September 1895 at Eastleigh, Hampshire. An apprentice at Cammell Laird in Birkenhead, he enlisted into the 16th (Service) Battalion, The Duke of Cambridge's Own (Middlesex Regiment) (Public Schools) in London on 25 October 1914. He was commissioned into The Duke of Cambridge's Own (Middlesex Regiment) Special Reserve on 21 April 1915 and was posted to the 6th (Reserve) Battalion, The Duke of Cambridge's Own (Middlesex Regiment) in Gillingham. Subsequently posted to the 2nd Battalion, The Duke of Cambridge's Own (Middlesex Regiment) in 23rd Brigade, 8th Division where he was **wounded** when shot in the neck and chest at Loos on 13 September 1916. He returned to the 2nd Battalion, The Duke of Cambridge's Own (Middlesex Regiment) on 23 December 1916. Promoted Captain 12 May 1917 and appointed Brigade Signalling Officer, 23rd Brigade until 10 July 1918, when he reverted to Lieutenant (seniority 1 July 1917). Attached to the 9th Royal Irish Fusiliers on 14 November 1918 as Signalling Officer. Released from service on 4 February 1919. Resigned his commission 6 March 1920. (WO 339/55293)

COOPER. Captain Richard George Born on 29 May 1889 at Dublin. An insurance clerk, he enlisted into the 12th (Reserve) Battalion, The Royal Inniskilling Fusiliers on 23 June 1915. Commissioned into Princess Victoria's (Royal Irish Fusiliers) on 6 January 1916 and joined the 10th (Reserve) Battalion. Joined the 9th Royal Irish Fusiliers on 16 March 1917. Lieutenant 6 July 1917. Applied to transfer to the Indian Army Reserve of Officers in July 1917 and left on 22 August 1917. Transferred to the Indian Army Reserve of Officers with seniority 25 September 1917. Joined 3/103rd Mahattra Light Infantry. Captain 1 September 1918. Joined the Indian Military Base Depot, Quetta in 1919. Released from service in October 1919. Resigned from the Indian Army Reserve of Officers 1 May 1922. (WO 339/51127)

H E Cowdy

COWDY. Second Lieutenant Harold Evans Born on 8 April 1897 at Portadown, County Armagh where he worked in the family business Messrs William Cowdy & Sons Ltd, manufacturers linen handkerchiefs. He joined 7th Officer Cadet Battalion in 1916. Commissioned into Royal Irish Fusiliers on 25 October 1916. Joined the 9th Royal Irish Fusiliers on 6 January 1917 and was posted to 'D' Company. **Killed in action** at the Battle of Langemarck on 16 August 1917, aged 20. (WO 339/64698)

CRAIG. Lieutenant George Daly Born on 8 November 1889 at Londonderry and attended Dublin University. A schoolmaster, he joined 3/6th Battalion, The Black Watch (Royal Highlanders) at Perth on 17 May 1915 (3309 - Private). Sergeant 10 June 1915. Commissioned into Princess Victoria's (Royal Irish Fusiliers) on 15 August 1915. To France May 1916 and joined the 9th Royal Irish Fusiliers on 20 June 1916. **Wounded** when he suffered concussion and was deafened by a shell during the attack at Hamel on 1 July 1916. Evacuated to hospital in England 7 July 1916. Subsequently declared fit for home service only and was posted to the 3rd (Reserve) Garrison Battalion 28 February 1917, where he spent the rest of the war. Lieutenant 28 June 1917. Captain 2 October 1918. Relinquished the rank of Captain 6 June 1919. Released from service 25 June 1919. Relinquished his commission in the Special Reserve of Officers 1 April 1920. Emigrated to the United States and lived at Seattle, Washington. (WO 339/38286)

CROSBIE MC*. Captain Thomas Edward Chapman Born on 30 May 1897 at Ballintaggart, Portadown. Attended Lurgan College prior to studying medicine at Queen's University, Belfast. Enlisted into the 10th (Reserve) Battalion (23653 - Private) 5 January 1916 then joined 7th

T E C Crosbie

Officer Cadet Battalion and was commissioned into Princess Victoria's (Royal Irish Fusiliers) on 19 December 1916. Joined the 9th Royal Irish Fusiliers on 19 March 1917. Awarded an **MC** for a raid near Havrincourt on 3 November 1917. Commanded 'C' Company November 1917 to April 1918. Awarded a Bar to his **MC** for his actions at St Quentin on 21 March 1918. Mortally **wounded** at Regent Street Dugouts one mile north of Wulverghem on 15 April 1918, he **died of wounds** that night in dressing station near Kemmel, aged 20. (WO 339/67922)

CROSS. Captain George Herbert Born in 1893 at County Cork. Lived in Dublin. Enlisted into The Royal Dublin Fusiliers (15389 - Private) on1 October 1914. Commissioned into the Army Service Corps on 28 November 1914. Captain 15 July 1915. To France 15 November 1915. 1914-15 Star. Served primarily with 32nd Division. **Mention in Despatches**. Transferred for infantry service and joined 2nd Infantry School on 25 January 1918. Joined the 11th (Service) Battalion, Princess Victoria's (Royal Irish Fusiliers). Posted to the 9th Royal Irish Fusiliers in August 1918 when the 11th (Service) Battalion was disbanded and joined on 29 August 1918. Appointed Officer Commanding 'C' Company. **Killed in action** during the attack at Vijfwegen on 30 September 1918, aged 25. (WO 339/16835)

CROTHERS. Captain Albert Victor Born on 22 January 1891 at Belfast. Enlisted into 2/6th (Perthshire) Battalion, The Black Watch (Royal Highlanders) (2561) on 16 November 1914. Commissioned into Princess Victoria's (Royal Irish Fusiliers) on 16 November 1915. He served with the 10th (Reserve) Battalion before landing in France on 28 August 1916. Joined the 9th Royal Irish Fusiliers on 9 September 1916 and was posted to 'B' Company. Lieutenant 16 November 1916. Attached to Headquarters 108th Brigade on 10 April 1917. He was accepted for the Indian Army Reserve of Officers in October 1917 left the 9th Royal Irish Fusiliers on 4 November 1917. He sailed for India on 21 December 1917. Lieutenant Indian army 9 February 1918 (seniority 16 November 1916). Served as a Captain with 2/30th (Punjab) Regiment of Bengal Infantry. (WO 339/46661)

CRYMBLE. Second Lieutenant John Gordon Born on 4 February 1897 at Belfast. Educated at the Royal Belfast Academical Institution and then as a medical student at Queen's University, Belfast. He enlisted into the 19th (Service) Battalion, The Royal Fusiliers (City of London Regiment) (2nd Public Schools) on 16 March 1915. Commissioned into Princess Victoria's (Royal Irish Fusiliers) on 5 August 1916. Joined the 9th Royal Irish Fusiliers on 7 October 1916 and was posted to 'B' Company. **Wounded** by a shrapnel bullet in the right leg on 22 December 1916 and **died of wounds** on 28 December 1916, aged 19, in 2nd Casualty Clearing Station. (WO 339/60747)

DARLING MC*. Second Lieutenant John (Jack) Born on 18 June 1897 at Enniskillen, County Fermanagh, the son of a civil engineer and the eldest of seven children. A student he enlisted at the Curragh into the 5th (Reserve) Battalion, The Royal Munster Fusiliers on 15 October 1916. Joined 7th Officer Cadet Battalion on 21 May 1917 and was commissioned into Princess Victoria's (Royal Irish Fusiliers) on 26 September 1917. Joined the 9th Royal Irish Fusiliers on 30 October 1917 and was posted to 'A' Company. Posted soon after to the 7th/8th (Service) Battalion in 49th Brigade, 16th (Irish) Division where he served until its disbandment. Returned to the 9th Royal Irish Fusiliers on 16 February 1918. He was posted to 'C' Company. **Wounded** near Erches during the retreat on 27 March 1918 and was awarded the **MC**. Evacuated to hospital in England 29 March 1918. He spent 5 months in hospital. Posted to, and served briefly with, the 1st Battalion in early October 1918. After returning to the 9th Royal Irish Fusiliers, he led the attack to capture Goldflake Farm on Hill 41 on 11 October 1918 and was awarded a Bar to his **MC**. **Died of wounds** on 26 October 1918 in 3rd Australian Casualty Clearing Station, aged 21, having been shot in the neck, thigh and groin during an attack the day before at the River Lys. He was the last officer to be killed while serving with the 9th Royal Irish Fusiliers. (WO 339/86932)

DARLING. Lieutenant Lionel Scott Born on 4 April 1895 at Lurgan, County Armagh, the son of a doctor. Enlisted into the 6th Reserve Cavalry Regiment at Dublin (4446 - Trooper) on 1 September 1914. Commissioned into Princess Victoria's (Royal Irish Fusiliers) on 11 January 1916. Joined the 9th Royal Irish Fusiliers on 29 October 1916. To hospital sick with rheumatic fever on 7 February 1917 and was evacuated to hospital in England on 20 March 1917. When he recovered he was held on the strength of the 3rd (Reserve) Battalion and was employed as an instructor in the Officer Training Corps at Belfast. Lieutenant 6 July 1917. Declared unfit for military service in February 1919 while employed by the Ministry of Labour, he relinquished his commission on account of ill-health contracted on active service 7 March 1919. Silver War Badge, number 143246. (WO 339/51130)

DAVIDSON. Lieutenant Albert A regular soldier or mobilised reservist, he served in France from December 1914 with the 2nd Battalion. 1914-15 Star. Commissioned into Princess Victoria's (Royal Irish Fusiliers) on 19 December 1916. Joined the 9th Royal Irish Fusiliers on 19 March 1917 and was posted to 'A' Company. Attached to the 11th (Service) Battalion, The Royal Irish Rifles (South Antrim) in 108th Brigade on 30 June 1917 where he spent most of that year before rejoining the 9th Royal Irish Fusiliers. Commanded 'A' Company for a period in April 1918. Lieutenant 19 June 1918. Tried at Field General Court Martial at Proven on 21 June 1918 on charges desertion and leaving his post; found not guilty. To hospital sick 6 September 1918 and evacuated to hospital in England 17 September 1918. He relinquished his commission on 4 September 1919.

DAVIES. Second Lieutenant Harold Lyndon Born on 7 December 1896 at Harts Hill, Staffordshire. Enlisted into the 7th (Service) Battalion, The South Staffordshire Regiment on 18 August 1914 (10516 - Private). Joined the Mediterranean Expeditionary Force with 33rd Brigade, 11th Division on 2 July 1915. 1914-15 Star. **Wounded** on 22 August 1915 while in the Dardanelles. The 7th (Service) Battalion, The South Staffordshire Regiment returned to France on 28 June 1916, where he served until 20 December 1916. Joined 2nd Officer Cadet Battalion at Pembroke College, Cambridge on 8 January 1917 but transferred to 6th Officer Cadet Battalion at Balliol College, Oxford on 15 May 1917. Commissioned into Princess Victoria's (Royal Irish Fusiliers) on 29 August 1917. Joined the 9th Royal Irish Fusiliers on 27 January 1918. **Wounded** at Guiscard on 24 March 1918 when he was hit in both legs by shrapnel. Evacuated to hospital in England 27 March 1918. He returned to the 9th Royal Irish Fusiliers on 15 August 1918 and was **wounded** again on 24 August 1918 near Bailleul when a shell buried him in a dug out causing injury to his back and head. He was evacuated to hospital in England on 30 August 1918. Relinquished his commission on account of ill-health contracted on active service 22 February 1919. Silver War Badge, number 165157. (WO 339/83327)

DAVIS. Second Lieutenant Vivian Alfred Born on 24 November 1898 and attended Dublin University before joining 7th Officer Cadet Battalion at Fermoy on 5 July 1917. Commissioned into The Prince of Wales's Leinster Regiment (Royal Canadians) on 31 October 1917. Attached to the 9th Royal Irish Fusiliers 17 April 1918. Posted to the 2nd Battalion, The Prince of Wales's Leinster Regiment (Royal Canadians) on 19 June 1918. **Killed in action** on 4 September 1918 while serving with the 2nd Battalion, The Prince of Wales's Leinster Regiment (Royal Canadians), aged 19. (WO 339/18889)

DAY. Second Lieutenant Henry Vivian Born on 23 January 1894 at Leicestershire. An engineer. Enlisted into the Leicestershire Yeomanry (Prince Albert's Own) (1741 - Corporal). To France 2 November 1914 in 7th Cavalry Brigade, 3rd Cavalry Division. 1914 Star. Commissioned into The Leicestershire Regiment 28 October 1915. Transferred to a Reserve Regiment of Cavalry and served with the Service Squadron of 6th (Inniskilling) Dragoons in 36th (Ulster) Division until June 1916 when it was absorbed by the 2nd North Irish Horse, X Corps Cavalry Regiment. Lieutenant 1 July 1917. Transferred to Princess Victoria's (Royal Irish Fusiliers) and joined the 9th Royal Irish Fusiliers in early October 1917. Left the 9th Royal Irish Fusiliers on 27 October 1917 for duty with the Royal Flying Corps. Relinquished his commission 12 February 1919. Founded a family haulage company (H V Day and Sons) at Glenfield, Leicestershire. Died in 1992, aged 98. (WO 339/45600)

DEAN OBE, MC. Lieutenant Colonel Herbert Shelton Born on 17 July 1896. Commissioned into the Service Squadron of the 6th (Inniskilling) Dragoons on 28 March 1916. Lieutenant 10

May 1916. Served with the 2nd North Irish Horse, X Corps Cavalry Regiment in France from 9 August 1916. Transferred to Princess Victoria's (Royal Irish Fusiliers) and joined the 9th Royal Irish Fusiliers on 2 October 1917. Acting Captain 22 October 1917. Commanded 'D' Company February 1918, vice Captain C B Despard. Awarded an **MC** for his actions during the withdrawal from St Quentin. **Wounded** on 12 April 1918 near Wulverghem and evacuated to hospital in England on 18 April 1918. He saw no further service with the 9th Royal Irish Fusiliers. When recovered he served with the Reserve Regiment of the North Irish Horse and relinquished his commission on 1 April 1920. Joined The Royal Ulster Rifles on 3 March 1921 as a Lieutenant (seniority 21 January 1918) and was posted to the 1st Battalion. Captain 1 April 1926. Adjutant of the Auxiliary Force, India from 1 October 30 to late 1932 when he rejoined the 1st Battalion. Posted to the 2nd Battalion in June 1937. Major 15 January 1938. Served in Palestine. **Mention in Despatches**. General Service Medal 1918-1962 and clasp 'Palestine'. Temporary Lieutenant Colonel 24 November 1940. Lieutenant Colonel 15 November 1944. **OBE (Military)**. Retired 30 July 1948. Retired from the Reserve of Officers 17 July 1951. Died at Eton, Buckinghamshire in 1969, aged 72.

DESPARD DSO, MC. Captain Charles Beauclerk Born on 31 December 1880 at Cultra, County Down. Educated at the Royal Belfast Academical Institution. Enlisted into The Duke of Cornwall's Light Infantry in 1899 and served as a Private and Corporal. Joined the Imperial Yeomanry (9364 - Corporal) for service in the South African War and served with 46th (Belfast) Company, 13th Battalion, Imperial Yeomanry. One of 400 men captured and subsequently released at Lindley in May 1900. Commissioned into the Imperial Yeomanry and served with 74th Battalion. **Mention in Despatches**, Queen's South Africa Medal, King's South Africa Medal. Emigrated to Canada in 1909 and settled as a rancher near Lloydminster, Saskatchewan. Returned to England on 28 September 1914 onboard the Lusitania. Commissioned into the Service Squadron of the 6th (Inniskilling) Dragoons as a Lieutenant on 19 October 1914 and served in 36th (Ulster) Division until June 1916 and then in the 2nd North Irish Horse, X Corps Cavalry Regiment. Captain 30 October 1915. 1914-15 Star. Transferred to Princess Victoria's (Royal Irish Fusiliers) and joined the 9th Royal Irish Fusiliers on 17 October 1917. Appointed Officer Commanding 'D' Company. Fought at Cambrai in October 1917 and Moeuvres in November 1917, his actions at the latter earned an **MC**. Battalion Second-in-Command February 1918. Earned a **DSO** at St Quentin. The last surviving Captain in 108th Brigade, he was **killed in action** at Kemmel Hill on 18 April 1918, aged 37. He was wounded by shell-fire and died soon after at a casualty post nearby. Buried in Kemmel Cemetery, his grave was lost subsequently and he is commemorated on the Tyne Cot Memorial as an officer of the 6th (Inniskilling) Dragoons, and on the Lloydminster War Memorial, Saskatchewan. He had applied to transfer to the Indian Army Reserve of Officers. (WO 339/12487)

DICKSON. Captain George Clawson Born on 26 September 1893 at Tandragee, County Armagh. Educated at Campbell College, Belfast. Commissioned into Princess Victoria's (Royal Irish Fusiliers) on 22 May 1915. To France with 36th (Ulster) Division in October 1915 as scout officer and a platoon commander in 'C' Company. 1914-15 Star. **Wounded** by machine-gun fire in No 14 Sap at Hamel on 18 May 1916, when a bullet lodged under his right arm, and evacuated to hospital in England on 2 June 1916. He took five months to recover and did not serve with the 9th Royal Irish Fusiliers again. Lieutenant 1 July 1917. Transferred to the Labour Corps on 19 November 1918. Captain 30 January 1919. Transferred to the General List, reverted to Lieutenant and was employed as an Assistant Military Landing Officer 26 August 1919. Released from service on 2 September 1919. Served with the Ulster Special Constabulary. Adjutant of 2nd Armagh (Portadown) Battalion, Ulster Home Guard during the Second World War. Worked for the County Armagh Education Committee. Died in 1955. His brother, Lieutenant James Henry Dickson, served with the 9th Royal Irish Fusiliers before being commissioned - see below. (WO 339/1257)

DOBBYN MC*, MB. Lieutenant Alexander Lee Born on 20 April 1897 at Waterford, County Waterford. Commissioned into Princess Victoria's (Royal Irish Fusiliers) on 5 October 1915, aged 18. To France 21 July 1916 and served with 8th (Service) Battalion in 49th Brigade, 16th (Irish) Division. **Wounded** at Leuze (Bouleaux) Wood near Combles on 6 September 1916 when he was shot through the left lung. Awarded an **MC** for his actions there. Lieutenant 1 January 1917. After sick leave and home service, during which time he was presented his MC at Buckingham Palace, he joined the 9th Royal Irish Fusiliers in September 1917. Detached throughout the early part of 1918 to the 10th (Reserve) Battalion he rejoined the 9th Royal Irish Fusiliers on 28 June 1918. Earned a Bar to his **MC** on a raid at Meulenhouck near Bailleul on 14 August 1918. Posted to the 1st Battalion later that month, where he was **wounded** on 12 October 1918 on Hill 41 by a gas shell that landed near 1st Battalion Headquarters. He recovered and rejoined the 9th Royal Irish Fusiliers on 13 November 1918. He was released from service on 14 February 1919. Relinquished his commission on 1 September 1921. He studied medicine at Trinity College, Dublin and graduated MB in 1924. He practiced in Hockley, Essex from 1928 and at Winton, Bournemouth in Dorset from 1933 to 1962. He died in Bournemouth on 20 May 1974, aged 77. His brother, Lieutenant William Augustus Nelson Dobbyn, was accidentally killed during instruction with grenades on 4 January 1917 while serving with the 15th (Service) Battalion, The Lancashire Fusiliers (2nd Salford). His cousin, Lieutenant R N Dobbyn Royal Flying Corps, was killed a flying accident on 23 November 1916. (WO 339/43890)

DOBSON. Second Lieutenant James Robinson Born in October 1889 at Mohill, County Leitrim. A student at Dublin University, he enlisted into the 1/9th (Highlanders) Battalion, The Royal Scots (Lothian Regiment) (2617 - Private) in Edinburgh in November 1914 and served at home until he deployed to France with 81st Brigade, 27th Division on 24 February 1915. 1914-15 Star. Awarded 28 days Field Punishment Number 1 on 17 March 1915 for drunkenness. Joined Officer Cadet School GHQ on 11 December 1915 and was commissioned into Princess Victoria's (Royal Irish Fusiliers) on 23 January 1916. He returned home to get new uniforms and fell ill with gastro-enteritis. Redeployed to France in April 1916. Tried at Field General Court Martial in October 1916 on a charge of drunkenness when serving in the base area; found not guilty. Joined the 9th Royal Irish Fusiliers on 7 November 1916 and was posted to 'D' Company. **Died of wounds** in 2nd Casualty Clearing Station on 19 February 1917, aged 27, having been shot in the chest and abdomen that day when out with stretcher bearers. (WO 339/53945)

DONALDSON. Second Lieutenant Francis Lawrence Hamilton Born on 16 June 1896 at Jordanstown, Belfast. A railway clerk, he enlisted into the Corps of Royal Engineers (64587) on 2 July 1915 and deployed to France with 150th Field Company in 36th (Ulster) Division on 5 October 1915. 1914-15 Star. Joined 6th Officer Cadet Battalion at Balliol College, Oxford on 5 July 1917. Commissioned into Princess Victoria's (Royal Irish Fusiliers) on 31 November 1917. Joined the 9th Royal Irish Fusiliers on 10 January 1918 and was posted to 'C' Company. **Captured** on 27 March 1918 at Erches. Repatriated on 25 December 1918. Released from service in 1919 and relinquished his commission on 20 November 1920. (WO 339/116567)

DOUGAN. Second Lieutenant James Hamilton Born in 1895 at Londonderry. Commissioned into The Royal Irish Rifles on 26 January 1917 and was posted to the 16th (Service) Battalion, The Royal Irish Rifles (2nd County Down) (Pioneers), arriving in France in April 1917. Attached to 'B' Company, 9th Royal Irish Fusiliers from 20 May 1917. He left later that year to rejoin the 16th (Service) Battalion, The Royal Irish Rifles (2nd County Down) (Pioneers). **Wounded** on 23 October 1917. Later in the war served with the Ministry of Labour. Joined the Royal Irish Constabulary in 1920 and in March 1922 was a District Inspector in command at Birr Barracks, King's County (later renamed County Offaly). His journal, which records the events of the times and concludes with the evacuation and handing over of his barracks to representatives of the Provisional Government of the Irish Free State, is in the museum of the Police Service of Northern Ireland. Appointed as a Captain in 8th (Belfast) Heavy Anti-Aircraft

Regiment, Royal Regiment of Artillery (Supplementary Reserve) 1 April 1939. Major 11 April 1942.

DUNCAN. Second Lieutenant Robert Stephens Born on 17 May 1899 at Buncrana, County Donegal. A medical student at Trinity College, Dublin, he served in the Officer Training Corps and joined 4th Officer Cadet Battalion in Oxford on 7 February 1918. Commissioned into Princess Victoria's (Royal Irish Fusiliers) on 31 July 1918. Joined the 9th Royal Irish Fusiliers on 21 September 1918 where he served for the remainder of the war. Left on 6 February 1919 for demobilisation and was released from service on 14 February 1919. Relinquished his commission in the Special Reserve of Officers 1 April 1920. He joined the Northern Ireland Civil Service. (WO 374/21185)

DUNWOODY. Second Lieutenant Hugh Henderson Born on 26 November 1889 at Strandtown, Belfast. Educated at Campbell College and Queen's University, Belfast where he studied Civil Engineering and joined the Officer Training Corps. He worked as an assistant master at Larne Grammar School. Commissioned into Princess Victoria's (Royal Irish Fusiliers) on 18 February 1916. Posted to the 10th (Reserve) Battalion for additional training but was one of six officers sent out early to France. Joined the 9th Royal Irish Fusiliers on 20 June 1916 and was posted to 'A' Company. **Killed** on the night of 31 July/1 August 1916 when accidentally shot in the head in front of a listening post, aged 27. (WO 339/54631)

ELLIOTT MM. Lieutenant William Born on 1 September 1891 in Clyhannagh, County Fermanagh. A farmer, he enlisted into the 11th (Service) Battalion, The Royal Inniskilling Fusiliers (Donegal and Fermanagh) on 18 November 1914 (17308). To France in 109th Brigade in October 1915. 1914-15 Star. Earned an **MM** as a Lance Corporal in 'A' Company, 11th (Service) Battalion, The Royal Inniskilling Fusiliers (Donegal and Fermanagh) at the Battle of Langemarck on 16 August 1917 and was promoted to Corporal. Sergeant 18 November 1917. **Mention in Despatches**. Joined 7th Officer Cadet Battalion on 5 April 1918. Commissioned into Princess Victoria's (Royal Irish Fusiliers) on 25 September 1918. Joined the 9th Royal Irish Fusiliers on 16 November 1918 where he served until March/April 1919 when he was attached to the 5th (Service) Battalion, The Royal Irish Regiment (Pioneers) in the Light Division in the British Army of the Rhine. Relinquished his commission on 20 September 1919. (WO 374/22477)

EMERSON. Major Richard Leslie Born on 3 January 1891 at London. Commissioned into Princess Victoria's (Royal Irish Fusiliers) on 25 March 1911 and served in India with the 2nd Battalion. Lieutenant 7 June 1913. Served with the 2nd Battalion in France from December 1914 to November 1915. 1914-15 Star. Captain 1 September 1915. Served in Macedonia and Serbia from November 1915 to September 1916. Attached to an Officer Cadet Battalion in early 1917 where he was appointed Second-in-Command on 4 March 1918. Major 4 March 1918. Posted to the 1st Battalion on 18 October 1918. Joined the 9th Royal Irish Fusiliers on 8 November 1918 as Second-in-Command. Posted to the 2nd Battalion in April 1919 pending service with the West Africa Frontier Force. Served with the West Africa Frontier Force from 30 April 1919 to 2 November 1920. Retired 7 July 1922. Served during the Second World War. Lieutenant 27 May 1941. Captain 20 March 1943. Retired on account of ill health 10 October 1944. Died at Lyme Regis, Dorset in August 1949, aged 58.

ENSOR OBE, DL. Colonel Charles Howard Born on 3 August 1878 at Clayton, Contra Costa County, California, United States. The family home in Ireland was Ardress House, Loughgall, County Armagh. Having been a company commander in the Armagh Regiment, Ulster Volunteer Force for 10 months, he enlisted into the 9th Royal Irish Fusiliers on its formation

and was commissioned as a Second Lieutenant on 15 September 1914. To France with 36th (Ulster) Division in October 1915 as Officer Commanding 'A' Company. 1914-15 Star. **Wounded** in the right leg when commanding his company during the attack at Hamel on 1 July 1916. He lay in a shell hole for four days (for the last ten hours up to his armpits in water) before being found. He was evacuated to hospital in England on 9 July 1916 where he remained until 20 October 1916. His wounds demanded five operations; two in France and three in Netley Hospital and they precluded general service. He served with the 10th (Reserve) Battalion until released from service in 1919. Silver War Badge, number B80412. On the formation of the Ulster Special Constabulary in November 1921 he was appointed County Commandant for County Armagh. **OBE (Civil)**. During the Second World War he was appointed Commandant of the four County Armagh Battalions of the Ulster Home Guard in the rank of Colonel. Appointed Deputy Lord Lieutenant of County Armagh. He held the post of County Commandant in the Ulster Special Constabulary until he retired in 1952, aged 74. In addition to his OBE, First World War medals and Defence Medal 1945, he was entitled to the Jubilee Medal 1935 and the Coronation Medal 1937. Ardress House was sold to the National Trust in 1961. He died at Rostrevor, County Down on 29 January 1963, aged 85 and was buried at Annaghmore Parish Church, County Armagh. Brother of Captain Ernest Nash Ensor. His brother, Private George Clarke Ensor, served as a Corporal with the 1st Battalion, Princess Victoria's (Royal Irish Fusiliers) during the South African war, ending his service as a Quartermaster Sergeant. Having emigrated to Canada, he enlisted into the 7th Battalion (British Columbia Regiment), Canadian Infantry in 2nd Infantry Brigade, 1st Canadian Division. He was wounded during the Battle of Saint Julien between 23 and 25 April 1915 and died of wounds on 28 April 1915; he is buried in Bailleul Communal Cemetery Extension (Nord). His brother, Private Edward Ensor, also emigrated to Canada and also enlisted into the 7th Battalion (British Columbia Regiment). His brother, Francis Oliver Ensor, served as a Lieutenant in the Royal Naval Reserve in the First World War and as a pilot with the Lighthouse and Pilotage Authorities during the Second World War. He was killed on 14/15 February 1940 when the SS Giorgio Ohlsen, on which he was pilot, struck a mine laid a few days previously by German destroyers off the coast of Norfolk; he is commemorated on Tower Hill Memorial to the Mercantile Marine. His brother, Captain Robert Weld Ensor, served with the Royal Northwest Mounted Police in Alberta, Canada and with the Canadian Brigade of the North Russia Expeditionary Force. His son, David George Ensor GM, DSM, earned a Distinguished Service Medal at sea serving as a Lance Sergeant with Third Regiment, Maritime Royal Artillery during the Second World War. He then earned a George Medal tackling armed robbers in Dungannon and Donaghmore, County Tyrone in 1952. (WO 339/14261)

ENSOR. Captain Ernest Nash Born on 26 March 1891 at Ardress House, Loughgall, County Armagh. Joined the Imperial Chinese Maritime Customs Service early in 1909. His service included four years in China. Left the Customs Service to join the Army. Enlisted into the 9th Royal Irish Fusiliers on 21 December 1914 (17720 - Private) and joined 'B' Company. Appointed Lance Corporal. Commissioned into Princess Victoria's (Royal Irish Fusiliers) on 7 March 1915. To France with 36th (Ulster) Division in October 1915 as a platoon commander. 1914-15 Star. Commanded 'B' Company September 1916 to March 1917. **Mention in Despatches**. Left 9th Royal Irish Fusiliers on 18 March 1917 for service with the Chinese Labour Corps. Transferred to the General List 20 May 1917. Acting Captain 1 July 1917, Temporary Captain Labour Corps 22 September 1917. Arrived in England from France on leave on 5 November 1918 having contracted influenza and pneumonia. Ordered to the

Joint Labour Centre, 27th Company Chinese Labour Corps at Newtownards. Released from service 6 July 1919. Relinquished his commission 4 March 1921. **Order of *Wen-Hu* (Order of the Striped Tiger)**. He rejoined the Imperial Chinese Maritime Customs Service. His later appointments included Officer in Charge (Commissioner) at Hankow from 17 April 1937 and in 1948, when the London office officially closed, he became the London representative. He died in Oxfordshire in 1979, aged 88. Brother of Captain Charles Howard Ensor. (WO 339/26863)

EYRE. Second Lieutenant Basil Joseph Born on 14 March 1896 at Dublin. A bank clerk, he was commissioned into Princess Victoria's (Royal Irish Fusiliers) on 14 December 1915. To France in July 1916 and joined the 9th Royal Irish Fusiliers on 16 August 1916. One of the first three Roman Catholic officers to join the 9th Royal Irish Fusiliers. Left on 23 October 1916 when posted to the 1st Battalion. **Wounded** at Arras on 11 May 1917 by shrapnel. Lieutenant 1 July 1917. When recovered he joined the 7th/8th (Service) Battalion. When the 7th/8th (Service) Battalion was disbanded he rejoined the 1st Battalion on 15 February 1918 and was posted to 'D' Company. **Captured** at Erches during the withdrawal on 27 March 1918. Repatriated on 25 December 1918 and was released from service on 4 March 1919. Resigned his commission 3 February 1920. (WO 339/50396)

FARIS. Major Arthur Percy Born on 31 July 1893 at Cathedral Close, Armagh. Educated at Campbell College, Belfast from 1908 to 1911. Commissioned from the Royal Military College, Sandhurst into Princess Victoria's (Royal Irish Fusiliers) on 4 September 1912 and joined the 2nd Battalion. Lieutenant 15 April 1914. Joined the 1st Battalion in France on 11 December 1915. 1914-15 Star. Captain 11 December 1915. **Wounded**. Seconded to the Infantry School as an instructor. Acting Major 22 July 1918. Reverted to Captain and rejoined the 1st Battalion on 12 November 1918 and was posted immediately to the 9th Royal Irish Fusiliers where he joined 'D' Company. Posted back to the 1st Battalion 28 November 1918. Commanded 'A' Company. Served in Iraq October 1919 to May 1921. General Service Medal 1918-1962 with clasps 'Iraq' and 'NW Persia'. Served at the Depot, Armagh 1922. Rejoined the 1st Battalion in 1925 and served with it in Cairo in 1927. Major 24 November 1932. Retired 4 April 1935. Set up in business as a mushroom grower at Farnham, Surrey. Recalled from the Regular Army Reserve of Officers in 1939 but relinquished his commission in 1942. Subsequently served in the Air Ministry. Retired from the Regular Army Reserve of Officers 11 December 1946. Lived at Hemingford, Fleet, Hampshire where he died on 4 January 1961, aged 67. His brother, Lieutenant Colonel John George Faris OBE, *Croix de Guerre* (France), served with the Gurkha Rifles. His brother, Second Lieutenant Sturton Johnston Faris, was killed in action on 30 July 1916 serving with the 17th (Service) Battalion, The King's (Liverpool Regiment). His brother, Second Lieutenant Romney Robinson Faris, served with the Corps of Royal Engineers.

FERGUSON MC, DCM. Major Alexander Born in 1868. Enlisted into The Royal Scots Fusiliers (1481) on 7 April 1886. Corporal September 1888, Lance Sergeant March 1890, Sergeant 17 July 1891. Served in South Africa as a Colour Sergeant with the 2nd Battalion. **DCM** and **Mention in Despatches**. Queen's South Africa Medal with clasps 'Cape Colony', 'Relief of Ladysmith', 'Wittebergen' and 'Tugela Heights' and the King's South Africa Medal with clasps '1901' and '1902'. Quarter Master Sergeant 9 July 1903. Discharged 6 April 1911. Joined the 9th Royal Irish Fusiliers on 20 September 1914 and was appointed Honorary Lieutenant and Quartermaster. To France with 36th (Ulster) Division in October 1915. 1914-15 Star. Appointed Adjutant 3 July 1916. Captain 19 February 1917. **Mention in Despatches**. Major 26 June 1917. **MC**. Left the 9th Royal Irish Fusiliers on 18 December 1917 to attend a medical board and was released from service, aged 50. Relinquished his commission 1 May 1920. He subsequently lived in Piershill, Edinburgh and was appointed to a post in the Navy Army and Air Force Institute. (WO 339/14264)

FITZGERALD MC. Major James Gerald Edward Born in 1883 at Clones, County Monaghan. A solicitor by profession in Monaghan town. Served in the North of Ireland Imperial Yeomanry

J G E Fitzgerald

(later the North Irish Horse). Member of the Armagh Regiment, Ulster Volunteer Force. Joined the 9th Royal Irish Fusiliers on its formation and was commissioned on 15 September 1914. Lieutenant 1 December 1914. To France with 36th (Ulster) Division in October 1915 as a platoon commander and the Machine-Gun Officer. 1914-15 Star. Joined 108th Brigade Machine Gun Company on 26 January 1916 and subsequently transferred to the Machine Gun Corps, continuing to serve with 108th Brigade Machine Gun Company. Company Second-in-Command during the Somme attack 1 July 1916. Captain 2 July 1916 and Officer Commanding the Brigade Machine Gun Company. **MC**. Major 1 January 1917. Subsequently served at the Command Depot and as an instructor in England in 1917-18. Returned to France in 1918. Deployed to Russia with the Machine Gun Corps in 1919 as part of the international mission assisting the White Russians. Released from service mid-1919. Relinquished his commission 9 July 1920. Died February 1951.

FITZGERALD OBE, JP, DL. Colonel William Coulson Born on 6 September 1865 at Portadown, County Armagh. Commissioned into the 3rd Battalion (Militia), Princess Victoria's (Royal Irish Fusiliers) as a Lieutenant on 16 August 1884. Captain 29 October 1887. Major 18 August 1897. Embodied 14 May - 4 December 1900. Lieutenant Colonel 20 January 1904 and appointed Commanding Officer of the 3rd Battalion (Militia). Coronation Medal 1911. Retired and relinquished his commission 20 January 1912 and granted the honorary rank of Colonel. Member of the Ulster Volunteer Force as second-in-command of the Armagh Regiment and commanding officer of the 1st (Armagh) Battalion, Armagh Regiment. Joined the 9th Royal Irish Fusiliers on its formation as Second-in-Command. Attached to the 12th (Reserve) Battalion, The Royal Inniskilling Fusiliers from 19 November 1914 as Second-in-Command. Appointed Commanding Officer of the 10th (Reserve) Battalion on its formation. **'B List' Press Mention**. Relinquished his commission on 1 June 1918 and granted the honorary rank of Lieutenant Colonel. **OBE (Military)**. President of the Armagh branch, Royal British Legion. JP. Deputy Lieutenant County Armagh 18 October 1924. Died 5 October 1937, aged 72, at Clantilew, County Armagh. (WO 339/20514)

FITZ-SIMON MC. Lieutenant Colonel Christopher Richard Manners Daniel O'Connell Born on 30 May 1898 at Glencullen, County Dublin. Educated at St Edmund's College, Ware. Commissioned into The Prince of Wales's Leinster Regiment (Royal Canadians) on 21 December 1917 and served with the 2nd Battalion. Attached to the 9th Royal Irish Fusiliers from 17 April 1918 to 16 June 1918. Posted back to the 2nd Battalion, The Prince of Wales's Leinster Regiment (Royal Canadians) and joined 'C' Company. **Wounded** and earned an **MC** at Gheleuwe on 30 September 1918. Lieutenant 21 June 1919. When The Prince of Wales's Leinster Regiment (Royal Canadians) was disbanded in 1922 he transferred to the 2nd Battalion, King's Own Royal Regiment (Lancaster) (seniority 21 June 1919). Lieutenant 6 September 1922. Captain 5 February 1930. Adjutant Auxiliary Force, India 1 April 1936 to 31 March 1939. Major 1 August 1938. Served with the 2nd Battalion in the Western Desert in the Second World War. Commanded the 1st Battalion, The East Surrey Regiment from May to September 1942 when he relinquished command due to ill health. He retired from the Army on medical grounds on 3 June 1943 with the honorary rank of Lieutenant Colonel. In 1953 he repurchased the old family home and lived there until he died in 1984, aged 86.

FLOOD MC. Captain Robert Samuel Born on 14 April 1891 at Ashfield, Cootehill, County Cavan. Worked as an assistant factory manager at Bessbrook Spinning Company and lived at Mullaghglass near Newry. Enlisted into the 9th Royal Irish Fusiliers on 14 December 1914 and was commissioned on 31 December 1914. Lieutenant 2 September 1915. To France with 36th

R S Flood

(Ulster) Division in October 1915 as bombing officer. 1914-15 Star. Commanded 'D' Company for a period in November 1916. Captain 23 February 1917. Commanded 'B' Company for a period in February 1917. Commanded 'A' Company in March 1917. Commanded 'D' Company June 1917 to October 1917. Awarded an **MC** for his actions when Officer Commanding 'D' Company at the Battle of Langemarck on 16 August 1917. **Killed in action** on 5 December 1917 at Marcoing by shrapnel, aged 26. At the time of his death his brother, Lieutenant William James Lowe Flood, was serving with 108th Trench Mortar Battery. His brother, Private Samuel Bailey Flood, served with the 5th (Reserve) Battalion, The King's Royal Rifle Corps. (WO 339/16416)

FULLERTON. Second Lieutenant David John Born in 1898 at Lisburn. Worked at Island Spinning Company Threadworks and was a prize-winning student at Belfast Municipal Technical Institute. Enlisted into The Royal Inniskilling Fusiliers Special Reserve (6741). Promoted Company Sergeant Major. 1914-15 Star. Commissioned into Princess Victoria's (Royal Irish Fusiliers) on 19 December 1916. Joined the 9th Royal Irish Fusiliers on 19 March 1917 and was posted to 'D' Company. **Wounded** in the neck on 24 May 1917 at Messines. **Wounded** at the Battle of Langemarck on 16 August 1917. Evacuated to hospital in England 20 August 1917. He did not serve with the 9th Royal Irish Fusiliers again. Lieutenant 19 June 1918. Released from service mid-1919.

GALLOWAY. Second Lieutenant Arthur James Born on 8 June 1892 at Marchfield, Mid-Lothian. A bank clerk, he served with the 1/4th Battalion (Queen's Edinburgh Rifles), The Royal Scots (Lothian Regiment), a Territorial Force battalion, from January 1910 to January 1914. Enlisted into the 1/9th (Highlanders) Battalion, The Royal Scots (Lothian Regiment) on 21 February 1914 (1624 - Private). Served in France from 18 March 1916 to 14 September 1916 in 154th Brigade, 51st (Highland) Division. As a Lance Corporal he joined 2nd Officer Cadet Battalion at Pembroke College, Cambridge on 14 October 1916 and was commissioned into Princess Victoria's (Royal Irish Fusiliers) on 1 March 1917. Joined the 9th Royal Irish Fusiliers on 24 April 1917 and was posted to 'A' Company. Attached to 122nd Field Company, Corps of Royal Engineers in May & June 1917. Returned home on leave on 22 December 1917, fell ill and was hospitalised. Discharged from hospital on 26 March 1918, he rejoined the 9th Royal Irish Fusiliers on 26 June 1918. Left on 22 August 1918 to report to the Air Ministry. Lieutenant 1 September 1918. Released from service 11 March 1919. Relinquished his commission 1 September 1921. (WO 339/64157)

GARNHAM. Second Lieutenant George Commissioned into the Reserve Regiment of Cavalry 28 November 1916. Transferred to the Service Squadron, 6th (Inniskilling) Dragoons 17 February 1917. Served with 2nd North Irish Horse, X Corps Cavalry Regiment. Joined the 9th Royal Irish Fusiliers on 8 November 1917 but left on 16 November 1917 when he returned to England to transfer to the Tank Corps and join the Tank Corps Depot, Wareham, Dorset for training. Lieutenant 28 May 1918. Promoted Acting Captain 2 August 1918, to command a Tank Section, which he relinquished on 17 August 1918. **Wounded**. Relinquished his commission on account of ill-health caused by wounds 1 August 1919. Silver War Badge, number 451730. (WO 339/67246)

GIBSON. Captain Gordon Hugh Born in July 1893 in Australia. A farmer, he served for three years in the Australian Light Horse. Enlisted into 2nd Dragoon Guards (Queen's Bays) (5707 - Trooper) on 6 August 1914. Posted to 2nd Reserve Cavalry Regiment at the Curragh on 6 November 1914 and deployed to France on 22 April 1915 to join the 6th (Inniskilling) Dragoons on 29 April 1915. 1914-15 Star. Commissioned into The Royal Inniskilling Fusiliers on 23 January 1916 and joined the 10th (Service) Battalion, The Royal Inniskilling Fusiliers (Derry) in 109th Brigade. **Wounded** during the attack at Thiepval on 1 July 1916 by shell fragments and when buried by a high explosive shell. Returned to Australia on compassionate leave in August 1916 while he was recuperating. On his return the ship was torpedoed off Crete and survivors were evacuated via Malta. Served as a Railway Transport Officer in Belfast from November 1916 to January 1917. Attached to the 9th Royal Irish Fusiliers from 5 March 1917 and acted as Officer Commanding 'D' Company before being posted to the 3rd (Reserve)

Garrison Battalion, which he joined at Bere Island, Bantry Bay on 20 April 1917. Transferred to Princess Victoria's (Royal Irish Fusiliers) 27 April 1917. Attached to the British West Indies Regiment where he served as Adjutant of the 9th (Service) Battalion, British West Indies Regiment from 21 July 1917 until August 1918. Lieutenant 23 July 1917. Rejoined the 9th Royal Irish Fusiliers on 1 August 1918, where he remained for the rest of the war. Commanded 'D' Company October 1918. Proceeded on leave to England on 7 November 1918 and was arrested for drunkenness. Attached to the 3rd (Reserve) Battalion, Scots Guards at Wellington Barracks, London pending court martial. Tried by court martial on 2 December 1918 charged with drunkenness; found not guilty. Relinquished his commission on 11 February 1919 (gazetted as British West Indies Regiment). He became a broker for Butterfield & Swire in Hong Kong. Returned to England on 18 August 1926. He relinquished the rank of Captain when he enlisted as a Trooper in a Regiment of Dragoons on 5 October 1926. He died in Australia in 1964. (WO 339/54659)

GIBSON. Captain John Edgar Born on 16 June 1889 at Portadown, County Armagh. Member of the 4th (Portadown) Battalion, Armagh Regiment, Ulster Volunteer Force. A linen merchant, he enlisted into the 9th Royal Irish Fusiliers on 15 September 1914 (14228) and appointed a Lance Sergeant in 'B' Company before being commissioned on 31 December 1914. Lieutenant 2 September 1915. To France with 36th (Ulster) Division in October 1915 in 'D' Company. **Wounded** by shellfire at Mesnil on 31 May 1916. **Wounded** on the left shoulder by a machine gun bullet during the attack at Hamel on 1 July 1916. He was evacuated to hospital in England on 4 July 1916 with Shillington and Jackson. His wound allowed home service only for some time with the 10th (Reserve) Battalion, which he joined on 26 October 1916. Captain 14 February 1917. To France 27 February 1917 and rejoined the 9th Royal Irish Fusiliers 4 March 1917, where he served for the rest of that year. Sent home for a rest on 26 December 1917 and served at the Command Depot, Tipperary. He returned to France on 22 November 1918 and rejoined the 9th Royal Irish Fusiliers on 26 November 1918 as Officer Commanding 'C' Company. Attached to the 5th (Service) Battalion, The Royal Irish Regiment (Pioneers) in the Light Division in the British Army of the Rhine in March/April 1919. Commanded the Light Division College, in the British Army of the Rhine September - October 1919. Released from service 12 November 1919. Relinquished his commission on 1 September 1921. (WO 339/16419)

GILLIARD. Second Lieutenant Thomas Arthur Born in 1887 at Newry, County Armagh. A clerk in a linen factory and a Salvation Army officer, he enlisted into The Royal Munster Fusiliers on 5 September 1914 (2998 - Corporal). Posted to the 6th (Service) Battalion, The Royal Munster Fusiliers. Embarked with the Mediterranean Expeditionary Force in July 1915 with 30th Brigade, 10th (Irish) Division. **Wounded** in the left arm on 26 August 1915. Sergeant 29 May 1916. Joined 2nd Officer Cadet Battalion at Pembroke College, Cambridge on 16 December 1916. Commissioned into Princess Victoria's (Royal Irish Fusiliers) on 27 March 1917. Joined the 9th Royal Irish Fusiliers on 26 June 1917 and was posted to 'A' Company. **Wounded** in the face on 23 November 1917 during the attack at Moeuvres. Evacuated to hospital in England 2 December 1917. Held on the strength of the 3rd (Reserve) Battalion until he recovered, when he transferred to the Tank Corps. Joined the Tank Corps Depot, Wareham, Dorset for training. Relinquished his commission 2 February 1919. Worked for the Land Purchase Commission in Northern Ireland and the Post Office. (WO 339/83278)

GILMER. Lieutenant Eric Hope Born on 28 December 1895 at Dublin. A worker in the flour trade, he joined the 10th (Reserve) Battalion at Lurgan on 17 November 1915. Lance Corporal 28 February 1916. Joined 7th Officer Cadet Battalion at Fermoy on 7 August 1916. Commissioned into Princess Victoria's (Royal Irish Fusiliers) on 19 December 1916. To France 27 February 1917 and joined 9th Royal Irish Fusiliers on 19 March 1917 and was posted to 'C' Company. Attached to HQ 108th Brigade as Assistant Signalling Officer on 10 July 1917. While serving with HQ 108th Brigade he was **wounded and captured** on the night of 26 March 1918 at Davenescourt. Lieutenant 19 June 1918. Repatriated 25 December 1918. Joined 46th

(Service) Battalion, The Royal Fusiliers (City of London Regiment) for service in North Russia in 1919. **Mention in Despatches**. Relinquished his commission 11 October 1919. Emigrated to Canada, where he died in 1962, aged 66. (WO 339/67926)

GIVEN DSO, OBE, MC. Brigadier Thomas Frederick Born on 25 January 1894. Educated at St Columbia's College, Rathfarnham and Trinity College, Dublin. Member of Masonic Lodge 223 in Monaghan. Joined the 9th Royal Irish Fusiliers on its formation and was commissioned dated 29 September 1914. To France with 36th (Ulster) Division in October 1915 in 'D' Company. 1914-15 Star. Captain 19 June 1916. Commanded 'D' Company in mid-1917. **Mention in Despatches**. When acting as Second-in-Command of the 9th Royal Irish Fusiliers he was **wounded** at the Battle of Langemarck on 16 August 1917. **MC**. He was evacuated to hospital in England on 19 August 1917 and saw no further service with the 9th Royal Irish Fusiliers. When recovered he joined the 10th (Reserve) Battalion and later served with 116th Training Reserve Battalion. Released from service mid-1919. Joined The Royal Munster Fusiliers as a Lieutenant 21 January 1921. Transferred to The East Yorkshire Regiment 13 September 1922 after The Royal Munster Fusiliers was disbanded. Captain 26 February 1923. Adjutant of the 1st Battalion 1 March 1926. Adjutant of the 4th Battalion (Territorial Army) 31 January 1935 to 16 February 1936. Major 16 February 1936. Acting Lieutenant Colonel 1940. **DSO**. Lieutenant Colonel 1 August 1942. Commanded the Home Forces 218th Independent Infantry Brigade. Retired 23 July 1946 with the honorary rank of Brigadier. Joined the Diplomatic Service. **OBE (Civil)** 1950 for services as Political Secretary, British Administration, Somalia. Shot and killed while trying to stop tribesmen looting on the border between British Somaliland and Ogaden (south-eastern Ethiopia) on 1 November 1952, aged 58.

GODSON MC*. Captain Edwin Alfred Born on 17 March 1889 at Upper Egdon, Tenbury Wells, Worcestershire. Educated at Winchester College and Trinity College, Oxford where he read law and where he joined the Officer Training Corps. A lawyer, he also worked in the stock exchange. He was commissioned into the 4th (Queen's Own) Hussars Special Reserve of Officers on 10 July 1912. Mobilised on the outbreak of war and deployed with the 4th (Queen's Own) Hussars to France on 20 November 1914 in 3rd Cavalry Brigade. 1914-15 Star. **Wounded** that month. He joined the Irish Cavalry Depot, Dublin in May 1915. Transferred to Princess Victoria's (Royal Irish Fusiliers) in January 1916. Joined the 9th Royal Irish Fusiliers on 18 March 1916 and was posted to 'A' Company. Awarded **MC** for a fighting patrol on 14 August 1916. Commanded 'A' Company in September & November 1916. Attached to Headquarters 108th Brigade on 13 January 1917 as Intelligence Officer and then acting Brigade Major. Returned to the 9th Royal Irish Fusiliers in July 1917, promoted to Acting Captain on 20 July 1917. Commanded 'A' Company from late August 1917 to 5 December 1917 when he was **wounded** at Couillet Wood, Marcoing, shot in the left thigh. He described his wounding: '*I asked the B'de Major when he arrived to come upstairs (to ground level), and look at a shaft to see if that might be what he wanted in talking about an ammunition store. I got out before him, and 'Whack'! And I shouted to the darkness "who hit me with that rock?" Fell over. Found a small hole only in my breeches above the knee and blood flowing. Could not get up. A machine gun bullet had got me. One would think the feeling would be a real smart stinging pain. No, it was more like a Tank hitting you.*' Evacuated to hospital in England 9 December 1917. **Mention in Despatches**. ***Croix de Guerre* (Belgium)**. Captain 19 April 1918. Briefly rejoined the 9th Royal Irish Fusiliers from 27 April 1918. Attached to HQ 36th (Ulster) Division and appointed General Staff Officer Grade 3 on 1 June 1918 then Brigade Major 107th Brigade. Awarded a Bar to his **MC** at the crossing of the River Lys. Transferred to the General List 11

November 1918 for service on the Staff. General Staff Officer Grade 3 in II Corps 16 January to 15 April 1919 when he returned to Ireland and was released from service. Relinquished his commission 1 April 1920. Returned to work as a barrister at Lincoln's Inn. Author of *'Digest of Cinematograph Films Act, 1927, and Other Legislation'*. He also printed a short journal of his exploits during the war. Died in London in late 1978, aged 89. His brother, Captain Frederick Phillip Godson MC, served with The East Yorkshire Regiment. His brother, Lieutenant Claude Lionel Godson, served with the Corps of Royal Engineers. (WO 339/25846)

GRAHAM. Captain William George Born on 10 October 1896 at Rostrevor, County Down. A linen stock keeper, he enlisted into Princess Victoria's (Royal Irish Fusiliers) on 9 February 1916 (23945 - Private). Corporal 31 October 1916. Joined the 9th Royal Irish Fusiliers in France in December 1916 and was posted to 'A' Company. Joined 7th Officer Cadet Battalion on 9 March 1917. Commissioned into Princess Victoria's (Royal Irish Fusiliers) on 26 June 1917. Joined the 9th Royal Irish Fusiliers in September 1917 and served there for the remainder of the war. Transferred to the General List while an instructor at First Army Infantry School from 29 January 1918 to 1 April 1918. Commanded 'B' Company (acting Captain) from 17 October 1918. ***Croix de Guerre* (Belgium)**. Attached to 7th (South Irish Horse) Battalion, The Royal Irish Regiment, in 21st Brigade, 30th Division in 1918. Lieutenant 27 December 1918. Attached to the 5th (Service) Battalion, The Royal Irish Regiment (Pioneers) in the Light Division in the British Army of the Rhine in March/April 1919. Served with 2nd Battalion, Princess Victoria's (Royal Irish Fusiliers) until released from service on 23 October 1919. Relinquished his commission 1 September 1921. He sailed for the United States in April 1920 and lived at Mount Clemens, Michigan, USA and in Wayne County with his sister, Bessie. Brother of Corporal Robert Wallace Graham. His sister, Miss Aileen Graham, served in France as a nurse with the Red Cross. (WO 339/98842)

GRAHAM. Lieutenant William Rennie Born on 16 May 1892 at Newry, County Down. Educated at Royal Belfast Academical Institution and Queen's University, Belfast. Worked for Vinolia Manufacturing Company in Belfast. Enlisted into Princess Victoria's (Royal Irish Fusiliers) as an officer cadet on 4 October 1916 (24914 - Cadet). Commissioned on 28 February 1917 and joined the 10th (Reserve) Battalion on 3 April 1917. Married Kathleen Prenter, the sister of Lieutenant D Prenter on 23 April 1917. Joined the 9th Royal Irish Fusiliers on 16 June 1917 and was posted to 'D' Company. He fell ill on 24 June 1917 and was evacuated to hospital in England on 29 July 1917. Joined the 1st Battalion on 14 June 1918. Recorded as **killed in action** on 1 October 1918, aged 26, during the attack at Vijfwegen; having been badly wounded, he died on his way to the dressing station. (WO 339/73108)

GRANT. Major John Born in 1884 at Belfast. Commissioned into the North Irish Horse on 9 March 1910. Lieutenant 22 April 1913. To France by 20 August 1914 as GHQ Troops. 1914 Star. Captain 30 August 1915. Served with the 2nd North Irish Horse, X Corps Cavalry Regiment. Transferred to Princess Victoria's (Royal Irish Fusiliers) and joined the 9th Royal Irish Fusiliers 30 September 1917. While on leave in December 1917 he was injured when he sprained his ankle leaving a taxi. He attended a Medical Board and did not return to the 9th Royal Irish Fusiliers. He was attached to IV Corps Cyclist Battalion from April 1918, seconded to the Army Cyclist Corps. **Mention In Despatches**. He rejoined the North Irish Horse 7 November 1919. Relinquished his commission in the North Irish Horse 28 May 1929. (WO 374/28602)

GRAVES. Lieutenant Colonel Thomas Francis Howard Born on 12 May 1897. Commissioned into Princess Victoria's (Royal Irish Fusiliers) on 11 August 1915. To France 4 July 1916 and joined the 1st Battalion on 20 July 1916. **Wounded** 26 August 1916. Lieutenant 17 November 1916. When recovered he joined 36 Infantry Base Depot on 2 May 1917 and rejoined the 1st

T F H Graves

Battalion on 5 May 1917. Sent to hospital suffering from appendicitis, he returned to the 1st Battalion in February 1918. **Wounded** 16 April 1918 at Wulverghem. When he recovered he joined the 9th Royal Irish Fusiliers on 31 October 1918. Posted to the 1st Battalion on 10 January 1919. Served in Iraq from 9 January 1920 to 31 December 1921. General Service Medal 1918-1962 with clasp 'NW Persia'. Served with the West Africa Frontier Force 18 March 1923 to 25 May 1927. Temporary Captain 2 October 1923. Captain 15 September 1926. 9 April 1929. Retired 9 November 1932. Recalled from the Regular Army Reserve of Officers just prior to the outbreak of the Second World War as a Captain. Brevet Major 1 September 1939. Acting Lieutenant Colonel 12 December 1941. Temporary Lieutenant Colonel 1 November 1945. Served in Northern Ireland during the Second World War. Died in Carmarthenshire, Wales in mid-1970, aged 73.

GREENAWAY MC. Second Lieutenant William George Born on 23 August 1896 at Minmurry, County Tyrone and lived in Tynan, County Armagh. A chemist's assistant, he enlisted into the Royal Army Medical Corps (31907 - Private) on 6 September 1914. Corporal 8 January 1915, Sergeant 13 November 1915. Served with the BEF from 22 November 1915 to 24 January 1917. 1914-15 Star. Reduced to the ranks 18 August 1916. Joined 7th Officer Cadet Battalion on 3 March 1917 (his character reference came from Sir James Stronge, father of Lieutenant J M Stronge). Commissioned into Princess Victoria's (Royal Irish Fusiliers) on 1 August 1917 and served with the 7th/8th (Service) Battalion in 49th Brigade, 16th (Irish) Division. Joined the 9th Royal Irish Fusiliers on 16 February 1918 from the 7th/8th (Service) Battalion on its disbandment and was posted to 'A' Company. Earned an **MC** for his actions near St Quentin on 9 March 1918. Left the 9th Royal Irish Fusiliers on 13 March 1918 for training as a Flying Officer (Observer) with the Royal Flying Corps. Transferred to the Royal Air Force on 22 June 1918. Relinquished his commission on account of ill-health caused by wounds on 11 November 1919. Joined the Indian Police Service in 1923. Served in the Royal Air Force in the Second World War. Pilot Officer 20 November 1939. Flying Officer 20 November 1940. Flight Lieutenant 1 March 1942. (WO 339/97039)

GREENWOOD. Second Lieutenant Charles Fenwick William Born on 5 December 1888 at Kingston-Upon-Thames, Surrey. Lived in Vancouver, Canada for nine years, spending six years as a mail clerk with the Canadian Civil Service. He enlisted on 15 March 1916 and served with the 31st Regiment, British Columbia Horse. Joined the 72nd Infantry Battalion in 12th Canadian Brigade, 4th Canadian Division (687306 - Corporal) and deployed with the Canadian Expeditionary Force. Having conducted officer cadet training in Canada, and after intervention from his father, a Royal Navy officer, he was commissioned into Princess Victoria's (Royal Irish Fusiliers) on 28 August 1917. Joined the 9th Royal Irish Fusiliers on 27 April 1918. To hospital sick on 15 August 1918 and evacuated to hospital in England 25 August 1918. Attached to the 2nd Battalion, The Royal Irish Rifles, he then applied to transfer to the Indian Army Reserve of Officers. Served with Queen Victoria's Own Corps of Guides (Frontier Force) (Lumsden's Cavalry). Lieutenant 1 March 1919. Relinquished his commission on 12 October 1919. Returned to Canada and lived in Ontario. (WO 339/88113)

GREGORY OBE MD. Lieutenant Joseph Richard Born on 14 July 1897 at Kiltegan, County Wicklow. A student, he enlisted into the South Irish Horse (1756 - Trooper) on 11 November 1915. Appointed Lance Corporal, he joined 7th (South Irish Horse) Battalion, The Royal Irish Regiment on the amalgamation and served in 49th Brigade, 16th (Irish) Division in France until late 1917. Joined 7th Officer Cadet Battalion and was rated one of the best cadets of his batch. Commissioned into Princess Victoria's (Royal Irish Fusiliers) on 26 June 1918. Joined the 9th Royal Irish Fusiliers on 14 October 1918 where he served for the remainder of the war. Applied for a permanent commission but, although regarded highly by Lieutenant Colonel Tamplin, he was not selected. Attached to the 5th (Service) Battalion, The Royal Irish Regiment (Pioneers) in the Light Division in the British Army of the Rhine in March/April 1919. Released from service on 13 December 1919. Relinquished his commission on 1 September 1921. Graduated MB from Trinity College, Dublin in 1925. Practised in South Wales for three years then took up practice in Kenya. MD. President of the Kenya Branch of the British Medical Association. During the Second World War he was the Director of the British Red Cross Society in the East African Territories and was appointed **OBE (Civil)**. Served for a year a mayor of Nairobi. Authored '*Under The Sun*' in 1951, a memoir of Dr R W Burkitt of Kenya. After retirement he served as Chairman of the Cancer Council of Kenya. Died at his home in Nairobi, Kenya on 5 March 1979, aged 81. (WO 374/29220)

GRUNDY. Second Lieutenant Frederick William David Born on 25 March 1892 at Shelton Halewood, Liverpool. Worked for the Royal Insurance Company. Played for Liverpool Cricket Club. Enlisted into the 1/10th (Scottish) Battalion, The King's (Liverpool Regiment) on 29 August 1914 (3821 - Private). Commissioned into Princess Victoria's (Royal Irish Fusiliers) on 2 June 1915 and served with the 7th (Service) Battalion in 49th Brigade, 16th (Irish) Division. Joined the 9th Royal Irish Fusiliers on 17 August 1916. Posted to the 1st Battalion on 22 January 1917. Suffered multiple gunshot wounds on 19 February 1917. Admitted to 8th General Hospital in Rouen but subsequently caught tetanus and **died of wounds** at 7.40pm on 26 February 1917, aged 24. (WO 339/5556)

HALL. Second Lieutenant Francis Henry Born on 23 August 1893 at Glenanne, County Armagh. A teacher, he enlisted into the 20th (Reserve) Battalion, The Royal Irish Rifles on 3 January 1916. Lance Corporal 3 March 1916. Joined the 11th (Service) Battalion, The Royal Irish Rifles (South Antrim) in 108th Brigade in France on 21 June 1916. Sergeant 27 July 1916. Joined 7th Officer Cadet Battalion on 8 February 1918 and was commissioned into The Royal Irish Rifles on 26 June 1918. Attached to the 9th Royal Irish Fusiliers on 14 September 1918. **Killed in action** during the attack at Vijfwegen on 30 September 1918, aged 25. (WO 374/30174)

HAMILL. Captain Harry Born on 3 August 1891. A teacher at the Royal Academical Institution, Belfast, he Joined Queen's University, Belfast Officer Training Corps and was commissioned for service with the Officer Training Corps on 25 April 1915. Commissioned into Princess Victoria's (Royal Irish Fusiliers) on 3 June 1916. Served with the 10th (Reserve) Battalion before joining the 9th Royal Irish Fusiliers on 19 March 1917; posted to 'A' Company. **Wounded** at the Battle of Langemarck on 16 August 1917 by a slight gun-shot wound to the right shoulder. He left the 9th Royal Irish Fusiliers that night having been transferred to the General List for service with the Indian Army Reserve of Officers. He embarked for India on 26 November 1917. Seniority as Lieutenant Indian Army Reserve of Officers from 6 June 1917. Served with 102nd Prince of Wales's Own Grenadiers. Promoted Acting Captain to command a company 16 February 1918 and reverted to Lieutenant 19 May 1918. Retired from the Indian Army Reserve of Officers 1 May 1922. Subsequently worked in India for the Indian Education Service. (WO 339/61616)

HAMILTON. Lieutenant Edward Born on 9 September 1893 at Ballymacarrett, County Down. A clerk, he enlisted into the 17th (Reserve) Battalion, The Royal Irish Rifles on 5 June 1915 (1059 - Private). Joined 7th Officer Cadet Battalion on 5 April 1916 and was commissioned into Princess Victoria's (Royal Irish Fusiliers) on 7 July 1916. To France 25 September 1916 and joined the 9th Royal Irish Fusiliers 14 October 1916. Commanded 6 Platoon, 'B' Company. Commanded 'B' Company from late March 1918 until he was **killed in action** near Wulverghem on 12 April 1918, aged 24. His death was registered as being on 14 April 1918. Brother of Second Lieutenant J I Hamilton. (WO 339/57718)

HAMILTON. Second Lieutenant James Ireland Born on 30 July 1891 at Belfast. The manager of a linen warehouse in Dunfermline, Scotland he returned to Ireland to join Queen's University, Belfast Officer Training Corps. He joined 7th Officer Cadet Battalion on 3 July 1916. Commissioned into Princess Victoria's (Royal Irish Fusiliers) on 25 October 1916. To France 1 January 1917 and joined the 9th Royal Irish Fusiliers on 6 January 1917. Posted to 'D' Company. **Wounded** at the Battle of Langemarck on 16 August 1917, being shot in the right thigh and left shoulder. Evacuated to hospital in England 20 August 1917. Relinquished his commission on account of ill-health caused by wounds 1 March 1919. Silver War Badge, number B80791. He subsequently joined the Northern Ireland Civil Service and lived in Belfast. Brother of Second Lieutenant E Hamilton. (WO 339/64724)

HARDY. Second Lieutenant Gathorne Born on 5 June 1898 at Wood Green, London. Enlisted into The Essex Regiment (37781 - Private) in early 1917. Joined 17th Officer Cadet Battalion at Rhyl on 5 May 1917 and was commissioned into Princess Victoria's (Royal Irish Fusiliers) on 29 August 1917. Served with the 7th/8th (Service) Battalion in 49th Brigade, 16th (Irish) Division until it was disbanded. Joined the 9th Royal Irish Fusiliers on 16 February 1918 and was posted to 'C' Company. **Wounded** in the head by a grenade and **captured** near Wulverghem on 12 April 1918. **Died of wounds** in captivity in a German Field Hospital at Courtrai on 30 April 1918, aged 19. (WO 339/100185)

HARTNESS. Lieutenant Frederick Carson Born on 2 May 1881 at Ballybay, County Monaghan. Worked as a farmer in Australia. Enlisted into the 18th (Service) Battalion, The Royal Fusiliers (City of London Regiment) (1st Public Schools) on 12 December 1914 (1598 - Private). Deployed to France in 98th Brigade, 33rd Division on 14 November 1915. 1914-15 Star. Corporal 15 December 1915. Served in the Transport Section. Joined 1st Officer Cadet Battalion at Newton Ferrers, Devon on 24 March 1916 and was commissioned into Princess Victoria's (Royal Irish Fusiliers) on 5 August 1916. Joined the 9th Royal Irish Fusiliers on 3 October 1916 and was posted to 'C' Company. Lieutenant 5 February 1918. Left the 9th Royal Irish Fusiliers in March 1918 for a rest but returned on 26 November 1918 and was posted to 'D' Company. Evacuated to hospital in England sick (pleurisy) on 9 January 1919. Relinquished his commission on 19 October 1919. Lived in Belfast. (WO 339/60788)

HENAHAN MC. Captain Michael Born on 12 January 1896 at County Cork. Joined the Irish Guards on 15 December 1914 (6192 - Guardsman). Serjeant 20 July 1915 and deployed to France with the 2nd Battalion on 17 August 1915. 1914-15 Star. Commissioned into Princess Victoria's (Royal Irish Fusiliers) on 7 July 1916. Joined the 9th Royal Irish Fusiliers on 31 October 1916 and was posted to 'A' Company. **Wounded** slightly 13 February 1917 north of Ploegsteert Wood. Captain 19 February 1917. Commanded 'C' Company February 1917 to November 1917. **Mention in Despatches**. Awarded an **MC** for a raid on 4 June 1917. **Wounded** by a bomb on 3 November 1917 during a raid at Havrincourt Wood. Adjutant from mid-November 1917 and **captured** on 21 March 1918 near Grand Seraucourt. Repatriated 18 December 1918. Relinquished his commission 16 October 1919. (WO 339/54496)

HENRY. Lieutenant Albert William Born on 20 March 1894 at Ely, Cambridgeshire. A clerk, he enlisted into 2nd Life Guards on 24 November 1914. Lance Corporal 29 October 1916. Joined 1st Cavalry Cadet Squadron at Netheravon on 6 December 1916 and was commissioned into the 2nd Reserve Cavalry Regiment on 17 February 1917. To France 14 April 1917 and joined the 2nd North Irish Horse, X Corps Cavalry Regiment. Transferred to Princess Victoria's (Royal Irish Fusiliers) and joined the 9th Royal Irish Fusiliers on 4 November 1917. Posted to 'A' Company. **Captured** on 27 March 1918 near Erches having been Officer Commanding 'A' Company for the last three days of the withdrawal of the 9th Royal Irish Fusiliers. Lieutenant 17 August 1918. Repatriated 25 December 1918 and rejoined the 2nd Reserve Cavalry Regiment at the Curragh on 26 February 1919. Relinquished his commission 11 June 1919. Lived at Windsor, Berkshire. Subsequently served with the 4th Battalion, Princess Charlotte of Wales's (Royal Berkshire Regiment) from 13 April 1921 to 12 May 1921, when he relinquished his commission. (WO 339/80330)

A C Hollywood

HOLLYWOOD. Lieutenant Arthur Carson Born on 29 December 1891 at Ballymacarrett, Belfast. Attended Friend's School, Lisburn 1903-06 and the Royal Belfast Academical Institution. A rent agent, he lived in Helens Bay, County Down and was the company commander of 'F' Company, Willowfield Battalion, Belfast Regiment,

Ulster Volunteer Force 1913-14. Joined 108th Field Ambulance in 36th (Ulster) Division on 12 September 1914. Promoted to Staff Sergeant. Commissioned into Princess Victoria's (Royal Irish Fusiliers) on 19 April 1915. Served with the 9th Royal Irish Fusiliers but did not sail with the Battalion in October 1915. Remained at Borden until he joined the 10th (Reserve) Battalion on 10 October 1915 (with Richardson and 132 men). Rejoined the 9th Royal Irish Fusiliers in January 1916 and was posted to 'A' Company. **Wounded** in the left arm by a bomb while on patrol near Hamel on 22 February 1916 and evacuated to hospital in England 3 March 1916. Lieutenant 29 February 1916. Rejoined the 9th Royal Irish Fusiliers on 1 May 1916. **Killed in action** during the attack at Hamel on 1 July 1916, aged 24. Although it was reported that his body was brought back and buried behind Hamel Village, he now has no known grave. His brother, Second Lieutenant James Hollywood, served with the 12th (Service) Battalion, The Royal Irish Rifles (Central Antrim) and was also killed in action on 1 July 1916, aged 23. (WO 339/4060)

HULSE. Major Adrian Born on 26 February 1882 at Kensington, London. Served in the Buckinghamshire Yeomanry (34026 Trooper). Served in the South Africa War 1901-02 with 57th (Buckinghamshire) Company, 15th Battalion, Imperial Yeomanry. Queen's South Africa Medal with clasps 'Cape Colony', 'Orange Free State', 'Transvaal', 'South Africa 1901', 'South Africa 1902'. Served with the Cape Mounted Riflemen in South Africa 1903-11. Worked then in Federated Malaysia for Morgan's Agency, a rubber and produce broker. Served in the Malay States Volunteer Rifles 1912-14. Commissioned (Captain) into the 16th (Service) Battalion, The Royal Irish Rifles (2nd County Down) (Pioneers) 2 November 1914. Transferred to the Service Squadron, 6th (Inniskilling) Dragoons as a Captain on 8 January 1915. To France with 36th (Ulster) Division in October 1915. 1914-15 Star. Served in the 2nd North Irish Horse, X Corps Cavalry Regiment from June 1916. Appointed Officer Commanding 'A' Squadron 7 July 1917. Transferred to Princess Victoria's (Royal Irish Fusiliers) and joined the 9th Royal Irish Fusiliers 5 October 1917. Served there until 16 November 1917 when he was attached to the 9th (Service) Battalion, The Royal Inniskilling Fusiliers (County Tyrone) in 109th Brigade. Town Major of Artemps from 6 February 1918 to 21 March 1918. Promoted to Acting Major and attached again to the 9th (Service) Battalion, The Royal Inniskilling Fusiliers (County Tyrone) as Second-in-Command on 21 April 1918. Senior Officers' Course at Aldershot 6 July 1918. Rejoined 109th Brigade on 11 October 1918 and served with the 2nd Battalion, The Royal Inniskilling Fusiliers then joined the 9th (Service) Battalion, The Royal Inniskilling Fusiliers (County Tyrone) on 7 November 1918, again as Second-in-Command. Temporary Major 15 December 1918. ***Croix de Guerre*** **(Belgium)**. Contracted bronchitis and influenza and saw no further service. Released from service 30 April 1919. Relinquished his commission 22 Oct 1920. Major Regular Army Reserve of Officers 8 December 1920. He joined the Auxiliary Division of the Royal Irish Constabulary as Second Class District Inspector 19 January 1921. Appointed Second-in-Command of 'O' Company. Promoted to First Class District Inspector and appointed Officer Commanding 'A' Company in County Kilkenny until January 1922. Retired from the Reserve of Officers on 26 February 1932. Died in 1964 at Leicester, Leicestershire, aged 82. (WO 339/14050)

HUMPHREYS. Second Lieutenant Frederick David Ritchie Born on 26 July 1895 at Ballycastle, County Antrim. A bank clerk, he joined the 9th Royal Irish Fusiliers on 16 September 1914 (14289 - Private). Corporal 29 May 1915. To France with 36th (Ulster) Division in October 1915 where he served until he was **wounded** in the arm during the attack at Hamel on 1 July 1916. 1914-15 Star. Discharged from hospital on 27 April 1917. Acting Sergeant 25 May 1917. Having served at home since leaving hospital, he joined 7th Officer Cadet Battalion on 8 February 1918. Commissioned into Princess Victoria's (Royal Irish Fusiliers) (County Armagh) on 25 June 1918 and joined the 9th Royal Irish Fusiliers on 14 September 1918. **Wounded** (shrapnel wound to the head) on 7 October 1918 at Hill 41 near Dadizeele. He caught influenza in the Casualty Clearing Station and was evacuated to hospital in England. He saw no further service and was released from service on 6 April 1919. Relinquished his commission on 1 September 1921. (WO 339/118303)

HUTCHINSON. Lieutenant William Henry Born on 11 November 1883 at Dublin. Joined the 1st Imperial Light Horse, South African Union Defence Force on 3 May 1914 and was commissioned. Served in German South West Africa. 1914-15 Star. Lieutenant 1 July 1916. Subsequently transferred to the North Irish Horse Special Reserve of Officers and served in 2nd North Irish Horse, X Corps Cavalry Regiment. Injured when thrown from a car on 29 May 1917 while on duty at X Corps HQ at Samer. Transferred to Princess Victoria's (Royal Irish Fusiliers) and joined the 9th Royal Irish Fusiliers on 2 October 1917. Posted to 'C' Company. **Wounded** on 3 November 1917 on a raid when shot in the chest and legs. Evacuated to hospital in England 3 December 1917. The severity of his wounds precluded further service and he remained in Ireland, joining the Reserve Regiment, North Irish Horse on 11 June 1918. Released from service on 1 March 1919. Resigned from the Special Reserve of Officers 1 April 1920. (WO 339/44013)

HUTSON. Lieutenant Eyre Massey Born in 1892 at Cork, County Cork. An insurance clerk, he was commissioned into Princess Victoria's (Royal Irish Fusiliers) on 5 October 1915. Joined the 9th Royal Irish Fusiliers on 17 August 1916. To hospital sick on 24 September 1916. When recovered he transferred to The London Regiment. Lieutenant 1 July 1917. Released from service mid-1919. Relinquished his commission 31 August 1920. Died on 21 September 1964 in Ireland.

INGLIS. Second Lieutenant James Malcolm Born on 6 July 1899 at Cultra, County Down. Educated at Shrewsbury School. A clerk, he enlisted as a cadet in The Royal Irish Rifles on 27 December 1917. Joined 5th Officer Cadet Battalion at Trinity College, Cambridge and was commissioned into Princess Victoria's (Royal Irish Fusiliers) on 23 June 1918. To France 7 September 1918 and joined the 9th Royal Irish Fusiliers on 22 September 1918. **Died of wounds** in 8th Stationary Hospital on 26 October 1918, aged 19, having been wounded during the fighting at Courtrai on the River Lys on 16 October 1918. He was the youngest officer to die while serving with the 9th Royal Irish Fusiliers. (WO 374/36333)

IRVINE MBE. Major Walter Frederick Born on 2 June 1897 at Belfast. A bank official with Belfast Banking Company, he enlisted into the 12th (Reserve) Battalion, The Royal Inniskilling Fusiliers on 13 March 1916 as a Cadet. Joined 7th Officer Cadet Battalion on 14 November 1916 and was commissioned into Princess Victoria's (Royal Irish Fusiliers) on 1 March 1917. Joined the 9th Royal Irish Fusiliers on 14 May 1917. Attached to the 12th (Service) Battalion, The Royal Irish Rifles (Central Antrim) in 108th Brigade on 30 June 1917 and transferred to The Royal Irish Rifles. **Wounded** at the Battle of Langemarck 16 August 1917. Served in 'A' Company and was gassed and **captured** near St Quentin on 21 March 1918. Lieutenant 1 September 1918. Repatriated on 11 December 1918. Relinquished his commission on 20 September 1919. Lieutenant Home Guard (National Defence Companies) 5 September 1939. Served with The Royal Ulster Rifles and The Inniskilling Fusiliers. Captain 30 April 1941. Granted the honorary rank of Major when he relinquished his commission on 16 June 1945. **MBE (Civil)** for service as the treasurer of the Northern Ireland Area of the British Legion 1969. (WO 339/76223)

IRWIN CSI, OBE. Captain George Robert Born on 2 April 1855. From Tynan, County Armagh. Educated at Uppingham School and Christ Church, Oxford; First in Classical Moderations. Joined the Indian Civil Service in 1878. He was appointed First Assistant and Secretary for Berar to the Resident at Hyderabad in 1892, Political Agent at Jhalawar in 1893, Resident of Jaipur in 1897 and Head of the Thuggy & Dacoity Department from 1900 - 1903. Retired 1903. **CSI**. Signed the Ulster Covenant 28 September 1912. Acted as Adjutant to Major Blacker in the 1st (Armagh) Battalion, Armagh Regiment, Ulster Volunteer Force. Joined the 9th Royal Irish Fusiliers on its formation. Captain 16 September 1914. Considered too old for active service he transferred to the General List 18 May 1915. Assistant Provost Marshal, Marseilles

Base 18 May 1915. 1914-15 Star. Fell ill in late 1915 and was asked to resign his commission on grounds of ill health. He refused and was sent to Egypt as a Staff Captain. He fell ill again, had a tumour removed from his mouth and returned to Ireland in July 1916. Resigned his commission 10 May 1917, aged 62. Silver War Badge, number 240893. Served as Head of Section of the Contraband Department at the Foreign Office. **OBE (Civil)**. Died at Penzance, Cornwall 4 March 1933, aged 87. (WO 339/14269)

JACK. Lieutenant Henry Dallas Born on 14 August 1892 at Yorkshire. Enlisted into 1/1st Lanarkshire Yeomanry on 24 September 1914 (5814 - Private) at Cupar, Fife. Commissioned into The Queen's Own Cameron Highlanders on 24 September 1915 and was posted to the 8th (Reserve) Battalion, The Queen's Own Cameron Highlanders. Transferred to the 2nd Reserve Cavalry Regiment and joined the 2nd North Irish Horse, X Corps Cavalry Regiment in July 1916. Lieutenant 1 July 1917. Transferred to Princess Victoria's (Royal Irish Fusiliers) and joined the 9th Royal Irish Fusiliers on 30 September 1917. He was attached to 13th (Service) Battalion, The Royal Irish Rifles (1st County Down). He applied to transfer to the Indian Army Reserve of Officers and left on 13 December 1917. His application was refused and he transferred to the General List for service on the Staff (Staff Lieutenant Class II) 27 January 1918. Relinquished his commission on 7 October 1919. Lived in Rock Ferry, Cheshire. (WO 339/43628)

JACKSON. Lieutenant Henry Kellett Born in 1895 at Cara House, Clones, County Monaghan, the son of Samuel Kidd Jackson JP, High Sheriff of County Monaghan and County Longford. Educated at Rossall School, Lancashire and at Trinity College, Dublin. Commissioned into Princess Victoria's (Royal Irish Fusiliers) on 9 October 1914. To France with 36th (Ulster) Division in October 1915 as a platoon commander in 'D' Company. 1914-15 Star. **Wounded** by a machine gun bullet in the right arm during the attack at Hamel on 1 July 1916. Evacuated to hospital in London with Shillington and Gibson on 4 July 1916. Lieutenant 23 July 1917. Relinquished his commission on account of ill-health caused by wounds and was employed subsequently with the Ministry of National Service. Silver War Badge, number 407256. On the evening of 13 July 1921 while staying with his mother at Cara House in Clones, he went out with his gun to a small plantation nearby. He did not return for supper and his body was found the next morning. He had been shot in the chest and an inquest found that he had died accidentally. He was aged 26. He was buried at Clogh Parish Church. (WO 339/66074)

JOHNSTON. Captain Charles Moore Born on 17 April 1886 at Portadown, County Armagh. Attended Lurgan College. Signed the Ulster Covenant 28 September 1912. Played a prominent part in the 4th (Portadown) Battalion, Armagh Regiment, Ulster Volunteer Force. Captain of Portadown Rugby Club. Married on 3 June 1914, 2 children (16 months and 3 weeks old when he died). Educated at Lurgan College and the Royal School of Mines, Commissioned into the 9th Royal Irish Fusiliers on 15 September 1914. Captain 1 December 1914. To France with 36th (Ulster) Division in October 1915. 1914-15 Star. Commanded 'C' Company January 1916, vice S J Scott. **Killed in action** during the attack at Hamel on 1 July 1916, aged 30. His body was recovered on 4 July. His son, Charles Collier Johnston, served in the Royal Regiment of Artillery in the Second World War. He was knighted in 1973 and created a life peer - Baron Johnston of Rockport, of Caversham in the Royal County of Berkshire. (WO 339/14271)

JOHNSTON OBE, MD. Lieutenant Joseph Alexander Love (Lex) Born on 10 June 1896 at County Londonderry. A medical student at Foyle College, Londonderry, he joined Queen's University, Belfast Officer Training Corps in November 1914. Joined 7th Officer Cadet Battalion on 30 March 1916. Commissioned into Princess Victoria's (Royal Irish Fusiliers) on 7 July 1916. Joined the 9th Royal Irish Fusiliers on 7 October 1916 and was posted to 'D' Company. **Wounded** in the jaw, leg and foot by shellfire at Havrincourt Wood on 11 September 1917 and evacuated to hospital in England on 21 October 1917. His wounds were severe and he attended hospital on and off until 27 March 1919. He relinquished his commission on account of ill-health caused by wounds 9 October 1919. Silver War Badge, number B230749. He returned to his medical studies at Queen's University, Belfast and graduated MB in 1923. MD 1926. Initially practiced at the Royal Victoria Hospital, Belfast. Appointed pathologist to the Northern Ireland Ministry of Home Affairs in 1934. Fellow of the British Medical Association in 1962. Made **OBE (Civil)** for his services as Consultant Physician, North-west Hospitals Group, Londonderry. High Sheriff of Londonderry City 1962-64. He died on 2 February 1966, aged 69. (WO 339/57724)

JOHNSTON. Captain Joseph Allen Born on 2 May 1891 at Portadown, the son of James Johnston JP. Worked in the linen trade with his father. Signed the Ulster Covenant 28 September 1912. Acted as an officer in the 4th (Portadown) Battalion, Armagh Regiment, Ulster Volunteer Force for 18 months. Commissioned into the 9th Royal Irish Fusiliers on 15 September 1914. To France with 36th (Ulster) Division in October 1915 in 'C' Company, where he was appointed Second-in-Command. 1914-15 Star. Commanded 'C' Company from July 1916 until he was **killed in action** near Wulverghem by a sniper on 18 February 1917, aged 25. His brother, Lieutenant James Andrew Johnston, served with The Royal Irish Rifles. (WO 339/14272)

JOHNSTON. Second Lieutenant Robert William Born on 8 June 1891. A school master, born in Fermanagh, he enlisted into 30th (Reserve) Battery, Royal Field Artillery on 6 April 1915. After four months he was transferred to the 12th (Reserve) Battalion, The Royal Inniskilling Fusiliers. Commissioned into Princess Victoria's (Royal Irish Fusiliers) on 5 January 1916. Joined the 9th Royal Irish Fusiliers on 17 August 1916. Commanded 'A' Company for a period in December 1916. Lieutenant 24 February 1917. **Wounded** at the Battle of Langemarck on 16 August 1917 by machine gun bullets in the chest and left arm and evacuated to hospital in England 21 September 1917. His wounds were severe and he was treated in hospital until late 1918. He relinquished his commission on account of ill-health caused by wounds 12 March 1920. (WO 339/51125)

KEMP MM. Lieutenant Henry Born on 22 December 1886. Enlisted into The East Yorkshire Regiment on 4 July 1905 (8295 - Private). Served with the 2nd Battalion in India. Sergeant 14 February 1914. Posted as an instructor to the 10th (Service) Battalion, The East Yorkshire Regiment (1st Hull) in Hull on the outbreak of war, then served in the 3rd (Reserve) Battalion, The East Yorkshire Regiment at Hull as a Company Quartermaster Sergeant in 'C' Company from 12 May 1916 and then as Acting Company Sergeant Major. Volunteered for active service four times but was refused on medical grounds due to deafness. To France 9 September 1917 and transferred to the 1st Battalion, The Royal Inniskilling Fusiliers as a Company Quartermaster Sergeant (renumbered 42517) on 27 September 1917. Awarded an **MM** for his conduct during the withdrawal from St Quentin after the 1st Battalion, The Royal Inniskilling Fusiliers had joined 109th Brigade. Acting Company Sergeant Major 23 March 1918. Commissioned directly into Princess Victoria's (Royal Irish Fusiliers) and joined the 9th Royal Irish Fusiliers on 24 July 1918, where he served for the remainder of the war. Lieutenant 24 January 1920. Retired 3 November 1920. Rejoined from the Reserve of Officers and joined 'B' Company, 2nd Battalion 10 April 1921. (WO 374/39104)

KERNAGHAN. Second Lieutenant John Born on 26 September 1891 at Muckamore, County Antrim. A clerk, he enlisted into the 11th (Service) Battalion, The Royal Irish Rifles (South Antrim) (19583 - Private) on 18 September 1914. Corporal 2 December 1914. Sergeant 17

August 1915. Deployed to France with the 11th (Service) Battalion, The Royal Irish Rifles (South Antrim) in 107th Brigade on 3 October 1915. 1914-15 Star. **Wounded** during the attack at Hamel on 1 July 1916. Returned to France on 18 January 1917. **Wounded** - gassed four times between 11 and 27 August 1917. Joined 7th Officer Cadet Battalion on 8 February 1918. Commissioned into Princess Victoria's (Royal Irish Fusiliers) on 26 June 1918. Joined the 9th Royal Irish Fusiliers on 22 September 1918. **Died of wounds** in 87th Field Ambulance on 1 October 1918, aged 27, having been shot in the chest and head during the attack at Vijfwegen on 30 September 1918. (WO 374/39358)

KERR DSO, MD. Colonel Cecil Hugh Born on 21 March 1898 at Strabane, County Tyrone. Educated at the Royal Belfast Academical Institution. A medical student at Queen's University, Belfast, he was commissioned into Princess Victoria's (Royal Irish Fusiliers) on 19 December 1916. Joined the 9th Royal Irish Fusiliers on 29 March 1917 and was posted to 'D' Company. **Mention in Despatches**. Lieutenant 19 June 1918. Acting Captain 13 June 1918. Commanded 'A' Company from June 1918 for the remainder of the war. **Mentioned in Despatches** for a second time. ***Croix de Guerre (étoile en bronze)* (France)**. Attached to the 5th (Service) Battalion, The Royal Irish Regiment (Pioneers) in the Light Division in the British Army of the Rhine in March/April 1919. Relinquished his commission 9 November 1920. He resumed his medical studies and graduated in 1923. Practiced in Belfast, Oswestry and London. MD in 1928. Commissioned as a Lieutenant in the Royal Army Medical Corps on 5 September 1939. Served with a Field Ambulance in France and was evacuated at Dunkirk. Earned a **DSO** as an acting Lieutenant Colonel commanding 176th Field Ambulance, 51st Highland Division at the Second Battle of El Alamein in 1942. **Mentioned in Despatches** for his services in Sicily in 1944. Appointed Colonel, Assistant Director Medical Services of 51st Highland Division. After the war he continued to practice medicine in London. Died on 8 October 1975, aged 77. His brother, Captain Robert Andrew Kerr MC, served with the Royal Army Medical Corps. His brother, Corporal Frederick John Kerr, served with the New Zealand Expeditionary Force and was wounded twice.

KERR MC. Lieutenant Colonel Robert Goodman Born on 23 November 1889 at Dublin. Lived at Delgany, County Wicklow. Educated at Campbell College, Belfast and Trinity College, Dublin. Commissioned into The Royal Inniskilling Fusiliers on 12 September 1914. Captain 25 November 1914. To France 9 March 1916 and commanded 'B' Company, 7th (Service) Battalion, The Royal Inniskilling Fusiliers in 49th Brigade, 16th (Irish) Division. **Wounded** 29 May 1916. Major 4 September 1916. **MC**. Acting Lieutenant Colonel 31 October 1916 to 1 January 1917, commanding the 7th (Service) Battalion, The Royal Inniskilling Fusiliers. Acting Lieutenant Colonel 10 April 1918, commanding the 7th/8th (Service) Battalion, The Royal Inniskilling Fusiliers. Joined 9th Royal Irish Fusiliers as Second-in-Command on 30 May 1918. **Killed in action** on 11 July 1918, aged 28, at Hoogenacker while on a reconnaissance of the front line with the Commanding Officer, Lieutenant Colonel G M Forde. (WO 339/13064)

KIELY. Second Lieutenant Florence Patrick Born on 7 March 1893 at Cork, County Cork. Worked as an insurance agent. Commissioned into Princess Victoria's (Royal Irish Fusiliers) on 14 December 1915 and served in the 4th (Extra Reserve) Battalion until he joined the 9th Royal Irish Fusiliers on 17 August 1916. One of the first three Roman Catholic officers to join the 9th Royal Irish Fusiliers. **Wounded** in the arms and legs during a raid on La Petite Douve Farm on 12 October 1916. Evacuated to hospital in England 25 October 1916. When recovered, he joined the 1st Battalion on 27 April 1917. 'C' Company. Battalion Intelligence Officer during the attack at the Chemical Works, Roeux. On 24 June 1917 he was part of a raiding party of four officers and sixty men ordered to attack an enemy system of occupied shell holes near Roeux. The British and German lines were about 1,000 yards apart and he had gone about 700 yards, with shells falling around him, when he was hit in the head and **killed in action**, aged 24. Privates Wylie and O'Brien went to his aid and found him dead in a shallow shell-hole but a search party that went out later failed to find his body. (WO 339/50392)

LAIRD MM*. Second Lieutenant Willie Born on 20 December 1893. A farmer from Raphoe, County Donegal, he enlisted into the 11th (Service) Battalion, The Royal Inniskilling Fusiliers (Donegal and Fermanagh) (14695) on 14 September 1914. Corporal November 1914. Sergeant October 1915. To France with 36th (Ulster) Division in October 1915. Earned an **MM**, a Bar to the **MM** and the ***Medaille Militaire* (France)** with 11th (Service) Battalion, The Royal Inniskilling Fusiliers (Donegal and Fermanagh). Warrant Officer Class II, Company Sergeant Major June 1917. Joined 16th Officer Cadet Battalion at Rhyl and was commissioned into Princess Victoria's (Royal Irish Fusiliers) on 29 May 1918. Joined the 11th (Service) Battalion. Posted to the 9th Royal Irish Fusiliers in August 1918 when the 11th (Service) Battalion was disbanded and joined on 28 August 1918. **Wounded** between 2-5 September 1918 near Wulverghem and evacuated to hospital in England. He saw no further service with the 9th Royal Irish Fusiliers and was released from service on 10 January 1919. Relinquished his commission on enlistment in the Army Reserve 9 April 1921. (WO 374/40405)

LARTER. Major Charles Brunskill Served as a Squadron Sergeant Major (1607) in the Queen's Own Royal Glasgow Yeomanry. Territorial Force Efficiency Medal. Served in France from 13 May 1915 with 'B' Squadron in 9th (Scottish) Division. 1914-15 Star. Commissioned into the 1st Reserve Cavalry Regiment on 20 December 1916. Served with the 4th Reserve Regiment of Cavalry at Aldershot. Joined the 2nd North Irish Horse, X Corps Cavalry Regiment on 7 May 1917. Transferred to Princess Victoria's (Royal Irish Fusiliers) and joined the 9th Royal Irish Fusiliers on 2 October 1917. Left on 16 November 1917 to transfer to the Tank Corps and joined the Tank Corps Depot, Wareham, Dorset for training. Lieutenant 21 June 1918. Acting Captain 28 July 1918 to command a Tank Section. **Wounded** in the knee and hip in August 1918. Released from service mid-1919. Relinquished his commission when he re-enlisted in the Territorial Force 20 May 1920. Served with the Home Guard in the Second World War. Second Lieutenant (102356) Argyll and Sutherland Highlanders 23 September 1939. Adjutant of a Home Guard battalion. Temporary Major 1944. Died at Glasgow on 8 February 1966.

LEAHY MC. Lieutenant Thomas Cecil Born on 9 May 1891. Son of a farmer in Newcastle West, County Limerick, he worked in Argentina until February 1916. Enlisted into the Royal Field Artillery (130329 - Gunner) on 16 March 1916. Transferred to 12th Reserve Cavalry Regiment at Aldershot on 2 August 1916. Lance Corporal 2 August 1916. Transferred to The Royal Dublin Fusiliers (renumbered 28187 - Corporal) on 2 December 1916 and deployed to France that month. Commissioned into Princess Victoria's (Royal Irish Fusiliers) on 31 October 1917 and joined the 9th Royal Irish Fusiliers on 10 January 1918. Posted to 'B' Company. Awarded an **MC** for his actions on a raid at Meulenhouck, near Bailleul on 22 July 1918. Lieutenant 1 May 1919. Released from service 17 June 1919. Relinquished his commission 1 September 1921. Died at Newcastle, County Down in 1943, aged 52. (WO 339/110989)

LEE. Second Lieutenant Samuel Born on 20 September 1891 at Belfast. A bank clerk with the Imperial Bank of Persia, he trained with the Inns of Court Officer Training Corps from 9 September to 19 November 1915 when he was commissioned into Princess Victoria's (Royal Irish Fusiliers). Served with the 4th (Extra Reserve) Battalion before he joined the 9th Royal Irish Fusiliers on 17 August 1916. Posted to the 1st Battalion on 21 October 1916. His behaviour under shell-fire on 11 April 1917 in Fampoux caused the Commanding Officer to have him removed from command. The Commanding Officer, Lieutenant Colonel A B Inceldon-Webber, sent him to the rear with a memo stating: *'Bearer is useless as a platoon commander in action and request that he is evacuated.'* He was requested to resign his commission for military inefficiency, which he did on 28 July 1917. His application for a Silver War Badge was refused. (WO 339/48142)

R L Lees

LEES. Second Lieutenant Robert Lindsay Born in 1896 at London. Enlisted into the 18th (Reserve) Battalion, The Royal Irish Rifles (1609). Commissioned into The Royal Irish Rifles on 26 June 1918. Served with the 3rd (Reserve) Battalion, The Royal Irish Rifles until he joined the 9th Royal Irish Fusiliers on 15 October 1918. He remained with the 9th Royal Irish Fusiliers until released from service in early 1919. Relinquished his commission 1 September 1921. Worked as a merchant in Nigeria between the wars.

LENDRUM JP, DL. Captain Marcus Beresford (Marc) Born on 11 October 1883 the son of George Lendrum, Deputy Lieutenant for Counties Tyrone and Fermanagh. Before the war he worked for the Hong Kong and Shanghai Bank in Malaysia and served with the Malay States Volunteer Rifles (Federated Malaysia). Joined the 9th Royal Irish Fusiliers and was commissioned on 6 March 1915. To France with 36th (Ulster) Division in October 1915. 1914-15 Star. Joined 108th Brigade Machine Gun Company on 26 January 1916. **Wounded** during the attack at Hamel on 1 July 1916. When he recovered he transferred to the Tank Corps and joined the Tank Corps Depot, Wareham, Dorset for training. Married his first wife (his nurse when he was in a nursing home in Brighton) in 1916. Lieutenant 1 October 1916. Acting Captain 1 March 1917. Served with the Tank Corps Officer Cadet Battalion throughout 1918. He deployed to Russia as part of the international mission assisting the White Russians in 1919. He was released from service later that year. Relinquished his commission 8 February 1921. Rejoined the Hong Kong and Shanghai Bank, this time in Yokohama in Japan until made manager of the corporation's silk interests in Lyons, France, where he remained for seventeen years. His wife died in 1935. On the outbreak of war he stayed in France until the last moment, when he was evacuated by Royal Navy ship from a southern port. On his return to Northern Ireland he rejoined the Army as a Captain and served as the Adjutant of one of the County Antrim battalions of the Ulster Home Guard. He also served with the Ulster Home Guard in County Tyrone (he commented that his most hostile encounter over this period was with an empty Guinness bottle thrown in Kilskeery Church Hall). Married twice more. JP County Tyrone. Deputy Lieutenant County Tyrone 1944. High Sheriff County Tyrone 1949. Member of the Orange Order. Served on the Select Vestry of Kilskeery Parish Church. Died 11 March 1969, aged 85. Buried at Kilskeery Parish Church. Brother of Captain George Waller Vesey. His brother, Captain Alan Cane Lendrum MC, was murdered by the Irish Republican Army on 22 September 1920.

LINDSAY. Captain Robert Henry Born in 1888 at Dromore, County Down. Enlisted into The Royal Irish Rifles on 6 January 1909 (9238 - Private) and served with the 2nd Battalion. Corporal 15 November 1911. Sergeant 28 August 1914. Served in France from 1 September to 25 November 1914. 1914 Star. Posted to the 6th (Service) Battalion, The Royal Irish Rifles in 31st Brigade, 10th (Irish) Division and deployed with the Mediterranean Expeditionary Force on 10 July 1915. Served at Gallipoli and Salonika. Acting Warrant Officer Class II, Company Sergeant Major 8 August 1915. Commissioned directly for service in the field into Princess Victoria's (Royal Irish Fusiliers) on 2 March 1916 and joined the 2nd Battalion, Princess Victoria's (Royal Irish Fusiliers) in 31st Brigade, 10th (Irish) Division in Macedonia. Evacuated to Malta with enteric fever on 9 December 1916. Joined the 3rd (Reserve) Battalion on 10 May 1917. Joined the 1st Battalion on 20 April 1918 as a company commander. Acting Captain 28 April 1918. Joined the 9th Royal Irish Fusiliers 18 July 1918 and appointed Officer Commanding 'D' Company on 7 August 1918. **Wounded** during the attack at Vijfwegen on 1 October 1918. **Wounded** on 18 October 1918 at the crossing of the Lys and evacuated to hospital in England. When recovered he rejoined the 3rd (Reserve) Battalion on 18 December 1918 at Southend. Served briefly with the 52nd (Graduated) Battalion, The South Wales Borderers at Ipswich from March 1919 until he rejoined the 2nd Battalion, Princess Victoria's (Royal Irish Fusiliers) on 9 September 1919. Placed on the half pay list on account of ill-health caused by wounds 19 May 1921. Retired on account of ill-health caused by wounds 4 March 1922. (WO 339/59075)

LOCKE. Lieutenant Henry Oscar Born in 1891 (the illegitimate son of Louisa Rosina Price who was one of over twenty children of William Samuel Price). He was placed in the Home for Little Boys, Horton Kirby, Kent. Joined the Inns of Court Officer Training Corps 7 June 1915. Commissioned (on probation) into Princess Victoria's (Royal Irish Fusiliers) Special Reserve of Officers on 7 October 1915. Joined the 9th Royal Irish Fusiliers on 18 June 1916. To hospital sick on 29 September 1916. Posted to the 1st Battalion on 21 October 1916. Lieutenant 1 July 1917. He was deemed unfit for general service on account of ill-health contracted on active service and placed on the retired list 26 January 1918. Served with the Ministry of Labour.

LOGAN MC*. Second Lieutenant Simon Born in 1888 at Lisburn. A compositor and foreman printer at the Lisburn Standard. Enlisted into the North Irish Horse (2230 - Corporal) in August 1916. Served with 2nd North Irish Horse, X Corps Cavalry Regiment. Transferred to Princess Victoria's (Royal Irish Fusiliers) and joined the 9th Royal Irish Fusiliers (renumbered 41358 - Corporal). Commissioned into Princess Victoria's (Royal Irish Fusiliers) on 26 June 1918. Served briefly with the 1st Battalion and joined the 9th Royal Irish Fusiliers as a platoon commander on 14 September 1918. Awarded an **MC** for his actions during the attack at Vijfwegen on 30 September 1918 and a Bar to his **MC** at the crossing of the Lys Canal on 16 October 1918. Released from service in early 1919. Relinquished his commission 1 September 1921. Lived in Belfast. Served in the Second World War with The Royal Irish Fusiliers (Princess Victoria's), Second Lieutenant (142577) 29 July 1940. One of his brothers served with the American Expeditionary Forces and a brother served with The Royal Irish Rifles.

LUTTON. Captain George Elliott Born on 29 March 1885 at Breagh, Portadown, County Armagh. A company commander in the 4th (Portadown) Battalion, Armagh Regiment, Ulster Volunteer Force. Enlisted into the 9th Royal Irish Fusiliers on 15 September 1914 (14402 - Private) and was immediately commissioned. To France with 36th (Ulster) Division in October 1915 as Signalling Officer. 1914-15 Star. Commanded 'C' Company for a period in October 1916. Transferred to the General List for service with the Signal Service, Corps of Royal Engineers on 14 February 1917 and promoted Captain. Joined 108th Brigade as Signalling Officer. Served the remainder of the war with the Signal Service, Corps of Royal Engineers. Relinquished his commission on 17 February 1919. He returned to Portadown after the war and became the manager of Spence Bryson & Company linen manufacturer. He founded the Clonavon Factory Choir from employees of the firm and, in 1926, founded the Portadown Male Voice Choir of which he was the first chairman from 1926-28 and then first president. (WO 339/14289)

LYNESS. Second Lieutenant Harold Born on 17 May 1896 at Belfast. Educated at the Royal Belfast Academical Institution before joining William Liddell and Company, Belfast. Enlisted into the 2/5th (Angus and Dundee) Battalion, The Black Watch (Royal Highlanders) at Forfar on 30 December 1914 (2689 - Private). Commissioned on 27 August 1915 into Princess Victoria's (Royal Irish Fusiliers) and joined the 5th (Service) Battalion in 31st Brigade, 10th (Irish) Division in Salonika. Joined the 9th Royal Irish Fusiliers on 20 June 1916. Suffered gunshot wounds to the back when bringing a wiring party home along Spring Trench to Red Lodge on the night of 31 August/1 September 1916 and **died of wounds** in 2nd Casualty Clearing Station at Bailleul in the early hours of 2 September 1916, aged 20. (WO 339/49026)

LYONS. Lieutenant Stewart Born on 13 October 1895 at Portrush, County Antrim. Enlisted as an officer cadet into 12th (Reserve) Battalion, The Royal Inniskilling Fusiliers on 21 June 1915. Commissioned into The Royal Inniskilling Fusiliers on 4 October 1915 and served with the 9th (Service) Battalion, The Royal Inniskilling Fusiliers (County Tyrone) in 109th Brigade. Suffered from shell-shock and trench fever in October 1916. When recovering he joined 12th (Reserve) Battalion, The Royal Inniskilling Fusiliers. Lieutenant 1 July 1917. Attached to the

11th (Service) Battalion, Princess Victoria's (Royal Irish Fusiliers). Posted to the 9th Royal Irish Fusiliers in August 1918 when the 11th (Service) Battalion was disbanded and joined on 29 August 1918. **Wounded** on 3 September 1918 at Kemmel when he was shot in the neck and back. He was evacuated to hospital in England on 20 September 1918. Released from service on 4 April 1919. Relinquished his commission 1 September 1921. (WO 339/50888)

MacLEAN. Captain Peter Easton Born on 30 April 1881 at Dublin. He served with the 6th (Volunteer) Battalion, The Royal Scots (Lothian Regiment) from 1896 to 1899 and with the Lothian and Berwickshire Yeomanry as a Trooper from 1905 to 1909. An accountant, educated in Scotland, he worked as a statistics clerk in King George V Hospital, Dublin. Commissioned into The Royal Irish Regiment Special Reserve of Officers on 1 January 1916. Served with the 3rd (Reserve) Battalion, The Royal Irish Regiment before being attached to the 10th (Service) Battalion, The Royal Irish Rifles (South Belfast) in 107th Brigade on 29 June 1916. Appointed Adjutant. Captain 9 May 1917. **Mention in Despatches**. To hospital in Manchester with an injured knee November 1917 then to Dublin. Transferred to Princess Victoria's (Royal Irish Fusiliers) 9 July 1918 and joined the 11th (Service) Battalion. Posted to the 9th Royal Irish Fusiliers in August 1918 when the 11th (Service) Battalion was disbanded and joined on 29 August 1918. Acting Second-in-Command for a period around October 1918. Adjutant from 4 February 1919 until the 9th Royal Irish Fusiliers was disbanded. Commanded 260th Prisoner of War Company, and briefly 306th Prisoner of War Company, from 20 June 1919 until he was released from service on 7 November 1919. Relinquished his commission 1 April 1920. (WO 339/51182)

MACK. Major Cyril Hugh Born in 1899 at Belfast. Educated at the Royal Belfast Academical Institution and Weymouth College, Dorset. Worked for Henry Matier Company Ltd, Belfast. Commissioned into Princess Victoria's (Royal Irish Fusiliers) on 8 January 1916. Joined the 9th Royal Irish Fusiliers on 13 April 1917 and was posted to 'A' Company. **Wounded** on 23 April 1917 by shrapnel while with a working party. Having recovered he transferred to the Indian Army Reserve of Officers on 25 September 1917 and joined 123rd Outram's Rifles. Captain Indian Army Reserve of Officers 8 January 1920. Resigned from the Indian Army Reserve of Officers 1 May 1922. During the Second World War he was involved in organising ARP Services and was commissioned from the Officers' Emergency Reserve as a Lieutenant (146575) 30 August 1940. Captain 1943. Major 1945. Served in Northern Ireland with the 5th (Northern Ireland) Battalion, The Royal Irish Fusiliers (Princess Victoria's) and as an instructor with Queen's University, Belfast Officer Training Corps. Commanded the Officer Training Corps October 1945 to September 1947. Retired October 1947. Died 5 June 1963.

MAGILL. Lieutenant Charles William Sinton Born on 21 May 1876 at Lisburn, County Antrim. Educated at Ulster Provincial School, Lisburn (now Friend's School). Member of the Lisburn Company, Ulster Volunteer Force. Joined Queen's University, Belfast Officer Training Corps on 18 October 1915. Commissioned into Princess Victoria's (Royal Irish Fusiliers) on 8 January 1916. Joined the 9th Royal Irish Fusiliers on 30 October 1916 and was posted to 'D' Company. Lieutenant 21 May 1917. **Wounded** at the Battle of Langemarck on 16 August 1917, suffering a severe wound to his left leg, which shortened it by over an inch, and was evacuated to hospital in England. He was then treated at the Ulster Volunteer Force Hospital in Gilford, County Down on and off until September 1918 and he saw no further service. Relinquished his commission on 16 November 1919. Joined the Ulster Special Constabulary and served as a District Inspector in County Londonderry. He died on 6 January 1969, aged 92. His cousin, Brigadier John Alexander Sinton VC, OBE, served with the Indian Medical Service during the First World War. (WO 339/51978)

W Mahoney

MAHONEY. Second Lieutenant William Enlisted into the Corps of Royal Engineers (15789 - Corporal) and deployed to France on 18 August 1914. 1914 Star and clasp. Acting Sergeant. **Mention in Despatches**. Commissioned into The Connaught Rangers on 27 February 1918. Attached to the 9th Royal Irish Fusiliers from 10 November 1918. He left on 3 March 1919 and joined the 2nd Battalion,

The Connaught Rangers. Lieutenant 27 August 1919. Retired 31 July 1922 when The Connaught Rangers was disbanded.

MALONE. Second Lieutenant Bristow Miniss Born on 28 October 1881 in Belfast. Educated at Campbell College. A flax and yarn agent, he enlisted initially into the 24th Battalion, The Royal Fusiliers (City of London Regiment) (2nd Sportsman's) (2124 - Private) in 99th Brigade, 33rd Division. To France 15 November 1915. 1914-15 Star. Commissioned into Princess Victoria's (Royal Irish Fusiliers) on 4 September 1916. Joined the 9th Royal Irish Fusiliers on 31 October 1916 as Officer Commanding 4 Platoon, 'A' Company. **Missing** at the Battle of Langemarck 16 August 1917 and later declared **killed in action** on that date, aged 35. His brother, Second Lieutenant William Adolph Malone, was captured on 16 May 1917 while serving with The Cheshire Regiment. (WO 339/55437)

MARTIN. Second Lieutenant Lawrence Henry Born on 7 August 1897 at County Cavan. A student at Dublin University, he joined 7th Officer Cadet Battalion on 4 November 1916. Commissioned into Princess Victoria's (Royal Irish Fusiliers) on 26 April 1917 and joined the 9th Royal Irish Fusiliers on 5 July 1917. **Killed in action** on 23 November 1917, aged 20, during the attack at Moeuvres. (WO 339/76241)

MATEER. Lieutenant Norman Cooper Born on 14 October 1885 at Belfast. Educated variously in Hastings, Belfast, Courtrai (Belgium) and Bonn, he spoke and wrote French, Flemish, Dutch and German. An official with the Imperial Chinese Maritime Customs Service, he arrived in London from China on 21 September 1915 and enlisted into the Army Service Corps (129632 - Private). To France 27 November 1915. 1914-15 Star. He subsequently served a probationary period with 3rd Army Intelligence Police before transferring to The Royal Irish Rifles (renumbered 9509 - Corporal) on 18 July 1916. He joined the 9th (Service) Battalion, The Royal Irish Rifles (West Belfast) on 20 October 1916 and was appointed Company Quartermaster Sergeant in 'B' Company. Joined 5th Officer Cadet Battalion at Trinity College, Cambridge on 6 February 1917. Commissioned into Princess Victoria's (Royal Irish Fusiliers) on 30 May 1917. Joined 9th Royal Irish Fusiliers on 27 April 1918. **Wounded** by shell-fire on 16 July 1918 and admitted to hospital with shell-shock. When recovered he joined 14th Conversion Camp as censor officer. Lieutenant 30 November 1918. Tried at Field General Court Martial at Trouville on 17 January 1919 on a charge of being absent without leave; found guilty and awarded a severe reprimand. Attached to the 5th (Service) Battalion, The Royal Irish Regiment (Pioneers) in the Light Division in the British Army of the Rhine in March/April 1919. Sailed for Shangai on 29 January 1920. Released from service on 8 March 1920. He rejoined the Imperial Chinese Maritime Customs Service and was caught up in the revolution in China when his customs station was looted and burned. Joined the British Australian and New Zealand Antarctic Research Expedition (BANZARE) (1929-31) on board the Royal Research Ship Discovery (Able Seaman). During the expedition Mount Mateer was named after him. **Polar Medal (Bronze) with clasp 1930-31**, presented by King George V in June 1934. Subsequently served as a merchant seaman, including as bosun on HMS Queen of Bermuda (F73) an armed merchant cruiser and troopship, during the Second World War. Died in Thurrock, Essex in late 1979, aged 94. (WO 339/91109)

MAXWELL. Lieutenant Arthur Frederick Born on 13 September 1884 at Londonderry. A chemist, he enlisted into the 10th (Reserve) Battalion, Princess Victoria's (Royal Irish Fusiliers) on 28 December 1915 (23593 - Private). Joined 7th Officer Cadet Battalion on 7 August 1916 and was commissioned into Princess Victoria's (Royal Irish Fusiliers) on 19 December 1916. Joined the 9th Royal Irish Fusiliers on 19 March 1917 and was posted to 'D' Company. **Wounded** in the back and arm on 24 March 1918 near Guiscard. Evacuated to hospital in England 31 March 1918. Lieutenant 19 June 1918. To hospital at Chatham 15 July 1918 from which he was discharged on 28 August 1919. Released from service on 23 September 1919. Relinquished his commission 1 September 1921. (WO 339/67941)

McCALL. Captain Robert George Born on 7 February 1896. From Keady, County Armagh. Educated at the Royal School, Armagh and Queen's University, Belfast. A teacher, he enlisted into The Royal Irish Rifles on 30 May 1916. Joined 7th Officer Cadet Battalion on 7 August 1916 and was commissioned into Princess Victoria's (Royal Irish Fusiliers) on 19 December 1916. Joined the 9th Royal Irish Fusiliers on 17 April 1917 and was posted to 'C' Company.

Attached to the 12th (Service) Battalion, The Royal Irish Rifles (Central Antrim) in 108th Brigade on 1 July 1917. **Wounded** at the Battle of Langemarck on 16 August 1917 when hit by shrapnel in the thigh. Evacuated to hospital in England 18 August 1917. When recovered he transferred to the General List for service on probation with the Indian Army; he sailed for India on 3 July 1918. Appointed Second Lieutenant 29 July 1918 (to rank from 19 September 1917). Served with 7th Duke of Connaught's Rajputs. Captain 12 September 1922. Returned to Great Britain on 17 November 1922. Retired from the Indian Army 27 March 1923. Started in business making wireless radios. Died in 1963 at Kent, aged 67. (WO 339/67935)

McCARTHY-O'LEARY DSO*, MC. Brigadier Heffernan William Dennis (Donogh) Born on 2 August 1885 to a landed family from Coomlagane, Millstreet, County Cork. Commissioned from the Royal Military College, Sandhurst into the 1st Battalion, Princess Victoria's (Royal Irish Fusiliers) on 16 August 1905. Lieutenant 24 February 1907. Posted to the 2nd Battalion in India 1912. Captain 3 August 1912. Adjutant 1913-16 in India, France and Salonika. 1914-15 Star. Attached temporarily to Headquarters 82nd Brigade as Brigade Major. **Wounded** near the Sturma River October 1916. **MC**. Twice **Mentioned in Despatches**. When recovered, joined the 9th Royal Irish Fusiliers on 24 June 1917. Attached to the Divisional Depot as Commanding Officer 20 July 1917 then attached to the 1st Battalion, The Royal Irish Rifles in August 1917 as Commanding Officer. Awarded the **DSO** for his actions at the Battle of Langemarck on 16 August 1917, where he was **wounded**. **Mention in Despatches**. Rejoined the 1st Battalion, The Royal Irish Rifles December 1917. Acting Lieutenant Colonel 12 January 1918. Transferred with the 1st Battalion, The Royal Irish Rifles to 107th Brigade, 36th (Ulster) Division. Earned a Bar to the **DSO** during the fighting on 27 March 1918 near Erches, where he was **wounded** twice. When recovered, joined the 1st Battalion, Princess Victoria's (Royal Irish Fusiliers) as Commanding Officer on 5 November 1918. Twice more **Mentioned in Despatches**. **Officer of the *Ordre de La Couronne* (Belgium)**. Posted to the 2nd Battalion August 1919. Commanded the guard of honour provided by the 2nd Battalion for the arrival in England of the Unknown Warrior on 15 November 1921. Company commander on amalgamation of the 1st and 2nd Battalions in October 1922. Served with the 1st Battalion in Egypt February 1925. Major and Brevet Lieutenant Colonel 15 March 1925. Commanding officer of the Depot, Omagh 1925-26. Rejoined the 1st Battalion at Cairo 1926. Commanding officer of the 1st Battalion 14 March 1929. Colonel 15 March 1929. Commander 158th (Royal Welch) Infantry Brigade 18 October 1933. Retired on half pay 18 October 1937. His final regular appointment was as Commander, Headquarters Blackdown and Deepcut, Aldershot Command in 1940. He also served with the Ulster Home Guard. President of the Old Comrades Association, Dublin Branch. Died at home in County Cork 23 February 1948, aged 62. Buried at Glasnevin Cemetery, Dublin.

McCAUSLAND. Lieutenant Ivan Edward (Jack) Born on 11 November 1895 at Belfast. Educated at the Royal Belfast Academical Institution. Enlisted into the 19th (Service) Battalion, The Royal Fusiliers (City of London Regiment) (2nd Public Schools) in 98th Brigade, 33rd Division (6696 - Private) and served in France from 15 November 1915. 1914-15 Star. Commissioned into Princess Victoria's (Royal Irish Fusiliers) on 5 August 1916. Joined the 9th Royal Irish Fusiliers on 7 October 1916 and was posted to 'B' Company. Commanded 'B' Company after the Battle of Langemarck until December 1917. Lieutenant 5 February 1918. Posted to England on duty from 8 February 1918 to 5 June 1918, when he rejoined the 9th Royal Irish Fusiliers. Left on 20 July 1918 on transfer to the Machine Gun Corps, where he spent the rest of the war. Served with 86th Battalion, Machine Gun Corps. Released from service in 1919. Died at Belfast on 6 March 1957, aged 62.

R I McCrum

McCRUM. Captain Robert Ivan Born in 1897 at Belfast. Enlisted into the Royal Army Medical Corps (63111 - Private) and served briefly in Egypt from 19 December 1915. 1914-15 Star. Commissioned into Princess Victoria's (Royal Irish Fusiliers) on 6 January 1916. Served with the 10th (Reserve) Battalion at home until he joined the 9th Royal Irish Fusiliers on 16 March 1917. To hospital sick on 24 April 1917 and evacuated to hospital in

England 30 April 1917. Lieutenant 6 July 1917. Rejoined the 9th Royal Irish Fusiliers 5 January 1918 as a platoon commander and then Second-in-Command 'C' Company. Attached to the 5th (Service) Battalion, The Royal Irish Regiment (Pioneers) in the Light Division in the British Army of the Rhine in March/April 1919. Relinquished his commission 19 February 1920. Worked for the family company in the linen trade. Lived in Canada for a period between the wars. Served in the Second World War; General List, Lieutenant (152246) 5 October 1940. Relinquished his commission 28 March 1946 on account of disability and was granted the honorary rank of Captain.

McELVAINE. Lieutenant Andrew Floyd Born on 11 January 1895 at Scarva, County Down. A bank clerk, he joined the Royal Navy on 30 December 1914 and served with the Royal Naval Air Service Armoured Car Section (Petty Officer 1st Class). To France June 1915. 1914-15 Star. Commissioned into Princess Victoria's (Royal Irish Fusiliers) on 8 January 1916 and served with the 9th Royal Irish Fusiliers from 20 June 1916 before transferring to the Heavy Brigade, Machine Gun Corps on 10 December 1916 for service with tanks. Served with Number 1 Section, 10 Company, 'D' Battalion, 1st Brigade. He commanded tank number D9 (770) on 3 May 1917 in support of 21st Division in the Third Battle of the Scarpe during the Arras offensive. During the attack the camouflage on his tank was set on fire which drew artillery fire. The driver moved off course but the tank was able to engage the enemy before ditching in the German front line. After becoming freed, D9 attacked along the rear of the German line before it re-crossed the front line and broke a track. He was **wounded** during this attack and rejoined 'D' Battalion on 18 June 1917. Lieutenant 1 August 1917. Evacuated to hospital in England sick on 25 September 1917 and treated at hospital in Manchester. He was declared fit in March 1918 and joined 18th Battalion, Tank Corps on 3 October 1918, one of the last Tank Corps Battalions to be formed and the last to deploy to France. Appointed as an Instructor and served in South Russia from mid-March to October 1919. Relinquished his commission on 4 January 1920. After the war became a banker in London, Colombia and Argentina. (WO 339/52000)

McFARLAND MC. Second Lieutenant Francis John Elliott Born on 11 August 1887 at Howth, Dublin. A civil engineer, he enlisted into the North Irish Horse (2207 - Trooper) on 28 June 1916 and joined 'E' (later 'B') Squadron. Commissioned into Princess Victoria's (Royal Irish Fusiliers) on 1 August 1917 he joined the 5th/6th (Service) Battalion in 31st Brigade, 10th (Irish) Division in Palestine where he earned an **MC** and was **wounded**. When recovered he joined the 9th Royal Irish Fusiliers on 28 June 1918 and was posted to 'D' Company. Reported **missing** on 22 July 1918 during a raid at Meulenhouck, near Bailleul. In March 1919 he was declared **killed in action** on that date, aged 30. (WO 339/103248)

MENAUL MC. Captain William John Born on 28 November 1886 at Drogheda, County Louth. An assistant factory manager with Thomas Sinton Ltd, Laurelvale, he lived in Tandragee, County Armagh. Signed the Ulster Covenant 28 September 1912 and was a company commander in the Armagh Regiment, Ulster Volunteer Force for a year. Joined the 9th Royal Irish Fusiliers on its formation. Second Lieutenant 15 September 1914. To France with 36th (Ulster) Division in October 1915 in 'B' Company. 1914-15 Star. He was also the intelligence and sniping officer. He led a valuable series of patrols in the Hamel area in May 1916 prior to the attack on 1 July 1916. Awarded an **MC** for his actions over this period and during the attack at Hamel on 1 July 1916. **Wounded** while rescuing wounded men on 2 July 1916. Hospitalised with shell shock on 12 August 1916, he returned to the 9th Royal Irish Fusiliers on 1 September 1916. **Wounded** on 11 October 1916 near Messines. Captain 26 June 1917. Appointed as Staff Captain at HQ

109th Brigade on 13 July 1917. In November 1917 he was appointed Assistant Staff Captain at HQ 108th Brigade and, subsequently, Staff Captain on 16 March 1918. Reverted to Assistant Staff Captain until 10 November 1918 when he was appointed Staff Captain vice Major V B Rogers MC. **Mention in Despatches. *Croix de Guerre* (Belgium)**. Released from service on 29 March 1919. Relinquished his commission 26 October 1920. Paintings made during his time in France are in the regimental museum in Armagh. He died after a heart attack on 29 July 1933, aged 46, and was buried at Mullavilly Parish Church, Tandragee. One of his two sons was Air Vice Marshall Stewart William Blacker Menaul CB, CBE, DFC, AFC. (WO 339/14278)

MIDGLEY. Second Lieutenant Benjamin Herbert Born on 22 December 1889 at Cradock, Eastern Cape, South Africa. A secretary, he served in the 2nd Mounted Rifles, Natal Carabiners (Z/235) from October 1914 to July 1915, and saw service in German South West Africa. 1914-15 Star. Arrived in England aboard the MV Norman on 8 June 1916. Enlisted into the South Irish Horse (2109 - Trooper) on 12 July 1916. Joined 2nd Cavalry Cadet Squadron on 13 July 1917 and then 2nd Officer Cadet Battalion at Pembroke College, Cambridge on 9 December 1917. Commissioned into The Prince of Wales's Leinster Regiment (Royal Canadians) on 30 January 1918. Attached briefly to the 7th (Service) Battalion, The Royal Irish Rifles in 48th Brigade, 16th (Irish) Division and then attached to the 9th Royal Irish Fusiliers from 17 April 1918 to 16 June 1918. Posted to 'D' Company, 2nd Battalion, The Prince of Wales's Leinster Regiment (Royal Canadians). Relinquished his commission on 12 October 1919. He returned to South Africa and became a farmer. He returned with his family to England on 31 July 1948 and lived in Devizes. He died at Poulshot, Wiltshire on 22 January 1957, aged 67 and is buried at St Peter's Church, Poulshot. (WO 339/103509)

MILES MC. Second Lieutenant Richard Douglas Born on 6 September 1888 at Kingston, Jamaica the son of Alfred Henry Miles CMG, ISO, Collector General, Jamaica. Moved to Canada where he worked in the Canadian Bank of Commerce. Joined 31st Battalion, the Canadian Infantry (Alberta) in 6th Canadian Brigade, 2nd Canadian Division, Canadian Expeditionary Force on 18 November 1914 (79350 - Lance Sergeant). Acting Company Sergeant Major. Commissioned into Princess Victoria's (Royal Irish Fusiliers) on 1 October 1915. Joined the 9th Royal Irish Fusiliers on 17 August 1916. Served with 'C' Company. Slightly **wounded** during a raid on 12 October 1916 for which he was awarded an **MC**. **Wounded** when shot in the abdomen during the Battle of Langemarck on 16 August 1916. **Died of wounds** on 17 August 1917, aged 28, in 3rd Australian Casualty Clearing Station. (WO 339/42675)

MILLER. Second Lieutenant David Joseph Born on 24 January 1895 at Banbridge, County Down. Worked as a designer for William Ewart & Sons, Belfast. Member of the Ulster Volunteer Force. Enlisted into the North Irish Horse on 22 May 1915 (1567 - Trooper). Served in France from 11 January 1916 to 6 May 1917. Lance Corporal 27 November 1916. Corporal 5 July 1917. Joined 12th Officer Cadet Battalion at Newmarket on 5 July 1917. Commissioned into Princess Victoria's (Royal Irish Fusiliers) on 30 October 1917. Posted initially to the 7th/8th (Service) Battalion in 49th Brigade, 16th (Irish) Division, he joined the 9th Royal Irish Fusiliers on 16 February 1918 when the former was disbanded and was posted to 'B' Company. **Killed in action** on 12 April 1918 near Wulverghem, aged 23. (WO 339/114644)

MITCHEL. Captain Frederick David Born on 16 August 1889 at Enniskillen, County Fermanagh, the son of Reverend S C Mitchel, Minister of Enniskillen Presbyterian Church. An accountant in the Lurgan branch of the Ulster Bank, he was commissioned into The Royal Inniskilling Fusiliers on 19 April 1915 but transferred to Princess Victoria's (Royal Irish Fusiliers) and joined the 10th (Reserve) Battalion on 19 October 1916. To France 12 June 1916 and joined the 9th Royal Irish Fusiliers on 21 June 1917 (Lieutenant) and was posted to 'D' Company as Second-in-Command. Captain October 1917. **Wounded** in the face by a machine gun bullet at Moeuvres on 23 November 1917 and **died of wounds** in 29th Casualty Clearing Station on 24 November 1917, aged 28. His brother, Lieutenant Victor Mitchel, served with the 1st Battalion during the First World War and in Iraq and North West Persia and served in the Second World War. His brother, Private George Cuthbert Mitchel, served with a Canadian home defence unit. (WO 339/4063)

MONTGOMERY. Lieutenant Eldred Merwin Born on 21 January 1888 at Kells, County Antrim. A bank clerk with Ulster Bank, he joined Queen's University, Belfast Officer Training Corps on 5 June 1916 and then 7th Officer Cadet Battalion on 5 October 1916. Commissioned into Princess Victoria's (Royal Irish Fusiliers) on 1 March 1917. He joined the 9th Royal Irish Fusiliers on 26 June 1917 and was posted to 'D' Company. Attached to the 12th (Service) Battalion, The Royal Irish Rifles (Central Antrim) in 108th Brigade on 3 July 1917. Soon after, he applied to transfer to the Indian Army Reserve of Officers and was accepted. He left for England on 28 October 1917 and sailed for India on 28 January 1918. Second Lieutenant (on probation) Indian Army Reserve of Officers 28 February 1918. Resigned his commission in the Indian Army Reserve of Officers 1 May 1922. His brother, Captain Verus Calvin Montgomery MB, served with the Royal Army Medical Corps. (WO 339/73124)

MONTGOMERY. Second Lieutenant Robert Taylor Born on 1 April 1885 at Portadown, County Armagh. Commandant of the Portadown Company, Ulster Volunteer Force Medical Corps. Enlisted into the 9th Royal Irish Fusiliers on 15 September 1914 (14452 - Private). Corporal 1 October 1914. Sergeant 1 January 1915. Commissioned into Princess Victoria's (Royal Irish Fusiliers) on 22 May 1915 and joined the 9th Royal Irish Fusiliers as a platoon commander in 'A' Company. To France with 36th (Ulster) Division in October 1915. 1914-15 Star. **Missing** during the attack at Hamel on 1 July 1916 and later declared **killed in action** on that date, aged 31. (WO 339/1262)

MOORE. Second Lieutenant William Born on 15 December 1892 at Belfast. Attended Campbell College and Queen's University, Belfast. Commissioned into Princess Victoria's (Royal Irish Fusiliers) on 8 January 1916 and served with the 10th (Reserve) Battalion (including service with the Ulster composite battalion during the Irish Republican attacks in Dublin) until he joined the 9th Royal Irish Fusiliers on 17 June 1917. Served with 'C' Company. **Killed in action** at the Battle of Langemarck on 16 August 1917, aged 24. His brother, Second Lieutenant Archibald Main Moore, served with the North Irish Horse and was commissioned into The Royal Irish Rifles; he was wounded twice. (WO 339/51980)

MORAN. Second Lieutenant Samuel Frederick Born on 23 November 1889 at Dublin. Joined the South Irish Horse in September 1914 (1177 - Corporal). Served in France with 'B' Squadron, IX Corps Cavalry Regiment from 23 November 1915 to 14 January 1917. 1914-15 Star. Joined 7th Officer Cadet Battalion at Fermoy on 9 March 1917. Commissioned into Princess Victoria's (Royal Irish Fusiliers) on 27 June 1917. Joined the 9th Royal Irish Fusiliers on 20 October 1917 and was attached to 13th (Service) Battalion, The Royal Irish Rifles (1st County Down). **Wounded** when shot in the back and head at Marcoing on 6 December 1917. He was evacuated to hospital in England on 31 December 1917 and remained in hospital until March 1918. He rejoined the 9th Royal Irish Fusiliers on 14 June 1918. He **died of wounds** on 1 October 1918, aged 28, in 3rd Australian Casualty Clearing Station, having been wounded during the attack at Vijfwegen the previous day. (WO 339/98873)

MORROW. Captain James Boyd Kenneth Born in 1894. Employed in the linen business, he enlisted into The Royal Irish Rifles in August 1914 at Newtownards. Commissioned into The Royal Irish Rifles on 14 October 1914 and joined the 13th (Service) Battalion, The Royal Irish Rifles (1st County Down) in 108th Brigade. To France with 36th (Ulster) Division in October 1915. 1914-15 Star. Lieutenant 14 December 1915. Acting Captain 1 September 1917 to 15 November 1917. Attached to the 9th Royal Irish Fusiliers on 12 April 1918 as Transport Officer. Acting Captain 3 July 1918 to 26 January 1919. Left for demobilisation on 19 January 1919. Relinquished his commission 26 January 1919. He settled in Canada. (WO 339/14237)

MURPHY MC*, DCM. Captain John Joseph Born on 24 May 1886 at Bruff, County Limerick. Enlisted into the Royal Marine Artillery on 4 January 1902. Served on HMS Commonwealth in 3rd Battle Squadron during the Balkan States War. Promoted to Corporal before he was discharged at the end of his service on 12 January 1914. Enlisted into Princess Victoria's (Royal Irish Fusiliers) (20071 - Private) on 29 May 1915. Served in France as a Sergeant with the 8th (Service) Battalion in 49th Brigade, 16th (Irish) Division from 19 February 1916. **Wounded** and earned a **DCM** during a raid on 11 July 1916. Joined Princess Victoria's (Royal Irish Fusiliers) Depot in Armagh on 30 January 1917 and 20th Officer Cadet Battalion at Crookham, Aldershot on 10 March 1917. Commissioned into Princess Victoria's (Royal Irish Fusiliers) on 27 June 1917. He joined the 9th Royal Irish Fusiliers on 16 September 1917. Recommended for the DSO but awarded an **MC** for a raid at Havrincourt on 3 November 1917. Suffered from trench fever and was evacuated to hospital in England 7 December 1917. Rejoined the 9th Royal Irish Fusiliers on 27 April 1918 and was appointed Officer Commanding 'B' Company. Acting Captain 24 June 1918. Again recommended for the DSO but awarded a Bar to his **MC** for a raid at Meulenhouck, near Bailleul on 22 July 1918. **Wounded** at Wulverghem on 4 September 1918. On 7 October 1918 he was accused by the Commanding Officer (Lieutenant Colonel P E Kelly) of being drunk. He was removed from command that month, returned to England on 16 December 1918 and was eventually ordered to resign his commission, which he did on 10 April 1919. Volunteered for service with the North Russia Relief Force and re-enlisted into the 45th (Service) Battalion, The Royal Fusiliers (City of London Regiment) as a company sergeant major (renumbered 133076) on 4 June 1919. Sailed for Russia on 3 July and landed on 12 July 1919. Transferred to the Class Z Reserve on 23 November 1919. Re-enlisted on 7 January 1920 for Regular Army service with The Prince of Wales's Leinster Regiment (Royal Canadians) (40099, renumbered 7178313 - Private). He joined the 2nd Battalion and was discharged as a Corporal on 4 July 1922, aged 36, when the Regiment was disbanded. On his return home to Kilballyowen, Bruff, County Limerick he worked breaking and carrying stone for a quarry until it closed. Unemployed in 1929, he wrote to the King requesting a War Gratuity for his commissioned service; it was refused by the War Office. He subsequently found work in the cement factory in Mungret, Limerick, and lived in a house in Bengal Terrace, Limerick, provided by the Irish Soldiers and Sailors Land Trust. He was killed in an explosion at the cement works on 10 April 1938, aged 51. Two of his brothers served during the First World War, one of whom was killed at the Battle of Loos. (WO 339/97762)

MURPHY. Captain William Maurice Born in May 1873 at Raithfriland, County Down. Enlisted into the 2nd Battalion, Princess Victoria's (Royal Irish Fusiliers) on 12 November 1892 (4347). Corporal 16 January 1896. Sergeant 23 October 1899. Served in South Africa from 23 October 1899 to 16 January 1903. Wounded 16 July 1900 when shot in the right arm. Queen's South Africa Medal with clasps 'Cape Colony', 'Transvaal', 'Tugela Heights' & 'Relief of Ladysmith'. King's South Africa Medal with clasps '1901' and '1902'. Colour Sergeant 17 September 1902. Moved with the 2nd Battalion to Quetta in India at the end of the South African War. Posted to the 1st Battalion in Dublin on 6 February 1907. Regimental Sergeant Major 2 October 1908. Long Service and Good Conduct Medal 1911. Coronation Medal 1911. To France with the 1st Battalion 22 August 1914. 1914 Star and clasp. Commissioned into the 1st Battalion on 23 October 1914. Lieutenant 4 September 1915. Captain 25 September 1915. Served with the 1st Battalion until he joined the 9th Royal Irish Fusiliers on 25 August 1918. Transferred to the General List for service on the Staff 4 September 1918. Subsequently Armagh Area Recruiting Officer. Retired and transferred to the Reserve of Officers 12 February 1920. Retired from the Reserve of Officers on 12 March 1923. Died on 30 November 1957, aged 84. (WO 339/11302)

NOLAN. Lieutenant Alexander Shelley Born on 15 September 1896 at Tipperary. A student, he enlisted into the 21st (Service) Battalion, The Royal Fusiliers (City of London Regiment) (4th Public Schools) in 98th Brigade, 33rd Division on 6 September 1914, aged 17, giving his year of birth as 1895. Commissioned into Princess Victoria's (Royal Irish Fusiliers) on 15 May 1915 and was posted to the 7th (Service) Battalion in 49th Brigade, 16th (Irish) Division. Joined the 9th Royal Irish Fusiliers on 16 August 1916 and was posted to 'B' Company. Suffered from appendicitis 13 September 1916 and was evacuated to hospital in England. Lieutenant 23 February 1917. Rejoined the 9th Royal Irish Fusiliers 8 March 1917. **Wounded** at the Battle of

Langemarck on 16 August 1917 when he was shot in the throat (the bullet exited his back by his lower ribs, having penetrated his left lung). He was evacuated to hospital in England on 15 October 1917. Having recovered by mid-1918, he served the remainder of the war with the Egyptian Labour Corps. Released from service on 6 April 1922. Relinquished his commission 8 May 1922. He subsequently served with the Colonial Service. Died of a heart attack at Brighton, Sussex in 1947, aged 51. (WO 339/3783)

O'FLAHERTY JOHNSTONE. Lieutenant George Irwin Born in 1896 at Inishmore, County Galway. Commissioned into Princess Victoria's (Royal Irish Fusiliers) on 19 October 1915. Joined the 9th Royal Irish Fusiliers on 16 August 1916 and was posted to 'D' Company. One of the first three Roman Catholic officers to join the 9th Royal Irish Fusiliers. Evacuated to hospital in England sick on 27 September 1916. Rejoined the 9th Royal Irish Fusiliers on 28 June 1917. Lieutenant 1 July 1917. **Captured** on the night of 21 March 1918 crossing the River Somme on the withdrawal from St Quentin. Repatriated on 10 December 1918. Relinquished his commission on account of ill-health contracted on active service. Silver War Badge, number 451977. Subsequently worked in Liverpool as a civil servant.

O'NEILL. Lieutenant Samuel Born on 15 May 1890 at County Carlow. Enlisted into the 9th Royal Irish Fusiliers on 11 March 1915. Commissioned into The Royal Inniskilling Fusiliers on 19 April 1915. Attached to the 9th Royal Irish Fusiliers. To France with 36th (Ulster) Division in October 1915. 1914-15 Star. Transferred to the General List for service with 108th Trench Mortar Battery and promoted to Acting Lieutenant 9 March 1916. **Missing** during the attack at Hamel on 1 July 1916 and subsequently declared **killed in action** on that date, aged 26. (WO 339/4072)

ORR BEM, JP. Major Robert Albert Born on 28 May 1888 near Plumbridge, County Tyrone. Commissioned into Princess Victoria's (Royal Irish Fusiliers) on 19 December 1916. To France 5 September 1917 and joined the 9th Royal Irish Fusiliers on 29 September 1917. Probably 'B' Company. **Wounded** on 12 April 1918 near Wulverghem and evacuated to hospital in England on 30 April 1918. He did not serve with the 9th Royal Irish Fusiliers again. Lieutenant 19 June 1918. Relinquished his commission 16 January 1920. Lived at Plumbridge, County Tyrone. Commissioned as a Second Lieutenant (361710) 25 February 1946 for service with the Army Cadet Force, Northern Ireland Command. Lieutenant 25 August 1947. Resigned his commission 28 June 1951 and appointed Honorary Major. Justice of the Peace. In 1965 he was awarded the **British Empire Medal** for his service as the Sub-Postmaster at Newtownstewart, County Tyrone.

OWLES MC. Captain Ernest Trafford Born on 24 August 1889 at Brentwood, London, he enlisted into Princess Victoria's (Royal Irish Fusiliers) on 29 August 1914. Commissioned into Princess Victoria's (Royal Irish Fusiliers) Special Reserve on 17 March 1915. Served in France from 24 May 1915 with the 2nd Battalion until **wounded** (gun-shot wound to the right leg) near Bois Grenier, south-west of Armentieres on 6 August 1915. 1914-15 Star. When fit for general service he joined the 3rd (Reserve) Battalion on 28 October 1915. Lieutenant 12 February 1916. Joined the 9th Royal Irish Fusiliers on 18 March 1916 as a platoon commander in 'C' Company. Attached to the Royal Flying Corps on 13 May 1916 for training as a Flying Officer (Observer). Appointed Flying Officer (Observer) 4 October 1916. Converted to Flying Officer 3 May 1917. Served with 12 Squadron. Awarded an **MC** for his reconnaissance over Bourlon Village on 22 November 1917 during the attack at Cambrai. Appointed Flight Commander and Temporary Captain Royal Flying Corps 5 December 1917. **Wounded** (gun-shot wound to the face) 21 March 1918 and was evacuated to hospital in England. Transferred to the Royal Air Force as a Captain 1 April 1918. His wounds precluded further service and he relinquished his commission on account of ill-health caused by wounds 23 January 1920. Studied at St Catherin's College, Cambridge 1920-23. Emigrated to Kenya where he married in 1923. Part owner and operator of Komassai Coffee Estate, Ruiru, of which he took ownership in 1959. He returned to England and died in Tunbridge Wells on 11 September 1974, aged 85. (WO 339/30947)

OZZARD MC. Second Lieutenant Harold Tronson Born on 29 December 1892 at Georgetown, Demerara, British Guiana. Enlisted firstly into The Gordon Highlanders in September 1914 but was discharged on 10 October 1914 as being unlikely to become an efficient soldier in that he was considered medically unfit for service. Enlisted secondly into 2nd King Edward's Horse (The King's Overseas Dominions Regiment) (1256 - Private) and deployed to France on 4 May 1915 with the Canadian Cavalry Brigade. 1914-15 Star. Commissioned into Princess Victoria's (Royal Irish Fusiliers) on 15 March 1916 and joined the 9th Royal Irish Fusiliers. Posted to 'A' Company. To hospital sick on 20 November 1916 and evacuated to hospital in England 27 November 1916. Rejoined the 9th Royal Irish Fusiliers 24 April 1917. Awarded an **MC** for a raid at Spanbroekmolen on 4 June 1917. Left the 9th Royal Irish Fusiliers on 25 August 1917 having transferred to the Tank Corps and joined the Tank Corps Depot, Wareham, Dorset for training. Returned to France and was severely **wounded**. Relinquished his commission on account of ill-health caused by wounds on 17 October 1917. Silver War Badge, number 290547. In 1927 he was appointed as Assistant Commissioner of the National Savings Committee. Died in Sussex in 1945, aged 53.

PARTRIDGE MC. Captain James Henry Born in May 1886 at Waltham Abbey, Essex. Enlisted into the 20th Hussars on 20 June 1906 and was discharged on 16 June 13. Mobilised on 5 August 1914 (5075 - Trooper), rejoined the 20th Hussars and deployed to France on 16 August 1914. 1914 Star. Corporal 13 March 1915. Sergeant 26 August 1916. Attended Officer Cadet School in France and was commissioned into Princess Victoria's (Royal Irish Fusiliers) on 25 December 1916. Joined the 9th Royal Irish Fusiliers on 27 December 1916 as Intelligence Officer. Adjutant of the Divisional Depot Battalion 20 July to 20 August 1917. Returned to the 9th Royal Irish Fusiliers as Intelligence Officer and earned an **MC** at Moeuvres on 23 November 1917. Commanded 'B' Company from December 1917 until he was **killed in action** in the rearguard fighting at Guiscard 24 March 1918, aged 31. (WO 339/121515)

PASCOE. Lieutenant Frank Guy Buckingham Born in October 1897 at Dalton-in-Furness, Lancashire. Commissioned into Princess Victoria's (Royal Irish Fusiliers) on 27 March 1915 and served with the 7th (Service) Battalion in 49th Brigade, 16th (Irish) Division before joining the 9th Royal Irish Fusiliers on 16 August 1916. Posted to the 1st Battalion on 10 January 1917. Admitted to 21st Casualty Clearing Station on 5 March 1917. Attached to the Royal Flying Corps as a Flying Officer (Observer) on 31 March 1917 and joined 53 Squadron. On his first operational flight he was **killed in action**, aged 20. At 8.40 am on 2 July 1917 near Comines while escorting a photographic patrol he was the observer in an RE8 of 53 Squadron piloted by Sergeant H A Whatley, aged 19. Their aircraft was shot down by Rittmeister Manfred von Richthofen; his 57th air victory. (WO 339/37189)

PEACOCK. Second Lieutenant Walter Born on 28 December 1895 at Ballymacarrett, Belfast. A clerk with the Prudential Assurance Company Ltd, Belfast, he joined 17th (Reserve) Battalion Royal Irish Rifles (1054 - Private) on 4 June 1915. Lance Corporal 7 December 1915. Joined 7th Officer Cadet Battalion on 5 April 1916 and was commissioned into Princess Victoria's (Royal Irish Fusiliers) on 7 July 1916. Joined the 9th Royal Irish Fusiliers on 7 October 1916 and was posted to 'A' Company. **Killed in action** on 22 December 1916 by shellfire while in the line at La Plus Douve Farm, aged 20. (WO 339/57737)

PERKINS. Lieutenant Charles James Thomas Born on 29 May 1897 at Wellingborough, Northamptonshire. Enlisted into the 3/1st Northamptonshire Yeomanry (2208 - Trooper) on 23 February 1916. Was promoted to Corporal before joining 1st Cavalry Cadet Squadron at Netheravon on 6 December 1916. Commissioned into 6th (Inniskilling) Dragoons on 17 February 1917 and served with the 2nd North Irish Horse, X Corps Cavalry Regiment. Transferred to Princess Victoria's (Royal Irish Fusiliers) and joined the 9th Royal Irish Fusiliers on 5 October 1917. Appointed as Officer Commanding 6 Platoon, 'B' Company. **Captured** with most of his platoon at Essigny on 22 March 1918. Lieutenant 17 August 1918. Repatriated on

11 December 1918. Relinquished his commission on 4 April 1919. Died in Wellingborough, Northamptonshire in January 1991, aged 93. (WO 339/80367)

POLLOCK. Lieutenant John James McElnay Born on 26 October 1896 at Cavan. A bank clerk, he enlisted into 7th (Service) Battalion, The Prince of Wales's Leinster Regiment (Royal Canadians) on 2 July 1915, where he joined 'A' Company and served in 16th (Irish) Division until mid-1917. Commissioned into Princess Victoria's (Royal Irish Fusiliers) on 1 August 1917. Joined the 9th Royal Irish Fusiliers on 4 November 1917. While attached to 108th Trench Mortar Battery, he commanded the remnants of the 12th (Service) Battalion, The Royal Irish Rifles (Central Antrim) at Erches on 27 March 1918 and was **captured** fighting alongside the 9th Royal Irish Fusiliers. Repatriated on 4 December 1918. Lieutenant 1 February 1919. Relinquished his commission on account of ill-health contracted on active service 31 October 1919. Silver War Badge, number B230695. Died in 1974 in Newport, Gwent. (WO 339/103344)

POOLE. Lieutenant Frank Tarbett Born on 3 December 1886 at Bishops Castle, Shropshire. A farmer, he enlisted into the 3rd (Reserve) Battalion, The King's (Shropshire Light Infantry) (19930 - Private) on 29 January 1915. Joined 1st Cavalry Cadet Squadron at Netheravon on 2 August 1916. Commissioned into the 4th Reserve Cavalry Regiment on 20 December 1916. Joined the 2nd North Irish Horse, X Corps Cavalry Regiment on 1 February 1917. Transferred to Princess Victoria's (Royal Irish Fusiliers) and joined the 9th Royal Irish Fusiliers 8 November 1917. Left on 15 December 1917 to return to England to transfer to the Tank Corps and joined the Tank Corps Depot, Wareham, Dorset for training. Served with 17th (Armoured Car) Battalion, Tank Corps. **Wounded** during a gas attack in August 1918 and was evacuated to hospital in Woolwich. Released from service on 20 February 1919. Died at Barry Island, Pembrokeshire on 20 January 1940, aged 43. (WO 339/67259)

PRATT DSO. Lieutenant Colonel Audley Charles Born on 13 May 1874 at Cabra Castle, Enniscoe, County Mayo. Educated at Harrow, he was commissioned into The Royal Scots (Lothian Regiment) on 7 December 1895. Served with the 1st Battalion, The Royal Scots (Lothian Regiment) in the South African War 1900-02. Queen's South Africa Medal with three clasps, King's South Africa Medal with clasps '1901' and '1902'. **Mention in Despatches**. Captain 3 November 1902. Retired 20 August 13. Reserve of Officers, Remount Service. Recalled from the Reserve of Officers and joined the 9th Royal Irish Fusiliers soon after its formation. Appointed Second-in-Command 19 November 1914. To France with 36th (Ulster) Division in October 1915. 1914-15 Star. Left on 22 August 1916 to take command of 11th (Service) Battalion, The Royal Inniskilling Fusiliers (Donegal and Fermanagh) in 109th Brigade vice Lieutenant Colonel G H Brush. **DSO**. **Mention in Despatches**. Attended the Senior Officers' Course in early 1917 before returning to command 11th (Service) Battalion, The Royal Inniskilling Fusiliers (Donegal and Fermanagh). **Wounded** June 1917 at Messines. **Killed in action** while in command at the Battle of Langemarck on 16 August 1917, aged 43. **Mention in Despatches**. His brother, Major Mervyn Pratt DSO, served with the King's Royal Rifle Corps.

D Prenter

PRENTER. Second Lieutenant Dalton Born in 1892 at Belfast. Member of the Ulster Volunteer Force. Worked for Moore & Weinberg linen manufacturers, Belfast. Enlisted into 14th (Service) Battalion, The Royal Irish Rifles (Young Citizens) (16946 - Private). To France with 36th (Ulster) Division in October 1915. 1914-15 Star. Commissioned into Princess Victoria's (Royal Irish Fusiliers) on 27 June 1917. Joined the 9th Royal Irish Fusiliers on 16 September 1917. **Killed in action** 21 March 1918 at Essigny, aged 27. His sister, Kathleen, married Lieutenant W R Graham. His brother, Thomas Prenter, served with the Canadian Expeditionary Force.

RADBOURNE. Captain Percy Charles Born on 7 May 1883 at Bray, Berkshire. Lived in Durban, South Africa. Served during the Bambatha Zulu rebellion with the Natal Mounted Police and as a Senior Lieutenant and company commander in 2nd Battalion, Durban Light Infantry during the campaign in German South West Africa. 1914-15 Star. Commissioned into Princess Victoria's (Royal Irish Fusiliers) as a Captain in April 1916 and joined the 9th Royal Irish Fusiliers on 25 July 1916 from the 10th (Reserve) Battalion. **Wounded** at Ypres on 1 August 1916 when hit in the knee by shrapnel and evacuated to hospital in England on 12 August 1916. When recovered, he was appointed Officer Commanding 143rd Labour Company, Chinese Labour Corps in August 1917. **Wounded** during an air raid on 3 May 1918. Commanded 8th Labour Company, Middlesex Regiment on 23 December 1918. Released from service on 5 March 1920. He returned to Durban after the war. Served as a Lieutenant with the South African Internment Corps during the Second World War. He died on 9 April 1944 and is one of thirty-three casualties who were cremated and have no grave and are commemorated on the Durban (Stellawood) Cremation Memorial. (WO 339/58265)

RATCLIFFE. Second Lieutenant Clifford Stanley Parents lived at Bellair, Durban, Natal, South Africa. Enlisted (details not known) and deployed to France on 13 July 1916. Commissioned into Princess Victoria's (Royal Irish Fusiliers) on 28 November 1917. Joined the 9th Royal Irish Fusiliers on 29 April 1918 and was posted to 'B' Company. **Missing** during a raid on Shoddy Farm, Meulenhouck, near Bailleul on 22 July 1918 and later declared **killed in action** on that date, aged 28.

REA. Lieutenant Norman Kerr Born on 1 May 1894 at Belfast. Enlisted into 2/6th (Perthshire) Battalion, The Black Watch (Royal Highlanders) (2510 - Private) in November 1914. Commissioned into Princess Victoria's (Royal Irish Fusiliers) on 16 November 1915 and served with the 10th (Reserve) Battalion before he joined the 9th Royal Irish Fusiliers on 25 July 1916. Appointed Assistant Adjutant. To hospital sick (bronchitis and asthma) on 21 November 1916 and evacuated to hospital in England 24 November 1916. Rejoined the 10th (Reserve) Battalion on 18 January 1917. Employed with the Ministry of Labour until he relinquished his commission on account of ill-health 10 January 1919. Silver War Badge, number B143149. (WO 339/46664)

REID. Lieutenant William Fitzgerald Born on 3 August 1896. A clerk, he joined the 9th Royal Irish Fusiliers on 16 September 1914. Commissioned into Princess Victoria's (Royal Irish Fusiliers) on 22 May 1915. To France with 36th (Ulster) Division in October 1915 as a platoon commander in 'B' Company. 1914-15 Star. Left on 14 November 1915 to command and exercise the 9th Royal Irish Fusiliers' details arriving at the Base Depot. After returning to the 9th Royal Irish Fusiliers he was transferred to the General List on 22 April 1916 for duty with 108th Trench Mortar Battery. To hospital sick and evacuated to hospital in England in September 1916. Returned to France in June 1917. Lieutenant 1 July 1917. Served again with 108th Trench Mortar Battery and was subsequently posted to the 7th/8th (Service) Battalion in 49th Brigade, 16th (Irish) Division, where he served until it was disbanded. Rejoined the 9th Royal Irish Fusiliers on 16 February 1918 and was posted to 'B' Company. **Wounded** in the left arm on 27 March 1918 at Erches and evacuated to hospital in England 29 March 1918. Transferred to the Indian Army (on probation) on 12 October 1918. Served with the 31st Punjabis in the Army of Occupation in Turkey. Transferred back to Princess Victoria's (Royal Irish Fusiliers) at his own request on 27 December 1919 and attached to the 10th (Service) Battalion, The Hampshire Regiment in 82nd Brigade, 27th Division in Turkey. Relinquished his commission on 29 January 1920. Applied to join the Officers' Emergency Reserve on 2 September 1939 but was not accepted. Died in Sussex in February 1989, aged 92. (WO 339/1264)

REYNOLDS MC. Lieutenant Edwin Wright Born on 14 June 1894 at Bessbrook, County Armagh. Enlisted into the 1/1st City of London Yeomanry on 17 March 1914 (1748 - Private). Lance Corporal 3 August 1914. Served in Egypt from 5 November 1914 to August 1915. 1914-15 Star. Landed at Gallipoli on 30 November 1915. Served at Dabaa in Egypt and on the Suez Canal with the Western Frontier Force from 11 December 1915 until returned to England in mid-1916. Joined 2nd Officer Cadet Battalion at Pembroke College, Cambridge and was commissioned into Princess Victoria's (Royal Irish Fusiliers) on 26 April

1917. Joined the 9th Royal Irish Fusiliers on 9 July 1917 and was posted to 'A' Company. To hospital sick on 11 August 1917 and evacuated to hospital in England 16 August 1917. Rejoined the 9th Royal Irish Fusiliers 21 April 1918 and was posted to 'B' Company. Commanded 'C' Company for a period in September 1918. Awarded an **MC** during the attacks near Dadizeele on 30 September and 1 October 1918. Sought a transfer to the Indian Army Reserve of Officers and left the 9th Royal Irish Fusiliers on 9 November 1918 for a Medical Board in London. He did not join the Indian Army Reserve of Officers and returned to the 9th Royal Irish Fusiliers. He embarked for demobilisation on 18 February 1919 and was released from service on 10 April 1919. He was gazetted as relinquishing his commission with effect from 19 February 1919. Died in Sussex in 1963, aged 69. His sister, Miss Harriet Eleanor Reynolds, served as a nurse during the First World war and earned the Royal Red Cross 2nd Class. (WO 339/83301)

RICHARDSON. Lieutenant Gerald Henry Born in 1894 near Newry, County Down. Commissioned into The Royal Inniskilling Fusiliers on 19 April 1915. Transferred to Princess Victoria's (Royal Irish Fusiliers) and joined the 10th (Reserve) Battalion from Borden on 10 October 1915 (with Hollywood and 132 men). Joined the 9th Royal Irish Fusiliers in France in November 1915 and was posted to 'B' Company. 1914-15 Star. While on leave in December 1916 he fell ill and was admitted to hospital. To France 13 April 1917 and rejoined the 9th Royal Irish Fusiliers on 20 April 1917. Lieutenant 1 July 1917. Served as a platoon commander with the Divisional Depot Battalion at Merckeghem from 20 July 1917 before rejoining the 9th Royal Irish Fusiliers in August 1917. Acting Captain and Officer Commanding 'A' Company throughout May 1918. Served with the 9th Royal Irish Fusiliers until 9 September 1918 when he went on leave. He was ordered to a medical board whilst on leave and did not return to the 9th Royal Irish Fusiliers. Served with the 3rd (Reserve) Battalion until released from service 9 April 1919. Became an engineer with the Bengal and North Western Railway in India. (WO 339/32229)

RICHEY. Second Lieutenant Robert Alexander Born in 1897 at Belfast. Enlisted into Princess Victoria's (Royal Irish Fusiliers) (23757). Commissioned into Princess Victoria's (Royal Irish Fusiliers) on 26 June 1918. Joined the 9th Royal Irish Fusiliers on 14 September 1918. **Captured** during the attack at Vijfwegen on 30 September 1918. Repatriated on 13 December 1918. Relinquished his commission 1 September 1921. Subsequently lived in Dungannon, County Tyrone.

ROBINSON MC. Captain George Born on 3 September 1895 at Annaghmore, County Armagh. A student, he enlisted into Princess Victoria's (Royal Irish Fusiliers) (21501 - Private) on 4 September 1915 and served in the 10th (Reserve) Battalion and at the School of Musketry, Dollymount. Lance Corporal 30 November 1915. Corporal 22 January 1916. Joined 7th Officer Cadet Battalion on 7 August 1916 and was commissioned into Princess Victoria's (Royal Irish Fusiliers) on 19 December 1916. Joined the 9th Royal Irish Fusiliers on 28 February 1917 and was posted to 'B' Company. **Wounded** when shot in the chest on 4 June 1917. Evacuated to hospital in England 12 June 1917. Rejoined the 9th Royal Irish Fusiliers 27 April 1918. Lieutenant 19 June 1918. **Wounded** at Bailleul on 24 August 1918. Evacuated to hospital in England 26 August 1918. **MC**. Rejoined the 9th Royal Irish Fusiliers on 22 November 1918. Attached to the 5th (Service) Battalion, The Royal Irish Regiment (Pioneers) in the Light Division in the British Army of the Rhine in March/April 1919. Released from service on 26 September 1919. Silver War Badge, number B230642. Relinquished his commission 1 September 1921. Emigrated to Canada and joined the Canadian Civil Service. (WO 339/67956)

ROCHE. Second Lieutenant William Henry Born on 12 May 1893 at Tralee, County Kerry. A merchant in Limerick, he was appointed Second Lieutenant (on probation) in The Royal Munster Fusiliers on 14 April 1915. Considered inefficient, he resigned his commission on 23 January 1916. Enlisted into The Royal Dublin Fusiliers (26580) on 12 March 1916. Promoted to Corporal before joining 16th Officer Cadet Battalion at Rhyl on 5 May 1917. Commissioned into Princess Victoria's (Royal Irish Fusiliers) on 29 July 1917 and was posted to the $7^{th}/8^{th}$ (Service) Battalion in 49th Brigade, 16th (Irish) Division. Joined the 9th Royal Irish Fusiliers on 16 February 1918 from $7^{th}/8^{th}$ (Service) Battalion on its disbandment, and was posted to 'D' Company. **Killed in action** on 27 March 1918, aged 25, at Erches. Found by German infantry and buried at Hattencourt; he was reinterred at Roye New British Cemetery. (WO 339/103063)

ROSS. Lieutenant Cecil Acheson Born in 1891 at Dublin. A government clerk, he enlisted into the $1/6^{th}$ (Perthshire) Battalion, The Black Watch (Royal Highlanders) (2488 - Private) on 29 October 1914. Served in France from 2 May 1915 to 2 January 1917 in 153rd Brigade, 51st (Highland) Division. 1914-15 Star. Lance Corporal 13 September 1916. Commissioned into Princess Victoria's (Royal Irish Fusiliers) on 29 August 1917. Joined the 9th Royal Irish Fusiliers on 27 April 1918. Battalion Intelligence Officer from 6 July 1918 to the end of the war. Lieutenant 1 March 1919. Released from service 12 April 1919. Relinquished his commission 1 September 1921. (WO 374/59151)

SAUNDERSON MC. Lieutenant William Robert Born on 24 May 1890. A horticultural instructor at the Department of Agricultural and Technical Instruction, he enlisted into The Royal Inniskilling Fusiliers (23846 - Private) on 7 June 1915. Joined 7th Officer Cadet Battalion on 2 June 1916. Commissioned into Princess Victoria's (Royal Irish Fusiliers) on 5 September 1916. To France 21 October 1916 and joined the 9th Royal Irish Fusiliers on 31 October 1916. Posted to 'D' Company. Transferred to the General List for service with 108th Trench Mortar Battery on 5 May 1917. **Mention in Despatches**. Lieutenant 5 March 1918. **MC**. Left France for demobilisation on 23 January 1919 and was released from service on 25 January 1919. Lived in Ballymena and continued to work as a horticultural instructor. Emigrated to the United States. Died on 2 December 1974, aged 84, in Owensboro, Kentucky. His son, Flying Officer (Air Gunner) Christopher William Joffre Saunderson was killed in action on 13 May 1944 when Halifax MZ575 of 76 Squadron, Royal Air Force was shot down by Oberleutnant Frederick Tober. (WO 339/61876)

SCOTT. Lieutenant John Eric Enlisted into the 16th (Service) Battalion, The Royal Irish Rifles (2nd County Down) (Pioneers) (913 - Private). To France with 36th (Ulster) Division in October 1915. 1914-15 Star. Promoted to Sergeant. Commissioned into Princess Victoria's (Royal Irish Fusiliers) on 30 May 1917. Joined the 9th Royal Irish Fusiliers on 30 September 1917. **Wounded** near Essigny on 22 February 1918 by a shell splinter. **Captured** on 22 March 1918 near Grand Seraucourt. Repatriated on 25 December 1918. Lived in Belfast.

SCOTT. Captain Samuel Jervois Born in 1872 at County Cork. Educated at the Royal College of Surgeons, Dublin and graduated in 1896. Member of the Royal College of Physicians Ireland. He was a doctor in Chapeltown (near Sheffield, Yorkshire) and was resident surgeon at Drumcondra Hospital, Dublin before becoming the doctor for Bessbrook Spinning Company. Joined the 9th Royal Irish Fusiliers on its formation and was immediately commissioned. Captain 25 September 1914. To France with 36th (Ulster) Division in October 1915 as Officer Commanding 'C' Company. 1914-15 Star. Transferred to the Royal Army Medical Corps 11 January 1916. Served with 108th Field Ambulance for the remainder of the war. Relinquished his commission with the honorary rank of Captain 12 April 1918. **Died** in Ireland on 27 May 1920, aged 48, of injuries or illness sustained on or aggravated by active service.

SEGGIE. Second Lieutenant Alexander Born on 9 July 1892 at Tunbridge Wells. A student at Reading University, he joined 19th (Service) Battalion, The Royal Fusiliers (City of London Regiment) (2nd Public Schools) at Epsom on 14 September 1914. Commissioned into Princess Victoria's (Royal Irish Fusiliers) on 16 May 1915. Joined the 3rd (Reserve) Battalion before joining the 9th Royal Irish Fusiliers on 12 December 1915 and was posted to 'B' Company as a platoon commander. 1914-15 Star. **Missing** during the attack at Hamel on 1 July 1916 and later declared **killed in action** on that date, aged 23. (WO 339/50183)

A Seggie

SETON. Captain Henry Winton Born on 1 August 1887. Commissioned into the Indian Army on 25 January 1908 and served with 1/9th Gurkha Rifles. Served on the North West Frontier in 1908 at the engagement at Matta. India General Service Medal and clasp 'North West Frontier 1908'. Lieutenant 25 April 1910. Attached to the 9th Royal Irish Fusiliers as Adjutant in November 1914. Captain 1 September 1915. To France with 36th (Ulster) Division in October 1915. 1914-15 Star. Left on 6 December 1915 to return to 1/9th Gurkha Rifles, but joined 20th (Reserve) Battalion, The Royal Irish Rifles on 19 June 1916 as Adjutant to Lieutenant Colonel S W W Blacker. Relinquished his appointment 15 May 1918. Retired on account of ill-health 25 July 1923. Died in Cornwall in 1976, aged 89.

SEYMOUR. Second Lieutenant William Matthew Born on 4 October 1896, the son of a former sergeant in the Royal Irish Constabulary from Andersonstown in Belfast. Educated at the Royal Belfast Academical Institution, he became a bank clerk with the Northern Bank, Belfast. He joined 7th Officer Cadet Battalion on 7 August 1916. Commissioned into Princess Victoria's (Royal Irish Fusiliers) on 19 December 1916. Joined the 9th Royal Irish Fusiliers on 1 July 1917 and was posted to 8 Platoon, 'B' Company. **Missing** at the Battle of Langemarck 16 August 1917 and later declared **killed in action** on that date, aged 20. (WO 339/67958)

SHEEHAN. Second Lieutenant Michael Thomas Served with The Royal Irish Regiment (7657 - Sergeant) and deployed to France on 29 August 1916. Commissioned into The Royal Irish Rifles on 26 June 1918. Attached to the 9th Royal Irish Fusiliers on 23 October 1918 where he spent the rest of the war in 'D' Company. To hospital injured and evacuated to hospital in England on 6 February 1919. Attached to the 5th (Service) Battalion, The Royal Irish Regiment (Pioneers) in the Light Division in the British Army of the Rhine in March/April 1919. Relinquished his commission 1 September 1921.

SHILLINGTON PC, JP, DL, MP. Right Honourable Major David Graham (Do) Born on 10 December 1872 at Drumcree, County Armagh into a prominent local family. Educated at Methodist College and Rydalmount, Colwyn Bay. Employed in the family business (T Shillington and Son, Portadown). An influential member of the Orange Order, he was a company commander in the 4th (Portadown) Battalion, Armagh Regiment, Ulster Volunteer Force. Joined the 9th Royal Irish Fusiliers on its formation and was immediately commissioned. Captain 16 September 1914. To France with 36th (Ulster) Division in October 1915 as Officer Commanding 'D' Company. 1914-15 Star. To hospital sick on 18 December 1915 and was evacuated to England on 30 December 1915. Returned to the 9th Royal Irish

Fusiliers on 23 June 1916 but was not forward with the Battalion during the attack on 1 July 1916. Commanded 'B' Company in July and August 1916. Appointed Battalion Second-in-Command 21 August 1916. Suffered from illness through late 1916 and early 1917. He returned to Ireland in February 1917 and after some time in hospital he joined the 10th (Reserve) Battalion on 16 March 1917. Major 2 July 1917. During the latter part of the war he transferred to The Royal Irish Rifles and served with the 20th (Reserve) Battalion, The Royal Irish Rifles. Released from service on 4 June 1919. Relinquished his commission 1 September 1921. Founder member and later President of the Portadown Branch, Royal British Legion. Member of Parliament for County Armagh 1921-29 and Central Armagh 1929-41. Minister of Labour 1937-38 in the Parliament of Northern Ireland. Privy Councillor 1937. Deputy Lord Lieutenant, County Armagh. Justice of the Peace. District Master of Portadown Loyal Orange Lodge Number 1 1926-1944. Died 22 January 1944, aged 71. Father of Captain T G Shillington. Uncle of Lieutenant G St G S Cather. His second son, born on 2 April 1911, joined the Royal Ulster Constabulary in 1933 and became Sir (Robert Edward) Graham Shillington CBE, DL, Chief Constable 1970-73. (WO 339/14284)

SHILLINGTON. Captain Thomas Graham Born on 9 October 1897 at Portadown, County Armagh. Attended Castle Park School, Dublin, Methodist College, Belfast and Rossall School in Blackpool. Underage, he was commissioned into Princess Victoria's (Royal Irish Fusiliers) on 7 January 1915, aged 17. To France with 36th (Ulster) Division in October 1915 as a platoon commander in 'B' Company. 1914-15 Star. Lieutenant 12 January 1916. Understudy as Adjutant to Lieutenant Cather March 1916. **Wounded** in both legs by machine-gun fire during the attack at Hamel on 1 July 1916. To hospital in London with Gibson and Jackson. Joined the 10th (Reserve) Battalion on his recovery on 26 September 1916. Rejoined the 9th Royal Irish Fusiliers on 12 December 1916 and was posted back to 'B' Company. Commanded 'A' Company from April 1917. Attended Adjutants' course at 2nd Army Central School May 1917. **Died of wounds** on 18 August 1917, aged 19, in 3rd Australian Casualty Clearing Station, having been shot in the throat during the Battle of Langemarck on 16 August 1917. Son of Major D G Shillington. Cousin of Lieutenant G St G S Cather. (WO 339/17419)

SLATTER. Second Lieutenant Thomas Born on 31 May 1895 at Manchester. A student school master, he enlisted into the 4th (Reserve) Battalion, The Lancashire Fusiliers on 4 November 1916. Corporal 26 July 1916. Lance Sergeant 20 January 1917. Joined 17th Officer Cadet Battalion at Rhyl on 24 May 1917 (joined the course late having been in hospital). Commissioned into Princess Victoria's (Royal Irish Fusiliers) on 29 August 1917 and was posted to the 7th/8th (Service) Battalion in 49th Brigade, 16th (Irish) Division until it was disbanded. Joined the 9th Royal Irish Fusiliers on 23 February 1918. **Captured** on 24 March 1918 at Guiscard. Repatriated on 1 December 1918. Released from service on 2 March 1919. Relinquished his commission on 1 September 1921. (WO 339/88338)

R.J.Sleator

SLEATOR. Second Lieutenant Robert John Born on 21 April 1881 at Armagh. Armagh Company, 1st (Armagh) Battalion, Ulster Volunteer Force. Member of Masonic Lodge 39. A travelling salesman. Enlisted into the 9th Royal Irish Fusiliers on 16 September 1914 (14691). Sergeant 23 September 1914. Company Sergeant Major 24 September 1915. To France with 36th (Ulster) Division in October 1915 as Company Sergeant Major 'B' Company. 1914-15 Star. On the recommendation of the Commanding Officer and commander 108th Brigade, he was appointed directly to a commission on 1 November 1916 and was posted to 'C' Company. Suffered from effects of eighteen months in the trenches and was sent to hospital suffering from severe depression on 15 February

1917. Rejoined the 9th Royal Irish Fusiliers on 19 March 1917 and was made Assistant Quartermaster. **Died** at 7.20pm on 8 May 1917, aged 36, after shooting himself with his revolver in the Quartermaster's store. (WO 339/79131)

SLOAN. Lieutenant Norman Ernest Woods Born on 31 October 1888 at Dublin. An electrical engineer, he was commissioned into Princess Victoria's (Royal Irish Fusiliers) on 9 December 1915. Joined the 9th Royal Irish Fusiliers on 17 August 1916. Posted to the 1st Battalion on 21 October 1916. Lieutenant 1 July 1917. **Wounded** in the right arm on 23 November 1917 during the attack on Lock Number 5/Round Trench east of Moeuvres. Admitted to 3rd General Hospital and evacuated to hospital in England. He had recovered by March 1918 and he transferred to the Machine Gun Corps. Served with 36th Battalion, Machine Gun Corps from 11 September 1918. Evacuated to hospital in England sick in October 1918. He subsequently served with the Machine Gun Corps Training Centre at Grantham from 10 January 1919. Released from service 30 October 1919. Subsequently lived in Rugby, where he died in early 1976, aged 87. (WO 339/50088)

SMALL. Second Lieutenant Alexander Born on 21 October 1882 at Loughgall, County Armagh. An architect, he joined the 9th Royal Irish Fusiliers on its formation as a Second Lieutenant on 15 September 1914. Fell ill with tuberculosis in February 1915 and was found unfit for service. He relinquished his commission on account of ill-health on 23 April 1915. Silver War Badge, number 341995. (WO 339/14285)

SMITH. Second Lieutenant Charles Born in 1879 at Dublin. Enlisted into The Prince of Wales's Leinster Regiment (Royal Canadians) on 29 January 1898 and served with the 1st Battalion in the South African War. Transferred to the Army Reserve as a Lance Corporal on 28 January 1905 and served with the Army Cyclist Corps (352 - Private) from 17 May 1911. To France 29 July 1915. A motor mechanic by trade, he transferred to the Army Service Corps (M/39584, renumbered M/229434) on 3 October 1915. Sergeant 3 December 1916. Attached to the Royal Garrison Artillery from 1 January 1917 to 16 March 1917. Joined 16th Officer Cadet Battalion at Rhyl on 7 June 1917. Commissioned into The Prince of Wales's Leinster Regiment (Royal Canadians) on 26 September 1917 and joined the 2nd Battalion. Attached to the 9th Royal Irish Fusiliers 17 April 1918. Posted back to the 2nd Battalion, The Prince of Wales's Leinster Regiment (Royal Canadians) in 88th Brigade, 29th Division on 19 June 1918. Attached to the 7th (Service) Battalion, The Royal Irish Regiment on 7 September 1918. Tried at Field General Court Martial at Boulogne on 25 February 1919 on a charge of allowing a prisoner to escape; found not guilty. Attached to 84th Labour Company on 12 October 1919. Released from service 10 January 1920. Lived in Dublin. (WO 339/110527)

SMITH. Lieutenant Edgar Montague Born on 10 April 1887 at Kent. Commissioned into Princess Victoria's (Royal Irish Fusiliers) on 27 March 1915 and served with the 4th (Extra Reserve) Battalion before joining the 9th Royal Irish Fusiliers on 31 March 1916. Posted to 'C' Company. Lieutenant 7 February 1916. **Wounded** by machine-gun bullets in his left arm and in both legs during the attack at Hamel on 1 July 1916. Evacuated to hospital in England 4 July 1916. When he recovered he re-joined the 4th (Extra Reserve) Battalion on 25 November 1916 as an instructor. Acting Captain 17 November 1918. Reverted to Lieutenant 18 December 1918. Released from service 4 January 1919. Worked for Blyth Green Jourdain, an international trading house and regularly worked in Peru. (WO 374/63300)

SMITH MC. Captain James Irwin Born on 4 May 1897. A bank clerk from Cornakinnegar, County Armagh. He enlisted into the 10th (Reserve) Battalion (23366 - Cadet) on 6 December 1915. Joined 7th Officer Cadet Battalion on 7 August 1916. Commissioned into Princess Victoria's (Royal Irish Fusiliers) on 19 December 1916. Joined the 9th Royal Irish Fusiliers on 19 March 1917. Attached to 12th (Service) Battalion, The Royal Irish Rifles (Central Antrim) in 108th Brigade from 30 June 1917 to late April 1918, when he rejoined the 9th Royal Irish Fusiliers. Acting Captain 3 May 1918 and was appointed Officer Commanding 'D' Company until June 1918. Reverted to Lieutenant on 19 June 1918 when he was posted to the 1st Battalion. Joined the 1st Battalion 13 July 1918, where he spent the rest of the war. Awarded an **MC** for his actions on a raid at Meulenhouck near Bailleul on 14 August 1918. Released from service on 27 January 1919. Relinquished his commission 1 September 1921. Subsequently spent time in Canada as a civil servant. (WO 339/67961)

SMITH. Lieutenant Robert Leslie Born on 22 March 1897 at Donaghmore, County Tyrone. Orphaned at a young age, he was educated at St Andrew's College, Dublin. He was serving an apprenticeship at Parkside Weaving Factory, Portadown. Enlisted into the Army Service Corps (103893 - Private) on 25 May 1915. A dispatch rider and car driver, he deployed to France on with 34th Division Field Ambulance Workshop Unit on 10 January 1916. Joined 104th Field Ambulance in 34th Division on 29 August 1916. Corporal 31 October 1916. Joined 88th Field Ambulance in 29th Division on 30 November 1916. Joined 7th Officer Cadet Battalion at Fermoy on 10 March 1917. Commissioned into Princess Victoria's (Royal Irish Fusiliers) on 27 June 1917. Joined the 9th Royal Irish Fusiliers on 30 September 1917 and was posted to 'A' Company. **Wounded** and **captured** on 27 March 1918 at Erches. Repatriated on 19 December 1918. Relinquished his commission 4 March 1919. Married in Dublin in 1919 and lived in Donaghmore before emigrating to Australia in 1929. He continued to work in the linen industry. Died in Queensland, Australia on 24 November 1971 aged 74. His brother, Second Lieutenant Stanley Herd Smith, died of wounds on 27 May 1918, aged 20, serving with 2nd Battalion, Tank Corps. His son, Captain John Vincent Stanley Smith, served with The Royal Irish Fusiliers (Princess Victoria's) in the Second World War. (WO 339/97870)

SPARKS MC. Captain Walter Born on 8 August 1894. An accountant, he joined the Inns of Court Officer Training Corps on 17 December 1914. Commissioned into Princess Victoria's (Royal Irish Fusiliers) Special Reserve of Officers on 31 March 1915 and joined the 2nd Battalion in France in May 1915. 1914-15 Star. Evacuated to hospital in England sick in October 1915. Joined the 8th (Service) Battalion in 49th Brigade, 16th (Irish) Division in January 1916. Lieutenant 12 February 1916. **Wounded** on 6 September 1916 when shot in the right thigh at Leuze (or Bouleaux) Wood near Combles. Evacuated to hospital in England. He was fit by January 1917 and returned to the 7th/8th (Service) Battalion. Awarded an **MC** for his actions at the Battle of Langemarck on 16 August 1917. Acting Captain 20 July 1917. Company commander from 22 September 1917 until 24 December 1917, when he was appointed Adjutant. Reverted to Lieutenant and proceeded on leave when the 7th/8th (Service) Battalion was disbanded in February 1918. Joined the 9th Royal Irish Fusiliers 2 May 1918 as Adjutant. Captain 22 April 1918. ***Croix de Guerre* (Belgium)**. He was released from service on 1 April 1919. Relinquished his commission in the Special Reserve of Officers 1 April 1920. (WO 339/30946)

STEELE MC*. Lieutenant Charles Henry Born on 22 April 1894 at Kilkenny, where his father was a serving soldier. He had three brothers and seven sisters. Enlisted into the 1st Battalion, Princess Victoria's (Royal Irish Fusiliers) as a boy soldier (10235 - Private) on 22 January 1909, aged 14. He deployed to France with the 1st Battalion on 22 August 1914. 1914 Star and clasp. Corporal 20 March 1915. Sergeant 7 January 1916. Commissioned into Princess Victoria's (Royal Irish Fusiliers) on 26 June 1918. Joined the 9th Royal Irish Fusiliers on 21 September 1918 and was posted to 'D' Company. Awarded an **MC** for his conduct during the attack at Vijfwegen on 30 September 1918 a Bar to his **MC** during the crossing of the Lys on 16 October 1918. Left to join the 1st Battalion 19 December 1918. Sailed with the 1st Battalion for the Middle-East 21 September 1919. Served in Iraq from October 1919 to May 1921 in 'D' (MG) Company. Lieutenant 26 December 1919. General Service Medal 1918-1962 with clasps 'Iraq' and 'NW Persia'. Retired and transferred to the Reserve of Officers 24 September 1922. Served as the aide-de-camp to the Governor and Commander-in-Chief Hong Kong from 13 November 1925 to 23 July 1927 in the local rank of Captain. Settled in London and became the secretary of the London branch of the Royal Irish Fusiliers Old Comrades Association. Active in the British Union of Fascists and became its prospective parliamentary candidate for Guildford. He became a journalist on a weekly newspaper (the Sunday Referee) but, because of its Jewish ownership, he left and became a steward with the Peninsular and Oriental Steam Navigation Company. Died 25 January 1939 soon after an accident (allegedly from a blow from a stone thrown at a British Union of Fascists rally), aged 44. Buried in London. His father was 3254 Pioneer Sergeant Albert Louis William Steele, who served with Princess Victoria's (Royal Irish Fusiliers) from 18 May 1889 to 17 May 1911. He served in South Africa with the 2nd Battalion. Queen's South Africa Medal with clasps 'Relief of Lady Smith', 'Tugela Heights' and 'Cape Colony'. He later joined the 1st Battalion and was awarded the Army Long Service and Good Conduct Medal in 1907. He died on 14 March 1948. His brother, Colour Sergeant Douglas William John Steele, was a regular soldier who served with the 9th Royal Irish Fusiliers; see Appendix 6. His brother, Private Percy Giles Steele, enlisted into The Prince of Wales's Leinster Regiment (Royal Canadians) in April 1908 and transferred to Princess Victoria's (Royal Irish Fusiliers) in May 1909. He joined the 2nd Battalion in India and spent a considerable amount of time in detention before being discharged in February 1914 for misconduct.

Captain C H Steele MC in the uniform of the British Union of Fascists

STEWART. Second Lieutenant William Johnston Born on 25 May 1893 at Glasgow. Joined 1/8th (The Argyllshire) Battalion, Princess Louise's (Argyll and Sutherland Highlanders) on 29 September 1914 (2113 - Private) and served with 51st (Highland) Division Cyclist Company in France from 1 May 1915. 1914-15 Star. **Wounded** on 19 June 1915 when shot in the back. Joined an Officer Cadet Battalion on 15 July 1915. Commissioned into Princess Victoria's (Royal Irish Fusiliers) on 21 December 1915. Joined the 9th Royal Irish Fusiliers on 2 April 1916 and was posted to 'B' Company as Officer Commanding 8 Platoon, 'B' Company. **Wounded** by shellfire 26 June 1916. **Missing** during the attack at Hamel on 1 July 1916 and later declared **killed in action** on that date, aged 23. (WO 339/51128)

STOKES. Second Lieutenant John Alan Born on 8 October 1894 at Belfast. A gas engineer, he enlisted into the 20th (Service) Battalion, The Royal Fusiliers (City of London Regiment) (3rd Public Schools) on 17 September 1914 (PS/5697 - Private) and served with 98th Brigade, 33rd Division from 14 November 1915. 1914-15 Star. Lance Corporal 15 May 1916. Returned from France on 22 July 1916. Posted to the 6th (Reserve) Battalion, The Royal Fusiliers (City of London Regiment) on 2 September 1916 (renumbered 49919 - Lance Corporal). Joined 16th Officer Cadet Battalion at Rhyl in late 1916 and was commissioned into Princess Victoria's (Royal Irish Fusiliers) on 28 March 1917. Joined the 9th Royal Irish Fusiliers on 26 June 1917 and was posted to 'C' Company. Attached to 12th (Service) Battalion, The Royal Irish Rifles (Central Antrim) in 108th Brigade on 3 July 1917 and was **killed in action** at the Battle of Langemarck on 16 August 1917, aged 22. (WO 339/79937)

STRONGE. Lieutenant James Matthew Born on 10 January 1891 at Tynan Abbey, County Armagh, the son and heir of the 5th Baronet, Sir James Stronge. Signed the Ulster Covenant 28 September 1912. An officer in the Dispatch Riding Corps, Ulster Volunteer Force. Joined the 9th Royal Irish Fusiliers on 14 September 1914. Second Lieutenant 12 October 1914. Lieutenant 1 May 1915. To France with 36th (Ulster) Division in October 1915. 1914-15 Star. Transport officer until he was **killed in action** at the Battle of Langemarck on 16 August 1917, aged 26. At the time of his death he had been married for a little over one month. (WO 339/14288)

TEES. Lieutenant Ernest Simpson Lowry Born on 5 May 1896 at Belfast. A student at Queen's University, Belfast, he was commissioned into The Oxfordshire and Buckinghamshire Light Infantry on 3 June 1915. Served in Salonika from December 1915. 1914-15 Star.

Transferred to Princess Victoria's (Royal Irish Fusiliers) in mid-1916 and was posted to the 6th (Service) Battalion in 31st Brigade, 10th (Irish) Division in Macedonia. Lieutenant 1 July 1917. Joined the 9th Royal Irish Fusiliers on 11 July 1918. **Wounded** by shell fragments on 24 August 1918 at Bailleul. He also suffered rheumatic fever and was evacuated to hospital in England on 15 September 1918. He saw no further service in France. He served in India from 15 August 1919 with 2nd Battalion, The Prince of Wales Own (West Yorkshire Regiment). Relinquished his commission 11 July 1920. Emigrated to the United States 3 November 1922. Lived in Wichita Falls, Texas and worked in the linen industry. Became a US citizen. Died at Comal, Texas in January 1974, aged 77. (WO 339/1986)

TOWNSEND. Captain Arthur Barry Born on 17 October 1880 at Armagh. Was an officer in the Armagh Regiment, Ulster Volunteer Force. Joined the 9th Royal Irish Fusiliers on its formation and was commissioned on 24 September 1914. Unfit for general service, he was attached to the 12th (Reserve) Battalion, The Royal Inniskilling Fusiliers where he served for the first part of 1915. Captain 24 September 1915. Joined the 10th (Reserve) Battalion, Princess Victoria's (Royal Irish Fusiliers) as Adjutant on its formation and served there for most of the war. Relinquished his appointment on account of ill-health 1 June 1918 and relinquished his commission on account of ill-health on 17 April 1919. Silver War Badge, number 167018. He lived in Dublin. He died on 29 September 1939, aged 58. Brother of Lieutenant Richard Stapleton Barry Townsend. (WO 339/14292)

TOWNSEND. Lieutenant Richard Stapleton Barry Born on 23 April 1884 at Armagh. Acted for a year as an officer in the Armagh Company, 1st (Armagh) Battalion, Ulster Volunteer Force. Joined the 9th Royal Irish Fusiliers on its formation on 15 September 1914 and was immediately commissioned. Lieutenant 1 December 1914. Remaining initially in Ireland, he joined the 9th Royal Irish Fusiliers on 17 February 1916 and was posted to 'C' Company. **Killed in action** during the attack at Hamel on 1 July 1916, aged 32. His body was recovered in early August 1916 by men of the 2nd Battalion, Irish Guards and is now buried in Ancre British Cemetery. Brother of Captain Arthur Barry Townsend. (WO 339/14291)

TRINDER. Second Lieutenant Samuel Levis Born on 23 March 1883 at Cork, the son of the then Commanding Officer of the 2nd Battalion, The Royal Inniskilling Fusiliers, Lieutenant Colonel J Trinder. Served as a Trooper in the South Irish Horse for 12 months then travelled to South Africa where he served in the Natal Police from 1904-10 (including the Bambatha Zulu Rebellion in 1906). Joined the 1st Imperial Light Horse on 28 September 1914 as a Trooper and served in German South West Africa. Left on 10 August 1915 to return home to seek a commission and joined 7th Officer Cadet Battalion on 6 April 1916. Commissioned into Princess Victoria's (Royal Irish Fusiliers) on 4 August 1916. Joined the 9th Royal Irish Fusiliers on 31 October 1916 and was posted to 'B' Company. Assistant Brigade Signalling Officer 4 April 1917. He returned to the 9th Royal Irish Fusiliers in July 1917. **Died of wounds** on 17 August 1917, aged 31, in 44th Casualty Clearing Station having been shot in the head and back the previous day during the Battle of Langemarck. (WO 339/57748)

TURNER MC. Lieutenant Edward John Lowry Born on 20 July 1877 at Belfast. Served in Princess Victoria's (Royal Irish Fusiliers) as a regular soldier from 2 February 1899 to 2 February 1910, transferred to the Army Reserve as a Sergeant. Signed the Ulster Covenant 28 September 1912. Enlisted on 23 October 1914 into the Service Squadron, 6th (Inniskilling) Dragoons (UD/99). Promoted Sergeant. Joined 7th Officer Cadet Battalion on 29 May 1916 and was commissioned into Princess Victoria's (Royal Irish Fusiliers) on 26 September 1916. Joined the 9th Royal Irish Fusiliers on 20 December 1916 and was posted to 'B' Company. Transport officer from August 1917 after the Battle of Langemarck. Awarded an **MC** for his actions during the withdrawal from St Quentin from 21 to 26 March 1918. Lieutenant 26 March 1918. **Wounded** on 12 April 1918 near Wulverghem when he was shot through the chest. Evacuated to hospital in England 3 May 1918. Treated at 5th London General Hospital before returning to Belfast. Relinquished his commission on account of ill-health caused by wounds 1 May 1919. After the war he lived at Benfleet, Essex before returning to Belfast. President of the North of Ireland Bands' Association from 1923. Chaired the Belfast Board of Guardians. (WO 339/61883)

TWEEDIE MM. Second Lieutenant Robert Enlisted into the 9th (Service) Battalion, The Royal Irish Rifles (West Belfast) 11 September 1914 (13751). Sergeant 13 September 1914. Tried by District Court Martial on 3 June 1915 on a charge of being absent without leave from Ballykinler training camp; found guilty and reduced in rank to Corporal. To France with 36th (Ulster) Division in October 1915. 1914-15 Star. **Wounded** by a trench mortar at Messines October 1916. Treated at 9th General Hospital, Rouen and evacuated to hospital in England. treated at the Royal County Surrey Hospital, Guildford. **MM**. When recovered, joined 7th Officer Cadet Battalion 9 March 1917. Commissioned into Princess Victoria's (Royal Irish Fusiliers) on 27 June 1917. Joined the 9th Royal Irish Fusiliers mid-1917. Evacuated to hospital in England (neurasthenia) 2 February 1918 and treated at Reading War Hospital. Referred to Craiglockhart War Hospital on 22 May 1918. Relinquished his commission on account of ill-health contracted on active service 25 September 1918. Silver War Badge, number B13454. Subsequently became an assistant foreman at Falls Flax Mills, Belfast. Charged with obtaining money by false pretences, he admitted seven charges at Belfast Assizes on 19 July 1920. Sentenced to four months in prison. Died of pneumonia 23 November 1929, leaving a widow and six children. (WO 339/98896)

UPRICHARD. Captain Forster Green Born on 27 June 1883 at Laurencetown, County Down. The son of a wealthy linen maker, he was commissioned into the North Irish Horse on 9 August 1914. To France 4 April 1915. 1914-15 Star. Captain 8 November 1915. He served with 2nd North Irish Horse, X Corps Cavalry Regiment from June 1916. Joined the 9th Royal Irish Fusiliers on 30 September 1917 but left on 14 October 1917 and transferred to The Royal Irish Rifles. Served with the 11th (Service) Battalion, The Royal Irish Rifles (South Antrim) in 108th Brigade and the 15th (Service) Battalion, The Royal Irish Rifles (North Belfast) in 107th Brigade. Released from service on 9 February 1919. Relinquished his commission 1 April 1920. He returned to the family linen business. Died 19 June 1945. His brother, Major Henry Albert Uprichard, was killed in action on 1 July 1916 serving with the 13th (Service) Battalion, The Royal Irish Rifles (1st County Down). (WO 339/10355)

VANSTON. Captain Henry William Frederick Mortimer Born in 1884 at Dublin. Commissioned into the 5th Battalion (Militia), The Royal Munster Fusiliers on 30 March 1903. Lieutenant 23 July 1903. On the formation of the Territorial Force and Special Reserve, transferred to the Special Reserve of Officers 2 August 1908. Transferred to Princess Victoria's (Royal Irish Fusiliers) Special Reserve as a Captain on 3 December 1913 and joined the 4th (Extra Reserve) Battalion. Mobilised with the 4th (Extra Reserve) Battalion in August 1914. To France and joined the 1st Battalion on 16 May 1915. 1914-15 Star. Returned to England 6 August 1915 and then joined the 9th Royal Irish Fusiliers on 31 March 1916. Appointed as Officer Commanding 'D' Company April 1916. Evacuated to hospital in England sick 19 June 1916. When recovered he returned to the 9th Royal Irish Fusiliers and again took command of 'D' Company until March 1917. Attached to 1/4th Battalion, The Essex Regiment from 30 June 1917, he joined it on 22 July 1917 in Alexandria for service with the Egyptian Expeditionary Force. Admitted to Narieh Schools Military Hospital, Cairo with dysentery on 1 September 1917 and **died** on 4 September 1917, aged 33. (WO 339/9391)

VESEY MC. Captain George Waller Born George Waller Lendrum on 5 August 1882 at Dublin. The family home and estate was at Corkhill, County Tyrone. He assumed his wife's surname to enable him to inherit Derrybard House, Fintona, County Tyrone. Commissioned on 10 April 1915 into the North Irish Horse. To France with 'F' Squadron in 33rd Division 17 November 1915. 1914-15 Star. Lieutenant 18 November 1915. Served with 2nd North Irish Horse, X Corps Cavalry Regiment. Transferred to Princess Victoria's (Royal Irish Fusiliers) and joined the 9th Royal Irish Fusiliers on 17 October 1917. Posted to 'A' Company. Awarded an **MC** for an action at Marcoing on 15 December 1917. Commanded 'A' Company from December 1917 until he was **wounded** on 24 March 1918 near Guiscard. He **died of wounds** in a French field hospital (*Ambulance 4/51*) on 26 March 1918, aged 35. Commemorated at Kilsheery Parish Church, County Tyrone. Brother of Captain Marcus Beresford Lendrum. His brother, Captain Alan Cane Lendrum MC*, was murdered by the IRA on 22 September 1920. (WO 339/33685)

VINT OStJ MD. Lieutenant Francis William Born on 10 July 1897 at Ballymena, County Armagh. Educated at Ballymena Academy and Queen's University, Belfast. Served with Queen's University, Belfast Officer Training Corps and was commissioned into Princess Victoria's (Royal Irish Fusiliers) on 25 August 1915. Joined the 7th (Service) Battalion in 49th Brigade, 16th (Irish) Division in France. **Wounded** on 26 June 1916 at Loos when shot by a sniper in the left arm. His wound was severe and, although recovered and on the strength of the 1st Battalion from 16 May 1917, he was held at the Infantry Base Depot at Havre from November 1917 until fully fit. Lieutenant 1 July 1917. Joined the 9th Royal Irish Fusiliers on 14 September 1918. **Wounded** during the attack near Bergstraat, 8 miles east of Courtrai, on 25 October 1918 when shot in the right thigh. One of the last two officers to be wounded. Evacuated to hospital in England 9 November 1918. He remained in hospital until mid-1919. Relinquished his commission on account of ill-health caused by wounds 3 September 1919. Silver War Badge, number B313277. Studied medicine at Queen's University, Belfast; MB 1924, MD 1930. Joined the East African Medical Service and conducted work of importance as a bacteriologist in the medical research laboratory, coming to the notice of Parliament. Some of his work has been quoted in controversial eugenics literature. Appointed Serving Brother, Venerable Order of the Hospital of St. John of Jerusalem (**MStJ**) 1939. Promoted to Officer, Venerable Order of the Hospital of St. John of Jerusalem (**OStJ**) 1944. Died on 10 June 1980, aged 82. His brother, Captain James Vint MC, served with the Royal Garrison Artillery. (WO 339/41791)

WALLACE. Lieutenant Samuel Wright Born on 4 July 1895. Joined Queen's University, Belfast Officer Training Corps. Commissioned into Princess Victoria's (Royal Irish Fusiliers) on 6 January 1916. Joined the 9th Royal Irish Fusiliers on 20 June 1916 where he served until January 1917. He was unfit to return from leave and did not rejoin the 9th Royal Irish Fusiliers. Lieutenant 6 July 1917. When recovered that summer, he sailed to Salonika but before joining his unit fell ill again and was admitted to 43rd General Hospital, Salonika. He was evacuated on 13 November 1917 via Malta and arrived in England on 7 January 1918. When recovered, he joined 3rd (Reserve) Garrison Battalion in England on 13 September 1918. Released from service on 28 May 1919. Relinquished his commission 1 September 1921. (WO 339/51123)

WARREN. Lieutenant Arthur Henry Born on 11 June 1895 at Dungiven, County Londonderry. A bank clerk, he enlisted into the 19th (Reserve) Battalion, The Royal Irish Rifles on 17 May 1916. Joined 7th Officer Cadet Battalion on 9 January 1917 and was commissioned into The Royal Irish Rifles on 26 April 1917. Joined the 14th (Service) Battalion, The Royal Irish Rifles (Young Citizens) in 109th Brigade in France in May 1917. **Wounded** by shrapnel on 16 August 1917 at the Battle of Langemarck. While recovering he acted as a Railway Transport Officer in Ireland. He returned to France on 25 September 1918 and was attached to the 9th Royal Irish Fusiliers on 15 October 1918. Lieutenant 26 October 1918. Embarked for demobilisation 12 February 1919 and released from service 14 February 1919. Relinquished his commission 1 September 1921. Subsequently worked for the Hong Kong and Shanghai Bank in the Philippines.(WO 339/83526)

WHALEN. Lieutenant Frederick Joseph Born on 23 November 1888 at Woodford, Essex. Served with the Surrey Yeomanry (Queen Mary's Regiment) from February 1909 to early 1914. Re-enlisted into the Surrey Yeomanry (Queen Mary's Regiment) on 9 August 1914 (1849 - Private) and served with 'A' Squadron in France from 21 December 1914 to 12 November 1915. 1914-15 Star. Commissioned directly into The King's (Shropshire Light Infantry) on 3 December 1915. Transferred to a Reserve Cavalry Regiment on 28 March 1916 and joined the 2nd North Irish Horse, X Corps Cavalry Regiment on 24 March 1917. Lieutenant 1 July 1917. Transferred to Princess Victoria's (Royal Irish Fusiliers) and joined the 9th Royal Irish Fusiliers on 2 October 1917. Left on 16 November 1917 to transfer to the Tank Corps and joined the Tank Corps Depot, Wareham, Dorset for training. Served with the 10th Battalion, Tank Corps (with Second Lieutenant G T L Bayliff) until he was evacuated to hospital in England sick in March 1918. Released from service 23 January 1919. Relinquished his commission 1 April 1920. Became a clerk in the Ministry of Agriculture and Fisheries. Enrolled in the Officers' Emergency Reserve in 1939. Died at Edmonton, Middlesex in 1963, aged 74. (WO 339/49691)

WHITE. Second Lieutenant Thomas Wilfred Born on 8 May 1898 at Londonderry. A student at Foyle College, he joined the Inns of Court Officer Training Corps on 27 April 1917 and remained there after it became 14th Officer Cadet Battalion at Berkhamstead, Hertfordshire on 7 September 1917. Commissioned on 18 December 1917 into Princess Victoria's (Royal Irish Fusiliers), he joined the 9th Royal Irish Fusiliers on 27 April 1918. To hospital sick (trench fever) 20 July 1918 and evacuated to hospital in England 10 August 1918. He saw no further service and was released from service on 28 May 1919. Relinquished his commission 1 September 1921. (WO 339/121859)

WHITLA OBE. Major Valentine George Born on 12 March 1863. Appointed Midshipman in the Royal Navy 15 January 1876. He served during the Egyptian Expedition of 1882, taking part in the bombardment of Alexandria and the landing with the Naval Brigade. Egypt Medal 1882-89. Khedive's Star. Commissioned as a Lieutenant in the 3rd Battalion, the Duke of Wellington's (West Riding Regiment) 20 July 1883. Commissioned into the 2nd Dragoon Guards (Queen's Bays) from the Militia on 6 May 1885. Captain 9 December 1892. Took part in the Expedition to Dongola in 1896. **Mention in Despatches**. Queen's Sudan Medal. Adjutant of 2nd Dragoon Guards (Queen's Bays) 1 November 1893 to 31 October 1897. Major 3rd (King's Own) Hussars 15 October 1898. South African War 1901. Queen's South Africa Medal with four clasps. Retired 6 June 1906 and spent some time hunting in Kenya. On the outbreak of war, he joined the North Irish Horse. To France June 1916. Served with 2nd North Irish Horse, X Corps Cavalry Regiment. **Mention in Despatches**. Joined the 9th Royal Irish Fusiliers on 30 September 1917. Left on 24 October 1917 to join the 11th (Service) Battalion, The Royal Inniskilling Fusiliers (Donegal and Fermanagh). Subsequently served in appointments as an Aide de Camp from 23 May 1918, which he finally relinquished on 18 April 1919. **OBE (Military)**. Died in Buckinghamshire in 1943, aged 80.

WIGHTMAN. Second Lieutenant Alexander Born on 24 April 1890 at Londonderry. A jeweller by profession. Signed the Ulster Covenant 28 September 1912. He enlisted into the 1/4th (City of Dundee) Battalion, The Black Watch (Royal Highlanders) (2709 - Private) on 28 December 1914. Deployed to France on 2 May 1915. 1914-15 Star. **Wounded** on 4 November 1916 at Thiepval by rifle grenade fragments in an accident. Lance Corporal 6 April 1917. **Wounded** on 23 April 1917 near Kemmel when shot in the left shoulder and evacuated to hospital in England. Joined 17th Officer Cadet Battalion at Rhyl on 5 April 1918. Commissioned into Princess Victoria's (Royal Irish Fusiliers) on 25 September 1918. Joined the 9th Royal Irish Fusiliers on 16 November 1918. Released from service on 22 February 1919. His brother, Air Mechanic Class 2, William Dysart Wightman, served briefly with the Royal Flying Corps from July to September 1915, when he was discharged as no longer physically fit for war service due to sickness. (WO 374/74226)

WILDING MC. Lieutenant Archibald Born on 19 January 1886 at Blackburn, Lancashire. Served with The Loyal North Lancashire Regiment from November 1906 to August 1908. Promoted Corporal. Joined the 3rd Battalion, The Royal Fusiliers (City of London Regiment) in 85th Brigade, 28th Division on 31 May 1915 (17599 - Private) and served in Salonika. 1914-15 Star. Joined 18th Officer Cadet Battalion at Bath on 7 April 1917. Commissioned into Princess Victoria's (Royal Irish Fusiliers) on 1 August 1917 and was posted to the 7th/8th (Service) Battalion in 49th Brigade, 16th (Irish) Division. Awarded an **MC** for his conduct at Fontaine Les Croisilles, near Cambrai on 20 November 1917. **Wounded** on 22 November 1917 - he was in charge of two Lewis guns when a shell fell in the trench and blew up the guns; he carried on at his post for 48 hours. When the 7th/8th (Service) Battalion was disbanded he joined the 9th Royal Irish Fusiliers on 16 February 1918. Due to the residual effect of his wound and having spent nearly three years at the front he was sent home for a rest on 3 March 1918 and spent the rest of the war with the 10th (Reserve) Battalion. Released from service on 12 December 1919. Relinquished his commission on 1 September 1921. Emigrated in February 1920 with his wife and daughter to the United States (where his brother lived) on the SS Bohemian (the ship sank off Nova Scotia on its return journey on 1 March 1920). He lived initially in Fall River, Massachusetts and then became a garage owner in The Bronx, New York. His son, Flying Officer John Archibald Wilding DFC, served as an air gunner and then a pilot with the Royal Canadian Air Force. He was killed on his twentieth sortie flying a Halifax III with 426 Squadron, Royal Canadian Air Force on 9 September 1944, aged 23. The aircraft was hit by flak over Le Havre. Flying Officer Wilding remained at the controls after it caught fire to allow his crew to bale out as it returned to Linton-on-Ouse. He and the flight engineer, Sergeant J F Andrew, were killed as they avoided crashing into the village of Wallingford, Oxfordshire. Both men were awarded a posthumous Mention in Despatches. Flying Officer Wilding is buried in Brookwood Military Cemetery, Surrey and commemorated in Wallingford. (WO 339/103222)

WILSON. Lieutenant Charles Rountree Born on 10 August 1885 at Richhill, County Armagh. Employed by the Department of Agriculture, he enlisted into the Army Service Corps on 19 August 1915. Staff Sergeant Major 3 February 1916. Commissioned into the Army Service Corps on 6 April 1916. Employed in the Forage Department in Ireland as an Assistant Purchasing Officer. Lieutenant 6 October 1917. Transferred for infantry service to Princess Victoria's (Royal Irish Fusiliers) on 19 May 1918 and joined the 9th Royal Irish Fusiliers on 20 July 1918. **Wounded** during the attack at Vijfwegen on 1 October 1918 and to hospital on 2 October 1918 and evacuated to hospital in England 6 October 1918. When recovered he joined the 3rd (Reserve) Battalion until he was released from service on 8 April 1919. Relinquished his commission on 1 September 1921. Died 16 February 1972, aged 86 in Richhill. He and his wife, who died in 1994 aged 102, are buried in Friends Burial Ground, Richhill. (WO 339/58001)

WILSON. Honorary Lieutenant and Quartermaster George Wade Born on 8 January 1889. From Portadown, County Armagh. A member of 4th (Portadown) Battalion, Armagh Regiment, Ulster Volunteer Force. An auctioneer's clerk in Dublin. Signed the Ulster Covenant 28 September 1912. He enlisted into the 9th Royal Irish Fusiliers on its formation on 15 September 1914 (14792 - Private). Corporal 22 September 1914. Appointed Warrant Officer Class 2 and Regimental Quartermaster Sergeant on 22 February 1915 vice Thwaites. To France with 36th (Ulster) Division in October 1915. 1914-15 Star. Appointed Honorary Lieutenant and Quartermaster 15 September 1916 and acted in this role until the end of the war. **Mention in Despatches**. **Knight of the *Ordre de La Couronne* (Belgium)**. ***Croix de Guerre* (Belgium)**. Released from service in late 1919. (WO 374/75592)

WINGFIELD. Group Captain Cecil Percy Born on 8 October 1896 at Streatham, London. Commissioned into Princess Victoria's (Royal Irish Fusiliers) on 8 April 1915, aged 18, and was posted to the 4th (Extra Reserve) Battalion. Lieutenant 7 February 1916. Joined the 9th Royal Irish Fusiliers on 31 March 1916 and was posted to 'D' Company. **Wounded** in the buttocks and abdomen while with a wiring party on 23 August 1916. Evacuated to hospital in England 7 September 1916. Discharged from hospital on 16 October 1916. Served again with the 4th (Extra Reserve) Battalion until attached to Number 2 Training School, Northolt for training as a Flying Officer on 19 May 1917. Transferred to the Royal Flying Corps on 16 July 1917. He redeployed to France in October 1917 but his wounds prevented general service and he was passed fit for flying below 10,000 feet only. Released from service on 18 April 1919. Joined the Royal Air Force, for employment in the Stores (later renamed Equipment) Branch, on 2 January 1923 (21037 - Pilot Officer). Flying Officer 9 February 1925. Flight Lieutenant 1 February 1932. Served with the Electrical and Wireless School and 503 (Bombing) Squadron. Then served in Iraq with Number 1 Armoured Car Company from 4 March 1932 to 24 July 1934. Posted to RAF Manston and also served at Number 11 Equipment Depot. Squadron Leader 1 December 1937. Served in the Air Ministry from 10 January 1938 and throughout the war. Wing Commander 1 January 1940. Group Captain 1 September 1942. Retired 22 May 1948, aged 52. Died 1977 in New Forest, Hampshire, aged 80. (WO 339/46966)

WOOD. Second Lieutenant Reginald Nixon Born in Dublin on 27 January 1889. Educated at The King's Hospital, Dublin. A secretary on the staff of Canadian News, he enlisted into the Honourable Artillery Company on 4 August 1914 (1138 - Private). Served in France from 29 December 1914. 1914-15 Star. Lance Corporal 5 August 1915. Attended an Officer Cadet School from October 1915 and was commissioned into Princess Victoria's (Royal Irish Fusiliers) on 23 January 1916 and joined the 9th Royal Irish Fusiliers on 29 January 1916. **Killed in action** on patrol near Hamel on 22 February 1916, aged 27. He was the first officer of the 9th Royal Irish Fusiliers to be killed in France. (WO 339/54682)

J Woods

WOODS. Lieutenant James Born on 3 November 1893 at Belfast. A ship's draughtsman, he joined Queen's University, Belfast Officer Training Corps on 12 December 1914 and then 7th Officer Cadet Battalion on 6 April 1916. Commissioned into Princess Victoria's (Royal Irish Fusiliers) on 7 July 1916, he joined the 9th Royal Irish Fusiliers on 7 October 1916 and was posted to 'C' Company. Detached from late 1917. Lieutenant 7 January 1918. He fell ill with influenza in April 1918 and was evacuated to hospital in England on 24 April 1918. He did not recover fully until early 1919. Released from service 25 January 1919. Relinquished his commission on 1 September 1921. (WO 339/57753)

WRIGHT. Lieutenant David Hamilton Born on 25 March 1889 at Fahan, County Donegal. An accountant, with the Londonderry and Lough Swilly Railway. He enlisted into the 12th (Reserve) Battalion, The Royal Inniskilling Fusiliers and was commissioned into Princess Victoria's (Royal Irish Fusiliers) on 19 April 1915. Initially, served at home with the 10th (Reserve) Battalion. Lieutenant 1 September 1916. Joined the 9th Royal Irish Fusiliers on 11 December 1916. Commanded 'B' Company from March 1917 until he was **captured** at the Battle of Langemarck on 16 August 1917. Repatriated 14 December 1918. Relinquished his commission on 20 March 1919. (WO 339/32232)

YOUNG MC. Second Lieutenant John Bruce Alan Born on 27 June 1897 at Ballymena, County Antrim. A musician, he enlisted into The Royal Irish Rifles on 2 September 1915 and joined the 5th (Extra Reserve) Battalion, The Royal Irish Rifles at Holywood. Joined 7th Officer Cadet Battalion on 29 May 1916. Commissioned into Princess Victoria's (Royal Irish Fusiliers) on 5 September 1916. Joined the 9th Royal Irish Fusiliers on 27 December 1916 and was posted to 'A' Company. **Wounded** at Moeuvres on 23 November 1917 when shot in the left arm. Evacuated to hospital in England 2 December 1917. **Mention in Despatches**. When recovered he rejoined the 9th Royal Irish Fusiliers on 26 April 1918 and was attached to 108th Trench Mortar Battery, with which he was **wounded** during the attack at Vijfwegen on 30 September 1918 and earned an **MC**. He was evacuated to hospital in England on 14 October 1918 and saw no further service. Released from service on 22 May 1919. Relinquished his commission on 1 September 1921. Died in Westminster, London February 1988, aged 90. (WO 339/61892)

Medical Officers

BERRY OBE, MB Royal Army Medical Corps. Major Winslow Seymour Sterling (He also used the surname Sterling Berry.) Born on 8 June 1880. Son of Thomas Sterling Berry, Bishop of Killaloe and Clonfert. Graduated from Trinity College, Dublin in 1904. An officer of the 1st (Armagh) Battalion, Armagh Regiment, Ulster Volunteer Force. Commissioned into the Royal Army Medical Corps as a Lieutenant on 29 October 1914. Joined the 9th Royal Irish Fusiliers as Medical Officer in early 1915. To France with 36th (Ulster) Division in October 1915. 1914-15 Star. Captain 29 October 1915. **Mention in Despatches**. Left in May 1917 to take up an appointment on the Staff of X Corps as Deputy Assistant Director of Medical Services. Major 25 February 1918. Served in the Army of Occupation at Headquarters British Army of the Rhine. **OBE (Military).** ***Croix de Guerre*** **(Belgium).** Relinquished his commission 14 October 1919. Served as the chief medical inspector to the Irish Local Government Board from December 1919 and later the Deputy Chief Medical Adviser to the Department of Local Government and Public Health in the Irish Free State and Ireland until his retirement in April 1946. Died 9 January 1948, aged 67, at Clonfert, County Galway. Uncle of Private Charles Seymour Gallogly, who lived with Berry and his family at Richhill, County Armagh in the years before the war.

BROWN MB Royal Army Medical Corps. Captain C R Commissioned into the Royal Army Medical Corps as a Lieutenant 9 October 1916. Captain 15 January 1918. Served as the Medical Officer with 9th Royal Irish Fusiliers throughout July 1918 vice Lieutenant F G McGuinness.

BURROWS MC, MB Royal Army Medical Corps. Captain Oswald Vincent Born in 1884 at Dublin. Graduated MB from Trinity College, Dublin in 1912. Commissioned into the Royal Army Medical Corps as a Lieutenant on 2 December 1915 and joined 108th Field Ambulance on 6 February 1916. Captain 2 December 1916. Succeeded Captain W S S Berry as Medical Officer for the 9th Royal Irish Fusiliers in May 1917. Awarded an **MC** for his actions at the Battle of Langemarck on 16 August 1917. He remained with the 9th Royal Irish Fusiliers until January 1918. Practised medicine in Sheffield and Wakefield after the war. Died in early 1953 in Nottingham.

McGUINNESS MD Canadian Army Medical Corps. Lieutenant Frederick Gallagher Born on 25 October 1891 at Ottawa, Ontario, Canada. Lived in Winnipeg, Manitoba, Canada. Graduated MD in 1917 from the University of Manitoba and was a Lieutenant in the Officer Training Corps. Commissioned as a Lieutenant into the Canadian Army Medical Corps 3 December 1917. Appointed Lieutenant, Royal Army Medical Corps on 19 February 1918 and deployed to France on 23 March 1918. Joined 108th Field Ambulance and served as the Medical Officer with 9th Royal Irish Fusiliers throughout May and June 1918. Relinquished his commission 14 April 1919. After the war studied in Dublin and Glasgow. Lecturer in Obstetrics

H S Morgan

1923-24; Assistant Professor 1929-38; Associate Professor 1939-40; Professor 1941-45; Professor and Director 1946-51 in the Department of Obstetrics, Winnipeg General Hospital. Died in Brandon, Manitoba, Canada on 21 May 1968, aged 77.

MORGAN MC, MD United States Army Medical Reserve Corps. Lieutenant Harold Sydney (Syd) Born on 2 May 1890 at Winton, Pennsylvania to Welsh and English parents. Studied at Stanford University School of Medicine, Palo Alto, California until 1912 (Phi Delta Theta) and at Johns Hopkins University School of Medicine, Baltimore, from which he graduated as a doctor in 1915. Practised at Bellview Hospital, New York. Commissioned as a Lieutenant in the United States Army Medical Reserve Corps in New York on 9 August September 1917. Posted first to United States Army Base Hospital Number 2, France and then Presbyterian Base Hospital Unit Number 1, France. Joined the 9th Royal Irish Fusiliers as the Medical Officer in February 1918 vice Captain O V Burrows. Awarded an **MC** for his actions with the 9th Royal Irish Fusiliers during the withdrawal from St Quentin in March 1918. **Killed in action** at Wulverghem on 12 April 1918, aged 28. Commemorated on the City of San Diego and San Diego County Memorial Roll.

RICHMAN MD United States Army Medical Reserve Corps. Captain Samuel Herbert Born in 1884 at Oak Forest, Chicago, Illinois. Studied medicine at Northwestern University. MD 1909. Served as a physician at South Dakota State Hospital (Insane Asylum), Yankton. Commissioned as a Lieutenant in the United States Army Medical Reserve Corps 29 July 1916. Served in France from mid-1917 and was attached to the Royal Army Medical Corps in an orthopaedic unit from 12 August 1917. He then joined 108th Field Ambulance and was attached to the 9th Royal Irish Fusiliers as Medical Officer throughout September 1917 while Captain O V Burrows was on leave. He also served with 13th (Service) Battalion, The Royal Irish Rifles (1st County Down), 110th Field Ambulance and 2nd Battalion, The Inniskilling Fusiliers. In February 1919 he requested permission to remain in Great Britain to study medicine at Edinburgh or London. After the war he practised in Kansas City, Missouri, before returning to Chicago and taking up a post at the University of Illinois as an Assistant in Radiography and subsequently an instructor in the Department of Roentgenology.

SOWERBY MC, MB Royal Army Medical Corps. Major Edward Seguier Born in 1889 in China to missionary parents. Schooled in Bristol and graduated MB from London University 1913. Served as a doctor at Bristol Royal Infirmary, Portsmouth Royal Hospital and, briefly, in China. Commissioned into the Royal Army Medical Corps as a Lieutenant on 30 August 1915. Joined 108th Field Ambulance on 29 July 1916. Captain 30 August 1916. Attached as Medical Officer throughout December 1916 while Captain W S S Berry was on leave. He served with all of the battalions in 108th Brigade at some time. Awarded an **MC** for his actions as a Medical Officer with 108th Field Ambulance during the Battle of Langemarck on 16 August 1917. Recommended, unsuccessfully, for a Bar to his MC by the Commanding Officer of 108th Field Ambulance for his conduct during the withdrawal in March 1918. Major 2 September 1918 and posted to 109th Field Ambulance. Relinquished his commission on 8 August 1919. He emigrated to South Africa in 1919 to take advantage of the climate due to a gas injury. Although seriously ill, he practised as a doctor at Peddie and Stutterheim. Returned to England in May 1932 but his injuries forced his return to South Africa. Died in Walmer, Port Elizabeth, South Africa 20 November 1933, aged 44.

SUTCLIFFE MC, MB Royal Army Medical Corps. Captain William Henry Born in 1884 at County Kildare. Graduated MB from Trinity College, Dublin in 1908. Travelled in South Africa before the war, returned to England in 1914 and was commissioned into the Royal Army Medical Corps as a Lieutenant on 21 September 1914. Deployed to France in June 1915. 1914-15 Star. Captain 21 September 1915. Served with 104th Field Ambulance in 34th Division. Awarded an **MC** for his actions when attached to 103rd Field Ambulance in 34th Division on 27/28 July 1918. Joined the 9th Royal Irish Fusiliers as Medical Officer in August 1918 vice Captain C R Brown, and remained there until the end of the war. Practiced medicine in Pembrokeshire and in Wimbledon, the latter throughout the Second World War. Subsequently in 1947 took up a practice in Raglan, Monmouthshire. Retired in 1958. Died at Romsey, Kent 23 January 1964, aged 79. His eldest son, Lieutenant Charles Francis (Chug) Sutcliffe died, aged 21, in North Africa on 5 January 1943 serving with the 1st Battalion, The Royal Irish Fusiliers (Princess Victoria's). His younger son, Brigadier M W Sutcliffe OBE, also served with the 1st Battalion, The Royal Irish Fusiliers (Princess Victoria's) during the Second World War and had a distinguished career thereafter.

Chaplains

ALLMAN. Chaplain to the Forces 4th Class William Brown Born in 1877 at Belfast. Studied at Trinity College, Dublin. Curate Armagh City 1902-05, Rector of Killeavy 1905-06, Rector of Milltown 1906-14, Rector of Clonfeacle 1914-18. Chaplain of Royal Black Preceptory 502 1909-1919. Signed the Ulster Covenant 28 September 1912. Commanded 'I' Company, 1st (Armagh) Battalion, Armagh Regiment, Ulster Volunteer Force. Volunteered for service with the Army Chaplains Department after a request from Reverend F J Halahan MC, an old friend. Chaplain in 36th (Ulster) Division to the Machine Gun Corps from 4 to 25 June 1918. Succeeded Reverend H S Bally as Chaplain to the 9th Royal Irish Fusiliers from 26 June 1918, where he served for the remainder of the war. Released from service on 3 March 1919 and returned to his parish at Clonfeacle. Relinquished his commission on 3 June 1919 and was appointed Honorary Chaplain to the Forces, 4th Class. Died in 1958, aged 81. (WO 374/1273)

BALLY MC. Chaplain to the Forces 4th Class Harold Spencer Born in July 1877 at Walton on the Hill, Lancashire. Schooled at the Birkenhead Institute. Graduated BSc from the University of Manchester in 1898 and granted the same degree from the University of Liverpool 1911. A Church of England priest, he volunteered for service with the Army Chaplains Department and was appointed Chaplain to the Forces 4th Class on 7 January 1918. Succeeded Reverend S Mayes as Chaplain to the 9th Royal Irish Fusiliers from 26 January 1918 to 25 June 1918. Awarded an **MC** for his actions at Wulverghem on 13 April 1918. Continued to serve in the Ulster Division as the Chaplain with 110th Field Ambulance from the end of June 1918. He was released from service on 22 November 1919 and relinquished his commission on 19 January 1920. Appointed Honorary Chaplain to the Forces 4th Class. Canon and Rector of Burgh St Margaret, Norfolk 1920-1927. Rector at Needham, St. Peter's Church, Norfolk 1927. Retired to Haywards Heath, West Sussex. Died in 1949. His son, Captain John Harold Bally, was killed in action in Germany on 25 April 1945 serving with the 6th Battalion, The Royal Sussex Regiment. (WO 374/3610)

HALAHAN MC*. Chaplain to the Forces 3rd Class Francis Johnston (Frank) Born on 18 November 1870 at Berehaven, County Cork. Studied at Trinity College, Dublin. Captain University Rowing Club 1892-93. Curate Assistant of Drumcree, County Armagh 1894-95. Rector of Mullaglass, County Down 1895-1905. Rector of Drumcree, County Armagh 1905-48. Signed the Ulster Covenant 28 September 1912. Having volunteered for service with the Army Chaplains Department, he joined the 9th Royal Irish Fusiliers in England on 23 September 1915. To France with 36th (Ulster) Division in October 1915. 1914-15 Star. Appointed Chaplain to the Forces 3rd Class and Senior Divisional Chaplain on 28 November 1916. Left the 9th Royal Irish Fusiliers on 22 March 1917 for Chaplains' School and then Divisional Headquarters. **Mention in Despatches** and awarded an **MC** for his gallantry during his service with the 9th Royal Irish Fusiliers. Praised for his courage while with 110th Field Ambulance in June 1917. Awarded a Bar to his **MC** for

his actions at the Battle of Langemarck on 16 August 1917 when the Divisional Chaplain. **Wounded** (gassed) at Neuve Eglise on 6 September 1918 and evacuated to hospital in England. **Mention in Despatches**. Relinquished his commission 1 September 1921 and appointed Honorary Chaplain to the Forces 4th Class. Returned to Drumcree Rectory where he served until he retired in 1948. He married on 11 August 1948, aged 77. Died 6 October 1951, aged 80. Buried at Drumcree Parish Church. (WO 374/30060)

MAYES. Chaplain to the Forces 4th Class Samuel Born in 1877. Rector at Kilmore Rectory, Richhill, County Armagh. An officer of the Crossmaglen Company, 2nd (South Armagh) Battalion, Armagh Regiment, Ulster Volunteer Force. Signed the Ulster Covenant 28 September 1912. Volunteered for service with the Army Chaplains Department and was appointed Chaplain to the Forces 4th Class in December 1916. Joined 110th Field Ambulance on 18 January 1917. Succeeded Reverend F J Halahan as Chaplain to the 9th Royal Irish Fusiliers on 22 March 1917. Chaplain during the Battle of Langemarck. Returned to Ireland and was released from service on 9 January 1918. Became the curate of Diamond Grange Parish Church, County Armagh from 1917 until his retirement in 1946. Canon of Armagh Cathedral. (WO 339/134484)

Soldiers of the Battalion Commissioned and Served Elsewhere

Below are listed twenty-five men who were commissioned from ranks of the 9th Royal Irish Fusiliers and who served elsewhere. The details of the service of five men who were commissioned after the war are contained in their entries in Appendix 6:

Former Private R A Dynes was commissioned in 1953 into The Black Watch (Royal Highland Regiment) of Canada.

Former Company Quartermaster Sergeant T Gray was commissioned into the Ulster Home Guard during the Second World War.

Former Sergeant F S Homersham DCM, MM* was commissioned in 1925 into the Royal Air Force.

Former Lance Corporal R D Meredith was commissioned in 1943 into the Territorial Army Reserve of Officers Special List for service in Northern Ireland with the Army Cadet Force.

Former Lance Corporal H J Uprichard was commissioned in 1943 into the Territorial Army Reserve of Officers Special List for service in Northern Ireland with the Army Cadet Force.

ANNESLEY. Second Lieutenant Hugh Alexander Born on 12 February 1891 at Belfast. He was employed as a warehouseman when he enlisted on 23 May 1915 into the North Irish Horse (1589). To France with 'F' Squadron in 33rd Division 17 November 1915. 1914-15 Star. Served with 2nd North Irish Horse, X Corps Cavalry Regiment. Joined the 9th Royal Irish Fusiliers from 36 Infantry Base Depot and transferred to Princess Victoria's (Royal Irish Fusiliers) in September/October 1917 (renumbered 41538 - Private). He joined 7th Officer Cadet Battalion at Fermoy on 8 February 1918. He was commissioned into The Royal Irish Rifles on 26 June 1918 and joined the 12th (Service) Battalion, The Royal Irish Rifles (Central Antrim). Released from service 5 February 1919. He relinquished his commission on 1 September 1921. (WO 374/1891)

ARMSTRONG. Second Lieutenant Henry Tottenham (Tottie) Born on 28 October 1897 the son of a farmer from Fivemiletown, County Tyrone. Enlisted in November 1914 into the Service Squadron of the 6th (Inniskilling) Dragoons (UD/162). To France with 36th (Ulster) Division in

October 1915. 1914-15 Star. Served with 2nd North Irish Horse, X Corps Cavalry Regiment. Joined the 9th Royal Irish Fusiliers from 36 Infantry Base Depot and transferred to Princess Victoria's (Royal Irish Fusiliers) in September/October 1917 (renumbered 41122 - Lance Corporal). Commissioned into Princess Victoria's (Royal Irish Fusiliers) on 26 June 1918. He died in Belfast on 19 December 1985, aged 88. His younger brother, Captain John Andrew Armstrong, served with the Royal Regiment of Artillery in the Second World War; he was evacuated from Dunkirk and later Mentioned in Despatches.

BROWN. Second Lieutenant William Born in 1886. From Cootehill, County Cavan. A bank clerk, he enlisted on 28 May 1915 into the 9th Royal Irish Fusiliers (19947) and joined 'C' Company. To France with 36th (Ulster) Division in October 1915. 1914-15 Star. To hospital April/May 1916. Detached to the Quartermaster's Stores and did not take part in the attack at Hamel on 1 July 1916. Corporal 17 July 1916. To England in December 1916 and joined 2nd Officer Cadet Battalion at Pembroke College, Cambridge. Commissioned into The Royal Munster Fusiliers on 1 March 1917. **Killed in action** on 1 March 1918 while attached to the 2nd Battalion, The Royal Inniskilling Fusiliers in 109th Brigade, aged 22. (WO 339/83295)

BYRNE. Second Lieutenant Edward Enlisted into the 6th (Inniskilling) Dragoons (4989). To France 1 July 1916. Served with 2nd North Irish Horse, X Corps Cavalry Regiment. Joined the 9th Royal Irish Fusiliers from 36 Infantry Base Depot and transferred to Princess Victoria's (Royal Irish Fusiliers) in September/October 1917 (renumbered 41634). Commissioned directly for service in the field into The Duke of Edinburgh's (Wiltshire Regiment) on 23 August 1918. **Wounded**. Lieutenant 23 February 1920. Placed on the half pay list 26 May 1920 on account of ill-health caused by wounds. He emigrated to Verdun, Montreal, Canada.

DICKSON. Lieutenant James Henry Born in 1887. From Portadown, County Armagh. Member of 4th (Portadown) Battalion, Armagh Regiment, Ulster Volunteer Force. Enlisted into the 9th Royal Irish Fusiliers (14127) in September 1914. To France with 36th (Ulster) Division in October 1915. 1914-15 Star. 'C' Company. Promoted Sergeant. Survived the attack at Hamel on 1 July 1916 unwounded. Commissioned into Princess Victoria's (Royal Irish Fusiliers) on 29 May 1917 and joined the 7th/8th (Service) Battalion. **Wounded** by a gunshot to the hand and **captured** at the Battle of Langemarck 16 August 1917. Lieutenant 30 November 1918. Repatriated 12 December 1918. Relinquished his commission 6 March 1919. He lived in Tandragee after the war. Brother of Captain George Clawson Dickson.

DUNWOODY. Lieutenant John Myles Born on 20 October 1896 at County Monaghan. From Bessbrook, County Armagh. He enlisted on 16 September 1914 into the 9th Royal Irish Fusiliers (14151). Promoted Corporal. Commissioned into The Royal Dublin Fusiliers on 9 April 1915. **Died** on 4 May 1917, aged 20. He was en route to Salonika to join the 6th (Service) Battalion, The Royal Dublin Fusiliers when the troopship SS Transylvania was sunk by two torpedoes from U63 off Cape Vado, Italy. There were 412 casualties: 402 military and ten crew members. (WO 339/41011)

ELLISON. Second Lieutenant Joseph From Belfast. Enlisted into the North Irish Horse (1017) in August 1914, probably a re-enlistment. To France 20 August 1914 with 'C' Squadron as 5th Division Cavalry and then as GHQ Troops. 1914 Star with clasp. Served with 2nd North Irish Horse, X Corps Cavalry Regiment. Joined the 9th Royal Irish Fusiliers from 36 Infantry Base Depot and transferred to Princess Victoria's (Royal Irish Fusiliers) in September/October 1917 (renumbered 41566 - Sergeant). Commissioned into The Royal Inniskilling Fusiliers on 14 October 1918. Relinquished his commission 21 January 1920.

ESPIE. Lieutenant Thomas Fletcher Born on 2 June 1895 at Portadown, County Armagh. Attended Lurgan College and on leaving became an apprentice in the handkerchief trade. Signed the Ulster Covenant on 28 September 1912. Member of 4th (Portadown) Battalion, Armagh Regiment, Ulster Volunteer Force. Enlisted into the 9th Royal Irish Fusiliers (14155) in September 1914. To France with 36th (Ulster) Division in October 1915 in 5 Platoon, 'B' Company. 1914-15 Star. Survived the Somme attack unwounded. Promoted Sergeant on 2 July

1916. Joined 2nd Officer Cadet Battalion at Pembroke College, Cambridge in early December 1916. Commissioned into Princess Victoria's (Royal Irish Fusiliers) on 28 March 1917. Joined the 5th/6th (Service) Battalion, Princess Victoria's (Royal Irish Fusiliers) in the Middle East in May/June 1917. Attached to the Royal Flying Corps, he was in flight training at Number 3 School of Aeronautics, Aboukir, Egypt when he fell ill with malaria and dysentery. After a stay in hospital in Cairo he returned to 5th/6th (Service) Battalion, Princess Victoria's (Royal Irish Fusiliers) in France. Lieutenant 28 September 1918. After returning to Ireland he fell ill again with malaria in early 1919, developed pneumonia and **died** on 6 February 1919, aged 23. (WO 339/83269)

FULTON OBE. Lieutenant Colonel James Norman Born on 24 April 1895 at Woodvale, Belfast. He enlisted on 8 February 1915 into 'E' Squadron, North Irish Horse (1442). To France with 'F' Squadron in 33rd Division 17 November 1915. 1914-15 Star. Served with 2nd North Irish Horse, X Corps Cavalry Regiment. Joined the 9th Royal Irish Fusiliers from 36 Infantry Base Depot and transferred to Princess Victoria's (Royal Irish Fusiliers) in September/October 1917 (renumbered 41207). 'D' Company. **Wounded** at Moeuvres on 23 November 1917 and evacuated to hospital in Ireland. He joined 7th Officer Cadet Battalion at Fermoy on 5 April 1918 and was commissioned into The Royal Inniskilling Fusiliers on 25 September 1918. Released from service on 25 January 1919. Served as an officer with Queen's University, Belfast Officer Training Corps. Stood as an Ulster Unionist candidate in Belfast Shankill in 1933 and 1938. As Lieutenant Colonel commanded the 4th Belfast Battalion of the Ulster Home Guard. **OBE (Military)**. (WO 374/26050)

GORDON. Lieutenant Arthur John Born in 1880. From Belfast, married with nine children. He enlisted into the 9th Royal Irish Fusiliers on 31 October 1914 (17149). To France with 36th (Ulster) Division in October 1915. 'A' Company. 1914-15 Star. Lance Corporal 11 November 1915. Corporal 30 September 1916. Spent some time at 108th Field Ambulance in 1916/17 with influenza and appendicitis. Joined 20th Officer Cadet Battalion at Crookham, Aldershot on 17 April 1917 and was commissioned into The Royal Inniskilling Fusiliers on 31 July 1917. Relinquished his commission 1 September 1921. (WO/339/103313)

GORRIE. Second Lieutenant Thomas Robert Born on 5 December 1891 at Oban, Scotland. He served with Forth Royal Garrison Artillery (Territorial Force) in Edinburgh from 1908 to 1913. A certified accountant in Paris, he enlisted there on 22 February 1916 and joined the North Irish Horse (2122) in Antrim in March 1916. Joined 2nd North Irish Horse, X Corps Cavalry Regiment on 3 April 1917. Transferred to Princess Victoria's (Royal Irish Fusiliers) in September/October 1917 and joined the 9th Royal Irish Fusiliers (renumbered 41313 - Private). 'C' Company. He joined 9th Officer Cadet Battalion in Gailes, Ayrshire on 24 March 1918 and was commissioned into the Machine Gun Corps on 29 October 1918. Released from service 9 February 1919. Relinquished his commission 1 September 1921. Spent some time in Brussels. Died in Westminster, London in 1973, aged 81. (WO 374/28175)

HOOD. Second Lieutenant Samuel Victor Born on 26 June 1897 at Dungannon, County Tyrone; he worked in the linen trade in Belfast. He enlisted on 25 November 1915 into the North Irish Horse (1967). Served with 2nd North Irish Horse, X Corps Cavalry Regiment. Lance Corporal 29 November 1916. Joined the 9th Royal Irish Fusiliers from 36 Infantry Base Depot and transferred to Princess Victoria's (Royal Irish Fusiliers) in September/October 1917 (renumbered 41558 - Lance Corporal). He joined 7th Officer Cadet Battalion at Fermoy and was commissioned into The Royal Inniskilling Fusiliers on 30 July 1918. Transferred to The Hampshire Regiment. Lieutenant 31 January 1920. Relinquished his commission 3 April 1920. (WO 374/34499)

MILNE MC. Captain Charles William Born on 24 December 1884 at Applegarth, Dumfriesshire. He enlisted into the 9th Royal Irish Fusiliers on 7 October 1914 (15865). Lance Corporal 1 December 1914. Corporal 20 March 1915. Company Quartermaster Sergeant 26 June 1915. To France with 36th (Ulster) Division in October 1915. 1914-15 Star. Warrant Officer Class II, Regimental Quartermaster Sergeant 15 September 1916 (vice RQMS G W Wilson). Recommended for a commission by Lieutenant Colonel Blacker in January 1917. He left the 9th Royal Irish Fusiliers in February 1917 and joined 11th Officer Cadet Battalion at

Pirbright on 14 March 1917. Commissioned into The Royal Inniskilling Fusiliers on 27 June 1917. Served with the 9th (Service) Battalion, The Royal Inniskilling Fusiliers (County Tyrone) and then 109th Brigade Trench Mortar Battery. Acting Captain 25 March 1918 to command 109th Brigade Trench Mortar Battery. Lieutenant 27 December 1918. Released from service 31 October 1919. Relinquished his commission on 1 January 1921. **MC**, **Mention in Despatches**, ***Croix de Guerre* (Belgium)**. (WO 339/97797)

PALMER MM. Captain William Herbert (Herbie) Born on 11 November 1894 at Portadown, County Armagh. 4th (Portadown) Battalion, Armagh Regiment, Ulster Volunteer Force. Played football for Portadown Olympic (vice-captain/captain). Worked as a clerk for Hamilton Robb Ltd. He enlisted into the 9th Royal Irish Fusiliers on 15 September 1914 (14601). Initially served in 'D' Company as a signaller. Lance Corporal 3 April 1915. Corporal 29 May 1915. To France with 36th (Ulster) Division in October 1915. 1914-15 Star. Sergeant 2 April 1916. 'C' Company. Appointed Battalion Scout Sergeant. Earned an MM at Hamel in May 1916, the first award to a man of the 9th Royal Irish Fusiliers for his work as a Scout (see Sergeant F Foster). He returned to Ireland and joined the 10th (Reserve) Battalion on 26 October 1916. He joined 7th Officer Cadet Battalion on 9 November 1917 and was commissioned into The Royal Irish Regiment on 26 March 1918. Joined the 7th (South Irish Horse) Battalion in 21st Brigade, 30th Division, where he spent the remainder of the war. Relinquished his commission 19 September 1919. After the war he became an accountant and lived at Finaghy, Belfast (he named his house 'Garryowen'). During the Second World War he was promoted to Captain and served as Officer Commanding 'C' Company, 4th (Belfast) Battalion, Ulster Home Guard. Died on 18 February 1974, aged 79. Buried at Dundonald Cemetery. His brother, Private Wesley George Palmer, served with The Royal Irish Rifles. (WO 339/118297)

PAMENTER DCM. Second Lieutenant Walter Richard Born in February 1889 at London. A tailor's cutter in Walthamstow, he enlisted into 1/7th (City of London) Battalion, The London Regiment (Territorial Force) (1201) on 16 February 1912. Mobilised and joined 1/7th (City of London) Battalion, The London Regiment (renumbered 350085). Remained in England as an instructor (Acting Sergeant). To France 3 November 1916. At the Infantry Base Depot he was attached to Princess Victoria's (Royal Irish Fusiliers) on 23 November 1916 and joined the 9th Royal Irish Fusiliers (renumbered 43351 – Lance Corporal). 'C' Company. Discharged from the Territorial Force and transferred to Princess Victoria's (Royal Irish Fusiliers) in March/April 1917. Corporal 12 April 1917. Sergeant 17 August 1917 (vice Sergeant R J Wolfe who was killed). Earned a **DCM** during the Havrincourt raid on 3 November 1917. To England on 15 January 1918 and joined 5th Officer Cadet Battalion at Cambridge on 5 April 1918. Commissioned into the Machine Gun Corps on 29 October 1918. Died in London in late-1966, aged 77. His father, Driver Walter Richard Pamenter, enlisted into the Commissariat Transport Corps in 1883, served in Egypt in 1884/5 (Egypt Medal) and was discharged to the Army Reserve in 1895. He re-enlisted in February 1915 into the Army Service Corps and was discharged in April 1917 as no longer physically fit for war service. Silver War Badge (number 270761). His brother, Rifleman Thomas George Pamenter, was wounded serving with the King's Royal Rifle Corps and discharged in February 1917 as no longer physically fit for war service. Silver War Badge (number 140730). He died in 1918. His brother, Private Edwin John Pamenter, served with The London regiment and the Labour Corps. (WO 374/52038)

PERCY. Second Lieutenant Samuel Ernest Born on 13 February 1898 at Shankhill, Belfast. He enlisted on 9 November 1914 into the Service Squadron of 6th (Inniskilling) Dragoons (UD/121). To France with 36th (Ulster) Division in October 1915. 1914-15 Star. Lance Corporal 17 November 1915. Served with 2nd North Irish Horse, X Corps Cavalry Regiment. Joined the 9th Royal Irish Fusiliers from 36 Infantry Base Depot and transferred to Princess Victoria's (Royal Irish Fusiliers) in September/October 1917 (renumbered 41150). 'B' Company. He joined 7th Officer Cadet Battalion at Fermoy on 8 February 1918 and was commissioned into Princess

Victoria's (Royal Irish Fusiliers) on 30 July 1918. Attached to the 1st (Reserve) Garrison Battalion, The Highland Light Infantry. Transferred to the General List 14 November 1918 for employment as a Staff Lieutenant Class III. Staff Lieutenant Class II 29 March 1919. Lieutenant 12 May 1919 (with seniority 1 September 1918). Relinquished his commission 1 September 1921. Lived in Belfast. (WO 374/53451)

PLEASANCE. Second Lieutenant Wilfred Born on 24 February 1878 and worked as a commercial clerk in London. He enlisted on 14 July 1916 into 3/7th Battalion, The London Regiment (6699). At the Infantry Base Depot, he was attached to Princess Victoria's (Royal Irish Fusiliers) on 23 November 1916 and joined the 9th Royal Irish Fusiliers (renumbered 43317). Discharged from the Territorial Force and transferred to Princess Victoria's (Royal Irish Fusiliers) in March/April 1917. He joined 5th Officer Cadet Battalion at Cambridge on 7 December 1917 and was commissioned into The Royal Fusiliers (City of London Regiment) on 1 May 1918. He joined the 6th (Reserve) Battalion, The Royal Fusiliers (City of London Regiment) in Carrickfergus, County Antrim. Relinquished his commission 24 May 1919. Died in London in 1952, aged 74. (WO 374/54428)

SHEPHERD. Second Lieutenant Oliver Bertrand Born in 1892 at Londonderry, County Londonderry and worked as a clerk in a shirt factory. He enlisted in January 1915 into the 9th Royal Irish Fusiliers (17777). 'C' Company. To France with 36th (Ulster) Division in October 1915. 1914-15 Star. Appointed Lance Corporal. **Wounded** during the attack at Hamel 1 July 1916. Transferred to the Machine Gun Corps (renumbered 106495 - Lance Corporal). Commissioned into the Machine Gun Corps 18 December 1917. Lieutenant Regular Army Reserve of Officers 1 July 1921 (seniority 29 January 1921). He worked in the clothing industry for the Belfast Collar Company and in 1937 he patented a version of the now-common cardboard 'shirt board' that retains shirts in a folded condition.

SMITH. Second Lieutenant James Tennent Born in 1896 at Galashiels and was employed as an engineer. He enlisted on 26 May 1915 into the North Irish Horse (1629). To France with 'F' Squadron in 33rd Division 17 November 1915. 1914-15 Star. Served with 2nd North Irish Horse, X Corps Cavalry Regiment. Joined the 9th Royal Irish Fusiliers from 36 Infantry Base Depot and transferred to Princess Victoria's (Royal Irish Fusiliers) in September/October 1917 (renumbered 41189). Subsequently commissioned into The London Regiment on 25 June 1918. He was released from service on 13 April 1919. (WO 374/63606)

THOMPSON. Second Lieutenant Robert Kirk Enlisted in October 1914 into the Service Squadron of 6th (Inniskilling) Dragoons (UD/73). To France with 36th (Ulster) Division in October 1915. 1914-15 Star. Served with 2nd North Irish Horse, X Corps Cavalry Regiment. Joined the 9th Royal Irish Fusiliers from 36 Infantry Base Depot and transferred to Princess Victoria's (Royal Irish Fusiliers) in September/October 1917 (renumbered 41375). Commissioned on the General List on 2 June 1918. Relinquished his commission 28 April 1919.

TINLEY. Second Lieutenant Cecil Cris Born on 16 May 1892 at Nottingham. He enlisted at Derby into The Sherwood Foresters (Nottinghamshire and Derbyshire Regiment) on 25 September 1914 (17293). To France 14 July 1915. 1914-15 Star. Served with the 13th (Service) and 10th (Service) Battalions, The Sherwood Foresters (Nottinghamshire and Derbyshire Regiment). Attached to the 1st Battalion, The Lincolnshire Regiment. **Wounded** when shot in the thigh on 15 July 1916 and was evacuated via 65th Field Ambulance and 34th Casualty Clearing Station to hospital in Huddersfield. Transferred to Princess Victoria's (Royal Irish Fusiliers) 31 August 1916 having joined the 9th Royal Irish Fusiliers on 8 August 1916 from the Infantry Base Depot (renumbered 43251). Corporal 29 September 1916. **Wounded** in the arm in a grenade accident during the final tests on a bombing course at 36th (Ulster) Division Specialist School on 15 December 1916. Lance Sergeant 25 May 1917. He joined 7th Officer Cadet Battalion at Fermoy on 10 November 1917 and was commissioned into The Sherwood Foresters (Nottinghamshire and Derbyshire Regiment) on 26 March 1918. Joined the 15th (Service) Battalion, The Sherwood Foresters (Nottinghamshire and Derbyshire Regiment) (Nottingham) in 105th Brigade, 35th Division. **Wounded** at Courtrai 20 October 1918 and was evacuated to hospital in London. Released from service 13 January 1919. Relinquished his commission 1 September 1921. He died in Derby in 1949, aged 57. (WO 374/68892)

TURKINGTON MM. Second Lieutenant Alfred Born on 26 December 1892 at Lurgan, County Armagh. He enlisted into the 9th Royal Irish Fusiliers in September 1914 (14720). To France with 36th (Ulster) Division in October 1915. 1914-15 Star. 'C' Company. Company runner during the attack at Hamel on 1 July 1916, which he survived unwounded. Corporal 2 July 1916. Sergeant 7 July 1916 (vice J Bryans who was killed). Earned an **MM** at the Battle of Langemarck on 16 August 1917. He joined 7th Officer Cadet Battalion at Fermoy on 5 April 1918 and was commissioned into The Queen's (Royal West Surrey Regiment) on 25 September 1918. He joined the 11th (Service) Battalion, The Queen's (Royal West Surrey Regiment) (Lambeth) in 123rd Brigade, 41st Division. Released from service on 9 November 1919. Married in Ontario, Canada on 7 June 1922. Settled in New Jersey, USA and became a carpet weaver. Died in London in late 1976, aged 84. Brother of Corporal Ernest Turkington. His brother, Lieutenant Colonel Albert Turkington OBE, served as a regular soldier with the 1st Battalion, Princess Victoria's (Royal Irish Fusiliers) from 1913 and served post war at Dover. He later served in the Ulster Special Constabulary and commanded a battalion of the Ulster Home Guard. (WO 374/69770)

WIDDESS. Second Lieutenant Abraham John Born in 1890. Enlisted into the North Irish Horse (2236) in August 1916. Served with 2nd North Irish Horse, X Corps Cavalry Regiment. Joined the 9th Royal Irish Fusiliers from 36 Infantry Base Depot and transferred to Princess Victoria's (Royal Irish Fusiliers) in September/October 1917 (renumbered 41219). Commissioned into The Prince of Wales's Own (West Yorkshire Regiment) on 25 June 1918. Initially joined the 14th (Reserve) Battalion, The Prince of Wales's Own (West Yorkshire Regiment). Relinquished his commission on 4 September 1919. Died in Surrey in 1964, aged 74.

WILLIAMSON. Lieutenant Hugh Albert Born in 1887 at Withington, Manchester. Lived at Mullabrack House, Markethill, County Armagh. Member of Markethill Company, 4th (Portadown) Battalion, Armagh Regiment, Ulster Volunteer Force. Enlisted into the 9th Royal Irish Fusiliers in September 1914 (14780). Promoted Sergeant. Commissioned (probationary) into The Manchester Regiment Special Reserve of Officers on 3 March 1915; confirmed as Second Lieutenant 4 October 1915. To France 30 June 1915. 1914-15 Star. Attached to the Royal Flying Corps and served with 34 Squadron. **Mentioned in Despatches. Missing** during an operational flight in a BE2e of 9 Squadron on 2 July 1916 and later declared **killed in action** on that date. With him and also killed was Lieutenant I C Macdonell Lord Strathcona's Horse (Royal Canadians), the son of Lieutenant General Sir Archibald Cameron Macdonell KCB, CMG, DSO, Canadian Army and Superintendent, Royal North West Mounted Police. His brother, Major George William Williamson OBE, MC served with The Manchester Regiment and the Royal Air Force. He served during the Second World War and retired as a Group Captain in 1942. (WO 339/5441)

WIMPEY. Second Lieutenant Alan Brooke Born on 16 September 1895 at Hammersmith, London. Enlisted into the 1/7th (City of London) Battalion, The London Regiment (2902 - Corporal). At the Infantry Base Depot, he was attached to Princess Victoria's (Royal Irish Fusiliers) on 23 November 1916 and joined the 9th Royal Irish Fusiliers (renumbered 43372). 'B' Company. Discharged from the Territorial Force and transferred to Princess Victoria's (Royal Irish Fusiliers) in March/April 1917. **Wounded** at the Battle of Langemarck on 16 August 1917. Joined 16th Officer Cadet Battalion at Rhyl on 7 December 1917 and was commissioned into The London Regiment on 29 May 1918. Relinquished his commission 30 September 1921. Lived in London. Commissioned into The Royal Fusiliers (City of London Regiment) 16 November 1939. Lieutenant 26 August 1940. Died at Bromley, Kent in 1983, aged 88. (WO 339/13568)

Officers Posted In But Did Not Join

The following are known to have been posted to the 9th Royal Irish Fusiliers but did not join. Some appear on the nominal rolls attached to the war diary. Ranks are as at the date of posting in:

BAILLIE. Second Lieutenant Peter 2nd North Irish Horse. Posted to the 9th Royal Irish Fusiliers in September 1917 and although it appears that he may have joined on 8 November 1917, he left for England on 13 November 1917 to transfer to the Indian Army Reserve of Officers.

BALLANTINE. Second Lieutenant Frederick Princess Victoria's (Royal Irish Fusiliers). Posted to the 9th Royal Irish Fusiliers but at 'L' Infantry Base Depot fell ill with bronchitis and was evacuated to hospital in England on 25 January 1918.

BEDDINGTON. Captain Frank Maurice Princess Victoria's (Royal Irish Fusiliers). Posted to the 9th Royal Irish Fusiliers in mid-1917 but was attached to 51st (Prisoner of War) Company, Labour Corps.

BENSON. Lieutenant Geoffrey The Royal Irish Rifles. Posted to the 9th Royal Irish Fusiliers on attachment in May 1918 but was evacuated to hospital in England suffering the effects of an old wound.

BRAMSTON-NEWMAN MVO. Major Richard Griffith Oliver 2nd North Irish Horse. Posted to the 9th Royal Irish Fusiliers in September 1917 but was ordered to a Medical Board on 26 October 1917.

CLARK. Lieutenant William James Princess Victoria's (Royal Irish Fusiliers). To France 6 December 1916 posted for duty with the 9th Royal Irish Fusiliers but attached immediately to 108th Brigade Trench Mortar Battery, which he joined after training on 17 March 1917.

EIGHTEEN. Second Lieutenant William George 2nd North Irish Horse. Posted to the 9th Royal Irish Fusiliers in September 1917 but was ordered to a Medical Board on 26 October 1917.

FILGATE. Captain Richard Alexander Baillie 2nd North Irish Horse. Posted to the 9th Royal Irish Fusiliers in September 1917 but at a Medical Board on 10 October 1917 was classified Permanently Unfit.

FORREST. Lieutenant P L F (Not positively identified) Posted to the 9th Royal Irish Fusiliers 4 October 1917 but fell ill and was evacuated to hospital in England on 24 November 1917.

GOULDING. Second Lieutenant Frederick Ernest The Royal Irish Rifles. Posted on attachment to the 9th Royal Irish Fusiliers and joined 'A' Infantry Base Depot on 1 August 1918 where he was accidentally **killed** on 5 August 1918.

HILL-LOWE. Lieutenant Arthur Noel Vernon 2nd North Irish Horse. Posted to the 9th Royal Irish Fusiliers in September 1917 but returned to England on 5 October 1917 injured.

JOHNSTON. Second Lieutenant James Herdman The Royal Irish Rifles. Posted on attachment to the 9th Royal Irish Fusiliers in October 1918 but fell ill and was evacuated to hospital in England on 2 November 1918.

LEADER. Lieutenant Thomas Henry Mowbray 2nd North Irish Horse. Posted to the 9th Royal Irish Fusiliers in September 1917 but returned to England on 15 November 1917 to transfer to the Tank Corps.

MacWILLIAMS. Lieutenant Thomas Alexander 2nd North Irish Horse. Posted to the 9th Royal Irish Fusiliers in September 1917 but returned to England on 22 September 1917 to transfer to the Indian Army Reserve of Officers.

OECKEN. Second Lieutenant Charles Albert John 2nd North Irish Horse. Posted to the 9th Royal Irish Fusiliers but returned to England on 20 September 1917 to transfer to the Indian Army Reserve of Officers.

PALLANT. Second Lieutenant Herbert Charles 2nd North Irish Horse. Posted to the 9th Royal Irish Fusiliers in September 1917 but returned to England on 29 October 1917 to transfer to the Indian Army Reserve of Officers. **Died** at Kain, East Persia 21 February 1920 while serving with the Indian Army Supply and Transport Corps.

SEYMOUR. Second Lieutenant F D 2nd North Irish Horse. Posted to the 9th Royal Irish Fusiliers in September 1917 but at a Medical Board on 10 October 1917 was classified Permanent Unfit.

STEPHENS. Second Lieutenant Frederick William 2nd North Irish Horse. Posted to the 9th Royal Irish Fusiliers in September 1917 but at a Medical Board on 24 September 1917 was classified Permanent Base.

WEBB. Second Lieutenant Richard John Princess Victoria's (Royal Irish Fusiliers). Posted to the 9th Royal Irish Fusiliers in April 1918 but was injured and was evacuated to hospital in England on 1 May 1918.

WILSON. Second Lieutenant F Princess Victoria's (Royal Irish Fusiliers). Posted to the 9th Royal Irish Fusiliers but fell ill and was evacuated to hospital in England on 7 March 1917.

APPENDIX 6

Roll of Warrant Officers, Non-Commissioned Officers & Other Ranks

This appendix lists the men who served with the 9th (Service) Battalion, Princess Victoria's (Royal Irish Fusiliers) (County Armagh) from its formation in September 1914 until the demise of the 9th (North Irish Horse) Battalion, Princess Victoria's (Royal Irish Fusiliers) in June 1919. The make-up of the Battalion changed significantly as the war progressed. That change is explained here.

In describing the movement of men between units, the terminology used is that of the time. Men could be *'detached from'* the 9th Royal Irish Fusiliers and *'attached to'* another unit. In this case a man was temporarily attached to another unit for a particular purpose, but remained on the strength of the 9th Royal Irish Fusiliers. Men were attached to other units for diverse tasks such as service at the headquarters of 36th (Ulster) Division, duty with 108th Brigade Trench Mortar Battery, or service as railway guards. *'Posted'* meant that a man was moved to another battalion or unit of his corps. For men of the 9th Royal Irish Fusiliers this meant joining another battalion of Princess Victoria's (Royal Irish Fusiliers). Those who were evacuated to the United Kingdom sick or wounded, were posted to the 10th (Reserve) Battalion. Those who joined after the disbandment of the 7th/8th Royal Irish Fusiliers were posted to the 9th Royal Irish Fusiliers. *'Transferred'* meant that a man was permanently moved to another corps. The men from other regiments who joined as reinforcement drafts were transferred from their regiments to Princess Victoria's (Royal Irish Fusiliers) and posted to the 9th Royal Irish Fusiliers. Finally, men were *'enlisted'* into the Army or the Territorial Force and *'discharged'* from them. This is pertinent to the Territorial Force reinforcements from The London Regiment. In accordance with the Military Service Acts 1916, they were discharged from the Territorial Force and re-enlisted into the Regular Army for service with Princess Victoria's (Royal Irish Fusiliers) before being formally posted to the 9th Royal Irish Fusiliers, to which many had been attached for some time.

Enlistments in September 1914

The first men to enlist into the County Armagh Battalion did so over six days beginning on 15 September 1914. The men of this draft were allocated regimental numbers in the batch 13950 to 14817 (866 men; two men serving with other battalions were allocated numbers towards the end of this batch). The reported strength of the new battalion formed at Clandeboye Camp on 21 September 1914 was 842 men. Assuming that all of the numbers were allocated, it is likely that some men arrived in the days after the first tally was taken at Clandeboye and before regimental numbers were issued. Of this first draft, 780 men have been identified.

The men of this first draft were all Protestant and many were members of the Ulster Volunteer Force. They were mainly from County Armagh, with the majority from the north of the county around Lurgan and Portadown. There were some men from Counties Cavan and Monaghan, the other traditional recruiting areas for Princess Victoria's (Royal Irish Fusiliers), and some from Counties Down and Antrim, and from Belfast.

Service records show that sixty-six men were discharged before the 9th Royal Irish Fusiliers embarked for France in October 1915. These discharges, in accordance with King's Regulations Paragraph 392, fell into three categories: The first (fifty-six men) were those considered medically unfit for service. For most this was in the first three months of service and resulted from a more detailed medical examination than the cursory check when they attested. These men were discharged as *'not being likely to become an efficient soldier'*. Subsequent to three months in service those considered medically unfit were discharged as *'no longer physically fit for war service'*. The second category were those who enlisted underage. It is evident that many underage (and also overage) enlistments went unremarked, but there were nine discharges for *'having made a mis-statement as to age on enlistment'*. Some of these were as a consequence of parents or their representatives writing to the commanding officer with an entreaty to release the recruit. One man was discharged in accordance with King's Regulations Paragraph 392 for *'misconduct'*.

One man died before the 9th Royal Irish Fusiliers sailed for France—Private J Topley, who drowned in an accident at Seaford. Two men, Privates G A Anderson and S G Dillon, fell ill and did not deploy to France; both died in early 1916.

Six men were commissioned from the ranks of the Battalion before October 1915. Eleven men were found to be unfit for general service as infantry and were posted to the 10th (Reserve) Battalion, to one of the garrison battalions or to the Labour Corps. One man transferred for duty with the Signal Service of the Corps of Royal Engineers and one transferred to the Military Foot Police. For a further forty-one men who enlisted in this batch, there is no record of their deployment to France with 36th (Ulster) Division in October 1915; some may have done so.

Eighty-six of the men in this number batch have not been identified. They have neither a medal index card nor a service record. The other men in this batch for whom there is no medal index card but where a service record does exist, were discharged under King's Regulation Paragraph 392. It is likely that the majority of this group of eighty-eight men was also discharged sometime in the months that followed their enlistment. Others may have been amongst the first officers commissioned, or amongst those listed below by name as serving with the 9th Royal Irish Fusiliers but where no regimental number has been identified.

The remaining 651 men sailed for France in October 1915. 189 of them were killed in action, died of wounds or died of illness, injury or accident.

Enlistments between October 1914 and July 1915

Following the arrival of the first volunteers at Clandeboye, recruiting continued apace. Like the early volunteers, these men were all Protestants—in February 1915 in a Parliamentary written answer, Mr Harold Tennant, the Undersecretary of State, recorded that there were one Roman Catholic officer and thirteen Roman Catholic other ranks in the Ulster Division. Initially, recruits joined the 9th Royal Irish Fusiliers at Clandeboye directly until the formation of the depot company, which became responsible for the basic training of recruits after the Battalion left for Seaford in July 1915. This responsibility passed to the 10th (Reserve) Battalion when it was formed in September 1915. In general, men who enlisted before the 9th Royal Irish Fusiliers moved to Seaford in July 1915, embarked for France with the Battalion in October 1915. Those who enlisted after July

1915 joined as reinforcements from the 10th (Reserve) Battalion.

The absence of complete records makes it impossible to determine exactly the number of men who enlisted into the 9th Royal Irish Fusiliers or the number discharged under King's Regulations in the months that followed their enlistment. The enlistments in this period that have been identified are:

Men who were allocated regimental numbers in the 15000 series (23 men):

- Three former regular soldiers who re-enlisted in September 1914 (15711 Russell, 15718 Mckane and 15719 Cross). All three embarked with the 9th Royal Irish Fusiliers in October 1915.
- Twenty men from County Armagh who enlisted in October 1914 and were allocated regimental numbers in the batch 15848 to 15872 (five other men in this batch are unidentified). Three men were discharged under King's Regulations 392 (one sick, one underage, and one for reasons that remain unknown). Sixteen men embarked with the Battalion in October 1915. One man joined the 9th Royal Irish Fusiliers in France in November 1915.

Men who were allocated regimental numbers in the 16000 series (79 men):

- Sixty men, mainly from Counties Cavan and Monaghan, who enlisted in September/October 1914 and were allocated regimental numbers in the batch 16087 to 16154 (eight other men in this batch are unidentified). The men from Cavan and Monaghan joined 'D' Company. Fifty-seven men deployed to France with the Battalion in October 1915. Two others served in France but their date of embarkation is not known. One man did not serve with the Battalion in France, for reasons that remain unknown.
- Sixteen men, mainly from County Armagh, who enlisted at Clandeboye in the first days of November 1914 and were allocated regimental numbers in the batch 16421 to 16436. One man was unfit for general service and transferred to a garrison battalion. Fourteen men embarked with the 9th Royal Irish Fusiliers in October 1915. One man served in France but his date of embarkation is not known.
- Three other men who enlisted in mid-November 1914; two embarked with the Battalion in October 1915. The service record of one man is unknown.

Men who were allocated regimental numbers in the 17000 series (95 men):

- Four men who enlisted in October 1914 and who were allocated regimental numbers 17069 to 17072; all embarked with the Battalion in October 1915.
- Eight men who enlisted in October/November 1914 and who were allocated regimental numbers 17147 to 17154; seven men embarked with the 9th Royal Irish Fusiliers in October 1915. One man served in France but his date of embarkation is not known.
- Eleven men who enlisted in November/December 1914 and who were allocated regimental numbers in the batch 17395 to 17409 (two other men in this batch are unidentified and two numbers were allocated to men who enlisted into other battalions). Ten men embarked with the Battalion in October 1915. One man served in France but his date of embarkation is not known.
- Fifteen men who enlisted in November/December 1914 and who were allocated regimental numbers in the batch 17540 to 17559 (five other men in this batch are unidentified). One man transferred to the Corps of Royal Engineers. Eleven men

embarked with the 9th Royal Irish Fusiliers in October 1915. One man joined the 9th Battalion in France in November 1915 and two men served in France, but their dates of embarkation are not known.

- Fifteen men who enlisted in December 1914/January 1915 and who were allocated regimental numbers in the batch 17655 to 17672 (three other men in this batch are unidentified). Twelve men embarked with the Battalion in October 1915. Three men served in France, but their dates of embarkation are not known.
- Four men who enlisted in January 1915 and who were allocated regimental numbers 17912 to 17915; all embarked with the Battalion in October 1915.
- Ten men, mainly from County Monaghan, who enlisted in January 1915 and who were allocated regimental numbers in the batch 17927 to 17937 (one number in this batch was allocated to a man who served with the 1st Battalion). Nine men embarked with the Battalion in October 1915. One man served in France, but his date of embarkation is not known.
- Ten men who enlisted in February 1915 and who were allocated regimental numbers 17944 to 17953. One man does not appear to have served in France and was discharged under King's Regulations 392 as no longer physically fit for war service due to sickness. Six men embarked with the Battalion in October 1915. Three men served in France, but their dates of embarkation are not known.
- Eighteen other men who enlisted between October 1914 and April 1915. One man was immediately commissioned. One man was discharged under King's Regulations 392 (sick). Sixteen men embarked with the Battalion in October 1915.

Men who were allocated regimental numbers in the 18000 series (155 men):

- Twenty-three men who enlisted in February 1915 and who were allocated regimental numbers in the batch 18043 to 18070 (five other men in this batch are unidentified but were probably 9th Royal Irish Fusiliers). All embarked with the Battalion in October 1915.
- Five men who enlisted in February 1915 and who were allocated regimental numbers in the batch 18089 to 18094 (one other man in this batch is unidentified). Two men were discharged under King's Regulations 392 (one sick, one underage). Two men embarked with the Battalion in October 1915. One man served in France, but his date of embarkation is not known.
- Twenty-two men who enlisted in February/March 1915 and who were allocated regimental numbers in the batch 18238 to 18261 (two other men in this batch are unidentified but were probably 9th Royal Irish Fusiliers). Nineteen men embarked with the Battalion in October 1915. One man joined the Battalion in France in November 1915 and two men served in France, but their dates of embarkation are not known.
- Three men who enlisted in March 1915 and who were allocated regimental numbers 18273 to 18275; all embarked with the Battalion in October 1915.
- Sixteen men who enlisted in April 1915 and who were allocated regimental numbers in the batch 18548 to 18566 (two other men in this batch are unidentified and one number was allocated to a man who enlisted into the 8th Royal Irish Fusiliers). One man remained behind with the 10th (Reserve) Battalion. Twelve men embarked with the Battalion in October 1915. One man joined the Battalion in France in November 1915 and two men served in France, but their dates of embarkation are not known.
- Four men who enlisted in April 1914 and who were allocated regimental numbers 18607 to 18610; all embarked with the Battalion in October 1915.

- Three men who enlisted in April 1915 and who were allocated regimental numbers 18631 to 18633. Two men embarked with the Battalion in October 1915 and one man joined it in France in November 1915.
- One man who enlisted in April 1915 and who was allocated the regimental number 18649. He served in France, but his date of embarkation is not known.
- Three men who enlisted in April 1915 and who were allocated regimental numbers 18652 to 18654. Two men embarked with the Battalion in October 1915 and one man served in France, but his date of embarkation is not known.
- Five men who enlisted in April 1915 and who were allocated regimental numbers in the batch 18671 to 18676 (one other man in this batch is unidentified); all embarked with the Battalion in October 1915.
- Twenty other men who enlisted between February and April 1915. One man does not appear to have served in France and was discharged under King's Regulations 392 as no longer physically fit for war service due to sickness. Eighteen men embarked with the 9th Royal Irish Fusiliers in October 1915. One man served in France, but his date of embarkation is not known.

Men who were allocated regimental numbers in the 19000 series (30 men):

- Six men who enlisted in April 1915 and who were allocated regimental numbers in the batch 19728 to 19735 (two men in this batch are unidentified); five embarked with the Battalion in October 1915. The other man served in France, but his date of embarkation is not known.
- Five men who enlisted in April 1915 and who were allocated regimental numbers in the batch 19762 to 19766. Two men embarked with the Battalion in October 1915. Three men served in France, but their dates of embarkation are not known.
- Four men who enlisted in May 1915 and who were allocated regimental numbers in the batch 19792 to 19798 (three other men in this batch are unidentified). Two men embarked with the Battalion in October 1915. Two men served in France, but their dates of embarkation are not known.
- Three men who enlisted in May 1915 and who were allocated regimental numbers in the batch 19888 to 19891 (one other man in this batch is unidentified); all embarked with the Battalion in October 1915.
- Twelve other men who enlisted in April and May 1915. Six men embarked with the Battalion in October 1915. Three men joined the 9th Royal Irish Fusiliers in France in November 1915 and three men served in France, but their dates of embarkation are not known.

Men who were allocated regimental numbers in the 20000 series (107 men):

- Nine men who enlisted at the end of May/early June 1915 and who were allocated regimental numbers in the batch 20024 to 20034 (two other men in this batch are unidentified). One man did not serve in France and was discharged under King's Regulations 392 as no longer physically fit for war service due to sickness. Seven men embarked with the Battalion in October 1915. One man served in France, but his date of embarkation is not known.
- Five men who enlisted in June 1915 and who were allocated regimental numbers in the batch 20066 to 20070. All embarked with the Battalion in October 1915.
- Three men who enlisted in June 1915 and who were allocated regimental numbers

20124 to 20126. One was discharged under King's Regulations 392 (underage) and two embarked with the Battalion in October 1915.

- Four men who enlisted in June 1915 and who were allocated regimental numbers in the batch 20212 to 20217 (two other men in this batch are unidentified). One man was discharged under King's Regulations 392 (underage). Three men embarked with the Battalion in October 1915.
- Sixty-eight men who enlisted in May and June 1915. They were allocated regimental numbers in the batch 20292 to 20367 (eight other men in this batch are unidentified but were probably 9th Royal Irish Fusiliers). Many of these men were from Glasgow and County Durham. Twenty-two of these men are known to have transferred from The Royal Inniskilling Fusiliers and one from The Royal Irish Rifles. The other men of this draft are recorded here as having *'enlisted in May/June 1915 and joined the 9th (Service) Battalion with the draft of men from The Royal Inniskilling Fusiliers who transferred to Princess Victoria's (Royal Irish Fusiliers) on 30 June 1915'*. One man was discharged under King's Regulations 392 (underage). Fifty-three men embarked with the Battalion in October 1915. Four men joined the Battalion in France in November 1915 and one in February 1916. Nine men served in France, but their dates of embarkation are not known.
- Eighteen other men who enlisted between May and July 1915. Eight men embarked with the Battalion in October 1915. One man did not deploy to France until February 1916. Nine men served in France, but their dates of embarkation are not known.

In summary, 489 men are definitely known to have enlisted between October 1914 and July 1915 and joined the 9th Royal Irish Fusiliers. Of these, 357 are known to have embarked with the Battalion in October 1915. A further sixty-four men served with the Battalion in France but they rejoined after the main body had arrived, or their dates of embarkation are not known. One hundred and forty-three of these men were killed in action, died of wounds, or died of illness, injury or accident.

Summary of Enlistments Between September 1914 and July 1915

Based on the reported strength of the new battalion formed at Clandeboye Camp on 21 September 1914 (842 men) and the number of enlistments between October 1914 and July 1915 (489 men), the lowest estimate of enlistments up to July 1915 is 1,331 men. Given the block of numbers allocated to the original batch of men and the number of missing records amongst the remainder, the total number of enlistments is likely to have been greater.

Of the 1,331 known enlistments between September 1914 and July 1915, 1,269 men have been identified. The remainder were discharged, or transferred, or were posted elsewhere. Of the men identified, 1,008 are known to have embarked with 36th (Ulster) Division in October 1915, with a further sixty-four men joining later. The war diary of the 9th Royal Irish Fusiliers reported that it landed in France with a strength of 995 other ranks; the discrepancy is a small one and likely to be explained by men on the advance party or detached for duty elsewhere. It is noteworthy that 332 of these men, a little under one third, were killed in action, died of wounds, or died of illness, injury or accident.

Reinforcement Drafts

Until the attack at Hamel on 1 July 1916, small drafts and individual reinforcements arrived from the 10th (Reserve) Battalion. These new men had enlisted in the latter half of 1915 and early 1916 and were from the same Ulster Protestant background as the Battalion's original members. In January 1916 the Military Service Act had been introduced. It allowed for the conscription of men in Great Britain but it did not apply in Ireland. As the number of recruits from Ireland reduced, and the demand for reinforcements increased after 1 July 1916, drafts were found for 36th (Ulster) Division from English regiments and from men compulsorily transferred from the cavalry and support corps for duty as infantry. Nevertheless, the 9th Royal Irish Fusiliers received men from the reserve battalions of Princess Victoria's (Royal Irish Fusiliers) in smaller drafts throughout the war. All the other battalions of Princess Victoria's (Royal Irish Fusiliers) were represented in their numbers. These men were a mix of regular soldiers, men recalled from the Army Reserve, men who had enlisted as Special Reservists, and wartime volunteers. They also represented both Catholic and Protestant communities and, although mainly from County Armagh, they came from all over Ireland. They also reflected the drafts from English regiments that had been transferred to other battalions of Princess Victoria's (Royal Irish Fusiliers), such as the men from The Bedfordshire Regiment who had transferred to the 5th (Service) Battalion in November 1915. Many of those who had seen previous service had recovered from wounds, injury or sickness.

There were nine drafts of reinforcements from men who were transferred to Princess Victoria's (Royal Irish Fusiliers) and who were posted to the 9th Royal Irish Fusiliers.

Draft 1

The Sherwood Foresters (Nottinghamshire and Derbyshire Regiment)

After the attack at Hamel on 1 July 1916, less than 300 men remained to regenerate the 9th Royal Irish Fusiliers. On 8 August 1916 the first draft of English soldiers arrived. This draft comprised men of The Sherwood Foresters (Nottinghamshire and Derbyshire Regiment). The Battalion's war diary reported it as being ninety-men strong. The known men of this draft were allocated regimental numbers in the batch 43195 to 43282 (eighty-eight men); eighty-four men have been identified. Some were newly trained men and others were recovered wounded or sick who had served previously in France, or with the Mediterranean Expeditionary Force. They arrived at the Infantry Base Depot in July 1916 from the 3rd (Reserve) Battalion, The Sherwood Foresters (Nottinghamshire and Derbyshire Regiment) at Sunderland. They were posted from the Infantry Base Depot to the 9th Royal Irish Fusiliers on 8 August 1916, pending transfer, and transferred to Princess Victoria's (Royal Irish Fusiliers) on 31 August 1916.

Draft 2

The London Regiment

The second draft of English soldiers to arrive comprised men of The London Regiment. The war diary records that the full draft was made up of *'34 Irishmen, 102 Englishmen and 1 Russian'*. It is known that the 'Russian' was from The London Regiment. The known men of this batch were allocated regimental numbers in the batch 43305 to 43402 (ninety-eight men). There are sufficient missing regimental numbers on the Medal Roll either side of this batch to indicate that a further five men could have joined and been posted elsewhere later. Ninety-one men of this batch have been identified; eighty-nine from The London Regiment, one from the Machine Gun Corps and one from the Army Service Corps.

Most of this draft were newly trained men from The London Regiment. They were Territorial Force soldiers who had elected to serve overseas—*'to accept liability, in the event of national emergency, to serve in any place outside the United Kingdom, in accordance with the provisions of Section XIII (2) (a) of the Territorial and Reserve Forces Act, 1907.'* They were from either the 3/7th or 3/9th Battalions, The London Regiment, and had been posted to the 1/7th (City of London) Battalion, The London Regiment or to the 1/9th (County of London) Battalion, The London Regiment (Queen Victoria's Rifles). This draft joined the 9th Royal Irish Fusiliers from the Infantry Base Depot on 26 November 1916. In accordance with the Military Service Acts 1916, they were discharged from the Territorial Force and re-enlisted into the Regular Army for service with Princess Victoria's (Royal Irish Fusiliers), most in March or April 1917. Although twelve men are not recorded on medal index cards as being from The London Regiment, it is likely that they were. They are recorded here as having *'joined the 9th (Service) Battalion, Princess Victoria's (Royal Irish Fusiliers) with the draft of men from The London Regiment in November 1916'.*

Draft 3

The Prince of Wales's Own (West Yorkshire Regiment)

The third draft of English soldiers to arrive comprised men of The Prince of Wales's Own (West Yorkshire Regiment). The men of this draft were allocated regimental numbers in the batch 40001 to 40089 (eighty-nine men); all have been identified. Some were newly trained men and others were recovered wounded or sick who had served previously in France or in Egypt. This draft transferred to Princess Victoria's (Royal Irish Fusiliers) at the Infantry Base Depot on 30 November 1916 and joined the 9th Royal Irish Fusiliers on 12 December 1916. Although eighteen men are not recorded on medal index cards as being from The Prince of Wales's Own (West Yorkshire Regiment), it is likely that they were. They are recorded here as having *'joined the 9th (Service) Battalion, Princess Victoria's (Royal Irish Fusiliers) with the draft of men from The Prince of Wales's Own (West Yorkshire Regiment) on 12 December 1916'.*

Draft 4

2nd North Irish Horse

The largest draft to join the 9th Royal Irish Fusiliers since the first men enlisted in September 1914 comprised the men compulsorily transferred for duty as infantry from the disbanded 2nd North Irish Horse, X Corps Cavalry Regiment. The men of this draft were allocated regimental numbers in the batch 41071 to 41645 (575 men); 562 men have been identified. In addition, five men were numbered 41694 to 41698, one man was numbered 41896 and one man was numbered 42295. These men originated in three distinct unit groups. The first comprised those who enlisted directly into the North Irish Horse, either as pre-war Special Reservists or as volunteers after the declaration of war. The second comprised those men who enlisted into the Service Squadron of 6th (Inniskilling) Dragoons and who deployed to France with 36th (Ulster) Division in October 1915 or who had been posted as reinforcements to the Squadron. The third group comprised those who had enlisted into other cavalry regiments and had been posted for duty with 2nd North Irish Horse, X Corps Cavalry Regiment, after it was formed. The majority of this draft joined 36 Infantry Base Depot at Harfleur on 25 August 1917 and joined the 9th Royal Irish Fusiliers in September 1917. A smaller detachment embarked for Egypt with the Regiment's horses on 25 August 1917. With the exception of a few sick men who were evacuated to hospital in England, these men left Egypt in late September 1917 and joined the renamed 9th (North Irish Horse) Battalion on 12 October 1917. All but a few men (those sick or injured who joined later) had transferred to Princess Victoria's (Royal Irish Fusiliers) by mid-October 1917.

Draft 5

7th/8th (Service) Battalion, Princess Victoria's (Royal Irish Fusiliers)

The 7th (Service) and 8th (Service) Battalions, Princess Victoria's (Royal Irish Fusiliers) in 49th Brigade, 16th (Irish) Division had amalgamated in October 1916. The 7th/8th Royal Irish Fusiliers was disbanded in February 1918 and many of its men made up a draft that reinforced the 9th Royal Irish Fusiliers. The war diary of the 9th Royal Irish Fusiliers records that this draft was of 213 men (the war diary of the 7th/8th Royal Irish Fusiliers records it being 220 men). Only 213 men of this draft have been identified due to incomplete medal index cards and service records. This draft comprised men of varying experience, reflecting the make-up of the 7th/8th Royal Irish Fusiliers in early 1918. There were pre-war Special Reservists, men who had enlisted into the 7th and 8th Royal Irish Fusiliers at the beginning of the war, men who had enlisted in the 5th and 6th Royal Irish Fusiliers in 10th (Irish Division) and served with the Mediterranean Expeditionary Force, and new men who had just arrived in France. This draft also included men from the Army Service Corps and English soldiers from The Buffs (East Kent Regiment) who had been transferred previously to the 7th/8th Royal Irish Fusiliers.

Draft 6

The London Regiment

The fourth draft of English soldiers to reinforce the 9th Royal Irish Fusiliers was the second draft from The London Regiment. The men of this draft were allocated regimental numbers in the batches 43431 to 43477 and 45731 to 45821 (138 men); 122 men have been identified. Some were newly trained men and others were recovered wounded or sick who had served previously in France. They arrived in France in March 1918 from the 22nd (Reserve) Battalion, The London Regiment. All were posted for duty with the 1/22nd and 1/24th (County of London) Battalions, The London Regiment (The Queen's). They transferred at 36 Infantry Base Depot to Princess Victoria's (Royal Irish Fusiliers) on 2 April 1918 and joined the 9th Royal Irish Fusiliers on 4 April 1918. Although forty-six men are not recorded on medal index cards as being from The London Regiment, it is likely that most were; however, two are known to have enlisted into the Royal Flying Corps and another had transferred to The Royal Irish Rifles. They are all recorded here as having *'joined the 9th (North Irish Horse) Battalion, Princess Victoria's (Royal Irish Fusiliers) with the draft of men from The London Regiment in April 1918'*.

Draft 7

The Royal Irish Rifles

In April 1918 the 9th Royal Irish Fusiliers also received a small draft of men who had been transferred from The Royal Irish Rifles. The men of this draft were allocated regimental numbers in the batch 49735 to 49748; all fourteen men have been identified. Seven men in this draft are not recorded on medal index cards as being from The Royal Irish Rifles. They are recorded here as having *'joined the 9th (North Irish Horse) Battalion, Princess Victoria's (Royal Irish Fusiliers) with the draft of men transferred from The Royal Irish Rifles in April 1918'*.

Draft 8

Army Service Corps and Army Veterinary Corps

The fifth draft of English soldiers to reinforce the 9th Royal Irish Fusiliers comprised men compulsorily transferred for duty as infantry from the Army Service Corps and the Army Veterinary Corps. The men of this draft were allocated regimental numbers in the batch 42077 to 42289 (213 men); 186 men have been identified. They were allocated regimental numbers in six batches (three Army Service Corps and three Army Veterinary Corps) when they transferred to Princess Victoria's (Royal Irish Fusiliers) at the Infantry Base depot on or about 8 May 1918. They joined the 9th Royal Irish Fusiliers on 8 June 1918. Of the 186 men identified in this draft, 105 were Army Service Corps and sixty-eight were Army Veterinary Corps. Most were experienced soldiers, some being pre-war regulars, and many had served in France with the Mediterranean Expeditionary Force, or in Egypt. Thirteen men in this draft are not recorded on medal index cards as being from either Corps. They comprise one man who served previously with The Duke of Cambridge's Own (Middlesex Regiment), one who served with The Royal Irish Rifles, and eleven of unknown background. They are recorded here as having *'joined the 9th (North Irish Horse) Battalion, Princess Victoria's (Royal Irish Fusiliers) with the draft of men transferred from the Army Service Corps and the Army Veterinary Corps in May 1918'.* A number of men in this draft were transferred to The Royal Irish Rifles on 19 June 1918 having served with the 9th Royal Irish Fusiliers for about ten days.

Draft 9

The Royal Irish Rifles

The last large reinforcement draft comprised men held at the Infantry Base Depot for service with The Royal Irish Rifles (most had been posted to the 2nd Battalion). The men of this draft were allocated regimental numbers in the batch 42430 to 42574 (145 men); 137 men have been identified. This draft transferred to Princess Victoria's (Royal Irish Fusiliers) on 14 September 1918 and joined the 9th Royal Irish Fusiliers on 22 September 1918. Most men of this draft were experienced soldiers, both direct enlistments into The Royal Irish Rifles and men transferred into The Royal Irish Rifles from English regiments and from the Support Corps. Thirty-six men of this draft were new men, most from Ireland, who enlisted into The Royal Irish Rifles in early/mid-1918 and arrived in France in September 1918 from the 3rd (Reserve) Battalion, The Royal Irish Rifles at Larkhill in Wiltshire. Six men in this draft are not recorded on medal index cards as being from The Royal Irish Rifles. They are recorded here as having *'joined the 9th (North Irish Horse) Battalion, Princess Victoria's (Royal Irish Fusiliers) with the draft of men transferred from The Royal Irish Rifles in September 1918'.*

Casualties, Prisoners, Transfers, Postings, Attachments, Commissioning and Discharge

The turnover of men was largely due to casualties; most men left the 9th Royal Irish Fusiliers due to wounds or illness. Having been evacuated to hospital in the United Kingdom, those whose wounds or illness prevented further service were discharged in accordance with King's Regulations Paragraph 392. They were awarded the Silver War Badge (see Appendix 4). Those who recovered from their wounds or illness returned to duty via one of two Irish Command Depots: at Randalstown in County Antrim or Tipperary in County Tipperary, where they were tested for fitness. Once fit for general service, they joined one of the Reserve Battalions of Princess Victoria's (Royal Irish Fusiliers). Some returned to the 9th Royal Irish Fusiliers but many were posted to other battalions, including Garrison Battalions, of Princess Victoria's (Royal Irish Fusiliers) or transferred to other infantry or cavalry regiments for general service. Those not fully fit for general service were transferred to the Corps of Royal Engineers and the supporting services: the Labour Corps, the Army Service Corps, the Army Ordnance Corps, the Army Veterinary Corps, the Royal Army Medical Corps and the Royal Defence Corps.

Some men were captured. Most of those shown below as *'missing'* were captured during the retreat in March 1918. Some, however, found their way back to the 9th Royal Irish Fusiliers after the casualty record was compiled, and others were discovered wounded in the British or French medical systems. Some were later declared as having been killed in action. Those confirmed as having been prisoners of war are indicated as such. Those annotated as *'Captured in 1918'* were captured after March 1918.

Men also left having been attached, posted or transferred to other units. In addition to the transfers of recovered wounded and sick, there were four occasions when batches of men transferred out of the 9th Royal Irish Fusiliers. The men in these batches are shown at the end of this appendix.

Transfer 1

108th Brigade Machine Gun Company

In January 1916 thirty-four men were attached to the new 108th Brigade Machine Gun Company and later transferred to the Machine Gun Corps. These men were allocated new regimental numbers in the batch 17775 to 17808. With the exception of the men who took the Machine Gun Corps regimental numbers 17779 and 17784, all of these men have been identified.

Transfer 2

The Tank Corps

Thirty-nine men left in December 1917 to join the Tank Corps Depot at Wareham in Dorset.

Transfer 3

The Royal Irish Rifles

Sixteen men were transferred to The Royal Irish Rifles in June 1918 to balance numbers across the Battalions of the Ulster Division. Fourteen of these men had joined at the beginning of the month having transferred from the Army Service Corps.

Transfer 4

5th (Service) Battalion, The Royal Irish Regiment (Pioneers)

The final transfer of men was to The Royal Irish Regiment for service with the 5th (Service) Battalion, The Royal Irish Regiment (Pioneers) in the Army of Occupation. Sixty-nine men transferred from the 9th Royal Irish Fusiliers.

Other men left to attend an Officer Training Battalion prior to being commissioned. The pressure caused by officer casualties resulted in a significant number of potential officers being selected from the ranks. Although most of the Battalion's first officers were commissioned immediately on enlistment, some spent a short time in the 9th Royal Irish Fusiliers before their commissions were confirmed. During the course of the war thirty-six soldiers served at some time with the Battalion and were commissioned subsequently. Fourteen were commissioned into Princess Victoria's (Royal Irish Fusiliers) with most of the remainder joining other Irish regiments —six to The Royal Inniskilling Fusiliers, and one each to The Royal Irish Regiment, The Royal Irish Rifles, The Royal Munster Fusiliers and the Royal Dublin Fusiliers. Eight men were commissioned into English regiments—one each into The Queen's (Royal West Surrey Regiment), The Royal Fusiliers (City of London Regiment), The Prince of Wales's Own (West Yorkshire Regiment) and The Sherwood Foresters (Nottinghamshire and Derbyshire Regiment), The Duke of Edinburgh's (Wiltshire Regiment) and The Manchester Regiment, and two into The London Regiment. Three men were commissioned into the Machine Gun Corps and one to the General List. The details for each are at Appendix 5.

Some men were discharged to the Class W, Class T or Class P Reserves during the course of the war. The Class W Reserve (and the Territorial Force Class W(T) Reserve) was introduced in June 1916 for *'those soldiers whose services are deemed to be more valuable to the country in civil rather than military employment'*. The men in these categories were not paid or pensioned by the Army and were liable to be recalled. The Class T Reserve (no Territorial equivalent) was introduced in October 1916 for men in specific skilled trades related largely to munitions production. Similarly, they were not paid or pensioned by the Army and were liable to be recalled. The Class P Reserve (and the Territorial Force Class P(T)) was also introduced in October 1916. These men were *'deemed to be temporarily of more value to the country in civil life rather than in the Army'*. Men in this category, as a result of having served in the Army or Territorial Force, were eligible for a pension on the grounds of disability or length of service. The men transferred to all of these reserve categories were discharged from service in December 1918.

Some men had reached the upper age limit for general service and were also discharged under King's Regulations Paragraph 392. A few men were discharged as part of a disciplinary process, normally following court martial or conviction by a civil court, under the same regulation.

Those who survived the war and were fit enough for continued service, went through the process of demobilisation and were transferred to the Army Reserve (regular soldiers), Special Reserve (special reservists), Territorial Force Reserve (Territorial Force soldiers) or, for the majority, the Class Z Reserve (war duration soldiers). The Class Z Reserve was established on 3 December 1918 to ensure that those who had been engaged for the duration of the war remained available for service in the event of the Armistice failing. It ceased to exist on 31 March 1920 and the men of the Class Z Reserve were discharged as of that date.

In early 1919 some men volunteered for service in the Regular Army. Others re-enlisted after demobilisation; on doing so they were discharged from the Class Z Reserve. Men who had not been transferred to the Class Z reserve or discharged, continued to serve with their original regimental number. Those who had been transferred to the Class Z Reserve or discharged were allocated a new regimental number. In August 1920 Army Order 338 instructed that new army numbers were to be issued to all men from a single series of numbers broken down into regimental blocks. Those serving in The Royal Irish Fusiliers (Princess Victoria's) (renamed in 1920) in the Regular Army or Special Reserve were renumbered in the block of numbers beginning 7040001. Those who re-enlisted but were not renumbered were, therefore, discharged (or had deserted) before September 1920. 104 men are known to have re-enlisted into (or remained in) the Regular Army for service with Princess Victoria's (Royal Irish Fusiliers); they are shown at the end of this appendix, as are twenty-four men who re-enlisted into other regiments.

THE ROLL

The roll below is compiled by surname, rank, forenames and regimental number (the regimental number is that with which the man served in the 9th Royal Irish Fusiliers). Some service numbers have not been identified. The names of former and subsequent units are given in full in order to avoid confusion. Details of previous and subsequent service outside this Battalion are shown within brackets [ ]. In most cases these details are scant, particularly for men who enlisted early in the war and transferred to the 9th Royal Irish Fusiliers much later. All of these records are incomplete. Some men will have served with another battalion before or after being posted to the 9th Royal Irish Fusiliers without it being recorded here. Some men recorded as being posted to the 9th (Service) Battalion may have joined after the Battalion was renamed in September 1917. Some of the men indicated as having served elsewhere may have only received a notice of posting and may not have joined their units before being posted or transferred to the 9th Royal Irish Fusiliers while at the Base Depot. Many men on this roll will have been wounded or fallen ill, but are not recorded as such because there are no surviving records to confirm it. Although it cannot be assumed in every case, those men who transferred to a support corps are likely to have been found unfit for general service as infantry due to wounds or illness. For those killed in action, died of wounds, illness or accident, the place of burial or commemoration by the Commonwealth War Graves Commission is shown in Appendix 2.

Regimental Sergeant Major

(Listed in order of appointment. Note that the rank of Warrant Officer Class I was not established until 1915.)

A STILWELL	22 September 1914 - 23 September 1915	Reduced in rank by District Court Martial
T McKANE	29 September 1915 - 8 November 1916	Evacuated to hospital in England sick.
C H TURNER	8 November 1916 - August 1918	Posted to the 3rd (Reserve) Battalion.
H HICKIE	August 1918	Posted.
G A WILLIAMS	August 1918 - June 1919	

STILWELL Warrant Officer Class II Albert 13524. (On a medal index card his number is recorded incorrectly as 13527.) Born in 1868 at Wandsworth, London. [Enlisted 5 December 1885 into The Royal Irish Regiment (2232). Joined the 1st Battalion 20 July 1888. Lance Corporal 21 July 1888. Corporal 14 December 1888. Lance Sergeant 1 August 1890. Sergeant 25 February 1891. Posted to the 2nd Battalion 10 December 1894. Served in India from 1894 to 1897. Posted back to the 1st Battalion 25 March 1897. Colour Sergeant 19 September 1897. Posted to the Depot as an instructor 15 June 1899. Served with The Royal Irish Regiment contingent at the coronation of King Edward VII. Coronation Medal 1902. Posted to the 4th (Extra Reserve) Battalion on promotion to Company Sergeant Major 17 June 1903. Long Service & Good Conduct Medal 1 October 1904. Discharged at the end of his service 24 June 1908.] Became and innkeeper at The Queen's Head, Dodford, Weedon, Northamptonshire. Re-enlisted 9 September 1914. Appointed Regimental Sergeant Major on the formation of the 9th (Service) Battalion, Princess Victoria's (Royal Irish Fusiliers) (County Armagh) on 22 September 1914. In arrest awaiting trial 18 September

1915 to 23 September 1915. Tried by District Court Martial at Bordon, charged with *'when on active service, drunkenness'*; found guilty and sentenced to be reduced in rank to Warrant officer Class II. [Joined the 10th (Reserve) Battalion 9 October 1915 as a Company Sergeant Major. Posted to the 3rd (Reserve) Garrison Battalion 19 December 1916. Attached to the 1st (Home Service) Garrison Battalion, The Royal Munster Fusiliers at Cork 4 July 1917 as a Company Sergeant Major. Transferred to the Labour Corps (renumbered 336040 Company Sergeant Major) 7 July 1917 and served with 659 Home Service Labour Company. Posted to the Labour Corps Irish Command Labour Centre 12 January 1918 as Company Sergeant Major 'B' Company.] Discharged as no longer physically fit for war service due to sickness 22 May 1918, aged 50. Silver War Badge, number 367847.

McKANE Warrant Officer Class I Thomas 15718. Born in 1871 at Belfast. [Served as a regular soldier for 21 years with The Royal Warwickshire Regiment (5586) and was discharged on 11 March 1910.] A postman in Belfast, he re-enlisted on 12 September 1914. Joined the 9th (Service) Battalion, Princess Victoria's (Royal Irish Fusiliers) (County Armagh) with the rank of Sergeant. Acting Company Sergeant Major 22 September 1914. Promoted Warrant Officer Class II 29 January 1915. Regimental Sergeant Major 29 September 1915 (vice Stilwell). To France with 36th (Ulster) Division in October 1915. Confirmed in rank December 1915. 1914-15 Star. Having been regularly sick but able to remain at duty he was sent to the Field Ambulance hospital in April 1916 (myalgia and rheumatism) and again on 19 October 1916. Evacuated to hospital in England 8 November 1916, when he relinquished his appointment. Posted to the Depot as Regimental Sergeant Major on 9 November 1916 before being posted to the 10th (Reserve) Battalion on 29 November 1916 (there is no indication that RSM E G Tuck relinquished his appointment in the 10th (Reserve) Battalion at this time; see below). Appointed Regimental Sergeant Major of the 3rd (Reserve) Battalion 23 May 1918 where he served briefly until he fell ill again. Discharged as no longer physically fit for war service due to sickness 6 September 1918, aged 46. Silver War Badge, number B8088. Long Service & Good Conduct Medal. Settled in South Norwood, London.

TURNER MC Warrant Officer Class I Charles Henry 17397. Born in 1879 at Birmingham, Warwickshire. [Enlisted into the 4th Battalion (Militia), The Royal Warwickshire Regiment. Re-enlisted in the Regular Army 6 October 1896 (4843). Joined the 2nd Battalion, The Royal Warwickshire Regiment 7 January 1897. Served in South Africa 24 November 1899 to 4 October 1902. Queen's South Africa Medal with clasps - 'Cape Colony', 'Paardeberg', 'Relief of Kimberly', 'Driefontein', 'Johannesburg', 'Diamond Hill' and 'Belfast'. King's South Africa Medal with clasps 'South Africa 1901' and 'South Africa 1902'. Served in Bermuda 5 October 1902 to 29 March 1903, Gibraltar 30 March 1904 to 12 June 1905 and South Africa 13 June 1905 to 16 February 1907. Lance Corporal 7 April 1906. Reverted to Private at his own request 23 May 1907. Transferred to The Cheshire Regiment 9 July 1908 (renumbered 9053 Private). Lance Corporal 21 July 1908. Corporal 29 October 1909. Discharged to the Army Reserve 3 December 1911.] Married 13 December 1910. Settled in Ballynafeigh, Belfast and was employed as a pottery worker. Enlisted into the 9th (Service) Battalion, Princess Victoria's (Royal Irish Fusiliers) (County Armagh) on 2 November 1914 and was immediately promoted Sergeant. Company Sergeant Major, 'C' Company 4 December 1914. To France with 36th (Ulster) Division in October 1915. Regimental Sergeant Major 8 November 1916 (vice McKane). **Wounded** near the right eye 19 February 1917. Regimental Sergeant Major during the Battle of Langemarck 16 August 1917 – **MC**. [Appointed Regimental Sergeant Major at the Depot 16 September 1918. Appointed Regimental Sergeant Major of the 3rd (Reserve) Battalion 15 October 1918 (vice Tuck).] Transferred to the Class Z Reserve 1 December 1919. 1914-15 Star. Long Service & Good Conduct Medal 1 April 1919. During the Second World war he served with 200th Territorial Army Reserve National Defence Company, which became the 6th (Home Defence) Battalion, The Royal Ulster Rifles on 1 November 1939. Company Sergeant Major (numbered D/24706). Died in the Ulster Volunteer Force Hospital, Belfast on 16 April 1940, aged 61, as a result of cardiac failure. Carnmoney Cemetery. H.135.

HICKIE Warrant Officer Class I Henry 42574 & 7042209. Born 9 February 1886 at Bury, Lancashire, the son of Colour Sergeant Henry Hickie The Lancashire Fusiliers. [Enlisted as a regular soldier into The Lancashire Fusiliers (9024). In 1911 he was a Sergeant with the 1st Battalion in India. To France 22 August 1914 with 2nd Battalion, The Lancashire Fusiliers in 12th Brigade, 4th Division as Regimental Sergeant Major. Served in 36th (Ulster) Division when 12th Brigade was attached from November 1915. Transferred to The Royal Irish Rifles (renumbered

9286) 13 February 1916 and joined the 8th (Service) Battalion, The Royal Irish Rifles (East Belfast).] Transferred to Princess Victoria's (Royal Irish Fusiliers) (renumbered 42574) and joined the 9th (Service) Battalion in August 1918 as Regimental Sergeant Major (vice Turner). Posted away soon afterwards. Continued to serve with Princess Victoria's (Royal Irish Fusiliers) after the war with the 2nd Battalion (renumbered 7042209). By 1923 he had transferred to The Gordon Highlanders (retained number 7042209), and was serving with the 2nd Battalion, The Gordon Highlanders.] 1914 Star and clasp. Died at Cambridge on 16 May 1954, aged 68.

WILLIAMS MM Warrant Officer Class I George Alfred 9428 & 7040183. Born on 12 September 1884 at Newport, Monmouthshire. Enlisted in Birmingham 23 October 1906 and joined the 1st Battalion, Princess Victoria's (Royal Irish Fusiliers) in Dublin February 1909. Lance Corporal 15 August 1907. Battalion saddler. Corporal 3 March 1909. Instructor at the Depot, Armagh. Lance Sergeant 20 March 1912. Sergeant 16 January 1914. To France 22 August 1914 as Saddler Sergeant. Requested to join a rifle company. To hospital with hepatitis March 1915. Discharged from hospital in England August 1915 and joined the 3rd (Reserve) Battalion as an instructor with junior officers. Appointed Drill Sergeant Major at Portobello Barracks, Dublin until 23 July 1917. Rejoined the 1st Battalion. Company Sergeant Major 24 March 1918. **MM** – St Quentin March 1918. On the request of Lieutenant Colonel Kelly he joined the 9th (North Irish Horse) Battalion in August 1918. Became Regimental Sergeant Major 16 September 1918 (vice Hickie) until the 9th (North Irish Horse) Battalion was disbanded in June 1919. 1914 Star. ***Chevalier de Ordre de Leopold II*** and ***Croix de Guerre* (Belgium)**. Continued to serve with Princess Victoria's (Royal Irish Fusiliers) after the war as a Warrant Officer Class I (renumbered 7040183). Discharged 22 November 1922. Settled in Walsall, Staffordshire. ***Kruis van de Veteranen van Koning Albert I* (Cross of the Veterans of King Albert I) (Belgium)**. Died 28 June 1975.

Regimental Quartermaster Sergeant

(Listed in order of appointment. Note that the rank of Warrant Officer Class II was not established until 1915.)

T A THWAITES	September 1914 - February 1915	Posted.
G W WILSON	22 February 1915 - 15 September 1916	Appointed Quartermaster.
C W MILNE	15 September 1916 - 3 February 1917	Commissioned.
H FOX	3 February 1917 - 26 August 1917	Wounded & to hospital.
J BARBOUR	27 August 1917 - February 1919	Demobilised.
W GRAY	February 1919 - June 1919	

THWAITES Regimental Quartermaster Sergeant Thomas Albert 3324. Born in 1872 at Portslade, Brighton, Sussex. A baker. Served with the 1st Volunteer Battalion, The Royal Sussex Regiment. Enlisted into The Royal Inniskilling Fusiliers (3324) 18 July 1890. Tried by District Court Martial on 17 February 1891 charged with *'fraudulent enlistment'*; found guilty and sentenced to eighty-four days imprisonment with hard labour. Lance Corporal 21 April 1892. Posted to the 2nd Battalion, The Royal Inniskilling Fusiliers 2 September 1892 and served in India from October 1892 to January 1902. Reverted to Private 25 May 1893. Lance Corporal 19 September 1893. Reverted to Private 7 May 1894. Lance Corporal 27 October 1894. Corporal 28 July 1896. Served in the operations in Tirah Valley on the North West Frontier in 1897-98. Lance Sergeant 9 November 1899. Sergeant 20 March 1900. India Medal with clasps 'Punjab Frontier 1897-98' and 'Tirah 1897-98'. Served in South Africa from January 1902 until April 1902. Evacuated to hospital in England sick (stricture urethra) 12 April 1902. Queen's South Africa Medal with three clasps. Posted to the Depot 16 October 1902. Posted to the 1st Battalion, The Royal Inniskilling Fusiliers 15 October 1904. Posted to the 2nd Battalion, The Royal Inniskilling Fusiliers 27 September 1905 in Egypt, where he served until January 1908. Colour Sergeant 28 February 1907. Posted to the 4th (Militia) Battalion, The Royal Inniskilling Fusiliers. Long Service & Good Conduct Medal 1909. Discharged to pension 20 January 1912. Lived in Belfast. Rejoined in September 1914 and served with the 9th (Service) Battalion, Princess Victoria's (Royal Irish

Fusiliers) (County Armagh) as the Regimental Quartermaster Sergeant. Served until February 1915, when he was replaced by Wilson. Appointed Company Sergeant Major in The London Regiment 29 February 1916. Transferred to The Worcestershire Regiment (203860) 12 March 1917. Served as a Company Sergeant Major in the 1st (Reserve) Garrison Battalion, with the 5th (Reserve) Battalion and at then at the Depot from 12 October 1918. Discharged 29 April 1919.

WILSON Warrant Officer Class II George Wade 14792. Subsequently Lieutenant and Quartermaster - see Appendix 5.

MILNE MC Warrant Officer Class II Charles William 15865. Commissioned into The Royal Inniskilling Fusiliers - see Appendix 5.

FOX Warrant Officer Class II Henry Joseph 14191. Born 17 September 1896 in County Wicklow into a farming family. Moved to Portadown and joined Great Northern Railway as a clerk in late-1912. Enlisted 16 September 1914 (falsified year of birth as 1894). 'C' Company. Sergeant 1914. To France with 36th (Ulster) Division in October 1915. Company Quartermaster Sergeant 1916. Regimental Quartermaster Sergeant 3 February 1917 (vice Milne). **Wounded** when trapped by barbed wire in a water-filled shell hole during the Battle of Langemarck 16 August 1917. He subsequently collapsed during the move of the 9th (Service) Battalion to Havrincourt. Admitted to 110th Field Ambulance on 26 August 1917. Moved to 48th Casualty Clearing Station and then 1st Australian General Hospital at Rouen. Admitted to hospital in Exeter 2 October 1917 then Bicton House Hospital Devon 11 December 1917. Discharged to the Irish Command Depot, Tipperary 18 February 1918. Joined 3rd (Reserve) Battalion at Rugeley, Staffordshire 22 May 1918. Seriously ill, he was readmitted to hospital in Cannock Chase 13 June 1918. Moved to hospital at Bray near Dublin 17 February 1919. S.M.S. Hospital, Blackrock 30 September 1919. Discharged as no longer physically fit for war service due to wounds 9 October 1919. Silver War Badge, number B321658. 1914-15 Star. Rejoined Great Northern Railway and became Deputy Chief Accountant. Retired 1958. Died 24 April 1972, aged 75.

BARBOUR MC Warrant Officer Class II John (Jack) 13994. Born in 1882 in Londonderry. Worked as a railway ticket collector with the Great Northern Railway. Lived at Dungannon, County Tyrone and then at Portadown, County Armagh. 4th (Portadown) Battalion, Armagh Regiment, Ulster Volunteer Force. Enlisted 15 September 1914. To France with 36th (Ulster) Division in October 1915. Promoted and appointed Pioneer Sergeant 21 January 1916. As Sergeant **Mention in Despatches** for his conduct on 1 July 1916. **36th (Ulster) Division Certificate for Gallantry** 1 July 1916. His wife died of typhoid in May 1917. Acting Regimental Quartermaster Sergeant 27 August 1917 (vice Fox). Promoted Warrant Officer Class II 2 October 1917. **MC**. Transferred to the Class Z Reserve 18 March 1919. 1914-15 Star. His brother, Lieutenant James Barbour served with The Royal Irish Regiment and was attached to The Royal Munster Fusiliers.

GRAY Warrant Officer Class II William 14202 & 7040580. Born in 1891 at Bessbrook, County Armagh. A clerk in Bessbrook linen mill. Enlisted September 1914. To France with 36th (Ulster) Division in October 1915. Evacuated to hospital in England 27 April 1916. Returned to France 23 May 1917. Regimental Quartermaster Sergeant from early-1919 (vice Barbour). 1914-15 Star. Re-enlisted on 11 March 1919 for Regular Army service with Princess Victoria's (Royal Irish Fusiliers) (renumbered 7040580). Served with the 2nd Battalion then on the staff of the Inter-Allied Control Commission in Berlin until 1925. Served at the Depot, Armagh from January to August 1925. Posted to the Central Training School (renamed in 1929 the Army Technical School (Boys)) at Chepstow as its first Regimental Quartermaster Sergeant. Died at Mount Pleasant Hospital, Chepstow on 19 October 1931, aged 40, as a result of a gangrenous appendix and peritonitis. Brother of Company Quartermaster Sergeant Reynold Gray and Company Quartermaster Sergeant (later Major) Thomas Gray. His brother, Private James Gray, enlisted in November 1915, aged 16, into Princess Victoria's (Royal Irish Fusiliers) Special Reserve. He was discharged in December 1915 having made a mis-statement as to age on enlistment.

Warrant Officers, Non-Commissioned Officers and Other Ranks

ABBOTT Private Charles 45761. Joined the 9th (North Irish Horse) Battalion, Princess Victoria's (Royal Irish Fusiliers) with the draft of men from The London Regiment in April 1918.

ABERCROMBIE Private William James 41507. Born in 1893 in County Fermanagh. From Blacklion, County Cavan. A farm servant. [Enlisted in August 1915 into the Service Squadron, 6th (Inniskilling) Dragoons (UD/279). Served with 2nd North Irish Horse, X Corps Cavalry Regiment.] Joined the renamed 9th (North Irish Horse) Battalion from 36 Infantry Base Depot and transferred to Princess Victoria's (Royal Irish Fusiliers) in September/October 1917 (renumbered 41507). **Killed in action** during the attack at Vijfwegen 30 September 1918. He is recorded as being aged 30 years at the time of his death, but was actually 25.

ABRAHAM Private Absalom 13974. Born in 1897. From Henry Street, Portadown, County Armagh. Enlisted September 1914, aged 17. To France with 36th (Ulster) Division in October 1915. **Killed in action** during the attack at Hamel 1 July 1916, aged 19. 1914-15 Star. Brother of Private James William Abraham. His brother, Private Thomas Robert Abraham, died of wounds on 17 April 1917 at Vimy Ridge while serving with the 102nd (North British Columbia) Battalion, Canadian Infantry.

ABRAHAM Private James William 20292. Born in Portadown, County Armagh. Living in Clydebank, Glasgow when he enlisted. [Enlisted into The Royal Inniskilling Fusiliers (22376).] Transferred to Princess Victoria's (Royal Irish Fusiliers) on 30 June 1915 (renumbered 20292) and joined the 9th (Service) Battalion. 'C' Company. To France with 36th (Ulster) Division in October 1915. **Killed in action** during the attack at Hamel 1 July 1916. 1914-15 Star. Brother of Private Absalom Abraham. His brother, Private Thomas Robert Abraham, died of wounds on 17 April 1917 at Vimy Ridge while serving with the 102nd (North British Columbia) Battalion, Canadian Infantry.

ADAIR Private Allen 13964. From Tandragee, County Armagh. A farmer. Member of Loyal Orange Lodge 110. Enlisted September 1914. To France with 36th (Ulster) Division in October 1915. Evacuated to hospital in England sick 19 February 1916. [Joined the 10th (Reserve) Battalion 31 July 1916.] Discharged as no longer physically fit for war service 27 September 1919.] Silver War Badge, number 506380. 1914-15 Star.

ADAIR Private Ernest 41206. Born in 1895 at Belfast. [Enlisted in February 1915 into the North Irish Horse (1440). To France with 'F' Squadron in 33rd Division 17 November 1915. Served with 2nd North Irish Horse, X Corps Cavalry Regiment.] Joined the renamed 9th (North Irish Horse) Battalion from 36 Infantry Base Depot and transferred to Princess Victoria's (Royal Irish Fusiliers) in September/October 1917 (renumbered 41206). Transferred to the Class Z Reserve 21 February 1919. 1914-15 Star.

ADAIR Private Henry Harrison 41496. Born in 1887 at Belfast. Lived at Holywood, County Down. A printer. [Enlisted in June 1915 into the North Irish Horse (1674). Served with 2nd North Irish Horse, X Corps Cavalry Regiment.] Joined the renamed 9th (North Irish Horse) Battalion from 36 Infantry Base Depot and transferred to Princess Victoria's (Royal Irish Fusiliers) in September/October 1917 (renumbered 41496).

ADAIR Private Robert 42547. [Served previously with The Royal Irish Rifles (1761).] Transferred at the Base Depot to Princess Victoria's (Royal Irish Fusiliers) 14 September 1918 (renumbered 42547) and joined the 9th (North Irish Horse) Battalion 22 September 1918. [Transferred to 5th (Service) Battalion, The Royal Irish Regiment (Pioneers) in the Light Division in the British Army of the Rhine in March/June 1919 (renumbered 41255).]

ADAMS Private Alexander R 25099. [Enlisted into the Army Service Corps (2750). To France 15 October 1914. Served with 2nd Remount Depot. Transferred to Princess Victoria's (Royal Irish Fusiliers) in May 1916 (renumbered 25099) and joined the 7th/8th (Service) Battalion in 49th Brigade 16th (Irish) Division.] Joined the 9th (North Irish Horse) Battalion when the 7th/8th (Service) Battalion was disbanded in February 1918. 'D' Company. **Missing** in the period 21-28 March 1918 during the retreat from St Quentin believed **captured**. 1914 Star.

ADAMS MBE MM* Sergeant John 13971. Born 7 December 1892. Apprentice mechanic. Member of Belleek Company, Armagh Regiment, Ulster Volunteer Force. Enlisted 14 September 1914.

Lance Corporal June 1915, 3 Section, 13 Platoon, 'D' Company. To France with 36th (Ulster) Division in October 1915. **Wounded** 1 May 1916 at Aveluy Wood (accidentally shot in the left hand). Treated at the Royal Alexandra Infirmary, Paisley, Scotland. Joined the Irish Command Depot, Tipperary in December 1916. Joined the 10th (Reserve) Battalion January/February 1917. To France end May 1917 and joined 36 Infantry Base Depot. Rejoined the 9th (Service) Battalion a few days later. **MM** – Battle of Langemarck 16 August 1917. To hospital sick November 1917 and then remained at the Base Depot as an instructor through early 1918. **MM Bar** – Shoddy Farm raid 22 July 1918. **Wounded** by a shrapnel ball to the right leg during the attack at Vijfwegen 30 September 1918. To England October 1918, to the 2/1st Southern General Hospital, Birmingham, then to the Mater Misericordiae Hospital, Dublin and then to the Royal Victoria Hospital, Belfast in mid-November 1918. Discharged from hospital 17 February 1919. Transferred to the Class Z Reserve 18 February 1919. 1914-15 Star. Trained and then worked as a motor mechanic for Rowland and Harris Ltd, Newry. Served with the Ulster Special Constabulary from 23 February 1922 to 1952, initially with Class 'A'. Sergeant 8 June 1922 and Head Constable 1 October 1924. Joined the Class 'B' Ulster Special Constabulary 21 May 1926 as a Sergeant Instructor. King's Jubilee Medal 1935. Adjutant of Armagh Ulster Special Constabulary from 20 June 1941. Defence Medal 1945. Ulster Special Constabulary Long Service Medal 1952. Retired 25 October 1952. Awarded **MBE** for his service as Adjutant, Ulster Special Constabulary in 1953. Died January 1971, aged 79.

ADAMS Private Robert 18069. From Keady, County Armagh. Enlisted into the 9th (Service) Battalion in February 1915. To France with 36th (Ulster) Division in October 1915. 'C' Company. **Captured** in the period 21-28 March 1918 during the retreat from St Quentin. Transferred to the Class Z Reserve 25 March 1919. 1914-15 Star.

ADAMS Private Thomas 20035. From Newry, County Down. [Enlisted in June 1915 and joined the 8th (Service) Battalion in 49th Brigade, 16th (Irish) Division.] Joined the 9th (North Irish Horse) Battalion when the 7th/8th (Service) Battalion was disbanded in February 1918. **Captured** in the period 11-18 April 1918 in the actions between Wulverghem and Kemmel. **Died** while a prisoner of war 15 July 1918.

ADAMSON Private John 22986. Enlisted in November 1915. Posted to the 9th (Service) Battalion. 'A' Company. **Missing** in the period 21-28 March 1918 during the retreat from St Quentin believed **captured**.

ADAMSON Private Leslie 13959. Born in 1888. From Portadown, County Armagh. 4th (Portadown) Battalion, Armagh Regiment, Ulster Volunteer Force. A damask weaver. Enlisted September 1914. To France with 36th (Ulster) Division in October 1915. **Wounded**. Discharged as no longer physically fit for war service due to wounds 7 September 1916. Silver War Badge, number 51699. 1914-15 Star.

ADAMSON MM Private William 41271. From Ballynahinch. [Enlisted in early September 1914 into the North Irish Horse (1088). Served with 2nd North Irish Horse, X Corps Cavalry Regiment.] Joined the renamed 9th (North Irish Horse) Battalion from 36 Infantry Base Depot and transferred to Princess Victoria's (Royal Irish Fusiliers) in September/October 1917 (renumbered 41271). **MM** – St Quentin 21-28 March 1918. **Wounded** (third time) in the period 11-18 April 1918 in the actions between Wulverghem and Kemmel. Treated at St George's Hospital, Weybridge, Surrey. Transferred to the Class Z Reserve 18 March 1919. 1914-15 Star. His brother, Corporal Edward McConkey Adamson, served with the Corps of Royal Engineers. A sister served as a nurse in Manchester and another worked in a munitions factory in Belfast.

ADDIS Private Robert 13972. Born in 1892 at Belfast. From Lurgan, County Armagh. Enlisted September 1914. A gardener. To France with 36th (Ulster) Division in October 1915. 'C' Company. **Killed in action** during the attack at Hamel 1 July 1916. 1914-15 Star. Brother of Private William John Addis.

ADDIS Private William John 13950. From Lurgan, County Armagh. A farmer. Enlisted September 1914. 'C' Company. To France with 36th (Ulster) Division in October 1915. Lewis gunner and **wounded** during the attack at Hamel 1 July 1916. [Transferred to the Labour Corps (renumbered 230551).] Transferred to the Class Z Reserve 17 February 1919. 1914-15 Star. Brother of Private Robert Addis.

AGNEW Corporal Joseph 42178. [Enlisted into the Army Service Corps (S4/093814).] Transferred to Princess Victoria's (Royal Irish Fusiliers) 8 May 1918 (renumbered 42178) and joined the 9th (North Irish Horse) Battalion. [Transferred to The Royal Inniskilling Fusiliers (renumbered 49820).]

AKAM Private Archibald Ernest 42542. Born 24 December 1888. [Enlisted into The London Regiment (6247) and served with 1/21st (County of London) Battalion, The London Regiment (First Surrey Rifles). Transferred to The Royal Irish Rifles (renumbered 43717).] Transferred at the Base Depot to Princess Victoria's (Royal Irish Fusiliers) 14 September 1918 (renumbered 42542) and joined the 9th (North Irish Horse) Battalion 22 September 1918. Died in Camberwell, London 1975, aged 86.

ALBOROUGH Private Charles Henry 42190. [Enlisted into the Army Service Corps (T4/44682). To France 15 January 1915. Attached to Headquarters 28th Division as a driver.] Transferred to Princess Victoria's (Royal Irish Fusiliers) 8 May 1918 (renumbered 42190) and joined the 9th (North Irish Horse) Battalion. Transferred to the Class Z Reserve 25 February 1919. 1914-15 Star.

ALDERDICE Private Thomas 24284. From Maytown, Bessbrook, County Armagh. Enlisted 26 April 1916. Posted to the 9th (Service) Battalion. 'A' Company. **Missing** in the period 21-28 March 1918 during the retreat from St Quentin believed **captured** and **wounded**. Discharged as no longer physically fit for war service due to wounds 1 April 1919. Silver War Badge, number B195563. His brother, Driver Archibald Alderdice, served with 13th Field Artillery Brigade, Australian Imperial Forces.

ALDERSON Lance Corporal Thomas 40049. [Enlisted into The Prince of Wales's Own (West Yorkshire Regiment) (12006).] Transferred to Princess Victoria's (Royal Irish Fusiliers) 30 November 1916 (renumbered 40049) and joined the 9th (Service) Battalion 12 December 1916. 'D' Company. **Missing** in the period 21-28 March 1918 during the retreat from St Quentin believed **captured**. Transferred to the Class Z Reserve 21 March 1919. 1914-15 Star.

ALEXANDER Sergeant Moses 30467. Born on 28 April 1878 at Ballykelly, County Down. A linen weaver from Portadown, County Armagh. [Re-enlisted into or transferred to Princess Victoria's (Royal Irish Fusiliers) in mid-1918. Posted to the 11th (Service) Battalion.] Posted to the 9th (North Irish Horse) Battalion in August 1918.

ALEXANDER Lance Corporal William 41404. [Enlisted in June 1915 into the North Irish Horse (1676). Served with 2nd North Irish Horse, X Corps Cavalry Regiment.] Joined the renamed 9th (North Irish Horse) Battalion from 36 Infantry Base Depot and transferred to Princess Victoria's (Royal Irish Fusiliers) in September/October 1917 (renumbered 41404). 'A' Company. **Missing** in the period 21-28 March 1918 during the retreat from St Quentin believed **captured**.

ALLELY Private Robert 17540. Born 17 September 1873. From Newbliss, County Monaghan. Enlisted into the 9th (Service) Battalion in November/December 1914. No record of date of deployment to France with 36th (Ulster) Division. Discharged as no longer physically fit for war service 6 December 1916, aged 43. 1914-15 Star. Died at Belfast in 1917, aged 43.

ALLEN Private A C 43349. From London. [Enlisted into The London Regiment.] Attached to the 9th (Service) Battalion, Princess Victoria's (Royal Irish Fusiliers) 26 November 1916. 'C' Company. Discharged from the Territorial Force, re-enlisted and transferred to Princess Victoria's (Royal Irish Fusiliers) in March/April 1917 (renumbered 43349). **Wounded** at the Battle of Langemarck 16 August 1917.

ALLEN Private Ernest 42257. [Served previously with The Royal Irish Rifles (22337).] Joined the 9th (North Irish Horse) Battalion, Princess Victoria's (Royal Irish Fusiliers) with the draft of men transferred from the Army Service Corps and the Army Veterinary Corps in May 1918 (renumbered 42257). [Transferred to the Army Service Corps (renumbered EMT/57049).]

ALLEN Private George 13957. Enlisted September 1914. To France with 36th (Ulster) Division in October 1915. Transferred to the Class Z Reserve 26 February 1919. 1914-15 Star.

ALLEN Lance Corporal George 13969. Enlisted September 1914. To France with 36th (Ulster) Division in October 1915. Transferred to the Class Z Reserve 23 March 1919. 1914-15 Star.

ALLEN Private George 24164. From Waringstown, County Down. Enlisted in March 1916. Posted to the 9th (Service) Battalion. 'A' Company. **Wounded** during the retreat from St Quentin 21-28 March 1918. **Captured** in 1918.

ALLEN Private George 41982. From Fulham, London. [Enlisted in 1917 and joined the 22nd (Reserve) Battalion, The London Regiment (685514).] Transferred to Princess Victoria's (Royal Irish Fusiliers) 2 April 1918 (renumbered 41982) and joined the 9th (North Irish Horse) Battalion 4 April 1918. **Missing** during the attack at Vijfwegen on 30 September or 1 October 1918; recorded as **killed in action** on 3 October 1918, aged 19.

ALLEN Private Henry 13973. From Drumgask, County Armagh. Enlisted September 1914. To France with 36th (Ulster) Division in October 1915. 'C' Company. Stretcher-bearer during the attack at Hamel 1 July 1916 during which he was **wounded**. Discharged as no longer physically fit for war service 9 September 1919. Silver War Badge, number 251968. 1914-15 Star.

ALLEN Private James 41074. [Enlisted in November 1914 into the Service Squadron, 6th (Inniskilling) Dragoons (UD/137). To France with 36th (Ulster) Division in October 1915. Served with 2nd North Irish Horse, X Corps Cavalry Regiment.] Joined the renamed 9th (North Irish Horse) Battalion from 36 Infantry Base Depot and transferred to Princess Victoria's (Royal Irish Fusiliers) in September/October 1917 (renumbered 41074). [Transferred to the Royal Garrison Artillery (renumbered 217887).] 1914-15 Star.

ALLEN Private John 13951. Enlisted September 1914. To France with 36th (Ulster) Division in October 1915. Discharged as no longer physically fit for war service due to sickness 28 February 1919, aged 28. Silver War Badge, number 251968. 1914-15 Star.

ALLEN Private John 41149. [Enlisted 23 November 1914 into the Service Squadron, 6th (Inniskilling) Dragoons (UD/182). To France with 36th (Ulster) Division in October 1915. Served with 2nd North Irish Horse, X Corps Cavalry Regiment.] Joined the renamed 9th (North Irish Horse) Battalion from 36 Infantry Base Depot and transferred to Princess Victoria's (Royal Irish Fusiliers) in September/October 1917 (renumbered 41149). **Wounded**. Discharged as no longer physically fit for war service due to wounds 2 October 1918, aged 24. Silver War Badge, number B22499. 1914-15 Star.

ALLEN Private Joseph 24847. Born 9 November 1897. From Scotch Street, Portadown, County Armagh. Enlisted in September 1916. Posted to the 9th (Service) Battalion. 'A' Company. **Killed in action** at the Battle of Langemarck 16 August 1917, aged 20.

ALLEN Private Robert 13952. From Bleary, County Armagh. Enlisted September 1914. To France with 36th (Ulster) Division in October 1915. 'C' Company. **Wounded** at the Battle of Langemarck 16 August 1917. Discharged as no longer physically fit for war service due to wounds 19 September 1919, aged 23. Silver War Badge, number B5078. 1914-15 Star.

ALLEN Private Thomas 13955. Born in Lurgan in 1879. Served pre-war in the 3rd Battalion (Militia), Princess Victoria's (Royal Irish Fusiliers). A labourer. Enlisted 18 September 1914. To France with 36th (Ulster) Division in October 1915. **Wounded** during the attack at Hamel 1 July 1916. Evacuated to hospital in England on 8 July 1916. Treated at 1st Northern General Hospital, Newcastle-upon-Tyne. Held strength at the Depot from 9 July 1916 and the 10th (Reserve) Battalion from 24 September 1917. [Transferred to the Royal Defence Corps (renumbered 73189) 4 May 1918.] Transferred to the Class Z Reserve 9 March 1919. 1914-15 Star. Lived in Portadown, County Armagh.

ALLEN Sergeant William 25050 & 7040775. From Armagh, County Armagh. A mill worker. Enlisted 15 November 1916. To France 17 May 1917 and joined the 9th (Service) Battalion. 'C' Company. **Wounded** by a gunshot to the right leg during the retreat from St Quentin 21-28 March 1918 and evacuated to hospital in England 1 April 1918. Re-enlisted in early-1919 for Regular Army service with Princess Victoria's (Royal Irish Fusiliers) (renumbered 7040775). Served with the 1st Battalion in Persia and Mesopotamia in 1919/20. General Service Medal 1918-1962 with clasps 'Iraq' & 'NW Persia'. Discharged 16 November 1922.

ALLEN Private William James 20531. Originally from Portadown, County Armagh. Came from the United States to enlist. Enlisted into the 9th (Service) Battalion in June 1915. 'B' Company. **Killed in action** during the attack at Hamel 1 July 1916, aged 28. His wife and children were provided with free passage to sail to the United States in September 1919 and settled in Three Rivers, Massachusetts.

ALLEN Private William McCreight 22018. Enlisted in October 1915. Posted to the 9th (Service) Battalion. 'D' Company. **Missing** in the period 21-28 March 1918 during the retreat from St

Quentin believed **captured**.

ALLINSON Private Frederick James 22025. Enlisted 6 October 1915. Posted to the 9th (Service) Battalion. Discharged as no longer physically fit for war service due to sickness 14 November 1918. Silver War Badge, number B41650.

ALLISON Private Thomas William 40050. Born in 1879. From West Hartlepool, County Durham. Worked as a labourer in Selby, Yorkshire. [Enlisted 18 November 1914 into The Prince of Wales's Own (West Yorkshire Regiment) (16229). Served with the 12th (Service) Battalion, The Prince of Wales's Own (West Yorkshire Regiment) but did not deploy to France. Transferred to the 13th (Reserve) and then 3rd (Reserve) Battalions.] To Infantry Base Depot, France 29 November 1916. Transferred to Princess Victoria's (Royal Irish Fusiliers) 30 November 1916 (renumbered 40050) and joined the 9th (Service) Battalion 12 December 1916. 'B' Company. **Killed in action** at the Battle of Langemarck 16 August 1917.

AMOS Private George Henry 42269. [Enlisted into the Army Veterinary Corps (10469). Served with 15th Veterinary Hospital, Salonika.] Transferred to Princess Victoria's (Royal Irish Fusiliers) 8 May 1918 (renumbered 42269) and joined the 9th (North Irish Horse) Battalion. Transferred to the Class Z Reserve 1 March 1919. 1914-15 Star.

ANDERSON Private Francis 17340. Born at Mullabrack, County Armagh. A farmer's son from Markethill, County Armagh. Enlisted into the 9th (Service) Battalion in November 1914. To France with 36th (Ulster) Division in October 1915. 'C' Company. **Wounded** during the attack at Hamel 1 July 1916 and **died of wounds** 3 July 1916, aged 36. 1914-15 Star.

ANDERSON Lance Corporal George Alex 13970. Born in 1896 at Armagh, County Armagh. Armagh Company, 1st (Armagh) Battalion, Armagh Regiment, Ulster Volunteer Force. Played cricket for Armagh Cricket Club in 1913 and 1914. Enlisted September 1914. Recommended for a commission, which he refused. He fell ill in 1915 and was discharged as no longer physically fit for war service due to sickness. **Died** in Ireland 8 January 1916. Brother of Sergeant Herbert Anderson.

ANDERSON Sergeant Herbert 13968. Born in 1893 in Armagh. Armagh Company, 1st (Armagh) Battalion, Armagh Regiment, Ulster Volunteer Force. Enlisted September 1914. To France with 36th (Ulster) Division in October 1915. 'A' Company. **Wounded** at the Battle of Langemarck 16 August 1917. Transferred to the Class Z Reserve 17 February 1919. 1914-15 Star. Brother of Lance Corporal George Alexander Anderson.

ANDERSON MM Private James 49974. From Glasgow. [Enlisted into The Royal Inniskilling Fusiliers. Transferred to Princess Victoria's (Royal Irish Fusiliers) in May 1918 (renumbered 49974) with the draft of men from The Royal Inniskilling Fusiliers and joined the 1st Battalion.] Posted to the 9th (North Irish Horse) Battalion in August 1918. **MM** – River Lys mid-October 1918. Re-enlisted in 1919 for Regular Army service with The Royal Inniskilling Fusiliers (28922).

ANDERSON Private James 41506. [Enlisted 13 December 1915 and joined 10th Reserve Cavalry Regiment (21297) at The Curragh. Posted to 2nd North Irish Horse, X Corps Cavalry Regiment.] Joined the renamed 9th (North Irish Horse) Battalion from 36 Infantry Base Depot and transferred to Princess Victoria's (Royal Irish Fusiliers) in September/October 1917 (renumbered 41506). **Wounded**. Discharged as no longer physically fit for war service due to wounds 9 May 1919. Silver War Badge, number B234836.

ANDERSON Private James 41519. [Enlisted in early-1915 into the Service Squadron, 6th (Inniskilling) Dragoons (UD/194). To France with 36th (Ulster) Division in October 1915. Served with 2nd North Irish Horse, X Corps Cavalry Regiment.] Joined the renamed 9th (North Irish Horse) Battalion from 36 Infantry Base Depot and transferred to Princess Victoria's (Royal Irish Fusiliers) in September/October 1917 (renumbered 41519). Listed as **missing** in the period 21-28 March 1918 during the retreat from St Quentin. Transferred to the Class Z Reserve 25 February 1919. 1914-15 Star.

ANDERSON Private John 13967. Enlisted September 1914. To France with 36th (Ulster) Division in October 1915. 'C' Company. To hospital mid-1916 and did not take part in the attack at Hamel on 1 July 1916. Transferred to the Class Z Reserve 23 March 1919. 1914-15 Star.

ANDERSON Private Johnston 13965. Born in 1891 at Derryscollop, Moy, County Armagh. A farm labourer. Enlisted September 1914. To France with 36th (Ulster) Division in October 1915. 'A' Company. **Captured** in the period 21-28 March 1918 during the retreat from St Quentin. Transferred to the Class Z Reserve 27 March 1919. 1914-15 Star. Served with the Class 'A' Ulster Special Constabulary in Armagh. Lived at Derryscollop, Moy, County Armagh. Died in 1959, aged 68.

ANDERSON Private Thomas John 24893. From Newtownards, County Down. Enlisted in October 1916. Posted to the 9th (Service) Battalion. 'C' Company. **Wounded** during the retreat from St Quentin 21-28 March 1918. [Transferred to the Labour Corps (renumbered 445704).] British War Medal and Victory Medal forfeit under Royal Warrant 1914 Article 1236 (b), that is: *'liable to trial on confession of desertion, or fraudulent enlistment, but whose trial has been dispensed with'.*

ANDERSON Private William 41563. [Enlisted in April 1913 into the North Irish Horse (834). To France 17 August 1914 with 'A' Squadron as GHQ Troops. Served with 2nd North Irish Horse, X Corps Cavalry Regiment.] Joined the renamed 9th (North Irish Horse) Battalion from 36 Infantry Base Depot and transferred to Princess Victoria's (Royal Irish Fusiliers) in September/October 1917 (renumbered 41563). [Transferred to the Labour Corps (renumbered 516690).] 1914 Star.

ANDREWS Private Francis (Frank) 24735. Born at Magherana, Waringstown, County Down. A damask weaver. Enlisted 28 August 1916 and joined the 10th (Reserve) Battalion. Joined the 9th (Service) Battalion 8 December 1916. 'B' Company. **Missing** at the Battle of Langemarck 16 August 1917 and later declared **killed in action** on that date, aged 40.

ANDREWS Private James 23592. Born in 1889. A farmer from Ballynabeck, County Armagh, he enlisted on 28 December 1915 and joined the 10th (Reserve) Battalion. To France 13 June 1916 and joined the 9th (Service) Battalion. 'D' Company. **Wounded** in the left leg, face and hand on 12 October 1916 during the raid on La Petite Douve Farm. Evacuated through 110th Field Ambulance and admitted to Charing Cross Hospital 17 November 1916. To Irish Command Depot, Tipperary 10 February 1917. To the 10th (Reserve) Battalion 21 May 1917. Rejoined the 9th (Service) Battalion 14 June 1917. To 40th Stationary Hospital and Number 4 Convalescence Depot because of his previous leg wound between 26 June 1917 and 24 August 1917, when he returned to the 9th (Service) Battalion. To 2nd Western General Hospital, Manchester 25 November 1917. Rejoined the 10th (Reserve) Battalion 31 January 1918. **Deserted** 23 August 1918. British War Medal and Victory Medal forfeit.

ANDREWS Private John William 43207. From Matlock Bath, Derbyshire. [Enlisted 29 November 1915 into The Sherwood Foresters (Nottinghamshire and Derbyshire Regiment).] Transferred to Princess Victoria's (Royal Irish Fusiliers) 31 August 1916 (renumbered 43207) having joined the 9th (Service) Battalion on 8 August 1916. 'A' Company. **Wounded** at the Battle of Langemarck 16 August 1917. Discharged as no longer physically fit for war service due to wounds 3 December 1918. Silver War Badge, number B55045.

ANDREWS Private Joseph 40097. Enlisted 23 February 1916. Transferred to Princess Victoria's (Royal Irish Fusiliers) in November 1916 (renumbered 40097). Posted to the 9th (Service) Battalion in mid-1917. **Wounded**. Discharged as no longer physically fit for war service due to wounds 16 April 1918, aged 21. Silver War Badge, number 343685.

ANDREWS Private Maurice Walker 40047. Born 28 May 1896 at North Bierley, Yorkshire. [Enlisted into the 18th (Service) Battalion, The Prince of Wales's Own (West Yorkshire Regiment) (2nd Bradford) (828). To Egypt 6 December 1915 with 93rd Brigade in 31st Division.] Transferred to Princess Victoria's (Royal Irish Fusiliers) 30 November 1916 (renumbered 40047) and joined the 9th (Service) Battalion 12 December 1916. 'D' Company. **Wounded** slightly during the Battle of Messines 9 June 1917. **Missing** in the period 21-28 March 1918 during the retreat from St Quentin believed **captured**. Transferred to the Class Z Reserve 26 March 1919. 1914-15 Star. Died in Yorkshire in late-1969, aged 73.

ANGUS Private Thomas 41191. Born in 1898 at Donaghadee, County Down. [Enlisted in November 1915 into the North Irish Horse (1927). Served with 2nd North Irish Horse, X Corps Cavalry Regiment.] Joined the renamed 9th (North Irish Horse) Battalion from 36 Infantry Base Depot and transferred to Princess Victoria's (Royal Irish Fusiliers) in September/October 1917 (renumbered 41191). 'D' Company. **Captured** in the period 21-28 March 1918 during the retreat from St Quentin.

ANNESLEY Private Hugh Alexander 41538. Commissioned into The Royal Irish Rifles - see Appendix 5.

ANNETT Lance Corporal Thomas James 22985. Born in 1898 at Belfast. Enlisted in November 1915. Posted to the 9th (Service) Battalion. **Wounded** twice.

ARCHER Corporal James 13962. Born in 1884 in Lurgan, County Armagh. A weaver. Enlisted September 1914. To France with 36th (Ulster) Division in October 1915. 'C' Company. Battalion bomb carrier during the attack at Hamel 1 July 1916, which he survived unwounded. [Transferred to the Royal Defence Corps (renumbered 84888).] Discharged as no longer physically fit for war service due to sickness 11 April 1919. Silver War Badge, number 475090. 1914-15 Star. Father of Private William John Archer.

ARCHER Private William John 13966. Born in 1901 in Lurgan, County Armagh. Enlisted 15 September 1914, considerably underage. He did not deploy overseas with 36th (Ulster) Division. Discharged as no longer physically fit for war service due to sickness 16 January 1917. Silver War Badge, number 95504. Son of Corporal James Archer.

ARCHIBALD Private William A 42431. [Enlisted 26 June 1916 into The Royal Irish Rifles (11477). Served with the 2nd Battalion, The Royal Irish Rifles.] Transferred at the Base Depot to Princess Victoria's (Royal Irish Fusiliers) 14 September 1918 (renumbered 42431) and joined the 9th (North Irish Horse) Battalion 22 September 1918. Discharged as no longer physically fit for war service due to sickness 14 May 1919. Silver War Badge, number B234838.

ARGUE Private William Thomas 26098. Born in 1895 at Derrynoose, County Armagh. A farmer's son, one of ten children. Enlisted in January 1917. Posted to the 9th (Service) Battalion. 'D' Company. **Captured** in the period 21-28 March 1918 during the retreat from St Quentin.

ARMOUR Private William J 42558. [Served previously with The Royal Irish Rifles (564).] Transferred at the Base Depot to Princess Victoria's (Royal Irish Fusiliers) 14 September 1918 (renumbered 42558) and joined the 9th (North Irish Horse) Battalion 22 September 1918. [Transferred back to The Royal Irish Rifles (renumbered 19/46093).]

ARMSTRONG Private Alexander 41624. [Enlisted in November 1914 into the Service Squadron, 6th (Inniskilling) Dragoons (UD/147). To France with 36th (Ulster) Division in October 1915. Served with 2nd North Irish Horse, X Corps Cavalry Regiment.] Joined the renamed 9th (North Irish Horse) Battalion from 36 Infantry Base Depot and transferred to Princess Victoria's (Royal Irish Fusiliers) in September/October 1917 (renumbered 41624). **Wounded** at Moeuvres 22/23 November 1917 and evacuated to hospital in England 22 December 1917. Treated at Edinburgh War Hospital. [Transferred to the Army Service Corps (renumbered T/454320).] 1914-15 Star. Lived in Belfast.

ARMSTRONG Lance Corporal Henry Tottenham 41122. Commissioned into Princess Victoria's (Royal Irish Fusiliers) - see Appendix 5.

ARMSTRONG DCM Lance Corporal Robert 41695. [Enlisted in February 1912 into the North Irish Horse (674). To France 20 August 1914 with 'C' Squadron as 5th Division Cavalry and then as GHQ Troops. Served with 2nd North Irish Horse, X Corps Cavalry Regiment.] Joined the renamed 9th (North Irish Horse) Battalion from 36 Infantry Base Depot and transferred to Princess Victoria's (Royal Irish Fusiliers) in September/October 1917 (renumbered 41695). **DCM** – Courtrai 16 October 1918. 1914 Star and clasp.

ARMSTRONG Private Thomas 17902. From Castleblayney, County Monaghan. Enlisted into the 9th (Service) Battalion in January 1915. 'A' Company. To France with 36th (Ulster) Division in October 1915. **Wounded** during the attack at Hamel 1 July 1916. **Wounded** at the Battle of Langemarck 16 August 1917. **Captured** in 1918. Transferred to the Class Z Reserve 26 March 1919. 1914-15 Star.

ARMSTRONG Private Thomas 40002. Joined the 9th (Service) Battalion, Princess Victoria's (Royal Irish Fusiliers) with the draft of men from The Prince of Wales's Own (West Yorkshire Regiment) on 12 December 1916. [Posted to the 1st Battalion.]

ARMSTRONG Private William John 41152. [Enlisted in November 1914 into the Service Squadron, 6th (Inniskilling) Dragoons (UD/184). To France with 36th (Ulster) Division in October 1915. Served with 2nd North Irish Horse, X Corps Cavalry Regiment.] Joined the renamed 9th (North Irish Horse) Battalion from 36 Infantry Base Depot and transferred to Princess Victoria's (Royal

Irish Fusiliers) in September/October 1917 (renumbered 41152). Transferred to the Class Z Reserve 16 February 1919. 1914-15 Star.

ARNELL Private James Thomas 45797. Born 1899. From Canning Town, London. [Enlisted in August 1917 and joined the 22nd (Reserve) Battalion, The London Regiment.] To France and joined 36 Infantry Base Depot 29 March 1918. Transferred to Princess Victoria's (Royal Irish Fusiliers) 2 April 1918 (renumbered 45797) and joined the 9th (North Irish Horse) Battalion 4 April 1918. **Killed in action** during the advance to Anseghem 25 October 1918, aged 19.

ARNOTT Lance Corporal Frederick James 43457. [Enlisted into The London Regiment (6039). To France and joined the 1/24th (County of London) Battalion, The London Regiment (The Queen's).] To France and joined 36 Infantry Base Depot 29 March 1918. Transferred to Princess Victoria's (Royal Irish Fusiliers) 2 April 1918 (renumbered 43457) and joined the 9th (North Irish Horse) Battalion 4 April 1918.

ARTHUR Private William Frederick Christy 41366. Born in 1897 at Douglas Bridge, County Tyrone. [Enlisted in November 1915 into the North Irish Horse (1873). Served with 2nd North Irish Horse, X Corps Cavalry Regiment.] Joined the renamed 9th (North Irish Horse) Battalion from 36 Infantry Base Depot and transferred to Princess Victoria's (Royal Irish Fusiliers) in September/October 1917 (renumbered 41366). **Killed in action** during the raid on Shoddy Farm near Meulenhouck 22 July 1918.

ASHFIELD Private Theophilus 41378. Born in 1890, a postman and farmhand from Sixmilecross, County Tyrone. [Enlisted 12 November 1915 into the Service Squadron, 6th (Inniskilling) Dragoons (UD/308). Served with 2nd North Irish Horse, X Corps Cavalry Regiment.] Joined the renamed 9th (North Irish Horse) Battalion from 36 Infantry Base Depot and transferred to Princess Victoria's (Royal Irish Fusiliers) in September/October 1917 (renumbered 41378). **Wounded**. Discharged as no longer physically fit for war service due to wounds 27 November 1918. Silver War Badge, number B48533. His brother, Private William James Ashfield, was wounded twice and captured while serving with The Royal Inniskilling Fusiliers.

ASHMAN Private Reginald John 41617. [Enlisted for service with cavalry (6080). Posted to 2nd North Irish Horse, X Corps Cavalry Regiment.] Joined the renamed 9th (North Irish Horse) Battalion from 36 Infantry Base Depot and transferred to Princess Victoria's (Royal Irish Fusiliers) in September/October 1917 (renumbered 41617).

ATKINS MM Sergeant Bertie 43461. Born 23 March 1893. From Bermondsey, London. A warehouseman. [Enlisted 17 September 1914 into The London Regiment (2433). To France 14 March 1915 and served with 1/22nd (County of London) Battalion, The London Regiment (The Queen's). **Wounded** by shellfire (both arms and buttocks) 24 May 1915 and evacuated to hospital in England. To France 20 December 1916 and rejoined 1/22nd (County of London) Battalion, The London Regiment (The Queen's) (renumbered 680909 in March 1917). **Wounded** 1 December 1917 (gassed and gunshot wound to the right foot) and evacuated to hospital in England. Joined the 22nd (Reserve) Battalion, The London Regiment 18 February 1918.] To France and joined 36 Infantry Base Depot 29 March 1918. Transferred to Princess Victoria's (Royal Irish Fusiliers) 2 April 1918 (renumbered 43461) and joined the 9th (North Irish Horse) Battalion 4 April 1918. Lance Corporal 21 May 1918. Corporal (vice Kelly) 17 August 1918 & Lance Sergeant (vice Porter) 17 August 1918. **MM** –Wulverghem 4 September 1918. **Wounded**, gunshot wound to the right buttock 16 October 1918 at Courtrai. Treated at 53rd General Hospital and evacuated to hospital in England. Discharged as no longer physically fit for war service due to wounds 23 May 1919. Silver War Badge, number B283771. [Re-enlisted 28 July 1919 and joined the Labour Corps, London District (renumbered 714307). To France 21 August 1919 and joined the Chinese Labour Corps Base Depot. Joined 183rd Labour Company 27 August 1919. To hospital sick (venereal disease - syphilis) 28 January 1920 and evacuated to hospital in England. Treated at Cherry Hinton Military Hospital, Cambridge. Posted to Eastern Command Labour Corps 28 April 1920. Discharged as no longer physically fit for service due to wounds 15 May 1920.] 1914-15 Star. Died at London in 1971, aged 78.

ATKINS Lance Corporal George Sydney 41073. [Served previously with the 2nd Dragoon Guards (Queen's Bays) in 1st Cavalry Division (4235). Posted to 2nd North Irish Horse, X Corps Cavalry Regiment.] Joined the renamed 9th (North Irish Horse) Battalion from 36 Infantry Base Depot and transferred to Princess Victoria's (Royal Irish Fusiliers) in September/October 1917 (renumbered 41073). 'A' Company. **Missing** in the period 21-28 March 1918 during the retreat from St Quentin believed **captured**.

ATKINSON Private Herbert 13954. Born in 1892 in Portadown, County Armagh. Enlisted September 1914. To France with 36th (Ulster) Division in October 1915. **Wounded** during the attack at Hamel 1 July 1916. Discharged as no longer physically fit for war service due to wounds 12 July 1917. Silver War Badge, number 208323. 1914-15 Star.

ATKINSON Private Matthew 13958. Born in 1879 at Seagoe, County Armagh. From Portadown, County Armagh. 4th (Portadown) Battalion, Armagh Regiment, Ulster Volunteer Force. A shoemaker. Enlisted September 1914. Discharged as not being likely to become an efficient soldier in that he was considered medically unfit for service (epilepsy) 3 October 1914.

ATKINSON Private Ralph 20338. From Washington Station, County Durham. [Enlisted into The Royal Inniskilling Fusiliers (23470).] Transferred to Princess Victoria's (Royal Irish Fusiliers) on 30 June 1915 (renumbered 20338) and joined the 9th (Service) Battalion. **Killed in action** during the attack at Hamel 1 July 1916, aged 18.

ATKINSON Corporal Robert 18255. Enlisted into the 9th (Service) Battalion in February/March 1915. To France with 36th (Ulster) Division in October 1915. Transferred to the Class Z Reserve 19 February 1919. 1914-15 Star.

ATWELL Private Edward 13956. Born in 1892. From Tandragee, County Armagh. Enlisted September 1914. To France with 36th (Ulster) Division in October 1915. **Wounded** during the attack at Hamel 1 July 1916, which resulted in his right foot and later his right leg being amputated. Discharged as no longer physically fit for war service due to wounds 5 February 1919. Silver War Badge, number 55049. 1914-15 Star. Brother of Private John Atwell.

ATWELL Private John 13960. Born in 1894 at Tandragee, County Armagh. 4th (Portadown) Battalion, Armagh Regiment, Ulster Volunteer Force. Enlisted September 1914. To France with 36th (Ulster) Division in October 1915. 'B' Company. **Wounded** 21 April 1916. **Wounded** at the Battle of Langemarck 16 August 1917. **Missing** in the period 21-28 March 1918 during the retreat from St Quentin believed **captured**. Transferred to the Class Z Reserve 4 April 1919. 1914-15 Star. Brother of Private Edward Atwell.

AUSTIN Corporal Leslie Dyson 25133. [Enlisted 30 May 1916 and joined the 7th/8th (Service) Battalion in 49th Brigade, 16th (Irish) Division. **16th (Irish) Division Parchment Certificate for Gallantry and Devotion to Duty** - Battle of Langemarck 16 August 1917.] Joined the 9th (North Irish Horse) Battalion when the 7th/8th (Service) Battalion was disbanded in February 1918. 'D' Company. **Wounded** during the retreat from St Quentin 21-28 March 1918. Discharged as no longer physically fit for war service due to wounds 9 August 1919. Silver War Badge, number B296142.

AUSTIN Private Thomas 27714. Enlisted in June 1917. Posted to the 9th (North Irish Horse) Battalion.

AVERELL Private Andrew 41584. Born in 1895 at Clonmacken, County Monaghan. An engine cleaner with the Great Northern Railway. [Enlisted 17 December 1915 into the North Irish Horse (2046). To France 28 January 1917. Served with 2nd North Irish Horse, X Corps Cavalry Regiment. To the field ambulance and casualty clearing station sick (bronchial catarrh) 1-31 May 1917. Embarked at Marseilles for Egypt with the Regiment's horses on Horse Transport SS Bohemian 25 August 1917.] Joined the renamed 9th (North Irish Horse) Battalion and transferred to Princess Victoria's (Royal Irish Fusiliers) in October 1917 (renumbered 41584). [Transferred to the Tank Corps 28 December 1917 (renumbered 304875) and posted for training to the Tank Corps Depot, at Bovington near Wareham, Dorset. To France 8 July 1918 and joined the 15th Battalion, Tank Corps. **Wounded** by a gunshot to the right arm 30 August 1918. Treated at 47th General Hospital. Rejoined the 15th Battalion, Tank Corps 11 November 1918.] Transferred to the Class Z Reserve 26 February 1919.

AVERELL MM Private Robert 41534. Born 24 May 1890. From Magherafelt, County Londonderry. Member of O'Hara Purple Guards Loyal Orange Lodge 310. A groom and chauffeur. [Enlisted 11 March 1910 into the North Irish Horse (485). To France 20 August 1914 with 'C' Squadron as 5th Division Cavalry and then as GHQ Troops. Served with 2nd North Irish Horse, X

Corps Cavalry Regiment.] Joined the renamed 9th (North Irish Horse) Battalion from 36 Infantry Base Depot and transferred to Princess Victoria's (Royal Irish Fusiliers) in September/October 1917 (renumbered 41534). 'C' Company. **MM** – Havrincourt raid 3 November 1917. [Transferred to the Tank Corps 28 December 1917 (renumbered 304872) and posted for training to the Tank Corps Depot, at Bovington near Wareham, Dorset. To France 8 July 1918 and joined 'C' Company, 15th Battalion. Injured (sprained ankle playing football) 3 September 1918 and evacuated to hospital in England. Treated at the South African Hospital, Richmond Park, London.] Transferred to the Class Z Reserve 21 February 1919. 1914 Star.

AVINGTON Private John 26091. From Ballynadrentagh, County Antrim. Enlisted in January 1917. Posted to the 9th (Service) Battalion. 'D' Company. Believed **wounded** in the period 21-28 March 1918 during the retreat from St Quentin. [Transferred to The Royal Irish Regiment (renumbered 18800).]

BAGG Private George Henry 18822. [Enlisted 3 September 1914. Transferred to Princess Victoria's (Royal Irish Fusiliers) in April 1915. To France 19 July 1915 and joined the 1st Battalion. Posted to the 6th (Service) Battalion.] Posted to the 9th (Service) Battalion. **Wounded**. Discharged as no longer physically fit for war service due to wounds 13 March 1919. 1914-15 Star.

BAILEY Corporal Albert George 25250. Born in 1891 in Sahm Toney, Norfolk. A footman in London. [Enlisted in August 1914 and joined 11th (Prince Albert's Own) Hussars (15745) on 20 October 1914. Lance Corporal 23 February 1915. Served in 1st Cavalry Division. **Wounded** by shellfire 8 January 1916 in the legs and feet. To 1st Cavalry Field Ambulance and Lahore British General Hospital, Calais then evacuated to hospital in England on 18 January 1916. To 16 Infantry Base Depot 10 December 1916. Transferred to Princess Victoria's (Royal Irish Fusiliers) (renumbered 25250) and posted to the 7th/8th (Service) Battalion in 49th Brigade, 16th (Irish) Division 11 December 1916.] Joined the 9th (North Irish Horse) Battalion when the 7th/8th (Service) Battalion was disbanded in February 1918. Lance Corporal (vice Knaggs) 30 March 1918. To 110th Field Ambulance 4 June 1918 due to his previous wound. **Killed in action** during the attack north of Bailleul 24 August 1918, aged 27. 1914-15 Star.

BAILEY Corporal John 24708. From Glasgow. [Enlisted in August 1916 and joined the 1st Battalion.] Posted to the 9th (Service) Battalion. 'A' Company. **Wounded** at the Battle of Langemarck 16 August 1917. [Posted back to the 1st Battalion.]

BAILEY Corporal Horace John 40037. Born in 1893 at Handsworth, Birmingham. [Enlisted 8 September 1914 into the 11th (Service) Battalion, The Prince of Wales's Own (West Yorkshire Regiment) (14630). Corporal 28 December 1914. To France in 69th Brigade, 23rd Division. **Wounded** by a gunshot to the neck. Evacuated to Queen Mary's Royal Naval Hospital, Southend. Held strength at the Depot from 8 July 1916. Posted to the 3rd (Reserve) Battalion, The Prince of Wales's Own (West Yorkshire Regiment) 6 September 1916.] Transferred to Princess Victoria's (Royal Irish Fusiliers) 30 November 1916 (renumbered 40037) and joined the 9th (Service) Battalion 12 December 1916. 'A' Company. **Killed in action** at the Battle of Langemarck 16 August 1917. 1914-15 Star.

BAILEY Lance Corporal John Thomas 25275 & 7040776. From Pontypridd, Glamorganshire (now Rhondda Cynon Taf). A coal miner. [Enlisted 13 February 1913 into the 11th (Prince Albert's Own) Hussars (9789). To France in 1st Cavalry Division 15 August 1914. **Wounded** by a gunshot to the right shoulder 30 July 1916 and evacuated to hospital in England 7 August 1916. To France 11 December 1916. Transferred to Princess Victoria's (Royal Irish Fusiliers) December 1916 (renumbered 25275) and posted to the 7th/8th (Service) Battalion in 49th Brigade, 16th (Irish) Division.] Joined the 9th (North Irish Horse) Battalion when the 7th/8th (Service) Battalion was disbanded in February 1918. 'A' Company. **Captured** in the period 21-28 March 1918 during the retreat from St Quentin. Repatriated 3 January 1919. 1914 Star. Transferred to the Section B Army Reserve, Princess Victoria's (Royal Irish Fusiliers) (renumbered 7040776). Discharged 12 February 1925. Re-enlisted into the 5th Battalion, The Welch Regiment (Territorial Army) 17 March 1925.

BAILIE Private William John 14029. Enlisted September 1914. To France with 36th (Ulster) Division in October 1915. [Transferred to the Labour Corps (renumbered 396573).] Transferred to the Class Z Reserve 8 April 1919. 1914-15 Star.

BAILLIE Private James 24627 & 7040751. From Belfast. Enlisted 26 July 1916. To France 16 December 1916 and joined the 9th (Service) Battalion. 'D' Company. **Captured** in the period 21-28 March 1918 during the retreat from St Quentin. Re-enlisted 1 August 1919 for Regular Army service with Princess Victoria's (Royal Irish Fusiliers) (renumbered 7040751). Served with the 1st Battalion in Persia and Mesopotamia in 1919/20. General Service Medal 1918-1962 with clasps 'Iraq' & 'NW Persia'. Discharged 23 December 1921.

BAINES Private William 41360. [Enlisted in November 1915 into the North Irish Horse (1833). Served with 2nd North Irish Horse, X Corps Cavalry Regiment.] Joined the renamed 9th (North Irish Horse) Battalion from 36 Infantry Base Depot and transferred to Princess Victoria's (Royal Irish Fusiliers) in September/October 1917 (renumbered 41360). 'B' Company. **Missing** in the period 21-28 March 1918 during the retreat from St Quentin believed **captured**.

BAIRD Private Albert James 18273. Born in 1896. Lived at Newry, County Down. Enlisted into the 9th (Service) Battalion in March 1915. To France with 36th (Ulster) Division in October 1915. Transferred to the Class Z Reserve 30 March 1919. 1914-15 Star.

BAIRD Private Charles 24301. [Enlisted in September 1914 into the North Irish Horse (1094). To France 18 December 1914. Served with 2nd North Irish Horse, X Corps Cavalry Regiment.] Transferred to Princess Victoria's (Royal Irish Fusiliers) in April/May 1916 (renumbered 24301) and was posted to the 9th (Service) Battalion. 'C' Company. Lewis gun ammunition carrier during the attack at Hamel 1 July 1916 during which he was **wounded**. Discharged as no longer physically fit for war service due to wounds 27 July 1918. Silver War Badge, number 379045. 1914 Star.

BAIRD Private Hugh 27650. From Ballylane, County Armagh. Enlisted in June 1917. Posted to the 9th (North Irish Horse) Battalion. 'A' Company. **Missing** in the period 21-28 March 1918 during the retreat from St Quentin believed **captured**.

BAIRD Private J 24618. Enlisted in August 1916. Posted to the 9th (Service) Battalion. 'C' Company. **Wounded** during the retreat from St Quentin 21-28 March 1918.

BAIRD Private John 17937. From Lurton, Cootehill, County Cavan. Enlisted into the 9th (Service) Battalion in January 1915. 'C' Company. To France with 36th (Ulster) Division in October 1915. Company signaller and **killed in action** during the attack at Hamel 1 July 1916, aged 20. 1914-15 Star.

BAIRD Lance Corporal Robert 13998. Born at Waringstown, County Down. From Lurgan, County Armagh. Enlisted September 1914. To France with 36th (Ulster) Division in October 1915. 'C' Company. **Killed in action** during the attack at Hamel 1 July 1916, aged 41. 1914-15 Star.

BAIRD MM Sergeant Thomas Henry 5581. Enlisted into the 3rd Battalion (Militia), Princess Victoria's (Royal Irish Fusiliers) Special Reserve. Served elsewhere before being **wounded** and posted to the 9th (North Irish Horse) Battalion. **MM** - Wulverghem, April 1918. Re-enlisted in 1919 for Regular Army service with The Norfolk Regiment (renumbered 72973, renumbered 5765352.) Discharged in 1925.

BAIRD Private William 21577. Born in 1897 at Shankill, Belfast. Enlisted in August 1915. Posted to the 9th (Service) Battalion in mid/late 1916. 'A' Company. **Killed in action** at the Battle of Langemarck 16 August 1917.

BAKER Private Walter Herbert 43312. Born in 1892 at Walthamstow, Essex. [Enlisted 18 July 1916 and joined 3/7th Battalion, The London Regiment. To France 9 November 1916.] Attached to the 9th (Service) Battalion, Princess Victoria's (Royal Irish Fusiliers) 26 November 1916. 'A' Company. Discharged from the Territorial Force, re-enlisted and transferred to Princess Victoria's (Royal Irish Fusiliers) in March/April 1917 (renumbered 43312). **Killed in action** at the Battle of Langemarck 16 August 1917.

BALDWIN Private Albert William 41153. Born in 1893 at County Cork. [Enlisted into 6th (Inniskilling) Dragoons (20005). Served with 2nd North Irish Horse, X Corps Cavalry Regiment.] Joined the renamed 9th (North Irish Horse) Battalion from 36 Infantry Base Depot and transferred to Princess Victoria's (Royal Irish Fusiliers) in September/October 1917 (renumbered 41153). 'B' Company. **Missing** in the period 21-28 March 1918 during the retreat from St Quentin believed **captured**.

BALES Private John 43229. Born in 1893 at Nottingham. A hosiery folder by occupation. [Enlisted 10 December 1915 and transferred to the Army Reserve. Mobilised 22 February 1916 and joined The Sherwood Foresters (Nottinghamshire and Derbyshire Regiment) (36090). To France 22 July 1916.] Transferred to Princess Victoria's (Royal Irish Fusiliers) 31 August 1916 (renumbered 43229) having joined the 9th (Service) Battalion on 8 August 1916. 'B' Company. **Wounded** at the Battle of Langemarck 16 August 1917 by a gunshot to the right forearm. Treated at Graylingwell War Hospital, Chichester. Joined the 3rd (Reserve) Battalion 26 October 1917 and the 10th (Reserve) Battalion 13 November 1917. Rejoined the 9th (North Irish Horse) Battalion 3 April 1918. **Wounded** in the period 9-18 April 1918 in the actions between Wulverghem and Kemmel and **died of wounds** 18 April 1918.

BALL Private Henry 43212. [Enlisted into The Sherwood Foresters (Nottinghamshire and Derbyshire Regiment) (35957).] Transferred to Princess Victoria's (Royal Irish Fusiliers) 31 August 1916 (renumbered 43212) having joined the 9th (Service) Battalion on 8 August 1916. [Transferred to the Machine Gun Corps (renumbered 73272).]

BALLAM Private James W 20066. Enlisted into the 9th (Service) Battalion in June 1915. To France with 36th (Ulster) Division in October 1915. 'C' Company. Survived the attack at Hamel on 1 July 1916 unwounded. [Transferred to the Machine Gun Corps (renumbered 162296).] 1914-15 Star.

BALLAM Lance Corporal Richard Cecil 22977. Born on 4 April 1898 at Salt Hill, County Galway. From Enfield, County Meath. Enlisted into Princess Victoria's (Royal Irish Fusiliers) 4 November 1915, aged 17. Joined the 9th (Service) Battalion in May 1917. Company and Battalion Signaller. **Wounded** at the Battle of Langemarck 16 August 1917. Returned to the 9th (North Irish Horse) Battalion in September 1918. Fell ill with influenza and **died** 5 December 1918 at Number 10 Stationary Hospital, Arneke, aged 20.

BALLANTINE Sergeant Thomas 18322. Born in 1884. From Ballynahone, County Armagh. Member of Loyal Orange Lodge 347. Armagh Regiment, Ulster Volunteer Force. A bread server. Enlisted into the 9th (Service) Battalion in March 1915. **Killed in action** at Moeuvres 23 November 1917, aged 33.

BALLENTINE Private Daniel 41545 & 7042140. Born in 1895 at Belfast. A book-keeper. [Enlisted 9 November 1915 into the North Irish Horse (1827). To France 30 June 1916. Served with 2nd North Irish Horse, X Corps Cavalry Regiment.] Joined the renamed 9th (North Irish Horse) Battalion from 36 Infantry Base Depot and transferred to Princess Victoria's (Royal Irish Fusiliers) in September/October 1917 (renumbered 41545). **Wounded** by a gunshot to the right leg and **captured** in late-1917. Also suffered frostbite to three toes. He was repatriated in August 1918 due to his wounds. Re-enlisted in early-1919 for Regular Army service with Princess Victoria's (Royal Irish Fusiliers) (renumbered 7042140). Discharged 9 November 1920 (King's Certificate 87/3119).

BALLIE Lancc Corporal James Hamilton 22796. Born in 1895 at Belfast. Enlisted 6 November 1915. Posted to the 9th (Service) Battalion. 'B' Company. **Wounded** at the Battle of Langemarck 16 August 1917. Discharged as no longer physically fit for war service due to wounds 10 October 1918. Silver War Badge, number B34280.

BALMER Corporal (Acting Sergeant) Joseph 13986. Born in 1894 at Ballylisk, Tandragee, County Armagh. A linen weaver. 4th (Portadown) Battalion, Armagh Regiment, Ulster Volunteer Force. Enlisted September 1914. To France with 36th (Ulster) Division in October 1915. 'D' Company. **Wounded** during the attack at Hamel 1 July 1916. **Killed in action** at the Battle of Langemarck 16 August 1917. 1914-15 Star.

BANKS Private Percy Albert 43323. Joined the 9th (Service) Battalion, Princess Victoria's (Royal Irish Fusiliers) with the draft of men from The London Regiment in November 1916.

BARBOUR Private James 41586. [Enlisted in May 1915 into the North Irish Horse (1614). Served with 2nd North Irish Horse, X Corps Cavalry Regiment.] Joined the renamed 9th (North Irish Horse) Battalion from 36 Infantry Base Depot and transferred to Princess Victoria's (Royal Irish Fusiliers) in September/October 1917 (renumbered 41586).

BARBOUR MC Warrant Officer Class II John 13994. Regimental Quartermaster Sergeant - see above.

BARK Private Herbert Ruddick 43431. Born in 1890 at Peckham, London. [Enlisted 31 May 1915 and joined the 3/24th Battalion, The London Regiment (4085). To France 9 October 1915 and joined 1/24th (County of London) Battalion, The London Regiment (The Queen's). **Wounded** by a gunshot to the right arm and to hospital in England 22 September 1916. Treated at Wharncliffe War Hospital, Sheffield. To 22nd (Reserve) Battalion, The London Regiment 8 January 1917. To Infantry Base Depot, France 24 February 1917 (renumbered 721539 in March 1917). Joined Number 1 Entrenching Battalion 17 March 1917. Rejoined 1/24th (County of London) Battalion, The London Regiment (The Queen's) 25 June 1917. **Wounded** by a gunshot to the buttock 22 August 1917 and evacuated to hospital in England. To 22nd (Reserve) Battalion, The London Regiment 5 February 1918.] To France and joined 36 Infantry Base Depot 29 March 1918. Transferred to Princess Victoria's (Royal Irish Fusiliers) 2 April 1918 (renumbered 43431) and joined the 9th (North Irish Horse) Battalion 4 April 1918. **Missing** in the period 11-18 April 1918 in the actions between Wulverghem and Kemmel; subsequently declared **killed in action** 19 April 1918, aged 27. 1914-15 Star. His brother, Private Edward J Bark, served with Princess Charlotte of Wales's (Royal Berkshire Regiment).

BARKER Private Frank 10910. [Enlisted into Princess Victoria's (Royal Irish Fusiliers) as a regular soldier in December 1911/January 1912 and served with the 1st Battalion.] Posted to the 9th (Service) Battalion. 'B' Company. **Wounded** at the Battle of Langemarck 16 August 1917.

BARKLEY Private Robert James 23191. Enlisted 20 November 1915. Posted to the 9th (Service) Battalion. **Wounded**. Discharged as no longer physically fit for war service due to wounds 26 February 1918. Silver War Badge, number 334281.

BARKLEY Private Patrick 20925, 33315 & 7041506. Born in 1885 at Shankill, Belfast. A rover drawer. [Enlisted in September 1915 and joined the 7th or 8th (Service) Battalion in 49th Brigade, 16th (Irish) Division.] Joined the 9th (North Irish Horse) Battalion when the 7th/8th (Service) Battalion was disbanded in February 1918. 'D' Company. **Wounded** during the retreat from St Quentin 21-28 March 1918. Re-enlisted 25 August 1919 for Regular Army service with Princess Victoria's (Royal Irish Fusiliers) (renumbered 33315, renumbered 7041506). Transferred to the Section D Reserve 24 August 1921. Discharged 16 August 1925.

BARLOW Private Arthur 45809. Joined the 9th (North Irish Horse) Battalion, Princess Victoria's (Royal Irish Fusiliers) with the draft of men from The London Regiment in April 1918. [Transferred to 5th (Service) Battalion, The Royal Irish Regiment (Pioneers) in the Light Division in the British Army of the Rhine in March/June 1919 (renumbered 41258).]

BARNES Private Joseph 11454. From Dublin. [Enlisted into Princess Victoria's (Royal Irish Fusiliers) as a regular soldier in early-1914. To France 7 November 1914 and joined the 1st Battalion.] Posted to the 9th (Service) Battalion. 'D' Company. **Killed in action** at the Battle of Langemarck 16 August 1917, aged 27. 1914 Star.

BARNES Lance Corporal William Thomas 41466. [Enlisted into the 6th (Inniskilling) Dragoons (9676). Served with 2nd North Irish Horse, X Corps Cavalry Regiment.] Joined the renamed 9th (North Irish Horse) Battalion from 36 Infantry Base Depot and transferred to Princess Victoria's (Royal Irish Fusiliers) in September/October 1917 (renumbered 41466).

BARR Sergeant Arthur 13979. Born 15 November 1884 at Drumcree, Portadown, County Armagh, one of ten children. 4th (Portadown) Battalion, Armagh Regiment, Ulster Volunteer Force. A clerk. Enlisted September 1914. 'B' Company. Sergeant 22 September 1914. Pioneer Sergeant 21 October 1914. To France with 36th (Ulster) Division in October 1915. Evacuated sick to hospital in England 21 January 1916. Joined the 10th (Reserve) Battalion 26 February 1916. To France 24 May 1916 and rejoined the 9th (Service) Battalion. **Wounded** by a gunshot to the right wrist during the attack at Hamel 1 July 1916. Evacuated to Huddersfield War Hospital, Yorkshire 9 November 1917. Joined the 10th (Reserve) Battalion 31 January 1918 and appointed Pioneer Sergeant (vice Pepper). To the 3rd (Reserve) Battalion 23 May 1918. Rejoined the 9th (North Irish Horse) Battalion 4 September 1918. Evacuated to hospital in England 10 October 1918. Joined the 3rd (Reserve) Battalion 20 November 1918. Discharged as no longer physically fit for war service due to wounds 12 December 1918. Silver War Badge, number B51554. 1914-15 Star. Became Master of Loyal Orange Lodge 89 in 1930. Died on 27 May 1940, aged 55. Brother of Private Edward Barr. His two brothers, John George and Joseph, also served during the war.

BARR Private Edward 13990. Born 2 May 1894 at Lurgan, County Armagh, one of ten children. From Portadown, County Armagh. A linen weaver. Enlisted September 1914. To France with 36th (Ulster) Division in October 1915. [Transferred to the Corps of Royal Engineers (renumbered 338832, renumbered WR/205588, renumbered 602048, renumbered WR/101045).] 1914-15 Star. Died on 27 February 1966, aged 71. Brother of Sergeant Arthur Barr. His two brothers, John George and Joseph, also served during the war.

BARRETT Private Peter 14945. [To France 21 April 1915 and served with the 2nd Battalion.] Posted to the 9th (North Irish Horse) Battalion. 'C' Company. **Missing** in the period 21-28 March 1918 during the retreat from St Quentin believed **captured**. Transferred to the Class Z Reserve 19 March 1919. 1914-15 Star.

BARRETT Lance Corporal St Clair Edward John 23761. Commissioned into Princess Victoria's (Royal Irish Fusiliers) - see Appendix 5.

BARRY Lance Corporal Lennox 45776. [Enlisted into The London Regiment (4395).] To France and joined 36 Infantry Base Depot 29 March 1918. Transferred to Princess Victoria's (Royal Irish Fusiliers) 2 April 1918 (renumbered 45776) and joined the 9th (North Irish Horse) Battalion 4 April 1918. British War Medal and Victory Medal forfeit (having been convicted by the civil power); their issue was authorised in 1931.

BARTON Private Alexander (Jock) 20829. From Loch Lomond. Enlisted 9 August 1915. To France 10 November 1915 and joined the 9th (Service) Battalion. **Wounded** on 11 April 1918 in the actions between Wulverghem and Kemmel. [Transferred to the Labour Corps (renumbered 618031).] Discharged as no longer physically fit for war service due to sickness 6 August 1919. Silver War Badge, number B272020. 1914-15 Star.

BARTON DCM Sergeant Harold 14040. Born in 1894. A boiler fireman from Cloghinny, County Armagh. Enlisted September 1914. To France with 36th (Ulster) Division in October 1915. 'C' Company. Survived the attack at Hamel on 1 July 1916 unwounded. **Wounded** during the Battle of Messines and to hospital 9 June 1917. **Wounded** and **captured** during the retreat from St Quentin 21-28 March 1918. **DCM**. Transferred to the Class Z Reserve 5 April 1919. 1914-15 Star.

BARTON Lance Corporal Samuel Boyd 41208. Born in 1887 at Shankill, Belfast. A damask weaver. [Enlisted 8 February 1915 into the North Irish Horse (1445). Served with 2nd North Irish Horse, X Corps Cavalry Regiment.] Joined the renamed 9th (North Irish Horse) Battalion from 36 Infantry Base Depot and transferred to Princess Victoria's (Royal Irish Fusiliers) in September/October 1917 (renumbered 41208). **Wounded**. Discharged as no longer physically fit for war service due to wounds 13 May 1919. Silver War Badge, number B234835. 1914-15 Star.

BATES Private Thomas 13991. From Portadown, County Armagh. 4th (Portadown) Battalion, Armagh Regiment, Ulster Volunteer Force. Enlisted September 1914. No record of date of deployment to France with 36th (Ulster) Division. Discharged as no longer physically fit for war service due to sickness 28 September 1917, aged 37. Silver War Badge, number 252000.

BATTERBEE Private Charles 43374. Born in 1878 at Jarrow, County Durham. From Canning Town, London. [Enlisted 4 December 1915 and joined the 3/7th Battalion, The London Regiment (6777).] Attached to the 9th (Service) Battalion, Princess Victoria's (Royal Irish Fusiliers) 26 November 1916. 'C' Company. Discharged from the Territorial Force, re-enlisted and transferred to Princess Victoria's (Royal Irish Fusiliers) in March/April 1917 (renumbered 43374). **Killed in action** during the Battle of Messines 9 June 1917.

BAXTER Private Alexander 14009. Born in 1890 at Lurgan, County Armagh. A linen weaver. Enlisted September 1914. To France with 36th (Ulster) Division in October 1915. 'C' Company. To hospital mid-1916, struck off strength when evacuated to hospital in England and did not take part in the attack at Hamel on 1 July 1916. [Transferred to The Northumberland Fusiliers (renumbered 49824).] Discharged as no longer physically fit for war service due to sickness 3 January 1918. Silver War Badge, number 306112. 1914-15 Star. Brother of Private William Edmond Baxter.

BAXTER Lance Corporal Albert 22973. Enlisted in November 1915. Posted to the 9th (Service) Battalion. As a Private in 'B' Company **wounded** at the Battle of Messines and to hospital 9 June 1917. Rejoined the 9th (North Irish Horse) Battalion and served in 'C' Company. **Wounded** in the period 21-28 March 1918 during the retreat from St Quentin.

BAXTER Corporal Bert 42160. Born in 1894 at St Neots, Cambridgeshire. A baker. [Enlisted 30 April 1915 into the Army Service Corps for service as a baker (S4/093500). To France 24 August 1915 and joined 23rd Field Bakery. To 12th Field Bakery 2 September 1916. Corporal 4 July 1917.] Transferred to Princess Victoria's (Royal Irish Fusiliers) 8 May 1918 (renumbered 42160) and joined the 9th (North Irish Horse) Battalion. Tried by Field General Court Martial on 11 January 1919 charged with *'absenting himself without leave'*; found not guilty. Transferred to the Class Z Reserve 4 April 1919. 1914-15 Star.

BAXTER Private George 13983. From Lurgan, County Armagh. Enlisted September 1914. To France with 36th (Ulster) Division in October 1915. **Wounded** during the attack at Hamel 1 July 1916. [Transferred to the Labour Corps (renumbered 545499). Transferred to The Northumberland Fusiliers (renumbered 99504).] Discharged as no longer physically fit for war service due to wounds 19 June 1918, aged 42. Silver War Badge, number 411710. 1914-15 Star.

BAXTER Private Joseph 23657. From Belfast. Enlisted in January 1916. Posted to the 9th (Service) Battalion. 'C' Company. **Wounded** during the attack at Hamel 1 July 1916. **Captured** in the period 21-28 March 1918 during the retreat from St Quentin.

BAXTER Corporal William 14026 & 28963. Enlisted September 1914. To France with 36th (Ulster) Division in October 1915. Transferred or discharged (reason unknown). Re-enlisted in January 1918 (renumbered 28963) and rejoined 9th (North Irish Horse) Battalion. Promoted Corporal. Transferred to the Class Z Reserve 27 January 1919. 1914-15 Star.

BAXTER Private William (Billy) 23216. Born 20 December 1898 at Belfast. From Portadown, County Armagh. A weaver. Enlisted 22 November 1915, aged 15 giving his age as 19 years and 5 months. Joined the 10th (Reserve) Battalion. Lance Corporal 5 September 1917. To 'A' Infantry Base Depot 15 March 1918. To hospital sick (not yet diagnosed) 21 March 1918. Treated at 39th General Hospital (effects of poison irritant drugs - sulphur. i.e. injured during gas training). Joined the 9th (North Irish Horse) Battalion 8 April 1918. Although recorded as posted to the 5th (Service) Battalion, The Royal Irish Regiment (Pioneers) in the Light Division in the British Army of the Rhine on 20 March 1919, he remained with the 9th (North Irish Horse) Battalion cadre. Departed France 13 June 1919. Transferred to the Class Z Reserve 15 July 1919. Died 31 August 1993, aged 94. Buried at Seagoe Cemetery, Portadown, County Armagh.

BAXTER Private William Edmond 14010. Born in 1898 at Lurgan, County Armagh. Enlisted September 1914, aged 16. To France with 36th (Ulster) Division in October 1915. 'C' Company. To hospital mid-1916, struck off strength when evacuated to hospital in England and did not take part in the attack at Hamel on 1 July 1916. [Transferred to The Royal Irish Regiment (renumbered 5839). Transferred to the Corps of Royal Engineers (renumbered 368055).] 1914-15 Star. Brother of Private Alexander Baxter.

BEAMISH Private John Joseph 42514. A railway brakeman. [Enlisted 8 March 1918 into The Royal Irish Rifles (22327).] Transferred at the Base Depot to Princess Victoria's (Royal Irish Fusiliers) 14 September 1918 (renumbered 42514) and joined the 9th (North Irish Horse) Battalion 22 September 1918. [Transferred to 5th (Service) Battalion, The Royal Irish Regiment (Pioneers) in the Light Division in the British Army of the Rhine 22 February 1919 (renumbered 41395). To hospital injured (broken leg) 27 March 1919 and evacuated to hospital in England.] Discharged as no longer physically fit for war service due to wounds 11 September 1919. Silver War Badge, number B314326.

BEARNS Private Robert 41697. Born in 1898. From Aughnacloy, County Fermanagh. [Enlisted 14 November 1914, aged 16, into the Service Squadron, 6th (Inniskilling) Dragoons (UD/164). To France with 36th (Ulster) Division in October 1915. Served with 2nd North Irish Horse, X Corps Cavalry Regiment.] Joined the renamed 9th (North Irish Horse) Battalion from 36 Infantry Base Depot and transferred to Princess Victoria's (Royal Irish Fusiliers) in September/October 1917 (renumbered 41697). **Wounded**. Discharged as no longer physically fit for war service due to wounds 23 November 1918. Silver War Badge, number B44352. 1914-15 Star.

BEASLEY Private Ernest Alfred 42113. [Enlisted into the Army Veterinary Corps (17749).] Transferred to Princess Victoria's (Royal Irish Fusiliers) 8 May 1918 (renumbered 42113) and joined the 9th (North Irish Horse) Battalion.

BEATTIE Private Alexander 19763. From Bessbrook, County Armagh. Enlisted into the 9th

(Service) Battalion in April 1915. **Wounded** during the attack at Hamel 1 July 1916 and **died of wounds** 9 July 1916. His brother, Private James Beattie, was killed in action at Thiepval on 1 July 1916 serving with 13th (Service) Battalion, The Royal Irish Rifles (1st County Down). His brother, Private John Beattie, served with Princess Victoria's (Royal Irish Fusiliers).

BEATTIE Private Harold 41124. Born in 1884 at Belfast. [Enlisted in November 1914 into the Service Squadron, 6th (Inniskilling) Dragoons (UD/139). To France with 36th (Ulster) Division in October 1915. Trained as a signaller. Served with 2nd North Irish Horse, X Corps Cavalry Regiment.] Joined the renamed 9th (North Irish Horse) Battalion from 36 Infantry Base Depot and transferred to Princess Victoria's (Royal Irish Fusiliers) in September/October 1917 (renumbered 41124). Transferred to the Class Z Reserve 31 March 1919. 1914-15 Star.

BEATTIE Private John 8936. [Enlisted into Princess Victoria's (Royal Irish Fusiliers) as a regular soldier in 1905. To France with the 1st Battalion 22 August 1914.] Posted to the 9th (Service) Battalion. [Subsequently rejoined the 1st Battalion.] 1914 Star & clasp.

BEATTIE Private John James 14041. Born in 1881 at Dungannon, County Tyrone. From Belfast. A flax dresser. Enlisted September 1914. Discharged as not being likely to become an efficient soldier in that he was considered medically unfit for service (bronchitis) 26 March 1915, aged 33.

BEATTIE Corporal Robert 20652. Enlisted July 1915. Posted to the 9th (Service) Battalion.

BEATTIE Private William George 14007. Enlisted September 1914. To France with 36th (Ulster) Division in October 1915. 'C' Company. In hospital just prior to the attack at Hamel 1 July 1916, he rejoined and served as a signaller and Battalion runner during the attack, which he survived unwounded. Later **wounded**. Discharged as no longer physically fit for war service due to wounds 15 March 1919. Silver War Badge, number B162471. 1914-15 Star.

BEATTY Private Robert 14006. Born 1880 at Ballyshannon, County Donegal. From Armagh, County Armagh. A compositor at the Armagh Guardian. Enlisted September 1914. To France with 36th (Ulster) Division in October 1915. 'A' Company. **Wounded** by a gunshot to the shoulder during the attack at Hamel 1 July 1916. Evacuated to hospital in England and treated at the 3rd Western General Hospital, Cardiff. To 36 Infantry Base Depot 2 May 1917 and rejoined the 9th (Service) Battalion 23 May 1917. **Wounded** at the Battle of Langemarck 16 August 1917 and evacuated to hospital in England. Irish Command Depot, Tipperary 9 February 1918. Transferred to the Class Z Reserve 6 February 1919. 1914-15 Star.

BEAUMONT Private William Charles 42285. [Enlisted 16 March 1915 into the Army Veterinary Corps (5095). To France 1 September 1915.] Transferred to Princess Victoria's (Royal Irish Fusiliers) 8 May 1918 (renumbered 42285) and joined the 9th (North Irish Horse) Battalion. **Wounded**. Discharged as no longer physically fit for war service due to wounds 30 August 1919. Silver War Badge, number B301537.

BECK Private John 41585. [Enlisted in September 1914 into the North Irish Horse (1114). Served with 2nd North Irish Horse, X Corps Cavalry Regiment.] Joined the renamed 9th (North Irish Horse) Battalion from 36 Infantry Base Depot and transferred to Princess Victoria's (Royal Irish Fusiliers) in September/October 1917 (renumbered 41585). Transferred to the Class Z Reserve 8 March 1919. 1914-15 Star.

BEER Lance Corporal Frank 43442. Born 14 July 1887 at London. From Bermondsey, London. A clerk. [Enlisted 15 September 1914 into The London Regiment (2403). To France 15 March 1915 and joined 1/22nd (County of London) Battalion, The London Regiment (The Queen's). To hospital sick (fever) 12-25 October 1915. **Wounded** by gunshots to the chest and leg 28 January 1916. Treated at 5th General Hospital, Rouen and evacuated to hospital in England 8 February 1916. Lance Corporal 23 February 1916. Renumbered 680886, The London Regiment in March 1917.] To France and joined 36 Infantry Base Depot 29 March 1918. Transferred to Princess Victoria's (Royal Irish Fusiliers) 2 April 1918 (renumbered 43442) and joined the 9th (North Irish Horse) Battalion 4 April 1918. To 63rd Casualty Clearing Station sick (dysentery) 20 September 1918. To 30th General Hospital 24 September and then evacuated to hospital in England. Treated at 2nd Western General Hospital, Manchester from 28 September 1918. Transferred to the Class Z Reserve 5 April 1919.

BEGGS Private Joseph 41075. [Enlisted 18 November 1914 into the Service Squadron, 6th (Inniskilling) Dragoons (UD/107). To France with 36th (Ulster) Division in October 1915. Served with 2nd North Irish Horse, X Corps Cavalry Regiment.] Joined the renamed 9th (North Irish Horse)

Battalion from 36 Infantry Base Depot and transferred to Princess Victoria's (Royal Irish Fusiliers) in September/October 1917 (renumbered 41705). **Wounded**. Discharged as no longer physically fit for war service due to wounds 27 March 1919. Silver War Badge, number B165705. 1914-15 Star.

BEHAN Private Patrick 18369 & 27637. Born in 1892 at Dublin. [Enlisted on 18 March 1915 and joined the 7th (Service) Battalion in 49th Brigade, 16th (Irish) Division (18369). 'A' Company. **Wounded** accidentally by grenade fragments to the shoulder 14 April 1916 during training with rifle grenades. Evacuated to hospital in Scotland. Treated at the War Hospital, Dundee. Posted to the 4th (Extra Reserve) Battalion 9 June 1916. Transferred to The Royal Irish Regiment 13 October 1916 (renumbered 2G/1892) and joined the 2nd (Home Service) Garrison Battalion, The Royal Irish Regiment. Transferred back to Princess Victoria's (Royal Irish Fusiliers) 26 May 1917 (renumbered 27637). Sentenced to twenty-one days detention for *'breaking out of barracks when under orders for overseas'*. To France 7 August 1917. Rejoined the 7th/8th (Service) Battalion.] Joined the 9th (North Irish Horse) Battalion when the 7th/8th (Service) Battalion was disbanded in February 1918. **Killed in action** by shellfire at Poperinghe railway station 9 April 1918.

BELL Private Edwin Victor 41190. Born 9 February 1897 at Belfast. A clerk. [Enlisted 20 September 1915 into the North Irish Horse (1726). To France 22 March 1916 and joined 'F' Squadron. Served with 2nd North Irish Horse, X Corps Cavalry Regiment.] Joined the renamed 9th (North Irish Horse) Battalion from 36 Infantry Base Depot and transferred to Princess Victoria's (Royal Irish Fusiliers) in September/October 1917 (renumbered 41190). 'D' Company. [Transferred to the Tank Corps (renumbered 304883 Tank Mechanic) 28 December 1917 and posted for training to the Tank Corps Depot, at Bovington near Wareham, Dorset. To France 19 June 1918 and joined the 1st Battalion, Tank Corps.] Transferred to the Class Z Reserve 24 February 1919.

BELL Corporal Francis 8586. [Enlisted into Princess Victoria's (Royal Irish Fusiliers) as a regular soldier in 1904. To France with the 1st Battalion 22 August 1914.] Posted to the 9th (North Irish Horse) Battalion. 'A' Company. **Captured** in the period 21-28 March 1918 during the retreat from St Quentin. 1914 Star.

BELL Private Isaac 15857. Enlisted into the 9th (Service) Battalion in October 1914. To France with 36th (Ulster) Division in October 1915. [Transferred to the Labour Corps (renumbered 516666).] Transferred to the Class Z Reserve 22 March 1919. 1914-15 Star.

BELL Private James Alexander 14027. Born at Shankill, Belfast. From Aghalee, County Antrim. Enlisted September 1914. To France with 36th (Ulster) Division in October 1915. 'C' Company. **Killed in action** during the attack at Hamel 1 July 1916, aged 19. 1914-15 Star.

BELL Private John 17541. Enlisted into the 9th (Service) Battalion in November/December 1914. To France with 36th (Ulster) Division in October 1915. **Wounded** during the attack at Hamel 1 July 1916. [Transferred to The Royal Fusiliers (City of London Regiment) (renumbered 144019). Transferred to the Labour Corps (renumbered 420838).] Transferred to the Class Z Reserve. 1914-15 Star.

BELL Lance Corporal John 21601. Enlisted 16 September 1915. Posted to the 9th (Service) Battalion in mid/late 1916. 'B' Company. **Wounded** during the retreat from St Quentin 21-28 March 1918. Discharged as no longer physically fit for war service due to wounds 29 July 1918, aged 35. Silver War Badge, number 379049.

BELL Private John 41411. [Enlisted into the Army Service Corps (059077 – Driver). Transferred to the North Irish Horse (renumbered 2674) in September 1917. Served with 2nd North Irish Horse, X Corps Cavalry Regiment.] Joined the renamed 9th (North Irish Horse) Battalion from 36 Infantry Base Depot and transferred to Princess Victoria's (Royal Irish Fusiliers) in September/October 1917 (renumbered 41411). 'A' Company. **Missing** in the period 21-28 March 1918 during the retreat from St Quentin believed **captured**.

BELL Private John A 41333. From Newry, County Down. [Enlisted in August 1916 into the North Irish Horse (2245). Served with 2nd North Irish Horse, X Corps Cavalry Regiment.] Joined the renamed 9th (North Irish Horse) Battalion from 36 Infantry Base Depot and transferred to Princess Victoria's (Royal Irish Fusiliers) in September/October 1917 (renumbered 41333). 'B' Company. Separated from the 9th (North Irish Horse) Battalion in the period 21-28 March 1918 during the retreat from St Quentin; rejoined 3 April 1918. **Missing** in the period 11-18 April 1918 in the actions between Wulverghem and Kemmel; subsequently declared **killed in action** 19 April 1918.

BELL Private P. Tried by Field General Court Martial on 19 June 1917 charged with an unknown act *'to the prejudice of good order and military discipline'*; found not guilty. Soldier not identified.

BELL Private Randal 41458. Born 8 December 1894 at Lurgan, County Armagh. [Enlisted in November 1915 into the North Irish Horse (2004). Served with 2nd North Irish Horse, X Corps Cavalry Regiment.] Joined the renamed 9th (North Irish Horse) Battalion from 36 Infantry Base Depot and transferred to Princess Victoria's (Royal Irish Fusiliers) in September/October 1917 (renumbered 41458).

BELL Private Robert 14035. Born in Crilly, County Tyrone. From Dunmurry, County Antrim. Enlisted September 1914. To France with 36th (Ulster) Division in October 1915. 'C' Company. **Killed in action** during the attack at Hamel 1 July 1916.

BELL Private Thomas James 18674. Enlisted into the 9th (Service) Battalion in April 1915. To France with 36th (Ulster) Division in October 1915. **Wounded**. Discharged as no longer physically fit for war service due to wounds 10 October 1918. Silver War Badge, number B34912. 1914-15 Star.

BELL Private Victor Nelson 41254. Born at Londonderry, County Londonderry. A clerk in the shipping office of G & J Burns. [Enlisted 5 September 1914 into the North Irish Horse (1154). To France 19 January 1915. Served with 2nd North Irish Horse, X Corps Cavalry Regiment.] Joined the renamed 9th (North Irish Horse) Battalion from 36 Infantry Base Depot and transferred to Princess Victoria's (Royal Irish Fusiliers) in September/October 1917 (renumbered 41254). **Killed in action** 26 October 1917 at Havrincourt, aged 20. 1914-15 Star.

BELL Private William 41629. [Enlisted in June 1915 into the North Irish Horse (1682). Served with 2nd North Irish Horse, X Corps Cavalry Regiment.] Joined the renamed 9th (North Irish Horse) Battalion from 36 Infantry Base Depot and transferred to Princess Victoria's (Royal Irish Fusiliers) in September/October 1917 (renumbered 41629). 'D' Company. **Wounded** during the retreat from St Quentin 21-28 March 1918.

BELL Lance Corporal William George 23725. From Hamiltonsbawn, County Armagh. Enlisted 13 January 1916. Posted to the 9th (Service) Battalion. 'C' Company. **Wounded** at the Battle of Langemarck 16 August 1917. Discharged as no longer physically fit for war service due to wounds 18 February 1918. Silver War Badge, number 318451.

BELLAMY Private Samuel 40052. [Enlisted into the, The Prince of Wales's Own (West Yorkshire Regiment) (8622). To France and joined the 1st Battalion 13 July 1915.] Transferred to Princess Victoria's (Royal Irish Fusiliers) 30 November 1916 (renumbered 40052) and joined the 9th (Service) Battalion 12 December 1916. Discharged 14 December 1918. 1914-15 Star.

BELLINGER Private Harry Fowler 42130. Born 1 August 1888. [Enlisted into the Army Veterinary Corps (8845). To France 5 June 1915.] Transferred to Princess Victoria's (Royal Irish Fusiliers) 8 May 1918 (renumbered 42130) and joined the 9th (North Irish Horse) Battalion. Transferred to the Class Z Reserve. Died in Oxfordshire in 1972, aged 83.

BENNETT Private Robert 41117. [Enlisted into the 8th (King's Royal Irish) Hussars (6539). To France 11 November 1914 in the Ambala Cavalry Brigade, 1st Indian Cavalry Division. Served with 2nd North Irish Horse, X Corps Cavalry Regiment.] Joined the renamed 9th (North Irish Horse) Battalion from 36 Infantry Base Depot and transferred to Princess Victoria's (Royal Irish Fusiliers) in September/October 1917 (renumbered 41117). 1914 Star.

BERESFORD Private Samuel 41430. [Enlisted in November 1915 into the North Irish Horse (1982). Served with 2nd North Irish Horse, X Corps Cavalry Regiment.] Joined the renamed 9th (North Irish Horse) Battalion from 36 Infantry Base Depot and transferred to Princess Victoria's (Royal Irish Fusiliers) in September/October 1917 (renumbered 41430).

BERESFORD Private Thomas H 41363. [Enlisted in June 1915 into the North Irish Horse (1709). Served with 2nd North Irish Horse, X Corps Cavalry Regiment.] Joined the renamed 9th (North Irish Horse) Battalion from 36 Infantry Base Depot and transferred to Princess Victoria's (Royal Irish Fusiliers) in September/October 1917 (renumbered 41363). [Transferred to The Royal Irish Rifles (renumbered 47499) and served with the 12th (Service) Battalion, The Royal Irish Rifles (Central Antrim).]

BERRILL Private George 41231. From Newry, County Down. [Enlisted 18 January 1916 into the

North Irish Horse (2067) (enlistment date is erroneously recorded on the Silver War Badge roll). Served with 2nd North Irish Horse, X Corps Cavalry Regiment.] Joined the renamed 9th (North Irish Horse) Battalion from 36 Infantry Base Depot and transferred to Princess Victoria's (Royal Irish Fusiliers) in September/October 1917 (renumbered 41231). 'D' Company. **Captured** in the period 21-28 March 1918 during the retreat from St Quentin. Discharged as no longer physically fit for war service due to sickness 12 April 1919. Silver War Badge, number B211234.

BERRINGTON Lance Corporal Charles Edwin 43264. Born in 1879 at Bestwood, Nottingham. [Enlisted into The Sherwood Foresters (Nottinghamshire and Derbyshire Regiment).] Transferred to Princess Victoria's (Royal Irish Fusiliers) 31 August 1916 having joined the 9th (Service) Battalion on 8 August 1916 (renumbered 43264). 'D' Company. **Wounded** at the Battle of Langemarck 16 August 1917. Died at Nottingham in 1950, aged 70.

BERRY Private Francis William 42491. Born in 1899 at Gloucester. Worked as a labourer in National Filling Factory Number 5 at Quedgeley. [Enlisted 10 February 1917, aged 17, and transferred to the Army Reserve. Mobilised 30 May 1917 and joined 45th Training Reserve Battalion. Transferred to The Rifle Brigade (The Prince Consorts Own) (35926) 11 October 1917. To 'A' Infantry Base Depot 31 March 1918 and transferred to the 2nd Battalion, The Royal Irish Rifles (renumbered 54224) 2 April 1918. **Wounded** by a gas shell 16 August 1918. Treated at 62 Casualty Clearing Station, Arneke and 83rd General Hospital, Boulogne.] Transferred at the Base Depot to Princess Victoria's (Royal Irish Fusiliers) 14 September 1918 (renumbered 42491) and joined the 9th (North Irish Horse) Battalion 22 September 1918. **Missing** during the attack at Vijfwegen on 30 September or 1 October 1918; recorded as **killed in action** during the period 30 September to 3 October 1918.

BERRY Corporal James 42161. Born in Stratford-upon-Avon, Warwickshire. [Enlisted into the Army Service Corps (S4/038970). To France 18 May 1915.] Transferred to Princess Victoria's (Royal Irish Fusiliers) 8 May 1918 (renumbered 42161) and joined the 9th (North Irish Horse) Battalion. [Transferred to The Royal Inniskilling Fusiliers (renumbered 48656) 31 August 1918 and joined the 2nd Battalion. **Killed in action** 8 September 1918 at Hill 63.] 1914-15-Star.

BEST Private Frank 13988. Born in 1879. From Portadown, County Armagh. 4th (Portadown) Battalion, Armagh Regiment, Ulster Volunteer Force. A shoemaker. Enlisted September 1914. To France with 36th (Ulster) Division in October 1915. 5 Platoon, 'B' Company in 1916. **Wounded** during the attack at Hamel 1 July 1916. Employed and paid as a Battalion cobbler. Transferred to the Class Z Reserve 11 March 1919. 1914-15 Star.

BEST Private Frank 41396. From Richhill, County Armagh. [Enlisted in September 1914 into the North Irish Horse (1115) To France 1 May 1915. Served with 2nd North Irish Horse, X Corps Cavalry Regiment.] Joined the renamed 9th (North Irish Horse) Battalion from 36 Infantry Base Depot and transferred to Princess Victoria's (Royal Irish Fusiliers) in September/October 1917 (renumbered 41396). 'D' Company. Believed **wounded** in the period 21-28 March 1918 during the retreat from St Quentin. **Wounded** during the attack at Vijfwegen on 30 September or 1 October 1918 and **died of wounds** 3 October 1918. 1914-15 Star.

BEST Private Thomas Henry 13980. From Portadown, County Armagh. 4th (Portadown) Battalion, Armagh Regiment, Ulster Volunteer Force. Enlisted September 1914. To France with 36th (Ulster) Division in October 1915. **Wounded** in the face and leg during the attack at Hamel 1 July 1916. Transferred to the Class Z Reserve 25 February 1919. 1914-15 Star. He died after the war and is buried in Seagoe Cemetery, Portadown, County Armagh and commemorated on Portadown War Memorial.

BEST Private William Henry 13977. Born in 1882 at Armagh. From Clounagh, Portadown, County Armagh. Worked for the Portadown Cooperative Society. Enlisted September 1914. To France with 36th (Ulster) Division in October 1915. **Killed in action** during the attack at Hamel 1 July 1916. 1914-15 Star.

BETHEL Sergeant David Henry 16093. Born in 1896 at County Monaghan. Enlisted into the 9th (Service) Battalion in October 1914. 'D' Company. To France with 36th (Ulster) Division in October 1915. **Wounded** at the Battle of Langemarck 16 August 1917. [Posted to the 1st Battalion. **Captured** in March/April 1918.] Transferred to the Class Z Reserve 2 April 1919. 1914-15 Star.

BICKETT Private Robert 41474. [Enlisted in August 1910 into the North Irish Horse (531). To

France 20 August 1914 with 'C' Squadron as 5th Division Cavalry and then as GHQ Troops. Served with 2nd North Irish Horse, X Corps Cavalry Regiment.] Joined the renamed 9th (North Irish Horse) Battalion from 36 Infantry Base Depot and transferred to Princess Victoria's (Royal Irish Fusiliers) in September/October 1917 (renumbered 41474). 'B' Company. **Missing** in the period 21-28 March 1918 during the retreat from St Quentin believed **captured**. 1914 Star.

BIGGART Private William 41388. Born in 1896 at Bendooragh, Ballymoney, County Antrim. A farm labourer on the Leslie Hill estate, Ballymoney. [Enlisted 19 November 1915 into the North Irish Horse (1932). To France 5 August 1916. Served with 2nd North Irish Horse, X Corps Cavalry Regiment.] Joined the renamed 9th (North Irish Horse) Battalion from 36 Infantry Base Depot and transferred to Princess Victoria's (Royal Irish Fusiliers) in September/October 1917 (renumbered 41388). 'A' Company. **Wounded** and **captured** during the retreat from St Quentin 21-28 March 1918 and **died of wounds** 3 April 1918 in captivity.

BINGHAM Private Joseph 41357. [Enlisted in November 1915 into the North Irish Horse (1869). Served with 2nd North Irish Horse, X Corps Cavalry Regiment.] Joined the renamed 9th (North Irish Horse) Battalion from 36 Infantry Base Depot and transferred to Princess Victoria's (Royal Irish Fusiliers) in September/October 1917 (renumbered 41357). [Transferred back to the North Irish Horse (renumbered Corps of Hussars 71606). Served with 5th Cyclist Battalion (North Irish Horse), V Corps.]

BINNS Private Thomas Wilkinson 40054. Born on 14 June 1895 at Keighley, Yorkshire. [Enlisted 11 January 1915 into the 15th (Service) Battalion, The Prince of Wales's Own (West Yorkshire Regiment) (1st Leeds) (1138). To Egypt 30 December 1915 with 93rd Brigade in 31st Division. **Wounded**.] Transferred to Princess Victoria's (Royal Irish Fusiliers) 30 November 1916 (renumbered 40054) and joined the 9th (Service) Battalion 12 December 1916. 'B' Company. Initially reported **missing**, he was **wounded** at the Battle of Langemarck 16 August 1917. Discharged as no longer physically fit for war service due to wounds 6 December 1918. Silver War Badge, number B54750. 1914-15 Star. After the war he worked for Leeds City Council and Chesterfield Rural District Council. He lived at Barlow, Derbyshire. Died at Glusburn near Keighley, Yorkshire on 27 December 1972, aged 77. His brother, Private Arthur Binns MM, also served with the 15th (Service) Battalion, The Prince of Wales's Own (West Yorkshire Regiment) (1st Leeds) and was captured in March 1918.

BINSLEY Private Harold 20339. (His name was actually spelled Binningsley but the family used the shortened version.) Born 25 January 1899 at Penshaw, Houghton-le-Spring, County Durham. A miner. Enlisted into The Royal Inniskilling Fusiliers 17 May 1915, aged 16, and joined the 12th (Reserve) Battalion. Transferred to Princess Victoria's (Royal Irish Fusiliers) 30 June 1915 (renumbered 20339). To France with 36th (Ulster) Division in October 1915. **Wounded** by a gunshot to the right leg 29 February 1916 and evacuated to hospital in England 8 March 1916. Treated at the Red Cross Hospital, Southampton. In May 1916 his mother wrote requesting his release from service on account of his age, by then 17 years. Posted to the 10th (Reserve) Battalion 30 June 1916. Classified as 'A4' - fit for general service but underage. [Transferred to The Royal Irish Rifles 30 June 1917. Transferred back to Princess Victoria's (Royal Irish Fusiliers) 18 January 1918 and posted to the 10th (Reserve) Battalion. Transferred to the Labour Corps (renumbered 545516) 6 April 1918.] Transferred to the Class P Reserve 3 July 1918 as a coal miner. 1914-15 Star. Died in 1928 in County Durham, aged 29.

BIRD Private Frederick Arthur 45821. Enlisted 8 May 1915. Joined the 9th (North Irish Horse) Battalion, Princess Victoria's (Royal Irish Fusiliers) with the draft of men from The London Regiment in April 1918. **Wounded**. Discharged as no longer physically fit for war service due to wounds 25 October 1918. Silver War Badge, number B34894.

BIRD Sergeant Herbert Alfred 43343. Joined the 9th (Service) Battalion, Princess Victoria's (Royal Irish Fusiliers) with the draft of men from The London Regiment in November 1916. **Mention in Despatches**.

BIRD Private James 40003. From Sunderland, County Durham. [Enlisted 1 May 1913 into The Prince of Wales's Own (West Yorkshire Regiment) (7883). Served with the 11th (Service) Battalion, The Prince of Wales's Own (West Yorkshire Regiment).] Transferred to Princess Victoria's (Royal Irish Fusiliers) 30 November 1916 (renumbered 40003) and joined the 9th (Service) Battalion 12

December 1916. 'A' Company. **Wounded** at the Battle of Langemarck 16 August 1917. Discharged as no longer physically fit for war service due to wounds 16 January 1919. Silver War Badge, number 510782. 1914-15 Star.

BIRNIE Private Robert Turner 41526. Born in 1896 in Cumbria. [Enlisted 9 November 1915 into the North Irish Horse (1832). Served with 2nd North Irish Horse, X Corps Cavalry Regiment.] Joined the renamed 9th (North Irish Horse) Battalion from 36 Infantry Base Depot and transferred to Princess Victoria's (Royal Irish Fusiliers) in September/October 1917 (renumbered 41526). [Transferred to the Machine Gun Corps (renumbered 143851). **Wounded**.] Discharged as no longer physically fit for war service due to wounds 12 June 1919, aged 23. Silver War Badge, number B244162.

BISHOP Lance Corporal Wallace Edward 27841. Born in 1884 at Bridgwater, Somerset. From Bedminster, Bristol. A storeman & tobacco weigher. Enlisted 30 November 1915 and transferred to the Army Reserve. Mobilised 2 June 1916 and joined the Army Ordnance Corps. Transferred to Princess Victoria's (Royal Irish Fusiliers) 25 July 1917 and joined the 10th (Reserve) Battalion. Lance Corporal 5 September 1917. To France 24 January 1918 and joined the 9th (North Irish Horse) Battalion 27 January 1918. 'B' Company. **Wounded** by a gunshot to the left arm on at Erches on 27 March during the retreat from St Quentin. Discharged as no longer physically fit for war service due to wounds 25 November 1918. Silver War Badge, number B46746. Died at Bristol in 1974, aged 89.

BITTLE Private Samuel 42499. [Enlisted into The Royal Irish Rifles (20123).] Transferred at the Base Depot to Princess Victoria's (Royal Irish Fusiliers) 14 September 1918 (renumbered 42499) and joined the 9th (North Irish Horse) Battalion 22 September 1918.

BLACK Private Alexander 20067. Enlisted into the 9th (Service) Battalion 2 June 1915. To France with 36th (Ulster) Division in October 1915. **Wounded**. Discharged as no longer physically fit for war service due to sickness 12 November 1916. Silver War Badge, number 509027. 1914-15 Star.

BLACK Private David 16094. From Bannaghroe, County Monaghan. A farmer's son. Enlisted into the 9th (Service) Battalion in October 1914. To France with 36th (Ulster) Division in October 1915. **Killed in action** during the attack at Hamel 1 July 1916, aged 19. 1914-15 Star. Brother of Privates John and Samuel Black.

BLACK Lance Corporal Hugh 16096. From Newbliss, County Monaghan. Enlisted into the 9th (Service) Battalion in October 1914. To France with 36th (Ulster) Division in October 1915. **Wounded** during the attack at Hamel 1 July 1916. Transferred to the Class Z Reserve 3 April 1919. 1914-15 Star.

BLACK Private Isaac 15858. From Portadown, County Armagh. Enlisted into the 9th (Service) Battalion 14 October 1914. To France with 36th (Ulster) Division in October 1915. **Wounded**. [Transferred to The Gloucestershire Regiment (renumbered 53417).] Discharged as no longer physically fit for war service 11 July 1916, aged 30. Silver War Badge, number 447122. 1914-15 Star.

BLACK Sergeant James 14045, 33638 & 7041723. Born in 1892 at Bessbrook, County Armagh. A wood turner. Enlisted September 1914. To France with 36th (Ulster) Division in October 1915. 'A' Company. **Wounded** at the Battle of Langemarck 16 August 1917. [Transferred to the Machine Gun Corps (renumbered 136938) and served with 19th Battalion, Machine Gun Corps.] 1914-15 Star. Re-enlisted 27 November 1919 for Regular Army service with Princess Victoria's (Royal Irish Fusiliers) (renumbered 33638, renumbered 7041723). Served with the 1st Battalion in Persia and Mesopotamia in 1919/20. General Service Medal 1918-1962 with clasps 'Iraq' & 'NW Persia'. Discharged 25 April 1922. His brother, Sergeant William Black, a regular soldier, was killed in action on 16 December 1914 serving with the 2nd Battalion, The Royal Irish Rifles.

BLACK Private John 17913. From Bannaghroe, County Monaghan. Enlisted into the 9th (Service) Battalion 29 January 1915. 3 Section, 13 Platoon, 'D' Company. To France with 36th (Ulster) Division in October 1915. **Wounded** during the attack at Hamel 1 July 1916. Discharged as no longer physically fit for war service due to sickness 3 July 1918, aged 26. Silver War Badge, number 415885. 1914-15 Star. Brother of Private David and Samuel Black.

BLACK Private John Edward 18862. Born in Sunderland. [Enlisted into the Hussars of the Line (10532).] Transferred to Princess Victoria's (Royal Irish Fusiliers) in April 1915 (renumbered

18862). Posted to the 1st Battalion.] Posted to the 9th (North Irish Horse) Battalion. **Killed in action** 25 September 1917 by shellfire at Havrincourt, aged 27.

BLACK Corporal Joseph 41387. From Coleraine, County Londonderry. [Enlisted in November 1915 into the North Irish Horse (1939). Served with 2nd North Irish Horse, X Corps Cavalry Regiment.] Joined the renamed 9th (North Irish Horse) Battalion from 36 Infantry Base Depot and transferred to Princess Victoria's (Royal Irish Fusiliers) in September/October 1917 (renumbered 41387). 'A' Company. **Captured** in the period 21-28 March 1918 during the retreat from St Quentin.

BLACK Private Samuel 16095. From Bannaghroe, County Monaghan. A farmer's son. Enlisted into the 9th (Service) Battalion in October 1914. 'D' Company. To France with 36th (Ulster) Division in October 1915. **Wounded** and **captured** in the period 21-28 March 1918 during the retreat from St Quentin. Transferred to the Class Z Reserve 20 March 1919. 1914-15 Star. Brother of Private David and John Black.

BLACK Private Thomas Henry 14002. Born in Waringstown, County Down. From Lurgan, County Armagh. Enlisted September 1914. To France with 36th (Ulster) Division in October 1915. 'C' Company. Lewis gunner. **Killed in action** during the attack at Hamel 1 July 1916, aged 29. 1914-15 Star.

BLACKBURN Private Robert 22016. Enlisted 6 October 1915. Posted to the 9th (Service) Battalion. 'D' Company. **Wounded** during the Battle of Messines on 8 or 9 June 1917. To hospital 9 June 1917. Discharged as no longer physically fit for war service due to wounds 18 June 1918, aged 31. Silver War Badge, number 387957.

BLAIR Private John 41517. [Enlisted on 1 September 1914 into the North Irish Horse (1078). To France 13 April 1915. Served with 2nd North Irish Horse, X Corps Cavalry Regiment.] Joined the renamed 9th (North Irish Horse) Battalion from 36 Infantry Base Depot and transferred to Princess Victoria's (Royal Irish Fusiliers) in September/October 1917 (renumbered 41517). [Subsequently attached to 12th (Service) Battalion, The Royal Irish Rifles (Central Antrim).] Transferred to the Class Z Reserve 11 March 1919. 1914-15 Star.

BLAIR Private Joseph 5525. [Enlisted into Princess Victoria's (Royal Irish Fusiliers) Special Reserve. Mobilised from the Special Reserve and to France 22 August 1914 with the 1st Battalion. Posted to the 2nd Battalion.] Posted to the 9th (Service) Battalion. [Posted to the 2nd Garrison Battalion in Salonika.]

BLAIR Private Joseph 22635. From Portadown, County Armagh. Enlisted in November 1915. Posted to the 9th (Service) Battalion. 'B' Company. **Wounded** at the Battle of Langemarck 16 August 1917. **Captured** in the period 21-28 March 1918 during the retreat from St Quentin.

BLAIR Private Michael 19981, 33700 & 7041767. Born in 1898 at Newry, County Down. Enlisted into the 9th (Service) Battalion in May 1915. [Posted to the 1st Battalion. **Captured** in March or April 1918.] Re-enlisted 29 December 1919 for Regular Army service with Princess Victoria's (Royal Irish Fusiliers) (renumbered 33700, renumbered 7041767). Discharged 31 March 1921. Enlisted into the Air Raid Precautions Corps 18 December 1939.

BLAIR Private William Robert 41370. [Enlisted into 'E' Squadron, North Irish Horse (1391). To France with 'F' Squadron in 33rd Division 17 November 1915.] Joined the renamed 9th (North Irish Horse) Battalion from 36 Infantry Base Depot and transferred to Princess Victoria's (Royal Irish Fusiliers) in September/October 1917 (renumbered 41370). Transferred to the Class Z Reserve 26 January 1919. 1914-15 Star.

BLAKE Private James 25943. From Belfast. [Enlisted in December 1916 and joined the 7th/8th (Service) Battalion in 49th Brigade, 16th (Irish) Division.] Joined the 9th (North Irish Horse) Battalion when the 7th/8th (Service) Battalion was disbanded in February 1918. 'A' Company. **Captured** in the period 21-28 March 1918 during the retreat from St Quentin.

BLAKE Private Leopold Ernest William 42500. Born in 1899 at Battersea, London. [Enlisted 19 May 1916, aged 17, and transferred to the Army Reserve. Mobilised 13 February 1917. Joined 110th Training Reserve Battalion (70360). To France 15 November 1917 and posted to 1/18th (County of London) Battalion, The London Regiment (London Irish Rifles) (renumbered 71522). Transferred to The Royal Irish Rifles (renumbered 45573) and joined the 2nd Battalion. **Wounded**

by a gunshot to the back 20 February 1918. Treated at 1st South African General Hospital, where he was recorded as 1/18th (County of London) Battalion, The London Regiment (London Irish Rifles) (71522), causing considerable administrative confusion. Evacuated to Belmont Road Auxiliary Hospital, London.] To France 6 September 1918 for service with the 2nd Battalion, The Royal Irish Rifles. Transferred at the Base Depot to Princess Victoria's (Royal Irish Fusiliers) 14 September 1918 and joined the 9th (North Irish Horse) Battalion 22 September 1918. **Killed in action** at Hill 41 11 October 1918, aged 19.

BLAKELY Private James 14039. Born in 1891 at Bessbrook, County Armagh. Enlisted September 1914. To France with 36th (Ulster) Division in October 1915. **Wounded** by shrapnel at Hamel in February 1916. **Killed in action** during the attack at Hamel 1 July 1916. 1914-15 Star. Brother of Private Robert John Blakely.

BLAKELY Private Robert John 14023. Born at Bessbrook, County Armagh. Enlisted September 1914. To France with 36th (Ulster) Division in October 1915. Transferred to the Class Z Reserve 22 March 1919. 1914-15 Star. Brother of Private James Blakely.

BLAKEMAN Private John 27564 & 7040806. From Stoke-on-Trent. A miner. Enlisted 30 July 1915. Transferred to the Army Reserve or served elsewhere before mobilising or transferring to Princess Victoria's (Royal Irish Fusiliers) in May 1917. To France 12 June 1917 and joined the 9th (Service) Battalion. **Wounded** 29 September 1917. Evacuated to hospital in England (probably sick) 27 July 1918. Transferred to the Section B Army Reserve, Princess Victoria's (Royal Irish Fusiliers) (renumbered 7040806). Discharged 29 July 1927.

BLAKEY Private Gordon 23809. Enlisted in January 1916. Posted to the 9th (Service) Battalion.

BLAZEY Corporal Ernest 42165. [Enlisted into the Army Service Corps (S4/39083). Served with 8th Field Bakery.] Transferred to Princess Victoria's (Royal Irish Fusiliers) 8 May 1918 (renumbered 42165) and joined the 9th (North Irish Horse) Battalion. Transferred to the Class Z Reserve.

BLENKIN Private John 40041. [Enlisted into the 11th (Service) Battalion, The Prince of Wales's Own (West Yorkshire Regiment) (15746). To France 26 August 1915 in 69th Brigade, 23rd Division.] Transferred to Princess Victoria's (Royal Irish Fusiliers) 30 November 1916 (renumbered 40041) and joined the 9th (Service) Battalion 12 December 1916. 'A' Company. **Missing** in the period 21-28 March 1918 during the retreat from St Quentin believed **captured**. Transferred to the Class Z Reserve 14 March 1919. 1914-15 Star.

BLEVINS Private George 24371. From Derrylee, County Tyrone. Enlisted 18 May 1916. Posted to the 9th (Service) Battalion. 'B' Company. **Wounded** at the Battle of Langemarck 16 August 1917. Separated from the 9th (North Irish Horse) Battalion in the period 21-28 March 1918 during the retreat from St Quentin; rejoined 3 April 1918. Discharged as no longer physically fit for war service due to wounds 21 July 1919. Silver War Badge, number B283770.

BLOOMFIELD Private Michael 42451. Born in 1899 at Dublin. [Enlisted into The Royal Irish Rifles (20241).] Transferred at the Base Depot to Princess Victoria's (Royal Irish Fusiliers) 14 September 1918 (renumbered 42451) and joined the 9th (North Irish Horse) Battalion 22 September 1918. **Missing** during the attack at Vijfwegen on 30 September or 1 October 1918; recorded as **killed in action** during the period 30 September to 3 October 1918.

BLOOMFIELD Corporal Robert 41508. [Enlisted in November 1914 into the Service Squadron, 6th (Inniskilling) Dragoons (UD/148). To France with 36th (Ulster) Division in October 1915. Served with 2nd North Irish Horse, X Corps Cavalry Regiment.] Joined the renamed 9th (North Irish Horse) Battalion from 36 Infantry Base Depot and transferred to Princess Victoria's (Royal Irish Fusiliers) in September/October 1917 (renumbered 41508). Transferred to the Class Z Reserve 26 February 1919. 1914-15 Star.

BLYTHE Private Edward 40004. From Yorkshire. [Enlisted 10 December 1915 into The Prince of Wales's Own (West Yorkshire Regiment).] Transferred to Princess Victoria's (Royal Irish Fusiliers) 30 November 1916 (renumbered 40004) and joined the 9th (Service) Battalion 12 December 1916. 'B' Company. **Wounded** at the Battle of Langemarck 16 August 1917. Discharged as no longer physically fit for war service due to wounds 16 January 1919. Silver War Badge, number B84700.

BOGIE Private David 42148. [Enlisted into the Army Veterinary Corps (26049).] Transferred to Princess Victoria's (Royal Irish Fusiliers) 8 May 1918 (renumbered 42148) and joined the 9th (North

Irish Horse) Battalion.

BOLINGBROKE Private James Arthur 42502. Born 12 September 1878. From Brighton. A wholesale newsagent. [Enlisted 26 June 1916 and transferred to the Army Reserve. Mobilised 12 October 1916 and joined the 4th (Reserve) Battalion, The Royal Sussex Regiment. To France 12 January 1917. Transferred to the 15th (Service) Battalion, The Royal Irish Rifles (North Belfast) (renumbered 44857). **Wounded** by shrapnel in the right knee 7 August 1917. Treated in hospital at Etaples. **Wounded** by a gunshot to the right thigh during the retreat from St Quentin in the period 21-23 March 1918. Treated at 14th General Hospital, Boulogne and evacuated to hospital in England.] To 'A' Infantry Base Depot 14 September 1918 and transferred to Princess Victoria's (Royal Irish Fusiliers) (renumbered 42502). Joined the 9th (North Irish Horse) Battalion 22 September 1918. **Wounded** by a gunshot to the right leg at Hill 41 on 11 October 1918. Treated at 14th General Hospital, Boulogne and evacuated to hospital in England. Joined the 3rd (Reserve) Battalion 27 December 1918. Transferred to the Class Z Reserve 19 March 1919.

BOND Private Alexander 42515. Born in 1899 at Strabane, County Londonderry. A farm labourer. [Enlisted 13 May 1918 into The Royal Irish Rifles (22648) and joined the 3rd (Reserve) Battalion, The Royal Irish Rifles.] Transferred at the Base Depot to Princess Victoria's (Royal Irish Fusiliers) 14 September 1918 (renumbered 42515) and joined the 9th (North Irish Horse) Battalion 22 September 1918. **Wounded** by a gunshot to the left leg during the attack at Vijfwegen 2 October 1918. When recovered he joined 'A' Infantry Base Depot but fell ill with influenza. Rejoined the 9th (North Irish Horse) Battalion 4 December 1918. Attached to 20th (Service) Battalion, The Duke of Cambridge's Own (Middlesex Regiment) for duty as a train guard 28 February 1919. Although posted to the 5th (Service) Battalion, The Royal Irish Regiment (Pioneers) in the Light Division in the British Army of the Rhine on 20 March 1919, he elected to re-enlist and remained with the 9th (North Irish Horse) Battalion. Re-enlisted 30 March 1919 for Regular Army service with Princess Victoria's (Royal Irish Fusiliers). Served with the 2nd Battalion at Dover. **Deserted** 6 September 1919.

BONSER Private Sydney Joseph 45782. Born 21 February 1890 at London. [Enlisted into the Royal Flying Corps (25859). Second Class Air Mechanic.] Joined the 9th (North Irish Horse) Battalion, Princess Victoria's (Royal Irish Fusiliers) with the draft of men from The London Regiment in April 1918 (renumbered 45782) (see Private S J K Eames). Died at Southend-on-Sea in 1969, aged 79.

BOOTH Private John 41528. [Enlisted in late-September/October 1914 into the Service Squadron, 6th (Inniskilling) Dragoons (UD/5). Served with 2nd North Irish Horse, X Corps Cavalry Regiment.] Joined the renamed 9th (North Irish Horse) Battalion from 36 Infantry Base Depot and transferred to Princess Victoria's (Royal Irish Fusiliers) in September/October 1917 (renumbered 41528).

BOOTH Private Joshua Myers 40055. Born in 1895 at Bradford, Yorkshire. [Enlisted 21 September 1914 into the 16th (Service) Battalion, The Prince of Wales's Own (West Yorkshire Regiment) (1st Bradford) (382). To Egypt 30 December 1915 with 93rd Brigade in 31st Division.] Transferred to Princess Victoria's (Royal Irish Fusiliers) 30 November 1916 (renumbered 40055) and joined the 9th (Service) Battalion 12 December 1916. 'D' Company. **Wounded** at the Battle of Langemarck 16 August 1917. Discharged as no longer physically fit for war service due to wounds 14 February 1919. Silver War Badge, number B129723. 1914-15 Star. He later worked for the Post Office.

BOSTON Private John 41309. Born in 1896. From Ballyclare, County Antrim. [Enlisted 11 January 1915 into the North Irish Horse (1393). Attached to 54th (East Anglian) Division Military Mounted Police 12 July 1915 and appointed Lance Corporal. Joined the Mediterranean Expeditionary Force in Egypt 27 July 1915. Served at Gallipoli. To 19th General Hospital, Alexandria sick (jaundice) 5 December 1915. Evacuated to hospital in England from Alexandria 15 January 1916. Reverted to Private 26 January 1916. To France 19 January 1917 and joined 2nd North Irish Horse, X Corps Cavalry Regiment. Awarded five days Field Punishment Number 2 for making an improper reply to an NCO 3 August 1917.] Joined the renamed 9th (North Irish Horse) Battalion from 36 Infantry Base Depot and transferred to Princess Victoria's (Royal Irish Fusiliers) in September/October 1917 (renumbered 41309). 'C' Company. **Wounded** by a gunshot to the right thigh and treated at 3rd Stationary Hospital. Evacuated to hospital in England 14 November

1917 and treated at Edinburgh War Hospital. Joined the 10th (Reserve) Battalion 31 January 1918. To 'A' Infantry Base Depot 1 April 1918 and rejoined the 9th (North Irish Horse) Battalion. **Wounded** by a gunshot to the right knee and thigh in the period 11-18 April 1918 in the actions between Wulverghem and Kemmel. Treated at 53rd General Hospital. Evacuated to hospital in England 21 April 1918. Posted to the 3rd (Reserve) Battalion 2 October 1918. Transferred to the Army Service Corps (renumbered M/416975) 3 December 1918. Transferred to the Class Z Reserve 8 March 1919. 1914-15 Star.

BOSWELL Lance Corporal Benjamin James 42501. Born in 1890 at London. A wheelwright and painter. [Enlisted 11 December 1915 and transferred to the Army Reserve. Mobilised 3 June 1916 and joined the 3/22nd Battalion, The London Regiment (7127). To France 30 September 1916. Transferred to The Royal Irish Rifles (renumbered 44084) and joined the 1st Battalion, The Royal Irish Rifles 29 October 1916. Lance Corporal 18 October 1917. **8th Division Certificate for Gallantry**. **Wounded** right forearm March 1918 during the retreat from St Quentin and evacuated to hospital in England. Treated at Lord Derby War Hospital, Winwick until 11 May 1918. Reverted to Private due to absence August 1918.] To France 7 September 1918. Transferred at 'A' Infantry Base Depot to Princess Victoria's (Royal Irish Fusiliers) 14 September 1918 (renumbered 42501) and joined the 9th (North Irish Horse) Battalion 22 September 1918. Transferred to the Class Z Reserve 19 March 1919. Died in Surrey 1966, aged 76.

BOWDEN Private Joseph Arthur 41287. Born 25 March 1897 at Cortober House, Cootehill, County Cavan. [Enlisted in November 1915 into the North Irish Horse (1965). Served with 2nd North Irish Horse, X Corps Cavalry Regiment.] Joined the renamed 9th (North Irish Horse) Battalion from 36 Infantry Base Depot and transferred to Princess Victoria's (Royal Irish Fusiliers) in September/October 1917 (renumbered 41287). **Missing** in the period 11-18 April 1918 in the actions between Wulverghem and Kemmel; subsequently declared **killed in action** 19 April 1918, aged 21.

BOWENS Private Walter 21581. Enlisted in August 1915. Posted to the 9th (Service) Battalion in mid/late 1916.

BOWERS Private John 27903, 33767, 7041816. From Shankill, Belfast. Enlisted in August 1917. Posted to the 9th (North Irish Horse) Battalion in early-1918. 'B' Company. Believed **wounded** in the period 21-28 March 1918 during the retreat from St Quentin. [Transferred to 5th (Service) Battalion, The Royal Irish Regiment (Pioneers) in the Light Division in the British Army of the Rhine in March/June 1919 (renumbered 41261).] Re-enlisted 31 December 1919 for Regular Army service with Princess Victoria's (Royal Irish Fusiliers) (renumbered 33767, renumbered 7041816). Served with the 1st Battalion in Persia and Mesopotamia in 1919/20. General Service Medal 1918-1962 with clasps 'Iraq' & 'NW Persia'. Discharged 25 April 1922.

BOWLES Private William 13976. From Montague Street, Portadown, County Armagh. 4th (Portadown) Battalion, Armagh Regiment, Ulster Volunteer Force. Enlisted September 1914. To France with 36th (Ulster) Division in October 1915. **Killed in action** during the attack at Hamel 1 July 1916. 1914-15 Star.

BOWMAN Private James 24271. From Belfast. Enlisted in April 1916. Posted to the 9th (Service) Battalion. **Wounded**. Tried by Field General Court Martial 25 May 1918 charged with *'drunkenness'*; found guilty and sentenced to twenty-eight days Field Punishment Number 1.

BOWMAN Private John 21651. Enlisted in September 1915. Posted to the 9th (Service) Battalion. 'A' Company. **Missing** in the period 21-28 March 1918 during the retreat from St Quentin believed **captured**.

BOYCE Lance Corporal David 22888 & 7040715. Born in 1892 at Portadown, County Armagh. Member of Edenderry Temperance and Benefit Loyal Orange Lodge 322. A linen weaver. Enlisted 13 November 1915. To France 2 November 1916 and joined the 9th (Service) Battalion. 'B' Company. **Wounded** at the Battle of Langemarck 16 August 1917 and evacuated to hospital in England 25 August 1917. Re-enlisted in early-1919 for Regular Army service with Princess Victoria's (Royal Irish Fusiliers) (renumbered 7040715). Discharged 22 October 1920 (King's Certificate 87/3112). Brother of Private Thomas Henry Boyce.

BOYCE Private Joseph 17308. From Portadown, County Armagh. Enlisted in November 1914 (probably a former soldier or special reservist). To France 1 February 1915. [Transferred to the

Labour Corps (renumbered 472391).] Transferred to the Class Z Reserve 11 July 1919.

BOYCE Private Joseph 29582. Enlisted in March 1918. Posted to the 9th (North Irish Horse) Battalion.

BOYCE Private Robert 3883 & 7040043. From Portadown. A weaver. Enlisted on 23 November 1915 into Princess Victoria's (Royal Irish Fusiliers) Special Reserve. [To France 10 May 1916 and joined the 8th (Service) Battalion in 49th Brigade, 16th (Irish) Division.] Joined the 9th (North Irish Horse) Battalion when the 7th/8th (Service) Battalion was disbanded in February 1918. Transferred to Princess Victoria's (Royal Irish Fusiliers) Special Reserve on 11 March 1919 (renumbered 7040043). Discharged 22 November 1922.

BOYCE Private Samuel John 19896. Enlisted into the 9th (Service) Battalion 19 May 1915. To France 17 November 1915 and rejoined the 9th (Service) Battalion. **Wounded**. Discharged as no longer physically fit for war service due to wounds 13 February 1919. Silver War Badge, number B140388. 1914-15 Star.

BOYCE Private Thomas Henry 13989. Born in 1895 at Portadown, County Armagh. 4th (Portadown) Battalion, Armagh Regiment, Ulster Volunteer Force. A linen weaver. Enlisted September 1914. To France with 36th (Ulster) Division in October 1915. **Wounded** by shellfire at Hamel 26 June 1916 (and erroneously reported as killed in action). Evacuated to hospital in England and treated at King George Hospital, London. To France 23 March 1917. **Wounded** in the period 9-18 April 1918 in the actions between Wulverghem and Kemmel. Evacuated to hospital in England and treated at the 1st Northern General Hospital, Newcastle-upon-Tyne. To the 3rd (Reserve) Battalion 30 September 1918. Transferred to the Class Z Reserve 26 March 1919. 1914-15 Star. Brother of Private David Boyce.

BOYD Private Alexander 14014. Born 1884 at Armagh, County Armagh. 1st (Armagh) Battalion, Armagh Regiment, Ulster Volunteer Force. A timber merchant. Enlisted September 1914. Forfeit twenty-four days pay for absence 19 December 1914. Discharged as no longer physically fit for war service due to sickness 28 June 1915. Silver War Badge was not awarded (his name appears on List B1516).

BOYD Private Ernest 14046. Born in 1892 at Armagh, County Armagh. 1st (Armagh) Battalion, Armagh Regiment, Ulster Volunteer Force. A chauffeur. Enlisted September 1914. Discharged as not being likely to become an efficient soldier in that he was considered medically unfit for service 7 November 1914. [He re-enlisted on 30 July 1915 into the Army Service Corps (Mechanical Transport) (numbered M2/116567) and did not declare his previous enlistment. Served with the Mediterranean Expeditionary Force from 15 September 1915. Served with the Egyptian Field Ambulance and Workshop Unit. Lance Corporal 9 August 1918. Acting Sergeant 15 July 1919. Embarked for the United Kingdom 9 February 1920.] 1914-15 Star. Transferred to the Class Z Reserve 25 March 1920.

BOYD Sergeant James 41564. From Ballinagall, County Monaghan. [Enlisted in September 1908 into the North Irish Horse (203). To France 17 August 1914 with 'A' Squadron as GHQ Troops. Served with 2nd North Irish Horse, X Corps Cavalry Regiment.] Joined the renamed 9th (North Irish Horse) Battalion from 36 Infantry Base Depot and transferred to Princess Victoria's (Royal Irish Fusiliers) in September/October 1917 (renumbered 41564). 'D' Company. **Captured** in the period 21-28 March 1918 during the retreat from St Quentin and held at a prisoner of war camp in Germany. 1914 Star.

BOYD Private Robert 14000. From Armagh, County Armagh. A printer's compositor. Enlisted September 1914. To France with 36th (Ulster) Division in October 1915. 'A' Company. **Killed in action** at the Battle of Langemarck 16 August 1917, aged 43. 1914-15 Star.

BOYD Private Thomas 14011. Enlisted September 1914. Discharged as no longer physically fit for war service due to sickness 25 May 1915. Silver War Badge was not awarded (his name appears on List B1516).

BOYD Private William Allan Nesbitt 23897. Born in 1896 at Tullamore, King's County. From Emyvale, County Monaghan. Enlisted in January 1916. Posted to the 9th (Service) Battalion. **Wounded** by shellfire at Spanbroekmolen on the night of 24/25 May 1917 and **died of wounds** 25 May 1917, aged 21.

BOYLE Private Michael 22036. [Enlisted in November 1915 and joined the 8th (Service) Battalion in 49th Brigade, 16th (Irish) Division.] Joined the 9th (North Irish Horse) Battalion when the 7th/8th (Service) Battalion was disbanded in February 1918. 'A' Company. **Missing** in the period 21-28 March 1918 during the retreat from St Quentin believed **captured**.

BOYLES Private William John 22644. From Belfast. Enlisted in October 1915. Posted to the 9th (Service) Battalion. **Killed in action** during the attack at Hamel 1 July 1916.

BRADFORD Private Christopher Walter 42282. Born in 1884 at Hertfordshire. [Enlisted into the Army Veterinary Corps (5511). Served in the Dardanelles with 11th Veterinary Hospital from 11 April 1915.] Transferred to Princess Victoria's (Royal Irish Fusiliers) 8 May 1918 (renumbered 42282) and joined the 9th (North Irish Horse) Battalion. Transferred to the Class Z Reserve 17 February 1919. 1914-15 Star. Died in 1953, aged 69.

BRADFORD Private Charles 45763. Joined the 9th (North Irish Horse) Battalion, Princess Victoria's (Royal Irish Fusiliers) with the draft of men from The London Regiment in April 1918. [Transferred to 5th (Service) Battalion, The Royal Irish Regiment (Pioneers) in the Light Division in the British Army of the Rhine in March/June 1919 (renumbered 41264).] Discharged on the completion of his period of service 15 May 1920.

BRADLEY Private George 14025. Enlisted September 1914. To France with 36th (Ulster) Division in October 1915. Transferred to the Class Z Reserve 23 March 1919. 1914-15 Star.

BRADLEY Private James 42454 & 7042383. From Holywood, County Down. [Enlisted into The Royal Irish Rifles (6009) 28 October 1915.] To France 13 July 1918. Transferred at the Base Depot to Princess Victoria's (Royal Irish Fusiliers) 14 September 1918 (renumbered 42454) and joined the 9th (North Irish Horse) Battalion 22 September 1918. Transferred to Princess Victoria's (Royal Irish Fusiliers) Special Reserve (renumbered 7042383). Discharged 27 October 1921.

BRADLEY Private Henry 41255. [Enlisted in August 1914 into the North Irish Horse (978). Served with 2nd North Irish Horse, X Corps Cavalry Regiment.] Joined the renamed 9th (North Irish Horse) Battalion from 36 Infantry Base Depot and transferred to Princess Victoria's (Royal Irish Fusiliers) in September/October 1917 (renumbered 41255).

BRADY Private Gerald 25291. From Belfast. [Enlisted in November 1916 and served with the 1st Battalion.] Posted to the 9th (Service) Battalion. Discharged for misconduct. Medals forfeit.

BRADY Private James 14024. Enlisted September 1914. No record of deployment to France with 36th (Ulster) Division in October 1915. [Transferred to the Labour Corps (renumbered 620779). Transferred to the Army Service Corps (renumbered EMT/64724).]

BRADY Private Patrick 9713. From Ballybay, County Monaghan. [Enlisted into Princess Victoria's (Royal Irish Fusiliers) as a regular soldier 8 May 1907. To France with the 1st Battalion 22 August 1914.] Posted to the 9th (Service) Battalion. 'B' Company. **Wounded** at the Battle of Langemarck 16 August 1917. [Transferred to the Labour Corps (renumbered 641531). Discharged as no longer physically fit for war service due to sickness 7 May 1919. Silver War Badge, number B280576.] 1914 Star.

BRANAGAN Private Bernard 20171. [Enlisted into the 5th (Service) Battalion in 31st Brigade, 10th (Irish) Division on 14 June 1915. Served with the Mediterranean Expeditionary Force from 22 September 1915. Posted to the 1st Battalion.] Posted to the 9th (North Irish Horse) Battalion. **Wounded**. Discharged as no longer physically fit for war service due to wounds 7 March 1919. 1914-15 Star.

BRANDON Private John 42206. Born 16 April 1886. From Bethnal Green, London. A toy maker for the Wholesale Toy Company. [Enlisted 11 December 1915 and transferred to the Army Reserve. Mobilised 8 June 1916 and posted to the 2nd (Home Service) Garrison Battalion, The Northamptonshire Regiment (29174). Transferred to the Army Service Corps.] Transferred to Princess Victoria's (Royal Irish Fusiliers) 8 May 1918 (renumbered 42206) and joined the 9th (North Irish Horse) Battalion. **Wounded** by a gunshot to the right foot during the attack south of Wulverghem 4 September 1918. Evacuated and treated at the Edinburgh War Hospital until 22 October 1918. Discharged as no longer physically fit for war service due to wounds 10 January 1919. Silver War Badge, number B84707.

BRANNAN Private James 40051. Joined the 9th (Service) Battalion, Princess Victoria's (Royal Irish

Fusiliers) with the draft of men from The Prince of Wales's Own (West Yorkshire Regiment) on 12 December 1916.

BRATTON Sergeant James 14017. Born 25 January 1896 at Armagh, County Armagh. Armagh Regiment, Ulster Volunteer Force. Enlisted September 1914. To France with 36th (Ulster) Division in October 1915. 'B' Company. **Wounded** by a grenade during the retreat from St Quentin 21-28 March 1918. **Mention in Despatches**. Joined the 3rd (Reserve) Battalion. Transferred to the Class Z Reserve 15 May 1919. 1914-15 Star. Served in the Second World War with the Royal Army Service Corps in North Africa. 1939-45 Star. North Africa Star. Worked as a quarry man and a grain thresher.

BRATTY Private Thomas David 41475. Born 1894. From Lurgan, one of ten children. [Enlisted in November 1915 into the North Irish Horse (1958). Served with 2nd North Irish Horse, X Corps Cavalry Regiment.] Joined the renamed 9th (North Irish Horse) Battalion from 36 Infantry Base Depot and transferred to Princess Victoria's (Royal Irish Fusiliers) in September/October 1917 (renumbered 41475). 'B' Company. **Captured** in the period 21-28 March 1918 during the retreat from St Quentin. As a prisoner of war he worked in the salt mines in Silesia. Repatriated in 1918 and transferred to the Class Z Reserve in early-1919. Emigrated to New Zealand, married and had five children. Died there 13 May 1971, aged 77.

BREEN Sergeant John 14012. Born in 1892. From Garrison, County Fermanagh. A grocer. Enlisted September 1914. To France with 36th (Ulster) Division in October 1915. 'A' Company. Took part in the fighting patrol 14 August 1916 with Lieutenant Godson. **Wounded** during the attack at Hamel 1 July 1916. Tried by Field General Court Martial on 11 July 1917 charged with *'drunkenness'*; found guilty and sentenced to a reduction of seniority to 1 July 1917. **Captured** in the period 21-28 March 1918 during the retreat from St Quentin. Held at Munster Prisoner of War Camp. Transferred to the Class Z Reserve 11 April 1919. 1914-15 Star.

BREEN Private Thomas George 28894. Enlisted 2 November 1917. Posted to the 9th (North Irish Horse) Battalion. Served there briefly before being discharged as no longer physically fit for war service due to sickness 19 January 1918. Silver War Badge, number B44360.

BRENNAN Private John 18410. From Glasgow. [Enlisted in April 1915. To France 5 July 1917 and joined the 1st Battalion]. Posted to the 9th (Service) Battalion. **Wounded** and evacuated to hospital in England. Transferred to the Class Z Reserve 11 January 1919. 1914-15 Star.

BRENNAN Corporal William 41568. [Enlisted in May 1915 into the North Irish Horse (1643). To France with 'F' Squadron in 33rd Division 17 November 1915. Served with 2nd North Irish Horse, X Corps Cavalry Regiment.] Joined the renamed 9th (North Irish Horse) Battalion from 36 Infantry Base Depot and transferred to Princess Victoria's (Royal Irish Fusiliers) in September/October 1917 (renumbered 41568). Transferred to the Class Z Reserve 11 March 1919. 1914-15 Star.

BREW Private John George 13975. Commissioned into Princess Victoria's (Royal Irish Fusiliers) - see Appendix 5.

BREWER Private Cecil 41272. [Enlisted in April 1913 into the North Irish Horse (837). To France 20 August 1914 with 'C' Squadron as 5th Division Cavalry and then as GHQ Troops. Served with 2nd North Irish Horse, X Corps Cavalry Regiment.] Joined the renamed 9th (North Irish Horse) Battalion from 36 Infantry Base Depot and transferred to Princess Victoria's (Royal Irish Fusiliers) in September/October 1917 (renumbered 41272). **Wounded** in December 1917 at Marcoing. 1914 Star.

BRIDGE Private Charles 27918. [Enlisted in August 1917 and posted to the 7th/8th (Service) Battalion in 49th Brigade, 16th (Irish) Division.] Joined the 9th (North Irish Horse) Battalion when the 7th/8th (Service) Battalion was disbanded in February 1918. 'D' Company. **Missing** in the period 21-28 March 1918 during the retreat from St Quentin believed **captured**.

BRIDGER Private George 42149. [Enlisted into the Army Veterinary Corps (23740).] Transferred to Princess Victoria's (Royal Irish Fusiliers) 8 May 1918 (renumbered 42149) and joined the 9th (North Irish Horse) Battalion.

BRIDGETT Private James 13993. Born in 1877. From Lurgan, County Armagh. A former regular soldier with the 2nd Battalion, Princess Victoria's (Royal Irish Fusiliers). Re-enlisted September 1914. To France with 36th (Ulster) Division in October 1915. 'C' Company. Battalion bomb carrier during the attack at Hamel 1 July 1916, which he survived unwounded. Transferred to the Class Z Reserve 15 March 1919. 1914-15 Star.

BRIDGSTOCK Private Edward 42284. [Enlisted into the Army Veterinary Corps (5428). Served in the Dardanelles from 11 April 1915.] Transferred to Princess Victoria's (Royal Irish Fusiliers) 8 May 1918 (renumbered 42284) and joined the 9th (North Irish Horse) Battalion. Transferred to the Class Z Reserve 6 April 1919. 1914-15 Star.

BRIEN Private Joseph 42455. From Bray, County Wicklow. [Enlisted into the 7th (Service) Battalion, The Royal Irish Rifles (4451). To France with 48th Brigade, 16th (Irish) Division 19 December 1915.] Transferred at the Base Depot to Princess Victoria's (Royal Irish Fusiliers) 14 September 1918 (renumbered 42455) and joined the 9th (North Irish Horse) Battalion 22 September 1918. **Missing** during the attack at Vijfwegen on 30 September or 1 October 1918; recorded as **killed in action** on 3 October 1918, aged 20. 1914-15 Star.

BRIGGS Private Charles 24262 & 7040740. From Belfast. [Enlisted 22 April 1916. To France 9 August 1917 and joined the 7th/8th (Service) Battalion in 49th Brigade, 16th (Irish) Division.] Joined the 9th (North Irish Horse) Battalion when the 7th/8th (Service) Battalion was disbanded in February 1918. Re-enlisted 19 January 1919 for Regular Army service with Princess Victoria's (Royal Irish Fusiliers) (renumbered 7040740). Served with the 1st Battalion in Mesopotamia and Egypt in 1919/20.

BRIGGS Corporal Isaac Alexander 24781. Born in 1897 at Loughgall, County Armagh. A cabinet maker. Enlisted 9 September 1916 and joined the 10th (Reserve) Battalion. To France and joined the 9th (Service) Battalion 21 December 1916. [Transferred to the Tank Corps (renumbered 304861) 28 December 1917 and posted for training to the Tank Corps Depot, at Bovington near Wareham, Dorset. To France in mid-1919 and joined the 12th Battalion, Tank Corps. Lance Corporal 13 June 1916. Corporal 7 September 1919.] Transferred to the Class Z Reserve 23 October 1919.

BRIGGS Private Robert J 24726. Enlisted in August 1916. Posted to the 9th (Service) Battalion. 'B' Company. Believed **wounded** in the period 21-28 March 1918 during the retreat from St Quentin. [Transferred to 5th (Service) Battalion, The Royal Irish Regiment (Pioneers) in the Light Division in the British Army of the Rhine in March/June 1919 (renumbered 41155).] Transferred to the Class Z Reserve.

BRIGGS Corporal Thomas Harrison 42092. Born in 1889. From Stanwix, Carlisle. A butcher. Served pre-war for four years with the Westmorland and Cumberland Yeomanry. Joined 18th (Victoria Mary, Princess of Wales's Own) Hussars in 1908 but purchased his discharge after two months service. [Enlisted 15 June 1915 into the Army Veterinary Corps (9676). To France 28 September 1915. Lance Corporal 4 July 1917. Corporal 29 September 1917.] Transferred to Princess Victoria's (Royal Irish Fusiliers) 5 May 1918 (renumbered 42092) and joined the 9th (North Irish Horse) Battalion. Reverted to Private at his own request 19 October 1918. **Killed in action** during the advance to Anseghem 25 October 1918, aged 31. 1914-15 Star.

BRINDLEY Private John 42128. [Enlisted into the Army Veterinary Corps (8938). To France 5 June 1915.] Transferred to Princess Victoria's (Royal Irish Fusiliers) 8 May 1918 (renumbered 42128) and joined the 9th (North Irish Horse) Battalion. Transferred to the Class Z Reserve 19 February 1919. 1914-15 Star.

BRITCHFORD Private Alfred John 42443. [Probably transferred from another corps to The Royal Irish Rifles (42486). Served with the 2nd Battalion, The Royal Irish Rifles.] Transferred at the Base Depot to Princess Victoria's (Royal Irish Fusiliers) 14 September 1918 (renumbered 42443) and joined the 9th (North Irish Horse) Battalion 22 September 1918.

BRITTAIN Sergeant Ernest 14015. Born at Armagh, County Armagh. Enlisted September 1914. To France with 36th (Ulster) Division in October 1915. **Wounded** during the attack at Hamel 1 July 1916. [Transferred to the Labour Corps (renumbered 654652).] 1914-15 Star.

BRITTEN Private Albert William 43352. Born in 1891 at Shoreditch, London. [Enlisted into The London Regiment (353167).] Attached to the 9th (Service) Battalion, Princess Victoria's (Royal Irish Fusiliers) 26 November 1916. 'A' Company. Discharged from the Territorial Force, re-enlisted and transferred to Princess Victoria's (Royal Irish Fusiliers) in March/April 1917 (renumbered 43352). **Missing** in the period 21-28 March 1918 during the retreat from St Quentin believed **captured**. Died at Sidcup, Kent in 1956, aged 65.

BRITTON Private Arthur 41154. [Enlisted into Corps of Dragoons (D/11312). Served with 2nd North Irish Horse, X Corps Cavalry Regiment.] Joined the renamed 9th (North Irish Horse) Battalion from 36 Infantry Base Depot and transferred to Princess Victoria's (Royal Irish Fusiliers) in September/October 1917 (renumbered 41154). [Transferred back to the Corps of Dragoons (again numbered D/11312).]

BRITTON Private James William 41601. [Enlisted in late-September/October 1914 into the Service Squadron, 6th (Inniskilling) Dragoons (UD/6). Served with 2nd North Irish Horse, X Corps Cavalry Regiment. **Wounded** by shellfire at Aveluy Wood when two troops engaged in salvage duty were subject to heavy bombardment 5 July 1916.] Joined the renamed 9th (North Irish Horse) Battalion from 36 Infantry Base Depot and transferred to Princess Victoria's (Royal Irish Fusiliers) in September/October 1917 (renumbered 41601). 'C' Company. **Missing** in the period 21-28 March 1918 during the retreat from St Quentin believed **captured**.

BROGGI Lance Corporal Guiliano Douglas 19119 & 7040651. Born 24 March 1898 at Kingston-upon-Thames. A carman. [Enlisted 11 May 1915. To France 8 June 1917 and joined the 7th/8th (Service) Battalion in 49th Brigade, 16th (Irish) Division.] Joined the 9th (North Irish Horse) Battalion when the 7th/8th (Service) Battalion was disbanded in February 1918. **Wounded** in the back 20 October 1918 and evacuated to hospital in England 25 October 1918. [Transferred to the Labour Corps (renumbered 382123). Served with 121st Company.] Transferred to the Section B Army Reserve, Princess Victoria's (Royal Irish Fusiliers) (renumbered 7040651). Discharged 10 May 1928. Died at Kingston-upon-Thames in 1979, aged 81.

BROLLY Private Thomas Paul 40118. Born in 1898 at Crindle, Myroe, County Londonderry. A shop assistant. [Enlisted 29 February 1916 and joined 10th Reserve Cavalry Regiment at the Curragh for service with Hussars of the Line (24760).] Transferred to Princess Victoria's (Royal Irish Fusiliers) 21 November 1916 (renumbered 40118). To 36 Infantry Base Depot 8 December 1916. Joined the 1st Battalion. 'C' Company. To hospital sick (trench foot) 31 December 1916. To 36 Infantry Base Depot 16 January 1917 and rejoined the 1st Battalion. To hospital injured (sprained ankle) 24 March 1917. Evacuated to hospital in England and treated at Lord Derby War Hospital, Winwick.] Joined 36 Infantry Base Depot 14 June 1917. Posted to the 9th (Service) Battalion. 'A' Company. **Missing** at the Battle of Langemarck 16 August 1917 and later declared **killed in action** on that date.

BROOKES Corporal Alfred 43455. [Enlisted into The London Regiment.] To France and joined 36 Infantry Base Depot 29 March 1918. Transferred to Princess Victoria's (Royal Irish Fusiliers) 2 April 1918 (renumbered 43455) and joined the 9th (North Irish Horse) Battalion 4 April 1918. As a Sergeant he was tried by Field General Court Martial on 23 August 1918 charged with an unknown act *'to the prejudice and good order of military discipline'*; found guilty and sentenced to be reduced to the Ranks. Ended his service as Corporal.

BROOKS Private David 14005. Born in 1893 at Armagh, County Armagh. Enlisted September 1914. To France with 36th (Ulster) Division in October 1915. **Killed in action** during the attack at Hamel 1 July 1916. 1914-15 Star. Brother of Private Frederick Brooks.

BROOKS Private Frederick 14008. Born 16 June 1895 at Armagh, County Armagh. 1st (Armagh) Battalion, Armagh Regiment, Ulster Volunteer Force. A saddler. Enlisted September 1914. Discharged as no longer physically fit for war service due to sickness 25 May 1915. Silver War Badge was not awarded (his name appears on List B1516). Brother of Private David Brooks.

BROOMFIELD Private Samuel 28687. Born in 1889 at Moneyquin, Lislea, County Armagh. A draper. Enlisted 24 September 1917 and joined the 10th (Reserve) Battalion. To 'A' Infantry Base Depot 5 April 1918. Posted to the 9th (North Irish Horse) Battalion 9 May 1918. **Killed in action** during the attack south of Wulverghem 4 September 1918, aged 19.

BROWN Private Albert 14020. Born in 1893. From Bessbrook, County Armagh. Enlisted September 1914. To France with 36th (Ulster) Division in October 1915. 'A' Company. **Wounded** during the attack at Hamel 1 July 1916. **Wounded** at the Battle of Langemarck 16 August 1917. Discharged as no longer physically fit for war service due to wounds 4 June 1919. Silver War Badge, number B245856. 1914-15 Star.

BROWN Private Albert 45815. Joined the 9th (North Irish Horse) Battalion, Princess Victoria's (Royal Irish Fusiliers) with the draft of men from The London Regiment in April 1918.

BROWN Private Alfred 19128. [Enlisted 17 May 1916. Served previously with the 1st Battalion. Posted to the 7th/8th (Service) Battalion in 49th Brigade, 16th (Irish) Division.] Joined the 9th (North Irish Horse) Battalion when the 7th/8th (Service) Battalion was disbanded in February 1918. 'A' Company. **Missing** in the period 21-28 March 1918 during the retreat from St Quentin believed **captured** and **wounded**. Discharged as no longer physically fit for war service due to wounds 28 May 1919. Silver War Badge, number B243074.

BROWN Corporal David 13995. Enlisted September 1914. To France with 36th (Ulster) Division in October 1915. 'C' Company. Employed as a signaller linesman during the attack at Hamel on 1 July 1916. Transferred to the Class Z Reserve 18 February 1919. 1914-15 Star.

BROWN Private David 13996 & 29438. Enlisted September 1914. To France with 36th (Ulster) Division in October 1915. Transferred or discharged, reason unknown. Re-enlisted or transferred back to Princess Victoria's (Royal Irish Fusiliers) in March 1918 (renumbered 29438). Posted to the 9th (North Irish Horse) Battalion. Transferred to the Class Z Reserve 23 May 1919. 1914-15 Star.

BROWN Lance Corporal Ernest 41481. [Enlisted in August 1914 into the North Irish Horse (1055). To France with 'F' Squadron in 33rd Division 17 November 1915. Served with 2nd North Irish Horse, X Corps Cavalry Regiment.] Joined the renamed 9th (North Irish Horse) Battalion from 36 Infantry Base Depot and transferred to Princess Victoria's (Royal Irish Fusiliers) in September/October 1917 (renumbered 41481). 'A' Company. **Captured** in the period 21-28 March 1918 during the retreat from St Quentin. Transferred to the Class Z Reserve 31 March 1919. 1914-15 Star.

BROWN Private Francis 49815. [Enlisted in 1915 into the 10th (Service) Battalion, The Royal Inniskilling Fusiliers (Derry). Transferred to Princess Victoria's (Royal Irish Fusiliers) in May 1918 and posted to the 1st Battalion.] Joined the 9th (North Irish Horse) Battalion.

BROWN Private George Alexander 41288. [Enlisted in January 1914 into the North Irish Horse (898). To France 20 August 1914 with 'C' Squadron as 5th Division Cavalry and then as GHQ Troops. Served with 2nd North Irish Horse, X Corps Cavalry Regiment.] Joined the renamed 9th (North Irish Horse) Battalion from 36 Infantry Base Depot and transferred to Princess Victoria's (Royal Irish Fusiliers) in September/October 1917 (renumbered 41288). 1914 Star.

BROWN Corporal Jacob 14038, 32875 & 7041163. Enlisted September 1914. To France with 36th (Ulster) Division in October 1915. 'A' Company. **Wounded** during the Battle of Messines and to hospital 9 June 1917. **Wounded** during the retreat from St Quentin 21-28 March 1918. [Transferred to the Labour Corps (renumbered 606891). Served with 154th Prisoner of War Company.] 1914-15 Star. Re-enlisted in August/September 1919 for Regular Army service with Princess Victoria's (Royal Irish Fusiliers) (renumbered 32875, renumbered 7041163). Served with the 1st Battalion in Persia and Mesopotamia in 1919/20. General Service Medal 1918-1962 with clasps 'Iraq' & 'NW Persia'.

BROWN Private James 18560. From Bessbrook, County Armagh. Enlisted into the 9th (Service) Battalion in April 1915. 'A' Company. To France with 36th (Ulster) Division in October 1915. **Killed in action** during the attack at Hamel 1 July 1916, aged 22. 1914-15 Star. His brother, Thomas Brown, served with the Royal Air Force.

BROWN Lance Corporal James Robert 14013. Born in 1894 at Lurgan, County Armagh. Enlisted September 1914. To France with 36th (Ulster) Division in October 1915. 3 Section, 13 Platoon, 'D' Company. **Wounded** during the attack at Hamel 1 July 1916. **Missing** at the Battle of Langemarck 16 August 1917 and later declared **killed in action** on that date, aged 22. 1914-15 Star.

BROWN Private James Samuel 18121. Born in 1898 at Hamiltonsbawn, County Armagh. Enlisted into the 9th (Service) Battalion in February 1915. 'B' Company. Reported missing at the Battle of Langemarck 16 August 1917 but his body was found and buried by men of the 9th (Service) Battalion, The Royal Irish Rifles (West Belfast) and he was declared as **killed in action** on that date, aged 19.

BROWN Sergeant John 14033. From Waringstown, County Down. Enlisted September 1914. To France with 36th (Ulster) Division in October 1915. 'C' Company. **Killed in action** during the attack at Hamel 1 July 1916.

BROWN Private John 17542. Born at Ballymacarrett, County Down. Worked at Harland and

Wolff shipyard, Belfast. Enlisted into the 9th (Service) Battalion 9 December 1914. 'D' Company. Charged on eight occasions throughout 1915 with being absent from tattoo, out of barracks when a defaulter or out of barracks. To France with 36th (Ulster) Division in October 1915. Sentenced to four days Field Punishment Number 1 for being drunk in billets 28 October 1915. To hospital sick (impetigo) 8-18 June 1916. **Wounded** by shrapnel in the shoulder at Hamel 1 July 1916 and evacuated to hospital in England. In hospital until 22 September 1916. Joined the 10th (Reserve) Battalion. Charged on three occasions with being absent from tattoo or overstaying his pass. Joined 36 Infantry Base Depot 20 December 1916. Rejoined 'D' Company, 9th (Service) Battalion 25 December 1916. **Wounded** by gunshots to the arms and hands at the Battle of Langemarck 16 August 1917 and evacuated to hospital in England. In hospital until 8 October 1917. [To the 3rd (Reserve) Battalion 4 January 1918. Joined the 2nd Garrison Battalion in Salonika on 17 March 1918. To hospital with malaria 18 September 1918. Sentenced to fourteen days Field Punishment Number 1 for an irregularity on guard 20 October 1918. Sentenced to seven days confined to camp and forfeit one day's pay for being absent from tattoo 20 November 1918. To hospital with diarrhoea 25 February 1919. To Base Depot 24 March 1919 and embarked for England 7 April 1919.] Transferred to the Class Z Reserve 25 May 1919.] 1914-15 Star.

BROWN Private Robert 41210. From Corkeeran, County Monaghan. [Enlisted 1 March 1915 into the North Irish Horse (1458). To France with 'F' Squadron in 33rd Division 17 November 1915. Served with 2nd North Irish Horse, X Corps Cavalry Regiment.] Joined the renamed 9th (North Irish Horse) Battalion from 36 Infantry Base Depot and transferred to Princess Victoria's (Royal Irish Fusiliers) in September/October 1917 (renumbered 41210). 'D' Company. **Captured** in the period 21-28 March 1918 during the retreat from St Quentin.

BROWN Private Samuel Watson 40006. [Enlisted into The Prince of Wales's Own (West Yorkshire Regiment) and joined the 4th (Extra Reserve) Battalion.] Transferred to Princess Victoria's (Royal Irish Fusiliers) 30 November 1916 (renumbered 40006) and joined the 9th (Service) Battalion 12 December 1916.

BROWN Private William 14022. Enlisted September 1914. To France with 36th (Ulster) Division in October 1915. **Mention in Despatches**. Transferred to the Class Z Reserve 23 March 1919. 1914-15 Star.

BROWN Corporal William 19947. Commissioned into The Royal Munster Fusiliers - see Appendix 5.

BROWN Lance Corporal William 21045. [Enlisted in November 1914 and joined the 8th (Service) Battalion in 49th Brigade, 16th (Irish) Division.] Joined the 9th (North Irish Horse) Battalion when the 7th/8th (Service) Battalion was disbanded in February 1918.

BROWN Corporal William 23802. Enlisted in January 1916. Posted to the 9th (Service) Battalion.

BROWN Private William 41451. Born in 1895 at Belfast. A library assistant at the Central Library, Belfast. [Enlisted 10 November 1915 into the North Irish Horse (1839). To France 11 August 1916 and posted to 1st North Irish Horse, VII Corps Cavalry Regiment.] Joined the renamed 9th (North Irish Horse) Battalion from 36 Infantry Base Depot and transferred to Princess Victoria's (Royal Irish Fusiliers) in September/October 1917 (renumbered 41451). 'C' Company. To the field ambulance sick in December 1916 and rejoined the 9th (North Irish Horse) Battalion on 5 January 1918. **Wounded** by gunshots to the left thigh and right foot on 24 March 1918 during the during the retreat from St Quentin. Treated at 46th Casualty Clearing Station, 62nd Field Ambulance, 72nd General Hospital, 6th General Hospital, 74th General Hospital and 13th Convalescent Depot. To 'A' Infantry Base Depot 11 July 1918 and rejoined the 9th (North Irish Horse) Battalion on 19 July 1918. **Wounded** on the raid at Shoddy Farm near Meulenhouck on the night of 11/12 August 1918 and **died of wounds** on 12 August 1918, aged 23.

BROWN Private William George 14032. Enlisted September 1914. To France with 36th (Ulster) Division in October 1915. Transferred to the Class Z Reserve 20 March 1919. 1914-15 Star.

BROWN Private William Henry 40053. Born in Diss, Norfolk. [Enlisted into the 12th (Service) Battalion, The Prince of Wales's Own (West Yorkshire Regiment) (14466). To France 8 September 1915.] Transferred to Princess Victoria's (Royal Irish Fusiliers) 30 November 1916 (renumbered 40053) and joined the 9th (Service) Battalion 12 December 1916. 'D' Company. **Captured** in the period 21-28 March 1918 during the retreat from St Quentin and **died** while a prisoner of war 5

September 1918, aged 25. 1914-15 Star.

BROWN Sergeant William John 15859. From Jervis Street, Portadown, County Armagh. Enlisted into the 9th (Service) Battalion in October 1914. 'B' Company. To France with 36th (Ulster) Division in October 1915. [Joined 108th Brigade Machine Gun Company in January 1916. Transferred to the Machine Gun Corps (renumbered 17775). Promoted to Warrant Officer Class II, Company Sergeant Major. **Killed in action** by shellfire during the attack at Hamel 1 July 1916.] 1914-15 Star.

BROWNING Private Francis Ernest 42127. From Slough, Buckinghamshire. [Enlisted into the Army Veterinary Corps (63760). Transferred to the Royal Field Artillery (renumbered 2277).] Transferred to Princess Victoria's (Royal Irish Fusiliers) 8 May 1918 (renumbered 42127) and joined the 9th (North Irish Horse) Battalion. **Wounded** during the attack north of Bailleul on 24 August 1918 and **died of wounds** 25 August 1918, aged 22.

BROWNLEE Private Herbert 41100. Born in 1896 at Coolyermer, Letterbreen, County Fermanagh. [Enlisted in late-September/October 1914 into the Service Squadron, 6th (Inniskilling) Dragoons (UD/3). To France with 36th (Ulster) Division in October 1915. Served with 2nd North Irish Horse, X Corps Cavalry Regiment.] Joined the renamed 9th (North Irish Horse) Battalion from 36 Infantry Base Depot and transferred to Princess Victoria's (Royal Irish Fusiliers) in September/October 1917 (renumbered 41100). 'A' Company. **Captured** in the period 21-28 March 1918 during the retreat from St Quentin. Transferred to the Class Z Reserve 26 March 1919. 1914-15 Star.

BROWNLEE Private James 13992. Enlisted September 1914. Discharged as not being likely to become an efficient soldier in that he was considered medically unfit for service 3 October 1914. Silver War Badge, number 496776.

BROWNLEE Private John 14019. Born at Lurgan, County Armagh. From Belfast. Member of Loyal Orange Lodge 524. Enlisted September 1914. To France with 36th (Ulster) Division in October 1915. 'C' Company. Bangalore torpedo specialist during the attack at Hamel 1 July 1916 and was **killed in action**, aged 37.

BRYAN Sergeant Andrew George 10805 & 7040402. Born in 1893 at Staines, Middlesex. An outdoor porter. Enlisted into Princess Victoria's (Royal Irish Fusiliers) as a regular soldier 25 September 1911. [To France 2 June 1917 and joined the 5th (Service) Battalion, in 31st Brigade, 10th (Irish) Division. Evacuated to hospital in England (probably sick) 1 October 1917.] To France 10 August 1918. Posted to the 9th (North Irish Horse) Battalion. Returned to England 15 June 1919 and transferred to the Section B Army Reserve, Princess Victoria's (Royal Irish Fusiliers) (renumbered 7040402). Discharged 24 September 1927.

BRYAN Private Henry Benjamin 41471. Born in 1893 at in Reading, Berkshire. Enlisted 18 June 1909 into 2nd Life Guards (Trooper 3331). [To France with 2nd Life Guards 8 October 1914. Transferred to 6th (Inniskilling) Dragoons (3331) and served with 2nd North Irish Horse, X Corps Cavalry Regiment.] Joined the renamed 9th (North Irish Horse) Battalion from 36 Infantry Base Depot and transferred to Princess Victoria's (Royal Irish Fusiliers) in September/October 1917 (renumbered 41471). **Wounded**. Discharged as no longer physically fit for war service due to wounds 21 December 1918. Silver War Badge, number B51546. 1914 Star and clasp. Lived in Reading, Berkshire and died there in 1965, aged 72.

BRYANS Private Charles 14004. Born in 1896 at Armagh, County Armagh. A footman. Enlisted September 1914, aged 18 years but giving his age as 19 years. 'A' Company. To France with 36th (Ulster) Division in October 1915. **Wounded** by a machine-gun bullet in the back during a patrol at the mill at Hamel on 22 February 1916. Evacuated to hospital in England 25 February 1916. Discharged as no longer physically fit for war service due to wounds 27 September 1916. Silver War Badge, number 146243. 1914-15 Star. Brother of Privates David Frederick, George Alexander and Joseph Albert Bryans. His eldest brother Private Robert Bryans served with Princess Victoria's (Royal Irish Fusiliers) Special Reserve from 1908 and in France with the 1st Battalion from September 1914; he was discharged as no longer physically fit for war service due to sickness in 1915. Step-brother of Lance Corporal Alfred Camlin.

BRYANS Private David 14043. Born in 1896 at Armagh, County Armagh. Enlisted September 1914. To France with 36th (Ulster) Division in October 1915. **Wounded** during the attack at Hamel

1 July 1916. **Killed in action** at Moeuvres 23 November 1917. 1914-15 Star.

BRYANS Private David Frederick 14044, 43517 & 7042223. Born in 1899 at Armagh, County Armagh. Enlisted September 1914, aged 14. Did not deploy to France with 36th (Ulster) Division in 1915. [Transferred to The London Regiment and joined the 18th (Reserve) Battalion, The London Regiment (London Irish Rifles) (renumbered 602354 in March 1917). Transferred back to Princess Victoria's (Royal Irish Fusiliers) in April 1918 and joined the 1st Battalion (renumbered 43517).] Re-enlisted in early-1919 for Regular Army service with Princess Victoria's (Royal Irish Fusiliers) (renumbered 7042223). Served with the 1st Battalion in Persia and Mesopotamia in 1919/20. General Service Medal 1918-1962 with clasps 'Iraq' & 'NW Persia'. For brothers - see Private Charles Bryans.

BRYANS Private George Alexander 20616. Born in 1893 at Armagh, County Armagh. Enlisted into the 9th (Service) Battalion in June 1915. To France with 36th (Ulster) Division in October 1915. 1914-15 Star. Transferred to the Class Z Reserve. For brothers - see Private Charles Bryans.

BRYANS Corporal James 15848. From Armagh, County Armagh. Enlisted into the 9th (Service) Battalion 19 October 1914. Corporal 28 August 1915. **Wounded** during the attack at Hamel 1 July 1916. **Captured** in the period 21-28 March 1918 during the retreat from St Quentin.

BRYANS Sergeant John 13987. From Lurgan, County Armagh. Enlisted into the 9th (Service) Battalion in September 1914. To France with 36th (Ulster) Division in October 1915. 'C' Company. **Killed in action** during the attack at Hamel 1 July 1916.

BRYANS Private John 14042. Enlisted into the 9th (Service) Battalion in September 1914. No record of deployment to France with 36th (Ulster) Division in October 1915. [Transferred to the Labour Corps (renumbered 231590).]

BRYANS Private Joseph Albert 22690. Born in 1895 at Armagh, County Armagh. Enlisted in November 1915. Posted to the 9th (Service) Battalion. For brothers see Private Charles Bryans.

BRYERS Private John George 13978. From Portadown, County Armagh. Enlisted into the 9th (Service) Battalion in September 1914. No record of deployment to France with 36th (Ulster) Division in October 1915. [Transferred to The Royal Irish Rifles (renumbered 1289) and joined the 18th (Reserve) Battalion. Transferred to the Army Service Corps (renumbered M/380514).]

BUCHANAN Private David 41421. [Enlisted in November 1915 into the North Irish Horse (1837). Served with 2nd North Irish Horse, X Corps Cavalry Regiment.] Joined the renamed 9th (North Irish Horse) Battalion from 36 Infantry Base Depot and transferred to Princess Victoria's (Royal Irish Fusiliers) in September/October 1917 (renumbered 41421).

BUCHANAN Private James Allen 41201. Born in 1892. From Letterkenny, County Donegal. A farmer. [Enlisted 17 October 1913 into the North Irish Horse (868). To France 17 August 1914 with 'A' Squadron as GHQ Troops. To hospital sick (acute rheumatism) 27 October 1914 and evacuated to hospital in England. To France with 'F' Squadron in 33rd Division 17 November 1915. Served with 2nd North Irish Horse, X Corps Cavalry Regiment. Lance Corporal 20 June 1916.] Joined the renamed 9th (North Irish Horse) Battalion from 36 Infantry Base Depot and transferred to Princess Victoria's (Royal Irish Fusiliers) in September/October 1917 (renumbered 41201). [Transferred to the Tank Corps (renumbered 304880) 28 December 1917 and posted for training to the Tank Corps Depot, at Bovington near Wareham, Dorset. To France 8 July 1918 and joined the 15th Battalion, Tank Corps.] Transferred to the Class Z Reserve 21 February 1919. 1914 Star. After the war he was at the District Lunatic Asylum, Londonderry.

BUCHANAN Private William 41196. [Enlisted in late-September/October 1914 into the Service Squadron, 6th (Inniskilling) Dragoons (UD/31). To France with 36th (Ulster) Division in October 1915. Served with 2nd North Irish Horse, X Corps Cavalry Regiment. **Wounded** by shellfire at Aveluy Wood when two troops engaged in salvage duty were subject to heavy bombardment 5 July 1916.] Joined the renamed 9th (North Irish Horse) Battalion from 36 Infantry Base Depot and transferred to Princess Victoria's (Royal Irish Fusiliers) in September/October 1917 (renumbered 41196). 'B' Company. **Missing** in the period 21-28 March 1918 during the retreat from St Quentin believed **captured**. Transferred to the Class Z Reserve 30 March 1919. 1914-15 Star.

BUCK Private William Henry 42498. Born in 1893. A driver. From Bethnal Green, London. [Enlisted 7 December 1915 and transferred to the Army Reserve. Mobilised 7 September 1916 and joined 18th (Reserve) Battalion, The London Regiment (London Irish Rifles) (593885). Sentenced to ten days Field Punishment Number 2 on 13 December 1916. To France 26 January 1917. Transferred to 11th (Service) Battalion, The Royal Irish Rifles (South Antrim) (renumbered 44328) 15 February 1917. To hospital sick (scarlet fever) 18 February-1 April 1917. Rejoined 11th (Service) Battalion, The Royal Irish Rifles (South Antrim) 17 June 1917. Injured (badly sprained ankle) 10 August 1917 and treated at 22nd General Hospital. **Wounded** by a gunshot to the left ankle during the retreat from St Quentin on 28 March 1918. Evacuated to hospital in England 31 March 1918 and treated at 2nd Western General Hospital, Manchester until 25 May 1918. Joined the 3rd (Reserve) Battalion 26 July 1918.] To France 7 September 1918. Transferred at 'A' Infantry Base Depot to Princess Victoria's (Royal Irish Fusiliers) 14 September 1918 (renumbered 42498) and joined the 9th (North Irish Horse) Battalion 22 September 1918. Injured (badly sprained ankle) when he slipped into a shell hole when in action on 10 October 1918. Evacuated to hospital in England and treated at Colchester Hospital, Aldershot 27 October-20 November 1918. Posted to the Depot 30 November 1918. Transferred to the Class Z Reserve.

BUCKLAND Private Colin William Frederick 45784. Born 9 February 1889 at Kendal, Westmorland. [Enlisted into The London Regiment.] To France and joined 36 Infantry Base Depot 29 March 1918. Transferred to Princess Victoria's (Royal Irish Fusiliers) 2 April 1918 (renumbered 45784) and joined the 9th (North Irish Horse) Battalion 4 April 1918. Died 1979 at Isle of Wight, Hampshire, aged 90.

BUCKLEY MM Private Robert 14021. Born 1890. From Rich Hill, County Armagh. A cabinet maker. Enlisted September 1914. To France with 36th (Ulster) Division in October 1915. 'A' Company. **MM** – Moeuvres 23 November 1917. **Captured** in the period 21-28 March 1918 during the retreat from St Quentin. **Mention in Despatches**. Transferred to the Class Z Reserve 1 April 1919. 1914-15 Star.

BUCKLEY Private Robert John 27453. Born 1893 in County Armagh. Enlisted in March 1917. Posted to the 9th (North Irish Horse) Battalion. 'A' Company. **Missing** in the period 21-28 March 1918 during the retreat from St Quentin believed **captured**.

BUCKLEY Private Thomas 19935. Enlisted into the 9th (Service) Battalion in May 1915. 'C' Company. To France with 36th (Ulster) Division in October 1915. Company bombing team during the attack at Hamel 1 July 1916 where he was **wounded** (shellshock). [Transferred to the Labour Corps (renumbered 221589) in mid-1917.] Transferred to the Class Z Reserve 31 March 1919. 1914-15 Star.

BULMAN Private Joseph 20319. From Newcastle-upon-Tyne. [Enlisted into The Royal Inniskilling Fusiliers (22879).] Transferred to Princess Victoria's (Royal Irish Fusiliers) 30 June 1915 (renumbered 20319) and joined the 9th (Service) Battalion. To France with 36th (Ulster) Division in October 1915. **Wounded** by shellfire at Hamel and **died of wounds** 26 April 1916. 1914-15 Star. Brother of Private Robert Bulman.

BULMAN Private Robert 20308. Born in 1888 at Newcastle-upon-Tyne. Enlisted 27 May 1915 and joined the 9th (Service) Battalion with the draft of men from The Royal Inniskilling Fusiliers who transferred to Princess Victoria's (Royal Irish Fusiliers) on 30 June 1915. To France with 36th (Ulster) Division in October 1915. **Wounded** during the attack at Hamel 1 July 1916. Discharged as no longer physically fit for war service due to wounds 18 February 1917. Silver War Badge, number 31728. 1914-15 Star. Recorded as being held on the strength of Princess Victoria's (Royal Irish Fusiliers) Depot when he **died of wounds** at Newcastle-upon-Tyne 12 October 1920. Brother of Private Joseph Bulman.

BULMER Private Roland Stanley 42117. [Enlisted 12 February 1916 into the Army Veterinary Corps (25151).] Transferred to Princess Victoria's (Royal Irish Fusiliers) 8 May 1918 (renumbered 42117) and joined the 9th (North Irish Horse) Battalion. Discharged as no longer physically fit for war service due to sickness 28 May 1919. Silver War Badge, number B243080.

BUNTING Lance Sergeant Thomas 13997. Born at Kilmore, County Down. Enlisted at Lurgan in September 1914. To France with 36th (Ulster) Division in October 1915. 'D' Company. **Killed in action** during the attack at Hamel 1 July 1916. 1914-15 Star.

BURDEN Private James 13999. From Armagh, County Armagh. Enlisted September 1914. To France with 36th (Ulster) Division in October 1915. **Wounded** during the attack at Hamel 1 July

1916. [Transferred to the Machine Gun Corps (renumbered 133647).] 1914-15 Star. Served with the Class 'A' Ulster Special Constabulary in 'B' Platoon, Armagh.

BURDEN Private Robert 14016. Enlisted September 1914. To France with 36th (Ulster) Division in October 1915. [Transferred to the Machine Gun Corps (renumbered 73273).] 1914-15 Star.

BURDON Private James Heggie 45799. Born in March 1899. Joined the 9th (North Irish Horse) Battalion, Princess Victoria's (Royal Irish Fusiliers) with the draft of men from The London Regiment in April 1918. Died in Wiltshire in 1975, aged 76.

BURGESS Private William John 23064. Enlisted in November 1915. Posted to the 9th (Service) Battalion.

BURKE Private Ivan Stephen 41123. Born in 1895 at Drumbeg, County Down. [Enlisted 14 November 1914 into the Service Squadron, 6th (Inniskilling) Dragoons (UD/138). To France with 36th (Ulster) Division in October 1915. Served with 2nd North Irish Horse, X Corps Cavalry Regiment.] Joined the renamed 9th (North Irish Horse) Battalion from 36 Infantry Base Depot and transferred to Princess Victoria's (Royal Irish Fusiliers) in September/October 1917 (renumbered 41123). 'A' Company. **Missing** in the period 21-28 March 1918 during the retreat from St Quentin believed **captured** and **wounded**. Discharged as no longer physically fit for war service due to wounds 6 February 1919. Silver War Badge, number B226465. 1914-15 Star.

BURKE Private John 17543. From Clones, County Monaghan. Enlisted into the 9th (Service) Battalion in November/December 1914. To France with 36th (Ulster) Division in October 1915. **Killed in action** during the attack at Hamel 1 July 1916, aged 20. 1914-15 Star. Brother of Private Joseph Burke.

BURKE Private Joseph 17817. From Clones, County Monaghan. Enlisted into the 9th (Service) Battalion in January 1915. To France with 36th (Ulster) Division in October 1915. **Killed in action** during the attack at Hamel 1 July 1916. 1914-15 Star. Brother of Private John Burke.

BURKE MM Private Thomas 23108. [Enlisted in November 1915 and joined the 8th (Service) Battalion in 49th Brigade, 16th (Irish) Division. **MM** – earned during a German attack on 27 April 1916 near Loos, during which he was **wounded**.] Joined the 9th (North Irish Horse) Battalion when the 7th/8th (Service) Battalion was disbanded in February 1918.

BURKE Private William 20069. Enlisted into the 9th (Service) Battalion in June 1915. To France with 36th (Ulster) Division in October 1915. Transferred to the Class Z Reserve 11 March 1919. 1914-15 Star.

BURKE Private William 41465. Born in 1897 at Portstewart, County Antrim. A grocer's assistant. [Enlisted 20 November 1916 into the North Irish Horse (2310). To France 14 April 1917. Served with 2nd North Irish Horse, X Corps Cavalry Regiment.] Joined the renamed 9th (North Irish Horse) Battalion from 36 Infantry Base Depot and transferred to Princess Victoria's (Royal Irish Fusiliers) in September/October 1917 (renumbered 41465). 'B' Company. [Transferred to the Tank Corps (renumbered 304852) 28 December 1917 and posted for training to the Tank Corps Depot, at Bovington near Wareham, Dorset. Posted to the 17th Battalion, Tank Corps 8 January 1918. To hospital sick (influenza) June 1918. To France 5 September 1918 and joined the 9th Battalion, Tank Corps 22 November 1918.] Transferred to the Class Z Reserve 1 May 1919.

BURKE Private William John 43470. Joined the 9th (North Irish Horse) Battalion, Princess Victoria's (Royal Irish Fusiliers) with the draft of men from The London Regiment in April 1918.

BURNETT Private Thomas 20212. From Portadown, County Armagh. Member of Masonic Lodge 82. Enlisted into the 9th (Service) Battalion in June 1915. To France with 36th (Ulster) Division in October 1915. **Wounded** during the attack at Hamel 1 July 1916 and lost a leg. Discharged as no longer physically fit for war service due to wounds 19 June 1917. Silver War Badge, number 188810. 1914-15 Star.

BURNISON Private Harold 14003. Born in 1897 at Lurgan, County Armagh. Enlisted September 1914. To France with 36th (Ulster) Division in October 1915. 3 Section, 13 Platoon, 'D' Company. Transferred to the Class Z Reserve 20 March 1919. 1914-15 Star. A talented football player, he played 326 games for Distillery FC. His brother, Samuel 'Surefoot' Burnison, won eight caps for Ireland.

BURNS Private Alexander 20442. Enlisted into the 9th (Service) Battalion in June 1915. Tried by Field General Court Martial on 16 August 1918 charged with *'when on active service disobeying a lawful command given by his superior officer'* and *'when in arrest escaping'*; found guilty and sentenced to six months imprisonment with hard labour.

BURNS Private Alexander 26109. Born at Markethill, County Armagh. From Darlington, County Durham. Enlisted 13 January 1917, aged 19. To France 10 August 1917 and joined the 9th (Service) Battalion. [Posted to the 1st Battalion on 16 September 1917. He was one of six men **killed in action** by shellfire at Metz-en-Coutre on 27 September 1917, aged 20.]

BURNS Lance Corporal John 13981. From Lurgan, County Armagh. Enlisted September 1914. To France with 36th (Ulster) Division in October 1915. 'C' Company. **Killed in action** during the attack at Hamel 1 July 1916, aged 40. 1914-15 Star.

BURNS Private Joseph 20094. Enlisted 7 June 1915 into the 9th (Service) Battalion. **Wounded**. Discharged as no longer physically fit for war service due to wounds 8 May 1919. Silver War Badge, number B226468.

BURNS Private Richard 14030. From Lurgan, County Armagh. Enlisted September 1914. To France with 36th (Ulster) Division in October 1915. 'C' Company. **Killed in action** 29 March 1918 during the retreat from St Quentin. 1914-15 Star.

BURNS Private Robert 13984. Enlisted September 1914. To France with 36th (Ulster) Division in October 1915. 'C' Company. To hospital in mid-1916. He did not take part in the attack at Hamel on 1 July 1916. Discharged as no longer physically fit for war service due to sickness 6 March 1917. Silver War Badge, number 34594. 1914-15 Star.

BURNS Corporal Thomas 12668. From Durham. [Enlisted in September 1914 and joined the 6th (Service) Battalion in 31st Brigade, 10th (Irish) Division. Embarked with the Mediterranean Expeditionary Force July 1915. Evacuated wounded or sick.] Posted to the 9th (Service) Battalion. 'B' Company. **Wounded** at the Battle of Langemarck 16 August 1917. [Transferred to the Royal Flying Corps (renumbered 143129).]

BURNS Private Terence 26819. Enlisted in February 1917. Posted to the 9th (Service) Battalion. 'A' Company. **Missing** in the period 21-28 March 1918 during the retreat from St Quentin believed **captured**.

BURNSIDE Private Samuel 41289. From Kilrea, County Londonderry. [Enlisted in February 1914 into the North Irish Horse (912). To France 17 August 1914 with 'A' Squadron as GHQ Troops. Served with 2nd North Irish Horse, X Corps Cavalry Regiment.] Joined the renamed 9th (North Irish Horse) Battalion from 36 Infantry Base Depot and transferred to Princess Victoria's (Royal Irish Fusiliers) in September/October 1917 (renumbered 41289). **Captured** in 1918. 1914 Star.

BURRELL Private Edward 13982. Born 20 August 1865 at Lurgan, County Armagh. A linen warper. Enlisted September 1914, aged 49. To France with 36th (Ulster) Division in October 1915. 'C' Company. Detached to Battalion Transport and did not take part in the attack at Hamel on 1 July 1916. [Transferred to the Labour Corps (renumbered 393771).] Discharged as no longer physically fit for war service due to sickness 26 November 1918. Silver War Badge B171590. 1914-15 Star.

BURROWS Private David John 14028. From Thomas Street, Portadown, County Armagh. Enlisted September 1914. To France with 36th (Ulster) Division in October 1915. **Killed in action** during the attack at Hamel 1 July 1916, aged 22. 1914-15 Star. His brother, Private William Burrows, served with Princess Victoria's (Royal Irish Fusiliers) in 10th (Irish) Division.

BURROWS Private Frederick 23724. Born in 1897 at Armagh, County Armagh. Enlisted in January 1916. Posted to the 9th (Service) Battalion. 'A' Company. **Killed in action** at the Battle of Langemarck 16 August 1917, aged 19.

BURROWS Private Thomas 41226. [Enlisted December 1914 into the North Irish Horse (1359). To France with 'F' Squadron in 33rd Division 17 November 1915. Served with 2nd North Irish Horse, X Corps Cavalry Regiment.] Joined the renamed 9th (North Irish Horse) Battalion from 36 Infantry Base Depot and transferred to Princess Victoria's (Royal Irish Fusiliers) in September/October 1917 (renumbered 41226). 'D' Company. **Captured** in the period 21-28 March 1918 during the retreat from St Quentin. Transferred to the Class Z Reserve 2 April 1919. 1914-15 Star.

BURTNEY Private John 24229. Born in 1884 at Claragh, Castlewilliam, County Down. Enlisted in April 1916. Posted to the 9th (Service) Battalion. 'B' Company. **Wounded** at the Battle of Langemarck 16 August 1917.

BUSH Private Thomas 14001. From Lurgan, County Armagh. Enlisted September 1914. To France with 36th (Ulster) Division in October 1915. 'C' Company. **Wounded** during the attack at Hamel 1 July 1916. Discharged as no longer physically fit for war service due to sickness 4 July 1918, aged 29. Silver War Badge, number 415890. 1914-15 Star.

BUSHBY Private John R 42220. [Enlisted into the Army Service Corps (T3/026511 Driver).] Transferred to Princess Victoria's (Royal Irish Fusiliers) 8 May 1918 (renumbered 42220) and joined the 9th (North Irish Horse) Battalion. [Transferred back to the Army Service Corps (renumbered ET/48085 Driver).]

BUSHELL Private Albert 42144. [Enlisted into the Army Service Corps (S/359068). Served with 31st, 14th and 16th Line of Communications Companies.] Transferred to Princess Victoria's (Royal Irish Fusiliers) 8 May 1918 (renumbered 42144) and joined the 9th (North Irish Horse) Battalion.

BUSTEED Private Richard 41546. Born in 1895 at Belfast. [Enlisted 5 October 1916 into the North Irish Horse (2285). Served with 2nd North Irish Horse, X Corps Cavalry Regiment.] Joined the renamed 9th (North Irish Horse) Battalion from 36 Infantry Base Depot and transferred to Princess Victoria's (Royal Irish Fusiliers) in September/October 1917 (renumbered 41546). **Wounded**. Discharged as no longer physically fit for war service due to wounds 15 November 1918. Silver War Badge, number B44340.

BUTLER Private Andrew 42444. [A regular soldier with the 2nd Battalion, The Royal Irish Rifles (10135). To France 15 August 1914 in 7th Brigade, 3rd Division.] Transferred at the Base Depot to Princess Victoria's (Royal Irish Fusiliers) 14 September 1918 (renumbered 42444) and joined the 9th (North Irish Horse) Battalion 22 September 1918. 1914 Star and clasp.

BUTLER Private Ernest Stanley 49892. [Transferred to Princess Victoria's (Royal Irish Fusiliers) in May 1918 (renumbered 49892) with a draft of men from English regiments and joined the 1st Battalion.] Posted to the 9th (North Irish Horse) Battalion in August 1918.

BUTLER Private John 40005. Joined the 9th (Service) Battalion, Princess Victoria's (Royal Irish Fusiliers) with the draft of men from The Prince of Wales's Own (West Yorkshire Regiment) on 12 December 1916. [Transferred to The Royal Inniskilling Fusiliers (renumbered 32304).]

BUTTERS Lance Corporal Alex 43275. Born in 1895 at Nottingham. A factory hand. [Enlisted 1 September 1914 and joined the 4th (Extra Reserve) Battalion, The Sherwood Foresters (Nottinghamshire and Derbyshire Regiment) (14064). To France 4 January 1915 and joined the 1st Battalion, The Sherwood Foresters (Nottinghamshire and Derbyshire Regiment). To hospital sick (frost bite in his feet) and evacuated to hospital in England 5 February 1915. Treated at 1st Eastern General Hospital, Cambridge. Joined the 3rd (Reserve) Battalion, The Sherwood Foresters (Nottinghamshire and Derbyshire Regiment) 20 April 1915. To France and joined the 2nd Battalion, The Sherwood Foresters (Nottinghamshire and Derbyshire Regiment) 17 August 1915. To hospital sick (frost bite in his feet) and rejoined November 1915. To hospital sick (influenza) 4 April 1916 and evacuated to hospital in England 10 April 1916. Joined the 3rd (Reserve) Battalion 28 June 1916. To France 14 July 1916.] Transferred to Princess Victoria's (Royal Irish Fusiliers) 31 August 1916 (renumbered 43275) having joined the 9th (Service) Battalion on 8 August 1916. 'D' Company. To 108th Field Ambulance sick (tonsillitis) 25 January 1917. Rejoined the 9th (Service) Battalion 19 April 1917. To the field ambulance sick (injured foot) 6 September 1917. Rejoined the 9th (Service) Battalion 15 September 1917. **Missing** in the period 21-28 March 1918 during the retreat from St Quentin and later declared **killed in action** 29 March 1918. 1914-15 Star.

BUTTON Private Arthur Frederick 43206. Born in 1894 at Nottingham. Warehouseman. [Enlisted 10 December 1915 into The Sherwood Foresters (Nottinghamshire and Derbyshire Regiment) (36278). To France 23 July 1916.] Transferred to Princess Victoria's (Royal Irish Fusiliers) 31 August 1916 (renumbered 43206) having joined the 9th (Service) Battalion on 8 August 1916. 'A' Company. Admitted to 108th Field Ambulance in December 1916 with measles. **Killed in action** at the Battle of Langemarck 16 August 1917.

BYARD Private Albert 43236. [Enlisted into The Sherwood Foresters (Nottinghamshire and Derbyshire Regiment).] Transferred to Princess Victoria's (Royal Irish Fusiliers) 31 August 1916 (renumbered 43236) having joined the 9th (Service) Battalion on 8 August 1916.

BYERS Corporal Joseph 24516. Born in 1898 at Oldcastle, County Cavan. From Aghacashel, Ballyjamesduff, County Cavan. Enlisted in June 1916. Posted to the 9th (Service) Battalion. 'D' Company. **Wounded** at the Battle of Langemarck 16 August 1917. **Captured** in the period 21-28 March 1918 during the retreat from St Quentin.

BYRNE Sergeant Edward 41634. Commissioned into The Duke of Edinburgh's (Wiltshire Regiment) - see Appendix 5.

BYRNE Corporal Joseph 41438. [Enlisted in October 1915 into the North Irish Horse (1762). Served with 2nd North Irish Horse, X Corps Cavalry Regiment.] Joined the renamed 9th (North Irish Horse) Battalion from 36 Infantry Base Depot and transferred to Princess Victoria's (Royal Irish Fusiliers) in September/October 1917 (renumbered 41438).

CABLE Private James 40058. Born in 1895 at South Shields. A coal miner. [Enlisted into The Prince of Wales's Own (West Yorkshire Regiment) (19211) 7 April 1915. To France 6 October 1915 with the 12th (Service) Battalion in 9th Brigade. **Wounded** when attached to 9th Brigade mining section 7 December 1915 by a gunshot to the scalp. Treated in the Field Ambulance. **Wounded** by a gunshot to the right hip in July 1916. Evacuated to hospital in England 22 July 1916 and treated at Wharncliffe War Hospital, Sheffield until 10 August 1916. Posted to the 3rd (Reserve) Battalion, The Prince of Wales's Own (West Yorkshire Regiment).] To 36 Infantry Base Depot, France 28 November 1916. Transferred to Princess Victoria's (Royal Irish Fusiliers) 30 November 1916 (renumbered 40058) and joined the 9th (Service) Battalion 12 December 1916. 'D' Company. **Missing** at the Battle of Langemarck 16 August 1917 and later declared **killed in action** on that date, aged 22. 1914-15 Star.

CADDELL Private Albert 22970. From Killycomain, County Armagh. Enlisted in November 1915. Posted to the 9th (Service) Battalion. 'B' Company. **Missing** in the period 21-28 March 1918 during the retreat from St Quentin believed **captured**.

CAHAL Private John 24800. Born at Curragh, Dublin. [Enlisted 16 September 1916 and joined the 9th (Service) Battalion, The Royal Dublin Fusiliers (21283).] Transferred to Princess Victoria's (Royal Irish Fusiliers) in September 1916 (renumbered 24800) and was posted to the 9th (Service) Battalion. **Wounded** during the Battle of Messines 9 June 1917. Discharged as no longer physically fit for war service due to wounds 19 December 1917, aged 19. Silver War Badge, number 288657.

CAHILL Private Francis 14101. Enlisted September 1914. To France with 36th (Ulster) Division in October 1915. Transferred to the Class Z Reserve 30 March 1919. 1914-15 Star.

CAIRNS Private Herbert 14196. From Belfast. To France with 36th (Ulster) Division in October 1915. [Transferred to the Machine Gun Corps (renumbered 19484) and was **killed in action** with the 36th Battalion during the retreat from St Quentin 23 March 1918.] 1914-15 Star. This number was also allocated to Private T Troughton.

CAIRNS Private Samuel 23407. Enlisted in December 1915. Posted to the 9th (Service) Battalion.

CAIRNS Private William 23510. From Belfast. [Enlisted in December 1915 and joined the 7th (Service) Battalion in 49th Brigade, 16th (Irish) Division.] Joined the 9th (North Irish Horse) Battalion when the 7th/8th (Service) Battalion was disbanded in February 1918. **Captured** in 1918.

CALDWELL Private David 14112. Born in 1896 in Scotland. From Monbrief, Lurgan, County Armagh. Enlisted September 1914. To France with 36th (Ulster) Division in October 1915. 'C' Company. **Wounded** during the attack at Hamel 1 July 1916. **Wounded** at the Battle of Langemarck 16 August 1917. [Transferred to the Seaforth Highlanders (Ross-shire Buffs, The Duke of Albany's) (renumbered 30480).] 1914-15 Star.

CALLACHER Private Edward 25905. (His number is incorrectly shown on his medal index card as 16120.) Born on 9 April 1897 at Belfast. Enlisted in December 1916. 'C' Company. **Wounded** at the Battle of Langemarck 16 August 1917 while attached to 108th Trench Mortar Battery. [Transferred to The Royal Irish Rifles (renumbered 5/46120).] Died at Belfast of pulmonary tuberculosis on 8 March 1958, aged 60. His uncle, Second Lieutenant Edward Callacher, served with the 1st Battalion, Princess Victoria's (Royal Irish Fusiliers) as a Sergeant (3337) during the South Africa War; he was injured in an accident on 13 January 1902 at Springfontein. He re-enlisted into Princess Victoria's (Royal Irish Fusiliers) and served as a Warrant Officer Class 1 (renumbered 15218), transferred to the Labour Corps (renumbered 329755) and was commissioned into Princess Victoria's (Royal Irish Fusiliers) on 18 November 1917. He served with a Garrison Battalion. He relinquished his commission on grounds of ill health on 10 July 1918.

CALLAGHAN Private George 14117. From Hamiltonsbawn, County Armagh. Enlisted September 1914. To France with 36th (Ulster) Division in October 1915. 'A' Company. **Killed in action** at the Battle of Langemarck 16 August 1917, aged 20. 1914-15 Star.

CALLAN Private James 24541, 31747 & 7041752. [Enlisted in June 1916 and joined the 7th or 8th (Service) Battalion in 49th Brigade, 16th (Irish) Division.] Joined the 9th (North Irish Horse) Battalion when the 7th/8th (Service) Battalion was disbanded in February 1918. Re-enlisted in 1919 for Regular Army service with Princess Victoria's (Royal Irish Fusiliers) (renumbered 31747, renumbered 7041752, incorrectly recorded as 7047152).

CALLEN Private Robert 21653. Enlisted 18 September 1915. Posted to the 9th (Service) Battalion in mid/late 1916. 'C' Company. **Wounded** during the attack at Hamel 1 July 1916. Discharged as no longer physically fit for war service due to wounds 1 June 1917. Silver War Badge, number 191794.

CALLUM Private Andrew 42435. [Enlisted into The Royal Irish Rifles (1667). To France 16 March 1915 and joined the 1st Battalion, The Royal Irish Rifles. Posted to the 8th (Service) Battalion, The Royal Irish Rifles (East Belfast).] Transferred at the Base Depot to Princess Victoria's (Royal Irish Fusiliers) 14 September 1918 (renumbered 42435) and joined the 9th (North Irish Horse) Battalion 22 September 1918. Transferred to the Class Z Reserve 7 March 1919. 1914-15 Star.

CALVERT Lance Corporal Herbert James 17147. From Keady, County Armagh. Educated at The Royal School, Armagh. Enlisted into the 9th (Service) Battalion in October 1914. To France with 36th (Ulster) Division in October 1915. **Killed in action** during the attack at Hamel 1 July 1916. 1914-15 Star.

CALVERT Private William 40042. From Leeds, Yorkshire. [Enlisted into The Prince of Wales's Own (West Yorkshire Regiment) (13012).] Transferred to Princess Victoria's (Royal Irish Fusiliers) 30 November 1916 (renumbered 40042) and joined the 9th (Service) Battalion 12 December 1916. 'A' Company. **Wounded** at the Battle of Langemarck 16 August 1917. [Transferred to the Army Service Corps (renumbered M/354534).]

CAMERON Corporal William David 26126. Enlisted in February 1917. Posted to the 9th (Service) Battalion. [Posted to the 1st Battalion.]

CAMLIN Lance Corporal Alfred 14091. Born at Armagh, County Armagh. Enlisted September 1914. To France with 36th (Ulster) Division in October 1915. 'A' Company. **Wounded** twice including at the Battle of Langemarck 16 August 1917. **Killed in action** during the attack north of Bailleul 24 August 1918. 1914-15 Star. For step-brothers - see Private Charles Bryans.

CAMPBELL Private Alfred 42572. From Cootehill, County Cavan. [Enlisted into 9th (Service) Battalion, The Royal Irish Rifles (West Belfast) 22 June 1916 (521). Posted to the 12th (Service) Battalion, The Royal Irish Rifles (Central Antrim).] Transferred at the Base Depot to Princess Victoria's (Royal Irish Fusiliers) 14 September 1918 (renumbered 42572) and joined the 9th (North Irish Horse) Battalion 22 September 1918. **Captured** in October 1918. Discharged as no longer physically fit for war service due to sickness 2 April 1919. Silver War Badge, number B185286.

CAMPBELL Private Bruce 41395. Born in 1888 at Dromara, County Down. [Enlisted 18 November 1915 into the North Irish Horse (1914). Served with 2nd North Irish Horse, X Corps Cavalry Regiment.] Joined the renamed 9th (North Irish Horse) Battalion from 36 Infantry Base Depot and transferred to Princess Victoria's (Royal Irish Fusiliers) in September/October 1917 (renumbered 41395). 'A' Company. **Missing** in the period 21-28 March 1918 during the retreat from St Quentin believed **captured** and **wounded**. Discharged as no longer physically fit for war service due to wounds 29 January 1919. Silver War Badge, number B97849.

CAMPBELL Private Charles 24481. From Glasgow. Enlisted in June 1916. Posted to the 9th (Service) Battalion. 'A' Company. **Wounded** at the Battle of Langemarck 16 August 1917. [Transferred to the Labour Corps (renumbered 641532).]

CAMPBELL Corporal David Oliver 18238. From Silverstream, County Monaghan. Enlisted into the 9th (Service) Battalion in February 1915. 'C' Company. To France with 36th (Ulster) Division in October 1915. **Killed in action** at the Battle of Langemarck 16 August 1917, aged 22. 1914-15 Star.

CAMPBELL Private George 23193. Enlisted 20 November 1915. Posted to the 9th (Service) Battalion. **Wounded**. Discharged as no longer physically fit for war service due to wounds 18 June 1918, aged 21. Silver War Badge, number 387952.

CAMPBELL Private Henry 20333. From Glasgow. [Enlisted into The Royal Inniskilling Fusiliers (22697).] Transferred to Princess Victoria's (Royal Irish Fusiliers) 30 June 1915 (renumbered 20333) and joined the 9th (Service) Battalion. 'B' Company. To France with 36th (Ulster) Division in October 1915. **Wounded** during the attack at Hamel 1 July 1916. **Killed in action** at the Battle of Langemarck 16 August 1917. 1914-15 Star.

CAMPBELL MM Sergeant James 13501. From Belfast. [Enlisted in September 1914 and joined the 7th or 8th (Service) Battalion in 49th Brigade, 16th (Irish) Division. Sergeant March 1915. **Wounded** during the Battle of Cambrai in November 1917. **16th (Irish) Division Parchment Certificate for Gallantry and Devotion to Duty**.] Joined the 9th (North Irish Horse) Battalion when the 7th/8th (Service) Battalion was disbanded in February 1918. **MM** – River Lys mid-October 1918. ***Croix de Guerre* (France)**.

CAMPBELL Sergeant James Whittaker 14050. Commissioned into Princess Victoria's (Royal Irish Fusiliers) - see Appendix 5.

CAMPBELL Private John 14097. From Richhill, County Armagh. Enlisted September 1914. To France with 36th (Ulster) Division in October 1915. **Killed in action** 25 September 1917 by shellfire at Havrincourt. 1914-15 Star.

CAMPBELL Private John 20024. From Foybeg, Portadown, County Armagh. Enlisted into the 9th (Service) Battalion in May/June 1915. To France with 36th (Ulster) Division in October 1915. **Killed in action** during the attack at Hamel 1 July 1916.

CAMPBELL Private John 41350. From Carnmoney, County Antrim. A farm labourer. [Enlisted 14 December 1916 into the North Irish Horse (2332). To France 14 May 1917. Served with 2nd North Irish Horse, X Corps Cavalry Regiment.] Joined the renamed 9th (North Irish Horse) Battalion from 36 Infantry Base Depot and transferred to Princess Victoria's (Royal Irish Fusiliers) in September/October 1917 (renumbered 41350). **Wounded** by gunshot to the right knee during the attack south of Wulverghem on 4/5 September 1918 and evacuated to hospital in England 7 September 1918. Transferred to the Class P Reserve 7 December 1918. Discharged as no longer physically fit for war service due to wounds 14 December 1918. Silver War Badge, number 510783.

CAMPBELL Corporal Marcus 41098. [Enlisted in November 1914 into the Service Squadron, 6th (Inniskilling) Dragoons (UD/161). To France with 36th (Ulster) Division in October 1915. Served with 2nd North Irish Horse, X Corps Cavalry Regiment.] Joined the renamed 9th (North Irish Horse) Battalion from 36 Infantry Base Depot and transferred to Princess Victoria's (Royal Irish Fusiliers) in September/October 1917 (renumbered 41098). Transferred to the Class Z Reserve 24 March 1919. 1914-15 Star.

CAMPBELL Private Patrick 23333. Born in 1896 at Londonderry. Enlisted 29 November 1915 and joined the 3rd (Reserve) Battalion. Forfeit nine days pay for absence 19 December 1915. Sentenced to fourteen days Field Punishment Number 2 and forfeit thirteen days pay for being absent for thirteen days 4 February 1915. Sentenced to ten days Field Punishment Number 2 and forfeit fourteen days pay for being absent for twelve days until apprehended by the Military Police in Londonderry 5 September 1915. Sentenced to eight days confined to camp for being improperly dressed and being out of bounds 1 July 1916. Sentenced to ten days Field Punishment Number 2 and forfeit five days pay for breaking out of camp when a defaulter and remaining absent for four days 26 September 1916. Posted to 5th or 6th (Service) Battalion in 31st Brigade, 10th (Irish) Division in the Mediterranean Expeditionary Force and embarked for Salonika 29 September 1916. To hospital sick (enteric fever) 16 November 1916. Evacuated to Malta and treated at Imtarfa Hospital 21 December 1916. Evacuated to hospital in England 12 January 1917. Treated at the Auxiliary Military Hospital, Tranmere until 26 February. Then treated at Addington Park War Hospital until 22 March 1917. Then at an enteric fever convalescent depot until 27 April 1917.] To 36 Infantry Base Depot 13 June 1917 and posted to the 9th (Service) Battalion. 'D' Company. **Wounded** by a gunshot to the hand at the Battle of Langemarck 16 August 1917. Evacuated to hospital in England and treated at Number 2 Military Hospital, Canterbury, Kent until 19 September 1917. Then treated at Fernleigh VAD Convalescent Hospital in Kent until 17 October 1917. Joined the 3rd (Reserve) Battalion 29 October 1917 and was charged with overstaying his sick leave; sentenced to forfeit six days pay. Sentenced to seven days confined to camp for being absent from tattoo 5 November 1918. Posted to the 10th (Reserve) Battalion 13 November 1918. Admonished and forfeit two days pay for overstaying his pass by twenty-four hours 18 December 1918. **Deserted** 22 December 1918.

CAMPBELL Private Joseph 41446. [Enlisted in October 1915 into the North Irish Horse (1756). Served with 2nd North Irish Horse, X Corps Cavalry Regiment.] Joined the renamed 9th (North Irish Horse) Battalion from 36 Infantry Base Depot and transferred to Princess Victoria's (Royal Irish Fusiliers) in September/October 1917 (renumbered 41446). 'C' Company. Believed **wounded** in the period 21-28 March 1918 during the retreat from St Quentin. [Transferred to the Corps of Lancers (renumbered 20027).]

CAMPBELL Private Robert 20356. Enlisted in May/June 1915 and joined the 9th (Service) Battalion with the draft of men from The Royal Inniskilling Fusiliers who transferred to Princess Victoria's (Royal Irish Fusiliers) on 30 June 1915. To France 7 November 1915 and rejoined the 9th (Service) Battalion. 'C' Company. Attached to the Base Depot and did not take part in the attack at Hamel on 1 July 1916. [Transferred to the Royal Defence Corps (renumbered 73191).] 1914-15 Star.

CAMPBELL Lance Corporal Robert 41473. [Enlisted in November 1915 into the North Irish Horse (2012). Served with 2nd North Irish Horse, X Corps Cavalry Regiment.] Joined the renamed 9th (North Irish Horse) Battalion from 36 Infantry Base Depot and transferred to Princess Victoria's (Royal Irish Fusiliers) in September/October 1917 (renumbered 41473).

CAMPBELL Lance Corporal Thomas 41155. [Enlisted in late-1914/early-1915 into the Service Squadron, 6th (Inniskilling) Dragoons (UD/195). To France with 36th (Ulster) Division in October 1915. Served with 2nd North Irish Horse, X Corps Cavalry Regiment. **Wounded** by shellfire at Aveluy Wood when two troops engaged in salvage duty were subject to heavy bombardment 5 July 1916.] Joined the renamed 9th (North Irish Horse) Battalion from 36 Infantry Base Depot and transferred to Princess Victoria's (Royal Irish Fusiliers) in September/October 1917 (renumbered 41155). Transferred to the Class Z Reserve 8 March 1919. 1914-15 Star.

CAMPBELL Private William 14105. Born in 1882 at Shankill, County Armagh. An Insurance agent. Enlisted September 1914. Discharged as not being likely to become an efficient soldier in that he was considered medically unfit for service due to having tuberculosis 29 November 1914.

CAMPBELL Private William 41553. [Enlisted in November 1915 into the Service Squadron, 6th (Inniskilling) Dragoons (UD/302). Served with 2nd North Irish Horse, X Corps Cavalry Regiment.] Joined the renamed 9th (North Irish Horse) Battalion from 36 Infantry Base Depot and transferred to Princess Victoria's (Royal Irish Fusiliers) in September/October 1917 (renumbered 41553). 'D' Company. **Wounded** during the retreat from St Quentin 21-28 March 1918.

CAMPBELL Private William John 24952. From Mourneview Street, Portadown, County Armagh. Enlisted in November 1916. Posted to the 9th (Service) Battalion. 'B' Company. **Missing** at the Battle of Langemarck 16 August 1917 and later declared **killed in action** on that date.

CAMPKIN Private Ernest Sydney 43362. Born in 1897 at Poplar, Middlesex. [Enlisted 24 November 1914, aged 17. Joined 100th Training Reserve Battalion on 19 June 1916. Joined 3/7th Battalion, The London Regiment 13 September 1916 (3236). To Infantry Base Depot, France 11 November 1916 for service with 1/7th (City of London) Battalion, The London Regiment.] Attached to the 9th (Service) Battalion, Princess Victoria's (Royal Irish Fusiliers) 26 November 1916. Discharged from the Territorial Force, re-enlisted and transferred to Princess Victoria's (Royal Irish Fusiliers) in March/April 1917 (renumbered 43362). Initially listed as **missing** on 21 March 1918 on the retreat from St Quentin, he was declared **killed in action**, aged 20, after receipt in December 1918 of a German list of Commonwealth war dead.

CANAVAN Private Peter 21737. [Enlisted in October 1915 and joined the 8th (Service) Battalion in 49th Brigade, 16th (Irish) Division. Transferred to the Machine Gun Corps (renumbered 73501) and posted to 49th Brigade, Machine Gun Company. Transferred back to Princess Victoria's (Royal Irish

Fusiliers) and rejoined the 7th/8th (Service) Battalion.] Joined the 9th (North Irish Horse) Battalion when the 7th/8th (Service) Battalion was disbanded in February 1918.

CARBERRY Private Patrick 13454, 33241 & 7041446. From Belfast. [Enlisted in September 1914 and joined the 7th or 8th (Service) Battalion in 49th Brigade, 16th (Irish) Division.] Joined the 9th (North Irish Horse) Battalion when the 7th/8th (Service) Battalion was disbanded in February 1918. 'A' Company. **Missing** in the period 21-28 March 1918 during the retreat from St Quentin believed **captured**. Re-enlisted 12 August 1919 for Regular Army service with Princess Victoria's (Royal Irish Fusiliers) (renumbered 33241, renumbered 7041446). Served with the 1st Battalion in Persia and Mesopotamia in 1919/20. General Service Medal 1918-1962 with clasps 'Iraq' & 'NW Persia'. Discharged 22 December 1921.

CARMAN Lance Corporal Sidney 43416. [Enlisted into the 7th (Service) Battalion, The Royal Irish Rifles (41873). To 36 Infantry Base Depot and joined the Surplus Company November 1917. Transferred to Princess Victoria's (Royal Irish Fusiliers) in February 1918 (renumbered 43416). Posted to the 7th/8th (Service) Battalion in 49th Brigade, 16th (Irish) Division (probably did not join).] Joined the 9th (North Irish Horse) Battalion when the 7th/8th (Service) Battalion was disbanded in February 1918. 'A' Company. **Missing** in the period 21-28 March 1918 during the retreat from St Quentin believed **captured**.

CARMICHAEL Private Thomas 42456. [Enlisted into The Royal Irish Rifles (1631).] Transferred at the Base Depot to Princess Victoria's (Royal Irish Fusiliers) 14 September 1918 (renumbered 42456) and joined the 9th (North Irish Horse) Battalion 22 September 1918. Re-enlisted in 1919 for Regular Army service with Princess Victoria's (Royal Irish Fusiliers). Discharged for misconduct 4 August 1920.

CARRAGHAR Private John 3517 & 14072. From Portadown, County Armagh. A weaver. Previously served with Princess Victoria's (Royal Irish Fusiliers) Special Reserve (3517 Sergeant). Enlisted September 1914 (renumbered 14072). Discharged as not being likely to become an efficient soldier in that he was considered medically unfit for service 25 November 1914. Silver War Badge, number B142328.

CARRINGTON Private William Henry 43238. [Enlisted into The Sherwood Foresters (Nottinghamshire and Derbyshire Regiment).] Transferred to Princess Victoria's (Royal Irish Fusiliers) 31 August 1916 (renumbered 43238) having joined the 9th (Service) Battalion on 8 August 1916.

CARROLL Private George 42222. [Enlisted into the Army Service Corps (T/32676 Driver). To France 8 September 1914 with 6th Division Train.] Transferred to Princess Victoria's (Royal Irish Fusiliers) 8 May 1918 (renumbered 42222) and joined the 9th (North Irish Horse) Battalion. [Transferred back to the Army Service Corps (renumbered ET/48086 Driver).] 1914 Star.

CARROLL Private George Frederick 23230. Born in 1894 at Armagh, County Armagh. Worked in a linen mill. Enlisted in November 1915 and joined the 10th (Reserve) Battalion. Joined the 9th (Service) Battalion in May/June 1916. 'B' Company. **Wounded** on 1 July 1916 and **died of wounds** 3 July 1917, aged 23.

CARROLL Private John 27856, 33102 & 7041336. From Portadown, County Armagh. Enlisted 31 July 1917. To France 5 April 1918 and joined the 9th (North Irish Horse) Battalion. [Transferred to the Labour Corps (renumbered 609368). Served with 11th Company.] Re-enlisted in August/September 1919 for Regular Army service with Princess Victoria's (Royal Irish Fusiliers) (renumbered 33102, renumbered 7041336). Served with the 1st Battalion in Persia and Mesopotamia in 1919/20. General Service Medal 1918-1962 with clasps 'Iraq' & 'NW Persia'. Discharged 28 February 1922. Enlisted into the 5th (Northern Ireland) Battalion, The Royal Irish Fusiliers (Princess Victoria's) 6 July 1940. Discharged 6 September 1943.

CARSON Private Christopher 41076. From County Fermanagh. [Enlisted in late-September/October 1914 into the Service Squadron, 6th (Inniskilling) Dragoons (UD/80). To France with 36th (Ulster) Division in October 1915. Served with 2nd North Irish Horse, X Corps Cavalry Regiment.] Joined the renamed 9th (North Irish Horse) Battalion from 36 Infantry Base Depot and transferred to Princess Victoria's (Royal Irish Fusiliers) in September/October 1917 (renumbered 41076). 'A' Company. **Captured** in the period 21-28 March 1918 during the retreat from St Quentin. Transferred to the Class Z Reserve 20 March 1919. 1914-15 Star.

CARSON Private Isaac 14103. From Bleary, County Down. A damask weaver. Enlisted September 1914. To France with 36th (Ulster) Division in October 1915. 'C' Company. Lewis gunner. **Wounded** during the attack at Hamel 1 July 1916. **Captured** in the period 21-28 March 1918 during the retreat from St Quentin. Transferred to the Class Z Reserve 21 March 1919. 1914-15 Star.

CARSON Private Isaac 14104. From Lurgan, County Armagh. A damask weaver. Enlisted September 1914. To France with 36th (Ulster) Division in October 1915. 'C' Company. Detached during the attack at Hamel on 1916, in which he did not take part. Evacuated wounded or sick to England in March 1917 and treated at 2nd Western General Hospital, Manchester. To the 10th (Reserve) Battalion 3 June 1917. [Transferred to the Labour Corps (renumbered 231591). Posted to 666th Labour Company 7 July 1917, 668th Labour Company 17 November 1917 & 485th Home Service Employment Company 1 May 1918. Transferred to the Royal Defence Corps (renumbered 80131) 25 June 1918 for service with 200th Protection Company but posted immediately to 199th Protection Company. Posted to 155th Protection Company 17 August 1918. Transferred to the Class Z Reserve 3 March 1919. 1914-15 Star.

CARSON Lance Corporal James 3592. [Enlisted into Princess Victoria's (Royal Irish Fusiliers) Special Reserve 7 June 1915. Posted to the 1st Battalion then the 7th/8th (Service) Battalion.] Joined the 9th (North Irish Horse) Battalion when the 7th/8th (Service) Battalion was disbanded in February 1918. **Wounded** during the retreat from St Quentin 21-28 March 1918. [Posted to the 1st Battalion. **Wounded**.] Discharged as no longer physically fit for war service due to wounds 22 November 1919. Silver War Badge, number B349067.

CARSON Private James 12469. Born in 1876 at Belfast. A shipyard labourer. [Enlisted 7 September 1914 and joined the 6th (Service) Battalion in 31st Brigade, 10th (Irish) Division. Embarked with the Mediterranean Expeditionary Force July 1915. Evacuated sick (malaria) 17 September 1916. Treated at Spinola Hospital, Malta and a convalescent camp then evacuated to hospital in England. Treated at Runcorn Vicarage Hospital 17 May to 8 June 1917, then at the Tropical School, 1st Western General Hospital until 16 August 1917. At the Depot, Ballykinler from August 1917 until posted to the 4th (Extra Reserve) Battalion 26 October 1917.] To 'L' Infantry Base Depot 24 January 1918 to be posted to the 7th/8th (Service) Battalion but joined the 9th (North Irish Horse) Battalion when the 7th/8th (Service) Battalion was disbanded in February 1918. **Captured** at Roye on 27 March 1918 during the retreat from St Quentin. Held at Kassel Prisoner of War Camp, Hesse. Repatriated 13 January 1919. Transferred to the Class Z Reserve 2 April 1919. 1914-15 Star.

CARSON Private James 14102. From Lurgan, County Armagh. 1st (Armagh) Battalion, Armagh Regiment, Ulster Volunteer Force. Enlisted September 1914. Discharged as not being likely to become an efficient soldier in that he was considered medically unfit for service because of a gastric ulcer 8 March 1915.

CARSON Lance Sergeant James 14088. From Lurgan, County Armagh. Enlisted September 1914. To France with 36th (Ulster) Division in October 1915. Transferred to the Class Z Reserve 27 March 1919. 1914-15 Star.

CARSON Lance Corporal John 22031. Enlisted 11 October 1915. Posted to the 9th (Service) Battalion. 'C' Company. **Wounded**. Discharged as no longer physically fit for war service due to wounds 1 March 1919. Silver War Badge, number B154465.

CARSON Private Richard J 24849. Born in 1898 at Eglish, County Armagh. Enlisted in September 1916. Posted to the 9th (Service) Battalion. 'B' Company. **Missing** at the Battle of Langemarck 16 August 1917 and later declared **killed in action** on that date.

CARSON Private Robert 14061. From Lurgan, County Armagh. Enlisted September 1914. To France with 36th (Ulster) Division in October 1915. 3 Section, 13 Platoon, 'D' Company in 1915. **Killed in action** during the attack at Hamel 1 July 1916, aged 29. 1914-15 Star.

CARSON Private Robert 14096. Born in 1892 at County Down. From Milford, County Armagh. Enlisted September 1914. To France with 36th (Ulster) Division in October 1915. 'A' Company. **Wounded** at the Battle of Langemarck 16 August 1917. Discharged as no longer physically fit for war service due to wounds 6 February 1918, aged 22. Silver War Badge, number 325492. 1914-15 Star.

CARSON Private Thomas 14099. Enlisted September 1914. No record of deployment to France with 36th (Ulster) Division in October 1915. [Transferred to the Labour Corps (renumbered 504360). Served with 677th Labour Company.] Discharged as no longer physically fit for war service due to sickness 19 September 1919, aged 38. Silver War Badge, number B14463.

CARSWELL Private Peter 42259. [Enlisted into the Army Service Corps (T3/026824). Served with 3rd Company, 2nd Division Train.] Transferred to Princess Victoria's (Royal Irish Fusiliers) 8 May 1918 (renumbered 42259) and joined the 9th (North Irish Horse) Battalion.

CARTER Private Christopher 41400. Born in 1891 at Belfast. [Enlisted in January 1912 into the North Irish Horse (657). To France 20 August 1914 with 'C' Squadron as 5th Division Cavalry and then as GHQ Troops. Served with 2nd North Irish Horse, X Corps Cavalry Regiment.] Joined the renamed 9th (North Irish Horse) Battalion from 36 Infantry Base Depot and transferred to Princess Victoria's (Royal Irish Fusiliers) in September/October 1917 (renumbered 41400). 1914 Star and clasp.

CARTER Private Eli 42131. [Enlisted into the Army Veterinary Corps (8453). To France 13 August 1915.] Transferred to Princess Victoria's (Royal Irish Fusiliers) 8 May 1918 (renumbered 42131) and joined the 9th (North Irish Horse) Battalion. Transferred to the Class Z Reserve. 1914-15 Star.

CARTER Private John Thomas 43456. Joined the 9th (North Irish Horse) Battalion, Princess Victoria's (Royal Irish Fusiliers) with the draft of men from The London Regiment in April 1918.

CARTER Private William Henry 27843. Served elsewhere before transferring to Princess Victoria's (Royal Irish Fusiliers) in July 1917. Joined the 10th (Reserve) Battalion. To France January 1918 and joined the 9th (North Irish Horse) Battalion. 'B' Company. **Missing** in the period 21-28 March 1918 during the retreat from St Quentin believed **captured**.

CARTMILL Private David 27800. [Enlisted 9 December 1915. Served elsewhere before transferring to Princess Victoria's (Royal Irish Fusiliers) in July 1917. To France in early-1918 posted to the 7th/8th (Service) Battalion.] Joined the 9th (North Irish Horse) Battalion when the 7th/8th (Service) Battalion was disbanded in February 1918. 'B' Company. Believed **wounded** in the period 21-28 March 1918 during the retreat from St Quentin. Discharged as no longer physically fit for war service due to sickness 24 December 1918. Silver War Badge, number B71500.

CARTMILL Private Thomas Rowland 41523. Born in 1892 at Mullaglass, County Armagh. Lived at Newry, County Down. A plumber and gasfitter. [Enlisted in January 1915 into the North Irish Horse (1387). Served with 2nd North Irish Horse, X Corps Cavalry Regiment.] Joined the renamed 9th (North Irish Horse) Battalion from 36 Infantry Base Depot and transferred to Princess Victoria's (Royal Irish Fusiliers) in September/October 1917 (renumbered 41523). 'A' Company. **Killed in action** 29 March 1918 during the retreat from St Quentin, aged 26. 1914-15 Star.

CARVELL DCM Sergeant Samuel 17545. Born 1897. From Portadown, County Armagh. Worked for Messrs Workman, Clark and Company, shipbuilders. Enlisted into the 9th (Service) Battalion in November/December 1914. To France with 36th (Ulster) Division in October 1915. **Wounded** during the attack at Hamel 1 July 1916. **DCM** – Langemarck 16 August 1917. [Transferred to the Labour Corps (renumbered 519595).] Transferred to the Class Z Reserve 1 March 1919. 1914-15 Star.

CASH Private Stephen 43089. From Belfast. [Enlisted into or transferred to Princess Victoria's (Royal Irish Fusiliers) in August 1916 and joined the 8th (Service) Battalion in 49th Brigade, 16th (Irish) Division.] Joined the 9th (North Irish Horse) Battalion when the 7th/8th (Service) Battalion was disbanded in February 1918.

CASKEY Corporal Thomas 41286. [Enlisted in September 1914 into the North Irish Horse (1149). To France 20 January 1915. Served with 2nd North Irish Horse, X Corps Cavalry Regiment.] Joined the renamed 9th (North Irish Horse) Battalion from 36 Infantry Base Depot and transferred to Princess Victoria's (Royal Irish Fusiliers) in September/October 1917 (renumbered 41286). Transferred to the Class Z Reserve 11 June 1919. 1914-15 Star.

CASSELS Private Alexander 41215. [Enlisted in October 1915 into the North Irish Horse (1739). Served with 2nd North Irish Horse, X Corps Cavalry Regiment.] Joined the renamed 9th (North Irish Horse) Battalion from 36 Infantry Base Depot and transferred to Princess Victoria's (Royal Irish Fusiliers) in September/October 1917 (renumbered 41215). 'D' Company. **Missing** in the period

21-28 March 1918 during the retreat from St Quentin believed **captured**.

CASSIDY Private John 27462. [Enlisted 23 March 1917 and served with the 1st Battalion.] Posted to the 9th (North Irish Horse) Battalion. **Wounded**. Discharged as no longer physically fit for war service due to wounds 7 October 1919. Silver War Badge, number B321655.

CASSIDY Private John Patrick 24025. From Arva, County Cavan. [Enlisted in February 1916 and joined the 7th or 8th (Service) Battalion in 49th Brigade, 16th (Irish) Division.] Joined the 9th (North Irish Horse) Battalion when the 7th/8th (Service) Battalion was disbanded in February 1918. **Captured** in the period 21-28 March 1918 during the retreat from St Quentin.

CASSIDY Private Robert 41290. Born in 1893 at Enniskillen, County Fermanagh. Lived at Belfast. A yardman. [Enlisted 13 August 1914 into the North Irish Horse (1002) (probably a re-enlistment but his record indicates no previous service). To France 20 August 1914 with 'C' Squadron as 5th Division Cavalry and then as GHQ Troops. To hospital sick (tonsillitis) 20 September 1914. Served with 2nd North Irish Horse, X Corps Cavalry Regiment. Attached to General Headquarters, 2nd Echelon 18 October 1916 and rejoined the 2nd North Irish Horse 2 December 1916.] Joined the renamed 9th (North Irish Horse) Battalion from 36 Infantry Base Depot and transferred to Princess Victoria's (Royal Irish Fusiliers) in September/October 1917 (renumbered 41290). 'C' Company. [Transferred to the Tank Corps (renumbered 304846) 28 December 1917 and posted for training to the Tank Corps Depot, at Bovington near Wareham, Dorset. Posted to the 17th Battalion, Tank Corps (Gunner) 8 January 1918. To France 8 July 1918 and joined 15th Battalion, Tank Corps. Posted to Headquarters 3rd Battalion, Tank Corps 13 November 1918. Posted to Oswestry for demobilisation 5 February 1919.] Transferred to the North Irish Horse Special Reserve 7 March 1919. 1914 Star.

CASSIE Private Frederick Thomas 42191. [Enlisted into the Army Service Corps (T/331101).] Transferred to Princess Victoria's (Royal Irish Fusiliers) 8 May 1918 (renumbered 42191) and joined the 9th (North Irish Horse) Battalion.

CATANACH Private Thomas 16384. [Enlisted in October 1914 into the 6th (Service) Battalion in 31st Brigade, 10th (Irish) Division. Embarked with the Mediterranean Expeditionary Force July 1915.] Posted to the 9th (Service) Battalion. Transferred to the Class Z Reserve 26 February 1919. 1914-15 Star.

CATHCART Private William 41462. [Enlisted in January 1913 into the North Irish Horse (774). To France 20 August 1914 with 'C' Squadron as 5th Division Cavalry and then as GHQ Troops. Served with 2nd North Irish Horse, X Corps Cavalry Regiment.] Joined the renamed 9th (North Irish Horse) Battalion from 36 Infantry Base Depot and transferred to Princess Victoria's (Royal Irish Fusiliers) in September/October 1917 (renumbered 41462). [Posted to the 1st Battalion.] 1914 Star.

CATHER Private James 41291. From Castlederg, County Tyrone. [Enlisted in January 1913 into the North Irish Horse (777). Served with 2nd North Irish Horse, X Corps Cavalry Regiment.] Joined the renamed 9th (North Irish Horse) Battalion from 36 Infantry Base Depot and transferred to Princess Victoria's (Royal Irish Fusiliers) in September/October 1917 (renumbered 41291). 'C' Company. **Captured** in the period 21-28 March 1918 during the retreat from St Quentin. 1914 Star.

CATLIN Private Frederick 42207. [Enlisted 21 February 1916 and joined 3/9th Battalion, The London Regiment (26771). To France and joined 1/7th Battalion, The Duke of Cambridge's Own (Middlesex Regiment) (renumbered 6673).] Transferred to Princess Victoria's (Royal Irish Fusiliers) in April/May 1918 (renumbered 42207). Joined the 9th (North Irish Horse) Battalion, Princess Victoria's (Royal Irish Fusiliers) with the draft of men transferred from the Army Service Corps and the Army Veterinary Corps in May 1918. **Wounded**. Discharged as no longer physically fit for war service due to wounds 29 July 1919. Silver War Badge, number B302849.

CATLIN Private Frederick William 43383. Born in 1887. From Upton Park, London. Boot salesman. [Enlisted 24 April 1915 into The London Regiment (4355). To France 14 May 1916 and joined 1/9th (County of London) Battalion, The London Regiment (Queen Victoria's Rifles). To hospital sick (influenza and trench fever) June 1916 and evacuated to hospital in England 4 July 1916.] To France 11 November 1916. Attached to the 9th (Service) Battalion, Princess Victoria's (Royal Irish Fusiliers) 26 November 1916. 'D' Company. Discharged from the Territorial Force, re-enlisted and transferred to Princess Victoria's (Royal Irish Fusiliers) in March/April 1917 (renumbered 43383). **Killed in action** at the Battle of Langemarck 16 August 1917, aged 28.

CAUGHEY Private William 41273. [Enlisted (probably a re-enlistment) in August 1914 into the North Irish Horse (972). To France 20 August 1914 with 'C' Squadron as 5th Division Cavalry and then as GHQ Troops. Served with 2nd North Irish Horse, X Corps Cavalry Regiment.] Joined the renamed 9th (North Irish Horse) Battalion from 36 Infantry Base Depot and transferred to Princess Victoria's (Royal Irish Fusiliers) in September/October 1917 (renumbered 41273). 1914 Star.

CAULFIELD Sergeant James 14062. From Lurgan, County Armagh. Enlisted September 1914. To France with 36th (Ulster) Division in October 1915. 'B' Company. **Wounded** during the attack at Hamel 1 July 1916. Discharged as no longer physically fit for war service due to wounds 10 May 1917. Silver War Badge, number 168873. 1914-15 Star.

CAULFIELD Corporal John Charles 41193. [Enlisted in February 1916 into the North Irish Horse (2103). Served with 2nd North Irish Horse, X Corps Cavalry Regiment.] Joined the renamed 9th (North Irish Horse) Battalion from 36 Infantry Base Depot and transferred to Princess Victoria's (Royal Irish Fusiliers) in September/October 1917 (renumbered 41193).

CAUSBY Private Edward 42559. [Served previously with The Royal Irish Rifles (22119).] Transferred at the Base Depot to Princess Victoria's (Royal Irish Fusiliers) 14 September 1918 (renumbered 42559) and joined the 9th (North Irish Horse) Battalion 22 September 1918. [Transferred to the Army Ordnance Corps (renumbered S/11769).]

CAVANAGH Private James 18540. [Enlisted 6 April 1915 into the 5th (Service) Battalion in 31st Brigade, 10th (Irish) Division. Embarked with the Mediterranean Expeditionary Force July 1915. Posted to the 7th/8th (Service) Battalion in 49th Brigade, 16th (Irish) Division.] Joined the 9th (North Irish Horse) Battalion when the 7th/8th (Service) Battalion was disbanded in February 1918. 'D' Company. Believed **wounded** in the period 21-28 March 1918 during the retreat from St Quentin. Discharged as no longer physically fit for war service due to wounds 25 February 1919. Silver War Badge, number B154143. 1914-15 Star.

CAVANAGH Private James 42121. [Enlisted into the Army Veterinary Corps (29852).] Transferred to Princess Victoria's (Royal Irish Fusiliers) 8 May 1918 (renumbered 42121) and joined the 9th (North Irish Horse) Battalion.

CAVE Private George William 43209. Born in 1889 at Plymouth. From Derby. A coach painter. [Enlisted 18 March 1915 and transferred to the Army Reserve. Mobilised 21 February 1916 and joined The Sherwood Foresters (Nottinghamshire and Derbyshire Regiment) (36241). To France 23 July 1916.] Transferred to Princess Victoria's (Royal Irish Fusiliers) 31 August 1916 (renumbered 43209) having joined the 9th (Service) Battalion on 8 August 1916. To hospital with impetigo from 18 January to 1 March 1917. Rejoined the 9th (Service) Battalion from the Base Depot 23 March 1917. 'A' Company. **Killed in action** on a raid at Spanbroekmolen 4 June 1917, aged 27.

CEARNEY Private James 42534. [Enlisted April/May 1918 into The Royal Irish Rifles (22632).] Transferred at the Base Depot to Princess Victoria's (Royal Irish Fusiliers) 14 September 1918 (renumbered 42534) and joined the 9th (North Irish Horse) Battalion 22 September 1918.

CHAMBERS Private David 41452. [Enlisted in December 1916 into the North Irish Horse (2326). Served with 2nd North Irish Horse, X Corps Cavalry Regiment.] Joined the renamed 9th (North Irish Horse) Battalion from 36 Infantry Base Depot and transferred to Princess Victoria's (Royal Irish Fusiliers) in September/October 1917 (renumbered 41452). [Transferred to 5th (Service) Battalion, The Royal Irish Regiment (Pioneers) in the Light Division in the British Army of the Rhine in March/June 1919 (renumbered 41271).]

CHAMBERS Lance Corporal George 14065. Born in 1897 at Sherrygroom, Newmills, County Tyrone. From Milford, County Armagh. Enlisted September 1914, aged 17. To France with 36th (Ulster) Division in October 1915. **Killed in action** during the attack at Hamel 1 July 1916, aged 19. 1914-15 Star.

CHAMBERS Private James 14125. Worked at Bessbrook Spinning Company Ltd. Enlisted September 1914. To France with 36th (Ulster) Division in October 1915. **Wounded** during the attack at Hamel 1 July 1916. **Wounded** in November 1916. [Transferred to the Labour Corps (renumbered 231592).] Transferred to the Class Z Reserve 19 May 1919. 1914-15 Star.

CHAMBERS Private James Andrew 22623, 33416 & 7041579. Born in 1899 at Shankill,

Belfast. Enlisted in November 1915, aged 16. Posted to the 9th (Service) Battalion. **Captured** in the period 21-28 March 1918 during the retreat from St Quentin. Transferred to the Class Z Reserve. Re-enlisted 18 September 1919 for Regular Army service with Princess Victoria's (Royal Irish Fusiliers) (renumbered 33416, renumbered 7041579). Served with the 1st Battalion in Persia and Mesopotamia in 1919/20. General Service Medal 1918-1962 with clasps 'Iraq' & 'NW Persia'. Discharged 23 December 1921.

CHAMBERS Lance Corporal James Henry 14052. From Carleton Street, Portadown, County Armagh. 4th (Portadown) Battalion, Armagh Regiment, Ulster Volunteer Force. Member of Edenderry Temperance and Benefit Loyal Orange Lodge 322. Enlisted September 1914. To France with 36th (Ulster) Division in October 1915. 'B' Company. **Wounded** during the attack at Hamel 1 July 1916. Separated from the 9th (North Irish Horse) Battalion in the period 21-28 March 1918 during the retreat from St Quentin; rejoined 3 April 1918. **Wounded**. Discharged as no longer physically fit for war service due to wounds 30 March 1919. 1914-15 Star. **Died of wounds** in Ireland 29 July 1920, aged 26.

CHAMBERS Private John 14089. From Bessbrook, County Armagh. Enlisted September 1914. To France with 36th (Ulster) Division in October 1915. 3 Section, 13 Platoon, 'D' Company in 1915. **Killed in action** during the attack at Hamel 1 July 1916.

CHAMBERS Private John G 14063. From Portadown, County Armagh. Enlisted September 1914. To France with 36th (Ulster) Division in October 1915. **Wounded** during the attack at Hamel 1 July 1916. [Transferred to the Labour Corps (renumbered 641511).] 1914-15 Star.

CHAMBERS Private Joseph 14074. Born in 1892 at Bessbrook, County Armagh. Enlisted September 1914. To France with 36th (Ulster) Division in October 1915. 'D' Company. **Killed in action** at the Battle of Langemarck 16 August 1917, aged 25. 1914-15 Star.

CHAMBERS Private Joseph 23659. Enlisted in January 1916. Posted to the 9th (Service) Battalion.

CHAMBERS Sergeant Joseph 41522. [Enlisted in July 1908 into the North Irish Horse (14). Served with 2nd North Irish Horse, X Corps Cavalry Regiment.] Joined the renamed 9th (North Irish Horse) Battalion from 36 Infantry Base Depot and transferred to Princess Victoria's (Royal Irish Fusiliers) in September/October 1917 (renumbered 41522). 'B' Company. Separated from the 9th (North Irish Horse) Battalion in the period 21-28 March 1918 during the retreat from St Quentin; rejoined on 3 April 1918.

CHAMBERS Private Samuel 18068. Born in 1895 at Darkley near Keady, County Armagh. From Armagh, County Armagh. A mechanic. Enlisted into the 9th (Service) Battalion in February 1915. To France with 36th (Ulster) Division in October 1915. 'C' Company. **Wounded** during the attack at Hamel 1 July 1916. [Posted to the 1st Battalion in early-1918 and was **wounded**. Evacuated to hospital in England and treated at 2nd Western General Hospital, Manchester.] Rejoined the 9th (Service) Battalion and was **killed in action** during the attack south of Wulverghem 5 September 1918. 1914-15 Star.

CHAMBERS Private Thomas 21676. From Glenanne, County Armagh. Enlisted in September 1915. Posted to the 9th (Service) Battalion in May/June 1916. 'A' Company. **Killed in action** during the attack at Hamel 1 July 1916, aged 19.

CHAMBERS MM Corporal Thomas Clyde 41256. (Some records incorrectly show number 41297, which was issued to Private J McWilliams below). [Enlisted in July 1914 into the North Irish Horse (958). To France 20 August 1914 with 'C' Squadron as 5th Division Cavalry and then as GHQ Troops. Served with 2nd North Irish Horse, X Corps Cavalry Regiment.] Joined the renamed 9th (North Irish Horse) Battalion from 36 Infantry Base Depot and transferred to Princess Victoria's (Royal Irish Fusiliers) in September/October 1917 (renumbered 41256). 'C' Company. **MM** – Havrincourt raid 3 November 1917. **Wounded** during the retreat from St Quentin 21-28 March 1918. 1914 Star.

CHANEY Private Edward Martin 42223. [Enlisted into the Army Service Corps (T/041321). Served with 25th Division Train. To France 24 September 1915.] Transferred to Princess Victoria's (Royal Irish Fusiliers) 8 May 1918 (renumbered 42223) and joined the 9th (North Irish Horse) Battalion. Transferred to the Class Z Reserve 3 March 1919. 1914-15 Star.

CHAPMAN Private Edward 16097. Enlisted into the 9th (Service) Battalion in October 1914. To France with 36th (Ulster) Division in October 1915. [Transferred to the Corps of Royal Engineers (WR/277189).] 1914-15 Star.

CHAPMAN Private Samuel Hamilton 17934. Born at Aghabog, County Monaghan. Enlisted into the 9th (Service) Battalion in January 1915. To France with 36th (Ulster) Division in October 1915. **Killed in action** during the attack at Hamel 1 July 1916. 1914-15 Star.

CHAPMAN Private Walter Wilfred 41630. [Enlisted 23 December 1914 for service with cavalry (5542). Posted to 2nd North Irish Horse, X Corps Cavalry Regiment.] Joined the renamed 9th (North Irish Horse) Battalion from 36 Infantry Base Depot and transferred to Princess Victoria's (Royal Irish Fusiliers) in September/October 1917 (renumbered 41630). 'D' Company. **Wounded** during the retreat from St Quentin 21-28 March 1918. Discharged as no longer physically fit for war service due to wounds 31 October 1918. Silver War Badge, number B35685.

CHARLTON Lance Corporal Frank 40083. [Served previously as a regular soldier with The Prince of Wales's Own (West Yorkshire Regiment) (8751). To France 5 November 1914 with the 2nd Battalion, The Prince of Wales's Own (West Yorkshire Regiment).] Transferred to Princess Victoria's (Royal Irish Fusiliers) 30 November 1916 (renumbered 40083) and joined the 9th (Service) Battalion 12 December 1916. 'C' Company. **Wounded** at the Battle of Langemarck 16 August 1917. 1914 Star.

CHATTERTON Private Thomas 42224 & 7042175. From Colne, Lancashire. A reacher-in. [Enlisted into the Army Service Corps (T/36189) 4 January 1915. To France 2 May 1916. Served with 138th Field Ambulance and 4th Division Train.] Transferred to Princess Victoria's (Royal Irish Fusiliers) 8 May 1918 (renumbered 42224) and joined the 9th (North Irish Horse) Battalion. **Wounded** by a gunshot to the left forearm during the attack south of Wulverghem on 4/5 September 1918 and evacuated to hospital in England 9 September 1918. Transferred to the Section B Army Reserve, Princess Victoria's (Royal Irish Fusiliers) (renumbered 7042175). Mobilised 9 April 1921. Discharged 3 January 1927.

CHEESEMAN Private George Thomas 42270. Born in 1890 at Erith, Kent. A horse keeper. [Enlisted 13 November 1915 into the Army Veterinary Corps (13180). To Egypt 21 November 1915 and served with 20th Veterinary Hospital.] Transferred to Princess Victoria's (Royal Irish Fusiliers) 8 May 1918 (renumbered 42270) and joined the 9th (North Irish Horse) Battalion. **Wounded** by a gunshot and evacuated to hospital in England in August 1918. Treated at Norfolk War Hospital, Thorpe until 19 October 1918. Transferred to the Class Z Reserve 8 February 1919. 1914-15 Star.

CHEESEMAN Private William Henry 45774. [Enlisted into The London Regiment (4204).] To France and joined 36 Infantry Base Depot 29 March 1918. Transferred to Princess Victoria's (Royal Irish Fusiliers) 2 April 1918 (renumbered 45774) and joined the 9th (North Irish Horse) Battalion 4 April 1918.

CHEETHAM Private Ernest 23555. [Enlisted in December 1915 and joined the 7th (Service) Battalion in 49th Brigade, 16th (Irish) Division.] Joined the 9th (North Irish Horse) Battalion when the 7th/8th (Service) Battalion was disbanded in February 1918.

CHERRIE Private William John 41515. Born in 1894 near Downpatrick, County Down. [Enlisted in February 1912 into the North Irish Horse (677). To France 17 August 1914 with 'A' Squadron as GHQ Troops. Served with 2nd North Irish Horse, X Corps Cavalry Regiment.] Joined the renamed 9th (North Irish Horse) Battalion from 36 Infantry Base Depot and transferred to Princess Victoria's (Royal Irish Fusiliers) in September/October 1917 (renumbered 42515). 'B' Company. **Captured** in the period 21-28 March 1918 during the retreat from St Quentin. Repatriated and arrived in Belfast on 5 December 1918. 1914 Star.

CHESTNUT Private Thomas 41242. Born in 1889 at Knockantern, County Londonderry. A railway porter. [Enlisted in May 1915 into the North Irish Horse (1632). Served with 2nd North Irish Horse, X Corps Cavalry Regiment.] Joined the renamed 9th (North Irish Horse) Battalion from 36 Infantry Base Depot and transferred to Princess Victoria's (Royal Irish Fusiliers) in September/October 1917 (renumbered 41242). [Transferred to the Tank Corps (renumbered 304877) 28 December 1917 and posted for training to the Tank Corps Depot, at Bovington near Wareham, Dorset.]

CHILD Private Allan 40059. [Enlisted into the 18th (Service) Battalion, The Prince of Wales's Own

(West Yorkshire Regiment) (2nd Bradford) (1130). To Egypt 26 December 1915 with 93rd Brigade in 31st Division.] Transferred to Princess Victoria's (Royal Irish Fusiliers) 30 November 1916 (renumbered 40059) and joined the 9th (Service) Battalion 12 December 1916. 'B' Company. **Missing** in the period 21-28 March 1918 during the retreat from St Quentin believed **captured**. Transferred to the Class Z Reserve 4 April 1919. 1914-15 Star.

CHILDS Corporal Alfred 42177. [Enlisted into the Army Service Corps (S4/093514). To France 24 August 1915.] Transferred to Princess Victoria's (Royal Irish Fusiliers) 8 May 1918 (renumbered 42177) and joined the 9th (North Irish Horse) Battalion. [Transferred to The Royal Inniskilling Fusiliers (renumbered 43865).] Transferred to the Class Z Reserve. 1914-15 Star.

CHILDS Private Edmund 41340. Born in 1893 at Belfast. A compositor. [Enlisted in October 1915 into the North Irish Horse (1753). Served with 2nd North Irish Horse, X Corps Cavalry Regiment.] Joined the renamed 9th (North Irish Horse) Battalion from 36 Infantry Base Depot and transferred to Princess Victoria's (Royal Irish Fusiliers) in September/October 1917 (renumbered 41340). 'B' Company. Believed **wounded** in the period 21-28 March 1918 during the retreat from St Quentin. [Posted to the 11th (Service) Battalion. Served with the 5th/6th (Service) Battalion when the 11th (Service) Battalion was absorbed.]

CHRISTIAN Sergeant Thomas 18048. Enlisted into the 9th (Service) Battalion in February 1915. 'C' Company. To France with 36th (Ulster) Division in October 1915. Served as a Sergeant at the Base Depot mid-1916. Did not take part in the attack at Hamel on 1 July 1916. Transferred to the Class Z Reserve 1 April 1919. 1914-15 Star.

CHRISTIE Private James 14124. From Edenknappagh, County Armagh. Enlisted September 1914. To France with 36th (Ulster) Division in October 1915. [Joined 108th Brigade Machine Gun Company in January 1916. Transferred to the Machine Gun Corps (renumbered 17785). **Killed in action** 28 May 1918, aged 40, while serving with 47th Battalion, Machine Gun Corps.] 1914-15 Star.

CINNAMOND Private William 41187. [Enlisted 8 April 1915 into the North Irish Horse (1476). To France with 'F' Squadron in 33rd Division 17 November 1915. Served with 2nd North Irish Horse, X Corps Cavalry Regiment.] Joined the renamed 9th (North Irish Horse) Battalion from 36 Infantry Base Depot and transferred to Princess Victoria's (Royal Irish Fusiliers) in September/October 1917 (renumbered 41187). **Wounded**. Discharged as no longer physically fit for war service due to wounds 1 March 1919. Silver War Badge, number B154119. 1914-15 Star.

CLARK Private Albert Henry 43338. From Shadwell, London. A dock labourer. [Enlisted 20 November 1915 into The London Regiment (6810) and transferred to the Army Reserve. Mobilised 22 July 1916 and joined 3/7th Battalion, The London Regiment. To France 10 November 1916.] Attached to the 9th (Service) Battalion, Princess Victoria's (Royal Irish Fusiliers) 26 November 1916. 4 Platoon, 'A' Company. Renumbered 353178, The London Regiment in March 1917. Discharged from the Territorial Force, re-enlisted and transferred to Princess Victoria's (Royal Irish Fusiliers) in March 1917 (renumbered 43338). **Wounded** by gunshots to the arm and leg at the Battle of Langemarck 16 August 1917. He was carried to a dressing station by another man of the 9th (Service) Battalion who waited with him until his wounds were dressed and he was placed in an ambulance of 48th Field Ambulance. The ambulance was destroyed by shellfire. Clark was subsequently listed as **missing** at the Battle of Langemarck 16 August 1917 and was declared **killed in action** on that date, aged 20, in January 1919.

CLARK Private George William 40009. Born 1889 at Barlow, Yorkshire. Lived at Selby, Yorkshire. Employed as a horseman for a local storekeeper. [Enlisted 11 December 1915 into The Prince of Wales's Own (West Yorkshire Regiment) (34455).] Transferred to Princess Victoria's (Royal Irish Fusiliers) 30 November 1916 (renumbered 40009) and joined the 9th (Service) Battalion 12 December 1916. 'A' Company. **Killed in action** at the Battle of Langemarck 16 August 1917. Commemorated at the Parish Church of St Wilfred's, Brayton and at Selby Abbey.

CLARK Private John Herbert 45818. Joined the 9th (North Irish Horse) Battalion, Princess Victoria's (Royal Irish Fusiliers) with the draft of men from The London Regiment in April 1918.

CLARK Private Joseph Randolf 40010. From Pateley Bridge, Yorkshire. [Enlisted into The Prince of Wales's Own (West Yorkshire Regiment) (34465).] Transferred to Princess Victoria's (Royal Irish Fusiliers) 30 November 1916 (renumbered 40010) and joined the 9th (Service) Battalion 12

December 1916. **Killed in action** at the Battle of Langemarck 16 August 1917.

CLARKE MM Lance Corporal Alan George Hart 41483. From Belfast. [Enlisted in January 1915 into the North Irish Horse (1433). To France with 'F' Squadron in 33rd Division 17 November 1915. Served with 2nd North Irish Horse, X Corps Cavalry Regiment.] Joined the renamed 9th (North Irish Horse) Battalion from 36 Infantry Base Depot and transferred to Princess Victoria's (Royal Irish Fusiliers) in September/October 1917 (renumbered 41483). 'C' Company. **MM** – Marcoing 16 December 1917. Separated from the 9th (North Irish Horse) Battalion in the period 21-28 March 1918 during the retreat from St Quentin; rejoined 2 April 1918. Transferred to the Class Z Reserve 20 March 1919. 1914-15 Star.

CLARKE MM Corporal David 14077. From Bessbrook, County Armagh. Enlisted September 1914. To France with 36th (Ulster) Division in October 1915. **Wounded** in both arms during the attack at Hamel 1 July 1916. **MM** – Bailleul 24 August 1918. Transferred to the Class Z Reserve 30 March 1919. 1914-15 Star. Brother of Private George Clarke.

CLARKE Private George 14114. From Bessbrook, County Armagh. Enlisted September 1914. To France with 36th (Ulster) Division in October 1915. **Wounded** during the attack at Hamel 1 July 1916. Discharged as no longer physically fit for war service due to wounds 26 February 1918. Silver War Badge, number 334288. 1914-15 Star. Brother of Private David Clarke.

CLARKE Private George Harry 42154. [Enlisted into the Army Veterinary Corps (30716).] Transferred to Princess Victoria's (Royal Irish Fusiliers) 8 May 1918 (renumbered 42154) and joined the 9th (North Irish Horse) Battalion.

CLARKE Private Henry 22803. From Jaegersfontein, South Africa. Enlisted in November 1915. Posted to the 9th (Service) Battalion. 'A' Company. **Captured** in the period 21-28 March 1918 during the retreat from St Quentin.

CLARKE Private James 42146. Born in 1883 at Neath, Glamorganshire. A butcher. [Enlisted 15 April 1915 into the Army Veterinary Corps (85724). Arrived in Egypt 22 June 1915. Sailed for the Dardanelles 3 July 1915. Returned to Egypt from Mudros 11 February 1916. Joined Number 4 Line of Communication Supply Company 2 September 1916. Joined Army Service Corps Base Depot 28 April 1918.] Joined 'A' Infantry Base Depot 5 May 1918. Transferred to Princess Victoria's (Royal Irish Fusiliers) 8 May 1918 (renumbered 42146) and joined the 9th (North Irish Horse) Battalion. 'C' Company. To hospital sick (trench fever) 28 December 1918 and evacuated to hospital in England. Treated at the War Hospital, Bradford until 17 April 1919. Transferred to the Class Z Reserve 15 May 1919. 1914-15 Star.

CLARKE Private Jeremiah 41393. [Enlisted 28 May 1915 into the North Irish Horse (1635). Served with 2nd North Irish Horse, X Corps Cavalry Regiment.] Joined the renamed 9th (North Irish Horse) Battalion from 36 Infantry Base Depot and transferred to Princess Victoria's (Royal Irish Fusiliers) in September/October 1917 (renumbered 41393). **Wounded** severely in the arm on 22/23 November 1917 during the attack at Moeuvres. Discharged as no longer physically fit for war service due to wounds, 16 October 1918. Silver War Badge, number B34295.

CLARKE Private John 45808. Enlisted 3 July 1917. Joined the 9th (North Irish Horse) Battalion, Princess Victoria's (Royal Irish Fusiliers) with the draft of men from The London Regiment in April 1918. **Wounded**. Discharged as no longer physically fit for war service due to wounds. Silver War Badge, number B224710.

CLARKE Private John William 43228. [Enlisted into The Sherwood Foresters (Nottinghamshire and Derbyshire Regiment).] Transferred to Princess Victoria's (Royal Irish Fusiliers) 31 August 1916 (renumbered 43228) having joined the 9th (Service) Battalion on 8 August 1916.

CLARKE Corporal Joseph 23439. From Newbliss, County Monaghan. A farmer. Enlisted 6 December 1915 and joined the 10th (Reserve) Battalion. **Wounded** by a gunshot to the left leg 2 May 1916 while serving with the Ulster Composite Battalion during the Irish Republican attacks in Dublin. To France 13 June 1916. Posted to the 9th (Service) Battalion. **Wounded** by shrapnel to the abdomen 5 December 1917 at Marcoing. Evacuated to hospital in England 24 December 1918. Discharged as no longer physically fit for war service due to wounds 15 November 1918. Silver War Badge, number B44339.

CLARKE Private Thomas 14067. Enlisted September 1914. To France with 36th (Ulster) Division in October 1915. Transferred to the Class Z Reserve 22 March 1919. 1914-15 Star.

CLARKE Private William 14121. Enlisted September 1914. To France with 36th (Ulster) Division in October 1915. Transferred to the Class Z Reserve 8 March 1919. 1914-15 Star.

CLARKE Private William 17928. Born at Killeevan, County Monaghan. Enlisted into the 9th (Service) Battalion in January 1915. To France with 36th (Ulster) Division in October 1915. **Killed in action** during the attack at Hamel 1 July 1916. 1914-15 Star.

CLARKSON Private John 20321. From Bory, County Durham. [Enlisted into The Royal Inniskilling Fusiliers (23830).] Transferred to Princess Victoria's (Royal Irish Fusiliers) 30 June 1915 (renumbered 20321) and joined the 9th (Service) Battalion. To France with 36th (Ulster) Division in October 1915. 'C' Company. To hospital early/mid-1916 and did not take part in the attack at Hamel. Struck off strength when evacuated to hospital in England. **Died** in hospital in England 28 September 1916, aged 32. His grave in Gateshead Fell (St John) Churchyard shows the badge and title of The Royal Inniskilling Fusiliers. 1914-15 Star.

CLAY Private George Robert 21756, 33218 & 7041429. Born in 1895 at Killeshandra, County Cavan. Enlisted in October 1915. Posted to the 9th (Service) Battalion in mid/late 1916. 'C' Company. Officer's servant for Captain J A Johnston and did not take part in the attack at Hamel on 1 July 1916. [Transferred to the Tank Corps (renumbered 304848) 28 December 1917 and posted for training to the Tank Corps Depot, at Bovington near Wareham, Dorset. Served with 7th Battalion, Tank Corps.] Re-enlisted 22 August 1919 for Regular Army service with Princess Victoria's (Royal Irish Fusiliers) (renumbered 33218, renumbered 7041429). Served with the 1st Battalion in Mesopotamia and Egypt in 1919/20. Discharged 11 November 1922.

CLAYTON Private Arthur Victor 40008. Born in 1887 at Attercliffe, Sheffield, Yorkshire. From Rotherham, Yorkshire. [Enlisted into The Prince of Wales's Own (West Yorkshire Regiment) (6844). To France 13 July 1915.] Transferred to Princess Victoria's (Royal Irish Fusiliers) 30 November 1916 (renumbered 40008) and joined the 9th (Service) Battalion 12 December 1916. 1914-15 Star. Re-enlisted in 1919 for Regular Army service with The York and Lancaster Regiment (renumbered 52759, renumbered 4736687). Served with the 2nd Battalion, The York and Lancaster Regiment in Persia and Mesopotamia in 1919/20. General Service Medal 1918-1962 with clasps 'Iraq' & 'NW Persia'. Died at Sheffield, Yorkshire in 1956, aged 68.

CLAYTON Private David 26099. From Drumcree, Portadown, County Armagh. Enlisted in January 1917. Posted to the 9th (Service) Battalion. 'D' Company. **Wounded** at the Battle of Langemarck 16 August 1917. [Transferred to The Royal Irish Regiment (renumbered 5934).]

CLAYTON Private Percy 45805. Joined the 9th (North Irish Horse) Battalion, Princess Victoria's (Royal Irish Fusiliers) with the draft of men from The London Regiment in April 1918.

CLEMENTS Private Frederick William 40057. [Enlisted into the 11th (Service) Battalion, The Prince of Wales's Own (West Yorkshire Regiment) (14350). To France 26 August 1915 in 69th Brigade, 23rd Division.] Transferred to Princess Victoria's (Royal Irish Fusiliers) 30 November 1916 (renumbered 40057) and joined the 9th (Service) Battalion 12 December 1916. Transferred to the Class Z Reserve 19 March 1919. 1914-15 Star.

CLEMENTS Private James 41292. [Enlisted in September 1914 into the North Irish Horse (1107). To France 2 June 1915. Served with 2nd North Irish Horse, X Corps Cavalry Regiment.] Joined the renamed 9th (North Irish Horse) Battalion from 36 Infantry Base Depot and transferred to Princess Victoria's (Royal Irish Fusiliers) in September/October 1917 (renumbered 41292). 'C' Company. **Wounded** during the retreat from St Quentin 21-28 March 1918. Transferred to the Class Z Reserve. 1914-15 Star.

CLEMENTS MM Sergeant Thomas 17151. Born in 1898 at Ahorey, Portadown, County Armagh. Enlisted into the 9th (Service) Battalion in October/November 1914, aged 16. 'A' Company. To France with 36th (Ulster) Division in October 1915. As a Corporal took part in the fighting patrol 14 August 1916 with Lieutenant Godson – **MM**. **Wounded** at the Battle of Langemarck 16 August 1917. **Killed in action** 22 November 1917 at Moeuvres.

CLEMENTS Private William 14049. From Portadown, County Armagh. Enlisted September 1914. To France with 36th (Ulster) Division in October 1915. [Transferred to the Labour Corps (renumbered 412358).] Transferred to the Class Z Reserve 3 March 1919. 1914-15 Star.

CLIFFORD Private James 14079. Enlisted September 1914. To France with 36th (Ulster) Division in October 1915. 'C' Company. Bombing team during the attack at Hamel 1 July 1916 during which he was **wounded**. Discharged as no longer physically fit for war service due to wounds 30 May 1918, aged 36. Silver War Badge, number 394855. 1914-15 Star.

CLIFFORD Private Joseph 42436. [Enlisted into the 8th (Service) Battalion, The Royal Irish Rifles (East Belfast) (898) in 107th Brigade. To France 23 November 1915.] Transferred at the Base Depot to Princess Victoria's (Royal Irish Fusiliers) 14 September 1918 (renumbered 42436) and joined the 9th (North Irish Horse) Battalion 22 September 1918. Transferred to the Class Z Reserve 30 March 1919. 1914-15 Star.

CLIFFORD Private Roland 27546. Enlisted 23 April 1917. Posted to the 9th (North Irish Horse) Battalion. **Wounded**. Discharged as no longer physically fit for war service due to wounds 21 June 1919. Silver War Badge, number B272103.

CLIFTON Private William George 42280. Born in 1878. From Bexhill-on-Sea. Coachman. Pre-war service with the Royal Garrison Artillery (Volunteers). [Enlisted 30 July 1915 into the Army Veterinary Corps (11282) and served with the Mediterranean Expeditionary Force from 28 August 1915. 1914-15 Star. Served with 15th Veterinary Hospital, Salonika from July 1916. To hospital in November 1917 with contusions to the chest having been kicked by a horse while clipping it.] Transferred to Princess Victoria's (Royal Irish Fusiliers) 8 May 1918 (renumbered 42280) and joined the 9th (North Irish Horse) Battalion. 'D' Company. **Killed in action** during the attack north of Bailleul 24 August 1918, aged 39.

CLOUGHAN Private William 14120. Born on 21 May 1883 at County Monaghan. Worked as a coachman for the Stronge family at Tynan, County Armagh. Armagh Regiment, Ulster Volunteer Force. Enlisted in September 1914. To France with 36th (Ulster) Division in October 1915. 'A' Company. A drummer (his drum was found in 2005 being used as a plant pot and has since been restored). **Wounded** at the Battle of Langemarck 16 August 1917 when he lost his left arm. Discharged as no longer physically fit for war service due to wounds 3 September 1919. Silver War Badge, number B301540. Served with the Ulster Special Constabulary in the Armagh Platoon Headquarters. Died 14 February 1961, aged 77. Buried at Armagh (St Mark) Church of Ireland Churchyard.

CLOUGHLEY Private Robert 14076. Born in 1889 at Armagh, County Armagh. Enlisted September 1914. To France with 36th (Ulster) Division in October 1915. [Joined 108th Brigade Machine Gun Company in January 1916. Transferred to the Machine Gun Corps (renumbered 17782). **Wounded**.] Discharged as no longer physically fit for war service due to wounds 10 December 1917, aged 28. Silver War Badge, number 304174. 1914-15 Star.

CLOW Private James Moncrieff 14085. From Emyvale, County Monaghan. Enlisted September 1914. To France with 36th (Ulster) Division in October 1915. [Joined 108th Brigade Machine Gun Company in January 1916. Transferred to the Machine Gun Corps (renumbered 17781). **Killed in action** while serving with 18th Battalion, Machine Gun Corps 29 September 1918.] 1914-15 Star.

CLULOW Private Joseph 26914. Born in 1891 in South Africa. Lived at Portadown, County Armagh. A linen weaver. Enlisted in February 1917. Posted to the 9th (Service) Battalion. 'B' Company. **Missing** at the Battle of Langemarck 16 August 1917 and later declared **killed in action** on that date. His son, 7902378 Sergeant James Ernest Ivor Clulow, was killed in action, aged 28, on 4 August 1944 near Antella, Italy when the regimental headquarters of the North Irish Horse was hit by shellfire. He is buried in Arezzo War Cemetery, Italy. Both men are commemorated on the Portadown War Memorial.

COBAIN Lance Sergeant Robert 14068 & 15861. Born at Pomeroy, County Tyrone. From Portadown, County Armagh. A tailor. 4th (Portadown) Battalion, Armagh Regiment, Ulster Volunteer Force. Served briefly before the war with The Royal Inniskilling Fusiliers - bought out. Enlisted September 1914 (renumbered 15861 in October 1914). To France with 36th (Ulster) Division in October 1915. 8 Platoon, 'B' Company during the attack at Hamel 1 July 1916. **Wounded** during the attack at Hamel 1 July 1916. **Wounded** at the Battle of Langemarck 16 August 1917. Transferred to the Class Z Reserve. 1914-15 Star.

COBINE Private William Francis 24415. Born in 1896 at Lisnaveane, County Monaghan. Enlisted 27 May 1916. Posted to the 9th (Service) Battalion. **Wounded**. Discharged as no longer physically fit for war service due to wounds 26 March 1918, aged 22. Silver War Badge, number 246355.

COCHRANE Private George 41248. Born in 1881 at Belfast. A paper butter. [Enlisted 11 November 1915 into the North Irish Horse (1847). To France 14 May 1917. Served with 2nd North Irish Horse, X Corps Cavalry Regiment.] Joined the renamed 9th (North Irish Horse) Battalion from 36 Infantry Base Depot and transferred to Princess Victoria's (Royal Irish Fusiliers) in September/October 1917 (renumbered 41248). 'D' Company. [Transferred to the Tank Corps (renumbered 304864) 28 December 1917 and posted for training to the Tank Corps Depot, at Bovington near Wareham, Dorset. Posted to the 17th Battalion, Tank Corps 8 January 1918 and to France 27 April 1918 when it converted to 17th (Armoured Car) Battalion.] Transferred to the Class Z Reserve 27 May 1919.

COCHRANE Corporal John 14100. From Portadown, County Armagh. Enlisted September 1914. To France with 36th (Ulster) Division in October 1915. [Transferred to the Royal Defence Corps (Lance Sergeant - 94473).] 1914-15 Star.

COCHRANE Private Robert Dunn 24397. Born in 1894 at Mountnorris, County Armagh. A linen weaver. Enlisted in May 1916. Posted to the 9th (Service) Battalion. 'D' Company. **Wounded** at the Battle of Langemarck 16 August 1917. **Killed in action** 29 March 1918 during the retreat from St Quentin.

COLCLOUGH Private Thomas Lionel 43334. Born at Bangalore, India in July 1883. From Stratford, London. Worked as a carman. [Enlisted in The London Regiment on 10 December 1915 and transferred to the Army Reserve. Mobilised in July 1916 and joined the 3/7th Battalion, The London Regiment (6727).] Attached to the 9th (Service) Battalion, Princess Victoria's (Royal Irish Fusiliers) 26 November 1916. Discharged from the Territorial Force, re-enlisted and transferred to Princess Victoria's (Royal Irish Fusiliers) in March/April 1917 (renumbered 43334). On 23 May 1917 he accidentally fired his rifle while cleaning it and killed Private W Limbert and wounded Lance Corporal E W G Linzey. Tried by Field General Court Martial on 12 June 1917 charged with: *'Neglect to the prejudice of good order and military discipline in that he, in the field, on 23 May 1917 neglected to unload his rifle preparatory to cleaning it, and thereby caused the death of a soldier, and seriously wounding another'*; found guilty and sentenced to fifty-six days Field Punishment Number 1. **Killed in action** at the Battle of Langemarck 16 August 1917.

COLE Lance Corporal George 41487. [Enlisted June 1915 into the North Irish Horse (1677). Served with 2nd North Irish Horse, X Corps Cavalry Regiment.] Joined the renamed 9th (North Irish Horse) Battalion from 36 Infantry Base Depot and transferred to Princess Victoria's (Royal Irish Fusiliers) in September/October 1917 (renumbered 41487). 'B' Company. **Missing** in the period 21-28 March 1918 during the retreat from St Quentin believed **captured**.

COLE Lance Corporal Herbert 14056. From Portadown, County Armagh. 4th (Portadown) Battalion, Armagh Regiment, Ulster Volunteer Force. Enlisted September 1914. To France with 36th (Ulster) Division in October 1915. **Wounded** near River Douve August 1916. Battalion Colour Guard June 1919. 1914-15 Star.

COLE Private Joseph 18467. From Glaslough, County Monaghan. Enlisted into the 9th (Service) Battalion in March 1915. To France with 36th (Ulster) Division in October 1915. **Killed in action** during the attack at Hamel 1 July 1916. 1914-15 Star.

COLE Lance Corporal William 14087. Enlisted September 1914. To France with 36th (Ulster) Division in October 1915. **Wounded**. Discharged as no longer physically fit for war service due to wounds 8 July 1918, aged 23. Silver War Badge, number 415895. 1914-15 Star.

COLEMAN Private Thomas 23568. [Enlisted in December 1915 and joined the 7th (Service) Battalion in 49th Brigade, 16th (Irish) Division.] Joined the 9th (North Irish Horse) Battalion when the 7th/8th (Service) Battalion was disbanded in February 1918. 'B' Company. **Missing** in the period 21-28 March 1918 during the retreat from St Quentin believed **captured**.

COLLIN Private John Benjamin 43377. Born in 1893. From Kensington, London. A carpenter. [Enlisted 9 March 1916 and joined the 3/7th Battalion, The London Regiment (6814). To France 10 November 1916 for duty with the 1/7th (City of London) Battalion, The London Regiment.] Attached to the 9th (Service) Battalion, Princess Victoria's (Royal Irish Fusiliers) 26 November 1916. Discharged from the Territorial Force, re-enlisted and transferred to Princess Victoria's (Royal Irish

Fusiliers) in March 1917 (renumbered 43377). To hospital sick (influenza) July 1917. [Transferred to the Tank Corps (renumbered 304856) 28 December 1917 and posted for training to the Tank Corps Depot, at Bovington near Wareham, Dorset. Posted to the 17th Battalion, Tank Corps 8 January 1918. To hospital sick (boils on legs) April 1918. Transferred to the Tank Corps Reserve Unit 23 May 1918. To France 2 September 1918 and joined 14th Battalion, Tank Corps.] Transferred to the Class Z Reserve 23 February 1919. Died at London in 1965, aged 72.

COLLINS Private Henry Walter 45751. [Enlisted 17 October 1916 into The London Regiment.] To France and joined 36 Infantry Base Depot 29 March 1918. Transferred to Princess Victoria's (Royal Irish Fusiliers) 2 April 1918 (renumbered 45751) and joined the 9th (North Irish Horse) Battalion 4 April 1918. **Wounded**. Discharged as no longer physically fit for war service due to wounds 5 April 1919. Silver War Badge, number B191357.

COLLINS Corporal Reginald Percy 10054. Born in 1894 at Chatham, Kent. From Baldock, Hertfordshire. [Enlisted into Princess Victoria's (Royal Irish Fusiliers) as a regular soldier in August/September 1908 and served with the 1st Battalion. To France with the 1st Battalion 22 August 1914. **Wounded** November 1914.] Posted to the 9th (North Irish Horse) Battalion. **Killed in action** during the attack at Vijfwegen 30 September 1918. 1914 Star.

COLLINS Private Thomas 14047. Born in 1869 at Lurgan, County Armagh. Served with the Mid-Ulster Royal Garrison Artillery Militia for seven years. Armagh Regiment, Ulster Volunteer Force. A weaver. Enlisted September 1914, aged 45 and joined 'C' Company. Discharged as not being likely to become an efficient soldier in that he was considered medically unfit for service 1 October 1914.

COLLINS Private William 20329. Enlisted 27 May 1915 and joined the 9th (Service) Battalion with the draft of men from The Royal Inniskilling Fusiliers who transferred to Princess Victoria's (Royal Irish Fusiliers) on 30 June 1915. To France with 36th (Ulster) Division in October 1915. Discharged as no longer physically fit for war service due to sickness 24 August 1917. Silver War Badge, number 231144. 1914-15 Star.

COLLISHAW Private James 43231. [Enlisted into The Sherwood Foresters (Nottinghamshire and Derbyshire Regiment).] Transferred to Princess Victoria's (Royal Irish Fusiliers) 31 August 1916 (renumbered 43231) having joined the 9th (Service) Battalion on 8 August 1916.

COLVILLE Private John 14057. Enlisted September 1914. To France with 36th (Ulster) Division in October 1915. [Transferred to the Labour Corps (renumbered 200465).] Transferred to the Class Z Reserve 24 February 1919. 1914-15 Star.

COLVIN Private Joseph 14064. From Tandragee, County Armagh. Enlisted September 1914. Discharged having made a mis-statement as to age on enlistment; soldier under 17 years of age at date of application for discharge 11 November 1914.

COMER Private Edward 12637. Born in 1894 at Belfast. [Enlisted in September 1914 and joined 6th (Service) Battalion, Princess Victoria's (Royal Irish Fusiliers) in 31st Brigade, 10th (Irish) Division. Embarked with the Mediterranean Expeditionary Force July 1915.] Posted to the 9th (Service) Battalion. 'A' Company. **Wounded** at the Battle of Langemarck 16 August 1917. [Transferred to the Royal Flying Corps (renumbered 148006).] 1914-15 Star. His brother, Private Walter Comer, enlisted into The Royal Irish Rifles and also served with the Seaforth Highlanders (Ross-shire Buffs, The Duke of Albany's) and The Cheshire Regiment.

CONATY Private Thomas 26853. [Enlisted 15 February 1917 and served with the 7th/8th (Service) Battalion in 49th Brigade, 16th (Irish) Division.] Joined the 9th (North Irish Horse) Battalion when the 7th/8th (Service) Battalion was disbanded in February 1918. **Wounded**. Discharged as no longer physically fit for war service due to wounds 27 March 1919. Silver War Badge, number B165703.

CONLEY Private William James 14115. Born in 1887. From Ballymacawley, County Armagh. Enlisted September 1914. To France with 36th (Ulster) Division in October 1915. To 109th Field Ambulance and 54th General Hospital injured (contusion to the buttocks due to being knocked over by a horse) 7 April 1918. Rejoined the 9th (North Irish Horse) Battalion 14 May 1918. Proceeded on leave on 15 January 1919 and while on leave was demobilised. Transferred to the Class Z Reserve 16 February 1919. (Due to a clerical error he was posted to the 5th (Service) Battalion, The Royal Irish Regiment (Pioneers) in the Light Division in the British Army of the Rhine on 20 March 1919.) 1914-15 Star.

CONLON Lance Corporal Michael 22112. [Enlisted in October 1915 and joined the 8th (Service) Battalion in 49th Brigade, 16th (Irish) Division.] Joined the 9th (North Irish Horse) Battalion when the 7th/8th (Service) Battalion was disbanded in February 1918. [Posted to the 1st Battalion.]

CONLON Private Thomas 43041. Born in 1886. From Geevagh, County Sligo. [Enlisted at Liverpool 17 December 1915 into The Connaught Rangers (7050). To France and joined 16 Infantry Base Depot 24 July 1916. Transferred to Princess Victoria's (Royal Irish Fusiliers) 31 August 1916 (renumbered 43041) and served with the 8th (Service) Battalion in 49th Brigade, 16th (Irish) Division. To the field ambulance and casualty clearing station in December 1916 (teeth). While there forfeit fourteen days pay for drunkenness in barracks. Rejoined the 7th/8th (Service) Battalion 8 February 1917. Forfeit fourteen days pay for drunkenness February 1917. Attached to 157th Field Company Royal Engineers 11 May 1917. Rejoined the 7th/8th (Service) Battalion 17 June 1917. Attached to 49th Brigade Trench Mortar Battery 25 June 1917. **Wounded** by a gunshot to the finger during the Battle of Langemarck on 16 August 1917.] Joined the 9th (North Irish Horse) Battalion when the 7th/8th (Service) Battalion was disbanded in February 1918. 'A' Company. **Killed in action** on the retreat from St Quentin 21 March 1918, aged 37.

CONN Lance Sergeant Alexander 14093. From Portadown, County Armagh. Enlisted September 1914. To France with 36th (Ulster) Division in October 1915. Transferred to the Class Z Reserve 26 February 1919. 1914-15 Star. Brother of Private Robert Conn.

CONN Private Henry 14095. Born in 1879. From Grange, County Armagh. A beetler in the linen trade. Enlisted September 1914. Did not serve overseas with 36th (Ulster) Division. [Posted to the 10th (Reserve) Battalion 9 October 1915. Transferred to The Royal Irish Regiment (renumbered G/1682) and posted to the 2nd (Home Service) Garrison Battalion at Dublin 19 September 1916. Transferred to the 15th (Transport Workers) Battalion, The Worcestershire Regiment (renumbered 39242) 24 December 1916 on its formation at Swindon.] Discharged as no longer physically fit for war service 28 November 1918.

CONN Private Jonathan 41293. [Enlisted 29 May 1915 into the North Irish Horse (1689). Served with 2nd North Irish Horse, X Corps Cavalry Regiment.] Joined the renamed 9th (North Irish Horse) Battalion from 36 Infantry Base Depot and transferred to Princess Victoria's (Royal Irish Fusiliers) in September/October 1917 (renumbered 41293). **Wounded**. Discharged as no longer physically fit for war service due to wounds 29 May 1918, aged 22. Silver War Badge, number 391436.

CONN Private Robert. From Portadown, County Armagh. Brother of Lance Sergeant Alexander Conn. Soldier not identified.

CONNOLLY Private Alfred 18676. Enlisted into the 9th (Service) Battalion 10 April 1915. To France with 36th (Ulster) Division in October 1915. **Wounded** during the attack at Hamel 1 July 1916. Discharged as no longer physically fit for war service due to wounds 19 October 1916, aged 20. Silver War Badge, number 447048. 1914-15 Star.

CONNOLLY Private John 14075. Enlisted September 1914. To France with 36th (Ulster) Division in October 1915. 'C' Company. Having been detached he returned to the Battalion just before the attack at Hamel on 1 July 1916 during which he was **wounded**. [Transferred to the Army Service Corps (renumbered T/425072).]

CONNOLLY Private Robert Montgomery 14081. Enlisted September 1914. To France with 36th (Ulster) Division in October 1915. 'C' Company. Signaller. Battalion runner during the attack at Hamel 1 July 1916, which he survived unwounded. 1914-15 Star. Transferred to the Class Z Reserve 15 March 1919.

CONNOR Lance Corporal James 41602. [Enlisted in early-1915 into the Service Squadron, 6th (Inniskilling) Dragoons (UD/212). To France with 36th (Ulster) Division in October 1915. Served with 2nd North Irish Horse, X Corps Cavalry Regiment.] Joined the renamed 9th (North Irish Horse) Battalion from 36 Infantry Base Depot and transferred to Princess Victoria's (Royal Irish Fusiliers) in September/October 1917 (renumbered 41602). Transferred to the Class Z Reserve 22 March 1919. 1914-15 Star.

CONNOR Private Michael 17322. From Glasgow. [Enlisted 12 December 1914 into the 5th (Service) or 6th (Service) Battalion. Served in the Mediterranean Expeditionary Force from 11 December 1915.] Joined the 9th (Service) Battalion. 'B' Company. **Wounded** at the Battle of Langemarck 16 August 1917. Discharged as no longer physically fit for war service due to wounds

3 September 1918, aged 26. Silver Badge Number, 445730. 1914-15 Star.

CONNOR Private Michael Patrick 42566 & 7042208. Joined the 9th (North Irish Horse) Battalion, Princess Victoria's (Royal Irish Fusiliers) with the draft of men transferred from The Royal Irish Rifles in September 1918. Re-enlisted in early-1919 for Regular Army service with Princess Victoria's (Royal Irish Fusiliers) (renumbered 7042208).

CONNOR Private Thomas George 23671. Enlisted in January 1916. Posted to the 9th (Service) Battalion.

CONWAY Private John 41486, 33956 & 7041937. From Shorncliffe, Kent. A clerk. [Enlisted in January 1915 into the North Irish Horse (1395). Served with 2nd North Irish Horse, X Corps Cavalry Regiment.] Joined the renamed 9th (North Irish Horse) Battalion from 36 Infantry Base Depot and transferred to Princess Victoria's (Royal Irish Fusiliers) in September/October 1917 (renumbered 41486). 'A' Company. **Captured** in the period 21-28 March 1918 during the retreat from St Quentin. 1914-15 Star. Re-enlisted 20 February 1920 for Regular Army service with Princess Victoria's (Royal Irish Fusiliers) (renumbered 33956, renumbered 7041937). Discharged 19 February 1922.

COOKE Private Clarence Walter Edward 45795. Born 29 March 1899. From Brixton, Surrey. [Enlisted 31 January 1917 and transferred to the Army Reserve. Mobilised 9 May 1917 and joined 110th Training Reserve Battalion for service with 22nd (County of London) Battalion, The London Regiment (The Queen's) (66989). Posted to 1/22nd (County of London) Battalion, The London Regiment (The Queen's) 1 December 1917.] To France and joined 36 Infantry Base Depot 29 March 1918. Transferred to Princess Victoria's (Royal Irish Fusiliers) 2 April 1918 (renumbered 45795) and joined the 9th (North Irish Horse) Battalion 4 April 1918. **Missing** during the attack at Vijfwegen on 30 September or 1 October 1918; recorded as **killed in action** on 3 October 1918.

COOKE Private Frederick St George 41694. Born in 1886 at Carrigallen, County Leitrim. From Lisburn. A grocer. Member of Masonic Lodge 313. [Enlisted into 6th (Inniskilling) Dragoons (2182). To France 28 January 1917. Served with 2nd North Irish Horse, X Corps Cavalry Regiment. To 25th Stationary Hospital sick (measles) 17 February 1917. Rejoined 2nd North Irish Horse 13 March 1917. To hospital sick (haemorrhoids) from 10 October to 7 December 1917. Renumbered H/71709.] Transferred to Princess Victoria's (Royal Irish Fusiliers) and joined the renamed 9th (North Irish Horse) Battalion on 1 January 1918 (renumbered 41694). **Missing** in the period 11-18 April 1918 in the actions between Wulverghem and Kemmel; subsequently declared **killed in action** 19 April 1918.

COOKE Corporal James 7989 & 24412. Born in 1889 at Portadown, County Armagh. [Enlisted into Princess Victoria's (Royal Irish Fusiliers) Special Reserve (7989). To France 22 August 1914 with the 1st Battalion. Discharged at the end of his service in 1915.] Re-enlisted in May 1916 for war service and posted to the 9th (Service) Battalion (renumbered 24412). 'B' Company. **Wounded** at the Battle of Langemarck 16 August 1917. [Transferred to The Royal Irish Rifles (renumbered 23920).] Discharged in 1919 at the end of his engagement. 1914 Star.

COOKE Private John 14055. From Portadown, County Armagh. Enlisted September 1914. To France with 36th (Ulster) Division in October 1915. 'B' Company. **Wounded** at the Battle of Langemarck 16 August 1917. [Transferred to the Army Service Corps (renumbered M/380129).] 1914-15 Star. Transferred to the Class Z Reserve.

COOKE Sergeant Robert 14082. Enlisted September 1914. Did not serve overseas with 36th (Ulster) Division. Discharged as no longer physically fit for war service due to sickness 7 October 1916. Silver War Badge, number B97868.

COOLE Private Thomas John 16098. From Mallinacross, Smithborough, County Monaghan. Enlisted into the 9th (Service) Battalion in October 1914. To France with 36th (Ulster) Division in October 1915. **Killed in action** during the attack at Hamel 1 July 1916, aged 25. 1914-15 Star.

COOPER Lance Corporal Alfred Thomas 40007. [Enlisted into The Prince of Wales's Own (West Yorkshire Regiment).] Transferred to Princess Victoria's (Royal Irish Fusiliers) 30 November 1916 (renumbered 40007) and joined the 9th (Service) Battalion 12 December 1916. 'A' Company. **Missing** in the period 21-28 March 1918 during the retreat from St Quentin believed **captured**.

COOPER Private Frederick 18566. From Armagh, County Armagh. Enlisted into the 9th (Service)

Battalion in April 1915. 'A' Company. To France with 36th (Ulster) Division in October 1915. **Captured** in the period 21-28 March 1918 during the retreat from St Quentin. Transferred to the Class Z Reserve 26 March 1919. 1914-15 Star. Served with the Ulster Special Constabulary. Served in the Ulster Home Guard during the Second World War. Died 14 March 1966.

COOPER Private George Ernest 43197. [Enlisted into The Sherwood Foresters (Nottinghamshire and Derbyshire Regiment).] Transferred to Princess Victoria's (Royal Irish Fusiliers) 31 August 1916 having joined the 9th (Service) Battalion on 8 August 1916 (renumbered 43197). 'A' Company. **Missing** in the period 21-28 March 1918 during the retreat from St Quentin believed **captured**.

COPELAND Private Samuel 20345. Enlisted in May/June 1915 and joined the 9th (Service) Battalion with the draft of men from The Royal Inniskilling Fusiliers who transferred to Princess Victoria's (Royal Irish Fusiliers) on 30 June 1915. 'D' Company. To France with 36th (Ulster) Division in October 1915. **Wounded** during the Battle of Messines and to hospital 9 June 1917. [Transferred to the King's Royal Rifle Corps (renumbered 52194).] 1914-15 Star.

COPELAND Corporal Thomas 41504. [Enlisted in March/April 1915 into the Service Squadron, 6th (Inniskilling) Dragoons (UD/238). To France with 36th (Ulster) Division in October 1915. Served with 2nd North Irish Horse, X Corps Cavalry Regiment.] Joined the renamed 9th (North Irish Horse) Battalion from 36 Infantry Base Depot and transferred to Princess Victoria's (Royal Irish Fusiliers) in September/October 1917 (renumbered 41504). 'C' Company. **Missing** in the period 21-28 March 1918 during the retreat from St Quentin believed **captured**. Transferred to the Class Z Reserve 18 March 1919. 1914-15 Star.

COPLETON Private Robert John 18632. Born in 1882. From Armagh, County Armagh. An ironworker. Enlisted into the 9th (Service) Battalion 19 April 1915. To France with 36th (Ulster) Division in October 1915. **Wounded** by a gunshot to the right shoulder at Hamel 1 July 1916 and evacuated to hospital in England. [To the 10th (Reserve) Battalion 30 September 1916. Posted to the 3rd (Reserve) Garrison Battalion at Bere Island, Bantry Bay 29 March 1917. Posted to the 2nd Garrison Battalion in Salonika on 10 October 1917. Transferred to the Labour Corps (renumbered 488869) 28 February 1918. Returned to England 31 March 1919.] Transferred to the Class Z Reserve 11 May 1919. 1914-15 Star.

CORBETT Private H S 41520. [Served as a regular soldier with the 3rd (King's Own) Hussars (306). To France 15 August 1914 with 4th Cavalry Brigade, The Cavalry Division. Served with 2nd North Irish Horse, X Corps Cavalry Regiment.] Joined the renamed 9th (North Irish Horse) Battalion from 36 Infantry Base Depot and transferred to Princess Victoria's (Royal Irish Fusiliers) in September/October 1917 (renumbered 41520). 1914 Star and clasp.

CORDNER Company Quartermaster Sergeant Frederick 22805. Born in 1892 at Lurgan, County Armagh. Enlisted in November 1915. Posted to the 9th (Service) Battalion in mid/late 1916. Company Quartermaster Sergeant.

CORDNER Private Stewart 22809. Born in 1897 at Shankill, County Armagh. Enlisted in November 1915. Posted to the 9th (Service) Battalion. 'C' Company. **Missing** at the Battle of Langemarck 16 August 1917 and later declared **killed in action** on that date, aged 20.

CORDNER Private William 14069. From Lurgan, County Armagh. Enlisted September 1914. To France with 36th (Ulster) Division in October 1915. 3 Section, 13 Platoon, 'D' Company in 1915. **Wounded** by a gunshot to the left arm during the attack at Hamel 1 July 1916. Evacuated to hospital in England and treated at Northamptonshire War Hospital, Northampton. To the 10th (Reserve) Battalion 11 December 1916. To France 24 May 1917 and rejoined the 9th (Service) Battalion. Injured (back) and evacuated to hospital in England 6 December 1917. To the 10th (Reserve) Battalion 15 February 1918. Discharged as no longer physically fit for war service due to sickness 28 August 1918, aged 26. Silver War Badge, number 445779. 1914-15 Star.

CORDNER Private William 14111. From Lurgan, County Armagh. Enlisted September 1914. To France with 36th (Ulster) Division in October 1915. 'C' Company. Released from hospital just prior to the attack at Hamel 1 July 1916, during which he was **killed in action**, aged 19. 1914-15 Star.

CORDY Private William James 14048. From Sandy Row, Portadown, County Armagh. 4th (Portadown) Battalion, Armagh Regiment, Ulster Volunteer Force. 'B' Company. To France with 36th (Ulster) Division in October 1915. **Wounded** by shellfire at Hamel while carrying rations forward and **died of wounds** 26 June 1916, aged 36. 1914-15 Star.

CORKIN Private James 14106. From Lurgan, County Armagh. Enlisted September 1914. To France with 36th (Ulster) Division in October 1915. **Killed in action** during the attack at Hamel 1 July 1916, aged 45. 1914-15 Star. Brother of Private John Corkin.

CORKIN Private John 14054. Born 20 May 1881 at Portadown, County Armagh. 4th (Portadown) Battalion, Armagh Regiment, Ulster Volunteer Force. A yarn dresser & drawer-in. Enlisted September 1914, falsifying his age as 29 years. To France with 36th (Ulster) Division in October 1915. 'B' Company. **Wounded** at the Battle of Langemarck 16 August 1917. Discharged as no longer physically fit for war service due to wounds 29 May 1918. Silver War Badge, number 394848. 1914-15 Star. Died 14 October 1972, aged 91. Buried at Seagoe Cemetery, Portadown, County Armagh. Brother of Private James Corkin.

CORKIN Lance Corporal Samuel Joseph 23876. From Jervis Street, Portadown, County Armagh. A yarn dresser for Spence Bryson Ltd, Portadown. Enlisted 24 January 1916 and joined the 10th (Reserve) Battalion. Joined the 9th (Service) Battalion in May/June 1916. 'B' Company. **Wounded** near the River Douve in the right leg by an explosive bullet 11 August 1916. Discharged as no longer physically fit for war service due to wounds 14 November 1916. Silver War Badge, number 508733. He died after the war and is commemorated on Portadown War Memorial.

CORR Private James 28786. From Dungannon, County Tyrone. Enlisted in October 1917. Posted to the 9th (North Irish Horse) Battalion. **Captured** in 1918.

COSTELLO Private Daniel J 24848. Born in 1887 at County Meath. Worked as a groom for a priest in Rowlestown, County Dublin and then at Mullingar, County West Meath (he married the priest's servant Catherine Korrigan). Enlisted in the Irish Guards but was discharged as no longer physically fit for service due to sickness. Re-enlisted on 10 August 1916 into Princess Victoria's (Royal Irish Fusiliers) and joined the 10th (Reserve) Battalion. To France 3 March 1917 and joined the 9th (Service) Battalion. 'A' Company. **Wounded** by a gunshot to the right wrist at the Battle of Langemarck 16 August 1917 and evacuated to hospital in England. Posted to the Irish Command Depot in November 1917. Attached to the Army Service Corps April 1918. To France April 1918. Discharged to the Class Z Reserve 15 July 1919.

COSTLEY Private James Albert 14060. Born in 1893 at Lurgan, County Armagh. A draper's assistant. Enlisted September 1914. To France with 36th (Ulster) Division in October 1915. 'C' Company. To hospital mid-1916 and struck off strength when evacuated to hospital in England; did not attack at Hamel on 1 July 1916. **Wounded** at the Battle of Langemarck 16 August 1917. Discharged as no longer physically fit for war service due to sickness 16 July 1918, aged 24. Silver War Badge, number 425683. 1914-15 Star. His brother, Sergeant Thomas Costley, was killed in action on 23 November 1917 serving with the 2nd Battalion, The Royal Irish Rifles.

COULSON Private William 17547. From Tyranny, Stonebridge, County Monaghan. Enlisted into the 9th (Service) Battalion in November/December 1914. To France with 36th (Ulster) Division in October 1915. **Wounded** during the attack at Hamel 1 July 1916. [Transferred to the Labour Corps (renumbered 425458).] 1914-15 Star.

COULTER MM Private Joseph 41530. Born 8 December 1893. A farmer from Mullaghfad, County Fermanagh. [Enlisted in November 1914 into the Service Squadron, 6th (Inniskilling) Dragoons (UD/150). To France with 36th (Ulster) Division in October 1915. Served with 2nd North Irish Horse, X Corps Cavalry Regiment.] Joined the renamed 9th (North Irish Horse) Battalion from 36 Infantry Base Depot and transferred to Princess Victoria's (Royal Irish Fusiliers) in September/October 1917 (renumbered 41530). **MM** – Bailleul 24 August 1918. **Killed in action** during the attack at Vijfwegen 1 October 1918, aged 24. 1914-15 Star.

COULTER Private Percy 41349. From Lisburn, County Antrim. [Enlisted in January 1917 into the North Irish Horse (2341). Served with 2nd North Irish Horse, X Corps Cavalry Regiment.] Joined the renamed 9th (North Irish Horse) Battalion from 36 Infantry Base Depot and transferred to Princess Victoria's (Royal Irish Fusiliers) in September/October 1917 (renumbered 41349).

COUPLAND Lance Corporal Leonard 43247. Born in 1890 at Long Sutton, Lincolnshire. Worked in the printing trade. [Enlisted 8 December 1915 into The Sherwood Foresters (Nottinghamshire and Derbyshire Regiment) (36574).] To France 23 July 1916. Transferred to Princess Victoria's (Royal Irish Fusiliers) 31 August 1916 (renumbered 43247) having joined the 9th (Service) Battalion on 8 August 1916. 'A' Company. Lance Corporal 20 October 1916. **Killed in action** at the Battle of

Langemarck 16 August 1917.

COURTNEY Sergeant Hugh William 14108. From Armagh, County Armagh. Enlisted September 1914. To France with 36th (Ulster) Division in October 1915. Platoon Sergeant 8 Platoon, 'B' Company when he was **wounded** during the attack at Hamel 1 July 1916 and evacuated to hospital in England. **Captured** in the period 21-28 March 1918 during the retreat from St Quentin. Transferred to the Class Z Reserve 23 February 1919. 1914-15 Star. After the war worked as a mechanic. Retired aged 80. Died 10 March 1961, aged 81. Buried in Aghavilly Churchyard.

COURTNEY Private John 14123. From Mulladry, Richhill, County Armagh. Member of Loyal Orange Lodge 371. Enlisted September 1914. To France with 36th (Ulster) Division in October 1915. [Joined 108th Brigade Machine Gun Company in January 1916. Transferred to the Machine Gun Corps (renumbered 17783). **Killed in action** during the attack at Hamel 1 July 1916.] 1914-15 Star.

COUSER Lance Corporal John Dobbin 17987. From Milford, County Armagh. Enlisted into the 9th (Service) Battalion in February 1915. To France with 36th (Ulster) Division in October 1915. [Transferred to the Royal Flying Corps (renumbered 143217) 8 March 1918 (with Privates W Muir and J Sands).] 1914-15 Star.

COUSINS Private Isaac 22641. Born in 1897 at Belfast. Enlisted 29 October 1915. To France 7 April 1916 and joined the 9th (Service) Battalion 19 May 1916. Initially declared **missing** at Hamel on 1 July 1916, his body was found in August 1916 and he was declared as **killed in action**.

COWAN Sergeant William 24395. Served in the Royal Irish Constabulary at Newry. Enlisted in May 1916. Posted to the 9th (Service) Battalion. 'A' Company. **Wounded** in the shoulder at the Battle of Langemarck 16 August 1917. Treated at Lincoln City Hospital.

COWAN Lance Corporal William Percival Graham 41532. [Enlisted in November 1915 into the North Irish Horse (1993). Served with 2nd North Irish Horse, X Corps Cavalry Regiment.] Joined the renamed 9th (North Irish Horse) Battalion from 36 Infantry Base Depot and transferred to Princess Victoria's (Royal Irish Fusiliers) in September/October 1917 (renumbered 41532).

COX Corporal Herbert Charles 45748. Enlisted 7 February 1916. Joined the 9th (North Irish Horse) Battalion, Princess Victoria's (Royal Irish Fusiliers) with the draft of men from The London Regiment in April 1918. **Wounded**. Discharged as no longer physically fit for war service due to wounds 12 December 1918. Silver War Badge, number B61026.

COX Private Thomas Albert 42091. [Enlisted 6 December 1901 into 7th (Princess Royal's) Dragoon Guards (5787). To France 13 August 1914. Transferred to the Army Veterinary Corps (renumbered 517).] Transferred to Princess Victoria's (Royal Irish Fusiliers) 8 May 1918 (renumbered 42091) and joined the 9th (North Irish Horse) Battalion. Discharged as no longer physically fit for war service due to sickness 13 February 1919. Silver War Badge, number B150010. 1914 Star.

COX Corporal William 16092. Enlisted into the 9th (Service) Battalion in October 1914. 'C' Company. **Wounded** during the attack at Hamel 1 July 1916. [Transferred to The Royal Irish Regiment (renumbered 5844).]

COYLE Private John 21214. [Enlisted in February 1915 and joined the 8th (Service) Battalion in 49th Brigade, 16th (Irish) Division.] Joined the 9th (North Irish Horse) Battalion when the 7th/8th (Service) Battalion was disbanded in February 1918.

CRAIG Private David 41554. [Enlisted into the 6th (Inniskilling) Dragoons (21321). Served with 2nd North Irish Horse, X Corps Cavalry Regiment.] Joined the renamed 9th (North Irish Horse) Battalion from 36 Infantry Base Depot and transferred to Princess Victoria's (Royal Irish Fusiliers) in September/October 1917 (renumbered 41554). 'D' Company. **Missing** in the period 21-28 March 1918 during the retreat from St Quentin believed **captured**.

CRAIG MM Lance Sergeant George 23438. Born at Shankill, County Armagh. [Enlisted into the Royal Field Artillery (101466).] Transferred to Princess Victoria's (Royal Irish Fusiliers) in December 1915 (renumbered 23438). Posted to the 9th (Service) Battalion and joined 'C' Company. **MM** – Havrincourt raid 3 November 1917. **Killed in action** 29 March 1918 during the retreat from St Quentin.

CRAIG Private Joseph 14066. From Portadown, County Armagh. 4th (Portadown) Battalion,

Armagh Regiment, Ulster Volunteer Force. Enlisted September 1914. To France with 36th (Ulster) Division in October 1915. **Wounded** during the attack at Hamel 1 July 1916. [Transferred to The King's (Liverpool Regiment) (renumbered 101571).] 1914-15 Star.

CRAIG Private John 41377 & 7042137. From Newbliss, Clones, County Monaghan. [Enlisted 3 November 1914 into the Service Squadron, 6th (Inniskilling) Dragoons (UD/105). To France with 36th (Ulster) Division in October 1915. Served with 2nd North Irish Horse, X Corps Cavalry Regiment. **Wounded** by shellfire at Aveluy Wood when two troops engaged in salvage duty were subject to heavy bombardment 5 July 1916.] Joined the renamed 9th (North Irish Horse) Battalion from 36 Infantry Base Depot and transferred to Princess Victoria's (Royal Irish Fusiliers) in September/October 1917 (renumbered 41377). Evacuated to hospital in England 1 February 1918. To France 29 July 1918 and rejoined the 9th (North Irish Horse) Battalion. **Wounded** (left leg) 27 September 1918. Re-enlisted 16 May 1919 for Regular Army service with Princess Victoria's (Royal Irish Fusiliers) (renumbered 7042137). Discharged for misconduct 30 June 1921; medals forfeit.

CRAIG Private Richard 22826. From Lurgan, County Armagh. Enlisted in November 1915. Posted to the 9th (Service) Battalion. **Wounded** in the face and right arm in November 1916. Treated at 13th General Hospital, Boulogne.

CRAIG Lance Corporal Robert 41380. [Enlisted in early-1915 into the Service Squadron, 6th (Inniskilling) Dragoons (UD/204). To France with 36th (Ulster) Division in October 1915. Served with 2nd North Irish Horse, X Corps Cavalry Regiment.] Joined the renamed 9th (North Irish Horse) Battalion from 36 Infantry Base Depot and transferred to Princess Victoria's (Royal Irish Fusiliers) in September/October 1917 (renumbered 41380). Transferred to the Class Z Reserve 5 March 1919. 1914-15 Star.

CRAIG Private William 14116. Enlisted September 1914. To France with 36th (Ulster) Division in October 1915. Transferred to the Class Z Reserve 5 February 1919. 1914-15 Star.

CRAMPTON Private Thomas 24927. Born in 1898 at Mountcharles, County Donegal. An electrician. Enlisted 20 October 1916. Joined the 9th (Service) Battalion 30 March 1917. 'C' Company. To hospital sick (impetigo) June 1917. **Missing** at the Battle of Langemarck 16 August 1917 and later declared **killed in action** on that date, aged 19.

CRANSTON Private William 29436. Enlisted 27 November 1915 and joined the 10th (Reserve) Battalion. Transferred or discharged, reason unknown. Re-enlisted or transferred to Princess Victoria's (Royal Irish Fusiliers) in March 1918 (renumbered 29436). Posted to the 9th (North Irish Horse) Battalion. Discharged as no longer physically fit for war service due to sickness 1 October 1918, aged 21. Silver War Badge, number B22500.

CRAVEN MM Lance Corporal Joseph 43276. Born at Armley, Leeds, Yorkshire. From Bulwell, Nottinghamshire. A coal miner at Gedling Colliery. [Enlisted into The Sherwood Foresters (Nottinghamshire and Derbyshire Regiment) (4473) 26 September 1912 and joined the 4th (Special Reserve) Battalion. To France 27 December 1914 and joined the 2nd Battalion. **Wounded** by a gunshot to the head 29 February 1916. Evacuated to hospital in England.] Transferred to Princess Victoria's (Royal Irish Fusiliers) 31 August 1916 (renumbered 43276) having joined the 9th (Service) Battalion on 8 August 1916. 'D' Company. **MM –** La Petite Douve Farm raid 12 October 1916. Lance Corporal 27 October 1916. **Wounded** by shrapnel to the left thigh, which fractured his femur, at the Battle of Langemarck 16 August 1917. Evacuated to hospital in England 22 September 1917 and treated at King George Hospital, London. [Joined the 10th (Reserve) Battalion January 1918. Reverted to Private at his own request 8 February 1918. Absent without leave 13 February to 5 March 1918. Forfeit twenty-one days pay and sentenced to fourteen days detention. Transferred to the Labour Corps (renumbered 545517) 6 April 1918. Transferred to the Class P Reserve 6 July 1918 as a coal miner.] Discharged as surplus to military requirements having suffered impairment since entry into the service 6 February 1919. Silver War Badge, number 462025. 1914-15 Star.

CRAWFORD Private Arthur Sydney 11185. Born in 1891 at Mount Merion, Blackrock, County Dublin. A cabinet maker. [Enlisted in November 1914 into the North Irish Horse (1345). To France with 'F' Squadron in 33rd Division 17 November 1915. Served with 2nd North Irish Horse, X Corps Cavalry Regiment.] Joined the renamed 9th (North Irish Horse) Battalion from 36 Infantry Base Depot and transferred to Princess Victoria's (Royal Irish Fusiliers) in September/October 1917 (renumbered 41485). 'A' Company. **Missing** in the period 21-28 March 1918 during the retreat from St Quentin and later declared **killed in action** 29 March 1918, aged 23 (his age is incorrectly recorded on the Commonwealth War Graves Commission commemoration details). 1914-15 Star.

CRAWFORD Private John 41470. From Lisbellaw, County Fermanagh. [Enlisted in April 1912 into the North Irish Horse (716). To France 20 August 1914 with 'C' Squadron as 5th Division Cavalry and then as GHQ Troops. Served with 2nd North Irish Horse, X Corps Cavalry Regiment.] Joined the renamed 9th (North Irish Horse) Battalion from 36 Infantry Base Depot and transferred to Princess Victoria's (Royal Irish Fusiliers) in September/October 1917 (renumbered 41470). **Captured** in the period 11-18 April 1918 in the actions between Wulverghem and Kemmel. 1914 Star and clasp.

CRAWFORD Private Matthew 41209. [Enlisted in February 1915 into the North Irish Horse (1456). To France with 'F' Squadron in 33rd Division 17 November 1915. Served with 2nd North Irish Horse, X Corps Cavalry Regiment.] Joined the renamed 9th (North Irish Horse) Battalion from 36 Infantry Base Depot and transferred to Princess Victoria's (Royal Irish Fusiliers) in September/October 1917 (renumbered 41209). Transferred to the Class Z Reserve 3 April 1919. 1914-15 Star.

CRAWFORD Private William 20302. From Glasgow. Enlisted in May/June 1915 and joined the 9th (Service) Battalion with the draft of men from The Royal Inniskilling Fusiliers who transferred to Princess Victoria's (Royal Irish Fusiliers) on 30 June 1915. 'B' Company. To France with 36th (Ulster) Division in October 1915. **Wounded** during the attack at Hamel 1 July 1916. **Wounded** at the Battle of Langemarck 16 August 1917. [Transferred to the Labour Corps (renumbered 642950).] 1914-15 Star.

CRAWFORD Private William George 41488. [Enlisted 23 July 1913 into the North Irish Horse (857). To France 20 August 1914 with 'C' Squadron as 5th Division Cavalry and then as GHQ Troops. Served with 2nd North Irish Horse, X Corps Cavalry Regiment.] Joined the renamed 9th (North Irish Horse) Battalion from 36 Infantry Base Depot and transferred to Princess Victoria's (Royal Irish Fusiliers) in September/October 1917 (renumbered 41488). **Wounded**. Discharged as no longer physically fit for war service due to wounds 29 August 1918, aged 26. Silver War Badge, number 445708. 1914 Star.

CRAWFORD Corporal William James 17672. Enlisted into the 9th (Service) Battalion in December 1914/January 1915. No record of date of deployment to France with 36th (Ulster) Division.

CRAWLEY Private John J 42221. [Enlisted into the Army Service Corps (T1/399). To France 4 October 1914.] Transferred to Princess Victoria's (Royal Irish Fusiliers) 8 May 1918 (renumbered 42221) and joined the 9th (North Irish Horse) Battalion. [Transferred to the Seaforth Highlanders (Ross-shire Buffs, The Duke of Albany's) (renumbered S/43768).] 1914 Star.

CREANEY Private James 14118. Enlisted September 1914. To France with 36th (Ulster) Division in October 1915. **Wounded** during the attack at Hamel 1 July 1916. [Posted to the 2nd Garrison Battalion in Salonika.] Transferred to the Class Z Reserve 31 March 1919.] 1914-15 Star.

CREANEY Private John 14113. Born at Shankill, Belfast. Enlisted September 1914. To France with 36th (Ulster) Division in October 1915. **Killed in action** during the attack at Hamel 1 July 1916. 1914-15 Star.

CREIGHTON Corporal Robert 41385. [Enlisted in May 1915 into the Service Squadron, 6th (Inniskilling) Dragoons (UD/262). Served with 2nd North Irish Horse, X Corps Cavalry Regiment.] Joined the renamed 9th (North Irish Horse) Battalion from 36 Infantry Base Depot and transferred to Princess Victoria's (Royal Irish Fusiliers) in September/October 1917 (renumbered 41385).

CRERIN Private John 22871. [Enlisted in November 1915. Served with the 1st Battalion.] Posted to the 9th (Service) Battalion.

CRICHTON MM Sergeant Daniel 11864. From Armagh, County Armagh. Enlisted August 1914. [To France 1 April 1915 and joined the 1st Battalion.] Posted to the 9th (North Irish Horse) Battalion. **MM** – Bailleul 24 August 1918. [Transferred to the Army Service Corps (ES/58143).] Transferred to the Class Z Reserve 3 May 1919. 1914-15 Star.

CRILLY Private Alexander 14078, 33685 & 7041758. From Bessbrook, County Armagh. Enlisted September 1914. To France with 36th (Ulster) Division in October 1915. 1914-15 Star. Re-enlisted 4 December 1919 for Regular Army service with Princess Victoria's (Royal Irish Fusiliers) (renumbered 33685, renumbered 7041758). Discharged 3 December 1921.

CRILLY MM Private John 14090. From Bessbrook, County Armagh. Enlisted September 1914. To France with 36th (Ulster) Division in October 1915. **Wounded** twice, once in November 1917. **MM** – Bailleul 24 August 1918. Transferred to the Class Z Reserve. 1914-15 Star.

CROOK Private Alfred Charles 42519. Born in 1896. From Dublin. A dairyman. [Enlisted 26 April 1918 into The Royal Irish Rifles (22565) and joined the 3rd (Reserve) Battalion.] To 'A' Infantry Base Depot, France 7 September 1918. Transferred to Princess Victoria's (Royal Irish Fusiliers) 14 September 1918 (renumbered 42519) and joined the 9th (North Irish Horse) Battalion 22 September 1918. 'A' Company. **Wounded** by a gunshot to the elbow during the advance to Anseghem 25 October 1918. Treated at 2nd Australian General Hospital, Boulogne and evacuated to hospital in England 9 November 1918. Posted to the 3rd (Reserve) Battalion 6 December 1918. Transferred to the Class Z Reserve 24 April 1919.

CROOK Private George T 42192. [Enlisted into the Army Service Corps (S/356634 Driver).] Transferred to Princess Victoria's (Royal Irish Fusiliers) 8 May 1918 (renumbered 42192) and joined the 9th (North Irish Horse) Battalion. [Transferred back to the Army Service Corps (renumbered S/356634 Driver).]

CROOK Private Leonard Walter 45754. Born in 1899 at West Ham, London. [Enlisted 19 September 1916 and transferred to the Army Reserve. Mobilised 19 March 1917 and joined 18th Training Reserve Battalion for service with 22nd (County of London) Battalion, The London Regiment (The Queen's) 8 December 1916 (67320). Posted to 1/22nd (County of London) Battalion, The London Regiment (The Queen's).] To France and joined 36 Infantry Base Depot 29 March 1918. Transferred to Princess Victoria's (Royal Irish Fusiliers) 2 April 1918 (renumbered 45754) and joined the 9th (North Irish Horse) Battalion 4 April 1918. **Missing** in the period 11-18 April 1918 in the actions between Wulverghem and Kemmel; subsequently declared **killed in action** 19 April 1918, aged 18.

CROOKS Private William 41257. (Some records incorrectly show number 41297, which was issued to Private J McWilliams below). From Cookstown, County Tyrone. [Enlisted in January 1913 into the North Irish Horse (782). To France 20 August 1914 with 'C' Squadron as 5th Division Cavalry and then as GHQ Troops. Served with 2nd North Irish Horse, X Corps Cavalry Regiment.] Joined the renamed 9th (North Irish Horse) Battalion from 36 Infantry Base Depot and transferred to Princess Victoria's (Royal Irish Fusiliers) in September/October 1917 (renumbered 41257). [Transferred to the Tank Corps 28 December 1917 (renumbered 304869) and posted for training to the Tank Corps Depot, at Bovington near Wareham, Dorset.] 1914 Star and clasp.

CRORKIN Private Charles 49760. Enlisted into or transferred to Princess Victoria's (Royal Irish Fusiliers) in April/May 1918 and joined the 9th (North Irish Horse) Battalion. Tried by Field General Court Martial on 10 June 1918 charged with *'losing by neglect'* (detail not known); found guilty and sentenced to fifty-six days Field Punishment Number 1. Tried by Field General Court Martial on 9 August 1918 charged with *'when on active service **deserting** His Majesty's service'*; found guilty and sentenced to ten years (reduced to five years) imprisonment. Tried by Field General Court Martial on 18 September 1918 charged with *'when on active service using insubordinate language to his superior officer'*; found guilty and sentenced to fifty-six days Field Punishment Number 1. Discharged as surplus to military requirements having suffered impairment since entry into the service 27 March 1919. Silver War Badge, B168542.

CROSBY Lance Corporal Albert 15651. Born in 1891 at Tooting, London. [Enlisted in September 1914 into the 6th (Service) Battalion in 31st Brigade, 10th (Irish) Division. Embarked with the Mediterranean Expeditionary Force July 1915.] Posted to the 9th (Service) Battalion. 'A' Company. **Wounded** at the Battle of Langemarck 16 August 1917. Transferred to the Class Z Reserve 19 April 1919. 1914-15 Star.

CROSS Warrant Officer Class II Francis Edward 15719. Born in Manchester. From Stonebridge, Middlesex. A former regular soldier; served in India. Enlisted into the 9th (Service) Battalion in September 1914. Company Sergeant Major 1915. To France with 36th (Ulster) Division in October 1915. **Killed in action** by shellfire at Hamel 8 May 1916. 1914-15 Star.

CROWTHER Private Joseph 40056. Joined the 9th (Service) Battalion, Princess Victoria's (Royal

Irish Fusiliers) with the draft of men from The Prince of Wales's Own (West Yorkshire Regiment) on 12 December 1916.

CROZIER Corporal George 41384. From Lurgan, County Armagh. [Enlisted into the North Irish Horse (693). To France 20 August 1914 with 'C' Squadron as 5th Division Cavalry and then as GHQ Troops. Served with 2nd North Irish Horse, X Corps Cavalry Regiment.] Joined the renamed 9th (North Irish Horse) Battalion from 36 Infantry Base Depot and transferred to Princess Victoria's (Royal Irish Fusiliers) in September/October 1917 (renumbered 41384). 'B' Company. **Captured** in the period 21-28 March 1918 during the retreat from St Quentin. 1914 Star.

CROZIER Corporal James Henry 27495. From Belfast. [To France with 36th (Ulster) Division Cyclist Company (7157) 3 October 1915.] Transferred to Princess Victoria's (Royal Irish Fusiliers) in April 1917 (renumbered 27495). Posted to the 9th (North Irish Horse) Battalion. 'A' Company. **Wounded** at the Battle of Langemarck 16 August 1917 and evacuated to hospital in England. Rejoined the 9th (North Irish Horse) Battalion. Transferred to the Class Z Reserve 19 February 1919. 1914-15 Star.

CROZIER Staff Sergeant John A/1999 Army Ordnance Corps. Joined the 9th (Service) Battalion, Princess Victoria's (Royal Irish Fusiliers) in 1915 as an Armourer Sergeant. 'C' Company. Detached to the Quartermaster during the attack at Hamel on 1 July 1916. Transferred to the Class Z Reserve 13 April 1919. 1914-15 Star.

CROZIER Private John 14053. From Portadown, County Armagh. Enlisted September 1914. No record of deployment to France with 36th (Ulster) Division in October 1915.

CROZIER Lance Corporal Robert John 14107. Enlisted September 1914. To France with 36th (Ulster) Division in October 1915. As a Private, 3 Section, 13 Platoon, 'D' Company. Transferred to the Class Z Reserve 18 February 1919. 1914-15 Star. After the war he became a police officer. His son, Lance Corporal David Alexander Crozier, was killed in action on 11 September 1944 serving with the 2nd Battalion, Irish Guards.

CROZIER Private Samuel 41476. [Enlisted in November 1915 into the North Irish Horse (1961). Served with 2nd North Irish Horse, X Corps Cavalry Regiment.] Joined the renamed 9th (North Irish Horse) Battalion from 36 Infantry Base Depot and transferred to Princess Victoria's (Royal Irish Fusiliers) in September/October 1917 (renumbered 41476).

CROZIER Acting Corporal William 24004. Born in 1898 at Drumarg or Downs, County Armagh. A farm labourer. Enlisted 23 February 1916, giving his age as 20 years, and joined the 10th (Reserve) Battalion. To France 2 November 1916 and joined the 9th (North Irish Horse) Battalion 26 November 1916. 'A' Company. To 110th Field Ambulance sick (influenza) 16-22 December 1916. Lance Corporal 5 may 1917. To 108th Field Ambulance sick (scabies) 16 June 1917 **Wounded** at the Battle of Langemarck 16 August 1917. Acting Corporal 2 April 1918. He is officially recorded as being **killed in action** on 24 July 1918. His service record, however, records his date of death as 25 July 1918. A letter from the chaplain, Reverend Allman, to his mother indicated that he had been killed on 12 July. There is no mention of his death in the war diary.

CROZIER Private William Robert Henry 41390. [Enlisted in November 1912 into the North Irish Horse (756). To France 1 May 1915. Served with 2nd North Irish Horse, X Corps Cavalry Regiment.] Joined the renamed 9th (North Irish Horse) Battalion from 36 Infantry Base Depot and transferred to Princess Victoria's (Royal Irish Fusiliers) in September/October 1917 (renumbered 41390). Transferred to the Class Z Reserve 8 March 1919. 1914-15 Star.

CRUTE Private Edwin Webber 43375. Born 7 July 1893 at Babbicombe, Devon. [Enlisted into 3/7th Battalion, The London Regiment (6695). To France 10 November 1916 and posted to 1/7th (City of London) Battalion, The London Regiment.] Attached to the 9th (Service) Battalion, Princess Victoria's (Royal Irish Fusiliers) 26 November 1916. Discharged from the Territorial Force, re-enlisted and transferred to Princess Victoria's (Royal Irish Fusiliers) in March/April 1917 (renumbered 43375). [Transferred to 5th (Service) Battalion, The Royal Irish Regiment (Pioneers) in the Light Division in the British Army of the Rhine in March/June 1919 (renumbered 41274).] Died at Decorum, Hertfordshire 1974, aged 81.

CULBERT Sergeant Samuel 14098. Born in 1896 at Lurgan, County Armagh. Enlisted September 1914. To France with 36th (Ulster) Division. 'D' Company. **Missing** at the Battle of Langemarck 16 August 1917 and later declared **killed in action** on that date, aged 21.

CULL Private John 14070. From Portadown, County Armagh. A linen weaver. Enlisted September 1914. Did not deploy to France with 36th (Ulster) Division in October 1915. Posted to the 2nd Garrison Battalion. Discharged as no longer physically fit for war service due to sickness 25 November 1918. Silver War Badge, number B46745. Brother of Private William Cull.

CULL Private William 14094. From Portadown, County Armagh. A linen weaver. Enlisted September 1914. To France with 36th (Ulster) Division in October 1915. 'C' Company. [Transferred to the Labour Corps (renumbered 409634).] Brother of Private John Cull.

CULLEN Lance Corporal Lindsay Cyril Vivian 23694. Born in 1899 at Londonderry, the son of Reverend Edward Benjamin Cullen, President of the Methodist Church in Ireland. A student at Methodist College, Belfast he enlisted on 10 January 1916, aged 16 and joined the 10th (Reserve) Battalion. Joined 7th Officer Cadet Battalion at Fermoy as an Officer Cadet. Identified as underage for a commission he rejoined the 10th (Reserve) Battalion 30 December 1916 and volunteered for service in France. Lance Corporal 1 January 1917. To France 1 February 1917 and almost immediately went to hospital with measles. Joined the 9th (Service) Battalion 20 March 1917. 'B' Company. Initially reported **missing** he was later found and listed as **killed in action** at the Battle of Langemarck 16 August 1917, aged 18.

CULLEN Private George 24672. From Portadown, County Armagh. Enlisted in August 1916. Posted to the 9th (Service) Battalion. 'A' Company. **Wounded** at the Battle of Langemarck 16 August 1917. Believed **wounded** in the period 21-28 March 1918 during the retreat from St Quentin. [Transferred to the Army Ordnance Corps (renumbered 048803).] Known to have been **captured** in 1918.

CULLEN Private Gerald 41616. [Enlisted for service with cavalry (5963). Posted to 2nd North Irish Horse, X Corps Cavalry Regiment.] Joined the renamed 9th (North Irish Horse) Battalion from 36 Infantry Base Depot and transferred to Princess Victoria's (Royal Irish Fusiliers) in September/October 1917 (renumbered 41616). 'D' Company. **Missing** in the period 21-28 March 1918 during the retreat from St Quentin believed **captured**.

CULLEN Private William James 14080. Born in 1887 at Derryaghy, County Antrim. Enlisted September 1914. To France with 36th (Ulster) Division in October 1915. 'A' Company. **Wounded** at the Battle of Langemarck 16 August 1917. [Unfit for general service due to shellshock he transferred to The Northumberland Fusiliers (renumbered TR/9/82163) and served with a Training Reserve Battalion. Discharged as no longer physically fit for war service due to wounds 21 September 1918.] Silver War Badge, number B18993. 1914-15 Star.

CULLEY Private William 17816. From Tullyallen, Mountnorris, County Armagh. Enlisted into the 9th (Service) Battalion in January 1915. To France with 36th (Ulster) Division in October 1915. 'C' Company. **Killed in action** during the attack at Hamel 1 July 1916. 1914-15 Star.

CUMMINGS Private William 41527. [Enlisted in January 1915 into the North Irish Horse (1424). To France with 'F' Squadron in 33rd Division 17 November 1915. Served with 2nd North Irish Horse, X Corps Cavalry Regiment.] Joined the renamed 9th (North Irish Horse) Battalion from 36 Infantry Base Depot and transferred to Princess Victoria's (Royal Irish Fusiliers) in September/October 1917 (renumbered 41527). Transferred to the Class Z Reserve 20 March 1919. 1914-15 Star.

CUMMINS Sergeant Samuel 14059. Born in 1889 at Lurgan. A linen weaver. Enlisted September 1914. To France with 36th (Ulster) Division in October 1915. Platoon Sergeant 'A' Company. 1914-15 Star. Battalion Colour Guard June 1919. His brother, Sergeant James Cummins, served as a Special Reservist with 3rd Battalion (Militia), Princess Victoria's (Royal Irish Fusiliers) (5675) in Ireland until he was discharged as no longer physically fit for war service on 31 March 1916. His brother, Corporal Moses Cummins, also a Special Reservist, was killed in action on 19 July 1915 serving with the 1st Battalion, The Royal Irish Rifles. His brother, Private Thomas Cummins, served as a regular soldier with the 1st Battalion, Princess Victoria's (Royal Irish Fusiliers) until he was discharged as no longer physically fit for war service due to sickness on 3 September 1917.

CUNNINGHAM Private Arthur John 24171. Born in 1898 at County Monaghan. The son of a farmer at Cormeen, County Monaghan. Enlisted in March 1916. Posted to the 9th (Service) Battalion. **Wounded** by shrapnel in the chest. Died suddenly in 1923, aged 25, as a consequence of his wound while working in the vegetable garden of the family farm. He is buried at Christ Church, Church of Ireland Churchyard, Aughnamullen, County Monaghan.

13971 Sergeant
John ADAMS MM*

24847 Private
Joseph ALLEN

41191 Private
Thomas ANGUS

22985 Lance Corporal
Thomas James ANNETT

13960 Private
John ATWELL

41534 Private
Robert AVERELL MM

22977 Lance Corporal
Richard Cecil BALLAM

13994 Regimental
Quartermaster Sergeant
John BARBOUR MC

23216 Private
William BAXTER

41388 Private
William BIGGART

40054 Private
Thomas Wilkinson
BINNS

41526 Private
Robert Turner BIRNIE

14017 Sergeant
James BRATTON

41475 Private
Thomas David BRATTY

15859 Sergeant
William John BROWN
(17775 Company Sergeant Major
W J BROWN Machine Gun Corps)

13987 Sergeant
John BRYANS

13999 Private
James BURDEN

25905 Private
Edward CALLACHER

17147 Lance Corporal
Herbert James CALVERT

18068 Private
Samuel CHAMBERS

22623 Private
James Andrew CHAMBERS

41486 Private
John CONWAY

14054 Private
John CORKIN

15719 Company
Sergeant Major
Francis Edward CROSS

14098 Sergeant
Samuel CULBERT

17816 Private
William CULLEY

24171 Private
Arthur John CUNNINGHAM

14086 Private
Albert CUST

20441 Lance Corporal
Ingram DICK MM

41364 Corporal
Albert Victor Spence DUNSEITH

14142 Private
Ralph Alfred DYNES
(Captain R A Dynes MBE)

41159 Private
William Thomas ELLIOTT

15255 Company
Quartermaster Sergeant
Robert George ELLISON

41103 Private
Henry EMERSON

14174 Private
George FERRIS

41229 Lance Corporal
Hugh Edmond FLANAGAN

41447 Private
Thomas FOREMAN

14191 Regimental
Quartermaster Sergeant
Henry Joseph FOX

22416 Private
Leonard FOX

Brothers

27477 Corporal
David FRAZER
(left, with his future
wife Elizabeth Stringer,
sister of Lance Corporal
William Stringer

and

14192 Private
Henry FRAZER (right)

41413 Private
Joseph GIBSON

15258 Private
George GILROY

49739 Private
James GLENN

23215 Lance Corporal
William James GRAHAM

14201 Private
Edmund GRAY

21645 Private
Thomas John Gerald HAIRE

17556 Private
James GREGG

22875 Lance Sergeant
Joseph GRAY

14260 Private
James HALL

23344 Private
Robert HANLEY

24347 Private
Isaac HANNA

41362 Private
Nathaniel HARVEY

24942 Private
James HAUGH

41401 Lance Sergeant
George Adams HENRY MM

41373 Private
Hugh HIGGINS

14299 Private
Moore HILL

14302 Sergeant
Robert HOBBS

14259 Private
Andrew HOBBS

14305 Private
David HOBBS

14273 Private
Herbert HOBBS

45807 Sergeant
Francis Stanhope
HOMERSHAM
DCM, MM*

41449 Lance Corporal
Samuel HOUSTON

13080 Sergeant
Charles INGLEDEW

41263 Private
Robert William JAMISON

41169 Private
George JOHNSTON

CUNNINGHAM Private Bernard 42217. From Birmingham. A cycle frame builder. [Enlisted 5 September 1913 into The Waggoners Special Reserve (T/33645). To France 20 August 1914 with 12th Company, Army Service Corps (5th Reserve Park).] Transferred to Princess Victoria's (Royal Irish Fusiliers) 8 May 1918 (renumbered 42217) and joined the 9th (North Irish Horse) Battalion. 1914 Star. Transferred to the Section B Army Reserve, Princess Victoria's (Royal Irish Fusiliers) 16 April 1919. Discharged 4 September 1925.

CUNNINGHAM Private Daniel 42527 & 7042389. From Burnbank, Lanarkshire. A puddler. [Enlisted 19 February 1917 into The Royal Irish Rifles (22639).] To France 6 September 1918 and transferred at the Base Depot to Princess Victoria's (Royal Irish Fusiliers) 14 September 1918 (renumbered 42527) and joined the 9th (North Irish Horse) Battalion 22 September 1918. **Wounded** by a gunshot to the right knee during the advance to Anseghem 25 October 1918 and evacuated to hospital in England 25 November 1918. Re-enlisted in early-1919 for Regular Army service with Princess Victoria's (Royal Irish Fusiliers) (renumbered 7042389). Discharged 25 August 1920 (King's Certificate 87/3126).

CUNNINGHAM Sergeant Joseph 14122. Enlisted September 1914. To France with 36th (Ulster) Division in October 1915. **Wounded** during the attack at Hamel 1 July 1916. [Transferred to the Labour Corps (renumbered 512017).] Discharged Transferred to the Class Z Reserve 6 March 1919. 1914-15 Star.

CUNNINGHAM Private William Francis 19093. From Walthamstow, Middlesex. [Enlisted 13 May 1915 into the Royal Field Artillery (146783). Transferred to Princess Victoria's (Royal Irish Fusiliers) in December 1915 (renumbered 19093) and served with the 1st Battalion. Posted to the 7th/8th (Service) Battalion in 49th Brigade, 16th (Irish) Division. **Wounded** (not known whether with 1st or 7th/8th). Discharged as no longer physically fit for war service due to wounds 23 July 1917. Silver War Badge, number 214468.] Rejoined and posted to the 9th (North Irish Horse) Battalion sometime in 1918 (retained number 19093). **Killed in action** during the attack south of Wulverghem 4 September 1918.

CUNNINGTON Private William 25150. Born in 1877 in Canada. A horse trainer. Sailed to Great Britain in December 1914 to enlist. [Enlisted into the Army Service Corps (RTS/5083). To France 22 January 1915 and served with 3rd Remount Depot. Transferred to Princess Victoria's (Royal Irish Fusiliers) in May 1916 and posted to 7th/8th (Service) Battalion in 49th Brigade, 16th (Irish) Division.] Joined the 9th (North Irish Horse) Battalion when the 7th/8th (Service) Battalion was disbanded in February 1918.] Transferred to the Class Z Reserve 4 April 1919. 1914-15 Star. Lived in Ulceby, Lincolnshire and requested repatriation to Loverna, Saskatchewan, Canada, in 1919.

CURRAN Private James. From Portadown, County Armagh. Soldier not identified.

CURRAN Private Patrick 42510. [Enlisted into The Royal Irish Rifles (22707).] Transferred at the Base Depot to Princess Victoria's (Royal Irish Fusiliers) 14 September 1918 (renumbered 42510) and joined the 9th (North Irish Horse) Battalion 22 September 1918.

CURRIE Private Allen 22647. From Lurgan, County Armagh. Enlisted in November 1915. Posted to the 9th (Service) Battalion. **Wounded** during the attack at Hamel 1 July 1916.

CURRIE Private David 42513. Born in 1899 at Belfast. [Enlisted 4 May 1918 into The Royal Irish Rifles (22571) and joined the 3rd (Reserve) Battalion.] Transferred at the Base Depot to Princess Victoria's (Royal Irish Fusiliers) 14 September 1918 (renumbered 42513) and joined the 9th (North Irish Horse) Battalion 22 September 1918. 'D' Company. **Wounded** on the attacks near Hill 41 on 6 October 1918 by a gunshot to the chest and **died of wounds** in 62nd (1/2nd London) Casualty Clearing Station at Remy Siding on 8 October 1918, aged 19.

CURRIE Private Robert 28964. Enlisted 12 January 1918. Posted to the 9th (North Irish Horse) Battalion. **Wounded**. Discharged as no longer physically fit for war service due to wounds 6 December 1918. Silver War Badge, number B54743.

CURRIE Private Thomas George 14071. From Portadown, County Armagh. Enlisted September 1914. To France with 36th (Ulster) Division in October 1915. [Transferred to The Northumberland Fusiliers (renumbered 99530). Transferred to the Army Service Corps (renumbered T/405274, renumbered M/354535).] 1914-15 Star.

CURRY Private Andrew 20316. From County Durham. [Enlisted into The Royal Inniskilling

Fusiliers (20883).] Transferred to Princess Victoria's (Royal Irish Fusiliers) 30 June 1915 (renumbered 20316) and joined the 9th (Service) Battalion. **Killed in action** during the attack at Hamel 1 July 1916, aged 23.

CURRY Lance Corporal Harry 41569. [Enlisted in May 1915 into the North Irish Horse (1646). Served with 2nd North Irish Horse, X Corps Cavalry Regiment.] Joined the renamed 9th (North Irish Horse) Battalion from 36 Infantry Base Depot and transferred to Princess Victoria's (Royal Irish Fusiliers) in September/October 1917 (renumbered 41569).

CURRY Private Robert 20318. Enlisted in May/June 1915 and joined the 9th (Service) Battalion with the draft of men from The Royal Inniskilling Fusiliers who transferred to Princess Victoria's (Royal Irish Fusiliers) on 30 June 1915. To France with 36th (Ulster) Division in October 1915. 3 Section, 13 Platoon, 'D' Company in 1915. [Transferred to 5th (Service) Battalion, The Royal Irish Regiment (Pioneers) in the Light Division in the British Army of the Rhine in March/June 1919 (renumbered 41275).] 1914-15 Star.

CURRY Private Robert. (Not positively identified as 20318 Private Robert Curry.) Tried by Field General Court Martial on 19 November 1918 charged with *'when on active service **deserting** His Majesty's service'*; found guilty and sentenced to ten years imprisonment. Soldier not positively identified.

CURTIS Private William 16099. From Arva, County Cavan. Enlisted into the 9th (Service) Battalion in October 1914. To France with 36th (Ulster) Division in October 1915. **Killed in action** during the attack at Hamel 1 July 1916, aged 22. 1914-15 Star.

CUSACK Private James 40088. Enlisted 10 March 1916. Joined the 9th (Service) Battalion, Princess Victoria's (Royal Irish Fusiliers) with the draft of men from The Prince of Wales's Own (West Yorkshire Regiment) on 12 December 1916. **Wounded**. Discharged as no longer physically fit for war service due to wounds 7 June 1918, aged 25. Silver War Badge, number 396907.

CUST Private Albert 14086. Born in 1894. A farmer from Milford, County Armagh. Signed the Ulster Covenant 28 September 1912. 1st (Armagh) Battalion, Armagh Regiment, Ulster Volunteer Force. Enlisted 16 September 1914. [Transferred to the Corps of Royal Engineers (renumbered 57997 Pioneer) for service with 36th (Ulster) Division Signal Company as a Telegraphist (Field Line) 6 February 1915. Trained at Dunstable Signal Depot then deployed to France 16 December 1915. Returned to Great Britain on 17 May 1918 and discharged as no longer physically fit for war service due to sickness 20 December 1918.] Silver War Badge, number B72067. 1914-15 Star. Served with the Class 'A' Ulster Special Constabulary in 'B' Platoon, Armagh.

CUTHBERTSON Private Thomas 20293. From Newcastle-upon-Tyne. Enlisted in May/June 1915 and joined the 9th (Service) Battalion with the draft of men from The Royal Inniskilling Fusiliers who transferred to Princess Victoria's (Royal Irish Fusiliers) on 30 June 1915. 'C' Company. To France with 36th (Ulster) Division in October 1915. **Wounded** at Hamel 30 June 1916. **Wounded** at the Battle of Langemarck 16 August 1917. Transferred to the Class Z Reserve 26 March 1919. 1914-15 Star.

CUTTS Lance Corporal George William 40038. [Enlisted into the 12th (Service) Battalion, The Prince of Wales's Own (West Yorkshire Regiment) (16257).] Transferred to Princess Victoria's (Royal Irish Fusiliers) 30 November 1916 (renumbered 40038) and joined the 9th (Service) Battalion 12 December 1916.

DALE Private Arthur W 41102. [Enlisted into the 6th (Inniskilling) Dragoons (GS/23330). Served with 2nd North Irish Horse, X Corps Cavalry Regiment.] Joined the renamed 9th (North Irish Horse) Battalion from 36 Infantry Base Depot and transferred to Princess Victoria's (Royal Irish Fusiliers) in September/October 1917 (renumbered 41102). [Transferred to the Corps of Dragoons (renumbered D/34448).]

DALZELL Private Hugh 24114. Born at Newtownards, County Down. Worked as a labourer for a blacksmith. Enlisted 17 March 1916 and joined the 10th (Reserve) Battalion. To France 30 June 1916 and joined the 9th (Service) Battalion. 'D' Company. **Killed in action** at the Battle of Langemarck 16 August 1917, aged 20.

DANIELL Private Percival Thomas 42281. [Enlisted 8 January 1915 into the Army Veterinary Corps (3303). To France 18 March 1915.] Transferred to Princess Victoria's (Royal Irish Fusiliers) 8

May 1918 (renumbered 42281) and joined the 9th (North Irish Horse) Battalion. **Wounded**. Discharged as no longer physically fit for war service due to wounds 25 January 1919. Silver War Badge, number B103525. 1914-15 Star.

DANIELS Private Henry Percy 45812. Born in 1898 at Woolwich, London. Enlisted 5 November 1916. Joined the 9th (North Irish Horse) Battalion, Princess Victoria's (Royal Irish Fusiliers) with the draft of men from The London Regiment in April 1918. **Wounded**. Discharged as no longer physically fit for war service 9 April 1919. Silver War Badge, number B209599.

DARLING Sergeant James 17071. Enlisted into the 9th (Service) Battalion in October 1914. To France with 36th (Ulster) Division in October 1915. Transferred to the Class Z Reserve 10 March 1919. 1914-15 Star.

DAVEY Private Allan 41589. Born in 1888 at Carrickfergus, County Antrim. [Enlisted in October 1914 into the North Irish Horse (1312). Served with 2nd North Irish Horse, X Corps Cavalry Regiment.] Joined the renamed 9th (North Irish Horse) Battalion from 36 Infantry Base Depot and transferred to Princess Victoria's (Royal Irish Fusiliers) in September/October 1917 (renumbered 41589). **Missing** in the period 11-18 April 1918 in the actions between Wulverghem and Kemmel; subsequently declared **killed in action** 19 April 1918, aged 30. 1914-15 Star.

DAVEY Private Robert 3842. Enlisted into Princess Victoria's (Royal Irish Fusiliers) Special Reserve in late-1915. Posted to the 9th (Service) Battalion. **Deserted** 20 October 1918. Medals initially forfeit, they were restored and issued by the Admiralty (for reasons unknown).

DAVIDSON Lance Corporal Matthew 14152. Enlisted September 1914. To France with 36th (Ulster) Division in October 1915. Transferred to the Class Z Reserve 2 April 1919. 1914-15 Star.

DAVIDSON Private Robert 14141. From Armagh, County Armagh. Enlisted September 1914. To France with 36th (Ulster) Division in October 1915. 'A' Company. **Captured** in the period 21-28 March 1918 during the retreat from St Quentin. Transferred to the Class Z Reserve 2 April 1919. 1914-15 Star.

DAVIDSON Private Samuel 41536. Born in 1891. From Belfast. A school teacher at a national school in Belfast. [Enlisted 2 December 1915 into the North Irish Horse (2027). Served with 2nd North Irish Horse, X Corps Cavalry Regiment.] Joined the renamed 9th (North Irish Horse) Battalion from 36 Infantry Base Depot and transferred to Princess Victoria's (Royal Irish Fusiliers) in September/October 1917 (renumbered 41536). 'C' Company. To hospital sick (impetigo) October 1917. [Attached to Depot Field Survey Company 5 May 1918. Transferred to the Corps of Royal Engineers (renumbered 362501) 1 August 1918. Posted to Depot Field Survey Company and then 2nd Field Survey Battalion as a survey post observer.] Transferred to the Class Z Reserve 4 February 1919.

DAVIDSON Private Walter 41274. [Enlisted in April 1915 into the North Irish Horse (1485). To France 22 September 1915. Served with 2nd North Irish Horse, X Corps Cavalry Regiment.] Joined the renamed 9th (North Irish Horse) Battalion from 36 Infantry Base Depot and transferred to Princess Victoria's (Royal Irish Fusiliers) in September/October 1917 (renumbered 41274). 'C' Company. Separated from the 9th (North Irish Horse) Battalion in the period 21-28 March 1918 during the retreat from St Quentin; rejoined 2 April 1918. Transferred to Princess Victoria's (Royal Irish Fusiliers) Special Reserve on 28 February 1919. 1914-15 Star.

DAVIDSON Private William 41444. [Enlisted 19 August 1916 into the North Irish Horse (2239). Served with 2nd North Irish Horse, X Corps Cavalry Regiment.] Joined the renamed 9th (North Irish Horse) Battalion from 36 Infantry Base Depot and transferred to Princess Victoria's (Royal Irish Fusiliers) in September/October 1917 (renumbered 41444). **Wounded**. Discharged as no longer physically fit for war service due to wounds 1 October 1918, aged 21. Silver War Badge, number B22494.

DAVIES Private Harold 41618. [Enlisted for service with cavalry (21277). Posted to 2nd North Irish Horse, X Corps Cavalry Regiment.] Joined the renamed 9th (North Irish Horse) Battalion from 36 Infantry Base Depot and transferred to Princess Victoria's (Royal Irish Fusiliers) in September/October 1917 (renumbered 41618).

DAVIS Private James 41461. [Enlisted 16 November 1911 into the North Irish Horse (637). To France 17 August 1914 with 'A' Squadron as GHQ Troops. Served with 2nd North Irish Horse, X

Corps Cavalry Regiment.] Joined the renamed 9th (North Irish Horse) Battalion from 36 Infantry Base Depot and transferred to Princess Victoria's (Royal Irish Fusiliers) in September/October 1917 (renumbered 41461). 'C' Company. Separated from the 9th (North Irish Horse) Battalion in the period 21-28 March 1918 during the retreat from St Quentin; rejoined 6 April 1918. 1914 Star.

DAVIS Private James E 42458. [Enlisted into The Royal Irish Rifles (22732).] Transferred at the Base Depot to Princess Victoria's (Royal Irish Fusiliers) 14 September 1918 (renumbered 42458) and joined the 9th (North Irish Horse) Battalion 22 September 1918. [Transferred to 5th (Service) Battalion, The Royal Irish Regiment (Pioneers) in the Light Division in the British Army of the Rhine in March/June 1919 (renumbered 41278).]

DAVIS Private John 19735. From Clones, County Monaghan. Enlisted into the 9th (Service) Battalion in April 1915. **Killed in action** during the attack at Hamel 1 July 1916.

DAVIS Private John Charles 41570. From Belfast. [Enlisted in January 1915 into the North Irish Horse (1384). To France with 'F' Squadron in 33rd Division 17 November 1915. Served with 2nd North Irish Horse, X Corps Cavalry Regiment.] Joined the renamed 9th (North Irish Horse) Battalion from 36 Infantry Base Depot and transferred to Princess Victoria's (Royal Irish Fusiliers) in September/October 1917 (renumbered 41570). 'D' Company. **Captured** in the period 21-28 March 1918 during the retreat from St Quentin. Transferred to the Class Z Reserve 31 March 1919. 1914-15 Star.

DAVIS Private Thomas Henry 16100. Born at Cootehill, County Cavan. Enlisted into the 9th (Service) Battalion in October 1914. To France with 36th (Ulster) Division in October 1915. **Killed in action** during the attack at Hamel 1 July 1916. 1914-15 Star.

DAVISON Lance Corporal Frank 43471. Joined the 9th (North Irish Horse) Battalion, Princess Victoria's (Royal Irish Fusiliers) with the draft of men from The London Regiment in April 1918.

DAVISON Private John 42532. [Enlisted April/May 1918 into The Royal Irish Rifles (22626).] Transferred at the Base Depot to Princess Victoria's (Royal Irish Fusiliers) 14 September 1918 (renumbered 42532) and joined the 9th (North Irish Horse) Battalion 22 September 1918.

DAWSON Private Arthur 20344. Born at Northwich, Cheshire. [Enlisted into The Royal Inniskilling Fusiliers (23903).] Transferred to Princess Victoria's (Royal Irish Fusiliers) on 30 June 1915 (renumbered 20344) and joined the 9th (Service) Battalion. To France with 36th (Ulster) Division in October 1915. **Wounded** during the attack at Hamel 1 July 1916. **Captured**. **Died** while a prisoner of war 8 July 1918. 1914-15 Star.

DAWSON Sergeant Edward 13389. Born in 1862 at Armagh, County Armagh. A former regular soldier and Army pensioner. Worked as a Gateman for the Great Northern Railway. Re-enlisted in September 1914. Later posted to the 9th (Service) Battalion. Evacuated to hospital in England sick. **Died** in Ireland 1 January 1917, aged 55.

DAWSON Private Thomas William 22176. From Cormeen, Clones, County Monaghan. Enlisted in October 1915. Posted to the 9th (Service) Battalion. 'C' Company. **Killed in action** at the Battle of Langemarck 16 August 1917, aged 20.

DEERY Lance Corporal Joseph 41244. Born in 1894 at Castlederg, County Tyrone. Worked as a clerk for Ulster Bank. [Enlisted in November 1915 into the North Irish Horse (2013). Served with 2nd North Irish Horse, X Corps Cavalry Regiment.] Joined the renamed 9th (North Irish Horse) Battalion from 36 Infantry Base Depot and transferred to Princess Victoria's (Royal Irish Fusiliers) in September/October 1917 (renumbered 41244). 'D' Company. Believed **wounded** in the period 21-28 March 1918 during the retreat from St Quentin. **Killed in action** at Hill 41 11 October 1918, aged 24.

DELL Private Edward Henry Valentine 45796. Born 14 February 1899 at London. Enlisted 1 May 1912. Joined the 9th (North Irish Horse) Battalion, Princess Victoria's (Royal Irish Fusiliers) with the draft of men from The London Regiment in April 1918. **Wounded**. Discharged as no longer physically fit for war service due to wounds 20 December 1918. Silver War Badge, number B64256. Died at London in 1969, aged 70.

DENANY Private John James 15553. [Enlisted in September 1914 into the 6th (Service) Battalion in 31st Brigade, 10th (Irish) Division. Embarked with the Mediterranean Expeditionary Force July 1915.] Posted to the 9th (North Irish Horse) Battalion. [Posted to the 1st Battalion.] Transferred to the Class Z Reserve 2 May 1919. 1914-15 Star.

DENBRIDGE Private William George 43315. Joined the 9th (Service) Battalion, Princess Victoria's (Royal Irish Fusiliers) with the draft of men from The London Regiment in November 1916.

DENNY Lance Corporal Cecil Arthur 45736. [Enlisted 20 November 1915 into The London Regiment (6164). Posted to 1/24th (County of London) Battalion, The London Regiment (The Queen's).] To France and joined 36 Infantry Base Depot 29 March 1918. Transferred to Princess Victoria's (Royal Irish Fusiliers) 2 April 1918 (renumbered 45736) and joined the 9th (North Irish Horse) Battalion 4 April 1918. **Wounded**. Discharged as no longer physically fit for war service due to wounds 14 February 1919. Silver War Badge, number B150014.

DENVER Private Alexander 14147. From Lurgan, County Armagh. A clerk in the linen trade; worked for Johnston, Allen & Co, Lurgan. Enlisted September 1914. To France with 36th (Ulster) Division in October 1915. **Wounded** during the attack at Hamel 1 July 1916. Discharged as no longer physically fit for war service due to wounds 30 June 1917. Silver War Badge, number 203184. 1914-15 Star.

DEVANE Lance Corporal John 29419. Enlisted, re-enlisted or transferred to Princess Victoria's (Royal Irish Fusiliers) in March 1918. Posted to the 9th (North Irish Horse) Battalion.

DEVINE Lance Corporal James 9386. [Enlisted into Princess Victoria's (Royal Irish Fusiliers) as a regular soldier in mid-1906. To France with the 1st Battalion 22 August 1914.] Posted to the 9th (North Irish Horse) Battalion. 1914 Star.

DEVINE Private Rodger 43285. Born at Ardstraw, County Tyrone. From Castlederg, County Tyrone. [Enlisted 14 December 1915 into The Royal Inniskilling Fusiliers (22782). To France 16 February 1916 with the 7th (Service) Battalion, The Royal Inniskilling Fusiliers. To hospital sick (trench foot) March 1916 and evacuated to hospital in England. To France 7 July 1916 and posted to the 11th (Service) Battalion, The Royal Inniskilling Fusiliers (Donegal and Fermanagh). Attached to the 2nd Battalion, The Royal Irish Rifles 20 July 1916. To hospital sick (boil on his right leg) August 1916.] Transferred to Princess Victoria's (Royal Irish Fusiliers) in August 1916 (renumbered 43285) and joined the 9th (Service) Battalion, Princess Victoria's (Royal Irish Fusiliers) 9 September 1916. 'A' Company. Sentenced to twenty-eight days Field Punishment Number 1 for being absent from a working party at Ypres 31 October 1916. To Casualty Clearing Station sick (inflammation of the foot) November 1916. To hospital sick (tonsillitis) January 1917. Treated at 13th General Hospital. Rejoined the 9th (North Irish Horse) Battalion 29 March 1917. Attached to 108th Brigade Machine Gun Company 25 May 1917. **Wounded** at the Battle of Langemarck 16 August 1917 by a gunshot to the right arm and hand. Rejoined the 9th (North Irish Horse) Battalion 9 October 1917. **Killed in action** during the attack at Vijfwegen 30 September 1918, aged 34.

DEVINE Private Samuel 41156. Born at Liverpool. From Brookeborough, County Fermanagh. [Enlisted in September/October 1915 into the Service Squadron, 6th (Inniskilling) Dragoons (UD/56). To France with 36th (Ulster) Division in October 1915. Served with 2nd North Irish Horse, X Corps Cavalry Regiment.] Joined the renamed 9th (North Irish Horse) Battalion from 36 Infantry Base Depot and transferred to Princess Victoria's (Royal Irish Fusiliers) in September/October 1917 (renumbered 41156). **Died of wounds** in England 24 February 1918. 1914-15 Star.

DEVLIN Private John 14145. Born in 1887 at Portadown, County Armagh. 4th (Portadown) Battalion, Armagh Regiment, Ulster Volunteer Force. A weaver. Enlisted September 1914. To France with 36th (Ulster) Division in October 1915. **Wounded** by gunshots to the thighs during the attack at Hamel 1 July 1916. Evacuated to hospital in England 2 October 1916. [Joined the 10th (Reserve) Battalion 14 August 1917. Transferred to the Labour Corps (renumbered 545501) 6 April 1918. Served with 361, 657 and 655 Home Service Employment Companies.] Transferred to the Class Z Reserve 22 May 1919. 1914-15 Star.

DEVLIN Private Robert 18553. Enlisted into the 9th (Service) Battalion in April 1915. To France with 36th (Ulster) Division in October 1915. 1914-15 Star.

DEVLIN Lance Corporal Samuel 14136. Born in 1891. Enlisted September 1914. To France with 36th (Ulster) Division in October 1915. **Wounded** by a gunshot to the leg and foot during the attack at Hamel 1 July 1916. Evacuated to hospital in England 8 July 1916 and was treated at 1st Southern General Hospital, Birmingham until November 1916. To France 2 May 1917 and rejoined the 9th (Service) Battalion 23 May 1917. **Wounded**. Evacuated to hospital in England 29 November

1917. Joined the 10th (Reserve) Battalion 25 February 1918. Transferred to the Class Z Reserve 5 February 1919. 1914-15 Star.

DEVOY Corporal John Forbes 41199. Born in 1894 at Newtownards, County Down. [Enlisted in January 1915 into the North Irish Horse (1431). Served with 2nd North Irish Horse, X Corps Cavalry Regiment.] Joined the renamed 9th (North Irish Horse) Battalion from 36 Infantry Base Depot and transferred to Princess Victoria's (Royal Irish Fusiliers) in September/October 1917 (renumbered 41199). Transferred to the Class Z Reserve. 1914-15 Star. His brother, Sergeant Samuel Devoy, was killed in action at Thiepval on 1 July 1916 serving with 13th (Service) Battalion, The Royal Irish Rifles (1st County Down). He is commemorated on the Thiepval Memorial.

DEWAR Corporal Alexander 42171. [Enlisted into the Army Service Corps (S2/22439 Lance Corporal). To France 18 July 1915. Served with 19th and 12th Field Bakeries.] Transferred to Princess Victoria's (Royal Irish Fusiliers) 8 May 1918 (renumbered 42171) and joined the 9th (North Irish Horse) Battalion. Transferred to the Class Z Reserve. 1914-15 Star.

DICK MM Lance Corporal Ingram 20441. Born at Belfast on 3 June 1882. Son of a maritime engineer he became an engine fitter. Enlisted into the 9th (Service) Battalion in June 1915. **MM** – Wulverghem 4 September 1918. ***Croix de Guerre* (Belgium)**. He was found drowned at Queen's Quay, Belfast on 30 December 1919, aged 37. The inquest was held by the Coroner for Belfast, Dr James Graham, on 31 December 1919. The inquest heard evidence that he had gone to the quay with another man in order to find a boat on which to work his passage to Glasgow. As he left one of the ships he fell into the water. The inquest found that he was accidentally drowned. He was buried on 2 January 1920 in a family plot at City Cemetery.

DICKENS Private Charles Henry 43355. Born 9 September 1897 at London. [Enlisted 18 November 1914, aged 17. Joined the 3/7th Battalion, The London Regiment (3192). To France 10 November 1916 for duty with the 1/7th (City of London) Battalion, The London Regiment.] Attached to the 9th (Service) Battalion, Princess Victoria's (Royal Irish Fusiliers) 26 November 1916. Renumbered 351045, The London Regiment in March 1917. Discharged from the Territorial Force, re-enlisted and transferred to Princess Victoria's (Royal Irish Fusiliers) in March 1917 (renumbered 43355). **Wounded** and evacuated to hospital in England 11 March 1917. Discharged as no longer physically fit for war service due to wounds 14 December 1918. Silver War Badge, number B63625. Died at Dartford, Kent in 1977, aged 79.

DICKENS Private Francis Albert 45278. [Enlisted 31 July 1916. Transferred to Princess Victoria's (Royal Irish Fusiliers) in December 1916 and joined the 7th/8th (Service) Battalion in 49th Brigade, 16th (Irish) Division.] Joined the 9th (North Irish Horse) Battalion when the 7th/8th (Service) Battalion was disbanded in February 1918. 'A' Company. **Missing** in the period 21-28 March 1918 during the retreat from St Quentin believed **captured**. Discharged as no longer physically fit for war service due to sickness 4 June 1919. Silver War Badge, number B256305.

DICKINSON Private Thomas 41078. From Galashiels, Selkirk. [Enlisted into the 6th (Inniskilling) Dragoons (6214). Served with 2nd North Irish Horse, X Corps Cavalry Regiment.] Joined the renamed 9th (North Irish Horse) Battalion from 36 Infantry Base Depot and transferred to Princess Victoria's (Royal Irish Fusiliers) in September/October 1917 (renumbered 41078). **Killed in action** 26 October 1917 at Havrincourt, aged 28.

DICKSON Private Adam 40093. Enlisted 8 May 1916. **Wounded**. Discharged as no longer physically fit for war service due to wounds 5 May 1919. Silver War Badge, number B224711.

DICKSON Private Edgar 41118. From Devenish, Enniskillen, County Fermanagh. A farmer. [Enlisted 2 October 1914 into the Service Squadron, 6th (Inniskilling) Dragoons (UD/7). To France with 36th (Ulster) Division in October 1915.] Joined the renamed 9th (North Irish Horse) Battalion from 36 Infantry Base Depot and transferred to Princess Victoria's (Royal Irish Fusiliers) in September/October 1917 (renumbered 41118). 'A' Company. Evacuated sick (trench fever) to hospital in England 4 January 1918. Posted to the North Irish Horse Depot, Randalstown 4 May 1918. Posted to the 3rd (Reserve) Battalion, Princess Victoria's (Royal Irish Fusiliers) 24 May 1918. [Transferred to the 53rd (Young Soldier) Battalion, The Sherwood Foresters (Nottinghamshire and Derbyshire Regiment) (renumbered 53031) at Rugeley, Cannock Chase 9 July 1918.] Transferred to the Class Z Reserve 13 February 1919. 1914-15 Star.

DICKSON Sergeant James Henry 14127. Commissioned into Princess Victoria's (Royal Irish

Fusiliers) - see Appendix 5.

DICKSON Private Stewart 17548. Born in 1893 at Portadown, County Armagh. Enlisted into the 9th (Service) Battalion 21 November 1914. Transferred to the Corps of Royal Engineers (renumbered 361330 Sapper Telegraph Operator) and posted to 36th (Ulster) Division Signal Company. To France with 36th (Ulster) Division in October 1915. To hospital 29 July to 26 September 1919 sick (gonorrhoea). Transferred to the Class Z Reserve 24 October 1919.

DICKSON Sergeant Thomas Robert 41120 & 7042386. Born in 1891 at Drumee, Enniskillen, County Fermanagh. A farmer. [Enlisted 11 November 1914 into the Service Squadron, 6th (Inniskilling) Dragoons (UD/166). Promoted to Lance Corporal. Served with 2nd North Irish Horse, X Corps Cavalry Regiment. **Wounded** by shellfire at Aveluy Wood when two troops engaged in salvage duty were subject to heavy bombardment 5 July 1916.] Joined the renamed 9th (North Irish Horse) Battalion from 36 Infantry Base Depot and transferred to Princess Victoria's (Royal Irish Fusiliers) in September/October 1917 (renumbered 41120). Platoon Sergeant 7 Platoon, 'B' Company. **Wounded** by a gunshot to the chest in the period 11-18 April 1918 in the actions between Wulverghem and Kemmel and evacuated to hospital in England 2 June 1918. 1914-15 Star. Re-enlisted in early-1919 for Regular Army service with Princess Victoria's (Royal Irish Fusiliers) (renumbered 7042386). Discharged 30 November 1920 (King's Certificate 87/3118).

DICKSON Lance Corporal Thomas John Ingram 23697. Born in 1899 at Madden, County Armagh. A farm labourer, he enlisted on 10 January 1916, aged 17, and joined the 10th (Reserve) Battalion. To France 16 May 1917 and joined the 9th (Service) Battalion 21 June 1917. 'A' Company. **Wounded** in the period 9-18 April 1918 in the actions between Wulverghem and Kemmel and **died of wounds** 18 April 1918, aged 19.

DILLON Lance Corporal David Oliver 19728. Enlisted into the 9th (Service) Battalion in April 1915. To France with 36th (Ulster) Division in October 1915. Transferred to the Class Z Reserve 7 May 1919. 1914-15 Star.

DILLON Private John Charles 23625, 29749 & 34073. Born in 1897 at Dundalk, County Louth. Enlisted 31 December 1915. Posted to the 9th (Service) Battalion. 'D' Company. **Wounded** at the Battle of Langemarck 16 August 1917. [Discharged or transferred. Re-enlisted or transferred back to Princess Victoria's (Royal Irish Fusiliers) (renumbered 29749). Posted to the 1st Battalion. Discharged as no longer physically fit for war service due to wounds 11 December 1918.] Re-enlisted in April/May 1920 for Regular Army service with Princess Victoria's (Royal Irish Fusiliers) (renumbered 34073). He was not renumbered again; discharged before September 1920.

DILLON Private Joseph Albert 14132. From Lurgan, County Armagh. Enlisted September 1914. To France with 36th (Ulster) Division in October 1915. **Wounded** during the attack at Hamel 1 July 1916. Discharged as no longer physically fit for war service due to wounds 8 September 1917. Silver War Badge, number 238598. 1914-15 Star. Brother of Sergeant Victor Samuel Dillon.

DILLON Private Samuel George 14130. Born September 1895. From Bridge Street, Portadown, County Armagh. 4th (Portadown) Battalion, Armagh Regiment, Ulster Volunteer Force. Enlisted September 1914. Sickness prevented deployment to France. Posted to the 10th (Reserve) Battalion 9 October 1915. **Died** of pleurisy in Belfast War Hospital on 7 January 1916, aged 21. The ceremony at his funeral at Seagoe was conducted by the band and a detachment of the 10th (Reserve) Battalion commanded by Colonel W G Fitzgerald.

DILLON Private Samuel Victor Johnston 14135. From Lurgan, County Armagh. Enlisted September 1914. To France with 36th (Ulster) Division in October 1915. 'C' Company. **Killed in action** during the attack at Hamel 1 July 1916, aged 20. 1914-15 Star. Brother of Private Joseph Dillon.

DITCHBURN Private Thomas 20300. From County Durham. Enlisted in May/June 1915 and joined the 9th (Service) Battalion with the draft of men from The Royal Inniskilling Fusiliers who transferred to Princess Victoria's (Royal Irish Fusiliers) on 30 June 1915. Posted to the 10th (Reserve) Battalion in October 1915. To France 12 November 1915 and rejoined the 9th (Service) Battalion. Discharged 14 December 1918. 1914-15 Star.

DITTON Lance Corporal Charles Edward 43387. Born in 1888 at Truro, Cornwall, one of fourteen children. A warehouseman from Kentish Town, London. [Enlisted 22 November 1915 and joined the 3/9th Battalion, The London Regiment (5711). Posted to the 1/9th (County of London)

Battalion, The London Regiment (Queen Victoria's Rifles). Lance Corporal.] Attached to the 9th (Service) Battalion, Princess Victoria's (Royal Irish Fusiliers) 26 November 1916. Discharged from the Territorial Force, re-enlisted and transferred to Princess Victoria's (Royal Irish Fusiliers) in March/April 1917 (renumbered 43387). Lance Corporal 18 April 1917. To hospital sick (influenza) 18 May 1917 and evacuated to hospital in England. Joined the 10th (Reserve) Battalion 7 September 1917. To France 9 May 1918 and rejoined the 9th (North Irish Horse) Battalion 25 May 1918. To hospital sick (influenza) 6 July 1918. Rejoined the 9th (North Irish Horse) Battalion 26 September 1918. **Killed in action** 16 October 1918 at Courtrai, aged 32.

DIXON Private David 18654. From Loughgilly, County Armagh. Enlisted into the 9th (Service) Battalion in April 1915. To France with 36th (Ulster) Division in October 1915. **Killed in action** during the attack at Hamel 1 July 1916. 1914-15 Star.

DIXON Private George John 43353. [Enlisted into The London Regiment (6732). Posted to the 1/7th (City of London) Battalion, The London Regiment.] Attached to the 9th (Service) Battalion, Princess Victoria's (Royal Irish Fusiliers) 26 November 1916. 'A' Company. Discharged from the Territorial Force, re-enlisted and transferred to Princess Victoria's (Royal Irish Fusiliers) in March/April 1917 (renumbered 43353). **Missing** in the period 21-28 March 1918 during the retreat from St Quentin believed **captured**.

DIXON Private James Alexander 41171. [Enlisted into the Service Squadron, 6th (Inniskilling) Dragoons (UD/315). Served with 2nd North Irish Horse, X Corps Cavalry Regiment.] Joined the renamed 9th (North Irish Horse) Battalion from 36 Infantry Base Depot and transferred to Princess Victoria's (Royal Irish Fusiliers) in September/October 1917 (renumbered 41171).

DIXON Lance Corporal Thomas George 24019. Born at Ballymoney, County Antrim. From Belfast. [Enlisted 29 February 1916. Joined 'A' Company of the 1st Battalion in France 26 September 1916. To hospital sick (influenza) 24 November 1916 and evacuated to hospital in England 15 December 1916. Rejoined the 1st Battalion 24 February 1917. **Wounded** by a gunshot to the right thigh 9 April 1917 on the first day of the Battle of Arras. Evacuated to hospital in England 28 April 1917 and then to the Ulster Volunteer Force Hospital, Belfast. To France 9 September 1917 and joined the 7th/8th (Service) Battalion, 'B' Company. To hospital with trench fever 21 December 1917 and evacuated to hospital in England. Joined the 3rd (Reserve) Battalion 6 July 1918.] To France 11 August 1918 and joined the 9th (North Irish Horse) Battalion 29 August 1918. **Killed in action** during the attack at Vijfwegen on 30 September 1918, aged 20.

DOAK Private John 14133. Enlisted September 1914. To France with 36th (Ulster) Division in October 1915. 'C' Company. To hospital mid-1916, he was discharged and joined the Base Depot in June 1916. Did not take part in the attack at Hamel on 1 July 1916. [Transferred to the Army Service Corps (renumbered M/331536).] Discharged as no longer physically fit for war service due to sickness 9 May 1918. Silver War Badge, number 363188. 1914-15 Star.

DOBBIN Lance Corporal James 42457. Born in 1900. [Enlisted 19 June 1916, aged 16, into The Royal Inniskilling Fusiliers (29436) and joined the 4th (Extra Reserve) Battalion. Posted to the 2nd Battalion, The Royal Inniskilling Fusiliers in France 16 May 1917 and then to the 1st Battalion, The Royal Inniskilling Fusiliers 9 June 1917. Evacuated to hospital in England October 1917.] At the Infantry Base Depot posted to the 2nd Battalion, The Royal Irish Rifles (renumbered 22730) but was transferred to Princess Victoria's (Royal Irish Fusiliers) 14 September 1918 (renumbered 42457) and joined the 9th (North Irish Horse) Battalion 22 September 1918. Lance Corporal 19 October 1918. Transferred to the Class Z Reserve 30 March 1919.

DOBSON Private Edmund 42226. [Enlisted into the Army Service Corps (T/259849).] Transferred to Princess Victoria's (Royal Irish Fusiliers) 8 May 1918 (renumbered 42226) and joined the 9th (North Irish Horse) Battalion.

DOBSON Private Oswald 40060 & 7042127. From Yorkshire. [Enlisted 12 April 1915 into the 12th (Service) Battalion, The Prince of Wales's Own (West Yorkshire Regiment) (19379). To France 12 October 1915. **Wounded** by a gunshot to the back and evacuated to hospital in England 21 May 1916.] To France 29 November 1916. Transferred to Princess Victoria's (Royal Irish Fusiliers) 30 November 1916 (renumbered 40060) and joined the 9th (Service) Battalion 12 December 1916. **Wounded** by a gunshot to the right forearm in the period 14/15 August 1917 immediately prior to the Battle of Langemarck and evacuated to hospital in England 22 August 1917. To France 14

March 1918 and rejoined the 9th (North Irish Horse) Battalion. **Wounded** by a gunshot to the right forearm 22 May 1918. 1914-15 Star. Re-enlisted 6 March 1919 for Regular Army service with Princess Victoria's (Royal Irish Fusiliers) (renumbered 7042127). Discharged 1 November 1924.

DODDS Private James 14148. Enlisted September 1914. Discharged as no longer physically fit for war service due to sickness 28 June 1915. Silver War Badge was not awarded (his name appears on List B1516).

DODDS Private William 14149. Enlisted September 1914. To France with 36th (Ulster) Division in October 1915. Transferred to the Class Z Reserve 11 March 1919. 1914-15 Star.

DONAGHY Private Wilson 41489. Born in 1892 at Shankill, Belfast. Worked for the Belfast Evening Telegraph. [Enlisted in September 1914 into the North Irish Horse (1181). To France 19 December 1914. Served with 2nd North Irish Horse, X Corps Cavalry Regiment.] Joined the renamed 9th (North Irish Horse) Battalion from 36 Infantry Base Depot and transferred to Princess Victoria's (Royal Irish Fusiliers) in September/October 1917 (renumbered 41489). Transferred to the Class Z Reserve 13 April 1919. 1914-15 Star.

DONALD Private Gordon 17659. Enlisted into the 9th (Service) Battalion in December 1914/January 1915. To France with 36th (Ulster) Division in October 1915. Transferred to the Class Z Reserve 15 March 1919. 1914-15 Star.

DONALD Private James 14128. From Portadown, County Armagh. 4th (Portadown) Battalion, Armagh Regiment, Ulster Volunteer Force. Enlisted September 1914. To France with 36th (Ulster) Division in October 1915. **Captured** in 1918. Transferred to the Class Z Reserve 23 April 1919. 1914-15 Star.

DONALD Private James 14138. Born in 1895. From Glenanne, County Armagh. A weaver. 1st (Armagh) Battalion, Armagh Regiment, Ulster Volunteer Force. Enlisted September 1914. To France with 36th (Ulster) Division in October 1915. 'A' Company. **Wounded** at the Battle of Langemarck 16 August 1917. Rejoined the 9th (Service) Battalion 27 August 1917. Absent off leave 3 March 1918 (**deserted**). Posted (in state of absence) to the Details Battalion 21 April 1919 and then held strength as a supernumerary at the Depot. 1914-15 Star.

DONALD Private Thomas 14150. Born in 1891 at Armagh, County Armagh. Enlisted September 1914. To France with 36th (Ulster) Division in October 1915. 'A' Company. **Wounded** by a gunshot to the back during the attack at Hamel 1 July 1916. To France 23 March 1917 and rejoined the 9th (Service) Battalion 20 April 1917. 'B' Company. **Wounded** by a gunshot to the left hip during a work party near Wieltje 4 August 1917. Evacuated to hospital in England 8 August 1917 and joined the 10th (Reserve) Battalion 21 October 1917. [To France 18 January 1918 and posted to the 1st Battalion. **Captured** in the period 21-28 March 1918 during the retreat from St Quentin. Repatriated via the prisoners of war reception camp at Ripon 12 January 1919.] Transferred to the Class Z Reserve 15 April 1919. 1914-15 Star.

DONALDSON Private David 14143. Born in 1895 at Portadown, County Armagh. A weaver. Enlisted September 1914. 'C' Company. Sentenced to forfeit three days pay and confined to barracks for seven days for wilfully absenting himself from parade and not complying with an order 25 February 1915. Sentenced to be confined to barracks for seven days for not complying with an order 15 March 1915. Posted to the 10th (Reserve) Battalion 9 September 1915. To France 2 December 1916 and joined the 9th (Service) Battalion. Evacuated to hospital in England 27 February 1917. Joined the 10th (Reserve) Battalion 26 April 1917. Between May and December 1917 charged on three occasions with being absent and once with not complying with an order forfeiting a total of twenty-two days pay. [Transferred to the Labour Corps (renumbered 545500) 6 April 1918. Posted to 375th Home Service Labour Company 15 January 1919.] Transferred to the Class Z Reserve 12 April 1919.

DONALDSON Private Joseph 10707 & 7040376. Born in 1892 at Seagoe, County Armagh. A weaver. [Enlisted into Princess Victoria's (Royal Irish Fusiliers) as a regular soldier 17 July 1911, aged 18. To France with the 1st Battalion 22 August 1914.] Posted to the 9th (North Irish Horse) Battalion. 1914 Star and clasp. Continued to serve with Princess Victoria's (Royal Irish Fusiliers) (renumbered 7040376). Discharged 7 January 1931. Enlisted into the Corps of Royal Engineers. Discharged 16 July 1932.

DONALDSON Private William 14137. Born in 1891 at Lurgan, County Armagh. A shoemaker.

Enlisted September 1914. To France with 36th (Ulster) Division in October 1915. 'C' Company. **Wounded** during the attack at Hamel 1 July 1916. **Wounded** at the Battle of Langemarck 16 August 1917. [Transferred to the Army Ordnance Corps (renumbered 040062).] 1914-15 Star.

DONALDSON Private William James 14134. From Portadown, County Armagh. 4th (Portadown) Battalion, Armagh Regiment, Ulster Volunteer Force. A weaver. Enlisted September 1914. 'B' Company. Discharged as not being likely to become an efficient soldier in that he was considered medically unfit for service due to a varicocele 15 December 1914.

DONNELL Private William 18091. From Bessbrook, County Armagh. Enlisted into the 9th (Service) Battalion in February 1915. To France with 36th (Ulster) Division in October 1915. 'A' Company. Listed as **wounded** at the Battle of Langemarck 16 August 1917 and later declared **killed in action** on that date. 1914-15 Star.

DONNERY Corporal Franciscus 18976. Born 18 December 1891 at Liverpool. [Enlisted into the Dragoons of the Line (6028). Transferred to Princess Victoria's (Royal Irish Fusiliers) in April 1915 (renumbered 18976). To France 28 June 1915 and posted to the 1st Battalion.] Posted to the 9th (Service) Battalion. 'A' Company. **Killed in action** at the Battle of Langemarck 16 August 1917, aged 25.

DONOVAN Private Edward 45022. [Enlisted in November/December 1916 and served with the 7th/8th (Service) Battalion in 49th Brigade, 16th (Irish) Division.] Joined the 9th (North Irish Horse) Battalion when the 7th/8th (Service) Battalion was disbanded in February 1918. 'D' Company. Believed **wounded** in the period 21-28 March 1918 during the retreat from St Quentin. [Transferred to the Army Ordnance Corps (renumbered 13064).]

DORRIAN Private Hugh 8065. Born in 1884 in the Falls area, Belfast. [Enlisted into Princess Victoria's (Royal Irish Fusiliers) in 1904. To France with the 1st Battalion 22 August 1914.] Posted to the 9th (Service) Battalion. 'A' Company. **Killed in action** at the Battle of Langemarck 16 August 1917.

DOUCH Private Joseph Ernest 50046. Born in 1899 at Hastings, Sussex. [Transferred to Princess Victoria's (Royal Irish Fusiliers) in May 1918 (renumbered 50046) with a draft of men from English regiments and joined the 1st Battalion.] Posted to the 9th (North Irish Horse) Battalion in August 1918. Died at Essex in 1948, aged 48.

DOUGAN Private Thomas 22764. Born in 1899 at Dundalk, County Louth. A groom. Enlisted 8 November 1915, aged 16, and joined the 4th (Extra Reserve) Battalion. To France 5 July 1916 and joined the 9th (Service) Battalion. **Wounded** by shrapnel in the groin that severed his urethra. Evacuated to hospital in England September 1916. [To France 20 January 1917 and joined the 7th/8th (Service) Battalion in 49th Brigade, 16th (Irish) Division. Evacuated to hospital in England 18 July 1917. Discharged as no longer physically fit for war service 26 September 1917 due to epilepsy. Re-enlisted into the Army Service Corps Remounts (renumbered 442028) 28 September 1918. Discharged as no longer physically fit for war service 12 February 1919 due to epilepsy.] Silver War Badge, number 261225.

DOUGHERTY Private James 17148. From Belfast. Enlisted into the 9th (Service) Battalion in October 1914. To France with 36th (Ulster) Division in October 1915. **Wounded** during the attack at Hamel 1 July 1916. [Transferred to the Army Service Corps (renumbered M/354536).] Transferred to the Class Z Reserve. 1914-15 Star.

DOWDS Private James 41551. [Enlisted into the Service Squadron, 6th (Inniskilling) Dragoons (UD/81). Served with 2nd North Irish Horse, X Corps Cavalry Regiment.] Joined the renamed 9th (North Irish Horse) Battalion from 36 Infantry Base Depot and transferred to Princess Victoria's (Royal Irish Fusiliers) in September/October 1917 (renumbered 41551). 'D' Company. **Captured** in the period 21-28 March 1918 during the retreat from St Quentin. Transferred to the Class Z Reserve 23 May 1919. 1914-15 Star.

DOWNES Private Percy 42227. [Enlisted into the Army Service Corps (T4/250672). To France 16 April 1915.] Transferred to Princess Victoria's (Royal Irish Fusiliers) 8 May 1918 (renumbered 42227) and joined the 9th (North Irish Horse) Battalion. Transferred to the Class Z Reserve 11 February 1919. 1914-15 Star.

DOWNEY Private Henry A 41113. Born in 1894 at Lisbellaw, County Fermanagh. [Enlisted into

'A' Squadron, North Irish Horse (724). To France 17 August 1914 as GHQ Troops. Served with 2nd North Irish Horse, X Corps Cavalry Regiment.] Transferred to Princess Victoria's (Royal Irish Fusiliers) and joined the 9th (North Irish Horse) Battalion 9 January 1917 (renumbered 41113). [Transferred to the Army Service Corps (renumbered M/40641).] 1914 Star. Joined the Royal Irish Constabulary in 1920.

DOWNEY Private Victor George Wilson 41181. Born in 1884 at Belfast. [Enlisted in December 1914 into the North Irish Horse (1354). To France with 'F' Squadron in 33rd Division 17 November 1915.] Joined the renamed 9th (North Irish Horse) Battalion from 36 Infantry Base Depot and transferred to Princess Victoria's (Royal Irish Fusiliers) in September/October 1917 (renumbered 41181). Transferred to the Class Z Reserve 11 February 1919. 1914-15 Star.

DOWNEY Private William 14126. Born at Portadown, County Armagh. An apprentice. Enlisted in September 1914, aged 16. Discharged having made a mis-statement as to age on enlistment; soldier under 17 years of age at date of application for discharge 19 October 1914.

DOWNEY Private Woolsey 18049. From Portadown, County Armagh. Enlisted into the 9th (Service) Battalion in February 1915, aged 17. To France with 36th (Ulster) Division in October 1915. 'C' Company. **Wounded** during the attack at Hamel 1 July 1916. Transferred to the Class Z Reserve 11 March 1919. 1914-15 Star.

DOYLE Corporal Edward 18643. Enlisted in April 1915 and joined the 7th (Service) or 8th (Service) Battalions in 49th Brigade, 16th (Irish) Division.] Joined the 9th (North Irish Horse) Battalion when the 7th/8th (Service) Battalion was disbanded in February 1918. 'D' Company. **Missing** in the period 21-28 March 1918 during the retreat from St Quentin believed **captured**. Re-enlisted in 1919 for Regular Army service with The Connaught Rangers (renumbered 40098 Lance Corporal) and served with the 1st Battalion.

DOYLE Private James 28998. [Enlisted in November 1917 and posted to the 1st Battalion.] Posted to the 9th (North Irish Horse) Battalion.

DRAFFIN Private Samuel 24947. Born in 1895 at Kirkestown, County Tyrone. [A farmer, he enlisted at Hull into the Royal Field Artillery (128029). Joined Number 1 Depot Royal Field Artillery, Newcastle-upon-Tyne. Served with 35th Reserve Battery, Royal Field Artillery.] Transferred to Princess Victoria's (Royal Irish Fusiliers) 8 November 1916 (renumbered 24947) and joined the 10th (Reserve) Battalion. To France 3 March 1917 and joined the 9th (Service) Battalion 28 March 1917. 'A' Company. **Killed in action** at the Battle of Langemarck 16 August 1917.

DRURY Private George 20240. Born at Killygany, County Wexford. From Cootehill, County Cavan. Enlisted into the 9th (Service) Battalion in June 1915. To France with 36th (Ulster) Division in October 1915. 'C' Company. Lewis gunner. **Killed in action** during the attack at Hamel 1 July 1916, aged 22. 1914-15 Star. Brother of Private James William Drury.

DRURY Private James William 20239. A postman from Cootehill, County Cavan. Enlisted into the 9th (Service) Battalion 23 June 1915. To France with 36th (Ulster) Division in October 1915. 'C' Company. Replaced 14213 Private W H Guy on a bombing team for the attack at Hamel 1 July 1916. **Wounded** during the attack at Hamel 1 July 1916. **Wounded** at the Battle of Langemarck 16 August 1917. [Posted to the 2nd Garrison Battalion in Salonika.] Discharged as no longer physically fit for war service due to wounds 23 May 1919. Silver War Badge, number B243072. Brother of Private George Drury.

DUFF Private Thomas Edward 20332. Born in 1876 at Gateshead, County Durham. A metal cleaner in a foundry. [Enlisted into The Royal Inniskilling Fusiliers (20282).] Transferred to Princess Victoria's (Royal Irish Fusiliers) on 30 June 1915 (renumbered 20332) and joined the 9th (Service) Battalion. To France with 36th (Ulster) Division in October 1915. 'B' Company. **Missing** at the Battle of Langemarck 16 August 1917 and later declared **killed in action** on that date. 1914-15 Star.

DUFF Private William J 14139. Enlisted September 1914. To France with 36th (Ulster) Division in October 1915. [Transferred to The Northumberland Fusiliers (renumbered 99552).] 1914-15 Star.

DUFFY Private Francis 18393. From Castleblayney, County Monaghan. [Enlisted in March 1915 into the 8th (Service) Battalion in 49th Brigade, 16th (Irish) Division.] Joined the 9th (North Irish Horse) Battalion when the 7th/8th (Service) Battalion was disbanded in February 1918. **Missing** in the period 21-28 March 1918 during the retreat from St Quentin and later declared **killed in action** 29 March 1918.

DUFFY Lance Corporal James 23879. Born at Darkley, County Armagh. From Motherwell, Scotland. A foundry labourer. Enlisted 11 December 1915 and joined the 10th (Reserve) Battalion. Lance Corporal 28 February 1916. To France 30 June 1916 and joined the 9th (Service) Battalion. 'D' Company. **Wounded** by gunshots to the head and back at the Battle of Langemarck 16 August 1917 and evacuated to hospital in England. Treated at Greylingwell War Hospital, Chichester. Rejoined the 10th (Reserve) Battalion 28 November 1917. To hospital in Armagh sick (eczema) 1-21 January 1918. To France 15 March 1918 and rejoined the 9th (North Irish Horse) Battalion. **Captured** in the period 21-28 March 1918 during the retreat from St Quentin. When repatriated to Ireland, he was suffering from eczema of the face and head. Discharged as no longer physically fit for war service due to sickness 24 January 1919. Silver War Badge, number B78593.

DUFFY Private James 20692 & 27737. Enlisted in July 1915 (20692). Joined the 6th (Service) Battalion in the Mediterranean Expeditionary Force at Salonika 3 December 1915. Evacuated to hospital in England sick or wounded. Transferred to The Royal Irish Regiment 27 January 1917. Transferred back to Princess Victoria's (Royal Irish Fusiliers) in June 1917 (renumbered 27737) and joined the 9th (Service) Battalion. **Deserted**, medals forfeit.

DUFFY Lance Corporal William 14140. From Lurgan, County Armagh. Enlisted September 1914. To France with 36th (Ulster) Division in October 1915. 'C' Company. **Wounded** during the attack at Hamel 1 July 1916. Discharged as no longer physically fit for war service due to wounds 10 April 1918. Silver War Badge, number 377961. 1914-15 Star.

DUGDALE Private William 42518. [Enlisted April/May 1918 into The Royal Irish Rifles (D/22623).] Transferred at the Base Depot to Princess Victoria's (Royal Irish Fusiliers) 14 September 1918 (renumbered 42518) and joined the 9th (North Irish Horse) Battalion 22 September 1918. [Transferred to the Corps of Royal Engineers (renumbered WR/210090).]

DUNCAN Private John 17760. From Glasgow. [Enlisted 12 January 1915. To France 25 May 1915.] Posted to the 9th (Service) Battalion. 'A' Company. **Wounded** and **captured** during the Battle of Langemarck 16 August 1917. Discharged as no longer physically fit for war service due to wounds 2 April 1919. Silver War Badge, number B170672. 1914-15 Star.

DUNDAS Private Johnston David 16101. From Fartagh, County Cavan. Enlisted into the 9th (Service) Battalion 7 October 1914. To France with 36th (Ulster) Division in October 1915. Discharged as no longer physically fit for war service due to sickness 5 March 1917. Silver War Badge, number 34598. 1914-15 Star.

DUNDAS Private William Henry 41399. From Belleek, County Fermanagh. [Enlisted 2 October 1911 into the North Irish Horse (620). To France 20 August 1914 with 'C' Squadron as 5th Division Cavalry and then as GHQ Troops. To hospital in February 1916 with scabies and bronchitis. To hospital November 1916 influenza. Served with 2nd North Irish Horse, X Corps Cavalry Regiment.] Joined the renamed 9th (North Irish Horse) Battalion from 36 Infantry Base Depot and transferred to Princess Victoria's (Royal Irish Fusiliers) in September/October 1917 (renumbered 41399). [Posted to the 1st Battalion 8 January 1918. 'C' Company. To hospital sick March 1918. Rejoined the 1st Battalion 25 May 1918. **Killed in action** during the attack at Vijfwegen 1 October 1918, aged 30, while serving with the 1st Battalion.] 1914 Star.

DUNLAVY Private Edward 20346. Enlisted 12 May 1915 and joined the 9th (Service) Battalion with the draft of men from The Royal Inniskilling Fusiliers who transferred to Princess Victoria's (Royal Irish Fusiliers) on 30 June 1915. To France with 36th (Ulster) Division in October 1915. **Wounded**. Discharged as no longer physically fit for war service due to wounds 2 January 1918. Silver War Badge, number 298032. 1914-15 Star.

DUNLOP Private David 41423. [Enlisted into 'A' Squadron, North Irish Horse (766). To France 17 August 1914 as GHQ Troops. Served with 2nd North Irish Horse, X Corps Cavalry Regiment.] Joined the renamed 9th (North Irish Horse) Battalion from 36 Infantry Base Depot and transferred to Princess Victoria's (Royal Irish Fusiliers) in September/October 1917 (renumbered 41423). [Transferred to The Royal Inniskilling Fusiliers (renumbered 32790).] 1914 Star.

DUNLOP Private Robert 20310. Enlisted in May/June 1915 and joined the 9th (Service) Battalion with the draft of men from The Royal Inniskilling Fusiliers who transferred to Princess Victoria's

(Royal Irish Fusiliers) on 30 June 1915. To France with 36th (Ulster) Division in October 1915. **Wounded**. [Posted to the 2nd Garrison Battalion in Salonika.] Transferred to the Class Z Reserve 11 March 1919. 1914-15 Star.

DUNN Private Albert 26101. Enlisted in January 1917. Posted to the 9th (Service) Battalion. 'A' Company. **Missing** in the period 21-28 March 1918 during the retreat from St Quentin believed **captured**.

DUNN Lance Corporal Frederick 40113. [Enlisted in December 1916 and served with the 1st Battalion.] Posted to the 9th (North Irish Horse) Battalion. 'A' Company. **Wounded** during the retreat from St Quentin 21-28 March 1918. Discharged as no longer physically fit for war service due to wounds 17 October 1918. Silver War Badge, number B34301.

DUNN Private John 41077. Born at London. Lived at Llandebie, Carmarthenshire. [Enlisted into the Dragoons of the Line (11390). Joined 6th (Inniskilling) Dragoons (renumbered 4390). Served with 2nd North Irish Horse, X Corps Cavalry Regiment.] Joined the renamed 9th (North Irish Horse) Battalion from 36 Infantry Base Depot and transferred to Princess Victoria's (Royal Irish Fusiliers) in September/October 1917 (renumbered 41077). **Killed in action** 26 October 1917 at Havrincourt, aged 36.

DUNN Private John 42545. [Enlisted 29 December 1914 into 14th (Service) Battalion, The Royal Irish Rifles (Young Citizens) (2737). To France with 36th (Ulster) Division 3 October 1915.] Transferred at the Base Depot to Princess Victoria's (Royal Irish Fusiliers) 14 September 1918 (renumbered 42545) and joined the 9th (North Irish Horse) Battalion 22 September 1918. **Wounded**. Discharged as no longer physically fit for war service due to wounds 11 January 1919. Silver War Badge, number B77849. 1914-15 Star.

DUNNE Lance Corporal James 9210. From Dublin. [Enlisted into Princess Victoria's (Royal Irish Fusiliers) as a regular soldier in June 1906. To France with the 1st Battalion 22 August 1914. Posted to the 7th/8th (Service) Battalion in 49th Brigade, 16th (Irish) Division.] Joined the 9th (North Irish Horse) Battalion when the 7th/8th (Service) Battalion was disbanded in February 1918. **Killed in action** 14 March 1918 near St Quentin.

DUNNE Private Patrick 15950. [Enlisted in September 1914 into the 8th (Service) Battalion in 49th Brigade, 16th (Irish) Division.] Joined the 9th (North Irish Horse) Battalion when the 7th/8th (Service) Battalion was disbanded in February 1918.

DUNSEITH Corporal Albert Victor Spence (Bertie) 41364. Born on 31 October 1898 at Belfast. Educated at the Royal Belfast Academical Institution. [Enlisted in April 1916 into the North Irish Horse (2137), aged 17. Served with 2nd North Irish Horse, X Corps Cavalry Regiment.] Joined the renamed 9th (North Irish Horse) Battalion from 36 Infantry Base Depot and transferred to Princess Victoria's (Royal Irish Fusiliers) in September/October 1917 (renumbered 41364). Served as a signaller in 'B' Company. Transferred to the Class Z Reserve in 1919. He travelled to Canada on 13 July 1922 and decided to remain there. He worked as a travelling salesman and lived in Ontario, where he married in 1923. He divorced in 1934, remarried and then returned to England with his family on 13 September 1937. He lived at Swiss Cottage, London. He died of a cerebral haemorrhage on 10 September 1939, aged 40. Buried in Carnmoney Cemetery, Section U, Grave 183.

DUNWOODY Corporal John Myles 14151. Commissioned into The Royal Dublin Fusiliers - see Appendix 5.

DWYER Private Timothy 42432. [Enlisted into The Royal Irish Rifles (11249). Served with the 2nd Battalion, The Royal Irish Rifles.] Transferred at the Base Depot to Princess Victoria's (Royal Irish Fusiliers) 14 September 1918 (renumbered 42432) and joined the 9th (North Irish Horse) Battalion 22 September 1918.

DYAS Private Walter Ernest 42225. Born 30 April 1899 at Stourbridge, Worcestershire. [Enlisted into the Army Service Corps (327406).] Transferred to Princess Victoria's (Royal Irish Fusiliers) 8 May 1918 (renumbered 42225) and joined the 9th (North Irish Horse) Battalion. [Transferred to 5th (Service) Battalion, The Royal Irish Regiment (Pioneers) in the Light Division in the British Army of the Rhine in March/June 1919 (renumbered 41280).] Died at Sandwell, West Midlands in 1980, aged 81.

DYE Private William J 45760. [Enlisted into The London Regiment (684238). Posted to 1/22nd (County of London) Battalion, The London Regiment (The Queen's).] To France and joined 36 Infantry Base Depot 29 March 1918. Transferred to Princess Victoria's (Royal Irish Fusiliers) 2 April 1918 (renumbered 45760) and joined the 9th (North Irish Horse) Battalion 4 April 1918. [Transferred to 5th (Service) Battalion, The Royal Irish Regiment (Pioneers) in the Light Division in the British Army of the Rhine in March/June 1919 (renumbered 41281).]

DYER Private Henry Edward 43325. Enlisted 19 July 1916. Joined the 9th (Service) Battalion, Princess Victoria's (Royal Irish Fusiliers) with the draft of men from The London Regiment in November 1916. 'A' Company. **Missing** in the period 21-28 March 1918 during the retreat from St Quentin believed **captured** and **wounded**. Discharged as no longer physically fit for war service due to wounds 5 July 1919. Silver War Badge, number B274250.

DYER Private T 43311. From Leeds. Joined the 9th (Service) Battalion, Princess Victoria's (Royal Irish Fusiliers) with the draft of men from The London Regiment in November 1916. 'D' Company. **Wounded** at the Battle of Langemarck 16 August 1917.

DYNES MBE Captain Ralph Alfred, formerly Private 14142. Born 5 November 1897 at Bleary, County Armagh. Enlisted September 1914. To France with 36th (Ulster) Division in October 1915. Transferred to the Class Z Reserve 1 March 1919. 1914-15 Star. Served with the Ulster Special Constabulary Class 'A' in the 31st Platoon at Clogher, County Tyrone. Emigrated to Montreal, Canada in March 1928. Enlisted into The Black Watch (Royal Highland Regiment) of Canada (numbered D81001). Became Regimental Sergeant Major. **MBE (Military)** for his service during the Second World War. Became the first leader of the Boys Pipes and Drums of the Black Watch. Proposed the establishment of Cadet Corps 2497, was commissioned and appointed Chief Instructor in 1953. He returned to Great Britain on 24 September 1956. Died 21 December 1967, aged 70, and is buried at St Matthias Parish Church, Knocknamuckley, County Down.

EADE Private George Charles 25169. [Enlisted in May 1916 and joined the 7th/8th (Service) Battalion in 49th Brigade, 16th (Irish) Division.] Joined the 9th (North Irish Horse) Battalion when the 7th/8th (Service) Battalion was disbanded in February 1918. 'A' Company. **Missing** in the period 21-28 March 1918 during the retreat from St Quentin believed **captured**.

EAMES Private Sidney James Knight 45781. Born in 1882 at Midhurst, Sussex. A farm manager. [Enlisted 26 April 1916 and joined the Royal Flying Corps (27158). To France 20 November 1916. Second Class Air Mechanic. Transferred for infantry service and posted to 112th Training Reserve Battalion 10 June 1917 for service with 22nd (County of London) Battalion, The London Regiment (The Queen's) (renumbered 61552). Posted to 1/22nd (County of London) Battalion, The London Regiment (The Queen's).] To France and joined 36 Infantry Base Depot 29 March 1918. Transferred to Princess Victoria's (Royal Irish Fusiliers) 2 April 1918 (renumbered 45781) and joined the 9th (North Irish Horse) Battalion 4 April 1918. **Wounded** by a gunshot to the left shoulder and face late in the period 9-18 April 1918 in the actions between Wulverghem and Kemmel and evacuated to hospital in England. Discharged as no longer physically fit for war service due to wounds 13 November 1918. Silver War Badge, number B112562. He returned to employment as a farm manager. Died in Chichester, Sussex in 1961, aged 79. His son, Flight Lieutenant Richard Knight Eames Royal Air Force Volunteer Reserve, died on 12 December 1944. He was flying a Lancaster of 1662 Heavy Conversion Unit conducting practice circuits when he crashed, killing five crewmembers. Flight Lieutenant R K Eames is buried at Apuldram (St Mary the Virgin) Churchyard, Chichester, Sussex.

EARL Private John Cecil 40150. [Enlisted in December 1916 and joined the 7th/8th (Service) Battalion in 49th Brigade, 16th (Irish) Division.] Joined the 9th (North Irish Horse) Battalion when the 7th/8th (Service) Battalion was disbanded in February 1918. 'A' Company. **Missing** in the period 21-28 March 1918 during the retreat from St Quentin believed **captured**.

EARLE Lance Corporal Leslie Marriott 43434. Born on 16 November 1894 at Lewisham, London. [Enlisted into The London Regiment (2250). To France 15 March 1915 and posted to the 1/24th (County of London) Battalion, The London Regiment (The Queen's).] To France and joined 36 Infantry Base Depot 29 March 1918. Transferred to Princess Victoria's (Royal Irish Fusiliers) 2 April 1918 (renumbered 43434) and joined the 9th (North Irish Horse) Battalion 4 April 1918. Discharged (disembodied) 16 March 1919. 1914-15 Star. He returned to education and studied at the School of Building Brixton, London and qualified as an architect. He emigrated to South Africa in 1922 and became a prominent architect in Capetown. He died there on 26 February 1971, aged 76.

ECCLES Private Thomas Edward 42231. [Enlisted 25 November 1915 into the Army Service Corps (T4/159582). Served with 223rd Company in 31st Division.] Transferred to Princess Victoria's (Royal Irish Fusiliers) 8 May 1918 (renumbered 42231) and joined the 9th (North Irish Horse) Battalion. **Wounded**. Discharged as no longer physically fit for war service due to wounds 7 October 1919. Silver War Badge, number B321656.

EDEN MM* Sergeant Robert Henry 43346. Born in 1898 at Fulham, London. [Enlisted into The London Regiment.] Attached to the 9th (Service) Battalion, Princess Victoria's (Royal Irish Fusiliers) 26 November 1916. 'C' Company. Discharged from the Territorial Force, re-enlisted and transferred to Princess Victoria's (Royal Irish Fusiliers) in March/April 1917 (renumbered 43346). **Wounded** (Private) at the Battle of Langemarck 16 August 1917. **MM** (Lance Corporal) - Wulverghem 4 September 1918. **MM Bar** (Sergeant) – Vijfwegen/Hill 41 between 30 September and 14 October 1918. [Transferred to the Royal Air Force (renumbered 351724).] Died in Fulham, London in 1963, aged 64.

EDEN Private Wilfred J 42229. [Enlisted into the Army Service Corps (T4/088602).] Transferred to Princess Victoria's (Royal Irish Fusiliers) 8 May 1918 (renumbered 42229) and joined the 9th (North Irish Horse) Battalion. [Transferred to 5th (Service) Battalion, The Royal Irish Regiment (Pioneers) in the Light Division in the British Army of the Rhine in March/June 1919 (renumbered 41282).]

EDEN Private William 43335. Born in 1896 at South Hackney, London. [Enlisted 20 July 1916 into The London Regiment (6779). Posted to the 1/7th (City of London) Battalion, The London Regiment.] Attached to the 9th (Service) Battalion, Princess Victoria's (Royal Irish Fusiliers) 26 November 1916. 'A' Company. Discharged from the Territorial Force, re-enlisted and transferred to Princess Victoria's (Royal Irish Fusiliers) in March/April 1917 (renumbered 43335). **Killed in action** at the Battle of Langemarck 16 August 1917, aged 20.

EDGAR Private James 42497. [Served with the 1st Battalion, The Royal Irish Rifles (827).] Transferred at the Base Depot to Princess Victoria's (Royal Irish Fusiliers) 14 September 1918 (renumbered 42497) and joined the 9th (North Irish Horse) Battalion 22 September 1918.

EDGAR Private Leslie Stewart 19731. From Portadown, County Armagh. Worked in his father's hardware shop. Enlisted into the 9th (Service) Battalion in April 1915. To France with 36th (Ulster) Division in October 1915. [Transferred to the Corps of Royal Engineers (renumbered 207334).] Transferred to the Class Z Reserve 20 April 1919. 1914-15 Star.

EDGAR Private Matthew 41431. Born in 1895. From Belfast. A clerk. [Enlisted 2 June 1915 into the North Irish Horse (1654). To France 22 February 1916. Served with 2nd North Irish Horse, X Corps Cavalry Regiment.] Joined the renamed 9th (North Irish Horse) Battalion from 36 Infantry Base Depot and transferred to Princess Victoria's (Royal Irish Fusiliers) in September/October 1917 (renumbered 41431). 'C' Company. **Captured** at Erches on 27 March 1918 during the retreat from St Quentin. Held at Limburg and Giessen Prisoner of War Camps. Repatriated 9 December 1918. Transferred to the Class Z Reserve 11 March 1919.

EDGAR Private William John 17903. From Armagh, County Armagh. Enlisted into the 9th (Service) Battalion in January 1915, aged 17. To France with 36th (Ulster) Division in October 1915. 'A' Company. Tried by Field General Court Martial on 5 January 1917 charged with *'when on active service* ***deserting*** *His Majesty's service'*; found guilty of *'absenting himself without leave'* and sentenced to six months imprisonment with hard labour. **Captured** at the Battle of Langemarck 16 August 1917.

EDWARDS Private Charles Bertram 42129. [Enlisted 8 March 1916 into the Army Veterinary Corps (28195).] Transferred to Princess Victoria's (Royal Irish Fusiliers) 8 May 1918 (renumbered 42129) and joined the 9th (North Irish Horse) Battalion. **Wounded**. Discharged as no longer physically fit for war service due to wounds 14 January 1919. Silver War Badge, number B84710.

EDWARDS Corporal Charles Griffith 14153. Born 23 March 1893. From Drumcairne, County Armagh. A motor engineer. Enlisted September 1914. To France with 36th (Ulster) Division in October 1915. Lance Corporal 18 January 1915. Served with the 9th (Service) Battalion Transport.

To the field ambulance sick (bronchial catarrh) 20 January 1916. Treated at 1st General Hospital, Rouen. Rejoined the 9th (Service) Battalion 22 March 1916. To hospital with impetigo 1-5 April 1916. Corporal 2 July 1916. To the field ambulance sick (influenza) 11-15 April 1917. Transferred to the Class Z Reserve 20 March 1919. 1914-15 Star. ***Croix de Guerre* (Belgium)**. After the war he was a driver with the Ulster Transport Authority. Died 7 February 1951, aged 57. His brother, Private David Edwards, served with The Black Watch (Royal Highlanders).

EDWARDS Private George 42101. [Enlisted into the Army Veterinary Corps (15858).] Transferred to Princess Victoria's (Royal Irish Fusiliers) 8 May 1918 (renumbered 42101) and joined the 9th (North Irish Horse) Battalion.

EDWARDS Private Leslie 42228. Born in 1893. From Merthyr Tydfil, Wales. A coal miner. [Enlisted 12 July 1915 into the Army Service Corps (T4/123205) for service with 38th (Welsh) Division Train. To France 30 June 1916 and joined 11th (Northern) Division Train. Subsequently served at 10th Reserve Park and 5th Cavalry Reserve Park. To hospital sick between 7 January 1918 and 9 February 1918. Joined 5th Army Auxiliary Horse Transport Company.] Transferred to Princess Victoria's (Royal Irish Fusiliers) 8 May 1918 (renumbered 42228) and joined the 9th (North Irish Horse) Battalion. **Wounded** by a gunshot to the right wrist during the attack south of Wulverghem 5 September 1918. Treated at 22nd General Hospital and rejoined the 9th (North Irish Horse) Battalion 27 October 1918. Being a coal miner, he left the 9th (North Irish Horse) Battalion for demobilization on 12 December 1918 and left France on 17 December 1918. He was the first man of the Battalion to be demobilised. Transferred to the Class Z Reserve 19 January 1919.

EDWARDS Private Robert John 41310. [Enlisted in November 1915 into the North Irish Horse (1946). Served with 2nd North Irish Horse, X Corps Cavalry Regiment.] Joined the renamed 9th (North Irish Horse) Battalion from 36 Infantry Base Depot and transferred to Princess Victoria's (Royal Irish Fusiliers) in September/October 1917 (renumbered 41310). 'C' Company. **Missing** in the period 21-28 March 1918 during the retreat from St Quentin believed **captured**.

EDWARDS Private William Glover 41158. From Cavantillycormick, County Fermanagh. A farmer's son. [Enlisted 23 July 1915 into the Service Squadron, 6th (Inniskilling) Dragoons (UD/270). Served with 2nd North Irish Horse, X Corps Cavalry Regiment.] Joined the renamed 9th (North Irish Horse) Battalion from 36 Infantry Base Depot and transferred to Princess Victoria's (Royal Irish Fusiliers) in September/October 1917 (renumbered 41158). **Wounded**. Discharged as no longer physically fit for war service due to wounds 28 August 1918, aged 27. Silver War Badge, number 445781.

EGAN Private Albert 27695. [Enlisted 8 June 1917 and posted to the 1st Battalion.] Posted to the 9th (North Irish Horse) Battalion. 'D' Company. **Wounded** during the retreat from St Quentin 21-28 March 1918. Discharged as no longer physically fit for war service due to wounds 5 April 1919. Silver War Badge, number B207388.

EGAN Private John 16217 & 7042306. From County Waterford. A tailor. [Enlisted 22 August 1914 and joined the 7th (Service) Battalion in 49th Brigade, 16th (Irish) Division. To France 18 February 1916.] Joined the 9th (North Irish Horse) Battalion when the 7th/8th (Service) Battalion was disbanded in February 1918. 'A' Company. **Captured** in the period 21-28 March 1918 during the retreat from St Quentin. Repatriated 8 December 1918. Re-enlisted 4 March 1919 for Regular Army service with Princess Victoria's (Royal Irish Fusiliers) (renumbered 7042306). Served with the 1st Battalion in Persia and Mesopotamia in 1919/20. General Service Medal 1918-1962 with clasps 'Iraq' & 'NW Persia'. Discharged 31 March 1922.

EGAN Lance Corporal Patrick 45338. From Ardnaculla North, Ennistymon, County Clare. [Served with the 1st Battalion, The Royal Munster Fusiliers (7350) in 86th Brigade, 29th Division. Embarked for Gallipoli March 1915.] Transferred to Princess Victoria's (Royal Irish Fusiliers) (renumbered 45338) and joined the 9th (North Irish Horse) Battalion in early-1918. 1914-15 Star.

ELKIN Private Frederick Ernest 41230. [Enlisted in May 1915 into the North Irish Horse (1583). Served with 2nd North Irish Horse, X Corps Cavalry Regiment.] Joined the renamed 9th (North Irish Horse) Battalion from 36 Infantry Base Depot and transferred to Princess Victoria's (Royal Irish Fusiliers) in September/October 1917 (renumbered 41230).

ELLIOTT Private Andrew 41157. [Enlisted into the Service Squadron, 6th (Inniskilling) Dragoons (UD/240). To France with 36th (Ulster) Division in October 1915. Served with 2nd North Irish Horse,

X Corps Cavalry Regiment.] Joined the renamed 9th (North Irish Horse) Battalion from 36 Infantry Base Depot and transferred to Princess Victoria's (Royal Irish Fusiliers) in September/October 1917 (renumbered 41157). Transferred to the Class Z Reserve 5 February 1919. 1914-15 Star.

ELLIOTT Lance Corporal Henry (Harry) 14158. From Armagh, County Armagh. Worked as an attendant at Armagh asylum. Enlisted September 1914. To France with 36th (Ulster) Division in October 1915. **Wounded** during the attack at Hamel 1 July 1916 and **died of wounds** 4 July 1916, aged 22. 1914-15 Star. Brother of 14154 Private James Elliott and Private Robert Elliott.

ELLIOTT Private Herbert 14159. Born in 1893 at Portadown, County Armagh. A carpenter. Enlisted September 1914. To France with 36th (Ulster) Division in October 1915. 'B' Company. **Wounded** at the Battle of Langemarck 16 August 1917. **Captured** in the period 21-28 March 1918 during the retreat from St Quentin. Transferred to the Class Z Reserve 8 April 1919. 1914-15 Star.

ELLIOTT MM Private James 14154. From Armagh, County Armagh. Worked in a linen mill. Enlisted September 1914. To France with 36th (Ulster) Division in October 1915. **36th (Ulster) Division Certificate for Gallantry** 1 July 1916. **MM** – Battle of Langemarck 16 August 1917. [Transferred to the Labour Corps (renumbered 666570).] 1914-15 Star. Brother of Privates Harry Elliott and Robert Elliott.

ELLIOTT Private James 14161. Enlisted September 1914. To France with 36th (Ulster) Division in October 1915. **Wounded** at Hamel on 10 February 1916. Discharged as no longer physically fit for war service due to wounds 13 June 1916. Silver War Badge, number 49540. 1914-15 Star.

ELLIOTT Private James 24113. Enlisted 14 March 1916. Posted to the 9th (Service) Battalion. **Wounded**. Discharged as no longer physically fit for war service due to wounds 29 August 1918, aged 38. Silver War Badge, number 445725.

ELLIOTT Private James 41294. [Enlisted 9 December 1912 into the North Irish Horse (761). To France 20 August 1914 with 'C' Squadron as 5th Division Cavalry and then as GHQ Troops. Served with 2nd North Irish Horse, X Corps Cavalry Regiment.] Joined the renamed 9th (North Irish Horse) Battalion from 36 Infantry Base Depot and transferred to Princess Victoria's (Royal Irish Fusiliers) in September/October 1917 (renumbered 41294). 'C' Company. **Wounded** during the retreat from St Quentin 21-28 March 1918. Discharged as no longer physically fit for war service due to wounds 30 January 1919. Silver War Badge, number B107073. 1914 Star and clasp.

ELLIOTT Private James A 41514. [Enlisted in November 1911 into the North Irish Horse (636). To France 17 August 1914 with 'A' Squadron as GHQ Troops. Served with 2nd North Irish Horse, X Corps Cavalry Regiment.] Joined the renamed 9th (North Irish Horse) Battalion from 36 Infantry Base Depot and transferred to Princess Victoria's (Royal Irish Fusiliers) in September/October 1917 (renumbered 41514). [Transferred to The Royal Irish Regiment (renumbered 3198).] 1914 Star.

ELLIOTT Private John 14157. Enlisted September 1914. To France with 36th (Ulster) Division in October 1915. **Wounded** during the attack at Hamel 1 July 1916. [Transferred to the Labour Corps (renumbered 231596).] Transferred to the Class Z Reserve 8 March 1919. 1914-15 Star. Lived at Desert, County Armagh.

ELLIOTT Private John 41175. From Armagh, County Armagh. [Enlisted 22 September 1914 into the Service Squadron, 6th (Inniskilling) Dragoons (UD/82). To France with 36th (Ulster) Division in October 1915. Served with 2nd North Irish Horse, X Corps Cavalry Regiment.] Joined the renamed 9th (North Irish Horse) Battalion from 36 Infantry Base Depot and transferred to Princess Victoria's (Royal Irish Fusiliers) in September/October 1917 (renumbered 41175). **Wounded**. Discharged as no longer physically fit for war service due to wounds 11 December 1918. Silver War Badge, number B57473. 1914-15 Star.

ELLIOTT Private Robert 19733. From Armagh, County Armagh. Enlisted into the 9th (Service) Battalion 29 April 1915. To France with 36th (Ulster) Division in October 1915. **Wounded** in March/April 1918. Discharged as no longer physically fit for war service due to wounds 7 November 1918. Silver War Badge, number B38708. 1914-15 Star. Worked as a postman after the war and died 15 April 1966. Brother of Private Harry Elliott and 14154 Private James Elliott.

ELLIOTT Private Thomas 14160. Born in 1894 at Ardress, County Armagh. A farmer's son. Enlisted September 1914. To France with 36th (Ulster) Division in October 1915. 'A' Company.

Wounded during the attack at Hamel 1 July 1916. **Wounded** at the Battle of Langemarck 16 August 1917. [Transferred to the Army Veterinary Corps (renumbered 35212).] 1914-15 Star. His brother, Sapper John Elliott, served with the Corps of Royal Engineers. His brother, Gunner William Elliott, was wounded serving with the Royal Garrison Artillery.

ELLIOTT Private William Thomas 41159. From Letterbreen, County Fermanagh. [Enlisted into the Service Squadron, 6th (Inniskilling) Dragoons (UD/284). Served with 2nd North Irish Horse, X Corps Cavalry Regiment.] Joined the renamed 9th (North Irish Horse) Battalion from 36 Infantry Base Depot and transferred to Princess Victoria's (Royal Irish Fusiliers) in September/October 1917 (renumbered 41159). **Missing** in the period 11-18 April 1918 in the actions between Wulverghem and Kemmel; subsequently declared **killed in action** 19 April 1918.

ELLIS Private Henry 23354. Born in 1897 at Portadown, County Armagh. Enlisted in December 1915. Posted to the 9th (Service) Battalion. 'B' Company. **Wounded** at the Battle of Langemarck 16 August 1917. [Transferred to the Labour Corps (renumbered 575044).] His brother, Rifleman Thomas Ellis, The Royal Irish Rifles, died on 24 June 1918 while a prisoner of war at Stendal Prisoner of War Camp, Saxony, Germany.

ELLISON Sergeant Joseph 41566. Commissioned into The Royal Inniskilling Fusiliers - see Appendix 5.

ELLISON Company Quartermaster Sergeant Robert George 15255. Born in 1894 at Shankill, Belfast. A butcher. [Enlisted 21 September 1914 and joined the 7th (Service) Battalion in 49th Brigade, 16th (Irish) Division. Lance Corporal 10 November 1914. Corporal 24 November 1914. Sergeant 1 April 1915. Company Quartermaster Sergeant 4 October 1915. To France 18 February 1916. Evacuated to hospital in England 25 January 1917. Joined the 4th (Extra Reserve) Battalion 1 June 1917.] To Infantry Base Depot, France 12 March 1918 and joined the 9th (North Irish Horse) Battalion as a Company Quartermaster Sergeant. **Wounded** by a gunshot to the right side 15 April 1918 in the actions between Wulverghem and Kemmel. Evacuated to hospital in England 21 April 1918. Posted to the 3rd (Reserve) Battalion 13 July 1918. To 36 Infantry Base Depot 30 September 1918 and rejoined the 9th (North Irish Horse) Battalion 8 October 1918 as a Company Quartermaster Sergeant. Transferred to the Class Z Reserve 30 March 1919.

ELLISON Private William Holland Kennedy 49736. Born in 1898 at Comber, County Down. [Enlisted 29 August 1916, aged 18, and joined the 19th (Reserve) Battalion, The Royal Irish Rifles (671) at Newcastle, County Down.] To 36 Infantry Base Depot, France 13 April 1918. Transferred to Princess Victoria's (Royal Irish Fusiliers) (renumbered 49736) and joined the 9th (North Irish Horse) Battalion. 'C' Company. **Missing** during the attack at Vijfwegen on 30 September or 1 October 1918; recorded as **killed in action** 2 October 1918, aged 20.

EMERSON Private Henry 41103. From Foglish, Fivemiletown, County Tyrone. [Enlisted into the Service Squadron, 6th (Inniskilling) Dragoons (UD/23). To France with 36th (Ulster) Division in October 1915. Served with 2nd North Irish Horse, X Corps Cavalry Regiment.] Joined the renamed 9th (North Irish Horse) Battalion from 36 Infantry Base Depot and transferred to Princess Victoria's (Royal Irish Fusiliers) in September/October 1917 (renumbered 41103). 'A' Company. **Captured** in the period 21-28 March 1918 during the retreat from St Quentin. Badly treated in captivity, he escaped from Fresnoy-le-Grand on 15 September 1918 with Lance Corporal Bennett of 1st Battalion, The Royal Irish Rifles. Transferred to the Class Z Reserve 11 March 1919. 1914-15 Star.

ENGLISH Private William 14156. Born in 1897 at Kinnegoe, County Armagh. Enlisted September 1914. To France with 36th (Ulster) Division in October 1915. 'A' Company. Promoted to Lance Corporal. As a result of the accidental death of Private W Limbert and the wounding of Lance Corporal E W G Linzey, he was tried by Field General Court Martial on 12 June 1917 charged with: *'Neglect to the prejudice of good order and military discipline in that he, in the field, on 23 May 1917 neglected to ensure that his section obeyed the procedures for rifle discipline in the trenches, resulting the death of a soldier, and the seriously wounding of another.'* Found guilty and sentenced to twenty-eight days Field Punishment Number 2 and reduced in rank. **Wounded** at the Battle of Langemarck 16 August 1917. Discharged as no longer physically fit for war service due to wounds 18 June 1918, aged 23. Silver War Badge, number 411847. 1914-15 Star.

ENSOR Private Ernest Nash 17720. Commissioned into Princess Victoria's (Royal Irish Fusiliers) - see Appendix 5.

ERSKINE Lance Corporal Alexander 41235. From Belfast. [Enlisted on 5 October 1914 into 'E' Squadron, North Irish Horse (1284). To France with 'F' Squadron in 33rd Division 17 November 1915. Served with 2nd North Irish Horse, X Corps Cavalry Regiment.] Joined the renamed 9th (North Irish Horse) Battalion from 36 Infantry Base Depot and transferred to Princess Victoria's (Royal Irish Fusiliers) in September/October 1917 (renumbered 41235). **Wounded** at Vijfwegen/Hill 41 and **died of wounds** 10 October 1918, aged 22. 1914-15 Star.

ERVIN Private. 'A' Company. Reported by Lieutenant Godson as taking part in the fighting patrol on 14 August 1916. Name mis-spelled, probably Erwin or Irvine.

ERWIN Private Andrew 21404. Born in 1898 at Ballymena, County Antrim. From Belfast. Enlisted 25 August 1915. Posted to the 9th (Service) Battalion. **Wounded**. [Posted to the 2nd Garrison Battalion in Salonika. Discharged as no longer physically fit for war service due to sickness 14 December 1918.] Silver War Badge, number 512024.

ESCOTT Lance Corporal Henry Walker 43384. Born in 1893 at London. [Enlisted into The London Regiment (4752). Posted to the 1/9th (County of London) Battalion, The London Regiment (Queen Victoria's Rifles).] Attached to the 9th (Service) Battalion, Princess Victoria's (Royal Irish Fusiliers) 26 November 1916. 'D' Company. Discharged from the Territorial Force, re-enlisted and transferred to Princess Victoria's (Royal Irish Fusiliers) in March/April 1917 (renumbered 43384). **Missing** in the period 21-28 March 1918 during the retreat from St Quentin believed **captured**. Died in London in 1952, aged 59.

ESPIE Lance Corporal Samuel 41386. [Enlisted in August/September 1912 into North Irish Horse (730). To France 20 August 1914 with 'C' Squadron as 5th Division Cavalry and then as GHQ Troops. Served with 2nd North Irish Horse, X Corps Cavalry Regiment.] Joined the renamed 9th (North Irish Horse) Battalion from 36 Infantry Base Depot and transferred to Princess Victoria's (Royal Irish Fusiliers) in September/October 1917 (renumbered 41386). [Transferred to The Royal Inniskilling Fusiliers (renumbered 42667).] 1914 Star.

ESPIE Corporal Thomas Fletcher 14155. Commissioned into The Royal Inniskilling Fusiliers - see Appendix 5.

EVANS Private Frank 42230 & 7042176. From Barrow-in-Furness, Lancashire (now Cumbria). [Enlisted as a regular soldier into the Army Service Corps (T/33395 – Driver) 26 November 1911. To France 17 August 1914 with 3rd Division Train. **Wounded** by a gunshot to the head 6 July 1915.] Transferred to Princess Victoria's (Royal Irish Fusiliers) 8 May 1918 (renumbered 42230) and joined the 9th (North Irish Horse) Battalion. **Wounded** by a gunshot to the hand during the attack south of Wulverghem 4 September 1918 and evacuated to hospital in England 7 September 1919. 1914 Star. Transferred to the Section B Army Reserve, Princess Victoria's (Royal Irish Fusiliers) (renumbered 7042176). Discharged 25 November 1925.

EVANS Private Robert 41311. Born in 1896. [Enlisted 16 February 1912 into the North Irish Horse (673). To France 13 April 1915. Served with 2nd North Irish Horse, X Corps Cavalry Regiment.] Joined the renamed 9th (North Irish Horse) Battalion from 36 Infantry Base Depot and transferred to Princess Victoria's (Royal Irish Fusiliers) in September/October 1917 (renumbered 41311). **Wounded** by a gunshot to the left hand. Discharged as no longer physically fit for war service due to wounds 19 January 1919. Silver War Badge, number B84713. 1914-15 Star. After the war he worked for the London, Midland and Scottish Railway Company.

EVERITT Private Harry 40061. Joined the 9th (Service) Battalion, Princess Victoria's (Royal Irish Fusiliers) with the draft of men from The Prince of Wales's Own (West Yorkshire Regiment) on 12 December 1916.

EWART Private David 21762. Born in 1898 at Drumcree, Portadown, County Armagh. Enlisted 2 October 1915. Posted to the 9th (Service) Battalion. 'B' Company. **Wounded** during the retreat from St Quentin 21-28 March 1918. Discharged as no longer physically fit for war service due to wounds 10 October 1918. Silver War Badge, number B34928. Brother of Sergeant Thomas Ewart. His brother, Private Joseph Henry Ewart, enlisted into Princess Victoria's (Royal Irish Fusiliers) Special Reserve in February 1915 but was discharged as not being likely to become an efficient soldier in that he was considered medically unfit for service. His brother, Private James Hall Ewart, served with the 2nd Battalion, Princess Victoria's (Royal Irish Fusiliers) and was discharged as no longer physically fit for war service due to sickness.

EWART Sergeant Thomas 11988. Born in 1891 at Drumcree, Portadown, County Armagh. A yarn dresser. [Enlisted in September 1914 and joined the 5th (Service) Battalion in 31st Brigade, 10th (Irish) Division. Embarked with the Mediterranean Expeditionary Force July 1915.] Posted to the 9th (North Irish Horse) Battalion. Platoon Sergeant 'C' Company. Transferred to the Class Z Reserve 18 February 1919. 1914-15 Star. Brother of Private David Ewart. For other brothers see above.

EYTON Private Charles George 43359. Born in 1881 at Kensington, London. Served previously as a regular soldier with 3rd Battalion, The King's Royal Rifle Corps (8412). Discharged in March 1908 as medially unfit for further service. [Re-enlisted 21 July 1916 into The London Regiment (6790).] Attached to the 9th (Service) Battalion, Princess Victoria's (Royal Irish Fusiliers) 26 November 1916. 'C' Company. Discharged from the Territorial Force, re-enlisted and transferred to Princess Victoria's (Royal Irish Fusiliers) in March/April 1917 (renumbered 43359). **Wounded** by shellfire on 24 May 1917 near Spanbroekmolen and **died of wounds** 30 May 1917 in 108th Field Ambulance.

FARLEY Private James 40043. [Enlisted 9 September 1914 into the 11th (Service) Battalion, The Prince of Wales's Own (West Yorkshire Regiment) (14029). To France 26 August 1915 in 69th Brigade, 23rd Division.] Transferred to Princess Victoria's (Royal Irish Fusiliers) 30 November 1916 (renumbered 40043) and joined the 9th (Service) Battalion 12 December 1916. 'D' Company. **Wounded** during the retreat from St Quentin 21-28 March 1918. Discharged as no longer physically fit for war service due to wounds 16 January 1919. Silver War Badge, number B84670. 1914-15 Star.

FARLEY Private Richard William 42479. Born in 1881 at Notting Hill, London. [Enlisted 7 December 1915 and transferred to the Army Reserve. Mobilised and joined the 10th (Reserve) Battalion, The London Regiment (4848). To France for service with the 1/7th (City of London) Battalion, The London Regiment but transferred to the 15th (Service) Battalion, The Royal Irish Rifles (North Belfast) (renumbered 43260). To hospital sick 8 August 1917; treated at Endell Street Military Hospital, London. Joined the 18th (Reserve) Battalion, The Royal Irish Rifles. Joined 'A' Infantry Base Depot 18 February 1918. Rejoined the 15th (Service) Battalion, The Royal Irish Rifles (North Belfast). **Wounded** by a gunshot to the leg during the retreat from St Quentin 21-28 March 1918. Evacuated to hospital in England. Joined the 3rd (Reserve) Battalion, The Royal Irish Rifles 22 May 1918.] Joined 'A' Infantry Base Depot 22 July 1918. Transferred at the Base Depot to Princess Victoria's (Royal Irish Fusiliers) 14 September 1918 (renumbered 42479) and joined the 9th (North Irish Horse) Battalion 22 September 1918. 'B' Company. Transferred to the Class Z Reserve 6 April 1919. Died in London in 1935, aged 54.

FARQUHAR Private John Henry 24689. From Annaghmore, County Armagh. Enlisted in August 1916. Posted to the 9th (Service) Battalion. 'A' Company. **Wounded** at the Battle of Langemarck 16 August 1917.

FARQUHAR Private Samuel 19773. [Enlisted into the 5th or 6th (Service) Battalion in April 1915. Served at Gallipoli with the Mediterranean Expeditionary Force from 24 August 1915.] Posted to the 9th (Service) Battalion. 'C' Company. Believed **wounded** in the period 21-28 March 1918 during the retreat from St Quentin. [Transferred to the Labour Corps (renumbered 573119).]

FARR Private Robert 14171. From Armagh, County Armagh. Enlisted September 1914. To France with 36th (Ulster) Division in October 1915. **Wounded** during the attack at Hamel 1 July 1916. Transferred to the Class Z Reserve 20 March 1919. 1914-15 Star.

FARR Private Thomas 23790. From Armagh, County Armagh. A plasterer. Enlisted 18 January 1916 and joined the 10th (Reserve) Battalion. To France 9 April 1916. Joined the 9th (Service) Battalion 19 May 1916. **Killed in action** during the attack at Hamel 1 July 1916, aged 29.

FARRELL Private Michael 23774. [Enlisted in January 1916. Served with the 1st Battalion and 7th/8th (Service) Battalion.] Joined the 9th (North Irish Horse) Battalion when the 7th/8th (Service) Battalion was disbanded in February 1918.

FARRELL Private Patrick 11176. [Enlisted into Princess Victoria's (Royal Irish Fusiliers) as a regular soldier 23 December 1912. To France with the 1st Battalion 22 August 1914.] Joined the 9th (Service) Battalion. [Posted back to the 1st Battalion, where he was **wounded**.] Discharged as no longer physically fit for war service due to wounds 17 September 1919. Silver War Badge, number B313359. 1914 Star.

FARRELL Private Roger 20474. [Enlisted into the 8th (Service) Battalion in 49th Brigade 16th (Irish) Division in June 1915. May have served with the 1st Battalion also.] Joined the 9th (North Irish Horse) Battalion when the 7th/8th (Service) Battalion was disbanded in February 1918.

FARRELL Private William John 18261. From Keady, County Armagh. A warper in a linen factory. Enlisted into the 9th (Service) Battalion in March 1915. To France with 36th (Ulster) Division in October 1915. 'C' Company. **Killed in action** during the attack at Hamel 1 July 1916, aged 26. 1914-15 Star.

FARSON Private Alexander (Sandy) 14183. Enlisted September 1914. To France with 36th (Ulster) Division in October 1915. [Transferred to the Labour Corps (renumbered 231585).] Discharged 28 February 1919. 1914-15 Star.

FARSON Lance Sergeant David 14180. Born in 1889 at Armagh, County Armagh. Enlisted September 1914. 'B' Company. Posted to the 10th (Reserve) Battalion 23 September 1915. Corporal 22 January 1916. Acting Sergeant 25 March 1916. To 36 Infantry Base Depot 2 May 1917 and joined the 9th (Service) Battalion (Corporal). 'B' Company. **Wounded** by a gunshot on his right side at the Battle of Langemarck 16 August 1917. Treated at 1st South African General Hospital. **Wounded** by a gunshot to the chest 2 November 1917. Lance Sergeant 31 December 1917. Believed **wounded** in the period 21-28 March 1918 during the retreat from St Quentin. **Wounded** by a gunshot to the forearm 14 April 1918 in the actions between Wulverghem and Kemmel. Evacuated to hospital in England from 46th Stationary Hospital, Etaples. Posted to the 3rd (Reserve) Battalion 27 July 1918. To 'A' Infantry Base Depot 15 August 1918 and rejoined 'B' Company, 9th (North Irish Horse) Battalion. **Wounded** by a gunshot to the left hand during the attack south of Wulverghem on 4 September 1918. Evacuated to Mile End Military Hospital, London from 22nd General Hospital, Camiers and then to the Military Hospital, Armagh in October 1918. Posted to the 3rd (Reserve) Battalion 24 October 1918. Reduced in rank to Corporal for drunkenness 30 October 1918. Transferred to the Class Z Reserve 20 March 1919. Joined the Royal Ulster Constabulary in 1923.

FAUL Lance Corporal James 21735. [Enlisted 16 April 1915 and joined the 8th (Service) Battalion in 49th Brigade, 16th (Irish) Division.] Joined the 9th (North Irish Horse) Battalion when the 7th/8th (Service) Battalion was disbanded in February 1918. 'D' Company. **Wounded** during the retreat from St Quentin 21-28 March 1918. Discharged as no longer physically fit for war service due to wounds 10 October 1918. Silver War Badge, number B34286.

FAULKNER Private James 18050. Born in 1895 at Belfast. Enlisted into the 9th (Service) Battalion 10 February 1915. To France with 36th (Ulster) Division in October 1915. **Wounded** by a gunshot to the chest at Moeuvres 22/23 November 1917 and evacuated to hospital in England 5 December 1917. Treated at Perth War Hospital, Perth. Joined the 10th (Reserve) Battalion 9 February 1918. [Transferred to the Royal Defence Corps (renumbered 73193) 4 May 1918. Served with 166th Protection Company in Staffordshire.] Transferred to the Class Z Reserve 6 April 1919. 1914-15 Star.

FAULKNER Private Thomas 14187. Enlisted September 1914. No record of deployment to France with 36th (Ulster) Division in October 1915. [Transferred to The Prince of Wales's Leinster Regiment (Royal Canadians) (renumbered 40015).] Re-enlisted in 1919 for Regular Army service with The King's Own (Royal Lancaster Regiment) (3702179).

FEARON Private Thomas 14167. Born on 5 July 1894 at Tandragee, County Armagh. A farm labourer. Enlisted September 1914. Posted to the 10th (Reserve) Battalion 23 September 1915. Posted to the 1st Garrison Battalion on 7 October 1915 and served in India and Burma. Transferred to the Class Z Reserve 31 December 1919.

FEETHAM Lance Corporal William 43203. [Served in France with the 1st Battalion, The Sherwood Foresters (Nottinghamshire and Derbyshire Regiment) (6014), possibly as a mobilised reservist from 18 May 1915.] Transferred to Princess Victoria's (Royal Irish Fusiliers) 31 August 1916 (renumbered 43203) having joined the 9th (Service) Battalion on 8 August 1916. 1914-15 Star.

FEGAN MM Corporal John 21059. From Belfast. [Enlisted in November 1914 and joined the 7th or 8th (Service) Battalion in 49th Brigade, 16th (Irish) Division.] Joined the 9th (North Irish Horse) Battalion when the 7th/8th (Service) Battalion was disbanded in February 1918. **MM** – River Lys mid-October 1918.

FENLON Private James 41914. [Served as a regular soldier of Special Reservist with the Army Service Corps (T/28888 Driver). To France 23 August 1914. Served with 280 Auxiliary Horse Transport Company. Attached to 10th Field Ambulance.] Transferred to Princess Victoria's (Royal Irish Fusiliers) in late-1917 and joined the 9th (North Irish Horse) Battalion. 1914 Star.

FERGUSON Private David John 49743. Joined the 9th (North Irish Horse) Battalion, Princess Victoria's (Royal Irish Fusiliers) with the draft of men transferred from The Royal Irish Rifles in April 1918.

FERGUSON Private Edward 27534. [From Cookstown, County Tyrone. Enlisted in April 1917. Posted to the 1st Battalion.] Posted to the 9th (North Irish Horse) Battalion. **Killed in action** near Terhand 14 October 1918, aged 20.

FERGUSON Private James 14199. Born in 1896 at Armagh, County Armagh. From Ballynahonemore, County Armagh. An apprentice painter. Enlisted in September 1914, aged 16. Discharged having made a mis-statement as to age on enlistment; soldier between 17 and 18 years of age at date of application for discharge 22 October 1914.

FERGUSON Private James 18258. From Clones, County Monaghan. Enlisted into the 9th (Service) Battalion in February/March 1915. 'D' Company. **Killed in action** at the Battle of Langemarck 16 August 1917.

FERGUSON Private John 15159. Enlisted into the 9th (Service) Battalion in September 1914. [Posted to the 2nd Battalion.]

FERGUSON Private John 18607. From Tandragee, County Armagh. Enlisted into the 9th (Service) Battalion in April 1915. To France with 36th (Ulster) Division in October 1915. 'B' Company. **Missing** in the period 21-28 March 1918 during the retreat from St Quentin and later declared **killed in action** 29 March 1918. 1914-15 Star.

FERGUSON Private John Anthony 14166. Enlisted September 1914. To France with 36th (Ulster) Division in October 1915. Transferred to the Class Z Reserve 20 March 1919. 1914-15 Star.

FERGUSON MM Sergeant Robert 14188. From Lurgan, County Armagh. Enlisted September 1914. To France with 36th (Ulster) Division in October 1915. 'D' Company. **MM** – Bailleul August 1918. Acting Company Quartermaster Sergeant. 1914-15 Star.

FERGUSON MM Private Robert J 22994. From Tandragee, County Armagh. Enlisted in November 1915. Posted to the 9th (Service) Battalion. 'B' Company. **Wounded** at the Battle of Langemarck 16 August 1917. **MM** – St Quentin 21-28 March 1918.

FERGUSON Private Stephen Alexander 23726. Born in 1897 at Ballynahonemore, County Armagh. Enlisted 12 January 1916. Posted to the 9th (Service) Battalion. 'A' Company. **Wounded** at the Battle of Langemarck 16 August 1917. Discharged as no longer physically fit for war service due to wounds 17 June 1918. Silver War Badge, number 395882.

FERGUSON Private William 14197. Born in 1899 at Balleer, Tassagh, County Armagh. Enlisted September 1914. To France with 36th (Ulster) Division in October 1915. 'D' Company. **Killed in action** during the attack at Hamel 1 July 1916, aged 17. 1914-15 Star.

FERGUSON Private William 42550. [Enlisted into The Royal Irish Rifles (21887).] Transferred at the Base Depot to Princess Victoria's (Royal Irish Fusiliers) 14 September 1918 (renumbered 42550) and joined the 9th (North Irish Horse) Battalion 22 September 1918.

FERGUSON Private William Victor 41312. Born in 1896 at Lisburn, County Down. Worked as a painter for his father. [Enlisted 16 February 1915 into the North Irish Horse (1448). To France 22 September 1915. Served with 2nd North Irish Horse, X Corps Cavalry Regiment.] Joined the renamed 9th (North Irish Horse) Battalion from 36 Infantry Base Depot and transferred to Princess Victoria's (Royal Irish Fusiliers) in September/October 1917 (renumbered 41312). 'C' Company. **Wounded** during the retreat from St Quentin 21-28 March 1918. Discharged as no longer physically fit for war service due to wounds 14 August 1918, aged 23. Silver War Badge, number 435821. 1914-15 Star.

FERRIE Private James 40099. From Belfast. [Enlisted on 25 May 1916 for service with 8th (King's Royal Irish) Hussars (21960) and joined 10th Reserve Regiment of Cavalry at The Curragh.]

Transferred to Princess Victoria's (Royal Irish Fusiliers) 6 December 1916 (renumbered 40099). To France 8 December 1916 and joined the 1st Battalion. To England 24 March 1917. To 36 Infantry Base Depot 13 June 1917 and posted back to the 1st Battalion.] Posted to the 9th (Service) Battalion 10 July 1917. **Wounded** by accident in the left leg and evacuated to hospital in England. Reported as a **deserter** 9 November 1917. Rejoined 8 February 1918. Tried by District Court Martial in February 1918 charged with *'absenting himself without leave'*; found guilty and sentenced to 112 days detention. Released from detention (eighteen days remitted) 27 May 1918. Posted to the 3rd (Reserve) Battalion 7 June 1918. Discharged to the Class P Reserve 12 August 1918, aged 28. Silver War Badge, number 435813.

FERRIN Corporal John 14184. Formerly a regular soldier with the 2nd Battalion, The Connaught Rangers. Enlisted into Princess Victoria's (Royal Irish Fusiliers) September 1914. Corporal 23 September 1914. Lance Sergeant 1 November 1914. Reprimanded for not complying with an order 12 November 1914. Reduced to Corporal for disobedience of orders 3 March 1915. Severely reprimanded for neglect of duty when on canteen duty 4 June 1915. Discharged as no longer physically fit (attributed to his age and having poor feet) for military service 28 June 1915. Did not receive a Silver War Badge.

FERRIS Corporal Edward 41269. [Enlisted 12 May 1915 into the North Irish Horse (1540). Served with 2nd North Irish Horse, X Corps Cavalry Regiment.] Joined the renamed 9th (North Irish Horse) Battalion from 36 Infantry Base Depot and transferred to Princess Victoria's (Royal Irish Fusiliers) in September/October 1917 (renumbered 41269). 'C' Company. **Wounded** during the retreat from St Quentin 21-28 March 1918. Discharged as no longer physically fit for war service due to wounds 17 November 1918. Silver War Badge, number B44342.

FERRIS Private George 14174. From Tandragee, County Armagh. Member of Loyal Orange Lodge 110. 4th (Portadown) Battalion, Armagh Regiment, Ulster Volunteer Force. Enlisted September 1914. To France with 36th (Ulster) Division in October 1915. **Killed in action** during the attack at Hamel 1 July 1916, aged 18. 1914-15 Star.

FERRIS Private James Patrick 23827. Born in 1898 at Lurgan, County Armagh. A weaver. [Enlisted 26 January 1916 and joined the 4th (Extra Reserve) Battalion. To 36 Infantry Base Depot 17 December 1917 and joined the 7th/8th (Service) Battalion in 49th Brigade, 16th (Irish) Division.] Joined the 9th (North Irish Horse) Battalion when the 7th/8th (Service) Battalion was disbanded in February 1918. **Wounded** by a gunshot to the left leg during the attack south of Wulverghem 5 September 1918 and evacuated to hospital in England. Discharged as no longer physically fit for war service due to wounds 14 March 1919. Silver War Badge, number B162482.

FERRIS Private John 14162. From Tandragee, County Armagh. 4th (Portadown) Battalion, Armagh Regiment, Ulster Volunteer Force. Enlisted September 1914. To France with 36th (Ulster) Division in October 1915. **Captured** in the period 11-18 April 1918 in the actions between Wulverghem and Kemmel. Repatriated January 1919. Transferred to the Class Z Reserve 2 April 1919. 1914-15 Star.

FERRIS Private Joseph 41588. [Enlisted 23 February 1916 into the North Irish Horse (1483). Served with 2nd North Irish Horse, X Corps Cavalry Regiment.] Joined the renamed 9th (North Irish Horse) Battalion from 36 Infantry Base Depot and transferred to Princess Victoria's (Royal Irish Fusiliers) in September/October 1917 (renumbered 41588). **Wounded**. Discharged as no longer physically fit for war service due to wounds 2 November 1918. Silver War Badge, number B38734.

FERRIS Private William 14169. Born in September 1879. From Tullyhue, Portadown, County Armagh. An engine driver. Enlisted September 1914. Discharged as not being likely to become an efficient soldier in that he was considered medically unfit for service 1 October 1914.

FIELD Private William 43366. [Enlisted 8 August 1914 into The London Regiment (2054). Posted to 1/7th (City of London) Battalion, The London Regiment.] Attached to the 9th (Service) Battalion, Princess Victoria's (Royal Irish Fusiliers) 26 November 1916. Discharged from the Territorial Force, re-enlisted and transferred to Princess Victoria's (Royal Irish Fusiliers) in March/April 1917 (renumbered 43366). **Wounded**. Discharged as no longer physically fit for war service due to wounds 21 February 1919. Silver War Badge, number B154139.

FINCH Lance Corporal George Frederick Sexton 41176. [Enlisted into the 6th (Inniskilling) Dragoons (21193). Served with 2nd North Irish Horse, X Corps Cavalry Regiment.] Joined the renamed 9th (North Irish Horse) Battalion from 36 Infantry Base Depot and transferred to Princess Victoria's (Royal Irish Fusiliers) in September/October 1917 (renumbered 41176).

FINCH Private Charles Frederick 45798. Joined the 9th (North Irish Horse) Battalion, Princess Victoria's (Royal Irish Fusiliers) with the draft of men from The London Regiment in April 1918.

FINCHAM Private George W 42102. [Enlisted into the Army Veterinary Corps (27194).] Transferred to Princess Victoria's (Royal Irish Fusiliers) 8 May 1918 (renumbered 42102) and joined the 9th (North Irish Horse) Battalion. [Transferred to 5th (Service) Battalion, The Royal Irish Regiment (Pioneers) in the Light Division in the British Army of the Rhine in March/June 1919 (renumbered 41284).]

FINDLAY Private Henry 18575. [Enlisted April 1915 into the 7th or 8th (Service) Battalion in 49th Brigade, 16th (Irish) Division.] Joined the 9th (North Irish Horse) Battalion when the 7th/8th (Service) Battalion was disbanded in February 1918. 'C' Company. Believed **wounded** in the period 21-28 March 1918 during the retreat from St Quentin. [Transferred to the Royal Air Force (Leading Aircraftman - 310055). **Deserted** 14 October 1918.] Lived at 63 Brown Street, Glasgow.

FINLAY Private Reginald 11500. Enlisted into Princess Victoria's (Royal Irish Fusiliers) as a regular soldier in July/August 1914. [To France 29 November 1914 and joined the 1st Battalion.] Posted to the 9th (North Irish Horse) Battalion. 'B' Company. **Missing** in the period 21-28 March 1918 during the retreat from St Quentin believed **captured**. [Transferred to the Corps of Royal Engineers (renumbered 603888).] 1914-15 Star.

FINNERTY Private Joseph 19993. Enlisted in May 1915 into the 8th (Service) Battalion in 49th Brigade, 16th (Irish) Division.] Joined the 9th (North Irish Horse) Battalion when the 7th/8th (Service) Battalion was disbanded in February 1918.

FINNIMORE Lance Corporal Charles Albert 13655. Born 29 November 1897 at Boyton, Cornwall. [Enlisted in September 1914 and joined the 6th (Service) Battalion in 31st Brigade, 10th (Irish) Division. Embarked with the Mediterranean Expeditionary Force July 1915.] Posted to the 9th (North Irish Horse) Battalion. 'C' Company. **Wounded** during the retreat from St Quentin 21-28 March 1918. Transferred to the Class Z Reserve. 1914-15 Star. After the war he emigrated to Canada. Died at McCreary, Manitoba, Canada on 28 December 1967, aged 70.

FIRTH Private Benson 40063. Born 17 May 1894 at Bradford, Yorkshire. [Enlisted 2 June 1915 into the 12th (Service) Battalion, The Prince of Wales's Own (West Yorkshire Regiment) (1453).] Transferred to Princess Victoria's (Royal Irish Fusiliers) 30 November 1916 (renumbered 40063) and joined the 9th (Service) Battalion 12 December 1916. 'B' Company. **Wounded** at the Battle of Langemarck 16 August 1917. Discharged as no longer physically fit for war service due to wounds 21 February 1919. Silver War Badge, number B154127. Died in 1979, aged 85 at Bradford, Yorkshire.

FIRTH Sergeant Herbert 43469. Born in 1882. From Brixton Hill, Surrey. [Enlisted 9 June 1915 into 3/24th Battalion, The London Regiment (4265). Lance Corporal 24 June 1915. Corporal 31 July 1915. Lance Sergeant 28 August 1915. Pioneer Sergeant 16 October 1915. Served at the 22nd (Reserve) Battalion, The London Regiment, Chiseldon (renumbered 721651 in March 1917) until March 1918.] To France and joined 36 Infantry Base Depot 29 March 1918. Transferred to Princess Victoria's (Royal Irish Fusiliers) 2 April 1918 (renumbered 43469) and joined the 9th (North Irish Horse) Battalion 4 April 1918. **Missing** in the period 11-18 April 1918 in the actions between Wulverghem and Kemmel; subsequently declared **killed in action** 19 April 1918. His brother, Lance Corporal E Firth, served with The East Yorkshire Regiment and the Royal Flying Corps.

FIRTH Private Thomas 25172. [Enlisted into the Army Service Corps (4898). To France 2 January 1915. Served with 4th Remount Depot.] Transferred to Princess Victoria's (Royal Irish Fusiliers) 8 May 1917 (25172) and joined the 7th/8th (Service) Battalion in 49th Brigade 16th (Irish) Division. Joined the 9th (North Irish Horse) Battalion when the 7th/8th (Service) Battalion was disbanded in February 1918. 'B' Company. **Missing** in the period 21-28 March 1918 during the retreat from St Quentin believed **captured**. Transferred to the Class Z Reserve 3 April 1919. 1914-15 Star.

FISHER Private Ernest Charles 43503. Born in 1889 at Peckham, Surrey. [Enlisted 17 November 1915 into The King's Royal Rifle Corps (16942). To France 20 June 1916. Transferred to The Royal

Irish Rifles (renumbered 16942) and joined 14th (Service) Battalion, The Royal Irish Rifles (Young Citizens) 13 July 1916. To the field ambulance and casualty clearing station (injured foot) 29 September to 19 October 1916. To the field ambulance and casualty clearing station (injured leg and neck) 22 March to 11 April 1917. To the field ambulance and casualty clearing station (injured leg) 24 May 1917. Rejoined 14th (Service) Battalion, The Royal Irish Rifles (Young Citizens) 8 June 1917. To hospital with an ulcer on his leg 19 December 1917. Joined the 16th (Service) Battalion, The Royal Irish Rifles (2nd County Down) (Pioneers) 12 April 1918.] Transferred to Princess Victoria's (Royal Irish Fusiliers) 15 June 1918 (renumbered 43503) and joined the 9th (North Irish Horse) Battalion 23 June 1918. **Killed in action** during the attack south of Wulverghem 4 September 1918.

FISHER Private James Irvine 14168. Born in 1897. From Lurgan, County Armagh. A clerk. Enlisted September 1914. Posted to the 10th (Reserve) Battalion 9 October 1915. Lance Corporal 28 February 1916. To France 26 October 1916 and joined the 9th (Service) Battalion. Acting Corporal 31 April 1918. **Wounded** by gunshot to the left shoulder and back during the attack south of Wulverghem 4 September 1918. Evacuated to hospital in England. Posted to the 3rd (Reserve) Battalion 10 January 1919. Forfeit eleven days pay and reduced in rank to Private for being absent without leave from 31 December 1918 to 10 January 1919. Transferred to the Class Z Reserve 17 February 1919. 1914-15 Star.

FISHER Private Stanley Charles 41936. Born in 1899 at Surrey. [Enlisted 21 April 1917 and transferred to the Army Reserve. Mobilised 27 November 1917 and joined 22nd (Reserve) Battalion, The London Regiment (685536).] To 'B' Infantry Base Depot 5 April 1918. Transferred to Princess Victoria's (Royal Irish Fusiliers) (renumbered 41936) and posted to the 1st Battalion. Joined the 9th (North Irish Horse) Battalion 9 May 1918. **Wounded** by a gunshot to the right hand during the attack south of Wulverghem 4 September 1918 and treated at 108th Field Ambulance. **Wounded** by a gunshot to the left leg during the attack at Vijfwegen 30 September 1918. Evacuated to hospital in England from 35th General Hospital, Calais. Joined the 3rd (Reserve) Battalion 16 December 1918. Transferred to the Class Z Reserve 21 April 1919.

FISHER Private William 14182. Enlisted September 1914. To France with 36th (Ulster) Division in October 1915. Transferred to the Class Z Reserve 7 February 1919. 1914-15 Star.

FITZGERALD Private Henry George 45741. [Enlisted into The London Regiment (5490). Posted to 1/24th (County of London) Battalion, The London Regiment (The Queen's).] To France and joined 36 Infantry Base Depot 29 March 1918. Transferred to Princess Victoria's (Royal Irish Fusiliers) 2 April 1918 (renumbered 45741) and joined the 9th (North Irish Horse) Battalion 4 April 1918.

FITZGERALD Private Marshall 41603. From Clonavilla, County Monaghan. [Enlisted into the Service Squadron, 6th (Inniskilling) Dragoons (UD/35). To France with 36th (Ulster) Division in October 1915. Served with 2nd North Irish Horse, X Corps Cavalry Regiment.] Joined the renamed 9th (North Irish Horse) Battalion from 36 Infantry Base Depot and transferred to Princess Victoria's (Royal Irish Fusiliers) in September/October 1917 (renumbered 41603). Transferred to the Class Z Reserve 23 March 1919. 1914-15 Star.

FITZGERALD Private Matthew 40087. Joined the 9th (Service) Battalion, Princess Victoria's (Royal Irish Fusiliers) with the draft of men from The Prince of Wales's Own (West Yorkshire Regiment) on 12 December 1916. [Transferred to the Corps of Hussars (renumbered 24239).] Lived at Finglas Bridge, Dublin.

FITZPATRICK Private Martin 3897 & 7040045. Born in 1895 at Painestown, County Meath. A farm labourer. Enlisted 10 December 1915 into Princess Victoria's (Royal Irish Fusiliers) Special Reserve. [Served with the 7th/8th (Service) Battalion in 49th Brigade, 16th (Irish) Division.] Joined the 9th (North Irish Horse) Battalion when the 7th/8th (Service) Battalion was disbanded in February 1918. 'A' Company. **Captured** in the period 21-28 March 1918 during the retreat from St Quentin. Repatriated 23 December 1918. Transferred to Princess Victoria's (Royal Irish Fusiliers) Special Reserve (renumbered 7040045) in early-1919. Discharged 9 December 1921.

FITZPATRICK Private William 20871. [Enlisted in August 1915 and joined the 8th (Service) Battalion in 49th Brigade, 16th (Irish) Division.] Joined the 9th (North Irish Horse) Battalion when the 7th/8th (Service) Battalion was disbanded in February 1918. **Deserted** 21 October 1918.

FITZSIMMONS Private William John 42551. Born in 1898 at Shankill, Belfast. [Enlisted 19

February 1918. To France 15 June 1918 and posted to the 1st Battalion, The Royal Irish Rifles (22093).] Transferred at the Base Depot to Princess Victoria's (Royal Irish Fusiliers) 14 September 1918 (renumbered 42551) and joined the 9th (North Irish Horse) Battalion 22 September 1918. **Killed in action** during the advance to Anseghem 25 October 1918.

FITZSIMONS MM Private James 14176. From Lurgan, County Armagh. Enlisted September 1914. To France with 36th (Ulster) Division in October 1915. [Joined 108th Brigade Machine Gun Company in January 1916. Transferred to the Machine Gun Corps (renumbered 17787). **Wounded** during the attack at Hamel 1 July 1916. Promoted Sergeant. **MM**.] 1914-15 Star. Brother of Private Robert Fitzsimons. Died at Lurgan 14 May 1952.

FITZSIMONS Private John 3956. Enlisted in late 1915 into Princess Victoria's (Royal Irish Fusiliers) Special Reserve. Mobilised and later posted to the 9th (Service) Battalion. 'B' Company. **Missing** in the period 21-28 March 1918 during the retreat from St Quentin believed **captured**.

FITZSIMONS Lance Corporal John 40001. From Woodhouse, Leeds, Yorkshire. [Enlisted into The Prince of Wales's Own (West Yorkshire Regiment).] Transferred to Princess Victoria's (Royal Irish Fusiliers) 30 November 1916 (renumbered 40001) and joined the 9th (Service) Battalion 12 December 1916. 'A' Company. **Wounded** at the Battle of Langemarck 16 August 1917.

FITZSIMONS Private Robert 14177. Born at Shankill, County Armagh. From Lurgan, County Armagh. Enlisted September 1914. To France with 36th (Ulster) Division in October 1915. To hospital at Rouen sick and **died** on 20 February 1916, aged 18. 1914-15 Star. Brother of Private James Fitzsimons.

FLAHERTY Private Patrick 7487 & 7040012. From Kingstown, Dun Laoghaire, Dublin. [Enlisted as a regular soldier into Princess Victoria's (Royal Irish Fusiliers) 9 April 1902. Mobilised from the Army Reserve and joined the 1st Battalion in France 12 September 1914. Evacuated to hospital in England 18 January 1915. To France 29 June 1916 and joined the 8th (Service) Battalion in 49th Brigade, 16th (Irish) Division. Evacuated to hospital in England 2 March 1917. To France 7 September 1917.] Joined the 9th (North Irish Horse) Battalion when the 7th/8th (Service) Battalion was disbanded in February 1918. Believed **wounded** in the period 11-18 April 1918 in the actions between Wulverghem and Kemmel and evacuated to hospital in England. 1914 Star and clasp. Re-enlisted 25 February 1919 for Regular Army service with Princess Victoria's (Royal Irish Fusiliers) (renumbered 7040012). Served with the 1st Battalion in Persia and Mesopotamia in 1919/20. General Service Medal 1918-1962 with clasps 'Iraq' & 'NW Persia'. Discharged 28 June 1922.

FLANAGAN Lance Corporal Hugh Edmond 41229. Born in 1896 at Ballymena, County Antrim. A teacher in the Ulster Institute for the Deaf, Dumb and Blind in Belfast. [Enlisted in May 1915 into the North Irish Horse (1508). To France with 'F' Squadron in 33rd Division 17 November 1915. Served with 2nd North Irish Horse, X Corps Cavalry Regiment.] Joined the renamed 9th (North Irish Horse) Battalion from 36 Infantry Base Depot and transferred to Princess Victoria's (Royal Irish Fusiliers) in September/October 1917 (renumbered 41229). **Missing** on 22 November 1917 at Moeuvres, aged 21, he was later declared **killed in action** on that date. 1914-15 Star. His older brother, Rifleman William Henry Murray Flanagan, was killed in action on 13 April 1918 while serving with the 12th (Service) Battalion, The Royal Irish Rifles (Central Antrim). His younger brother, Guardsman Thomas Jamison Flanagan, served with the Irish Guards.

FLANAGAN Private Richard 41604. From Belfast. A carpenter. [Enlisted 25 August 1915 into the Service Squadron, 6th (Inniskilling) Dragoons (UD/280). To France 27 December 1916. Served with 2nd North Irish Horse, X Corps Cavalry Regiment. Embarked at Marseilles for Egypt with the Regiment's horses on Horse Transport SS Bohemian 25 August 1917.] Joined the renamed 9th (North Irish Horse) Battalion and transferred to Princess Victoria's (Royal Irish Fusiliers) in October 1917 (renumbered 41604). [Transferred to the Tank Corps (renumbered 304866) 28 December 1917 and posted for training to the Tank Corps Depot, at Bovington near Wareham, Dorset.] Transferred to the Class Z Reserve 28 March 1919.

FLAVELLE Private Luke 14165. From Portadown, County Armagh. 4th (Portadown) Battalion, Armagh Regiment, Ulster Volunteer Force. Enlisted September 1914. To France with 36th (Ulster) Division in October 1915. **Wounded** during the attack at Hamel 1 July 1916. Discharged as no longer physically fit for war service due to wounds 19 March 1917. Silver War Badge, 146249. 1914-15 Star. Brother of Private William Flavelle. His brother, Private Thomas Flavelle, served with the Duke of Lancaster's Own Yeomanry and died of pneumonia on 6 November 1918.

FLAVELLE Private William 14164. Born in 1884 at Portadown, County Armagh. 4th (Portadown) Battalion, Armagh Regiment, Ulster Volunteer Force. Enlisted September 1914. Admonished for being absent without leave 4 November 1914. Sentenced to forfeit eight days pay for being absent off pass 2 June 1915. Sentenced to forty-eight hours Field Punishment Number 2 for being out of barracks when confined to camp, disobeying an order and drunk 30 June 1915. To France with 36th (Ulster) Division in October 1915. Sentenced to twenty-one days Field Punishment Number 1 for *'when on active service – drunkenness'* 21 January 1916. Transferred to the Class Z Reserve 15 March 1919. 1914-15 Star. Brother of Private Luke Flavelle. His brother, Private Thomas Flavelle, served with the Duke of Lancaster's Own Yeomanry and died of pneumonia on 6 November 1918.

FLEMING Private John 49737. [Enlisted into The Royal Irish Rifles (463).] Transferred to Princess Victoria's (Royal Irish Fusiliers) in April 1918 (renumbered 49737) and joined the 9th (North Irish Horse) Battalion. [Transferred to The Corps of Royal Engineers (renumbered 624672).]

FLEMING Lance Corporal Matthew 11299. Born in 1895 at Drogheda, County Louth. [Enlisted 28 July 1913 into Princess Victoria's (Royal Irish Fusiliers) as a regular soldier. To France with the 1st Battalion 22 August 1914.] Posted to the 9th (Service) Battalion. 'B' Company. **Wounded** at the Battle of Langemarck 16 August 1917. [Transferred to the Labour Corps (renumbered 411293, renumbered 618754).] Discharged as no longer physically fit for war service due to wounds 25 January 1919. Silver War Badge, number B106122. 1914 Star.

FLEMING Sergeant Patrick 7839 & 7040119. From Muckno, Castleblayney, County Monaghan. [Enlisted into Princess Victoria's (Royal Irish Fusiliers) as a regular soldier 3 January 1903. To France with the 2nd Battalion 19 December 1914. **Wounded** by a gunshot to the face 13 May 1915 and evacuated to hospital in England. Posted to the 6th (Service) Battalion and joined the Mediterranean Expeditionary Force 31 August 1916. Acting Company Sergeant Major.] Posted to the 9th (North Irish Horse) Battalion. 1914-15 Star. Continued to serve with Princess Victoria's (Royal Irish Fusiliers) (renumbered 7040119). Discharged 2 January 1924.

FLEMING Private William 14190. From Portadown, County Armagh. Enlisted September 1914. To France with 36th (Ulster) Division in October 1915. **Wounded** during the attack at Hamel 1 July 1916. [Transferred to the Labour Corps (renumbered 231597). Discharged 26 January 1919.] 1914-15 Star. His brother, Private George Fleming served with the 5th (Service) Battalion.

FLEMING Private William James 16154. From Stranooden, County Monaghan. Enlisted into the 9th (Service) Battalion in October 1914. To France with 36th (Ulster) Division in October 1915. **Killed in action** during the attack at Hamel 1 July 1916. 1914-15 Star.

FLEMING Private William John 11634. From Portadown, County Armagh. [Enlisted 20 August 1914 and joined the 5th (Service) Battalion in 31st Brigade, 10th (Irish) Division. Embarked with the Mediterranean Expeditionary Force July 1915.] Posted to the 9th (Service) Battalion. **Wounded**. Discharged as no longer physically fit for war service due to wounds 16 May 1917. Silver War Badge, number 173222. 1914-15 Star.

FLEMING Private William 41104. [Enlisted into the Service Squadron, 6th (Inniskilling) Dragoons (UD/36). To France with 36th (Ulster) Division in October 1915. Served with 2nd North Irish Horse, X Corps Cavalry Regiment.] Joined the renamed 9th (North Irish Horse) Battalion from 36 Infantry Base Depot and transferred to Princess Victoria's (Royal Irish Fusiliers) in September/October 1917 (renumbered 41104). 1914-14 Star. Transferred to the Class Z Reserve.

FLOOD Private Arthur 43216. Born in 1897 in Chesterfield, Derbyshire. A tailor. [Enlisted 13 January 1916 into The Sherwood Foresters (Nottinghamshire and Derbyshire Regiment) (35507). To France 14 June 1916. Attached to the 1st Battalion, The South Staffordshire Regiment 8 July 1916. **Wounded** 14 July 1916. Treated in 65th Field Ambulance and 2nd General Hospital.] Transferred to Princess Victoria's (Royal Irish Fusiliers) 31 August 1916 (renumbered 43216) having joined the 9th (Service) Battalion on 8 August 1916. 'C' Company. Admitted to hospital with influenza 13-22 September 1916 and then to the Base Depot. Rejoined 17 February 1917. **Wounded** (back and head) at the Battle of Langemarck 16 August 1917. Evacuated to hospital in England via 22nd General Hospital. [Transferred to the Corps of Royal Engineers (renumbered 327185) from 20 May 1918. Served at Chatham.] Transferred to the Class Z Reserve 19 February 1919.

FLOOD Corporal William Alexander 42181. [Enlisted into the Army Service Corps (S4/42680). To France 7 July 1915 and served with 15th and 13th Field Bakeries.] Transferred to Princess Victoria's (Royal Irish Fusiliers) 8 May 1918 (renumbered 42181) and joined the 9th (North Irish Horse) Battalion. Transferred to the Class Z Reserve 17 February 1919. 1914-15 Star.

FLYNN MM Lance Sergeant Bernard 6328. Born 1887. From Doncaster, Yorkshire. A chemist. [Enlisted into Princess Victoria's (Royal Irish Fusiliers) Special Reserve in mid-1914. Mobilised on 27 November 1914. Lance Corporal 8 February 1915. To France 6 March 1915 and joined the 2nd Battalion. Reduced to Private 16 March 1916. Evacuated to hospital in England 7 December 1916. Treated at 1st Western General Hospital, Fazackerley, Liverpool. Lance Corporal 25 July 1917. To 36 Infantry Base Depot 18 October 1917 and posted to the 7th/8th (Service) Battalion in 49th Brigade, 16th (Irish) Division. **MM** – late-1917. Corporal 21 November 1917. Lance Sergeant 24 December 1917.] Joined the 9th (North Irish Horse) Battalion when the 7th/8th (Service) Battalion was disbanded in February 1918. 'C' Company. **Wounded** by a gunshot to the left foot 23 March 1918 during the retreat from St Quentin. Evacuated to hospital in England and treated at Chester War Hospital until September 1918. Joined the 3rd (Reserve) Battalion 20 September 1918. Transferred to the Class Z Reserve 21 March 1919. 1914-15 Star.

FOGG Private Sidney 43208. [Enlisted into The Sherwood Foresters (Nottinghamshire and Derbyshire Regiment).] Transferred to Princess Victoria's (Royal Irish Fusiliers) 31 August 1916 having joined the 9th (Service) Battalion on 8 August 1916 (renumbered 43208). [Transferred to 5th (Service) Battalion, The Royal Irish Regiment (Pioneers) in the Light Division in the British Army of the Rhine in March/June 1919 (renumbered 41289).]

FORBES Private Cecil 17152. Enlisted 23 November 1914 into the 9th (Service) Battalion. To France with 36th (Ulster) Division in October 1915. [Joined 108th Brigade Machine Gun Company in January 1916. Transferred to the Machine Gun Corps (renumbered 17786).] Discharged as no longer physically fit for war service due to sickness 16 October 1918. Silver War Badge, number B56287. 1914-15 Star.

FORBES Private John 41453. From Ahoghill, Ballymena, County Antrim. A clerk with Frazer & Haughton Ltd, dyers, Ballymena. [Enlisted 19 November 1915 into the North Irish Horse (1924). To France 27 July 1916. Served with 'D' Squadron. 1st North Irish Horse, VII Corps Cavalry Regiment. To 99 Field Ambulance sick (diarrhoea) 20 September 1916. Returned to duty 24 September 1916.] Joined the renamed 9th (North Irish Horse) Battalion from 36 Infantry Base Depot and transferred to Princess Victoria's (Royal Irish Fusiliers) in September/October 1917 (renumbered 41453). 'C' Company. Reportedly killed in action on 22 March 1918 attempting to rescue another man of the Battalion who had been captured. He is recorded as **killed in action** 29 March 1918 during the retreat from St Quentin, aged 22.

FORBES Private Michael 25171. [Enlisted into the Army Service Corps RTS/5678. To France 13 March 1915. Served with 3rd Remount Depot.] Transferred to Princess Victoria's (Royal Irish Fusiliers) in May 1916 and joined the 7th/8th (Service) Battalion in 49th Brigade 16th (Irish) Division. Joined the 9th (North Irish Horse) Battalion when the 7th/8th (Service) Battalion was disbanded in February 1918. 'B' Company. 1914-15 Star. Transferred to the Class Z Reserve.

FORD Private John 41535. From Lisbellaw, County Fermanagh. [Enlisted 21 December 1912 into the North Irish Horse (772). To France 20 August 1914 with 'C' Squadron as 5th Division Cavalry and then as GHQ Troops. Served with 2nd North Irish Horse, X Corps Cavalry Regiment.] Joined the renamed 9th (North Irish Horse) Battalion from 36 Infantry Base Depot and transferred to Princess Victoria's (Royal Irish Fusiliers) in September/October 1917 (renumbered 41535). 'C' Company. **Killed in action** on a raid at Havrincourt 3 November 1917. 1914 Star.

FORDE Private James Henry 22551. From Mullavilly, County Armagh. Enlisted in November 1915. Posted to the 9th (Service) Battalion. 'A' Company. **Wounded** during the attack at Hamel 1 July 1916. **Wounded** at Moeuvres 22/23 November 1917. **Wounded** and **captured** in the period 21-28 March 1918 during the retreat from St Quentin. Repatriated December 1918.

FORDE Private Samuel James 17671. From Portadown, County Armagh. Enlisted into the 9th (Service) Battalion in December 1914/January 1915. To France with 36th (Ulster) Division in October 1915. **Killed in action** 22 February 1916 while on patrol near Hamel, aged 30. 1914-15 Star.

FORDE Private Thomas 16632. From Portadown, County Armagh. Enlisted into the 9th (Service) Battalion in November 1914. No record of service outside the United Kingdom. [Transferred to the Royal Defence Corps (renumbered 67450).]

FOREMAN Private Thomas 41447. From Belfast. [Enlisted 16 October 1916 into the North Irish Horse (2294). Served with 2nd North Irish Horse, X Corps Cavalry Regiment.] Joined the renamed 9th (North Irish Horse) Battalion from 36 Infantry Base Depot and transferred to Princess Victoria's (Royal Irish Fusiliers) in September/October 1917 (renumbered 41447). 'C' Company. **Captured** in the period 21-28 March 1918 during the retreat from St Quentin. Discharged as no longer physically fit for war service due to sickness 5 July 1919. Silver War Badge, number B274243.

FORREST Private Robert Henry 42271. From Padiham, Lancashire. A coachman. [Enlisted 14 July 1915 into the Army Veterinary Corps (10766). To Egypt 30 October 1915. Served with 15th Veterinary Hospital, Salonika. To hospital in Salonika (malaria) 22 August 1916. Evacuated to Malta. Returned to Base Depot Salonika 27 November 1916. To hospital (malaria) 23 March -3 April 1917. To hospital (venereal sores) 20 June - 27 July 1917. Embarked for France via Taranto 18 January 1918. Landed at Marseilles 27 January 1918.] Transferred to Princess Victoria's (Royal Irish Fusiliers) 8 May 1918 (renumbered 42271) and joined the 9th (North Irish Horse) Battalion 13 May 1918. **Died** at 36th Casualty Clearing Station of pneumonia 27 June 1918, aged 31. 1914-15 Star.

FORSYTHE Private Henry 14163. Born in 1888 in Portadown, County Armagh. A labourer at Portadown golf links. 4th (Portadown) Battalion, Armagh Regiment, Ulster Volunteer Force. Enlisted September 1914. To France with 36th (Ulster) Division in October 1915. 'B' Company. **Wounded** by gunshots to his right side and thigh during the attack at Hamel 1 July 1916. Evacuated to hospital in England. Returned to France 23 February 1917 and rejoined the 9th (Service) Battalion. **Wounded** by gunshot to his back and left arm at the Battle of Langemarck 16 August 1917. Evacuated to hospital in England. Discharged as no longer physically fit for war service due to wounds 18 June 1918, aged 29. Silver War Badge, number 411845. 1914-15 Star.

FORSYTHE Private James 41490. [Enlisted in January 1913 into the North Irish Horse (797). To France 20 August 1914 with 'C' Squadron as 5th Division Cavalry and then as GHQ Troops. Served with 2nd North Irish Horse, X Corps Cavalry Regiment.] Joined the renamed 9th (North Irish Horse) Battalion from 36 Infantry Base Depot and transferred to Princess Victoria's (Royal Irish Fusiliers) in September/October 1917 (renumbered 41490). 1914 Star and clasp.

FOSTER Private Alfred 41509. [Enlisted 6 November 1914 into the Service Squadron, 6th (Inniskilling) Dragoons (UD/151). To France with 36th (Ulster) Division in October 1915. Served with 2nd North Irish Horse, X Corps Cavalry Regiment.] Joined the renamed 9th (North Irish Horse) Battalion from 36 Infantry Base Depot and transferred to Princess Victoria's (Royal Irish Fusiliers) in September/October 1917 (renumbered 41509). **Wounded**. Discharged as no longer physically fit for war service due to wounds 11 October 1918. Silver War Badge, number B34764. 1914-15 Star.

FOSTER MM Sergeant Frederick 14175. Born 21 March 1896. From Shankill, County Armagh. A clerk. Enlisted September 1914. To France with 36th (Ulster) Division in October 1915. 'B' Company. **MM** – Hamel May/June 1916, the first award to a man of the 9th (Service) Battalion (see Sergeant W H Palmer). **Killed in action** by shellfire at Hamel in the early hours of 1 July 1916 as the 9th (Service) Battalion went back into the line, aged 21. 1914-15 Star.

FOSTER Sergeant John McKelvey 22800. From Belfast. Enlisted in November 1915, aged 16. Served with the Ulster Composite Battalion during the Irish Republican attacks in Dublin. Posted to the 9th (Service) Battalion in August/September 1918. **Captured** in September 1918.

FOSTER Private Joseph 14198. Enlisted September 1914. To France with 36th (Ulster) Division in October 1915. [Transferred to the Labour Corps (renumbered 605180).] 1914-15 Star.

FOSTER Private Robert 14181. Enlisted September 1914. Did not serve overseas with 36th (Ulster) Division. Discharged as no longer physically fit for war service due to sickness 18 October 1916. Silver War Badge, number 506381.

FOSTER Private Robert 15450. Born at Poolstock, Lancashire. [Enlisted into The Lancashire Fusiliers (5797). Transferred to Princess Victoria's (Royal Irish Fusiliers) in September 1914 (renumbered 15450) and served with the 7th (Service) Battalion in 49th Brigade, 16th (Irish) Division.] Joined the 9th (North Irish Horse) Battalion when the 7th/8th (Service) Battalion was disbanded in February 1918. 'C' Company. **Missing** in the period 21-28 March 1918 during the retreat from St Quentin and later declared **killed in action** 29 March 1918.

FOSTER Sergeant William 8343. From Belfast. [Enlisted 22 February 1904 into Princess Victoria's (Royal Irish Fusiliers) as a regular soldier. To France with the 1st Battalion 22 August 1914.] Posted to the 9th (Service) Battalion. 4 Platoon, 'C' Company. **Wounded** at the Battle of Langemarck 16 August 1917. [Transferred to the Army Ordnance Corps (renumbered 10206).] Discharged as no longer physically fit for war service due to wounds 14 January 1918, aged 32. Silver War Badge, number 314841. 1914 Star and clasp.

FOWLER Lance Corporal Richard 41275. [Enlisted in May 1914 into the North Irish Horse (945). Served with 2nd North Irish Horse, X Corps Cavalry Regiment.] Joined the renamed 9th (North Irish Horse) Battalion from 36 Infantry Base Depot and transferred to Princess Victoria's (Royal Irish Fusiliers) in September/October 1917 (renumbered 41275).

FOWLER Private William E 45786. From Lambeth, London. Joined the 9th (North Irish Horse) Battalion, Princess Victoria's (Royal Irish Fusiliers) with the draft of men from The London Regiment in April 1918. [Transferred to 5th (Service) Battalion, The Royal Irish Regiment (Pioneers) in the Light Division in the British Army of the Rhine in March/June 1919 (renumbered 41290).]

FOX Lance Sergeant George Ross 14173. From Lurgan, County Armagh. Enlisted September 1914. To France with 36th (Ulster) Division in October 1915. 'C' Company. **Killed in action** during the attack at Hamel 1 July 1916, aged 35. 1914-15 Star.

FOX Warrant Officer Class II Henry Joseph 14191. Regimental Quartermaster Sergeant - see above.

FOX Private Leonard 22416. Born in 1894 at Redbourn, Hertfordshire. [Enlisted 31 August 1914 into The Bedfordshire Regiment (13179). To France 11 March 1915. Transferred to Princess Victoria's (Royal Irish Fusiliers) in November 1915 (renumbered 22416) and joined the 5th (Service) Battalion in 31st Brigade, 10th (Irish) Division in the Mediterranean Expeditionary Force.] Posted to the 9th (Service) Battalion. 'A' Company. **Wounded** at the Battle of Langemarck 16 August 1917. Discharged as no longer physically fit for war service due to wounds 3 December 1918. Silver War Badge, number B55042.

FOX Private Samuel 14195. Born in 1862 at Seagoe, County Armagh. Enlisted 27 December 1881 into The Royal Munster Fusiliers (153). He transferred to Princess Victoria's (Royal Irish Fusiliers) 31 March 1882 (renumbered 758). Served in the East Indies from 12 September 1883 and returned to Ireland on 13 February 1889. Lance Corporal 12 November 1886. Transferred to the Army Reserve 17 February 1889. Discharged from the Army Reserve 26 December 1893. Served a one year engagement with The Reserve Regiment from 13 March 1900 to 12 March 1901. Enlisted into the 3rd Battalion, Royal Garrison Regiment (renumbered 2912) 15 July 1901. Served in Malta from 20 September 1901 and returned to Ireland on 8 August 1903. Discharged at the end of his engagement 10 August 1903. Worked as a platelayer for the Great Northern Railway. He signed the Ulster Covenant on 28 September 1912. Armagh Regiment, Ulster Volunteer Force. Enlisted in September 1914, aged 52, giving his age as 44. To France with 36th (Ulster) Division in October 1915. Evacuated to hospital in England 6 October 1916. Joined the 10th (Reserve) Battalion on 21 October 1916. Lance Corporal 21 October 1916. Acting Corporal 25 May 1917. [Transferred to the Labour Corps (renumbered 231577 Corporal) 7 July 1917 and served with various Home Service Employment Companies. Reduced to Private on 14 August 1918 for neglect of duty by failing to conduct a man to hospital. Discharged as surplus to military requirements having suffered impairment since entry into the service (myalgia, valvular disease of the heart and shell-shock) 4 October 1918, aged 56.] 1914-15 Star. Brother of Private Simpson Walker Fox. His son, 11664 Private Samuel James Fox, died of wounds on 12 December 1916, aged 19, at a casualty clearing station at Meaulte, near Albert, while serving with the 1st Battalion.

FOX Private Simpson Walker 14185. Born 1882 at Seagoe, County Armagh. A linen weaver in Portadown, County Armagh. Enlisted into the Mid-Ulster Royal Garrison Artillery Militia on 9 May 1901 (1414 Gunner) and then the Royal Field Artillery Special Reserve on 9 August 1908 (renumbered 5146 Acting Bombardier). Discharged as no longer physically fit for service due to sickness (teeth) in 1910.] Enlisted in September 1914. To France with 36th (Ulster) Division in October 1915. [Joined 108th Brigade Machine Gun Company. Transferred to the Machine Gun

Corps (renumbered 17790).] Brother of Private Samuel Fox.

FRAME Private James 24907. Born in 1895 in Dromore, County Down. Lived in the United States and returned to Ireland and enlisted in October 1916. Posted to the 9th (Service) Battalion. 'C' Company. **Wounded** when shot in the throat during a raid at Spanbroekmolen 4 June 1917. **Missing** at the Battle of Langemarck 16 August 1917 and later declared **killed in action** on that date, aged 22. His brother, Rifleman David Frame, died of wounds on 29 June 1916 while serving with 13th (Service) Battalion, The Royal Irish Rifles (1st County Down). He was one of the men killed or injured by shellfire at Martinsart as the 13th (Service) Battalion, The Royal Irish Rifles (1st County Down) moved into the line on the night of 28 June 1916.

FRAMPTON Private George 25176. [Enlisted in May 1916 and joined the 7th/8th (Service) Battalion in 49th Brigade, 16th (Irish) Division.] Joined the 9th (North Irish Horse) Battalion when the 7th/8th (Service) Battalion was disbanded in February 1918.

FRANCE Private John A 42122. [Enlisted into the Army Veterinary Corps (30609).] Transferred to Princess Victoria's (Royal Irish Fusiliers) 8 May 1918 (renumbered 42122) and joined the 9th (North Irish Horse) Battalion. [Transferred to 5th (Service) Battalion, The Royal Irish Regiment (Pioneers) in the Light Division in the British Army of the Rhine in March/June 1919 (renumbered 41286).]

FRANCEY Private James 41424. From Ballymena, County Antrim. [Enlisted in September 1916 into the North Irish Horse (2268). Served with 2nd North Irish Horse, X Corps Cavalry Regiment.] Joined the renamed 9th (North Irish Horse) Battalion from 36 Infantry Base Depot and transferred to Princess Victoria's (Royal Irish Fusiliers) in September/October 1917 (renumbered 41424). **Captured** in the period 9-18 April 1918 in the actions between Wulverghem and Kemmel.

FRANCEY Private William 41415. From Ballymena, County Antrim. A hotel waiter. [Enlisted 19 October 1915 into the North Irish Horse (1750). To France 19 May 1916 and joined 5th General Base Depot. Posted to 1st North Irish Horse, VII Corps Cavalry Regiment 19 July 1916. Awarded ten days Field Punishment Number 1 for absence and drunkenness 1 October 1916. Tried by Field General Court Martial on 20 November 1916 charged with *'drunkenness'*; found guilty and sentenced to ninety days Field Punishment Number 1. Served with 2nd North Irish Horse, X Corps Cavalry Regiment.] Joined the renamed 9th (North Irish Horse) Battalion from 36 Infantry Base Depot and transferred to Princess Victoria's (Royal Irish Fusiliers) in September/October 1917 (renumbered 41415). To hospital sick (trench fever) 15 December 1917 and evacuated to hospital in England. Joined 'A' Infantry Base Depot 3 April 1918 and rejoined the 9th (North Irish Horse) Battalion 8 April 1918. **Wounded** by a gunshot to the thigh during the raid on Shoddy Farm near Meulenhouck 22 July 1918. Rejoined the 9th (North Irish Horse) Battalion 10 August 1918. Transferred to the 43rd (Garrison) Battalion, The Royal Fusiliers (City of London Regiment) (renumbered GS/84279) 16 September 1918. Forfeit seven days pay for being dirty on guard mounting parade 12 October 1918. Served with 34th (Garrison) Company.] Transferred to the Class Z Reserve 26 February 1919. Transferred to the Class Z Reserve 26 February 1919.

FRAZER Private Alexander 41644. [Enlisted in January 1913 into the North Irish Horse (799). To France 17 August 1914 with 'A' Squadron as GHQ Troops. Served with 2nd North Irish Horse, X Corps Cavalry Regiment.] Joined the renamed 9th (North Irish Horse) Battalion from 36 Infantry Base Depot and transferred to Princess Victoria's (Royal Irish Fusiliers) in September/October 1917 (renumbered 41644). 1914 Star.

FRAZER Corporal David 14186. Born 3 December 1872 at Armagh, County Armagh. A newspaper compositor. 1st (Armagh) Battalion, Armagh Regiment, Ulster Volunteer Force. Enlisted September 1914. To France with 36th (Ulster) Division in October 1915. 'A' Company. Corporal 23 September 1916. Reduced in rank to Private; *'not fit for duties of rank in field'* 24 June 1918. Transferred to the Class Z Reserve 15 March 1919. 1914-15 Star. Died 15 August 1951, aged 78. Brother of Private William Frazer. Father of Corporal David and Private Henry Frazer. His eldest son, Sergeant John (Johnny) Frazer, served pre-war with the 3rd Battalion (Militia), Princess Victoria's (Royal Irish Fusiliers) (5680). He became Transport Sergeant of the 5th/6th (Service) Battalion.

FRAZER Corporal David 20360 & 27477. Born 11 August 1898 at Armagh, County Armagh. Enlisted into the 9th (Service) Battalion on 9 June 1915, aged 16 (20360). Discharged having made a mis-statement as to age on enlistment; soldier under 17 years of age at date of application for discharge 30 July 1915. Travelled to Dublin and enlisted as a drummer in The Queen's Own (Royal West Kent Regiment). Transferred to Princess Victoria's (Royal Irish Fusiliers) in March 1917 (renumbered 27477) and was posted back to the 9th (Service) Battalion. **Wounded** by gas. Evacuated to hospital in England. Joined the 3rd (Reserve) Battalion in Rugeley, Staffordshire. Discharged as no longer physically fit for war service due to sickness 14 August 1918, aged 20. Silver War Badge, number 435837. After the war served with the Royal Irish Constabulary from 1919 and then the Royal Ulster Constabulary. Married one of the sisters (Elizabeth) of Lance Corporal William Stringer in 1920. Died in 1981, aged 82. Son of Corporal David Frazer (14186) and brother of Private Henry Frazer. Cousin of Private Richard Stewart.

FRAZER Private Henry (Harry) 14192. Born 14 September 1895. From Armagh, County Armagh. Worked as a motor mechanic. 1st (Armagh) Battalion, Armagh Regiment, Ulster Volunteer Force. Enlisted September 1914. To France with 36th (Ulster) Division in October 1915. 'A' Company. **Wounded** during the retreat from St Quentin 21-28 March 1918. Discharged as no longer physically fit for war service due to wounds 10 October 1918. Silver War Badge, number B34288. 1914-15 Star. Worked as a clerk after the war. Secretary of the Armagh branch, Old Comrades Association. Died 30 April 1950, aged 55. Son of Corporal David Frazer (14186) and brother of Corporal David Frazer (27477). Cousin of Private Richard Stewart.

FRAZER Private Robert 41491. From Belfast. [Enlisted in September 1914 into the North Irish Horse (1080). Served with 2nd North Irish Horse, X Corps Cavalry Regiment.] Joined the renamed 9th (North Irish Horse) Battalion from 36 Infantry Base Depot and transferred to Princess Victoria's (Royal Irish Fusiliers) in September/October 1917 (renumbered 41491). 'C' Company. **Captured** in the period 21-28 March 1918 during the retreat from St Quentin.

FRAZER Private William 14179. From Lonsdale Street, County Armagh. Enlisted September 1914. Discharged as no longer physically fit for war service due to sickness 28 June 1915, aged 33. Enrolled as a munitions worker June 1915. Initially denied a Silver War Badge, he later applied on the basis of having served as a munitions worker and was awarded badge number 520484. Brother of Corporal David Frazer (14186).

FRAZER Private Willoughby 9852. Born in 1887 at Portadown, County Armagh. A linen weaver. [Enlisted into Princess Victoria's (Royal Irish Fusiliers) as a regular soldier in 1907. To France with the 2nd Battalion 19 December 1914. **Wounded**.] Joined the 9th (Service) Battalion. **Wounded**. **Died of wounds** 16 August 1918, aged 30. 1914-15 Star.

FREAR Sergeant George 40062. Born in 1895 Hull, Yorkshire. A railway porter with North Eastern Railway. [Enlisted 9 September 1914 into the 12th (Service) Battalion, The Prince of Wales's Own (West Yorkshire Regiment) (13949). To France 10 September 1915. Evacuated to hospital in England sick (synovitis knee) 4 January 1916. Posted to the 13th (Reserve) Battalion, The Prince of Wales's Own (West Yorkshire Regiment) August 1916. Posted to the 3rd (Reserve) Battalion, The Prince of Wales's Own (West Yorkshire Regiment) 10 October 1916.] Transferred to Princess Victoria's (Royal Irish Fusiliers) 30 November 1916 (renumbered 40062) and joined the 9th (Service) Battalion 12 December 1916. 'D' Company. **Wounded** at the Battle of Langemarck 16 August 1917. Evacuated to hospital in England and treated at 1st London General Hospital. To 'A' Infantry Base Depot 3 April 1918 and rejoined the 9th (North Irish Horse) Battalion. Lance Corporal 27 October 1918. Corporal 5 November 1918. Lance Sergeant 13 November 1918. Sergeant November 1918. [Transferred to 5th (Service) Battalion, The Royal Irish Regiment (Pioneers) in the Light Division in the British Army of the Rhine in March/June 1919 (renumbered 41287).] Transferred to the Class Z Reserve 20 January 1920.

FREEBURN Private Frank 14172. From Portadown, County Armagh. 4th (Portadown) Battalion, Armagh Regiment, Ulster Volunteer Force. Enlisted September 1914. To France with 36th (Ulster) Division in October 1915. **Wounded** (shellshock) during the attack at Hamel 1 July 1916. **Wounded** in the period 9-18 April 1918 in the actions between Wulverghem and Kemmel. Transferred to the Class Z Reserve 30 March 1919. 1914-15 Star.

FREEDMAN Private Elkan 40011. Born on 24 April 1897 at Leeds, Yorkshire of Russian parents. [Enlisted into The Prince of Wales's Own (West Yorkshire Regiment) (33928).] Transferred to Princess Victoria's (Royal Irish Fusiliers) 30 November 1916 (renumbered 40011) and joined the 9th (Service) Battalion 12 December 1916. [Transferred to The Royal Fusiliers (City of London

Regiment) (renumbered J/9338).] He became a gentleman's outfitter. Died at Leeds, Yorkshire in 1965, aged 67.

FREELAND Private Joseph 18257. Enlisted into the 9th (Service) Battalion in February/March 1915. To France with 36th (Ulster) Division in October 1915. Transferred to the Class Z Reserve 30 May 1919. 1914-15 Star.

FREEMAN Private Sydney Wilfred 43241. Born in 1895 in Glinton, Huntingdonshire. A chemist's porter. [Enlisted 11 December 1915 and transferred to the Army Reserve. Mobilised on 16 February 1916 and joined The Sherwood Foresters (Nottinghamshire and Derbyshire Regiment) (35780).] To France 23 July 1916. Transferred to Princess Victoria's (Royal Irish Fusiliers) 31 August 1916 having joined the 9th (Service) Battalion on 8 August 1916 (renumbered 43241). 'B' Company. To the field ambulance sick (scabies). **Wounded** (gunshot wounds to the legs) at the Battle of Langemarck 16 August 1917 and evacuated to hospital in England. Treated in East Leeds War Hospital. To France 18 January 1918 and posted to the 1st Battalion. **Missing** during the retreat from St Quentin and declared **killed in action** 21 March 1918, aged 23.

FREEMAN Private William 23688. Enlisted 3 January 1916. Posted to the 9th (Service) Battalion. Discharged as no longer physically fit for war service due to sickness 18 June 1918, aged 37. Silver War Badge, number 387955.

FRIEND Corporal Walter Harvey 45026. [Enlisted in December 1916 and served with the 7th/8th (Service) Battalion in 49th Brigade, 16th (Irish) Division.] Joined the 9th (North Irish Horse) Battalion when the 7th/8th (Service) Battalion was disbanded in February 1918.

FRY Private William Albert (Bertie) 24759. From Portadown, County Armagh. Member of Masonic Lodge 82. Enlisted 4 September 1916. Joined the 9th (Service) Battalion. 'C' Company. Incorrectly reported **killed in action** during the retreat from St Quentin in March 1918; he was **wounded**. Discharged as no longer physically fit for war service due to wounds 16 October 1918. Silver War Badge, number B34292.

FUGARD Private Thomas 11164 & 7040488. From Shankill, County Armagh. [Enlisted into Princess Victoria's (Royal Irish Fusiliers) as a regular soldier 9 December 1912. To France with the 2nd Battalion 19 December 1914. Evacuated to hospital in England 27 May 1915. To France 7 July 1916 and posted to the 8th (Service) Battalion in 49th Brigade, 16th (Irish) Division.] Posted to the 9th (North Irish Horse) Battalion. 'A' Company. **Captured** in the period 21-28 March 1918 during the retreat from St Quentin. Transferred to the Section B Army Reserve, Princess Victoria's (Royal Irish Fusiliers) (renumbered 7040488). Fraudulent enlistment into the Royal Army Ordnance Corps; held to serve.

FULTON Private David 23194. Enlisted 19 November 1915. Posted to the 9th (Service) Battalion. 'C' Company. To hospital mid-1916. Did not take part in the attack at Hamel on 1 July 1916. Discharged as no longer physically fit for war service due to sickness 28 May 1919. Silver War Badge, number 179439.

FULTON Private Hugh 14178. From Ballinagarrick, Lurgan, County Armagh. A weaver. Member of 5th (Lurgan) Battalion, Armagh Regiment, Ulster Volunteer Force. Enlisted September 1914. To France with 36th (Ulster) Division in October 1915. **Wounded** by shellfire 31 May 1916 at Mesnil. **Died of wounds** 1 June 1916, aged 33. 1914-15 Star.

FULTON Private James 14170. From Mary Street, Portadown, County Armagh. 4th (Portadown) Battalion, Armagh Regiment, Ulster Volunteer Force. Enlisted September 1914. To France with 36th (Ulster) Division in October 1915. 'B' Company. **Killed in action** during the attack at Hamel 1 July 1916, aged 19. 1914-15 Star.

FULTON Private James Norman 41207. Commissioned into The Royal Inniskilling Fusiliers - see Appendix 5.

FULTON Private Nicholas 14193. Born in 1871 at Portadown, County Armagh. 4th (Portadown) Battalion, Armagh Regiment, Ulster Volunteer Force. A weaver. Served pre-war in the 3rd Battalion (Militia), Princess Victoria's (Royal Irish Fusiliers). Enlisted September 1914. Discharged as not being likely to become an efficient soldier in that he was considered medically unfit for service 15 December 1914.

FULTON Private Richard 14269. Born at Drumcree, County Armagh. From Henry Street,

Portadown, County Armagh. Worked in the linen trade. 4th (Portadown) Battalion, Armagh Regiment, Ulster Volunteer Force. Enlisted September 1914. To France with 36th (Ulster) Division in October 1915. [Joined 108th Brigade Machine Gun Company in January 1916. Transferred to the Machine Gun Corps (renumbered 17788). **Killed in action** with 36th Battalion, Machine Gun Corps 21 March 1918 during the retreat from St Quentin, aged 31.] 1914-15 Star.

GABBEY Private Thomas 49738. Enlisted 30 August 1916. Joined the 9th (North Irish Horse) Battalion, Princess Victoria's (Royal Irish Fusiliers) with the draft of men transferred from The Royal Irish Rifles in April 1918. **Wounded**. Discharged as no longer physically fit for war service due to wounds 8 May 1919. Silver War Badge, number B242664.

GAGEBY Lance Corporal James Percy Neill 24320. Born in 1898 at Belfast. [Enlisted in May 1916 and joined the 7th or 8th (Service) Battalion in 49th Brigade, 16th (Irish) Division.] Joined the 9th (North Irish Horse) Battalion when the 7th/8th (Service) Battalion was disbanded in February 1918. 'A' Company. **Captured** in the period 21-28 March 1918 during the retreat from St Quentin. After the war he emigrated to the United States and worked as an iron moulder in New Jersey and became a US citizen. He died in New Jersey, United States.

GALBRAITH Private George 41188. From Glengormley, County Antrim. [Enlisted in May 1915 into the North Irish Horse (1601). To France with 'F' Squadron in 33rd Division 17 November 1915. Served with 2nd North Irish Horse, X Corps Cavalry Regiment.] Joined the renamed 9th (North Irish Horse) Battalion from 36 Infantry Base Depot and transferred to Princess Victoria's (Royal Irish Fusiliers) in September/October 1917 (renumbered 41188). **Wounded** at Moeuvres on 23 November 1917 and **died of wounds** 24 November 1917.

GALBRAITH Private Joseph 42571 & 33607. Born in 1899 at Ballymacarrett, Belfast. [Enlisted 29 November 1917 into The Royal Irish Rifles (20951). To France 26 August 1918.] Transferred at the Base Depot to Princess Victoria's (Royal Irish Fusiliers) 14 September 1918 (renumbered 42571) and joined the 9th (North Irish Horse) Battalion 22 September 1918. Re-enlisted in 1919 for Regular Army service with Princess Victoria's (Royal Irish Fusiliers) (renumbered 33607). **Deserted** 1 January 1920.

GALBRAITH Private Patrick 24581. Born in 1894 at Claudy, County Londonderry. A farm labourer from Dungiven, County Londonderry. Enlisted 17 July 1916 and joined the 3rd (Reserve) Battalion. To 36 Infantry Base Depot, France 9 December 1916. Joined the 9th (Service) Battalion 22 December 1916. 'B' Company. **Killed in action** at the Battle of Langemarck 16 August 1917, aged 23.

GALLAGHER Private Philip 21962. [Enlisted in October 1915 and joined the 8th (Service) Battalion in 49th Brigade, 16th (Irish) Division.] Joined the 9th (North Irish Horse) Battalion when the 7th/8th (Service) Battalion was disbanded in February 1918.

GALLAGHER Lance Corporal Thomas E 42541. [Enlisted 10 December 1915 into The Royal Irish Rifles (10826). Served with 2nd Battalion, The Royal Irish Rifles.] Transferred at the Base Depot to Princess Victoria's (Royal Irish Fusiliers) 14 September 1918 (renumbered 42541) and joined the 9th (North Irish Horse) Battalion 22 September 1918. **Wounded**. Discharged as no longer physically fit for war service due to wounds 27 March 1919. Silver War Badge, number B168536.

GALLERY Private William 14216. Enlisted September 1914. To France with 36th (Ulster) Division in October 1915. Tried by Field General Court Martial on 12 July 1918 charged with *'absenting himself without leave'* and *'drunkenness'*; found guilty and sentenced to twenty-eight days Field Punishment Number 1. [Transferred to the Labour Corps (renumbered 604038).] 1914-15 Star.

GALLOGLY Private Charles Seymour 14200. Born 10 March 1896 at Tullamore, Edenderry, King's County. A student. Enlisted September 1914. Discharged as not being likely to become an efficient soldier in that he was considered medically unfit for service 1 October 1914. [Re-enlisted into The Royal Irish Rifles (17/340) and joined the 17th (Reserve) Battalion, The Royal Irish Rifles. Posted to the 10th (Service) Battalion, The Royal Irish Rifles (South Belfast). To France with 36th (Ulster) Division in October 1915. Evacuated to hospital in England. Transferred to The Northumberland Fusiliers (renumbered 50038) and served in Ireland with the 3rd (Home Service) Garrison Battalion, The Northumberland Fusiliers.] Discharged as no longer physically fit for war service 6 September 1918. Silver War Badge, number 506282. 1914-15 Star. Nephew of Major W S S Berry, the Medical Officer. In 1950 he emigrated to the United States, where he died in Glendale,

California on 24 November 1951, aged 55. Buried at Glendale Memorial Park.

GALLOWAY Private Charles Henry 29532. Enlisted, re-enlisted or transferred to Princess Victoria's (Royal Irish Fusiliers) in March 1918. Posted to the 9th (North Irish Horse) Battalion.

GALWEY Private Patrick 20430. [Enlisted in July 1915 and joined the 8th (Service) Battalion in 49th Brigade, 16th (Irish) Division.] Joined the 9th (North Irish Horse) Battalion when the 7th/8th (Service) Battalion was disbanded in February 1918. 'D' Company. **Missing** in the period 21-28 March 1918 during the retreat from St Quentin believed **captured**.

GARMONY Private Robert 14219. Born on 31 August 1894 at Killylea, County Armagh. From Tynan, County Armagh. Enlisted September 1914. To France with 36th (Ulster) Division in October 1915. **Wounded** by a gunshot to the left hand (losing two fingers) during the attack at Hamel 1 July 1916. Evacuated to hospital in England. Joined the 10th (Reserve) Battalion. Discharged as no longer physically fit for war service due to wounds 4 July 1917. Silver War Badge, number 208329. 1914-15 Star.

GARNER Private William A 43319. Joined the 9th (Service) Battalion, Princess Victoria's (Royal Irish Fusiliers) with the draft of men from The London Regiment in November 1916. [Transferred to the Labour Crops (renumbered 599190).]

GARNHAM Corporal Leonard 45804. Joined the 9th (North Irish Horse) Battalion, Princess Victoria's (Royal Irish Fusiliers) with the draft of men from The London Regiment in April 1918.

GARRETT Private Frank 45747. [Enlisted into The London Regiment (6204). Posted to 1/24th (County of London) Battalion, The London Regiment (The Queen's).] To France and joined 36 Infantry Base Depot 29 March 1918. Transferred to Princess Victoria's (Royal Irish Fusiliers) 2 April 1918 (renumbered 45747) and joined the 9th (North Irish Horse) Battalion 4 April 1918.

GASKIN Private James 6391. Born in 1896 at Shankill, County Armagh. A weaver. Enlisted 19 July 1915 into Princess Victoria's (Royal Irish Fusiliers) Special Reserve and joined the 3rd (Reserve) Battalion. To 36 Infantry Base Depot, France 10 June 1917. Joined the 9th (Service) Battalion 26 June 1917. 'B' Company. Listed as **missing** at the Battle of Langemarck 16 August 1917 and later declared as **killed in action** on that date, aged 19.

GASTON Private George Francis 50016. Born in 1899 at London. From Battersea, London. [Enlisted into The London Regiment (557178) and joined the 16th (Reserve) Battalion, The London Regiment.] Transferred to Princess Victoria's (Royal Irish Fusiliers) in May 1918 (renumbered 50016) and joined the 9th (North Irish Horse) Battalion. **Killed in action** during the attack south of Wulverghem 4 September 1918, aged 18.

GATES Private David 14211. From Bridge Street, Portadown, County Armagh. Enlisted September 1914. To France with 36th (Ulster) Division in October 1915. **Wounded** during the attack at Hamel 1 July 1916. **Wounded** (shell shock) in November 1917. Transferred to the Class Z Reserve 21 March 1919. 1914-15 Star.

GAUL Private William James 43437. [Enlisted into The London Regiment. Posted to 1/24th (County of London Battalion) Battalion, The London Regiment (The Queen's) (7011). Transferred to The Royal Irish Rifles (renumbered 43838).] Transferred to Princess Victoria's (Royal Irish Fusiliers) (renumbered 43437) and joined the 9th (North Irish Horse) Battalion with the draft of men from The London Regiment in April 1918.

GAYNOR Private Robert 9202 & 25198. Enlisted into Princess Victoria's (Royal Irish Fusiliers) as a regular soldier 22 June 1906 (9202). [To France with the 2nd Battalion 19 December 1914. Discharged at the termination of his service.] Re-enlisted for war service in November 1916 (renumbered 25198) and joined the 9th (Service) Battalion. 'C' Company. **Wounded** at the Battle of Langemarck 16 August 1917. Transferred to the Class P Reserve 5 July 1918, aged 31. Silver War Badge, number 447040.

GEAR Corporal Edward 42088. From Southsea, Hampshire. A baker. [Enlisted 5 August 1915 into the Army Service Corps (S4/125686). To France 2 May 1916 and posted to 39th Field Bakery. Posted to 8th Field Bakery, Dieppe. Corporal 16 February 1917.] Transferred to Princess Victoria's (Royal Irish Fusiliers) 8 May 1918 (renumbered 42088) and joined the 9th (North Irish Horse) Battalion. **Captured** during the attack south of Wulverghem 4 September 1918. Transferred to the Class Z Reserve 14 May 1919.

GEARY Private George Edmund Clugston 25210. Born in 1896 at Johnstone, Renfrewshire. [Enlisted 27 February 1916 and transferred to the Army Reserve. Mobilised 27 November 1916 and joined the 4th (Extra Reserve) Battalion. Charged on 3 March 1917 with: *'When under orders for British Expeditionary Force absent from tattoo on 22 February 1917 until apprehended by the civil power on 25 February 1917 thereby evading embarkation'*; found guilty and sentenced to fourteen days detention and forfeit four days pay. To 36 Infantry Base Depot 17 March 1917 and joined the 1st Battalion 22 April 1917. **Wounded** at Moeuvres 22/23 November 1917 and evacuated to hospital in England. Posted to the 10th (Reserve) Battalion. Fined six days pay for overstaying his pass 15 February 1918. Fined ten days pay for breaking out of barracks 8 April 1918. Tried by District Court Martial on 16 July 1918 charged with: *'**Deserting** His Majesty's Service from 13 April 1918 until apprehended by the civil power at Armagh on 6 July 1918 in plain clothes.'* Found guilty and sentenced to fifty-six days detention. Posted to the 3rd (Reserve) Battalion 26 July 1918.] To 36 Infantry Base Depot 25 August 1918 and joined the 9th (North Irish Horse) Battalion 9 September 1918. 'D' Company. **Wounded** when shot in the left arm at Courtrai on 16 October 1918. Treated at 54th General Hospital, Aubergue then evacuated to hospital in England 24 October 1918. Treated at 5th Northern General Hospital, Leicester until 1 March 1919. Discharged as no longer physically fit for war service due to wounds 5 April 1919. Silver War Badge, number B207385.

GEDDES Private Thomas 14234. Enlisted September 1914. No record of deployment to France with 36th (Ulster) Division in October 1915. [Transferred to the Labour Corps (renumbered 231599). Served with 666th Labour Company.]

GEDDIS Private John 41510. [Enlisted 7 June 1915 into the Service Squadron, 6th (Inniskilling) Dragoons (UD/264). Served with 2nd North Irish Horse, X Corps Cavalry Regiment.] Joined the renamed 9th (North Irish Horse) Battalion from 36 Infantry Base Depot and transferred to Princess Victoria's (Royal Irish Fusiliers) in September/October 1917 (renumbered 41510). **Wounded**. Discharged as no longer physically fit for war service due to wounds 14 August 1918, aged 22. Silver War Badge, number 435820.

GENTLES Private William 15840. Born in 1888 at St Thomas, Dublin. A painter. [Enlisted 27 October 1914 and joined the 6th (Service) Battalion in 31st Brigade, 10th (Irish) Division. Embarked with the Mediterranean Expeditionary Force July 1915. **Wounded** by a gunshot to the scalp 9 August 1915 at Gallipoli. Evacuated to hospital in England September 1915. Joined the 3rd (Reserve) Battalion 17 December 1915. To Infantry Depot France and joined the 7th (Service) Battalion 19 April 1916. **Wounded** by shrapnel to the right ankle at Langemarck 16 August 1917. Evacuated to hospital in England and treated at 2nd Western General Hospital, Manchester.] To 36 Infantry Base Depot 21 January 1918 and joined the 9th (North Irish Horse) Battalion in February 1918 with the draft from the disbanded 7th/8th (Service) Battalion. Transferred to the Class Z Reserve 16 March 1919. 1914-15 Star.

GEOFFROY Private Francis Lewis 41571. Born 16 January 1894 at Ballymahon, County Longford. Lived at Edgeworthstown, County Longford, where his father ran the Imperial Hotel. He emigrated to the United States on 26 April 1911, where he worked as a clerk in Brooklyn, New York. He returned to the United Kingdom on 16 December 1915. [Enlisted 29 January 1916 into the North Irish Horse (2104). Served with 2nd North Irish Horse, X Corps Cavalry Regiment.] Joined the renamed 9th (North Irish Horse) Battalion from 36 Infantry Base Depot and transferred to Princess Victoria's (Royal Irish Fusiliers) in September/October 1917 (renumbered 41571). **Wounded**. Discharged as no longer physically fit for war service due to wounds 12 December 1918. Silver War Badge, number B71387. After the war he returned to the United States and lived in Delaware County, Pennsylvania, where he died in 1975, aged 81.

GEORGE Lance Corporal Thomas 24908. Born in 1899 at Armagh, County Armagh. Enlisted in October 1916, aged 17. Posted to the 9th (Service) Battalion.

GERAGHTY Private Peter 43178. Enlisted into or transferred to Princess Victoria's (Royal Irish Fusiliers) in August 1916 and joined the 7th (Service) Battalion in 49th Brigade 16th (Irish) Division.] Joined the 9th (North Irish Horse) Battalion when the 7th/8th (Service) Battalion was disbanded in February 1918.

GERVIN Private John Joseph 16153. Enlisted into the 9th (Service) Battalion in October 1914. To France with 36th (Ulster) Division in October 1915. Transferred to the Class Z Reserve 5 March 1919. 1914-15 Star.

GIBSON Private Duncan Clarke 42232. From Haddington, Scotland. [Enlisted 9 November 1915 into the Army Service Corps (T4/124094). To France 29 February 1916 and served with 21st Reserve Park and 19th Mobile Veterinary Station.] Transferred to Princess Victoria's (Royal Irish Fusiliers) 8 May 1918 (renumbered 42232) and joined the 9th (North Irish Horse) Battalion. Transferred to the Class Z Reserve 10 March 1919.

GIBSON Private Henry 14239. From Lurgan, County Armagh. Enlisted September 1914. To France with 36th (Ulster) Division in October 1915. **Killed in action** during the attack at Hamel 1 July 1916, aged 20. 1914-15 Star. Brother of Lance Corporal William John Gibson.

GIBSON Private Henry 42162. [Enlisted into the Army Service Corps (S4/090282). To France 11 September 1915.] Transferred to Princess Victoria's (Royal Irish Fusiliers) 8 May 1918 (renumbered 42162) and was posted to the 9th (North Irish Horse) Battalion. [Part of the draft transferred on 19 June 1918 to The Royal Irish Rifles (renumbered 45865).] 1914-15 Star. Transferred to the Class Z Reserve.

GIBSON Lance Sergeant John Edgar 14228. Commissioned into Princess Victoria's (Royal Irish Fusiliers) - see Appendix 5.

GIBSON Private John Henry 14222. Enlisted September 1914. To France with 36th (Ulster) Division in October 1915. 'B' Company. **Wounded** (shellshock) during the attack at Hamel 1 July 1916. Posted to the 5th (Service) Battalion and later back to the 9th (North Irish Horse) Battalion. **Missing** in the period 21-28 March 1918 during the retreat from St Quentin believed **captured**. Transferred to the Class Z Reserve 11 March 1919. 1914-15 Star. Emigrated to Canada.

GIBSON Private Joseph 6123. [Enlisted in July 1914 into Princess Victoria's (Royal Irish Fusiliers) Special Reserve. Mobilised from the Special Reserve and joined the 1st Battalion in France 31 October 1914.] 'C' Company. Believed **wounded** in the period 21-28 March 1918 during the retreat from St Quentin. [Transferred to The Northumberland Fusiliers (renumbered 89301).] 1914 Star.

GIBSON Private Joseph 41413. From Ashfield, Cootehill, County Cavan. [Enlisted in November 1915 into the North Irish Horse (1966). Served with 2nd North Irish Horse, X Corps Cavalry Regiment.] Joined the renamed 9th (North Irish Horse) Battalion from 36 Infantry Base Depot and transferred to Princess Victoria's (Royal Irish Fusiliers) in September/October 1917 (renumbered 41413). 'A' Company. **Captured** in the period 21-28 March 1918 during the retreat from St Quentin. His brother, Cadet George Arthur Gibson, served with The Royal Irish Rifles and was wounded.

GIBSON Lance Corporal William John 14225. From Lurgan, County Armagh. Enlisted September 1914. To France with 36th (Ulster) Division in October 1915. 'C' Company. **Killed in action** with a bombing team during the attack at Hamel 1 July 1916, aged 27. 1914-15 Star. Brother of Private Henry Gibson.

GIBSON Private William John 18254. From Tullyvin, Cootehill, County Cavan. Enlisted into the 9th (Service) Battalion in February/March 1915. To France with 36th (Ulster) Division in October 1915. 'D' Company. **Missing** at the Battle of Langemarck 16 August 1917 and later declared **killed in action** on that date, aged 23. 1914-15 Star.

GIFFEN Private David 17297. From Ballynahonemore, County Armagh. Enlisted into the 9th (Service) Battalion in November 1914. To France with 36th (Ulster) Division in October 1915. 'A' Company. **Wounded** in the legs during the attack at Hamel 1 July 1916. Listed as **wounded** at the Battle of Langemarck 16 August 1917 and later declared **killed in action** on that date, aged 22. 1914-15 Star.

GIFFEN Private William 17655. From Derryraine, Armagh, County Armagh. Enlisted into the 9th (Service) Battalion in December 1914/January 1915. To France with 36th (Ulster) Division in October 1915. 'A' Company. **Wounded** during the attack at Hamel 1 July 1916. **Wounded** at the Battle of Langemarck 16 August 1917. [Transferred to the Labour Corps (renumbered 575358).] 1914-15 Star.

GILBERT Private Alfred Bartholomew 42546. Born 14 May 1895. From Pentonville, London. [Enlisted 10 December 1915 and transferred to the Army Reserve. Mobilised in early-1916 and joined the 12th (Service) Battalion, The Rifle Brigade (The Prince Consorts Own) (15803). To France

24 April 1917. Transferred to The Royal Irish Rifles (renumbered 41941) and joined the 10th (Service) Battalion, The Royal Irish Rifles (South Belfast). Evacuated to England sick (bronchitis) 29 July 1917.] Transferred at the Base Depot to Princess Victoria's (Royal Irish Fusiliers) 14 September 1918 (renumbered 42546) and joined the 9th (North Irish Horse) Battalion 22 September 1918. **Wounded** by gunshot to the left arm and abdomen during the advance to Anseghem 25 October 1918. Treated at 2nd Australian General Hospital, Boulogne and evacuated to England. Joined the 3rd (Reserve) Battalion 30 December 1918. Transferred to the Class Z Reserve 17 February 1919. Died in 1968, aged 73 at Stepney, London.

GILBERT Lance Corporal Alfred William 18957. Born in 1893 at Bournemouth, Hampshire. A greengrocer's assistant. [Enlisted or transferred to Princess Victoria's (Royal Irish Fusiliers) April 1915. To France 28 June 1915 and joined the 1st Battalion.] Posted to the 9th (Service) Battalion. 'C' Company. **Wounded** at the Battle of Langemarck 16 August 1917. Transferred to the Class Z Reserve. 1914-15 Star.

GILBERT Private John R 45738. [Enlisted into The London Regiment (5451). Posted to 1/24th (County of London) Battalion, The London Regiment (The Queen's).] To France and joined 36 Infantry Base Depot 29 March 1918. Transferred to Princess Victoria's (Royal Irish Fusiliers) 2 April 1918 (renumbered 45738) and joined the 9th (North Irish Horse) Battalion 4 April 1918. [Posted to the 1/9th (County of London) Battalion, The London Regiment (The Queen's).]

GILCHRIST Private Thomas 24358. Born in 1893 at Lurgan, County Armagh. A weaver. Enlisted in May 1916. Posted to the 9th (Service) Battalion. 'C' Company. **Wounded** at the Battle of Langemarck 16 August 1917. [Transferred to the Labour Corps (renumbered 571605).]

GILCHRIST Private William 7688. [Enlisted into Princess Victoria's (Royal Irish Fusiliers) as a regular soldier in 1902. To France with the 1st Battalion 22 August 1914.] Posted to the 9th (North Irish Horse) Battalion. Tried by Field General Court Martial on 6 November 1918 charged with *'allowing to escape a person committed to his charge whom it was his duty to keep guard'*; found not guilty. 1914 Star.

GILKINSON Private Edward 14231. Born 1888. A tailor from Pomeroy, County Tyrone. [Enlisted into The Royal Inniskilling Fusiliers 12 July 1908 (3092). Bought out 23 May 1913.] Re-enlisted September 1914 and joined the 9th (Service) Battalion, Princess Victoria's (Royal Irish Fusiliers). To France with 36th (Ulster) Division in October 1915. [Joined 108th Brigade Machine Gun Company in January 1916. Transferred to the Machine Gun Corps (renumbered 17789).] 1914-15 Star.

GILKINSON Private James 14235. Born at Derrytagh, County Armagh. Enlisted September 1914. To France with 36th (Ulster) Division in October 1915. 'D' Company. **Wounded** during the attack at Hamel 1 July 1916. **Killed in action** 29 March 1918 during the retreat from St Quentin. 1914-15 Star.

GILLAN MM Warrant Officer Class II Thomas F 9458 & 7040186. From Dublin. A gardener's assistant. [Enlisted into Princess Victoria's (Royal Irish Fusiliers) as a regular soldier 5 November 1906. To France with the 2nd Battalion (Sergeant) 19 December 1914). Served with the 2nd Battalion in Salonika from 11 December 1915. **MM**. Served in Egypt from 21 September 1917 to 5 July 1918.] Posted to the 9th (North Irish Horse) Battalion. 'D' Company. 1914-15 Star. Continued to serve with Princess Victoria's (Royal Irish Fusiliers) (renumbered 7040186) and served with the 2nd Battalion. Long Service & Good Conduct Medal. Discharged 4 November 1924 and lived in Maidstone.

GILLANDERS Corporal Edward Robert 16103. From Aughnaseda, County Monaghan. Enlisted into the 9th (Service) Battalion in October 1914. To France with 36th (Ulster) Division in October 1915. **Wounded** during the attack at Hamel 1 July 1916. **Captured** in 1918. Transferred to the Class Z Reserve 23 March 1919. 1914-15 Star.

GILLANDERS MM Private Robert Hugh 16105. Born in 1893 at Aughbrick, Castleshane, County Monaghan. Enlisted into the 9th (Service) Battalion in October 1914. 'D' Company. To France with 36th (Ulster) Division in October 1915. **Wounded** at the Battle of Langemarck 16 August 1917. **MM** – Wulverghem 4 September 1918. Transferred to the Class Z Reserve 18 March 1919. 1914-15 Star.

GILLESPIE Corporal Cyril 14220. Enlisted September 1914. To France with 36th (Ulster) Division in October 1915. Discharged as no longer physically fit for war service due to sickness 13 June

1916. Silver War Badge, number 175799. 1914-15 Star.

GILLESPIE Private David 20331. Enlisted in May/June 1915 and joined the 9th (Service) Battalion with the draft of men from The Royal Inniskilling Fusiliers who transferred to Princess Victoria's (Royal Irish Fusiliers) on 30 June 1915. To France with 36th (Ulster) Division in October 1915. [Transferred to the Machine Gun Corps (renumbered 73274).] 1914-15 Star.

GILLESPIE Private James 14242. From Armagh, County Armagh. Enlisted September 1914. To France with 36th (Ulster) Division in October 1915. 'A' Company. **Wounded** by shellfire during the attack at Hamel 1 July 1916. Crawled back after four days in a water-filled shell-hole. **Missing** in the period 11-18 April 1918 in the actions between Wulverghem and Kemmel; subsequently declared **killed in action** 19 April 1918, aged 33. 1914-15 Star. His brother-in-law, Private John Trimble, was killed in action on 24 October 1914 serving with The Prince of Wales's Volunteers (South Lancashire Regiment). His brother-in-law, Assistant Storekeeper William Trimble was killed in action on 25 May 1917 while serving with the Royal Navy.

GILLESPIE Corporal John 14218. Enlisted September 1914. To France with 36th (Ulster) Division in October 1915. [Transferred to the Labour Corps (renumbered 603803).] 1914-15 Star.

GILLESPIE Private Samuel 22810. Enlisted in November 1915. Posted to the 9th (Service) Battalion.

GILLESPIE Private William J 17072. From Portadown, County Armagh. Enlisted into the 9th (Service) Battalion in October 1914. To France with 36th (Ulster) Division in October 1915. **Wounded** during the attack at Hamel 1 July 1916. [Transferred to the Labour Corps (renumbered 309990).] Transferred to the Class Z Reserve 16 April 1919. 1914-15 Star.

GILLILAND Private Alexander 41249. [Enlisted in May 1915 into the North Irish Horse (1600). To France with 'F' Squadron in 33rd Division 17 November 1915. Served with 2nd North Irish Horse, X Corps Cavalry Regiment.] Joined the renamed 9th (North Irish Horse) Battalion from 36 Infantry Base Depot and transferred to Princess Victoria's (Royal Irish Fusiliers) in September/October 1917 (renumbered 41249). Transferred to the Class Z Reserve 26 March 1919. 1914-15 Star.

GILLILAND Private Charles 22553. Enlisted in November 1915. Posted to the 9th (Service) Battalion.

GILLILAND Private James 14205. From Portadown, County Armagh. Member of Edenderry Temperance and Benefit Loyal Orange Lodge 322. Enlisted September 1914. To France with 36th (Ulster) Division in October 1915. 'D' Company. **Captured** in the period 21-28 March 1918 during the retreat from St Quentin. Transferred to the Class Z Reserve 21 March 1919. 1914-15 Star.

GILMANEY Private John 20343. From Washington, County Durham. [Enlisted into The Royal Inniskilling Fusiliers (23475).] Transferred to Princess Victoria's (Royal Irish Fusiliers) on 30 June 1915 (renumbered 20343) and joined the 9th (Service) Battalion. To France with 36th (Ulster) Division in October 1915. **Killed in action** during the attack at Hamel 1 July 1916. 1914-15 Star.

GILMORE Private Joseph 3017. From Enniskillen, County Fermanagh. [Enlisted 25 July 1912 into the 4th Battalion (Militia), Princess Victoria's (Royal Irish Fusiliers) Special Reserve. Mobilised 6 August 1914. Reported as having **deserted** 5 September 1914. Tried by District Court Martial at Carrickfergus on 12 November 1914 charged with *'absenting himself without leave'*, *'loosing by neglect his equipment'* and *'fraudulent enlistment'*; he pleaded guilty and was sentenced to 120 days detention with thirty days remission. To France 16 February 1915. To hospital 26 February 1916 and evacuated to hospital in England. Treated at Mill Road Infirmary, Liverpool. To France 31 August 1916. Returned to Ireland where he served throughout 1917, during which time he was charged five times for being absent from tattoo or absent without leave.] To Infantry Base Depot, France 24 January 1918 and posted to the 7th/8th (Service) Battalion; probably did not join. Joined the 9th (North Irish Horse) Battalion when the 7th/8th (Service) Battalion was disbanded in February 1918. 'A' Company. **Captured** in the period 21-28 March 1918 during the retreat from St Quentin. **Died** of pneumonia on 18 October 1918 at Merseburg Prisoner of War Camp, Saxony aged 26. He was interred in the camp cemetery and reinterred at Berlin South-Western Cemetery in 1925. 1914-15 Star.

GILMORE Private McClelland 18633. From Mowhan, County Armagh. Armagh Regiment, Ulster Volunteer Force. Enlisted into thc 9th (Service) Battalion in April 1915. To France with 36th (Ulster)

Division in October 1915. **Wounded** during the attack at Hamel 1 July 1916 and **died of wounds** in hospital in England 28 July 1916, aged 20. 1914-15 Star.

GILROY Private George 15258. Born at Ballymacarrett, County Down. [Enlisted September 1914 into the 7th (Service) Battalion in 49th Brigade, 16th (Irish) Division.] Joined the 9th (North Irish Horse) Battalion when the 7th/8th (Service) Battalion was disbanded in February 1918. **Killed in action** 27 March 1918 during the retreat from St Quentin, aged 31.

GIRLING Private Henry 42089. [Enlisted into the Army Service Corps (T4/035583). To France 12 January 1915 and served with 28th, 5th, 23rd and 8th Field Bakeries.] Transferred to Princess Victoria's (Royal Irish Fusiliers) 8 May 1918 (renumbered 42089) and joined the 9th (North Irish Horse) Battalion. Transferred to the Class Z Reserve 24 February 1919. 1914-15 Star.

GIRVAN Warrant Officer Class II Francis 14210. From Tarson, County Armagh. Enlisted September 1914. To France with 36th (Ulster) Division in October 1915. 'D' Company. **Wounded** 26 June 1916. Company Sergeant Major. Transferred to the Class Z Reserve 11 March 1919. 1914-15 Star. Brother of Lance Sergeant Joseph Girvan. His brother, Private John Girvan, a regular soldier with the 1st Battalion, was killed in action on 15/16 September 1916.

GIRVAN Private James 19796. Born at Armagh, County Armagh. Enlisted into the 9th (Service) Battalion in May 1915. 'A' Company. **Died** in Ireland 18 March 1917, aged 18. Armagh (St Mark) Church of Ireland Churchyard. 4. 30.

GIRVAN Lance Sergeant Joseph 14241. Born at Derryadd, County Armagh. From Lurgan, County Armagh. Enlisted September 1914. To France with 36th (Ulster) Division in October 1915. **Wounded** during the attack at Hamel 1 July 1916 and **died of wounds** 4 July 1916, aged 30. 1914-15 Star. Brother of Company Sergeant Major Francis Girvan. His brother, Private John Girvan, a regular soldier with the 1st Battalion, was killed in action on 15/16 September 1916.

GIRVAN Private Robert 16106. Born in 1893 at Annahagh, County Monaghan. A tailor. Enlisted into the 9th (Service) Battalion 25 September 1914. To France with 36th (Ulster) Division in October 1915. **Wounded** by a gunshot to the chest during the attack at Hamel 1 July 1916 and evacuated to hospital in England. Joined the 10th (Reserve) Battalion 24 October 1916. [Transferred to the Labour Corps (renumbered 545513) 6 April 1918. Served with 657th and 655th Home Service Employment Companies.] Transferred to the Class Z Reserve 24 April 1919. 1914-15 Star.

GIRVAN Private Robert James 19762, 33969 & 7041947. From Milford, County Armagh. Enlisted into the 9th (Service) Battalion in April 1915. Re-enlisted in February 1920 for Regular Army service with Princess Victoria's (Royal Irish Fusiliers) (renumbered 33969, renumbered 7041947). Discharged 7 March 1922.

GIRVIN Private William 14206. From Lurgan, County Armagh. A weaver. Enlisted into the 9th (Service) Battalion September 1914. To France with 36th (Ulster) Division in October 1915. A cook in 'C' Company. **Killed in action** by shellfire at Mesnil on 12 February 1916, the first soldier of the 9th (Service) Battalion to be killed in France. 1914-15 Star.

GLASS Lance Corporal Frederick Hugh 21827. Enlisted in October 1915 and joined the 7th (Service) Battalion in 49th Brigade, 16th (Irish) Division.] Joined the 9th (North Irish Horse) Battalion when the 7th/8th (Service) Battalion was disbanded in February 1918.

GLASS Private Joseph 22982. From Bessbrook, County Armagh. Enlisted in November 1915. Posted to the 9th (Service) Battalion. **Killed in action** during the attack at Hamel 1 July 1916.

GLASS Private Patrick John 3428. Born at Ballymoney, County Antrim. From Hordle, Hampshire. [Enlisted in early-1915 into Princess Victoria's (Royal Irish Fusiliers) Special Reserve. Joined the 6th (Service) Battalion in 31st Brigade, 10th (Irish) Division. Served with the Mediterranean Expeditionary Force from September 1915.] Joined the 9th (North Irish Horse) Battalion in early-1918. **Missing** in the period 11-18 April 1918 in the actions between Wulverghem and Kemmel; subsequently declared **killed in action** 19 April 1918, aged 26. 1914-15 Star.

GLENN Private James 49739. Born in 1899. [Enlisted 31 May 1915, aged 16, and joined the 19th (Reserve) Battalion, The Royal Irish Rifles. Posted to the 20th (Reserve) Battalion, The Royal Irish Rifles 3 July 1917. Rejoined the 19th (Reserve) Battalion, The Royal Irish Rifles 27 March 1918.] Transferred at 'G' Infantry Base Depot to Princess Victoria's (Royal Irish Fusiliers) 15 April 1918 (renumbered 49739) and joined the 9th (North Irish Horse) Battalion. 'C' Company. **Wounded** by a gunshot to the right knee August 1918. Evacuated to England from 4th General Hospital. Posted to the 3rd (Reserve) Battalion 16 November 1918. Discharged as no longer physically fit for war service due to wounds 1 April 1919. Silver War Badge, number B170670.

GLENN Lance Corporal Samuel 18556. Enlisted into the 9th (Service) Battalion in April 1915. To France with 36th (Ulster) Division in October 1915. 'C' Company. Bombing team. **Wounded** during the attack at Hamel 1 July 1916. **Wounded** during the retreat from St Quentin 21-28 March 1918. **Captured** later in 1918. Discharged as no longer physically fit for war service due to wounds 31 March 1920. 1914-15 Star.

GLENN Private William 14209. From Lurgan, County Armagh. Enlisted September 1914. To France with 36th (Ulster) Division in October 1915. **Killed in action** during the attack at Hamel 1 July 1916. 1914-15 Star.

GLENVILLE Private Alfred 43328. Born in 1883. From Deptford, Kent. [Joined the 3/7th Battalion, The London Regiment (352936) 28 June 1916. To France 10 November 1916.] Attached to the 9th (Service) Battalion, Princess Victoria's (Royal Irish Fusiliers) 26 November 1916. 'B' Company. Discharged from the Territorial Force, re-enlisted and transferred to Princess Victoria's (Royal Irish Fusiliers) in March/April 1917 (renumbered 43328). **Wounded** by shrapnel at the Battle of Langemarck 16 August 1917. Evacuated to hospital in England and treated at Bagthorpe Military Hospital, Nottinghamshire until 8 September 1917. [To France 18 January 1918 and posted to the 1st Battalion. **Captured** while serving with the 1st Battalion during the retreat from St Quentin and held for a time at Limburg Prisoner of War Camp. **Died** of intestinal catarrh in hospital at Avesnes-sur-Helpe on 29 May 1918 while a prisoner of war.]

GODDARD Private Charles 42208. Joined the 9th (North Irish Horse) Battalion, Princess Victoria's (Royal Irish Fusiliers) with the draft of men transferred from the Army Service Corps and the Army Veterinary Corps in May 1918.

GODDARD Private Herbert Edward Stannard 42234. Born 18 October 1896 at Woolwich, London. [Enlisted into the Army Service Corps (T4/037586). To France 18 January 1915 and served with 28th Division Train.] Transferred to Princess Victoria's (Royal Irish Fusiliers) 8 May 1918 (renumbered 42234) and joined the 9th (North Irish Horse) Battalion. Transferred to the Class Z Reserve 23 February 1919. 1914-15 Star. Died 1980, aged 83 at Worthing, West Sussex.

GODFREY Corporal George 42173. [Enlisted into the Army Service Corps (S4/093509).] Transferred to Princess Victoria's (Royal Irish Fusiliers) 8 May 1918 (renumbered 42173) and joined the 9th (North Irish Horse) Battalion. [Transferred to The Royal Inniskilling Fusiliers (renumbered 49821).]

GOGGINS Private Joseph 16212. [Enlisted in October 1914 into the 5th (Service) Battalion in 31st Brigade, 10th (Irish) Division. Embarked with the Mediterranean Expeditionary Force July 1915. Posted to the 7th/8th (Service) Battalion in 49th Brigade, 16th (Irish) Division.] Joined the 9th (North Irish Horse) Battalion when the 7th/8th (Service) Battalion was disbanded in February 1918. **Missing** in the period 21-28 March 1918 during the retreat from St Quentin believed **captured**.

GOLDMAN Private Harry 45765. Joined the 9th (North Irish Horse) Battalion, Princess Victoria's (Royal Irish Fusiliers) with the draft of men from The London Regiment in April 1918.

GOOCH Corporal Maurice Stanley 42182. [Enlisted into the Army Service Corps (S3/025151). To France 28 July 1918 and served with 49th and 16th Field Bakeries.] Transferred to Princess Victoria's (Royal Irish Fusiliers) 8 May 1918 (renumbered 42182) and joined the 9th (North Irish Horse) Battalion. Transferred to the Class Z Reserve 24 February 1919. 1914-15 Star.

GOODFELLOW Private Albert 20340. From County Durham. Enlisted in May/June 1915 and joined the 9th (Service) Battalion with the draft of men from The Royal Inniskilling Fusiliers who transferred to Princess Victoria's (Royal Irish Fusiliers) on 30 June 1915. To France with 36th (Ulster) Division in October 1915. 'D' Company. **Wounded** at the Battle of Langemarck 16 August 1917. **Wounded** during the retreat from St Quentin 21-28 March 1918. Discharged as no longer physically fit for war service due to wounds 14 December 1918. 1914-15 Star.

GOODFELLOW Private William G 18067. Enlisted into the 9th (Service) Battalion in February 1915. To France with 36th (Ulster) Division in October 1915. 'C' Company. To hospital mid-1916.

Discharged just before the attack at Hamel on 1 July 1916 when he acted as a company runner and survived unwounded. **Wounded** when shot in the head near Spanbroekmolen on the night of 4/5 June 1917. [Transferred to 5th (Service) Battalion, The Royal Irish Regiment (Pioneers) in the Light Division in the British Army of the Rhine in March/June 1919 (renumbered 41293). Re-enlisted in 1919 for Regular Army service with the Corps of Royal Engineers (renumbered 2206222).] 1914-15 Star.

GORDON Lance Sergeant Arthur John 17149. Commissioned into The Royal Inniskilling Fusiliers - see Appendix 5.

GORDON Private George James 43376. [Enlisted 2 December 1915 into The London Regiment (6769). Posted for service with the 1/7th (City of London) Battalion, The London Regiment.] Attached to the 9th (Service) Battalion, Princess Victoria's (Royal Irish Fusiliers) 26 November 1916. 'C' Company. Discharged from the Territorial Force, re-enlisted and transferred to Princess Victoria's (Royal Irish Fusiliers) in March/April 1917 (renumbered 43376). **Wounded** during the retreat from St Quentin 21-28 March 1918. Discharged as no longer physically fit for war service due to wounds 14 July 1919. Silver War Badge, number B294629.

GORDON Private James 14217. From Carrickblacker Road, Portadown, County Armagh. 4th (Portadown) Battalion, Armagh Regiment, Ulster Volunteer Force. Member of Clounagh Loyal Orange Lodge 9. Enlisted September 1914. To France with 36th (Ulster) Division in October 1915. 'C' Company. **Killed in action** during the attack at Hamel 1 July 1916. 1914-15 Star. Related to Sergeant William Gordon. Private Gordon and Private Ephraim Sherman (1st Battalion, killed in action on 6 July 1916) appear on the Clounagh Loyal Orange Lodge banner unfurled in July 1921).

GORDON Lance Corporal James 41184. [Enlisted 14 January 1915 into the North Irish Horse (1402). To France with 'F' Squadron in 33rd Division 17 November 1915. Served with 2nd North Irish Horse, X Corps Cavalry Regiment.] Joined the renamed 9th (North Irish Horse) Battalion from 36 Infantry Base Depot and transferred to Princess Victoria's (Royal Irish Fusiliers) in September/October 1917 (renumbered 41184). **Wounded**. Discharged as no longer physically fit for war service due to wounds 9 August 1918, aged 27. Silver War Badge, number 435797. 1914-15 Star.

GORDON Lance Corporal Robert 14232. Born in 1881 at Lurgan, County Armagh. A handkerchief printer. Enlisted September 1914. To France with 36th (Ulster) Division in October 1915. 'C' Company. Detached to Battalion Headquarters and did not take part in the attack at Hamel on 1 July 1916. [Transferred to the Royal Defence Corps (renumbered 84895).] Discharged as no longer physically fit for war service due to sickness 1 February 1919. Silver War Badge, number B191655. 1914-15 Star.

GORDON Private Thomas 14244. Enlisted September 1914. To France with 36th (Ulster) Division in October 1915. [Transferred to The Northumberland Fusiliers (renumbered 49818) and served with the 3rd (Home Service) Garrison Battalion, The Northumberland Fusiliers at Belfast.] Discharged as no longer physically fit for war service due to sickness (haemorrhoids) 5 June 1918, aged 27. Silver War Badge, number 380406. 1914-15 Star.

GORDON Sergeant William 14221. From Castle Avenue, Portadown, County Armagh. Enlisted September 1914. To France with 36th (Ulster) Division in October 1915. 'D' Company. **Wounded** during the attack at Hamel 1 July 1916 and **died of wounds** 2 July 1916, aged 27. 1914-15 Star. Related to Private James Gordon (14217).

GORDON Private William 41574. [Enlisted in January 1915 into the North Irish Horse (1403). To France with 'F' Squadron in 33rd Division 17 November 1915. Served with 2nd North Irish Horse, X Corps Cavalry Regiment.] Joined the renamed 9th (North Irish Horse) Battalion from 36 Infantry Base Depot and transferred to Princess Victoria's (Royal Irish Fusiliers) in September/October 1917 (renumbered 41574). 'D' Company. **Wounded** during the retreat from St Quentin 21-28 March 1918. Transferred to the Class Z Reserve 27 March 1919. 1914-15 Star.

GORMAN MM Private Matthew 20938. Enlisted into the 9th (Service) Battalion in September 1915. Posted to the 10th (Reserve) Battalion. Posted to the 9th (Service) Battalion in April/May 1916. 'B' Company. **MM** – attack at Hamel 1 July 1916. Believed **wounded** in the period 21-28 March 1918 during the retreat from St Quentin. [Transferred to the Royal Air Force (renumbered 332200).]

GORMAN Private William 42561. [Served previously with The Royal Irish Rifles (20645).] Transferred at the Base Depot to Princess Victoria's (Royal Irish Fusiliers) 14 September 1918 (renumbered 42561) and joined the 9th (North Irish Horse) Battalion 22 September 1918. [Transferred to 5th (Service) Battalion, The Royal Irish Regiment (Pioneers) in the Light Division in the British Army of the Rhine in March/June 1919 (renumbered 41294).]

GORRIE Private Thomas Robert 41313. Commissioned into the Machine Gun Corps - see Appendix 5.

GOTTEN Private D. From Portadown, County Armagh. Soldier not identified.

GOULDING Private James 15533. [Enlisted in September 1915 into the 5th (Service) Battalion in 31st Brigade, 10th (Irish) Division. Embarked with the Mediterranean Expeditionary Force July 1915. Transferred to the Machine Gun Corps (renumbered 31397). Transferred back to Princess Victoria's (Royal Irish Fusiliers) (again numbered 15533) and posted to the 7th/8th (Service) Battalion.] Joined the 9th (North Irish Horse) Battalion when the 7th/8th (Service) Battalion was disbanded in February 1918. Transferred to the Class Z Reserve.

GOURLEY Private Thomas 27571. Born in 1895 at Ballyrena, County Down. A farm labourer at Newtownards. Enlisted 1 May 1917 and joined the 10th (Reserve) Battalion. To 36 Infantry Base Depot 9 August 1917 and posted to the 9th (Service) Battalion 10 August 1917; he may not have joined. [Posted to the 1st Battalion 1 September 1917. 'A' Company.] Re-enlisted 17 February 1919 for Regular Army service with Princess Victoria's (Royal Irish Fusiliers). Returned to Ireland on leave and was reported as **deserted** on 5 July 1919 (his due return date).

GOVENLOCK Lance Corporal George 42438. [Enlisted into the Army Service Corps (T2/14435 – Driver). To France 24 September 1915 and served with 7th Reserve Park. Acting Sergeant. Deprived of rank for misconduct in a theatre of war. Transferred to The Royal Irish Rifles (renumbered 47303) and posted to the 1st Battalion.] Transferred at the Base Depot to Princess Victoria's (Royal Irish Fusiliers) 14 September 1918 (renumbered 42438) and joined the 9th (North Irish Horse) Battalion 22 September 1918. Transferred to the Class Z Reserve 15 March 1919. 1914-15 Star.

GRACEY DCM Corporal James 41572. [Enlisted in May 1915 into the North Irish Horse (1504). To France with 'F' Squadron in 33rd Division 17 November 1915. Served with 2nd North Irish Horse, X Corps Cavalry Regiment.] Joined the renamed 9th (North Irish Horse) Battalion from 36 Infantry Base Depot and transferred to Princess Victoria's (Royal Irish Fusiliers) in September/October 1917 (renumbered 41572). **DCM** – Wulverghem 4 September 1918. Transferred to the Class Z Reserve. 1914-15 Star.

GRACEY Private Samuel 14230. Born in 1881 at Lurgan, County Armagh. A mechanic for Spence Bryson Ltd, Portadown. Enlisted September 1914. To France with 36th (Ulster) Division in October 1915. Evacuated to hospital in England sick (haemorrhoids) 3 March 1916. [Posted to the 10th (Reserve) Battalion. Lance Corporal 28 June 1916. Acting Corporal 25 May 1917. Posted to the 3rd (Reserve) Battalion 24 May 1918. Posted to the 11th (Service) Battalion 19 June 1918. Transferred to the Army Service Corps (renumbered M/403183) 1 August 1918 and reverted to Private.] Transferred to the Class Z Reserve 12 February 1919. 1914-15 Star.

GRACEY Corporal Thomas 23378. Born at Kilmore, County Down. Enlisted in December 1915. Posted to the 9th (Service) Battalion. 'C' Company. **Killed in action** at the Battle of Langemarck 16 August 1917.

GRACEY Private William 20125. Born in 1900 at Portadown, County Armagh. A weaver. Enlisted into the 9th (Service) Battalion 11 June 1915, aged 15 but giving his age as 19 years. Discharged having made a mis-statement as to age on enlistment being under 17 years of age 17 June 1915.

GRACEY Corporal William Harrison 22760. From Portadown, County Armagh. Enlisted 8 November 1915. Posted to the 9th (Service) Battalion. 'B' Company. **Wounded** at the Battle of Langemarck 16 August 1917. Discharged as no longer physically fit for war service due to wounds 18 July 1918, aged 21. Silver War Badge, number 425698.

GRAFTON Private John Elliott 4857. Born in 1879 at Woolwich, Kent. [Enlisted into Princess Victoria's (Royal Irish Fusiliers) 8 March 1894, aged 14, as a drummer. Posted to the Depot 7 March 1906. Corporal 8 March 1906. Reverted to Lance Corporal 1 April 1906. Posted to the 2nd Battalion in India 9 March 1907. Reverted to Private at his own request 29 April 1907. To France

19 December 1914 with the 2nd Battalion. **Wounded** by a gunshot to the chest and then evacuated to hospital in England 17 January 1915. Posted to the 3rd (Reserve) Battalion 31 March 1915. To 36 Infantry Base Depot 7 September 1917 and posted to the 7th/8th (Service) Battalion in 49th Brigade, 16th (Irish) Division.] Joined the 9th (North Irish Horse) Battalion when the 7th/8th (Service) Battalion was disbanded in February 1918. **Wounded** by a gunshot to the right thigh in the period 9-14 April 1918 in the actions between Wulverghem and Kemmel and evacuated to hospital in England 14 April 1918. To 36 Infantry Base Depot 15 September 1918. **Wounded** at Vijfwegen/Hill 41 and then evacuated to hospital in England 15 October 1918. Discharged as no longer physically fit for war service due to wounds 21 February 1919 after nearly twenty-five years service, aged 39. Silver War Badge, number B154110. 1914-15 Star. Long Service & Good Conduct Medal.

GRAHAM Private Abraham 14204. From Richhill, County Armagh. Enlisted September 1914. To France with 36th (Ulster) Division in October 1915. **Died of wounds** 22 March 1917, aged 22. 1914-15 Star.

GRAHAM Private Albert 14214. Enlisted September 1914. To France with 36th (Ulster) Division in October 1915. 'C' Company. **Wounded** during the attack at Hamel 1 July 1916. **Wounded** during the retreat from St Quentin 21-28 March 1918. Discharged as no longer physically fit for war service due to wounds 16 January 1919. Silver War Badge, number B84669. 1914-15 Star.

GRAHAM Private Andrew 14208. From Richhill, County Armagh. Enlisted September 1914. To France with 36th (Ulster) Division in October 1915. **Killed in action** during the attack at Hamel 1 July 1916.

GRAHAM Corporal Charles 17406. From Killeshandra, County Cavan. [Enlisted into The Royal Irish Rifles (14446).] Transferred to Princess Victoria's (Royal Irish Fusiliers) in November/December 1914 (renumbered 17406) and joined the 9th (Service) Battalion. To France with 36th (Ulster) Division in October 1915. 'C' Company. Survived the attack at Hamel on 1 July 1916 unwounded. **Died** 3 February 1917 in an accident with a grenade at a bombing school. 1914-15 Star.

GRAHAM Lance Corporal Isaac 41573. [Enlisted in October 1914 into the North Irish Horse (1320). To France with 'F' Squadron in 33rd Division 17 November 1915. Served with 2nd North Irish Horse, X Corps Cavalry Regiment.] Joined the renamed 9th (North Irish Horse) Battalion from 36 Infantry Base Depot and transferred to Princess Victoria's (Royal Irish Fusiliers) in September/October 1917 (renumbered 41573). Transferred to the Class Z Reserve 11 March 1919. 1914-15 Star.

GRAHAM Private James 41247. [Enlisted in November 1915 into the North Irish Horse (1983). Served with 2nd North Irish Horse, X Corps Cavalry Regiment.] Joined the renamed 9th (North Irish Horse) Battalion from 36 Infantry Base Depot and transferred to Princess Victoria's (Royal Irish Fusiliers) in September/October 1917 (renumbered 41247).

GRAHAM MM Corporal John 14233. From Lurgan, County Armagh. Armagh Regiment, Ulster Volunteer Force. Enlisted September 1914, aged 17. To France with 36th (Ulster) Division in October 1915. 'C' Company. Attached to 108th Trench Mortar Battery prior to the attack at Hamel 1 July 1916, which he survived unwounded – **MM**. Later **wounded**. Discharged as no longer physically fit for war service due to wounds 27 July 1918. Silver War Badge, number 379043. 1914-15 Star.

GRAHAM Private Joseph 6405 & 7040084. From Darkley, County Armagh. Enlisted on 6 November 1915 into Princess Victoria's (Royal Irish Fusiliers) Special Reserve, aged 17. To France 27 March 1918 and joined the 9th (North Irish Horse) Battalion. Remained in Princess Victoria's (Royal Irish Fusiliers) Special Reserve (renumbered 7040084) after the war. Discharged 5 November 1921.

GRAHAM Private Robert Wellington 14229. Born in 1895 at Portadown, County Armagh. 4th (Portadown) Battalion, Armagh Regiment, Ulster Volunteer Force. A baker. Enlisted September 1914. To France with 36th (Ulster) Division in October 1915. Evacuated to hospital in England and treated at 5th Northern General Hospital, Leicester until 6 March 1917. [Transferred to the Royal Army Medical Corps (renumbered 136748).] 1914-15 Star.

GRAHAM Corporal Robert Wallace 23321. Born 10 October 1879 at Rostrevor, County Down. 4th (Portadown) Battalion, Armagh Regiment, Ulster Volunteer Force. Enlisted November 1915. Posted to the 9th (Service) Battalion. To hospital at Le Havre sick and **died** of meningitis 5 August 1917, aged 37. Brother of Captain (formerly 23945 Corporal) William George Graham. His sister, Miss Aileen Graham, served in France as a nurse with the Red Cross.

GRAHAM Private Samuel 18239. Enlisted into the 9th (Service) Battalion in February 1915. To France with 36th (Ulster) Division in October 1915. [Transferred to the Labour Corps (renumbered 231600).] Transferred to the Class Z Reserve 28 April 1919. 1914-15 Star.

GRAHAM Private Thomas 14240. Born in 1894 at Armagh, County Armagh. 1st (Armagh) Battalion, Armagh Regiment, Ulster Volunteer Force. Enlisted September 1914. Lance Corporal 30 May 1915. To France with 36th (Ulster) Division in October 1915. [Transferred to The Machine Gun Corps (renumbered 86882) 5 January 1916. **Wounded** by a gunshot to the shoulder at Hamel on 1 July 1916 and evacuated to hospital in England. Treated at the 2nd Southern General Hospital, Bristol and at the Military Convalescent Hospital, Holywood, County Down. Corporal 2 April 1917. Sergeant 25 April 1917. To Egypt 1 June 1917. Served with 158th (North Wales) Brigade Machine Gun Company and 53rd (Welsh) Division Machine Gun Battalion in the Palestine Campaign. **Wounded** by a gunshot 6 November 1917 at Tell Khuweilfe. Embarked at Alexandria for hospital in England 3 June 1919.] Transferred to the Class Z Reserve 23 July 1919. 1914-15 Star.

GRAHAM Sergeant Thomas 14245. Enlisted September 1914. Did not serve overseas with 36th (Ulster) Division. Discharged as no longer physically fit for war service due to sickness 10 October 1918. Silver War Badge, number 506382.

GRAHAM Private Thomas R 42512. Joined the 9th (North Irish Horse) Battalion, Princess Victoria's (Royal Irish Fusiliers) with the draft of men transferred from The Royal Irish Rifles in September 1918. [Transferred to 5th (Service) Battalion, The Royal Irish Regiment (Pioneers) in the Light Division in the British Army of the Rhine in March/June 1919 (renumbered 41413).]

GRAHAM Private William 8360. [Enlisted into Princess Victoria's (Royal Irish Fusiliers) as a regular soldier in 1904. To France with the 1st Battalion 22 August 1914. Posted to the 7th/8th (Service) Battalion in 49th Brigade, 16th (Irish) Division.] Joined the 9th (North Irish Horse) Battalion when the 7th/8th (Service) Battalion was disbanded in February 1918. 1914 Star and clasp.

GRAHAM MM Lance Corporal William 18926. From Bawnboy, County Cavan. [Enlisted or transferred to Princess Victoria's (Royal Irish Fusiliers) April 1915. To France 28 June 1915 and joined the 1st Battalion.] Posted to the 9th (Service) Battalion. 'A' Company. **MM** – 1917. **Captured** in the period 21-28 March 1918 during the retreat from St Quentin. Transferred to the Class Z Reserve 18 March 1919. 1914-15 Star.

GRAHAM Private William 23217. From Portadown, County Armagh. Enlisted in November 1915. Posted to the 9th (Service) Battalion. 'B' Company. **Wounded** at the Battle of Langemarck 16 August 1917.

GRAHAM Private William 41295. [Enlisted in February/March 1913 into the North Irish Horse (811). To France 20 August 1914 with 'C' Squadron as 5th Division Cavalry and then as GHQ Troops. Served with 2nd North Irish Horse, X Corps Cavalry Regiment.] Joined the renamed 9th (North Irish Horse) Battalion from 36 Infantry Base Depot and transferred to Princess Victoria's (Royal Irish Fusiliers) in September/October 1917 (renumbered 41295). 1914 Star and clasp.

GRAHAM Private William George 20336. From Pelaw, County Durham. [Enlisted into The Royal Inniskilling Fusiliers (22527).] Transferred to Princess Victoria's (Royal Irish Fusiliers) on 30 June 1915 (renumbered 20336) and joined the 9th (Service) Battalion. To France with 36th (Ulster) Division in October 1915. **Killed in action** during the attack at Hamel 1 July 1916, aged 19. 1914-15 Star.

GRAHAM Corporal William George 23945. Commissioned into Princess Victoria's (Royal Irish Fusiliers) - see Appendix 5. Brother of Corporal Robert Wallace Graham.

GRAHAM Lance Corporal William James 23215. Born in 1898 at Crann, Middletown, County Armagh. Enlisted in November 1915. Posted to the 9th (Service) Battalion. 'C' Company. Killed in action at the Battle of Langemarck 16 August 1917.

GRANT Private Albert 19015. [Enlisted in December 1915 and served previously with the 1st Battalion.] Posted to the 9th (Service) Battalion.

GRANT Private John 23595. Enlisted 29 December 1915. Posted to the 9th (Service) Battalion.

Discharged as no longer physically fit for war service due to sickness 6 September 1917. Silver War Badge, number 233721.

GRANT Private Thomas James 17153. From Cabra, Tandragee, County Armagh. Enlisted into the 9th (Service) Battalion in November 1914. To France with 36th (Ulster) Division in October 1915. 'A' Company. **Missing** during the attack at Hamel 1 July 1916 and later declared **killed in action** on that day, aged 21. 1914-15 Star.

GRANTHAM Private William John 43388. Born in 1880 at Cuxton, Kent. A solicitor's clerk. [Enlisted 16 February 1916 and transferred to the Army Reserve. Mobilised 29 May 1916 and joined the 3/9th Battalion, The London Regiment (6171).] Attached to the 9th (Service) Battalion, Princess Victoria's (Royal Irish Fusiliers) 26 November 1916. Discharged from the Territorial Force, re-enlisted and transferred to Princess Victoria's (Royal Irish Fusiliers) in March/April 1917 (renumbered 43388). **Wounded** by a gunshot to the hand at the Battle of Langemarck 16 August 1917. Evacuated to England and treated at 2nd London General Hospital and the Great Northern Hospital, London. Posted to the 3rd (Reserve) Battalion 10 December 1917. [Transferred to the 28th (Home Service) Battalion, The Durham Light Infantry (renumbered 99639 Lance Corporal) 21 September 1918.] Transferred to the Class Z Reserve 17 January 1919.

GRAY Private Edmund 14201. Born in 1889 at Mullaghglass, County Armagh. Member of Bessbrook Company, Armagh Regiment, Ulster Volunteer Force. Enlisted September 1914. To France with 36th (Ulster) Division in October 1915. 'A' Company. Commended for his work as a stretcher-bearer during the raid at La Petite Douve Farm on 12 October 1916. **Killed in action** at the Battle of Langemarck 16 August 1917, aged 27. 1914-15 Star.

GRAY Private Herbert James 14212. Born in 1896 at Killeen, Armagh, County Armagh. A farmer's son. Enlisted September 1914. To France with 36th (Ulster) Division in October 1915. 'B' Company. Reportedly **wounded** three times including being **wounded** during the attack at Hamel 1 July 1916 and **wounded** at the Battle of Langemarck 16 August 1917. Discharged as no longer physically fit for war service due to wounds 3 March 1919. Silver War Badge, number B154471. 1914-15 Star.

GRAY Lance Sergeant Joseph 22875. From Milford, County Armagh. A damask designer. Enlisted on 12 November 1915 and joined the 10th (Reserve) Battalion. To 36 Infantry Base Depot 3 March 1916. Lance Sergeant 16 June 1916. Joined the 9th (Service) Battalion 1 September 1916 and reverted to Lance Corporal. 'C' Company. **Wounded** when he had his back crushed as a result of shellfire near Spanbroekmolen on the night of 4/5 June 1917. Treated at 8th Stationary Hospital and rejoined the 9th (Service) Battalion 14 July 1917. Corporal 17 August 1917. To 48th Casualty Clearing Station sick (epididymitis) and evacuated to England. Treated at the Red Cross Hospital, Torquay. To 'A' Infantry Base Depot 14 March 1918 and rejoined the 9th (North Irish Horse) Battalion. Treated at 5th General Hospital (injured feet) in April & May 1918. Treated at 54th General Hospital for trench fever in August & September 1918. Transferred to the Class Z Reserve 25 February 1919.

GRAY Private Robert 11899. Born in 1885 at Barrack Hill, County Cavan. [Enlisted 28 August 1914 and served with the 5th (Service) Battalion in 31st Brigade, 10th (Irish) Division. Embarked with the Mediterranean Expeditionary Force July 1915.] Posted to the 9th (Service) Battalion. 'D' Company. **Wounded** at the Battle of Langemarck 16 August 1917. Discharged as no longer physically fit for war service due to wounds 20 March 1918, aged 30. Silver War Badge, number 355869. 1914-15 Star.

GRAY Sergeant (Acting Company Quartermaster Sergeant) Reynold (Rennie) 12242. Born in 1894 at Bessbrook, County Armagh. A mechanic in Bessbrook linen mill. [Enlisted in September 1914 and joined the 5th or 6th (Service) Battalion in 31st Brigade, 10th (Irish) Division.] Posted to the 9th (Service) Battalion. To France with 36th (Ulster) Division in October 1915. Transferred to the Class Z Reserve 13 March 1919. 1914-15 Star. Brother of Company Quartermaster Sergeant Thomas Gray and Warrant Officer Class II William Gray. His brother, Private James Gray, enlisted in November 1915 into Princess Victoria's (Royal Irish Fusiliers) Special Reserve aged 16. He was discharged in December 1915 having made a mis-statement as to age on enlistment.

GRAY Major Thomas, formerly Company Quartermaster Sergeant 14236. Born in 1897 at Bessbrook, County Armagh. A clerk in Bessbrook linen mill. Enlisted September 1914, aged 17.

Promoted to Company Quartermaster Sergeant in 1915. To hospital sick (enteric fever) and treated at 25th Stationary Hospital, Rouen from 12 September 1917. **Wounded** in the right leg in September 1918. Posted to the 10th (Reserve) Battalion. Transferred to the Class Z Reserve 21 March 1919. After the war he worked initially as an audit clerk for Atkinson and Boyd chartered accountants in Newry. During the Second World War he was commissioned for service with the Ulster Home Guard. On 13 March 1946 he was granted the honorary rank of Major. Brother of Company Quartermaster Sergeant Reynold Gray and Warrant Officer Class II William Gray. His brother, Private James Gray, enlisted in November 1915 into Princess Victoria's (Royal Irish Fusiliers) Special Reserve aged 16. He was discharged in December 1915 having made a mis-statement as to age on enlistment.

GRAY Warrant Officer Class II William 14202. Regimental Quartermaster Sergeant - see above.

GRAY Private William 14243. Born 16 June 1880. From Armagh, County Armagh. Enlisted September 1914. Discharged as not being likely to become an efficient soldier in that he was considered medically unfit for service 1 October 1914.

GREEN Private Albert V J 43475. Born 15 February 1898 at Lambeth, London. [Enlisted into The London Regiment (4896). Posted to the 1/24th (County of London) Battalion, The London Regiment (The Queen's).] To France and joined 36 Infantry Base Depot 29 March 1918. Transferred to Princess Victoria's (Royal Irish Fusiliers) 2 April 1918 (renumbered 43475) and joined the 9th (North Irish Horse) Battalion 4 April 1918. [Transferred to 5th (Service) Battalion, The Royal Irish Regiment (Pioneers) in the Light Division in the British Army of the Rhine in March/June 1919 (renumbered 41296).] Died at Ipswich, Suffolk in 1977, aged 79.

GREEN Private Ernest Harold 43256. [A regular soldier with 7th (Princess Royal's) Dragoon Guards (8974). To France 13 October 1914 as part of the 9th Secunderabad Cavalry Brigade, 1st Indian Cavalry Division. Transferred for infantry service to The Sherwood Foresters (Nottinghamshire and Derbyshire Regiment) (renumbered 32638, renumbered 11336) and posted to the 2nd Battalion.] Transferred to Princess Victoria's (Royal Irish Fusiliers) 31 August 1916 (renumbered 43256) having joined the 9th (Service) Battalion on 8 August 1916. Tried by Field General Court Martial on 3/4 March 1917 on eight counts of *'disgraceful conduct of an indecent kind'*; found guilty on seven counts (eighth count dismissed) and sentenced to five years penal servitude, reduced to the ranks and discharged. 1914 Star and clasp, no record of medals forfeit.

GREEN Private John 15863. Enlisted into the 9th (Service) Battalion in October 1914. To France with 36th (Ulster) Division in October 1915. Transferred to the Class Z Reserve 15 March 1919. 1914-15 Star.

GREEN Private John William 42233. [Enlisted into the Army Service Corps (T/024172). To France 17 November 1915 and served with 29th Division Train.] Transferred to Princess Victoria's (Royal Irish Fusiliers) 8 May 1918 (renumbered 42233) and joined the 9th (North Irish Horse) Battalion. Transferred to the Class Z Reserve 11 March 1919. 1914 15 Star.

GREEN Lance Corporal Thomas 41105. [Enlisted into the Service Squadron, 6th (Inniskilling) Dragoons (UD/130). To France with 36th (Ulster) Division in October 1915. Served with 2nd North Irish Horse, X Corps Cavalry Regiment.] Joined the renamed 9th (North Irish Horse) Battalion from 36 Infantry Base Depot and transferred to Princess Victoria's (Royal Irish Fusiliers) in September/October 1917 (renumbered 41105). Transferred to the Class Z Reserve 21 March 1919. 1914-15 Star.

GREEN Private William 41441. [Enlisted into the Irish Horse (2062). Served with 2nd North Irish Horse, X Corps Cavalry Regiment.] Joined the renamed 9th (North Irish Horse) Battalion from 36 Infantry Base Depot and transferred to Princess Victoria's (Royal Irish Fusiliers) in September/October 1917 (renumbered 41441).

GREENLEE Private Thomas 14223. Enlisted September 1914. To France with 36th (Ulster) Division in October 1915. Transferred to the Class Z Reserve 17 February 1919. 1914-15 Star.

GREENLEES Private Samuel 27859. Enlisted in July 1917. Posted to the 9th (North Irish Horse) Battalion. 'B' Company. Separated from the 9th (North Irish Horse) Battalion in the period 21-28 March 1918 during the retreat from St Quentin; rejoined 3 April 1918. [Posted to the 5th/6th (Service) Battalion.]

GREENWOOD Private Ralph 27819. Born in 1895 at Queensbury, Bradford, Yorkshire. Served elsewhere before transferring to Princess Victoria's (Royal Irish Fusiliers) in July 1917. Posted to the 9th (North Irish Horse) Battalion. 'D' Company. **Missing** in the period 21-28 March 1918 during the retreat from St Quentin believed **captured**.

GREER Private Charles 49744. Born on 9 July 1899 at Belfast. [Enlisted 27 July 1917 and joined the 20th (Reserve) Battalion, The Royal Irish Rifles (2517). Posted to the 18th (Reserve) Battalion, The Royal Irish Rifles 28 March 1918.] To France 11 April 1918. At the Infantry Base Depot transferred to Princess Victoria's (Royal Irish Fusiliers) (renumbered 49744) and joined the 9th (North Irish Horse) Battalion 22 April 1918. **Wounded** by gunshots to the face and abdomen during the attack at Vijfwegen on 30 September or 1 October 1918 and **died of wounds** 4 October 1918 at 3rd Australian Casualty Clearing Station, aged 19.

GREER Private James 23783. Born in 1896 at Rathfriland, County Down. A blacksmith. Enlisted 19 January 1916. To France 5 July 1916 and joined the 9th (Service) Battalion. **Wounded**. **Wounded** again on 3 August 1917 and **died of wounds** 4 August 1917, aged 21. His father, Private John Greer, served during the South Africa War and in the First World War with The Royal Irish Rifles, including with the Ulster Composite Battalion during the Irish Republican attacks in Dublin. His brother, Private William Greer, was wounded serving with The Royal Irish Rifles.

GREER Private William 21405. From Newtownhamilton, County Armagh. [Enlisted into The Royal Inniskilling Fusiliers (23523).] Transferred to Princess Victoria's (Royal Irish Fusiliers) in August 1915 (renumbered 21405). Posted to the 9th (Service) Battalion. 'C' Company. **Missing** at the Battle of Langemarck 16 August 1917 and later declared **killed in action** on that date, aged 26.

GREGG Private James 17556. From John Street, Portadown, County Armagh. Enlisted into the 9th (Service) Battalion in November/December 1914. 'C' Company. **Killed in action** during the attack at Hamel 1 July 1916.

GREGG Sergeant Thomas 14237. Enlisted September 1914. To France with 36th (Ulster) Division in October 1915. **Wounded** during the attack at Hamel 1 July 1916. [Transferred to the Labour Corps (renumbered 426978).] Transferred to the Class Z Reserve 18 July 1919. 1914-15 Star.

GREGG Lance Sergeant Thomas Alfred 41550. [Enlisted into the Service Squadron, 6th (Inniskilling) Dragoons (UD/9). To France with 36th (Ulster) Division in October 1915. Served with 2nd North Irish Horse, X Corps Cavalry Regiment.] Joined the renamed 9th (North Irish Horse) Battalion from 36 Infantry Base Depot and transferred to Princess Victoria's (Royal Irish Fusiliers) in September/October 1917 (renumbered 41550). Transferred to the Class Z Reserve 5 February 1919. 1914-15 Star.

GREGG DCM Lance Corporal William 11216. Born at Ballymacarrett, Belfast. [Enlisted into Princess Victoria's (Royal Irish Fusiliers) as a regular soldier in early-1913. To France with the 1st Battalion 22 August 1914.] Posted to the 9th (North Irish Horse) Battalion. **DCM** – Vijfwegen 30 September 1918. **Killed in action** during the attack at Vijfwegen 1 October 1918.

GREGSON Sergeant Thomas 14207. From Drumgor, County Armagh. Enlisted September 1914. To France with 36th (Ulster) Division in October 1915. 'C' Company. Lance Corporal in bombing team during the attack at Hamel on 1 July 1916, which he survived unwounded. Transferred to the Class Z Reserve 16 February 1919. 1914-15 Star.

GREGSON Private Thomas 20147. From Seagoe. Enlisted into the 9th (Service) Battalion in June 1915. Related to Private William Gregson.

GREGSON Private William 14226. From Seagoe. Enlisted September 1914. No record of deployment to France with 36th (Ulster) Division in October 1915. [Transferred to the Labour Corps (renumbered 487919).] Discharged as no longer physically fit for war service due to sickness 19 October 1918. Silver War Badge, number B53006. Related to Private Thomas Gregson.

GREY Private George 14227. Born in 1880 at Portadown, County Armagh. 4th (Portadown) Battalion, Armagh Regiment, Ulster Volunteer Force. Enlisted September 1914. Discharged as not being likely to become an efficient soldier in that he was considered medically unfit for service 27 February 1915.

GRIBBEN Private Samuel 41381. From Lisburn, County Antrim. [Enlisted into the Service

Squadron, 6th (Inniskilling) Dragoons (UD/37). To France with 36th (Ulster) Division in October 1915. Served with 2nd North Irish Horse, X Corps Cavalry Regiment.] Joined the renamed 9th (North Irish Horse) Battalion from 36 Infantry Base Depot and transferred to Princess Victoria's (Royal Irish Fusiliers) in September/October 1917 (renumbered 41381). 'A' Company. **Captured** in the period 21-28 March 1918 during the retreat from St Quentin. Transferred to the Class Z Reserve 25 March 1919. 1914-15 Star.

GRIBBEN Private William 20986. From Clough, County Down. [Enlisted in September 1915 and joined the 8th (Service) Battalion in 49th Brigade, 16th (Irish) Division.] Joined the 9th (North Irish Horse) Battalion when the 7th/8th (Service) Battalion was disbanded in February 1918. **Missing** in the period 11-18 April 1918 in the actions between Wulverghem and Kemmel; subsequently declared **killed in action** 19 April 1918.

GRIBBIN Private Arthur 23011. Born at Dromore, County Down. [Enlisted in November 1915 and joined the 8th (Service) Battalion in 49th Brigade, 16th (Irish) Division.] Joined the 9th (North Irish Horse) Battalion when the 7th/8th (Service) Battalion was disbanded in February 1918. **Missing** in the period 11-18 April 1918 in the actions between Wulverghem and Kemmel; subsequently declared **killed in action** 19 April 1918.

GRIFFIN Lance Corporal Walter 19085. Enlisted 4 December 1915. Posted to the 9th (Service) Battalion. Discharged as no longer physically fit for war service due to sickness 2 March 1919. Silver War Badge, number B154469.

GRIFFITHS Private Thomas Owen 13771. [Enlisted in September 1914 and joined the 6th (Service) Battalion in 31st Brigade, 10th (Irish) Division. Embarked with the Mediterranean Expeditionary Force July 1915.] Posted to the 9th (North Irish Horse) Battalion. 'C' Company. **Missing** in the period 21-28 March 1918 during the retreat from St Quentin believed **captured**. Transferred to the Class Z Reserve 18 March 1919. 1914-15 Star.

GRIMASON Private Joseph 17395. Enlisted into the 9th (Service) Battalion in November 1914. To France with 36th (Ulster) Division in October 1915. Discharged 6 September 1916. 1914-15 Star.

GRIMASON Private Robert 14238. From Lurgan, County Armagh. Enlisted September 1914. To France with 36th (Ulster) Division in October 1915. 'C' Company. Released from hospital just prior to the attack at Hamel 1 July 1916, during which he was **killed in action**, aged 26. 1914-15 Star.

GRIMES Private James 21401. Enlisted in August 1915. Posted to the 9th (Service) Battalion. 'B' Company. **Missing** in the period 21-28 March 1918 during the retreat from St Quentin believed **captured**.

GRIMLEY Private Thomas 21755. From Portadown, County Armagh. Signed the Ulster Covenant 28 September 1912. Enlisted 2 October 1915. Posted to the 9th (Service) Battalion in May/June 1916. **Wounded** during the attack at Hamel 1 July 1916. [After he recovered he was posted to the 2nd Garrison Battalion in Salonika.] Discharged as no longer physically fit for war service due to sickness 23 November 1918. Silver War Badge, number B46714.

GROVE Private Thomas Richard 45801. Joined the 9th (North Irish Horse) Battalion, Princess Victoria's (Royal Irish Fusiliers) with the draft of men from The London Regiment in April 1918.

GROVES Corporal David Edward 43333. Born in 1893 at Hackney, London. Joined the 9th (Service) Battalion, Princess Victoria's (Royal Irish Fusiliers) with the draft of men from The London Regiment in November 1916. 'A' Company. **Wounded** and **missing** during the retreat from St Quentin 21-28 March 1918 believed **captured**. Died at London in 1959, aged 66.

GROVES Private Joseph 27746. Born at Born Clontibret, County Monaghan. Lived at Castleblayney, County Monaghan. A salesman. Enlisted 20 June 1917 and joined the 10th (Reserve) Battalion. Lance Corporal 21 July 1917. To France 14 March 1918 and joined the 9th (North Irish Horse) Battalion. **Captured** in the period 11-18 April 1918 in the actions between Wulverghem and Kemmel. **Died** of intestinal catarrh in the Bavarian War Hospital, Hautmont while a prisoner of war 3 August 1918, aged 41.

GRUNDLE Sergeant Albert 17154. Born in 1897. From Mullaghead, County Armagh. Enlisted into the 9th (Service) Battalion 23 November 1914. 'D' Company. **Wounded** during the attack at Hamel 1 July 1916. Commended for his coolness as a Sergeant on the raid at La Petite Douve Farm on 12 October 1916. **Wounded** at Messines in June 1917. Discharged as no longer physically fit for war service due to wounds 11 December 1917, aged 22. Silver War Badge, number 279284.

GUMBLE Private Kenzer 43321. Born in 1895 at Belvedere, London into a Romany family. [Enlisted into The London Regiment. Posted to 1/7th (City of London) Battalion, The London Regiment (352873).] Attached to the 9th (Service) Battalion, Princess Victoria's (Royal Irish Fusiliers) 26 November 1916. 'B' Company. Discharged from the Territorial Force, re-enlisted and transferred to Princess Victoria's (Royal Irish Fusiliers) in March/April 1917 (renumbered 43321). **Captured** in the period 21-28 March 1918 during the retreat from St Quentin. After he was repatriated he returned to Belvedere. **Died** on 9 June 1920 of pulmonary tuberculosis and haemoptysis as a result of being gassed. His brother, Driver Levi Gumble, served with the Royal Field Artillery. His brother, Private Herbert Gumble, served with 49th Training Reserve Battalion but was discharged as no longer physically fit for war service due to sickness (epilepsy). His brother, Private Randal Gumble, served with The Middlesex Regiment.

GUNTRIP Lance Corporal Frederick 41619. [Enlisted 29 May 1915 for service with cavalry (21247). Posted to 2nd North Irish Horse, X Corps Cavalry Regiment.] Joined the renamed 9th (North Irish Horse) Battalion from 36 Infantry Base Depot and transferred to Princess Victoria's (Royal Irish Fusiliers) in September/October 1917 (renumbered 41619). **Wounded**. Discharged as no longer physically fit for war service due to wounds 14 April 1919. Silver War Badge, number B214596.

GUY Private William 16938. Born in 1894 at Portadown, County Armagh. Enlisted September 1914 into the 9th (Service) Battalion. To France 4 November 1915 and rejoined the 9th (Service) Battalion. **Wounded** by shellshock concussion at Hamel late-June 1916. Evacuated to hospital in England and treated at King George Hospital, London. Private W Guy and Private W H Guy were enlisted at the same time and allocated the same regimental number (14213). Private W Guy was allocated a new number (16983) at Clandeboye. Confusion continued after both were wounded at Hamel and evacuated to hospitals in England; no record of Private W Guy could be found. The confusion was rectified by confirming that he had been allocated a new number (16983) and he was re-attested after joining the Irish Command Depot, Tipperary on discharge from hospital in August 1916. [Transferred to The Worcestershire Regiment (renumbered 47653) and joined the 5th (Reserve) Battalion, The Worcestershire Regiment.] Transferred to the Class Z Reserve 20 February 1919. 1914-15 Star.

GUY Private William Harry 14213. See Private William Guy. Born in 1892 at Lurgan, County Armagh. A weaver. Enlisted September 1914. To France with 36th (Ulster) Division in October 1915. 'C' Company. Bombing team. **Wounded** by a shrapnel ball to the back at Hamel 24 June 1916. Evacuated to hospital in England and treated at East Leeds War Hospital. **Wounded** at the Battle of Langemarck 16 August 1917. Discharged as no longer physically fit for war service due to wounds 6 April 1918. Silver War Badge, number 342083. 1914-15 Star.

HACK Private Victor 41079. [Enlisted into the 6th (Inniskilling) Dragoons (GS/21610). Served with 2nd North Irish Horse, X Corps Cavalry Regiment.] Joined the renamed 9th (North Irish Horse) Battalion from 36 Infantry Base Depot and transferred to Princess Victoria's (Royal Irish Fusiliers) in September/October 1917 (renumbered 41079). 'A' Company. **Missing** in the period 21-28 March 1918 during the retreat from St Quentin believed **captured**. Re-enlisted in 1919 for Regular Army service with the 3rd (Prince of Wales's) Dragoon Guards (renumbered 34450, renumbered 392549).]

HADDEN Private James 14251. Born in 1894 at Portadown, County Armagh. 4th (Portadown) Battalion, Armagh Regiment, Ulster Volunteer Force. Member of Loyal Orange Lodge 110. Enlisted September 1914. 'B' Company. Discharged as no longer physically fit for war service due to sickness (valvular disease - heart) 28 June 1915. Silver War Badge, number 238601.

HADDEN Lance Corporal Robert Henry Knowles (Harry) 14314. Born in 1894 at Tullyheron, County Armagh. Enlisted September 1914. To France with 36th (Ulster) Division in October 1915. 'A' Company. **Wounded** during the retreat from St Quentin 21-28 March 1918. Transferred to the Class Z Reserve 5 April 1919. 1914-15 Star. His brothers, Gunner Marcus Albert Hadden and Trooper John Girvan Hadden, served with the Canadian Expeditionary Force.

HADDOCK Private George Albert 20126. Born in 1895 at Lurgan, County Armagh. Enlisted into the 9th (Service) Battalion 10 June 1915. To France with 36th (Ulster) Division in October 1915.

Discharged as no longer physically fit for war service due to sickness 5 June 1916. Silver War Badge, number 95492. 1914-15 Star.

HADDOCK Private Samuel 14328. Enlisted September 1914. To France with 36th (Ulster) Division in October 1915. Transferred to the Class Z Reserve 13 April 1919. 1914-15 Star.

HADDOCK Private Thomas 18671. From Portadown, County Armagh. Enlisted into the 9th (Service) Battalion 21 April 1915. To France with 36th (Ulster) Division in October 1915. 5 Platoon, 'B' Company. Believed **wounded** in the period 21-28 March 1918 during the retreat from St Quentin. Discharged as no longer physically fit for war service due to wounds 5 November 1918. Silver War Badge, number B38736. 1914-15 Star.

HAGUE Private Henry Charles 31273. Born in 1880 at Alcester Lanes End, Birmingham. Enlisted 24 June 1916 and transferred to the Army Reserve. Mobilised 14 April 1917 and joined a Reserve Regiment of Cavalry (35246). Transferred to The Loyal North Lancashire Regiment (renumbered 39349) 11 July 1917. Transferred to The Royal Irish Regiment (renumbered 3925) 9 May 1918. To France 14 May 1918 and posted to the 2nd Garrison Guard Battalion, The Royal Irish Regiment.] Transferred to Princess Victoria's (Royal Irish Fusiliers) (renumbered 31273). Joined the 9th (North Irish Horse) Battalion in late-1918. Transferred to the Class Z Reserve 9 April 1919.

HAGUE Lance Corporal Isaac 43265. Born in 1892 at Radford, Nottingham. [Served with the 3rd Battalion (Militia), The Sherwood Foresters (Nottinghamshire and Derbyshire Regiment). Enlisted in the Regular Army 6 April 1912 and joined the 2nd Battalion, The Sherwood Foresters (Nottinghamshire and Derbyshire Regiment) (11840) on 30 May 1912. Posted to the 1st Battalion 9 October 1913 and served in India. When the 1st Battalion returned he was posted to the 3rd (Reserve) Battalion, The Sherwood Foresters (Nottinghamshire and Derbyshire Regiment) on 19 November 1914. Sentenced to twelve days detention for two counts of *'breaking out of camp and remaining absent'* 25 November 1914. To France 11 December 1914 and joined the 1st Battalion, The Sherwood Foresters (Nottinghamshire and Derbyshire Regiment). **Wounded** 3 January 1915. Sentenced to fourteen days Field Punishment Number 2 for being absent for parade for the trenches and remaining absent on 10 January 1915. Evacuated to hospital in England 30 April 1915 and posted to the Depot. Sentenced to twenty-one days detention and forfeit thirty-one days pay for absence from 14 June to 14 July 1915. Posted to the 3rd (Reserve) Battalion, The Sherwood Foresters (Nottinghamshire and Derbyshire Regiment) 14 August 1915. Declared a **deserter** on 27 December 1915. Rejoined 11 February 1916. Sentenced to forfeit forty-seven days pay and fourteen days detention.] To France 14 July 1916. Transferred to Princess Victoria's (Royal Irish Fusiliers) 31 August 1916 (renumbered 43265) having joined the 9th (Service) Battalion on 8 August 1916. Lance Corporal 2 October 1916. **Wounded** by shellfire near Wieltje and **died of wounds** in 114th Casualty Clearing Station on 13 August 1917. 1914-15 Star.

HAIN Private John 45783. Born in 1899 at Edinburgh. From Newcastle. Enlisted 11 January 1917. Joined the 9th (North Irish Horse) Battalion, Princess Victoria's (Royal Irish Fusiliers) with the draft of men from The London Regiment in April 1918. **Wounded** and **captured** in the period 11-18 April 1918 in the actions between Wulverghem and Kemmel. One eye was removed in a German hospital in Ghent. Subsequently held in Soltau Prisoner of War Camp. Repatriated December 1918. Discharged as no longer physically fit for war service due to wounds 15 January 1919. Silver War Badge, number B84697.

HAIRE Private James 14331. Enlisted September 1914. To France with 36th (Ulster) Division in October 1915. Transferred to the Class Z Reserve 12 March 1919. 1914-15 Star.

HAIRE Private Joseph 19732. Enlisted 27 April 1915 into the 9th (Service) Battalion. To France with 36th (Ulster) Division in October 1915. 'C' Company. Attached to 36th (Ulster) Division Signal Company during the attack at Hamel 1 July 1916 and did not take part in the attack. **Wounded** at the Battle of Langemarck 16 August 1917. **Wounded** during the retreat from St Quentin 21-28 March 1918. Discharged as no longer physically fit for war service due to wounds 4 October 1918, aged 22. Silver War Badge, number B22501. 1914-15 Star.

HAIRE Lance Corporal Leonard 17953. From Bridge Street, Portadown, County Armagh. Enlisted into the 9th (Service) Battalion in February 1915. To France with 36th (Ulster) Division in October 1915. 'C' Company. Detached as a signaller at headquarters signalling station during the attack at Hamel 1 July 1916 and did not take part in the attack. Transferred to the Class Z Reserve 5 March

1919. 1914-15 Star.

HAIRE Private Thomas John Gerald 21645. Born in 1898 at Hillhead, Stewartstown, County Tyrone. From Cloverhill, County Cavan. Worked for the Great Northern Railway at Belturbet Station. Enlisted in September 1915, aged 17. Posted to the 9th (Service) Battalion. 'D' Company. **Killed in action** 27 March 1918 during the retreat from St Quentin, aged 20.

HALE Private Richard 18507. [Enlisted April 1915 into the 8th (Service) Battalion in 49th Brigade, 16th (Irish) Division.] Joined the 9th (North Irish Horse) Battalion when the 7th/8th (Service) Battalion was disbanded in February 1918. 'D' Company. **Missing** in the period 21-28 March 1918 during the retreat from St Quentin believed **captured**.

HALES Private Charles Joseph 17399. From Belturbet, County Cavan. Enlisted into the 9th (Service) Battalion in November/December 1914. To France with 36th (Ulster) Division in October 1915. **Killed in action** during the attack at Hamel 1 July 1916.

HALES Private Clarence Oswald 42090. Born 18 January 1892 at Wolverhampton, Shropshire. [Enlisted into the Army Veterinary Corps (4005). To France 26 January 1915.] Transferred to Princess Victoria's (Royal Irish Fusiliers) 8 May 1918 (renumbered 42090) and joined the 9th (North Irish Horse) Battalion. Transferred to the Class Z Reserve 15 February 1919. 1914-15 Star. Died at Wolverhampton, West Midlands in 1992, aged 100.

HALL Private Arthur James 45745. Born in 1895. From Finsbury Park, London. Worked as a stitching machine operator. [Enlisted 25 February 1916 and transferred to the Army Reserve. Mobilised and joined 3/24th Battalion, The London Regiment (5615) in April 1916. To France 14 July 1916 and joined Number 1 Entrenching Battalion. Joined 1/24th (County of London) Battalion, The London Regiment (The Queen's) 23 September 1916. **Wounded** by a gunshot to the left thigh 4 November 1916 and evacuated to hospital in England. Treated at Northumberland War Hospital until 4 May 1917. Posted to 22nd (Reserve) Battalion, The London Regiment.] To 'K' Infantry Base Depot, France 30 March 1918. Transferred to Princess Victoria's (Royal Irish Fusiliers) 2 April 1918 (renumbered 45745) and joined the 9th (North Irish Horse) Battalion 4 April 1918. **Missing** in the period 11-18 April 1918 in the actions between Wulverghem and Kemmel; subsequently declared **killed in action** 19 April 1918.

HALL Private George 42286. [Enlisted into the Army Veterinary Corps (3512). To France 23 January 1915.] Transferred to Princess Victoria's (Royal Irish Fusiliers) 8 May 1918 (renumbered 42286) and joined the 9th (North Irish Horse) Battalion. Transferred to the Class Z Reserve 7 February 1919. 1914-15 Star.

HALL Private Herbert 41225. Born in 1898 at Ballynacree, County Wexford. A farmer's son. [Enlisted 23 October 1914 into the North Irish Horse (1330). To France 23 January 1915. Served with 2nd North Irish Horse, X Corps Cavalry Regiment.] Joined the renamed 9th (North Irish Horse) Battalion from 36 Infantry Base Depot and transferred to Princess Victoria's (Royal Irish Fusiliers) in September/October 1917 (renumbered 41225). Discharged as no longer physically fit for war service due to sickness 28 September 1918. Silver War Badge, number B18094. 1914-15 Star.

HALL Private James 14246. From Portadown, County Armagh. 4th (Portadown) Battalion, Armagh Regiment, Ulster Volunteer Force. Enlisted September 1914. To France with 36th (Ulster) Division in October 1915. 'C' Company. Detached to the Battalion Transport and did not take part in the attack at Hamel on 1 July 1916. Transferred to the Class Z Reserve 6 March 1919. 1914-15 Star.

HALL Private James 14260. Born in 1896. From Clare, County Armagh. Member of the Tandragee Company, Armagh Regiment, Ulster Volunteer Force. Enlisted September 1914. To France with 36th (Ulster) Division in October 1915. 'B' Company. **Killed in action** 3 April 1916 by shellfire near Mesnil, aged 20.

HALL Private James 16939. Enlisted 28 September 1914. To France with 36th (Ulster) Division in October 1915. Discharged as no longer physically fit for war service due to sickness 1 March 1917. Silver War Badge, number 34601. 1914-15 Star.

HALL Private James 20092. From Armagh, County Armagh. Enlisted into the 9th (Service) Battalion in June 1915. To France with 36th (Ulster) Division in October 1915. **Killed in action** during the attack at Hamel 1 July 1916. 1914-15 Star.

HALL Private Joseph 17386. Born at St Saviours, County Armagh. From Battlehill, Portadown,

County Armagh. Enlisted into the 9th (Service) Battalion in November 1914. To France with 36th (Ulster) Division in October 1915. **Killed in action** during the attack at Hamel 1 July 1916. His body was recovered in September 1916. 1914-15 Star.

HALL Private Robert 16107. Enlisted into the 9th (Service) Battalion in October 1914. To France with 36th (Ulster) Division in October 1915. [Joined 108th Brigade Machine Gun Company in January 1916. Transferred to the Machine Gun Corps (renumbered 17793).] 1914-15 Star.

HALL Private Robert 21652 & 33331. Born in 1890. From Shankill, Belfast. Enlisted 17 September 1915 and joined the 9th (Service) Battalion. Posted to the 10th (Reserve) Battalion 23 September 1915. To France and rejoined the 9th (Service) Battalion 19 February 1916. Evacuated to hospital in England injured or sick in early-1916. Posted to the 10th (Reserve) Battalion in the latter half of 1916. **Deserted** 10 September 1916 and was apprehended in Belfast by the police on 18 September 1916. Returned to France 16 December 1916 and rejoined the 9th (Service) Battalion. Evacuated to hospital in England sick (hernia) 2 March 1917 and treated at 2nd Northern General Hospital, Leeds until 24 April 1917. Forfeit six days pay for absence from 11 to 16 June 1916. Forfeit six days pay for absence from 10 to 16 June 1916. Joined the 10th (Reserve) Battalion 26 July 1917. To France 7 September 1917 and rejoined the 9th (North Irish Horse) Battalion. 'C' Company. Evacuated to hospital in England (injured foot) and treated at the Military Hospital, Tidworth from 10-29 December 1917. Joined the 10th (Reserve) Battalion 7 January 1918. To 'A' Infantry Base Depot 1 April 1918 and rejoined the 9th (North Irish Horse) Battalion. Transferred to the Class Z Reserve 22 March 1919. Re-enlisted 1 September 1919 for Regular Army service with Princess Victoria's (Royal Irish Fusiliers) (renumbered 33331) and joined the 2nd Battalion at Eastchurch, Kent. **Deserted** 21 December 1919.

HALL Private Robert 22770. From Aghavoory, Fivemiletown, County Tyrone. Enlisted in November 1915. Posted to the 9th (Service) Battalion. 'C' Company. **Missing** at the Battle of Langemarck 16 August 1917 and later declared **killed in action** on that date, aged 25.

HALL Private Robert 26060 & 31825. From Lurgan, County Armagh. A weaver. Enlisted 22 December 1916 and joined the 10th (Reserve) Battalion. To 36 Infantry Base Depot 21 March 1917 and joined the 9th (Service) Battalion. **Wounded** at the Battle of Langemarck 16 August 1917 and evacuated to hospital in England. [Transferred to the Labour Corps (renumbered 545514) 6 April 1918.] Transferred back to Princess Victoria's (Royal Irish Fusiliers) (renumbered 31825) 7 October 1918 and joined the 3rd (Reserve) Battalion. Discharged as no longer physically fit for war service due to sickness (corneal ulcer) 11 December 1918. Silver War Badge, number B61034.

HALL Private Robert 41516. [Enlisted into the Service Squadron, 6th (Inniskilling) Dragoons (UD/171). To France with 36th (Ulster) Division in October 1915. Served with 2nd North Irish Horse, X Corps Cavalry Regiment.] Joined the renamed 9th (North Irish Horse) Battalion from 36 Infantry Base Depot and transferred to Princess Victoria's (Royal Irish Fusiliers) in September/October 1917 (renumbered 41516). [Transferred to the Tank Corps (renumbered 304851) 28 December 1917 and posted for training to the Tank Corps Depot, at Bovington near Wareham, Dorset.] 1914-15 Star.

HALL Private Robert James 41542. [Enlisted in September 1912 into the North Irish Horse (736). To France 17 August 1914 with 'A' Squadron as GHQ Troops. Served with 2nd North Irish Horse, X Corps Cavalry Regiment.] Joined the renamed 9th (North Irish Horse) Battalion from 36 Infantry Base Depot and transferred to Princess Victoria's (Royal Irish Fusiliers) in September/October 1917 (renumbered 41542). 1914 Star.

HALL Private William 14332. From Armagh, County Armagh. Enlisted September 1914. To France with 36th (Ulster) Division in October 1915. **Killed in action** during the attack at Hamel 1 July 1916. 1914-15 Star.

HALL Private William R 14275. From Lurgan, County Armagh. Enlisted September 1914. To France with 36th (Ulster) Division in October 1915. 'C' Company. Survived the attack at Hamel on 1 July 1916 unwounded. **Wounded** at the Battle of Langemarck 16 August 1917. [Transferred to The Bedfordshire Regiment (renumbered 64277).] Transferred to the Class Z Reserve.

HALLAM Private Albert William Francis 45750. Born in 1892. An electrical engineer with the County of London Electrical Supply Company. [Enlisted 14 February 1916 and transferred to the Army Reserve. Mobilised 21 June 1916 and joined the 3/24th Battalion, The London Regiment

(723174).] To France and joined 36 Infantry Base Depot 29 March 1918. Transferred to Princess Victoria's (Royal Irish Fusiliers) 2 April 1918 (renumbered 45750) and joined the 9th (North Irish Horse) Battalion 4 April 1918. **Wounded** by gunshots to the right arm and leg on 18 April 1918 in the actions between Wulverghem and Kemmel. Treated at 3rd Canadian General Hospital and then in England at Bradford War Hospital. Transferred to the Class Z Reserve 10 March 1919.

HALLEY Private Patrick 17022. [Enlisted 17 August 1914. Served previously with the 7th (Service) Battalion in 49th Brigade, 16th (Irish) Division.] Joined the 9th (North Irish Horse) Battalion when the 7th/8th (Service) Battalion was disbanded in February 1918. **Wounded**. Discharged as no longer physically fit for war service due to wounds 5 July 1919. Silver War Badge, number B265552.

HALLIDAY Private Robert 18226. From Drumconnick, County Cavan. Enlisted into the 9th (Service) Battalion in February 1915. To France with 36th (Ulster) Division in October 1915. 'C' Company. **Killed in action** during the attack at Hamel 1 July 1916, aged 19. 1914-15 Star.

HALLIGAN Private Robert 14285. Born in 1895 at Richhill, County Armagh. A cabinet maker. Enlisted September 1914. Discharged as not being likely to become an efficient soldier in that he was considered medically unfit for service 9 November 1914.

HALLIGAN Private Robert 14326. Born in 1890 at Loughgall, County Armagh. Enlisted September 1914. To France with 36th (Ulster) Division in October 1915. **Died** of pneumonia 10 December 1916, aged 26. 1914-15 Star. Brother of Private Thomas William Hogg Halligan.

HALLIGAN Private Robert James 22011. Born in 1894 at Loughgall, County Armagh. Enlisted 4 October 1915 and joined the 10th (Reserve) Battalion. Posted to the 9th (Service) Battalion. 'C' Company. **Wounded** during the attack at Hamel 1 July 1916. Discharged after service overseas in the armed forces of the Crown, on account of disablement or ill-health caused otherwise than by misconduct 10 October 1917, aged 24. Silver War Badge, number 134662.

HALLIGAN Private Thomas William Hogg 14335. Born in 1888 at Loughgall, County Armagh. Enlisted September 1914. To France with 36th (Ulster) Division in October 1915. 'B' Company. **Wounded** and later **died of wounds** during the advance to Anseghem 25 October 1918. 1914-15 Star. Brother of 14326 Private Robert Halligan.

HALPIN Private Thomas 24468. Born in 1896 at Kilfinane, County Limerick. Enlisted in June 1916. Posted to the 9th (Service) Battalion. 'B' Company. **Wounded** (shell-shock) at the Battle of Langemarck 16 August 1917. [Transferred to The Northumberland Fusiliers (renumbered 87382).]

HAMILTON Private Albert 17950. From Lurgan, County Armagh. Enlisted into the 9th (Service) Battalion in February 1915. To France with 36th (Ulster) Division in October 1915. Brother of Corporal James Hamilton and Privates John and Joseph Hamilton.

HAMILTON Private Alexander 14287. From Lurgan, County Armagh. Enlisted September 1914. To France with 36th (Ulster) Division in October 1915. **Killed in action** during the attack at Hamel 1 July 1916, aged 20. 1914-15 Star.

HAMILTON Private George Armstrong 19906. Enlisted in May 1915.

HAMILTON Private Harry 14280. Enlisted September 1914. To France with 36th (Ulster) Division in October 1915. To France with 36th (Ulster) Division in October 1915. 'C' Company. Vickers ammunition carrier during the attack at Hamel on 1 July 1916, which he survived unwounded. [Transferred to the Labour Corps (renumbered 668528).] 1914-15 Star.

HAMILTON Corporal James 14288. From Lurgan, County Armagh. Enlisted September 1914. To France with 36th (Ulster) Division in October 1915. 'C' Company. **Killed in action** during the attack at Hamel 1 July 1916. 1914-15 Star. Brother of Privates Albert, John and Joseph Hamilton.

HAMILTON Private James Hans 14308. Born 14 June 1879 at Drumachee, Hamilton's Bawn, County Armagh. A carpenter. Enlisted September 1914. Did not deploy to France with 36th (Ulster) Division in October 1915. [Transferred to the Corps of Royal Engineers (renumbered 248677 Pioneer). Served in France with 51st Artisan Works Company.] Discharged as no longer physically fit for war service due to sickness 19 March 1918, age 39. Silver War Badge, number 369745.

HAMILTON Private John 14255. Enlisted September 1914. No record of date of deployment to France with 36th (Ulster) Division.

HAMILTON MM Private John 14282. From Lurgan, County Armagh. Enlisted September 1914. To France with 36th (Ulster) Division in October 1915. 'C' Company. Survived the attack at Hamel on 1 July 1916 unwounded. **MM** – La Petite Douve Farm raid 12 October 1916. **Missing** at the Battle of Langemarck 16 August 1917 and later declared **killed in action** on that date. 1914-15 Star. Brother of Corporal James Hamilton and Privates Albert and Joseph Hamilton.

HAMILTON Private John 22854. From Ballymena, County Antrim. [Enlisted in November 1915 and joined the 8th (Service) Battalion in 49th Brigade, 16th (Irish) Division.] Joined the 9th (North Irish Horse) Battalion when the 7th/8th (Service) Battalion was disbanded in February 1918. 'A' Company. **Captured** in the period 21-28 March 1918 during the retreat from St Quentin.

HAMILTON Warrant Officer Class II Joseph 14271. From Shankill, County Armagh. Enlisted September 1914. To France with 36th (Ulster) Division in October 1915. 'C' Company. Lance Corporal and Bangalore torpedo specialist during the attack at Hamel 1 July 1916, which he survived unwounded. Promoted Corporal after the attack at Hamel on 1 July 1916. Company Sergeant Major 1918. **Killed in action** during the advance to Anseghem 25 October 1918, aged 26. 1914-15 Star.

HAMILTON Private Joseph 14283 & 29529. From Lurgan, County Armagh. Enlisted September 1914. To France with 36th (Ulster) Division in October 1915. 'C' Company. **Wounded** during the attack at Hamel 1 July 1916. Transferred or discharged. Subsequently re-enlisted into or transferred back to Princess Victoria's (Royal Irish Fusiliers) in March 1918 (renumbered 29529) and rejoined the 9th (North Irish Horse) Battalion. Transferred to the Class Z Reserve 11 March 1919. 1914-15 Star. Brother of Corporal James Hamilton and Privates Albert and John Hamilton.

HAMILTON Private Robert 18259. From Ballinode, County Monaghan. Enlisted into the 9th (Service) Battalion in February/March 1915. To France with 36th (Ulster) Division in October 1915. **Missing** in the period 11-18 April 1918 in the actions between Wulverghem and Kemmel; subsequently declared **killed in action** 19 April 1918, aged 24. 1914-15 Star.

HAMILTON Lance Corporal Samuel 14264. From Lurgan, County Armagh. Enlisted September 1914. To France with 36th (Ulster) Division in October 1915. 'C' Company. **Killed in action** during the attack at Hamel 1 July 1916. 1914-15 Star.

HAMILTON Private Thomas 16429. Born in 1894. Enlisted into the 9th (Service) Battalion on 2 November 1914. [Transferred to the Royal Army Medical Corps (renumbered 136749).] Discharged as no longer physically fit for war service due to sickness 24 April 1918, aged 23. Silver War Badge, number 404393.

HAMILTON Lance Corporal Thomas J 14307. From Corcreaney, County Armagh. Enlisted September 1914. To France with 36th (Ulster) Division in October 1915. 'C' Company. **Wounded** during the attack at Hamel 1 July 1916. [Transferred to the Labour Corps (Corporal 518497).] Transferred to the Class Z Reserve 28 March 1919. 1914-15 Star.

HAMILTON Private William Claud 41463. [Enlisted in December 1912 into the North Irish Horse (770). To France 20 August 1914 with 'C' Squadron as 5th Division Cavalry and then as GHQ Troops. Served with 2nd North Irish Horse, X Corps Cavalry Regiment.] Joined the renamed 9th (North Irish Horse) Battalion from 36 Infantry Base Depot and transferred to Princess Victoria's (Royal Irish Fusiliers) in September/October 1917 (renumbered 41463). 'B' Company. **Captured** in the period 21-28 March 1918 during the retreat from St Quentin. 1914 Star.

HAMMERSLEY Sergeant Harold William 27840 & 7042315. Born 27 October 1897 at Burslem, Staffordshire. Enlisted 27 April 1914, aged 17. He served elsewhere before transferring to Princess Victoria's (Royal Irish Fusiliers) in July 1917. Joined the 10th (Reserve) Battalion. To France January 1918 and joined the 9th (North Irish Horse) Battalion. In April 1919 he volunteered for service with the North Russia Relief Force and enlisted into the 46th (Service) Battalion, The Royal Fusiliers (City of London Regiment) (renumbered 131713 Sergeant). Awarded the **MSM** for his service in North Russia. Re-enlisted in February/March 1920 for Regular Army service with Princess Victoria's (Royal Irish Fusiliers) (renumbered 7042315 Sergeant). Transferred to the Royal Army Ordnance Corps (7042315 Sergeant) 5 September 1921. Long Service & Good Conduct Medal. Died 14 August 1944, aged 46 at Nottinghamshire; he took his own life after a period of illness.

HAMMOND Private Henry Walter 45740. Born 1897. From Stepney, London. A glass worker.

[Enlisted 30 November 1915, aged 18, and transferred to the Army Reserve. Mobilised on 18 April 1916 and joined The London Regiment (5723). To France 14 July 1916 and joined the 1/24th (County of London) Battalion, The London Regiment (The Queen's). 'A' Company. **Wounded** (gassed) 14 September 1917. Evacuated to Bermondsey Military Hospital, London 23 September 1917.] To France and joined 36 Infantry Base Depot 29 March 1918. Transferred to Princess Victoria's (Royal Irish Fusiliers) 2 April 1918 (renumbered 45740) and joined the 9th (North Irish Horse) Battalion 4 April 1918. **Captured** 12 April 1918 (reported 14 April 1918) at La Petite Douve Farm in the actions between Wulverghem and Kemmel. **Died** in hospital at Le Cateau while a prisoner of war 27 September 1918, aged 21.

HAMPTON Private Samuel 24850. Born in 1893 at Belfast. Enlisted in September 1916. Posted to the 9th (Service) Battalion.

HANDFORD Private Thomas 43222. Born in 1890 at Newmills, Derbyshire. A builders labourer. [Enlisted 11 December 1915. Served with the 1st Battalion, The Sherwood Foresters (Nottinghamshire and Derbyshire Regiment) (35591).] Transferred to Princess Victoria's (Royal Irish Fusiliers) 31 August 1916 (renumbered 43222) having joined the 9th (Service) Battalion on 8 August 1916. 'C' Company. **Wounded** by a gunshot to the right buttock at the Battle of Langemarck 16 August 1917 and **captured**. Discharged as no longer physically fit for war service due to wounds 2 April 1919. Silver War Badge, number B185279.

HANLEY Corporal David 41531. [Enlisted in June 1915 into the North Irish Horse (1680). Served with 2nd North Irish Horse, X Corps Cavalry Regiment.] Joined the renamed 9th (North Irish Horse) Battalion from 36 Infantry Base Depot and transferred to Princess Victoria's (Royal Irish Fusiliers) in September/October 1917 (renumbered 41531).

HANLEY Private Robert 23344. From Belfast. [Enlisted in November 1915. Served with the 7th/8th (Service) Battalion in 49th Brigade, 16th (Irish) Division.] Joined the 9th (North Irish Horse) Battalion when the 7th/8th (Service) Battalion was disbanded in February 1918. 'C' Company. **Captured** in the period 21-28 March 1918 during the retreat from St Quentin.

HANLEY Private Thomas 8992. [Enlisted into Princess Victoria's (Royal Irish Fusiliers) as a regular soldier 3 October 1905. To France with the 1st Battalion 22 August 1914.] Posted to the 9th (North Irish Horse) Battalion. Discharged as no longer physically fit for war service due to sickness 26 July 1919. Silver War Badge, number B296137. 1914 Star.

HANLON Private Joshua 23920. Born in 1895. From Poyntzpass, County Armagh. A groom. [Enlisted 19 November 1915 at Cork into the Irish Guards (10457). Transferred to Princess Victoria's (Royal Irish Fusiliers) 4 February 1916 (renumbered 23920) and joined the 10th (Reserve) Battalion. Lance Corporal 28 February 1916. Corporal 27 May 1916. To hospital sick (hernia) 5 July to 1 August 1916.] To France 15 October 1916, reverted to Private and joined the 9th (Service) Battalion. To a casualty clearing station sick (impetigo) June 1917. [Transferred to the Tank Corps (renumbered 304874) 28 December 1917 and posted for training to the Tank Corps Depot, at Bovington near Wareham, Dorset. To France 8 July 1918 and joined 15th Battalion, Tank Corps. **Wounded** by shrapnel to the thigh and back 21 August 1918. Treated at 2nd Canadian General Hospital. Rejoined 15th Battalion, Tank Corps 24 October 1918.] Transferred to the Class Z Reserve 17 March 1919.

HANNA Private Charles 41160. [Enlisted into the Service Squadron, 6th (Inniskilling) Dragoons (UD/123). To France with 36th (Ulster) Division in October 1915. Served with 2nd North Irish Horse, X Corps Cavalry Regiment.] Joined the renamed 9th (North Irish Horse) Battalion from 36 Infantry Base Depot and transferred to Princess Victoria's (Royal Irish Fusiliers) in September/October 1917 (renumbered 41160). Transferred to the Class Z Reserve 14 March 1919. 1914-15 Star.

HANNA Private Herbert 41236. [Enlisted in October 1914 into the North Irish Horse (1298). To France with 'F' Squadron in 33rd Division 17 November 1915. Served with 2nd North Irish Horse, X Corps Cavalry Regiment.] Joined the renamed 9th (North Irish Horse) Battalion from 36 Infantry Base Depot and transferred to Princess Victoria's (Royal Irish Fusiliers) in September/October 1917 (renumbered 41236). Transferred to the Class Z Reserve 20 February 1919. 1914-15 Star.

HANNA Private Isaac 24347. Born 30 April 1896 at Lurgan, County Armagh. Lived at Ballynarry, County Armagh. Enlisted 13 May 1916. Posted to the 9th (Service) Battalion. 'B' Company. **Wounded** at the Battle of Langemarck 16 August 1917. Discharged as no longer physically fit for war service due to wounds 30 January 1918, aged 21. Silver War Badge, number 310233. Died 12 November 1938, aged 42.

HANNA Private John 14316. Enlisted September 1914. To France with 36th (Ulster) Division in October 1915. Transferred to the Class Z Reserve 22 March 1919. 1914-15 Star.

HANNA Private John 18248. Enlisted 22 February 1915 into the 9th (Service) Battalion. To France with 36th (Ulster) Division in October 1915. **Wounded**. Discharged as no longer physically fit for war service due to wounds 18 June 1918, aged 22. Silver War Badge, number 411846. 1914-15 Star.

HANNA Lance Corporal Robert 23220. From Crobane, Newry, County Down. A farm labourer. Enlisted in November 1915. Posted to the 9th (Service) Battalion. 'C' Company. **Wounded** at the Battle of Langemarck 16 August 1917.

HANNA Lance Corporal Robert 27446. Born in 1899. From Bessbrook, County Armagh. Enlisted 22 March 1917. Posted to the 9th (Service) Battalion. 'B' Company. **Wounded** at the Battle of Langemarck 16 August 1917. Discharged as no longer physically fit for war service due to wounds 16 January 1919. Silver War Badge, number B84673. Brother of Private William Hanna.

HANNA Private Robert James 14261. Enlisted September 1914. To France with 36th (Ulster) Division in October 1915. 'C' Company. Stretcher-bearer during the attack at Hamel 1 July 1916, which he survived unwounded. Transferred to the Class Z Reserve 28 February 1919. 1914-15 Star.

HANNA Private Samuel Joseph 41203. [Enlisted in December 1914 into the North Irish Horse (1355). Served with 2nd North Irish Horse, X Corps Cavalry Regiment.] Joined the renamed 9th (North Irish Horse) Battalion from 36 Infantry Base Depot and transferred to Princess Victoria's (Royal Irish Fusiliers) in September/October 1917 (renumbered 41203).

HANNA Private William 14281. Born at Bessbrook, County Armagh. Enlisted September 1914. To France with 36th (Ulster) Division in October 1915. 'A' Company. **Wounded** (leg amputated) at the Battle of Langemarck 16 August 1917. **Died of wounds** 10 September 1917. 1914-15 Star. Brother of Lance Corporal Robert Hanna.

HANNA Private William 42524, 33418 & 7041580. From Newry, County Down. [Served previously with The Royal Irish Rifles (22658).] Transferred at the Base Depot to Princess Victoria's (Royal Irish Fusiliers) 14 September 1918 (renumbered 42524) and joined the 9th (North Irish Horse) Battalion 22 September 1918. Re-enlisted 18 September 1919 for Regular Army service with Princess Victoria's (Royal Irish Fusiliers) (renumbered 33418, renumbered 7041580). Discharged 17 September 1926. Enlisted into The Cameronians (Scottish Rifles) 25 January 1927. Transferred to the Class A Reserve 5 November 1927.

HANNA Private William Henry 20856. Born in 1883 at Lurgan, County Armagh. A weaver. Enlisted 7 June 1915 into the 9th (Service) Battalion. To France with 36th (Ulster) Division in October 1915. 'C' Company. Bangalore torpedo carrier during the attack at Hamel 1 July 1916, which he survived unwounded. Discharged as no longer physically fit for war service due to sickness 19 August 1917. Silver War Badge, number 228755. 1914-15 Star.

HANRAHAN Private Michael 27871. [Enlisted in August 1917. To France and posted to the 7th/8th (Service) Battalion in 49th Brigade, 16th (Irish) Division.] Joined the 9th (North Irish Horse) Battalion when the 7th/8th (Service) Battalion was disbanded in February 1918. 'A' Company. **Missing** in the period 21-28 March 1918 during the retreat from St Quentin believed **captured**.

HANSON Private William 27447. Enlisted in March 1917. Posted to the 9th (North Irish Horse) Battalion. [Posted to the 1st Battalion. **Captured** in March/April 1918.]

HARDINGTON Lance Corporal Joseph James 43363. Born in 1898 at Laytonstone, Essex. A shop assistant. [Enlisted 9 December 1915, aged 17, and transferred to the Army Reserve. Mobilised 21 July 1916 and joined the 3/7th Battalion, The London Regiment (353177). To France 10 November 1916 for service with the 1/7th (City of London) Battalion, The London Regiment.] Attached to the 9th (Service) Battalion, Princess Victoria's (Royal Irish Fusiliers) 26 November 1916. 'C' Company. Discharged from the Territorial Force, re-enlisted and transferred to Princess Victoria's (Royal Irish Fusiliers) in March/April 1917 (renumbered 43363). Lance Corporal 24 October 1917. **Captured** in the period 21-28 March 1918 during the retreat from St Quentin. **Died**

of erysipelas of the face and cardiac weakness 14 August 1918 in the Bavarian War Hospital, Hautmont while a prisoner of war.

HARDWIDGE Lance Corporal Alfred 43255. [Enlisted into The Sherwood Foresters (Nottinghamshire and Derbyshire Regiment).] Transferred to Princess Victoria's (Royal Irish Fusiliers) 31 August 1916 (renumbered 43255) having joined the 9th (Service) Battalion on 8 August 1916.

HARE Private Henry 41106. [Enlisted into the Service Squadron, 6th (Inniskilling) Dragoons (UD/170). To France with 36th (Ulster) Division in October 1915. Served with 2nd North Irish Horse, X Corps Cavalry Regiment.] Joined the renamed 9th (North Irish Horse) Battalion from 36 Infantry Base Depot and transferred to Princess Victoria's (Royal Irish Fusiliers) in September/October 1917 (renumbered 41106). Transferred to the Class Z Reserve 18 March 1919. 1914-15 Star.

HARE Sergeant Thomas 14286 & 7040581. Born in 1892 at Bessbrook, County Armagh. Enlisted September 1914. To France with 36th (Ulster) Division in October 1915. 'D' Company. **Wounded** during the attack at Hamel 1 July 1916 and evacuated to hospital in England on 3 July 1916. To France 22 December 1916 and rejoined the 9th (Service) Battalion. Evacuated to hospital in England 28 April 1917. To France 7 September 1917 and rejoined the 9th (Service) Battalion. **Wounded** during the raid at Havrincourt on 3 November 1917 and evacuated to hospital in England on 5 November 1917. 1914-15 Star. Re-enlisted on 6 March 1919 for Regular Army service with Princess Victoria's (Royal Irish Fusiliers) (renumbered 7040581) and joined the 2nd Battalion. Discharged 31 March 1921 on the termination of his period of engagement. He returned to live in Bessbrook, County Armagh. His brother, Rifleman William John Wallace Hare, served with The Royal Irish Rifles.

HARGREAVES Corporal Arthur Broughton 17280. Born 23 August 1898 in Burnley, Lancashire. [Enlisted in November 1914 into the 7th or 8th (Service) Battalion in 49th Brigade, 16th (Irish) Division.] Joined the 9th (North Irish Horse) Battalion when the 7th/8th (Service) Battalion was disbanded in February 1918. 'B' Company. Believed **wounded** in the period 21-28 March 1918 during the retreat from St Quentin. Tried by Field General Court Martial on 10 June 1918 charged with an unknown act *'to the prejudice and good order of military discipline'*; found guilty and sentenced to forty-two days Field Punishment Number 1. Tried by Field General Court Martial on 10 December 1918 charged with *'absenting himself without leave'*; found guilty and sentenced to forty-two days Field Punishment Number 1. Died in 1982, aged 83.

HARKNESS Private Andrew John 41296. [Enlisted in November 1915 into the North Irish Horse (1935). Served with 2nd North Irish Horse, X Corps Cavalry Regiment.] Joined the renamed 9th (North Irish Horse) Battalion from 36 Infantry Base Depot and transferred to Princess Victoria's (Royal Irish Fusiliers) in September/October 1917 (renumbered 41296). 'C' Company. **Missing** in the period 21-28 March 1918 during the retreat from St Quentin believed **captured**.

HARKNESS Private Thomas 41182. [Enlisted in January 1915 into the North Irish Horse (1380). To France with 'F' Squadron in 33rd Division 17 November 1915. Served with 2nd North Irish Horse, X Corps Cavalry Regiment.] Joined the renamed 9th (North Irish Horse) Battalion from 36 Infantry Base Depot and transferred to Princess Victoria's (Royal Irish Fusiliers) in September/October 1917 (renumbered 41182). [Transferred to The Inniskilling Fusiliers (renumbered 48188).] Transferred to the Class Z Reserve. 1914-15 Star.

HARLAND Lance Sergeant George 14262. Born at Lurgan in 1886. Served pre-war in the 3rd Battalion (Militia), Princess Victoria's (Royal Irish Fusiliers). A weaver in the linen trade. Enlisted at Lurgan on 15 September 1915. Corporal 14 August 1915. To France with 36th (Ulster) Division in October 1915. Admitted to 12th General Hospital, Rouen in February 1916 and evacuated to hospital in England. Discharged from hospital and joined the 10th (Reserve) Battalion on 3 June 1916. Lance Sergeant 25 May 1917. Posted to the 3rd (Reserve) Battalion 20 May 1918. [Transferred to Alexandra Princess of Wales's Own (Yorkshire Regiment) (renumbered 63433) and joined the 13th (Service) Battalion at Aldeburgh.] 1914-15 Star. Transferred to the Class Z Reserve 25 July 1919.

HARLOW Private Frederick Charles 45743. [Enlisted into The London Regiment. Posted to 1/24th (County of London) Battalion, The London Regiment (The Queen's) (4167).] To France and joined 36 Infantry Base Depot 29 March 1918. Transferred to Princess Victoria's (Royal Irish

Fusiliers) 2 April 1918 (renumbered 45743) and joined the 9th (North Irish Horse) Battalion 4 April 1918.

HARPER Private Henry 21119. From Holywood, County Down. [Enlisted into The Connaught Rangers (2306). Transferred to Princess Victoria's (Royal Irish Fusiliers) in December 1914/January 1915 (renumbered 21119). Joined the 7th or 8th (Service) Battalion in 49th Brigade, 16th (Irish) Division.] Joined the 9th (North Irish Horse) Battalion when the 7th/8th (Service) Battalion was disbanded in February 1918.] **Missing** in the period 11-18 April 1918 in the actions between Wulverghem and Kemmel; subsequently declared **killed in action** 19 April 1918.

HARPER Private Robert 41467. [Enlisted in November 1915 into the North Irish Horse (1980). Served with 2nd North Irish Horse, X Corps Cavalry Regiment.] Joined the renamed 9th (North Irish Horse) Battalion from 36 Infantry Base Depot and transferred to Princess Victoria's (Royal Irish Fusiliers) in September/October 1917 (renumbered 41467).

HARPER Private William John 14247. Born at Glasgow. 4th (Portadown) Battalion, Armagh Regiment, Ulster Volunteer Force. Enlisted September 1914. To France with 36th (Ulster) Division in October 1915. 'C' Company. **Killed in action** during the attack at Hamel 1 July 1916, aged 28. 1914-15 Star.

HARPUR Private Thompson 41433. Born in 1897 at Londonderry. Lived in Belfast. [Enlisted in September 1914 into the North Irish Horse (1084). Served with 2nd North Irish Horse, X Corps Cavalry Regiment.] Joined the renamed 9th (North Irish Horse) Battalion from 36 Infantry Base Depot and transferred to Princess Victoria's (Royal Irish Fusiliers) in September/October 1917 (renumbered 41433). 'C' Company. **Wounded** and **captured** in the period 21-28 March 1918 during the retreat from St Quentin. **Died of wounds** 18 May 1918 while a prisoner of war, aged 21.

HARRIS Private Arthur M 42287. [Enlisted into the Army Veterinary Corps (32998).] Transferred to Princess Victoria's (Royal Irish Fusiliers) 8 May 1918 (renumbered 42287) and joined the 9th (North Irish Horse) Battalion. [Transferred to 5th (Service) Battalion, The Royal Irish Regiment (Pioneers) in the Light Division in the British Army of the Rhine in March/June 1919 (renumbered 41302).] Transferred to the Class Z Reserve.

HARRIS Private Percy John 45766. From London. [Enlisted in 1917 and in 1917 and joined the 22nd (Reserve) Battalion, The London Regiment (684222).] To France and joined 36 Infantry Base Depot 29 March 1918. Transferred to Princess Victoria's (Royal Irish Fusiliers) 2 April 1918 (renumbered 45766) and joined the 9th (North Irish Horse) Battalion 4 April 1918. **Wounded** in the period 11-15 April 1918 in the actions in the actions between Wulverghem and Kemmel and **died of wounds** 15 April 1918, aged 33.

HARRIS Lance Corporal Reginald Herbert 43453. [Enlisted 12 September 1914 into The London Regiment and joined 2/24th (County of London) Battalion, The London Regiment (The Queen's) (2984).] To France and joined 36 Infantry Base Depot 29 March 1918. Transferred to Princess Victoria's (Royal Irish Fusiliers) 2 April 1918 (renumbered 43453) and joined the 9th (North Irish Horse) Battalion 4 April 1918. Discharged as no longer physically fit for war service due to sickness 7 April 1919. Silver War Badge, number B207394.

HARRISON Private Arthur R 43382. Born in 1890 at Stratford, London. Joined the 9th (Service) Battalion, Princess Victoria's (Royal Irish Fusiliers) with the draft of men from The London Regiment in November 1916. 'D' Company. Transferred to Princess Victoria's (Royal Irish Fusiliers) in March 1917 (renumbered 43382). **Wounded** at the Battle of Langemarck 16 August 1917. Evacuated to hospital in England 20 August 1917. Discharged as no longer physically fit for war service due to wounds 7 June 1918. Silver War Badge, number 395828. Died at Stratford, London on 11 November 1927, aged 37.

HARRISON Private Charles 43326. From Walthamstow, London. [Enlisted 17 July 1916 into The London Regiment.] Attached to the 9th (Service) Battalion, Princess Victoria's (Royal Irish Fusiliers) 26 November 1916. 'A' Company. Discharged from the Territorial Force, re-enlisted and transferred to Princess Victoria's (Royal Irish Fusiliers) in March/April 1917 (renumbered 43326). **Wounded** at the Battle of Langemarck 16 August 1917. Discharged as no longer physically fit for war service due to wounds 24 July 1918, aged 28. Silver War Badge, number 379061.

HARRISON Corporal Corrie 14958. [Enlisted into the 5th (Service) Battalion in 31st Brigade, 10th (Irish) Division. Embarked with the Mediterranean Expeditionary Force July 1915. Posted to the 1st

Battalion.] Posted to the 9th (North Irish Horse) Battalion. Transferred to the Class Z Reserve 4 February 1919. 1914-15 Star.

HARRISON Private James 14258. Enlisted September 1914. No record of deployment to France with 36th (Ulster) Division in October 1915.

HARRISON Private Thomas Andrew 41183. From Castleblayney, County Monaghan. [Enlisted in January 1915 into the North Irish Horse (1381). To France with 'F' Squadron in 33rd Division 17 November 1915. Served with 2nd North Irish Horse, X Corps Cavalry Regiment.] Joined the renamed 9th (North Irish Horse) Battalion from 36 Infantry Base Depot and transferred to Princess Victoria's (Royal Irish Fusiliers) in September/October 1917 (renumbered 41183). **Captured** in 1918. Transferred to the Class Z Reserve 26 March 1919. 1914-15 Star.

HARRISON Private William H 14325. Enlisted September 1914. No record of deployment to France with 36th (Ulster) Division in October 1915. [Transferred to The Royal Munster Fusiliers (renumbered G/1443). Served with the 1st Garrison Battalion, The Royal Munster Fusiliers in Italy.]

HARRISON Private William 43266. [Enlisted in 1904 as a regular soldier into The Sherwood Foresters (Nottinghamshire and Derbyshire Regiment) (9357). Served with the 2nd Battalion, The Sherwood Foresters (Nottinghamshire and Derbyshire Regiment).] Transferred to Princess Victoria's (Royal Irish Fusiliers) 31 August 1916 (renumbered 43266) having joined the 9th (Service) Battalion on 8 August 1916.

HART Private Joseph 25181. Born at Armagh, County Armagh. Lived in Glasgow. Enlisted in November 1916. Posted to the 9th (Service) Battalion. 'D' Company. **Missing** at the Battle of Langemarck 16 August 1917 and later declared **killed in action** on that date, aged 30.

HARTE Private Dominick 20689, 33964 & 7041944. From Keady, County Armagh. A postman. [Enlisted in July 1915 and joined the 7th or 8th (Service) Battalion in 49th Brigade, 16th (Irish) Division.] Joined the 9th (North Irish Horse) Battalion when the 7th/8th (Service) Battalion was disbanded in February 1918. Re-enlisted 25 February 1920 for Regular Army service with Princess Victoria's (Royal Irish Fusiliers) (renumbered 33964, renumbered 7041944). **Deserted** 28 December 1922.

HARTE Lance Corporal D 28746. Enlisted in October 1917. Posted to the 9th (North Irish Horse) Battalion in early-1918. 'B' Company. **Missing** in the period 21-28 March 1918 during the retreat from St Quentin believed **captured**.

HARTLEY Private James Clegg 45793 & 7042238. Born in 1899 at Burnley, Lancashire. [Enlisted 16 March 1917. Served previously with The Royal Irish Rifles (28746).] To France 29 March 1918. Joined the 9th (North Irish Horse) Battalion, Princess Victoria's (Royal Irish Fusiliers) with the draft of men from The London Regiment in April 1918 (renumbered 45793). Evacuated to hospital in England 13 July 1918. Re-enlisted in early-1920 for Regular Army service with Princess Victoria's (Royal Irish Fusiliers) (renumbered 7042238). Discharged 15 March 1925.

HARTROPP Lance Corporal William Thomas 43211. Born 28 April 1891. [Enlisted 24 November 1915 into The Sherwood Foresters (Nottinghamshire and Derbyshire Regiment).] Transferred to Princess Victoria's (Royal Irish Fusiliers) 31 August 1916 having joined the 9th (Service) Battalion on 8 August 1916 (renumbered 43211). 'A' Company. **Wounded** during the retreat from St Quentin 21-28 March 1918. Discharged as no longer physically fit for war service due to wounds 21 March 1919. Silver War Badge, number B167276. Died at Derby in 1971, aged 80.

HARVEY Private Frederick Wright 45771. [Enlisted into The London Regiment (5839). Posted to 1/22nd (County of London) Battalion, The London Regiment (The Queen's).] To France and joined 36 Infantry Base Depot 29 March 1918. Transferred to Princess Victoria's (Royal Irish Fusiliers) 2 April 1918 (renumbered 45771) and joined the 9th (North Irish Horse) Battalion 4 April 1918.

HARVEY Private George 14265. Enlisted September 1914. To France with 36th (Ulster) Division in October 1915. 'C' Company. Survived the attack at Hamel on 1 July 1916 unwounded. Transferred to the Class Z Reserve 29 April 1919. 1914-15 Star.

HARVEY Private Nathaniel 41362. Born in 1882 at Belfast. A shipyard labourer. [Enlisted in August 1914 into the North Irish Horse (1032). To France 1 May 1915. Served with 2nd North Irish Horse, X Corps Cavalry Regiment.] Joined the renamed 9th (North Irish Horse) Battalion from 36

Infantry Base Depot and transferred to Princess Victoria's (Royal Irish Fusiliers) in September/October 1917 (renumbered 41362). 'B' Company. **Captured** in the period 21-28 March 1918 during the retreat from St Quentin. Transferred to the Class Z Reserve 27 March 1919. 1914-15 Star.

HARVEY Private Peter 21120. Born in 1894 at Bessbrook, County Armagh. [Enlisted into The Connaught Rangers (4279) 6 May 1915. Transferred to Princess Victoria's (Royal Irish Fusiliers) in August 1915 (renumbered 21120) and joined the 8th (Service) Battalion in 49th Brigade, 16th (Irish) Division. 'B' Company. To France 19 February 1916. **Wounded** (gas) 29 April 1916. Treated at 112 Field ambulance and 1st General Hospital. Rejoined the 8th (Service) Battalion 1 June 1916. Sentenced to seven days Field Punishment Number 1 for not complying with an order 3 March 1917. **Wounded** by a gunshot to the scalp 7 June 1917 and evacuated to hospital in Ireland. Treated at hospital in Dublin and at the Princess Patricia Hospital, Bray. **Mention in Despatches**.] Joined the 9th (North Irish Horse) Battalion when the 7th/8th (Service) Battalion was disbanded in February 1918. **Wounded** by shrapnel to the right hand and left foot in the period 11-18 April 1918 in the actions between Wulverghem and Kemmel. Evacuated to hospital in England and treated at the City of London Military Hospital, at the Irish Counties War Hospital, Dublin and at the Military Convalescent Hospital, Holywood, County Down. Joined the 3rd (Reserve) Battalion 13 August 1918. Sentenced to fourteen days Field Punishment Number 2 for drunkenness 7 November 1918. Sentenced to fourteen days Field Punishment Number 2 for *'whilst a prisoner in arrest, breaking his arrest on 22 November 1918 and remaining absent till 9pm same date'* 26 November 1918. Sentenced to twenty-eight days Field Punishment Number 2 for breaking out of the guardroom 30 November 1918. Transferred to the Class Z Reserve 29 March 1919.

HARVEY Private Thomas 14248. (Documents show his number as 14246, corrected to 14248). From Drumgor, Portadown, County Armagh. 4th (Portadown) Battalion, Armagh Regiment, Ulster Volunteer Force. A saddler. Enlisted September 1914. Discharged as not being likely to become an efficient soldier in that he was considered medically unfit for service 3 October 1914.

HARVEY Private William 22975. Born in 1875. From Keady, County Armagh. A linen worker. Enlisted 12 November 1915 and joined the 10th (Reserve) Battalion. To France 8 July 1917 and joined the 9th (Service) Battalion. 'C' Company. **Wounded** at the Battle of Langemarck 16 August 1917 and evacuated to hospital in England. Treated at Reading War Hospital. Posted to the 10th (Reserve) Battalion 27 September 1917. [Transferred to the Royal Army Medical Corps (renumbered 136750) in 1918. Served in the Army of Occupation and then with 8th Company at York.] Transferred to the Class Z Reserve 27 July 1920.

HARVISON Private Andrew 16152. Enlisted into the 9th (Service) Battalion in October 1914. To France with 36th (Ulster) Division in October 1915. **Wounded** during the attack at Hamel 1 July 1916. [Transferred to the Labour Corps (renumbered 599188).] 1914-15 Star.

HASLETT Private Frederick J 45790. Joined the 9th (North Irish Horse) Battalion, Princess Victoria's (Royal Irish Fusiliers) with the draft of men from The London Regiment in April 1918. [Transferred to 5th (Service) Battalion, The Royal Irish Regiment (Pioneers) in the Light Division in the British Army of the Rhine in March/June 1919 (renumbered 41304).]

HASSARD Private Joseph 41632. [Enlisted into the Service Squadron, 6th (Inniskilling) Dragoons (UD/197). To France with 36th (Ulster) Division in October 1915. Served with 2nd North Irish Horse, X Corps Cavalry Regiment.] Joined the renamed 9th (North Irish Horse) Battalion from 36 Infantry Base Depot and transferred to Princess Victoria's (Royal Irish Fusiliers) in September/October 1917 (renumbered 41632). Transferred to the Class Z Reserve 20 February 1919. 1914-15 Star.

HASSARD Private Frank 17405. Enlisted into the 9th (Service) Battalion in November/December 1914. To France with 36th (Ulster) Division in October 1915. 'C' Company. **Wounded** during the attack at Hamel 1 July 1916. Transferred to the Class Z Reserve 20 March 1919. 1914-15 Star.

HASSETT Private John 29032. From Belfast. Enlisted 7 September 1914. Served elsewhere before transferring to Princess Victoria's (Royal Irish Fusiliers) in early-1918 (renumbered 29032). Posted to the 9th (North Irish Horse) Battalion. **Wounded**. Discharged as no longer physically fit for war service due to wounds 2 April 1919. Silver War Badge, number B202545.

HASTIE Private Richard 40013. [Enlisted into The Prince of Wales's Own (West Yorkshire Regiment) in 1905 (8008). To France and joined the 1st Battalion, The Prince of Wales's Own (West

Yorkshire Regiment) 1 April 1915.] Transferred to Princess Victoria's (Royal Irish Fusiliers) 30 November 1916 (renumbered 40013) and joined the 9th (Service) Battalion 12 December 1916. Transferred to the Class Z Reserve 14 March 1919. 1914-15 Star.

HATHAWAY Corporal Richard 43436. From London. [Enlisted 15 July 1915 into The London Regiment (4565). To France 10 November 1915 and joined Number 1 Entrenching Battalion 24 December 1915. Admitted to 18th Casualty Clearing Station with impetigo in July 1916. **Wounded** by a gunshot to the face on 27 July 1916 and evacuated to hospital in England. Treated at 3rd Western General Hospital, Cardiff. Joined the 22nd (Reserve) Battalion, The London Regiment 6 February 1917. Lance Corporal 9 July 1917.] To France and joined 36 Infantry Base Depot 29 March 1918. Transferred to Princess Victoria's (Royal Irish Fusiliers) 2 April 1918 (renumbered 43436) and joined the 9th (North Irish Horse) Battalion 4 April 1918. Admitted to 110th Field Ambulance with influenza 17 June 1918. **Wounded** by gunshot to the neck and chest during the attacks on Hill 41 and **died of wounds** in 3rd Australian Casualty Clearing Station on 7 October 1918. 1914-15 Star.

HATHWAY Private Gilbert Francis 42272. [Enlisted into the Army Veterinary Corps (20203).] Transferred to Princess Victoria's (Royal Irish Fusiliers) 8 May 1918 (renumbered 42272) and joined the 9th (North Irish Horse) Battalion.

HATTER Lance Corporal Arthur 43240. Born in 1890 at Nottingham. A lace warehouseman. [Enlisted 8 December 1915 into The Sherwood Foresters (Nottinghamshire and Derbyshire Regiment).] Transferred to Princess Victoria's (Royal Irish Fusiliers) 31 August 1916 having joined the 9th (Service) Battalion on 8 August 1916 (renumbered 43240). 'B' Company. **Wounded** at the Battle of Langemarck 16 August 1917. Discharged as no longer physically fit for war service due to wounds 2 August 1918. Silver War Badge, number 379985.

HAUGH Private James 24942. Born in 1897 at Mullartown, Annalong, County Down. Enlisted 1 November 1916. Posted to the 9th (Service) Battalion. [Posted to the 1st Battalion. **Wounded**.] Discharged as no longer physically fit for war service due to wounds 4 December 1919. Silver War Badge, number B349069. His brother, Private George Haugh, served with The Royal Irish Rifles.

HAWKINS Sergeant Douglas Norman 19065. Enlisted 10 December 1915. **Wounded**. Discharged as no longer physically fit for war service due to wounds 2 April 1919. Silver War Badge, number B195568.

HAWKINS Corporal Frederick 43430. [Enlisted into the 7th (Service) Battalion, The Royal Irish Rifles (7816). To France with 48th Brigade, 16th (Irish) Division 19 December 1915.] To 36 Infantry Base Depot and joined the Surplus Company November 1917. Transferred to Princess Victoria's (Royal Irish Fusiliers) (renumbered 43430) in February 1918. Posted to the 7th/8th (Service) Battalion in 49th Brigade, 16th (Irish) Division (probably did not join).] Joined the 9th (North Irish Horse) Battalion when the 7th/8th (Service) Battalion was disbanded in February 1918. 1914-15 Star.

HAWKINS Corporal Frederick Louis 43444. [Enlisted 22 April 1915 into The London Regiment (3422). Posted to 1/22nd (County of London) Battalion, The London Regiment (The Queen's).] To France and joined 36 Infantry Base Depot 29 March 1918. Transferred to Princess Victoria's (Royal Irish Fusiliers) 2 April 1918 (renumbered 43444) and joined the 9th (North Irish Horse) Battalion 4 April 1918. Discharged as no longer physically fit for war service due to sickness 11 June 1919. Silver War Badge, number 458692.

HAWTHORNE Private John 18065. From Bradford, Yorkshire. Enlisted into the 9th (Service) Battalion in February 1915. To France with 36th (Ulster) Division in October 1915. 'C' Company. **Wounded** during the attack at Hamel 1 July 1916. **Missing** at the Battle of Langemarck 16 August 1917 and later declared **killed in action** on that date. 1914-15 Star.

HAWTHORNE Sergeant Robert G 18554. Enlisted into the 9th (Service) Battalion in April 1915. Posted to the 10th (Reserve) Battalion and did not serve overseas.

HAWTHORNE Private Thomas Charles 41432. Born in 1895 at Ballyhone, Larne, County Antrim. [Enlisted 13 December 1916 into the North Irish Horse (2329). To France 12 May 1917. Served with 2nd North Irish Horse, X Corps Cavalry Regiment.] Joined the renamed 9th (North Irish Horse) Battalion from 36 Infantry Base Depot and transferred to Princess Victoria's (Royal Irish Fusiliers) in September/October 1917 (renumbered 41432). 'C' Company. **Wounded** by a gunshot to the abdomen on a raid at Havrincourt 3 November 1917. Evacuated to hospital in England 19 November 1917. Joined the 10th (Reserve) Battalion February 1918. To France 9 May 1918 and rejoined the 9th (North Irish Horse) Battalion. [Transferred to 5th (Service) Battalion, The Royal Irish Regiment (Pioneers) in the Light Division in the British Army of the Rhine in March/June 1919 (renumbered 41305). Served as a Regimental Bugler. Transferred to The Royal Warwickshire Regiment (renumbered 44579) 30 November 1919 and served with the 51st (Graduated) Battalion at Southwold, Suffolk.] Transferred to the Class Z Reserve 14 March 1920.

HAYES Private Isaac 14322. Born in 1884 at Portadown, County Armagh. Served pre-war in the 3rd Battalion (Militia), Princess Victoria's (Royal Irish Fusiliers). Enlisted September 1914. To France with 36th (Ulster) Division in October 1915. **Wounded** by shrapnel in the right foot 31 May 1916. Treated at 4th Casualty Clearing Station and 2nd General Hospital. Rejoined the 9th (Service) Battalion on 14 August 1916. **Wounded** at the Battle of Langemarck 16 August 1917. Treated at 3rd Canadian Casualty Clearing Station and 22nd General Hospital. Rejoined the 9th (Service) Battalion on 16 September 1917. **Captured** at Erches 27 March 1918 during the retreat from St Quentin. Repatriated 28 November 1918. Transferred to the Class Z Reserve 26 March 1919. 1914-15 Star.

HAYES Private John 14303. From Sarah Street, Portadown, County Armagh. Enlisted September 1914. To France with 36th (Ulster) Division in October 1915. 'B' Company. **Killed in action** during the attack at Hamel 1 July 1916, aged 37. 1914-15 Star. Both of his brothers also died: Private William Hayes was killed in action on 12 October 1916 while serving with the 1st Battalion at Le Transloy. Private Alexander Hayes died in France on 31 July 1918 while serving with the 2nd (Garrison) Battalion, The Royal Irish Regiment.

HAYES Corporal Richard 42183. From Newcastle-upon-Tyne. [Enlisted into the Army Service Corps (S4/056242). To France 25 July 1915.] Transferred to Princess Victoria's (Royal Irish Fusiliers) 8 May 1918 (renumbered 42183) and joined the 9th (North Irish Horse) Battalion. [Transferred to The Royal Inniskilling Fusiliers (renumbered 43335). **Wounded** near Terhand/Vijfwegen and **died of wounds** 2 October 1918 while serving with the 1st Battalion, The Royal Inniskilling Fusiliers.] 1914-15 Star.

HAYES Private Wesley 18558. From Clonroot, Portadown, County Armagh. Armagh Regiment, Ulster Volunteer Force. Enlisted into the 9th (Service) Battalion in April 1915. To France with 36th (Ulster) Division in October 1915. **Killed in action** during the attack at Hamel 1 July 1916. 1914-15 Star.

HAYNES Lance Corporal Maurice Frederick 45753. Born on 30 October 1898 at London. [Enlisted into The London Regiment.] To France and joined 36 Infantry Base Depot 29 March 1918. Transferred to Princess Victoria's (Royal Irish Fusiliers) 2 April 1918 (renumbered 45753) and joined the 9th (North Irish Horse) Battalion 4 April 1918. Died in 1971, aged 72.

HAYNES Private William 42164. [Enlisted into the Army Service Corps (S4/11399).] Transferred to Princess Victoria's (Royal Irish Fusiliers) 8 May 1918 (renumbered 42164) and joined the 9th (North Irish Horse) Battalion. [Part of the draft transferred on 19 June 1918 to The Royal Irish Rifles (renumbered 45854).]

HAYWARD Sergeant Thomas Henry 43439. [Enlisted into The London Regiment (3224). To France 29 June 1915 and joined 1/24th (County of London) Battalion, The London Regiment (The Queen's).] To France and joined 36 Infantry Base Depot 29 March 1918. Transferred to Princess Victoria's (Royal Irish Fusiliers) 2 April 1918 (renumbered 43439) and joined the 9th (North Irish Horse) Battalion 4 April 1918. Discharged 10 March 1919. 1914-15 Star.

HAYWOOD Private Horace Edgar 43233. Born in 1890. From Chesterfield, Derbyshire. A joiner. [Enlisted 20 November 1915 and transferred to the Army Reserve. Mobilised 14 February 1916 and joined the 3rd (Reserve) Battalion, The Sherwood Foresters (Nottinghamshire and Derbyshire Regiment) (35504).] To France 23 July 1917. Transferred to Princess Victoria's (Royal Irish Fusiliers) 31 August 1916 (renumbered 43233) having joined the 9th (Service) Battalion on 8 August 1916. 'B' Company. **Missing** at the Battle of Langemarck on 16 August 1917; in 1920 he was declared **killed in action** on that date.

HAZLETT Private John Alexander 16108. From Edenisland, County Monaghan. Enlisted into the 9th (Service) Battalion in October 1914. To France with 36th (Ulster) Division in October 1915.

Killed in action during the attack at Hamel 1 July 1916, aged 30. 1914-15 Star.

HEALY Private Patrick 43082. [Enlisted into or transferred to Princess Victoria's (Royal Irish Fusiliers) in August 1916 and joined the 8th (Service) Battalion in 49th Brigade, 16th (Irish) Division.] Joined the 9th (North Irish Horse) Battalion when the 7th/8th (Service) Battalion was disbanded in February 1918. 'D' Company. **Missing** in the period 21-28 March 1918 during the retreat from St Quentin believed **captured**.

HEATHFIELD Private William 43249. Born in 1894 at Normanton, Derbyshire. A coal miner. [Enlisted 7 November 1914 into The Sherwood Foresters (Nottinghamshire and Derbyshire Regiment) (18637) and joined the 3rd (Reserve) Battalion. Posted to the 13th (Reserve) Battalion 5 December 1914. To France 24 August 1915. Posted to the 1st Battalion, The Sherwood Foresters (Nottinghamshire and Derbyshire Regiment). To hospital sick (eczema) and evacuated to hospital in England 17 March 1916. To France 4 July 1916.] Transferred to Princess Victoria's (Royal Irish Fusiliers) 31 August 1916 (renumbered 43249) having joined the 9th (Service) Battalion on 8 August 1916. [Transferred to the Tank Corps (renumbered 304850) 28 December 1917 and posted for training to the Tank Corps Depot, at Bovington near Wareham, Dorset. Posted to the 17th Battalion, Tank Corps 8 January 1918. Posted to the Tank Corps Reserve Unit at Wareham and attached to 18th Battalion, Tank Corps 29 May 1918. To France and joined 11th Battalion, Tank Corps 2 September 1918.] 1914-15 Star. Transferred to the Class Z Reserve May 1919.

HEATHWOOD Private Robert 41285. Born in 1894 at Belfast. Worked in the linen industry. [Enlisted in September 1914 into the North Irish Horse (1135). To France 18 January 1915. Served with 2nd North Irish Horse, X Corps Cavalry Regiment.] Joined the renamed 9th (North Irish Horse) Battalion from 36 Infantry Base Depot and transferred to Princess Victoria's (Royal Irish Fusiliers) in September/October 1917 (renumbered 41285). 'C' Company. **Killed in action** on a raid at Havrincourt 3 November 1917. 1914-15 Star. He has no known grave but is probably buried in an unmarked grave in Cambrai East Military Cemetery.

HEFFERNAN Private Albert Francis 43316. Born in 1883 at Carlisle, Cumberland. A stick mounter (walking stick decorator) from Stoke Newington, London. [Enlisted 19 July 1916 and joined 3/7th Battalion, The London Regiment (6764).] To 8 Infantry Base Depot, France 11 November 1916. Attached to the 9th (Service) Battalion, Princess Victoria's (Royal Irish Fusiliers) 26 November 1916. 'C' Company. **Wounded** 7 February 1917 by a gunshot to the arm and evacuated via 110th Field Ambulance to 3rd Canadian General Hospital. To 36 Infantry Base Depot 19 March 1917 and rejoined the 9th (Service) Battalion 28 March 1917. Discharged from the Territorial Force, re-enlisted and transferred to Princess Victoria's (Royal Irish Fusiliers) in April 1917 (renumbered 43316). **Wounded** at the Battle of Langemarck 16 August 1917 by gunshot to the right side that penetrated his abdomen and **died of wounds** 31 August 1917 in 12th General Hospital, Rouen aged 32.

HEGAN Sergeant Joseph Alexander 14336. From Portadown, County Armagh. Member of Masonic Lodge 82. Enlisted September 1914. To France with 36th (Ulster) Division in October 1915. 'A' Company. **Wounded** during the attack at Hamel 1 July 1916. Transferred to the Class Z Reserve 27 March 1919. 1914-15 Star.

HEMPHILL Lance Corporal John 41394. [Enlisted in April 1915 into the North Irish Horse (1478). Served with 2nd North Irish Horse, X Corps Cavalry Regiment.] Joined the renamed 9th (North Irish Horse) Battalion from 36 Infantry Base Depot and transferred to Princess Victoria's (Royal Irish Fusiliers) in September/October 1917 (renumbered 41394).

HENDERSON Private Alexander 42193. [Enlisted into the Army Service Corps (T2/22920).] Transferred to Princess Victoria's (Royal Irish Fusiliers) 8 May 1918 (renumbered 42193) and joined the 9th (North Irish Horse) Battalion.

HENNESEY Sergeant George 14333. Born in 1892 at Drumadd, County Armagh. Armagh Regiment, Ulster Volunteer Force. Worked for a grocer. Enlisted September 1914. To France with 36th (Ulster) Division in October 1915. 'C' Company. **Wounded** in the leg during the attack at Hamel 1 July 1916. **Wounded** at the Battle of Langemarck 16 August 1917. Discharged as no longer physically fit for war service due to wounds 4 September 1919. Silver War Badge, number 445737. 1914-15 Star. Served on the Headquarters Staff of the Ulster Special Constabulary and then at the Ministry of Labour. During the Second World War served with the 4th Armagh (Armagh)

Battalion, Ulster Home Guard. His injured leg was amputated in February 1965. He did not recover from this and died on 14 October 1965, aged 73.

HENNING Private George 14292. Enlisted September 1914. To France with 36th (Ulster) Division in October 1915. **Wounded**. Discharged as no longer physically fit for war service due to wounds 19 September 1918, aged 24. Silver War Badge, number B5075. 1914-15 Star.

HENNING Lance Corporal Samuel Joseph 14252. Born in 1880 at Portadown, County Armagh. 4th (Portadown) Battalion, Armagh Regiment, Ulster Volunteer Force. A steam roller driver. Enlisted September 1914. To France with 36th (Ulster) Division in October 1915. 'B' Company. **Wounded** at the Battle of Langemarck 16 August 1917. [Transferred to the Army Service Corps (renumbered M/380354).]

HENRY Private Edward 43410. [To France 29 November 1915 and joined the 2nd Battalion, The Royal Irish Rifles (7590 Private). To 36 Infantry Base Depot and joined the Surplus Company November 1917. Transferred to Princess Victoria's (Royal Irish Fusiliers) in February 1918 (renumbered 43410). Posted to the 7th/8th (Service) Battalion in 49th Brigade, 16th (Irish) Division (probably did not join).] Joined the 9th (North Irish Horse) Battalion when the 7th/8th (Service) Battalion was disbanded in February 1918. 'A' Company. **Missing** in the period 21-28 March 1918 during the retreat from St Quentin believed **captured**. Transferred to the Class Z Reserve 9 May 1919. 1914-15 Star.

HENRY MM Lance Sergeant George Adams 41401. Born in 1894 at Cloghog, County Londonderry. A grocer at Ballyhackamore, County Down. [Enlisted in March 1912 into the North Irish Horse (683). To France 20 August 1914 with 'C' Squadron as 5th Division Cavalry and then as GHQ Troops. Detached for duty as the bodyguard of General Sir John French and later General Sir Horace Smith-Dorrien. Served with 2nd North Irish Horse, X Corps Cavalry Regiment.] Joined the renamed 9th (North Irish Horse) Battalion from 36 Infantry Base Depot and transferred to Princess Victoria's (Royal Irish Fusiliers) in September/October 1917 (renumbered 41401). 'C' Company. **MM** – Marcoing 16 December 1917. **Wounded** on 14 March 1918 and **died of wounds** 26 March 1918 at the Australian General Hospital, Rouen. 1914 Star.

HENRY Private John (Jack) 41575. [Enlisted 3 March 1915 into the North Irish Horse (1461). To France with 'F' Squadron in 33rd Division 17 November 1915. Served with 2nd North Irish Horse, X Corps Cavalry Regiment.] Joined the renamed 9th (North Irish Horse) Battalion from 36 Infantry Base Depot and transferred to Princess Victoria's (Royal Irish Fusiliers) in September/October 1917 (renumbered 41575). 'D' Company. Believed **wounded** in the period 21-28 March 1918 during the retreat from St Quentin. Discharged as no longer physically fit for war service due to wounds 4 March 1919. Silver War Badge, number B162472. 1914-15 Star.

HENRY Private James 14257. From Portadown, County Armagh. Enlisted September 1914. To France with 36th (Ulster) Division in October 1915. 'B' Company. **Wounded** during the attack at Hamel 1 July 1916. [Transferred to the Labour Corps (renumbered 231602).] 1914-15 Star. Transferred to the Class Z Reserve 7 April 1919.

HENRY Private John 14312. From Lurgan, County Armagh. Enlisted September 1914. To France with 36th (Ulster) Division in October 1915. 'C' Company. Attached to Headquarters 108th Brigade and did not take part in the attack at Hamel on 1 July 1916. **Missing** at the Battle of Langemarck 16 August 1917 and later declared **killed in action** on that date. 1914-15 Star.

HENRY Private Robert 15647. [Enlisted in September 1914 into the 6th (Service) Battalion in 31st Brigade, 10th (Irish) Division. Embarked with the Mediterranean Expeditionary Force July 1915. Posted to the 7th/8th (Service) Battalion in 49th Brigade, 16th (Irish) Division.] Joined the 9th (North Irish Horse) Battalion when the 7th/8th (Service) Battalion was disbanded in February 1918. 1914-15 Star.

HENRY Private Thomas 41425. [Enlisted in December 1915 into the North Irish Horse (2052). Served with 2nd North Irish Horse, X Corps Cavalry Regiment.] Joined the renamed 9th (North Irish Horse) Battalion from 36 Infantry Base Depot and transferred to Princess Victoria's (Royal Irish Fusiliers) in September/October 1917 (renumbered 41425).

HENRY Private William. Tried by Field General Court Martial on 18 February 1919 charged with *'theft'*; found guilty and sentenced to fourteen days Field Punishment Number 2. Soldier not identified.

HENRY Private William George 14276. From Charles Street, Portadown, County Armagh. Married with four children. 4th (Portadown) Battalion, Armagh Regiment, Ulster Volunteer Force. Enlisted September 1914. To France with 36th (Ulster) Division in October 1915. **Killed in action** during the attack at Hamel 1 July 1916. 1914-15 Star.

HENRY Private William Robert 24645. Born in 1884. Lived at Shankill, Belfast. An oiler by trade. Enlisted 14 August 1916. To France 8 December 1916 and was posted to the 9th (Service) Battalion. Spent most of his time in France in hospital suffering from bronchitis and asthma. Evacuated to hospital in England 10 February 1917. Discharged as no longer physically fit for war service due to sickness (bronchitis and emphysema) 22 March 1917. Recorded as having transferred to the Labour Corps (renumbered 364647), this is unlikely to have been completed. **Died** 10 February 1919 at Carnmoney, County Antrim.

HERRING Private James William 43215. Born in 1889. From New Houghton, Nottinghamshire. A coal miner. [Enlisted 2 December 1914 and joined the 9th (Service) Battalion, The Sherwood Foresters (Nottinghamshire and Derbyshire Regiment) (20325). Sailed with the Mediterranean Expeditionary Force 1 July 1915. **Wounded** at Suvla Bay by a gunshot to the leg on 9 August 1915. Treated at 16th Stationary Hospital on the island of Lemnos. Evacuated to hospital in England 16 September 1915 and posted to the 3rd (Reserve) Battalion, The Sherwood Foresters (Nottinghamshire and Derbyshire Regiment) 5 October 1915. To France 29 March 1916 and immediately admitted to hospital with impetigo. Joined 7 Platoon, 'B' Company, 1st Battalion, The Sherwood Foresters (Nottinghamshire and Derbyshire Regiment) 28 March 1916. **Wounded** 7 July 1916 by a gunshot to the back. Treated at 22nd General Hospital, Camiers and then at Number 6 Convalescent Depot, Etaples.] Joined 14 Infantry Base Depot 25 July 1916. Transferred to Princess Victoria's (Royal Irish Fusiliers) 31 August 1916 (renumbered 43215) having joined the 9th (Service) Battalion on 8 August 1916. 'A' Company. Lance Corporal 29 September 1916. Private 11 August 1917. Listed as **wounded** at the Battle of Langemarck 16 August 1917 and later declared **killed in action** on that date, aged 28. 1914-15 Star.

HERRON Private Robert 14295. Born in 1884. From Summerisland, County Armagh. A mill worker. Enlisted September 1914. To France with 36th (Ulster) Division in October 1915. 'A' Company. Evacuated to hospital in England sick (scalded foot) October 1916. Joined the 10th (Reserve) Battalion 15 December 1916. To France 27 July 1917 and rejoined the 9th (Service) Battalion. **Captured** in the period 21-28 March 1918 during the retreat from St Quentin. Repatriated 5 December 1918. Transferred to the Class Z Reserve 1 April 1919. 1914-15 Star.

HERRON Private Robert 41348. [Enlisted in April 1915 into the North Irish Horse (1486). Served with 2nd North Irish Horse, X Corps Cavalry Regiment.] Joined the renamed 9th (North Irish Horse) Battalion from 36 Infantry Base Depot and transferred to Princess Victoria's (Royal Irish Fusiliers) in September/October 1917 (renumbered 41348). 'B' Company. Separated from the 9th (North Irish Horse) Battalion in the period 21-28 March 1918 during the retreat from St Quentin; rejoined 3 April 1918.

HERRON Private William 18051. Enlisted into the 9th (Service) Battalion in February 1915. To France with 36th (Ulster) Division in October 1915. 'C' Company. Survived the attack at Hamel on 1 July 1916 unwounded. **Wounded** during the Battle of Messines and to hospital 9 June 1917. Transferred to the Class Z Reserve 2 April 1919. 1914-15 Star.

HETHERINGTON Private John 42289. [Enlisted into the Army Veterinary Corps (16573).] Transferred to Princess Victoria's (Royal Irish Fusiliers) 8 May 1918 (renumbered 42289) and joined the 9th (North Irish Horse) Battalion.

HEWITT Corporal Adam 14324. From Lurgan, County Armagh. Enlisted September 1914. 'D' Company. Discharged as no longer physically fit for war service due to sickness 25 May 1915. Silver War Badge, number B349064.

HEWITT Lance Corporal Albert 14300. Enlisted September 1914. To France with 36th (Ulster) Division in October 1915. Transferred to the Class Z Reserve 11 March 1919. 1914-15 Star.

HEWITT Lance Corporal Frances (Frank) 14334. Born in 1894 at Richhill. Enlisted September 1914. To France with 36th (Ulster) Division in October 1915. **Wounded** during the attack at Hamel 1 July 1916. Discharged as no longer physically fit for war service due to wounds 27 September 1917, aged 23. Silver War Badge, number 261228. 1914-15 Star.

HEWITT Private James 14306. From Portadown, County Armagh. Enlisted September 1914. To France with 36th (Ulster) Division in October 1915. **Wounded** during the attack at Hamel 1 July 1916. [Posted to the 1st Battalion and was **killed in action** during the attack south of Wulverghem on 4 September 1918.] 1914-15 Star.

HEWITT Private James 14309. From Portadown, County Armagh. Married with four children. Enlisted September 1914. To France with 36th (Ulster) Division in October 1915. **Killed in action** during the attack at Hamel 1 July 1916. 1914-15 Star. Brother of 22755 Private Thomas Hewitt.

HEWITT Lance Corporal James 16423. From Clounagh, Portadown, County Armagh. Enlisted into the 9th (Service) Battalion in November 1914. To France with 36th (Ulster) Division in October 1915. 'B' Company. **Killed in action** during the attack at Hamel 1 July 1916, aged 18. 1914-15 Star.

HEWITT Private Joseph 22790. From Ballintaggart, County Armagh. Enlisted in November 1915. Posted to the 9th (Service) Battalion. **Wounded** during the attack at Hamel 1 July 1916. [Posted to the 2nd Garrison Battalion in Salonika.]

HEWITT Private Robert 14297. Born in 1890 at Drumcree, County Armagh. A farmer. Enlisted September 1914. Discharged as not being likely to become an efficient soldier in that he was considered medically unfit for service 4 November 1914.

HEWITT Private Robert 17669. Enlisted into the 9th (Service) Battalion in December 1914/January 1915. To France with 36th (Ulster) Division in October 1915. 1914-15 Star.

HEWITT Private Thomas 14315. Attended Seagoe School. From Bridge Street, Portadown, County Armagh. 4th (Portadown) Battalion, Armagh Regiment, Ulster Volunteer Force. Enlisted September 1914. To France with 36th (Ulster) Division in October 1915. **Killed in action** during the attack at Hamel 1 July 1916, aged 19.

HEWITT Private Thomas 14256. Enlisted September 1914. To France with 36th (Ulster) Division in October 1915. Transferred to the Class Z Reserve 26 March 1919. 1914-15 Star.

HEWITT Private Thomas 22755. Born in 1891 at Kilmore, Portadown, County Armagh. Enlisted 8 November 1915 and joined the 10th (Reserve) Battalion. To France 19 February 1916 and joined the 9th (Service) Battalion. **Killed in action** during the attack at Hamel 1 July 1916, aged 24. Brother of 14309 Private James Hewitt.

HEWITT Private Walter James 25284. [Enlisted in December 1916. Posted to the 1st Battalion. Served then with the 7th/8th (Service) Battalion in 49th Brigade, 16th (Irish) Division.] Joined the 9th (North Irish Horse) Battalion when the 7th/8th (Service) Battalion was disbanded in February 1918. 'C' Company. **Missing** in the period 21-28 March 1918 during the retreat from St Quentin believed **captured**.

HICKEY Private William 20018. From Youghal, County Cork. Enlisted in May 1915, aged 16. Posted to the 9th (Service) Battalion in late 1916. **Wounded** when shot while looking over the parapet in the line west of Messines and **died of wounds** 7 February 1917, aged 18.

HICKIE Warrant Officer Class I Henry 42574. Regimental Sergeant Major - see above.

HICKS Private Frederick Hugh 23854. From Ward End, Birmingham. [Enlisted into The Oxfordshire and Buckinghamshire Light Infantry (19177).] Transferred to Princess Victoria's (Royal Irish Fusiliers) in January 1916 (renumbered 23854). Posted to the 9th (Service) Battalion. 'B' Company. **Wounded** during the attack at Hamel 1 July 1916. Initially reported as **missing** at the Battle of Langemarck 16 August 1917. His body was found and buried by men of the 9th (Service) Battalion, The Royal Irish Rifles (West Belfast) and he was declared **killed in action** on that date, aged 22.

HIGGINS Private David 14330. From Belfast. Enlisted September 1914. To France with 36th (Ulster) Division in October 1915. 'A' Company. **Wounded** at the Battle of Langemarck 16 August 1917. Transferred to the Class Z Reserve 30 March 1919. 1914-15 Star. Re-enlisted in 1919 for Regular Army service with The Royal Inniskilling Fusiliers. Died at Ballynabeck, Scarva, County Down in 1930.

HIGGINS Corporal Henry 14278. Born in 1890. Enlisted September 1914. To France with 36th (Ulster) Division in October 1915. [Joined 108th Brigade Machine Gun Company in January 1916.

Transferred to the Machine Gun Corps (renumbered 17792). **Wounded**. Discharged as no longer physically fit for war service due to wounds 9 September 1918.] Silver War Badge, number B36398. 1914-15 Star.

HIGGINS Private Hugh 41373. Born in 1897 at Belfast. Worked as a shop assistant for John Rea Ltd. [Enlisted 27 December 1916 into the North Irish Horse (2337). To France 14 May 1917. Served with 2nd North Irish Horse, X Corps Cavalry Regiment.] Joined the renamed 9th (North Irish Horse) Battalion from 36 Infantry Base Depot and transferred to Princess Victoria's (Royal Irish Fusiliers) in September/October 1917 (renumbered 41373). **Captured** at Roye on 27 March 1918 during the retreat from St Quentin. Worked in a coal mine in Germany as a prisoner of war and spent some time at Limburg Prisoner of War Camp.

HILL Private Ernest 41322. From Belfast. [Enlisted in July 1916 into the North Irish Horse (2213). Served with 2nd North Irish Horse, X Corps Cavalry Regiment.] Joined the renamed 9th (North Irish Horse) Battalion from 36 Infantry Base Depot and transferred to Princess Victoria's (Royal Irish Fusiliers) in September/October 1917 (renumbered 41322). 'C' Company. **Captured** in the period 21-28 March 1918 during the retreat from St Quentin.

HILL Private John 14263. Enlisted September 1914. To France with 36th (Ulster) Division in October 1915. 'C' Company. **Wounded** during the attack at Hamel 1 July 1916. [Transferred to the Corps of Royal Engineers (renumbered 311042).] Transferred to the Class Z Reserve 20 July 1919. 1914-15 Star.

HILL Private John 14311. From Lurgan, County Armagh. Enlisted September 1914. To France with 36th (Ulster) Division in October 1915. 'C' Company. Bombing team during the attack during the attack at Hamel on 1 July 1916 during which he was **wounded**. **Missing** at the Battle of Langemarck 16 August 1917 and later declared **killed in action** on that date. 1914-15 Star.

HILL Private Moore 14299. From Carleton Street, Portadown, County Armagh. Student at Portadown Technical College. Enlisted September 1914. To France with 36th (Ulster) Division in October 1915. 'D' Company. Became seriously ill and was evacuated to Edinburgh Military Hospital where he **died** on 10 May 1916, aged 19. His remains were returned home and he is buried in a shared grave with his brother, Private Robert Hill (16431), in Drumcree Church of Ireland Churchyard. 1914-15 Star.

HILL Private Robert 16431. From Carleton Street, Portadown, County Armagh. Enlisted into the 9th (Service) Battalion in November 1914. To France with 36th (Ulster) Division in October 1915. 'B' Company. **Wounded** during the attack at Hamel 1 July 1916 and **died of wounds** on 17 July 1916, aged 22, in Norfolk War Hospital, Thorpe. His remains were returned home and he was buried in Drumcree Church of Ireland Churchyard on 21 July 1916, where his brother, Private Moore Hill, was later interred. 1914-15 Star.

HILL Private Robert J 14266. From Portadown, County Armagh. Enlisted September 1914. To France with 36th (Ulster) Division in October 1915. [Joined 108th Brigade Machine Gun Company in January 1916. Transferred to the Machine Gun Corps (renumbered 17791).] 1914-15 Star.

HILL Private Thomas 14301. Born in 1879. From Milford, County Armagh. Enlisted September 1914. 'A' Company. Discharged as not being likely to become an efficient soldier in that he was considered medically unfit for service 20 October 1914. Silver War Badge, number 228756.

HILTON Private William 23491. From Hackney, Middlesex. [Enlisted into The Duke of Cornwall's Light Infantry (22319). Transferred to Princess Victoria's (Royal Irish Fusiliers) in December 1915 (renumbered 23491) and posted to the 7th (Service) Battalion in 49th Brigade, 16th (Irish) Division.] Joined the 9th (North Irish Horse) Battalion when the 7th/8th (Service) Battalion was disbanded in February 1918. **Killed in action** near St Quentin 19 February 1918.

HIND Private James 43277. [Enlisted into The Sherwood Foresters (Nottinghamshire and Derbyshire Regiment) (791). To France 16 March 1915.] Transferred to Princess Victoria's (Royal Irish Fusiliers) 31 August 1916 (renumbered 43277) having joined the 9th (Service) Battalion on 8 August 1916. [Transferred to the Army Service Corps (renumbered M/40944). **Deserted** 7 June 1918; medals forfeit.]

HIND Private John Henry 43199. From Nottingham. A carriage hand. [Enlisted 10 December 1915 and transferred to the Army Reserve. Mobilised 16 February 1916 and joined the 3rd

(Reserve) Battalion, The Sherwood Foresters (Nottinghamshire and Derbyshire Regiment) (35533). To France 22 July 1916.] Transferred to Princess Victoria's (Royal Irish Fusiliers) 31 August 1916 (renumbered 43199) having joined the 9th (Service) Battalion on 8 August 1916. 'A' company. [Transferred to the Tank Corps (renumbered 304858) 28 December 1917 and posted for training to the Tank Corps Depot, at Bovington near Wareham, Dorset. Posted to the 17th Battalion, Tank Corps 8 January 1918 and to France 27 April 1918 when it converted to 17th (Armoured Car) Battalion.] Transferred to the Class Z Reserve 8 October 1919.

HINE Private Thomas Arthur 42019. Born at Morley, Yorkshire. Lived at West Ham, London. [Enlisted into The London Regiment. Posted to 1/22nd (County of London) Battalion, The London Regiment (The Queen's) in December 1917.] To France and joined 'B' Infantry Base Depot in early-April 1918. Transferred to Princess Victoria's (Royal Irish Fusiliers) April 1918 and posted to the 1st Battalion. Posted to the 9th (North Irish Horse) Battalion in May 1918.

HISTON Private Daniel 42103. [Enlisted into the Army Veterinary Corps (SE/15554).] Transferred to Princess Victoria's (Royal Irish Fusiliers) 8 May 1918 (renumbered 42103) and joined the 9th (North Irish Horse) Battalion. [Transferred to the Seaforth Highlanders (Ross-shire Buffs, The Duke of Albany's) (renumbered S/43790).]

HOAR MM Private William 43341. From London. [Enlisted into The London Regiment (3598). Posted to 1/7th (City of London) Battalion, The London Regiment.] Attached to the 9th (Service) Battalion, Princess Victoria's (Royal Irish Fusiliers) 26 November 1916. 'B' Company. Discharged from the Territorial Force, re-enlisted and transferred to Princess Victoria's (Royal Irish Fusiliers) in March/April 1917 (renumbered 43341). **Wounded** at the Battle of Langemarck 16 August 1917. [Posted to the 1st Battalion. **MM.**]

HOBBS Private Andrew 14259. From Union Street, Lurgan, County Armagh. Enlisted September 1914. To France with 36th (Ulster) Division in October 1915. 'C' Company. Company runner during the attack at Hamel 1 July 1916. **Killed in action** during the attack at Hamel 1 July 1916, aged 38. 1914-15 Star. Brother of Sergeant Robert Hobbs and Privates David and Herbert Hobbs.

HOBBS Private David 14305. From Union Street, Lurgan, County Armagh. Enlisted September 1914. To France with 36th (Ulster) Division in October 1915. 'C' Company. **Killed in action** during the attack at Hamel 1 July 1916. 1914-15 Star. Brother of Sergeant Robert Hobbs and Privates Andrew and Herbert Hobbs.

HOBBS Private Herbert George 14273. From Union Street, Lurgan, County Armagh. Enlisted September 1914. To France with 36th (Ulster) Division in October 1915. **Wounded** during the attack at Hamel 1 July 1916. Returned to Lurgan in August 1916. Discharged as no longer physically fit for war service due to wounds 28 July 1917. Silver War Badge, number 218112. 1914-15 Star. Died at home in Lurgan in 1947. Brother of Sergeant Robert Hobbs and Privates Andrew and David Hobbs.

HOBBS Sergeant Robert 14302. From Union Street, Lurgan, County Armagh. Enlisted September 1914. To France with 36th (Ulster) Division in October 1915. 'C' Company. **Killed in action** during the attack at Hamel 1 July 1916. 1914-15 Star. Brother of Privates Andrew, David and Herbert Hobbs.

HOBSON Private Evelyn Peate 40012. Born 23 July 1882 at West Yorkshire. [Enlisted 6 December 1915 into The Prince of Wales's Own (West Yorkshire Regiment).] Transferred to Princess Victoria's (Royal Irish Fusiliers) 30 November 1916 (renumbered 40012) and joined the 9th (Service) Battalion 12 December 1916. **Wounded**. Discharged as no longer physically fit for war service due to wounds 6 September 1918, aged 36. Silver War Badge, number 445745. Died in Yorkshire in 1980, aged 98.

HOBSON Corporal Leonard 14293. Born in 1884 at Doncaster, Yorkshire. An engine driver. Enlisted September 1914 at Armagh. 'B' Company. Corporal 22 September 1914. Lance Sergeant 1 January 1915. Reverted to Corporal for falling out without permission during a march 8 May 1915. To France with 36th (Ulster) Division in October 1915. [Transferred to the Labour Corps (renumbered 519658) 27 February 1918. Served with 80th Company. Reprimanded for neglect of duty whilst in charge of a working party and improperly dressed whilst on duty 30 May 1918. Reprimanded for refusing to comply with an order given by the Military Police 8 November 1918. Promoted Sergeant.] Transferred to the Class Z Reserve 18 July 1919. 1914-15 Star.

HODGEN Private Abraham 14249. Born 10 September 1895 at Brackagh, County Armagh. 4th (Portadown) Battalion, Armagh Regiment, Ulster Volunteer Force. A farmer. Enlisted September 1914. To France with 36th (Ulster) Division in October 1915. **Wounded** during the attack at Hamel 1 July 1916. Transferred to the Class Z Reserve 22 March 1919. 1914-15 Star. Emigrated to Canada in 1927. Died 20 May 1982 at Niagara Falls, Canada and is buried with his wife Edith in Lundy's Cemetery. Brother of Private William Henry Hodgen.

HODGEN Private William Henry 14277. Born 1890 at Brackagh, County Armagh. Enlisted September 1914. 'B' Company. Discharged as no longer physically fit for war service due to sickness (rheumatism) 24 April 1915. Brother of Private Abraham Hodgen.

HODGSON Private Herbert John 43463. [Enlisted into The London Regiment (1752). Posted to 1/24th (County of London) Battalion, The London Regiment (The Queen's).] To France and joined 36 Infantry Base Depot 29 March 1918. Transferred to Princess Victoria's (Royal Irish Fusiliers) 2 April 1918 (renumbered 43463) and joined the 9th (North Irish Horse) Battalion 4 April 1918. Transferred to the Class Z Reserve 13 March 1919. 1914-15 Star.

HODGSON Private Jacob 41383. [Enlisted into the 6th (Inniskilling) Dragoons (5498). Served with 2nd North Irish Horse, X Corps Cavalry Regiment.] Joined the renamed 9th (North Irish Horse) Battalion from 36 Infantry Base Depot and transferred to Princess Victoria's (Royal Irish Fusiliers) in September/October 1917 (renumbered 41383).

HOEY Private William 41125. From County Tyrone. [Enlisted into the Service Squadron, 6th (Inniskilling) Dragoons (UD/152). Served with 2nd North Irish Horse, X Corps Cavalry Regiment.] Joined the renamed 9th (North Irish Horse) Battalion from 36 Infantry Base Depot and transferred to Princess Victoria's (Royal Irish Fusiliers) in September/October 1917 (renumbered 41125). [Transferred to the Labour Corps.]

HOGAN Private John 42459. [Enlisted into the 15th (Service) Battalion, The Cheshire Regiment (1st Birkenhead) (23170). Transferred to The Royal Irish Rifles (renumbered 40281) and served with the 13th (Service) Battalion, The Royal Irish Rifles (1st County Down).] Transferred at the Base Depot to Princess Victoria's (Royal Irish Fusiliers) 14 September 1918 (renumbered 42459) and joined the 9th (North Irish Horse) Battalion 22 September 1918.

HOGG Private Henry 27613, 7040809 & 7043094. Born in 1897 at Butlersbridge, County Cavan. Enlisted 15 May 1917. To France 5 October 1917 and joined the 9th (North Irish Horse) Battalion. 'A' Company. **Captured** in the period 21-28 March 1918 during the retreat from St Quentin. Repatriated 25 November 1918. Re-enlisted in August/September 1919 for Regular Army service with Princess Victoria's (Royal Irish Fusiliers) (renumbered 7040809). Served with the 1st Battalion in Persia and Mesopotamia in 1919/20. General Service Medal 1918-1962 with clasps 'Iraq' & 'NW Persia'. Discharged 21 November 1922. Re-enlisted into The Cameronians (Scottish Rifles) 14 September 1923. Transferred to The Royal Irish Fusiliers (Princess Victoria's) 12 February 1924 (renumbered 7043094). Discharged 21 March 1934. Re-enlisted into the 5th (Home Defence) Battalion, The Royal Inniskilling Fusiliers 28 October 1940.

HOLBROOK Private John 20349. Born at Enniskillen, County Fermanagh. Lived at County Durham. Enlisted in May/June 1915 and joined the 9th (Service) Battalion with the draft of men from The Royal Inniskilling Fusiliers who transferred to Princess Victoria's (Royal Irish Fusiliers) on 30 June 1915. 'D' Company. **Wounded** at the Battle of Langemarck 16 August 1917. **Captured** in the period 21-28 March 1918 during the retreat from St Quentin.

HOLDEN-HATTON Private James 19776. Enlisted on 3 May 1915 into the 9th (Service) Battalion. **Wounded**. [Posted to the 2nd Garrison Battalion in Salonika.] Discharged as no longer physically fit for war service due to sickness 23 November 1918. Silver War Badge, number B77838.

HOLLAND Private Albert 14310. From Lurgan, County Armagh. Enlisted September 1914. To France with 36th (Ulster) Division in October 1915. 'C' Company. Replaced 14699 Private W J Sands on a bombing team for the attack at Hamel 1 July 1916, during which he was **killed in action**. 1914-15 Star.

HOLLAND Private Phillip 42636. Born in 1889 at Ballymacarrett, County Armagh. Worked at Harland and Wolff shipyard, Belfast. Served briefly with 4th Battalion (Militia), The Royal Irish Rifles then enlisted into The Royal Irish Rifles 9 March 1907 (8557). Joined the 2nd Battalion, The Royal Irish Rifles. Tried by District Court Martial on 20 August 1907 charged with *'absenting* *himself without leave'*; found guilty and sentenced to twenty-one days detention. Tried by a civil court on 31 October 1907 charged with stealing a bicycle; found guilty and sentenced to two months imprisonment with hard labour. Tried by District Court Martial on 5 June 1909 charged with ***'deserting** His Majesty's service'*; found guilty and sentenced to forty-two days imprisonment with hard labour. All previous service was forfeit on conviction of desertion. Tried by a civil court on 15 January 1910 charged with stealing a bicycle; found guilty and sentenced to one month imprisonment with hard labour. Discharged from the Army due to conviction by the civil power 1 February 1910. [Enlisted 13 August 1914 into the North Irish Horse (1005). To France 20 August 1914 with 'C' Squadron as 5th Division Cavalry and then as GHQ Troops. To hospital with scabies 9-20 March 1915. To hospital sick (haemorrhoids) three times from October to December 1915 and evacuated to hospital in England 11 December 1915. To France 5 March 1917 and posted to 'A' Squadron, North Irish Horse. Served with 2nd North Irish Horse, X Corps Cavalry Regiment.] Transferred to Princess Victoria's (Royal Irish Fusiliers) 24 October 1917 (renumbered 42636) and joined the 9th (North Irish Horse) Battalion 6 November 1917. 'C' Company. [Posted to the Cavalry Base Depot 22 November 1917. Transferred back to the North Irish Horse (renumbered Corps of Hussars 71195) 4 December 1917 and served in V Corps Cavalry Regiment and then 5th Cyclist Battalion (North Irish Horse), V Corps. To hospital sick (myalgia) 7 September 1918 and evacuated to hospital in England.] Discharged as no longer physically fit for war service due to sickness 4 March 1919, aged 30. Silver War Badge, number B206257. 1914 Star. Emigrated to Canada.

HOLLAND Private Thomas 18062. From Woodview, County Armagh. Enlisted into the 9th (Service) Battalion in February 1915. To France with 36th (Ulster) Division in October 1915. 'C' Company. **Killed in action** during the attack at Hamel 1 July 1916, aged 23.

HOLLAND Corporal Thomas H 14320. From Lurgan, County Armagh. Enlisted September 1914. To France with 36th (Ulster) Division in October 1915. 'D' Company. Transferred to the Class Z Reserve 15 March 1919. 1914-15 Star. Re-enlisted in 1919 for Regular Army service with The Hampshire Regiment.

HOLLYWOOD Private Alexander 22749. From Lurgan, County Armagh. A weaver. Enlisted 10 November 1915 and joined the 10th (Reserve) Battalion. Joined the 9th (Service) Battalion on 13 June 1916. **Wounded** on the raid at La Petite Douve Farm on 12 October 1916 by a gunshot to the back and **died of wounds** 18 October 1916, aged 30, in 1st Canadian Casualty Clearing Station. Brother of Private John Hollywood.

HOLLYWOOD Private John 14318. Born in 1886. From Lurgan, County Armagh. A shoemaker. Enlisted September 1914. To France with 36th (Ulster) Division in October 1915. Transferred to the Class Z Reserve 23 March 1919. 1914-15 Star. Brother of Private Alexander Hollywood.

HOLMES Private George 49742. From Strandtown, Belfast. [Enlisted into The Royal Irish Rifles (688).] Transferred to Princess Victoria's (Royal Irish Fusiliers) in April 1918 (renumbered 49742) and joined the 9th (North Irish Horse) Battalion. [Transferred to The Royal Inniskilling Fusiliers (renumbered 22304).]

HOLMES Private Thomas Henry 14250. Born on 13 April 1888 at Killicomain, Portadown, County Armagh. 4th (Portadown) Battalion, Armagh Regiment, Ulster Volunteer Force. Enlisted September 1914. To France with 36th (Ulster) Division in October 1915. 'B' Company. **Killed in action** during the attack at Hamel 1 July 1916, aged 27. His brother, Driver Norman Sydney Holmes, was killed in action on 21 March 1918 serving with 15th (Scottish) Division Ammunition Column, Army Service Corps.

HOLMES Corporal William John 14254. From Portadown, County Armagh. 4th (Portadown) Battalion, Armagh Regiment, Ulster Volunteer Force. Enlisted September 1914. No record of deployment to France with 36th (Ulster) Division in October 1915. [Posted to the 1st Garrison Battalion and served in India and Burma. Discharged as no longer physically fit for war service due to sickness 17 July 1918, aged 30.] Silver War Badge, number 425705.

HOLMES Private William John 14270. From Portadown, County Armagh. 4th (Portadown) Battalion, Armagh Regiment, Ulster Volunteer Force. Enlisted September 1914. To France with 36th (Ulster) Division in October 1915. **Wounded** during the attack at Hamel 1 July 1916. [Transferred to The Royal Irish Regiment and posted to the 1st Garrison Battalion, The Royal Irish Regiment in Egypt (renumbered 5837).] 1914-15 Star.

HOLT Private Tom Schofield 25979. Born in 1886 at Summerseat, Lancashire. A weaver. [Enlisted 2 March 1916 and joined 4th Reserve Cavalry Regiment for service with 4th (Royal Irish) Dragoon Guards (21753). To hospital sick in October and November 1916 (boils) and treated at the Military Hospital, Tidworth. To 36 Infantry Base Depot 1 January 1917. Transferred to Princess Victoria's (Royal Irish Fusiliers) January 1917 (renumbered 25979) and joined the 1st Battalion. To hospital sick (impetigo) in January and March 1918.] Posted to the 9th (North Irish Horse) Battalion 1 May 1918. To the field ambulance sick (impetigo) in June 1918. **Wounded** by shrapnel through the left hand during the attack north of Bailleul 24 August 1918 and evacuated to hospital in England. Treated at the Special Military Surgical Hospital, Edmonton, London. Transferred to the Class Z Reserve 3 March 1919. Lived in Summerseat, Lancashire.

HOMERSHAM AFC, DCM, MM* Wing Commander Francis Stanhope, formerly Sergeant 45807. Born 21 January 1899 at Hungerford, Berkshire. Lived in Murrayshire and studied at Elgin Academy 1905 – 1915. Then became an engineering student at a polytechnic in London until 1916. [Enlisted into The London Regiment in 1917. Trained as an Assistant Instructor, Physical and Bayonet Training at the Headquarters Gymnasium, Aldershot on Course Number 18 in December 1917.] To France and joined 36 Infantry Base Depot 29 March 1918. Transferred to Princess Victoria's (Royal Irish Fusiliers) 2 April 1918 (renumbered 45807) and joined the 9th (North Irish Horse) Battalion 4 April 1918. **MM** – (Lance Corporal) Wulverghem 4 September 1918. **MM Bar** – (Sergeant) Vijfwegen/Hill 41, 30 September to 14 October 1918. **DCM** – Courtrai 16 October 1918. [Transferred to 5th (Service) Battalion, The Royal Irish Regiment (Pioneers) in the Light Division in the British Army of the Rhine in March/June 1919 (renumbered 41301).] Transferred to the Class Z Reserve October 1919. After the war he returned to engineering college in London from 1922–24 and then joined the Royal Air Force. Commissioned as a Pilot Officer 6 January 1925. Completed his flight training at Number 4 Flying Training School, Egypt, 2 January 1926. Flying Officer 6 August 1926. Involved in an accident on 22 July 1927 at El Tabbin, near the River Nile, when a DH9A of 47 (Bombing) Squadron, based at Helwan, Egypt, crashed. 355883 Aircraftman Class 1 Harold Kauntze Bacon was killed. Flying Officer Homersham, the pilot, was uninjured. Served in Egypt until September 1929. Transferred to the Reserve of Air Force Officers 6 January 1930. Flight Lieutenant 4 February 1931. Mobilised in 1939. Squadron Leader. **AFC** (as Acting Wing Commander). Wing Commander 1 June 1942. Commanded Number 15 Elementary Flying Training School at RAF Kingstown, Carlisle. Took part in raids over Mannheim. (During his period in command of Number 15 Elementary Flying Training School, two German prisoners of war (Oberleutnant Harry Wappler, whose Heinkel He111 of KG 27 crashed into a barrage balloon over Newport in Monmouthshire and Leutnant Heinz Schnabel, a fighter pilot of 1/JG3 Jagdstaffell, who was among over 80 pilots shot down in September 1940) escaped from their prisoner of war camp at Shap by hiding in laundry baskets. They stowed away on a train bound for Carlisle. Posing as Dutch airmen they successfully stole a Miles Magister training aircraft. Later, seriously low on fuel, they spotted an aerodrome and refuelled but on taking off again they got lost in bad weather, ran low on fuel again and had to land in a meadow five miles north of Great Yarmouth. Still pretending to be Dutch airmen they were taken to Horsham, St Faith. By this time, news of escape had broken. Both men were arrested and later moved to a camp in Canada.) Transferred to the Royal Air Force Reserve of Officers 1946. Became a commercial salesman for Cadbury Fry's. Retired from the Royal Air Force Reserve of Officers 10 February 1954. Died at Freedom Fields Hospital, Birmingham on 2 January 1955, aged 56.

HONEY Private George 43230. Born at Mapperley, Derbyshire. [Enlisted into The Sherwood Foresters (Nottinghamshire and Derbyshire Regiment) (36126).] Transferred to Princess Victoria's (Royal Irish Fusiliers) 31 August 1916 (renumbered 43230) having joined the 9th (Service) Battalion on 8 August 1916. **Wounded** by shellfire on the night of 24/25 May 1917 near Spanbroekmolen and is recorded as having **died of wounds** on 25 May 1917. The burial was conducted by Reverend Mayes and his return (Army Form W3314) shows a burial date of 24 May 1917.

HONEYFORD Private Benjamin 14323. Enlisted September 1914. To France with 36th (Ulster) Division in October 1915. **Wounded**. [Transferred to the Labour Corps (renumbered 615238).] Transferred to the Class Z Reserve 27 April 1919. 1914-15 Star.

41161 Private
Oliver JOHNSTON

22152 Private
William James JOHNSTON

14355 Private
James JOYCE

Company Quartermaster
Sergeant
J KANE

41577 Private
James KELLY

15464 Company
Sergeant Major
Samuel Joseph
KEMBLE

3481 Private
John LAPPIN

41420 Private
David LAW

41108 Private
James LENAGHAN

41324 Private
William LIPSETT

24692 Private
Dominick LIVINGSTONE

14414 Company
Sergeant Major
Robert LUCAS
DCM, MM

14419 Private
Thomas LYNESS

41567 Company Quartermaster Sergeant
Francis Joseph Aloysius MacMAHON

41592 Private
Charles MAGILL

22734 Private
Thomas MALONEY

41698 Private
William Joseph MATCHETT

23410 Lance Corporal
George MATTHEWS

22029 Private
George McBRIDE

17951 Private
William McCALLUM

41329 Private
William McCARLEY MM

14556 Company
Sergeant Major
William John McCLEAN DCM

20444 Sergeant
James Campbell Hall
McCONKEY MM

41607 Private
William McCORMICK

14554 Sergeant
David McCULLOUGH

14502 Corporal
Johnston McCULLOUGH

41367 Lance Corporal
Isaac Baxter McDOWELL

41464 Private
John McFETRIDGE

41612 Sergeant
William John McKEOWN

14546 Private
John Samuel McKNIGHT

42152 Private
Daniel Scott McLEISH

41549 Private
Alexander McLELLAN

41426 Private
George McLORN

14534 Lance Corporal
Herbert McLOUGHLIN

42492 Private
Samuel MEEKE

14458 Lance Corporal
Robert Douglas MEREDITH

27574 Private
Robert MILLER

19059 Corporal
Francis Robert MINTER

16127 Corporal
John Stewart MITCHELL

41511 Sergeant
William Thomas MOFFIT

14442 Private
Robert Andrew MOORHEAD
(304862 Private R A
Moorhead MM Tank Corps)

21150 Corporal
John MORTON

17948 Private
Robert NEILL

42295 Private
James NESBITT

13231 Private
Bernard O'CALLAGHAN

14577 Sergeant
William NEILL DCM

41119 Sergeant
John O'NEILL

43268 Private
George OSTICK

42241 Private
Frederick OWENS

HONEYSETT Private Charles Edward 45778. Born 26 January 1899 at Thornton Heath, Surrey. Worked as a clerk. [Enlisted 26 January 1917 at Wimbledon and transferred to the Army Reserve. Mobilised 26 April 1917 and joined 110th Training Reserve Battalion at Wimbledon (73025) for service with 22nd (County of London) Battalion, The London Regiment (The Queen's). Joined 22nd (Reserve) Battalion, The London Regiment in 2nd London Reserve Brigade at Chiseldon Camp, Wiltshire 20 November 1917.] To France and joined 36 Infantry Base Depot 29 March 1918. Transferred to Princess Victoria's (Royal Irish Fusiliers) 2 April 1918 (renumbered 45778) and joined the 9th (North Irish Horse) Battalion 4 April 1918. Lewis Gunner, 6 Platoon, 'B' Company. Evacuated sick via 109th Field Ambulance to hospital in Boulogne 22 April 1918. Rejoined 23 July 1918. To hospital sick 18 August 1918 and evacuated to hospital in England 9 October 1918. Transferred to the Class Z Reserve 24 February 1919. Re-enlisted in 1939. Corporal Royal Army Service Corps (S/2081298). Served at the War Office. Accompanied the delegation to the Quebec Conference in 1943 that lay the foundations of the United Nations. Died 19 January 1982, aged 82, at St Martin, Cornwall.

HOOD Private Samuel Victor 41558. Commissioned into The Royal Inniskilling Fusiliers - see Appendix 5.

HOOKER Sergeant George Henry 43390. Born in 1886 in London. A commercial traveller. [Enlisted 11 December 1915 and transferred to the Army Reserve. Mobilised 2 June 1916 and joined 3/9th Battalion, The London Regiment (6199). Lance Corporal 12 November 1916.] Attached to the 9th (Service) Battalion, Princess Victoria's (Royal Irish Fusiliers) 26 November 1916. Discharged from the Territorial Force, re-enlisted and transferred to Princess Victoria's (Royal Irish Fusiliers) in March/April 1917 (renumbered 43390). Corporal 17 August 1917. Sergeant 3 May 1918. **Missing** during the attack at Vijfwegen on 30 September or 1 October 1918; recorded as **killed in action** on 3 October 1918, aged 31.

HOOKS Private John 18250. From Markethill, County Armagh. Enlisted into the 9th (Service) Battalion in February/March 1915. To France with 36th (Ulster) Division in October 1915. 'C' Company. Bombing team during the attack at Hamel 1 July 1916, when he was **wounded**. **Captured** in the period 21-28 March 1918 during the retreat from St Quentin. Transferred to the Class Z Reserve. 1914-15 Star. Died at Markethill 5 April 63, aged 69.

HOOPER Corporal Arthur Montague 16150 & 7040590. Born in 1895 at Ventnor, Isle of Wight, Hampshire. Enlisted 15 October 1914 into the 9th (Service) Battalion. To France with 36th (Ulster) Division in October 1915. 'A' Company. **Wounded** by a gunshot to the left leg at the Battle of Langemarck 16 August 1917. Evacuated to hospital in England 20 August 1917. To France 31 March 1918. **Wounded** in the hands 13 April 1918. 1914-15 Star. Re-enlisted in early-1919 for Regular Army service with Princess Victoria's (Royal Irish Fusiliers) (renumbered 7040590) and promoted to Corporal while serving with the 1st Battalion. Discharged 27 January 1931. Died at Southampton, Hampshire 29 March 1960, aged 64.

HOPKINS Private Alfred William 43451. [Enlisted into The London Regiment (1698). To France 15 March 1915 and posted to 1/24th (County of London) Battalion, The London Regiment (The Queen's).] To France and joined 36 Infantry Base Depot 29 March 1918. Transferred to Princess Victoria's (Royal Irish Fusiliers) 2 April 1918 (renumbered 43451) and joined the 9th (North Irish Horse) Battalion 4 April 1918. 1914-15 Star.

HORNER Private William Robert 27754 & 7040817. From Shankill, Belfast. Enlisted 8 December 1915. Served elsewhere/transferred to the Army Reserve before transferring to or re-enlisting into Princess Victoria's (Royal Irish Fusiliers) in June 1917. To France 5 October 1917 and joined the 9th (North Irish Horse) Battalion. Re-enlisted in August/September 1919 for Regular Army service with Princess Victoria's (Royal Irish Fusiliers) (renumbered 7040817). Discharged for misconduct 16 March 1921. Enlisted into the Royal Regiment of Artillery 3 October 1939.

HOUSTON Private David 14290. From Lurgan, County Armagh. A linen weaver. Enlisted September 1914. To France with 36th (Ulster) Division in October 1915. 3 Section, 13 Platoon, 'D' Company in 1915. Discharged as no longer physically fit for war service due to sickness 20 February 1919. Silver War Badge, number B154124. 1914-15 Star.

HOUSTON Private Frederick 20342. Born at Castledawson, County Londonderry. [Enlisted in Scotland into The Royal Inniskilling Fusiliers (22369).] Transferred to Princess Victoria's (Royal

Irish Fusiliers on 30 June 1915 (renumbered 20342) and joined the 9th (Service) Battalion. To France with 36th (Ulster) Division in October 1915. **Killed in action** during the attack at Hamel 1 July 1916. 1914-15 Star.

HOUSTON Private John 14319. From Lurgan, County Armagh. Enlisted September 1914. To France with 36th (Ulster) Division in October 1915. **Wounded** during the attack at Hamel 1 July 1916. [Transferred to the Labour Corps (renumbered 231601).] Transferred to the Class Z Reserve 12 April 1919. 1914-15 Star.

HOUSTON Private Joseph Frederick 17150. From Armagh, County Armagh. Enlisted into the 9th (Service) Battalion in October/November 1914. To France with 36th (Ulster) Division in October 1915. 'C' Company. **Died of wounds** 22 June 1918, aged 25. 1914-15 Star.

HOUSTON Private Ross 20033. Born at Portadown, County Armagh. Served pre-war with the Mid-Ulster Royal Garrison Artillery Militia. Enlisted into the 9th (Service) Battalion 1 June 1915. Posted to the 10th (Reserve) Battalion 9 October 1915. Did not serve overseas with 36th (Ulster) Division. Discharged as no longer physically fit for war service due to sickness 3 May 1916. Silver War Badge, number 509025.

HOUSTON Private Samuel 22154. From Lurgan, County Armagh. Enlisted in October 1915. Posted to the 9th (Service) Battalion in May/June 1916. **Killed in action** during the attack at Hamel 1 July 1916, aged 18.

HOUSTON Lance Corporal Samuel 41449. From Belfast. [Enlisted in September 1916 into the North Irish Horse (2281). Served with 2nd North Irish Horse, X Corps Cavalry Regiment.] Joined the renamed 9th (North Irish Horse) Battalion from 36 Infantry Base Depot and transferred to Princess Victoria's (Royal Irish Fusiliers) in September/October 1917 (renumbered 41449). **Wounded**.

HOUSTON Private Thomas 20305. Born at Eglish, County Armagh. From Glasgow. [Enlisted into The Royal Inniskilling Fusiliers (20914).] Transferred to Princess Victoria's (Royal Irish Fusiliers) on 30 June 1915 (renumbered 20305) and joined the 9th (Service) Battalion. To France with 36th (Ulster) Division in October 1915. 'B' Company. **Wounded** by shellfire near Mesnil and **died of wounds** 10 April 1916, aged 40. 1914-15 Star.

HOUSTON Private Thomas William 23964. From Monaghan, County Monaghan. Enlisted 14 February 1916 and joined the 10th (Reserve) Battalion. To France 15 June 1916 and joined the 9th (Service) Battalion. **Wounded** in October 1916 by shrapnel to the left leg that resulted in it being amputated. Evacuated to hospital in England 5 November 1916. Discharged as no longer physically fit for war service due to wounds 11 April 1918, aged 20. Silver War Badge, number 343320.

HOUSTON Private William Robert 14304. Born at Lurgan, County Armagh. A plumber. Enlisted 19 September 1914. No record of deployment to France with 36th (Ulster) Division in October 1915. [Transferred to the Labour Corps (renumbered 369480).] Discharged as no longer physically fit for war service due to sickness 26 January 1918, aged 34. Silver War Badge, number 312294.

HOWARD Lance Corporal Robert 23199. Enlisted 20 November 1915. Posted to the 9th (Service) Battalion. 'C' Company. **Wounded** in the period 21-28 March 1918 during the retreat from St Quentin. Evacuated to hospital in England. Transferred to the Class P Reserve 25 July 1918, aged 23. Silver War Badge, number 379040. Lived in Knock, Belfast.

HOWARD Private Harry 42104. [Enlisted into the Army Veterinary Corps (19878).] Transferred to Princess Victoria's (Royal Irish Fusiliers) 8 May 1918 (renumbered 42104) and joined the 9th (North Irish Horse) Battalion.

HOWE Private John 41300. [Enlisted 24 January 1914 into the North Irish Horse (891). Served with 2nd North Irish Horse, X Corps Cavalry Regiment.] Joined the renamed 9th (North Irish Horse) Battalion from 36 Infantry Base Depot and transferred to Princess Victoria's (Royal Irish Fusiliers) in September/October 1917 (renumbered 41300). **Wounded**. Discharged as no longer physically fit for war service due to wounds 7 March 1919. Silver War Badge, number B154450.

HOWE Private William Henry 41419. [Enlisted in January 1916 into the North Irish Horse (2092). Served with 2nd North Irish Horse, X Corps Cavalry Regiment.] Joined the renamed 9th (North Irish Horse) Battalion from 36 Infantry Base Depot and transferred to Princess Victoria's (Royal Irish Fusiliers) in September/October 1917 (renumbered 41419). 1914 Star.

HOY Private Alfred 22691. Enlisted in November 1915. Posted to the 9th (Service) Battalion.

HOY Private William C 43441. [Enlisted into The London Regiment (2215). To France 15 March 1915 and posted to 1/24th (County of London) Battalion, The London Regiment (The Queen's) (renumbered 720506 in March 1917).] To France and joined 36 Infantry Base Depot 29 March 1918. Transferred to Princess Victoria's (Royal Irish Fusiliers) 2 April 1918 (renumbered 43441) and joined the 9th (North Irish Horse) Battalion 4 April 1918. 1914-15 Star.

HOY Private William John 6093. Born at Shankill, County Armagh. [Enlisted on 16 July 1914 into Princess Victoria's (Royal Irish Fusiliers) Special Reserve. Served with the 5th (Service) or 6th (Service) Battalion in 31st Brigade, 10th (Irish) Division with the Mediterranean Expeditionary Force from 11 September 1915. Evacuated to hospital in England wounded or sick.] To 36 Infantry Base Depot 14 June 1917 and posted to the 9th (Service) Battalion 'B' Company. **Wounded** (shell-shock, injured back and knee) at the Battle of Langemarck 16 August 1917. Treated at 14th General Hospital and evacuated to hospital in England. Discharged as no longer physically fit for war service due to wounds 12 January 1918. Silver War Badge, number 304117. 1914-15 Star.

HOYNES Private Daniel 40169. [Enlisted into the 7th (Service) Battalion, The Royal Inniskilling Fusiliers (21113). Transferred in December 1916 to Princess Victoria's (Royal Irish Fusiliers) (renumbered 40169) and posted to the 7th/8th (Service) Battalion in 49th Brigade, 16th (Irish) Division.] Joined the 9th (North Irish Horse) Battalion when the 7th/8th (Service) Battalion was disbanded in February 1918. 'B' Company. **Missing** in the period 21-28 March 1918 during the retreat from St Quentin believed **captured**. Re-enlisted in 1919 for Regular Army service with The Royal Inniskilling Fusiliers (renumbered 6974375). Medals forfeit due to misconduct.

HUDSON Lance Corporal John 42490. [Enlisted into the Army Service Corps (S4/125964). To France 1 September 1915 and served with 39th Railhead Supply Depot. Transferred to The Royal Irish Rifles (renumbered 47234) and joined the 13th (Service) Battalion, The Royal Irish Rifles (1st County Down).] Transferred at the Base Depot to Princess Victoria's (Royal Irish Fusiliers) 14 September 1918 (renumbered 42490) and joined the 9th (North Irish Horse) Battalion 22 September 1918. 1914-15 Star.

HUDSPETH Private William 20355. From County Durham. Enlisted in May/June 1915 and joined the 9th (Service) Battalion with the draft of men from The Royal Inniskilling Fusiliers who transferred to Princess Victoria's (Royal Irish Fusiliers) on 30 June 1915.

HUGGARD Private William 41623. [Enlisted into 'C' Squadron, North Irish Horse (816). To France 20 August 1914 with 'C' Squadron as 5th Division Cavalry and then as GHQ Troops. Served with 2nd North Irish Horse, X Corps Cavalry Regiment.] Joined the renamed 9th (North Irish Horse) Battalion from 36 Infantry Base Depot and transferred to Princess Victoria's (Royal Irish Fusiliers) in September/October 1917 (renumbered 41623). [Transferred to the Army Service Corps (renumbered EMT/54401).] 1914 Star.

HUGHES DCM, MM Company Quartermaster Sergeant James 4517. From John Street, Portadown, County Armagh. Armagh Regiment, Ulster Volunteer Force. [Enlisted into Princess Victoria's (Royal Irish Fusiliers) Special Reserve. To France with the 1st Battalion 22 August 1914. **Wounded** in the face in October 1916. **MM** – Chemical Works, Roeux, April/May 1917.] Posted to the 9th (North Irish Horse) Battalion. 'A' Company. **DCM** – St Quentin 23 March 1918. Company Quartermaster Sergeant. **Missing** in the period 21-28 March 1918 during the retreat from St Quentin and later declared **killed in action** 29 March 1918, aged 30. 1914 Star.

HUGHES Private James 42460 & 7042200. [Served with the 2nd Battalion, The Royal Irish Rifles (440).] Transferred at the Base Depot to Princess Victoria's (Royal Irish Fusiliers) 14 September 1918 (renumbered 42460) and joined the 9th (North Irish Horse) Battalion 22 September 1918. Re-enlisted in early-1919 for Regular Army service with Princess Victoria's (Royal Irish Fusiliers) (renumbered 7042200). Served with the 1st Battalion in Persia and Mesopotamia in 1919/20. General Service Medal 1918-1962 with clasps 'Iraq' & 'NW Persia'.

HUGHES Private John 14327. Enlisted September 1914. To France with 36th (Ulster) Division in October 1915. 'C' Company. To hospital 1916, struck off strength when evacuated to hospital in England and did not take part in the attack at Hamel on 1 July 1916. **Wounded** during the retreat from St Quentin 21-28 March 1918. [Transferred to the Army Service Corps (renumbered M/410566).] 1914-15 Star.

HUGHES Corporal John 20095. Enlisted into the 9th (Service) Battalion in June 1915.

HUGHES Lance Corporal Percy Albert 43350. [Enlisted into The London Regiment (5161). Posted to 1/7th (City of London) Battalion, The London Regiment.] Attached to the 9th (Service) Battalion, Princess Victoria's (Royal Irish Fusiliers) 26 November 1916. Discharged from the Territorial Force, re-enlisted and transferred to Princess Victoria's (Royal Irish Fusiliers) in March/April 1917 (renumbered 43350).

HUGHES Private Robert 18699. Enlisted into the 9th (Service) Battalion 26 April 1915. To France with 36th (Ulster) Division in October 1915. Discharged as no longer physically fit for war service due to sickness 11 September 1916. Silver War Badge, number 97502. 1914-15 Star.

HUGHES Private Robert 41216. [Enlisted 5 January 1916 into the North Irish Horse (2066). Served with 2nd North Irish Horse, X Corps Cavalry Regiment.] Joined the renamed 9th (North Irish Horse) Battalion from 36 Infantry Base Depot and transferred to Princess Victoria's (Royal Irish Fusiliers) in September/October 1917 (renumbered 41216). 'D' Company. Believed **wounded** in the period 21-28 March 1918 during the retreat from St Quentin. Discharged as no longer physically fit for war service due to wounds 27 March 1919. Silver War Badge, number B165693.

HUGHES Sergeant William 14321. From Mandeville Street, Portadown, County Armagh. Enlisted September 1914. To France with 36th (Ulster) Division in October 1915. 'D' Company. Sergeant March 1916. **Wounded** during the attack at Hamel 1 July 1916 and, although having made progress in hospital, he **died of wounds** 11 July 1916. 1914-15 Star.

HULETT Private Frank 45731. [Enlisted 22 November 1915 into The London Regiment (5523). Posted to 1/24th (County of London) Battalion, The London Regiment (The Queen's).] To France and joined 36 Infantry Base Depot 29 March 1918. Transferred to Princess Victoria's (Royal Irish Fusiliers) 2 April 1918 (renumbered 45731) and joined the 9th (North Irish Horse) Battalion 4 April 1918. **Wounded**. Discharged as no longer physically fit for war service due to wounds 5 June 1919. Silver War Badge, number B302853.

HULL Corporal Robert John 41576. Born in 1896 at Lambeg, County Down. An engine driver from Lisburn, County Antrim. [Enlisted 8 May 1915 into the North Irish Horse (1519). Lance Corporal 28 December 1915. To France 11 January 1916. Fractured his skull in an accident while grazing two horses in the village of Grouches on 11 May 1916; one of the horses bolted and kicked his head. Evacuated to hospital in England 30 May 1916 via 10th General Hospital, Rouen and treated at Beaufort War Hospital, Bristol. Corporal 1 August 1916. To France 20 September 1916. Reverted to Private 13 November 1916. Served with 2nd North Irish Horse, X Corps Cavalry Regiment.] Joined the renamed 9th (North Irish Horse) Battalion from 36 Infantry Base Depot and transferred to Princess Victoria's (Royal Irish Fusiliers) in September/October 1917 (renumbered 41576). 'D' Company. Believed **wounded** in the period 21-28 March 1918 during the retreat from St Quentin. **Killed in action** at Hill 41 on 11 October 1918, aged 31.

HULL Corporal William 14268. From Garvaghy Road, Portadown, County Armagh. Enlisted September 1914. To France with 36th (Ulster) Division in October 1915. **Killed in action** during the attack at Hamel 1 July 1916, aged 25. 1914-15 Star. His brother, Rifleman George Hull, was killed in action on 2 July 1916 while serving with 16th (Service) Battalion, The Royal Irish Rifles (2nd County Down) (Pioneers). A second brother, David, also served during the war.

HUMMERSTONE Private Charles Stephen 42188. Born 1891. From Norbury, Surrey. A book stall manager. [Enlisted 10 November 1915 into the Army Service Corps (T4/142275). To France 9 April 1916.] Transferred to Princess Victoria's (Royal Irish Fusiliers) 8 May 1918 (renumbered 42188) and joined the 9th (North Irish Horse) Battalion. **Killed in action** during the attack south of Wulverghem 4 September 1918, aged 27. His brother, Gunner Francis William Hummerstone, served in the Royal Garrison Artillery (134318).

HUMPHRIES Sergeant Frederick David Richie 14289. Commissioned into Princess Victoria's (Royal Irish Fusiliers) - see Appendix 5.

HUNN Private Ernest Herbert 45045. [Enlisted 8 May 1916. Transferred to Princess Victoria's (Royal Irish Fusiliers) with the draft of men from The Buffs (East Kent Regiment) in December 1916 (renumbered 45045) and joined the 7th/8th (Service) Battalion in 49th Brigade 16th (Irish) Division.] Joined the 9th (North Irish Horse) Battalion when the 7th/8th (Service) Battalion was disbanded in February 1918. 'B' Company. **Wounded** in the period 21-28 March 1918 during the retreat from St

Quentin and evacuated to hospital in England. Discharged as no longer physically fit for war service due to wounds 7 November 1918. Silver War Badge, number B38711.

HUNTER Private James Alexander 22799. Born in 1893 at Holywood, County Down. A linen manufacturer's clerk. Enlisted in November 1915. Posted to the 9th (Service) Battalion. 'B' Company. **Wounded** at the Battle of Langemarck 16 August 1917. [Transferred to the Army Service Corps (renumbered S/389989).]

HUNTER Private Joseph 41233. From Magherafelt, County Londonderry. [Enlisted in July 1916 into the North Irish Horse (2227). Served with 2nd North Irish Horse, X Corps Cavalry Regiment.] Joined the renamed 9th (North Irish Horse) Battalion from 36 Infantry Base Depot and transferred to Princess Victoria's (Royal Irish Fusiliers) in September/October 1917 (renumbered 41233). 'D' Company. **Captured** in the period 21-28 March 1918 during the retreat from St Quentin. 1914-15 Star.

HUNTER Private Joseph 41323. [Enlisted in August 1914 into the North Irish Horse (1045). Served with 2nd North Irish Horse, X Corps Cavalry Regiment.] Joined the renamed 9th (North Irish Horse) Battalion from 36 Infantry Base Depot and transferred to Princess Victoria's (Royal Irish Fusiliers) in September/October 1917 (renumbered 41323). Transferred to the Class Z Reserve. 1914-15 Star.

HUNTER Private William 14253. From Tandragee, County Armagh. Member of Loyal Orange Lodge 110. 4th (Portadown) Battalion, Armagh Regiment, Ulster Volunteer Force. Enlisted September 1914. To France with 36th (Ulster) Division in October 1915. 'B' Company. **Killed in action** during the attack at Hamel 1 July 1916, aged 19. 1914-15 Star.

HUNTER Corporal William Alexander 49733. Transferred to Princess Victoria's (Royal Irish Fusiliers) in April 1918 and joined the 9th (North Irish Horse) Battalion.

HUNTER Corporal William John 10917 & 7040427. Born in 1891 at Monaghan, County Monaghan. Worked in Glasgow as a labourer in a chemical works. [Enlisted as a regular soldier in Glasgow 19 January 1912 and joined the 1st Battalion. Evacuated to hospital in England 7 September 1914. Posted to the 3rd (Reserve) Battalion on 7 January 1915. To France 18 January 1915 and joined the 2nd Battalion. To 13th General Hospital with frostbite and evacuated to hospital in England 24 February 1915. Posted to the 3rd (Reserve) Battalion 26 May 1915. To France 1 June 1915 and rejoined the 1st Battalion. Corporal 7 January 1917. **Wounded** by shrapnel to the right arm 17 October 1916 and evacuated to hospital in England 20 October 1916. Treated at 5th Northern General Hospital, Leicester. Posted to the 3rd (Reserve) Battalion 21 May 1917.] To 36 Infantry Base Depot 13 June 1917 and joined the 9th (North Irish Horse) Battalion. 'D' Company. **Wounded** by a gunshot to the scrotum and right thigh at the Battle of Langemarck 16 August 1917. Treated at 14th General Hospital where a rifle bullet was removed from his leg and then evacuated to hospital in England. Treated at Queen Mary's Military Hospital, Whalley. Posted to the 10th (Reserve) Battalion 22 March 1918. To 36 Infantry Base Depot 12 April 1918 and rejoined the 9th (North Irish Horse) Battalion 25 April 1918. [Posted to the 1st Battalion 8 June 1918. **Wounded** by a gunshot to the left hand during the attack north of Bailleul 24 August 1918 and evacuated to hospital in England.] Transferred to the Section B Army Reserve, Princess Victoria's (Royal Irish Fusiliers) (renumbered 7040427) 29 January 1919. 1914-15 Star. Discharged 18 January 1928.

HURLOCK Private Joseph Henry 20054. From Union Street, Portadown, County Armagh. Enlisted into the 9th (Service) Battalion in June 1915. To France with 36th (Ulster) Division in October 1915. **Wounded** during the attack at Hamel 1 July 1916. Transferred to the Class Z Reserve 30 March 1919. 1914-15 Star.

HURREN Corporal James Samuel 43472. [Enlisted into The London Regiment (6166). Posted to 1/22nd (County of London) Battalion, The London Regiment (The Queen's).] To France and joined 36 Infantry Base Depot 29 March 1918. Transferred to Princess Victoria's (Royal Irish Fusiliers) 2 April 1918 (renumbered 43472) and joined the 9th (North Irish Horse) Battalion 4 April 1918.

HUSTON Private Samuel 28726. From Dunlargue, County Armagh. Enlisted in October 1917. Posted to the 9th (North Irish Horse) Battalion.

HUSTON Private William 14296. From Armagh, County Armagh. Enlisted September 1914. To France with 36th (Ulster) Division in October 1915. **Wounded** in the face and neck in May 1916.

Wounded during the attack at Hamel 1 July 1916. [Transferred to the Labour Corps (renumbered 231584).] Transferred to the Class Z Reserve 3 April 1919. 1914-15 Star.

HUSTWAYTE Private Frank 43263. Born 18 July 1887 at Nottingham. [A regular soldier with the 1st Battalion, The Sherwood Foresters (Nottinghamshire and Derbyshire Regiment) (10932). Sailed from India and to France 4 November 1914 in 24th Brigade, 8th Division.] Transferred to Princess Victoria's (Royal Irish Fusiliers) 31 August 1916 (renumbered 43263) having joined the 9th (Service) Battalion on 8 August 1916. Transferred to the Class Z Reserve. 1914 Star. Re-enlisted 6 August 1919 for Regular Army service with The Leicestershire Regiment (renumbered 4848898). **Died** due to a fractured spine while serving with the 1st Battalion, The Leicestershire Regiment at the Curragh, Dublin 15 September 1920.

HUTCHINSON Private George 18043. From Cloghan, County Armagh. Enlisted into the 9th (Service) Battalion 15 February 1915. To France with 36th (Ulster) Division in October 1915. Transferred to the Class Z Reserve 20 March 1919. 1914-15 Star. Brother of Privates Henry and William Hutchinson.

HUTCHINSON Private Hamilton Thomas 41492. Born in 1893 at Stewartstown, County Tyrone. [Enlisted in December 1915 into the North Irish Horse (2036). Served with 2nd North Irish Horse, X Corps Cavalry Regiment.] Joined the renamed 9th (North Irish Horse) Battalion from 36 Infantry Base Depot and transferred to Princess Victoria's (Royal Irish Fusiliers) in September/October 1917 (renumbered 41292). 'C' Company. **Captured** in the period 21-28 March 1918 during the retreat from St Quentin and held at Limburg Prisoner Of War Camp.

HUTCHINSON Private Henry 18045. From Cloghan, County Armagh. Enlisted into the 9th (Service) Battalion 15 February 1915. To France with 36th (Ulster) Division in October 1915. **Wounded** during the attack at Hamel 1 July 1916. **Wounded** by a gunshot to the right thigh at Moeuvres 22/23 November 1917 and evacuated to hospital in England 22 December 1917. Treated at Edinburgh War Hospital. Joined the Irish Command Depot, Randalstown 4 April 1918. Joined the 3rd (Reserve) Battalion 20 July 1918. [Transferred to the Labour Corps (renumbered 562422) 18 August 1918 and posted to 301st Home Service Labour Company. Joined 341st Home Service Works Company 2 September 1918.] Discharged as no longer physically fit for war service due to wounds 16 October 1918, aged 23. Silver War Badge, number B27834. 1914-15 Star. Brother of Privates George and William Hutchinson.

HUTCHINSON Private James Alexander 22151. From Hamiltonsbawn, County Armagh. Enlisted in November 1915. Posted to the 9th (Service) Battalion. **Killed in action** by shellfire at Hamel 25 April 1916, aged 18. Brother of Lance Corporal John Hutchinson.

HUTCHINSON Lance Corporal John Joseph 14272. From Hamiltonsbawn, County Armagh. 4th (Portadown) Battalion, Armagh Regiment, Ulster Volunteer Force. Enlisted September 1914. To France with 36th (Ulster) Division in October 1915. **Wounded** by shellfire at Hamel and **died of wounds** 28 June 1916, aged 21. 1914-15 Star. Brother of Private James Hutchinson.

HUTCHINSON Private Joseph 24230. Enlisted in April 1916. Posted to the 9th (Service) Battalion.

HUTCHINSON Private Samuel George 25973. From Armagh. Enlisted 8 December 1916. Posted to the 9th (Service) Battalion. 'A' Company. **Captured** at the Battle of Langemarck 16 August 1917. Discharged as no longer physically fit for war service due to sickness 7 July 1919. Silver War Badge, number B296134.

HUTCHINSON Private William John 18044. From Cloghan, County Armagh. Enlisted into the 9th (Service) Battalion 15 February 1915. To France with 36th (Ulster) Division in October 1915. 'A' Company. **Killed in action** at the Battle of Langemarck 16 August 1917, aged 23. 1914-15 Star. Brother of Privates George and Henry Hutchinson.

HUTTON Private Joseph 23651 & 7042511. Enlisted in January 1916. Posted to the 9th (Service) Battalion. Re-enlisted in mid-1920 for Regular Army service with Princess Victoria's (Royal Irish Fusiliers) (renumbered 7042511). Served with the 2nd Battalion. Medals forfeit due to a conviction by the civil power.

HYAMS Private Michael 45762. Joined the 9th (North Irish Horse) Battalion, Princess Victoria's (Royal Irish Fusiliers) with the draft of men from The London Regiment in April 1918.

HYDE Sergeant Thomas 14267. From Portadown, County Armagh. Member of Masonic Lodge 82.

4th (Portadown) Battalion, Armagh Regiment, Ulster Volunteer Force. Enlisted September 1914. To France with 36th (Ulster) Division in October 1915. **Wounded**. Discharged as no longer physically fit for war service due to wounds 9 May 1917. Silver War Badge, number 168876. 1914-15 Star.

HYDE Private William John 14313. From Born in 1894 at Milford, County Armagh. Enlisted September 1914. To France with 36th (Ulster) Division in October 1915. 'A' Company. **Wounded** at the Battle of Langemarck 16 August 1917. **Missing** in the period 21-28 March 1918 during the retreat from St Quentin believed **captured**. Transferred to the Class Z Reserve 23 March 1919. 1914-15 Star.

HYNES Private Henry 14329. Born at Loughgall, County Armagh. Enlisted September 1914. To France with 36th (Ulster) Division in October 1915. **Killed in action** during the attack at Hamel 1 July 1916. 1914-15 Star.

ILLING Private Benjamin 45770. [Enlisted into The London Regiment (4124). Posted to 1/22nd (County of London) Battalion, The London Regiment (The Queen's).] To France and joined 36 Infantry Base Depot 29 March 1918. Transferred to Princess Victoria's (Royal Irish Fusiliers) 2 April 1918 (renumbered 45770) and joined the 9th (North Irish Horse) Battalion 4 April 1918.

INGLEDEW Acting Company Quartermaster Sergeant Charles 13080. Born in 1895 at Belfast. [Enlisted in September 1914 and joined the 7th (Service) Battalion in 49th Brigade, 16th (Irish) Division.] Joined the 9th (North Irish Horse) Battalion when the 7th/8th (Service) Battalion was disbanded in February 1918. **Killed in action** during the attack south of Wulverghem 5 September 1918.

INGLIS Lance Corporal Thomas 41596. [Enlisted in November 1915 into the North Irish Horse (1945). Served with 2nd North Irish Horse, X Corps Cavalry Regiment.] Joined the renamed 9th (North Irish Horse) Battalion from 36 Infantry Base Depot and transferred to Princess Victoria's (Royal Irish Fusiliers) in September/October 1917 (renumbered 41596).

INNOCENT Private William 42140. [Enlisted into the Army Veterinary Corps (365430).] Transferred to Princess Victoria's (Royal Irish Fusiliers) 8 May 1918 (renumbered 42140) and joined the 9th (North Irish Horse) Battalion.

IRVINE Private Carson 14073. Enlisted September 1914. To France with 36th (Ulster) Division in October 1915. [Joined 108th Brigade Machine Gun Company in January 1916. Transferred to the Machine Gun Corps (renumbered 17780).] 1914-15 Star.

IRVINE Private Frederick 14342. See Private F Irwin below.

IRVINE Private H 11712. [Enlisted into Princess Victoria's (Royal Irish Fusiliers) as a regular soldier in August 1914. To France 27 December 1914 and joined the 1st Battalion.] 'C' Company. **Missing** in the period 21-28 March 1918 during the retreat from St Quentin believed **captured**. 1914-15 Star. Enlisted in Princess Louise's (Argyll and Sutherland Highlanders) (renumbered 31041). Medals forfeit due to fraudulent enlistment.

IRVINE Private John 20294. From Glasgow. Enlisted in May/June 1915 and joined the 9th (Service) Battalion with the draft of men from The Royal Inniskilling Fusiliers who transferred to Princess Victoria's (Royal Irish Fusiliers) on 30 June 1915. To France with 36th (Ulster) Division in October 1915. 'C' Company. **Wounded** during the attack at Hamel 1 July 1916. **Wounded** at the Battle of Langemarck 16 August 1917. Believed **wounded** in the period 21-28 March 1918 during the retreat from St Quentin. [Transferred to the Labour Corps (renumbered 575259).] 1914-15 Star.

IRVINE Private Kennedy 42530. From Belfast. [Enlisted April/May 1918 into The Royal Irish Rifles (22502).] Transferred at the Base Depot to Princess Victoria's (Royal Irish Fusiliers) 14 September 1918 (renumbered 42530) and joined the 9th (North Irish Horse) Battalion 22 September 1918. [Transferred to 5th (Service) Battalion, The Royal Irish Regiment (Pioneers) in the Light Division in the British Army of the Rhine in March/June 1919 (renumbered 41308).]

IRVING Corporal William 42077. Born in 1891 at Hurlford, Ayrshire. A baker. [Enlisted 23 October 1915 into the Army Service Corps (S4/143934).] Transferred to Princess Victoria's (Royal Irish Fusiliers) 8 May 1918 (renumbered 42077) and joined the 9th (North Irish Horse) Battalion. **Wounded** by a gunshot to the right thigh during the attack north of Bailleul 24 August 1918. Treated at Horton (County of London) War Hospital, Epsom and 3rd Scottish General Hospital,

Glasgow. Transferred to the Class Z Reserve 6 April 1919.

IRWIN Private David 16109. Born in 1869. Enlisted into the 9th (Service) Battalion in October 1914. Did not deploy to France with 36th (Ulster) Division in October 1915. [Transferred to The Sherwood Foresters (Nottinghamshire and Derbyshire Regiment) (renumbered 78162).] Discharged as no longer physically fit for war service due to sickness 27 May 1918, aged 48. Silver War Badge, number 396600.

IRWIN Private Frederick 14342. (Listed as Frederick Irvine on his 1914-15 Star medal index card). From Corcreaney, County Armagh. A solicitor's clerk. Enlisted 16 September 1914. To France with 36th (Ulster) Division in October 1915. 'C' Company. Lewis gunner during the attack at Hamel 1 July 1916, during which he was **wounded**. **Wounded** at the Battle of Langemarck 16 August 1917. Discharged as no longer physically fit for war service due to wounds 4 January 1918, aged 22. Silver War Badge, number 299450. 1914-15 Star. His brother, Private Thomas Irwin, was killed in action on 6 August 1917 serving with 4th Australian Pioneer Battalion, 4th Australian Division.

IRWIN Private John 42477. From Ligoniel, Belfast. [Served previously with The Royal Irish Rifles (17/2039).] Transferred at the Base Depot to Princess Victoria's (Royal Irish Fusiliers) 14 September 1918 (renumbered 42477) and joined the 9th (North Irish Horse) Battalion 22 September 1918. Re-enlisted in 1919 for Regular Army service with The Royal Irish Rifles (renumbered 25722, renumbered 7007303). Served with the 2nd Battalion, The Royal Irish Rifles in Mesopotamia in 1919/20. General Service Medal 1918-1962 with clasp 'Iraq'.

IRWIN Private John L 16110. From Tandragee, County Armagh. Enlisted into the 9th (Service) Battalion 5 October 1915. **Wounded**. Discharged as no longer physically fit for war service due to wounds 6 June 1918, aged 24. Silver War Badge, number 387961. 1914-15 Star. Emigrated to Canada after the war. During the Second World War he served with Royal Canadian Air Force, Royal Canadian Navy and Royal Air Force Ferry Command at Dorval, Quebec and in Korea.

IRWIN Private Richard 18241, 34083 & 7042031. From Armagh, County Armagh. A saddler. Enlisted into the 9th (Service) Battalion in February 1915. [Transferred to the Army Ordnance Corps (renumbered 20/476, renumbered 038863).] Re-enlisted 8 May 1920 for Regular Army service with Princess Victoria's (Royal Irish Fusiliers) (renumbered 34083, renumbered 7042031). Discharged 7 July 1921. Enlisted 7 September 1940 into the Royal Air Force (renumbered 1068033).

IRWIN Sergeant Richard 41268. Born in May 1885 in Donaghcloney, County Down. A linen weaver from Lurgan, County Armagh. Waringstown Company, Ulster Volunteer Force. Member of Loyal Orange Lodge 477. [Enlisted in August 1909 into the North Irish Horse (398). To France 20 August 1914 with 'C' Squadron as 5th Division Cavalry and then as GHQ Troops. Served with 2nd North Irish Horse, X Corps Cavalry Regiment.] Joined the renamed 9th (North Irish Horse) Battalion from 36 Infantry Base Depot and transferred to Princess Victoria's (Royal Irish Fusiliers) in September/October 1917 (renumbered 41268). 'C' Company. **Killed in action** 3 November 1917 on a raid at Havrincourt, aged 32. 1914 Star.

IRWIN Corporal Robert 14338. From Portadown, County Armagh. 4th (Portadown) Battalion, Armagh Regiment, Ulster Volunteer Force. Enlisted September 1914. To France with 36th (Ulster) Division in October 1915. **Captured** in the period 11-18 April 1918 in the actions between Wulverghem and Kemmel. Transferred to the Class Z Reserve 1 April 1919. 1914-15 Star.

IRWIN Private Robert 14344. From Mullaglass, County Armagh. A engine cleaner. Enlisted September 1914. Discharged as not being likely to become an efficient soldier in that he was considered medically unfit (tachycardia) for service 15 December 1914.

IRWIN Private Robert 41080. From Londonderry. [Enlisted into the Service Squadron, 6th (Inniskilling) Dragoons (UD/153). To France with 36th (Ulster) Division in October 1915. Served with 2nd North Irish Horse, X Corps Cavalry Regiment.] Joined the renamed 9th (North Irish Horse) Battalion from 36 Infantry Base Depot and transferred to Princess Victoria's (Royal Irish Fusiliers) in September/October 1917 (renumbered 41080). **Killed in action** 14 April 1918 in the actions between Wulverghem and Kemmel. 1914-15 Star.

IRWIN Sergeant Robert 41560. From Donaghcloney, County Down. A groom. Enlisted in January 1909 into the North of Ireland Imperial Yeomanry/North Irish Horse (263). [Re-enlisted 10 August

1914 into the North Irish Horse (renumbered 988). Lance Corporal 22 July 1915. Corporal 18 November 1915. To France 24 February 1916. Served with 2nd North Irish Horse, X Corps Cavalry Regiment. To hospital 22 February 1917. Sergeant 24 May 1917.] Joined the renamed 9th (North Irish Horse) Battalion from 36 Infantry Base Depot and transferred to Princess Victoria's (Royal Irish Fusiliers) in September/October 1917 (renumbered 41560). [Transferred to the Tank Corps (renumbered 304845) 28 December 1917 and posted for training to the Tank Corps Depot, at Bovington near Wareham, Dorset. Posted to the 17th Battalion, Tank Corps 8 January 1918. Posted to the Tank Corps Reserve Unit at Wareham. Posted to 18th Battalion, Tank Corps 31 August 1918 and deployed with it to France 2 October 1918.] Transferred to the Class Z Reserve 19 February 1919.

IRWIN Private Robert James 14340. From Armagh, County Armagh. Enlisted September 1914. To France with 36th (Ulster) Division in October 1915. **Wounded**. Transferred to the Class Z Reserve 20 March 1919. 1914-15 Star.

IRWIN Private Thomas 14339. Enlisted September 1914. To France with 36th (Ulster) Division in October 1915. **Wounded**. Discharged as no longer physically fit for war service due to wounds 31 May 1917. Silver War Badge, number 188817. 1914-15 Star.

IRWIN Private Thomas 14341. Enlisted September 1914. To France with 36th (Ulster) Division in October 1915. Transferred to the Class Z Reserve 27 March 1919. 1914-15 Star.

IRWIN Private William 14343. From Newry, County Down. Enlisted September 1914. To France with 36th (Ulster) Division in October 1915. 'D' Company. **Wounded** during the attack at Hamel 1 July 1916. **Wounded** at the Battle of Langemarck 16 August 1917. [Transferred to the Army Service Corps (renumbered 380593).] Transferred to the Class Z Reserve. 1914-15 Star.

IRWIN Private William 23285. Enlisted in November 1915. Posted to the 9th (Service) Battalion.

IRWIN Sergeant William Garnett Wolsey 41146. Born in 1896 at Dungannon, County Tyrone. [Enlisted into the Service Squadron, 6th (Inniskilling) Dragoons (UD/83). To France with 36th (Ulster) Division in October 1915. Served with 2nd North Irish Horse, X Corps Cavalry Regiment.] Joined the renamed 9th (North Irish Horse) Battalion from 36 Infantry Base Depot and transferred to Princess Victoria's (Royal Irish Fusiliers) in September/October 1917 (renumbered 41146). 'A' Company. **Wounded** during the attack north of Bailleul 24 August 1918 and **died of wounds** 26 August 1918, aged 22. 1914-15 Star.

IRWIN Private William Thomas 29440. From Lurgan, County Armagh. Enlisted, re-enlisted or transferred to Princess Victoria's (Royal Irish Fusiliers) in March 1918. Posted to the 9th (North Irish Horse) Battalion. **Captured**. **Died** in Ireland 16 May 1919, aged 19.

ISHERWOOD Private Gilbert 40048. Born in 1893 at Bradford, West Yorkshire. [Enlisted into the 16th (Service) Battalion, The Prince of Wales's Own (West Yorkshire Regiment) (1st Bradford) (526).] Transferred to Princess Victoria's (Royal Irish Fusiliers) 30 November 1916 (renumbered 40048) and joined the 9th (Service) Battalion 12 December 1916. Died at Bradford, West Yorkshire in 1966, aged 72.

JACK Private Gilbert 41600. Born in 1893 at Londonderry, County Londonderry. A shirt cutter. [Enlisted in September 1914 into the North Irish Horse (1152) 5 September 1914. To France 28 April 1915. Served with 2nd North Irish Horse, X Corps Cavalry Regiment.] Joined the renamed 9th (North Irish Horse) Battalion from 36 Infantry Base Depot and transferred to Princess Victoria's (Royal Irish Fusiliers) in September/October 1917 (renumbered 41600). 'D' Company. Believed **wounded** in the period 21-28 March 1918 during the retreat from St Quentin. Discharged as no longer physically fit for war service due to wounds 1 March 1919. Silver War Badge, number B154480.

JACK Private William 23454. [Enlisted in December 1915 and joined the 8th (Service) Battalion in 49th Brigade, 16th (Irish) Division.] Joined the 9th (North Irish Horse) Battalion when the 7th/8th (Service) Battalion was disbanded in February 1918.

JACKSON Private Archibald Moore 16112. From Tandrageebane, County Monaghan. Enlisted into the 9th (Service) Battalion in October 1914. To France with 36th (Ulster) Division in October 1915. **Wounded**. Transferred to the Class Z Reserve 23 March 1919. 1914-15 Star.

JACKSON MM Lance Corporal Edward 24174. Born in 1891 Rackeragh, County Monaghan. A tailor. Enlisted in March 1916. Posted to the 9th (Service) Battalion. **MM** – Battle of Langemarck 16 August 1917.

JACKSON Sergeant Francis P 22282. [A regular soldier with The Bedfordshire Regiment (7996). To Belgium 6 October 1914 with the 2nd Battalion, The Bedfordshire Regiment in 21st Brigade, 7th Division. Transferred to Princess Victoria's (Royal Irish Fusiliers) in November 1915 (renumbered 22282) and joined the 5th (Service) Battalion in 31st Brigade, 10th (Irish) Division in the Mediterranean Expeditionary Force.] Joined the 9th (Service) Battalion. 'A' Company. **Missing** in the period 21-28 March 1918 during the retreat from St Quentin believed **captured**. 1914 Star and clasp. Continued to serve with the Regular Army in The Bedfordshire & Hertfordshire Regiment (renumbered 42856, renumbered 5943565).

JACKSON Sergeant George Wesley 14361. Born in 1895 at Tandragee, County Armagh. 4th (Portadown) Battalion, Armagh Regiment, Ulster Volunteer Force. Enlisted September 1914. To France with 36th (Ulster) Division in October 1915. Platoon Sergeant 5 Platoon, 'B' Company. **Killed in action** during the attack at Hamel 1 July 1916, aged 21. 1914-15 Star.

JACKSON Private John H 43198. [Enlisted into The Sherwood Foresters (Nottinghamshire and Derbyshire Regiment).] Transferred to Princess Victoria's (Royal Irish Fusiliers) 31 August 1916 having joined the 9th (Service) Battalion on 8 August 1916 (renumbered 43198). [Transferred to the Labour Corps (renumbered 654110).]

JACKSON Private Noble William 16113. From Tandrageebane, County Monaghan. Enlisted into the 9th (Service) Battalion in October 1914. To France with 36th (Ulster) Division in October 1915. **Wounded** during the attack at Hamel 1 July 1916. Transferred to the Class Z Reserve 23 March 1919. 1914-15 Star. Brother of Private Thomas Henry Jackson.

JACKSON Private Robert 43108. [Enlisted into or transferred to Princess Victoria's (Royal Irish Fusiliers) in August 1916 and joined the 7th (Service) Battalion in 49th Brigade, 16th *Irish) Division. Posted to the 5th/6th (Service) Battalion.] Posted to the 9th (Service) Battalion. 'A' Company. **Wounded** during the Battle of Messines and to hospital 9 June 1917.

JACKSON Private Thomas Henry 17932. From Tandrageebane, County Monaghan. Enlisted into the 9th (Service) Battalion in January 1915. To France with 36th (Ulster) Division in October 1915. **Killed in action** during the attack at Hamel 1 July 1916, aged 23. 1914-15 Star. Brother of Private Noble William Jackson.

JACKSON Private William Adair 22983. Born in 1889 at Belfast. A French polisher. Enlisted 10 November 1915 and joined the 10th (Reserve) Battalion. To 16 Infantry Base Depot 15 October 1916. Joined the 9th (Service) Battalion 24 October 1916. To hospital sick (pterygium) 26 February 1917. Treated at 13th Stationary Hospital. To 36 Infantry Base Depot 17 March 1917 and rejoined the 9th (Service) Battalion 29 March 1917. To hospital sick (influenza) June 1917. To hospital sick (conjunctivitis and corneal ulcer) November 1917. To hospital sick (conjunctivitis) April 1918. **Wounded** in the period 9-18 April 1918 in the actions between Wulverghem and Kemmel. Treated at 13th General Hospital. To hospital sick (conjunctivitis) May 1918. To 'A' Infantry Base Depot 10 June 1918. To hospital sick (scabies) 14 June 1918. Rejoined the 9th (North Irish Horse) Battalion 24 June 1918. To the field ambulance sick (conjunctivitis) 17 July 1918. Rejoined the 9th (North Irish Horse) Battalion 25 July 1918. To the field ambulance sick (scabies) in late July 1918. To the field ambulance (injured hand) September 1918. Transferred to the Class Z Reserve 11 March 1919. **Died** of pulmonary tuberculosis at Belfast on 7 April 1919, aged 31.

JAGGER Lance Corporal Jesse 41178. [Enlisted 14 December 1914 into 6th (Inniskilling) Dragoons (11311). Served with 2nd North Irish Horse, X Corps Cavalry Regiment.] Joined the renamed 9th (North Irish Horse) Battalion from 36 Infantry Base Depot and transferred to Princess Victoria's (Royal Irish Fusiliers) in September/October 1917 (renumbered 41178). **Wounded**. Discharged as no longer physically fit for war service due to wounds 11 March 1919. Silver War Badge, number B158473.

JAMESON Private James 14375. From Armagh, County Armagh. Enlisted September 1914. To France with 36th (Ulster) Division in October 1915. **Wounded** during the attack at Hamel 1 July 1916. [Transferred to the Labour Corps (renumbered 213605).] Discharged as no longer physically fit for war service due to wounds 5 February 1919. Silver War Badge, number B122447. 1914-15 Star.

JAMISON Private Robert William 41263. Born in 1893 at Newcastle, County Down. Joined the Royal Irish Constabulary in 1912 and served in Belfast. [Enlisted 10 April 1916 into the North Irish Horse (2144). Served with 2nd North Irish Horse, X Corps Cavalry Regiment.] Joined the renamed 9th (North Irish Horse) Battalion from 36 Infantry Base Depot and transferred to Princess Victoria's (Royal Irish Fusiliers) in September/October 1917 (renumbered 41263). 'C' Company. **Wounded** during the retreat from St Quentin 21-28 March 1918. Discharged as no longer physically fit for war service due to wounds 2 January 1919. Silver War Badge, number B71395.

JAMISON Private William John 27600. Enlisted into Princess Victoria's (Royal Irish Fusiliers) in May 1917. Posted to the 9th (North Irish Horse) Battalion.

JARVIS Sergeant. Battalion tailor in 1914. Soldier not identified.

JARVIS Private Harold Sherrick Richard 43381. Born 31 August 1897 at London. [Enlisted into The London Regiment (3516). Posted to the 1/9th (County of London) Battalion, The London Regiment (The Queen's).] Attached to the 9th (Service) Battalion, Princess Victoria's (Royal Irish Fusiliers) 26 November 1916. Discharged from the Territorial Force, re-enlisted and transferred to Princess Victoria's (Royal Irish Fusiliers) in March/April 1917 (renumbered 43381). Died at London in 1976, aged 78.

JARVIS Corporal William 42159. [Enlisted into the Army Service Corps (S4/055764). To France 28 February 1915.] Transferred to Princess Victoria's (Royal Irish Fusiliers) 8 May 1918 (renumbered 42159) and joined the 9th (North Irish Horse) Battalion. [Part of the draft transferred on 19 June 1918 to The Royal Irish Rifles (renumbered 45851).] 1914-15 Star.

JEANS Sergeant Jesse Cornelius 42079. Born in 1890 at Kington Magna, Dorset. [Enlisted into the Army Service Corps (S4/109537). To France 4 December 1915.] Transferred to Princess Victoria's (Royal Irish Fusiliers) 8 May 1918 (renumbered 42079) and joined the 9th (North Irish Horse) Battalion. [Part of the draft transferred on 19 June 1918 to The Royal Irish Rifles (renumbered 45852). Posted to the 1st Battalion, The Royal Irish Rifles. **Missing** in the fighting near Vijfwegen and recorded as **killed in action** 2 October 1918, aged 28.] 1914-15 Star.

JEFFERS Private Thomas 14359. From Portadown, County Armagh. 4th (Portadown) Battalion, Armagh Regiment, Ulster Volunteer Force. Enlisted September 1914. To France with 36th (Ulster) Division in October 1915. Transferred to the Class Z Reserve 11 March 1919. 1914-15 Star.

JELLY Private William 14354. From Portadown, County Armagh. 4th (Portadown) Battalion, Armagh Regiment, Ulster Volunteer Force. Member of Loyal Orange Lodge 32. Enlisted September 1914. To France with 36th (Ulster) Division in October 1915. Transferred to the Class Z Reserve 20 March 1919. 1914-15 Star. He became land steward on the estate of the Duke of Manchester at Tandragee. He died in 1933.

JENKINSON Corporal John 14350. From Portadown, County Armagh. 4th (Portadown) Battalion, Armagh Regiment, Ulster Volunteer Force. Enlisted 15 September 1914. To France with 36th (Ulster) Division in October 1915. **Wounded** in the stomach during the attack at Hamel 1 July 1916. Discharged as no longer physically fit for war service due to wounds 15 February 1917. Silver War Badge, number 21710. 1914-15 Star.

JENKINSON Private Samuel 17479. Born at Altrincham, Cheshire. [Enlisted 31 December 1914 into Princess Victoria's (Royal Irish Fusiliers). To France 26 July 1915 and joined the 1st Battalion. **Wounded** at Les Beoufs 12 October 1916. Rejoined the 1st Battalion 17 October 1916. To hospital sick (influenza) 30 April 1917. Rejoined the 1st Battalion 3 July 1917. To hospital (sprained ankle) 7 July 1917. To 36 Infantry Base Depot 31 August 1917. To hospital sick (scabies) 6 September 1917. Rejoined the 1st Battalion 28 September 1917. Injured by barbed wire that infected his right knee (synovitis) 16 November 1917 and evacuated to hospital in England 6 December 1917.] To 'L' Infantry Base Depot August 1918. Joined the 9th (North Irish Horse) Battalion 29 August 1918. **Wounded** by a gunshot to the left chest during the attack south of Wulverghem on 4 September 1918 that broke his third rib and scapula. Treated at 3rd Canadian General Hospital and evacuated to hospital in Britain. Treated at 3rd Scottish General Hospital, Glasgow. Discharged from hospital 5 February 1919. Transferred to the Class Z Reserve 4 March 1919.

JENNER Private Samuel Joseph 42235 & 7042177. Born in 1897 at Rotherhithe, London. [Enlisted 17 April 1915 into the Army Service Corps (T/36891), giving his age as 19 years. To France 13 July 1915 and served with 17th Division Train.] Transferred to Princess Victoria's (Royal

Irish Fusiliers) 8 May 1918 (renumbered 42235) and joined the 9th (North Irish Horse) Battalion. **Captured** during the attack at Vijfwegen 30 September 1918. Repatriated 16 December 1918. Transferred to the Section B Army Reserve, Princess Victoria's (Royal Irish Fusiliers) 20 March 1919 (renumbered 7042177). Mobilised 17 January 1921. Discharged 16 April 1927. 1914-15 Star. Died at Reading, Berkshire in 1952, aged 55.

JENNINGS Lance Corporal Albert Robert 43435. From Walworth, London. [Enlisted 3 September 1914 into The London Regiment (2507) and joined the 3/24th Battalion. To France 15 March 1915. To hospital sick (scabies) 30 March 1915. Joined the 1/24th (County of London) Battalion, The London Regiment (The Queen's) 3 July 1915. **Wounded** in the eye by shellfire 23 May 1916 and evacuated to hospital in England. Joined the 22nd (Reserve) Battalion, The London Regiment 24 February 1917.] To France and joined 36 Infantry Base Depot 29 March 1918. Transferred to Princess Victoria's (Royal Irish Fusiliers) 2 April 1918 (renumbered 43435) and joined the 9th (North Irish Horse) Battalion 4 April 1918. Lance Corporal 21 May 1918. **Wounded** by gunshots to the hand, stomach and neck during the attack at Vijfwegen on 1 October 1918 and **died of wounds** 14 October 1918 in 3rd Australian Casualty Clearing Station.

JENNINGS Private Arthur Edward 42445. [Enlisted into the 14th (Service) Battalion, The Royal Irish Rifles (Young Citizens) (42560).] Transferred at the Base Depot to Princess Victoria's (Royal Irish Fusiliers) 14 September 1918 (renumbered 42245) and joined the 9th (North Irish Horse) Battalion 22 September 1918.

JENNINGS MM Lance Corporal Francis 41338. [Enlisted in November 1915 into the North Irish Horse (1879). Served with 2nd North Irish Horse, X Corps Cavalry Regiment.] Joined the renamed 9th (North Irish Horse) Battalion from 36 Infantry Base Depot and transferred to Princess Victoria's (Royal Irish Fusiliers) in September/October 1917 (renumbered 41338). **MM**.

JENNINGS Private Rowan 14360. From Portadown, County Armagh. Enlisted September 1914. To France with 36th (Ulster) Division in October 1915. **Wounded** during the attack at Hamel 1 July 1916. [Transferred to the Tank Corps (renumbered 304860) 28 December 1917 and posted for training to the Tank Corps Depot, at Bovington near Wareham, Dorset.] 1914-15 Star.

JOHNSON Sergeant Arthur 43252. From Rotherham. [Enlisted 31 August 1914 into The Sherwood Foresters (Nottinghamshire and Derbyshire Regiment) (19879). To France 3 May 1915 and joined the 2nd Battalion, The Sherwood Foresters (Nottinghamshire and Derbyshire Regiment).] Transferred to Princess Victoria's (Royal Irish Fusiliers) 31 August 1916 (renumbered 43252) having joined the 9th (Service) Battalion on 8 August 1916. 'A' Company. **Wounded** at the Battle of Langemarck 16 August 1917. Discharged as no longer physically fit for war service due to wounds 8 December 1919. Silver War Badge, number 01286.

JOHNSON Lance Corporal Charles Thomas 42439. [Enlisted into The London Regiment (4605). Posted to the 1/17th (County of London) Battalion, The London Regiment (Poplar and Stepney Rifles). Transferred to The Royal Irish Rifles (renumbered 13538) and posted to the 9th (Service) Battalion, The Royal Irish Rifles (West Belfast).] Transferred at the Base Depot to Princess Victoria's (Royal Irish Fusiliers) 14 September 1918 (renumbered 42439) and joined the 9th (North Irish Horse) Battalion 22 September 1918.

JOHNSON Private Reginald 43367. From Leyton, Essex. [Enlisted into The London Regiment (3379). Posted to the 1/7th (City of London) Battalion, The London Regiment.] Attached to the 9th (Service) Battalion, Princess Victoria's (Royal Irish Fusiliers) 26 November 1916. 'A' Company. Discharged from the Territorial Force, re-enlisted and transferred to Princess Victoria's (Royal Irish Fusiliers) in March/April 1917 (renumbered 43367). **Wounded** at the Battle of Langemarck 16 August 1917.

JOHNSTON Private Andrew 14349. From West Street, Portadown, County Armagh. 4th (Portadown) Battalion, Armagh Regiment, Ulster Volunteer Force. Enlisted September 1914. To France with 36th (Ulster) Division in October 1915. **Killed in action** during the attack at Hamel 1 July 1916. 1914-15 Star.

JOHNSTON Private Archibald 14371. From Dumfries. Enlisted September 1914. To France with 36th (Ulster) Division in October 1915. **Wounded** during the attack at Hamel 1 July 1916 and **died of wounds** 16 July 1916, aged 23. 1914-15 Star.

JOHNSTON Sergeant Arthur 14372. From Lurgan, County Armagh. An apprentice linen weaver.

Enlisted September 1914. Lance Corporal 1 January 1915. Did not deploy to France with the 9th (Service) Battalion. Posted to the 10th (Reserve) Battalion 9 October 1915. Sergeant 20 November 1915. Posted to the 3rd (Reserve) Battalion 1 June 1918 and then to 7th Officer Cadet Battalion, Fermoy. Rejoined the 3rd (Reserve) Battalion 26 July 1918. Discharged as no longer physically fit for war service due to sickness (severe stammering) 5 December 1918. Silver War Badge, number B107078.

JOHNSTON Private Daniel 18060. From Portadown, County Armagh. A tinsmith. Enlisted into the 9th (Service) Battalion in February 1915. To France with 36th (Ulster) Division in October 1915. 'C' Company. **Wounded** during the attack at Hamel 1 July 1916. **Wounded** at the Battle of Langemarck 16 August 1917. **Captured**. Transferred to the Class Z Reserve 11 March 1919. 1914-15 Star.

JOHNSTON Private David 14346. From Portadown, County Armagh. 4th (Portadown) Battalion, Armagh Regiment, Ulster Volunteer Force. A blacksmith. Enlisted September 1914. To France with 36th (Ulster) Division in October 1915. **Wounded** in the back in May/June 1918. Transferred to the Class Z Reserve 13 April 1919. 1914-15 Star.

JOHNSTON Private David 17549. Enlisted into the 9th (Service) Battalion in November/December 1914. To France with 36th (Ulster) Division in October 1915. [Transferred to the Machine Gun Corps (renumbered 162291).] 1914-15 Star.

JOHNSTON Private George 41169. From Drumgarrow, County Fermanagh. A farmer's son. [Enlisted in late-September/October 1914 into the Service Squadron, 6th (Inniskilling) Dragoons (UD/39). To France with 36th (Ulster) Division in October 1915. Served with 2nd North Irish Horse, X Corps Cavalry Regiment.] Joined the renamed 9th (North Irish Horse) Battalion from 36 Infantry Base Depot and transferred to Princess Victoria's (Royal Irish Fusiliers) in September/October 1917 (renumbered 41169). 'B' Company. Believed **wounded** in the period 21-28 March 1918 during the retreat from St Quentin. **Died** 13 October 1918, aged 27. It is presumed that he died in a French medical unit at the Chateau de Perreuse. There is no recorded explanation for his death and burial so far from where the 9th (North Irish Horse) Battalion was located throughout 1918. 1914-15 Star.

JOHNSTON Private George Uriah 41359. Born 20 February 1898 at Shankill, Belfast. [Enlisted 1 January 1917 into the North Irish Horse (2338). Served with 2nd North Irish Horse, X Corps Cavalry Regiment.] Joined the renamed 9th (North Irish Horse) Battalion from 36 Infantry Base Depot and transferred to Princess Victoria's (Royal Irish Fusiliers) in September/October 1917 (renumbered 41359). **Wounded**. Discharged as no longer physically fit for war service due to wounds 17 June 1918, aged 20. Silver War Badge, number 387928. Emigrated to the United States in November 1920, where he worked as a clerk in Chicago, Illinois. He became a United States citizen in 1928 and died in Arizona in November 1968.

JOHNSTON Private Hamilton 22564. From Belfast. Enlisted in November 1915. Posted to the 9th (Service) Battalion. **Wounded** during the attack at Hamel 1 July 1916. [Posted to the 1st Garrison Battalion and served in India and Burma.]

JOHNSTON Corporal Herbert Corry 22761. Born at Lurgan, County Armagh. A farmer. Enlisted 8 November 1915 and joined the 10th (Reserve) Battalion. Lance Corporal 21 January 1916. Corporal 1 February 1916. Lance Sergeant 18 February 1916. Sergeant 25 March 1916. To hospital in Belfast sick (scabies) May 1916. Posted as an Officer Cadet to 21st Officer Cadet Battalion, Crookham 17 March 1917. Returned to the 10th (Reserve) Battalion 25 April 1917. Reverted to Corporal 22 May 1917. To 36 Infantry Base Depot, France 24 May 1917. Promoted to Acting Lance Sergeant. While at the Base Depot he was charged with not complying with an order given by a Senior NCO and reverted to Corporal 9 June 1917. Joined the 9th (Service) Battalion 15 June 1917. 'C' Company. **Missing** at the Battle of Langemarck 16 August 1917 and later declared **killed in action** on that date, aged 19. His brother, Second Lieutenant John Ernest Johnston, was killed in action on 10 July 1916 serving with The South Staffordshire Regiment. His brother, Lieutenant David Percival Johnston, served with the Corps of Royal Engineers (Corporal) before being commissioned into the Royal Garrison Artillery.

JOHNSTON Company Quartermaster Sergeant James 14348. Born in 1895 at Seagoe, Portadown, County Armagh. 4th (Portadown) Battalion, Armagh Regiment, Ulster Volunteer Force.

Member of Edenderry Temperance and Benefit Loyal Orange Lodge 322. Worked as a clerk in the linen trade at Portadown Spinning Company. Enlisted September 1914. To France with 36th (Ulster) Division in October 1915. **Wounded** by a gunshot to the left arm during the attack at Hamel 1 July 1916. Treated at 24th General Hospital, Etaples. Rejoined the 9th (Service) Battalion 16 July 1916. Company Quartermaster Sergeant 'B' Company 30 August 1916. Wounded by gas January 1917. To hospital (injured leg) 29 March 1917 and evacuated to hospital in England 5 April 1917. Continued to suffer headaches and defective vision as a result of his wounds. Transferred to the Class Z Reserve 18 July 1919. 1914-15 Star.

JOHNSTON Lance Corporal James 23447. Born in 1880 at Seagoe, County Armagh. A weaver. Enlisted 18 December 1915 and joined the 10th (Reserve) Battalion. Lance Corporal 25 May 1917. To France 7 August 1917 and joined the 9th (Service) Battalion. To hospital sick (nephritis) and evacuated to hospital in England 31 January 1918. [Transferred to the Labour Corps (renumbered 657864). To France 24 September 1918. Served with 1043rd Area Employment Company.] Transferred to the Class Z Reserve 6 August 1919.

JOHNSTON Private James Frazer 41126. Born in 1897 at Clogher, County Tyrone. Lived at Blacklion, County Cavan. [Enlisted in March 1915 into the Service Squadron, 6th (Inniskilling) Dragoons (UD/229). Served with 2nd North Irish Horse, X Corps Cavalry Regiment.] Joined the renamed 9th (North Irish Horse) Battalion from 36 Infantry Base Depot and transferred to Princess Victoria's (Royal Irish Fusiliers) in September/October 1917 (renumbered 41126). 'A' Company. **Wounded** during the retreat from St Quentin and **died of wounds** 25 March 1918, aged 20.

JOHNSTON Private John 41107. Born at Enniskillen. [Enlisted into The Royal Inniskilling Fusiliers (14073). Transferred in October 1914 to the Service Squadron, 6th (Inniskilling) Dragoons (renumbered UD/84). To France with 36th (Ulster) Division in October 1915. Served with 2nd North Irish Horse, X Corps Cavalry Regiment.] Joined the renamed 9th (North Irish Horse) Battalion from 36 Infantry Base Depot and transferred to Princess Victoria's (Royal Irish Fusiliers) in September/October 1917 (renumbered 41107). **Wounded** by sniper fire near St Quentin and **died of wounds** 11 February 1918, aged 22. 1914-15 Star.

JOHNSTON Private Oliver 41161. Born in 1892 at Enniskillen, County Fermanagh. Lived in Belfast and worked as a porter in an iron store (probably in the shipyards). Member of Royal Black Preceptory 873 and Loyal Orange Lodge 428. Member of the Special Service Section, Willowfield Battalion, East Belfast Regiment, Ulster Volunteer Force. [Enlisted in August 1915 into the Service Squadron, 6th (Inniskilling) Dragoons (UD/281). Served with 2nd North Irish Horse, X Corps Cavalry Regiment.] Joined the renamed 9th (North Irish Horse) Battalion from 36 Infantry Base Depot and transferred to Princess Victoria's (Royal Irish Fusiliers) in September/October 1917 (renumbered 41161). **Wounded** twice, including in November 1917 when he was wounded in the abdomen.

JOHNSTON Private Richard 14365. From Lurgan, County Armagh. Enlisted September 1914. To France with 36th (Ulster) Division in October 1915. 'C' Company. Company bomb carrier during the attack at Hamel 1 July 1916 during which he was **killed in action**. 1914-15 Star.

JOHNSTON MM Sergeant Robert 14358. From Portadown, County Armagh. 4th (Portadown) Battalion, Armagh Regiment, Ulster Volunteer Force. Enlisted September 1914. To France with 36th (Ulster) Division in October 1915. 'B' Company. **Wounded** accidentally in September 1916. **Wounded** at the Battle of Langemarck 16 August 1917. **MM** – Shoddy Farm raid 22 July 1918. **Wounded**. Discharged as no longer physically fit for war service due to wounds 18 February 1919. Silver War Badge, number B97851. 1914-15 Star.

JOHNSTON Lance Sergeant Robert 16111. Enlisted into the 9th (Service) Battalion in October 1914. To France with 36th (Ulster) Division in October 1915. 'D' Company. **Wounded** during the Battle of Messines and to hospital 9 June 1917. **Missing** in the period 21-28 March 1918 during the retreat from St Quentin believed **captured**. Transferred to the Class Z Reserve 11 April 1919. 1914-15 Star.

JOHNSTON Private Robert 18682. Enlisted into the 9th (Service) Battalion in April 1915. To France with 36th (Ulster) Division in October 1915. Transferred to the Class Z Reserve 27 March 1919. 1914-15 Star.

JOHNSTON Private Robert 41454. [Enlisted in November 1915 into the North Irish Horse (1789). Served with 2nd North Irish Horse, X Corps Cavalry Regiment.] Joined the renamed 9th (North Irish

Horse) Battalion from 36 Infantry Base Depot and transferred to Princess Victoria's (Royal Irish Fusiliers) in September/October 1917 (renumbered 41454).

JOHNSTON Private Thomas 18563. From Portadown, County Armagh. Enlisted into the 9th (Service) Battalion in April 1915. To France with 36th (Ulster) Division in October 1915. [Posted to the 1st Battalion. **Captured** in March/April 1918.] Transferred to the Class Z Reserve 25 March 1919. 1914-15 Star.

JOHNSTON Private Walter 20032. Enlisted in June 1915.

JOHNSTON Private William 12872. [Enlisted in September 1914 and joined the 6th (Service) Battalion in 31st Brigade, 10th (Irish) Division. Embarked with the Mediterranean Expeditionary Force July 1915.] Posted to the 9th (Service) Battalion.

JOHNSTON Private William 14373. From Lisbellaw, County Fermanagh. Enlisted September 1914. To France with 36th (Ulster) Division in October 1915. 'C' Company. Lewis gunner. **Killed in action** during the attack at Hamel 1 July 1916, aged 21. 1914-15 Star.

JOHNSTON Private William 14464, 33274 & 7041472. From Killeshandra, County Cavan. (This number, which appears on his Medal Index Card, is incorrect. It was issued to 14464 Lance Corporal S J Magee below. His correct number has not been identified.) Enlisted September 1914. To France with 36th (Ulster) Division in October 1915. [Transferred to The King's (Liverpool Regiment) and was posted to the 2nd Garrison Battalion, The King's (Liverpool Regiment) (renumbered 90137). Transferred to the Labour Corps (renumbered 393786) and served with 820th Area Employment Company.] 1914-15 Star. Re-enlisted 1 September 1919 for Regular Army service with Princess Victoria's (Royal Irish Fusiliers) (renumbered 33274, renumbered 7041472). Discharged 14 April 1923. Medals forfeit due to misconduct.

JOHNSTON Private William 17408. Enlisted in November/December 1914. 'C' Company. To hospital in June 1916, struck off strength when evacuated to hospital in England and did not take part in the attack at Hamel on 1 July 1916.

JOHNSTON Lance Corporal William 18061. Born at Liverpool. From Tassagh, County Armagh. Enlisted into the 9th (Service) Battalion in February 1915. To France with 36th (Ulster) Division in October 1915. 'C' Company. Survived the attack at Hamel on 1 July 1916 unwounded. **Wounded** during the retreat from St Quentin 21-28 March 1918. **Wounded** during the attack south of Wulverghem on 4/5 September 1918 and **died of wounds** 9 September 1918. 1914-15 Star.

JOHNSTON Private William James 22152. Born at Kirkcubbin, County Down. From Belfast. Enlisted in November 1915. Posted to the 9th (Service) Battalion. 'B' Company. **Killed in action** at the Battle of Langemarck 16 August 1917, aged 34.

JONES Sergeant Albert Halligan 14345. From Portadown, County Armagh. Enlisted September 1914. To France with 36th (Ulster) Division in October 1915. [Transferred to the Labour Corps (renumbered 231571 Sergeant).] Transferred to the Class Z Reserve 3 June 1919. 1914-15 Star.

JONES Corporal Alfred 42078. [Enlisted into the Army Service Corps (S4/144073). Served with 2nd Australian Division Supply Column and 17th Field Bakery.] Transferred to Princess Victoria's (Royal Irish Fusiliers) 8 May 1918 (renumbered 42078) and joined the 9th (North Irish Horse) Battalion. [Posted to the 1st Battalion. ***Croix de Guerre* (Belgium)**.]

JONES Private David 17069. From Portadown, County Armagh. Enlisted into the 9th (Service) Battalion in October 1914. To France with 36th (Ulster) Division in October 1915. **Wounded**. [Transferred to the Labour Corps (renumbered 445555).] Transferred to the Class Z Reserve 14 May 1919. Brother of Private Edward Jones, Corporal Henry Jones and Private Joseph Jones. Another brother, James Jones, served with 44th (Manitoba) Battalion, Canadian Infantry.

JONES Private Edward 14363. From South Street, Portadown, County Armagh. 4th (Portadown) Battalion, Armagh Regiment, Ulster Volunteer Force. Enlisted September 1914. To France with 36th (Ulster) Division in October 1915. 'C' Company. Stretcher-bearer. **Wounded** in June 1917. **Killed in action** at the Battle of Langemarck 16 August 1917, aged 38, when he was shot in the back while carrying a wounded man back from the line. 1914-15 Star. Brother of Private David Jones, Corporal Henry Jones and Private Joseph Jones. Another brother, James Jones, served with 44th (Manitoba) Battalion, Canadian Infantry.

JONES Corporal Henry 14364. From Portadown, County Armagh. 4th (Portadown) Battalion,

Armagh Regiment, Ulster Volunteer Force. Enlisted September 1914. To France with 36th (Ulster) Division in October 1915. **Wounded** during the attack at Hamel 1 July 1916. **Wounded** in January 1918. Discharged as no longer physically fit for war service due to wounds 30 August 1918, aged 34. Silver War Badge, number 445714. 1914-15 Star. Married the sister of Sergeant William Gordon. Brother of Private David Jones, Private Edward Jones and Private Joseph Jones. Another brother, James Jones, served with 44th (Manitoba) Battalion, Canadian Infantry.

JONES Private Herbert 41638. [Enlisted in November 1915 into the North Irish Horse (1807). Served with 2nd North Irish Horse, X Corps Cavalry Regiment.] Joined the renamed 9th (North Irish Horse) Battalion from 36 Infantry Base Depot and transferred to Princess Victoria's (Royal Irish Fusiliers) in September/October 1917 (renumbered 41638).

JONES Private James 14353. From Lurgan, County Armagh. Enlisted September 1914. To France with 36th (Ulster) Division in October 1915. 'C' Company. **Wounded** during the attack at Hamel 1 July 1916 and **died of wounds** 2 July 1916. 1914-15 Star. Brother of the future wife of Private Thomas Lyness.

JONES Sergeant James 14367. Enlisted September 1914. To France with 36th (Ulster) Division in October 1915. **Wounded** during the attack at Hamel 1 July 1916. Discharged as no longer physically fit for war service due to wounds 2 April 1917. 1914-15 Star. Subsequently became an instructor with the Ulster Special Constabulary. During the Second World War served as a storeman at Ballymena camp. Later worked as a storeman with the Territorial Army in Armagh until his death on 22 March 1952, aged 65. Member of Loyal Orange Lodge 1249 and Royal Black Preceptory 691.

JONES Private Joseph 14347. Born in 1880. Enlisted September 1914. To France with 36th (Ulster) Division in October 1915. [Transferred to the Machine Gun Corps (renumbered 73275). **Wounded**.] Discharged as no longer physically fit for war service due to wounds 7 July 1919, aged 38. Silver War Badge, number B337578. 1914-15 Star. Brother of Private David Jones, Private Edward Jones and Corporal Henry Jones. Another brother, James Jones, served with 44th (Manitoba) Battalion, Canadian Infantry.

JONES Private Joseph Henry 42073. [Enlisted 16 August 1917 into The London Regiment. Posted to 1/22nd (County of London) Battalion, The London Regiment (The Queen's) in December 1917.] To France and joined 'B' Infantry Base Depot in early-April 1918. Transferred to Princess Victoria's (Royal Irish Fusiliers) April 1918 and posted to the 1st Battalion. Posted to the 9th (North Irish Horse) Battalion in mid-1918. **Wounded**. Discharged as no longer physically fit for war service due to wounds 2 September 1919. Silver War Badge, number B301539.

JONES Private Samuel 14368. From Lurgan, County Armagh. Enlisted September 1914. To France with 36th (Ulster) Division in October 1915. **Killed in action** during the attack at Hamel 1 July 1916, aged 19.

JONES Private Thomas 14352. From Portadown, County Armagh. A baker. Enlisted September 1914. No record of deployment to France with 36th (Ulster) Division in October 1915. [Transferred to the Labour Corps (renumbered 120718).] Discharged as no longer physically fit for war service due to sickness 18 October 1918, aged 35. Silver War Badge, number B53224.

JONES Private Thomas 14370. Enlisted 16 September 1916. Did not serve overseas with 36th (Ulster) Division. Discharged as no longer physically fit for war service due to sickness 25 April 1916. Silver War Badge, number 95494.

JORDAN Private Ernest John 26852. Enlisted 1 August 1916 and transferred to the Army Reserve. Mobilised in February 1917. Posted to the 9th (Service) Battalion. Discharged as no longer physically fit for war service due to sickness 23 October 1919. Silver War Badge, number B326059.

JOSEPHS Private Wolf 42141. [Enlisted into the Army Service Corps (T4/216251). Served with 4th Line of Communications Company.] Transferred to Princess Victoria's (Royal Irish Fusiliers) 8 May 1918 (renumbered 42141) and joined the 9th (North Irish Horse) Battalion.

JOURNET Sergeant C 43427 & 7042216. From Camden Town, London. [Enlisted and joined a Training Reserve Battalion for service with The Rifle Brigade (The Prince Consort's Own) (1298). Transferred to The Royal Irish Rifles (renumbered 42135). Promoted Sergeant. To 36 Infantry Base

Depot and joined the Surplus Company November 1917. Transferred to Princess Victoria's (Royal Irish Fusiliers) (renumbered 43427) in February 1918. Posted to the 7th/8th (Service) Battalion in 49th Brigade, 16th (Irish) Division (probably did not join).] Joined the 9th (North Irish Horse) Battalion when the 7th/8th (Service) Battalion was disbanded in February 1918. 'A' Company. **Missing** in the period 21-28 March 1918 during the retreat from St Quentin believed **captured**. Re-enlisted in early-1919 for Regular Army service with Princess Victoria's (Royal Irish Fusiliers) (renumbered 7042216).

JOWETT Private William Arthur 42114. [Enlisted into the Army Veterinary Corps (30705).] Transferred to Princess Victoria's (Royal Irish Fusiliers) 8 May 1918 (renumbered 42114) and joined the 9th (North Irish Horse) Battalion.

JOYCE Corporal Andrew 14362. From Tandragee, County Armagh. Enlisted in September 1914. No record of deployment to France with 36th (Ulster) Division in October 1915. Posted to the 1st Garrison Battalion and served in India and Burma. Died 17 October 1951 and is buried at Mullavilly Parish Church.

JOYCE Private James 14355. From West Street, Portadown, County Armagh the son of a former soldier of Princess Victoria's (Royal Irish Fusiliers). 4th (Portadown) Battalion, Armagh Regiment, Ulster Volunteer Force. Enlisted September 1914, aged 16. To France with 36th (Ulster) Division in October 1915. **Killed in action** during the attack at Hamel 1 July 1916, aged 18. 1914-15 Star.

JOYCE Private Thomas James 16114. From Portmore Street, Portadown, County Armagh. Enlisted into the 9th (Service) Battalion in October 1914. To France with 36th (Ulster) Division in October 1915. **Killed in action** during the attack at Hamel 1 July 1916. 1914-15 Star.

JOYCE Private William 17945. Enlisted into the 9th (Service) Battalion 4 February 1915. Discharged as no longer physically fit for war service due to sickness 11 September 1916. Silver War Badge, number 92463.

JOYCE Private William James 14357. Enlisted September 1914. To France with 36th (Ulster) Division in October 1915. Discharged as no longer physically fit for war service due to sickness 6 June 1918, aged 38. Silver War Badge, number 396908. 1914-15 Star.

JUDD Private Arthur 43243. [Enlisted into The Sherwood Foresters (Nottinghamshire and Derbyshire Regiment).] Transferred to Princess Victoria's (Royal Irish Fusiliers) 31 August 1916 (renumbered 43243) having joined the 9th (Service) Battalion on 8 August 1916.

JUDGE Private Cecil 43360. Born in 1889 at Newington, London. A clerk. [Enlisted 10 December 1915 and transferred to the Army Reserve. Mobilised 18 July 1916 and joined the 3/7th Battalion, The London Regiment (6736). Posted to the 1/7th (City of London) Battalion, The London Regiment.] Attached to the 9th (Service) Battalion, Princess Victoria's (Royal Irish Fusiliers) 26 November 1916. 'C' Company. Discharged from the Territorial Force, re-enlisted and transferred to Princess Victoria's (Royal Irish Fusiliers) in March/April 1917 (renumbered 43360). **Missing** at the Battle of Langemarck 16 August 1917 and later declared **killed in action** on that date, aged 28.

JUKES Private Alfred 20323. (This is his correct number. The number on his medal index card (23818) is that allocated when he enlisted.) Born in 1881 at Gateshead, County Durham. Served for six years in the Militia. [Enlisted 4 June 1915 and joined the 12th (Reserve) Battalion, The Royal Inniskilling Fusiliers (23818).] Transferred to Princess Victoria's (Royal Irish Fusiliers) 30 June 1915 (renumbered 20323) and joined the 9th (Service) Battalion. 'C' Company. To France with 36th (Ulster) Division in October 1915. Discharged from hospital just before the attack at Hamel on 1 July 1916, which he survived unwounded. **Wounded** by a gunshot to the wrist at the Battle of Langemarck 16 August 1917 and evacuated to hospital in England 7 September 1917. [Joined the 10th (Reserve) Battalion, Princess Victoria's (Royal Irish Fusiliers) 29 September 1917 and posted immediately to the 2nd (Home Service) Garrison Battalion, The Royal Irish Regiment in Dublin. Transferred to The Royal Irish Regiment (renumbered 3252 Private) 6 March 1918. Embarked with this unit for France 15 May 1918 and remained with it when it became the 8th (Service) Battalion, The Royal Irish Regiment in 121st Brigade, 40th Division.] Transferred to the Class Z Reserve 10 February 1919. 1914-15 Star. Re-enlisted 10 June 1919 for service with the Labour Corps (renumbered 702844). Served in France from 7 July 1919 to 21 April 1920 with 200th Labour Company employed in the exhumation of war graves, including those around Gommecourt Wood. Discharged from service 30 April 1920.

JULIAN Private John W 45787. [Joined 110th Training Reserve Battalion for service with 22nd (County of London) Battalion, The London Regiment (The Queen's) (66984).] To France and joined 36 Infantry Base Depot 29 March 1918. Transferred to Princess Victoria's (Royal Irish Fusiliers) 2 April 1918 (renumbered 45787) and joined the 9th (North Irish Horse) Battalion 4 April 1918. [Transferred to 5th (Service) Battalion, The Royal Irish Regiment (Pioneers) in the Light Division in the British Army of the Rhine in March/June 1919 (renumbered 41310).]

KANE Private Francis Joseph 26834. From Dublin. Enlisted 14 February 1917 and joined the 3rd (Reserve) Battalion. Posted to the 9th (Service) Battalion in mid-1917. 'C' Company. **Wounded** in the left arm and leg at the Battle of Langemarck 16 August 1917 and **captured**. Held at Freiderichsfeld Prisoner of War Camp. Discharged as no longer physically fit for war service due to wounds 5 April 1919. Silver War Badge, number B214598.

KANE Sergeant (Acting Company Quartermaster Sergeant) John 12330. A former regular soldier. [Enlisted 9 September 1914 and joined the 5th or 6th (Service) Battalion in 31st Brigade, 10th (Irish) Division. Company Quartermaster Sergeant.] Posted to the 9th (Service) Battalion in late-1914 and then to a reserve battalion. Did not serve overseas with 36th (Ulster) Division. Discharged having reached the age for discharge 4 June 1918, aged 52.

KANE Company Quartermaster Sergeant J. (Not a duplicate with above). 'C' Company. Company Quartermaster Sergeant. Soldier not identified.

KANE Private Stephen 26289. [Enlisted in January/February 1917 and joined the 7th/8th (Service) Battalion in 49th Brigade, 16th (Irish) Division.] Joined the 9th (North Irish Horse) Battalion when the 7th/8th (Service) Battalion was disbanded in February 1918.

KANE Private W James 14382. From Lurgan, County Armagh. Enlisted September 1914. To France with 36th (Ulster) Division in October 1915. **Killed in action** during the attack at Hamel 1 July 1916, aged 28. 1914-15 Star.

KANE Private William 14377. From Portadown, County Armagh. 4th (Portadown) Battalion, Armagh Regiment, Ulster Volunteer Force. Enlisted September 1914. To France with 36th (Ulster) Division in October 1915. Transferred to the Class Z Reserve 23 March 1919. 1914-15 Star.

KAVANAGH Lance Corporal William J 24429. From Dublin. Enlisted in May 1916. Posted to the 9th (Service) Battalion. 'D' Company. **Wounded** at the Battle of Langemarck 16 August 1917. [Transferred to the Labour Corps (renumbered 612738).]

KEARNEY Private Patrick 12354. Born at Armagh, County Armagh. Worked in the iron works at Coatbridge, Lanarkshire with his brother William. [Enlisted in September 1914 and joined the 5th (Service) Battalion in 31st Brigade, 10th (Irish) Division. Embarked with the Mediterranean Expeditionary Force July 1915. Evacuated to hospital in England.] Posted to the 9th (Service) Battalion. 'A' Company. **Killed in action** at the Battle of Langemarck 16 August 1917. His brother, Private William Kearney, served with him in the 5th Battalion and, having been partially deafened by a shell, was transferred to the 2nd (Home Service) Garrison Battalion, The Royal Irish Regiment before being transferred to the Class W Reserve. His brother, Private James Kearney, also served with the 5th or 6th Battalion in the Mediterranean Expeditionary Force and was wounded twice. His brother, Sergeant Joseph Kearney, served with the Australian Imperial Force. Another brother (Hendry or Henry) served with The Royal Inniskilling Fusiliers. His brother-in-law, Gunner Joseph Daly, served with the Royal Field Artillery.

KEASKIN Private James 17376 & 7040600. Born in 1900 at Carrickmacross, County Monaghan. Enlisted 23 December 1914, aged 14 and giving his age as 18 years. [To France 7 June 1915 and joined the 1st Battalion. **Wounded** by a gunshot to the thigh 2 December 1917 and evacuated to hospital in England.] To France 4 May 1918 and joined the 9th (Service) Battalion. 1914-15 Star. Re-enlisted in early-1919 for Regular Army service with Princess Victoria's (Royal Irish Fusiliers) (renumbered 7040600). Served with the 1st Battalion in Persia and Mesopotamia in 1919/20. General Service Medal 1918-1962 with clasps 'Iraq' & 'NW Persia'. Discharged 22 December 1926.

KEEGAN Private Michael 20547. Enlisted into the 9th (Service) Battalion in June 1915. 'D' Company. **Missing** in the period 21-28 March 1918 during the retreat from St Quentin believed **captured**.

KEENAN Private John Francis 42549. Born 15 February 1887 at Kilkenny, County Kilkenny. A painter for Gerald Stokes, Bagenalstown, County Carlow. [Enlisted 14 March 1917 into The Royal Irish Rifles (10525) (His medal index card shows his regimental numbers incorrectly). To 36 Infantry Base Depot 7 July 1917 and joined the 1st Battalion, The Royal Irish Rifles. Injured in action (bruised foot) 27 October 1917 and returned to duty. **Wounded** by shrapnel to the left foot 17 November 1917. Treated at 26th General Hospital and evacuated to hospital in England. To France 14 June 1918 and posted to the 1st Battalion, The Royal Irish Rifles.] Transferred to Princess Victoria's (Royal Irish Fusiliers) 14 September 1918 (renumbered 42549) and joined the 9th (North Irish Horse) Battalion 22 September 1918. **Wounded** by a gunshot to the thigh at Courtrai 16 October 1918. Treated at 53rd General Hospital. Rejoined the 9th (North Irish Horse) Battalion 25 November 1918. [Transferred to 5th (Service) Battalion, The Royal Irish Regiment (Pioneers) in the Light Division in the British Army of the Rhine in March/June 1919 (renumbered 41311).] Transferred to the Class Z Reserve 12 January 1920.

KEENAN Sergeant Samuel 18046. Enlisted into the 9th (Service) Battalion in February 1915. To France with 36th (Ulster) Division in October 1915. [Transferred to the Labour Corps (renumbered 519750).] 1914-15 Star.

KEITH Sergeant John 14391. From Portadown, County Armagh. Enlisted into the 3rd Battalion (Militia), Princess Victoria's (Royal Irish Fusiliers) 11 May 1908. Discharged at the termination of his engagement 10 May 1914. Enlisted September 1914 and joined the 9th (Service) Battalion. To France with 36th (Ulster) Division in October 1915. 'B' Company. **Wounded** when shot in the face during the attack at Hamel 1 July 1916. Recovered and rejoined the 9th (Service) Battalion. **Wounded** near River Douve August 1916. **MSM**. 1914-15 Star. Battalion Colour Guard June 1919. 1914-15 Star.

KELLER Private Albert Gordon 25103. Born in 1895 at Stavely, Derbyshire. A clerk. [Enlisted 28 October 1914 into the Army Service Corps (3482). To France 4 November 1914. Served with 1st Remount Depot. To England for transfer to infantry 12 August 1916. To 16 Infantry Base Depot December 1916 and transferred to Princess Victoria's (Royal Irish Fusiliers) (renumbered 25103). Joined the 7th/8th (Service) Battalion 3 December 1916. **Wounded** by a gunshot to the thigh at the Battle of Langemarck 16 August 1917 and evacuated to hospital in England. Treated at hospital in Bradford until 23 October 1917 and then in Ireland. Served at the Depot, Ballykinler.] To France 14 March 1918. Posted to the 9th (North Irish Horse) Battalion. **Killed in action** 14 April 1918 in the actions between Wulverghem and Kemmel.

KELLETT Private William 20314. Enlisted 15 May 1915 and joined the 9th (Service) Battalion with the draft of men from The Royal Inniskilling Fusiliers who transferred to Princess Victoria's (Royal Irish Fusiliers) on 30 June 1915. To France with 36th (Ulster) Division in October 1915. **Wounded**. Discharged as no longer physically fit for war service due to wounds 4 October 1917. Silver War Badge, number 255962, aged 22. 1914-15 Star.

KELLETT Private William 42268. [Enlisted 13 July 1915 into the Army Veterinary Corps (S/210639). To France 17 October 1915.] Transferred to Princess Victoria's (Royal Irish Fusiliers) 8 May 1918 (renumbered 42268) and joined the 9th (North Irish Horse) Battalion. [Transferred to The Royal Inniskilling Fusiliers (renumbered 48658). **Wounded**.] Discharged as no longer physically fit for war service due to wounds 18 August 1919. Silver War Badge, number B292361. 1914-15 Star.

KELLS Private John Joseph 16115. From Lisboduff, Cootehill, County Cavan. Enlisted into the 9th (Service) Battalion in October 1914. To France with 36th (Ulster) Division in October 1915. **Killed in action** during the attack at Hamel 1 July 1916, aged 30. 1914-15 Star.

KELLY Private Charles 18398. From Battlehill, Portadown, County Armagh. Enlisted into the 9th (Service) Battalion in March 1915. To France with 36th (Ulster) Division in October 1915. 'B' Company. **Killed in action** during the attack at Hamel 1 July 1916, aged 27. His body was recovered in September 1916 and buried in Hamel Military Cemetery. 1914-15 Star.

KELLY Private Christopher 11285 & 25199. [Enlisted as a regular soldier into Princess Victoria's (Royal Irish Fusiliers) 9 July 1913 (11285) and served with the 1st Battalion. To France 22 August 1914. **Wounded**. Transferred to The Royal Irish Regiment (renumbered 2G/623) and served with the 2nd (Home Service) Garrison Battalion, The Royal Irish Regiment at Dublin. Transferred back to Princess Victoria's (Royal Irish Fusiliers) in November 1916 (renumbered

25199).] Posted to the 9th (Service) Battalion. 'D' Company. **Wounded** at the Battle of Langemarck 16 August 1917. Discharged as no longer physically fit for war service due to wounds 20 May 1919. Silver War Badge, number 507822.

KELLY Private Edward 16116. Enlisted into the 9th (Service) Battalion in October 1914. To France with 36th (Ulster) Division in October 1915. [Transferred to the Labour Corps (renumbered 570278).] 1914-15 Star.

KELLY Private Henry 41361. From Belfast. [Enlisted in May 1915 into the North Irish Horse (1556). Served with 2nd North Irish Horse, X Corps Cavalry Regiment.] Joined the renamed 9th (North Irish Horse) Battalion from 36 Infantry Base Depot and transferred to Princess Victoria's (Royal Irish Fusiliers) in September/October 1917 (renumbered 41361). 'B' Company. **Captured** in the period 21-28 March 1918 during the retreat from St Quentin.

KELLY Private Hugh 41217. [Enlisted in January 1916 into the North Irish Horse (2063). Served with 2nd North Irish Horse, X Corps Cavalry Regiment.] Joined the renamed 9th (North Irish Horse) Battalion from 36 Infantry Base Depot and transferred to Princess Victoria's (Royal Irish Fusiliers) in September/October 1917 (renumbered 41217). 'D' Company. **Wounded** during the retreat from St Quentin 21-28 March 1918.

KELLY Private James 41577. From Belfast. [Enlisted in February 1915 into the North Irish Horse (1444). To France with 'F' Squadron in 33rd Division 17 November 1915. Served with 2nd North Irish Horse, X Corps Cavalry Regiment.] Joined the renamed 9th (North Irish Horse) Battalion from 36 Infantry Base Depot and transferred to Princess Victoria's (Royal Irish Fusiliers) in September/October 1917 (renumbered 41577). **Wounded** during the attack south of Wulverghem and **died of wounds** 5 September 1918, aged 24. 1914-15 Star.

KELLY Private John 27583. From Wigan, Lancashire. [Enlisted into The Manchester Regiment (48306).] Transferred to Princess Victoria's (Royal Irish Fusiliers) in May 1917 (renumbered 27583). Posted to the 9th (North Irish Horse) Battalion. 'B' Company. Declared **missing** at the Battle of Langemarck 16 August 1917; rejoined. **Killed in action** during the attack north of Bailleul 24 August 1918, aged 19.

KELLY Private Robert 14383 & 17579. Born in 1898 at Richhill, County Armagh. An apprentice cabinet maker. Enlisted in Armagh September 1914, aged 16. Discharged having made a mis-statement as to age on enlistment; soldier under 17 years of age at date of application for discharge 21 October 1914. He re-enlisted again at Armagh on 11 January 1915 and was allocated the number 17579. Discharged as not being likely to become an efficient soldier in that he was considered medically unfit for service 23 January 1915.

KELLY Private Robert 20031. Enlisted into the 9th (Service) Battalion 1 June 1915. To France with 36th (Ulster) Division in October 1915. 'C' Company. Lewis gun team during the attack at Hamel 1 July 1916, which he survived unwounded. [Transferred to the Labour Corps (renumbered 231607).] Discharged as no longer physically fit for war service due to sickness 18 June 1918, aged 45. Silver War Badge, number 410617. 1914-15 Star.

KELLY Private William 14378. Born at Bathgate, Edinburgh. From Lurgan, County Armagh. Enlisted September 1914. To France with 36th (Ulster) Division in October 1915. 'C' Company. Bombing team. **Killed in action** during the attack at Hamel 1 July 1916, aged 36.

KELLY MM Private William 14393. Enlisted September 1914. To France with 36th (Ulster) Division in October 1915. **MM** – Wulverghem April 1918. [Transferred to the Labour Corps (renumbered 642924).] 1914-15 Star.

KELLSO Private John 25206. Born in 1888. From Belfast. A postman. Enlisted 21 November 1916 and joined the 10th (Reserve) Battalion. To France 5 March 1917 and joined the 9th (Service) Battalion 23 March 1917. 'B' Company. **Wounded** by shrapnel to the left thigh at the Battle of Langemarck 16 August 1917. Treated at 1st Canadian General Hospital and evacuated to hospital in England. Treated at 2nd Southern General Hospital, Bristol. Joined the 10th (Reserve) Battalion 15 October 1917. [Transferred to the Royal Defence Corps (renumbered 73194) 5 April 1918 and posted to 199th Protection Company. Posted to 170th Protection Company 31 August 1918.] Transferred to the Class Z Reserve 30 March 1919.

KEMBLE Warrant Officer Class II Samuel Joseph 15464. Born in 1885 at Cardiff,

Glamorganshire. Worked in Guest Keen steel works at Cardiff docks. [Enlisted 8 September 1914 into The Lancashire Fusiliers. Transferred to Princess Victoria's (Royal Irish Fusiliers) 12 September 1914 and joined the 7th (Service) Battalion. Lance Corporal 10 November 1914. Corporal 7 February 1915. Lance Sergeant 21 June 1915. Sergeant 16 December 1915. To France in 49th Brigade, 16th (Irish) Division February 1916. **Wounded** by a gunshot 9 March 1916. Acting Company Sergeant Major 7 February 1917.] Joined the 9th (North Irish Horse) Battalion 19 July 1918. Company Sergeant Major. Posted to 4th Convalescent Depot as Company Sergeant Major. Transferred to the Class Z Reserve 27 February 1919. Died at Cardiff, Glamorganshire in 1947, aged 62.

KENDALL Private Sidney 43502. [Served with the 16th (Service) Battalion, The Royal Irish Rifles (2nd County Down) (Pioneers) (41213).] Transferred to Princess Victoria's (Royal Irish Fusiliers) 15 June 1918 (renumbered 43502) and joined the 9th (North Irish Horse) Battalion 23 June 1918.

KENNEDY Private Absalom 14384. From Armagh, County Armagh. A pastry baker. Enlisted September 1914. To France with 36th (Ulster) Division in October 1915. [Posted to the 5th/6th (Service) Battalion.] Transferred to the Class Z Reserve 13 April 1919. 1914-15 Star.

KENNEDY Lance Corporal Alfred Joseph 23313. From Cootehill, County Armagh. A farmer. Enlisted 19 November 1915 and joined the 10th (Reserve) Battalion. To France 10 July 1916 and joined the 9th (Service) Battalion. **Wounded** by a gunshot to the left thigh. Evacuated to hospital in England 18 March 1917 and treated at which King George Hospital, London where his left leg was amputated on 24 April 1917. Fitted with a false limb at the Ulster Volunteer Force Hospital, Belfast in September 1917. Discharged as no longer physically fit for war service due to wounds 17 June 1918, aged 22. Silver War Badge, number 387930.

KENNEDY Private James Walter 17931. From Dunraymond, County Monaghan. Enlisted into the 9th (Service) Battalion in January 1915. To France with 36th (Ulster) Division in October 1915. **Killed in action** during the attack at Hamel 1 July 1916. 1914-15 Star.

KENNEDY MM Private John 20947. From Ballindrait, County Donegal. [Enlisted in September 1915 and joined the 8th (Service) Battalion in 49th Brigade, 16th (Irish) Division.] Joined the 9th (North Irish Horse) Battalion when the 7th/8th (Service) Battalion was disbanded in February 1918. **MM** – River Lys mid-October 1918.

KENNEDY Private Joseph 24656. From Belfast. Enlisted in August 1916. Posted to the 9th (Service) Battalion. 'C' Company. **Wounded** at the Battle of Langemarck 16 August 1917.

KENNEDY Lance Corporal Robert 21079, 33311 & 7041504. From Shankill, Belfast. [Enlisted in November 1914 and joined the 8th (Service) Battalion in 49th Brigade, 16th (Irish) Division.] Joined the 9th (North Irish Horse) Battalion when the 7th/8th (Service) Battalion was disbanded in February 1918. Re-enlisted 25 August 1919 for Regular Army service with Princess Victoria's (Royal Irish Fusiliers) (renumbered 33311, renumbered 7041504). Served with the 1st Battalion in Persia and Mesopotamia in 1919/20. General Service Medal 1918-1962 with clasps 'Iraq' & 'NW Persia'. Discharged 23 December 1921.

KENNEDY Private Robert John 14386. From Armagh, County Armagh. Enlisted September 1914. To France with 36th (Ulster) Division in October 1915. **Wounded** during the attack at Hamel 1 July 1916. **Wounded** in the period 21-28 March 1918 during the retreat from St Quentin. Discharged as no longer physically fit for war service due to sickness 23 November 1918. Silver War Badge, number B44351. 1914-15 Star.

KENNEDY Private Robert John 41344. Born 27 March 1897. From Cullybackey, County Antrim. A farmer. [Enlisted 1 November 1915 into the North Irish Horse (1761). To France 19 May 1916 and joined 'A' Squadron. To hospital sick (blepharitis) 22 September 1916. To hospital sick (hernia) 13 June 1917. Served with 2nd North Irish Horse, X Corps Cavalry Regiment.] Joined the renamed 9th (North Irish Horse) Battalion from 36 Infantry Base Depot and transferred to Princess Victoria's (Royal Irish Fusiliers) in September/October 1917 (renumbered 41344). 'A' Company. **Wounded** by a gunshot to the left leg at Moeuvres 22/23 November 1917 and evacuated to hospital in England. To 'A' Infantry Base Depot. 15 May 1918 and rejoined the 9th (North Irish Horse) Battalion. **Wounded** by a shell fragment in the right shoulder 3 September 1918. Evacuated to hospital in England and treated at Croydon War Hospital. Joined the 3rd (Reserve) Battalion 30 October 1918. Transferred to the Class Z Reserve 19 February 1919.

KENNEDY Private Samuel Joseph 23200. Born in County Tyrone. Worked in the linen trade in Belfast. Enlisted 20 November 1915. Posted to the 9th (Service) Battalion. 'D' Company. **Wounded** at the Battle of Langemarck 16 August 1917. Discharged as no longer physically fit for war service due to wounds 27 March 1918. Silver War Badge, number 246308.

KENNEDY Private William 41442 & 7042139. From Lurgan, County Armagh. A weaver. [Enlisted in February 1914 into the North Irish Horse (902). To France 17 August 1914 with 'A' Squadron as GHQ Troops. Served with 2nd North Irish Horse, X Corps Cavalry Regiment.] Joined the renamed 9th (North Irish Horse) Battalion from 36 Infantry Base Depot and transferred to Princess Victoria's (Royal Irish Fusiliers) in September/October 1917 (renumbered 41442). 'C' Company. **Captured** in the period 21-28 March 1918 during the retreat from St Quentin. 1914 Star and clasp. Repatriated 4 December 1918. Re-enlisted 22 February 1919 for Regular Army service with Princess Victoria's (Royal Irish Fusiliers) (renumbered 7042139). Served with the 1st Battalion in Mesopotamia and Egypt in 1919-21. General Service Medal 1918-1962 with clasp 'Iraq'. **Died** (valvular disease of the heart) 30 August 1921 in Citadel Military Hospital, Cairo.

KENNY Private J J 26859. [Enlisted in January 1917 and joined the 7th/8th (Service) Battalion.] Joined the 9th (North Irish Horse) Battalion when the 7th/8th (Service) Battalion was disbanded in February 1918. 'C' Company. **Missing** in the period 21-28 March 1918 during the retreat from St Quentin believed **captured**.

KEOWN Private Walter Thomas Johnston 21674. Born in 1897 at Glenanne, County Armagh. Enlisted in September 1915. Posted to the 9th (Service) Battalion. 'A' Company. **Missing** in the period 21-28 March 1918 during the retreat from St Quentin believed **captured**.

KERNS Lance Corporal Robert 41503. Born in 1891 at Belfast. Worked in the linen trade. [Enlisted in October 1914 into the Service Squadron, 6th (Inniskilling) Dragoons (UD/71). To France with 36th (Ulster) Division in October 1915. Lance Corporal 18 November 1915. Served with 2nd North Irish Horse, X Corps Cavalry Regiment.] Joined the renamed 9th (North Irish Horse) Battalion from 36 Infantry Base Depot and transferred to Princess Victoria's (Royal Irish Fusiliers) in September/October 1917 (renumbered 41503). Lance Corporal 17 November 1917.] Transferred to the Class Z Reserve 18 February 1919. 1914-15 Star.

KERR Lance Sergeant Bernard 20949. Born in 1883 at Belfast. [Enlisted into The Connaught Rangers (3652) 5 December 1914 and joined the 6th (Service) Battalion. Transferred to Princess Victoria's (Royal Irish Fusiliers) 16 September 1915 (renumbered 20949) and joined the 8th (Service) Battalion in 49th Brigade, 16th (Irish) Division. Corporal and Lance Sergeant 15 November 1915. To France in 49th Brigade, 16th (Irish) Division February 1916. **Wounded** by a gunshot to the right shoulder 29 April 1916 and evacuated to hospital in England. Joined the 4th (Extra Reserve) Battalion 7 June 1916. Reverted to Private at own request 29 June 1916. Posted to the 7th/8th (Service) Battalion but did not join.] To France 24 January 1918. Joined the 9th (North Irish Horse) Battalion when the 7th/8th (Service) Battalion was disbanded in February 1918. 'D' Company. Believed **wounded** in the period 21-28 March 1918 during the retreat from St Quentin. **Killed in action** 12 April 1918 in the actions between Wulverghem and Kemmel.

KERR Private Charles 41339. [Enlisted in December 1916 into the North Irish Horse (2330). Served with 2nd North Irish Horse, X Corps Cavalry Regiment.] Joined the renamed 9th (North Irish Horse) Battalion from 36 Infantry Base Depot and transferred to Princess Victoria's (Royal Irish Fusiliers) in September/October 1917 (renumbered 41339).

KERR Private Hugh 41590. From Portaferry, County Down. [Enlisted January 1915 into the North Irish Horse (1419). To France 23 September 1915. Served with 2nd North Irish Horse, X Corps Cavalry Regiment.] Joined the renamed 9th (North Irish Horse) Battalion from 36 Infantry Base Depot and transferred to Princess Victoria's (Royal Irish Fusiliers) in September/October 1917 (renumbered 41590). 'D' Company. **Captured** in the period 21-28 March 1918 during the retreat from St Quentin. Transferred to the Class Z Reserve 15 April 1919. 1914-15 Star.

KERR Private John 14381. Born in Belfast in 1879. A labourer for Chapman's Ltd. Enlisted in Portadown on 15 September 1914. To France with 36th (Ulster) Division in October 1915. **Wounded** during the attack at Hamel 1 July 1916. Joined the 10th (Reserve) Battalion 23 August 1916. Posted to the 3rd (Reserve) Garrison Battalion at Bere Island, Bantry Bay 10 March 1917. Transferred to The Royal Irish Regiment (renumbered 5388) and served with a garrison battalion from 5 October 1917.] Transferred to the Class Z Reserve 17 July 1919.

KERR Private Robert William 41696. Born in 1888 at Beagh Little, Derrygonnelly, Enniskillen, County Fermanagh. A farmer's son. [Enlisted 10 November 1914 into the Service Squadron, 6th (Inniskilling) Dragoons (UD/175). To France 3 October 1915 and attached to 3rd (London) Battery, Royal Field Artillery in 36th (Ulster Division) as an officer's batman. Served with 2nd North Irish Horse, X Corps Cavalry Regiment.] Transferred to Princess Victoria's (Royal Irish Fusiliers) (renumbered 41696) and joined the 9th (North Irish Horse) Battalion January 1918. 'B' Company. **Captured** in the period 21-28 March 1918 during the retreat from St Quentin. **Died** of heart disease 4 December 1918, aged 30 in Reserve Hospital 2 at Hamburg before he could be repatriated. 1914-15 Star. His brother, Private Thomas Edward Kerr, was killed in action on 1 July 1916 while serving with 11th (Service) Battalion, The Royal Inniskilling Fusiliers (Donegal and Fermanagh).

KERR Private Samuel 23705. Enlisted in January 1915. Posted to the 9th (Service) Battalion. 'C' Company. Believed **wounded** in the period 21-28 March 1918 during the retreat from St Quentin. [Transferred to the Corps of Royal Engineers (renumbered 616454).]

KERR Private Thomas 41162. [Enlisted in February 1915 into the Service Squadron, 6th (Inniskilling) Dragoons (UD/218). To France with 36th (Ulster) Division in October 1915. Served with 2nd North Irish Horse, X Corps Cavalry Regiment.] Joined the renamed 9th (North Irish Horse) Battalion from 36 Infantry Base Depot and transferred to Princess Victoria's (Royal Irish Fusiliers) in September/October 1917 (renumbered 41162). 'B' Company. **Missing** in the period 21-28 March 1918 during the retreat from St Quentin believed **captured**. Transferred to the Class Z Reserve 24 March 1919. 1914-15 Star.

KERR Private William 41301. [Enlisted in March 1914 into the North Irish Horse (924). To France 20 August 1914 with 'C' Squadron as 5th Division Cavalry and then as GHQ Troops. Served with 2nd North Irish Horse, X Corps Cavalry Regiment.] Joined the renamed 9th (North Irish Horse) Battalion from 36 Infantry Base Depot and transferred to Princess Victoria's (Royal Irish Fusiliers) in September/October 1917 (renumbered 41301). [Transferred to the Tank Corps (renumbered 304863) 28 December 1917 and posted for training to the Tank Corps Depot, at Bovington near Wareham, Dorset.] 1914 Star.

KERSHAW Private Patrick 11247 & 7040502. Born at Tullamore, King's County (now County Offaly). Worked in London as a porter. [Enlisted into Princess Victoria's (Royal Irish Fusiliers) as a regular soldier in 1913. To France with the 1st Battalion 22 August 1914. **Wounded** and evacuated to hospital in England 8 November 1914. To France 10 May 1915 and rejoined the 1st Battalion. Evacuated to hospital in England 14 December 1916.] To France 16 February 1918 and joined the 9th (North Irish Horse) Battalion. [Posted back to the 1st Battalion. **Captured** in the period 21-28 March 1918 during the retreat from St Quentin.] Transferred to the Section B Army Reserve, Princess Victoria's (Royal Irish Fusiliers) (renumbered 7040502). 1914 Star and clasp.

KEYS Corporal John Henry 41502. Born in 1888 at Carrickreagh, County Fermanagh. [Enlisted in October 1914 into the Service Squadron, 6th (Inniskilling) Dragoons (UD/59). To France with 36th (Ulster) Division in October 1915. Lance Corporal 18 November 1915. Served with 2nd North Irish Horse, X Corps Cavalry Regiment.] Joined the renamed 9th (North Irish Horse) Battalion from 36 Infantry Base Depot and transferred to Princess Victoria's (Royal Irish Fusiliers) in September/October 1917 (renumbered 41502). 'C' Company. **Captured** in the period 21-28 March 1918 during the retreat from St Quentin. Transferred to the Class Z Reserve 1 April 1919. 1914-15 Star.

KIDBY Private Herbert 42446. [Enlisted into the Army Service Corps (233872). Transferred to The Royal Irish Rifles (renumbered 42976).] Transferred at the Base Depot to Princess Victoria's (Royal Irish Fusiliers) 14 September 1918 (renumbered 42446) and joined the 9th (North Irish Horse) Battalion 22 September 1918. [Transferred to 5th (Service) Battalion, The Royal Irish Regiment (Pioneers) in the Light Division in the British Army of the Rhine in March/June 1919 (renumbered 41312).]

KIDD Private Alexander 21656 & 31982. Enlisted in September 1915. Posted to the 9th (Service) Battalion. Re-enlisted in 1919 for Regular Army service with Princess Victoria's (Royal Irish Fusiliers) (renumbered 31982). Discharged as no longer physically fit for war service due to sickness 21 March 1919. Silver War Badge, number B167343.

KIDD Corporal Francis George 41270. Born in 1894 at Drumragh, County Tyrone. A farmer. [Enlisted 26 February 1913 into the North Irish Horse (805). To France 20 August 1914 with 'C' Squadron as 5th Division Cavalry and then as GHQ Troops. Served with 2nd North Irish Horse, X Corps Cavalry Regiment.] Joined the renamed 9th (North Irish Horse) Battalion from 36 Infantry Base Depot and transferred to Princess Victoria's (Royal Irish Fusiliers) in September/October 1917 (renumbered 41270). **Wounded** by a gunshot to the right thigh during the advance to Anseghem 25 October 1918. Treated at 2nd Australian General Hospital, where his leg was amputated on 29 October 1918, and evacuated to hospital in England. Treated at Whipps Cross War Hospital, Leytonstone and Hanover House, Buckhurst Hill. Fitted with a false limb at the Ulster Volunteer Force Hospital, Belfast in July 1919. Discharged as no longer physically fit for war service due to wounds 31 October 1919. Silver War Badge, number B334063. 1914 Star and clasp.

KIERANS Private Joseph 16344. From Clones, County Monaghan. [Enlisted in October 1914. Served with the 2nd Battalion.] Posted to the 9th (Service) Battalion. **Killed in action** at the Battle of Langemarck 16 August 1917.

KILFEDDER Private Edward James 41331. Born 1 April 1898 at Edenamohill Under, County Fermanagh. [Enlisted 13 December 1916 into the North Irish Horse (2331). Served with 2nd North Irish Horse, X Corps Cavalry Regiment.] Joined the renamed 9th (North Irish Horse) Battalion from 36 Infantry Base Depot and transferred to Princess Victoria's (Royal Irish Fusiliers) in September/October 1917 (renumbered 41331). **Wounded**. Discharged as no longer physically fit for war service due to wounds 16 July 1919. Silver War Badge, number B294633. In 1947 he became a postman. Died in County Fermanagh on 20 February 1977, aged 78.

KILFEDDER Private Robert. Tried by Field General Court Martial on 10 June 1918 charged with *'losing by neglect'* (detail not known); found guilty and sentenced to fifty-six days Field Punishment Number 1. No other details known.

KILPATRICK Private Thomas 14379. From Seagoe, Portadown, County Armagh. 4th (Portadown) Battalion, Armagh Regiment, Ulster Volunteer Force. Enlisted September 1914. To France with 36th (Ulster) Division in October 1915. **Wounded** at Hamel by shellfire at the end of June 1916 and **died of wounds** 11 July 1916, aged 20. 1914-15 Star. Brother of Private William James Kilpatrick. His brother, Robert, also served during the First World War.

KILPATRICK Private William James 14380. From Seagoe, Portadown, County Armagh. Enlisted September 1914. To France with 36th (Ulster) Division in October 1915. [Transferred to the Labour Corps (renumbered 231606).] Transferred to the Class Z Reserve 19 March 1919. 1914-15 Star. Brother of Private Thomas Kilpatrick. His brother, Robert, also served during the First World War.

KILSBY Private Richard 42440. [Enlisted into The Northamptonshire Regiment (7337) and served with the 2nd Battalion. Transferred to The Royal Irish Rifles (renumbered 41919) and joined the 7th (Service) Battalion, The Royal Irish Rifles.] Transferred at the Base Depot to Princess Victoria's (Royal Irish Fusiliers) 14 September 1918 (renumbered 42240) and joined the 9th (North Irish Horse) Battalion 22 September 1918.

KIMMITT Private Edward 14389. Enlisted September 1914. No record of deployment to France with 36th (Ulster) Division in October 1915. [Transferred to the Labour Corps (renumbered 407449).]

KING Company Quartermaster Sergeant. Company Quartermaster Sergeant 'C' Company 1914. Soldier not identified.

KING Private Albert 22974. Born in 1896 at Richhill, County Armagh. Enlisted in November 1915. Posted to the 9th (Service) Battalion. 'D' Company. **Wounded** at the Battle of Langemarck 16 August 1917.

KING Private David 15850. Enlisted into the 9th (Service) Battalion 19 October 1914. To France with 36th (Ulster) Division in October 1915. Discharged as no longer physically fit for war service due to sickness 18 February 1917. Silver War Badge, number 31734. 1914-15 Star.

KING Private G H 43339. From London. [Enlisted into The London Regiment.] Attached to the 9th (Service) Battalion, Princess Victoria's (Royal Irish Fusiliers) 26 November 1916. 'B' Company.

Discharged from the Territorial Force, re-enlisted and transferred to Princess Victoria's (Royal Irish Fusiliers) in March/April 1917 (renumbered 43339). **Wounded** at the Battle of Langemarck 16 August 1917.

KING Private George 14385. Enlisted September 1914. To France with 36th (Ulster) Division in October 1915. Transferred to the Class Z Reserve 16 February 1919. 1914-15 Star.

KING Private Henry James 42236. [Enlisted into the Army Service Corps (T2/13832). Served with 9th Division Train.] Transferred to Princess Victoria's (Royal Irish Fusiliers) 8 May 1918 (renumbered 42236) and joined the 9th (North Irish Horse) Battalion. Transferred to the Class Z Reserve 19 March 1919. 1914-15 Star.

KING Private John 14387. Enlisted September 1914. To France with 36th (Ulster) Division in October 1915. 'C' Company. Detached to the Battalion Transport and did not take part in the attack at Hamel on 1 July 1916. Transferred to the Class Z Reserve 11 March 1919. 1914-15 Star.

KING Private John Donaldson 41302. Born in 1892 at Whitecross, County Armagh. [Enlisted in September 1913 into the North Irish Horse (864). To France August 1914 as GHQ Troops. Served with 2nd North Irish Horse, X Corps Cavalry Regiment.] Joined the renamed 9th (North Irish Horse) Battalion from 36 Infantry Base Depot and transferred to Princess Victoria's (Royal Irish Fusiliers) in September/October 1917 (renumbered 41302). 'C' Company. **Killed in action** 3 November 1917 on a raid at Havrincourt, aged 25. 1914 Star. His brother, Private William Alexander King, was killed in action on 30 July 1916 serving with the 1/6th (Perthshire) Battalion, The Black Watch (Royal Highlanders).

KING Private Thomas 22042. [Enlisted 9 October 1915 and joined the 8th (Service) Battalion in 49th Brigade, 16th (Irish) Division.] Joined the 9th (North Irish Horse) Battalion when the 7th/8th (Service) Battalion was disbanded in February 1918. 'A' Company. **Missing** in the period 21-28 March 1918 during the retreat from St Quentin believed **captured** and **wounded**. Discharged as no longer physically fit for war service due to wounds 7 January 1919. Silver War Badge, number B77843.

KING Private William 26118. From Kilmacanogue, County Wicklow. Enlisted in January 1917. Posted to the 9th (North Irish Horse) Battalion. **Captured**.

KING Private William Michael 43153. From Loughgall, County Armagh. [Enlisted 9 January 1916. Transferred to Princess Victoria's (Royal Irish Fusiliers) in August 1916 and joined the 7th (Service) Battalion in 49th Brigade, 16th (Irish) Division.] Joined the 9th (North Irish Horse) Battalion when the 7th/8th (Service) Battalion was disbanded in February 1918. 'C' Company. **Captured** in the period 21-28 March 1918 during the retreat from St Quentin. Discharged as no longer physically fit for war service due to sickness 20 February 1919. Silver War Badge, number B154480.

KINSELLA Private Patrick 42506. Born in County Wicklow. Lived in County Wexford. Enlisted in Glasgow. [Enlisted April/May 1918 into The Royal Irish Rifles (22581).] Transferred at the Base Depot to Princess Victoria's (Royal Irish Fusiliers) 14 September 1918 (renumbered 42506) and joined the 9th (North Irish Horse) Battalion 22 September 1918. **Missing** during the attack at Vijfwegen on 30 September or 1 October 1918; recorded as **killed in action** 2 October 1918, aged 30.

KIRK Private James Alfred 40014. Born in 1890 at Leeds. [Enlisted 27 November 1915 and transferred to the Army Reserve. Mobilised 5 June 1916 and joined 4th (Extra Reserve) Battalion, The Prince of Wales's Own (West Yorkshire Regiment) (33857).] Transferred to Princess Victoria's (Royal Irish Fusiliers) 30 November 1916 (renumbered 40014) and joined the 9th (Service) Battalion 12 December 1916. 'B' Company. **Wounded** by a gunshot to the chest at the Battle of Langemarck 16 August 1917 and **died of wounds** 18 August 1917 in 32nd Casualty Clearing Station.

KIRKPATRICK Private David William 41605. [Enlisted in November 1914 into the Service Squadron, 6th (Inniskilling) Dragoons (UD/188). To France with 36th (Ulster) Division in October 1915. To France with 36th (Ulster) Division in October 1915. Served with 2nd North Irish Horse, X Corps Cavalry Regiment.] Joined the renamed 9th (North Irish Horse) Battalion from 36 Infantry Base Depot and transferred to Princess Victoria's (Royal Irish Fusiliers) in September/October 1917 (renumbered 41605). [Transferred to The Royal Irish Regiment (renumbered 32847).] Transferred to the Class Z Reserve. 1914-15 Star.

KIRKWOOD Sergeant George 14388. From Milford, County Armagh. Enlisted September 1914. To France with 36th (Ulster) Division in October 1915. 'A' Company. **Wounded** during the attack at Hamel 1 July 1916. Transferred to the Class Z Reserve 31 March 1919. 1914-15 Star.

KNAGGS MM Sergeant Robert William 16117. From Newbliss, County Monaghan. A chemist's assistant. Enlisted into the 9th (Service) Battalion in October 1914. To France with 36th (Ulster) Division in October 1915. **MM** – Battle of Langemarck 16 August 1917. ***Croix de Guerre* (Belgium)**. 1914-15 Star.

KNICHEL Corporal John 42174. Born in 1886 at London. [Enlisted into the Army Service Corps (S4/122959). To France 1 August 1915. Served with 61st and 13th Field Bakeries.] Transferred to Princess Victoria's (Royal Irish Fusiliers) 8 May 1918 (renumbered 42174) and joined the 9th (North Irish Horse) Battalion. Transferred to the Class Z Reserve. 1914-15 Star.

KNIGHT Lance Corporal Ernest 45820. Enlisted 1 January 1917. Joined the 9th (North Irish Horse) Battalion, Princess Victoria's (Royal Irish Fusiliers) with the draft of men from The London Regiment in April 1918. Discharged as no longer physically fit for war service due to wounds. Silver War Badge, number B150028.

KNIGHT Private John Henry 22483 & 43305. [Enlisted into Princess Victoria's (Royal Irish Fusiliers) in 1915 (22483). To Salonika 18 November 1915 and joined the 5th (Service) Battalion. Transferred to the Machine Gun Corps (renumbered 11684). Served with 42nd Machine Gun Company in 14th (Light) Division.] Transferred back to Princess Victoria's (Royal Irish Fusiliers) (renumbered 43305) and joined the 9th (Service) Battalion on 26 November 1916 with the draft of men from The London Regiment. 'D' Company. **Wounded** at the Battle of Langemarck 16 August 1917. Tried by Field General Court Martial on 16 August 1918 charged with *'when on active service using insubordinate language to his superior officer'*; found guilty and sentenced to ninety days Field Punishment Number 1. Transferred to the Class Z Reserve 10 February 1919. 1914-15 Star.

KNIGHT Private William Guy 41081. [Enlisted for service with cavalry. Posted to 2nd North Irish Horse, X Corps Cavalry Regiment (9980).] Joined the renamed 9th (North Irish Horse) Battalion from 36 Infantry Base Depot and transferred to Princess Victoria's (Royal Irish Fusiliers) in September/October 1917 (renumbered 41081).

KNIGHT Lance Sergeant William George Thomas 10461 & 7040311. Born in 1896 at Woking, Surrey. [Enlisted into Princess Victoria's (Royal Irish Fusiliers) as a regular soldier 19 July 1910, aged 14. Served with the 1st Battalion. To France 10 October 1916. Evacuated to hospital in England 14 December 1916.] To France 3 June 1917 and joined the 9th (Service) Battalion. **Wounded** by a gunshot to the right knee 20 August 1918 and evacuated to hospital 27 August 1918. Continued to serve with Princess Victoria's (Royal Irish Fusiliers) (renumbered 7040311). Discharged 30 May 1936. Died at Surrey in 1958, aged 62.

KNIPE Private Thomas 14392. Enlisted September 1914. To France with 36th (Ulster) Division in October 1915. Transferred to the Class Z Reserve 15 April 1919. 1914-15 Star.

KNOWLES Corporal Arthur 42080. [Enlisted into the Army Service Corps (694980).] Transferred to Princess Victoria's (Royal Irish Fusiliers) 8 May 1918 (renumbered 42080) and joined the 9th (North Irish Horse) Battalion. [Part of the draft transferred on 19 June 1918 to The Royal Irish Rifles (renumbered 45850). Posted to the 1st Battalion, The Royal Irish Rifles.]

KNOX Private John 20367. From Glasgow. Enlisted 7 May 1915 and joined the 9th (Service) Battalion with the draft of men from The Royal Inniskilling Fusiliers who transferred to Princess Victoria's (Royal Irish Fusiliers) on 30 June 1915. To France with 36th (Ulster) Division in October 1915. **Wounded** during the attack at Hamel 1 July 1916. Discharged as no longer physically fit for war service due to wounds 16 January 1918. Silver War Badge, number 314844. 1914-15 Star.

KNOX Private W 41342. [Enlisted in September 1914 into the North Irish Horse (1212). To France 1 May 1915. Served with 2nd North Irish Horse, X Corps Cavalry Regiment.] Joined the renamed 9th (North Irish Horse) Battalion from 36 Infantry Base Depot and transferred to Princess Victoria's (Royal Irish Fusiliers) in September/October 1917 (renumbered 41342). [Transferred to the Army Ordnance Corps (renumbered 052894).] 1914-15 Star.

KRAFTCHICK Private Segmund 45816. From London. Joined the 9th (North Irish Horse)

Battalion, Princess Victoria's (Royal Irish Fusiliers) with the draft of men from The London Regiment in April 1918.

KYLE Private Andrew 17396. Born 22 February 1884. From Ballymacarrett, Belfast. A brass moulder. Enlisted into the 9th (Service) Battalion 9 December 1914. To France with 36th (Ulster) Division in October 1915. To the field ambulance injured (shoulder) 2 February 1916. **Wounded** (shell shock and injured back) during the attack at Hamel 1 July 1916. Rejoined the 9th (Service) Battalion 16 July 1916. To 36 Infantry Base Depot 7 August 1917 for transfer to the Class W Reserve as a munitions worker. To England 16 August 1917. Recalled 22 April 1918. Joined the 3rd (Reserve) Battalion 1 May 1918. To 36 Infantry Base Depot 10 June 1918 and rejoined the 9th (North Irish Horse) Battalion. **Wounded** by a gunshot to the right wrist during the attack at Vijfwegen 30 September 1918. Treated at 32nd Stationary Hospital and evacuated to hospital in England. Transferred to the Class Z Reserve 27 January 1919. 1914-15 Star.

LACEY Corporal John W 24817. Enlisted in September 1916. Posted to the 9th (Service) Battalion. 'D' Company. **Wounded** during the retreat from St Quentin 21-28 March 1918. [Transferred to 5th (Service) Battalion, The Royal Irish Regiment (Pioneers) in the Light Division in the British Army of the Rhine in March/June 1919 (renumbered 41313).]

LADLEY Private Archibald 23181. Born in 1897 at Castletown, County Louth. [Enlisted in November 1915 and joined the 8th (Service) Battalion in 49th Brigade, 16th (Irish) Division.] Joined the 9th (North Irish Horse) Battalion when the 7th/8th (Service) Battalion was disbanded in February 1918. 'D' Company. **Wounded** during the retreat from St Quentin 21-28 March 1918.

LAIDLAW Private Robert 42523. [Served previously with The Royal Irish Rifles (173).] Transferred at the Base Depot to Princess Victoria's (Royal Irish Fusiliers) 14 September 1918 (renumbered 42523) and joined the 9th (North Irish Horse) Battalion 22 September 1918. [Transferred to The Royal Irish Regiment (renumbered 18982).]

LAKE Private Henry John 42237. Born in 1890. From South Acton, London. [Enlisted 23 March 1915 into the Army Service Corps (T4/059577 – Horsekeeper). To France 4 April 1915 and attached to 3rd Guards Brigade.] To 'A' Infantry Base Depot 6 May 1918. Sentenced to ten days Field Punishment Number 1 for drunkenness 10 May 1918. Transferred to Princess Victoria's (Royal Irish Fusiliers) 8 May 1918 (renumbered 42237) and joined the 9th (North Irish Horse) Battalion 8 June 1918. **Wounded** by shrapnel to the right arm 15 July 1918 and evacuated to hospital in England. Joined the 3rd (Reserve) Battalion 10 December 1918. Transferred to the Class Z Reserve 18 March 1919. 1914-15 Star.

LALLY Private George 42509. Born in 1900 at Enniskillen, County Fermanagh. [Enlisted 2 May 1918 into The Royal Irish Rifles (22569) and joined the 3rd (Reserve) Battalion, giving his age as nineteen years and eight months.] To 'A' infantry Base Depot France 7 September 1918. Transferred to Princess Victoria's (Royal Irish Fusiliers) (renumbered 42509) and joined the 9th (North Irish Horse) Battalion 22 September 1918. Initially declared **missing and wounded** during the attack at Vijfwegen on 30 September or 1 October 1918, he was subsequently recorded as **killed in action** on 30 September 1918, aged 18.

LAMB Private Jackson 22141 & 7040678. From Richhill, County Armagh. Enlisted 18 October 1915. To France 8 July 1916 and joined the 9th (Service) Battalion. Evacuated to hospital in England 7 February 1917. To France 27 July 1917 and rejoined the 9th (Service) Battalion. Re-enlisted 8 March 1919 for Regular Army service with Princess Victoria's (Royal Irish Fusiliers) (renumbered 7040678). Discharged 5 April 1912, medically unfit for further service.

LAMB Private Wesley 14400. From Portadown, County Armagh. A clerk. Enlisted September 1914. To France with 36th (Ulster) Division in October 1915. [Transferred to the Labour Corps (renumbered 231031).] Transferred to the Class Z Reserve 12 August 1919. 1914-15 Star.

LAMBERT Sergeant Charles 40015. Joined the 9th (Service) Battalion, Princess Victoria's (Royal Irish Fusiliers) with the draft of men from The Prince of Wales's Own (West Yorkshire Regiment) on 12 December 1916.

LAMOND Private Robert Thomas George Osmond 43332. Born 20 April 1890. From Walthamstow, London. A stock-keeper. [Enlisted 27 June 1916 into The London Regiment (6707). To 8 Infantry Base Depot 10 November 1916 for service with 1/7th (City of London) Battalion, The London Regiment.] Attached to the 9th (Service) Battalion, Princess Victoria's (Royal Irish Fusiliers)

26 November 1916. 'C' Company. Discharged from the Territorial Force, re-enlisted and transferred to Princess Victoria's (Royal Irish Fusiliers) in March 1917 (renumbered 43332). **Wounded** by a gunshot to the face during the retreat from St Quentin 27 March 1918. Treated at 9th General Hospital and 2nd Convalescent Depot. Did not rejoin the 9th (North Irish Horse) Battalion. To hospital sick (pneumonia) April 1918. To hospital sick (pleurisy) June 1918 and evacuated to hospital in England. Treated at Endell Street Military Hospital, London. Joined the 3rd (Reserve) Battalion. Lance Corporal 7 May 1919. Posted to the 2nd Battalion 26 July 1919. Transferred to the Class Z Reserve 23 September 1919. Died at Chichester, Sussex in 1958, aged 67.

LAMONT Private Alexander 41239. [Enlisted January 1915 into the North Irish Horse (1412). To France 8 November 1915. Served with 2nd North Irish Horse, X Corps Cavalry Regiment.] Joined the renamed 9th (North Irish Horse) Battalion from 36 Infantry Base Depot and transferred to Princess Victoria's (Royal Irish Fusiliers) in September/October 1917 (renumbered 41239). 'D' Company. **Missing** in the period 21-28 March 1918 during the retreat from St Quentin believed **captured**. Transferred to the Class Z Reserve 5 April 1919. 1914-15 Star.

LANDLES Private John 21763. From Berwick-upon-Tweed. Enlisted in October 1915. Posted to the 9th (Service) Battalion in May/June 1916. **Killed in action** during the attack at Hamel 1 July 1916.

LANFEAR Corporal Alfred 42267. Born 20 October 1877 at Eton Wick, Buckinghamshire. [Served with the Army Veterinary Corps (9719). Joined the Mediterranean Expeditionary Force 17 October 1915.] Transferred to Princess Victoria's (Royal Irish Fusiliers) 8 May 1918 (renumbered 42267) and joined the 9th (North Irish Horse) Battalion. Transferred to the Class Z Reserve 21 March 1919. 1914-15 Star. Died at Eton Wick, Buckinghamshire 2 May 1950, aged 72.

LAPPIN Private George 41163. [Enlisted in November 1914 into the Service Squadron, 6th (Inniskilling) Dragoons (UD/142). To France with 36th (Ulster) Division in October 1915. Served with 2nd North Irish Horse, X Corps Cavalry Regiment.] Joined the renamed 9th (North Irish Horse) Battalion from 36 Infantry Base Depot and transferred to Princess Victoria's (Royal Irish Fusiliers) in September/October 1917 (renumbered 41163). Transferred to the Class Z Reserve 16 March 1919. 1914-15 Star.

LAPPIN Private John 3481. From Belfast. Enlisted in 1915 into Princess Victoria's (Royal Irish Fusiliers) Special Reserve. Posted to the 9th (Service) Battalion. 'A' Company. **Wounded** at the Battle of Langemarck 16 August 1917.

LAPPIN Private John Joseph 18098. From Drumcree, Portadown, County Armagh. Member of Loyal Orange Lodge 20. Kilmagamish and Drumcree Company, 4th (Portadown) Battalion, Armagh Regiment, Ulster Volunteer Force. Enlisted into the 9th (Service) Battalion 17 February 1915. To France with 36th (Ulster) Division in October 1915. 'C' Company. Company runner during the attack at Hamel 1 July 1916, during which he was **wounded**. He was initially reported to his family as **missing**. Evacuated to hospital at Norwich. [Transferred to the Army Veterinary Corps (SE/35215) 16 April 1918.] Discharged as no longer physically fit for war service due to wounds 6 January 1919, aged 23. Silver War Badge, number B77740. 1914-15 Star.

LARKIN Private John 20580. Born in 1900 at Shankill, County Armagh. Lived at Lurgan, County Armagh. Enlisted 26 July 1915, aged 15, and joined the 12th (Reserve) Battalion, The Royal Inniskilling Fusiliers. Transferred to Princess Victoria's (Royal Irish Fusiliers) on 30 June 1915 (renumbered 20580) and joined the 9th (Service) Battalion. Joined the 10th (Reserve) Battalion 23 September 1915. To 36 Infantry Base Depot 13 February 1916 and rejoined the 9th (Service) Battalion 23 February 1916. To 109th Field Ambulance sick (incontinence) and treated at 2nd General Hospital before being evacuated to hospital in England 8 April 1916. Discharged as no longer physically fit for war service due to sickness 24 November 1916. Silver War Badge, number 107180. **Died** at home in Garland Avenue, Lurgan, County Armagh of pulmonary tuberculosis on 25 March 1917, aged 17.

LARTER Private Arthur W 45810. Joined the 9th (North Irish Horse) Battalion, Princess Victoria's (Royal Irish Fusiliers) with the draft of men from The London Regiment in April 1918. Re-enlisted in 1919 for Regular Army service with The Suffolk Regiment (renumbered 70977, renumbered 5820964). Served with the 1st Battalion, The Suffolk Regiment in operations against the Moplah Rebellion in Malabar, Western India between September 1921 and February 1922. India General

Service Medal 1918-1962 with clasp 'Malabar 1921-22'. Subsequently lived in Islington, North London.

LAURENCE Private Herbert 40017. Joined the 9th (Service) Battalion, Princess Victoria's (Royal Irish Fusiliers) with the draft of men from The Prince of Wales's Own (West Yorkshire Regiment) on 12 December 1916.

LAVERTY Private Alexander 42485. [Served previously with The Royal Irish Rifles (His number, 20517, is also listed for Private L H Ross below).] Transferred at the Base Depot to Princess Victoria's (Royal Irish Fusiliers) 14 September 1918 (renumbered 42485) and joined the 9th (North Irish Horse) Battalion 22 September 1918. [Transferred to 5th (Service) Battalion, The Royal Irish Regiment (Pioneers) in the Light Division in the British Army of the Rhine in March/June 1919 (renumbered 41411).]

LAVERTY Private Samuel 16427 & 7042608. From Portadown, County Armagh. Enlisted into the 9th (Service) Battalion in November 1914. To France with 36th (Ulster) Division in October 1915. **Wounded** during the attack at Hamel 1 July 1916. [Transferred to the Royal Flying Corps (renumbered 146276).] 1914-15 Star. Transferred to the Section D Army Reserve, Princess Victoria's (Royal Irish Fusiliers) (renumbered 7042608).

LAVERY Private Henry 26841. From Glasgow. [Enlisted 2 March 1916 and transferred to the Army Reserve. Mobilised 16 February 1917 and joined the 4th (Extra Reserve) Battalion. To 36 Infantry Base Depot, France 10 May 1917 and joined the 7th/8th (Service) Battalion 15 May 1917. Tried by Field General Court Martial on 26 January 1918 charged with: *'Conduct to the prejudice of good order and military discipline; causing the death of a comrade by negligently handling his rifle.'* Found guilty and sentenced to twenty-eight days Field Punishment Number 1. (The dead soldier was 3444 Private John Donnelly.)] Joined the 9th (North Irish Horse) Battalion when the 7th/8th (Service) Battalion was disbanded in February 1918. **Missing** in the period 11-18 April 1918 in the actions between Wulverghem and Kemmel; subsequently declared **killed in action** 19 April 1918, aged 32.

LAVERY Sergeant Michael 23162. [Enlisted in November 1915 and joined the 8th (Service) Battalion in 49th Brigade, 16th (Irish) Division. **Wounded** in 1916.] Joined the 9th (North Irish Horse) Battalion when the 7th/8th (Service) Battalion was disbanded in February 1918.

LAVERY Second Corporal Robert 20337. Born in 1875 at Lurgan, County Armagh. From Glasgow. A clerk with the Caledonian Railway Company. [Enlisted 31 May 1915 into the 12th (Reserve) Battalion, The Royal Inniskilling Fusiliers (23640).] Transferred to Princess Victoria's (Royal Irish Fusiliers) 30 June 1915 (renumbered 20337) and joined the 9th (Service) Battalion. To France with 36th (Ulster) Division in October 1915. Lance Corporal 29 November 1915. [Transferred to the Corps of Royal Engineers 20 June 1917 (renumbered 343098) and posted to 232nd Army Troops Company.] Transferred to the Class Z Reserve. 1914-15 Star.

LAW Private David 41420. From Belfast. A clerk. [Enlisted on 1 November 1915 into the North Irish Horse (1771). To France 18 May 1916 and joined 'A' Squadron. Served with 2nd North Irish Horse, X Corps Cavalry Regiment.] Joined the renamed 9th (North Irish Horse) Battalion from 36 Infantry Base Depot and transferred to Princess Victoria's (Royal Irish Fusiliers) in September/October 1917 (renumbered 41420). **Wounded** 12 April 1918 in the actions between Wulverghem and Kemmel and evacuated to hospital in England. Transferred to the Class Z Reserve 24 March 1919.

LAW Private James 14422. From Caledon, County Armagh. Enlisted 21 September 1914. To France with 36th (Ulster) Division in October 1915. **Wounded** during the attack at Hamel 1 July 1916. [Transferred to the Royal Army Medical Corps (renumbered 206924).] Discharged as no longer physically fit for war service due to wounds 4 March 1918. Silver War Badge, number 336277. 1914-15 Star.

LAW Private Robert Matthew 41082. Born in 1892 at Carn, Milltown, County Fermanagh. A farmer's son. [Enlisted in October 1914 into the Service Squadron, 6th (Inniskilling) Dragoons (UD/13). Served with 2nd North Irish Horse, X Corps Cavalry Regiment.] Joined the renamed 9th (North Irish Horse) Battalion from 36 Infantry Base Depot and transferred to Princess Victoria's (Royal Irish Fusiliers) in September/October 1917 (renumbered 41082). 'A' Company. **Wounded** during the retreat from St Quentin 21-28 March 1918. After the war he emigrated to Toronto,

Canada and became a police officer.

LAWLEY Private Edward 40016. From Leeds. [Enlisted into The Prince of Wales's Own (West Yorkshire Regiment) (33932).] Transferred to Princess Victoria's (Royal Irish Fusiliers) 30 November 1916 (renumbered 40016) and joined the 9th (Service) Battalion 12 December 1916. **Missing** in the period 11-18 April 1918 in the actions between Wulverghem and Kemmel; subsequently declared **killed in action** 19 April 1918, aged 35.

LAWLOR Private John 11946. [Enlisted 1 September 1914 and joined the 7th (Service) Battalion in 49th Brigade, 16th (Irish) Division.] Joined the 9th (North Irish Horse) Battalion when the 7th/8th (Service) Battalion was disbanded in February 1918. 'B' Company. Separated from the 9th (North Irish Horse) Battalion in the period 21-28 March 1918 during the retreat from St Quentin; rejoined 3 April 1918. **Wounded**. Discharged as no longer physically fit for war service due to wounds 16 March 1919. Silver War Badge, number B162491.

LAWRENCE Private Richard Charles 43373. [Enlisted into The London Regiment (3101). Posted to the 1/7th (City of London) Battalion, The London Regiment.] Attached to the 9th (Service) Battalion, Princess Victoria's (Royal Irish Fusiliers) 26 November 1916. Discharged from the Territorial Force, re-enlisted and transferred to Princess Victoria's (Royal Irish Fusiliers) in March/April 1917 (renumbered 43373).

LAWRENCE Private William Herbert 42155. Born in 1881. Lived in Chichester, Sussex. A stableman. [Enlisted 10 December 1915 and transferred to the Army Reserve. Mobilised 22 June 1917 and joined the Army Veterinary Corps (29986). To France 5 September 17. Suffered from lack of sleep after being bombed by aircraft at Bapaume on the night of 2/3 December 1917 and admitted to hospital 8 December 1917. Discharged from hospital 2 April 1918.] Transferred to Princess Victoria's (Royal Irish Fusiliers) 5 May 1918 (renumbered 42155) and joined the 9th (North Irish Horse) Battalion 8 June 1918. Declared **missing** after the raid on Shoddy Farm near Meulenhouck on 22 July 1918 and subsequently declared **killed in action** on that date, aged 34.

LAWSON Private Herbert James 24010. Born in 1897 at Ballyhalbert, County Down. Enlisted 24 February 1916. Posted to the 9th (Service) Battalion. Discharged as no longer physically fit for war service due to sickness 27 June 1917. Silver War Badge, number 198321.

LAY Lance Corporal Albert 42264. [Enlisted into the Army Service Corps (T4/071814, Driver). Served with 2nd Company, 29th Division Train at Gallipoli from May 1915 and 247th Company, attached to 1/3rd East Lancashire Field Ambulance in 42nd (East Lancashire) Division.] Transferred to Princess Victoria's (Royal Irish Fusiliers) 8 May 1918 (renumbered 42264) and joined the 9th (North Irish Horse) Battalion. Transferred to the Class Z Reserve 28 February 1919. 1914-15 Star.

LAY Lance Corporal Henry Leonard 20781. [Enlisted in July 1915 and joined the 5th (Service) Battalion in the Mediterranean Expeditionary Force in October 1915. Posted to the 7th/8th (Service) Battalion in 49th Brigade, 16th (Irish) Division.] Joined the 9th (North Irish Horse) Battalion when the 7th/8th (Service) Battalion was disbanded in February 1918. 'C' Company. Separated from the 9th (North Irish Horse) Battalion in the period 21-28 March 1918 during the retreat from St Quentin; rejoined 2 April 1918. Transferred to the Class Z Reserve. 1914-15 Star.

LEANEY Corporal Reginald Alfred 23877. Born in 1893 at Lambeth, London. Worked as a servant for William DeSalis Filgate at Lissrenny, County Louth. Enlisted in January 1916. Posted to the 9th (Service) Battalion. 'D' Company. **Wounded** at the Battle of Langemarck 16 August 1917. [Transferred to 5th (Service) Battalion, The Royal Irish Regiment (Pioneers) in the Light Division in the British Army of the Rhine in March/June 1919 (renumbered 41315).] Died in Dublin in 1944, aged 50.

LEARY Lance Corporal John Frazer 16119. From Killeevan, Clones, County Monaghan. Enlisted into the 9th (Service) Battalion in October 1914. To France with 36th (Ulster) Division in October 1915. **Killed in action** during the attack at Hamel 1 July 1916, aged 23. 1914-15 Star.

LEARY Private James Joseph 18253. From Kilcorran, Clones, County Monaghan. Enlisted into the 9th (Service) Battalion in February/March 1915. To France with 36th (Ulster) Division in October 1915. **Died of wounds** 4 December 1916, aged 20. 1914-15 Star.

LEATHERBY Sergeant Reuben Henry 43438. Born in 1885. From Yiewsley, Middlesex. [Enlisted 19 July 1915 into The London Regiment.] To France and joined 36 Infantry Base Depot 29 March

1918. Transferred to Princess Victoria's (Royal Irish Fusiliers) 2 April 1918 (renumbered 43438) and joined the 9th (North Irish Horse) Battalion 4 April 1918. **Wounded**. Discharged as no longer physically fit for war service due to wounds 15 October 1919. Silver War Badge, number B322819. Died at Middlesex in 1949, aged 63.

LEBURN MM Private Leonard Edwin 42447. Born 29 September 1897 at Portsea Island, Hampshire. From London. [Enlisted into The London Regiment (7396). Posted to the 1/12th (County of London) Battalion, The London Regiment (The Rangers). Transferred to The Royal Irish Rifles (43643). Posted to the 13th (Service) Battalion, The Royal Irish Rifles (1st County Down).] Transferred at the Base Depot to Princess Victoria's (Royal Irish Fusiliers) 14 September 1918 (renumbered 42447) and joined the 9th (North Irish Horse) Battalion 22 September 1918. **MM** – Wulverghem 4 September 1918. After the war joined the civil service as a clerk. Died at London in 1988, aged 90.

LEE Private Archibald 41552. Born in 1889 at Lisnaskea, County Fermanagh. An engine driver. [Enlisted in October 1914 into the Service Squadron, 6th (Inniskilling) Dragoons (UD/61). To France with 36th (Ulster) Division in October 1915. Served with 2nd North Irish Horse, X Corps Cavalry Regiment.] Joined the renamed 9th (North Irish Horse) Battalion from 36 Infantry Base Depot and transferred to Princess Victoria's (Royal Irish Fusiliers) in September/October 1917 (renumbered 41552). 'D' Company. **Captured** in the period 21-28 March 1918 during the retreat from St Quentin. Transferred to the Class Z Reserve 18 April 1919. 1914-15 Star. His brother, Private Francis Lee, served with The Royal Inniskilling Fusiliers.

LEE Private George 41127. [Enlisted in April 1915 into the Service Squadron, 6th (Inniskilling) Dragoons (UD/243). To France with 36th (Ulster) Division in October 1915. Served with 2nd North Irish Horse, X Corps Cavalry Regiment.] Joined the renamed 9th (North Irish Horse) Battalion from 36 Infantry Base Depot and transferred to Princess Victoria's (Royal Irish Fusiliers) in September/October 1917 (renumbered 41127). Transferred to the Class Z Reserve 20 March 1919. 1914-15 Star.

LEE Private John William 40064. From Manningham, York. Joined the 9th (Service) Battalion, Princess Victoria's (Royal Irish Fusiliers) with the draft of men from The Prince of Wales's Own (West Yorkshire Regiment) on 12 December 1916. **Wounded** at the Battle of Langemarck 16 August 1917. [Posted to the 11th (Service) Battalion. Served with the 5th/6th (Service) Battalion when the 11th (Service) Battalion was absorbed.]

LEE Private Mark 41642. Born in 1897 near Irvinestown, County Fermanagh. [Enlisted in October 1914 into the Service Squadron, 6th (Inniskilling) Dragoons (UD/42). To France with 36th (Ulster) Division in October 1915. To France with 36th (Ulster) Division in October 1915. Served with 2nd North Irish Horse, X Corps Cavalry Regiment.] Joined the renamed 9th (North Irish Horse) Battalion from 36 Infantry Base Depot and transferred to Princess Victoria's (Royal Irish Fusiliers) in September/October 1917 (renumbered 41642). 'B' Company. **Missing** in the period 21-28 March 1918 during the retreat from St Quentin and later declared **killed in action** on 29 March 1918, aged 20. 1914-15 Star.

LEE Private William 42505. [Enlisted 12 December 1915 into The London Regiment (6003). Joined the 2/22nd (County of London) Battalion, The London Regiment (The Queens). Transferred to The Royal Irish Rifles (renumbered 43912).] Transferred at the Base Depot to Princess Victoria's (Royal Irish Fusiliers) 14 September 1918 (renumbered 42505) and joined the 9th (North Irish Horse) Battalion 22 September 1918. **Wounded**. Discharged as no longer physically fit for war service due to wounds 20 May 1919. Silver War Badge, number B241031.

LEEMAN Private Albert 23195. Enlisted in November 1915. Posted to the 9th (Service) Battalion. 'C' Company. Battalion bomb carrier during the attack at Hamel on 1 July 1916, which he survived unwounded. [Transferred to The Royal Irish Regiment (renumbered 5737).]

LEEMAN Private Edward 14399. Enlisted September 1914. To France with 36th (Ulster) Division in October 1915. **Wounded** during the attack at Hamel 1 July 1916. [Transferred to the Labour Corps (renumbered 604296).] 1914-15 Star.

LEEMAN Private James 14423. Enlisted September 1914. To France with 36th (Ulster) Division in October 1915. Transferred to the Class Z Reserve 15 March 1919. 1914-15 Star.

LEEMAN Private Thomas 14394. From Portadown, County Armagh. Enlisted September 1914.

Discharged having made a mis-statement as to age on enlistment; soldier under 17 years of age at date of application for discharge 10 October 1914.

LEEMAN Private William James 14395. From Portadown, County Armagh. 4th (Portadown) Battalion, Armagh Regiment, Ulster Volunteer Force. Enlisted September 1914. To France to join 36th (Ulster) Division 17 November 1915. **Wounded** during the attack at Hamel 1 July 1916. **Wounded** twice more, including in October 1918. Transferred to the Class Z Reserve 26 February 1919. 1914-15 Star.

LEINSTER Private William George 41266. Born at Drumullan, County Cavan. From Lisburn, County Antrim. [Enlisted in April 1915 into the North Irish Horse (1469). Served with 2nd North Irish Horse, X Corps Cavalry Regiment.] Joined the renamed 9th (North Irish Horse) Battalion from 36 Infantry Base Depot and transferred to Princess Victoria's (Royal Irish Fusiliers) in September/October 1917 (renumbered 41266). **Missing** in the period 11-18 April 1918 in the actions between Wulverghem and Kemmel; subsequently declared **killed in action** 19 April 1918, aged 26. 1914-15 Star.

LENAGHAN Private James 41108. From Belfast. [Enlisted in November 1914 into the Service Squadron, 6th (Inniskilling) Dragoons (UD/143). To France with 36th (Ulster) Division in October 1915. Served with 2nd North Irish Horse, X Corps Cavalry Regiment.] Joined the renamed 9th (North Irish Horse) Battalion from 36 Infantry Base Depot and transferred to Princess Victoria's (Royal Irish Fusiliers) in September/October 1917 (renumbered 41108). 'D' Company. **Captured** in the period 21-28 March 1918 during the retreat from St Quentin. Transferred to the Class Z Reserve 21 March 1919. 1914-15 Star.

LENNON Private Alexander 18362. From Killylea, County Armagh. Enlisted into the 9th (Service) Battalion in March 1915. To France with 36th (Ulster) Division in October 1915. 'C' Company. **Wounded** during the attack at Hamel 1 July 1916. **Missing** at the Battle of Langemarck 16 August 1917 and later declared **killed in action** on that date. 1914-15 Star.

LENNON Private Arthur 14424. From Bleary, County Armagh. Enlisted September 1914. To France with 36th (Ulster) Division in October 1915. 'C' Company. Bangalore torpedo carrier during the attack at Hamel 1 July 1916, during which he was **killed in action**, aged 43. 1914-15 Star.

LEONARD Private William Thomas 16120. From County Monaghan. A postman. Enlisted into the 9th (Service) Battalion 25 September 1914. To France with 36th (Ulster) Division in October 1915. 'D' Company. **Wounded** at the Battle of Langemarck 16 August 1917. Discharged as no longer physically fit for war service due to wounds 20 August 1918, aged 38. Silver War Badge, number 437949. 1914-15 Star.

LESLIE Private William 24954. From Castledawson, County Londonderry. Enlisted in November 1916. Posted to the 9th (Service) Battalion. 'D' Company. **Missing** at the Battle of Langemarck 16 August 1917 and later declared **killed in action** on that date.

LESTER Private James 29535. [Enlisted 5 July 1916. Discharged or transferred. Re-enlisted into or transferred back to Princess Victoria's (Royal Irish Fusiliers) in March 1918 (renumbered 29535). Posted to the 1st Battalion.] Posted to the 9th (North Irish Horse) Battalion. **Wounded**. Discharged as no longer physically fit for war service due to wounds 21 August 1919. Silver War Badge, number B305333.

LESTER Sergeant Robert 14415. Enlisted September 1914. To France with 36th (Ulster) Division in October 1915. [Joined 108th Brigade Machine Gun Company in January 1916 (Private). Transferred to the Machine Gun Corps (renumbered 17794). Promoted Sergeant. **36th (Ulster) Division Certificate for Gallantry**. **MSM**. ***Croix de Guerre* (France)**.] 1914-15 Star.

LEWIS Private Andrew 41204. From Belfast. [Enlisted in January 1976 into the North Irish Horse (1376). To France with 'F' Squadron in 33rd Division 17 November 1915. Served with 2nd North Irish Horse, X Corps Cavalry Regiment.] Joined the renamed 9th (North Irish Horse) Battalion from 36 Infantry Base Depot and transferred to Princess Victoria's (Royal Irish Fusiliers) in September/October 1917 (renumbered 41204). 'D' Company. **Captured** in the period 21-28 March 1918 during the retreat from St Quentin. Transferred to the Class Z Reserve 26 March 1919. 1914-15 Star.

LEWIS Private George Alexander 41417. [Enlisted in May 1915 into the North Irish Horse (1569).

Served with 2nd North Irish Horse, X Corps Cavalry Regiment.] Joined the renamed 9th (North Irish Horse) Battalion from 36 Infantry Base Depot and transferred to Princess Victoria's (Royal Irish Fusiliers) in September/October 1917 (renumbered 41417). 'B' Company. **Missing** in the period 21-28 March 1918 during the retreat from St Quentin believed **captured**.

LEWIS Private James 17667. From Portadown, County Armagh. Enlisted into the 9th (Service) Battalion in December 1914/January 1915. To France with 36th (Ulster) Division in October 1915. 'A' Company. **Wounded** during the attack at Hamel 1 July 1916. **Captured** in the period 21-28 March 1918 during the retreat from St Quentin. 1914-15 Star.

LEWIS Lance Corporal William Achilles 41083. Born on 14 August 1894 at Newport, Monmouthshire. [Enlisted for service with cavalry (8647). Posted to 2nd North Irish Horse, X Corps Cavalry Regiment.] Joined the renamed 9th (North Irish Horse) Battalion from 36 Infantry Base Depot and transferred to Princess Victoria's (Royal Irish Fusiliers) in September/October 1917 (renumbered 41083). Died at Pontypridd, Mid-Glamorgan in 1981, aged 87.

LIGGETT Private George 24670. Born in 1893 at Portadown, County Armagh. A linen weaver. [Enlisted in July 1914 into Princess Victoria's (Royal Irish Fusiliers) Special Reserve (6130). Served with the 1st Battalion and discharged.] Re-enlisted 5 August 1916 (renumbered 24670). Posted to the 9th (Service) Battalion. **Wounded**. Discharged as no longer physically fit for war service due to wounds 8 July 1918, aged 25. Silver War Badge, number 415894.

LIMBERT Private William 40046. Born in 1896 at Leeds. A telephone operator. [Enlisted 14 June 1915 and joined 19th (Reserve) Battalion, The Prince of Wales's Own (West Yorkshire Regiment) (1463). To France and joined the 'Leeds Pals' - the 15th (Service) Battalion, The Prince of Wales's Own (West Yorkshire Regiment) (1st Leeds), 4 April 1916. **Wounded** by a gunshot to the right thigh on 1 July 1916 and evacuated to hospital in England. Treated at 2nd Southern General Hospital, Bristol until 31 August 1916. When recovered he joined the 3rd (Reserve) Battalion, The Prince of Wales's Own (West Yorkshire Regiment) 6 September 1916.] To France 29 November 1916. Transferred to Princess Victoria's (Royal Irish Fusiliers) (renumbered 40046) and joined the 9th (North Irish Horse) Battalion. 'A' Company. **Accidentally killed** at 4.00am on 23 May 1917, aged 20, when shot in the head by Private T L Colclough who fired his rifle when he was cleaning it. Lance Corporal E W G Linzey was wounded in the neck.

LINDSAY Private Albert 14427. Enlisted September 1914. To France with 36th (Ulster) Division in October 1915. Transferred to the Class Z Reserve 5 March 1919. 1914-15 Star.

LINDSAY Lance Corporal Alexander 42093. [Enlisted 11 December 1915 into the Army Veterinary Corps (16327).] Transferred to Princess Victoria's (Royal Irish Fusiliers) 8 May 1918 (renumbered 42093) and joined the 9th (North Irish Horse) Battalion. **Wounded**. Discharged as no longer physically fit for war service due to wounds 5 June 1919. Silver War Badge, number B242930.

LINDSAY Private Fred 14407. Enlisted September 1914. To France with 36th (Ulster) Division in October 1915. 'C' Company. Did not take part in the attack at Hamel on 1 July 1916. [Transferred to the Labour Corps (renumbered 231610).] Transferred to the Class Z Reserve 23 April 1919. 1914-15 Star.

LINDSAY Private Robert 23322. From Belfast. Enlisted in November 1915. Posted to the 9th (Service) Battalion. 'D' Company. **Wounded** at the Battle of Langemarck 16 August 1917. **Captured** in 1918.

LINDSAY Lance Corporal William 14412. Enlisted September 1914. To France with 36th (Ulster) Division in October 1915. 3 Section, 13 Platoon, 'D' Company. Transferred to the Class Z Reserve 14 April 1919. 1914-15 Star.

LINDSAY Private William 41084. From Letterbreen, County Fermanagh. [Enlisted in October 1914 into the Service Squadron, 6th (Inniskilling) Dragoons (UD/60). Served with 2nd North Irish Horse, X Corps Cavalry Regiment.] Joined the renamed 9th (North Irish Horse) Battalion from 36 Infantry Base Depot and transferred to Princess Victoria's (Royal Irish Fusiliers) in September/October 1917 (renumbered 41084). **Missing** in the period 11-18 April 1918 in the actions between Wulverghem and Kemmel; subsequently declared **killed in action** 19 April 1918, aged 31.

LINNELL Private Frederick William 43210. Born in 1895. From Sawley, Derbyshire. A baker. [Enlisted 23 November 1915 and transferred to the Army Reserve. Mobilised 15 February 1916 and joined the 3rd (Reserve) Battalion, The Sherwood Foresters (Nottinghamshire and Derbyshire Regiment) (35579).] To France 23 July 1916. Transferred to Princess Victoria's (Royal Irish Fusiliers) (renumbered 43210) and joined the 9th (Service) Battalion 31 August 1916. 'A' Company. To the field ambulance sick in December 1916 (dyspepsia) and in June 1917 (scabies). **Missing** at the Battle of Langemarck 16 August 1917 and later declared **killed in action** on that date, aged 22.

LINSELL Private Alfred J 22292. [Served with the 5th (Service) or 6th (Service) Battalion in the Mediterranean Expeditionary Force in Salonika from 6 November 1915.] 'C' Company. Believed **wounded** in the period 21-28 March 1918 during the retreat from St Quentin. [Transferred to the Royal Garrison Artillery (renumbered 39178).] 1914-15 Star.

LINTON Private Albin 20028. From Portadown, County Armagh. A gunsmith. Enlisted into the 9th (Service) Battalion 1 June 1915, aged 18. Discharged as no longer physically fit for war service due to sickness 26 February 1918. Silver War Badge, number 334282.

LINTON Private Alexander 41448. From Clough, County Down. [Enlisted in May 1916 into the North Irish Horse (2176). Served with 2nd North Irish Horse, X Corps Cavalry Regiment.] Joined the renamed 9th (North Irish Horse) Battalion from 36 Infantry Base Depot and transferred to Princess Victoria's (Royal Irish Fusiliers) in September/October 1917 (renumbered 41448). 'C' Company. **Captured** in the period 21-28 March 1918 during the retreat from St Quentin.

LINTON Private David Henry 14707 & 29059. From Camlough, County Armagh. Enlisted September 1914. To France with 36th (Ulster) Division in October 1915. **Wounded** during the attack at Hamel 1 July 1916. Discharged or transferred. Re-enlisted into or transferred back to Princess Victoria's (Royal Irish Fusiliers) in early-1918 (renumbered 29059). Posted to the 9th (North Irish Horse) Battalion. Transferred to the Class Z Reserve 1 March 1919. 1914-15 Star.

LINZEY Lance Corporal Edward William George 40039. Born on 13 November 1896 in Oxfordshire. [Enlisted into the 12th (Service) Battalion, The Prince of Wales's Own (West Yorkshire Regiment) (15521). To France 7 October 1915.] Transferred to Princess Victoria's (Royal Irish Fusiliers) 30 November 1916 (renumbered 40039) and joined the 9th (Service) Battalion 12 December 1916. 'A' Company. **Wounded** in the neck on 23 May 1917 by a shot accidentally fired by Private T L Colclough, which killed Private W Limbert. **Missing** in the period 21-28 March 1918 during the retreat from St Quentin believed **captured**. Transferred to the Class Z Reserve. Died in Eton, Buckinghamshire in 1973, aged 76.

LIPSETT Private William 41324. Born 7 May 1895 at Derrinloughan, County Leitrim. A farmer. [Enlisted in November 1913 into the North Irish Horse (879). To France 20 August 1914 with 'C' Squadron as 5th Division Cavalry and then as GHQ Troops. Served with 2nd North Irish Horse, X Corps Cavalry Regiment.] Joined the renamed 9th (North Irish Horse) Battalion from 36 Infantry Base Depot and transferred to Princess Victoria's (Royal Irish Fusiliers) in September/October 1917 (renumbered 41324). 1914 Star and clasp. Served with the Ulster Special Constabulary Class 'B' from 1920 and with Class 'A' from 27 February 1922 in 1 Platoon, Killkeel, County Down. Joined the Royal Ulster Constabulary 1 August 1922 and served in Londonderry. Retired from the Royal Ulster Constabulary 4 October 1954. Defence Medal 1945. Police Long Service & Good Conduct Medal. Settled with his family in Waterlooville, Hampshire where he died on 7 November 1983, aged 88.

LIVINGSTON Warrant Officer Class II Samuel James 8489 & 7040141. From Seagoe, County Armagh. A groom. [Enlisted into Princess Victoria's (Royal Irish Fusiliers) as a regular soldier 19 July 1904. Served with the 2nd Battalion.] To France 15 June 1916 and joined the 9th (Service) Battalion 20 June 1916. Company Sergeant Major. [Posted to the 1st Battalion. **Wounded** by a gunshot to the shoulder in the period 21-28 March 1918 during the retreat from St Quentin and evacuated to hospital in England.] Continued to serve after the war (renumbered 7040141). Discharged 31 August 1921. Lived at Portadown.

LIVINGSTON Private William 14410. Enlisted 5 September 1914. To France with 36th (Ulster) Division in October 1915. 'C' Company. Battalion bomb carrier during the attack at Hamel 1 July 1916, which he survived unwounded. Discharged as no longer physically fit for war service due to sickness 4 December 1916. Silver War Badge, number 100511. 1914-15 Star.

LIVINGSTON Private William 23190. Enlisted 23 November 1915. Posted to the 9th (Service) Battalion. 'C' Company. To hospital mid-1916 and did not take part in the attack at Hamel on 1 July 1916. Discharged as surplus to military requirements, not having suffered impairment since entry into the service, 11 January 1919. Silver War Badge, number B108573 (note: the Silver War Badge roll records his number erroneously as 23199).

LIVINGSTONE Private Dominick 24692. Born in 1897 at Shankill, Belfast. Enlisted 16 August 1916 and joined the 4th (Extra Reserve) Battalion. To France 20 December 1917 and posted to the 7th/8th (Service) Battalion but did not join. Joined the 9th (North Irish Horse) Battalion when the 7th/8th (Service) Battalion was disbanded in February 1918. 'B' Company. **Killed in action** by shellfire at Poperinghe railway station 9 April 1918.

LLOYD Sergeant Alfred 8754. [Enlisted into Princess Victoria's (Royal Irish Fusiliers) as a regular soldier in 1904. To France with the 1st Battalion 22 August 1914. **Wounded** August 1914. Evacuated to hospitals in Cambridge and Aldershot. Served also with the 6th (Service) Battalion in the Mediterranean Expeditionary Force.] Posted to the 9th (North Irish Horse) Battalion. 'A' Company. **Missing** in the period 21-28 March 1918 during the retreat from St Quentin believed **captured**. 1914 Star. He emigrated to Canada in 1926. Brother of Private Thomas Lloyd. His brother, Private Benjamin Lloyd (6031), was killed in action on 3 May 1917 at the Chemical Works, Roeux while serving with the 1st Battalion, Princess Victoria's (Royal Irish Fusiliers). He is buried in Crump Trench Cemetery. Two other brothers also served: John Henry Lloyd with the Army Service Corps and Private Joseph Lloyd (11470) Princess Victoria's (Royal Irish Fusiliers), who was wounded and lost an eye.

LLOYD Private Thomas 14404. From Tandragee, County Armagh. 4th (Portadown) Battalion, Armagh Regiment, Ulster Volunteer Force. Enlisted September 1914. To France with 36th (Ulster) Division in October 1915. **Killed in action** during the attack at Hamel 1 July 1916. 1914-15 Star. Brother of Sergeant Alfred Lloyd. His brother, Private Benjamin Lloyd (6031), was killed in action on 3 May 1917 at the Chemical Works, Roeux while serving with the 1st Battalion, Princess Victoria's (Royal Irish Fusiliers). Two other brothers also served: John Henry Lloyd with the Army Service Corps and Private Joseph Lloyd (11470) Princess Victoria's (Royal Irish Fusiliers), who was wounded and lost an eye.

LOCKER Private Charles 42273. [Enlisted into the Army Veterinary Corps (SE/31600).] Transferred to Princess Victoria's (Royal Irish Fusiliers) 8 May 1918 (renumbered 42273) and joined the 9th (North Irish Horse) Battalion.

LOCKHART DCM Sergeant John 41148. From Belfast. [Enlisted in November 1914 into the Service Squadron, 6th (Inniskilling) Dragoons (UD/133). To France with 36th (Ulster) Division in October 1915. Corporal 18 November 1915. Served with 2nd North Irish Horse, X Corps Cavalry Regiment.] Joined the renamed 9th (North Irish Horse) Battalion from 36 Infantry Base Depot and transferred to Princess Victoria's (Royal Irish Fusiliers) in September/October 1917 (renumbered 41148). 'B' Company. Sergeant 25 June 1918. **DCM** – Shoddy Farm raid 22 July 1918. ***Croix de Guerre* (Belgium)**. Transferred to the Class Z Reserve 8 March 1919. 1914-15 Star.

LOCKHART Private Robert 18559. From Tandragee, County Armagh. Enlisted into the 9th (Service) Battalion in April 1915. To France with 36th (Ulster) Division in October 1915. 'B' Company. **Wounded** during the attack at Hamel 1 July 1916. **Wounded** on the raid at La Petite Douve Farm on 12 October 1916 and **died of wounds** later that day, aged 26. 1914-15 Star.

LOCKHART Sergeant William 41543. Born 18 August 1888. A farmer from Jarrettspass, Newry, County Armagh. Member of Loyal Orange Lodge 225. [Enlisted in March 1909 into the North Irish Horse (346). To France 17 August 1914 with 'A' Squadron as GHQ Troops. Served with 2nd North Irish Horse, X Corps Cavalry Regiment.] Joined the renamed 9th (North Irish Horse) Battalion from 36 Infantry Base Depot and transferred to Princess Victoria's (Royal Irish Fusiliers) in September/October 1917 (renumbered 41543). **Captured** at Erches on 27 March 1918 during the retreat from St Quentin. Held in Gefangenlager 3, Camp III in Munster. 1914 Star. He returned to Jarrettspass after the war where he bought a farm, married (1922) and became an elder in the local church. Died 4 June 1964, aged 76. Buried at First Drumbanagher and Jarrettspass Presbyterian Church.

LOGAN Lance Corporal Charles Victor 22991. Born in 1896 at Newry, County Down. From Portadown, County Armagh. Enlisted in November 1915. Posted to the 9th (Service) Battalion. **Captured**. After the war he emigrated to Canada and worked as a ropemaker. He returned to Portadown with his family in 1934.

LOGAN Private John Wilson 41308. From Carrickfergus, County Antrim. Worked in the drapery business. [Enlisted in may 1915 into the North Irish Horse (1652). Served with 2nd North Irish Horse, X Corps Cavalry Regiment.] Joined the renamed 9th (North Irish Horse) Battalion from 36 Infantry Base Depot and transferred to Princess Victoria's (Royal Irish Fusiliers) in September/October 1917 (renumbered 41308). 'C' Company. **Missing** in the period 21-28 March 1918 during the retreat from St Quentin believed **captured**.

LOGAN Corporal Simon 41358. Commissioned into Princess Victoria's (Royal Irish Fusiliers) - see Appendix 5.

LOGUE Corporal Hugh 27818. Enlisted into/transferred to Princess Victoria's (Royal Irish Fusiliers) in July 1917. Posted to the 9th (North Irish Horse) Battalion.

LOMAS Private Thomas 42147. [Enlisted into the Army Veterinary Corps (19944).] Transferred to Princess Victoria's (Royal Irish Fusiliers) 8 May 1918 (renumbered 42147) and joined the 9th (North Irish Horse) Battalion.

LONEY Private Alfred 20027. Born at Richhill, County Armagh. From Tandragee, County Armagh. Member of Loyal Orange Lodge 371. Enlisted into the 9th (Service) Battalion in May/June 1915. To France with 36th (Ulster) Division in October 1915. 'B' Company. **Killed in action** during the attack at Hamel 1 July 1916, aged 21. 1914-15 Star.

LONEY Private Osmond Percy (Ossie) 17127. From Richhill, County Armagh. Enlisted into the 9th (Service) Battalion 27 November 1914. To France with 36th (Ulster) Division in October 1915. **Wounded** (lost an eye) during the attack at Hamel 1 July 1916. Discharged as no longer physically fit for war service due to wounds 28 December 1917, aged 22. Silver War Badge, number 296225. 1914-15 Star.

LONG Private Edward 14417. From, Lurgan, County Armagh. Enlisted September 1914. Did not serve overseas with 36th (Ulster) Division. Discharged as no longer physically fit for war service due to sickness 24 March 1916, aged 25. Silver War Badge, number 508789.

LONG Lance Corporal George 14397. Born in 1872 at Lurgan, County Armagh. A partner in a plumbing company (Messrs John Long & Sons). Armagh Regiment, Ulster Volunteer Force. Enlisted September 1914, aged 42. To France with 36th (Ulster) Division in October 1915. **Wounded** in the arm by shrapnel at Hamel in February 1916 and evacuated to hospital in England. [Posted to the 2nd Garrison Battalion in Salonika.] 1914-15 Star.

LONG Private George 41555. [Enlisted 9 September 1914 into the North Irish Horse (1193). To France 2 June 1915. Served with 2nd North Irish Horse, X Corps Cavalry Regiment.] Joined the renamed 9th (North Irish Horse) Battalion from 36 Infantry Base Depot and transferred to Princess Victoria's (Royal Irish Fusiliers) in September/October 1917 (renumbered 41555). Discharged as no longer physically fit for war service due to sickness 17 June 1918, aged 22. Silver War Badge, number 387960. 1914-15 Star.

LONG Private James 19888. From Lurgan, County Armagh. Enlisted into the 9th (Service) Battalion in May 1915. To France with 36th (Ulster) Division in October 1915. 'C' Company. **Killed in action** during the attack at Hamel 1 July 1916, aged 19. 1914-15 Star.

LONG MM Sergeant John Ernest 43464. From Clapham. [Enlisted into The London Regiment (2928). To France 15 March 1915 and posted to the 1/24th (County of London) Battalion, The London Regiment (The Queen's).] To France and joined 36 Infantry Base Depot 29 March 1918. Transferred to Princess Victoria's (Royal Irish Fusiliers) 2 April 1918 (renumbered 43464) and joined the 9th (North Irish Horse) Battalion 4 April 1918. **MM** – Wulverghem 4 September 1918. Disembodied 6 April 1919. Re-enlisted into The London Regiment Territorial Force (renumbered 2928 Sergeant, renumbered 6779573). 1914-15 Star.

LONGHEED Private Joseph 17409. See Private Joseph Lougheed below.

LORIMER Private John 41343. [Enlisted in August 1916 into the North Irish Horse (2232). Served with 2nd North Irish Horse, X Corps Cavalry Regiment.] Joined the renamed 9th (North Irish

Horse) Battalion from 36 Infantry Base Depot and transferred to Princess Victoria's (Royal Irish Fusiliers) in September/October 1917 (renumbered 41343). [Transferred to 5th (Service) Battalion, The Royal Irish Regiment (Pioneers) in the Light Division in the British Army of the Rhine in March/June 1919 (renumbered 41317).]

LOUDAN Private Robert 14411. Enlisted September 1914. To France with 36th (Ulster) Division in October 1915. Transferred to the Class Z Reserve 1 March 1919. 1914-15 Star.

LOUGHEED Private George 20651. Born in 1894 at Dungarvan, County Waterford. From Dunaweel, Killeshandra, County Cavan. A gamekeeper. Enlisted into the 9th (Service) Battalion in July 1915. 'C' Company. Lewis gun ammunition carrier during the attack at Hamel 1 July 1916, during which he was **wounded**. [Posted to the 1st Garrison Battalion and served in India and Burma.] Brother of Private Joseph Lougheed. His brother, Corporal Robert Lougheed, was killed in action on 12 May 1915 serving with the 1st Battalion, The Prince of Wales's Leinster Regiment (Royal Canadians).

LOUGHEED Private Joseph 17409. Born in 1892 at County Monaghan. From Dunaweel, Killeshandra, County Cavan. A gamekeeper. Enlisted into the 9th (Service) Battalion in November/December 1914. 'C' Company. **Killed in action** during the attack at Hamel 1 July 1916. He is recorded by the Commonwealth War Graves Commission as Private Joseph Longheed. Brother of Private George Lougheed. His brother, Corporal Robert Lougheed, was killed in action on 12 May 1915 serving with the 1st Battalion, The Prince of Wales's Leinster Regiment (Royal Canadians).

LOUGHLIN Lance Corporal Daniel 10100. [Enlisted into Princess Victoria's (Royal Irish Fusiliers) as a regular soldier 21 October 1908. To France with the 2nd Battalion 19 December 1914. Posted to the 7th (Service) Battalion in 49th Brigade, 16th (Irish) Division.] Joined the 9th (North Irish Horse) Battalion when the 7th/8th (Service) Battalion was disbanded in February 1918. 'A' Company. **Missing** in the period 21-28 March 1918 during the retreat from St Quentin believed **captured**. Discharged as no longer physically fit for war service due to sickness 5 February 1919. Silver War Badge, number B245849. 1914-15 Star.

LOUTH Private Francis 6207. [Enlisted on 28 August 1914 into Princess Victoria's (Royal Irish Fusiliers) Special Reserve. To France 6 April 1915 and joined the 2nd Battalion. Posted to the 6th (Service) Battalion.] Posted to the 9th (Service) Battalion. Evacuated to hospital in England wounded or sick on more than one occasion. Discharged as surplus to military requirements having suffered impairment since entry into the service 8 March 1919. Silver War Badge, number B256448. 1914-15 Star.

LOWE Private Thomas 14406. From Lurgan, County Armagh. Enlisted September 1914. To France with 36th (Ulster) Division in October 1915. **Wounded** during the attack at Hamel 1 July 1916. Discharged as no longer physically fit for war service due to wounds 14 December 1918, aged 27. Silver War Badge, number 263381. 1914-15 Star.

LOWTHER Private Matthew 41382. [Enlisted into the 6th (Inniskilling) Dragoons (21106). Served with 2nd North Irish Horse, X Corps Cavalry Regiment.] Joined the renamed 9th (North Irish Horse) Battalion from 36 Infantry Base Depot and transferred to Princess Victoria's (Royal Irish Fusiliers) in September/October 1917 (renumbered 41382).

LUCAS Private Joseph 41238. [Enlisted 30 December 1914 into the North Irish Horse (1364). To France with 'F' Squadron in 33rd Division 17 November 1915. Served with 2nd North Irish Horse, X Corps Cavalry Regiment.] Joined the renamed 9th (North Irish Horse) Battalion from 36 Infantry Base Depot and transferred to Princess Victoria's (Royal Irish Fusiliers) in September/October 1917 (renumbered 41238). [Transferred to the Tank Corps (renumbered 304878) 28 December 1917 and posted for training to the Tank Corps Depot, at Bovington near Wareham, Dorset. Returned to France with the Tank Corps. **Wounded** in the leg and evacuated to hospital in England.] Discharged as no longer physically fit for war service due to wounds 14 March 1919. Silver War Badge, number B156894.

LUCAS DCM, MM Warrant Officer Class II Robert 14414. Born at Loughgall, 8 January 1883. Farmer and postman. 4th (Portadown) Battalion, Armagh Regiment, Ulster Volunteer Force. Enlisted September 1914. To France with 36th (Ulster) Division in October 1915. One of the best shots in the 9th (Service) Battalion. 'C' Company. Battalion Scout Sergeant at Hamel 1 July 1916 –

MM. Promoted Company Sergeant Major vice Turner. **DCM** – St Quentin March 1918. Discharged as no longer physically fit for war service due to sickness 11 December 1918. Silver War Badge, number B61015. 1914-15 Star. He worked as a chauffeur for a doctor in Belfast. Died in January 1951, aged 68. Buried in Belfast.

LUNN Private James 14409. From Lurgan, County Armagh. A shoe maker. 5th (Lurgan) Battalion, Armagh Regiment, Ulster Volunteer Force. Enlisted September 1914. To France with 36th (Ulster) Division in October 1915. 'C' Company. Did not take part in the attack at Hamel on 1 July 1916. **Wounded** by shrapnel to the right leg at the Battle of Langemarck 16 August 1917 and evacuated to hospital in England. Posted to the Irish Command Depot 9 February 1918. To 36 Infantry Base Depot 31 May 1918. [Joined the 1st Battalion 7 June 1918. 'B' Company.] Transferred to the Class Z Reserve 24 March 1919. 1914-15 Star. He was one of six brothers who served during the First World War: Rifleman Robert Lunn was wounded serving with the 6th (Service) Battalion, The Royal Irish Rifles and, having lost an arm, was discharged as unfit for further service due to wounds; Rifleman Edward Lunn was wounded three times serving with The Royal Irish Rifles and subsequently served with the Royal Garrison Artillery; Privates Joseph and Henry Lunn were wounded serving with Princess Victoria's (Royal Irish Fusiliers); Private Samuel Lunn was killed in action on 12 October 1916 serving with the 1st Battalion, Princess Victoria's (Royal Irish Fusiliers).

LUNN Private William 14396. Born at Shankill, County Armagh. A van man. 5th (Lurgan) Battalion, Armagh Regiment, Ulster Volunteer Force. Enlisted September 1914. Posted to the 10th (Reserve) Battalion 15 September 1915. Posted to the 3rd (Reserve) Garrison Battalion at Bere Island, Bantry Bay 29 August 1917. Transferred to The Royal Irish Regiment 5 October 1917 and joined the 1st Garrison Battalion, The Royal Irish Regiment in Egypt.] Transferred to the Class Z Reserve 18 April 1919.

LUNN Private William 14405. Born at Dromore, County Down. Lived in Scarva, County Down. Married (Catherine) with seven children. Previous service during the South African War. Worked with the Great Northern Railway. Armagh Regiment, Ulster Volunteer Force. Enlisted September 1914. To France with 36th (Ulster) Division in October 1915. **Killed in action** by shellfire at Hamel just prior to the attack on 1 July 1916, aged 41. His son, Private William James Lunn, attended his funeral at Hamel Military Cemetery. 1914-15 Star.

LUNN Private William James 16435. From Scarva, County Down. Enlisted into the 9th Royal Irish Fusiliers 3 November 1914. To France with 36th (Ulster) Division in October 1915. **Wounded**. Discharged as no longer physically fit for war service due to wounds 27 July 1918, aged 23. Silver War Badge, number 379051. 1914-15 Star. Son of Private William Lunn (14405). 1914-15 Star.

LUTTON Private Charles 14401. From Portadown, County Armagh. 4th (Portadown) Battalion, Armagh Regiment, Ulster Volunteer Force. An iron moulder. Enlisted September 1914. To France with 36th (Ulster) Division in October 1915. 'B' Company. One of the few men unwounded during the attack at Hamel 1 July 1916. **Wounded** at the Battle of Langemarck 16 August 1917. Transferred to the Class Z Reserve 22 March 1919. 1914-15 Star.

LUTTON Private George Elliott 14402. Commissioned into Princess Victoria's (Royal Irish Fusiliers) - see Appendix 5.

LYE Private Walter John Thomas 43322. Born in 1893 at London. Joined the 9th (Service) Battalion, Princess Victoria's (Royal Irish Fusiliers) with the draft of men from The London Regiment in November 1916. Died at London in 1966, aged 73.

LYMER Private Frank 42238. [Enlisted into the Army Service Corps (291219).] Transferred to Princess Victoria's (Royal Irish Fusiliers) 8 May 1918 (renumbered 42238) and joined the 9th (North Irish Horse) Battalion. [Transferred to 5th (Service) Battalion, The Royal Irish Regiment (Pioneers) in the Light Division in the British Army of the Rhine in March/June 1919 (renumbered 41318).]

LYNAS Private Edward 14416. Born on 10 July 1898 at Armagh, County Armagh. Employed as a baker. Enlisted September 1914, aged 15. To France with 36th (Ulster) Division in October 1915. **Wounded** by shellfire during the attack at Hamel 1 July 1916. Crawled back after four days in a water-filled shell-hole. [Transferred to the Army Service Corps (renumbered S/393427).] Transferred to the Class Z Reserve. 1914-15 Star. Chairman of the Old Comrades Association (Armagh Branch). Died at Armagh, County Armagh 5 November 60, aged 62. He was survived by seven sons; all serving in the Royal Navy, Royal Marines or Army. Brother of Private James Lynas.

LYNAS Private James 11741. Born 3 August 1894 at Armagh, County Armagh. [Enlisted in August 1914 and joined the 5th (Service) or 6th (Service) Battalion in 31st Brigade, 10th (Irish) Division.] Posted to the 9th (Service) Battalion. To France with 36th (Ulster) Division in October 1915. 'A' Company. **Wounded** at the Battle of Langemarck 16 August 1917. Transferred to the Class Z Reserve 24 May 1919. 1914-15 Star. After the war he served with the Royal Ulster Constabulary. Died at Armagh, County Armagh 25 November 1971, aged 77. Buried at St Mark's Church of Ireland Churchyard, Armagh. Brother of Private Edward Lynas.

LYNAS Private Samuel 18247. From Tandragee, County Armagh. Enlisted 18 February 1915 into the 9th (Service) Battalion. To France 17 November 1915 and rejoined the 9th (Service) Battalion. Discharged as no longer physically fit for war service due to sickness 13 April 1918, aged 37. Silver War Badge, number 343326. 1914-15 Star. Lived in Canada for eight years from 1927 before returning to Northern Ireland.

LYNCH Private Charles 20362. Enlisted in May/June 1915 and joined the 9th (Service) Battalion with the draft of men from The Royal Inniskilling Fusiliers who transferred to Princess Victoria's (Royal Irish Fusiliers) on 30 June 1915. To France with 36th (Ulster) Division in October 1915. 'A' Company. Tried for *'drunkenness'* by Commander 108th Brigade on 21 April 1917.

LYNCH Private Michael 20592. From Knocklong, County Limerick. [Enlisted 14 June 1915 and joined the 8th (Service) Battalion in 49th Brigade, 16th (Irish) Division. To France 8 February 1916.] Joined the 9th (North Irish Horse) Battalion when the 7th/8th (Service) Battalion was disbanded in February 1918. 'A' Company. **Killed in action** 29 March 1918 during the retreat from St Quentin, aged 24.

LYNCH Private Patrick J 23690. Enlisted in January 1916. Posted to the 9th (Service) Battalion. 'B' Company. **Missing** in the period 21-28 March 1918 during the retreat from St Quentin believed **captured**.

LYNCH Private Robert 18713. Born at Clontibret, County Monaghan. From Castleshane, County Monaghan. Enlisted into the 9th (Service) Battalion in April 1915. To France with 36th (Ulster) Division in October 1915. **Wounded** on 1 July 1916 and **died of wounds** 2 July 1916. 1914-15 Star.

LYNCH Private Samuel George 41174. [Enlisted in October 1914 into the Service Squadron, 6th (Inniskilling) Dragoons (UD/85). To France with 36th (Ulster) Division in October 1915. Served with 2nd North Irish Horse, X Corps Cavalry Regiment.] Joined the renamed 9th (North Irish Horse) Battalion from 36 Infantry Base Depot and transferred to Princess Victoria's (Royal Irish Fusiliers) in September/October 1917 (renumbered 41174). Transferred to the Class Z Reserve 19 March 1919. 1914-15 Star.

LYNESS Private Frank 22969. Enlisted in November 1915. Posted to the 9th (Service) Battalion. 'D' Company. **Wounded** during the retreat from St Quentin 21-28 March 1918.

LYNESS Private John 14426. Enlisted September 1914. No record of deployment to France with 36th (Ulster) Division in October 1915. [Transferred to the Labour Corps (renumbered 394022).]

LYNESS Private Joseph 14421. From Lurgan, County Armagh. Enlisted September 1914. To France with 36th (Ulster) Division in October 1915. 'C' Company. Vickers gun ammunition carrier during the attack at Hamel 1 July 1916, during which he was **killed in action**, aged 21. 1914-15 Star.

LYNESS Private Thomas 14419. Born in 1893, at Drumgor, County Armagh. A farmer's son. Enlisted September 1914. To France with 36th (Ulster) Division in October 1915. 'C' Company. **Wounded** during the attack at Hamel on 1 July 1916. Served also in 'D' Company & the Battalion Transport. Transferred to the Class Z Reserve 20 March 1919. 1914-15 Star. Married Deborah Jones (sister of Private James Jones) in 1922. Worked as a quarryman and labourer in Lurgan until retirement in 1960. Died 1966, aged 73. His brother, Sergeant Archibald Lyness, served in 16th (Service) Battalion, The Royal Irish Rifles (2nd County Down) (Pioneers). Cousin of Privates Francis, John and William McKerr.

LYNESS Private Thomas 22801. (Some records show his name spelled Lynass.) Born in 1896 at Lurgan, County Armagh. Enlisted 10 November 1915 and joined the 10th (Reserve) Battalion. To France and joined the 9th (Service) Battalion. 'C' Company. Incorrectly reported **killed in action** in the period 21-28 March 1918 during the retreat from St Quentin but is believed **captured**. Discharged as no longer physically fit for war service due to sickness 20 February 1919. Silver War Badge, number B148889.

LYNESS Private William 27901. Enlisted 13 August 1917. Posted to the 9th (North Irish Horse) Battalion in early-1918. **Wounded**. Discharged as no longer physically fit for war service due to wounds 10 October 1918. Silver War Badge, number B34763.

LYNN Private John 24353. From Belfast. [Enlisted in May 1916 and served with the 1st Battalion.] Posted to the 9th (Service) Battalion. 'A' Company. **Captured** in the period 21-28 March 1918 during the retreat from St Quentin.

LYNN Private Samuel 14408. From Lurgan, County Armagh. A plumber. Enlisted September 1914. Discharged as not being likely to become an efficient soldier in that he was considered medically unfit (haemoptysis) for service 19 November 1914.

LYNN Private Samuel 26823. From Greenock, Renfrewshire. Enlisted 11 December 1915 and transferred to the Army Reserve. Mobilised 6 February 1917 and joined the 10th (Reserve) Battalion. To France 19 June 1917 and joined the 9th (Service) Battalion. 'B' Company. **Wounded** by a gunshot to the left arm at the Battle of Langemarck 16 August 1917 and evacuated to hospital in England. Joined the Irish Command Depot, Tipperary 9 February 1918. Joined the 10th (Reserve) Battalion 25 February 1918. [Transferred to the Labour Corps (renumbered 545515). 6 April 1918.] Discharged as no longer physically fit for war service due to wounds 19 June 1918, aged 29. Silver War Badge, number 411712. Lived in Ballyclare, County Antrim.

LYNN Private Thomas 41472. [Enlisted 13 November 1911 into the North Irish Horse (634). To France 20 August 1914 with 'C' Squadron as 5th Division Cavalry and then as GHQ Troops. Served with 2nd North Irish Horse, X Corps Cavalry Regiment.] Joined the renamed 9th (North Irish Horse) Battalion from 36 Infantry Base Depot and transferred to Princess Victoria's (Royal Irish Fusiliers) in September/October 1917 (renumbered 41472). **Wounded**. Discharged as no longer physically fit for war service due to wounds 18 June 1918, aged 26. Silver War Badge, number 387951. 1914 Star and clasp.

LYNN MM Private William John 15864. Enlisted into the 9th (Service) Battalion in October 1914. To France with 36th (Ulster) Division in October 1915. Served as a stretcher bearer on 1 July 1916. **MM** – Battle of Langemarck 16 August 1917. Transferred to the Class Z Reserve 15 March 1919. 1914-15 Star.

LYONS Private Thomas 41408. [Enlisted in November 1915 into the North Irish Horse (1928). Served with 2nd North Irish Horse, X Corps Cavalry Regiment.] Joined the renamed 9th (North Irish Horse) Battalion from 36 Infantry Base Depot and transferred to Princess Victoria's (Royal Irish Fusiliers) in September/October 1917 (renumbered 41408).

LYONS Private Thomas 41325. From Belfast. [Enlisted in November 1915 into the North Irish Horse (1846). Served with 2nd North Irish Horse, X Corps Cavalry Regiment.] Joined the renamed 9th (North Irish Horse) Battalion from 36 Infantry Base Depot and transferred to Princess Victoria's (Royal Irish Fusiliers) in September/October 1917 (renumbered 41325). 'C' Company. **Killed in action** 29 March 1918 during the retreat from St Quentin.

LYTTLE Private Isaac Victor 14403. Born in 1898 at Lurgan, County Armagh. Enlisted September 1914. To France with 36th (Ulster) Division in October 1915. **Wounded**. [Transferred to the Labour Corps (renumbered 213609).] Discharged as no longer physically fit for war service due to sickness 6 December 1917. Silver War Badge, number 300465. 1914-15 Star.

LYTTLE Private John 19948. From Tandragee, County Armagh. Enlisted into the 9th (Service) Battalion in May 1915. To France with 36th (Ulster) Division in October 1915. 5 Platoon, 'B' Company. **Killed in action** during the attack at Hamel 1 July 1916, aged 21. 1914-15 Star.

LYTTLE Lance Corporal Joseph Samuel 14398. Enlisted September 1914. To France with 36th (Ulster) Division in October 1915. 'C' Company. **Killed in action** during the attack at Hamel 1 July 1916. 1914-15 Star.

LYTTLE Private Samuel Ernest 22779. Born in 1893 at Portadown, County Armagh. Enlisted 9 November 1915. Posted to the 9th (Service) Battalion. 'C' Company. **Wounded** during the attack at Hamel 1 July 1916. **Wounded** at the Battle of Langemarck 16 August 1917. Discharged as no longer physically fit for war service due to wounds 29 August 1918, aged 25. Silver War Badge, number 445711.

LYTTLE Private Thomas Henry 14425. Born at Shankill, County Armagh in 1880. A weaver in the linen trade. Armagh Regiment, Ulster Volunteer Force. Enlisted September 1914. Discharged as not being likely to become an efficient soldier in that he was considered medically unfit for service 1 October 1914.

LYTTLE Private William John 14420. Enlisted September 1914.

MACK Private Robert James 42493. Born in 1899 at Bethnal Green, Middlesex. [Enlisted into The King's Royal Rifle Corps (26043). Transferred to The Royal Irish Rifles (renumbered 54194).] Transferred at the Base Depot to Princess Victoria's (Royal Irish Fusiliers) 14 September 1918 (renumbered 42493) and joined the 9th (North Irish Horse) Battalion 22 September 1918. **Killed in action** during the advance to Anseghem 25 October 1918.

MACKLE Sergeant Patrick 10175. Born in 1890 at Knockramer, Lurgan, County Armagh. [Enlisted 23 December 1908 into Princess Victoria's (Royal Irish Fusiliers) as a regular soldier. Mobilised from the Army Reserve and to France 7 November 1914. Joined the 1st Battalion. **Wounded** in March 1916.] Posted to the 9th (Service) Battalion. 'B' Company. **Wounded** in the face and arm at the Battle of Langemarck 16 August 1917. Discharged as no longer physically fit for war service due to wounds 8 May 1918. Silver War Badge, number 363630. 1914 Star.

MACKRELL Private James 22987. Enlisted 8 November 1915. Posted to the 9th (Service) Battalion. 'D' Company. **Captured** in the period 21-28 March 1918 during the retreat from St Quentin. Repatriated in December 1918. Discharged as no longer physically fit for war service due to sickness 2 April 1919. Silver War Badge, number B195564.

MADDOCK Private George Harry 43248. Born 20 September 1889 at Bakewell, Derbyshire. [Enlisted 29 November 1915 into The Sherwood Foresters (Nottinghamshire and Derbyshire Regiment) (35874).] Transferred to Princess Victoria's (Royal Irish Fusiliers) 31 August 1916 having joined the 9th (Service) Battalion on 8 August 1916 (renumbered 43248). 'B' Company. **Wounded** at the Battle of Langemarck 16 August 1917. [Transferred to the Army Ordnance Corps (renumbered 040063).] Discharged as no longer physically fit for war service due to wounds 18 July 1918, aged 28. Silver War Badge, number 428457. Died at Bakewell, Derbyshire in 1975, aged 85.

MAGEE Private Edward 14463. Enlisted September 1914. To France with 36th (Ulster) Division in October 1915. 'C' Company. Company trench storeman at Hamel in 1916. Did not take part in the attack at Hamel on 1 July 1916. [Transferred to the Labour Corps (renumbered 634019).] 1914-15 Star.

MAGEE Private James 14460. From Kilmoriarty, Portadown, County Armagh. Member of Loyal Orange Lodge 31. 4th (Portadown) Battalion, Armagh Regiment, Ulster Volunteer Force. Enlisted September 1914. To France with 36th (Ulster) Division in October 1915. **Killed in action** during the attack at Hamel 1 July 1916, aged 27. Related to Sergeant Robert Magee. His brother-in-law, Private Thomas Francis Whalley served with the 1st Battalion. He was wounded in 1915, discharged as unfit for further service (sickness) on 27 August 1918 and died on 24 February 1920.

MAGEE Private John 14459. From Tandragee, Portadown, County Armagh. 4th (Portadown) Battalion, Armagh Regiment, Ulster Volunteer Force. Enlisted September 1914. To France with 36th (Ulster) Division in October 1915. 'B' Company. Initially reported **wounded**, he was later declared **killed in action** at the Battle of Langemarck 16 August 1917, aged 32. 1914-15 Star.

MAGEE Sergeant Robert 14466. From Coronation Street, Portadown, County Armagh. 4th (Portadown) Battalion, Armagh Regiment, Ulster Volunteer Force. Enlisted September 1914. To France with 36th (Ulster) Division in October 1915. 'B' Company. **Killed in action** during the attack at Hamel 1 July 1916, aged 38. 1914-15 Star. Related to Private James Magee.

MAGEE Lance Corporal Samuel James 14464. (See Private W Johnston above.) Born in 1895 at Seagoe, County Armagh. 4th (Portadown) Battalion, Armagh Regiment, Ulster Volunteer Force. Enlisted September 1914. Lance Corporal 20 August 1915. To France with 36th (Ulster) Division 4 October 1915 but evacuated sick to hospital in England 25 October 1915 and treated at 1st Western General Hospital, Fazackerley, Liverpool. Joined the 10th (Reserve) Battalion 3 March

1916. Transferred to the Military Foot Police (renumbered P/6233) 23 December 1916. Transferred to the Class Z Reserve 27 August 1919. 1914-15 Star.

MAGEE Private Thomas 14487. Enlisted September 1914. To France with 36th (Ulster) Division in October 1915. Discharged as no longer physically fit for war service due to wounds 13 October 1918. Silver War Badge, number B35683. 1914-15 Star.

MAGEE Private William J 14435. Enlisted September 1914. To France with 36th (Ulster) Division in October 1915. [Transferred to the Labour Corps (renumbered 414765).] Transferred to the Class Z Reserve 23 April 1919. 1914-15 Star.

MAGEE Private William Houston 41218. Born in 1888 at Belfast. [Enlisted 3 May 1915 into the North Irish Horse (1514). Served with 2nd North Irish Horse, X Corps Cavalry Regiment.] Joined the renamed 9th (North Irish Horse) Battalion from 36 Infantry Base Depot and transferred to Princess Victoria's (Royal Irish Fusiliers) in September/October 1917 (renumbered 41218). **Wounded**. Discharged as no longer physically fit for war service due to wounds 24 June 1918, aged 29. Silver War Badge, number 414492.

MAGILL Private Charles 41592. Born 26 November 1896 at Cokermain, Cairncastle, County Antrim. [Enlisted 11 December 1915 into the North Irish Horse (2043). To France 26 November 1916 and joined 2nd North Irish Horse, X Corps Cavalry Regiment. Embarked at Marseilles for Egypt with the Regiment's horses on Horse Transport SS Bohemian 25 August 1917.] Joined the renamed 9th (North Irish Horse) Battalion and transferred to Princess Victoria's (Royal Irish Fusiliers) in October 1917 (renumbered 41592). [Transferred to the Tank Corps (renumbered 304865 Gunner) 28 December 1917 and posted for training to the Tank Corps Depot, at Bovington near Wareham, Dorset. Posted to the 17th Battalion, Tank Corps 8 January 1918 and to France 27 April 1918 when it converted to 17th (Armoured Car) Battalion. **Wounded** by a gunshot to the foot 21 August 1918 and evacuated to hospital in England. Posted to the 22nd (Light) Battalion, Tank Corps at Bovington, 4 January 1919. 'A' Company.] Transferred to the Class Z Reserve 13 March 1919. Joined the Royal Irish Constabulary in late-1919. Emigrated to the United States in July 1924. Lived in Yonkers, New York, where he died in October 1972, aged 75.

MAGILL Private James 16089. Enlisted into the 9th (Service) Battalion 14 October 1914. To France with 36th (Ulster) Division in October 1915. 'C' Company. Company storeman. Did not take part in the attack at Hamel on 1 July 1916. Discharged as no longer physically fit for war service due to sickness 9 January 1917. Silver War Badge, number 95500. 1914-15 Star.

MAGILL Private James 41435. Born in 1893 at Ballymena, County Antrim. A railway labourer. [Enlisted 8 November 1915 into the North Irish Horse (1805). To France 30 June 1916. Served with 2nd North Irish Horse, X Corps Cavalry Regiment.] Joined the renamed 9th (North Irish Horse) Battalion from 36 Infantry Base Depot and transferred to Princess Victoria's (Royal Irish Fusiliers) in September/October 1917 (renumbered 41435). 'C' Company. **Wounded** and **captured** in the period 21-28 March 1918 during the retreat from St Quentin. **Killed** 6 June 1918 by bombs dropped by French aircraft while a prisoner of war, aged 25. Five other men were killed in this attack, believed to be: Sergeant Matthewson Baillie 1st Battalion, Princess Victoria's (Royal Irish Fusiliers), Corporal John Martin 16th (Service) Battalion, The Royal Irish Rifles (2nd County Down) (Pioneers), Rifleman Anthony Moore 12th (Service) Battalion, The Royal Irish Rifles (Central Antrim) and Riflemen Alexander Gillespie and Archibald Larmour 15th (Service) Battalion, The Royal Irish Rifles (North Belfast).

MAGILL Lance Corporal Matthew 26082. From Markethill, County Armagh. [A regular soldier with the 1st Battalion, The Loyal North Lancashire Regiment (7094). To France 12 August 1914 in 2nd Brigade, 1st Division.] Transferred to Princess Victoria's (Royal Irish Fusiliers) 3 January 1917 (renumbered 26082). Posted to the 9th (Service) Battalion. 'A' Company. **Wounded** in the neck at the Battle of Langemarck 16 August 1917. Discharged as no longer physically fit for war service due to wounds 30 November 1917. Silver War Badge, number 274442. Died 29 May 1961, aged 78. Buried at First Presbyterian Church, Markethill.

MAGILL Private Robert Matthew 41282. [Enlisted 4 January 1916 into the North Irish Horse (2055). Served with 2nd North Irish Horse, X Corps Cavalry Regiment.] Joined the renamed 9th (North Irish Horse) Battalion from 36 Infantry Base Depot and transferred to Princess Victoria's (Royal Irish Fusiliers) in September/October 1917 (renumbered 41282). Discharged as no longer physically fit for war service due to sickness 7 August 1918, aged 29. Silver War Badge, number 434575.

MAGILL Private Thomas 17949. From Lurgan, County Armagh. Enlisted into the 9th (Service) Battalion in February 1915. To France with 36th (Ulster) Division in October 1915. **Wounded** during the attack at Hamel 1 July 1916. [Transferred to the Corps of Dragoons (renumbered D/33616).] Transferred to the Class Z Reserve. 1914-15 Star.

MAGILL Private William 23709. Born in 1897 at Belfast. Enlisted in January 1916. Posted to the 9th (Service) Battalion. 'A' Company. **Wounded** at the Battle of Langemarck 16 August 1917. When he recovered he rejoined the 9th (North Irish Horse) Battalion in 'B' Company. Separated from the 9th (North Irish Horse) Battalion in the period 21-28 March 1918 during the retreat from St Quentin; rejoined 3 April 1918.

MAGINNIS Sergeant Charles 14455. From Tandragee, County Armagh. A draper's assistant. 4th (Portadown) Battalion, Armagh Regiment, Ulster Volunteer Force. Enlisted September 1914. To France with 36th (Ulster) Division in October 1915. **Wounded** in the head by shellfire in January 1918. Discharged as no longer physically fit for war service due to wounds 25 March 1919. Silver War Badge, number B165690. 1914-15 Star. Died in 1960.

MAGOWAN MM Lance Corporal Andrew 18058. From Garvaghy Road, Portadown, County Armagh. Enlisted into the 9th (Service) Battalion in February 1915. To France with 36th (Ulster) Division in October 1915. 'C' Company. Lewis gunner; battle surplus and did not take part in the attack at Hamel on 1 July 1916. **MM** – Spanbroekmolen raid 4 June 1917. **Missing** at the Battle of Langemarck 16 August 1917 and later declared **killed in action** on that date, aged 18. 1914-15 Star.

MAGOWAN Private John 22142. From Ballybreagh, Portadown, County Armagh. Enlisted in October 1915. Posted to the 9th (Service) Battalion. 'A' Company. **Wounded** on 1 July 1916 and **died of wounds** 2 July 1916, aged 21.

MAGUIRE Private George 27508. [Enlisted 2 March 1916 and transferred to the Army Reserve. Mobilised from the Army Reserve or transferred to Princess Victoria's (Royal Irish Fusiliers) in April 1917. Joined the 7th/8th (Service) Battalion in 49th Brigade, 16th (Irish) Division.] Joined the 9th (North Irish Horse) Battalion when the 7th/8th (Service) Battalion was disbanded in February 1918. 'B' Company. **Wounded** during the retreat from St Quentin 21-28 March 1918. Discharged as no longer physically fit for war service due to wounds 20 February 1919. Silver War Badge, number B154138.

MAGUIRE Private James 15127, 33329 & 7041518. From Newry. [Enlisted in September 1914 into the 6th (Service) Battalion. Embarked with the Mediterranean Expeditionary Force July 1915.] Posted to the 9th (Service) Battalion. Re-enlisted 29 August 1919 for Regular Army service with Princess Victoria's (Royal Irish Fusiliers) (renumbered 33329, renumbered 7041518). Served with the 1st Battalion in Persia and Mesopotamia in 1919/20. General Service Medal 1918-1962 with clasps 'Iraq' & 'NW Persia'. Discharged 23 December 1921.

MAGUIRE Private John C 18318. [Enlisted or transferred to Princess Victoria's (Royal Irish Fusiliers) in March 1915. To France 25 May 1915 and joined the 1st or 2nd Battalion.] Posted to the 9th (Service) Battalion. 'C' Company. **Wounded** at the Battle of Langemarck 16 August 1917. [Transferred to The Prince of Wales's Own (West Yorkshire Regiment) (renumbered 88000).] 1914-15 Star.

MAGUIRE Sergeant Leslie 18245. From Moy, County Tyrone. Enlisted into the 9th (Service) Battalion in February 1915. To France with 36th (Ulster) Division in October 1915. 'A' Company. **Wounded** at the Battle of Langemarck 16 August 1917. [Transferred to 5th (Service) Battalion, The Royal Irish Regiment (Pioneers) in the Light Division in the British Army of the Rhine in March/June 1919 (renumbered 41321).] 1914-15 Star.

MAITLAND Private James 41591. [Enlisted 14 March 1913 into the North Irish Horse (807). To France 20 August 1914 with 'C' Squadron as 5th Division Cavalry and then as GHQ Troops. Served with 2nd North Irish Horse, X Corps Cavalry Regiment. Embarked at Marseilles for Egypt with the Regiment's horses on Horse Transport SS Bohemian 25 August 1917.] Joined the renamed 9th (North Irish Horse) Battalion and transferred to Princess Victoria's (Royal Irish Fusiliers) in October 1917 (renumbered 41591). **Wounded**. Discharged as no longer physically fit for war service due to wounds 21 March 1919. Silver War Badge, number B167275. 1914 Star.

MAJOR Private Thomas 14465. Served with the 1st Battalion, Princess Victoria's (Royal Irish Fusiliers) (354) during the South African War. Re-enlisted September 1914 (renumbered 14465). To France with 36th (Ulster) Division in October 1915. [Transferred to the Labour Corps (renumbered 445076).] 1914-15 Star. Died 1930s.

MAKINSON MM Lance Sergeant Harry 18869. Born at Burnley, Lancashire. From Clayon-le-Moors. [Enlisted into the Hussars of the Line (19522). Transferred to Princess Victoria's (Royal Irish Fusiliers) in April 1915 (renumbered 18869). To France 21 July 1915 and joined the 1st Battalion.] Posted to the 9th (Service) Battalion. 'C' Company. **MM** – Havrincourt raid 3 November 1917. **Wounded** by shellfire at Poperinghe railway station and **died of wounds** 11 April 1918.

MALAM Lance Corporal William 17095. From Salford, Lancashire. [Enlisted into The Lancashire Fusiliers (6274). Transferred to Princess Victoria's (Royal Irish Fusiliers) in October 1914 and joined the 6th (Service) Battalion. Embarked with the Mediterranean Expeditionary Force July 1915.] Posted to the 9th (Service) Battalion. 'B' Company. **Missing** at the Battle of Langemarck 16 August 1917 and later declared **killed in action** on that date, aged 24. 1914-15 Star.

MALCOLMSON Private Samuel 14454. From Jervis Street, Portadown, County Armagh. 4th (Portadown) Battalion, Armagh Regiment, Ulster Volunteer Force. Enlisted September 1914. To France with 36th (Ulster) Division in October 1915. 'B' Company. **Wounded** (shellshock) during the attack at Hamel 1 July 1916. **Killed in action** 23 November 1917 at Moeuvres, aged 23. 1914-15 Star.

MALLIN Private Joseph 41341. [Enlisted in September 1914 into the North Irish Horse (1119). To France 1 May 1915. Served with 2nd North Irish Horse, X Corps Cavalry Regiment.] Joined the renamed 9th (North Irish Horse) Battalion from 36 Infantry Base Depot and transferred to Princess Victoria's (Royal Irish Fusiliers) in September/October 1917 (renumbered 41341). Transferred to the Class Z Reserve 11 March 1919. 1914-15 Star.

MALLON Private Hugh 23433. [Enlisted in December 1915 and joined the 7th (Service) Battalion in 49th Brigade, 16th (Irish) Division.] Joined the 9th (North Irish Horse) Battalion when the 7th/8th (Service) Battalion was disbanded in February 1918. 'C' Company. **Missing** in the period 21-28 March 1918 during the retreat from St Quentin believed **captured**.

MALLON Lance Corporal James 3919 & 7040047. From Drumcree, County Armagh. A weaver. Enlisted on 12 January 1916 into Princess Victoria's (Royal Irish Fusiliers) Special Reserve. [To France 10 January 1918 and joined the 7th/8th (Service) Battalion in 49th Brigade, 16th (Irish) Division.] Joined the 9th (North Irish Horse) Battalion when the 7th/8th (Service) Battalion was disbanded in February 1918. **Wounded** by a gunshot to the left arm during the attack south of Wulverghem on 5 September 1918 and evacuated to hospital in England. Re-enlisted 26 February 1919 for Regular Army service with Princess Victoria's (Royal Irish Fusiliers) (renumbered 7040047). Volunteered for service with the North Russia Relief Force. Served in North Russia from 18 September 1919 with 45th (Service) Battalion, The Royal Fusiliers (City of London Regiment). Arrived in Egypt 20 May 1921 and served there to 17 December 1921. Discharged 31 March 1922.

MALONE Private John James 16122. From Clones, County Monaghan. Enlisted into the 9th (Service) Battalion in October 1914. To France with 36th (Ulster) Division in October 1915. 'D' Company. **Wounded** during the attack at Hamel 1 July 1916 and **died of wounds** 20 July 1916, aged 23. 1914-15 Star.

MALONE Corporal Thomas 14437. Born at Lurgan, County Armagh. Enlisted September 1914. To France with 36th (Ulster) Division in October 1915. 'C' Company. **Killed in action** during the attack at Hamel 1 July 1916. 1914-15 Star.

MALONEY Private Thomas 22734. Born at Shankill, Belfast. Enlisted in November 1915. Posted to the 9th (Service) Battalion. 'C' Company. Signaller. **Wounded** during the retreat from St Quentin and **died of wounds** 28 March 1918.

MANTON Private William 41521. [Enlisted for service with cavalry (15673). Served with 2nd North Irish Horse, X Corps Cavalry Regiment.] Joined the renamed 9th (North Irish Horse) Battalion from 36 Infantry Base Depot and transferred to Princess Victoria's (Royal Irish Fusiliers) in September/October 1917 (renumbered 41521). [Transferred to the Labour Corps (renumbered

511006). Transferred to a garrison battalion of The Royal Fusiliers (City of London Regiment) (renumbered GS/105759).]

MAPLES Private Edward Christopher 40018. Born on 12 December 1885 at New Wortley, Leeds, Yorkshire. [Enlisted on 15 October 1915 into The Prince of Wales's Own (West Yorkshire Regiment) (32993) and transferred to the Army Reserve. Mobilised 5 June 1916 and posted to the 4th (Extra Reserve) Battalion, The Prince of Wales's Own (West Yorkshire Regiment). Transferred to the Corps of Royal Engineers (185244) 4 August 1916 and was posted to 6th Provisional Field Company. He failed his trade test and was returned to The Prince of Wales's Own (West Yorkshire Regiment) at the end of August 1916.] Transferred to Princess Victoria's (Royal Irish Fusiliers) 30 November 1916 (renumbered 40018) and joined the 9th (Service) Battalion 12 December 1916. 'B' Company. To hospital sick (impetigo) 23 June 1917 and evacuated to hospital in England 27 July 1917. Posted to the 10th (Reserve) Battalion 12 October 1917. [Transferred to the Royal Army Medical Corps (136751) 28 January 1918 and was posted to the 6th Training Battalion, Royal Army Medical Corps. Posted to 8th Company, Royal Army Medical Corps for service at Keighley War Hospital.] Transferred to the Class Z Reserve 14 July 1919. Died in 1944 at Leeds, aged 59.

MARCHANT Private Alfred William 50042. Born 4 October 1899 at Mile End, London. [Transferred to Princess Victoria's (Royal Irish Fusiliers) in May 1918 (renumbered 50042) with a draft of men from English regiments and joined the 1st Battalion.] Posted to the 9th (North Irish Horse) Battalion in August 1918. Died at London 1 June 1939, aged 39.

MARK Private George 41562. Born in 1896 at Ballymena, County Antrim. [Enlisted 28 August 1916 into the North Irish Horse (2251). To France 20 March 1917 and joined 2nd North Irish Horse, X Corps Cavalry Regiment.] Joined the renamed 9th (North Irish Horse) Battalion from 36 Infantry Base Depot and transferred to Princess Victoria's (Royal Irish Fusiliers) in September/October 1917 (renumbered 41562). 'D' Company. **Wounded** by a gunshot to the face during the retreat from St Quentin 21-28 March 1918. **Killed in action** during the attack south of Wulverghem 4 September 1918, aged 22.

MARKS Private William 14453. From Portadown, County Armagh. 4th (Portadown) Battalion, Armagh Regiment, Ulster Volunteer Force. Member of Loyal Orange Lodge 110. Enlisted September 1914. To France with 36th (Ulster) Division in October 1915. Transferred to the Class Z Reserve 23 March 1919. 1914-15 Star. Died at Armagh on 1 March 1932, aged 38. Buried at Ballymore parish Churchyard.

MARRINER Private William 20320. Enlisted 24 May 1915 and joined the 9th (Service) Battalion with the draft of men from The Royal Inniskilling Fusiliers who transferred to Princess Victoria's (Royal Irish Fusiliers) on 30 June 1915. To France with 36th (Ulster) Division in October 1915. **Wounded**. Discharged as no longer physically fit for war service due to wounds 14 March 1919. Silver War Badge, number B162130.

MARSH Private Alexander 45811. Enlisted 24 January 1917. Joined the 9th (North Irish Horse) Battalion, Princess Victoria's (Royal Irish Fusiliers) with the draft of men from The London Regiment in April 1918. Discharged as no longer physically fit for war service due to sickness 12 December 1918. Silver War Badge, number B61019.

MARSH Private Milford 21865. Born in 1896 at St Peter Port, Guernsey, Channel Islands. Enlisted on 26 April 1915. Joined the 7th (Service) Battalion in 49th Brigade, 16th (Irish) Division.] Joined the 9th (North Irish Horse) Battalion when the 7th/8th (Service) Battalion was disbanded in February 1918. **Wounded**. Discharged as no longer physically fit for war service due to wounds 5 June 1919. Silver War Badge, number B242929.

MARSHALL MM Private John William 18252. Born in 1897 in Australia. From Ballyloughan, Armagh, County Armagh. Enlisted into the 9th (Service) Battalion in February/March 1915. To France with 36th (Ulster) Division in October 1915. 'A' Company. **Wounded** at the Battle of Langemarck 16 August 1917. **MM** – Moeuvres 23 November 1917. **Wounded** during the retreat from St Quentin 21-28 March 1918. **Killed in action** by shellfire on 25 July 1918 at Meulenhouck, aged 21. 1914-15 Star.

MARTIN Private Edward 14451. Enlisted September 1914. To France with 36th (Ulster) Division in October 1915. Discharged as no longer physically fit for war service due to sickness 19 April 1916. Silver War Badge, number B41652. 1914-15 Star.

MARTIN Private Henry 10544. [Enlisted into Princess Victoria's (Royal Irish Fusiliers) as a regular soldier in 23 November 1910. To France 26 January 1915 and joined the 2nd Battalion. Posted to the 1st Battalion.] Posted to the 9th (North Irish Horse) Battalion. [Posted back to the 1st Battalion.] Discharged as no longer physically fit for war service due to sickness 26 April 1918, aged 27. Silver War Badge, number 404428. 1914-15 Star.

MARTIN Private Hugh 24737. [Enlisted in August 1916 and served with the 1st Battalion.] Posted to the 9th (Service) Battalion.

MARTIN Private James 12951. From Belfast. [Enlisted in September 1914 and joined the 6th (Service) Battalion in 31st Brigade, 10th (Irish) Division. Embarked with the Mediterranean Expeditionary Force July 1915. Evacuated to hospital in England. Posted to the 8th (Service) Battalion in 49th Brigade, 16th (Irish) Division.] Joined the 9th (North Irish Horse) Battalion when the 7th/8th (Service) Battalion was disbanded in February 1918. **Wounded** at Anseghem on 25/26 October 1918 and **died of wounds** 27 December 1918, aged 33. 1914-15 Star.

MARTIN Private James Leabon 42461. [Enlisted into the 9th (Service) Battalion, The Royal Irish Rifles (West Belfast) (1247).] Transferred at the Base Depot to Princess Victoria's (Royal Irish Fusiliers) 14 September 1918 (renumbered 42461) and joined the 9th (North Irish Horse) Battalion 22 September 1918. Transferred to the Class Z Reserve 13 May 1919. 1914-15 Star.

MARTIN Private Leonard William 45062. Born in 1886 at Willesborough, Kent. A weights and measures inspector. [Enlisted 27 November 1915 into The Buffs (East Kent Regiment) (9965). To France 28 November 1916 and joined 16 Infantry Base Depot. Transferred to Princess Victoria's (Royal Irish Fusiliers) (renumbered 45062) 29 November 1916 and joined the 7th/8th (Service) Battalion 10 December 1916. 'C' Company. **Wounded** by a gunshot to the left arm 16 August 1917. Evacuated to hospital in England and treated at 4th Northern General Hospital, Lincoln. Discharged from hospital 19 September 1917 and posted to the 4th (Extra Reserve) Battalion 30 September 1917.] To 'L' Infantry Base Depot 11 January 1918. Joined the 9th (North Irish Horse) Battalion when the 7th/8th (Service) Battalion was disbanded in February 1918. **Wounded** in the period 9-18 April 1918 in the actions between Wulverghem and Kemmel. Treated at 62nd Casualty Clearing Station and 32nd Stationary Hospital. To Number 1 Convalescent Depot, Boulogne 20 May 1918. To 'A' Infantry Base Depot 7 June 1918 and rejoined the 9th (North Irish Horse) Battalion 27 July 1918. **Wounded** by a gunshot to the left leg that broke his fibula at Anseghem on 25/26 October 1918 and **died of wounds** 1 November 1918.

MARTIN Private William 26912. Enlisted in February 1917. Posted to the 9th (Service) Battalion. **Deserted** 23 March 1918 (this was two days into the withdrawal from St Quentin. There is no information as to where he deserted from, i.e. from the front line, from the Battalion's rear details or while on leave). Medals forfeit.

MARTIN Private William 41131. [Enlisted in November 1914 into the Service Squadron, 6th (Inniskilling) Dragoons (UD/156). To France with 36th (Ulster) Division in October 1915. Served with 2nd North Irish Horse, X Corps Cavalry Regiment.] Joined the renamed 9th (North Irish Horse) Battalion from 36 Infantry Base Depot and transferred to Princess Victoria's (Royal Irish Fusiliers) in September/October 1917 (renumbered 41131). 'A' Company. **Captured** in the period 21-28 March 1918 during the retreat from St Quentin. Transferred to the Class Z Reserve 2 April 1919. 1914-15 Star.

MARTIN Private William 41180. From Castleblayney, County Monaghan. A farmer. [Enlisted 5 February 1913 into the North Irish Horse (814). Mobilised August 1914 and **deserted** on 16 August 1914. Rejoined 16 October 1914. Tried by Field General Court Martial on 21 October 1914 charged with *'**deserting** His Majesty's service'* and *'losing by neglect his equipments'*; found guilty and sentenced to thirty-five days detention. Attended a course of cookery at Dublin 9-28 August 1915. To France with 'F' Squadron in 33rd Division 17 November 1915.] Joined the renamed 9th (North Irish Horse) Battalion from 36 Infantry Base Depot and transferred to Princess Victoria's (Royal Irish Fusiliers) in September/October 1917 (renumbered 41180). [Transferred to the Tank Corps (renumbered 304871) 28 December 1917 and posted for training to the Tank Corps Depot, at Bovington near Wareham, Dorset. To France 8 July 1918 and joined the 15th Battalion, Tank Corps.] Transferred to the Class Z Reserve 20 February 1919. 1914-15 Star.

MARTINDALE Private Henry David 13618. Born 21 October 1888. From Islington, London. A carman. [Enlisted 4 September 1914 at Bodmin into The Duke of Cornwall's Light Infantry (14898). Transferred to Princess Victoria's (Royal Irish Fusiliers) 18 September 1914 (renumbered 13618) and posted to the 6th (Service) Battalion. 'D' Company. **Deserted** 20 December 1914. Apprehended by the police in London on 18 April 1915. Tried by District Court Martial at Dublin on 29 April 1915 charged with ***'deserting** His Majesty's Service'* and *'losing by neglect his equipments'*; found guilty of absence without leave and sentenced to six months imprisonment with hard labour and to be discharged with ignominy. The finding was confirmed but the sentence was reduced to forty-two days imprisonment and discharge remitted. To France 31 May 1915 and joined the 1st Battalion. 15 Platoon, 'D' Company. **Wounded** by a gunshot to the right wrist 11 April 1917 and evacuated to hospital in England 21 April 1917. Joined the 3rd (Reserve) Battalion 30 May 1917.] To 36 Infantry Base Depot 14 June 1917 and joined the 9th (Service) Battalion 10 July 1917. 'C' Company. **Wounded** in his left hand by a bomb at the Battle of Langemarck 16 August 1917 and evacuated to hospital in England. Treated at Fulham Military Hospital, London. Absent 19 November 1917. Joined the 10th (Reserve) Battalion 29 November 1917. Forfeit eleven days pay for absence. Absent 15 January 1918. Rejoined 22 January 1918 and forfeit eight days pay for absence. Transferred to the Labour Corps (renumbered 545498) 6 April 1918 and posted to 361st Home Service Employment Company, Newtownards, County Down 25 July 1918. Absent 4 August 1918 and apprehended by the police in London on 12 August 1918; forfeit eighteen days pay for absence. To France 26 August 1918 and joined 84th Labour Company 31 August 1918. Transferred to the Class Z Reserve 24 February 1919. Died at Islington, London in 1934, aged 45.

MARTLE Private Hilary 43313. Born in 1897. From East Ham, London. [Enlisted 3 June 1916 into The London Regiment.] Attached to the 9th (Service) Battalion, Princess Victoria's (Royal Irish Fusiliers) 26 November 1916. 'A' Company. Discharged from the Territorial Force, re-enlisted and transferred to Princess Victoria's (Royal Irish Fusiliers) in March/April 1917 (renumbered 43313). **Wounded** at the Battle of Langemarck 16 August 1917. Discharged as no longer physically fit for war service due to wounds 21 June 1918, aged 20. Silver War Badge, number 411856. Worked as a lighterage contractor. Died at Romford, Essex in 1963, aged 65.

MASON Private Bertie Frederick 42274. Born in 1884. From Clapton, London. A garbage contractor. [Enlisted 1 May 1917 into the Army Veterinary Corps (27777). To hospital sick 6 September 1917.] To France 14 March 1918. Transferred to Princess Victoria's (Royal Irish Fusiliers) 8 May 1918 (renumbered 42274) and joined the 9th (North Irish Horse) Battalion. To 108th Field Ambulance sick (synovitis knee) 3 July 1918. To 62nd Casualty Clearing Station sick (bleeding haemorrhoid). Transferred to 3rd Canadian General Hospital 21 July 1918 where he developed trench fever. **Wounded** (shell shock) during bombing of the hospital. Evacuated to hospital in England 14 August 1918. Transferred to the Class Z Reserve 20 February 1919.

MASON Private Samuel Alexander 41635. Born in 1894 at Myroe near Limavady, County Londonderry. Worked in the linen trade in Belfast. [Enlisted in November 1914 into the Service Squadron, 6th (Inniskilling) Dragoons (UD/104). To France with 36th (Ulster) Division in October 1915. Served with 2nd North Irish Horse, X Corps Cavalry Regiment.] Joined the renamed 9th (North Irish Horse) Battalion from 36 Infantry Base Depot and transferred to Princess Victoria's (Royal Irish Fusiliers) in September/October 1917 (renumbered 41635). Transferred to the Class Z Reserve 20 March 1919. 1914-15 Star.

MATCHETT Private William 18673. Enlisted into the 9th (Service) Battalion 21 April 1915. To France with 36th (Ulster) Division in October 1915. Discharged as no longer physically fit for war service due to sickness 26 February 1918. Silver War Badge, number 334284. 1914-15 Star.

MATCHETT Private William Joseph 41698. Born in 1891 at Tandragee, County Armagh. A cashier with York Street Flax Spinning Company, Belfast. [Enlisted 18 August 1916 into the North Irish Horse (2237). To France 28 January 1917. Served with 2nd North Irish Horse, X Corps Cavalry Regiment. Embarked at Marseilles for Egypt with the Regiment's horses on Horse Transport SS Bohemian 25 August 1917. To 15th General Hospital, Alexandria, Egypt sick (malaria) 12 September 1917. Evacuated to hospital in England. Renumbered H/71719.] Transferred to Princess Victoria's (Royal Irish Fusiliers) 1 January 1918 and joined the 9th (North Irish Horse) Battalion (renumbered 41698). **Wounded** by a gunshot to the left forearm 12 April 1918 in the actions between Wulverghem and Kemmel. Transferred to the Class Z Reserve 10 February 1919.

MATEER Private John 21680. Enlisted in September 1915. Posted to the 9th (Service) Battalion in mid/late 1916.

MATHER Sergeant James 14962. [Enlisted 10 September 1914 into the 5th (Service) Battalion in 31st Brigade, 10th (Irish) Division. Embarked with the Mediterranean Expeditionary Force July 1915. Posted to the 7th/8th (Service) Battalion in 49th Brigade, 16th (Irish) Division.] Joined the 9th (North Irish Horse) Battalion when the 7th/8th (Service) Battalion was disbanded in February 1918. **Wounded**. Discharged as no longer physically fit for war service due to wounds 12 December 1918. Silver War Badge, number B61024.

MATHER Private James 15542. Born at Bury, Lancashire. [Enlisted into The Lancashire Fusiliers (6157). Transferred to Princess Victoria's (Royal Irish Fusiliers) in September 1914 (renumbered 15542) and joined the 6th (Service) Battalion. Embarked with the Mediterranean Expeditionary Force July 1915.] Joined the 9th (North Irish Horse) Battalion. 'D' Company. **Missing** in the period 21-28 March 1918 during the retreat from St Quentin and later declared **killed in action** 29 March 1918. 1914-15 Star.

MATHERS Sergeant Thomas 41479. [Enlisted in May 1914 into the North Irish Horse (946). To France with 'F' Squadron in 33rd Division 17 November 1915. Served with 2nd North Irish Horse, X Corps Cavalry Regiment.] Joined the renamed 9th (North Irish Horse) Battalion from 36 Infantry Base Depot and transferred to Princess Victoria's (Royal Irish Fusiliers) in September/October 1917 (renumbered 41479). Transferred to the Class Z Reserve 21 February 1919. 1914-15 Star.

MATHERS Private William 42517 & 7042204. [Enlisted April/May 1918 into The Royal Irish Rifles (22641).] Transferred at the Base Depot to Princess Victoria's (Royal Irish Fusiliers) 14 September 1918 (renumbered 42517) and joined the 9th (North Irish Horse) Battalion 22 September 1918. Re-enlisted in early-1919 for Regular Army service with Princess Victoria's (Royal Irish Fusiliers) (renumbered 7042204). Served with the 1st Battalion in Persia and Mesopotamia in 1919/20. General Service Medal 1918-1962 with clasps 'Iraq' & 'NW Persia'.

MATSON Private Frederick 15851. Born in 1898 at Armagh, County Armagh. Enlisted into the 9th (Service) Battalion in October 1914, aged 16. To France with 36th (Ulster) Division in October 1915. 1914-15 Star.

MATTHEWS Lance Corporal Arthur William 43465. [Enlisted 28 November 1914 into The London Regiment (6988). Posted to the 1/24th (County of London) Battalion, The London Regiment (The Queen's).] To France and joined 36 Infantry Base Depot 29 March 1918. Transferred to Princess Victoria's (Royal Irish Fusiliers) 2 April 1918 (renumbered 43465) and joined the 9th (North Irish Horse) Battalion 4 April 1918. **Wounded**. Discharged as no longer physically fit for war service due to wounds 21 March 1919. Silver War Badge, number B167277.

MATTHEWS Lance Corporal George 23410. From Belfast. Enlisted 10 December 1915. Posted to the 9th (Service) Battalion. **Wounded**. Discharged as no longer physically fit for war service due to wounds 27 November 1919. Silver War Badge, number B349063.

MATTHEWS Corporal Hugh 13102. From Blaris, Lisburn, County Antrim. Worked in a flax spinning room. [Enlisted 14 September 1914 and joined the 7th (Service) Battalion. Lance Corporal 13 January 1915. Corporal 10 July 1916.] Joined the 9th (North Irish Horse) Battalion when the 7th/8th (Service) Battalion was disbanded in February 1918. 'A' Company. **Captured** in the period 21-28 March 1918 during the retreat from St Quentin. Repatriated 6 January 1919. Transferred to the Class Z Reserve April 1919.

MATTHEWS Sergeant Reginald Edwin 43342. From Ongar, Essex. [Enlisted 31 May 1915 and joined the 3/7th Battalion, The London Regiment. Corporal 13 November 1915. To 8 Infantry Base Depot 12 November 1916 for service with 1/7th (City of London) Battalion, The London Regiment. Reverted to Private.] Attached to the 9th (Service) Battalion, Princess Victoria's (Royal Irish Fusiliers) 26 November 1916. Renumbered 352110, The London Regiment in March 1917. Discharged from the Territorial Force, re-enlisted and transferred to Princess Victoria's (Royal Irish Fusiliers) in March/April 1917 (renumbered 43342). To hospital sick (boils and influenza) throughout the latter half of 1917. To hospital (injured right foot) at the end of November 1917 and evacuated to hospital in England 24 December 1917. Discharged from hospital 6 March 1918 and joined the 10th (Reserve) Battalion 16 March 1918. To 'J' Infantry Base Depot 12 April 1918 and rejoined the 9th (North Irish Horse) Battalion. Sergeant 22 April 1918. **Wounded** by shell fragments to the back at Anseghem on 26 October 1918 and **died of wounds** on 1 November 1918 at 3rd

Australian Casualty Clearing Station, aged 24.

MATTHEWS Corporal Robert 14446. From Toberhuney, County Armagh. Enlisted September 1914. To France with 36th (Ulster) Division in October 1915. 'C' Company. Survived the attack at Hamel on 1 July 1916 unwounded. Transferred to the Class Z Reserve 19 March 1919. 1914-15 Star.

MATTOCK Private William Alfred 42194. Born in 1884 at Seend, Melksham, Wiltshire. A groom. [Enlisted 10 December 1915 and transferred to the Army Reserve. Mobilised 31 May 1916 and joined The Duke of Edinburgh's (Wiltshire Regiment) (427). Transferred to the Army Service Corps.] To France 18 April 1918 and joined 'A' Infantry Base Depot 6 May 1918. Transferred to Princess Victoria's (Royal Irish Fusiliers) 8 May 1918 (renumbered 42194) and joined the 9th (North Irish Horse) Battalion 8 June 1918. **Wounded** by barbed wire during the attack south of Wulverghem 4 September 1918 and treated at the field ambulance. To the Divisional Reinforcement Company 20 September 1918 and rejoined the 9th (North Irish Horse) Battalion. **Killed in action** at Hill 41 on 11 October 1918, aged 34.

MAWHIRST Private John 14448. Enlisted September 1914. No record of deployment to France with 36th (Ulster) Division in October 1915. [Transferred to the Labour Corps (renumbered 641551).]

MAWHIRT Private George E 14440. From Lurgan, County Armagh. Enlisted September 1914. To France with 36th (Ulster) Division in October 1915. 'C' Company. Signaller during the attack at Hamel on 1 July 1916, during which he was **wounded**. [Posted to the 1st Battalion.] Transferred to the Class Z Reserve.

MAXWELL Company Quartermaster Sergeant Allen 14439. From Lurgan, County Armagh. Enlisted September 1914. To France with 36th (Ulster) Division in October 1915. **Wounded** during the attack at Hamel 1 July 1916. Company Quartermaster Sergeant. 1914-15 Star. Brother of Private Ambrose Maxwell.

MAXWELL Private Ambrose (Amby) 14434. From Lurgan, County Armagh. A weaver. Enlisted September 1914, aged 16. To France with 36th (Ulster) Division in October 1915. Evacuated to hospital in England 1 September 1916. **Wounded** by a gunshot (minor) to the left arm during the attack at Hamel 1 July 1916. To hospital sick (diagnosed as adenitis) 19 July 1916 and evacuated to hospital in England. Joined the Irish Command Depot. To hospital sick (no diagnosis) 9 February 1917. To hospital sick (tuberculosis) 23 April 1917. Discharged as no longer physically fit for war service due to sickness (tuberculosis) 28 May 1917. Silver War Badge, number 183835. **Died** of pulmonary tuberculosis 3 July 1918. 1914-15 Star. Brother of Company Quartermaster Sergeant Allen Maxwell.

MAXWELL Private Joseph 14484. From Shankill, County Armagh. A weaver. Served pre-war with the 3rd Battalion (Militia), Princess Victoria's (Royal Irish Fusiliers). 5th (Lurgan) Battalion, Ulster Volunteer Force. Enlisted September 1914. Discharged as not being likely to become an efficient soldier in that he was considered medically unfit (chronic rheumatism) for service 8 March 1915.

MAXWELL Private Richard 14471. From Portadown, County Armagh. 4th (Portadown) Battalion, Armagh Regiment, Ulster Volunteer Force. Enlisted September 1914. To France with 36th (Ulster) Division in October 1915. **Wounded** during the attack at Hamel 1 July 1916. Discharged as no longer physically fit for war service due to wounds 19 December 1917. Silver War Badge, number 288661. 1914-15 Star.

MAXWELL Private Robert John 14483. Born in 1861 at Lurgan, County Armagh. Served for eight years in the 3rd Battalion (Militia), Princess Victoria's (Royal Irish Fusiliers). Armagh Regiment, Ulster Volunteer Force. A weaver. Enlisted September 1914, aged 53 years giving his age as 43 years. Discharged as not being likely to become an efficient soldier in that he was considered medically unfit for service 1 October 1914.

MAXWELL Private Thomas 42543. [Served with 9th (Service) Battalion, The Royal Irish Rifles (West Belfast) (15570).] Transferred at the Base Depot to Princess Victoria's (Royal Irish Fusiliers) 14 September 1918 and joined the 9th (North Irish Horse) Battalion 22 September 1918. Transferred to the Class Z Reserve.

MAXWELL Private William 14430. Enlisted September 1914. To France with 36th (Ulster) Division in October 1915. 'C' Company. Battalion bomb carrier during the attack at Hamel 1 July 1916, unwounded. Discharged as no longer physically fit for war service due to sickness 2 January 1917. Silver War Badge, number 107183. 1914-15 Star.

MAXWELL Private William Frederick 22756. Born in 1898 at Lurgan, County Armagh. Enlisted in November 1915, aged 17. Posted to the 9th (Service) Battalion in 1916. 'C' Company. To hospital sick in mid-1916 and evacuated to hospital in England. Did not take part in the attack at Hamel on 1 July 1916. [Transferred to The Royal Irish Rifles (renumbered 20/411) and joined the 20th (Reserve) Battalion, The Royal Irish Rifles. Transferred to the Royal Garrison Artillery (renumbered 226823 Gunner). Transferred to the Royal Navy (renumbered C/SS 8109 Ordinary Seaman) and held with the Fleet Reserve at Chatham.]

MAXWELL Sergeant William John 14485. Born in 1898 at Drumgor, Lurgan, County Armagh. Enlisted September 1914, aged 16. To France with 36th (Ulster) Division in October 1915. 'C' Company. **Wounded** and **captured** at the Battle of Langemarck 16 August 1917.

MAYO Private Arthur Frederick 45772. Born in 1898 at Southwark, London. A clerk. [Enlisted 11 September 1916 and transferred to the Army Reserve. Mobilised 30 December 1916 and joined the 22nd (Reserve) Battalion, The London Regiment (6417). To hospital sick (impetigo complicated by acne) 27 April to 13 June 1917. To France and joined the 1/22nd (County of London) Battalion, The London Regiment (The Queen's) (renumbered 683292) 21 November 1917. To hospital sick (trench feet) 24 December 1917 to 23 February 1918 and evacuated to hospital in England. Treated at the Military Hospital, Winchester.] To France and joined 36 Infantry Base Depot 29 March 1918. Transferred to Princess Victoria's (Royal Irish Fusiliers) 2 April 1918 (renumbered 45772) and joined the 9th (North Irish Horse) Battalion 4 April 1918. **Wounded** by a gunshot to his left hand 11 April 1918 in the actions between Wulverghem and Kemmel. Treated at 14th General Hospital and evacuated to hospital in England. To hospital (injured foot) 19 August 1918 to 6 February 1919. Transferred to the Class Z Reserve 7 March 1919. Died at London in 1951, aged 53.

McADAM Sergeant Wilson 14553. (Also spelled McCadam.) Born in 1891. Lived at Tandragee, County Armagh. Member of Clonmakate Company, Armagh Regiment, Ulster Volunteer Force. Member of Loyal Orange Lodge 110. Worked in the linen trade at Thomas Sinton's mill. Enlisted September 1914. To France with 36th (Ulster) Division in October 1915. 'C' Company. Evacuated sick to hospital in England in mid-1916. Did not take part in the attack at Hamel on 1 July 1916. Transferred to the Class Z Reserve 6 March 1919. 1914-15 Star.

McALEER Private Andrew 42433. Born at Omagh, County Tyrone. [Enlisted 5 September 1915 and joined F Company, 3rd (Reserve) Battalion, The Royal Irish Rifles (9726). **Deserted** 15 October 1916. Rejoined 19 January 1918. Tried by District Court Martial on 2 February 1918 charged with ***'deserting** His Majesty's service'*; found guilty and sentenced to six months detention. To France 27 June 1918 and joined the 2nd Battalion, The Royal Irish Rifles.] Transferred at the Base Depot to Princess Victoria's (Royal Irish Fusiliers) 14 September 1918 (renumbered 42433) and joined the 9th (North Irish Horse) Battalion 22 September 1918. **Killed in action** during the attack at Vijfwegen 1 October 1918, aged 24.

McALEER Private William Grey 27557. From Belfast. Enlisted 24 April 1917. Posted to the 9th (North Irish Horse) Battalion. **Wounded**. Discharged as no longer physically fit for war service due to wounds 15 May 1918, aged 21. Silver War Badge, number 365986.

McALEESE Private William 14532. From Richhill, County Armagh. Enlisted September 1914. To France with 36th (Ulster) Division in October 1915. **Wounded** during the attack at Hamel 1 July 1916. [Transferred to the Labour Corps (renumbered 564317).] 1914-15 Star.

McALESTER Sergeant John 14524. Enlisted September 1914. Did not serve overseas. Discharged as no longer physically fit for war service due to sickness 12 November 1916. Silver War Badge, number 113978.

McALISTER Private James 14531. From Kilmore, Richhill, County Armagh. Enlisted September 1914. To France with 36th (Ulster) Division in October 1915. [Transferred to the Labour Corps (renumbered 223617).] 1914-15 Star. He died on 12 March 1941, aged 85 and is buried in the Quaker Burial Ground at Kilmore, Richhill, County Armagh. His brother, Private Gabriel McAlister, was killed in action on 10 April 1917 serving with the 15th Canadian Battalion (48th Highlanders of

Canada), Canadian Infantry.

McALLISTER Private David 41512. [Enlisted in October/November 1914 into the Service Squadron, 6th (Inniskilling) Dragoons (UD/90). Served with 2nd North Irish Horse, X Corps Cavalry Regiment.] Joined the renamed 9th (North Irish Horse) Battalion from 36 Infantry Base Depot and transferred to Princess Victoria's (Royal Irish Fusiliers) in September/October 1917 (renumbered 41512). 'D' Company. **Wounded** during the retreat from St Quentin 21-28 March 1918. [Transferred to the Corps of Dragoons (renumbered D/33619).]

McALLISTER Private Edward 24119, 33734 & 7041797. From Templemore, County Londonderry. A hawker. [Enlisted in March 1916 and joined the 7th or 8th (Service) Battalion in 49th Brigade, 16th (Irish) Division.] Joined the 9th (North Irish Horse) Battalion when the 7th/8th (Service) Battalion was disbanded in February 1918. Re-enlisted 16 December 1919 for Regular Army service with Princess Victoria's (Royal Irish Fusiliers) (renumbered 33734, renumbered 7041797). Served with the 1st Battalion in Persia and Mesopotamia in 1919/20. General Service Medal 1918-1962 with clasps 'Iraq' & 'NW Persia'. Transferred to the Army Reserve 21 October 1926. Discharged 15 December 1931.

McALLISTER Private Joseph 27558. From Belfast. Enlisted in April 1917. Posted to the 9th (North Irish Horse) Battalion in early-1918. **Killed in action** during the advance to Anseghem 25 October 1918, aged 21.

McALLISTER Lance Corporal Robert 24272. Born in 1897 at Belfast. A printer. Enlisted 20 April 1916 and joined the 10th (Reserve) Battalion. Lance Corporal 14 August 1916. To France 21 December 1916 and joined the 9th (Service) Battalion. 'C' Company. **Wounded** by a gunshot to the right knee at the Battle of Langemarck 16 August 1917. Evacuated to hospital in England. Joined the 10th (Reserve) Battalion 9 March 1918. [Transferred to the Royal Defence Corps (73186) 4 May 1918 and posted to 500th Protection Company 15 June 1918.] Transferred to the Class Z Reserve 14 April 1919.

McALLISTER Private Thomas 41128. From Strandtown, Belfast. [Enlisted 12 April 1915 into the Service Squadron, 6th (Inniskilling) Dragoons (UD/249). Sentenced to three days confinement to barracks for '*absenting himself without leave*' 10 May 1915. Absent without leave from 3 July 1915 until apprehended by the police in Belfast on 9 July 1915. Tried by District Court Martial 22 July 1915; found guilty and sentenced to twenty-eight days detention. To France with 36th (Ulster) Division in October 1915. Attached to Headquarters 36th (Ulster) Division as batman for Captain H M Appleton (Assistant Provost Marshall) 3 October 1915. Sentenced to the loss of seven days' pay for neglect of duty for failing to clean his billet when told to do so 7 November 1915. Later that day he shot himself in the lower leg with Captain Appleton's revolver; the Board of Inquiry found that the wound was self-inflicted. Admitted to 109th Field Ambulance and treated at 2nd General Hospital. Discharged from hospital 25 December 1915. In his absence he was sentenced to forty-two days Field Punishment Number 1 but the sentence was quashed by Headquarters 3rd Army. Sentenced to the loss of fourteen days' pay for reporting sick without due cause 31 December 1915. Sentenced to the loss of three days pay for being '*absent off parade*' 13 March 1916. Sentenced to fourteen days Field Punishment Number 1 for not complying with an order 18 March 1916.] Joined 36 Infantry Base Depot 25 August 1917. Sentenced to 21 days Field Punishment Number 2 for not complying with an order and insolence to a non-commissioned officer 1 September 1916. Joined the renamed 9th (North Irish Horse) Battalion from 36 Infantry Base Depot and transferred to Princess Victoria's (Royal Irish Fusiliers) in September/October 1917 (renumbered 41128). 'A' Company. Evacuated to hospital in England sick and held strength at the Depot from 14 December 1917. Discharged from hospital to the Irish Command Depot 22 January 1918. Posted to the 10th (Reserve) Battalion but **deserted** 1 May 1918.

McALPINE Lance Corporal Wallace 42529. [Enlisted in May 1915 into the North Irish Horse (1648). Transferred to the Military Mounted Police (renumbered 13080).] Joined the 9th (North Irish Horse) Battalion, Princess Victoria's (Royal Irish Fusiliers) with the draft of men transferred from The Royal Irish Rifles in September 1918.

McANESPIE Private Harry 24744 & 32982. [Enlisted in August 1916 and joined the 7th/8th (Service) Battalion in 49th Brigade, 16th (Irish) Division.] Joined the 9th (North Irish Horse) Battalion when the 7th/8th (Service) Battalion was disbanded in February 1918. Re-enlisted in 1919 for

Regular Army service with Princess Victoria's (Royal Irish Fusiliers) (renumbered 32982). He was not renumbered again; discharged before September 1920.

McARTHUR Private John 20324. Born at Newcastle-upon-Tyne. Lived at Whitley Bay, Northumberland. [Enlisted into The Royal Inniskilling Fusiliers (21262).] Transferred to Princess Victoria's (Royal Irish Fusiliers) on 30 June 1915 (renumbered 20324) and joined the 9th (Service) Battalion. To France with 36th (Ulster) Division in October 1915. 'C' Company. Bombing team during the attack at Hamel 1 July 1916. **Wounded** during the attack at Hamel 1 July 1916. **Missing** at the Battle of Langemarck 16 August 1917 and later declared **killed in action** on that date. 1914-15 Star.

McATEER Private Thomas 14529. From Tartaraghan, County Armagh. Served pre-war as a regular soldier with the 1st Battalion, Princess Victoria's (Royal Irish Fusiliers); discharged for misconduct. Enlisted September 1914 and joined the 9th (Service) Battalion. Forfeit six days pay for absence 2 January 1915. Awarded twenty-eight days detention 16 March 1915. Discharged for misconduct 14 April 1915.

McATEER Private Thomas W 23080. Enlisted in November 1915. Posted to the 9th (Service) Battalion. 'C' Company. **Wounded** during the attack at Hamel 1 July 1916. Re-enlisted in 1919 for Regular Army service with the Seaforth Highlanders (Ross-shire Buffs, The Duke of Albany's) (32898, renumbered 2811432). Served with the 1st Battalion.

McAULEY Private John 42466. From Castlerock, County Londonderry. [Enlisted into The Royal Inniskilling Fusiliers (31032). Transferred to The Royal Irish Rifles (renumbered 381).] Transferred at the Base Depot to Princess Victoria's (Royal Irish Fusiliers) 14 September 1918 and joined the 9th (North Irish Horse) Battalion 22 September 1918. **Killed in action** during the advance to Anseghem 25 October 1918, aged 20.

McAULEY Private Thomas 41495. [Enlisted in September 1914 into the North Irish Horse (1174). To France 18 December 1914. Served with 2nd North Irish Horse, X Corps Cavalry Regiment.] Joined the renamed 9th (North Irish Horse) Battalion from 36 Infantry Base Depot and transferred to Princess Victoria's (Royal Irish Fusiliers) in September/October 1917 (renumbered 41495). Transferred to the Class Z Reserve. 1914-15 Star.

McAULEY Lance Corporal William John 41556. Born in 1894. From Randalstown, County Antrim. A farmer. [Enlisted 28 October 1915 into the North Irish Horse (1759). Lance Corporal 1 August 1916. Corporal 14 September 1916. To France 20 September 1916. Reverted to Private at his own request 13 November 1916. Admitted to the field ambulance sick (psoriasis) November 1916, (influenza) February 1917 and (tonsillitis) March 1917.] Joined the renamed 9th (North Irish Horse) Battalion from 36 Infantry Base Depot and transferred to Princess Victoria's (Royal Irish Fusiliers) in September/October 1917 (renumbered 41556). **Wounded** by shell shrapnel in the left thigh and right buttock at Poperinghe railway station and **died of wounds** in 10th Casualty Clearing Station at Remy Siding 11 April 1918.

McAVOY Private William 24418. From Belfast. Enlisted in May 1916. Posted to the 9th (Service) Battalion. 'A' Company. **Wounded** at the Battle of Langemarck 16 August 1917. [Transferred to the Army Service Corps (renumbered M/380519). **Deserted** 1 March 1918.]

McAVOY Private William Robert 42463 & 33566. [Enlisted into the 16th (Service) Battalion, The Royal Irish Rifles (2nd County Down) (Pioneers) (16/87). Posted to the 2nd Battalion, The Royal Irish Rifles.] Transferred at the Base Depot to Princess Victoria's (Royal Irish Fusiliers) 14 September 1918 (renumbered 42463) and joined the 9th (North Irish Horse) Battalion 22 September 1918. Transferred to the Class Z Reserve 13 April 1919. 1914-15 Star. Re-enlisted in 1919 for Regular Army service with Princess Victoria's (Royal Irish Fusiliers) (renumbered 33566). Transferred to The Cameronians (Scottish Rifles) (renumbered 3237412). Medals forfeit due to misconduct.

McBRIDE Private George 22029. Born at Belfast. [Enlisted in October 1915 and joined the 7th (Service) Battalion in 49th Brigade, 16th (Irish) Division.] Joined the 9th (North Irish Horse) Battalion when the 7th/8th (Service) Battalion was disbanded in February 1918. 'D' Company. **Missing** in the period 21-28 March 1918 during the retreat from St Quentin and later declared **killed in action** 29 March 1918.

McBRIDE Private James 41214. From Ballymoney, County Antrim. [Enlisted in May 1915 into the North Irish Horse (1615). Served with 2nd North Irish Horse, X Corps Cavalry Regiment.] Joined the renamed 9th (North Irish Horse) Battalion from 36 Infantry Base Depot and transferred to Princess Victoria's (Royal Irish Fusiliers) in September/October 1917 (renumbered 41214). **Captured** in 1918.

McBRIDE DCM Acting Warrant Officer Class II Robert John 23566. From Crieve, Ballybay, County Monaghan. Enlisted in December 1915. Posted to the 9th (Service) Battalion. **Wounded. DCM** – Wulverghem 12 April 1918 (Sergeant). ***Medaille Militaire* (France)**. Acting Company Sergeant Major. Brother of Lance Corporal William McBride MM.

McBRIDE Private William 14575. From Tandragee, Portadown, County Armagh. Enlisted September 1914. To France with 36th (Ulster) Division in October 1915. 'B' Company. **Wounded** at the Battle of Langemarck 16 August 1917. [Transferred to the Royal Army Medical Corps (136752).] 1914-15 Star.

McBRIDE MM Lance Corporal William 22935. From Crieve, Ballybay, County Monaghan. Enlisted in November 1915. Posted to the 9th (Service) Battalion. 'D' Company. **MM. Captured** in the period 21-28 March 1918 during the retreat from St Quentin. Repatriated in December 1918. Brother of Warrant Officer Class II Robert John McBride DCM.

McCABE Private Alexander 14573. Born 5 April 1896. From Seagoe, Portadown, County Armagh. 4th (Portadown) Battalion, Armagh Regiment, Ulster Volunteer Force. Enlisted September 1914. To France with 36th (Ulster) Division in October 1915. **Killed in action** during the attack at Hamel 1 July 1916, aged 20. 1914-15 Star.

McCABE Private Henry 23736. Enlisted in January 1916. Posted to the 9th (Service) Battalion. 'D' Company. **Missing** in the period 21-28 March 1918 during the retreat from St Quentin believed **captured**.

McCABE Private Stephen 14564. From Lurgan, County Armagh. Enlisted September 1914. To France with 36th (Ulster) Division in October 1915. 'D' Company. **Wounded** on 17 November 1916. **Wounded** at the Battle of Langemarck 16 August 1917. **Missing** in the period 21-28 March 1918 during the retreat from St Quentin believed **captured**.

McCAFFERY Private James 22851. Born at Armagh, County Armagh. From Strabane, County Tyrone. Enlisted in November 1915. Posted to the 9th (Service) Battalion. 'D' Company. **Missing** in the period 21-28 March 1918 during the retreat from St Quentin and later declared **killed in action** 29 March 1918.

McCAFFERY Private Vincent 3556. Born at Armagh, County Armagh. Enlisted in May/June 1915 into Princess Victoria's (Royal Irish Fusiliers) Special Reserve. [Served with the 8th (Service) Battalion in 49th Brigade, 16th (Irish) Division.] Joined the 9th (North Irish Horse) Battalion when the 7th/8th (Service) Battalion was disbanded in February 1918. 'C' Company. **Killed in action** 24 March 1918 during the retreat from St Quentin.

McCAIRNS Private David 33004 & 7041257. (Original number unknown; 33004 was issued on re-enlistment in September 1919.) From Glasgow, a miner. [To France 19 April 1916 and joined the 7th (Service) Battalion in 49th Brigade, 16th (Irish) Division. **Wounded** by a gunshot to the face 7 September 1916. **Wounded** by a gunshot to the back at the Battle of Langemarck 16 August 1917 and evacuated to hospital in England.] To France 19 March 1918 and joined the 9th (North Irish Horse) Battalion. Re-enlisted 6 September 1919 for Regular Army service with Princess Victoria's (Royal Irish Fusiliers) (renumbered 33004, renumbered 7041257). Served with the 1st Battalion in Persia and Mesopotamia in 1919/20. General Service Medal 1918-1962 with clasps 'Iraq' & 'NW Persia'. Discharged 30 December 1921. Lived at Glasgow.

McCALL Corporal James 22793. Enlisted 11 November 1915. Posted to the 9th (Service) Battalion. Discharged as no longer physically fit for war service due to sickness 12 December 1918. Silver War Badge, number B57480.

McCALL Private John 41165. [Enlisted in November 1914 into the Service Squadron, 6th (Inniskilling) Dragoons (UD/115). To France with 36th (Ulster) Division in October 1915. Served with 2nd North Irish Horse, X Corps Cavalry Regiment.] Joined the renamed 9th (North Irish Horse) Battalion from 36 Infantry Base Depot and transferred to Princess Victoria's (Royal Irish Fusiliers) in September/October 1917 (renumbered 41165). Transferred to the Class Z Reserve 23 March 1919. 1914-15 Star.

McCALLUM Private Joseph 42239. [Enlisted into the Army Service Corps Special Reserve (T4/241119 – Driver). To France 2 May 1915.] Transferred to Princess Victoria's (Royal Irish Fusiliers) 8 May 1918 (renumbered 42239) and joined the 9th (North Irish Horse) Battalion. Disembodied 7 February 1919. 1914-15 Star.

McCALLUM Private William 17951. Born at Lurgan, County Armagh. Enlisted into the 9th (Service) Battalion in February 1915. To France with 36th (Ulster) Division in October 1915. 'C' Company. Bombing team during the attack at Hamel 1 July 1916, after which he was declared **missing**. In May 1917 he was declared **killed in action** during the attack at Hamel 1 July 1916. 1914-15 Star.

McCAMBLEY Corporal James 14492. A labourer from Belfast. Enlisted September 1914. To France with 36th (Ulster) Division in October 1915. **Killed in action** during the attack at Hamel 1 July 1916.

McCAMMOND Corporal Archibald 14539. (The 1901 and 1911 census records show his name as McCammon.) From Milford, County Armagh. A linen weaver. Enlisted September 1914. To France with 36th (Ulster) Division in October 1915. 'C' Company. **Missing** at the Battle of Langemarck 16 August 1917 and later declared **killed in action** on that date, aged 20. 1914-15 Star.

McCANN Private A Edward 16087. Enlisted into the 9th (Service) Battalion in October 1914. To France with 36th (Ulster) Division in October 1915. [Transferred to the Labour Corps (renumbered 231617).] Discharged 15 July 1918. 1914-15 Star.

McCANN Private Alexander 22780. From Atkinson's Avenue, Portadown, County Armagh. A mechanic. Enlisted 9 November 1915 and joined the 10th (Reserve) Battalion. To France 13 June 1916 and joined the 9th (Service) Battalion. 'B' Company. **Missing** at the Battle of Langemarck 16 August 1917 and later declared **killed in action** on that date.

McCann Private Francis 5315. [Enlisted into Princess Victoria's (Royal Irish Fusiliers) Special Reserve. To France 31 October 1914 and joined the 1st Battalion. Posted to the 5th/6th (Service) Battalion.] Posted to the 9th (North Irish Horse) Battalion. 1914 Star.

McCANN Private Hugh 6403 & 7040083. Born in 1898 at Belfast. From Darkley, Keady, County Armagh. [Enlisted on 7 November 1915 into Princess Victoria's (Royal Irish Fusiliers) Special Reserve, aged 17. To France 5 November 1917 and joined the 7th/8th (Service) Battalion in 49th Brigade, 16th (Irish) Division.] Joined the 9th (North Irish Horse) Battalion when the 7th/8th (Service) Battalion was disbanded in February 1918. 'C' Company. **Captured** in the period 21-28 March 1918 during the retreat from St Quentin. Re-enlisted into Princess Victoria's (Royal Irish Fusiliers) Special Reserve on 2 April 1919 (renumbered 7040083). Discharged 6 November 1921. Emigrated to Montreal, Canada after the war but returned to Ireland in the 1930s and settled in Banbridge, County Down. Worked as a boiler-man at Thomas Ferguson's linen factory. His brother, Gunner Thomas McCann Royal Garrison Artillery, died of wounds on 22 September 1915 serving with 27th Trench Mortar Battery.

McCANN Private James 13319. [Enlisted in September 1914 and joined the 7th (Service) Battalion in 49th Brigade, 16th (Irish) Division.] Joined the 9th (North Irish Horse) Battalion when the 7th/8th (Service) Battalion was disbanded in February 1918.

McCANN Lance Sergeant John 25211. Enlisted in November 1916. Posted to the 9th (Service) Battalion. [Transferred to the Royal Air Force (renumbered 286810).]

McCANN Private Robert 14507. Born at Armagh, County Armagh. Enlisted September 1914. To France with 36th (Ulster) Division in October 1915. **Killed in action** during the attack at Hamel 1 July 1916. 1914-15 Star. 1914-15 Star.

McCAPPIN Sergeant John 14576. Born at Lurgan, County Armagh. Enlisted September 1914. To France with 36th (Ulster) Division in October 1915. **Killed in action** by shellfire at Hamel 26 June 1916. 1914-15 Star.

McCARLEY MM Private William 41329. From Harryville, Ballymena. [Enlisted in August 1916 into the North Irish Horse (2252). Served with 2nd North Irish Horse, X Corps Cavalry Regiment.] Joined the renamed 9th (North Irish Horse) Battalion from 36 Infantry Base Depot and transferred to Princess Victoria's (Royal Irish Fusiliers) in September/October 1917 (renumbered 41329). **MM** – Wulverghem April 1918.

McCARROLL Private George 14561. Enlisted September 1914. To France with 36th (Ulster) Division in October 1915. 'C' Company. Signaller at the forward visual transmitting station during the attack at Hamel 1 July 1916 and did not take part in the attack. Transferred to the Class Z Reserve 15 March 1919. 1914-15 Star.

McCARTNEY Corporal Alexander 14505. Born in 1890 at Armagh, County Armagh. Enlisted September 1914. To France with 36th (Ulster) Division in October 1915. 'A' Company. Forfeit six days pay for absence. **Wounded** during the attack at Hamel 1 July 1916. Lance Corporal 25 September 1916. **Wounded** by a gunshot to the face (injuries to his ear, mouth and tongue) at the Battle of Langemarck 16 August 1917 and evacuated to hospital in England. Joined the 10th (Reserve) Battalion 20 November 1917. [Transferred to the Royal Defence Corps (73188) 4 May 1918. Served with 200th, 500th and 455th Protection Companies. Corporal 13 February 1919.] 1914-15 Star. Transferred to the Class Z Reserve 27 March 1919.

McCARTNEY Private Edward 41170. [Enlisted in November 1915 into the Service Squadron, 6th (Inniskilling) Dragoons (UD/307). Served with 2nd North Irish Horse, X Corps Cavalry Regiment.] Joined the renamed 9th (North Irish Horse) Battalion from 36 Infantry Base Depot and transferred to Princess Victoria's (Royal Irish Fusiliers) in September/October 1917 (renumbered 41170).

McCARTNEY Private George 14522. From Armagh, County Armagh. Enlisted September 1914. To France with 36th (Ulster) Division in October 1915. **Wounded** during the attack at Hamel 1 July 1916. [Transferred to the Machine Gun Corps (136940).] 1914-15 Star.

MacCAULEY Private Richard 42511. [Enlisted April/May 1918 into The Royal Irish Rifles (22559).] Transferred at the Base Depot to Princess Victoria's (Royal Irish Fusiliers) 14 September 1918 (renumbered 42511) and joined the 9th (North Irish Horse) Battalion 22 September 1918.

McCAUSLAND Lance Corporal Joseph Ernest 42562 & 7042206. Born in 1901 at Clogherny, County Tyrone. [Enlisted into The Royal Inniskilling Fusiliers (29978). Transferred to The Royal Irish Rifles (renumbered 22762).] Transferred at the Base Depot to Princess Victoria's (Royal Irish Fusiliers) 14 September 1918 (renumbered 42562) and joined the 9th (North Irish Horse) Battalion 22 September 1918. Re-enlisted in early-1919 for Regular Army service with Princess Victoria's (Royal Irish Fusiliers) (renumbered 7042206). Served with the 1st Battalion in Persia and Mesopotamia in 1919/20. General Service Medal 1918-1962 with clasps 'Iraq' & 'NW Persia'. Died 8 November 1980, aged 79. Buried at Clogherny Presbyterian Church, County Tyrone.

McCLATCHEY Private George 16088. Born in 1896 at Lurgan, County Armagh. Enlisted into the 9th (Service) Battalion 12 October 1914. To France with 36th (Ulster) Division in October 1915. 'C' Company. Signaller at the forward visual transmitting station during the attack at Hamel 1 July 1916 and did not take part in the attack. **Wounded** at the Battle of Langemarck 16 August 1917. Discharged as no longer physically fit for war service due to wounds 8 May 1918. Silver War Badge, number 363628. 1914-15 Star. His brother, Bombardier Samuel McClatchey, was killed in action on 10 August 1917 serving with 92nd Battery, 17th Brigade, Royal Field Artillery in 29th Division.

McCLATCHEY Private George 23288. [Enlisted on 29 November 1915. Served with the 7th/8th (Service) Battalion in 49th Brigade, 16th (Irish) Division.] Joined the 9th (North Irish Horse) Battalion when the 7th/8th (Service) Battalion was disbanded in February 1918. 'C' Company. Believed **wounded** in the period 21-28 March 1918 during the retreat from St Quentin. Discharged as no longer physically fit for war service due to wounds 16 October 1918. Silver War Badge, number B34293.

McCLATCHEY Private Richard 18700. From Portadown, County Armagh. Enlisted 26 April 1915 into the 9th (Service) Battalion. To France with 36th (Ulster) Division in October 1915. **Wounded** during the attack at Hamel 1 July 1916. Discharged as no longer physically fit for war service due to wounds 18 June 1918, aged 23. Silver War Badge, number 411847. 1914-15 Star.

McCLATCHEY Private Samuel 14495. Born in 1897 at Portadown, County Armagh. Enlisted September 1914. To France with 36th (Ulster) Division in October 1915. 'B' Company. **Wounded** at the Battle of Langemarck 16 August 1917. [Posted to the 1st Battalion.] Transferred to the Class Z Reserve 31 March 1919. 1914-15 Star.

McCLATCHEY Private Samuel 21759. From Lurgan, County Armagh. Enlisted in October 1915. Posted to the 9th (Service) Battalion in May/June 1916. 'C' Company. Company bomb carrier during the attack at Hamel 1 July 1916. **Wounded** during the attack at Hamel 1 July 1916. [Transferred to the Labour Corps (renumbered 570452).]

McCLAY Private Allen 42482. Enlisted 11 February 1918. Joined the 9th (North Irish Horse) Battalion, Princess Victoria's (Royal Irish Fusiliers) with the draft of men transferred from The Royal Irish Rifles in September 1918. **Wounded**. Discharged as no longer physically fit for war service due to wounds 25 July 1919. Silver War Badge, number B302852.

McCLAY Lance Corporal Hamilton 41477. Born 4 March 1896 at Raneany East, County Donegal. [Enlisted in February 1914 into the North Irish Horse (897). To France 20 August 1914 with 'C' Squadron as 5th Division Cavalry and then as GHQ Troops. Served with 2nd North Irish Horse, X Corps Cavalry Regiment.] Joined the renamed 9th (North Irish Horse) Battalion from 36 Infantry Base Depot and transferred to Princess Victoria's (Royal Irish Fusiliers) in September/October 1917 (renumbered 41477). 1914 Star. Emigrated to the United States and lived in Woburn, Middlesex, Massachusetts where he died on 28 February 1973, aged 76.

McCLEAN Private Herbert William 41392. Born in 1891. From Ballymena, Country Antrim. A linen worker. [Enlisted 23 November 1915 into the North Irish Horse (1952). To France 5 August 1916. Served with 2nd North Irish Horse, X Corps Cavalry Regiment.] Joined the renamed 9th (North Irish Horse) Battalion from 36 Infantry Base Depot and transferred to Princess Victoria's (Royal Irish Fusiliers) in September/October 1917 (renumbered 41392). 'A' Company. **Captured** in the period 21-28 March 1918 during the retreat from St Quentin. Repatriated 25 November 1918. Transferred to the Class Z Reserve 10 April 1919. His brother, Private John Gerald McClean, served with The Royal Scots (Lothian Regiment).

McCLEAN Private Joseph Henry 29536. Born in 1899 at Lisburn, County Antrim. A miller from Dundonald, County Down. Enlisted 12 April 1916 and joined the 10th (Reserve) Battalion. Lance Corporal 21 May 1917. [Transferred to 20th (Reserve) Battalion, The Royal Irish Rifles 30 June 1917. Charged with absence from parade and reverted to Private 24 August 1917.] Transferred back to Princess Victoria's (Royal Irish Fusiliers) in March 1918 (renumbered 29536). To Infantry Base Depot, France 3 April 1918 and posted to the 9th (North Irish Horse) Battalion. **Wounded** by a gunshot to the chest during the attack south of Wulverghem on 4 September 1918 and **died of wounds** in 62nd Casualty Clearing Station 13 September 1918, aged 19.

McCLEAN Private Thomas James 24723 & 33965. Born in 1897 at Drumcree, Portadown, County Armagh. Enlisted 22 August 1916 and joined the 10th (Reserve) Battalion. To France 3 March 1917 and joined the 9th (Service) Battalion. **Wounded** by shrapnel to the left ear. [Transferred to the Labour Corps (renumbered 410841) 22 September 1917. Served with 888th and 961st Area Employment Companies. Transferred to The Royal Sussex Regiment (renumbered 30851) and joined the 17th (Service) Battalion, The Royal Sussex Regiment in France on 15 June 1918. Posted to the 3rd (Reserve) Battalion, The Royal Sussex Regiment 28 December 1918.] Transferred to the Class Z Reserve 20 February 1919. Re-enlisted 28 February 1920 for Regular Army service with Princess Victoria's (Royal Irish Fusiliers) (renumbered 33965). Joined the 2nd Battalion on 9 March 1920. 'C' Company. Sentenced to seven days confined to barracks for being absent without leave from 6 to 9 March 1920. To Dover Military Hospital due to the effects of his wound and referred to the Royal Herbert Hospital, Woolwich. He refused an operation and returned to the 2nd Battalion. **Deserted** 7 July 1920.

McCLEAN Private William John 14525. From Portadown, County Armagh. 4th (Portadown) Battalion, Armagh Regiment, Ulster Volunteer Force. Enlisted September 1914. To France with 36th (Ulster) Division in October 1915. 'C' Company. Attached to Headquarters 108th Brigade and did not take part in the attack at Hamel on 1 July 1916. **Captured** in the period 21-28 March 1918 during the retreat from St Quentin. Transferred to the Class Z Reserve 28 March 1919. 1914-15 Star.

McCLEAN DCM Acting Warrant Officer Class II William John 14556. Born in 1889 at Portadown, County Armagh. A linen weaver. Enlisted September 1914. To France with 36th (Ulster) Division in October 1915. 'B' Company. Battalion Bugler 1916. As a Lance Sergeant **36th (Ulster) Division Certificate for Gallantry** 1 July 1916. As a sergeant he was **wounded** when shot in the right arm near Spanbroekmolen 5 June 1917. Acting Company Sergeant Major. **Wounded** during the retreat from St Quentin 21-28 March 1918 but subsequently rejoined the 9th (North Irish

Horse) Battalion. **DCM** – Bailleul 24 August 1918. Discharged as no longer physically fit for war service due to wounds 16 April 1919. Silver War Badge, number B214558. 1914-15 Star. After the war he served as Sergeant in the Royal Ulster Constabulary at Camlough and in Belfast. He retired after six years service due to the impact of his wounds and returned to work as a tailor. He lived in Portadown. He died in 1962, aged 73, and is buried in Drumcree Church of Ireland Churchyard. His son served in the Royal Air Force during the Second World War.

McCLEARY Private Andrew Waring 14563. Born in 1897 at Lurgan, County Armagh. Enlisted September 1914. To France with 36th (Ulster) Division in October 1915. 'C' Company. Detached and did not take part in the attack at Hamel on 1 July 1916. **Wounded** at the Battle of Langemarck 16 August 1917. Discharged as no longer physically fit for war service due to wounds 21 February 1919. Silver War Badge, number B97869. 1914-15 Star. Brother of Privates John and Thomas Henry McCleary.

McCLEARY Private Hugh 21576. From Belfast. Enlisted in August 1915. Posted to the 9th (Service) Battalion in mid/late 1916. 'C' Company. **Wounded** in the left eye on a raid at Spanbroekmolen 4 June 1917. [Transferred to the Machine Gun Corps (renumbered 133189).]

McCLEARY Sergeant James 14549. From Lurgan, County Armagh. Enlisted September 1914. To France with 36th (Ulster) Division in October 1915. **Wounded** (shellshock) during the attack at Hamel 1 July 1916. [Transferred to the Labour Corps (renumbered 230550 Private).] Transferred to the Class Z Reserve 9 April 1919. 1914-15 Star.

McCLEARY Private John 14548. From Lurgan, County Armagh. A linen weaver. Enlisted September 1914. To France with 36th (Ulster) Division in October 1915. 'C' Company. Lewis gunner during the attack at Hamel on 1 July 1916, where he was **wounded**. **Wounded** at the Battle of Langemarck 16 August 1917. **Wounded** during the retreat from St Quentin 21-28 March 1918 and **died of wounds** in Ireland 10 May 1918. 1914-15 Star. Brother of Privates Andrew Waring and Thomas Henry McCleary.

McCLEARY Private Thomas Henry 14560. Born in 1896 at Lurgan, County Armagh. A printer in a linen mill. Enlisted September 1914, aged 18 giving his age as 19 years. To France with 36th (Ulster) Division in October 1915. 'C' Company. Bombing team during the attack at Hamel 1 July 1916, which he survived unwounded. [Transferred to The Royal Welch Fusiliers (57252).] Discharged as no longer physically fit for war service 13 October 1917, aged 21. Silver War Badge, number 429733. 1914-15 Star. Brother of Privates Andrew Waring and John McCleary.

McCLEERY Private Robert 41593. From Killyleagh, County Down. [Enlisted in June 1916 into the North Irish Horse (2198). Served with 2nd North Irish Horse, X Corps Cavalry Regiment.] Joined the renamed 9th (North Irish Horse) Battalion from 36 Infantry Base Depot and transferred to Princess Victoria's (Royal Irish Fusiliers) in September/October 1917 (renumbered 41593). 'D' Company. **Captured** in the period 21-28 March 1918 during the retreat from St Quentin.

McCLELLAND MM Private George B 49741. From Belfast. [Enlisted into The Royal Irish Rifles (964).] Transferred to Princess Victoria's (Royal Irish Fusiliers) in April 1918 (renumbered 49741) and joined the 9th (North Irish Horse) Battalion. **MM** – Bailleul August 1918. [Transferred to the Machine Gun Corps (renumbered 195792).]

McCLELLAND Private John 10417. [Enlisted into Princess Victoria's (Royal Irish Fusiliers) as a regular soldier in August 1910. Transferred to the Labour Corps (renumbered 200254) after January 1917. Served with 254th District Employment Company.] Transferred back to Princess Victoria's (Royal Irish Fusiliers) and joined the 9th (North Irish Horse) Battalion (retained number 10417). Tried by Field General Court Martial on 27 November 1918 charged with *'absenting himself without leave'*; found guilty and sentenced to forty-two days Field Punishment Number 2.

McCLELLAND Private Richard 42563 & 7042207. [Enlisted into The Royal Irish Rifles (21790).] Transferred at the Base Depot to Princess Victoria's (Royal Irish Fusiliers) 14 September 1918 (renumbered 42563) and joined the 9th (North Irish Horse) Battalion 22 September 1918. Re-enlisted in early-1919 for Regular Army service with Princess Victoria's (Royal Irish Fusiliers) (renumbered 7042207). Served with the 1st Battalion in Persia and Mesopotamia in 1919/20. General Service Medal 1918-1962 with clasps 'Iraq' & 'NW Persia'.

McCLELLAND MM Private Thomas Alexander 41307. From Armagh, County Armagh. [Enlisted in July 1916 into the North Irish Horse (2231). Served with 2nd North Irish Horse, X Corps Cavalry

Regiment.] Joined the renamed 9th (North Irish Horse) Battalion from 36 Infantry Base Depot and transferred to Princess Victoria's (Royal Irish Fusiliers) in September/October 1917 (renumbered 41307). **MM** – St Quentin 21-28 March 1918. After the war he joined the General Post Office and became Assistant Superintendent, Travelling Post Offices Section. **BEM (Civil)**.

McCLINTON Private John Harris 41436. [Enlisted in January 1915 into the North Irish Horse (1383). Attached to 54th (East Anglian) Division Military Mounted Police, appointed Lance Corporal and embarked with the Mediterranean Expeditionary Force July 1915. Evacuated to hospital in England. Served with 2nd North Irish Horse, X Corps Cavalry Regiment.] Joined the renamed 9th (North Irish Horse) Battalion from 36 Infantry Base Depot and transferred to Princess Victoria's (Royal Irish Fusiliers) in September/October 1917 (renumbered 41436). 1914-15 Star.

McCLURE Private Edward 41284. Born 14 August 1894 at Gracehill Moravian settlement, Ahoghill, County Antrim. [Enlisted in November 1915 into the North Irish Horse (1918). Served with 2nd North Irish Horse, X Corps Cavalry Regiment.] Joined the renamed 9th (North Irish Horse) Battalion from 36 Infantry Base Depot and transferred to Princess Victoria's (Royal Irish Fusiliers) in September/October 1917 (renumbered 41284). [Part of the draft transferred on 19 June 1918 to The Royal Irish Rifles (45841).] Died in 1969.

McCLURE Private John George 41559. Born 4 June 1896 at Larne, County Antrim. Lived with his parents in Dublin. A clerk. [Enlisted 17 November 1915 into the North Irish Horse (1948). To France 5 August 1916. Served with 2nd North Irish Horse, X Corps Cavalry Regiment.] To hospital from 36 Infantry Base Depot 19 September 1917 sick (impetigo). Transferred to Princess Victoria's (Royal Irish Fusiliers) 20 September 1917 (renumbered 41559). On discharge from hospital joined the renamed 9th (North Irish Horse) Battalion. 'D' Company. **Wounded** by a gunshot to the right ear and **captured** on 27 March 1918 during the retreat from St Quentin. Held at a prisoner of war camp in Germany. Repatriated 16 December 1918. Admitted to King George V Hospital, Dublin for treatment for his wounded ear. Discharged as no longer physically fit for war service due to wounds 25 April 1919. Silver War Badge, number B218362. After the war he became an accountant and worked in Honduras, Costa Rica and Nicaragua. He emigrated to the United States and lived at Jackson Heights, New York, working for Transfilm Inc. He became a US citizen in 1949. He died at Jackson Heights, New York in 1968.

McCLURE Private Samuel 14572. From Tamnaficarbet, Portadown, County Armagh. 4th (Portadown) Battalion, Armagh Regiment, Ulster Volunteer Force. Enlisted September 1914. To France with 36th (Ulster) Division in October 1915. 1914-15 Star.

McCLURG Private Charles 17550. From Belfast. Enlisted into the 9th (Service) Battalion in November/December 1914. To France with 36th (Ulster) Division in October 1915. **Wounded** during the attack at Hamel 1 July 1916. [Transferred to The Northumberland Fusiliers (49825).] Transferred to the Class Z Reserve. 1914-15 Star.

McCLURG Corporal James 14508. From Downpatrick, County Down. Formerly chauffeur to the Primate of Armagh. Enlisted September 1914. To France with 36th (Ulster) Division in October 1915. **Wounded** during the attack at Hamel 1 July 1916. Discharged as no longer physically fit for war service due to sickness 7 June 1918, aged 29. Silver War Badge, number 395832. 1914-15 Star.

McCOMBE Private James 14491. From Portadown, County Armagh. Enlisted September 1914. To France with 36th (Ulster) Division in October 1915. **Wounded** during the attack at Hamel 1 July 1916. Discharged as no longer physically fit for war service due to wounds 20 October 1916, aged 36. Silver War Badge, number 425673.

McCOMBRIE Private George 41518. See Private G McCoubrie below.

McCOMMICK Lance Corporal Samuel John 14541. Born in 1875 at Portadown, County Armagh. A mill foreman. Enlisted September 1914, aged 39, giving his age as 35. To France with 36th (Ulster) Division in October 1915. 'B' Company. **Wounded** near River Douve by machine-gun fire 11 August 1916. [Transferred to the Labour Corps (renumbered 231620).] Discharged as no longer physically fit for war service due to wounds 21 May 1918, aged 42. Silver War Badge, number, 390750. 1914-15 Star.

McCONKEY MM Sergeant James Campbell Hall 20444. Known as Campbell. Born 21 October 1896 in Monaghan, County Monaghan. From Newry, County Down. Enlisted into the 9th (Service)

Battalion in June 1915. 'C' Company. **MM** – Raid at Spanbroekmolen 4 June 1917. **Wounded** at the Battle of Langemarck 16 August 1917. Died in Dover, Kent 1971, aged 74. Brother of Corporal Thomas O'Loughlin McConkey.

McCONKEY Corporal Thomas O'Loughlin 20443. Born in 1895 in Monaghan, County Monaghan. From Newry, County Down. Enlisted into the 9th (Service) Battalion in June 1915. 'C' Company. **Wounded** at the Battle of Langemarck 16 August 1917. Brother of Sergeant James Campbell Hall McConkey.

McCONNELL Private Edward 14552. Enlisted September 1914. To France with 36th (Ulster) Division in October 1915. [Transferred to The Worcestershire Regiment (renumbered 47651).] 1914-15 Star.

McCONNELL Private Hugh 23449. From Bessbrook, County Armagh. Enlisted in December 1915. Posted to the 9th (Service) Battalion. **Wounded** in mid-1916. [Posted to the 2nd Garrison Battalion in Salonika.]

McCONNELL Private Robert 41445. Born at Cloughfin, County Antrim. [Enlisted in November 1915 into the North Irish Horse (1859). Served with 2nd North Irish Horse, X Corps Cavalry Regiment.] Joined the renamed 9th (North Irish Horse) Battalion from 36 Infantry Base Depot and transferred to Princess Victoria's (Royal Irish Fusiliers) in September/October 1917 (renumbered 41445). **Missing** in the period 11-18 April 1918 in the actions between Wulverghem and Kemmel; subsequently declared **killed in action** 19 April 1918, aged 23.

McCONNELL Private Robert 42564, 33495 & 7041633. From Ballymacarrett, County Down. [Enlisted 26 November 1917, aged 18, into The Royal Irish Rifles (21032).] Transferred at the Base Depot to Princess Victoria's (Royal Irish Fusiliers) 14 September 1918 (renumbered 42564) and joined the 9th (North Irish Horse) Battalion 22 September 1918. Re-enlisted 28 May 1919 for Regular Army service with Princess Victoria's (Royal Irish Fusiliers) (renumbered 33495, renumbered 7041633). Discharged 31 March 1922. Enlisted into the Royal Air Force 4 July 1939.

McCONVILLE Private Edward 3885 & 7040044. From Lurgan, County Armagh. A bottler. Enlisted on 23 November 1915 into Princess Victoria's (Royal Irish Fusiliers) Special Reserve, aged 18. [To France 13 March 1916 and joined the 8th (Service) Battalion in 49th Brigade, 16th (Irish) Division. **Wounded** in mid-1916.] Joined the 9th (North Irish Horse) Battalion when the 7th/8th (Service) Battalion was disbanded in February 1918. 'D' Company. **Captured** in the period 21-28 March 1918 during the retreat from St Quentin. Re-enlisted on 26 March 1919 for Regular Army service with Princess Victoria's (Royal Irish Fusiliers) (7040044). Discharged 4 March 1921.

McCONVILLE Private John 14570. Born at Ballinagarrick, County Armagh. 4th (Portadown) Battalion, Armagh Regiment, Ulster Volunteer Force. Enlisted September 1914. To France with 36th (Ulster) Division in October 1915. **Killed in action** during the attack at Hamel 1 July 1916. 1914-15 Star.

McCONVILLE Private Joseph 19808. Enlisted into the 9th (Service) Battalion 10 May 1915. To France 18 November 1915 and rejoined the 9th (Service) Battalion. A Field General Court Martial on 20 October 1916 quashed a charge of malingering, for which he had been sentenced to fourteen days Field Punishment Number 2 by the commanding officer. Tried by Field General Court Martial on 11 April 1917 charged with *'when on active service striking his superior officer'* and *'drunkenness'*; found guilty and sentenced to eighty-four days Field Punishment Number 1. Discharged as no longer physically fit for war service due to sickness 6 May 1918, aged 34. Silver War Badge, number 407199.

McCONVILLE Private Patrick 3279. [Enlisted on 24 July 1914 into Princess Victoria's (Royal Irish Fusiliers) Special Reserve. To France 1 February 1915 and joined the 2nd Battalion. Posted to the 7th/8th (Service) Battalion in 49th Brigade, 16th (Irish) Division.] Joined the 9th (North Irish Horse) Battalion when the 7th/8th (Service) Battalion was disbanded in February 1918. 'D' Company. Believed **wounded** in the period 21-28 March 1918 during the retreat from St Quentin. [Posted to the 2nd Battalion.] Discharged as no longer physically fit for war service due to sickness 11 December 1919. Silver War Badge, number 496777.

McCONVILLE Company Quartermaster Sergeant Thomas 14516. From Lurgan, County Armagh. Enlisted September 1914. Took part in the recruiting march in February 1915 (Lance Sergeant). To France with 36th (Ulster) Division in October 1915. Company Quartermaster

Sergeant. **MSM**. Battalion Colour Guard June 1919. 1914-15 Star. His brother, Private James McConville, also served with Princess Victoria's (Royal Irish Fusiliers) and with the 5th (Service) Battalion, The Royal Irish Regiment (Pioneers) in the Army of Occupation.

McCOO Private Joseph 27802. [Enlisted in July 1917 and joined the 7th/8th (Service) Battalion in 49th Brigade, 16th (Irish) Division.] Joined the 9th (North Irish Horse) Battalion when the 7th/8th (Service) Battalion was disbanded in February 1918.

McCORD Private Thomas James 23202. Born at Lurgan, County Armagh. Enlisted in November 1915. Posted to the 9th (Service) Battalion. 'C' Company. **Wounded** at the Battle of Langemarck 16 August 1917. Discharged as no longer physically fit for war service due to wounds 15 November 1918. Silver War Badge, number B44336.

McCORD Private William 14536. From Lurgan, County Armagh. Enlisted September 1914. To France with 36th (Ulster) Division in October 1915. 'D' Company. **Wounded** at the Battle of Langemarck 16 August 1917. **Captured** in the period 21-28 March 1918 during the retreat from St Quentin. Transferred to the Class Z Reserve 1 April 1919. 1914-15 Star.

McCORMACK Private Albert 41267. [Enlisted into the 6th (Service) Battalion (18292). Joined the Mediterranean Expeditionary Force 22 September 1915. Transferred to the North Irish Horse (renumbered 2210) in July 1916. Served with 2nd North Irish Horse, X Corps Cavalry Regiment.] Joined the renamed 9th (North Irish Horse) Battalion from 36 Infantry Base Depot and transferred to Princess Victoria's (Royal Irish Fusiliers) in September/October 1917 (renumbered 41267). 'C' Company. **Missing** in the period 21-28 March 1918 during the retreat from St Quentin believed **captured**. Transferred to the Class Z Reserve. 1914-15 Star.

McCORMACK Private Christopher 27799. Enlisted 16 July 1917. Posted to the 9th (North Irish Horse) Battalion. **Wounded**. Discharged as no longer physically fit for war service due to wounds 6 February 1919. Silver War Badge, number B115651.

McCORMICK MM Private Robert James 14566. From Portadown, County Armagh. A father of ten. Enlisted September 1914. To France with 36th (Ulster) Division in October 1915. 'B' Company. **Wounded** during the attack at Hamel 1 July 1916. **MM** – Battle of Langemarck 16 August 1917. Transferred to the Class Z Reserve 22 March 1919. 1914-15 Star.

McCORMICK Private Thomas Henry 23364. Born at Donaghcloney, County Down. Enlisted in December 1915. Posted to the 9th (Service) Battalion. 'B' Company. **Killed in action** at the Battle of Langemarck 16 August 1917.

McCORMICK Private William 41607. From Belfast. [Enlisted in early-1915 into the Service Squadron, 6th (Inniskilling) Dragoons (UD/208). To France with 36th (Ulster) Division in October 1915. Served with 2nd North Irish Horse, X Corps Cavalry Regiment.] Joined the renamed 9th (North Irish Horse) Battalion from 36 Infantry Base Depot and transferred to Princess Victoria's (Royal Irish Fusiliers) in September/October 1917 (renumbered 41607). **Wounded** at Anseghem on 25/26 October 1918 and **died of wounds** 3 November 1918. 1914-15 Star.

McCORRY Private Joseph 20627. From Lurgan, County Armagh. [Enlisted 28 July 1915 and joined the 8th (Service) Battalion in 49th Brigade, 16th (Irish) Division.] Joined the 9th (North Irish Horse) Battalion when the 7th/8th (Service) Battalion was disbanded in February 1918. **Captured** in the period 21-28 March 1918 during the retreat from St Quentin. Discharged as no longer physically fit for war service due to wounds 12 February 1919. Silver War Badge, number B140386.

McCOUBRIE Private George 41518. (The 1914 Star roll mis-spells his name as McCOMBRIE.) Born in 1889 at County Down. [Enlisted in August 1914 into the North Irish Horse (990) (probably a re-enlistment). To France 20 August 1914 with 'C' Squadron as 5th Division Cavalry and then as GHQ Troops. Served with 2nd North Irish Horse, X Corps Cavalry Regiment.] Joined the renamed 9th (North Irish Horse) Battalion from 36 Infantry Base Depot and transferred to Princess Victoria's (Royal Irish Fusiliers) in September/October 1917 (renumbered 41518). 1914 Star.

McCOURT Sergeant Henry 14497. From Bleary, County Armagh. Enlisted September 1914. To France with 36th (Ulster) Division in October 1915. 'A' Company. **Wounded** during the attack at Hamel 1 July 1916. **Wounded** again. Discharged as no longer physically fit for war service due to wounds 14 February 1919. Silver War Badge, number B150013. 1914-15 Star.

McCOY Private Robert 23353 & 29548. Born 14 March 1899. From Caledon, County Tyrone. Enlisted 6 December 1915, aged 16, and joined the 10th (Reserve) Battalion (23353). To France 9 July 1916 and joined the 9th (Service) Battalion. Returned to Ireland 27 October 1916 due to being under-age. Transferred to the 20th (Reserve) Battalion, The Royal Irish Rifles (renumbered 20/447 Rifleman) 30 June 1917. **Deserted** 7 July 1917. Rejoined 20 October 1917. Tried by District Court Martial for *'fraudulent enlistment'* in the Army Service Corps; found guilty and sentenced to fifty-six days detention. Transferred back to Princess Victoria's (Royal Irish Fusiliers) 26 March 1918 (renumbered 29548). Joined 'A' Infantry Base Depot 3 April 1918 and rejoined the 9th (North Irish Horse) Battalion. **Wounded** by a gunshot to the left hand (removed part of index finger) 11 April 1918 in the actions between Wulverghem and Kemmel. Evacuated to hospital in England 17 April 1918. Joined 3rd (Reserve) Battalion 30 July 1918. To France 30 September 1918 and rejoined the 9th (North Irish Horse) Battalion. **Wounded** by a gunshot to the left hand during the advance to Anseghem 25 October 1918 and evacuated to hospital in England. Treated at 5th Northern General Hospital, Leicester. Joined 3rd (Reserve) Battalion 10 December 1918. Discharged as no longer physically fit for war service due to wounds 21 March 1919. Silver War Badge, number 167345.

McCRACKEN Private George 24055. Enlisted in February 1916. Posted to the 9th (Service) Battalion. 'D' Company. **Missing** in the period 21-28 March 1918 during the retreat from St Quentin believed **captured**. Medals forfeit due to misconduct.

McCRACKEN Sergeant Joseph 24394. Enlisted in May 1916. Posted to the 9th (Service) Battalion.

McCRACKLE Private Arthur 43258. Born in 1889 at Nottingham. [Enlisted into The Sherwood Foresters (Nottinghamshire and Derbyshire Regiment) (36817).] Transferred to Princess Victoria's (Royal Irish Fusiliers) 31 August 1916 (renumbered 43258) having joined the 9th (Service) Battalion on 8 August 1916. [Transferred to the Labour Corps (renumbered 518669). Transferred to The Black Watch (Royal Highlanders) (renumbered S/30206).] Died in 1930 at Nottingham.

McCREADY Private David 18249. From Banbridge, County Down. Enlisted into the 9th (Service) Battalion in February/March 1915. To France with 36th (Ulster) Division in October 1915. 'C' Company. Company runner during the attack at Hamel 1 July 1916, during which he was **wounded**. **Captured** in the period 21-28 March 1918 during the retreat from St Quentin. Transferred to the Class Z Reserve 16 April 1919. 1914-15 Star.

McCREADY MM Private Ernest 21411. Born 1899 in Woodvale, Belfast. [Enlisted in August 1915. Joined the 7th or 8th (Service) Battalion in 49th Brigade, 16th (Irish) Division. **MM** and **16th (Irish) Division Parchment Certificate for Gallantry and Devotion to Duty** – earned with the 7th/8th (Service) Battalion at Messines 7 June 1917.] Joined the 9th (North Irish Horse) Battalion when the 7th/8th (Service) Battalion was disbanded in February 1918. 'B' Company. Separated from the 9th (North Irish Horse) Battalion in the period 21-28 March 1918 during the retreat from St Quentin; rejoined 3 April 1918. [Transferred to the Corps of Royal Engineers (renumbered 361164).]

McCREADY Private William 18093. From Newry, County Down. Enlisted into the 9th (Service) Battalion in February 1915. [Posted to the 11th (Service) Battalion. Served with the 5th/6th (Service) Battalion when the 11th (Service) Battalion was absorbed. **Died** on 23 September 1918 in 6th Casualty Clearing Station while serving with the 5th/6th (Service) Battalion.]

McCREARY Private Thomas 14499. From Markethill, County Armagh. Enlisted September 1914. To France with 36th (Ulster) Division in October 1915. 'A' Company. **Missing** in the period 21-28 March 1918 during the retreat from St Quentin believed **captured**. Transferred to the Class Z Reserve 5 April 1919. 1914-15 Star.

McCREIGHT Sergeant John 41402. [Enlisted in November 1915 into the North Irish Horse (1831). Served with 2nd North Irish Horse, X Corps Cavalry Regiment.] Joined the renamed 9th (North Irish Horse) Battalion from 36 Infantry Base Depot and transferred to Princess Victoria's (Royal Irish Fusiliers) in September/October 1917 (renumbered 41402).

McCRORY Private Samuel 49745. Born in 1899 at Broughdone, County Antrim. Joined the 9th (North Irish Horse) Battalion, Princess Victoria's (Royal Irish Fusiliers) with the draft of men transferred from The Royal Irish Rifles in April 1918. **Wounded**. His brother, Private Matthew McCrory, was captured while served with the 12th (Service) Battalion, The Royal Irish Rifles (Central Antrim).

McCRORY Private Thomas 14571. From Portadown, County Armagh. Enlisted September 1914. To France with 36th (Ulster) Division in October 1915. **Wounded** during the attack at Hamel 1 July 1916. [Posted to the 2nd Garrison Battalion in Salonika.] Transferred to the Class Z Reserve 3 June 1919. 1914-15 Star.

McCULLAGH Private Benjamin 41391. [Enlisted in October 1915 into the North Irish Horse (1738). Served with 2nd North Irish Horse, X Corps Cavalry Regiment.] Joined the renamed 9th (North Irish Horse) Battalion from 36 Infantry Base Depot and transferred to Princess Victoria's (Royal Irish Fusiliers) in September/October 1917 (renumbered 41391).

McCULLAGH Private Robert 20363. Enlisted in May/June 1915 and joined the 9th (Service) Battalion with the draft of men from The Royal Inniskilling Fusiliers who transferred to Princess Victoria's (Royal Irish Fusiliers) on 30 June 1915. To France with 36th (Ulster) Division in October 1915. [Joined 108th Brigade Machine Gun Company in January 1916. Transferred to the Machine Gun Corps (renumbered 17800).] 1914-15 Star.

McCULLOUGH Sergeant David 14554. Born on 2 June 1892 at Tandragee, County Armagh. 4th (Portadown) Battalion, Armagh Regiment, Ulster Volunteer Force. Member of Loyal Orange Lodge 110. Enlisted September 1914. To France with 36th (Ulster) Division in October 1915. 'D' Company. **Wounded** during the attack at Hamel 1 July 1916. **36th (Ulster) Division Certificate for Gallantry** 1 July 1916. **Captured** in the period 21-28 March 1918 during the retreat from St Quentin. Transferred to the Class Z Reserve 11 April 1919. 1914-15 Star. After the war he emigrated to Canada. During the Second World War he served with the Canadian Armed Forces. Died in 1957.

McCULLOUGH DCM, MM Sergeant James 14555. (The Honours and Awards appendix to Cyril Falls' history of 36th (Ulster) Division records his rank as Regimental Sergeant Major.) From Portadown, County Armagh. 4th (Portadown) Battalion, Armagh Regiment, Ulster Volunteer Force. Enlisted September 1914. To France with 36th (Ulster) Division in October 1915. Battalion Signal Sergeant. **MM** – Battle of Langemarck 16 August 1917. **DCM**. Transferred to the Class Z Reserve 7 March 1919. 1914-15 Star.

McCULLOUGH Corporal John 23232. Enlisted in November 1915. Posted to the 9th (Service) Battalion.

McCULLOUGH Corporal Johnston 14502. Born in 1890 at Bessbrook, County Armagh. Enlisted September 1914. To France with 36th (Ulster) Division in October 1915. **Killed in action** during the attack at Hamel 1 July 1916. 1914-15 Star. Brother of Private William James McCullough.

McCULLOUGH Private Samuel 14510. Born in 1896 at Lurgan, County Armagh. Enlisted September 1914, aged 18. To France with 36th (Ulster) Division in October 1915. 'C' Company. **Wounded** at the Battle of Langemarck 16 August 1917. Discharged as no longer physically fit for war service due to wounds 26 June 1918. Silver War Badge, number 414490.

McCULLOUGH Private William James 23299. Born in 1888 at Bessbrook, County Armagh. From Loughgilly, County Armagh. Enlisted in November 1915. Posted to the 9th (Service) Battalion. **Wounded** and **died of wounds** 21 November 1916, aged 27. Brother of Corporal Johnston McCullough.

McCURRY Private Thomas 41606. Born in 1890 at Shankill, Belfast. Worked in the bottling industry. [Enlisted in November 1914 into the Service Squadron, 6th (Inniskilling) Dragoons (UD/144). To France with 36th (Ulster) Division in October 1915. Served with 2nd North Irish Horse, X Corps Cavalry Regiment.] Joined the renamed 9th (North Irish Horse) Battalion from 36 Infantry Base Depot and transferred to Princess Victoria's (Royal Irish Fusiliers) in September/October 1917 (renumbered 41606). 'C' Company. **Captured** in the period 21-28 March 1918 during the retreat from St Quentin. Transferred to the Class Z Reserve. 1914-15 Star.

McDAID Private James 13513, 21010 & 7040671. Born in 1884 at Douglas Bridge, County Tyrone. From Letterkenny, County Donegal. A carpenter. [Enlisted 30 September 1914 into Princess Victoria's (Royal Irish Fusiliers) and joined the 8th (Service) Battalion (13513). Discharged as not being likely to become an efficient soldier in that he was considered medically unfit for service 16 November 1914. Re-enlisted 30 November 1914 (renumbered 21010) and joined the 7th or 8th (Service) Battalion in 49th Brigade, 16th (Irish) Division. To France 18 February 1916. **Wounded** (shellshock) 6 September 1916 and evacuated to hospital in England 22 October 1916.]

To France 2 January 1918 and joined the 9th (North Irish Horse) Battalion when the 7th/8th (Service) Battalion was disbanded in February 1918. 'D' Company. **Wounded** by gunshots to the knee and head in the period 21-28 March 1918 during the retreat from St Quentin. Re-enlisted 11 March 1919 for Regular Army service with Princess Victoria's (Royal Irish Fusiliers) (renumbered 7040671). Posted to the 1st Battalion July 1919. Posted to the 2nd Battalion 18 October 1919. Posted back to the 1st Battalion and served in Persia and Mesopotamia from 22 January 1920. General Service Medal 1918-1962 with clasps 'Iraq' & 'NW Persia'. To Egypt with the 1st Battalion May 1921. Tried by Field General Court Martial in Egypt on 29 June 1920 charged with *'when on active service using insubordinate language to a superior officer'*; found guilty and sentenced to twenty-one days detention. Embarked for England 4 December 1921. Discharged 31 March 1922. Enlisted 5 December 1939 into Princess Louise's (Argyll and Sutherland Highlanders) (2988411).

McDADE Private James 23284. From Shankill, Belfast. Enlisted in November 1915. Posted to the 9th (Service) Battalion. 'C' Company. Company bomb carrier during the attack at Hamel 1 July 1916, during which he was **wounded**. **Died of wounds** 20 July 1916, aged 33. Brother of Private Samuel Stockman McDade.

McDADE Private Samuel Stockman 24309. (His medal index card incorrectly spells his name as MacDade.) Born in 1889 at Belfast. A porter. Enlisted in May 1916. Posted to the 9th (Service) Battalion. 'C' Company. **Wounded** at the Battle of Langemarck 16 August 1917. Treated at the Royal Victoria Hospital, Netley. Brother of Private James McDade.

McDERMOTT Private Richard 41109. [Enlisted in early-1915 into the Service Squadron, 6th (Inniskilling) Dragoons (UD/215). To France with 36th (Ulster) Division in October 1915. Served with 2nd North Irish Horse, X Corps Cavalry Regiment.] Joined the renamed 9th (North Irish Horse) Battalion from 36 Infantry Base Depot and transferred to Princess Victoria's (Royal Irish Fusiliers) in September/October 1917 (renumbered 41109). Transferred to the Class Z Reserve. 1914-15 Star.

McDERMOTT Private Stephan 20577. [Enlisted in June 1915 and joined the 7th (Service) Battalion in 49th Brigade, 16th (Irish) Division.] Joined the 9th (North Irish Horse) Battalion when the 7th/8th (Service) Battalion was disbanded in February 1918.

McDONALD Private Alexander 14506. From Richhill, County Armagh. Enlisted September 1914. To France with 36th (Ulster) Division in October 1915. **Killed in action** during the attack at Hamel 1 July 1916, aged 22. 1914-15 Star.

McDONALD Lance Corporal Hugh 45755. Born at Woolwich. A bank clerk in London. [Enlisted 8 May 1917. Joined 110th Training Reserve Battalion (73147) for service with The London Regiment. To hospital sick (influenza) 13-18 March 1918. Treated at Chiseldon Camp Hospital, Wiltshire.] To France and joined 36 Infantry Base Depot 29 March 1918. Transferred to Princess Victoria's (Royal Irish Fusiliers) 2 April 1918 (renumbered 45755) and joined the 9th (North Irish Horse) Battalion 4 April 1918. **Captured** 12 April 1918 in the actions between Wulverghem and Kemmel. Repatriated 22 November 1918. To hospital sick (gastritis) and treated at Ripon Camp Hospital, Yorkshire and King George Hospital, London. Joined the 3rd (Reserve) Battalion 12 February 1919. Lance Corporal 16 April 1919. Posted to the 2nd Battalion 24 July 1919. Reverted to Private for neglect of duty - absent from his post. Transferred to the Class Z Reserve 29 November 1919.

McDONALD Corporal Ross 14509. Born 1885. A tailor from Armagh. Enlisted September 1914. Discharged as no longer physically fit for war service due to sickness 28 June 1915. Silver War Badge, number 179444. [Reenlisted into the Army Service Corps (renumbered T/328116) on 30 April 1917. Trained as a driver. Served with the Tractor Depot, Avonmouth and 10th Mobility Company.] Transferred to the Class Z Reserve 21 March 1919.

McDONALD Private William 41351. [Enlisted in August 1914 into the North Irish Horse (1049). Served with 2nd North Irish Horse, X Corps Cavalry Regiment.] Joined the renamed 9th (North Irish Horse) Battalion from 36 Infantry Base Depot and transferred to Princess Victoria's (Royal Irish Fusiliers) in September/October 1917 (renumbered 41351).

McDONNELL Private James 42522 & 7042205. From Belfast. [Served previously with The Royal Irish Rifles (22822).] Transferred at the Base Depot to Princess Victoria's (Royal Irish Fusiliers) 14 September 1918 (renumbered 42522) and joined the 9th (North Irish Horse) Battalion 22 September 1918. Re-enlisted in early-1919 for Regular Army service with Princess Victoria's (Royal Irish

Fusiliers) (renumbered 7042205). Served with the 1st Battalion in Persia and Mesopotamia in 1919/20. General Service Medal 1918-1962 with clasps 'Iraq' & 'NW Persia'.

McDOWELL Lance Corporal Isaac Baxter 41367. From Belfast. [Enlisted in December 1916 into the North Irish Horse (2333). Served with 2nd North Irish Horse, X Corps Cavalry Regiment.] Joined the renamed 9th (North Irish Horse) Battalion from 36 Infantry Base Depot and transferred to Princess Victoria's (Royal Irish Fusiliers) in September/October 1917 (renumbered 41367). 'B' Company. **Captured** in the period 21-28 March 1918 during the retreat from St Quentin.

McDOWELL Private James 18552. Enlisted into the 9th (Service) Battalion in April 1915. To France with 36th (Ulster) Division in October 1915. [Transferred to the Labour Corps (renumbered 640810).] Transferred to the Class Z Reserve. 1914-15 Star.

McDOWELL Private John 14538. Enlisted September 1914. To France with 36th (Ulster) Division in October 1915. [Joined 108th Brigade Machine Gun Company in January 1916. Transferred to the Machine Gun Corps (renumbered 17797). Transferred to The Northumberland Fusiliers (renumbered 90084).] 1914-15 Star.

McDOWELL Private John 42538. [Enlisted April/May 1918 into The Royal Irish Rifles (22355).] Transferred at the Base Depot to Princess Victoria's (Royal Irish Fusiliers) 14 September 1918 (renumbered 42538) and joined the 9th (North Irish Horse) Battalion 22 September 1918.

McDOWELL Sergeant Samuel John 23380. From Lurgan, County Armagh. Enlisted December 1915. Posted to the 9th (Service) Battalion. **Wounded**.

McDOWELL Sergeant Solomon 14550. Born in 1871 at Knocknamuckley, County Armagh. A weaver, he served in the 5th Battalion (Militia), The Royal Irish Rifles. Enlisted as a regular soldier into The Royal Inniskilling Fusiliers (1889) 13 March 1886 and joined the 2nd Battalion. Served in India and Burma from 12 February 1888 to 15 February 1894. Transferred to the Section A Army Reserve 21 February 1894. Transferred to the Section D Army Reserve 12 March 1898. Mobilised from the Army Reserve for service in the South African War. Joined the 1st Battalion 1 March 1900 in South Africa. Evacuated to England 18 September 1900. Joined the 2nd Battalion 2 June 1902 in South Africa. Queen's South Africa Medal. King's South Africa Medal. Discharged 9 September 1902. Worked as a railway carter. 5th (Lurgan) Battalion, Ulster Volunteer Force. Enlisted September 1914. Sergeant 29 September 1914 and appointed Sergeant Cook. To France with 36th (Ulster) Division in October 1915. 'C' Company. Detached to the Quartermaster's stores during the attack at Hamel on 1 July 1916. Evacuated to hospital in England 12 October 1916. Joined the 10th (Reserve) Battalion 16 March 1917. Joined the 3rd (Reserve) Battalion 25 May 1918. Discharged as no longer physically fit for war service due to sickness 29 October 1918. Silver War Badge, number B34901. 1914-15 Star. Father of Private William James McDowell.

McDOWELL Private William F 41524. [Enlisted in September 1914 into the North Irish Horse (1164). To France 19 January 1915. Served with 2nd North Irish Horse, X Corps Cavalry Regiment.] Joined the renamed 9th (North Irish Horse) Battalion from 36 Infantry Base Depot and transferred to Princess Victoria's (Royal Irish Fusiliers) in September/October 1917 (renumbered 41524). [Transferred to the Tank Corps (renumbered 304868) 28 December 1917 and posted for training to the Tank Corps Depot, at Bovington near Wareham, Dorset.] 1914-15 Star.

McDOWELL Private William James 14527. Worked for the Great Northern Railway at Lurgan. Born at Shankill, County Armagh. Enlisted September 1914. To France with 36th (Ulster) Division in October 1915. 'C' Company. Survived the attack at Hamel 1 July 1916 unwounded. **Wounded** by shellfire at Havrincourt on 25 September 1917 and **died of wounds** the same day. Son of Sergeant Solomon McDowell.

McDOWELL Private William John 20364. From Glasgow. Enlisted in May/June 1915 and joined the 9th (Service) Battalion with the draft of men from The Royal Inniskilling Fusiliers who transferred to Princess Victoria's (Royal Irish Fusiliers) on 30 June 1915. To France with 36th (Ulster) Division in October 1915. **Wounded** during the attack at Hamel 1 July 1916. [Posted to the 1st Battalion.] Transferred to the Class Z Reserve. 1914-15 Star.

McELROY Private Robert 18536. Enlisted into the 9th (Service) Battalion in April 1915. To France with 36th (Ulster) Division in October 1915. **Wounded**. [Posted to the 2nd Garrison Battalion in Salonika.] Transferred to the Class Z Reserve 18 April 1919. 1914-15 Star.

McEVOY Lance Sergeant James Joseph 20673. Born at Omagh, County Tyrone. Enlisted, underage, in 1914/early 1915 into the Royal Army Medical Corps (12544). Transferred to Princess Victoria's (Royal Irish Fusiliers) in July 1915 (renumbered 20673). Posted to the 9th (Service) Battalion in mid/late 1916. 'C' Company. **Killed in action** at the Battle of Langemarck 16 August 1917, aged 19.

McFADDEN Sergeant John 41179. From Portrush, County Antrim. [Enlisted in September 1914 into the North Irish Horse (1170). To France 28 January 1915. Served with 2nd North Irish Horse, X Corps Cavalry Regiment.] Joined the renamed 9th (North Irish Horse) Battalion from 36 Infantry Base Depot and transferred to Princess Victoria's (Royal Irish Fusiliers) in September/October 1917 (renumbered 41179). 'D' Company. **Captured** in the period 21-28 March 1918 during the retreat from St Quentin. Transferred to the Class Z Reserve 26 March 1919. 1914-15 Star.

McFADDEN Private Thomas 20296. Enlisted in May/June 1915 and joined the 9th (Service) Battalion with the draft of men from The Royal Inniskilling Fusiliers who transferred to Princess Victoria's (Royal Irish Fusiliers) on 30 June 1915. To France with 36th (Ulster) Division in October 1915. 'C' Company. Company bomb carrier during the attack at Hamel 1 July 1916, which he survived unwounded. [Transferred to the Labour Corps (renumbered 381413).] Transferred to the Class Z Reserve 16 February 1919. 1914-15 Star.

McFADDEN Private Thomas 24647. Enlisted August 1916. Posted to the 9th (Service) Battalion. [Transferred to the Machine Gun Corps (renumbered 146246).]

McFALLS Private Patrick 24582. An alias for Private Brown Vance - see below.

McFARLAND Private Ephraim 14567. From Tandragee, County Armagh. 4th (Portadown) Battalion, Armagh Regiment, Ulster Volunteer Force. Worked at White's Mill, Tandragee. Enlisted September 1914. To France with 36th (Ulster) Division in October 1915. **Wounded** in April 1916 and while in hospital he was commended for his gallantry by the Commandant of the Base Depot for rousing his comrades and evacuating the tents during a fire. **Wounded** during the attack at Hamel 1 July 1916. Discharged as no longer physically fit for war service due to wounds 28 February 1918. Silver War Badge, number 336281. 1914-15 Star. Brother of Private George McFarland.

McFARLAND Private George 14574. From Tandragee, County Armagh. From Portadown, County Armagh. Member of Loyal Orange Lodge 110. 4th (Portadown) Battalion, Armagh Regiment, Ulster Volunteer Force. Enlisted September 1914. To France with 36th (Ulster) Division in October 1915. 'B' Company. **Killed in action** during the attack at Hamel 1 July 1916, aged 17. 1914-15 Star. Brother of Private Ephraim McFarland.

McFERRAN Private James 42503. [Enlisted into the 10th (Service) Battalion, The Royal Irish Rifles (South Belfast) (922). To France 2 October 1915.] Transferred at the Base Depot to Princess Victoria's (Royal Irish Fusiliers) 14 September 1918 (renumbered 42503) and joined the 9th (North Irish Horse) Battalion 22 September 1918. Transferred to the Class Z Reserve 24 May 1919. 1914-15 Star.

McFETRIDGE Private John 41464. [Enlisted in November 1915 into the North Irish Horse (1941). Served with 2nd North Irish Horse, X Corps Cavalry Regiment.] Joined the renamed 9th (North Irish Horse) Battalion from 36 Infantry Base Depot and transferred to Princess Victoria's (Royal Irish Fusiliers) in September/October 1917 (renumbered 41464). 'B' Company. **Wounded** 12 April 1918 in the actions between Wulverghem and Kemmel.

McGAFFIN Private James 41599. [Enlisted in May/June 1915 into the North Irish Horse (1653). Served with 2nd North Irish Horse, X Corps Cavalry Regiment.] Joined the renamed 9th (North Irish Horse) Battalion from 36 Infantry Base Depot and transferred to Princess Victoria's (Royal Irish Fusiliers) in September/October 1917 (renumbered 41599). 'D' Company. **Wounded** during the retreat from St Quentin 21-28 March 1918.

McGAFFIN Private William John 24734. Born in 1888 at Knocknamuckley, County Down. Lived at Portadown, County Armagh. Enlisted in August 1916. Posted to the 9th (Service) Battalion. 'B' Company. **Killed in action** at the Battle of Langemarck 16 August 1917, aged 29.

McGAHEY Private John 14488. From Lurgan, County Armagh. Enlisted September 1914. To France with 36th (Ulster) Division in October 1915. 'C' Company. Vickers gun ammunition carrier during the attack at Hamel 1 July 1916 during which he was **wounded**. [Posted to the 2nd Garrison Battalion in Salonika.] Transferred to the Class Z Reserve 23 May 1919. 1914-15 Star.

McGAHEY Private Samuel 14521. Born at Armagh, County Armagh. Enlisted September 1914. To France with 36th (Ulster) Division in October 1915. 'C' Company. **Killed in action** during the attack at Hamel 1 July 1916. 1914-15 Star.

McGAHEY Private William 41609. From Blacklion, County Cavan. [Enlisted in September 1915 into the Service Squadron, 6th (Inniskilling) Dragoons (UD/292). Served with 2nd North Irish Horse, X Corps Cavalry Regiment.] Joined the renamed 9th (North Irish Horse) Battalion from 36 Infantry Base Depot and transferred to Princess Victoria's (Royal Irish Fusiliers) in September/October 1917 (renumbered 41609). **Missing** in the period 11-18 April 1918 in the actions between Wulverghem and Kemmel; subsequently declared **killed in action** 19 April 1918.

McGARRELL Private Hugh 14518. (Recorded as Megarrell on his medal index card.) Born in 1898 at Belfast. Lived at Mullaglass, County Armagh. Worked at Bessbrook Spinning Company Ltd. Enlisted September 1914, aged 16, giving his age as 19 years. To France with 36th (Ulster) Division in October 1915. **Wounded** in November 1916. [Transferred to the Royal Defence Corps (80156).] Discharged as no longer physically fit for war service due to sickness 21 November 1918. Silver War Badge, number B54928. 1914-15 Star.

McGAUGHEY Private James 24606. Born in 1898 at Lurgan, County Armagh. [Enlisted into The Suffolk Regiment (34436).] Transferred to Princess Victoria's (Royal Irish Fusiliers) in July 1916. Posted to the 9th (Service) Battalion. **Killed in action** during the advance to Anseghem 25 October 1918.

McGAUGHEY Private William 21754. From Glenanne, County Armagh. Enlisted in October 1915. Posted to the 9th (Service) Battalion in mid/late1916. **Wounded**.

McGEOWN Private Robert 14551. Born at Tandragee, County Armagh. Enlisted September 1914. To France with 36th (Ulster) Division in October 1915. 'B' Company. **Missing** at the Battle of Langemarck 16 August 1917 and later declared **killed in action** on that date. 1914-15 Star.

McGEOWN Private Robert Jackson 14511. From Kilmore, County Armagh. Enlisted September 1914. To France with 36th (Ulster) Division in October 1915. 'C' Company. Lewis gunner during the attack at Hamel, during which he was **wounded**. **Wounded** when shot in the ankle during a raid at Spanbroekmolen 4 June 1917. **Captured** in the period 21-28 March 1918 during the retreat from St Quentin. 1914-15 Star. Transferred to the Class Z Reserve.

McGIFFIN Private Joseph Stewart 3501. Born in 1899 at Carrickfergus, County Antrim. Enlisted in May/June 1915 into Princess Victoria's (Royal Irish Fusiliers) Special Reserve. Posted to the 9th (Service) Battalion in 1917. 'C' Company. **Killed in action** at the Battle of Langemarck 16 August 1917, aged 18.

McGILL Private Benjamin 20348. Born at Newcastle-upon-Tyne. Enlisted in May/June 1915 and joined the 9th (Service) Battalion with the draft of men from The Royal Inniskilling Fusiliers who transferred to Princess Victoria's (Royal Irish Fusiliers) on 30 June 1915. To France with 36th (Ulster) Division in October 1915. **Killed in action** during the attack at Hamel 1 July 1916, aged 24. 1914-15 Star.

McGINTY Private George 23062. Born at Shankill, Belfast. Enlisted in November 1915 and joined the 10th (Reserve) Battalion. Posted to the 9th (Service) Battalion in mid-1916. **Killed in action** during the attack at Hamel 1 July 1916.

McGIVERN Private Robert William 23947. From Poyntzpass, County Armagh. Worked at Drumbanagher House. Member of Drumbanagher Loyal Orange Lodge 253 and the Armagh Regiment, Ulster Volunteer Force. **Wounded** on the raid at La Petite Douve Farm on 12 October 1916 and **died of wounds** later that day, aged 20.

McGIVERN Private William 18457. From Poyntzpass, County Armagh. Enlisted into the 9th (Service) Battalion in March 1915. To France with 36th (Ulster) Division in October 1915. **Killed in action** during the attack at Hamel 1 July 1916, aged 19. 1914-15 Star.

McGLINCHEY Private J 21227. Enlisted in February 1915. 'D' Company. **Missing** in the period 21-28 March 1918 during the retreat from St Quentin believed **captured**.

McGOLDRICK Private James 26907. From Scotland. [Enlisted in January 1917. Posted to the 1st Battalion but may not have joined.] Posted to the 9th (Service) Battalion. 'D' Company. **Wounded** (shell-shock) at the Battle of Langemarck 16 August 1917. **Missing** in the period 21-28 March 1918 during the retreat from St Quentin believed **captured**.

McGOVERN Private John 22178. [Enlisted in October 1915 and joined the 8th (Service) Battalion in 49th Brigade, 16th (Irish) Division.] Joined the 9th (North Irish Horse) Battalion when the 7th/8th (Service) Battalion was disbanded in February 1918.

McGOWAN Drummer Robert 12884. From Portstewart, County Londonderry. [Enlisted into The Royal Irish Rifles 1 September 1914 but transferred immediately at the Depot to Princess Victoria's (Royal Irish Fusiliers) and joined the 6th (Service) Battalion on 6 September 1914. Joined the Mediterranean Expeditionary Force 7 August 1915. Evacuated to hospital in England 8 November 1915. Joined the 3rd (Reserve) Battalion 11 December 1915.] To 36 Infantry Base Depot 13 June 1917 and joined the 9th (Service) Battalion 10 July 1917. **Wounded** at the Battle of Langemarck 16 August 1917. Evacuated to hospital in England 23 August 1917. Joined the Irish Command Depot 27 February 1918. Joined the 3rd (Reserve) Battalion 3 September 1919. Transferred to the Class Z Reserve 20 March 1919. 1914-15 Star.

McGRANE Private William 10752. Born at Stamullen, County Meath. [Enlisted into Princess Victoria's (Royal Irish Fusiliers) as a regular soldier in 1911. To France 19 December 1914 with the 2nd Battalion. Served with the 7th/8th (Service) Battalion in 49th Brigade, 16th (Irish) Division.] Joined the 9th (North Irish Horse) Battalion when the 7th/8th (Service) Battalion was disbanded in February 1918. 'B' Company. **Missing** in the period 11-18 April 1918 in the actions between Wulverghem and Kemmel; subsequently declared **killed in action** 19 April 1918, aged 27. 1914-15 Star.

McGRANN MM Private David 7963. Born in 1881. From Lurgan, County Armagh. A labourer. [Enlisted into Princess Victoria's (Royal Irish Fusiliers) as a regular soldier in 1903. Mobilised from the Army Reserve and joined the 1st Battalion. To France 22 August 1914. Declared **missing** in November 1914. Rejoined and later joined 7th/8th (Service) Battalion in 49th Brigade, 16th (Irish) Division.] Joined the 9th (North Irish Horse) Battalion when the 7th/8th (Service) Battalion was disbanded in February 1918. 'B' Company. **MM** – Raid at Spanbroekmolen 4 June 1917. **Wounded** when shot in the face and chest at Messines on 6 June 1917. **Killed in action** at the Battle of Langemarck 16 August 1917, aged 36. 1914 Star.

McGRATH Private Robert 14520. Enlisted September 1914. To France with 36th (Ulster) Division in October 1915. 'C' Company. Company runner during the attack at Hamel 1 July 1916. **Wounded** (shellshock) during the attack at Hamel 1 July 1916. **Wounded** at the Battle of Langemarck 16 August 1917. Discharged as no longer physically fit for war service due to wounds 2 April 1918. Silver War Badge, number 373744. 1914-15 Star.

McGRAW Private James 17768. [Enlisted in November 1914. Served with the 1st Battalion. Served with the 7th/8th (Service) Battalion in 49th Brigade, 16th (Irish) Division.] Joined the 9th (North Irish Horse) Battalion when the 7th/8th (Service) Battalion was disbanded in February 1918.

McGRAW Private Patrick 42526. [Enlisted 22 January 1917 into The Royal Irish Rifles (22638).] Transferred at the Base Depot to Princess Victoria's (Royal Irish Fusiliers) 14 September 1918 (renumbered 42526) and joined the 9th (North Irish Horse) Battalion 22 September 1918. **Wounded**. Discharged as no longer physically fit for war service due to wounds 10 October 1919. Silver War Badge, number B321661.

McGRORY Private Michael 42544. [Served previously with The Royal Irish Rifles (11094).] Transferred at the Base Depot to Princess Victoria's (Royal Irish Fusiliers) 14 September 1918 (renumbered 42544) and joined the 9th (North Irish Horse) Battalion 22 September 1918. [Transferred to 5th (Service) Battalion, The Royal Irish Regiment (Pioneers) in the Light Division in the British Army of the Rhine in March/June 1919 (renumbered 41338).]

McGUIGAN Private John 41237. From Newry, County Down. A hardware merchant. [Enlisted 13 October 1914 into the North Irish Horse (1307) (with Francis MacMahon). To France with 'F' Squadron in 33rd Division 17 November 1915. Served with 2nd North Irish Horse, X Corps Cavalry Regiment. To the field ambulance sick (influenza) 7-14 February 1917.] Joined the renamed 9th (North Irish Horse) Battalion from 36 Infantry Base Depot and transferred to Princess Victoria's

(Royal Irish Fusiliers) in September/October 1917 (renumbered 41237). 'D' Company. Evacuated sick (trench fever) to hospital in England 9 December 1917. Treated at the County of Middlesex War Hospital, St Albans. Joined the 10th (Reserve) Battalion 8 April 1918. Joined the 3rd (Reserve) Battalion 25 May 1918. [Transferred to the Army Service Corps (renumbered S/424911) 16 July 1918 as a clerk. Posted for duty as a clerk with 6th Cyclist Brigade at the Curragh, Dublin 14 October 1918.] Transferred to the Class Z Reserve 23 July 1919. 1914-15 Star.

McGUINNESS Private Patrick 43182. {Enlisted in August 1916 and joined the 7th (Service) Battalion in 49th Brigade, 16th (Irish) Division.] Joined the 9th (North Irish Horse) Battalion when the 7th/8th (Service) Battalion was disbanded in February 1918. 'A' Company. **Missing** in the period 21-28 March 1918 during the retreat from St Quentin believed **captured**.

McGUINNESS Private Thomas 40068. From Leeds. [Enlisted into the 11th (Service) Battalion, The Prince of Wales's Own (West Yorkshire Regiment) (13980). To France 26 August 1915 in 69th Brigade, 23rd Division.] Transferred to Princess Victoria's (Royal Irish Fusiliers) 30 November 1916 (renumbered 40068) and joined the 9th (Service) Battalion 12 December 1916. 'D' Company. **Wounded** at the Battle of Langemarck 16 August 1917. Transferred to the Class Z Reserve 24 March 1919. 1914-15 Star.

McHUGH Private Patrick 20993. Born at Claremorris, County Mayo. [Enlisted into The Connaught Rangers (4250). Transferred to Princess Victoria's (Royal Irish Fusiliers) in September 1915 (renumbered 20993) and joined the 8th (Service) Battalion in 49th Brigade, 16th (Irish) Division.] Joined the 9th (North Irish Horse) Battalion when the 7th/8th (Service) Battalion was disbanded in February 1918. **Wounded** and **captured**. **Died of wounds** while a prisoner of war 21 October 1918.

McILDOON Lance Corporal George 41222. [Enlisted 2 December 1911 into the North Irish Horse (631). To France with 'F' Squadron in 33rd Division 17 November 1915. Served with 2nd North Irish Horse, X Corps Cavalry Regiment.] Joined the renamed 9th (North Irish Horse) Battalion from 36 Infantry Base Depot and transferred to Princess Victoria's (Royal Irish Fusiliers) in September/October 1917 (renumbered 41222). **Wounded**. Discharged as no longer physically fit for war service due to wounds 7 January 1919. Silver War Badge, number 73770. 1914-15 Star.

McILDOON Sergeant John 17946. Enlisted 4 February 1915 into the 9th (Service) Battalion. No record of date of deployment to France with 36th (Ulster) Division. Discharged as no longer physically fit for war service due to sickness 5 March 1917. Silver War Badge, number 34605.

McILRATH Private Robert Allen 16126. Born at Keady, County Armagh. Enlisted into the 9th (Service) Battalion in October 1914. To France with 36th (Ulster) Division in October 1915. [Joined 108th Brigade Machine Gun Company in January 1916. Transferred to the Machine Gun Corps (renumbered 17798). **Killed in action** during the attack at Hamel 1 July 1916.] 1914-15 Star.

McILRATH Private Thomas 41422. [Enlisted in November 1915 into the North Irish Horse (1917). Served with 2nd North Irish Horse, X Corps Cavalry Regiment.] Joined the renamed 9th (North Irish Horse) Battalion from 36 Infantry Base Depot and transferred to Princess Victoria's (Royal Irish Fusiliers) in September/October 1917 (renumbered 41422). 'B' Company. **Captured** in the period 21-28 March 1918 during the retreat from St Quentin. Repatriated and arrived in Belfast on 5 December 1918.

McILROY Private Alfred 14512. From Lurgan, County Armagh. Enlisted September 1914. To France with 36th (Ulster) Division in October 1915. **Wounded** during the attack at Hamel 1 July 1916. [Posted to the 1st Battalion and was **killed in action** during the attack at Vijfwegen 30 September 1918.] 1914-15 Star. Brother of Private James McIlroy.

McILROY Private James 14528. From Lurgan, County Armagh. Enlisted September 1914. To France with 36th (Ulster) Division in October 1915. 'C' Company. **Wounded** during the attack at Hamel 1 July 1916. Transferred to the Class Z Reserve 11 March 1919. 1914-15 Star. Brother of Private Alfred McIlroy.

McILROY Private Thomas 24150. From Mountnorris, County Armagh. Enlisted in March 1916. Posted to the 9th (Service) Battalion. 'C' Company. **Wounded** at the Battle of Langemarck 16 August 1917. **Missing** in the period 21-28 March 1918 during the retreat from St Quentin believed **captured**.

McILROY Private Thomas 42486. [Enlisted into The Royal Irish Rifles (21850).] Transferred at the Base Depot to Princess Victoria's (Royal Irish Fusiliers) 14 September 1918 (renumbered 42486) and joined the 9th (North Irish Horse) Battalion 22 September 1918.

McILROY Private William 22984. Born at Larne, County Antrim. From Kilwaughter, County Antrim. Enlisted in November 1915. Posted to the 9th (Service) Battalion. 'D' Company. **Killed in action** by shellfire near Spanbroekmolen, aged 20. His death is recorded as 4 June 1917 but it is likely that he was killed on 5 June 1917.

McILROY Lance Corporal William John 20357. Born at Armagh, County Armagh. Lived in Glasgow. Enlisted in May/June 1915 and joined the 9th (Service) Battalion with the draft of men from The Royal Inniskilling Fusiliers who transferred to Princess Victoria's (Royal Irish Fusiliers) on 30 June 1915. To France with 36th (Ulster) Division in October 1915. 'A' Company. **Missing** at the Battle of Langemarck 16 August 1917 and later declared **killed in action** on that date. 1914-15 Star.

McILWAIN Private Adam 12164. [Enlisted in September 1914 and joined the 7th (Service) Battalion in 49th Brigade, 16th (Irish) Division.] Joined the 9th (North Irish Horse) Battalion when the 7th/8th (Service) Battalion was disbanded in February 1918.

McILWAINE Private Robert 14517. Born in at Lurgan, County Armagh. A damask weaver. Enlisted September 1914. No record of deployment to France with 36th (Ulster) Division in October 1915. [Transferred to The King's (Liverpool Regiment) (90045).]

McINERNEY Private Thomas 18090. From Bessbrook, County Armagh. Enlisted into the 9th (Service) Battalion in February 1915. To France with 36th (Ulster) Division in October 1915. 'C' Company. Lewis gun ammunition carrier during the attack at Hamel 1 July 1916, which he survived unwounded. **Wounded** in November 1917. Transferred to the Class Z Reserve 27 March 1919. 1914-15 Star.

McINNES Private George 20358. From Glasgow. Enlisted in May/June 1915 and joined the 9th (Service) Battalion with the draft of men from The Royal Inniskilling Fusiliers who transferred to Princess Victoria's (Royal Irish Fusiliers) on 30 June 1915. To France with 36th (Ulster) Division in October 1915. **Wounded** during the attack at Hamel 1 July 1916. Transferred to the Class Z Reserve. 1914-15 Star.

McINTOSH Corporal Albert 41328. [Enlisted 19 September 1912 into the North Irish Horse (734). To France 20 August 1914 with 'C' Squadron as 5th Division Cavalry and then as GHQ Troops. Served with 2nd North Irish Horse, X Corps Cavalry Regiment.] Joined the renamed 9th (North Irish Horse) Battalion from 36 Infantry Base Depot and transferred to Princess Victoria's (Royal Irish Fusiliers) in September/October 1917 (renumbered 41328). 'C' Company. **Wounded** during the retreat from St Quentin 21-28 March 1918. Discharged as no longer physically fit for war service due to wounds 15 November 1918. Silver War Badge, number B115650. 1914 Star.

McINTOSH Private John 41086. [Enlisted in October 1914 into the Service Squadron, 6th (Inniskilling) Dragoons (UD/45). To France with 36th (Ulster) Division in October 1915. Promoted to Corporal. Reduced in rank to Private for misconduct (absent from duty and drunk) 12 October 1916. Served with 2nd North Irish Horse, X Corps Cavalry Regiment.] Joined the renamed 9th (North Irish Horse) Battalion from 36 Infantry Base Depot and transferred to Princess Victoria's (Royal Irish Fusiliers) in September/October 1917 (renumbered 41086). Transferred to the Class Z Reserve 22 March 1919. 1914-15 Star.

McINTYRE Private Richard 21639. From Dungannon, County Tyrone. Enlisted in September 1915. Posted to the 9th (Service) Battalion in May/June 1916. 'A' Company. **Killed in action** during the attack at Hamel 1 July 1916, aged 24.

McIVOR Private Joseph 19823. [Enlisted in May 1915 into the 7th (Service) Battalion in 49th Brigade, 16th (Irish) Division.] Joined the 9th (North Irish Horse) Battalion when the 7th/8th (Service) Battalion was disbanded in February 1918. 'C' Company. **Missing** in the period 21-28 March 1918 during the retreat from St Quentin believed **captured**.

McKAIG Private William James 24446. Born in 1898 at Shankill, Belfast. Enlisted 2 June 1916. Posted to the 9th (Service) Battalion. **Wounded**. Discharged as no longer physically fit for war service due to wounds 18 January 1919. Silver War Badge, number B88045.

McKANE Warrant Officer Class I Thomas 15718. Regimental Sergeant Major - see above.

McKEE Private James 18718. Enlisted into the 9th (Service) Battalion in April 1915. Medals forfeit due to misconduct.

McKEE Private Matthew 42472. [Enlisted into The Royal Irish Rifles (22121).] Transferred at the Base Depot to Princess Victoria's (Royal Irish Fusiliers) 14 September 1918 (renumbered 42472) and joined the 9th (North Irish Horse) Battalion 22 September 1918.

McKEE Private William 23807. Enlisted 21 January 1916. Posted to the 9th (Service) Battalion. **Wounded**. Discharged as no longer physically fit for war service due to wounds 13 September 1917. Silver War Badge, number 243180.

McKEEVER Private James 21152. From Ballymoney, County Antrim. [Enlisted in December 1914/January 1915 and joined the 8th (Service) Battalion in 49th Brigade, 16th (Irish) Division. **Wounded**.] Joined the 9th (North Irish Horse) Battalion when the 7th/8th (Service) Battalion was disbanded in February 1918. 'D' Company. **Captured** in the period 21-28 March 1918 during the retreat from St Quentin.

McKELVEY Private Thomas 14501. Enlisted September 1914. To France with 36th (Ulster) Division in October 1915. [Joined 108th Brigade Machine Gun Company in January 1916. Transferred to the Machine Gun Corps (renumbered 17799).] 1914-15 Star.

McKENNA Private Thomas 24720. [Enlisted 28 August 1916 and served with the 2nd and 1st Battalions.] Posted to the 9th (North Irish Horse) Battalion. [Subsequently posted back to the 1st Battalion. **Wounded**.] Discharged as no longer physically fit for war service due to wounds 2 April 1919. Silver War Badge, number B185281.

McKENZIE Private John 41172. [Enlisted in September/October 1915 into the Service Squadron, 6th (Inniskilling) Dragoons (297). Served with 2nd North Irish Horse, X Corps Cavalry Regiment.] Joined the renamed 9th (North Irish Horse) Battalion from 36 Infantry Base Depot and transferred to Princess Victoria's (Royal Irish Fusiliers) in September/October 1917 (renumbered 41172). [Transferred to the Labour Corps (renumbered 637557).] Re-enlisted in 1919 for Regular Army service with the Seaforth Highlanders (Ross-shire Buffs, The Duke of Albany's) (renumbered 32266, renumbered 2811007).

McKEOWN Private Frederick Victor 21681, 42301 & 7042184. Born in 1899 at Belfast. Enlisted in September 1915 into the 9th (Service) Battalion, aged 15 (21681). [Too young for service he was transferred to a Reserve Battalion of The Royal Irish Rifles (renumbered 479). To France in 1918 and transferred back to Princess Victoria's (Royal Irish Fusiliers) (renumbered 42301) and joined the 1st Battalion.] Re-enlisted in early-1919 for Regular Army service with Princess Victoria's (Royal Irish Fusiliers) (renumbered 7042184) and remained with the 1st Battalion. Served with the 1st Battalion in Persia and Mesopotamia in 1919/20. General Service Medal 1918-1962 with clasps 'Iraq' & 'NW Persia'. Lived in Belfast.

McKEOWN Private James 22552. From Gilford, County Armagh. Enlisted in November 1915. Posted to the 9th (Service) Battalion. **Captured**. Brother of Private John McKeown.

McKEOWN Private John 23302. From Gilford, County Armagh. Enlisted in November 1915. Posted to the 9th (Service) Battalion. 'B' Company. **Captured** in the period 21-28 March 1918 during the retreat from St Quentin. Brother of Private James McKeown.

McKEOWN Private Patrick 42465. [Served previously with The Royal Irish Rifles (6670). To France 5 January 1915.] Transferred at the Base Depot to Princess Victoria's (Royal Irish Fusiliers) 14 September 1918 and joined the 9th (North Irish Horse) Battalion 22 September 1918. 1914-15 Star.

McKEOWN Private Thomas James 23917. Born at Killeevan, County Monaghan. From Stone Bridge, Clones, County Monaghan. Enlisted in February 1916. Posted to the 9th (Service) Battalion. **Killed in action** by shellfire at Hamel 31 May 1916, aged 36.

McKEOWN Private William 21604. Enlisted in September 1915. Posted to the 9th (Service) Battalion. 'A' Company. **Captured** in the period 21-28 March 1918 during the retreat from St Quentin. Held as a prisoner of war in Germany. Died 12 December 1967. Buried at Seagoe Cemetery, Portadown, County Armagh.

McKEOWN Sergeant William John 41612. Served as William John Nixon. Born 1895. From Dungannon, County Tyrone. 'B' Company, Tyrone Battalion, Ulster Volunteer Force (Number 5411). [Enlisted 7 November 1914 into the Service Squadron, 6th (Inniskilling) Dragoons (UD/111). To France with 36th (Ulster) Division in October 1915. After the attack at Thiepval on 1 July 1916 he was **missing** for four days. Embarked at Marseilles for Egypt with the Regiment's horses on Horse Transport SS Bohemian 25 August 1917.] Transferred to Princess Victoria's (Royal Irish Fusiliers) 6 October 1917 (renumbered 41612) and joined the 9th (North Irish Horse) Battalion 12 October 1917. 'B' Company. **Wounded** during the retreat from St Quentin on 23 March 1918. Rejoined the 9th (North Irish Horse) Battalion and was **wounded** by a gunshot to the left wrist south of Wulverghem on 6 September 1918. Transferred to the Class Z Reserve 3 March 1919. 1914-15 Star. Joined the Ulster Special Constabulary in 1923 (Number 3285).

McKERR Private Francis 14542. From Drumgor, Portadown, County Armagh. Enlisted September 1914. To France with 36th (Ulster) Division in October 1915. 'D' Company. **Killed in action** during the attack at Hamel 1 July 1916, aged 35. 1914-15 Star. Brother of Privates John and William McKerr. Cousin of Private Thomas Lyness.

McKERR Private John 14562. From Drumgor, County Armagh. Enlisted September 1914. To France to join 36th (Ulster) Division 17 November 1915. 'C' Company. **Wounded** during the attack at Hamel 1 July 1916. [Transferred to the Royal Defence Corps (85520) and The York and Lancaster Regiment (64251).] 1914-15 Star. Brother of Privates Francis and William McKerr. Cousin of Private Thomas Lyness.

McKERR Private William 14494. From Drumgor, County Armagh. Enlisted September 1914. Discharged as no longer physically fit for war service due to sickness 25 May 1915, aged 20. Silver War Badge, number 508790. Brother of Privates Francis and John McKerr. Cousin of Private Thomas Lyness.

McKERR Sergeant William Robert 4859. Born in 1880 at Lurgan, County Armagh. Enlisted into Princess Victoria's (Royal Irish Fusiliers) Special Reserve. A linen weaver. [Served with the 8th (Service) Battalion in 49th Brigade, 16th (Irish) Division.] Joined the 9th (North Irish Horse) Battalion when the 7th/8th (Service) Battalion was disbanded in February 1918. Died at Lurgan in 1947.

McKEVITT Private Martin 41547. From Belfast. [Enlisted in November 1915 into the North Irish Horse (1816). Served with 2nd North Irish Horse, X Corps Cavalry Regiment.] Joined the renamed 9th (North Irish Horse) Battalion from 36 Infantry Base Depot and transferred to Princess Victoria's (Royal Irish Fusiliers) in September/October 1917 (renumbered 41547). 'C' Company. **Captured** in the period 21-28 March 1918 during the retreat from St Quentin.

McKIMM Private David 42473. [Enlisted into The Royal Irish Rifles (22078).] Transferred at the Base Depot to Princess Victoria's (Royal Irish Fusiliers) 14 September 1918 (renumbered 42473) and joined the 9th (North Irish Horse) Battalion 22 September 1918.

McKINLAY Private Anthony 23318. Born at Glasgow. Enlisted (or transferred to Princess Victoria's (Royal Irish Fusiliers)) in November 1915. Posted to the 9th (Service) Battalion. 'D' Company. **Wounded** at the Battle of Langemarck 16 August 1917 and **died of wounds** 9 September 1917, aged 23.

McKINLEY Sergeant Alexander Weir 41200. [Enlisted in November 1915 into the North Irish Horse (1984). Served with 2nd North Irish Horse, X Corps Cavalry Regiment.] Joined the renamed 9th (North Irish Horse) Battalion from 36 Infantry Base Depot and transferred to Princess Victoria's (Royal Irish Fusiliers) in September/October 1917 (renumbered 41200). 'D' Company. **Missing** in the period 21-28 March 1918 during the retreat from St Quentin believed **captured**.

McKINLEY Lance Corporal John (Jack) 14540. Born 11 May 1895 at Milford, County Armagh. Enlisted September 1914. To France with 36th (Ulster) Division in October 1915. 'A' Company. **Wounded** at the Battle of Langemarck 16 August 1917. Transferred to the Class Z Reserve 24 March 1919. 1914-15 Star.

McKINNEY Private Robert Henry 26082. Enlisted in January 1917. Posted to the 9th (Service) Battalion. Re-enlisted in 1919 for Regular Army service with Princess Victoria's (Royal Irish Fusiliers) (7040785). Served with the 1st Battalion in Persia and Mesopotamia in 1919/20. General Service Medal 1918-1962 with clasps 'Iraq' & 'NW Persia'.

McKINNEY Private William 19765. From Gilford, County Down. Enlisted into the 9th (Service)

Battalion in April 1915. To France with 36th (Ulster) Division in October 1915. **Wounded** during the attack at Hamel 1 July 1916. Transferred to the Class Z Reserve 20 March 1919. 1914-15 Star.

McKISSICK Private Maurice 21018. From Bangor, County Down. [Enlisted in November 1914 and joined the 8th (Service) Battalion in 49th Brigade, 16th (Irish) Division.] Joined the 9th (North Irish Horse) Battalion when the 7th/8th (Service) Battalion was disbanded in February 1918. 'A' Company. **Captured** in the period 21-28 March 1918 during the retreat from St Quentin.

McKNIGHT Private Alexander 29589 & 7040893. Born 14 September 1899 at Portadown, County Armagh. Enlisted 15 November 1917, aged 18. To France 1 April 1918. **Wounded** by a gunshot to the left foot in the period 11-18 April 1918 in the actions between Wulverghem and Kemmel and evacuated to hospital in England 22 April 1918. [To France 18 July 1918 and posted to the 11th (Service) Battalion in 1918. Served with the 5th/6th (Service) Battalion when the 11th (Service) Battalion was absorbed.] Re-enlisted in August/September 1919 for Regular Army service with Princess Victoria's (Royal Irish Fusiliers) (renumbered 7040893). Served with the 1st Battalion in Persia and Mesopotamia in 1919/20. General Service Medal 1918-1962 with clasps 'Iraq' & 'NW Persia'. Transferred to The Highland Light Infantry and served in India. Discharged 21 March 1922. Served during the Second World War. Died at Dover, Kent in 1970, aged 71.

McKNIGHT Lance Corporal John 43504. [Enlisted into the 13th (Service) Battalion, The Royal Irish Rifles (1st County Down) (19116). To France with 36th (Ulster) Division in October 1915.] Transferred to Princess Victoria's (Royal Irish Fusiliers) 15 June 1918 (renumbered 43504) and joined the 9th (North Irish Horse) Battalion 23 June 1918. Transferred to the Class Z Reserve 22 March 1919. 1914-15 Star.

McKNIGHT Private John Samuel 14546. Born at Newry, County Down. Enlisted September 1914. To France with 36th (Ulster) Division in October 1915. **Killed in action** during the attack at Hamel 1 July 1916, aged 26. 1914-15 Star.

McLAUGHLIN Private Joseph 41405. [Enlisted in January 1915 into the North Irish Horse (1377). To France with 'F' Squadron in 33rd Division 17 November 1915. Served with 2nd North Irish Horse, X Corps Cavalry Regiment.] Joined the renamed 9th (North Irish Horse) Battalion from 36 Infantry Base Depot and transferred to Princess Victoria's (Royal Irish Fusiliers) in September/October 1917 (renumbered 41405).

McLAVERTY Corporal William 24758, 33368 & 7041548. From Shankill, Belfast. A storeman. [Enlisted 4 September 1916 and served with the 1st Battalion.] Posted to the 9th (Service) Battalion. 'C' Company. **Wounded** at the Battle of Langemarck 16 August 1917. Re-enlisted 3 April 1919 for Regular Army service with Princess Victoria's (Royal Irish Fusiliers) (renumbered 33368, renumbered 7041548). Served with the 1st Battalion in Persia and Mesopotamia in 1919/20. General Service Medal 1918-1962 with clasps 'Iraq' & 'NW Persia'. Discharged 11 October 1921. Enlisted 26 January 1940 into The Royal Fusiliers (City of London Regiment).

McLEAN Private Samuel 18652. From Lislea, County Armagh. Enlisted into the 9th (Service) Battalion in April 1915. To France with 36th (Ulster) Division in October 1915. **Killed in action** during the attack at Hamel 1 July 1916, aged 20. 1914-15 Star.

McLEAN Private William John 14519. Enlisted September 1914. 'A' Company. To France with 36th (Ulster) Division in October 1915. **Missing** in the period 21-28 March 1918 during the retreat from St Quentin believed **captured**. Transferred to the Class Z Reserve 2 April 1919. 1914-15 Star.

McLEISH Private Daniel Scott 42152. Born 17 April 1898 in Perth, Scotland. [Enlisted into the Army Veterinary Corps (14149).] Transferred to Princess Victoria's (Royal Irish Fusiliers) 8 May 1918 (renumbered 42152) and joined the 9th (North Irish Horse) Battalion. Died in St Ninians, Stirling in 1971, aged 73. His brother, James McLeish, also served during the First World War.

McLELLAN Private Alexander 41549. From Belfast. A draper. [Enlisted in June 1915 into the North Irish Horse (1685). Served with 2nd North Irish Horse, X Corps Cavalry Regiment.] Joined the renamed 9th (North Irish Horse) Battalion from 36 Infantry Base Depot and transferred to Princess Victoria's (Royal Irish Fusiliers) in September/October 1917 (renumbered 41549). 'A' Company. **Captured** in the period 21-28 March 1918 during the retreat from St Quentin.

McLENAGHAN Company Quartermaster Sergeant William Samuel 41580. From Islandreagh, County Antrim. [Enlisted in January 1916 into the North Irish Horse (2065). Served with 2nd North

Irish Horse, X Corps Cavalry Regiment.] Joined the renamed 9th (North Irish Horse) Battalion from 36 Infantry Base Depot and transferred to Princess Victoria's (Royal Irish Fusiliers) in September/October 1917 (renumbered 41580). Company Quartermaster Sergeant.

MacLEOD Private Malcolm 40066. [Enlisted into The Prince of Wales's Own (West Yorkshire Regiment) (21798).] Transferred to Princess Victoria's (Royal Irish Fusiliers) 30 November 1916 (renumbered 40066) and joined the 9th (Service) Battalion 12 December 1916. [Transferred to the Royal Defence Corps (renumbered 96896).]

McLORN Private George 41426. [Enlisted in November 1915 into the North Irish Horse (1817). Served with 2nd North Irish Horse, X Corps Cavalry Regiment.] Joined the renamed 9th (North Irish Horse) Battalion from 36 Infantry Base Depot and transferred to Princess Victoria's (Royal Irish Fusiliers) in September/October 1917 (renumbered 41426). **Wounded** twice.

McLOUGHLIN Private Charles 14558. Enlisted September 1914. To France with 36th (Ulster) Division in October 1915. Transferred to the Class Z Reserve 8 March 1919. 1914-15 Star.

McLOUGHLIN Lance Corporal Herbert 14534. From Armagh, County Armagh. Enlisted September 1914. To France with 36th (Ulster) Division in October 1915. Battalion Signaller. **Wounded**. Transferred to the Class Z Reserve 3 March 1919. **MSM**. 1914-15 Star. Employed as a linesman with the General Post Office in Portadown, County Armagh. Died at Armagh Hospital 21 April 1966.

McLOUGHLIN Private William 14503. Enlisted September 1914. To France with 36th (Ulster) Division in October 1915. [Transferred to the Army Service Corps (renumbered R/310717).] Transferred to the Class Z Reserve 28 March 1919. 1914-15 Star.

McLOUGHLIN Private William 41129. [Enlisted in April 1915 into the Service Squadron, 6th (Inniskilling) Dragoons (UD/253). Served with 2nd North Irish Horse, X Corps Cavalry Regiment.] Joined the renamed 9th (North Irish Horse) Battalion from 36 Infantry Base Depot and transferred to Princess Victoria's (Royal Irish Fusiliers) in September/October 1917 (renumbered 41129). **Deserted** 16 July 1918; medals forfeit. Discharged having been convicted by the civil power.

MacMAHON Company Quartermaster Sergeant Francis Joseph Aloysius 41567. Born 2 August 1894 at Clough, County Down. [Enlisted 13 October 1914 into the North Irish Horse (1308). To France with 'F' Squadron in 33rd Division 17 November 1915. **Wounded** twice. Embarked at Marseilles for Egypt with the Regiment's horses on Horse Transport SS Bohemian 25 August 1917.] Joined the renamed 9th (North Irish Horse) Battalion from 36 Infantry Base Depot and transferred to Princess Victoria's (Royal Irish Fusiliers) in October 1917 (renumbered 41567). 'D' Company. Company Quartermaster Sergeant. **Captured** (escaped) and **wounded** (gunshot to the left arm) in the period 21-28 March 1918 during the retreat from St Quentin. [Served as a clerk in a British staging camp for the American Expeditionary Force at Harfleur.] Transferred to the Class Z Reserve 31 May 1919. 1914 Star. Unemployed, he sought work in Liverpool, briefly served in the police and as a barman. Returned to Ireland and joined the Great Northern Railway as the Locomotive Superintendent Clerk. He emigrated to Australia, arriving at Melbourne from London on 8 January 1923 on board SS Benalla. Enlisted into the Australian Army in the Second World War and served as the Regimental Sergeant Major, 16th Garrison Battalion, formed to guard the prisoner of war camps at Hay, New South Wales. Died 19 May 1971, aged 76 in Canberra, Australia.

McMAHON Corporal (Acting Sergeant) John 14513. Enlisted September 1914. To France with 36th (Ulster) Division in October 1915. 'C' Company. **Wounded** during the attack at Hamel 1 July 1916. **Wounded** at the Battle of Langemarck 16 August 1917. Discharged as no longer physically fit for war service due to wounds 27 July 1918, aged 24. Silver War Badge, number 379033. 1914-15 Star.

McMANUS Private Charles 20994. [Enlisted in September 1915 and joined the 8th (Service) Battalion in 49th Brigade, 16th (Irish) Division.] Joined the 9th (North Irish Horse) Battalion when the 7th/8th (Service) Battalion was disbanded in February 1918. 'A' Company. **Missing** in the period 21-28 March 1918 during the retreat from St Quentin believed **captured**.

McMANUS Private James 14504. From Armagh, County Armagh. Enlisted September 1914. To France with 36th (Ulster) Division in October 1915. **Wounded** in the period 11-18 April 1918 in the actions between Wulverghem and Kemmel and **died of wounds** 28 April 1918, aged 25. 1914-15

Star.

McMANUS Private James 21078. [Enlisted 17 November 1914 and joined the 8th (Service) Battalion in 49th Brigade, 16th (Irish) Division.] Joined the 9th (North Irish Horse) Battalion when the 7th/8th (Service) Battalion was disbanded in February 1918. 'C' Company. Separated from the 9th (North Irish Horse) Battalion in the period 21-28 March 1918 during the retreat from St Quentin; rejoined 4 April 1918. Discharged as no longer physically fit for war service due to sickness 18 October 1918. Silver War Badge, number B34769.

McMANUS Lance Corporal Randal Edmund 41505. From Dungannon, County Tyrone. Educated at Dungannon Royal School. Emigrated to Canada but returned to Ireland to enlist. [Enlisted 31 October 1914 into the Service Squadron, 6th (Inniskilling) Dragoons (UD/88). Lance Corporal 12 February 1915. Charged with refusing to obey an order and being absent off parade and reverted to Private 12 April 1915. To France with 36th (Ulster) Division in October 1915. Served with 2nd North Irish Horse, X Corps Cavalry Regiment. Lance Corporal 19 May 1917.] Joined the renamed 9th (North Irish Horse) Battalion from 36 Infantry Base Depot and transferred to Princess Victoria's (Royal Irish Fusiliers) in September/October 1917 (renumbered 41505). **Missing** in the period 11-18 April 1918 in the actions between Wulverghem and Kemmel; subsequently declared **killed in action** 19 April 1918, aged 26. 1914-15 Star. His brother, Second Lieutenant Hubert McManus, served with the North Irish Horse and the Machine Gun Corps before being commissioned into the Machine Gun Corps in October 1917.

McMASTER Private Francis 41533. [Recorded as having served with the North Irish Horse (3347) in 2nd North Irish Horse, X Corps Cavalry Regiment (this regimental number was probably allocated on his transfer to 6th (Inniskilling) Dragoons.] Joined the renamed 9th (North Irish Horse) Battalion from 36 Infantry Base Depot and transferred to Princess Victoria's (Royal Irish Fusiliers) in September/October 1917 (renumbered 41533).

McMASTER Private James Thomas 41194. [Enlisted in June 1916 into the North Irish Horse (2029). Served with 2nd North Irish Horse, X Corps Cavalry Regiment.] Joined the renamed 9th (North Irish Horse) Battalion from 36 Infantry Base Depot and transferred to Princess Victoria's (Royal Irish Fusiliers) in September/October 1917 (renumbered 41194). 'D' Company. **Missing** in the period 21-28 March 1918 during the retreat from St Quentin believed **captured**. Lived at Ballymoney, County Antrim.

McMASTER Private John 41608. [Enlisted in November 1914 into the Service Squadron, 6th (Inniskilling) Dragoons (UD/190). To France with 36th (Ulster) Division in October 1915. Served with 2nd North Irish Horse, X Corps Cavalry Regiment.] Joined the renamed 9th (North Irish Horse) Battalion from 36 Infantry Base Depot and transferred to Princess Victoria's (Royal Irish Fusiliers) in September/October 1917 (renumbered 41608). Transferred to the Class Z Reserve 18 March 1919. 1914-15 Star.

McMASTER Sergeant John Alexander 41243. [Enlisted in May 1915 into the North Irish Horse (1638). Served with 2nd North Irish Horse, X Corps Cavalry Regiment.] Joined the renamed 9th (North Irish Horse) Battalion from 36 Infantry Base Depot and transferred to Princess Victoria's (Royal Irish Fusiliers) in September/October 1917 (renumbered 41243).

McMENAMIN Private Edward 27647. Enlisted 24 May 1917. Posted to the 9th (North Irish Horse) Battalion. Discharged as no longer physically fit for war service due to sickness 14 February 1919. Silver War Badge, number B129717.

McMENAMIN Private James 42537. Joined the 9th (North Irish Horse) Battalion, Princess Victoria's (Royal Irish Fusiliers) with the draft of men transferred from The Royal Irish Rifles in September 1918. [Transferred to 5th (Service) Battalion, The Royal Irish Regiment (Pioneers) in the Light Division in the British Army of the Rhine in March/June 1919 (renumbered 41339).]

McMILLAN Private Archibald 17641. Enlisted into the 9th (Service) Battalion in December 1914/January 1915. To France with 36th (Ulster) Division in October 1915. 'C' Company. Signaller at the forward visual transmitting station during the attack at Hamel 1 July 1916 and did not take part in the attack. Transferred to the Class Z Reserve. 1914-15 Star.

McMILLAN Lance Corporal Hawthorn 41478. From Belfast. A grocer. [Enlisted in October 1914 into the North Irish Horse (1294). To France with 'F' Squadron in 33rd Division 17 November 1915. Served with 2nd North Irish Horse, X Corps Cavalry Regiment.] Joined the renamed 9th (North Irish

Horse) Battalion from 36 Infantry Base Depot and transferred to Princess Victoria's (Royal Irish Fusiliers) in September/October 1917 (renumbered 41478). Transferred to the Class Z Reserve 23 March 1919. 1914-15 Star.

McMORROW Sergeant Owen John 16192. Born at Drumlease, Manorhamilton, County Leitrim. A farmer. [Enlisted 16 October 1914 into the 6th (Service) Battalion, The Connaught Rangers (1370). Transferred to Princess Victoria's (Royal Irish Fusiliers) 16 November 1914 (renumbered 16192) and joined the 8th (Service) Battalion in 49th Brigade, 16th (Irish) Division. Lance Corporal 26 May 1915. To France 19 February 1916 in 16th (Irish) Division. **16th (Irish) Division Parchment Certificate for Gallantry and Devotion to Duty** - Ginchy September 1916. Corporal 5 January 1917. **Wounded** (shrapnel wound to the neck) at the Battle of Langemarck 16 August 1917. Treated at 2nd Canadian Casualty Clearing Station and 2nd Australian General Hospital. Rejoined the 7th/8th (Service) Battalion 10 September 1917. Sergeant 31 December 1917.] Joined the 9th (North Irish Horse) Battalion when the 7th/8th (Service) Battalion was disbanded in February 1918. 'A' Company. **Captured** in the period 21-28 March 1918 during the retreat from St Quentin. Repatriated 5 December 1918. Transferred to the Class Z Reserve 17 March 1919.

McMULLAN Private Adam 14569. Born in 1887 at Donaghcloney, County Down. From Park Road, Portadown, County Armagh. Edenderry Pipe Band. 4th (Portadown) Battalion, Armagh Regiment, Ulster Volunteer Force. Enlisted September 1914. To France with 36th (Ulster) Division in October 1915. 'B' Company. To hospital in England February 1916. **Missing** at the Battle of Langemarck 16 August 1917 and later declared **killed in action** on that date, aged 30. 1914-15 Star.

McMULLAN Private George 42123. [Enlisted into the Army Veterinary Corps (28236).] Transferred to Princess Victoria's (Royal Irish Fusiliers) 8 May 1918 (renumbered 42123) and joined the 9th (North Irish Horse) Battalion.

McMULLAN Private Matthew 22940. [Enlisted in November 1915 and joined the 7th (Service) Battalion in 49th Brigade, 16th (Irish) Division. Posted to the 1st Battalion.] Posted to the 9th (North Irish Horse) Battalion in late-1917/early-1918. 'D' Company. **Missing** in the period 21-28 March 1918 during the retreat from St Quentin believed **captured**.

McMULLAN Private William 42464. From Ballycastle, County Antrim. [Enlisted into The Royal Irish Rifles (20553).] Transferred at the Base Depot to Princess Victoria's (Royal Irish Fusiliers) 14 September 1918 (renumbered 42464) and joined the 9th (North Irish Horse) Battalion 22 September 1918. **Wounded** during the attack at Vijfwegen on 30 September or 1 October 1918 and **died of wounds** 5 October 1918, aged 20.

McMULLAN Private William John 14545. Born at Lurgan, County Armagh. Enlisted September 1914. To France with 36th (Ulster) Division in October 1915. 'C' Company. Company bomb carrier during the attack at Hamel 1 July 1916, during which he was **killed in action**. 1914-15 Star. His son, Corporal James McMullan, was wounded serving with The Royal Irish Rifles.

McMURRAY Private Samuel 41314. [Enlisted in October 1914 into the North Irish Horse (1289). Attached to 54th (East Anglian) Division Military Mounted Police 12 July 1915 and appointed Lance Corporal. Joined the Mediterranean Expeditionary Force in Egypt 27 July 1915. Served with 2nd North Irish Horse, X Corps Cavalry Regiment.] Joined the renamed 9th (North Irish Horse) Battalion from 36 Infantry Base Depot and transferred to Princess Victoria's (Royal Irish Fusiliers) in September/October 1917 (renumbered 41314). 'C' Company. **Missing** in the period 21-28 March 1918 during the retreat from St Quentin believed **captured**. Transferred to the Class Z Reserve 26 February 1919. 1914-15 Star.

McMURRAY Lance Corporal Thomas 14533. From Richhill, County Armagh. Enlisted September 1914. To France with 36th (Ulster) Division in October 1915. **Wounded** during the attack at Hamel 1 July 1916. He left hospital in January 1917. Discharged as no longer physically fit for war service due to wounds 10 October 1918. Silver War Badge, number B41684. 1914-15 Star.

McMURRAY Private Thomas 41164. Born in 1893 at Upper Tannybrake, near Kells, County Antrim. [Enlisted 13 August 1915 into the Service Squadron, 6th (Inniskilling) Dragoons (UD/277). To France 25 April 1917 and transferred to the Machine Gun Corps (Cavalry). Served with 2nd North Irish Horse, X Corps Cavalry Regiment.] Joined the renamed 9th (North Irish Horse) Battalion from 36 Infantry Base Depot and transferred to Princess Victoria's (Royal Irish Fusiliers) on 23

September 1917 (renumbered 41164). **Wounded** by a gunshot to the thigh at Marcoing 15 December 1917. Evacuated to hospital in England 20 December 1917 and treated at the War Hospital, Stratford-upon-Avon until February 1918. [Posted to the 3rd (Reserve) Garrison Battalion at Bere Island, Bantry Bay 18 March 1918. Transferred to The Royal Irish Regiment (renumbered 3547) 20 April 1918 and posted to the 2nd (Home Service) Garrison Battalion, The Royal Irish Regiment. To France (2nd Garrison Guard Battalion became 8th (Garrison) Battalion and then 8th (Service) Battalion, The Royal Irish Regiment). 'C' Company.] Transferred to the Class Z Reserve 22 April 1919. His brother, Lance Corporal George McMurray, was killed in action at Hamel on 1 July 1916 serving with the 12th (Service) Battalion, The Royal Irish Rifles (Central Antrim).

McMURRAY Private Thomas 41494. [Enlisted 25 May 1915 into the North Irish Horse (1613). Served with 2nd North Irish Horse, X Corps Cavalry Regiment.] Joined the renamed 9th (North Irish Horse) Battalion from 36 Infantry Base Depot and transferred to Princess Victoria's (Royal Irish Fusiliers) in September/October 1917 (renumbered 41494). **Wounded**. Discharged as no longer physically fit for war service due to wounds 1 October 1918, aged 24. Silver War Badge, number B22495.

McMURRAY Private William Henry 18274. Born 9 June 1896. From Poyntzpass, County Armagh. Enlisted into the 9th (Service) Battalion in March 1915. To France with 36th (Ulster) Division in October 1915. 6 Platoon, 'B' Company. **Killed in action** during the attack at Hamel 1 July 1916, aged 20. 1914-15 Star.

McNAIRNEY Private Patrick 26817. [Enlisted in February 1917 and joined the 7th/8th (Service) Battalion in 49th Brigade, 16th (Irish) Division.] Joined the 9th (North Irish Horse) Battalion when the 7th/8th (Service) Battalion was disbanded in February 1918.

McNALLY Private Frederick 14515. Born at Lurgan, County Armagh. Enlisted September 1914. To France with 36th (Ulster) Division in October 1915. 'C' Company. Lewis gunner during the attack at Hamel 1 July 1916 and was **killed in action**. 1914-15 Star.

McNALLY Private James 21654. From Belfast. Enlisted in September 1915. Posted to the 9th (Service) Battalion in May/June 1916. **Killed in action** during the attack at Hamel 1 July 1916, aged 24.

McNALLY Private James 23591. From Portadown, County Armagh. Enlisted in December 1915. Posted to the 9th (Service) Battalion. 'B' Company. **Captured** at the Battle of Langemarck 16 August 1917.

McNALLY Private Patrick. Tried by Field General Court Martial on 11 December 1918 charged with *'when on active service* ***deserting*** *His Majesty's service'*; found guilty and sentenced to three years imprisonment with hard labour. Soldier not identified.

McNALLY Private Thomas 14523. Born in 1894. From Lurgan, County Armagh. A weaver. Armagh Regiment, Ulster Volunteer Force. Enlisted September 1914. Joined the 10th (Reserve) Battalion 9 October 1915. Joined the 3rd (Reserve) Garrison Battalion at Bere Island, Bantry Bay 18 March 1918. [Transferred to The Royal Irish Regiment (renumbered 3525) 20 April 1918.] Transferred to the Class Z Reserve 24 May 1919.

McNALLY Private Thomas 14547. Born in 1882 at Portadown, County Armagh. A weaver. Enlisted September 1914. To France with 36th (Ulster) Division in October 1915. **Wounded** during the attack at Hamel 1 July 1916 by a gunshot wound to the back that fractured both hip bones. Evacuated to hospital in England 6 July 1916. Joined the 10th (Reserve) Battalion 4 October 1917. [Transferred to the Labour Corps (renumbered 545502) 6 April 1918 and served with the Irish Command Labour Centre.] Discharged as no longer physically fit for war service due to wounds 19 June 1918. Silver War Badge, number 410635. 1914-15 Star.

McNALLY Private William 14498. Born in Richhill, County Armagh in 1894. A labourer. Armagh Regiment, Ulster Volunteer Force. Enlisted September 1914. No record of deployment to France with 36th (Ulster) Division in October 1915; his name was removed from the 1914-15 Star roll.

McNALLY Private William James 21521. From Richhill, County Armagh. Enlisted in August 1915. Posted to the 9th (Service) Battalion in May/June 1916. **Killed in action** during the attack at Hamel 1 July 1916, aged 19.

McNAMARA Private Joseph 21480. From Belfast. [Enlisted in August 1915 and joined the 8th

(Service) Battalion in 49th Brigade, 16th (Irish) Division.] Joined the 9th (North Irish Horse) Battalion when the 7th/8th (Service) Battalion was disbanded in February 1918. 'C' Company. **Captured** in the period 21-28 March 1918 during the retreat from St Quentin.

McNAYE Private John 27798. Born at Killylea, County Armagh. Enlisted in July 1917. Posted to the 9th (North Irish Horse) Battalion. **Killed in action** during the attack south of Wulverghem 4 September 1918, aged 35.

McNEICE Private Albert 14526. Enlisted September 1914. No record of deployment to France with 36th (Ulster) Division in October 1915. **Injured** (fractured knee) in March 1917. [Transferred to the Labour Corps (renumbered 620925 Sergeant).]

McNEILANCE Private Samuel John 41493. From Belfast. A steel plater. [Enlisted in October 1914 into the North Irish Horse (1293). To France with 'F' Squadron in 33rd Division 17 November 1915. Served with 2nd North Irish Horse, X Corps Cavalry Regiment.] Joined the renamed 9th (North Irish Horse) Battalion from 36 Infantry Base Depot and transferred to Princess Victoria's (Royal Irish Fusiliers) in September/October 1917 (renumbered 41493). [Transferred to the Corps of Royal Engineers (WR/347334).]

McNEILL Private James Henry 14568. From Portadown, County Armagh. 4th (Portadown) Battalion, Armagh Regiment, Ulster Volunteer Force. Enlisted September 1914. To France with 36th (Ulster) Division in October 1915. Officer's Mess cook in 1916. Transferred to the Class Z Reserve 1 March 1919. 1914-15 Star.

McNEILL Private John 18551. Enlisted into the 9th (Service) Battalion in April 1915. To France November 1915 and rejoined the 9th (Service) Battalion. **Wounded**. [Transferred to the Labour Corps (renumbered 231586). Served with 581st Home Service Employment Company.] Discharged as no longer physically fit for war service due to wounds 26 September 1918. Silver War Badge, number B16463, aged 30. 1914-15 Star.

McNEILL Private John 21170. From Belfast. [Enlisted in December 1914/January 1915 and joined the 8th (Service) Battalion in 49th Brigade, 16th (Irish) Division.] Joined the 9th (North Irish Horse) Battalion when the 7th/8th (Service) Battalion was disbanded in February 1918. 'D' Company. **Captured** in the period 21-28 March 1918 during the retreat from St Quentin.

McNUTT Private John Andrew 41398. Born 24 June 1884 at Carnshanagh, Fohan, County Donegal. A bank official in Dublin. [Enlisted 24 November 1915 into the North Irish Horse (1964). To France 1 August 1916. Served with 2nd North Irish Horse, X Corps Cavalry Regiment.] Joined the renamed 9th (North Irish Horse) Battalion from 36 Infantry Base Depot and transferred to Princess Victoria's (Royal Irish Fusiliers) in September/October 1917 (renumbered 41398). To hospital sick (rheumatism and trench fever) 12 April 1918 and evacuated to hospital in England. Treated at 2nd Western General Hospital, Manchester. [Transferred to the Army Service Corps (renumbered S/4445403) 9 November 1918.] Transferred to the Class Z Reserve 18 February 1919. After the war he became a manager in the Northern Bank and lived at Bangor.

McPAKE Private William 42533. [Enlisted 7 May 1918 into The Royal Irish Rifles (22631).] Transferred at the Base Depot to Princess Victoria's (Royal Irish Fusiliers) 14 September 1918 (renumbered 42533) and joined the 9th (North Irish Horse) Battalion 22 September 1918. **Wounded**. Discharged as no longer physically fit for war service due to wounds 28 May 1919. Silver War Badge, number B243079.

McQUADE Private Thomas 42570. [Enlisted into The Royal Irish Rifles (21857).] Transferred at the Base Depot to Princess Victoria's (Royal Irish Fusiliers) 14 September 1918 (renumbered 42570) and joined the 9th (North Irish Horse) Battalion 22 September 1918. Tried by Field General Court Martial on 19 November 1918 charged with *'wilfully injuring himself with intent thereby to render himself unfit for service'*; found guilty and sentenced to ninety-one days Field Punishment Number 1. [Transferred to 5th (Service) Battalion, The Royal Irish Regiment (Pioneers) in the Light Division in the British Army of the Rhine in March/June 1919 (renumbered 41344).]

McQUAID Private Patrick 24815. [Enlisted 21 September 1914 and joined the 7th or 8th (Service) Battalion in 49th Brigade, 16th (Irish) Division.] Joined the 9th (North Irish Horse) Battalion when the 7th/8th (Service) Battalion was disbanded in February 1918. 'B' Company. **Wounded** during the retreat from St Quentin 21-28 March 1918. Discharged as no longer physically fit for war service due to wounds 3 December 1918. Silver War Badge, number B55044.

McQUEEN Private William 20366. From Belfast. [Enlisted 6 April 1915 into The Royal Inniskilling Fusiliers.] Transferred to Princess Victoria's (Royal Irish Fusiliers) on 30 June 1915 (renumbered 20366) and joined the 9th (Service) Battalion. To France with 36th (Ulster) Division in October 1915. **Wounded** during the attack at Hamel 1 July 1916. Discharged as no longer physically fit for war service due to wounds 8 November 1916. Silver War Badge, number 258755. 1914-15 Star.

McSTAY Corporal James 24698. Born in 1892 at Garvagh, County Armagh. An agricultural labourer. Enlisted in August 1916. Posted to the 9th (Service) Battalion. 'A' Company. **Wounded** at the Battle of Langemarck 16 August 1917. [Transferred to 5th (Service) Battalion, The Royal Irish Regiment (Pioneers) in the Light Division in the British Army of the Rhine in March/June 1919 (renumbered 41341).]

McSTAY Private Joseph 24699. Born in 1893 at Mullaghbrack, County Armagh. A shop assistant. Enlisted in August 1916. Posted to the 9th (Service) Battalion. 'A' Company. Listed as **wounded** after the Battle of Langemarck 16 August 1917 and later declared **killed in action** on that date.

McTEAGUE Private John 24329. (Also spelled McTaig.) Born in 1898 at Belfast. Enlisted in May 1916. Posted to the 9th (Service) Battalion. 'D' Company. **Missing** at the Battle of Langemarck 16 August 1917 and later declared **killed in action** on that date, aged 19.

McVEIGH Private Charles 19752. [Enlisted in April 1915 into the 7th (Service) Battalion in 49th Brigade, 16th (Irish) Division.] Joined the 9th (North Irish Horse) Battalion when the 7th/8th (Service) Battalion was disbanded in February 1918. 'A' Company. **Captured** in the period 21-28 March 1918 during the retreat from St Quentin.

McVEIGH Private Michael 41456. Born at Londonderry. [Enlisted in August 1914 into the North Irish Horse (1013). To France 1 May 1915. Served with 2nd North Irish Horse, X Corps Cavalry Regiment.] Joined the renamed 9th (North Irish Horse) Battalion from 36 Infantry Base Depot and transferred to Princess Victoria's (Royal Irish Fusiliers) in September/October 1917 (renumbered 41456). **Killed in action** during the advance to Anseghem 25 October 1918, aged 28. 1914-15 Star.

McVEIGH Private Thomas 41253. [Enlisted in September 1914 into the North Irish Horse (1163). To France 19 December 1915. Served with 2nd North Irish Horse, X Corps Cavalry Regiment.] Joined the renamed 9th (North Irish Horse) Battalion from 36 Infantry Base Depot and transferred to Princess Victoria's (Royal Irish Fusiliers) in September/October 1917 (renumbered 41253). Transferred to the Class Z Reserve 15 March 1919. 1914-15 Star.

McVEY Private Edward 14535. Born in Scotland. From Loughgall, County Armagh. A farm labourer. Enlisted September 1914. To France with 36th (Ulster) Division in October 1915. 1914-15 Star.

McVICKER Private James 41637. [Enlisted in January 1915 into the North Irish Horse (1426). To France with 'F' Squadron in 33rd Division 17 November 1915. Served with 2nd North Irish Horse, X Corps Cavalry Regiment.] Joined the renamed 9th (North Irish Horse) Battalion from 36 Infantry Base Depot and transferred to Princess Victoria's (Royal Irish Fusiliers) in September/October 1917 (renumbered 41637). Transferred to the Class Z Reserve 27 March 1919. 1914-15 Star.

McWHIRTER Private James 17660. From Lisdrumchor Lower, Glenanne, County Armagh. Enlisted into the 9th (Service) Battalion in December 1914/January 1915. To France 17 November 1915 and rejoined the 9th (Service) Battalion. 'D' Company. **Wounded** during the attack at Hamel 1 July 1916. **Wounded** at the Battle of Langemarck 16 August 1917. **Captured** in the period 21-28 March 1918 during the retreat from St Quentin. Brother of Privates Joseph and Samuel McWhirter.

McWHIRTER Private Joseph 14544. From Lisdrumchor Lower, Glenanne, County Armagh. Enlisted September 1914. To France with 36th (Ulster) Division in October 1915. **Wounded**. [Transferred to the Labour Corps (renumbered 231621).] Discharged as no longer physically fit for war service 19 June 1918. Silver War Badge, number 410641. 1914-15 Star. Brother of Privates James and Samuel McWhirter.

McWHIRTER Private Samuel 14543. Born in 1890 at Lisdrumchor Lower, Glenanne, County Armagh. Enlisted September 1914. To France with 36th (Ulster) Division in October 1915.

Wounded during the attack at Hamel 1 July 1916 and **died of wounds** that day, aged 25. 1914-15 Star. Brother of Privates James and Joseph McWhirter.

McWILLIAMS Private Christopher 41085. Born on 8 June 1898 at Cleenagh, County Fermanagh. [Enlisted in May 1915 into the Service Squadron, 6th (Inniskilling) Dragoons (UD/268). Served with 2nd North Irish Horse, X Corps Cavalry Regiment.] Joined the renamed 9th (North Irish Horse) Battalion from 36 Infantry Base Depot and transferred to Princess Victoria's (Royal Irish Fusiliers) in September/October 1917 (renumbered 41085). **Killed in action** 23 November 1917 at Moeuvres. His father, Private James McWilliams, served with the Corps of Royal Engineers.

McWILLIAMS Private John 41297. [Enlisted in April 1910 into the North Irish Horse (500). To France 17 August 1914 with 'A' Squadron as GHQ Troops. Served with 2nd North Irish Horse, X Corps Cavalry Regiment.] Joined the renamed 9th (North Irish Horse) Battalion from 36 Infantry Base Depot and transferred to Princess Victoria's (Royal Irish Fusiliers) in September/October 1917 (renumbered 41297). [Posted to the 5th/6th (Service) Battalion.] Posted back to 9th (North Irish Horse) Battalion. 1914 Star and clasp.

McWILLIAMS Private Robert John 19764. From Armagh, County Armagh. Enlisted into the 9th (Service) Battalion in April 1915. **Killed in action** during the attack at Hamel 1 July 1916, aged 19.

McWILLIAMS Private Samuel 16147. From Creeve, County Monahan. Enlisted into the 9th (Service) Battalion in October 1914. To France with 36th (Ulster) Division in October 1915. **Wounded**. [Transferred to the Royal Army Medical Corps (136753).] 1914-15 Star. Brother of Private Thomas McWilliams.

McWILLIAMS Lance Corporal Thomas 16124. From Creeve, County Monahan. Enlisted into the 9th (Service) Battalion in October 1914. To France with 36th (Ulster) Division in October 1915. **Wounded** during the attack at Hamel 1 July 1916. Transferred to the Class Z Reserve 24 March 1919. 1914-15 Star. Brother of Private Samuel McWilliams.

McWILLIAMS Lance Corporal William 41132. [Enlisted in September 1915 into the Service Squadron, 6th (Inniskilling) Dragoons (UD/293). Served with 2nd North Irish Horse, X Corps Cavalry Regiment.] Joined the renamed 9th (North Irish Horse) Battalion from 36 Infantry Base Depot and transferred to Princess Victoria's (Royal Irish Fusiliers) in September/October 1917 (renumbered 41132).

MEANEY Lance Corporal Patrick 3371. [Enlisted in late-1914/early-1915 into Princess Victoria's (Royal Irish Fusiliers) Special Reserve. Mobilised 1 May 1915. To France 25 May 1915 and joined the 1st Battalion. Posted to the 7th/8th (Service) Battalion in 49th Brigade, 16th (Irish) Division.] Joined the 9th (North Irish Horse) Battalion when the 7th/8th (Service) Battalion was disbanded in February 1918. **Wounded**. Discharged as no longer physically fit for war service due to wounds 15 August 1918, aged 23. Silver War Badge, number 435842. 1914-15 Star.

MEDDINGS Private William H 42265. [Enlisted into the Army Service Corps (172649).] Transferred to Princess Victoria's (Royal Irish Fusiliers) 8 May 1918 (renumbered 42265) and joined the 9th (North Irish Horse) Battalion. [Transferred to the Army Cyclist Corps (renumbered 23048).]

MEDLAND Warrant Officer Class II Wilfred Harold 9259. Born in 1884 at Cirencester, Gloucestershire. From Newtownards, County Down. [Enlisted into Princess Victoria's (Royal Irish Fusiliers) as a regular soldier in 1906.] Posted to the 9th (Service) Battalion. Company Sergeant Major 'C' Company. **Killed in action** at the Battle of Langemarck 16 August 1917.

MEDLOW Private David 24664. Born in 1894 at Kernan, Portadown, County Armagh. Member of Edenderry Temperance and Benefit Loyal Orange Lodge 322. Enlisted 11 August 1914. He either served elsewhere before transferring or was a Special Reservist when re-enlisted in August 1916 and renumbered. Posted to the 9th (Service) Battalion. 'D' Company. **Wounded** at the Battle of Langemarck 16 August 1917. Discharged as no longer physically fit for war service due to wounds 18 June 1918. Silver War Badge, number 387959.

MEEK Private William 42142. From London. A butcher. [Enlisted 24 June 1916 and transferred to the Army Reserve. Mobilised 2 November 1916 into the Army Service Corps (S4/218376). Served at Bulford. To France 23 September 1917 and served with 31st and 14th Line of Communication

Companies.] To 'A' Infantry Base Depot 4 May 1918. Transferred to Princess Victoria's (Royal Irish Fusiliers) 8 May 1918 (renumbered 42142) and joined the 9th (North Irish Horse) Battalion. **Wounded** by a gunshot to the chest during the attack south of Wulverghem on 4 September 1918. Treated at 3rd Canadian General Hospital and evacuated to hospital in England. Treated at Richmond War Hospital, Dublin. Transferred to the Class Z Reserve 3 February 1919. Lived at Newington Butts, London.

MEEKE Private Samuel 42492. Born 27 May 1899 at Ahoghill, County Antrim. Lived at Slatt, County Antrim. [Enlisted into the Seaforth Highlanders (Ross-shire Buffs, The Duke of Albany's) in 1915 but was discharged having made a mis-statement as to age on enlistment; soldier under 17 years of age at date of application for discharge. Enlisted into The Royal Irish Rifles (9049) 18 May 1916, aged 16, and joined the 4th (Extra Reserve) Battalion, The Royal Irish Rifles. His mother wrote to his Commanding Officer and informed him of Meeke's true age. The reply by the Adjutant acknowledges his previous underage enlistment and informs her that she could apply for his discharge. Sentenced on 25 September 1916 to twenty-one days detention for absence. Reported as **deserted** 22 January 1917. Rejoined 18 April 1917. Tried by District Court Martial on 9 May 1917 charged with *'when on active service, absenting himself without leave and losing by neglect his clothing and regimental necessaries.'* Found guilty and sentenced to 112 days detention, with twenty-eight days remitted. While in detention, posted to the 5th (Extra Reserve) Battalion, The Royal Irish Rifles 2 July 1917. Released from detention 17 July 1917. Reported as **deserted** 18 July 1917. Rejoined 6 September 1917. Tried by Regimental Court Martial at Holywood on 13 September 1917 charged with *'absenting himself without leave'*; found guilty and sentenced to forty-two days detention. Reported as **deserted** 14 October 1917. Rejoined 13 December 1917. Tried by District Court Martial on 29 December 1917 charged with *'when on active service, absenting himself without leave and losing by neglect his clothing and regimental necessaries.'* Found guilty and sentenced to six months detention. Released from detention 30 May 1918. To France 27 June 1918 and joined 'A' Infantry Base Depot 30 June 1918. Posted to the 2nd Battalion, The Royal Irish Rifles (did not join). On 31 July 1918 while at the Base Depot, he was admitted to 40th Stationary Hospital injured (contusion to neck caused by tripping over a tent peg).] Transferred at the Base Depot to Princess Victoria's (Royal Irish Fusiliers) 14 September 1918 (renumbered 42492) and joined the 9th (North Irish Horse) Battalion 22 September 1918. **Wounded** during the attack at Vijfwegen on 30 September or 1 October 1918 and **died of wounds** at 3rd Australian Casualty Clearing Station 6 October 1918, aged 19.

MEGARITY Lance Corporal Jackson 23727 & 7040726. Born in 1897 at Edenknappagh, County Armagh. The son of a farmer. Enlisted 31 January 1916. To France 21 July 1916 and joined the 9th (Service) Battalion. 'C' Company. **Wounded** during the retreat from St Quentin 21-28 March 1918 and evacuated to hospital in England 3 April 1918. Re-enlisted in early-1919 for Regular Army service with Princess Victoria's (Royal Irish Fusiliers) (renumbered 7040726). Served with the 1st Battalion in Persia and Mesopotamia in 1919/20. General Service Medal 1918-1962 with clasps 'Iraq' & 'NW Persia'. Discharged 31 March 1922.

MEGARRELL Private Hugh 14518. See Private H McGarrell above.

MELLOR Lance Corporal Ernest 43278. Born in 1889 at Nottingham. A tram driver. [Enlisted 29 August 1914 into The Leicestershire Regiment (12891). Transferred to the 4th (Extra Reserve) Battalion, The Sherwood Foresters (Nottinghamshire and Derbyshire Regiment) (19906) 11 September 1914. To France 15 March 1915 and joined the 1st Battalion. Evacuated to hospital in England. Joined the 3rd (Reserve) Battalion, The Sherwood Foresters (Nottinghamshire and Derbyshire Regiment) 10 June 1916.] To Infantry Base Depot, France 14 July 1916 and transferred to Princess Victoria's (Royal Irish Fusiliers) 31 August 1916 having joined the 9th (Service) Battalion on 8 August 1916. 14 Platoon, 'D' Company. Lance Corporal 1 December 1916. **Wounded** by gunshot to the buttock and thigh at the Battle of Langemarck 16 August 1917. Treated at 3rd Australian General Hospital and evacuated to hospital in England. Treated at the Lady Forester Auxiliary Hospital, Much Wenlock, Shropshire. Joined the 3rd (Reserve) Battalion 1 May 1918. To 'A' Infantry Base Depot 24 May 1918. Rejoined the 9th (North Irish Horse) Battalion. Declared **missing** at Hill 41 on 11 October 1918 and subsequently declared **killed in action** on that date. 1914-15 Star.

MELLOR Lance Corporal Stanley Hastings 27820. Born in 1892 at Orrell Park, Liverpool. A warehouse clerk. [Enlisted into the Army Ordnance Corps (912104).] Transferred to Princess Victoria's (Royal Irish Fusiliers) in July 1917 (renumbered 27820). Posted to the 9th (North Irish Horse) Battalion. **Killed in action** during the attack at Vijfwegen 30 September 1918, aged 26.

MELVIN Private John Tubman 40019. Born in 1896 at Burradon, Northumberland. [Enlisted into The Prince of Wales's Own (West Yorkshire Regiment) (36286).] Transferred to Princess Victoria's (Royal Irish Fusiliers) 30 November 1916 (renumbered 40019) and joined the 9th (Service) Battalion 12 December 1916. 'A' Company. Listed as **wounded** during at the Battle of Langemarck 16 August 1917 later declared **killed in action** on that date.

MENARY Private Henry William 24325. Born in 1886 at Milford, County Armagh. A harness mounter. Enlisted in May 1916. Posted to the 9th (Service) Battalion. **Captured**.

MENGHAM Private Thomas Alfred 42260. Born in 1883 at Portsea Island, Hampshire. [Mobilised from the Army Reserve into the Army Service Corps (T/26374). To France 5 October 1914. Served with 2nd Division Train and 280th Horsed Transport Company.] Transferred to Princess Victoria's (Royal Irish Fusiliers) 8 May 1918 (renumbered 42260) and joined the 9th (North Irish Horse) Battalion. Died at Portsmouth in 1967, aged 83.

MERCER Private David Henry 15866. Born in 1891 at Drumcree, County Armagh. From Portadown, County Armagh. A weaver & well-known footballer. Enlisted 13 August 1908 into the 3rd Battalion (Militia), Princess Victoria's (Royal Irish Fusiliers) (5144). Enlisted (fraudulently) into the 9th (Service) Battalion in October 1914. To France with 36th (Ulster) Division in October 1915. **Wounded** three times. Transferred to the Class Z Reserve. 1914-15 Star (initially forfeit due to fraudulent enlistment but restored).

MEREDITH Lieutenant Robert Douglas JP, formerly Lance Corporal 14458. From Tandragee, County Armagh. 4th (Portadown) Battalion, Armagh Regiment, Ulster Volunteer Force. Member of Loyal Orange Lodge 110. Enlisted in September 1914, aged 16. To France with 36th (Ulster) Division in October 1915. **Wounded** by a gunshot to the arm during the attack at Hamel 1 July 1916. **Wounded** in the wrist in the period 11-18 April 1918 in the actions between Wulverghem and Kemmel. Transferred to the Class Z Reserve 20 March 1919. 1914-15 Star. Opened a grocery shop after the war. Commissioned into the Territorial Army Reserve of Officers Special List as a Second Lieutenant for duty with the Army Cadet Force in Northern Ireland 23 June 1943. Promoted Lieutenant. Relinquished his commission 18 October 1945. Worshipful District Master of Tandragee District Number 4 from 1945 to 1974. JP. Died in 1980 and is buried at Ballymore Parish Churchyard.

MERVYN DCM Corporal Michael 5631. Born at Shankill, Belfast. Served briefly with the 3rd Battalion (Militia), The Royal Irish Rifles. Enlisted 13 March 1897 into Princess Victoria's (Royal Irish Fusiliers) as a regular soldier (5958) and joined the 2nd Battalion. Posted to the 1st Battalion in Egypt 11 February 1899. Sailed with the 1st Battalion for South Africa in September 1899. Corporal 1 January 1900. Tried by Field General Court Martial on 14 April 1902 charged with *'when on active service drunkenness on duty'* and *'neglect to the prejudice of good order and military discipline'*; found guilty and sentenced to six months imprisonment with hard labour and to be reduced to the ranks. Posted to the 2nd Battalion 12 September 1902, with which he remained in South Africa and took part in the Relief of Ladysmith. Lance Corporal 19 November 1902. Tried by Field General Court Martial on 15 December 1902 charged with *'drunkenness when on duty'*; found guilty and sentenced to forty-two days imprisonment with hard labour. Released 17 January 1903 with the remainder of his sentence remitted by the Captain of HMY Soudan when the 2nd Battalion arrived in India. Queen's South Africa Medal with clasps 'Orange Free State', 'Transvaal', 'Tugela Heights' and 'Relief of Ladysmith'. King's South Africa Medal with clasps 'South Africa 1901' and 'South Africa 1902'. Joined the Depot 29 January 1905. Transferred to the Army Reserve 1 May 1905. Discharged from the Army Reserve on termination of his engagement 12 May 1909. Enlisted 15 June 1911 into 3rd Battalion (Militia), Princess Victoria's (Royal Irish Fusiliers) Special Reserve (renumbered 5631). Worked as a carter for Messrs Wordie, Belfast. [Lance Corporal 11 September 1914. Corporal 16 September 1914. To France 8 February 1915 and joined the 2nd Battalion. Sergeant 18 June 1915. Tried by Field General Court Martial on 29 July 1915 charged with *'drunkenness'*; found guilty, reduced in rank to Corporal and fined £1. **DCM** - Armentieres 1915. To Salonika 27 November 1915. Evacuated to hospital in England 8 July 1916. Joined the 3rd (Reserve) Battalion 24 August 1916.] To France 8 December 1916 and joined the 9th

(Service) Battalion. 'B' Company. **Wounded** at the Battle of Langemarck 16 August 1917 and evacuated to hospital in England 20 August 1917. Joined the 10th (Reserve) Battalion 12 October 1917. [Transferred to The Royal Irish Rifles (renumbered 22221) 7 March 1918 and joined the 20th (Reserve) Battalion. Posted to the 3rd (Reserve) Battalion, The Royal Irish Rifles 15 May 1918.] Discharged as no longer physically fit for war service due to wounds 8 August 1918. Silver War Badge, number B6394. 1914-15 Star.

METCALFE Corporal Thomas 14490. Born in 1895 at Portadown, County Armagh. Worked in a linen mill. Enlisted September 1914. To France with 36th (Ulster) Division in October 1915. 'B' Company. Believed **wounded** in the period 21-28 March 1918 during the retreat from St Quentin. [Transferred to the Army Service Corps (renumbered S/41556).] Transferred to the Class Z Reserve 23 March 1919. 1914-15 Star.

MIDGLEY Private Thomas 20303. From Durham. Enlisted 18 May 1915 and joined the 9th (Service) Battalion with the draft of men from The Royal Inniskilling Fusiliers who transferred to Princess Victoria's (Royal Irish Fusiliers) on 30 June 1915. **Wounded** during the attack at Hamel 1 July 1916. [Posted to 3rd (Reserve) Garrison Battalion at Bere Island, Bantry Bay.] Discharged as no longer physically fit for war service due to wounds 8 October 1917. Silver War Badge, number 255995.

MIGHTON Sergeant Benjamin 14472. Born 1 December 1890 at Lurgan, County Armagh. A printer. Enlisted September 1914. To France with 36th (Ulster) Division in October 1915. Transferred to the Class Z Reserve 2 April 1919. 1914-15 Star. Son of Private John Mighton.

MIGHTON Private John 14449. From Lurgan, County Armagh. Enlisted September 1914. To France with 36th (Ulster) Division in October 1915. [Transferred to the Labour Corps (renumbered 213613).] Transferred to the Class Z Reserve 25 March 1919. 1914-15 Star. Father of Sergeant Benjamin Mighton.

MILES Sergeant Ernest Charles 43440. From Feckham, Surrey. [Enlisted into The London Regiment (721582).] To France and joined 36 Infantry Base Depot 29 March 1918. Transferred to Princess Victoria's (Royal Irish Fusiliers) 2 April 1918 (renumbered 43440) and joined the 9th (North Irish Horse) Battalion 4 April 1918. **Missing** in the period 11-18 April 1918 in the actions between Wulverghem and Kemmel; subsequently declared **killed in action** 19 April 1918.

MILLAR Private James 41228. Born in 1898 at Newtownards. A dairyman. [Enlisted 11 January 1915 into the North Irish Horse (1396), aged 16. To France with 'F' Squadron in 33rd Division 17 November 1915. Served with 2nd North Irish Horse, X Corps Cavalry Regiment.] Joined the renamed 9th (North Irish Horse) Battalion from 36 Infantry Base Depot and transferred to Princess Victoria's (Royal Irish Fusiliers) in September/October 1917 (renumbered 41228). 'A' Company. [Transferred to the Tank Corps (renumbered 304898) 28 December 1917 and posted for training to the Tank Corps Depot, at Bovington near Wareham, Dorset. To France 14 August 1918 and joined the 11th Battalion, Tank Corps 7 September 1918.] Transferred to the Class Z Reserve 16 February 1919. 1914-15 Star.

MILLAR Private Robert 41252. [Enlisted 10 June 1915 into the North Irish Horse (1691). Served with 2nd North Irish Horse, X Corps Cavalry Regiment.] Joined the renamed 9th (North Irish Horse) Battalion from 36 Infantry Base Depot and transferred to Princess Victoria's (Royal Irish Fusiliers) in September/October 1917 (renumbered 41252). **Wounded**. Discharged as no longer physically fit for war service due to wounds 16 July 1918, aged 32. Silver War Badge, number 425676.

MILLER MM Private George Frederick 43201. Born 10 October 1892 at Heanor, Derbyshire. [Enlisted into The Sherwood Foresters (Nottinghamshire and Derbyshire Regiment).] Transferred to Princess Victoria's (Royal Irish Fusiliers) 31 August 1916 having joined the 9th (Service) Battalion on 8 August 1916 (renumbered 43201). **MM** – Wulverghem April 1918. Died at Derbyshire 1974, aged 81.

MILLER Private Robert 27574. Enlisted in May 1917. Posted to the 9th (North Irish Horse) Battalion. [Posted to the 1st Battalion with which he was **killed in action** on 23 November 1917 during the attack on Round Trench and Lock No 5.]

MILLER Private Samuel 41437. Born in 1898 at Ballynoe, County Antrim. [Enlisted 17 October 1916 into the North Irish Horse (2293). To France 8 April 1917. Served with 2nd North Irish Horse, X Corps Cavalry Regiment.] Joined the renamed 9th (North Irish Horse) Battalion from 36 Infantry

Base Depot and transferred to Princess Victoria's (Royal Irish Fusiliers) in September/October 1917 (renumbered 41437). Separated from the 9th (North Irish Horse) Battalion in the period 21-28 March 1918 during the retreat from St Quentin; rejoined 6 April 1918. Evacuated to hospital in England 8 May 1918. Rejoined the 9th (North Irish Horse) Battalion October 1918. [Transferred to 5th (Service) Battalion, The Royal Irish Regiment (Pioneers) in the Light Division in the British Army of the Rhine in March/June 1919 (renumbered 41328).] Transferred to the Class Z Reserve 8 November 1919.

MILLER Private William 29555. From Derrylane, Killeshandra, County Cavan. A farm labourer. Enlisted 25 March 1918 and joined the 3rd (Reserve) Battalion. To France 10 August 1918 and joined the 9th (North Irish Horse) Battalion. **Killed in action** during the attack south of Wulverghem 4 September 1918, aged 20.

MILLER Private William James 45732. [Enlisted into The London Regiment (735024). Posted to the 1/24th (County of London) Battalion, The London Regiment (The Queen's).] To France and joined 36 Infantry Base Depot 29 March 1918. Transferred to Princess Victoria's (Royal Irish Fusiliers) 2 April 1918 (renumbered 45732) and joined the 9th (North Irish Horse) Battalion 4 April 1918.

MILLIGAN Private Francis William 42218. Born at Walton, Lancashire. [Enlisted into the Army Service Corps (S4/140215). To France 29 February 1916. Served with 39th Division Supply Column.] Transferred to Princess Victoria's (Royal Irish Fusiliers) 8 May 1918 (renumbered 42218) and joined the 9th (North Irish Horse) Battalion. **Killed in action** during the attack at Vijfwegen 30 September 1918.

MILLIGAN Private John James 41326. [Enlisted in January 1913 into the North Irish Horse (785). To France 20 August 1914 with 'C' Squadron as 5th Division Cavalry and then as GHQ Troops. Served with 2nd North Irish Horse, X Corps Cavalry Regiment.] Joined the renamed 9th (North Irish Horse) Battalion from 36 Infantry Base Depot and transferred to Princess Victoria's (Royal Irish Fusiliers) in September/October 1917 (renumbered 41326). 1914 Star.

MILLIGAN Sergeant Robert 14470. Enlisted September 1914. To France with 36th (Ulster) Division in October 1915. Discharged as no longer physically fit for war service due to sickness 28 February 1919. Silver War Badge, number B154466. 1914-15 Star.

MILLIGAN Private Robert 14489. From Portadown, County Armagh. Enlisted September 1914. To France with 36th (Ulster) Division in October 1915. 'B' Company. **Wounded** during the attack at Hamel 1 July 1916. **Wounded** at the Battle of Langemarck 16 August 1917. Discharged as no longer physically fit for war service due to wounds 29 May 1918, aged 23. Silver War Badge, number 391440. 1914-15 Star.

MILLIGAN Private William 14481. Born at Magheralin, County Armagh. From Century Street, Portadown, County Armagh. Enlisted September 1914. To France with 36th (Ulster) Division in October 1915. **Wounded** during the attack at Hamel 1 July 1916. [Joined the 1st Garrison Battalion and served in India and Burma. **Died** in a train crash in Burma on 10 February 1918. He was proceeding on leave to the United Kingdom following a serious illness.]

MILLIGAN Private William 20070. Born in 1880. From Portadown, County Armagh. Enlisted into the 9th (Service) Battalion 3 June 1915. 'B' Company. To France with 36th (Ulster) Division in October 1915. Evacuated to hospital in England 27 October 1916 and treated at Whittington Barracks, Lichfield. Discharged from hospital 18 November 1916 and posted to the Irish Command Depot. Joined the 10th (Reserve) Battalion 2 January 1917. [Transferred to the Royal Defence Corps (renumbered 73195) 4 May 1918 and served with 170th Protection Company.] Transferred to the Class Z Reserve 16 March 1919. 1914-15 Star.

MILLIKIN Private William 41443. [Enlisted in August 1915 into the North Irish Horse (1720). Served with 2nd North Irish Horse, X Corps Cavalry Regiment.] Joined the renamed 9th (North Irish Horse) Battalion from 36 Infantry Base Depot and transferred to Princess Victoria's (Royal Irish Fusiliers) in September/October 1917 (renumbered 41443).

MILLNS Lance Corporal John 43267. From Doncaster. [Enlisted 2 November 1914 into The Sherwood Foresters (Nottinghamshire and Derbyshire Regiment) (18364) and joined the 3rd (Reserve) Battalion. Lance Corporal 26 January 1915. Reverted to Private 17 April 1915. Sentenced to ten days detention for misconduct 7 August 1915. Awarded fourteen days detention for misconduct 10 March 1916. Qualified as a Signaller June 1916.] To France 14 July 1916 and transferred to Princess Victoria's (Royal Irish Fusiliers) 31 August 1916 having joined the 9th (Service) Battalion on 8 August 1916. 'D' Company, Signal Section. To hospital 19 August to 2 September 1916 with scabies. To hospital 3-6 November 1916 with scabies. To hospital 15 January 1917 with rheumatism. Joined 36 Infantry Base Depot 29 April 1917. Rejoined the 9th (Service) Battalion 9 May 1917. **Killed in action** at the Battle of Langemarck 16 August 1917, aged 24.

MILLS Private David 42462. [Enlisted into The Royal Irish Rifles (93).] Transferred at the Base Depot to Princess Victoria's (Royal Irish Fusiliers) 14 September 1918 (renumbered 42462) and joined the 9th (North Irish Horse) Battalion 22 September 1918.

MILLS Lance Corporal Henry 43446. [Enlisted 21 September 1914 into The London Regiment (3073). To France 29 June 1915. Posted to the 1/24th (County of London) Battalion, The London Regiment (The Queen's).] To France and joined 36 Infantry Base Depot 29 March 1918. Transferred to Princess Victoria's (Royal Irish Fusiliers) 2 April 1918 (renumbered 43446) and joined the 9th (North Irish Horse) Battalion 4 April 1918. Discharged as no longer physically fit for war service due to wounds 29 January 1919. Silver War Badge, number B302454. 1914-15 Star.

MILLS Private John 23708. Enlisted in January 1916. Posted to the 9th (Service) Battalion.

MILLS Private John Hugh 42520. Born 5 September 1900 at Ballynacaird, County Antrim. A farm labourer. [Enlisted into 11 May 1918 The Royal Irish Rifles (22645) and joined the 3rd (Reserve) Battalion, The Royal Irish Rifles.] To France 6 September 1918. Transferred at the Base Depot to Princess Victoria's (Royal Irish Fusiliers) 14 September 1918 (renumbered 42520) and joined the 9th (North Irish Horse) Battalion 22 September 1918. Found to be underage, he was posted to 'A' Infantry Base Depot 24 October 1918 and then 3rd Young Soldiers Battalion at Martin Eglise 5 November 1918. Rejoined the 9th (North Irish Horse) Battalion 25 December 1918. To 4th General Hospital sick (diarrhoea) 20 March 1919 and evacuated to hospital in England. Joined the 3rd (Reserve) Battalion, Princess Victoria's (Royal Irish Fusiliers) 8 July 1919. Posted to the 2nd Battalion 26 July 1919. Transferred to the Class Z Reserve 21 November 1919.

MILLS Private Robert 41087. Born in 1896 at Aghintain, County Tyrone. [Enlisted 6 November 1914 into the Service Squadron, 6th (Inniskilling) Dragoons (UD/155). To France with 36th (Ulster) Division in October 1915. Served with 2nd North Irish Horse, X Corps Cavalry Regiment.] Joined the renamed 9th (North Irish Horse) Battalion from 36 Infantry Base Depot and transferred to Princess Victoria's (Royal Irish Fusiliers) in September/October 1917 (renumbered 41087). Discharged as no longer physically fit for war service due to sickness 14 May 1919. Silver War Badge, number B234834. 1914-15 Star. **Died** at Fivemiletown, County Tyrone on 26 October 1919, aged 22.

MILLS Private Samuel 14476. Enlisted September 1914. To France with 36th (Ulster) Division in October 1915. [Joined 108th Brigade Machine Gun Company in January 1916. Transferred to the Machine Gun Corps (renumbered 17801). Promoted Sergeant.] **Deserted** 28 December 1917. 1914-15 Star.

MILNE Warrant Officer Class II Charles William 15865. Regimental Quartermaster Sergeant - see above.

MINTER Corporal Francis Robert 19059. Born 23 February 1896 at Huntingfield, Suffolk. [Enlisted into the Royal Field Artillery. Transferred to Princess Victoria's (Royal Irish Fusiliers) in December 1915. Served with the 7th/8th (Service) Battalion in 49th Brigade, 16th (Irish) Division.] Joined the 9th (North Irish Horse) Battalion when the 7th/8th (Service) Battalion was disbanded in February 1918. Transferred to the Class Z Reserve 5 March 1919. Emigrated to Alberta, Canada in 1920 and became a farmer. In 1946 he moved with his family to Elk Lake, Vancouver Island. Died at Victoria, British Columbia, Canada 25 June 1975, aged 79. His brother, Able Seaman Arthur Minter, was killed in action at Flesquieres on 22 March 1918 serving with the Anson Battalion in 188th Brigade, 63rd (Royal Naval) Division. He is commemorated on the Arras Memorial. His brothers, Privates Rufus Everett Minter, Percival Claude Minter and Reginald Minter served with the Army Service Corps; the latter in Mesopotamia and India. His sisters May and Lillian Minter served as Voluntary Aid Detachment nurses.

MISKIMMIN Private Cecil 41455. [Enlisted in October 1914 into the North Irish Horse (1237). To

France 1 May 1915. Served with 2nd North Irish Horse, X Corps Cavalry Regiment.] Joined the renamed 9th (North Irish Horse) Battalion from 36 Infantry Base Depot and transferred to Princess Victoria's (Royal Irish Fusiliers) in September/October 1917 (renumbered 41455). 'C' Company. **Missing** in the period 21-28 March 1918 during the retreat from St Quentin believed **captured**. Transferred to the Class Z Reserve 22 March 1919. 1914-15 Star.

MITCHELL Private George Nicholl 42094. [Enlisted 22 May 1915 into the Army Veterinary Corps (16327). To France 26 May 1915.] Transferred to Princess Victoria's (Royal Irish Fusiliers) 8 May 1918 (renumbered 42094) and joined the 9th (North Irish Horse) Battalion. **Wounded**. Discharged as no longer physically fit for war service due to wounds 12 March 1919. Silver War Badge, number B157590. 1914-15 Star.

MITCHELL Corporal John Stewart 16127. Born in 1889 at Latlurcan, County Monaghan. Enlisted into the 9th (Service) Battalion in October 1914. To France with 36th (Ulster) Division in October 1915. 'D' Company. **Wounded** at the Battle of Langemarck 16 August 1917. **Killed in action** 29 March 1918 during the retreat from St Quentin, aged 27. 1914-15 Star.

MITCHELL Private Joseph Henry 23411. Enlisted on 19 December 1915. Posted to the 9th (Service) Battalion. Discharged as no longer physically fit for war service due to sickness 16 January 1919. Silver War Badge, number B84694.

MITCHELL Sergeant Julien 45749. Joined the 9th (North Irish Horse) Battalion, Princess Victoria's (Royal Irish Fusiliers) with the draft of men from The London Regiment in April 1918.

MITCHELL Private Moses 14475. From Lurgan, County Armagh. Enlisted September 1914. To France with 36th (Ulster) Division in October 1915. 'C' Company. Attached to Divisional Headquarters during the attack at Hamel 1 July 1916 and did not take part in the attack. Later **wounded**. [Transferred to the Labour Corps (renumbered 381183).] Discharged as no longer physically fit for war service due to wounds 29 March 1919. Silver War Badge, number B184867. 1914-15 Star. Brother of Sergeant William James Mitchell MM.

MITCHELL Lance Corporal Robert Alexander 41223. From Londonderry. [Enlisted in September 1914 into the North Irish Horse (1194). To France 20 January 1915. Served with 2nd North Irish Horse, X Corps Cavalry Regiment.] Joined the renamed 9th (North Irish Horse) Battalion from 36 Infantry Base Depot and transferred to Princess Victoria's (Royal Irish Fusiliers) in September/October 1917 (renumbered 41223). 'D' Company. **Captured** in the period 21-28 March 1918 during the retreat from St Quentin. Transferred to the Class Z Reserve 3 April 1919. 1914-15 Star.

MITCHELL Private Thomas 29437. Enlisted, re-enlisted or transferred to Princess Victoria's (Royal Irish Fusiliers) in March 1918. Posted to the 9th (North Irish Horse) Battalion.

MITCHELL Private William 40067. From Bradford, Yorkshire. [Enlisted into the 18th (Service) Battalion, The Prince of Wales's Own (West Yorkshire Regiment) (2nd Bradford) (1276) with which he landed in Egypt in 93rd Brigade, 31 Division 22 December 1915.] Transferred to Princess Victoria's (Royal Irish Fusiliers) 30 November 1916 (renumbered 40067) and joined the 9th (Service) Battalion 12 December 1916. 'B' Company. **Wounded** at the Battle of Langemarck 16 August 1917. **Deserted** March 1918. 1914-15 Star.

MITCHELL MM Sergeant William James 14474. Born in 1891 at Lurgan, County Armagh. A clerk for Johnston, Allen and Company, linen manufacturer. Enlisted September 1914. To France with 36th (Ulster) Division in October 1915. 'C' Company. Lance Corporal July 1916. Detached to the Battalion Orderly Room and did not take part in the attack at Hamel on 1 July 1916. **MM** – Wulverghem April 1918. Transferred to the Class Z Reserve 19 February 1919. 1914-15 Star. Served with the Ulster Special Constabulary and was active in the British Legion. Died in 1940. Brother of Private Moses Mitchell.

MOFFAT Private James 20307. From Byker, Newcastle-on-Tyne. [Enlisted into The Royal Inniskilling Fusiliers (24063).] Transferred to Princess Victoria's (Royal Irish Fusiliers) on 30 June 1915 (renumbered 20307) and joined the 9th (Service) Battalion. **Killed in action** during the attack at Hamel 1 July 1916, aged 22. 1914-15 Star.

MOFFETT Private Robert William 14443. From Tullycorbett, County Monaghan. Enlisted September 1914. [Transferred to the Military Foot Police (renumbered P/4498). To France 18

November 1915.] Transferred to the Class Z Reserve 19 March 1919. 1914-15 Star.

MOFFITT Sergeant William Thomas 41511. [Enlisted in October 1914 into the Service Squadron, 6th (Inniskilling) Dragoons (UD/15). To France with 36th (Ulster) Division in October 1915. Served with 2nd North Irish Horse, X Corps Cavalry Regiment.] Joined the renamed 9th (North Irish Horse) Battalion from 36 Infantry Base Depot and transferred to Princess Victoria's (Royal Irish Fusiliers) in September/October 1917 (renumbered 41511). 'B' Company. **Missing** in the period 21-28 March 1918 during the retreat from St Quentin believed **captured**. 1914-15 Star.

MOIR Private Thomas Alexander 14431. Born in 1879 at Armagh, County Armagh. Served for one year with the North Irish Horse and purchased his discharge. 1st (Armagh) Battalion, Armagh Regiment, Ulster Volunteer Force. A horse dealer. Enlisted 16 September 1914. Did not serve overseas with 36th (Ulster) Division. Unfit for general service, he was posted to the 9th (Service) Battalion details on 3 October 1915 and posted to the 10th (Reserve) Battalion on 9 October 1915. [Transferred to the Labour Corps (renumbered 231612) 7 July 1917. Served with 666th and 668th Labour Companies and 485th Home Service Employment Company. Transferred to the Royal Defence Corps (renumbered 80159) 25 June 1918 and served with 200th and 155th Protection Companies. Transferred to the Class Z Reserve 26 March 1919.

MOLLOY Private Albert 14445. From Lurgan, County Armagh. Enlisted September 1914. Discharged as not being likely to become an efficient soldier in that he was considered medically unfit for service 1 October 1914.

MOLLOY Private Francis 14467. Born in 1898 at Drumcree, Portadown, County Armagh. Lived at John Street, Portadown, County Armagh. A weaver. Enlisted 1 December 1913 into the 3rd Battalion (Militia), Princess Victoria's (Royal Irish Fusiliers) (6011). Discharged having made a mis-statement as to age on enlistment; soldier under 17 years of age at date of application for discharge 7 January 1914. Enlisted again in September 1914, aged 16, and joined the 9th (Service) Battalion. To France with 36th (Ulster) Division in October 1915. [Joined 108th Brigade Machine Gun Company in January 1916. Transferred to the Machine Gun Corps (renumbered 17795).] Discharged as no longer physically fit for war service due to sickness 8 May 1918. Silver War Badge, number 386329. 1914-15 Star.

MOLLOY Private Henry Loughard (Harry) 17929. Born in 1899 at Newtownbutler, County Fermanagh. From Newbliss, County Monaghan. Enlisted into the 9th (Service) Battalion in January 1915. To France with 36th (Ulster) Division in October 1915. **Wounded** by shellfire at Hamel and **died of wounds** 25 June 1916, aged 17. 1914-15 Star.

MONAGHAN Private Robert 22981. From Bessbrook, County Armagh. Enlisted in November 1915. Posted to the 9th (Service) Battalion. 'D' Company. **Wounded** during the attack at Hamel 1 July 1916. **Captured** in the period 21-28 March 1918 during the retreat from St Quentin.

MONAGHAN Private William 14486. From Derryadd, County Armagh. Enlisted September 1914. To France with 36th (Ulster) Division in October 1915. 'C' Company. Released from hospital just before the attack at Hamel 1 July 1916, he did not take part in the attack. [Posted to the 13th (Service) Battalion, The Royal Irish Rifles (1st County Down).] Transferred to the Class Z Reserve 27 March 1919. 1914-15 Star. Served with the Ulster Special Constabulary. Emigrated to the United States in 1927 where he died in 1967.

MONAGHAN Private William 23300. Born at Newtownhamilton, County Armagh. Enlisted in November 1915. Posted to the 9th (Service) Battalion. 'D' Company. **Killed in action** at the Battle of Langemarck 16 August 1917, aged 32.

MONKS Private Frederick Albert 49991. Born in 1899 at Bristol. [Transferred to Princess Victoria's (Royal Irish Fusiliers) in May 1918 (renumbered 49991) with a draft of men from English regiments and joined the 1st Battalion.] Posted to the 9th (North Irish Horse) Battalion in August 1918. Died at Bristol in 1979, aged 79.

MONTGOMERY Private George 40089. Enlisted 25 May 1916. Joined the 9th (Service) Battalion, Princess Victoria's (Royal Irish Fusiliers) with the draft of men from The Prince of Wales's Own (West Yorkshire Regiment) on 12 December 1916. **Wounded**. Discharged as no longer physically fit for war service due to wounds 28 February 1918. Silver War Badge, number 334290.

MONTGOMERY Private James 20313. Born in Newtownards, County Down. [Enlisted into The

Royal Irish Rifles (3788).] Joined the 9th (Service) Battalion with the draft of men from The Royal Inniskilling Fusiliers who transferred to Princess Victoria's (Royal Irish Fusiliers) on 30 June 1915 (renumbered 20313). To France with 36th (Ulster) Division in October 1915. [Transferred to the Labour Corps (renumbered 545508).] **Died** in Ireland 1 May 1920.

MONTGOMERY Private John 41306. [Enlisted 26 February 1914 into the North Irish Horse (914). To France 20 August 1914 with 'C' Squadron as 5th Division Cavalry and then as GHQ Troops. Served with 2nd North Irish Horse, X Corps Cavalry Regiment.] Joined the renamed 9th (North Irish Horse) Battalion from 36 Infantry Base Depot and transferred to Princess Victoria's (Royal Irish Fusiliers) in September/October 1917 (renumbered 41306). **Wounded**. Discharged as no longer physically fit for war service due to wounds 14 December 1918. Silver War Badge, number B61022. 1914 Star.

MONTGOMERY Private Robert Taylor 14452. Commissioned into Princess Victoria's (Royal Irish Fusiliers) - see Appendix 5.

MONTGOMERY Private Samuel William 41410. From Ballymena, County Antrim. A solicitor's clerk. [Enlisted 8 November 1915 into the North Irish Horse (1815). To France 30 June 1916. Served with 'A' Squadron, 2nd North Irish Horse, X Corps Cavalry Regiment. Detached for duty at Number 4 German Prisoners of War Camp 1 November 1916.] Joined the renamed 9th (North Irish Horse) Battalion from 36 Infantry Base Depot and transferred to Princess Victoria's (Royal Irish Fusiliers) in September/October 1917 (renumbered 41410). 'A' Company. **Wounded** by a gunshot to the chest during the retreat from St Quentin 21 March 1918 and evacuated to hospital in England 27 March 1918. **Wounded** by shrapnel to the left shoulder at Hill 41 on 11 October 1918 and evacuated to hospital in England. Treated at the General Military Hospital, Colchester. Transferred to the Class Z Reserve 8 March 1919.

MONTGOMERY Private Thomas 41234. From Ballymena, County Antrim. [Enlisted in February 1912 into the North Irish Horse (672). To France with 'F' Squadron in 33rd Division 17 November 1915. Served with 2nd North Irish Horse, X Corps Cavalry Regiment.] Joined the renamed 9th (North Irish Horse) Battalion from 36 Infantry Base Depot and transferred to Princess Victoria's (Royal Irish Fusiliers) in September/October 1917 (renumbered 41234). **Wounded** in September 1918. Transferred to the Class Z Reserve 20 March 1919. 1914-15 Star.

MONTGOMERY Lance Corporal William 41251. From Belfast. [Enlisted in February 1915 into the North Irish Horse (1449). To France with 'F' Squadron in 33rd Division 17 November 1915. Served with 2nd North Irish Horse, X Corps Cavalry Regiment.] Joined the renamed 9th (North Irish Horse) Battalion from 36 Infantry Base Depot and transferred to Princess Victoria's (Royal Irish Fusiliers) in September/October 1917 (renumbered 41251). 'D' Company. **Captured** in the period 21-28 March 1918 during the retreat from St Quentin. Transferred to the Class Z Reserve. 1914-15 Star.

MOODY Private Robert 41303. [Enlisted in March 1913 into the North Irish Horse (812). To France 20 August 1914 with 'C' Squadron as 5th Division Cavalry and then as GHQ Troops. Served with 2nd North Irish Horse, X Corps Cavalry Regiment.] Joined the renamed 9th (North Irish Horse) Battalion from 36 Infantry Base Depot and transferred to Princess Victoria's (Royal Irish Fusiliers) in September/October 1917 (renumbered 41303). 1914 Star.

MOON Private John (Jack) 41412. Born in 1893 at Kilderry, Muff, County Donegal. Worked as a shop assistant in Londonderry. [Enlisted on 17 November 1915 into the North Irish Horse (1962). To France 3 August 1916. Served with 2nd North Irish Horse, X Corps Cavalry Regiment.] Joined the renamed 9th (North Irish Horse) Battalion from 36 Infantry Base Depot and transferred to Princess Victoria's (Royal Irish Fusiliers) in September/October 1917 (renumbered 41412). 'A' Company. **Killed in action** 29 March 1918 during the retreat from St Quentin, aged 24.

MOONEY Sergeant James 3868 & 7040041. From Muckno, Castleblayney, County Monaghan. Enlisted on 9 November 1915 into Princess Victoria's (Royal Irish Fusiliers) Special Reserve, aged 17. [To France 26 September 1916 and joined the 1st Battalion. **Wounded** in the buttocks 11 April 1917 and evacuated to hospital in England 16 April 1917. To France 1 August 1917 and joined the 7th/8th (Service) Battalion in 49th Brigade, 16th (Irish) Division.] Joined the 9th (North Irish Horse) Battalion when the 7th/8th (Service) Battalion was disbanded in February 1918. **Wounded** (gassed) during the attack south of Wulverghem on 4 September 1918. Re-enlisted in early-1919 for

Regular Army service with Princess Victoria's (Royal Irish Fusiliers) (renumbered 7040041). Served with the 1st Battalion in Persia in 1919/20. Discharged 17 April 1922 medically unfit for further service.

MOORE Sergeant Adam David 14438. Born in 1888 at Pettigo, County Donegal. Enlisted September 1914. To France with 36th (Ulster) Division in October 1915. 'A' Company. **Killed in action** during the attack at Hamel 1 July 1916. 1914-15 Star.

MOORE Private Albert 18565. Enlisted into the 9th (Service) Battalion in April 1915. To France with 36th (Ulster) Division in October 1915. Battalion Colour Guard June 1919. 1914-15 Star.

MOORE MBE Warrant Officer Class II Alfred 14436, 33502 & 7041638. Born in 1894 in County Tyrone. Worked for the General Post Office in Armagh. Enlisted September 1914. To France with 36th (Ulster) Division in October 1915. **Wounded** during the attack at Hamel 1 July 1916. When he recovered he served with the 10th (Reserve) Battalion and then 7th Officer Cadet Battalion as an instructor. Transferred to the Class Z Reserve 4 April 1919. 1914-15 Star. Re-enlisted in for Regular Army service with Princess Victoria's (Royal Irish Fusiliers) (renumbered 33502, renumbered 7041638) and joined the 2nd Battalion at Chatham. Served in Egypt, India and Sudan. Returned with the 2nd Battalion to Bordon in 1935. Became Regimental Quartermaster Sergeant at the Army Technical School (Boys) at Chepstow, where he served until he was discharged to the Army Reserve 25 April 1949 after thirty-five years service. War Medal 1939-45. Defence Medal. **MSM**. Long Service & Good Conduct Medal. Re-enlisted into the Territorial Army and joined the 5th Battalion, The Royal Irish Fusiliers (Princess Victoria's) (Territorial Army) as Regimental Quartermaster Sergeant (renumbered 22271769). **MBE (Military)**. Territorial Efficiency Medal and clasp. Employed as a civilian clerk with the Territorial Army Association. Chairman of the Old Comrades Association (Armagh). Died December 1963.

MOORE Private James 14461. From Killylea, County Armagh. Armagh Regiment, Ulster Volunteer Force. Enlisted September 1914. 'B' Company. Discharged as not being likely to become an efficient soldier in that he was considered medically unfit for service 10 October 1914.

MOORE Private James 18063. Enlisted into the 9th (Service) Battalion in February 1915. To France with 36th (Ulster) Division in October 1915. 'A' Company. **Missing** in the period 21-28 March 1918 during the retreat from St Quentin believed **captured**. Transferred to the Class Z Reserve 24 March 1919. 1914-15 Star.

MOORE Private James 18256. From Newbliss, County Monaghan. Enlisted into the 9th (Service) Battalion in February/March 1915. To France with 36th (Ulster) Division in October 1915. **Killed in action** during the attack at Hamel 1 July 1916, aged 19. 1914-15 Star.

MOORE Private James 41304. [Enlisted 12 December 1912 into the North Irish Horse (767). To France 20 August 1914 with 'C' Squadron as 5th Division Cavalry and then as GHQ Troops. Served with 2nd North Irish Horse, X Corps Cavalry Regiment.] Joined the renamed 9th (North Irish Horse) Battalion from 36 Infantry Base Depot and transferred to Princess Victoria's (Royal Irish Fusiliers) in September/October 1917 (renumbered 41304). **Wounded**. Discharged as no longer physically fit for war service due to wounds 3 June 1918, aged 20. Silver War Badge, number 394857. 1914 Star.

MOORE Private John 14433. Enlisted September 1914. To France with 36th (Ulster) Division in October 1915. 'A' Company. Separated from the 9th (North Irish Horse) Battalion in the period 21-28 March 1918 during the retreat from St Quentin and rejoined 6 April 1918. Transferred to the Class Z Reserve 24 March 1919. 1914-15 Star.

MOORE Private Maurice Victor 41620. [Enlisted 9 January 1915 for service with (11341). Posted to 2nd North Irish Horse, X Corps Cavalry Regiment.] Joined the renamed 9th (North Irish Horse) Battalion from 36 Infantry Base Depot and transferred to Princess Victoria's (Royal Irish Fusiliers) in September/October 1917 (renumbered 41620). **Wounded**. Discharged as no longer physically fit for war service due to wounds 2 April 1919. Silver War Badge, number B205729.

MOORE Private Richard James 20291. From Hamiltonsbawn, County Armagh. Enlisted 2 July 1915 into the 9th (Service) Battalion. To France with 36th (Ulster) Division in October 1915. **Wounded** during the attack at Hamel 1 July 1916. Discharged as no longer physically fit for war service due to wounds 7 June 1918, aged 23. Silver War Badge, number 395830. 1914-15 Star.

MOORE Private Rowland Gladstone S 45803. Born 14 November 1898 at Dartford, Kent. Joined the 9th (North Irish Horse) Battalion, Princess Victoria's (Royal Irish Fusiliers) with the draft of men from The London Regiment in April 1918. Battalion signaller. Died at Chichester, Sussex 1990, aged 91.

MOORE Private Samuel 18346. Enlisted into the 9th (Service) Battalion 18 March 1915. Discharged as no longer physically fit for war service due to sickness 18 September 1916. Silver War Badge, number 168877.

MOORE Private Thomas Henry 41283. From Belfast. [Enlisted in June 1915 into the North Irish Horse (1690). Served with 2nd North Irish Horse, X Corps Cavalry Regiment.] Joined the renamed 9th (North Irish Horse) Battalion from 36 Infantry Base Depot and transferred to Princess Victoria's (Royal Irish Fusiliers) in September/October 1917 (renumbered 41283).

MOORE Private Thomas John 14456. From Portadown, County Armagh. 4th (Portadown) Battalion, Armagh Regiment, Ulster Volunteer Force. A linen weaver. Enlisted September 1914. To France with 36th (Ulster) Division in October 1915. **Wounded** (shell-shock) during the attack at Hamel 1 July 1916. Transferred to the Class Z Reserve 5 February 1919. 1914-15 Star.

MOORE Private William 14428. Enlisted September 1914. To France with 36th (Ulster) Division in October 1915. **Wounded** in October/November 1916. Discharged as no longer physically fit for war service due to wounds 24 May 1918, aged 28. Silver War Badge, number 390973. 1914-15 Star.

MOORE Private William 14429. Enlisted September 1914. To France with 36th (Ulster) Division in October 1915. Transferred to the Class Z Reserve 11 March 1919. 1914-15 Star.

MOORE Lance Corporal William 15418 & 7040586. From Widnes, Lancashire. [Enlisted 14 October 1914 and to France 19 February 1916 with the 8th (Service) Battalion in 49th Brigade 16th (Irish) Division.] Joined the 9th (North Irish Horse) Battalion when the 7th/8th (Service) Battalion was disbanded in February 1918. 'A' Company. **Missing** in the period 21-28 March 1918 during the retreat from St Quentin believed **captured**. Re-enlisted in early-1919 for Regular Army service with Princess Victoria's (Royal Irish Fusiliers) (renumbered 7040586). Served with the 1st Battalion in Persia and Mesopotamia in 1919/20. General Service Medal 1918-1962 with clasps 'Iraq' & 'NW Persia'. Discharged 1 January 1923.

MOORE Private William 42478 & 7042400. From Donaghadee, County Down. Worked as a heater boy at Harland and Wolff shipyard, Belfast. [Enlisted 24 August 1914 into The Royal Irish Rifles (6978), age 17. To France 30 August 1916 and joined the 1st Battalion, The Royal Irish Rifles. To hospital sick (rheumatism) 23 October 1916. Rejoined the 1st Battalion 9 December 1916. 'A' Company. Evacuated to hospital in England sick (trench fever) 19 January 1917 and treated at Lord Derby War Hospital, Winwick. To 16 Infantry Base Depot 31 May 1917 and joined the 7th (Service) Battalion, The Royal Irish Rifles 22 June 1917. **Wounded** by a gunshot to the right thigh at the Battle of Langemarck 16 August 1917. Treated at 2nd Canadian Casualty Clearing Station. Rejoined the 7th (Service) Battalion, The Royal Irish Rifles 10 September 1917. Posted to the 2nd Battalion, The Royal Irish Rifles 14 November 1917. **Wounded** by a gunshot to the left hand 5 December 1917 at Marcoing and evacuated to hospital in England. Treated at 2nd Western General Hospital, Manchester and Irish Counties War Hospital, Dublin.] Transferred at the Base Depot to Princess Victoria's (Royal Irish Fusiliers) 14 September 1918 (renumbered 42478) and joined the 9th (North Irish Horse) Battalion 22 September 1918. **Wounded** by a gunshot to the left hand during the attack at Vijfwegen on 30 September or 1 October 1918 and evacuated to hospital in England. Treated at the War Hospital, Bradford. Joined the 3rd (Reserve) Battalion 5 December 1918. Transferred to the Class Z Reserve 30 March 1919. Enlisted into Princess Victoria's (Royal Irish Fusiliers) Special Reserve (renumbered 7042400). Discharged 23 August 1920. Re-enlisted 24 September 1924 into The Royal Inniskilling Fusiliers. Discharged 23 September 1936.

MOORE Corporal William John 41240. Born in 1895 at Bushmills, County Antrim. Employed as a valet. [Enlisted 24 August 1914 into the North Irish Horse 1 March 1915 (1457). To France with 'F' Squadron in 33rd Division 17 November 1915. Served with 2nd North Irish Horse, X Corps Cavalry Regiment.] Joined the renamed 9th (North Irish Horse) Battalion from 36 Infantry Base Depot and transferred to Princess Victoria's (Royal Irish Fusiliers) in September/October 1917 (renumbered 41240). 'A' Company. Corporal 3 October 1917. To hospital (injured arm) 4 May 1918 and evacuated to hospital in England 14 May 1918. Treated at Endell Street Military Hospital,

London. Posted to the 10th (Reserve) Battalion. To hospital in Ireland 3 June 1918 with diarrhoea. Discharged from hospital 26 August 1918. **Deserted** 18 September 1918.

MOOREY Lance Sergeant Alfred 45046. [Enlisted into The Buffs (East Kent Regiment) (8430) in 1907. Served with the 2nd Battalion. Mobilised from the Army Reserve. To France 8 June 1915. Transferred to Princess Victoria's (Royal Irish Fusiliers) in December 1916 (renumbered 45046) and joined the 7th/8th (Service) Battalion in 49th Brigade, 16th (Irish) Division.] Joined the 9th (North Irish Horse) Battalion when the 7th/8th (Service) Battalion was disbanded in February 1918. Transferred to the Class Z Reserve 10 March 1919. ***Croix de Guerre* (Belgium)**. 1914-15 Star.

MOORHEAD Lance Corporal Andrew 16121. Born at Smithborough, County Monaghan. Enlisted into the 9th (Service) Battalion in October 1914. To France with 36th (Ulster) Division in October 1915. **Killed in action** during the attack at Hamel 1 July 1916, aged 22. 1914-15 Star.

MOORHEAD MM Private Robert Andrew 14442. Born in 1895 at Ashton-under-Lyne, Manchester, Lancashire. From Bessbrook, County Armagh. Enlisted September 1914. To France with 36th (Ulster) Division in October 1915. 14 Platoon, 'D' Company. **Wounded** by a gunshot to the ankle during the attack at Hamel 1 July 1916 and evacuated to hospital in England. Joined the 10th (Reserve) Battalion 23 August 1916. To France 23 December 1916 and rejoined the 9th (Service) Battalion. [Transferred to the Tank Corps (304862) 28 December 1917 and posted for training to the Tank Corps Depot, at Bovington near Wareham, Dorset. Posted to the 17th Battalion, Tank Corps 8 January 1918 and to France 27 April 1918 when it converted to 17th (Armoured Car) Battalion. 'B' Company. **MM** - November 1918.] 1914-15 Star. Served in the British Army of the Rhine. Transferred to the Class Z Reserve 27 May 1919. Lived at Belfast.

MOORHEAD MM Sergeant William 14482. From Lurgan, County Armagh. Enlisted September 1914. To France with 36th (Ulster) Division in October 1915. 'C' Company. To hospital around June 1916. **Wounded** during the attack at Hamel 1 July 1916. **MM** – Vijfwegen/Hill 41 between 30 September and 14 October 1918. [Transferred to 5th (Service) Battalion, The Royal Irish Regiment (Pioneers) in the Light Division in the British Army of the Rhine in March/June 1919 (renumbered 41329).] Transferred to the Class Z Reserve. 1914-15 Star.

MORAGHAN Corporal John Joseph 21216. [Enlisted in February 1915 and joined the 8th (Service) Battalion in 49th Brigade, 16th (Irish) Division.] Joined the 9th (North Irish Horse) Battalion when the 7th/8th (Service) Battalion was disbanded in February 1918. 'A' Company. **Missing** in the period 21-28 March 1918 during the retreat from St Quentin believed **captured**.

MORAN MM Lance Corporal Daniel 41064. From Athleague, County Roscommon. [Enlisted into The Royal Welch Fusiliers (36134). Transferred to Princess Victoria's (Royal Irish Fusiliers) in early-1917. Posted to the 1st Battalion.] Joined the 9th (Service) Battalion. 'A' Company. **MM** – late-1917. **Missing** in the period 21-28 March 1918 during the retreat from St Quentin believed **captured**.

MORAN MM Private John 8895, 33070 & 7041310. From Arklow, County Wicklow. [Enlisted into Princess Victoria's (Royal Irish Fusiliers) as a regular soldier in 1905 and served with the 2nd Battalion. To France with the 2nd Battalion 19 December 1914.] Posted to the 9th (North Irish Horse) Battalion. **MM** – River Lys mid-October 1918. ***Croix de Guerre* (France)**. 1914-15 Star. Transferred to the Class Z Reserve. Re-enlisted in August/September 1919 for Regular Army service with Princess Victoria's (Royal Irish Fusiliers) (renumbered 33070, renumbered 7041310). Long Service & Good Conduct medal, 1924. Discharged 21 September 1926.

MORAN Private Richard 41305. (His medal index card incorrectly shows his regimental number as 41306 (issued to Private J Montgomery); his service records show the correct number.) Born in 1895 at Londonderry. Worked at Dumbarton, Dumbartonshire as a clothes salesman. [Enlisted 2 December 1915 and transferred to the Army Reserve. Mobilised 21 January 1916 and joined the North Irish Horse (2091). To France 26 November 1916. Served with 2nd North Irish Horse, X Corps Cavalry Regiment.] Joined the renamed 9th (North Irish Horse) Battalion from 36 Infantry Base Depot and transferred to Princess Victoria's (Royal Irish Fusiliers) in September/October 1917 (renumbered 41305). 'C' Company. [Transferred to the Tank Corps (renumbered 304849) 28 December 1917 and posted for training to the Tank Corps Depot, at Bovington near Wareham, Dorset. Posted to 5th Advanced Tank Workshop 23 February 1918. To France 28 June 1918.] Transferred to the Class Z Reserve 5 July 1919.

MORAN Private William 42560. [Enlisted into The Royal Inniskilling Fusiliers (22145). Transferred to The Royal Irish Rifles (renumbered 22741).] Transferred at the Base Depot to Princess Victoria's (Royal Irish Fusiliers) 14 September 1918 (renumbered 42560) and joined the 9th (North Irish Horse) Battalion 22 September 1918. [Transferred to the Corps of Royal Engineers (renumbered 624796).]

MORRIS Private George Edward 23408. Born in Belfast in 1885. Worked as a blouse manufacturers assistant. Enlisted in December 1915. Posted to the 9th (Service) Battalion.

MORRISH Private Frederick George 43253. Born in 1891 at Allerton, Derbyshire. A lace maker. [Enlisted into The Sherwood Foresters (Nottinghamshire and Derbyshire Regiment) (24416).] Transferred to Princess Victoria's (Royal Irish Fusiliers) 31 August 1916 (renumbered 43253) having joined the 9th (Service) Battalion on 8 August 1916. 'C' Company. **Missing** at the Battle of Langemarck 16 August 1917 and later declared **killed in action** on that date, aged 24.

MORRISON Private Francis James 41112. Born on 30 June 1895 at Brookeborough, County Fermanagh. [Enlisted in late-1914/early-1915 into the Service Squadron, 6th (Inniskilling) Dragoons (UD/198). To France with 36th (Ulster) Division in October 1915. Served with 2nd North Irish Horse, X Corps Cavalry Regiment.] Joined the renamed 9th (North Irish Horse) Battalion from 36 Infantry Base Depot and transferred to Princess Victoria's (Royal Irish Fusiliers) in September/October 1917 (renumbered 41112). **Killed in action** near Wieltje 25 May 1918, aged 22. 1914-15 Star. His brother, Private John Morrison, was killed in action at Thiepval on 1 July 1916 serving with the 11th (Service) Battalion, The Royal Inniskilling Fusiliers (Donegal and Fermanagh). His brother, Private Alexander (Sandy) Morrison, was a Special Reservist who served with the 2nd Battalion, The Royal Inniskilling Fusiliers. He was wounded in 1915 and 1916 and captured in 1918.

MORRISON Private George 18251. From Portadown, County Armagh. Enlisted into the 9th (Service) Battalion in February/March 1915. To France with 36th (Ulster) Division in October 1915. **Wounded** during the attack at Hamel 1 July 1916. [Transferred to 5th (Service) Battalion, The Royal Irish Regiment (Pioneers) in the Light Division in the British Army of the Rhine in March/June 1919 (renumbered 41331).] 1914-15 Star.

MORRISON Private George 41610. From Macosquin, County Londonderry. [Enlisted in June 1915 into the Service Squadron, 6th (Inniskilling) Dragoons (UD/266). To France with 36th (Ulster) Division in October 1915. Served with 2nd North Irish Horse, X Corps Cavalry Regiment.] Joined the renamed 9th (North Irish Horse) Battalion from 36 Infantry Base Depot and transferred to Princess Victoria's (Royal Irish Fusiliers) in September/October 1917 (renumbered 41610). 'C' Company. **Wounded** and **captured** in the period 21-28 March 1918 during the retreat from St Quentin. **Died of wounds** while a prisoner of war 22 April 1918, aged 24. 1914-15 Star.

MORRISON Private Henry 42525. [Enlisted April/May 1918 into with The Royal Irish Rifles (22634).] Transferred at the Base Depot to Princess Victoria's (Royal Irish Fusiliers) 14 September 1918 (renumbered 42525) and joined the 9th (North Irish Horse) Battalion 22 September 1918. [Transferred to 5th (Service) Battalion, The Royal Irish Regiment (Pioneers) in the Light Division in the British Army of the Rhine in March/June 1919 (renumbered 41332).]

MORRISON Private John 41110. [Enlisted 6 November 1914 into the Service Squadron, 6th (Inniskilling) Dragoons (UD/157). To France with 36th (Ulster) Division in October 1915. Served with 2nd North Irish Horse, X Corps Cavalry Regiment.] Joined the renamed 9th (North Irish Horse) Battalion from 36 Infantry Base Depot and transferred to Princess Victoria's (Royal Irish Fusiliers) in September/October 1917 (renumbered 41110). Discharged as no longer physically fit for war service due to sickness 19 March 1919. Silver War Badge, number B162031. 1914-15 Star.

MORRISON MM Private John 41327. From Whitehouse, County Antrim. [Enlisted in November 1915 into the North Irish Horse (1972). Served with 2nd North Irish Horse, X Corps Cavalry Regiment.] Joined the renamed 9th (North Irish Horse) Battalion from 36 Infantry Base Depot and transferred to Princess Victoria's (Royal Irish Fusiliers) in September/October 1917 (renumbered 41327). 'C' Company. **MM** – Havrincourt raid 3 November 1917. **Captured** in the period 21-28 March 1918 during the retreat from St Quentin.

MORRISON Private Neil Reid 20350. From Parkhead, Glasgow. [Enlisted into The Royal Inniskilling Fusiliers (20916).] Transferred to Princess Victoria's (Royal Irish Fusiliers) on 30 June

1915 (renumbered 20350) and joined the 9th (Service) Battalion. To France with 36th (Ulster) Division in October 1915. **Killed in action** during the attack at Hamel 1 July 1916, aged 27. 1914-15 Star.

MORRISON Private Peter 20295. From Glasgow. Enlisted in May/June 1915 and joined the 9th (Service) Battalion with the draft of men from The Royal Inniskilling Fusiliers who transferred to Princess Victoria's (Royal Irish Fusiliers) on 30 June 1915. To France with 36th (Ulster) Division in October 1915. 'C' Company. Bombing team during the attack at Hamel 1 July 1916, which he survived unwounded. **Wounded** at the Battle of Langemarck 16 August 1917. Transferred to the Class Z Reserve 1 April 1919. 1914-15 Star.

MORRISON Private Richard 14480. From Lurgan, County Armagh. Served briefly pre-war with 5th Battalion (Militia), The Royal Irish Rifles. Enlisted September 1914. Discharged as not being likely to become an efficient soldier in that he was considered medically unfit (hernia) for service 9 November 1914.

MORRISON Private Robert Boyd 23792. (His regimental number is listed incorrectly as 23791 on the Silver War Badge Roll.) Born in 1895 at Belfast. Enlisted 19 January 1916. Posted to the 9th (Service) Battalion. 'C' Company. **Wounded** during the Battle of Messines and to hospital 9 June 1917. Discharged as no longer physically fit for war service due to wounds 17 June 1918. Silver War Badge, number 387926.

MORRISON Lance Corporal Thomas 14450. From Tandragee, County Armagh. 4th (Portadown) Battalion, Armagh Regiment, Ulster Volunteer Force. Enlisted September 1914. To France with 36th (Ulster) Division in October 1915. 'B' Company. To hospital in March 1916 having been crushed by a horse. **Wounded** by shellfire during the raid at La Petite Douve Farm on 12 October 1916. **Wounded** at the Battle of Langemarck 16 August 1917. **Captured** in the period 21-28 March 1918 during the retreat from St Quentin. Transferred to the Class Z Reserve 21 March 1919. 1914-15 Star.

MORRISON Private William 22849. Born in 1873 at County Armagh. From Annaclare, County Armagh. Enlisted 13 November 1915 and joined the 10th (Reserve) Battalion. To France 13 June 1916 and joined the 9th (Service) Battalion. 'B' Company. **Missing** at the Battle of Langemarck 16 August 1917 and later declared **killed in action** on that date, aged 44.

MORROW Private George 23606. From Shankill, County Armagh. Enlisted in December 1915. Posted to the 9th (Service) Battalion. 'C' Company. **Killed in action** at the Battle of Langemarck 16 August 1917, aged 20.

MORROW Private Richard 15853. From Bangor, County Down. Enlisted into the 9th (Service) Battalion in October 1914. To France 17 November 1915 and rejoined the 9th (Service) Battalion. 'C' Company. **Wounded** during the attack at Hamel 1 July 1916. [Transferred to the Labour Corps (renumbered 231615).] Transferred to the Class Z Reserve 26 March 1919. 1914-15 Star.

MORROW Private Robert Edgar 41130. Born 7 March 1895 at Belfast. [Enlisted in November 1914 into the Service Squadron, 6th (Inniskilling) Dragoons (UD/179). To France with 36th (Ulster) Division in October 1915. Served with 2nd North Irish Horse, X Corps Cavalry Regiment.] Joined the renamed 9th (North Irish Horse) Battalion from 36 Infantry Base Depot and transferred to Princess Victoria's (Royal Irish Fusiliers) in September/October 1917 (renumbered 41130). Transferred to the Class Z Reserve 12 March 1919. 1914-15 Star. Died at Belfast 8 April 1951, aged 56.

MORROW Corporal William 14457. From Poyntzpass, County Armagh. 4th (Portadown) Battalion, Armagh Regiment, Ulster Volunteer Force. Enlisted September 1914. To France with 36th (Ulster) Division in October 1915. **Killed in action** during the attack at Hamel 1 July 1916. 1914-15 Star.

MORROW Lance Corporal William 18660 & 7040624. From Tallaght, Dublin. [Enlisted 19 April 1915 into the 7th (Service) Battalion in 49th Brigade 16th (Irish) Division. To France 19 February 1916.] Joined the 9th (North Irish Horse) Battalion when the 7th/8th (Service) Battalion was disbanded in February 1918. 'D' Company. **Captured** in the period 21-28 March 1918 during the retreat from St Quentin. Repatriated 10 December 1918. Re-enlisted in early-1919 for Regular Army service with Princess Victoria's (Royal Irish Fusiliers) (renumbered 7040624). Served with the 1st Battalion in Persia and Mesopotamia in 1919/20. General Service Medal 1918-1962 with clasps 'Iraq' & 'NW Persia'. Transferred to the Section D Army Reserve 25 April 1922. Discharged 18 April

1927.

MORTIMER Private Henry (Harry) 24909. Born in 1898 at Portadown, County Armagh. Lived at West Street, Portadown. [Enlisted in September 1916 into the North Irish Horse (2267).] Transferred to Princess Victoria's (Royal Irish Fusiliers) in October 1916. Posted to the 9th (Service) Battalion. 'C' Company. **Missing** at the Battle of Langemarck 16 August 1917 and later declared **killed in action** on that date, aged 19.

MORTON Private David 23878. From Keady, County Armagh. Enlisted in January 1916. Posted to the 9th (Service) Battalion. 'B' Company. **Wounded** during the Battle of Messines and to hospital 9 June 1917. **Captured** in the period 21-28 March 1918 during the retreat from St Quentin.

MORTON Private Edward 17407. From Killeshandra, County Cavan. [Enlisted into The Royal Irish Rifles (14907).] Transferred to Princess Victoria's (Royal Irish Fusiliers) in November/December 1914 (renumbered 17407) and joined the 9th (Service) Battalion. To France with 36th (Ulster) Division in October 1915. 'C' Company. **Killed in action** during the attack at Hamel 1 July 1916. 1914-15 Star.

MORTON Private Edward 28773. Born in April 1901 at Kilmore, County Cavan. Enlisted in October 1917, aged 16. Posted to the 9th (North Irish Horse) Battalion in early-1918. **Wounded** in the period 11-18 April 1918 in the actions between Wulverghem and Kemmel and **died of wounds** 18 April 1918, aged 17. Brother of Sergeant Robert John Morton and Private William Morton (22619).

MORTON Private Henry 42151. From West Hartlepool, County Durham. [Enlisted into the Army Veterinary Corps (19631).] Transferred to Princess Victoria's (Royal Irish Fusiliers) 8 May 1918 (renumbered 42151) and joined the 9th (North Irish Horse) Battalion. **Killed in action** during the attack south of Wulverghem 4 September 1918.

MORTON Corporal Hugh Victor 16125. From County Monaghan. Enlisted into the 9th (Service) Battalion in October 1914. To France with 36th (Ulster) Division in October 1915. 'D' Company. **Wounded**. Then **wounded** in the neck during the Battle of Messines and to hospital 9 June 1917. Transferred to the Class Z Reserve 12 March 1919. 1914-15 Star.

MORTON Corporal John 21150. From Belturbet, County Cavan. [Enlisted in December 1914/January 1915 and joined the 8th (Service) Battalion in 49th Brigade, 16th (Irish) Division.] Joined the 9th (North Irish Horse) Battalion when the 7th/8th (Service) Battalion was disbanded in February 1918. **Wounded** three times.

MORTON MM Private Joseph 14447. From Tamnificarbet, County Armagh. Enlisted September 1914. To France with 36th (Ulster) Division in October 1915. 'C' Company. Worked as one of the company grooms. Did not take part in the attack at Hamel on 1 July 1916. **MM** – Battle of Langemarck 16 August 1917. ***Decoration Militaire* (Belgium)**. Transferred to the Class Z Reserve 20 March 1919. 1914-15 Star.

MORTON Sergeant Robert John 18064. Born in 1890 at Kilmore, County Cavan. Enlisted into the 9th (Service) Battalion in February 1915. To France with 36th (Ulster) Division in October 1915. 'C' Company. In hospital mid-1916. Did not take part in the attack at Hamel on 1 July 1916. **Killed in action** during the attack south of Wulverghem 4 September 1918. 1914-15 Star. Brother of Privates Edward and William Morton.

MORTON Private William 14468. Born at Londonderry. Lived at Armagh, County Armagh. A printer's compositor with the Armagh Guardian. Armagh Regiment, Ulster Volunteer Force. Although diagnosed and treated for tuberculosis, he enlisted in September 1914. He refused to remain with the Depot details and deployed to France with 36th (Ulster) Division in October 1915. He was evacuated to hospital in England sick (pulmonary tuberculosis) on 10 November 1915. Discharged as no longer physically fit for war service due to sickness 24 December 1915, the same day that he **died** of pulmonary tuberculosis in Ireland, aged 21. 1914-15 Star.

MORTON Private William 22619. Born in 1893 at Kilmore, County Cavan. Worked at Armagh as a gardener. Enlisted 1 November 1915 and joined the 10th (Reserve) Battalion. To France 12 October 1916 and joined the 9th (Service) Battalion. 'B' Company. **Wounded** by a gunshot to the buttock at the Battle of Langemarck 16 August 1917. Treated at 2nd Canadian Casualty Clearing Station before being treated in hospital at Etaples. Rejoined the 9th (North Irish Horse) Battalion in late September 1917. To hospital sick (boils) 13 December 1917; he developed bronchitis and remained in hospital until 16 March 1918. **Captured** on 27 March 1918 during the retreat from St Quentin. Held at Geissen Prisoner of War Camp. **Died** of pulmonary tuberculosis 17 October 1918 in the hospital at Limburg Prisoner of War Camp. His death was first reported by W D Stubbs, a repatriated prisoner of war. Brother of Sergeant Robert John Morton and Private Edward Morton.

MOSES Private Abraham 14441. From Bessbrook, County Armagh. Enlisted September 1914. To France with 36th (Ulster) Division in October 1915. **Wounded** during the attack at Hamel 1 July 1916. [Transferred to the Labour Corps (renumbered 231614).] Transferred to the Class Z Reserve 28 March 1919. 1914-15 Star.

MOSES Private Harry 40065. From Leeds. [Enlisted into The Prince of Wales's Own (West Yorkshire Regiment) (35321).] Transferred to Princess Victoria's (Royal Irish Fusiliers) 30 November 1916 (renumbered 40065) and joined the 9th (Service) Battalion 12 December 1916. 'B' Company. **Missing** at the Battle of Langemarck 16 August 1917 and later declared **killed in action** on that date.

MOTTRAM Private George Edward 15503. Born in 1883 at Oldham, Lancashire. [Enlisted 5 September 1914 into The Lancashire Fusiliers (5882). Transferred to Princess Victoria's (Royal Irish Fusiliers) 24 September 1914 (renumbered 15503) and joined the 7th (Service) Battalion in 49th Brigade, 16th (Irish) Division. To hospital 14 September 1916 injured (scalded foot caused when he was boiling bacon for his company).] Joined the 9th (North Irish Horse) Battalion when the 7th/8th (Service) Battalion was disbanded in February 1918. Transferred to the Class Z Reserve 19 April 1919. Lived at Oldham.

MOUNTNEY Private Harry 45802. Enlisted 18 March 1917. Joined the 9th (North Irish Horse) Battalion, Princess Victoria's (Royal Irish Fusiliers) with the draft of men from The London Regiment in April 1918. **Wounded**. Discharged as no longer physically fit for war service due to wounds 24 October 1919. Silver War Badge, number B329767.

MOWBRAY Private Thomas 20301. Born 21 June 1883 at South Shields, County Durham. [Enlisted into The Royal Inniskilling Fusiliers (23838).] Transferred to Princess Victoria's (Royal Irish Fusiliers) on 30 June 1915 (renumbered 20301) and joined the 9th (Service) Battalion. To France with 36th (Ulster) Division in October 1915. 'B' Company. **Wounded** at the Battle of Langemarck 16 August 1917, aged 34. **Killed in action** during the attack south of Wulverghem 4 September 1918. 1914-15 Star.

MOY Private Frederick 41166. [Enlisted 10 July 1908 into the 6th Dragoon Guards (Carabiners) (2199). To France 16 December 1914 and joined 4th Cavalry Brigade. Served with 2nd North Irish Horse, X Corps Cavalry Regiment.] Joined the renamed 9th (North Irish Horse) Battalion from 36 Infantry Base Depot and transferred to Princess Victoria's (Royal Irish Fusiliers) in September/October 1917 (renumbered 41166). **Wounded**. Discharged as no longer physically fit for war service due to wounds 6 December 1918. Silver War Badge, number B54753. 1914-15 Star.

MOYLES MM Private Thomas 16024. From Navan, County Meath. [Enlisted 15 October 1914 and joined the 8th (Service) Battalion in 49th Brigade, 16th (Irish) Division. **MM** – late-1917.] Joined the 9th (North Irish Horse) Battalion when the 7th/8th (Service) Battalion was disbanded in February 1918. 'C' Company. Believed **wounded** in the period 21-28 March 1918 during the retreat from St Quentin. Discharged as no longer physically fit for war service due to wounds 10 April 1919. Silver War Badge, number B209600.

MOYSE Private Horace Kenneth 41625. Born 25 April 1886 at Windsor, Berkshire. Worked as a draper for Sinclaire and Sons in Belfast. [Enlisted 1 October 1914 into the North Irish Horse (1236). To France 2 June 1915. Served with 2nd North Irish Horse, X Corps Cavalry Regiment.] Joined the renamed 9th (North Irish Horse) Battalion from 36 Infantry Base Depot and transferred to Princess Victoria's (Royal Irish Fusiliers) in September/October 1917 (renumbered 41625). To hospital sick (hernia) October 1917. Treated at 5th General Hospital, Rouen. [Transferred to the Labour Corps (renumbered 443255) 22 November 1917. Transferred to The Royal Fusiliers (City of London Regiment) (renumbered GS/106911) 28 August 1918. Posted to 35th (Garrison) Company, 43rd (Garrison) Battalion, The Royal Fusiliers (City of London Regiment). Posted to 34th (Garrison) Company 13 February 1919.] Transferred to the Class Z Reserve 17 March 1919. 1914-15 Star.

Lived at Wimbledon, London.

MULDOON Private Samuel 24703. Born in 1893 at Killyman, County Armagh. Enlisted 16 August 1916. Posted to the 9th (Service) Battalion, where he served briefly before being evacuated to hospital in England sick. Discharged as no longer physically fit for war service due to sickness 5 March 1917. Silver War Badge, number 140089. Died at Killyman, County Armagh in 1921, aged 28.

MULHERON Private William 42528. [Enlisted April/May 1918 into The Royal Irish Rifles (22633).] Transferred at the Base Depot to Princess Victoria's (Royal Irish Fusiliers) 14 September 1918 (renumbered 42528) and joined the 9th (North Irish Horse) Battalion 22 September 1918.

MULHOLLAND Corporal John 22942. [Enlisted in November 1915. Served with the 1st Battalion. Served with the 7th/8th (Service) Battalion in 49th Brigade, 16th (Irish) Division.] Joined the 9th (North Irish Horse) Battalion when the 7th/8th (Service) Battalion was disbanded in February 1918. 'B' Company. **Missing** in the period 21-28 March 1918 during the retreat from St Quentin believed **captured**.

MULHOLLAND Private Samuel 14477. Enlisted September 1914. To France with 36th (Ulster) Division in October 1915. 'C' Company. Detached to the Battalion Transport and did not take part in the attack at Hamel on 1 July 1916. [Transferred to the Royal Garrison Artillery (285933).]

MUIR Private William 23698. Enlisted in January 1916. Posted to the 9th (Service) Battalion. [Transferred to the Royal Flying Corps (renumbered 144908) 8 March 1918 (with Privates J D Couser and J Sands).]

MULLAN Private Hugh 41626. From Garvagh, County Londonderry. [Enlisted in December 1915 into the North Irish Horse (2040). Served with 2nd North Irish Horse, X Corps Cavalry Regiment.] Joined the renamed 9th (North Irish Horse) Battalion from 36 Infantry Base Depot and transferred to Princess Victoria's (Royal Irish Fusiliers) in September/October 1917 (renumbered 41626). 'C' Company. **Captured** in the period 21-28 March 1918 during the retreat from St Quentin.

MULLAN Lance Corporal William 21086. [Enlisted in November 1914 and joined the 8th (Service) Battalion in 49th Brigade, 16th (Irish) Division.] Joined the 9th (North Irish Horse) Battalion when the 7th/8th (Service) Battalion was disbanded in February 1918. 'B' Company. **Missing** in the period 21-28 March 1918 during the retreat from St Quentin believed **captured**.

MULLEN Corporal John 16450. Born at Tullyherron, Waringstown, County Down. A weaver. Enlisted into the 9th (Service) Battalion 17 November 1914. To France with 36th (Ulster) Division in October 1915. 'D' Company. Forfeit seven days pay for drunkenness 10 November 1915. Lance Corporal 2 July 1916. Corporal 17 November 1916. **Wounded** by a gunshot to the right arm at the Battle of Langemarck 16 August 1917 and evacuated to hospital in England 22 August 1917. Joined the Irish Command Depot, Tipperary 9 February 1918. [Transferred to the Labour Corps (renumbered 561694) 9 August 1918.] Transferred to the Class Z Reserve 15 June 1919.

MULLEN Private James 42521. [Enlisted 11 December 1915 into The Royal Irish Rifles (22629).] Transferred at the Base Depot to Princess Victoria's (Royal Irish Fusiliers) 14 September 1918 (renumbered 42521) and joined the 9th (North Irish Horse) Battalion 22 September 1918. **Wounded**. Discharged as no longer physically fit for war service due to wounds 12 April 1919. Silver War Badge, number B211236.

MULLEN Sergeant William 16090. From Leagh, County Monaghan. Enlisted into the 9th (Service) Battalion in October 1914. To France with 36th (Ulster) Division in October 1915. 'D' Company. **Killed in action** during the attack at Hamel 1 July 1916. 1914-15 Star.

MULLIGAN Private Edwin 20142. Enlisted into the 9th (Service) Battalion in June 1915.

MULLIGAN Private Robert 27523. From Portadown, County Armagh. Enlisted in April 1917. Posted to the 9th (North Irish Horse) Battalion.

MULVENNA Private Samuel James 41264. From Craigywarren, County Antrim. An iron ore miner. [Enlisted in November 1915 into the North Irish Horse (1973). Served with 2nd North Irish Horse, X Corps Cavalry Regiment.] Joined the renamed 9th (North Irish Horse) Battalion from 36 Infantry Base Depot and transferred to Princess Victoria's (Royal Irish Fusiliers) in September/October 1917 (renumbered 41264).

MUNDEN Corporal Richard H 42082. [Enlisted into the Army Service Corps (G2/SR/102605). To France 30 April 1915.] Transferred to Princess Victoria's (Royal Irish Fusiliers) 8 May 1918 (renumbered 42082) and joined the 9th (North Irish Horse) Battalion. [Transferred to The Royal Inniskilling Fusiliers (renumbered 43998).] Transferred to the Class Z Reserve. 1914-15 Star.

MURDOCK Private Archibald Marshall Weir 24053. Born in 1889 at Saval More, Newry, County Down. A mechanic. Enlisted in February 1916. Posted to the 9th (Service) Battalion. 'D' Company. **Missing** at the Battle of Langemarck 16 August 1917 and later declared **killed in action** on that date, aged 28.

MURPHY Private Edward 18702. Enlisted in April 1915 into the 7th (Service) Battalion in 49th Brigade, 16th (Irish) Division.] Joined the 9th (North Irish Horse) Battalion when the 7th/8th (Service) Battalion was disbanded in February 1918.

MURPHY Private Felix 11737. From Carrickgallogly, Newry, County Down. A farmer's son. [Enlisted in August 1914 and joined the 7th (Service) Battalion in 49th Brigade, 16th (Irish) Division.] Joined the 9th (North Irish Horse) Battalion when the 7th/8th (Service) Battalion was disbanded in February 1918. **Killed in action** during the attack at Vijfwegen 30 September 1918, aged 30.

MURPHY Private Isaac 23222. From Newry, County Down. Enlisted in November 1915. Posted to the 9th (Service) Battalion. 'B' Company. **Wounded** at the Battle of Langemarck 16 August 1917. **Captured** in the period 21-28 March 1918 during the retreat from St Quentin.

MURPHY Private James 21704. [Enlisted 16 July 1915 and joined the 8th (Service) Battalion in 49th Brigade, 16th (Irish) Division.] Joined the 9th (North Irish Horse) Battalion when the 7th/8th (Service) Battalion was disbanded in February 1918. **Wounded**. Discharged as no longer physically fit for war service due to wounds 16 March 1919. Silver War Badge, number B162468.

MURPHY Private James 22917. [Enlisted 2 October 1915 and joined the 7th (Service) Battalion in 49th Brigade, 16th (Irish) Division.] Joined the 9th (North Irish Horse) Battalion when the 7th/8th (Service) Battalion was disbanded in February 1918. **Wounded**. Discharged as no longer physically fit for war service due to wounds 6 February 1919. Silver War Badge, number 233156.

MURPHY Private John 14444. From Milford, County Armagh. Enlisted September 1914. To France with 36th (Ulster) Division in October 1915. 'A' Company. **Wounded** while on a work party on the night of 16/17 May 1917 and **died of wounds** 18 May 1917. 1914-15 Star.

MURPHY Private John 41088. [Enlisted in early-1915 into the Service Squadron, 6th (Inniskilling) Dragoons (UD/202). To France with 36th (Ulster) Division in October 1915. Served with 2nd North Irish Horse, X Corps Cavalry Regiment.] Joined the renamed 9th (North Irish Horse) Battalion from 36 Infantry Base Depot and transferred to Princess Victoria's (Royal Irish Fusiliers) in September/October 1917 (renumbered 41088). Transferred to the Class Z Reserve 12 July 1919. 1914-15 Star.

MURPHY Corporal Joseph 17402. Enlisted into the 9th (Service) Battalion in November/December 1914. To France with 36th (Ulster) Division in October 1915. [Joined 108th Brigade Machine Gun Company in January 1916. Transferred to the Machine Gun Corps (renumbered 17796). **Mention in Despatches**. Promoted Sergeant.] 1914-15 Star.

MURPHY Lance Sergeant Richard 19998. [Enlisted on 30 May 1915 and joined the 8th (Service) Battalion in 49th Brigade, 16th (Irish) Division.] Joined the 9th (North Irish Horse) Battalion when the 7th/8th (Service) Battalion was disbanded in February 1918. **Wounded**. Discharged as no longer physically fit for war service due to wounds 19 June 1919. Silver War Badge, number B265557.

MURPHY Lance Corporal Thomas Alexander 41537. From Ballymoney, County Antrim. A plumber. [Enlisted 27 May 1915 into the North Irish Horse (1631). To France 23 March 1916 and joined 'E' Squadron. Served with 2nd North Irish Horse, X Corps Cavalry Regiment. To hospital sick (syphilis sores) 30 June 1916 and treated at 39th General Hospital, Havre. Joined 'D' Squadron 16 September 1916. To hospital sick (syphilis) 28 May 1917 and treated at 1st Stationary Hospital, Rouen.] Joined the renamed 9th (North Irish Horse) Battalion from 36 Infantry Base Depot and transferred to Princess Victoria's (Royal Irish Fusiliers) in September/October 1917 (renumbered 41537). 'C' Company. **Wounded** by shrapnel to a finger of his right hand 3 November 1917. Treated at 110th Field Ambulance. To hospital injured (sprained left ankle) and evacuated to 24th General Hospital in England. Treated at City of London Military Hospital. To 'A' Infantry Base

Depot 15 June 1918 and immediately to hospital. To 'A' Infantry Base Depot 9 August 1918 and rejoined the 9th (North Irish Horse) Battalion. Lance Corporal 15 September 1918. **Wounded** by a gunshot to the arm 9 October 1918 and evacuated to hospital in England. Treated (again) at City of London Military Hospital. Transferred to the Class Z Reserve 23 May 1919.

MURPHY Private William 24739. [Enlisted 31 August 1916. Served with the 1st Battalion.] Posted to the 9th (Service) Battalion. **Wounded**. Discharged as no longer physically fit for war service due to wounds 13 February 1918. Silver War Badge, number 327291.

MURRAY Private Arthur 42110. [Enlisted into the Army Veterinary Corps (22934).] Transferred to Princess Victoria's (Royal Irish Fusiliers) 8 May 1918 (renumbered 42110) and joined the 9th (North Irish Horse) Battalion.

MURRAY Private Bernard 19736. [Enlisted in April 1915 into the 7th (Service) Battalion in 49th Brigade, 16th (Irish) Division.] Joined the 9th (North Irish Horse) Battalion when the 7th/8th (Service) Battalion was disbanded in February 1918. 'C' Company. **Missing** in the period 21-28 March 1918 during the retreat from St Quentin believed **captured**.

MURRAY Lance Corporal David 23286. From Armagh, County Armagh. Enlisted in November 1915. Posted to the 9th (Service) Battalion. 'B' Company. **Captured** in the period 21-28 March 1918 during the retreat from St Quentin.

MURRAY Private Owen J 20288. Enlisted in June 1915 and joined the 7th or 8th (Service) Battalion in 49th Brigade, 16th (Irish) Division.] Joined the 9th (North Irish Horse) Battalion when the 7th/8th (Service) Battalion was disbanded in February 1918. 'D' Company. **Wounded** during the retreat from St Quentin 21-28 March 1918. [Transferred to the Labour Corps (renumbered 612586).]

MURRAY Private Patrick 22898. Enlisted in November 1915. Posted to the 9th (Service) Battalion. 'C' Company. Believed **wounded** in the period 21-28 March 1918 during the retreat from St Quentin. [Transferred to the Machine Gun Corps (renumbered 162299).] Re-enlisted in 1919 for Regular Army service with The Royal Dublin Fusiliers (renumbered 33174).

MURRAY Private Robert Scott 42434. [Enlisted into The Royal Irish Rifles (21938).] Transferred at the Base Depot to Princess Victoria's (Royal Irish Fusiliers) 14 September 1918 (renumbered 42434) and joined the 9th (North Irish Horse) Battalion 22 September 1918.

MURRAY Private Walter McClean 22891. Born at Rockcorry, County Monaghan. Enlisted in November 1915. Posted to the 9th (Service) Battalion. 'B' Company. Believed **wounded** in the period 21-28 March 1918 during the retreat from St Quentin. **Killed in action** during the attack at Vijfwegen 30 September 1918, aged 21.

MURRELL Private Stanley 41245. From Belfast. [Enlisted 1 October 1914 into the North Irish Horse (1238). To France 28 April 1915. Served with 2nd North Irish Horse, X Corps Cavalry Regiment.] Joined the renamed 9th (North Irish Horse) Battalion from 36 Infantry Base Depot and transferred to Princess Victoria's (Royal Irish Fusiliers) in September/October 1917 (renumbered 41245). **Wounded** in the right leg in the period 11-18 April 1918 in the actions between Wulverghem and Kemmel. Discharged as no longer physically fit for war service due to wounds 16 August 1919. Silver War Badge, number B302460. 1914-15 Star.

MURREY Lance Sergeant William John 20958. [Enlisted 1 October 1914 and joined the 8th (Service) Battalion in 49th Brigade, 16th (Irish) Division. **16th (Irish) Division Parchment Certificate for Gallantry and Devotion to Duty** – Messines 7 June 1917.] Joined the 9th (North Irish Horse) Battalion when the 7th/8th (Service) Battalion was disbanded in February 1918.

NAIRN Private William 11849. [Enlisted in August 1914 into the 6th (Service) Battalion. Posted to the 1st Battalion. Posted to the 7th (Service) Battalion in 49th Brigade, 16th (Irish) Division.] Joined the 9th (North Irish Horse) Battalion when the 7th/8th (Service) Battalion was disbanded in February 1918.

NAISBITT Private Henry 40084. [Enlisted into The Prince of Wales's Own (West Yorkshire Regiment) (8055). To France with the 1st Battalion 25 March 1915.] Transferred to Princess Victoria's (Royal Irish Fusiliers) 30 November 1916 (renumbered 40084) and joined the 9th (Service) Battalion 12 December 1916. Re-enlisted on 19 March 1919 into Princess Victoria's (Royal Irish Fusiliers) Special Reserve. 1914-15 Star.

NAPIER Corporal Robert 14578. Enlisted September 1914. To France with 36th (Ulster) Division in October 1915. 'C' Company. Lance Corporal attached to Headquarters 108th Brigade during the attack at Hamel 1 July 1916. **Mention in Despatches**. 1914-15 Star. Transferred to the Class Z Reserve 3 May 1919.

NASH Private John Albert 43347. From West Hampstead, London. [Enlisted into The London Regiment (6431). Posted to the 1/7th (City of London) Battalion, The London Regiment.] Attached to the 9th (Service) Battalion, Princess Victoria's (Royal Irish Fusiliers) 26 November 1916. 'C' Company. Discharged from the Territorial Force, re-enlisted and transferred to Princess Victoria's (Royal Irish Fusiliers) in March/April 1917 (renumbered 43347). **Wounded** at the Battle of Langemarck 16 August 1917.

NEESON MM Private John 22735, 33830 & 7041845. From Crumlin, County Antrim. Enlisted in November 1915, aged 16. Posted to the 9th (North Irish Horse) Battalion. **MM** – River Lys mid-October 1918. Re-enlisted 3 January 1920 for Regular Army service with Princess Victoria's (Royal Irish Fusiliers) (renumbered 33830, renumbered 7041845). Served with the 1st Battalion in Persia and Mesopotamia in 1919/20. General Service Medal 1918-1962 with clasps 'Iraq' & 'NW Persia'. Discharged 7 August 1922.

NEILL Private Hugh 27442. Enlisted 21 March 1917. Posted to the 9th (North Irish Horse) Battalion. Discharged as no longer physically fit for war service due to sickness 14 December 1918. Silver War Badge, number B63631.

NEILL Corporal James 14588. From Lurgan, County Armagh. A cabinet maker. Enlisted September 1914. To France with 36th (Ulster) Division in October 1915. 'C' Company. Signaller at the forward transmitting station on 1 July 1916 and did not take part in the attack. **Wounded** at the Battle of Langemarck 16 August 1917. Transferred to the Class Z Reserve 10 March 1919. 1914-15 Star.

NEILL Private Robert 17948. From Belfast. Enlisted into the 9th (Service) Battalion in February 1915. 'C' Company. **Captured** in the period 21-28 March 1918 during the retreat from St Quentin.

NEILL Private Samuel 14589. Enlisted September 1914. To France with 36th (Ulster) Division in October 1915. Attached to Number 9 Rest Camp. Transferred to the Class Z Reserve 24 March 1919. 1914-15 Star.

NEILL Private Samuel 16434. Born on 30 August 1894 at Tandragee, County Armagh. Enlisted into the 9th (Service) Battalion in November 1914. To France with 36th (Ulster) Division in October 1915. **Wounded** during the attack at Hamel 1 July 1916. [Transferred to the Labour Corps (renumbered 605287).] 1914-15 Star. Lived for some time in the United States but returned to run the family farm. Died in 1975 and is buried at Ballymore Parish Churchyard.

NEILL DCM Sergeant William 14577. Born 26 July 1879 at Ballymacateer, County Armagh. Armagh Regiment, Ulster Volunteer Force. Enlisted September 1914. To France with 36th (Ulster) Division in October 1915. 'C' Company. Promoted Sergeant and attached to the Battalion Transport, where he served during the attack at Hamel on 1 July 1916. Appointed Transport Sergeant 24 August 1916. **DCM**. Transferred to the Class Z Reserve 16 March 1919. 1914-15 Star. On behalf of the 9th (North Irish Horse) Battalion, planted the tree at the dedication of the Ulster Tower. Served with the Ulster Special Constabulary 'A' Class and became a Head Constable. Died at home 20 February 55, aged 75. He is buried at Lurgan New Cemetery.

NEILL Private William 17947. Enlisted into the 9th (Service) Battalion in February 1915. To France with 36th (Ulster) Division in October 1915. 'C' Company. **Wounded** during the attack at Hamel 1 July 1916. **Missing** in the period 21-28 March 1918 during the retreat from St Quentin believed **captured**. Transferred to the Class Z Reserve 26 March 1919. 1914-15 Star.

NEILLY Private Robert 42565. From Coleraine, County Londonderry. [Enlisted into The Royal Irish Rifles (21049).] Transferred at the Base Depot to Princess Victoria's (Royal Irish Fusiliers) 14 September 1918 (renumbered 42565) and joined the 9th (North Irish Horse) Battalion 22 September 1918. **Captured** in October 1918.

NEILSON Private Archibald 20325. Enlisted in May/June 1915 and joined the 9th (Service) Battalion with the draft of men from The Royal Inniskilling Fusiliers who transferred to Princess Victoria's (Royal Irish Fusiliers) on 30 June 1915. To France 17 November 1915. 'C' Company during the attack at Hamel, which he survived unwounded. **Wounded** during the retreat from St Quentin 21-28 March 1918. [Transferred to the Labour Corps (renumbered 516650).] Transferred to the Class Z Reserve 19 April 1919. 1914-15 Star.

NELSON Private George 19824. From Armagh, County Armagh. Enlisted into the 9th (Service) Battalion in May 1915. To France with 36th (Ulster) Division in October 1915. **Killed in action** during the attack at Hamel 1 July 1916. 1914-15 Star.

NELSON Private James 14579. Enlisted September 1914. To France with 36th (Ulster) Division in October 1915. **Wounded** during the attack at Hamel 1 July 1916. [Transferred to the Labour Corps (renumbered 231622).] Transferred to the Class Z Reserve 11 March 1919. 1914-15 Star.

NELSON Private James 14586. From Armagh, County Armagh. Enlisted September 1914. To France with 36th (Ulster) Division in October 1915. [Transferred to 5th (Service) Battalion, The Royal Irish Regiment (Pioneers) in the Light Division in the British Army of the Rhine in March/June 1919 (renumbered 41346).] 1914-15 Star. After the war he was employed as a plumber at St Luke's Hospital, Armagh. Retired 1953. Died 2 February 1963.

NELSON Private John 41641. [Enlisted in September 1914 into the North Irish Horse (1151). To France 28 April 1915. Served with 2nd North Irish Horse, X Corps Cavalry Regiment.] Joined the renamed 9th (North Irish Horse) Battalion from 36 Infantry Base Depot and transferred to Princess Victoria's (Royal Irish Fusiliers) in September/October 1917 (renumbered 41641). Transferred to the Class Z Reserve 16 March 1919. 1914-15 Star.

NELSON Private Thomas J 41434. [Enlisted in November 1915 into the North Irish Horse (1979). Served with 2nd North Irish Horse, X Corps Cavalry Regiment.] Joined the renamed 9th (North Irish Horse) Battalion from 36 Infantry Base Depot and transferred to Princess Victoria's (Royal Irish Fusiliers) in September/October 1917 (renumbered 41434). [Transferred to The Northumberland Fusiliers (87080).]

NELSON Private William A 41258. [Enlisted in March 1916 into the North Irish Horse (2136). Served with 2nd North Irish Horse, X Corps Cavalry Regiment.] Joined the renamed 9th (North Irish Horse) Battalion from 36 Infantry Base Depot and transferred to Princess Victoria's (Royal Irish Fusiliers) in September/October 1917 (renumbered 41258). 'C' Company. Believed **wounded** in the period 21-28 March 1918 during the retreat from St Quentin. [Transferred to 5th (Service) Battalion, The Royal Irish Regiment (Pioneers) in the Light Division in the British Army of the Rhine in March/June 1919 (renumbered 41347).]

NESBITT Private Abner 14590. From Richhill, County Armagh. Enlisted September 1914, aged 17. To France with 36th (Ulster) Division in October 1915. **Wounded** during the attack at Hamel 1 July 1916. Discharged as no longer physically fit for war service due to wounds 4 January 1918. Silver War Badge, number 299446. 1914-15 Star. Son of Private George Nesbitt. His brother, Private Jackson Nesbitt, served as a regular soldier with the 1st Battalion.

NESBITT Private George 14583. Born in 1856 at Richhill, County Armagh. A stonemason. Served pre-war with the 4th Battalion (Militia), Princess Victoria's (Royal Irish Fusiliers). Enlisted September 1914, aged 58, giving his age as 44 years. Discharged as not being likely to become an efficient soldier in that he was considered medically unfit for service 1 October 1914. Father of Private Abner Nesbitt.

NESBITT MM Sergeant George 41198. [Enlisted 12 October 1908 into the North Irish Horse (223). To France 17 August 1914 with 'A' Squadron as GHQ Troops. Served with 2nd North Irish Horse, X Corps Cavalry Regiment.] Joined the renamed 9th (North Irish Horse) Battalion from 36 Infantry Base Depot and transferred to Princess Victoria's (Royal Irish Fusiliers) in September/October 1917 (renumbered 41198). 'D' Company. **Wounded** during the retreat from St Quentin 21-28 March 1918 – **MM**. Discharged as no longer physically fit for war service due to wounds 28 November 1918. Silver War Badge, number B46747. 1914 Star.

NESBITT Private James 42295. Born in 1890 at Belfast. An auctioneer. [Enlisted on 3 September 1914 into the North Irish Horse (1089). To France 20 January 1915. Served with 2nd North Irish Horse, X Corps Cavalry Regiment.] Transferred to Princess Victoria's (Royal Irish Fusiliers) (renumbered 42295) and joined the 9th (North Irish Horse) Battalion in early-1918. [Transferred to the Labour Corps (renumbered 385227).] Transferred to the Class Z Reserve 28 February 1919. 1914-15 Star.

NESBITT Private Joseph 24411. From Carnagh, County Armagh. Enlisted in May 1916. Posted to the 9th (Service) Battalion. 'C' Company. **Captured** in the period 21-28 March 1918 during the retreat from St Quentin. After the war lived at Clogher, County Tyrone.

NESBITT Private Robert 14585. From Richhill, County Armagh. Enlisted September 1914. To France with 36th (Ulster) Division in October 1915. **Killed in action** during the attack at Hamel 1 July 1916, aged 24. 1914-15 Star. Brother of Private Thomas Adam Nesbitt.

NESBITT Private Thomas Adam 20026. From Richhill, County Armagh. Enlisted into the 9th (Service) Battalion in May/June 1915. To France with 36th (Ulster) Division in October 1915. 'C' Company. Bombing team during the attack at Hamel 1 July 1916, where he was **wounded**. Separated from the 9th (North Irish Horse) Battalion in the period 21-28 March 1918 during the retreat from St Quentin; rejoined 2 April 1918. Transferred to the Class Z Reserve 15 March 1919. 1914-15 Star. Brother of Private Robert Nesbitt.

NETTLINGHAM Private Louis James B 42112. Born in 1890 at Northfleet, Kent. [Enlisted into the Army Veterinary Corps (21893).] Transferred to Princess Victoria's (Royal Irish Fusiliers) 8 May 1918 (renumbered 42112) and joined the 9th (North Irish Horse) Battalion. Died at Dartford, Kent in 1960, aged 70.

NEVILLE Private John 14581. Enlisted September 1914. To France with 36th (Ulster) Division in October 1915. Transferred to the Class Z Reserve 24 March 1919. 1914-15 Star.

NEVILLE Lance Corporal John 14591. From Armagh, County Armagh. Enlisted September 1914. To France with 36th (Ulster) Division in October 1915. **Killed in action** during the attack at Hamel 1 July 1916. 1914-15 Star. Brother of Private Thomas Neville.

NEVILLE Private Richard Elgie 40020. Born in 1881 at Leeds, Yorkshire. Joined the 9th (Service) Battalion, Princess Victoria's (Royal Irish Fusiliers) with the draft of men from The Prince of Wales's Own (West Yorkshire Regiment) on 12 December 1916. Died at Leeds, Yorkshire in 1942, aged 61.

NEVILLE Private Thomas 14584. From Armagh, County Armagh. Worked at the Gillis linen mill. Enlisted September 1914. To France with 36th (Ulster) Division in October 1915. **Killed in action** during the attack at Hamel 1 July 1916, aged 22. 1914-15 Star. Brother of Private John Neville.

NEVILLE Private William 29537, 34021 & 7041985. Enlisted into or transferred to Princess Victoria's (Royal Irish Fusiliers) March 1918. Posted to the 9th (North Irish Horse) Battalion. Re-enlisted 31 March 1920 for Regular Army service with Princess Victoria's (Royal Irish Fusiliers) (renumbered 34021, renumbered 7041985). Discharged 30 March 1922.

NEWBURN Lance Corporal William Henry 41298. Born in 1894 at Belfast. [Enlisted in January 1916 into the North Irish Horse (2085). Served with 2nd North Irish Horse, X Corps Cavalry Regiment.] Joined the renamed 9th (North Irish Horse) Battalion from 36 Infantry Base Depot and transferred to Princess Victoria's (Royal Irish Fusiliers) in September/October 1917 (renumbered 41298). After the war he emigrated to the United States and worked as a salesman.

NEWELL Private Henry 41439. [Enlisted in May 1913 into the North Irish Horse (849). To France 20 August 1914 with 'C' Squadron as 5th Division Cavalry and then as GHQ Troops. Served with 2nd North Irish Horse, X Corps Cavalry Regiment.] Joined the renamed 9th (North Irish Horse) Battalion from 36 Infantry Base Depot and transferred to Princess Victoria's (Royal Irish Fusiliers) in September/October 1917 (renumbered 41439). 1914 Star and clasp.

NEWLAND Private Stanley Reuben 19060. Born on 2 July 1885 at Roughton, Norfolk. A farm labourer. Enlisted 8 December 1915. Posted to the 9th (Service) Battalion. 'C' Company. **Wounded** at the Battle of Langemarck 16 August 1917. Discharged as no longer physically fit for war service due to wounds 21 June 1918, aged 32. Silver War Badge, number 414486. Died at North Walsham, Norfolk in 1972, aged 86.

NEWMAN Private Walter John 45737. [Enlisted into The London Regiment. Posted to the 1/22nd (County of London) Battalion, The London Regiment (The Queen's) (6594).] To France and joined 36 Infantry Base Depot 29 March 1918. Transferred to Princess Victoria's (Royal Irish Fusiliers) 2 April 1918 (renumbered 45737) and joined the 9th (North Irish Horse) Battalion 4 April 1918.

NEWMAN Lance Corporal William Ewart 27821. Enlisted into or transferred to Princess Victoria's (Royal Irish Fusiliers) in July 1917. Posted to the 9th (North Irish Horse) Battalion.

NEWMAN Private William James 14582. Born in 1863 at County Down. From Tandragee, County Armagh. Tandragee Company, Armagh Regiment, Ulster Volunteer Force. An oatmeal miller. Enlisted September 1914. Did not serve overseas with 36th (Ulster) Division. Discharged as no longer physically fit for war service due to sickness 26 April 1916. Silver Wound Badge, number 55058. Father of Private William James Newman.

NEWMAN Private William James 17558. (His medal index card incorrectly shows him as The Royal Inniskilling Fusiliers.) Born in 1890 at Newtownards, County Down. From Tandragee, County Armagh. Worked in the linen industry. Enlisted into the 9th (Service) Battalion in November/December 1914. To France with 36th (Ulster) Division in October 1915. 'B' Company. **Wounded** 1 July 1916 at Hamel. **Wounded** at the Battle of Langemarck 16 August 1917. [Transferred to the Labour Corps (renumbered 518017). Transferred to the 43rd (Garrison) Battalion, The Royal Fusiliers (City of London Regiment) (GS/102055).] 1914-15 Star. Son of Private William James Newman.

NICOL Private John 42209. Joined the 9th (North Irish Horse) Battalion, Princess Victoria's (Royal Irish Fusiliers) with the draft of men transferred from the Army Service Corps and the Army Veterinary Corps in May 1918. [Transferred to 5th (Service) Battalion, The Royal Irish Regiment (Pioneers) in the Light Division in the British Army of the Rhine in March/June 1919 (renumbered 41345).]

NICHOLL Private John 41611. From Clones, County Monaghan. [Enlisted in October 1914 into the Service Squadron, 6th (Inniskilling) Dragoons (UD/47). To France with 36th (Ulster) Division in October 1915. Served with 2nd North Irish Horse, X Corps Cavalry Regiment.] **Wounded** by shellfire at Aveluy Wood when two troops engaged in salvage duty were subject to heavy bombardment 5 July 1916. Joined the renamed 9th (North Irish Horse) Battalion from 36 Infantry Base Depot and transferred to Princess Victoria's (Royal Irish Fusiliers) in September/October 1917 (renumbered 41611). 'C' Company. **Captured** in the period 21-28 March 1918 during the retreat from St Quentin. **Died** 22 July 1918 in the Bavarian War Hospital, Hautmont while a prisoner of war. 1914-15 Star.

NICHOLSON Private Anthony Dent 20297. Enlisted 13 May 1915 and joined the 9th (Service) Battalion with the draft of men from The Royal Inniskilling Fusiliers who transferred to Princess Victoria's (Royal Irish Fusiliers) on 30 June 1915. To France with 36th (Ulster) Division in October 1915. 'C' Company. To hospital mid-1916, struck off strength when evacuated to hospital in England and did not take part in the attack at Hamel on 1 July 1916. Discharged as no longer physically fit for war service due to sickness 27 February 1917. Silver War Badge, number 33219. 1914-15 Star.

NICHOLSON Private Henry 40069. Born in 1885 at Leeds, Yorkshire. From Bradford, Yorkshire. [Enlisted 2 September 1914 and joined the 10th (Service) Battalion, The Prince of Wales's Own (West Yorkshire Regiment) (12406). Joined the 13th (Reserve) Battalion 22 December 1914. To France 13 July 1915 and rejoined the 10th (Service) Battalion. To hospital sick (trench foot) and evacuated to hospital in England 19 November 1915. Treated at the Metropolitan Hospital, London. To France and rejoined the 10th (Service) Battalion, The Prince of Wales's Own (West Yorkshire Regiment) 10 March 1916. **Wounded** by a gunshot to the wrist at Fricourt on 1 July 1916 and evacuated to hospital in England. Rejoined the 13th (Reserve) Battalion, The Prince of Wales's Own (West Yorkshire Regiment) 7 August 1916. Posted to the 3rd (Reserve) Battalion, The Prince of Wales's Own (West Yorkshire Regiment) 10 October 1916.] To France 29 November 1916. Transferred to Princess Victoria's (Royal Irish Fusiliers) 30 November 1916 (renumbered 40069) and joined the 9th (Service) Battalion. **Missing** on 27 March 1918, he rejoined on 9 April 1918. **Wounded** by gunshots to both legs and **died of wounds** on 21 June 1918 at 5th Australian Casualty Clearing Station. 1914-15 Star.

NICHOLSON Sergeant Leonard 14580. Enlisted September 1914. To France with 36th (Ulster) Division in October 1915. As a Lance Corporal served in 3 Section, 13 Platoon, 'D' Company. Transferred to the Class Z Reserve 26 March 1919. 1914-15 Star.

NICHOLSON Private Thomas 16425. Born at Drumcree, County Armagh. Lived in Portadown, County Armagh. 4th (Portadown) Battalion, Armagh Regiment, Ulster Volunteer Force. Enlisted into the 9th (Service) Battalion in November 1914. To France with 36th (Ulster) Division in October 1915.

5 Platoon, 'B' Company. **Wounded** by shellfire at Mesnil on 12 February 1916 and **died of wounds** 13 February 1916, aged 40. 1914-15 Star.

NILAND Private Thomas 20311. Enlisted 15 May 1915 and joined the 9th (Service) Battalion with the draft of men from The Royal Inniskilling Fusiliers who transferred to Princess Victoria's (Royal Irish Fusiliers) on 30 June 1915. Discharged as no longer physically fit for war service due to sickness 3 August 1918, aged 22. Silver War Badge, number 434621.

NIXON Private Andrew 41089. [Enlisted in November 1914 into the Service Squadron, 6th (Inniskilling) Dragoons (UD/176). To France with 36th (Ulster) Division in October 1915. Served with 2nd North Irish Horse, X Corps Cavalry Regiment.] Joined the renamed 9th (North Irish Horse) Battalion from 36 Infantry Base Depot and transferred to Princess Victoria's (Royal Irish Fusiliers) in September/October 1917 (renumbered 41089). Transferred to the Class Z Reserve 26 April 1919. 1914-15 Star.

NIXON Private John 41621. [Enlisted in August 1914 into the North Irish Horse (1053). To France 18 December 1914. Served with 2nd North Irish Horse, X Corps Cavalry Regiment.] Joined the renamed 9th (North Irish Horse) Battalion from 36 Infantry Base Depot and transferred to Princess Victoria's (Royal Irish Fusiliers) in September/October 1917 (renumbered 41621). Transferred to the Class Z Reserve 22 February 1919. 1914-15 Star.

NIXON Corporal Robert George 22175. Enlisted in October 1915. Posted to the 9th (Service) Battalion.

NIXON Private Thomas 25183. Born 10 July 1879. Lived at Stramore, Glaslough, County Monaghan. A farmer's son. Enlisted in November 1916. Posted to the 9th (Service) Battalion. 'B' Company. **Wounded** at the Battle of Langemarck 16 August 1917. His twin brother, Private James Nixon, enlisted into The Royal Inniskilling Fusiliers in 1903, transferred to the Army Reserve in 1906 and transferred to the Royal Army Medical Corps in 1909. He was mobilised in 1914 and was discharged at the end of his engagement in 1916.

NIXON Private William John 41612. An alias for Private William John McKeown - see above.

NOBLE Private James 41090. [Enlisted in June 1915 into the Service Squadron, 6th (Inniskilling) Dragoons (UD/261). Served with 2nd North Irish Horse, X Corps Cavalry Regiment.] Joined the renamed 9th (North Irish Horse) Battalion from 36 Infantry Base Depot and transferred to Princess Victoria's (Royal Irish Fusiliers) in September/October 1917 (renumbered 41090).

NOBLE Private John William 40021. From Leeds. [Enlisted 11 December 1915 into The Prince of Wales's Own (West Yorkshire Regiment).] Transferred to Princess Victoria's (Royal Irish Fusiliers) 30 November 1916 (renumbered 40021) and joined the 9th (Service) Battalion 12 December 1916. 'A' Company. **Wounded** at the Battle of Langemarck 16 August 1917. Discharged as no longer physically fit for war service due to wounds 1 April 1918. Silver War Badge, number 373745.

NORMAN Corporal Harry 42184. [Enlisted into the Army Service Corps (S3/027531). To France 28 July 1915. Served with 49th and 16th Field Bakeries.] Transferred to Princess Victoria's (Royal Irish Fusiliers) 8 May 1918 (renumbered 42184) and joined the 9th (North Irish Horse) Battalion. Transferred to the Class Z Reserve 8 March 1919. 1914-15 Star.

NORRIS MM Private Robert 13447. From Armagh, County Armagh. [Enlisted in September 1914 and joined the 7th (Service) Battalion in 49th Brigade, 16th (Irish) Division.] Joined the 9th (North Irish Horse) Battalion when the 7th/8th (Service) Battalion was disbanded in February 1918. **MM** – Vijfwegen/Hill 41 between 30 September and 14 October 1918. Transferred to the Class Z Reserve.

NORRIS Private William 17551. From Gransha, Clones, County Monaghan. Enlisted 10 December 1914 into the 9th (Service) Battalion. To France with 36th (Ulster) Division in October 1915. **Wounded**. Discharged as no longer physically fit for war service due to wounds 21 February 1918. Silver War Badge, number 318457. 1914-15 Star.

NORRIS Private William Charles 42185. [Enlisted 12 February 1909 into the Army Service Corps (S/29286). To France 12 August 1914. Served with 22nd Depot Unit of Supply.] Transferred to Princess Victoria's (Royal Irish Fusiliers) 8 May 1918 (renumbered 42185) and was posted to the 9th (North Irish Horse) Battalion. [Part of the draft transferred on 19 June 1918 to The Royal Irish Rifles (renumbered 45866).] Discharged as surplus to military requirements having suffered impairment since entry into the service 6 May 1919. Silver War Badge, number B243234. 1914

Star.

NORTH Private John 23205. From Belturbet, County Cavan. Enlisted in November 1915. Posted to the 9th (Service) Battalion. 'D' Company. **Missing** at the Battle of Langemarck 16 August 1917 and later declared **killed in action** on that date.

NORTH Private William 20842. Born in 1893 at Killoughter, County Cavan. From Redhills, County Cavan. A blacksmith. Cavan Ulster Volunteer Force. Enlisted 6 August 1915 and joined the 9th (Service) Battalion. Joined the 10th (Reserve) Battalion 23 September 1915. To 16 Infantry Base Depot 15 October 1916 and rejoined the 9th (Service) Battalion. 'B' Company. Attached to 108th Brigade Trench Mortar Battery for a period in July 1917. **Missing** at the Battle of Langemarck 16 August 1917 and later declared **killed in action** on that date.

NORTH Private William 42240 & 7042179. From Islington, London. A car driver. [Enlisted 19 August 1914 into the Army Service Corps (T/34370). To France 28 August 1914 with 28th Division Train.] Transferred to Princess Victoria's (Royal Irish Fusiliers) 8 May 1918 (renumbered 42240) and joined the 9th (North Irish Horse) Battalion. **Wounded** by a gunshot to the right thigh during the attack at Vijfwegen 30 September 1918 and evacuated to hospital in England 1 October 1918. 1914 Star. Transferred to the Section B Army Reserve, Princess Victoria's (Royal Irish Fusiliers) (renumbered 7042179). Discharged 18 August 1926.

NORWOOD Sergeant Arnold 41924. Born 5 July 1896 at Mansfield, Nottinghamshire. A coal miner at Langwith Colliery, Mansfield. [Enlisted 5 November 1914 into the 11th (Service) Battalion, The Sherwood Foresters (Nottinghamshire and Derbyshire Regiment) (18742). Transferred to The Royal Irish Rifles and posted to the 13th (Service) Battalion, The Royal Irish Rifles (1st County Down) (renumbered 43119). **Wounded** 1 July 1916 at Hamel. Sergeant 2 July 1916. Rejoined 13th (Service) Battalion, The Royal Irish Rifles (1st County Down) 7 August 1916. To the field ambulance sick in June and July 1917 (scabies and impetigo). To 36 Infantry Base Depot 18 November 1917 following the amalgamation of the 11th and 13th (Service) Battalions.] Transferred to Princess Victoria's (Royal Irish Fusiliers) 12 December 1917 (renumbered 41924) and joined the 9th (North Irish Horse) Battalion 26 December 1917. 'D' Company. To the field ambulance sick (scabies) February 1918. **Wounded** by a gunshot to the right hand 12 April 1918 in the actions between Wulverghem and Kemmel. Treated at 11th Stationary Hospital, Rouen. **Wounded** by shrapnel in the right thigh and right arm during the attack at Vijfwegen on 30 September or 1 October (recorded as 3 October 1918). Treated at 2nd Canadian Casualty Clearing Station and 22nd Stationary Hospital. Evacuated to hospital in England and treated at Northamptonshire War Hospital, Northampton. Transferred to the Class Z Reserve 26 February 1919. 1914-15 Star. Died at Mansfield, Nottinghamshire in 1934, aged 38.

NOWELL Private William 45746. Born in 1892 at Battersea, London. A Tram conductor. [Enlisted 4 December 1915 and transferred to the Army Reserve. Mobilised 3 March 1916 and joined the 3/24th Battalion, The London Regiment (5416). To France 19 December 1916 and joined 1/24th (County of London) Battalion, The London Regiment (The Queen's) 21 January 1917 (renumbered 722363 in March 1917). Evacuated sick to England in December 1917 and treated at Southern General Hospital. When recovered, posted to the 22nd (Reserve) Battalion, The London Regiment.] To France 29 March 1918. Transferred to Princess Victoria's (Royal Irish Fusiliers) 2 April 1918 (renumbered 45746) and joined the 9th (North Irish Horse) Battalion 4 April 1918. 4 Platoon, 'A' Company. **Missing** in the period 11-18 April 1918 in the actions between Wulverghem and Kemmel; subsequently declared **killed in action** 19 April 1918, aged 26.

NUIR Corporal Alexander 42081. [Enlisted into the Army Service Corps (S4/111284). To France 3 October 1915.] Transferred to Princess Victoria's (Royal Irish Fusiliers) 8 May 1918 (renumbered 42081) and joined the 9th (North Irish Horse) Battalion. Transferred to the Class Z Reserve. 1914-15 Star.

O'BOYLE Private John 21245. [Enlisted 8 February 1915 and joined the 8th (Service) Battalion in 49th Brigade, 16th (Irish) Division.] Joined the 9th (North Irish Horse) Battalion when the 7th/8th (Service) Battalion was disbanded in February 1918. **Wounded** in left foot in August 1917 prior to the Battle of Langemarck. Discharged as no longer physically fit for war service due to wounds 17 September 1919. Silver War Badge, number B313356.

O'BRIEN Private Dennis 11108. Born at Galway. From Stechford, Birmingham. [Enlisted into

Princess Victoria's (Royal Irish Fusiliers) as a regular soldier in 1913. To France with the 2nd Battalion 19 December 1914. Posted to the 1st Battalion.] Posted to the 9th (Service) Battalion. 'C' Company. **Missing** in the preliminaries to the Battle of Langemarck and later declared **killed in action** by shellfire 14 August 1917. 1914-15 Star.

O'BRIEN Private James 41276. [Enlisted in February 1912 into the North Irish Horse (664). To France 20 August 1914 with 'C' Squadron as 5th Division Cavalry and then as GHQ Troops. Served with 2nd North Irish Horse, X Corps Cavalry Regiment.] Joined the renamed 9th (North Irish Horse) Battalion from 36 Infantry Base Depot and transferred to Princess Victoria's (Royal Irish Fusiliers) in September/October 1917 (renumbered 41276). 'C' Company. **Missing** in the period 21-28 March 1918 during the retreat from St Quentin believed **captured**. 1914 Star.

O'BRIEN Private Thomas 9654. [Enlisted into Princess Victoria's (Royal Irish Fusiliers) as a regular soldier in 1907 and served with the 2nd Battalion. Posted to the 1st Battalion.] Posted to the 9th (North Irish Horse) Battalion. Discharged 13 November 1918. 1914-15 Star.

O'BRIEN Private Thomas 22921. [Enlisted 3 August 1915 and joined the 7th (Service) Battalion in 49th Brigade, 16th (Irish) Division.] Joined the 9th (North Irish Horse) Battalion when the 7th/8th (Service) Battalion was disbanded in February 1918. 'B' Company. **Missing** in the period 21-28 March 1918 during the retreat from St Quentin believed **captured**. Discharged as no longer physically fit for war service due to sickness 1 September 1919. Silver War Badge, number 467194.

O'CALLAGHAN Private Bernard 13231. Born at Johnstone, Renfrewshire. Lived at Belfast and worked as a thread pinner. [Enlisted into The Royal Irish Rifles (11504). Transferred to Princess Victoria's (Royal Irish Fusiliers) and joined the 6th (Service) Battalion in 31st Brigade, 10th (Irish) Division. Embarked with the Mediterranean Expeditionary Force July 1915. **Wounded**.] Posted to the 9th (Service) Battalion. 'B' Company. **Killed in action** at the Battle of Langemarck 16 August 1917. 1914-15 Star.

O'DONNELL Private John 42555. [Enlisted into The Royal Inniskilling Fusiliers (28551) and joined the 7th (Service) Battalion, The Royal Inniskilling Fusiliers in 49th Brigade, 16th (Irish) Division. Transferred to The Royal Irish Rifles (renumbered 22731).] Transferred at the Base Depot to Princess Victoria's (Royal Irish Fusiliers) 14 September 1918 (renumbered 42555) and joined the 9th (North Irish Horse) Battalion 22 September 1918.

O'DONNELL Private Michael 29667. From Glasgow. [Served previously with the 5th (Service) Battalion. Discharged or transferred.] Enlisted, re-enlisted or transferred to Princess Victoria's (Royal Irish Fusiliers) in March 1918. Posted to the 9th (North Irish Horse) Battalion. **Missing** during the attack at Vijfwegen on 30 September or 1 October 1918; recorded as **killed in action** on 2 October 1918, aged 29.

OGDEN Private Richard 15518. Born in 1893 at Salford, Manchester. [Enlisted 1 September 1914 into The Lancashire Fusiliers (6146).] Transferred to Princess Victoria's (Royal Irish Fusiliers) 12 December 1914 and joined the 8th (Service) Battalion in 49th Brigade, 16th (Irish) Division. Lance Corporal. To France 19 February 1916. Reverted to Private due to repeated charges of having a *'dirty rifle on parade'*.] Joined the 9th (North Irish Horse) Battalion when the 7th/8th (Service) Battalion was disbanded in February 1918. 'C' Company. **Missing** in the period 21-28 March 1918 during the retreat from St Quentin and later declared **killed in action** 21 March 1918.

OGLE Private Matthew 14594. From Lurgan, County Armagh. Enlisted September 1914. To France with 36th (Ulster) Division in October 1915. 'C' Company. **Killed in action** by shellfire at Hamel 26 June 1916, aged 19. 1914-15 Star.

OGLESBY Private Albert 42448. Born in 1884 at Dublin. [Served as a regular soldier with the 2nd Battalion, The Royal Irish Rifles (10984).] Transferred at the Base Depot to Princess Victoria's (Royal Irish Fusiliers) 14 September 1918 (renumbered 42448) and joined the 9th (North Irish Horse) Battalion 22 September 1918. **Killed in action** during the attack at Vijfwegen 30 September 1918, aged 34. His brother, Lance Corporal Patrick Oglesby, was also a regular soldier with the 2nd Battalion, The Royal Irish Rifles. He was wounded and captured on 25 September 1915.

OGLESBY Private David 42516. [Enlisted into The Royal Irish Rifles (20240).] Transferred at the Base Depot to Princess Victoria's (Royal Irish Fusiliers) 14 September 1918 (renumbered 42516) and joined the 9th (North Irish Horse) Battalion 22 September 1918. [Transferred to 5th (Service) Battalion, The Royal Irish Regiment (Pioneers) in the Light Division in the British Army of the Rhine in March/June 1919 (renumbered 41348).]

O'HALLORAN Private Thomas 27728. Enlisted 19 June 1917. Posted to the 9th (North Irish Horse) Battalion. Discharged as no longer physically fit for war service due to sickness 12 December 1918. Silver War Badge, number B61025. Battalion in 49th Brigade, 16th (Irish) Division.] Joined the 9th (North Irish Horse) Battalion when the 7th/8th (Service) Battalion was disbanded in Company. **Missing** in the period 21-28 March 1918 during the retreat from St Quentin believed **captured. MM. *Croix de Guerre* (France)**.

OLDHAM Private John Byers 41346. Born in 1897 at Belfast. [Enlisted into the Army Service Corps (T4/159974). Served with 221st Company. Transferred to the North Irish Horse (renumbered 2665) in August 1917 and was immediately transferred for service as infantry.] Joined the renamed 9th (North Irish Horse) Battalion from 36 Infantry Base Depot and transferred to Princess Victoria's (Royal Irish Fusiliers) in September/October 1917 (renumbered 41346). His brother Second Lieutenant Thomas Hemphill Byers, served as a Lance Sergeant in The Royal Irish Rifles, transferred to the Machine Gun Corps and was promoted to Company Quartermaster Sergeant before being commissioned into the Machine Gun Corps in 1917. He later transferred to the Tank Corps. His brother, Second Lieutenant Edward Garr Oldham, enlisted into the 10th (Service) Battalion, The Royal Irish Rifles (South Belfast) and served in France with 36th (Ulster) Division from October 1915. He was commissioned into The Royal Irish Rifles in 1917.

O'NEILL Corporal Charles Bernard 18532 & 7042308. From Dublin. Served as a regular soldier with the 1st Battalion, Princess Victoria's (Royal Irish Fusiliers) during the South African War. Queen's South Africa Medal. King's South Africa Medal. Discharged to the Army Reserve. [Re-enlisted 7 April 1915, aged 31, (renumbered 18532). To France 20 May 1915 and joined the 2nd Battalion. Evacuated to hospital in England 30 November 1915.] To France 13 June 1917 and posted to the 9th (Service) Battalion. Section Commander 4 Section, 5 Platoon, 'B' Company. **Wounded** on 16 August 1917 during the Battle of Langemarck and evacuated to hospital in England 18 August 1917. To France 24 May 1918 and rejoined the 9th (North Irish Horse) Battalion. **Wounded** during the attack at Vijfwegen 30 September 1918 and evacuated to hospital in England 8 October 1918. 1914-15 Star. Re-enlisted 26 February 1919 for Regular Army service with Princess Victoria's (Royal Irish Fusiliers) (renumbered 7042308). Served with the 1st Battalion in Persia and Mesopotamia in 1919/20. General Service Medal 1918-1962 with clasps 'Iraq' & 'NW Persia'. Discharged 31 March 1922. Subsequently served in the Merchant Navy.

O'NEILL Private Francis 42573. [Served previously with the 1st Battalion, The Royal Irish Rifles (11499).] Transferred at the Base Depot to Princess Victoria's (Royal Irish Fusiliers) 14 September 1918 and joined the 9th (North Irish Horse) Battalion 22 September 1918.

O'NEILL Sergeant John 41119. [Enlisted in October 1914 into the Service Squadron, 6th (Inniskilling) Dragoons (UD/94). To France with 36th (Ulster) Division in October 1915. Served with 2nd North Irish Horse, X Corps Cavalry Regiment.] Joined the renamed 9th (North Irish Horse) Battalion from 36 Infantry Base Depot and transferred to Princess Victoria's (Royal Irish Fusiliers) in September/October 1917 (renumbered 41119). Transferred to the Class Z Reserve 19 March 1919. 1914-15 Star.

O'NEILL Private William 49746. Joined the 9th (North Irish Horse) Battalion, Princess Victoria's (Royal Irish Fusiliers) with the draft of men transferred from The Royal Irish Rifles in April 1918.

O'PREY Lance Corporal William 41347. [Enlisted in November 1915 into the North Irish Horse (1840). Served with 2nd North Irish Horse, X Corps Cavalry Regiment.] Joined the renamed 9th (North Irish Horse) Battalion from 36 Infantry Base Depot and transferred to Princess Victoria's (Royal Irish Fusiliers) in September/October 1917 (renumbered 41347).

ORCHARD Lance Corporal Robert 43202. [Enlisted 30 February 1912 and joined the 2nd Battalion, The Sherwood Foresters (Nottinghamshire and Derbyshire Regiment) (11809). To France 8 September 1914. Later posted to the 1st Battalion, The Sherwood Foresters (Nottinghamshire and Derbyshire Regiment).] Transferred to Princess Victoria's (Royal Irish Fusiliers) 31 August 1916 having joined the 9th (Service) Battalion on 8 August 1916 (renumbered 43202). Discharged as no longer physically fit for war service due to sickness 3 June 1918, aged 25. Silver War Badge, number 394856. 1914 Star.

O'REILLY Private Alexander Ernest 27874. From Speenoge, County Donegal. [Enlisted in August 1917. Posted to the 7th/8th (Service) Battalion in 49th Brigade, 16th (Irish) Division.] Joined the 9th (North Irish Horse) Battalion when the 7th/8th (Service) Battalion was disbanded in February 1918. 'A' Company. **Wounded** during the retreat from St Quentin and **died of wounds** 29 March 1918.

ORR Private Alexander 14593. From Portadown, County Armagh. Member of Edenderry Temperance and Benefit Loyal Orange Lodge 322. Enlisted September 1914. To France with 36th (Ulster) Division in October 1915. [Part of the draft transferred on 19 June 1918 to The Royal Irish Rifles (45839). **Wounded** by a gunshot to the right shoulder October 1918.] Discharged as no longer physically fit for war service 16 October 1919. Silver War Badge, number B327247. 1914-15 Star.

ORR Corporal David 14592. From Bridge Street, Portadown, County Armagh. Apprentice mechanic at Hamilton Robb Ltd. 4th (Portadown) Battalion, Armagh Regiment, Ulster Volunteer Force. Enlisted September 1914. To France with 36th (Ulster) Division in October 1915. Machine-gun Section. [Joined 108th Brigade Machine Gun Company January 1916. Transferred to the Machine Gun Corps (renumbered 17778). **Killed in action** during the attack at Hamel 1 July 1916, aged 22.] 1914-15 Star.

ORR Private Henry 41091. Born in 1893 at Brookeborough, County Fermanagh. A farm servant. [Enlisted in October 1914 into the Service Squadron, 6th (Inniskilling) Dragoons (UD/62). To France with 36th (Ulster) Division in October 1915. Served with 2nd North Irish Horse, X Corps Cavalry Regiment.] Joined the renamed 9th (North Irish Horse) Battalion from 36 Infantry Base Depot and transferred to Princess Victoria's (Royal Irish Fusiliers) in September/October 1917 (renumbered 41091). **Killed in action** 23 November 1917 at Moeuvres, aged 22. 1914-15 Star. Brother of Lance Corporal John Robert Orr and Private William Orr.

ORR Lance Corporal John Robert 41151. Born in 1892 at Brookeborough, County Fermanagh. An apprentice to his father, a carpenter. [Enlisted into the Service Squadron, 6th (Inniskilling) Dragoons (UD/48). To France with 36th (Ulster) Division in October 1915. Served with 2nd North Irish Horse, X Corps Cavalry Regiment.] Joined the renamed 9th (North Irish Horse) Battalion from 36 Infantry Base Depot and transferred to Princess Victoria's (Royal Irish Fusiliers) in September/October 1917 (renumbered 41151). 'A' Company. **Captured** in the period 21-28 March 1918 during the retreat from St Quentin. Transferred to the Class Z Reserve 26 March 1919. 1914-15 Star. Brother of Privates Henry and William Orr.

ORR Private William 41092. Born in 1895 at Brookeborough, County Fermanagh. An apprentice to his father, a carpenter. [Enlisted 26 October 1914 into the Service Squadron, 6th (Inniskilling) Dragoons (UD/63). To France with 36th (Ulster) Division in October 1915. Served with 2nd North Irish Horse, X Corps Cavalry Regiment.] Joined the renamed 9th (North Irish Horse) Battalion from 36 Infantry Base Depot and transferred to Princess Victoria's (Royal Irish Fusiliers) in September/October 1917 (renumbered 41092). **Wounded**. Discharged as no longer physically fit for war service due to wounds 29 July 1918, aged 22. Silver War Badge, number 379048. 1914-15 Star. Brother of Lance Corporal John Robert Orr and Private Henry Orr.

OSBORNE Private Robert 14595. Enlisted September 1914. Discharged as no longer physically fit for war service due to sickness 28 June 1915, aged 34. Silver War Badge, number 508791.

OSBORNE Private William 43386. [Enlisted into The London Regiment (4912). Posted to the 1/9th (County of London) Battalion, The London Regiment (The Queen's).] Attached to the 9th (Service) Battalion, Princess Victoria's (Royal Irish Fusiliers) 26 November 1916. Discharged from the Territorial Force, re-enlisted and transferred to Princess Victoria's (Royal Irish Fusiliers) in March/April 1917 (renumbered 43386).

OSCROFT Lance Sergeant William 43261. Born at Sutton-in-Ashfield, Nottinghamshire. A coal miner. [Enlisted 23 June 1903 into The Sherwood Foresters (Nottinghamshire and Derbyshire Regiment) (8795) and joined the 2nd Battalion. Posted to the 1st Battalion 3 November 1904 in Singapore. Served in India from December 1906 to March 1911. Transferred to the Section A Army Reserve 30 May 1911. Transferred to the Section B Army Reserve 31 May 1912. Mobilised from the Army Reserve 5 August 1914 and to France 4 November 1914 with the 1st Battalion, The Sherwood Foresters (Nottinghamshire and Derbyshire Regiment). **Wounded** by a gunshot to the left hand 20

November 1914 and evacuated to hospital in England 4 January 1915. Joined the 3rd (Reserve) Battalion, The Sherwood Foresters (Nottinghamshire and Derbyshire Regiment) 20 February 1915. Joined the 1st Battalion 18 May 1915. Posted to the 2nd Battalion 11 September 1915. **Wounded** by a gunshot to the neck 15 September 1915 and evacuated to hospital in England 25 September 1915. Joined the 3rd (Reserve) Battalion, The Sherwood Foresters (Nottinghamshire and Derbyshire Regiment) 5 November 1915. To France 14 July 1916.] Transferred to Princess Victoria's (Royal Irish Fusiliers) 31 August 1916 (renumbered 43261) having joined the 9th (Service) Battalion on 8 August 1916. Lance Corporal 29 September 1917. Corporal 3 October 1916. Lance Sergeant 11 January 1917. Transferred to the Class Z Reserve 19 February 1919. 1914 Star.

OSTICK Private George 43268. Born in 1890. From Retford, Nottinghamshire. [Enlisted 21 August 1914 and joined the 9th (Service) Battalion, The Sherwood Foresters (Nottinghamshire and Derbyshire Regiment) (13009). Embarked with the Mediterranean Expeditionary Force July 1915. Landed at Suvla Bay 17 August 1915. To hospital with enteric fever 6 November 1915. Evacuated to Malta and treated at Imtarfa Hospital. Evacuated to hospital in England 24 December 1915.] To France 14 July 1916. Transferred to Princess Victoria's (Royal Irish Fusiliers) 31 August 1916 (renumbered 43268) having joined the 9th (Service) Battalion on 8 August 1916. 'D' Company. **Missing** at the Battle of Langemarck 16 August 1917 and later declared **killed in action** on that date. 1914-15 Star. His brother, Private Harry Wright Ostick Royal Marine Light Infantry, was killed in action on 1 January 1915 when HMS Formidable was sunk by a torpedo fired by U24. His brother, Private Frederick Ostick, was killed in action on 16 September 1916 serving with 2nd Battalion, The Sherwood Foresters (Nottinghamshire and Derbyshire Regiment).

O'TOOLE Corporal John 21005. From Dublin. [Enlisted in November 1914 and joined the 8th (Service) Battalion in 49th Brigade, 16th (Irish) Division. Served with the 1st Battalion.] Posted to the 9th (Service) Battalion. 'A' Company. **Wounded** at the Battle of Langemarck 16 August 1917. **Wounded** during the retreat from St Quentin 21-28 March 1918.

OVERTON Private Herbert 42195. Joined the 9th (North Irish Horse) Battalion, Princess Victoria's (Royal Irish Fusiliers) with the draft of men transferred from the Army Service Corps and the Army Veterinary Corps in May 1918.

OWENS Private Frederick 42241. From Belfast. [Enlisted into the Army Service Corps (T4/058935 – Driver).] Transferred to Princess Victoria's (Royal Irish Fusiliers) 8 May 1918 (renumbered 42241) and joined the 9th (North Irish Horse) Battalion. **Wounded**.

OWENS Private Thomas 23033. [Enlisted in November 1915. Joined the 7th/8th (Service) Battalion in 49th Brigade, 16th (Irish) Division.] Joined the 9th (North Irish Horse) Battalion when the 7th/8th (Service) Battalion was disbanded in February 1918.

OWENS Private Thomas Francis 41594. Born in 1893. From Ballymoney, County Antrim. A rural postman. [Enlisted 10 May 1915 into the North Irish Horse (1525). Treated in Portobello Military Hospital, Dublin (gonorrhoea) September-December 1916 and January-February 1917. Served with 2nd North Irish Horse, X Corps Cavalry Regiment.] Joined the renamed 9th (North Irish Horse) Battalion from 36 Infantry Base Depot and transferred to Princess Victoria's (Royal Irish Fusiliers) in September/October 1917 (renumbered 41594). 'D' Company. **Captured** in the period 21-28 March 1918 during the retreat from St Quentin. Repatriated 16 December 1918. Transferred to the Class Z Reserve 8 April 1919.

PADDON Private Herbert Jasper Joseph 45791. Born 18 March 1899 at St Thomas, Devonshire. Joined the 9th (North Irish Horse) Battalion, Princess Victoria's (Royal Irish Fusiliers) with the draft of men from The London Regiment in April 1918. Died in Devon in 1977, aged 78.

PAGE Private John William 43370. From Middlesex. [Enlisted into The London Regiment (3623). Posted to the 1/7th (City of London) Battalion, The London Regiment.] Attached to the 9th (Service) Battalion, Princess Victoria's (Royal Irish Fusiliers) 26 November 1916. 'B' Company. Discharged from the Territorial Force, re-enlisted and transferred to Princess Victoria's (Royal Irish Fusiliers) in March/April 1917 (renumbered 43370). **Wounded** at the Battle of Langemarck 16 August 1917.

PAGE Lance Corporal Samuel 43279. [Enlisted 10 December 1915 into The Sherwood Foresters (Nottinghamshire and Derbyshire Regiment).] Transferred to Princess Victoria's (Royal Irish Fusiliers) 31 August 1916 having joined the 9th (Service) Battalion on 8 August 1916 (renumbered 43279). 'D' Company. **Wounded** during the Battle of Messines and evacuated to hospital in

England 9 June 1917. Discharged as no longer physically fit for war service due to wounds 5 July 1919. Silver War Badge, number B274250.

PAINE Private Samuel Albert 45775. From Maida Hill, London. [Enlisted 16 March 1916 and joined the 2/12th (County of London) Battalion, The London Regiment (The Rangers) (5420). Posted to the 1/22nd (County of London) Battalion, The London Regiment (The Queen's) 19 July 1916. Renumbered 684341 in March 1917. **Wounded** by gas poisoning early December 1917. Evacuated to hospital in England 8 December 1917 and treated at the Military Hospital, Boscombe. Discharged from hospital 15 January 1918.] To Infantry Base Depot 30 March 1918. Transferred to Princess Victoria's (Royal Irish Fusiliers) in April 1918 (renumbered 45775). Joined the 9th (North Irish Horse) Battalion 8 June 1918. **Wounded** by a shrapnel bullet to the elbow; treated at 110th Field Ambulance and returned to duty. **Wounded** by a gunshot to the head during the attack south of Wulverghem on 4/5 September 1918 and **died of wounds** 6 September 1918 in 18th Casualty Clearing Station, aged 21.

PALMER Private George Ernest 43219. [Enlisted into The Sherwood Foresters (Nottinghamshire and Derbyshire Regiment).] Transferred to Princess Victoria's (Royal Irish Fusiliers) 31 August 1916 having joined the 9th (Service) Battalion on 8 August 1916 (renumbered 43219).

PALMER Corporal James 16426. Enlisted into the 9th (Service) Battalion in November 1914. To France with 36th (Ulster) Division in October 1915. 1914-15 Star.

PALMER Sergeant John 15854. Enlisted into the 9th (Service) Battalion 19 October 1914. To France with 36th (Ulster) Division in October 1915. **Wounded** in the period 21-28 March 1918 during the retreat from St Quentin. Discharged as no longer physically fit for war service due to wounds 12 December 1918. Silver War Badge, number B51547. 1914-15 Star.

PALMER MM Sergeant William Herbert (Herbie) 14601. Commissioned into The Royal Irish Regiment - see Appendix 5.

PAMENTER DCM Sergeant Walter Richard 43351. Commissioned into the Machine Gun Corps - see Appendix 5.

PARFETT Private Herbert 42186. [Enlisted into the Army Service Corps (S/29559). To France 11 August 1914. Served with 5th Field Bakery.] Transferred to Princess Victoria's (Royal Irish Fusiliers) 8 May 1918 (renumbered 42186) and joined the 9th (North Irish Horse) Battalion. [Part of the draft transferred on 19 June 1918 to The Royal Irish Rifles (renumbered 45856).] 1914 Star.

PARK Private Robert 41353. (The family also spelled their name Parke.) Born in 1889 at Grange, Magherafelt, County Londonderry. Member of O'Hara Purple Guards Loyal Orange Lodge 310. [Enlisted in December 1916 into the North Irish Horse (2325). Served with 2nd North Irish Horse, X Corps Cavalry Regiment.] Joined the renamed 9th (North Irish Horse) Battalion from 36 Infantry Base Depot and transferred to Princess Victoria's (Royal Irish Fusiliers) in September/October 1917 (renumbered 41353). **Missing** in the period 11-18 April 1918 in the actions between Wulverghem and Kemmel; subsequently declared **killed in action** 19 April 1918, aged 29. His brother, Private William John Parke, was killed in action on 26 October 1917 serving with 58th (Central Ontario) Battalion, Canadian Infantry in 9th Infantry Brigade, 3rd Canadian Division at Belvue Spur on the first day of the Second Battle of Passchendaele.

PARKE Private William 41459. From Glarryford, County Antrim. [Enlisted in August 1916 into the North Irish Horse (2256). Served with 2nd North Irish Horse, X Corps Cavalry Regiment.] Joined the renamed 9th (North Irish Horse) Battalion from 36 Infantry Base Depot and transferred to Princess Victoria's (Royal Irish Fusiliers) in September/October 1917 (renumbered 41459). 'C' Company. **Captured** in the period 21-28 March 1918 during the retreat from St Quentin. Repatriated in December 1918.

PARKER Private E 17866. Enlisted into the 9th (Service) Battalion in January 1915. To France with 36th (Ulster) Division in October 1915. 'C' Company. Lewis gun team during the attack at Hamel 1 July 1916, during which he was **wounded**. [Transferred to the Military Foot Police (renumbered P/16046).] 1914-15 Star.

PARKER Private George 43205. [Enlisted into The Sherwood Foresters (Nottinghamshire and Derbyshire Regiment).] Transferred to Princess Victoria's (Royal Irish Fusiliers) 31 August 1916 (renumbered 43205) having joined the 9th (Service) Battalion on 8 August 1916. [Transferred to the

Labour Corps (renumbered 637566).]

PARKER Lance Corporal George Edward 43462. [Enlisted into The London Regiment (2143). To France 14 March 1915 with 1/22nd (County of London) Battalion, The London Regiment (The Queen's).] To France and joined 36 Infantry Base Depot 29 March 1918. Transferred to Princess Victoria's (Royal Irish Fusiliers) 2 April 1918 (renumbered 43462) and joined the 9th (North Irish Horse) Battalion 4 April 1918. Transferred to the Class Z Reserve 10 April 1919. 1914-15 Star.

PARKER Private Harry 40022. Born in 1880 at Leeds. [Enlisted 7 December 1915 and transferred to the Army Reserve. Mobilised 30 June 1916 and joined the 14th (Reserve) Battalion, The Prince of Wales's Own (West Yorkshire Regiment) (25265).] To France 28 November 1916. Transferred to Princess Victoria's (Royal Irish Fusiliers) 30 November 1916 (renumbered 40022) and joined the 9th (Service) Battalion 12 December 1916. **Wounded** by shellfire near Spanbroekmolen on the night of 24/25 May 1917 and is recorded as having **died of wounds** on 25 May 1917, aged 37. The burial was conducted by Reverend Mayes and his return (Army Form W3314) shows a burial date of 24 May 1917.

PARKER Private Harry 43259. From Derby. [Enlisted into The Sherwood Foresters (Nottinghamshire and Derbyshire Regiment).] Transferred to Princess Victoria's (Royal Irish Fusiliers) 31 August 1916 (renumbered 43259) having joined the 9th (Service) Battalion on 8 August 1916. 'C' Company. **Wounded** at the Battle of Langemarck 16 August 1917. Separated from the 9th (North Irish Horse) Battalion in the period 21-28 March 1918 during the retreat from St Quentin; rejoined 2 April 1918.

PARKER Private Herbert 15867. From Portadown, County Armagh. Enlisted into the 9th (Service) Battalion in October 1914. To France with 36th (Ulster) Division in October 1915. 'B' Company. **Captured** in 1918. Transferred to the Class Z Reserve 25 March 1919. 1914-15 Star.

PARKES Private Richard 42556. [Enlisted into the 7th (Service) Battalion, The Royal Irish Rifles (8425). To France with 48th Brigade, 16th (Irish) Division 19 December 1915.] Transferred at the Base Depot to Princess Victoria's (Royal Irish Fusiliers) 14 September 1918 and joined the 9th (North Irish Horse) Battalion 22 September 1918. Transferred to the Class Z Reserve 18 March 1919. 1914-15 Star.

PARKS Private John 14608. Born in 1895 at Lurgan, County Armagh. Enlisted September 1914. To France with 36th (Ulster) Division in October 1915. 'D' Company. **Wounded** in the left thigh at the Battle of Langemarck 16 August 1917. Discharged as no longer physically fit for war service due to wounds 6 June 1918, aged 23. Silver War Badge, number 395823. 1914-15 Star.

PARKS Private Joseph 14599. From Clounagh, Portadown, County Armagh. Enlisted September 1914. To France with 36th (Ulster) Division in October 1915. 'B' Company. **Killed in action** during the attack at Hamel 1 July 1916, aged 23. 1914-15 Star.

PARSONS Private Cyril Herbert 43369. From Manor Park, Essex. [Enlisted into The London Regiment (6757). Posted to the 1/7th (City of London) Battalion, The London Regiment.] Attached to the 9th (Service) Battalion, Princess Victoria's (Royal Irish Fusiliers) 26 November 1916. Discharged from the Territorial Force, re-enlisted and transferred to Princess Victoria's (Royal Irish Fusiliers) in March/April 1917 (renumbered 43369). **Wounded** at the Battle of Langemarck 16 August 1917.

PARSONS Corporal Wilfred 42083. From Essex. [Enlisted into the Army Service Corps (S2/11752). Served with the Mediterranean Expeditionary Force from June 1915. Served with 13th Field Bakery.] Transferred to Princess Victoria's (Royal Irish Fusiliers) 8 May 1918 (renumbered 42083) and joined the 9th (North Irish Horse) Battalion. 'A' Company. **Wounded** at the Battle of Langemarck 16 August 1917. Transferred to the Class Z Reserve 24 February 1919. 1914-15 Star.

PARTRIDGE Private John Ernest 45788. Born in 1899. From Streatham, London. [Enlisted 21 March 1917, aged 17, into The Queen's (Royal West Surrey Regiment) (67088). Posted to 1/22nd (County of London) Battalion, The London Regiment (The Queen's) 1 December 1917.] To 'K' Infantry Base Depot 31 March 1918. Transferred to Princess Victoria's (Royal Irish Fusiliers) 2 April 1918 (renumbered 45788) and joined the 9th (North Irish Horse) Battalion 6 April 1918. **Captured** (reported **wounded**) in the period 11-18 April 1918 (probably on 12 April) in the actions between Wulverghem and Kemmel. **Died** of *'general weakness'* at Heilsberg Prisoner of War Camp, East Prussia (now Lidzbark Warmiński, Poland) 27 October 1918, aged 19.

41594 Private
Thomas Francis OWENS

14601 Sergeant
William Herbert PALMER MM

42531 Private
George PENNELL

41406 Private
William Joseph PETTY

43340 Private
Laurence Gordon RANGER

41142 Private
Samuel QUINN

24600 Corporal
Ernest Hugh RAMSEY

22951 Private
Hugh REID

41403 Private
John Edward RIDDELL

29590 Sergeant
Dennis RODDY

41147 Lance Sergeant
Hubert ROE DCM

18453 Private
Frederick RYAN

14655 Private
Andrew ROWAN

(Centre) 14699 Private
William John SANDS

16134 Lance Corporal
John SCOTT

22556 Sergeant
Thomas SCOTT MM

15855 Private
Joseph SELBY

41428 Private
George Moorhead SHANNON

14708 Corporal
John SHARP MM

43281 Private
Silas George SHAW

41246 Private
Henry SIMMS

18345 Sergeant
Robert SLATOR

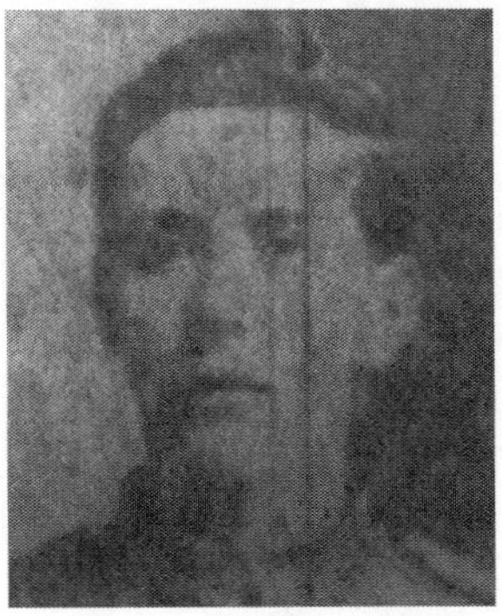

41418 Private
James SLEATOR

14698 Private
Joshua SLOAN

41279 Private
James SMITON

42474 Private
Isaac SMYTH

41192 Private
George STEWART

13527 Regimental
Sergeant Major
Albert STILWELL

14694 Sergeant
Thomas STRINGER

14687 Private
Richard STEWART

14704 Lance Corporal
William STRINGER

41213 Private
Robert THOMPSON

21185 Private
William TIGHE

15871 Private
Thomas Joseph TRUEMAN

17517 Regimental
Sergeant Major
Edward George TUCK

14196 Private
Thomas TROUGHTON

18564 Private
Joseph VENNARD

17397 Regimental
Sergeant Major
Charles Henry TURNER MC

14740 Company
Sergeant Major
Abraham VENARD MM

42066 Private
John William Bannister
WAKEFIELD

14812 Sergeant
William WARREN

19889 Private
David WATSON

41140 Private
Robert WEIR

9428 Regimental
Sergeant Major
George Alfred WILLIAMS MM

41501 Private
Clarence WILSON

43389 Private
Joseph WOOLF

18609 Sergeant
Richard John WOLFE MM

PATEMAN Private Rupert Stanley 45735. Born in 1891 at Peckham, London. [Enlisted 10 December 1915 into The London Regiment (6827). Posted to the 1/24th (County of London) Battalion, The London Regiment (The Queen's).] To France and joined 36 Infantry Base Depot 29 March 1918. Transferred to Princess Victoria's (Royal Irish Fusiliers) 2 April 1918 (renumbered 45735) and joined the 9th (North Irish Horse) Battalion 4 April 1918. **Wounded**. Discharged as no longer physically fit for war service due to wounds 13 May 1919. Silver War Badge, number B234839. Died at Southend-on-Sea in 1968.

PATTERSON Private David 25184. From Ballylintagh, Hillsborough, County Down. Enlisted in November 1916. Posted to the 9th (Service) Battalion. 'C' Company. **Wounded** by a gunshot to the right leg during a raid at Spanbroekmolen 4 June 1917. Believed **wounded** in the period 21-28 March 1918 during the retreat from St Quentin. Discharged as no longer physically fit for war service due to wounds 27 August 1919. Silver War Badge, number B305340. His brother, Private Robert James Patterson, was wounded serving with the Australian Imperial Force. His brother, William Morris Patterson, was wounded serving with the Canadian Infantry.

PATTERSON Private John 27634. Enlisted 24 May 1917. Posted to the 9th (North Irish Horse) Battalion. **Wounded**. Discharged as no longer physically fit for war service due to wounds 18 July 1918, aged 21. Silver War Badge, number 425700.

PATTERSON Private Joseph 18548. Enlisted into the 9th (Service) Battalion in April 1915. To France with 36th (Ulster) Division in October 1915. 'A' Company. **Wounded** during the Battle of Messines and to hospital 9 June 1917. Transferred to the Class Z Reserve 27 February 1919. 1914-15 Star.

PATTERSON Private Joseph 41134. [Enlisted 26 October 1914 into the Service Squadron, 6th (Inniskilling) Dragoons (UD/64). To France with 36th (Ulster) Division in October 1915. Served with 2nd North Irish Horse, X Corps Cavalry Regiment.] Joined the renamed 9th (North Irish Horse) Battalion from 36 Infantry Base Depot and transferred to Princess Victoria's (Royal Irish Fusiliers) in September/October 1917 (renumbered 41134). Discharged as no longer physically fit for war service due to sickness 17 January 1919. Silver War Badge, number B84701. 1914-15 Star.

PATTERSON Private Richard George Graham 14596. Born in 1893 at Boyle, County Roscommon. From Richhill, County Armagh. Enlisted September 1914. To France with 36th (Ulster) Division in October 1915. 'B' Company. **Missing** at the Battle of Langemarck 16 August 1917 and later declared **killed in action** on that date. 1914-15 Star.

PATTERSON Corporal Robert 41480. [Enlisted 19 January 1915 into the North Irish Horse (1408). To France with 'F' Squadron in 33rd Division 17 November 1915. Served with 2nd North Irish Horse, X Corps Cavalry Regiment.] Joined the renamed 9th (North Irish Horse) Battalion from 36 Infantry Base Depot and transferred to Princess Victoria's (Royal Irish Fusiliers) in September/October 1917 (renumbered 41480). 'C' Company. **Wounded** during the retreat from St Quentin 21-28 March 1918. Discharged as no longer physically fit for war service due to wounds 15 November 1918. Silver War Badge, number B44338. 1914-15 Star.

PATTERSON Private Robert Niven 17134. [Enlisted 16 November 1914. To France 27 July 1915 and joined the 1st Battalion.] Posted to the 9th (Service) Battalion. 'D' Company. **Missing** in the period 21-28 March 1918 during the retreat from St Quentin believed **captured**. Discharged as no longer physically fit for war service due to wounds 14 April 1919. Silver War Badge, number B211237. 1914-15 Star.

PATTERSON Private Thomas 14612. Born in 1874 at Seagoe, County Armagh. Enlisted 31 January 1893 as a regular soldier with 1st Battalion, The Royal Irish Rifles (3819). Sentenced to ten days imprisonment for absence 5 March 1894. Served in Malta from March to November 1894. Served in India from November 1894 to March 1905. Transferred to Section D Army Reserve 20 May 1905. Discharged from Section D Army Reserve 19 May 1909. A weaver. Armagh Regiment, Ulster Volunteer Force. Enlisted September 1914. To France with 36th (Ulster) Division in October 1915. 'C' Company. **Wounded** during the attack at Hamel 1 July 1916 and evacuated to hospital in England. Joined the 10th (Reserve) Battalion 11 September 1916. Joined the 3rd (Reserve) Battalion 10 March 1917. Posted to the 2nd Garrison Battalion in Salonika 5 May 1917. [Transferred to The King's (Liverpool Regiment) (90064) 17 August 1917.] Transferred to the Class Z Reserve 29 March 1919. 1914-15 Star.

PATTERSON Private William 14614 & 7040582. Born at Tullyallen, County Armagh. A linen weaver. Enlisted September 1914. To France with 36th (Ulster) Division in October 1915. 1914-15 Star. Re-enlisted on 9 January 1919 for Regular Army service with Princess Victoria's (Royal Irish Fusiliers) (renumbered 7040582). Served with the 1st Battalion in Persia and Mesopotamia in 1919/20. General Service Medal 1918-1962 with clasps 'Iraq' & 'NW Persia'. Served with the 1st Battalion in Egypt from June 1921 until 17 December 1921. Discharged 31 March 1922 on the termination of his period of engagement. Returned to live in Glenanne, County Armagh.

PATTERSON Private William 18610. Born at Hillsborough, County Down. From Park Road, Portadown, County Armagh. Enlisted into the 9th (Service) Battalion in April 1915. To France with 36th (Ulster) Division in October 1915. **Killed in action** during the attack at Hamel 1 July 1916. 1914-15 Star.

PATTERSON Private William James 41336. [Enlisted in September 1916 into the North Irish Horse (2269). Served with 2nd North Irish Horse, X Corps Cavalry Regiment.] Joined the renamed 9th (North Irish Horse) Battalion from 36 Infantry Base Depot and transferred to Princess Victoria's (Royal Irish Fusiliers) in September/October 1917 (renumbered 41336).

PATTISON Private John 6313. Born in 1887 at Ballymoney, County Antrim. Lived in Greenock, Scotland. [Enlisted in late-1914 into Princess Victoria's (Royal Irish Fusiliers) Special Reserve. Mobilised on 24 November 1914. To France 1 February 1915 and joined the 2nd Battalion. Evacuated to hospital in England and treated at 1st Western General Hospital, Fazackerley, Liverpool. Joined the 3rd (Reserve) Battalion 23 October 1916.] To 36 Infantry Base Depot, France 9 December 1916 and joined the 9th (Service) Battalion 12 December 1916. 'B' Company. Sentenced to seven days Field Punishment Number 1 for damaging government property. **Missing** at the Battle of Langemarck 16 August 1917 and later declared **killed in action** on that date. 1914-15 Star.

PATTON Private George 14618. From West Street, Portadown, County Armagh. Enlisted September 1914. To France with 36th (Ulster) Division in October 1915. **Killed in action** during the attack at Hamel 1 July 1916, aged 42. 1914-15 Star.

PATTON Lance Corporal William Andrews 41259. [Enlisted in September 1914 into the North Irish Horse (1196). To France 18 December 1914. Served with 2nd North Irish Horse, X Corps Cavalry Regiment.] Joined the renamed 9th (North Irish Horse) Battalion from 36 Infantry Base Depot and transferred to Princess Victoria's (Royal Irish Fusiliers) in September/October 1917 (renumbered 41259). **Captured**. Transferred to the Class Z Reserve 10 April 1919. 1914-15 Star.

PATTON Private William Lockhart 23314. Born at Belfast in 1897. Enlisted 26 November 1915 and joined the 10th (Reserve) Battalion. To France 26 October 1916 and joined the 9th (Service) Battalion. 'B' Company. **Wounded** at the Battle of Langemarck 16 August 1917. [Transferred to the Army Service Corps (renumbered S/405651) 9 February 1918 as a clerk.] Discharged as no longer physically fit for war service due to wounds 7 June 1918, aged 21. Silver War Badge, number 414285.

PAUL MM Private Joshua 41355. Born 1889. A farmer's son from Crew, Maghera, County Londonderry. [Enlisted in March 1914 into the North Irish Horse (922). To France 17 August 1914 with 'A' Squadron as GHQ Troops. Served with 2nd North Irish Horse, X Corps Cavalry Regiment.] Joined the renamed 9th (North Irish Horse) Battalion from 36 Infantry Base Depot and transferred to Princess Victoria's (Royal Irish Fusiliers) in September/October 1917 (renumbered 41355). **MM** – Bailleul 24 August 1918. 1914 Star.

PAWSEY Private Napier 40185. Born in 1880 at Stowmarket, Suffolk. [Enlisted into The Bedfordshire Regiment (47885). Transferred to Princess Victoria's (Royal Irish Fusiliers) in November 1915 and joined the 5th (Service) Battalion in 31st Brigade, 10th (Irish) Division in the Mediterranean Expeditionary Force.] Re-enlisted or transferred in December 1916 (renumbered 40185) and joined the 9th (Service) Battalion. **Deserted**. Tried at Field General Court Martial on 13 May 1918 charged with *'when on active service* ***deserting*** *His Majesty's service'*; found guilty and sentenced to two years imprisonment with hard labour. Died in Suffolk 29 November 1948, aged 68.

PEACOCK Lance Corporal James 20361. Enlisted 7 May 1915 and joined the 9th (Service) Battalion with the draft of men from The Royal Inniskilling Fusiliers who transferred to Princess

Victoria's (Royal Irish Fusiliers) on 30 June 1915. To France with 36th (Ulster) Division in October 1915. **Wounded** during the attack at Hamel 1 July 1916. Unfit to plead at Field General Court Martial on 21 February 1918 when charged with an unknown act *'to the prejudice and good order of military discipline'* and with *'wilfully injuring himself with intent thereby to render himself unfit for service'*. Discharged as no longer physically fit for war service due to sickness 30 August 1918, aged 26. Silver War Badge, number 445719. 1914-15 Star.

PEARCE Corporal Frank Lawrence 42187. [Enlisted into the Army Service Corps (S4/064505). To France 10 March 1915. Served with 52nd Field Bakery.] Transferred to Princess Victoria's (Royal Irish Fusiliers) 8 May 1918 (renumbered 42187) and joined the 9th (North Irish Horse) Battalion. Transferred to the Class Z Reserve. 1914-15 Star.

PEARSON Private David 14609. Born in 1880. From Clonroot, County Armagh. Enlisted September 1914. Discharged as not being likely to become an efficient soldier in that he was considered medically unfit for service 3 October 1914.

PEARSON Private Frederick 17586 & 22971. Born 22 August 1897 at Bamber Bridge, Lancashire. Lived at Rockmacraney, County Armagh. Enlisted into the 9th (Service) Battalion 11 January 1915. Discharged as not being likely to become an efficient soldier in that he was considered medically unfit for service (albuminuria) 13 January 1915. Re-enlisted in November 1915 (numbered 22971). Posted to the 9th (Service) Battalion. 'D' Company. **Wounded** at the Battle of Langemarck 16 August 1917. [Transferred to the Labour Corps (renumbered 637585) and Army Ordnance Corps (renumbered S/12285).]

PEARSON Private George 14597. Born in 1886 at Derryadd, Portadown, County Armagh. A weaver. Enlisted September 1914. Discharged as not being likely to become an efficient soldier in that he was considered medically unfit for service (missing all molars) 10 October 1914.

PEARSON Private John 5901. [Enlisted into Princess Victoria's (Royal Irish Fusiliers) Special Reserve. To France with the 1st Battalion 22 August 1914. Posted to the 7th/8th (Service) Battalion in 49th Brigade, 16th (Irish) Division.] Joined the 9th (North Irish Horse) Battalion when the 7th/8th (Service) Battalion was disbanded in February 1918. 1914 Star.

PEARSON Private John A 18549. From Richhill, County Armagh. Enlisted into the 9th (Service) Battalion in April 1915. To France with 36th (Ulster) Division in October 1915. 'C' Company. Attached to 108th Brigade Machine Gun Company in June 1916. Detached to the Base Depot and did not take part in the attack at Hamel on 1 July 1916. **Wounded** at the Battle of Langemarck 16 August 1917. [Transferred to the Corps of Royal Engineers (renumbered WR/332527).] 1914-15 Star.

PEARSON Private Robert 43225. [Enlisted into The Sherwood Foresters (Nottinghamshire and Derbyshire Regiment) (41824).] Transferred to Princess Victoria's (Royal Irish Fusiliers) 31 August 1916 (renumbered 43225) having joined the 9th (Service) Battalion on 8 August 1916. [Transferred to the Tank Corps (renumbered 304855) 28 December 1917 and posted for training to the Tank Corps Depot, at Bovington near Wareham, Dorset.]

PEARSON Private Victor 14607. Enlisted September 1914. Did not serve overseas with 36th (Ulster) Division. Discharged as no longer physically fit for war service due to sickness 3 May 1916, aged 21. Silver War Badge, number 508792.

PEDLOW Corporal Arthur William 22762. Born in 1894 at Lurgan, County Armagh. Enlisted 8 November 1915. Posted to the 9th (Service) Battalion. 'D' Company. **Wounded** at the Battle of Langemarck 16 August 1917. Discharged as no longer physically fit for war service due to wounds 1 October 1918, aged 23. Silver War Badge, number B22502.

PEERS MM Private Archibald 42244. Born in 1897. From West Kirby, Cheshire. [Enlisted into the Army Service Corps (T4/039520). To France 22 September 1915.] Transferred to Princess Victoria's (Royal Irish Fusiliers) 8 May 1918 (renumbered 42244) and joined the 9th (North Irish Horse) Battalion. **MM** – Bailleul 24 August 1918. [Transferred to the Royal Army Service Corps (renumbered MR/47801).] 1914-15 Star. Transferred to the Class Z Reserve. Died at Wirral, Cheshire 1960, aged 63.

PEMBERTON Private Francis Alexander 42243. Born in 1885 at London. [Enlisted into the Army Service Corps (T4/070493 – Driver). Served with 39th Division Train.] Transferred to Princess

Victoria's (Royal Irish Fusiliers) 8 May 1918 (renumbered 42243) and joined the 9th (North Irish Horse) Battalion. Died at Surrey in 1953, aged 68.

PENNELL Private George 42531. Born in 1899 at Crewe, Cheshire. [Enlisted on 16 May 1918 at Belfast into The Royal Irish Rifles (22669) and joined the 3rd (Reserve) Battalion.] To France 7 September 1918 and joined 'A' Infantry Base Depot. Transferred to Princess Victoria's (Royal Irish Fusiliers) 14 September 1918 (renumbered 42531) and joined the 9th (North Irish Horse) Battalion 22 September 1918. 'C' Company. **Killed in action** during the advance to Anseghem 25 October 1918, aged 19.

PENTLAND Sergeant Joshua 16424. Born in 1890 at Tandragee, County Armagh. Armagh Regiment, Ulster Volunteer Force. A linen weaver. Enlisted into the 9th (Service) Battalion in November 1914. To France with 36th (Ulster) Division in October 1915. Platoon Sergeant to Lieutenant W G Boyd on 16 August 1917. **Captured** 27 March 1918 during the retreat from St Quentin, serving in 'B' Company. Transferred to the Class Z Reserve 4 April 1919. 1914-15 Star. Served with the Ulster Special Constabulary at Poyntzpass, Tyrones Ditches, Tandragee and Clare, County Armagh. Later lived in the United States, returning to Northern Ireland in 1934. Served with the Ulster Home Guard in the Second World War. Died in 1974, aged 84.

PENTLAND Private Richard John 14615. Born in 1889 at Portadown, County Armagh. A linen weaver. Enlisted September 1914. To France with 36th (Ulster) Division in October 1915. 'B' Company. **Wounded** in the right arm during the attack at Hamel 1 July 1916. **Wounded** at the Battle of Langemarck 16 August 1917 when shot in the chest. Discharged as no longer physically fit for war service due to wounds 24 July 1918, aged 28. Silver War Badge, number 379057. 1914-15 Star. Died as a result of his wounds after the war and is commemorated on Portadown War Memorial; his date of death cannot be confirmed.

PENTLAND Private William Henry 17842. Born in 1870 at Aldershot, Hampshire, the son of a regular soldier, Private George A Pentland, who served with the 2nd Battalion, The Cheshire Regiment (on discharge his father returned with his family to Portadown, County Armagh). Enlisted into the 9th (Service) Battalion in January 1915. To France with 36th (Ulster) Division in October 1915. 'C' Company. Lewis gun ammunition carrier at Hamel attack. **Killed in action** during the attack at Hamel 1 July 1916, aged 46. 1914-15 Star.

PEPPER Private Andrew 41427. Born in 1885 at Banbridge, County Down. Lived at Belfast. An upholsterer. [Enlisted 6 November 1915 into the North Irish Horse (1797). To France 29 June 1916. To hospital with fever 7-19 August 1916. Served with 2nd North Irish Horse, X Corps Cavalry Regiment.] Joined the renamed 9th (North Irish Horse) Battalion from 36 Infantry Base Depot and transferred to Princess Victoria's (Royal Irish Fusiliers) in September/October 1917 (renumbered 41427). **Killed in action** on the night of 11/12 August 1918 during the raid at Shoddy Farm, Meulenhouck, aged 34. His death was recorded as being on 12 August 1918.

PERCY Private Robert 19891. From Moira, County Down. A weaver. Enlisted into the 9th (Service) Battalion 19 May 1915. To France with 36th (Ulster) Division in October 1915. 'C' Company. To the field ambulance sick (scabies) March 1916. Battalion bomb carrier during the attack at Hamel 1 July 1916. **Wounded** by a gunshot to his left thigh 1 July 1916. Treated at 41st Casualty Clearing Station. Joined 36 Infantry Base Depot 20 July 1917 and was one of the group attached to the 2nd Battalion, The Royal Irish Rifles. Rejoined the 9th (Service) Battalion, Princess Victoria's (Royal Irish Fusiliers) 9 September 1916. To 4th General Hospital sick (gastric ulcer) 17 September 1918 and evacuated to hospital in England. Posted to the 3rd (Reserve) Garrison Battalion at West Hartlepool. Transferred to the Class Z Reserve 3 April 1919.

PERCY Lance Corporal Samuel Ernest 41150. Commissioned into Princess Victoria's (Royal Irish Fusiliers) - see Appendix 5.

PERERA Private William 45814. Born in 1899 at Colombo, Ceylon. [Enlisted 26 February 1917 and joined the 110th Training Reserve Battalion (70795). Transferred to The Queen's (Royal West Surrey Regiment) (renumbered 66599) 15 November 1917. Posted to 1/22nd (County of London) Battalion, The London Regiment (The Queen's).] To France and joined 36 Infantry Base Depot 29 March 1918. Transferred to Princess Victoria's (Royal Irish Fusiliers) 2 April 1918 (renumbered 45814) and joined the 9th (North Irish Horse) Battalion 4 April 1918. **Wounded** by shell splinters 18 April 1918 during in the actions between Wulverghem and Kemmel. Treated at 3rd Canadian

General Hospital. Rejoined the 9th (North Irish Horse) Battalion 13 May 1918. To hospital sick (influenza) 29 June 1918. Rejoined the 9th (North Irish Horse) Battalion October 1918. Transferred to 5th (Service) Battalion, The Royal Irish Regiment (Pioneers) in the Light Division in the British Army of the Rhine in March/June 1919 (renumbered 35549). Re-enlisted 16 April 1919 for Regular Army service with The Royal Irish Regiment (renumbered 7110732). Posted to The Royal Irish Regiment Depot 3 August 1919. Posted to the 2nd Battalion, The Royal Irish Regiment 10 November 1919 and served in India from 13 February 1920. Discharged, his service no longer required, 3 September 1920.

PERKINS Private Ernest 42242. Born in 1881 at Egginton, Burton-on-Trent, Derbyshire. [Enlisted 24 January 1901 as a regular soldier in the Army Service Corps (T/17874 – Driver). Transferred to the Section A Army Reserve 23 January 1909. Transferred to the Section B Army Reserve 23 January 1910. Transferred to the Section D Army Reserve 24 January 1913. Mobilised from the Army Reserve 5 August 1914 and to France 19 August 1914 with 1st Reserve Park.] Transferred to Princess Victoria's (Royal Irish Fusiliers) 8 May 1918 (renumbered 42242) and joined the 9th (North Irish Horse) Battalion. **Wounded** by gunshots to the right thigh and left arm in the period 21-28 March 1918 during the retreat from St Quentin. Evacuated to hospital in England. Discharged as no longer physically fit for war service due to wounds 19 March 1919. Silver War Badge, number B167350. 1914 Star.

PETERS Frederick Richmond Strafford 41578. Born 17 April 1889 at Dublin. [Enlisted 5 November 1914 into the North Irish Horse (1341). Served with 2nd North Irish Horse, X Corps Cavalry Regiment.] Joined the renamed 9th (North Irish Horse) Battalion from 36 Infantry Base Depot and transferred to Princess Victoria's (Royal Irish Fusiliers) in September/October 1917 (renumbered 41578). **Wounded**. [Transferred to the Army Pay Corps (renumbered 22532).] Discharged as no longer physically fit for war service due to wounds 19 February 1919. Silver War Badge, number B205744.

PETTICREW Lance Corporal David John 41315. [Enlisted in March 1915 into the North Irish Horse (1463). To France 22 September 1915. Served with 2nd North Irish Horse, X Corps Cavalry Regiment.] Joined the renamed 9th (North Irish Horse) Battalion from 36 Infantry Base Depot and transferred to Princess Victoria's (Royal Irish Fusiliers) in September/October 1917 (renumbered 41315). Transferred to the Class Z Reserve 17 June 1919. 1914-15 Star.

PETTITT Private Frank 40183. Enlisted in December 1916. Posted to the 9th (Service) Battalion. 'B' Company. **Missing** in the period 21-28 March 1918 during the retreat from St Quentin believed **captured**.

PETTY Private William Joseph 41406. Born in 1891 at Belfast. A clerk. [Enlisted 23 November 1915 into the North Irish Horse (1944). Lance Corporal 10 December 1915. Reverted to Private at own request 4 April 1916. To France 2 August 1916. Served with 2nd North Irish Horse, X Corps Cavalry Regiment.] Joined the renamed 9th (North Irish Horse) Battalion from 36 Infantry Base Depot and transferred to Princess Victoria's (Royal Irish Fusiliers) in September/October 1917 (renumbered 41406). **Missing** 22 November 1917 at Moeuvres and later declared as **killed in action** on that date, aged 26.

PHELPS Private William 42119. [Enlisted into the Army Veterinary Corps (29065).] Transferred to Princess Victoria's (Royal Irish Fusiliers) 8 May 1918 (renumbered 42119) and joined the 9th (North Irish Horse) Battalion.

PHILLIPS Private Albert Geoffrey 45744. Born in 1890. A teacher. [Enlisted 12 January 1916 into The London Regiment (5503). To France 14 July 1916 and posted to the 1/24th (County of London) Battalion, The London Regiment (The Queen's). To hospital sick (influenza) 27 January 1917 and evacuated to hospital in England. Treated at Norfolk War Hospital, Thorpe. Attended the Signal School, Dunstable from November 1917 to March 1918. Lance Corporal 1 November 1917.] To France and joined 36 Infantry Base Depot 30 March 1918. Reverted to Private. Transferred to Princess Victoria's (Royal Irish Fusiliers) 2 April 1918 (renumbered 45744) and joined the 9th (North Irish Horse) Battalion 4 April 1918. **Wounded** by a gunshot to the back 11 April 1918 in the actions between Wulverghem and Kemmel. Treated at 32nd Stationary Hospital. To 'A' Infantry Base Depot 12 July 1918. Rejoined the 9th (North Irish Horse) Battalion 4 August 1918. 'D' Company. **Wounded** by gunshots to the legs at Courtrai 16 October 1918. Treated at 14th Stationary Hospital and rejoined the 9th (North Irish Horse) Battalion. To hospital sick (scarlet fever) 24 October 1918 and evacuated to hospital in England. Transferred to the Class Z Reserve 4 March 1919.

PHILLIPS Private Edward George 43364. Born at Hoxton, Middlesex. From Bethnal Green, London. [Enlisted into The London Regiment (6421). Posted to the 1/7th (City of London) Battalion, The London Regiment.] Attached to the 9th (Service) Battalion, Princess Victoria's (Royal Irish Fusiliers) 26 November 1916. Discharged from the Territorial Force, re-enlisted and transferred to Princess Victoria's (Royal Irish Fusiliers) in March/April 1917 (renumbered 43364). **Wounded** in the period 11-18 April 1918 in the actions between Wulverghem and Kemmel and **died of wounds** 25 April 1918, aged 34.

PHILLIPS Private John 18246. From Park Road, Portadown, County Armagh. Enlisted into the 9th (Service) Battalion in February 1915. To France with 36th (Ulster) Division in October 1915. 'C' Company. **Killed in action** during the attack at Hamel 1 July 1916. 1914-15 Star.

PHILLIPS Private Thomas Patrick 42552. [Enlisted into The Royal Irish Rifles (22092).] Transferred at the Base Depot to Princess Victoria's (Royal Irish Fusiliers) 14 September 1918 (renumbered 42552) and joined the 9th (North Irish Horse) Battalion 22 September 1918. Emigrated to Providence, Rhode Island, United States.

PHILPOTT Sergeant Thomas 17651. Born in 1888 at Milford, County Armagh. Enlisted into the 9th (Service) Battalion in December 1914/January 1915. To France with 36th (Ulster) Division in October 1915. 'B' Company. **Wounded** at the Battle of Langemarck 16 August 1917. 1914-15 Star.

PICKERING Private George William 43214. [Enlisted into The Sherwood Foresters (Nottinghamshire and Derbyshire Regiment).] Transferred to Princess Victoria's (Royal Irish Fusiliers) 31 August 1916 having joined the 9th (Service) Battalion on 8 August 1916 (renumbered 43214). 'A' Company. Believed **wounded** in the period 21-28 March 1918 during the retreat from St Quentin. [Transferred to 5th (Service) Battalion, The Royal Irish Regiment (Pioneers) in the Light Division in the British Army of the Rhine in March/June 1919 (renumbered 41352).]

PICKERING Private William 20359. From Glasgow. Enlisted in May/June 1915 and joined the 9th (Service) Battalion with the draft of men from The Royal Inniskilling Fusiliers who transferred to Princess Victoria's (Royal Irish Fusiliers) on 30 June 1915. To France with 36th (Ulster) Division in October 1915. 'A' Company. **Wounded** during the attack at Hamel 1 July 1916. **Wounded** during the retreat from St Quentin 21-28 March 1918. Transferred to the Class Z Reserve. 1914-15 Star.

PICKERING Private William 25240. [Enlisted into the Army Service Corps (RTS/3493). To France 20 August 1914. Served with 1st Remount Depot. Transferred to Princess Victoria's (Royal Irish Fusiliers) 8 May 1916 and joined the 1st Battalion.] Posted to the 9th (North Irish Horse) Battalion.

PIERPOINT Private Samuel 43254. Born in 1895. From Carlton, Nottinghamshire. A railwayman with the Great Northern Railway. [Enlisted 11 February 1915 and joined the 3rd (Reserve) Battalion, The Sherwood Foresters (Nottinghamshire and Derbyshire Regiment) (23195). Posted to the 9th (Service) Battalion, The Sherwood Foresters (Nottinghamshire and Derbyshire Regiment) 23 August 1915 and joined the Mediterranean Expeditionary Force 6 September 1915. Evacuated to hospital in England (frostbite) 24 January 1916. Posted to the 3rd (Reserve) Battalion, The Sherwood Foresters (Nottinghamshire and Derbyshire Regiment) 19 April 1916.] Transferred to Princess Victoria's (Royal Irish Fusiliers) 31 August 1916 (renumbered 43254) having joined the 9th (Service) Battalion on 8 August 1916. [Transferred to the Tank Corps (renumbered 304853) 28 December 1917 and posted for training to the Tank Corps Depot, at Bovington near Wareham, Dorset. Posted to the 17th Battalion, Tank Corps 8 January 1918 and to France 27 April 1918 when it converted to 17th (Armoured Car) Battalion.] Transferred to the Class Z Reserve 30 May 1919. 1914-15 Star. His brother, Private Ernest Pierpoint, served with the 1st Battalion, The Bedfordshire Regiment (wounded) and the Corps of Royal Engineers.

PIERSON Private Henry 16432. From Tandragee, County Armagh. A weaver. Enlisted into the 9th (Service) Battalion in November 1914. To France with 36th (Ulster) Division in October 1915. 1914-15 Star.

PIERSON Private James 14619. Born in 1889 at Portadown, County Armagh. Armagh Regiment, Ulster Volunteer Force. Enlisted September 1914. To France with 36th (Ulster) Division in October 1915. **Wounded** at Hamel by a shrapnel to the arm and chest on 31 May 1916. Evacuated to hospital in England then joined the 10th (Reserve) Battalion 15 June 1916. Posted to the 3rd

(Reserve) Battalion 22 May 1918. [Transferred to the Labour Corps (renumbered 562426) 18 August 1918. Served with 613th Labour Company.] 1914-15 Star. Transferred to the Class Z Reserve 2 April 1919.

PILBEAM Private George 40186. Enlisted, re-enlisted or transferred to Princess Victoria's (Royal Irish Fusiliers) in December 1916. Posted to the 9th (Service) Battalion.

PILKINGTON Private William 45817. From Camberwell, London. [Enlisted into The Queen's (Royal West Surrey Regiment) (60613). Posted to 1/22nd (County of London) Battalion, The London Regiment (The Queen's).] To France and joined 36 Infantry Base Depot 29 March 1918. Transferred to Princess Victoria's (Royal Irish Fusiliers) 2 April 1918 (renumbered 45817) and joined the 9th (North Irish Horse) Battalion 4 April 1918. **Missing** in the period 11-18 April 1918 in the actions between Wulverghem and Kemmel; subsequently declared **killed in action** 19 April 1918, aged 20.

PINKERTON Private John 41354. [Enlisted in early-1917 into the North Irish Horse (2358). Served with 2nd North Irish Horse, X Corps Cavalry Regiment.] Joined the renamed 9th (North Irish Horse) Battalion from 36 Infantry Base Depot and transferred to Princess Victoria's (Royal Irish Fusiliers) in September/October 1917 (renumbered 41354).

PINKERTON Private Samuel 41133. From Londonderry. [Enlisted in November 1914 into the Service Squadron, 6th (Inniskilling) Dragoons (UD/158). To France with 36th (Ulster) Division in October 1915. Served with 2nd North Irish Horse, X Corps Cavalry Regiment.] Joined the renamed 9th (North Irish Horse) Battalion from 36 Infantry Base Depot and transferred to Princess Victoria's (Royal Irish Fusiliers) in September/October 1917 (renumbered 41133). **Killed in action** during the attack south of Wulverghem 4 September 1918. 1914-15 Star.

PIPER Lance Corporal Herbert Alfred 43454. Born in 1893 at St Olave (Southwark), London. [Enlisted into The London Regiment (2002). To France 15 March 1915 and joined the 1/24th (County of London) Battalion, The London Regiment (The Queen's).] To France and joined 36 Infantry Base Depot 29 March 1918. Transferred to Princess Victoria's (Royal Irish Fusiliers) 2 April 1918 (renumbered 43454) and joined the 9th (North Irish Horse) Battalion 4 April 1918. Discharged 22 February 1919. 1914-15 Star.

PLANT Private Gordon 25108. [Enlisted into the Army Service Corps (3337). To France 20 August 1914. Served with 1st Remount Depot. Transferred to Princess Victoria's (Royal Irish Fusiliers) in May 1916 (renumbered 25108) joined the 7th/8th (Service) Battalion in 49th Brigade, 16th (Irish) Division.] Joined the 9th (North Irish Horse) Battalion when the 7th/8th (Service) Battalion was disbanded in February 1918. 1914 Star.

PLEASANCE Private Wilfred 43317. Commissioned into The Royal Fusiliers (City of London Regiment) - see Appendix 5.

PLESTED Corporal Johnny Jacobs 42166. Born 29 August 1884 at Buckinghamshire. [Enlisted into the Army Service Corps (S4/84630). To France 29 April 1915 and served with 54th and 11th Field Bakeries.] Transferred to Princess Victoria's (Royal Irish Fusiliers) 8 May 1918 (renumbered 42166) and joined the 9th (North Irish Horse) Battalion. Transferred to the Class Z Reserve. 1914-15 Star. Died in 1956, aged 72.

PLUNKETT Private Joseph 15041. [Enlisted in September 1914 into the 5th (Service) Battalion in 31st Brigade, 10th (Irish) Division. Embarked with the Mediterranean Expeditionary Force July 1915.] Posted to the 9th (Service) Battalion. 'B' Company. **Wounded** at the Battle of Langemarck 16 August 1917. Believed **wounded** in the period 21-28 March 1918 during the retreat from St Quentin. [Transferred to the Labour Corps (renumbered 575256).] 1914-15 Star.

POINTZ Private William 18675. See Private William Poyntz below.

POLI Private Frederick 40155. Born 1 October 1888 at Leicester. [Enlisted in December 1916 and joined the 7th/8th (Service) Battalion in 49th Brigade, 16th (Irish) Division.] Joined the 9th (North Irish Horse) Battalion when the 7th/8th (Service) Battalion was disbanded in February 1918. 'A' Company. **Missing** in the period 21-28 March 1918 during the retreat from St Quentin believed **captured**. Died at Leicester in 1975, aged 86.

POLLOCK Sergeant David 14606. From Portadown, County Armagh. A carpenter. Enlisted September 1914. To France with 36th (Ulster) Division in October 1915. 'B' Company. Rated as one of the best Sergeants in the 9th (Service) Battalion. **Wounded** in the shoulder by shellfire 4 May

1916. Discharged as no longer physically fit for war service due to wounds 15 October 1917, aged 26. Silver War Badge, number 258764. 1914-15 Star.

POLLOCK Private James 42467. [A regular soldier or mobilised Army Reservist with the 2nd Battalion, The Royal Irish Rifles (2333). To France December 1914.] Transferred at the Base Depot to Princess Victoria's (Royal Irish Fusiliers) 14 September 1918 and joined the 9th (North Irish Horse) Battalion 22 September 1918. **Wounded** at Anseghem on 25/26 October 1918 and **died of wounds** 7 December 1918 at 10th Stationary Hospital at Tourcoing.

POLLOCK Private Thomas 41277. From Donaghadee, County Down. [Enlisted in October 1915 into the North Irish Horse (1743). Served with 2nd North Irish Horse, X Corps Cavalry Regiment.] Joined the renamed 9th (North Irish Horse) Battalion from 36 Infantry Base Depot and transferred to Princess Victoria's (Royal Irish Fusiliers) in September/October 1917 (renumbered 41277). 'C' Company. **Captured** in the period 21-28 March 1918 during the retreat from St Quentin.

POLLOCK Lance Corporal Walter 41440. [Enlisted in July 1916 into the North Irish Horse (2225). Served with 2nd North Irish Horse, X Corps Cavalry Regiment.] Joined the renamed 9th (North Irish Horse) Battalion from 36 Infantry Base Depot and transferred to Princess Victoria's (Royal Irish Fusiliers) in September/October 1917 (renumbered 41440).

POOLE Private Robert 22630. From Portadown, County Armagh. Enlisted in November 1915. Posted to the 9th (Service) Battalion. **Wounded** during the attack at Hamel 1 July 1916. [Posted to the 2nd Garrison Battalion in Salonika.]

POOLMAN Private Percy Charles 42263. Born in 1891 at Dorney, Windsor. A farm labourer. [Enlisted 3 May 1909 into the Army Service Corps (T/27520). Transferred to the Army Reserve 2 May 1911. Mobilised 5 August 1914. To France with 3rd Division Train 13 August 1914. To hospital sick (scabies) July 1915. Posted to 10th Reserve Park, Army Service Corps 11 August 1916. To hospital in August 1916 with impetigo.] To 'A' Infantry Base Depot 6 May 1918. Transferred to Princess Victoria's (Royal Irish Fusiliers) 8 May 1918 (renumbered 42263) and joined the 9th (North Irish Horse) Battalion 26 June 1918. **Missing** during the attack at Vijfwegen on 30 September or 1 October 1918; recorded as **killed in action** on 3 October 1918, aged 27. 1914 Star.

POPE Lance Corporal Edward 20317. Enlisted in May/June 1915 and joined the 9th (Service) Battalion with the draft of men from The Royal Inniskilling Fusiliers who transferred to Princess Victoria's (Royal Irish Fusiliers) on 30 June 1915. To France with 36th (Ulster) Division in October 1915. Discharged as no longer physically fit for war service 14 December 1918. 1914-15 Star.

PORTER Private David 23965. From Portadown, County Armagh. Enlisted 20 November 1915. Posted to the 9th (Service) Battalion. 'B' Company. **Wounded** at the Battle of Langemarck 16 August 1917. Discharged as no longer physically fit for war service due to wounds 18 June 1918, aged 21. Silver War Badge, number 387952.

PORTER Sergeant John 14605. Enlisted September 1914. To France with 36th (Ulster) Division in October 1915. 'B' Company. **Missing** in the period 21-28 March 1918 during the retreat from St Quentin believed **captured**. Sergeant 30 March 1918. Transferred to the Class Z Reserve. 1914-15 Star.

PORTER Sergeant Samuel 14611. Born in 1862. From Glenanne, County Armagh. Enlisted 28 September 1880 as a regular soldier with the 51st (2nd Yorkshire, West Riding, The King's Own Light Infantry) Regiment (2334) (from 1881 the 1st Battalion, The King's Own Light Infantry (South Yorkshire Regiment)). Served in the East Indies from February 1883 to November 1887. Took part in the Burma campaign in 1886-87. India General Service Medal with clasp 'Burma 1885-7'. Transferred to the Section A Army Reserve November 1887 (conduct rated as *'Indifferent - addicted to drink'*). Transferred to the Section D Army Reserve 1892. Discharged from the Army Reserve 27 September 1896. Armagh Regiment, Ulster Volunteer Force. Enlisted September 1914, aged 52, falsifying his age as 46. Corporal 22 September 1914. Lance Sergeant 1 January 1915. Reduced in rank to Corporal for *'when in charge of an escort allowing a soldier under arrest to get drunk'* 17 June 1915. Attached to the 12th (Reserve) Battalion, The Royal Inniskilling Fusiliers 26 June 1915. Posted to the 10th (Reserve) Battalion, Princess Victoria's (Royal Irish Fusiliers) 23 September 1915. Sergeant 7 October 1915. Discharged as no longer physically fit for war service due to sickness (rheumatism) 13 April 1918, aged 56. Silver War Badge, number 343327. Father of Sergeant

Samuel George Porter.

PORTER Sergeant Samuel George 23316. Born in 1897. From Glenanne, County Armagh. Enlisted in November 1915. Posted to the 9th (Service) Battalion. 'A' Company. **Wounded** at the Battle of Langemarck 16 August 1917. Son of Sergeant Samuel Porter.

PORTER Sergeant Valentine Markham 40182. Born 11 November 1877 at York. 'B' Company. Enlisted in December 1916. Posted to the 9th (Service) Battalion. **Missing** in the period 21-28 March 1918 during the retreat from St Quentin believed **captured**. Died at Birmingham 29 November 1957, aged 80.

PORTER Private William 20650. Born in 1896 at Killeshandra, County Cavan. A postman. Enlisted 21 July 1915. To France 3 March 1916 and joined the 9th (Service) Battalion. 'C' Company. **Wounded** by shellfire in the left leg and left arm at Hamel 1 July 1916 and evacuated to hospital in England 17 July 1916. To France 3 March 1917 and rejoined the 9th (Service) Battalion 20 April 1917. 'C' Company. **Captured** at the Battle of Langemarck 16 August 1917. Held at Dulmen Prisoner of War Camp, Westphalia. Transferred to the Class Z Reserve 1 April 1919.

PORTER Lance Corporal William 41633. [Enlisted in November 1914 into the Service Squadron, 6th (Inniskilling) Dragoons (UD/96). To France with 36th (Ulster) Division in October 1915. Served with 2nd North Irish Horse, X Corps Cavalry Regiment.] Joined the renamed 9th (North Irish Horse) Battalion from 36 Infantry Base Depot and transferred to Princess Victoria's (Royal Irish Fusiliers) in September/October 1917 (renumbered 41633). Transferred to the Class Z Reserve 5 February 1919. 1914-15 Star.

POSNETT Private George 41168. [Enlisted in November 1914 into the Service Squadron, 6th (Inniskilling) Dragoons (UD/113). To France with 36th (Ulster) Division in October 1915. Served with 2nd North Irish Horse, X Corps Cavalry Regiment.] Joined the renamed 9th (North Irish Horse) Battalion from 36 Infantry Base Depot and transferred to Princess Victoria's (Royal Irish Fusiliers) in September/October 1917 (renumbered 41168). **Missing** in the period 21-28 March 1918 during the retreat from St Quentin believed **captured**. Transferred to the Class Z Reserve 5 April 1919. 1914-15 Star.

POTTER Corporal Frank 25109. [A regular soldier with the Army Service Corps (RTS/4034). To France 20 August 1914. Served with 1st Remount Depot. Transferred to Princess Victoria's (Royal Irish Fusiliers) in May 1916 joined the 7th/8th (Service) Battalion in 49th Brigade, 16th (Irish) Division.] Joined the 9th (North Irish Horse) Battalion when the 7th/8th (Service) Battalion was disbanded in February 1918. 'D' Company. **Missing** in the period 21-28 March 1918 during the retreat from St Quentin believed **captured**. 1914 Star.

POWELL Private J W 42210. [Enlisted into the Army Service Corps (248192 Driver). To France 29 March 1915.] Transferred to Princess Victoria's (Royal Irish Fusiliers) 8 May 1918 (renumbered 42210) and joined the 9th (North Irish Horse) Battalion. 1914-15 Star.

POWELL Private Joseph 14610. Enlisted September 1914. To France with 36th (Ulster) Division in October 1915. 'C' Company. Detached to the Battalion Transport and did not take part in the attack at Hamel on 1 July 1918. 1914-15 Star. Battalion Colour Guard June 1919.

POWELL Private Lewis J 42275. [Enlisted into the Army Veterinary Corps (14218).] Transferred to Princess Victoria's (Royal Irish Fusiliers) 8 May 1918 (renumbered 42275) and joined the 9th (North Irish Horse) Battalion. [Transferred to 5th (Service) Battalion, The Royal Irish Regiment (Pioneers) in the Light Division in the British Army of the Rhine in March/June 1919 (41354).]

POWER Corporal Stephen 17441. [Enlisted 1 January 1915. To France 6 April 1915 and joined the 2nd Battalion.] Posted to the 9th (Service) Battalion. 'C' Company. Separated from the 9th (North Irish Horse) Battalion in the period 21-28 March 1918 during the retreat from St Quentin; rejoined 6 April 1918. **Wounded**. Discharged as no longer physically fit for war service due to wounds 28 January 1919. Silver War Badge, number B97865. 1914-15 Star.

POYNTER Private Sydney John 42262. Born in 1881 at London. [Enlisted into the Army Service Corps (T4/243247 Driver). Served with 59th Division Train.] Transferred to Princess Victoria's (Royal Irish Fusiliers) 8 May 1918 (renumbered 42262) and joined the 9th (North Irish Horse) Battalion. Died at Battle, Sussex in 1942, aged 60.

POYNTZ Private William 18675. Born 18 February 1867 at Drung, County Cavan. Enlisted into the 9th (Service) Battalion in April 1915. To France with 36th (Ulster) Division in October 1915. **Killed in action** during the attack at Hamel 1 July 1916, aged 49. (The spelling of Poyntz is correct. It was corrected to Pointz on his medal index card. He is commemorated as Pointz on Ireland's Memorial Record.) 1914-15 Star.

PRATT Lance Corporal Thompson 21600. Born in 1895 at Belfast. Enlisted in September 1915. Posted to the 9th (Service) Battalion in mid/late 1916. 'D' Company. **Wounded** at the Battle of Langemarck 16 August 1917. [Posted to the 1st Battalion.]

PRENTER Private Ernest 23298. Born in 1898 at Lurgan, County Armagh. Enlisted in November 1915. Posted to the 9th (Service) Battalion.

PRESCOTT Private William 14620. Enlisted September 1914. To France with 36th (Ulster) Division in October 1915. Transferred to the Class Z Reserve 16 March 1919. 1914-15 Star.

PRESTON Private Thomas 14602. Enlisted September 1914. To France with 36th (Ulster) Division in October 1915. 'D' Company. **Wounded** during the retreat from St Quentin 21-28 March 1918. Discharged as no longer physically fit for war service due to wounds 12 September 1918, aged 31. Silver War Badge, number 449135. 1914-15 Star.

PRICE Private Henry 41409. [Enlisted in October 1914 into the North Irish Horse (1254). To France 1 May 1915. Served with 2nd North Irish Horse, X Corps Cavalry Regiment. **Mention in Despatches**.] Joined the renamed 9th (North Irish Horse) Battalion from 36 Infantry Base Depot and transferred to Princess Victoria's (Royal Irish Fusiliers) in September/October 1917 (renumbered 41409).

PRICE Lance Corporal Patrick 11123. [Enlisted into Princess Victoria's (Royal Irish Fusiliers) as a regular soldier in 1912. To France 26 October 1914 and joined the 1st Battalion. **Wounded** in the left arm and hand in August 1916.] Posted to the 9th (North Irish Horse) Battalion. **Wounded**. Discharged as no longer physically fit for war service due to wounds 24 February 1919. Silver War Badge, number B242938. 1914 Star.

PRICE Private Samuel 41167. Born at Ballymacarrett, County Down. [Enlisted in November 1914 into the Service Squadron, 6th (Inniskilling) Dragoons (UD/118). To France with 36th (Ulster) Division in October 1915. Served with 2nd North Irish Horse, X Corps Cavalry Regiment.] Joined the renamed 9th (North Irish Horse) Battalion from 36 Infantry Base Depot and transferred to Princess Victoria's (Royal Irish Fusiliers) in September/October 1917 (renumbered 41167). **Killed in action** 23 November 1917 at Moeuvres. 1914-15 Star.

PRINCE Private John Thomas 41093. [Enlisted into 6th (Inniskilling) Dragoons (21564). Served with 2nd North Irish Horse, X Corps Cavalry Regiment.] Joined the renamed 9th (North Irish Horse) Battalion from 36 Infantry Base Depot and transferred to Princess Victoria's (Royal Irish Fusiliers) in September/October 1917 (renumbered 41093).

PRITCHARD Lance Corporal Charles Henry 19066. Born in 1894 at Uckington, Shropshire. Worked for his father at Morrells Wood Farm, near Leighton, Shropshire. Enlisted into (or transferred to) Princess Victoria's (Royal Irish Fusiliers) in December 1915. Posted to the 9th (Service) Battalion. 'D' Company. **Wounded** at the Battle of Langemarck 16 August 1917. [Transferred to 5th (Service) Battalion, The Royal Irish Regiment (Pioneers) in the Light Division in the British Army of the Rhine in March/June 1919 (renumbered 41353).] Died at Bridgnorth, Shropshire in 1961, aged 67.

PRITCHARD Private Hugh Owen 25110. [A regular soldier with the Army Service Corps (A/1020). To France 20 August 1914 and served with 1st Remount Depot. Transferred to the Corps of Hussars (renumbered 30762). Transferred to Princess Victoria's (Royal Irish Fusiliers) in May 1916 and joined the 7th/8th (Service) Battalion in 49th Brigade, 16th (Irish) Division.] Joined the 9th (North Irish Horse) Battalion when the 7th/8th (Service) Battalion was disbanded in February 1918. 'C' Company. **Missing** in the period 21-28 March 1918 during the retreat from St Quentin believed **captured**. 1914 Star.

PROCTOR Private George 42106. [Enlisted into the Army Veterinary Corps (17750).] Transferred to Princess Victoria's (Royal Irish Fusiliers) 8 May 1918 (renumbered 42106) and joined the 9th (North Irish Horse) Battalion.

PROCTOR Private Isaac 14604. Born on 2 May 1869. From Armagh, County Armagh. A baker.

Enlisted September 1914. Discharged as no longer physically fit for war service due to sickness 28 June 1915. Silver War Badge, number 243183. Father of Private Isaac Proctor.

PROCTOR Private Isaac 23206. Born in 1894 at Armagh, County Armagh. Enlisted 22 November 1915. Posted to the 9th (Service) Battalion. 'D' Company. **Wounded** at the Battle of Langemarck 16 August 1917. Discharged as no longer physically fit for war service due to wounds 12 November 1917, aged 23. Silver War Badge, number 263383. Son of Private Isaac Proctor.

PROCTOR Private John Cars Logan 14621. Born in 1894 at Armagh, County Armagh. A painter. Armagh Regiment, Ulster Volunteer Force. Enlisted September 1914. To France with 36th (Ulster) Division in October 1915. To hospital sick (tuberculosis) and evacuated to hospital in England 10 November 1915. Posted to the 10th (Reserve) Battalion 29 December 1915. Discharged as no longer physically fit for war service due to sickness 25 May 1916, aged 22. Silver War Badge, number 508793. 1914-15 Star.

PROCTOR Private John 22655. Enlisted in November 1915. Posted to the 9th (Service) Battalion. 'A' Company. **Captured** in the period 21-28 March 1918 during the retreat from St Quentin.

PROCTOR Lance Corporal Joseph 20495. Born in 1899 at Kilmore, Richhill, County Armagh. A farm labourer. [Enlisted 15 July 1915, aged 16. To France 1 January 1916 and joined the 1st Battalion. 'A' Company. **Wounded** by a gunshot to the shoulder 26 January 1916. Treated at 11th Stationary Hospital, Rouen. Applied for discharge being underage; held to serve. Declared **missing** 11 April 1917 during the attacks at the Chemical Works, Roeux but rejoined. **Wounded** by shrapnel to the left thigh at Arras 8 May 1917 and evacuated to hospital in England. Treated at East Leeds War Hospital and St John VAD Hospital, Hull.] To France 5 May 1918 and joined the 9th (North Irish Horse) Battalion 8 May 1918. 'D' Company. To hospital 23 May 1918 due to his previous wound and evacuated to hospital in England. Treated at Mile End Military Hospital, London, the City of Dublin Hospital, the Royal Victoria Hospital, Belfast and Holywood Convalescent Hospital. Joined the 3rd (Reserve) Battalion 4 October 1918. Discharged as no longer physically fit for war service due to wounds 12 December 1918. Silver War Badge, number B51551.

PROCTOR Private William 23071. From Armagh, County Armagh. Enlisted in November 1915. Posted to the 9th (Service) Battalion in mid-1916. 'A' Company. **Killed in action** at the Battle of Langemarck 16 August 1917.

PURVIS Private Edward 41316. Born in 1891 at Belfast. A draper. [Enlisted in November 1915 into the North Irish Horse (1925). Served with 2nd North Irish Horse, X Corps Cavalry Regiment.] Joined the renamed 9th (North Irish Horse) Battalion from 36 Infantry Base Depot and transferred to Princess Victoria's (Royal Irish Fusiliers) in September/October 1917 (renumbered 41316). [Transferred to the Army Service Corps (renumbered M/403422).]

PUSHMAN Private Arthur 43324. Born in 1881 at London. A painter and decorator. [Enlisted 17 July 1916 and joined 3/7th Battalion, The London Regiment (6703).] To 8 Infantry Base Depot, France 10 November 1916. Attached to the 9th (Service) Battalion, Princess Victoria's (Royal Irish Fusiliers) 26 November 1916. 'C' Company. Discharged from the Territorial Force, re-enlisted and transferred to Princess Victoria's (Royal Irish Fusiliers) in March/April 1917 (renumbered 43324). To 108th Field Ambulance sick (boils) June 1917. **Missing** at the Battle of Langemarck 16 August 1917 and later declared **killed in action** on that date, aged 37.

PWYANEFSKY Private M J 43314. See Private M J Pyanowski below.

PYANOWSKI Private Mat J 43314. (His medal index card reads Twyansofky - probably a mis-spelling of Twyanofsky. He is reported in the 9th (Service) Battalion War Diary as '6816 Private M T Pwyanefsky'. Both are believed to mis-spellings/variations of the anglicised name Pyanowski.) [Enlisted into The London Regiment (6816).] Joined the 9th (Service) Battalion, Princess Victoria's (Royal Irish Fusiliers) with the draft of men from The London Regiment on 26 November 1916. Discharged from the Territorial Force, re-enlisted and transferred to Princess Victoria's (Royal Irish Fusiliers) in March/April 1917 (renumbered 43314). [Transferred to 5th (Service) Battalion, The Royal Irish Regiment (Pioneers) in the Light Division in the British Army of the Rhine in March/June 1919 (renumbered 41291).]

PYATT Private John J 43269. [Enlisted in 1907 into The Sherwood Foresters (Nottinghamshire and Derbyshire Regiment) (10295). Mobilised from the Army reserve and to France 11 December

1914.] Transferred to Princess Victoria's (Royal Irish Fusiliers) 31 August 1916 having joined the 9th (Service) Battalion on 8 August 1916. Discharged to the Class P Reserve as no longer physically fit for war service due to sickness 12 September 1917. Silver War Badge, number 224281. 1914-15 Star.

PYE MM Private Edward 43447. [Enlisted into The London Regiment (2345). To France 15 March 1915 and posted to the 1/24th (County of London) Battalion, The London Regiment (The Queen's).] To France and joined 36 Infantry Base Depot 29 March 1918. Transferred to Princess Victoria's (Royal Irish Fusiliers) 2 April 1918 (renumbered 43447) and joined the 9th (North Irish Horse) Battalion 4 April 1918. **MM** – Shoddy Farm north of Bailleul 22 July 1918. 1914-15 Star.

PYE Private Edward Thomas 9344. [Enlisted into Princess Victoria's (Royal Irish Fusiliers) as a regular soldier in 1906. To France 22 August 1914 with the 1st Battalion.] Posted to the 9th (North Irish Horse) Battalion.

QUAIL Private William Henry 14623. Born in 1884 at Shankill, County Armagh. Lived at Lurgan, County Armagh. A yarn dresser. 5th (Lurgan) Battalion, Armagh Regiment, Ulster Volunteer Force. Played for Glenavon Football Club. Enlisted September 1914. To France with 36th (Ulster) Division in October 1915. 'C' Company. Stretcher-bearer during the attack at Hamel 1 July 1916, which he survived unwounded. **Wounded** by gunshots to the back, right thigh and foot at the Battle of Langemarck 16 August 1917. Evacuated to hospital in England 1 September 1917. Joined the 10th (Reserve) Battalion 25 February 1918. [Transferred to the Labour Corps (renumbered 545503) 6 April 1918. Posted to 658th Home Service Employment Company 9 June 1918. Posted to 668th Home Service Employment Company 11 July 1918. Posted to 395th Home Service Employment Company 8 March 1919.] Transferred to the Class Z Reserve 11 April 1919. 1914-15 Star.

QUINN Private George 7426 & 32920. [Enlisted into Princess Victoria's (Royal Irish Fusiliers) as a regular soldier in 1902. Mobilised from the Army Reserve and joined the 1st Battalion. Posted to the 7th/8th (Service) Battalion in 49th Brigade, 16th (Irish) Division.] Joined the 9th (North Irish Horse) Battalion when the 7th/8th (Service) Battalion was disbanded in February 1918. Re-enlisted 26 May 1919 for Regular Army service with Princess Victoria's (Royal Irish Fusiliers) (renumbered 32920). Discharged as no longer physically fit for war service due to sickness 29 July 1919. Silver War Badge, number B293969.

QUINN Private John 14625. From Portadown, County Armagh. Enlisted September 1914. To France with 36th (Ulster) Division in October 1915. 'B' Company. **Wounded** during the attack at Hamel 1 July 1916. **Missing** at the Battle of Langemarck 16 August 1917 and later declared **killed in action** on that date, aged 21. 1914-15 Star.

QUINN Private John Thomas 14622. From Markethill, County Armagh. 4th (Portadown) Battalion, Armagh Regiment, Ulster Volunteer Force. Enlisted September 1914. To France with 36th (Ulster) Division in October 1915. **Killed in action** by shellfire at Hamel 27 June 1916, aged 20. 1914-15 Star.

QUINN Private Joseph 11144. [Enlisted into Princess Victoria's (Royal Irish Fusiliers) as a regular soldier in 1912. To France and joined the 2nd Battalion. Posted to the 1st Battalion.] Posted to the 9th (Service) Battalion. [Posted back to the 1st Battalion. Posted to the 3rd (Reserve) Battalion. Attached to 2nd Battalion, The Hampshire Regiment.]

QUINN Private Joseph 42507. [Enlisted April/May 1918 into The Royal Irish Rifles (22508).] Transferred at the Base Depot to Princess Victoria's (Royal Irish Fusiliers) 14 September 1918 (renumbered 42507) and joined the 9th (North Irish Horse) Battalion 22 September 1918. [Transferred to 5th (Service) Battalion, The Royal Irish Regiment (Pioneers) in the Light Division in the British Army of the Rhine in March/June 1919 (renumbered 41355).]

QUINN Private Samuel 41142. [Enlisted 28 October 1914 into the Service Squadron, 6th (Inniskilling) Dragoons (UD/68). To France with 36th (Ulster) Division in October 1915. Served with 2nd North Irish Horse, X Corps Cavalry Regiment.] Joined the renamed 9th (North Irish Horse) Battalion from 36 Infantry Base Depot and transferred to Princess Victoria's (Royal Irish Fusiliers) in September/October 1917 (renumbered 41142). **Wounded**. Discharged as no longer physically fit for war service due to wounds 8 October 1918. Silver War Badge, number 73762. 1914-15 Star.

QUINN Company Quartermaster Sergeant William Arthur 41097. Born in 1890 at Drumarky, County Fermanagh. A farmer. [Enlisted in October 1914 into the Service Squadron, 6th

(Inniskilling) Dragoons (UD/18). To France with 36th (Ulster) Division in October 1915. Served with 2nd North Irish Horse, X Corps Cavalry Regiment. **Wounded** by shellfire at Aveluy Wood when two troops engaged in salvage duty were subject to heavy bombardment 5 July 1916. Acting Squadron Quartermaster Sergeant.] Joined the renamed 9th (North Irish Horse) Battalion from 36 Infantry Base Depot and transferred to Princess Victoria's (Royal Irish Fusiliers) in September/October 1917 (renumbered 41097). Company Quartermaster Sergeant. Transferred to the Class Z Reserve 3 March 1919. 1914-15 Star. After the war he returned to his farm.

QUINN Private William Stanley 29588 & 7040892. Born in 1900 at Tullylish, Gilford, County Down. Enlisted 3 December 1917, aged 17, giving his age as 18. Transferred to Princess Victoria's (Royal Irish Fusiliers) in March 1918 (renumbered 29588). To France 3 April 1918 and joined the 9th (North Irish Horse) Battalion. Evacuated to hospital in England 8 May 1918. Re-enlisted in August/September 1919 for Regular Army service with Princess Victoria's (Royal Irish Fusiliers) (renumbered 7040892). Discharged 31 March 1922. Enlisted into the Royal Army Service Corps 12 January 1940.

QUIRK Private Patrick 40023. Joined the 9th (Service) Battalion, Princess Victoria's (Royal Irish Fusiliers) with the draft of men from The Prince of Wales's Own (West Yorkshire Regiment) on 12 December 1916.

RADCLIFFE Corporal David 18550. Enlisted into the 9th (Service) Battalion in April 1915. **Wounded** (shellshock) 1916.

RAE Private George 20326. Enlisted in May/June 1915 and joined the 9th (Service) Battalion with the draft of men from The Royal Inniskilling Fusiliers who transferred to Princess Victoria's (Royal Irish Fusiliers) on 30 June 1915. To France with 36th (Ulster) Division in October 1915. [Joined 108th Brigade Machine Gun Company in January 1916. Transferred to the Machine Gun Corps (renumbered 17802).] 1914-15 Star.

RADFORD Private William Edward 43217. Born in 1889 at Nottingham. An ale and stout bottler. [Enlisted 11 December 1915 and transferred to the Army Reserve. Mobilised 10 April 1916 and joined the 4th (Reserve) Battalion, The Sherwood Foresters (Nottinghamshire and Derbyshire Regiment) (42150). To France 15 July 1916.] Transferred to Princess Victoria's (Royal Irish Fusiliers) 31 August 1916 (renumbered 43217) having joined the 9th (Service) Battalion on 8 August 1916. 'A' Company. Attached to 36th (Ulster) Division Works Battalion 5-29 January 1917. Sentenced to fourteen days Field Punishment Number 1 for overstaying his leave. **Captured** in the period 21-28 March 1918 during the retreat from St Quentin. Transferred to the Class Z Reserve 15 March 1919. Re-enlisted 19 October 1919 for Regular Army service with the Royal Army Medical Corps (renumbered 207036). Posted to 20th Company, Royal Army Medical Corps at Tidworth.

RAFFERTY Private George 14648. Enlisted 16 September 1914. To France with 36th (Ulster) Division in October 1915. Discharged as no longer physically fit for war service due to sickness 11 May 1918, aged 41. Silver War Badge, number 361968.

RAFFERTY Private John 14656. From Richhill, County Armagh. Served pre-war with the 3rd Battalion (Militia), Princess Victoria's (Royal Irish Fusiliers). Enlisted September 1914. Discharged as not being likely to become an efficient soldier in that he was considered medically unfit for service (varicose veins) 20 October 1914.

RAFFERTY Private Thomas 21283 & 7040672. From Dublin. [Enlisted in 24 August 1915 and joined the 8th (Service) Battalion in 49th Brigade, 16th (Irish) Division. To France 18 February 1916.] Joined the 9th (North Irish Horse) Battalion when the 7th/8th (Service) Battalion was disbanded in February 1918. 'C' Company. **Missing** in the period 21-28 March 1918 during the retreat from St Quentin believed **wounded**. Re-enlisted in early-1919 for Regular Army service with Princess Victoria's (Royal Irish Fusiliers) (renumbered 7040672). Served with the 1st Battalion in Mesopotamia in 1919/20. Transferred to the Section B Army Reserve, Princess Victoria's (Royal Irish Fusiliers) 23 August 1922. Discharged 23 August 1927. Lived at Dublin.

RAFFERTY Private Thomas George 14647. From Richhill, County Armagh. Enlisted September 1914. Discharged as not being likely to become an efficient soldier in that he was considered medically unfit for service 4 November 1914.

RAINEY Private David 23918. Enlisted 6 November 1915. Posted to the 9th (Service) Battalion.

Discharged as no longer physically fit for war service due to sickness 27 March 1919. Silver War Badge, number B165700.

RAINEY Private John 17666. From Tandragee, County Armagh. Enlisted into the 9th (Service) Battalion in December 1914/January 1915. To France with 36th (Ulster) Division in October 1915. **Wounded** (shellshock) during the attack at Hamel 1 July 1916. **Wounded** in June 1917. 1914-15 Star. Died in 1944.

RAINEY Private John 41278. [Enlisted in January 1913 into the North Irish Horse (801). To France 20 August 1914 with 'C' Squadron as 5th Division Cavalry and then as GHQ Troops. Served with 2nd North Irish Horse, X Corps Cavalry Regiment.] Joined the renamed 9th (North Irish Horse) Battalion from 36 Infantry Base Depot and transferred to Princess Victoria's (Royal Irish Fusiliers) in September/October 1917 (renumbered 41278). 'C' Company. **Missing** in the period 21-28 March 1918 during the retreat from St Quentin believed **captured**. 1914 Star.

RAMSEY Corporal Ernest Hugh 24600. From Belfast. [Enlisted 21 July 1916 and joined the 7th/8th (Service) Battalion in 49th Brigade, 16th (Irish) Division.] Joined the 9th (North Irish Horse) Battalion when the 7th/8th (Service) Battalion was disbanded in February 1918. 'D' Company. **Wounded** during the retreat from St Quentin 21-28 March 1918. Discharged as no longer physically fit for war service due to wounds 29 August 1918, aged 20. Silver War Badge, number 445707.

RANCE Lance Corporal John 43218. Born in 1879. From Wellow, Nottinghamshire. A whipper-in at Rufford Hunt kennels. [Enlisted 7 December 1915 and transferred to the Army Reserve. Mobilised 5 April 1916 and joined the 4th (Extra Reserve) Battalion, The Sherwood Foresters (Nottinghamshire and Derbyshire Regiment) (41514). To France 16 July 1916.] Transferred to Princess Victoria's (Royal Irish Fusiliers) 31 August 1916 having joined the 9th (Service) Battalion on 8 August 1916 (renumbered 43218). To 3rd Canadian General Hospital sick (kidneys) and evacuated to hospital in England 30 October 1916. Posted to the Irish Command Depot, Tipperary 14 March 1917. Posted to the 10th (Reserve) Battalion 2 August 1917. [Transferred to the Royal Defence Corps (73202) 4 May 1918 and joined 200th Protection Company.] Transferred to the Class Z Reserve 12 March 1919.

RANDALL Private Charles 41917. Born in 1891 at Lavenham, Suffolk. An outdoor porter. [Enlisted 13 January 1910 into the Army Service Corps (T/28728). To France 14 August 1914 with 2nd Railway Supply Detachment. Transferred to Princess Victoria's (Royal Irish Fusiliers) 28 January 1915 (renumbered 41917) and joined the 1st Battalion. To hospital sick (scabies) in April 1916. To hospital injured (legs) 27 March 1918. Joined 12th Convalescent Depot 6 April 1918.] Joined the 9th (North Irish Horse) in mid-1918. **Wounded** by shrapnel to the left knee during the attack at Vijfwegen on 30 September or 1 October 1918 (recorded as 3 October 1918). Treated at 2nd Canadian Casualty Clearing Station and 32nd Stationary Hospital. Evacuated to hospital in England 9 October 1918. Treated at Northamptonshire War Hospital, Northampton. Discharged as no longer physically fit for war service due to wounds 18 March 1919. Silver War Badge, number B256302.

RANDALL Private Herbert 45806. Joined the 9th (North Irish Horse) Battalion, Princess Victoria's (Royal Irish Fusiliers) with the draft of men from The London Regiment in April 1918. [Transferred to 5th (Service) Battalion, The Royal Irish Regiment (Pioneers) in the Light Division in the British Army of the Rhine in March/June 1919 (renumbered 41356).]

RANDALL Private Walter A 42107. [Enlisted into the Army Veterinary Corps (16334).] Transferred to Princess Victoria's (Royal Irish Fusiliers) 8 May 1918 (renumbered 42107) and joined the 9th (North Irish Horse) Battalion. [Transferred to the Seaforth Highlanders (Ross-shire Buffs, The Duke of Albany's) (renumbered 44596). Transferred to the Royal Army Medical Corps (renumbered 170010).]

RANDERSON Private Thomas Henry 40026. Born in 1889 at Leeds. [Enlisted 15 June 1916 into The Prince of Wales's Own (West Yorkshire Regiment) (34378).] Transferred to Princess Victoria's (Royal Irish Fusiliers) 30 November 1916 (renumbered 40026) and joined the 9th (Service) Battalion 12 December 1916. 'C' Company. **Wounded** on 9 June 1917 during the Battle of Messines and **died of wounds** 12 June 1917, aged 27.

RANGER Private Laurence Gordon 43340. Born 28 October 1897 at Layton, Essex. [Enlisted into

The London Regiment.] Attached to the 9th (Service) Battalion, Princess Victoria's (Royal Irish Fusiliers) 26 November 1916. 'B' Company. Discharged from the Territorial Force, re-enlisted and transferred to Princess Victoria's (Royal Irish Fusiliers) in March/April 1917 (renumbered 43340). **Wounded** by shrapnel in the left thigh at the Battle of Langemarck 16 August 1917. Recovered by stretcher bearers on 17 August 1917 and was evacuated to hospital in England 22 August 1917. Joined the 3rd (Reserve) Battalion at Rugeley 6 July 1918. To France 11 August 1918 and rejoined the 9th (North Irish Horse) Battalion 29 August 1918. To the Field Ambulance injured (sprained ankle) 6 September 1918. Rejoined the 9th (North Irish Horse) Battalion 4 October 1918. Became servant to Second Lieutenant W Elliott MM 17 November 1918 (the day after Elliott joined the Battalion). Appointed an officers' mess cook 1 March 1919. Left the 9th (North Irish Horse) Battalion for demobilisation 9 May 1919. Transferred to the Class Z Reserve. Died at Brighton in 1977, aged 79.

RANKIN Private William John 42468. [Enlisted into the 8th (Service) Battalion, The Royal Inniskilling Fusiliers (24749). Transferred to The Royal Irish Rifles (renumbered 22719).] Transferred at the Base Depot to Princess Victoria's (Royal Irish Fusiliers) 14 September 1918 (renumbered 42468) and joined the 9th (North Irish Horse) Battalion 22 September 1918.

RAWLINGS Corporal Evan 30604. [A regular soldier with the 2nd Battalion, Royal Munster Fusiliers (5158). Transferred to Princess Victoria's (Royal Irish Fusiliers) and posted to the 11th (Service) Battalion in June 1918.] Joined the 9th (North Irish Horse) Battalion in August 1918.

RAYNOR Private John James 43273. Born in 1886. From Ilkeston, Derbyshire. A coal miner. [Enlisted 18 January 1915 and joined the 3rd (Reserve) Battalion, The Sherwood Foresters (Nottinghamshire and Derbyshire Regiment) (22385). Posted to the 9th (Service) Battalion, The Sherwood Foresters (Nottinghamshire and Derbyshire Regiment) at Suvla Bay in the Mediterranean Expeditionary Force 13 September 1915. Evacuated (probably sick) February 1916. Rejoined the 3rd (Reserve) Battalion 23 May 1916.] To France 14 July 1916. Transferred to Princess Victoria's (Royal Irish Fusiliers) 31 August 1916 (renumbered 43273) having joined the 9th (Service) Battalion on 8 August 1916. 'D' Company. Commended for his work as a stretcher-bearer during the raid at La Petite Douve Farm on 12 October 1916. **Wounded** by a gunshot to the jaw, causing a fracture and the loss of teeth. Treated at 3rd Western General Hospital, Cardiff from 15 October 1916 and then at West Bridgford Hospital, Nottinghamshire from 17 January 1917 to 2 February 1917. Joined the 10th (Reserve) Battalion 7 March 1918. To 'A' Infantry Base Depot, France 3 April 1917 and rejoined the 9th (Service) Battalion. **Missing** in the period 11-18 April 1918 in the actions between Wulverghem and Kemmel; subsequently declared **killed in action** 19 April 1918, aged 33. 1914-15 Star.

REA Private John 17403. Enlisted into the 9th (Service) Battalion 24 November 1914. To France with 36th (Ulster) Division in October 1915. 'C' Company. Company bomb carrier during the attack at Hamel 1 July 1916, during which he was **wounded**. Discharged as no longer physically fit for war service due to wounds 19 October 1916, aged 21. Silver War Badge, number 423991.

REANEY Private Robert 18070. From Darkley, County Armagh. Enlisted into the 9th (Service) Battalion in February 1915. To France with 36th (Ulster) Division in October 1915. 'C' Company. To hospital mid-1916. Rejoined and was a company runner during the attack at Hamel 1 July 1916, during which he was **wounded**. **Killed in action** during the raid on La Petite Douve Farm 12 October 1916. 1914-15 Star.

REAVEY Private Francis 8605. From Coatbridge, Lanarkshire. [Enlisted into Princess Victoria's (Royal Irish Fusiliers) as a regular soldier in 1905. To France with the 1st Battalion 22 August 1914.] Posted to the 9th (North Irish Horse) Battalion. 1914 Star & clasp.

REDMOND Private James Henry 14639. Born in 1894 at Portadown, County Armagh. 4th (Portadown) Battalion, Armagh Regiment, Ulster Volunteer Force. A linen weaver. Enlisted September 1914. To France with 36th (Ulster) Division in October 1915. 'D' Company. **Wounded** at the Battle of Langemarck 16 August 1917. Discharged as no longer physically fit for war service due to wounds 18 June 1918. Silver War Badge, number 387958. 1914-15 Star.

REDPATH Sergeant John 14633. From Portadown, County Armagh. 4th (Portadown) Battalion, Armagh Regiment, Ulster Volunteer Force. Member of Loyal Orange Lodge 110. Enlisted September 1914. To France with 36th (Ulster) Division in October 1915. 'D' Company. **Wounded** during the

Battle of Messines and to hospital 9 June 1917. **Captured** in the period 21-28 March 1918 during the retreat from St Quentin. Transferred to the Class Z Reserve 11 April 1919. 1914-15 Star.

REECE Private Harold 42261. Born in 1894 at Southport, Lancashire. [Enlisted 5 June 1913 into the Army Service Corps (966) for service with the West Lancashire Division Transport and Supply Column. Enlisted into the Army Service Corps (T4/252864).] Transferred to Princess Victoria's (Royal Irish Fusiliers) 8 May 1918 (renumbered 42261) and joined the 9th (North Irish Horse) Battalion. **Wounded** during the attack south of Wulverghem and **died of wounds** 4 September 1918.

REEVES Private Thomas W 43476. [Enlisted into The London Regiment (3986). Posted to the 1/22nd (County of London) Battalion, The London Regiment (The Queen's) (renumbered 681768).] To France and joined 36 Infantry Base Depot 29 March 1918. Transferred to Princess Victoria's (Royal Irish Fusiliers) 2 April 1918 (renumbered 43476) and joined the 9th (North Irish Horse) Battalion 4 April 1918.

REID Corporal Bristow 41877. [Enlisted 18 September 1914 into 11th (Service) Battalion, The Royal Irish Rifles (South Antrim) (19741) and deployed To France with 36th (Ulster) Division in October 1915.] Transferred to Princess Victoria's (Royal Irish Fusiliers) (renumbered 41877) and joined the 9th (North Irish Horse) Battalion in late-1917. 'D' Company. **Wounded** during the retreat from St Quentin 21-28 March 1918. Discharged as no longer physically fit for war service due to wounds 12 November 1918. Silver War Badge, number B41643. 1914-15 Star.

REID Lance Corporal David 14629. From Portadown, County Armagh. 4th (Portadown) Battalion, Armagh Regiment, Ulster Volunteer Force. Enlisted September 1914. To France with 36th (Ulster) Division in October 1915. Groom to Lieutenant Colonel Blacker. Transferred to the Class Z Reserve 22 March 1919. 1914-15 Star.

REID Sergeant George Christopher 41529. Born on 31 August 1885 at Boho, Enniskillen, County Fermanagh. A farmer. [Enlisted 22 September 1914 into The Royal Inniskilling Fusiliers (14165). Transferred in October/November 1914 to the Service Squadron, 6th (Inniskilling) Dragoons (renumbered UD/97). To France with 36th (Ulster) Division in October 1915. Served with 2nd North Irish Horse, X Corps Cavalry Regiment.] Joined the renamed 9th (North Irish Horse) Battalion from 36 Infantry Base Depot and transferred to Princess Victoria's (Royal Irish Fusiliers) in September/October 1917 (renumbered 41529). **Killed in action** 26 October 1917 at Havrincourt, aged 32. 1914-15 Star.

REID Private Hugh 22951. From Belfast. [Enlisted in November 1915 and joined the 8th (Service) Battalion in 49th Brigade, 16th (Irish) Division.] Joined the 9th (North Irish Horse) Battalion when the 7th/8th (Service) Battalion was disbanded in February 1918. 'B' Company. **Captured** in the period 21-28 March 1918 during the retreat from St Quentin.

REID Sergeant John 22978. Served with the Royal Irish Constabulary at Newry. Enlisted 8 November 1915. Posted to the 9th (Service) Battalion. 'D' Company. **Wounded** in the right shoulder and left leg at the Battle of Langemarck 16 August 1917. Discharged as no longer physically fit for war service due to wounds 14 March 1919. Silver War Badge, number B162481.

REID Private John Charles 21655. Enlisted in September 1915. Posted to the 9th (Service) Battalion in mid/late 1916.

REID Private Joseph Cooper 24852. Born in 1886 near Dungannon, County Tyrone. A farmer's son. Enlisted 28 September 1916. Posted to the 9th (Service) Battalion. 'B' Company. **Wounded** at the Battle of Langemarck 16 August 1917. Discharged as no longer physically fit for war service due to wounds 7 June 1918. Silver War Badge, number 395831.

REID Corporal Norman Hugh 14657. Born in 1898. From Waringstown, County Down. Enlisted September 1914. To France with 36th (Ulster) Division in October 1915. 'A' then 'B' Company. **Wounded** during the attack at Hamel 1 July 1916. Treated at Dunsdale Hospital, Westerham, Kent. **Wounded** at the Battle of Langemarck 16 August 1917 and **died of wounds** 17 August 1917, aged 19 in 32nd Casualty Clearing Station. 1914-15 Star.

REID Lance Corporal Percival Henry A 41548. Born in 1898 at Belfast. Lived at Newtownbreda, Belfast. Worked in the linen trade. [Enlisted 4 January 1916 into the North Irish Horse (2056). To France 26 November 1916. Served with 2nd North Irish Horse, X Corps Cavalry Regiment.] Joined the renamed 9th (North Irish Horse) Battalion from 36 Infantry Base Depot and transferred to Princess Victoria's (Royal Irish Fusiliers) in September/October 1917 (renumbered 41548). 'A' Company. **Wounded** by shrapnel during the retreat from St Quentin 21-28 March 1918. **Wounded** on patrol at Meulenhouck 10 August 1918. [Transferred to 5th (Service) Battalion, The Royal Irish Regiment (Pioneers) in the Light Division in the British Army of the Rhine in March/June 1919 (renumbered 41357). Transferred at his own request to the Royal Army Service Corps (renumbered T/453128) as a driver in the Transport Branch 24 July 1919. Served with 172nd Company in the Light Division Train. Lance Corporal 9 August 1919.] Transferred to the Class Z Reserve 2 October 1919. When discharged he was suffering from pulmonary tuberculosis, attributed to his Army service. He **died** of pulmonary tuberculosis at Lisburn on 24 May 1921.

REID Sergeant Robert 41484. [Enlisted in August 1914 into the North Irish Horse (961). To France 20 August 1914 with 'C' Squadron as 5th Division Cavalry and then as GHQ Troops. Served with 2nd North Irish Horse, X Corps Cavalry Regiment.] Joined the renamed 9th (North Irish Horse) Battalion from 36 Infantry Base Depot and transferred to Princess Victoria's (Royal Irish Fusiliers) in September/October 1917 (renumbered 41484). 1914 Star.

REID Private Thomas 14661. Enlisted September 1914. To France with 36th (Ulster) Division in October 1915. 3 Section, 13 Platoon, 'D' Company in 1915. [Transferred to The Royal Inniskilling Fusiliers (renumbered 43566).]

REID Lance Corporal Thomas Robinson 22989. Enlisted in November 1915. Posted to the 9th (Service) Battalion.

REILLY Sergeant James 14636. Enlisted September 1914. To France with 36th (Ulster) Division in October 1915. Transferred to the Class Z Reserve 22 March 1919. 1914-15 Star.

REILLY Private James 18499. [Enlisted in April 1915. To France 7 August 1915 and joined the 2nd Battalion. Posted to the 7th/8th (Service) Battalion in 48th Brigade, 16th (Irish) Division.] Joined the 9th (North Irish Horse) Battalion when the 7th/8th (Service) Battalion was disbanded in February 1918. Transferred to the Class Z Reserve 31 March 1919. 1914-15 Star.

REILLY Private John 41639. [Enlisted in November 1915 into the North Irish Horse (1930). Served with 2nd North Irish Horse, X Corps Cavalry Regiment.] Joined the renamed 9th (North Irish Horse) Battalion from 36 Infantry Base Depot and transferred to Princess Victoria's (Royal Irish Fusiliers) in September/October 1917 (renumbered 41639).

REILLY Private Michael 42487. [Enlisted into The Royal Irish Rifles (20943).] Transferred at the Base Depot to Princess Victoria's (Royal Irish Fusiliers) 14 September 1918 (renumbered 42487) and joined the 9th (North Irish Horse) Battalion 22 September 1918.

REILLY Private Peter 3228. Enlisted into Princess Victoria's (Royal Irish Fusiliers) Special Reserve. Posted to the 9th (Service) Battalion. [Posted to the 5th (Service) Battalion.]

REYNOLDS Corporal Frederick 42172. [Enlisted into the Army Service Corps (S4/090259). To France 5 September 1915. Served with 21st Field Bakery.] Transferred to Princess Victoria's (Royal Irish Fusiliers) 8 May 1918 (renumbered 42172) and joined the 9th (North Irish Horse) Battalion. Transferred to the Class Z Reserve 19 March 1919. 1914-15 Star.

REYNOLDS Private George 41185. [Enlisted 20 January 1915 into the North Irish Horse (1415). Served with 2nd North Irish Horse, X Corps Cavalry Regiment.] Joined the renamed 9th (North Irish Horse) Battalion from 36 Infantry Base Depot and transferred to Princess Victoria's (Royal Irish Fusiliers) in September/October 1917 (renumbered 41185). **Wounded**. Discharged as no longer physically fit for war service due to wounds 9 October 1918. Silver War Badge, number B41680. 1914-15 Star.

REYNOLDS Private James 14663. Enlisted September 1914. Discharged as no longer physically fit for war service due to sickness 28 June 1915, aged 28. Silver War Badge, number 508795.

REYNOLDS Lance Corporal William 14643 & 7040583. Born in 1891 at Shankill, County Armagh. A linen weaver. Enlisted on 15 September 1914. Did not deploy to France with 36th (Ulster) Division in October 1915. Posted to the 1st Garrison Battalion and served in India from 12 February 1916 to 31 January 1919. Re-enlisted on 1 February 1919 for Regular Army service with Princess Victoria's (Royal Irish Fusiliers) (renumbered 7040583). Discharged 18 November 1920 on the termination of his period of engagement. Returned to live at Shankill, County Armagh.

RICE Private Samuel Philip 43330. Born in London in 1885. Joined the 9th (Service) Battalion, Princess Victoria's (Royal Irish Fusiliers) with the draft of men from The London Regiment in November 1916. 'C' Company. **Missing** in the period 21-28 March 1918 during the retreat from St Quentin believed **captured**. Died at London in 1959, aged 74.

RICH Private Albert 42115. From Nether Stowey, Somerset. [Enlisted into the Army Veterinary Corps (16572).] Transferred to Princess Victoria's (Royal Irish Fusiliers) 8 May 1918 (renumbered 42115) and joined the 9th (North Irish Horse) Battalion. [Transferred to 5th (Service) Battalion, The Royal Irish Regiment (Pioneers) in the Light Division in the British Army of the Rhine in March/June 1919 (renumbered 41359).]

RICHARDS Lance Corporal E J 18307. From Dublin. [Enlisted in March 1915 into the 5th (Service) or 6th (Service) Battalion in 31st Brigade, 10th (Irish) Division. Embarked with the Mediterranean Expeditionary Force July 1915.] Posted to the 9th (Service) Battalion. 'A' Company. **Wounded** at the Battle of Langemarck 16 August 1917. [Transferred to the Corps of Royal Engineers (renumbered 623965).]

RICHARDS Private William 40139. From Llanda, Glamorganshire. [Served previously with Hussars of the Line (24611). Transferred to Princess Victoria's (Royal Irish Fusiliers) in December 1916 and posted to the 1st Battalion.] Joined the 9th (Service) Battalion in mid-1917. 'B' Company. **Killed in action** at the Battle of Langemarck 16 August 1917.

RICHARDS Private William H 45792. Joined the 9th (North Irish Horse) Battalion, Princess Victoria's (Royal Irish Fusiliers) with the draft of men from The London Regiment in April 1918. [Transferred to the Army Service Corps (renumbered M/47044).]

RICHARDSON Lance Corporal George 14664. From Loughgall, County Armagh. Enlisted September 1914. To France with 36th (Ulster) Division in October 1915. **Killed in action** during the attack at Hamel 1 July 1916. 1914-15 Star.

RICHARDSON Private George 23352, 34060 & 7042014. From Benburb, County Tyrone. A weaver. Enlisted in December 1915. Posted to the 9th (Service) Battalion. Re-enlisted 21 April 1920 for Regular Army service with Princess Victoria's (Royal Irish Fusiliers) (renumbered 34060, renumbered 7042014). Discharged 20 April 1922.

RICHARDSON Lance Corporal John 22890. Enlisted in November 1915. Posted to the 9th (Service) Battalion. **Wounded** by a gunshot wound and suffered a crushed back on a raid at Spanbroekmolen 4 June 1917.

RICHARDSON Private William Henry 24576. From Derrycorry, Moy, County Armagh. Enlisted 14 July 1916. Posted to the 9th (Service) Battalion. 'B' Company. **Wounded** at the Battle of Langemarck 16 August 1917. Discharged as no longer physically fit for war service due to wounds 18 June 1918, aged 33. Silver War Badge, number 411849.

RICHARDSON Private William James 24287. Enlisted 26 April 1916. Posted to the 9th (Service) Battalion. 'C' Company. **Missing** in the period 21-28 March 1918 during the retreat from St Quentin believed **captured**. Discharged as no longer physically fit for war service due to sickness 11 July 1919. Silver War Badge, number B283769.

RICHARDSON Private William L 14975. Born in 1891 at Stockton-on-Tees. [Enlisted 9 November 1914 into the 5th (Service) Battalion in 31st Brigade, 10th (Irish) Division. Embarked with the Mediterranean Expeditionary Force July 1915. **Wounded** by a gunshot to the shoulder 9 August 1915 and evacuated to hospital in England.] Posted to the 9th (Service) Battalion. 'C' Company. **Wounded** by a gunshot to the knee. **Captured** at Erches 27 March 1918 during the retreat from St Quentin. Transferred to the Class Z Reserve 19 March 1919. 31 March 1920. 1914-15 Star.

RICHEY Private Robert Alexander 23757. Commissioned into Princess Victoria's (Royal Irish Fusiliers) - see Appendix 5.

RICHMOND Private Alexander 24562. Enlisted 4 July 1916. Posted to the 9th (Service) Battalion. Tried by Field General Court Martial on 21 August 1917 on a charge of *'absenting himself without leave'*; found guilty and sentenced to fifty-six days Field Punishment Number 1. Discharged as no longer physically fit for war service due to sickness 21 June 1919. Silver War Badge, number B264844.

RICHMOND Private Robert 40661. [Enlisted in March 1913 into the North Irish Horse (821). To

France 20 August 1914 with 'C' Squadron as 5th Division Cavalry and then as GHQ Troops. Served with 2nd North Irish Horse, X Corps Cavalry Regiment.] Transferred to Princess Victoria's (Royal Irish Fusiliers) 9 January 1917 and joined the 9th (Service) Battalion. 1914 Star.

RIDDALLS Private Charles 43306. From London. [Enlisted 3 July 1916 into The London Regiment.] Attached to the 9th (Service) Battalion, Princess Victoria's (Royal Irish Fusiliers) 26 November 1916. 'D' Company. Discharged from the Territorial Force, re-enlisted and transferred to Princess Victoria's (Royal Irish Fusiliers) in March/April 1917 (renumbered 43306). **Wounded** at the Battle of Langemarck 16 August 1917. Discharged as no longer physically fit for war service due to wounds 6 March 1918, aged 34. Silver War Badge, number 339114.

RIDDELL Private John Edward 41403. Born in 1896. From Portrush, County Antrim. A clerk. [Enlisted 24 May 1915 into the North Irish Horse (1603). To France 12 January 1916. To hospital with a poisoned hand 12 April 1916. Joined 'A' Squadron 29 May 1916. Posted to 'E' Squadron 4 August 1916. Detached for duty at Number 4 German Prisoner of War Camp 1 November 1916. While there, sentenced to seven days Field Punishment Number 1 for quitting camp when under medical treatment and *'using highly obscene and insolent language to an NCO.'* Served with 2nd North Irish Horse, X Corps Cavalry Regiment.] Joined the renamed 9th (North Irish Horse) Battalion from 36 Infantry Base Depot and transferred to Princess Victoria's (Royal Irish Fusiliers) in September/October 1917 (renumbered 41403). **Wounded** by a gunshot to the right thigh 22/23 November 1917 at Moeuvres and evacuated to hospital in England. Joined the 10th (Reserve) Battalion 11 March 1918. To 'G' Infantry Base Depot 12 April 1918 and rejoined the 9th (North Irish Horse) Battalion 22 April 1918. **Killed in action** near Meulenhouck 2-3 August 1918, aged 21.

RIDGEWAY Private James Henry Frederick 43358. [Enlisted into The London Regiment. Posted to the 1/7th (City of London) Battalion, The London Regiment (3366).] Attached to the 9th (Service) Battalion, Princess Victoria's (Royal Irish Fusiliers) 26 November 1916. Discharged from the Territorial Force, re-enlisted and transferred to Princess Victoria's (Royal Irish Fusiliers) in March/April 1917 (renumbered 43358).

RILEY Private Frederick George 42116. [Enlisted into the Army Veterinary Corps (25374).] Transferred to Princess Victoria's (Royal Irish Fusiliers) 8 May 1918 (renumbered 42116) and joined the 9th (North Irish Horse) Battalion.

RILEY Private M. Tried by Field General Court Martial on 5 December 1918 charged with *'when on active service **deserting** His Majesty's service'*; found guilty of *'absenting himself without leave'* and sentenced to eighteen months imprisonment with hard labour. Soldier not identified.

RINGROSE Private Alfred 40024. From York. [Enlisted into The Prince of Wales's Own (West Yorkshire Regiment) (36092).] Transferred to Princess Victoria's (Royal Irish Fusiliers) 30 November 1916 (renumbered 40024) and joined the 9th (Service) Battalion 12 December 1916. 'B' Company. **Killed in action** 29 March 1918 during the retreat from St Quentin.

RISEBROOK Private Victor Ralph 45035. Born in 1897 at Norfolk. [Enlisted into or transferred to Princess Victoria's (Royal Irish Fusiliers) in December 1916 and served with the 7th/8th (Service) Battalion in 49th Brigade, 16th (Irish) Division.] Joined the 9th (North Irish Horse) Battalion when the 7th/8th (Service) Battalion was disbanded in February 1918. 'D' Company. **Missing** in the period 21-28 March 1918 during the retreat from St Quentin believed **captured**. Died at Norfolk in 1966, aged 69.

RITCHIE Corporal James 14646. Enlisted September 1914. Did not serve overseas with 36th (Ulster) Division. Discharged as no longer physically fit for war service due to sickness 29 January 1919. Silver War Badge, number B97870.

RITCHIE Private James Alexander 41356. [Enlisted in November 1916 into the North Irish Horse (2306). Served with 2nd North Irish Horse, X Corps Cavalry Regiment.] Joined the renamed 9th (North Irish Horse) Battalion from 36 Infantry Base Depot and transferred to Princess Victoria's (Royal Irish Fusiliers) in September/October 1917 (renumbered 41356).

ROACH Corporal John 13869. [Enlisted in September 1914 and joined the 6th (Service) Battalion in 31st Brigade, 10th (Irish) Division. Embarked with the Mediterranean Expeditionary Force July 1915. Posted to the 7th/8th (Service) Battalion in 49th Brigade, 16th (Irish) Division.] Joined the 9th (North Irish Horse) Battalion when the 7th/8th (Service) Battalion was disbanded in February 1918.

'C' Company. **Wounded** during the retreat from St Quentin 21-28 March 1918. Transferred to the Class Z Reserve 29 January 1919. 1914-15 Star.

ROBB Private Herbert 22804. Born in 1894. From Lurgan, County Armagh. A groom. Enlisted 15 November 1915 and joined the 10th (Reserve) Battalion. To France 20 July 1916 and joined the 9th (Service) Battalion 29 July 1916. 'D' Company. To the field ambulance sick (boils and an ear infection) November 1916. **Wounded** March 1917. Treated at 3rd Canadian General Hospital and then evacuated to Wharncliffe War Hospital, Sheffield 25 March 1917. Joined 36 Infantry Base Depot 26 July 1917 and rejoined the 9th (Service) Battalion 20 August 1917. **Wounded** 18 April 1918 by shrapnel in the actions between Wulverghem and Kemmel and **died of wounds** in 64th Casualty Clearing Station 20 April 1918, aged 23.

ROBB Private Henry Joseph 43307. From Battersea, London. [Enlisted 30 June 1916 into The London Regiment.] Attached to the 9th (Service) Battalion, Princess Victoria's (Royal Irish Fusiliers) 26 November 1916. 'D' Company. Discharged from the Territorial Force, re-enlisted and transferred to Princess Victoria's (Royal Irish Fusiliers) in March/April 1917 (renumbered 43307). **Wounded** at the Battle of Langemarck 16 August 1917. Discharged as no longer physically fit for war service due to wounds 7 June 1918, aged 32. Silver War Badge, number 395833.

ROBB Corporal William 14626. From Garvaghy Road, Portadown, County Armagh. 4th (Portadown) Battalion, Armagh Regiment, Ulster Volunteer Force. Enlisted September 1914. To France with 36th (Ulster) Division in October 1915. 'C' Company. **Killed in action** during the attack at Hamel 1 July 1916. 1914-15 Star.

ROBERTS Lance Corporal Albert 27827. Enlisted into or transferred to Princess Victoria's (Royal Irish Fusiliers) in July 1917. Posted to the 9th (North Irish Horse) Battalion. 'D' Company. **Missing** in the period 21-28 March 1918 during the retreat from St Quentin believed **captured**.

ROBERTS Private Henry John 45769. Born in 1878 at Bermondsey, Surrey. A furniture packer. [Enlisted 12 December 1915 and transferred to the Army Reserve. Mobilised 3 August 1917 and joined 22nd (Reserve) Battalion, The London Regiment (684098).] To France and joined 36 Infantry Base Depot 29 March 1918. Transferred to Princess Victoria's (Royal Irish Fusiliers) 2 April 1918 (renumbered 45769) and joined the 9th (North Irish Horse) Battalion 4 April 1918. **Killed in action** during the attack south of Wulverghem 4 September 1918.

ROBERTS Sergeant James William 11977. [Enlisted in September 1914 and joined the 5th (Service) Battalion in 31st Brigade, 10th (Irish) Division. Embarked with the Mediterranean Expeditionary Force July 1915. Posted to the 8th (Service) Battalion in 49th Brigade, 16th (Irish) Division.] Joined the 9th (North Irish Horse) Battalion when the 7th/8th (Service) Battalion was disbanded in February 1918. Transferred to the Class Z Reserve. 1914-15 Star.

ROBERTS Private Robert 17449. Born Brymbo, Denbighshire. From Tyseley, Warwickshire, enlisted in Birmingham in November/December 1914. Posted to the 9th (Service) Battalion. 'B' Company. **Missing** at the Battle of Langemarck 16 August 1917 and later declared **killed in action** on that date, aged 31.

ROBERTS Private Samuel 42126. [Enlisted into the Army Veterinary Corps (28496).] Transferred to Princess Victoria's (Royal Irish Fusiliers) 8 May 1918 (renumbered 42126) and joined the 9th (North Irish Horse) Battalion.

ROBERTS MM Corporal Thomas James 43428. Born in 1889 at Birmingham. [Enlisted 18 August 1914 and joined 10th Reserve Regiment of Cavalry at The Curragh for service with 4th (Queen's Own) Hussars (14365). Transferred to 8th Reserve Regiment of Cavalry for service with 16th (The Queen's) Lancers (renumbered 18018) 9 November 1914. Transferred to The Royal Irish Rifles and posted to the 3rd (Reserve) Battalion, The Royal Irish Rifles 2 June 1915 (renumbered 5121). To France 28 June 1915 and joined the 2nd Battalion, The Royal Irish Rifles. To hospital in the latter part of 1915 and returned to the 2nd Battalion, The Royal Irish Rifles 15 December 1915. 'A' Company. Attended 3rd Army Trench Mortar School 18 March 1916. Attached to 74th Brigade Trench Mortar Battery on its formation 24 March 1916. Lance Corporal and Acting Corporal 1 June 1916. Reverted to Private for being drunk in billets. Lance Corporal 11 August 1916. **Wounded** in the leg by shrapnel 7 October 1916. **MM**. Treated at 133rd Field Ambulance. Rejoined 74th Brigade Trench Mortar Battery 8 November 1916. Corporal 19 January 1917. To the field ambulance sick (scabies) March 1917. Rejoined 2nd Battalion, The Royal Irish Rifles 11 November

1916. To 36 Infantry Base Depot and joined the Surplus Company 14 November 1917.] Transferred to Princess Victoria's (Royal Irish Fusiliers) 8 February 1918 (renumbered 43428) and joined the 9th (Service) Battalion. 'A' Company. **Missing** in the period 21-28 March 1918 during the retreat from St Quentin and later declared **killed in action** 29 March 1918. 1914-15 Star.

ROBERTSON Sergeant Archibald 42100. [Enlisted into the Army Veterinary Corps (TT/0238 Sergeant).] Transferred to Princess Victoria's (Royal Irish Fusiliers) 8 May 1918 (renumbered 42100) and joined the 9th (North Irish Horse) Battalion.

ROBINSON Sergeant George 14641. Enlisted September 1914. To France with 36th (Ulster) Division in October 1915. [Joined 108th Brigade Machine Gun Company in January 1916. Transferred to the Machine Gun Corps (renumbered 17777 Sergeant).] 1914-15 Star.

ROBINSON MM Corporal George 17944. From Druminally, Portadown, County Armagh. Enlisted into the 9th (Service) Battalion in February 1915. To France with 36th (Ulster) Division in October 1915. 'C' Company. Detached to the Battalion Transport during the attack at Hamel on 1 July 1916. **MM** – Hamel. **Wounded** in the liver by a machine gun bullet 6 September 1916 in the River Douve area and **died of wounds** 12 September 1916, aged 30. 1914-15 Star.

ROBINSON Sergeant George Dickson 41143. Born in 1892 at Lurgan, County Armagh. (His service number is incorrectly recorded as 41133 on his medal index card.) [Enlisted in early-1915 into the Service Squadron, 6th (Inniskilling) Dragoons (UD/209). To France with 36th (Ulster) Division in October 1915. Served with 2nd North Irish Horse, X Corps Cavalry Regiment. **Wounded** by shellfire at Aveluy Wood when two troops engaged in salvage duty were subject to heavy bombardment 5 July 1916.] Joined the renamed 9th (North Irish Horse) Battalion from 36 Infantry Base Depot and transferred to Princess Victoria's (Royal Irish Fusiliers) in September/October 1917 (renumbered 41143). Transferred to the Class Z Reserve 23 March 1919. 1914-15 Star.

ROBINSON Private Hugh 14660. Born in 1878 at Portadown, County Armagh. A weaver. Enlisted September 1914. Posted to the 10th (Reserve) Battalion 9 October 1915. Appointed Drummer 1 November 1916. Transferred to the Royal Defence Corps (renumbered 73199) 4 May 1918 and served with 250th Protection Company. Transferred to The Black Watch (Royal Highlanders) (renumbered S/27392) 29 June 1918 and joined the 9th (Service) Battalion in 47th Brigade, 16th Division. Transferred to the Class Z Reserve 4 April 1919.

ROBINSON Private Hugh 41135. [Enlisted in April 1915 into the Service Squadron, 6th (Inniskilling) Dragoons (UD/257). To France with 36th (Ulster) Division in October 1915. Served with 2nd North Irish Horse, X Corps Cavalry Regiment.] Joined the renamed 9th (North Irish Horse) Battalion from 36 Infantry Base Depot and transferred to Princess Victoria's (Royal Irish Fusiliers) in September/October 1917 (renumbered 41135). Transferred to the Class Z Reserve 20 March 1919. 1914-15 Star.

ROBINSON Private James 14665. Enlisted September 1914. No record of date of deployment to France with 36th (Ulster) Division.

ROBINSON DCM Warrant Officer Class II John (Jack) 14642. Enlisted September 1914. To France with 36th (Ulster) Division in October 1915. **36th (Ulster) Division Certificate for Gallantry** 1 July 1916. **DCM** – Moeuvres 23 November 1917 as Company Quartermaster Sergeant in 'D' Company. Company Sergeant Major. Transferred to the Class Z Reserve 23 March 1919. 1914-15 Star. Served during the Second World War in the Ulster Home Guard.

ROBINSON Private Reginald 42245. [Enlisted 4 September 1915 into the Army Service Corps (T4/247656). Served with 66th Division Train.] Transferred to Princess Victoria's (Royal Irish Fusiliers) 8 May 1918 (renumbered 42245) and joined the 9th (North Irish Horse) Battalion. Discharged as no longer physically fit for war service due to sickness 18 July 1918, aged 22. Silver War Badge, number 425691.

ROBINSON MM Corporal Robert Edmund 20086. Born in 1899 at Poyntzpass, County Armagh. Worked at Cultra Manor, County Down. Enlisted in June 1915, aged 15. Posted to the 10th (Reserve) Battalion in October 1915. Joined the 9th (Service) Battalion in late-summer 1916. 'B' Company. [Attached to 108th Trench Mortar Battery. **Wounded** when he lost three fingers to shellfire on 30 November 1916. Treated at County of Middlesex War Hospital, Napsbury, St Albans. **MM**. While on leave in June 1917 at a function held by the people of Poyntzpass he was presented with a gold watch and chain. Subsequently transferred to The Royal Irish Rifles (renumbered

22223) and joined the 20th (Reserve) Battalion, The Royal Irish Rifles.] His brother, Lance Corporal William James Robinson, was killed in action on 22 March 1918 serving with the 1st Battalion, The Royal Muster Fusiliers.

ROBINSON Private Samuel 18243. From Markethill, County Armagh. Enlisted into the 9th (Service) Battalion in February 1915. To France with 36th (Ulster) Division in October 1915. 'C' Company. **Killed in action** during the attack at Hamel 1 July 1916, aged 24. 1914-15 Star.

ROBINSON Sergeant William 14631. Born in 1871 at Tandragee, County Armagh. A fireman. 3rd Battalion, Armagh Regiment, Ulster Volunteer Force. Enlisted September 1914, aged 43 but giving his age as 34. To France with 36th (Ulster) Division in October 1915. Transferred to the Class Z Reserve 31 March 1919. 1914-15 Star. A pension record exists for a man of this name and number indicating that he was discharged as not being likely to become an efficient soldier in that he was considered medically unfit for service on 1 October 1914. It is likely that this was a clerical error and the document was annotated in error. The relevant entry is the same as that for Private William John Robinson.

ROBINSON Private William 14652. Born at Lurgan, County Armagh. 5th (Lurgan) Battalion, Armagh Regiment, Ulster Volunteer Force. A weaver. Enlisted September 1914. Discharged as not being likely to become an efficient soldier in that he was considered medically unfit for service (varicose veins and unable to march) 7 November 1914.

ROBINSON Private William 18054. Enlisted into the 9th (Service) Battalion in February 1915. To France with 36th (Ulster) Division in October 1915. 'C' Company. Detached to Battalion Transport and did not take part in the attack on 1 July 1916. Transferred to the Class Z Reserve 21 February 1919. 1914-15 Star.

ROBINSON Private William 23596. Enlisted in December 1915. Posted to the 9th (Service) Battalion.

ROBINSON Private William John 14658. Born in 1870 at Shankill, County Armagh. A weaver. Served for twelve years in the 3rd Battalion (Militia), Princess Victoria's (Royal Irish Fusiliers) Enlisted September 1914, aged 44 but giving his age as 38 years. Discharged as not being likely to become an efficient soldier in that he was considered medically unfit for service 1 October 1914.

ROBINSON Private William John 18183 & 22750. From Armagh, County Armagh. A labourer. Enlisted 26 February 1915, giving his age as 35 years. Discharged as not being likely to become an efficient soldier in that he was considered medically unfit for service (very poor teeth) 13 April 1915. Re-enlisted 9 November 1915, again giving his age as 35 years (numbered 22750). Posted to the 3rd (Reserve) Battalion.

ROBSON Private Joseph 20335. Enlisted in May/June 1915 and joined the 9th (Service) Battalion with the draft of men from The Royal Inniskilling Fusiliers who transferred to Princess Victoria's (Royal Irish Fusiliers) on 30 June 1915. To France 17 November 1915 and rejoined the 9th (Service) Battalion. 'C' Company. Evacuated to hospital in England June 1916. Did not take part in the attack at Hamel on 1 July 1916. Transferred to the Class Z Reserve 9 March 1919. 1914-15 Star.

ROBSON Sergeant William 20312. Enlisted in May/June 1915 and joined the 9th (Service) Battalion with the draft of men from The Royal Inniskilling Fusiliers who transferred to Princess Victoria's (Royal Irish Fusiliers) on 30 June 1915.

RODDY Sergeant Dennis 29590. Born in 1897. From Londonderry. A clerk. [Enlisted 2 August 1915 into The Royal Irish Rifles (20656) and joined the 3rd (Reserve) Battalion, The Royal Irish Rifles. Lance Corporal 12 August 1916. Joined the 5th (Extra Reserve) Battalion, The Royal Irish Rifles 17 August 1917. Corporal 25 August 1917. Transferred to Princess Victoria's (Royal Irish Fusiliers) 27 March 1918 (renumbered 29590) and joined the 3rd (Reserve) Battalion. Reverted to Lance Corporal 28 March 1918.] To 'A' Infantry Base Depot, France 3 April 1918 and posted to the 9th (North Irish Horse) Battalion. Sergeant 8 April 1918. **Killed in action** during the attack south of Wulverghem 4 September 1918, aged 21.

RODGERS MM Private James 20353. From Glasgow. Enlisted in May/June 1915 and joined the 9th (Service) Battalion with the draft of men from The Royal Inniskilling Fusiliers who transferred to Princess Victoria's (Royal Irish Fusiliers) on 30 June 1915. To France with 36th (Ulster) Division in October 1915. **Wounded** during the attack at Hamel 1 July 1916. **MM** – Battle of Langemarck 16

August 1917. [Transferred to the Army Service Corps (renumbered S/389990).] 1914-15 Star.

RODGERS Private James 41540. [Enlisted in September 1912 into the North Irish Horse (732). To France 17 August 1914 with 'A' Squadron as GHQ Troops. Served with 2nd North Irish Horse, X Corps Cavalry Regiment.] Joined the renamed 9th (North Irish Horse) Battalion from 36 Infantry Base Depot and transferred to Princess Victoria's (Royal Irish Fusiliers) in September/October 1917 (renumbered 41540). 1914 Star.

RODGERS Private William Kiddy 43280. Born in 1891 at Milford, Derby. A painter. Served pre-war in the 5th Battalion (Militia), The Sherwood Foresters (Nottinghamshire and Derbyshire Regiment). [Enlisted 25 November 1915 and transferred to the Army Reserve. Mobilised 16 February 1916 and joined the 3rd (Reserve) Battalion, The Sherwood Foresters (Nottinghamshire and Derbyshire Regiment) (35831).] To France 16 July 1916. Transferred to Princess Victoria's (Royal Irish Fusiliers) 31 August 1916 having joined the 9th (Service) Battalion on 8 August 1916 (renumbered 43280). 'D' Company. **Wounded** by a gunshot to the chest and **captured** in the period 21-28 March 1918 during the retreat from St Quentin. **Died of wounds** in the War Hospital at Avesnes-sur-Helpe at 6.30am on 14 April 1918 while a prisoner of war, aged 27.

ROE DCM Lance Sergeant Hubert 41147. Born in 1892 at Horton, Yorkshire. From Wealdstone, Middlesex. [Served as a regular soldier with 2nd Dragoon Guards (Queen's Bays) (4392). To France in 1st Cavalry Division August 1914. Served with 6th (Inniskilling) Dragoons (4392) in 2nd North Irish Horse, X Corps Cavalry Regiment.] Joined the renamed 9th (North Irish Horse) Battalion from 36 Infantry Base Depot and transferred to Princess Victoria's (Royal Irish Fusiliers) in September/October 1917 (renumbered 41147). **DCM** – Moeuvres 23 November 1917 and **wounded**. [When recovered he joined the 1st Battalion where he was **wounded**. He **died of wounds** 8 April 1918 in 14th General Hospital, Wimereux.] His brother, Private George C Roe, served with The Hertfordshire Regiment and the Corps of Royal Engineers. His brother, Private William Arthur Roe, served with The King's Royal Rifle Corps (wounded) and the Labour Corps.

ROGERS Corporal Cecil Arthur 18162 & 7040614. From Islington, London. A groundsman. [Enlisted 16 February 1915, aged 18, into the 5th (Service) or 6th (Service) Battalion in 31st Brigade, 10th (Irish) Division. Served with the Mediterranean Expeditionary Force from 4 October 1915 to November 1915. Served in Salonika from 27 November 1915 to September 1917. Served in Egypt from 22 September 1917 to May 1918.] To France 18 May 1918. Posted to the 9th (North Irish Horse) Battalion. 1914-15 Star. Transferred to the Section B Army Reserve, Princess Victoria's (Royal Irish Fusiliers) (renumbered 7040614) 1 May 1919. Discharged 15 February 1927.

ROGERS MM* Private Frank C 23504. From Highbury, London. [Enlisted (or transferred to Princess Victoria's (Royal Irish Fusiliers)) in December 1915 and joined the 7th or 8th (Service) Battalion. **MM & 16th (Irish) Division Parchment Certificate for Gallantry and Devotion to Duty** – Battle of Langemarck 16 August 1917.] Joined the 9th (North Irish Horse) Battalion when the 7th/8th (Service) Battalion was disbanded in February 1918. **MM Bar** – St Quentin 21-28 March 1918.

ROGERS Private Joseph 43336. Born in 1890 at Littleport, Cambridgeshire. From Canning Town, London. A flour miller. [Enlisted 1 December 1915 and transferred to the Army Reserve. Mobilised 17 July 1916 and joined 3/7th Battalion, The London Regiment (6719). To France 10 November 1916 and posted to 1/7th (City of London) Battalion, The London Regiment.] Attached to the 9th (Service) Battalion, Princess Victoria's (Royal Irish Fusiliers) 26 November 1916. 'A' Company. Discharged from the Territorial Force, re-enlisted and transferred to Princess Victoria's (Royal Irish Fusiliers) 10 April 1917. **Wounded** (shell shock) at Messines 9 June 1917. Evacuated to hospital in England 5 March 1918. Joined the 3rd (Reserve) Battalion 7 May 1918. [Transferred to the Labour Corps 29 August 1918 and posted to 485th Home Service Employment Company. Served with 527th and 522nd Home Service Employment Companies. Corporal 29 April 1919. Transferred to Alexandra, Princess of Wales's Own (Yorkshire Regiment) (66288) 28 June 1919.] Transferred to the Class Z Reserve 8 November 1919.

ROLLINS Private Thomas Henry 41260. [Enlisted in August 1914 into the North Irish Horse (984). To France 9 February 1915. Served with 2nd North Irish Horse, X Corps Cavalry Regiment.] Joined the renamed 9th (North Irish Horse) Battalion from 36 Infantry Base Depot and transferred to Princess Victoria's (Royal Irish Fusiliers) in September/October 1917 (renumbered 41260). 'C'

Company. **Missing** in the period 21-28 March 1918 during the retreat from St Quentin believed **captured**. Transferred to the Class Z Reserve 15 April 1919. 1914-15 Star.

ROLSTON Private William 14640. Enlisted September 1914. To France with 36th (Ulster) Division in October 1915. 1914-15 Star.

ROONEY Private Samuel 20124. From Portadown, County Armagh. Enlisted into the 9th (Service) Battalion in June 1915. To France with 36th (Ulster) Division in October 1915. **Wounded** during the attack at Hamel 1 July 1916. Transferred to the Class Z Reserve 31 March 1919. 1914-15 Star.

ROONEY Private Terence 18332. From Dublin. Enlisted in March 1915. Later posted to the 9th (North Irish Horse) Battalion. **Killed in action** during the attack south of Wulverghem 4 September 1918, aged 30.

ROONEY MM Sergeant Thomas 23829. From Belfast. Enlisted in January 1916 and joined the 7th/8th (Service) Battalion in 49th Brigade, 16th (Irish) Division.] Joined the 9th (North Irish Horse) Battalion when the 7th/8th (Service) Battalion was disbanded in February 1918. **MM** late-1917.

ROONEY Private Thomas 24803. Enlisted in September 1916. Posted to the 9th (Service) Battalion. 'B' Company. **Missing** in the period 21-28 March 1918 during the retreat from St Quentin believed **captured**.

ROSE Lance Corporal Edgar Cecil 43380. Born in 1891 at Paddington, London. A railway clerk. [Enlisted 2 September 1914 and joined 1/9th (County of London) Battalion, The London Regiment (Queen Victoria's Rifles) (2924). To France 22 January 1915. To hospital (ulcerated toe) 20 January 1916 and evacuated to hospital in England 5 February 1916.] To France 11 November 1916. Attached to the 9th (Service) Battalion, Princess Victoria's (Royal Irish Fusiliers) 26 November 1916. 'D' Company. Discharged from the Territorial Force, re-enlisted and transferred to Princess Victoria's (Royal Irish Fusiliers) in March/April 1917 (renumbered 43380). Lance Corporal 25 April 1917. **Wounded** by gunshots to the left arm, right leg and face at the Battle of Langemarck 16 August 1917 and **died of wounds** in 32nd Stationary Hospital, Wimereux on 10 September 1917. 1914-15 Star.

ROSENBERG Private Barnet 40025. (Some military records show his name as Bernard.) Born in 1879 at Leeds, Yorkshire. [Enlisted into The Prince of Wales's Own (West Yorkshire Regiment) (34322).] Transferred to Princess Victoria's (Royal Irish Fusiliers) 30 November 1916 (renumbered 40025) and joined the 9th (Service) Battalion 12 December 1916. 'A' Company. **Killed in action** at the Battle of Langemarck 16 August 1917, aged 38.

ROSS Private George 43391. [Enlisted 10 November 1915 into The London Regiment (5909). Posted to the 1/9th (County of London) Battalion, The London Regiment (Queen Victoria's Rifles).] Attached to the 9th (Service) Battalion, Princess Victoria's (Royal Irish Fusiliers) 26 November 1916. Discharged from the Territorial Force, re-enlisted and transferred to Princess Victoria's (Royal Irish Fusiliers) in March/April 1917 (renumbered 43391). **Wounded**. Discharged as no longer physically fit for war service due to wounds 14 February 1919. Silver War Badge, number B150026.

ROSS Private George Victor 41330. [Enlisted 12 December 1916 into the North Irish Horse (2323). Served with 2nd North Irish Horse, X Corps Cavalry Regiment.] Joined the renamed 9th (North Irish Horse) Battalion from 36 Infantry Base Depot and transferred to Princess Victoria's (Royal Irish Fusiliers) in September/October 1917 (renumbered 41330). **Wounded**. Discharged as no longer physically fit for war service due to wounds 29 November 1919. Silver War Badge, number B349065.

ROSS Private Henry 41211. [Enlisted in March 1915 into the North Irish Horse (1464). To France with 'F' Squadron in 33rd Division 17 November 1915. Served with 2nd North Irish Horse, X Corps Cavalry Regiment.] Joined the renamed 9th (North Irish Horse) Battalion from 36 Infantry Base Depot and transferred to Princess Victoria's (Royal Irish Fusiliers) in September/October 1917 (renumbered 41211).

ROSS Private Isaac 23063. From Glasgow. Enlisted 15 November 1915. Posted to the 9th (Service) Battalion in mid-1916. **Wounded** during the attack at Hamel 1 July 1916. Discharged as no longer physically fit for war service due to sickness 25 December 1916. Silver War Badge, number 100521.

ROSS Private John 41317. [Enlisted 6 December 1915 into the North Irish Horse (2032). Served with 2nd North Irish Horse, X Corps Cavalry Regiment.] Joined the renamed 9th (North Irish Horse) Battalion from 36 Infantry Base Depot and transferred to Princess Victoria's (Royal Irish Fusiliers) in September/October 1917 (renumbered 41317). 'C' Company. Believed **wounded** in the period 21-28 March 1918 during the retreat from St Quentin. Discharged as no longer physically fit for war service due to wounds 14 March 1919. Silver War Badge, number B162122.

ROSS Private L H 42471. [Served previously with The Royal Irish Rifles (20517, this number is also listed for Private A Laverty above).] Transferred at the Base Depot to Princess Victoria's (Royal Irish Fusiliers) 14 September 1918 (renumbered 42471) and joined the 9th (North Irish Horse) Battalion 22 September 1918. [Transferred to the Seaforth Highlanders (Ross-shire Buffs, The Duke of Albany's) (renumbered 31992). **Deserted**.]

ROSS Private Stuart Gordon 42469. From Jersey. A farmer. [Enlisted 30 April 1917 and joined the 4th (Extra Reserve) Battalion, The Royal Irish Rifles (10814). To France 13 July 1918.] Transferred at the Base Depot to Princess Victoria's (Royal Irish Fusiliers) 14 September 1918 (renumbered 42469) and joined the 9th (North Irish Horse) Battalion 22 September 1918. **Wounded** by a gunshot to the left arm at Hill 41 11 October 1918 and evacuated to hospital in England. Posted to the 3rd (Reserve) Battalion. Discharged as no longer physically fit for war service due to wounds 6 June 1919. Silver War Badge, number B274248.

ROULSTON Private Willie 41261. Born in 1894 at Ramelton, County Donegal. From Londonderry. [Enlisted 5 September 1914 into the North Irish Horse (1153). To France 20 January 1915. **Wounded** by a gunshot to the chest 13 April 1915. Treated at 13th General Hospital, Boulogne and evacuated to hospital in England 27 April 1915. Treated at hospital in Liverpool. To France 4 August 1916. Served with 2nd North Irish Horse, X Corps Cavalry Regiment.] Joined the renamed 9th (North Irish Horse) Battalion from 36 Infantry Base Depot and transferred to Princess Victoria's (Royal Irish Fusiliers) in September/October 1917 (renumbered 41261). [Transferred to the Tank Corps (renumbered 304847) 28 December 1917 and posted for training to the Tank Corps Depot, at Bovington near Wareham, Dorset. Posted to the 17th Battalion, Tank Corps 12 January 1918. To the Tank Corps Reinforcement Depot, France 2 September 1918 and posted to the 11th Battalion, Tank Corps 7 November 1918.] Transferred to the Class Z Reserve 28 March 1919. 1914-15 Star.

ROUNTREE Private William 23880. Born at Belturbet, County Cavan. From Knockateery, Cloverhill, County Cavan. Enlisted in January 1916. Posted to the 9th (Service) Battalion. 'C' Company. **Killed in action** during the Battle of Messines 9 June 1917, aged 22.

ROUT Private Frederick George 43392. [Enlisted into The London Regiment (5254). Posted to the 1/9th (County of London) Battalion, The London Regiment (Queen Victoria's Rifles).] Attached to the 9th (Service) Battalion, Princess Victoria's (Royal Irish Fusiliers) 26 November 1916. 'D' Company. Discharged from the Territorial Force, re-enlisted and transferred to Princess Victoria's (Royal Irish Fusiliers) in March/April 1917 (renumbered 43392). **Missing** in the period 21-28 March 1918 during the retreat from St Quentin believed **captured**.

ROWAN Private Andrew 14655. Born at Loughgilly, County Armagh. Lived at Coronation Street, Portadown, County Armagh. A weaver in the linen trade. Enlisted September 1914. To France with 36th (Ulster) Division in October 1915. 'B' Company. **Killed in action** during the attack at Hamel 1 July 1916, aged 35. He is buried in the same grave as Private William Henry Pentland in Ancre British Cemetery. 1914-15 Star.

ROWAN Private Charles 22727. Enlisted 7 November 1915. Posted to the 9th (Service) Battalion. 'C' Company. **Wounded** during the attack at Hamel 1 July 1916. Discharged as no longer physically fit for war service due to wounds 26 November 1917. Silver War Badge, number 275448.

ROWEN Private Henry 41094. [Enlisted in March 1915 into the Service Squadron, 6th (Inniskilling) Dragoons (UD/222). To France with 36th (Ulster) Division in October 1915. Served with 2nd North Irish Horse, X Corps Cavalry Regiment.] Joined the renamed 9th (North Irish Horse) Battalion from 36 Infantry Base Depot and transferred to Princess Victoria's (Royal Irish Fusiliers) in September/October 1917 (renumbered 41094). Transferred to the Class Z Reserve 29 March 1919. 1914-15 Star.

ROWLAND Private John 14628. Enlisted September 1914. Discharged as no longer physically fit for war service due to sickness 25 May 1915, aged 34. Silver War Badge, number 508794.

ROWNTREE Private Robert 14644. (Some records show his name spelled Rountree) Born in 1889 at Loughgall, County Armagh. A gardener. Enlisted September 1914. To France with 36th (Ulster) Division in October 1915. 'A' Company. Accidentally shot and killed Second Lieutenant H H Dunwoody on 31 July 1916. [Transferred to the Tank Corps (renumbered 304873 Corporal) 28 December 1917 and posted for training to the Tank Corps Depot, at Bovington near Wareham, Dorset.] 1914-15 Star.

RUDDELL Sergeant Frederick 14635. From Portadown, County Armagh. 4th (Portadown) Battalion, Armagh Regiment, Ulster Volunteer Force. Enlisted September 1914. To France with 36th (Ulster) Division in October 1915. Transferred to the Class Z Reserve. 1914-15 Star.

RUDDELL Private Joseph 14645. Born in 1895. From Shankill, County Armagh. Enlisted September 1914. Discharged as not being likely to become an efficient soldier in that he was considered medically unfit for service 20 October 1914.

RUDDELL Private William 29547. Enlisted 18 October 1915 and served elsewhere. Re-enlisted or transferred to Princess Victoria's (Royal Irish Fusiliers) in March 1918 (renumbered 29547). Posted to the 9th (North Irish Horse) Battalion. Discharged as no longer physically fit for war service due to sickness 13 March 1919. Silver War Badge, number B162041.

RUDDY Private John 42361. [Enlisted 7 April 1915 into The Royal Irish Rifles Special Reserve (7556). Served with the 1st Battalion.] Transferred at the Base Depot to Princess Victoria's (Royal Irish Fusiliers) 14 September 1918 and joined the 9th (North Irish Horse) Battalion 22 September 1918. **Wounded**. Discharged as no longer physically fit for war service due to wounds 31 March 1919. Silver War Badge, number B185287.

RUSK Private John 14637. Enlisted September 1914. To France with 36th (Ulster) Division in October 1915. [Transferred to the Royal Flying Corps (renumbered 129237).] 1914-15 Star.

RUSK Private James 17553. Born at Kileevin, County Monaghan. Enlisted into the 9th (Service) Battalion in November/December 1914. To France with 36th (Ulster) Division in October 1915. **Killed in action** during the attack at Hamel 1 July 1916. 1914-15 Star.

RUSSELL Company Quarter Master Sergeant George 15711. A former regular soldier. Enlisted September 1914. To France with 36th (Ulster) Division in October 1915 and employed in a Divisional administrative post (Colour Sergeant). [Subsequently Acting Regimental Quartermaster Sergeant in The Northumberland Fusiliers (52382).] 1914-15 Star.

RUSSELL Private James 15869. Enlisted into the 9th (Service) Battalion in October 1914. No record of deployment to France with 36th (Ulster) Division.

RUSSELL Private John 27687. Enlisted in June 1917. Posted to the 9th (North Irish Horse) Battalion. 'D' Company. **Missing** in the period 21-28 March 1918 during the retreat from St Quentin believed **captured**.

RUSSELL Private John Francis 41460. [Enlisted 26 August 1916 into the North Irish Horse (2250). Served with 2nd North Irish Horse, X Corps Cavalry Regiment.] Joined the renamed 9th (North Irish Horse) Battalion from 36 Infantry Base Depot and transferred to Princess Victoria's (Royal Irish Fusiliers) in September/October 1917 (renumbered 41460). Discharged as no longer physically fit for war service due to sickness 7 August 1918, aged 22. Silver War Badge, number 434649.

RUSSELL Private Joseph 14632. From Portadown, County Armagh. 4th (Portadown) Battalion, Armagh Regiment, Ulster Volunteer Force. Enlisted September 1914. To France with 36th (Ulster) Division in October 1915. **Wounded** during the attack at Hamel 1 July 1916. [Posted to the 11th (Service) Battalion. Served with the 5th/6th (Service) Battalion when the 11th (Service) Battalion was absorbed.] 1914-15 Star. Brother of Lance Corporal Thomas James Russell. His brother Private William George Russell earned a DCM in 1914 serving with the Irish Guards; he was discharged in 1917 and died as a result of his war service in 1927.

RUSSELL Private Nicholas 41334. [Enlisted in March 1917 into the North Irish Horse (2399). Served with 2nd North Irish Horse, X Corps Cavalry Regiment.] Joined the renamed 9th (North Irish Horse) Battalion from 36 Infantry Base Depot and transferred to Princess Victoria's (Royal Irish Fusiliers) in September/October 1917 (renumbered 41334). 'B' Company. **Wounded** during the retreat from St Quentin 21-28 March 1918.

RUSSELL Lance Corporal Thomas James 14630. From Park Road, Portadown, County Armagh and the eldest of five sons. Enlisted into Princess Victoria's (Royal Irish Fusiliers) in 1893 and joined the 2nd Battalion. Rejoined from the Army Reserve at the beginning of the South African War and served in the Royal Field Artillery. Queen's South Africa Medal with five clasps, King's South Africa Medal with clasps 'South Africa 1901' and 'South Africa 1902'. 4th (Portadown) Battalion, Armagh Regiment, Ulster Volunteer Force. Enlisted September 1914. To France with 36th (Ulster) Division in October 1915. **Killed in action** during the attack at Hamel 1 July 1916. Brother of Private Joseph Russell. His brother Private William George Russell earned a DCM in 1914 serving with the Irish Guards; he was discharged in 1917 and died as a result of his war service in 1927.

RUSSELL Private William John 14659. Born in 1897 at Lurgan, County Armagh. Enlisted September 1914. To France with 36th (Ulster) Division in October 1915. **Wounded** during the attack at Hamel 1 July 1916 and **died of wounds** 3 July 1916, aged 19. 1914-15 Star. His father, Private William George Russell, and his brother, Private David Russell, served with The Royal Irish Rifles.

RUSSELL Private William Wilfred 22447. Born at St Pancras, London. [Mobilised from the Army Reserve or the Special Reserve and to France 27 December 1914. Joined the 2nd Battalion, The Bedfordshire Regiment (17851). Transferred to Princess Victoria's (Royal Irish Fusiliers) in November 1915 (renumbered 22447) and joined the 5th (Service) Battalion in 31st Brigade, 10th (Irish) Division in the Mediterranean Expeditionary Force.] Posted to the 9th (Service) Battalion. **Killed in action** during the attack north of Bailleul 24 August 1918, aged 26. 1914-15 Star.

RUTHERFORD Private William 41416. [Enlisted in January 1913 into the North Irish Horse (786). To France 20 August 1914 with 'C' Squadron as 5th Division Cavalry and then as GHQ Troops. Served with 2nd North Irish Horse, X Corps Cavalry Regiment.] Joined the renamed 9th (North Irish Horse) Battalion from 36 Infantry Base Depot and transferred to Princess Victoria's (Royal Irish Fusiliers) in September/October 1917 (renumbered 41416). 'B' Company. **Missing** in the period 21-28 March 1918 during the retreat from St Quentin believed **captured**. 1914 Star.

RYAN Lance Corporal David 18653. Enlisted into the 9th (Service) Battalion in April 1915.

RYAN Private Edward 20097. Enlisted on 8 June 1915 into the 9th (Service) Battalion. Discharged as no longer physically fit for war service due to sickness 31 July 1917. Silver War Badge, number 226565.

RYAN Private Frederick 18453. From Druminargle, Scarva, County Down. Enlisted into the 9th (Service) Battalion in March 1915. To France with 36th (Ulster) Division in October 1915. **Wounded** during the attack at Hamel 1 July 1916. [Posted to the 1st Battalion. **Captured** in the period 21-28 March 1918 during the retreat from St Quentin.] Transferred to the Class Z Reserve 1 April 1919. 1914-15 Star.

RYAN Lance Corporal William Patrick 43466. [Enlisted into The London Regiment (3985). Posted to the 1/24th (County of London) Battalion, The London Regiment (The Queen's).] To France and joined 36 Infantry Base Depot 29 March 1918. Transferred to Princess Victoria's (Royal Irish Fusiliers) 2 April 1918 (renumbered 43466) and joined the 9th (North Irish Horse) Battalion 4 April 1918.

SADLER Corporal James William 42134. Born in 1888 at Wokingham, Berkshire. [Enlisted into the Army Service Corps (S4/035590). To France 15 January 1915.] Transferred to Princess Victoria's (Royal Irish Fusiliers) 8 May 1918 (renumbered 42134) and joined the 9th (North Irish Horse) Battalion 8 June 1918. [Part of the draft transferred on 19 June 1918 to The Royal Irish Rifles (renumbered 45847) and joined the 12th (Service) Battalion, The Royal Irish Rifles (Central Antrim). **Killed in action** 3 September 1918.] 1914-15 Star.

SALLIS Private Sydney Herbert 19103. Born in 1897 at Littleport, Cambridgeshire. [Enlisted into the Royal Field Artillery (146876).] Transferred to Princess Victoria's (Royal Irish Fusiliers) in December 1915. Posted to the 9th (Service) Battalion. 'B' Company. **Missing** at the Battle of Langemarck 16 August 1917 and later declared **killed in action** on that date.

SALLOWAY Private George E 43274. Born in 1883 at Derby, Derbyshire. [Enlisted into The Sherwood Foresters (Nottinghamshire and Derbyshire Regiment) (18600).] Transferred to Princess Victoria's (Royal Irish Fusiliers) 31 August 1916 (renumbered 43274) having joined the 9th (Service) Battalion on 8 August 1916. [Transferred to the Machine Gun Corps (renumbered 159339).] Died at Derby in 1959, aged 76.

SALMON Corporal William John 22089. [Enlisted in October 1915 and joined the 7th or 8th (Service) Battalion in 49th Brigade, 16th (Irish) Division.] Joined the 9th (North Irish Horse) Battalion when the 7th/8th (Service) Battalion was disbanded in February 1918.

SAMUELS Private William N 42196. [Enlisted into the Army Service Corps (S/390536). Transferred to the Royal Field Artillery (renumbered 243196).] Transferred to Princess Victoria's (Royal Irish Fusiliers) 8 May 1918 (renumbered 42196) and joined the 9th (North Irish Horse) Battalion. [Transferred to the Seaforth Highlanders (Ross-shire Buffs, The Duke of Albany's) (renumbered S/44575).]

SANDERS Private James 45819. [Enlisted into The London Regiment. Posted to 1/22nd (County of London) Battalion, The London Regiment (The Queen's).] To France and joined 36 Infantry Base Depot 29 March 1918. Transferred to Princess Victoria's (Royal Irish Fusiliers) 2 April 1918 (renumbered 45819) and joined the 9th (North Irish Horse) Battalion 4 April 1918. [Transferred to the Army Service Corps (renumbered MT/43895).]

SANDERS Private Lawrie 43242. [Enlisted into The Sherwood Foresters (Nottinghamshire and Derbyshire Regiment) (15096).] Transferred to Princess Victoria's (Royal Irish Fusiliers) 31 August 1916 (renumbered 43242) having joined the 9th (Service) Battalion on 8 August 1916. [Transferred to the Royal Defence Corps (renumbered 73201).] Transferred to the Class Z Reserve.

SANDERSON Private Albert George 40029. Born on 1 December 1881 at York. [Enlisted 7 December 1915 and transferred to the Army Reserve. Mobilised 9 June 1916 and joined 14th (Reserve) Battalion, The Prince of Wales's Own (West Yorkshire Regiment) (33460).] Transferred to Princess Victoria's (Royal Irish Fusiliers) 30 November 1916 (renumbered 40029) and joined the 9th (Service) Battalion 12 December 1916. 'A' Company. To 110th Field Ambulance sick (influenza) 24 April 1917; rejoined 4 May 1917. To 109th Field Ambulance injured (knee) 8 November 1917; rejoined 15 November 1917. To hospital at Le Havre sick (diarrhoea) 5 December 1917; rejoined after leave on 3 March 1918. **Wounded** by gunshots to the legs 27 March 1918 during the retreat from St Quentin and evacuated to hospital in England. Treated at 1st Southern General Hospital, Birmingham, The Hollies Four Oaks Voluntary Aid Detachment Hospital, Birmingham and the North of Ireland Convalescent Depot, Randalstown, County Antrim. Posted to the 3rd (Reserve Garrison) Battalion 28 August 1918. [Transferred to the Labour Corps (renumbered 651743). To France 1 October 1918 and posted to 78th Labour Company.] Transferred to the Class Z Reserve 24 March 1919.

SANDERSON Private James 14682. Enlisted September 1914. To France with 36th (Ulster) Division in October 1915. [Transferred to the Labour Corps (renumbered 396445).] Transferred to the Class Z Reserve 1 April 1919. 1914-15 Star.

SANDS Private Alfred 42480. [Enlisted into The Royal Irish Rifles (5251). Served with the 6th (Service) Battalion, The Royal Irish Rifles in the Mediterranean Expeditionary Force from 16 October 1915.] Transferred at the Base Depot to Princess Victoria's (Royal Irish Fusiliers) 14 September 1918 (renumbered 42480) and joined the 9th (North Irish Horse) Battalion 22 September 1918. [Transferred to The Royal Inniskilling Fusiliers (48985).] 1914-15 Star.

SANDS Private David 41595. [Enlisted in April 1915 into the North Irish Horse (1482). To France 22 September 1915. Served with 2nd North Irish Horse, X Corps Cavalry Regiment.] Joined the renamed 9th (North Irish Horse) Battalion from 36 Infantry Base Depot and transferred to Princess Victoria's (Royal Irish Fusiliers) in September/October 1917 (renumbered 41595). 'D' Company. **Missing** in the period 21-28 March 1918 during the retreat from St Quentin believed **captured**. Transferred to the Class Z Reserve 7 March 1919. 1914-15 Star.

SANDS Private Joe 18094. From Ballymerattybeg, County Armagh. Enlisted into the 9th (Service) Battalion 16 February 1915. Discharged as not being likely to become an efficient soldier in that he was considered medically unfit (epilepsy) for service 24 April 1915. His illness came to light when he was examined by Lieutenant W S Berry in a post-epileptic coma.

SANDS Private Joseph 40071. [Enlisted into the 12th (Service) Battalion, The Prince of Wales's Own (West Yorkshire Regiment) (14693). To France 11 September 1915.] Transferred to Princess Victoria's (Royal Irish Fusiliers) 30 November 1916 (renumbered 40071) and joined the 9th (Service) Battalion 12 December 1916. [Transferred to the Royal Flying Corps (renumbered 144909) 8 March

1918 (with Privates J D Couser and W Muir).] 1914-15 Star.

SANDS Private William John 14699. Born 16 July 1893 in Clare, County Down. Lived in Bleary, County Armagh. A weaver. Enlisted September 1914. To France with 36th (Ulster) Division in October 1915. 'C' Company. Company bombing team. **Wounded** (shell-shock) at Hamel 24 June 1916. Transferred to the Class Z Reserve. 1914-15 Star. He became a civil servant in Lurgan working at the Employment Office. Died in Lurgan, County Armagh in November 1974, aged 81.

SAUNDERS Lance Corporal Alfred Charles 20767. [Enlisted 31 January 1915 into the 8th (Service) Battalion in 49th Brigade 16th (Irish) Division.] Joined the 9th (North Irish Horse) Battalion when the 7th/8th (Service) Battalion was disbanded in February 1918. 'D' Company. **Wounded** during the retreat from St Quentin 21-28 March 1918. Discharged as no longer physically fit for war service due to wounds 19 September 1918, aged 32. Silver War Badge, number B5076.

SAUNDERS Private George W 42568. [Enlisted into The Royal Sussex Regiment (4786). Transferred to The Royal Irish Rifles (renumbered 42837).] Transferred at the Base Depot to Princess Victoria's (Royal Irish Fusiliers) 14 September 1918 (renumbered 42568) and joined the 9th (North Irish Horse) Battalion 22 September 1918. [Transferred to 5th (Service) Battalion, The Royal Irish Regiment (Pioneers) in the Light Division in the British Army of the Rhine in March/June 1919 (renumbered 41361).]

SCANLON Lance Corporal Frederick 41482. Born in 1890 at Bagnalstown, County Carlow. A shop assistant. [Enlisted 3 March 1915 into the North Irish Horse (1460). To France with 'F' Squadron in 33rd Division 17 November 1915. Lance Corporal 12 August 1916. Served with 2nd North Irish Horse, X Corps Cavalry Regiment.] Joined 36 Infantry Base Depot 25 August 1917. Joined the renamed 9th (North Irish Horse) Battalion from 36 Infantry Base Depot and transferred to Princess Victoria's (Royal Irish Fusiliers) in September/October 1917 (renumbered 41482). **Killed in action** 23 November 1917 at Moeuvres, aged 28. 1914-15 Star.

SCARCE Lance Corporal William Frederick 43308. Born in 1881 at Brighton, Sussex. A hotel porter. [Enlisted 6 July 1916 into The London Regiment (5758).] To France 9 November 1916. Attached to the 9th (Service) Battalion, Princess Victoria's (Royal Irish Fusiliers) 26 November 1916. 'D' Company. Discharged from the Territorial Force, re-enlisted and transferred to Princess Victoria's (Royal Irish Fusiliers) in March/April 1917 (renumbered 43308). Lance Corporal 18 April 1917. **Missing** at the Battle of Langemarck 16 August 1917 and later declared **killed in action** on that date.

SCARLETT Private George Fleming 41497. Born 21 February 1891 at Castlepollard, County Westmeath. A groom for William Chaine at Cairncastle Lodge, County Antrim. [Enlisted in August 1914 into the North Irish Horse (967). To France 18 December 1914. Served with 2nd North Irish Horse, X Corps Cavalry Regiment.] Joined the renamed 9th (North Irish Horse) Battalion from 36 Infantry Base Depot and transferred to Princess Victoria's (Royal Irish Fusiliers) in September/October 1917 (renumbered 41497). **Deserted** 6 February 1918. [Re-enlisted for service as Private George Fleming in the South Irish Horse (H/74182). Transferred to the Army Service Corps (renumbered M/20820) and was discharged 31 August 1922 at the termination of his engagement.] 1914-15 Star.

SCHWENK Private Philip 45756. From Limehouse, London. A clerk. [Enlisted 9 September 1916, aged 17, and transferred to the Army Reserve. Mobilised 18 May 1917 and joined the 22nd (Reserve) Battalion, The London Regiment (683833). Unfit for overseas service, he was transferred to the Labour Corps 31 July 1917 (renumbered 342116) and served with 638th and 639th Home Service Employment Companies. Classed as fit for overseas service, he was transferred back to 22nd (Reserve) Battalion, The London Regiment 18 January 1918.] To France and joined 36 Infantry Base Depot 29 March 1918. Transferred to Princess Victoria's (Royal Irish Fusiliers) 2 April 1918 (renumbered 45756) and joined the 9th (North Irish Horse) Battalion 4 April 1918. To 110th Field Ambulance sick (scabies) 6-13 May 1918. **Killed in action** during the attack north of Bailleul 24 August 1918, aged 19.

SCOTT Corporal Eric John 11345 & 7042303. From Fermoy, County Cork. The son of a regular soldier. [Enlisted into Princess Victoria's (Royal Irish Fusiliers) as a regular soldier 8 September 1913, aged 15. To France 12 June 1916. Served with the 1st Battalion (Acting Sergeant). **Wounded** 17 October 1917 and evacuated to hospital in England 5 November 1917.] Posted to the 9th (North

Irish Horse) Battalion. Re-enlisted in early-1919 for Regular Army service with Princess Victoria's (Royal Irish Fusiliers) (renumbered 7042303). Served with the 1st Battalion in Persia and Mesopotamia in 1919/20. General Service Medal 1918-1962 with clasps 'Iraq' & 'NW Persia'. Joined the 2nd Battalion at Dover. Discharged 2 September 1925. Enlisted into the 5th Battalion, The Royal Inniskilling Fusiliers (Territorial Army).

SCOTT Private Frederick 41468. [Enlisted in November 1915 into the North Irish Horse (1977). Served with 2nd North Irish Horse, X Corps Cavalry Regiment.] Joined the renamed 9th (North Irish Horse) Battalion from 36 Infantry Base Depot and transferred to Princess Victoria's (Royal Irish Fusiliers) in September/October 1917 (renumbered 41468). [Posted to the 11th (Service) Battalion. Served with the 5th/6th (Service) Battalion when the 11th (Service) Battalion was absorbed.]

SCOTT Private Henry William 42488. [Served previously with the 8th (Service) Battalion, The Royal Irish Rifles (East Belfast) (1693).] Transferred at the Base Depot to Princess Victoria's (Royal Irish Fusiliers) 14 September 1918 (renumbered 42488) and joined the 9th (North Irish Horse) Battalion 22 September 1918. Emigrated to the United States and settled in Detroit, Michigan.

SCOTT Private James 42535. [Enlisted into the 10th (Service) Battalion, The Royal Irish Rifles (South Belfast) (13575). To France with 36th (Ulster) Division in October 1915.] Transferred at the Base Depot to Princess Victoria's (Royal Irish Fusiliers) 14 September 1918 and joined the 9th (North Irish Horse) Battalion 22 September 1918. 1914-15 Star.

SCOTT Lance Corporal John 16134. From Corlespratten, Arva, County Cavan. Arva Company, Ulster Volunteer Force. Enlisted into the 9th (Service) Battalion in October 1914. No record of date of deployment to France with 36th (Ulster) Division. 'D' Company. **Wounded** during the attack at Hamel 1 July 1916. **Killed in action** 4 June 1917 on a raid at Spanbroekmolen, aged 27.

SCOTT Private John W 42111. [Enlisted into the Army Veterinary Corps (21923).] Transferred to Princess Victoria's (Royal Irish Fusiliers) 8 May 1918 (renumbered 42111) and joined the 9th (North Irish Horse) Battalion. [Transferred to 5th (Service) Battalion, The Royal Irish Regiment (Pioneers) in the Light Division in the British Army of the Rhine in March/June 1919 (renumbered 41362).]

SCOTT Lance Corporal Sidney James 43445. [Enlisted into The London Regiment (3332). To France 15 March 1915 and posted to the 1/24th (County of London) Battalion, The London Regiment (The Queen's) (8400).] To France and joined 36 Infantry Base Depot 29 March 1918. Transferred to Princess Victoria's (Royal Irish Fusiliers) 2 April 1918 (renumbered 43445) and joined the 9th (North Irish Horse) Battalion 4 April 1918. Company runner, 'B' Company. Discharged 17 February 1919. 1914-15 Star.

SCOTT Private Thomas 18749 & 7040626. From Dublin. A clerk. [Enlisted 17 October 1914. Transferred to Princess Victoria's (Royal Irish Fusiliers) April 1915. To France 2 January 1916 and joined the 1st Battalion. Evacuated to hospital in England 2 December 1917.] To France 4 May 1918 and joined the 9th (North Irish Horse) Battalion. Re-enlisted in early-1919 for Regular Army service with Princess Victoria's (Royal Irish Fusiliers) (renumbered 7040626). Discharged 31 March 1921.

SCOTT MM Sergeant Thomas 22556. From Tynan, County Armagh. [Enlisted in November 1915. Posted to the 7th/8th (Service) Battalion in 49th Brigade, 16th (Irish) Division.] Joined the 9th (North Irish Horse) Battalion when the 7th/8th (Service) Battalion was disbanded in February 1918. **MM** – Bailleul 24 August 1918. **Killed in action** during the attack south of Wulverghem 4 September 1918, aged 21.

SCOTT Private William 17952. From Lurgan, County Armagh. Enlisted into the 9th (Service) Battalion in February 1915. To France with 36th (Ulster) Division in October 1915. 'C' Company. Bombing team during the attack at Hamel 1 July 1916, which he survived unwounded. **Wounded** at the Battle of Langemarck 16 August 1917. **Captured**. Transferred to the Class Z Reserve 15 April 1919. 1914-15 Star. Joined the Royal Irish Constabulary in 1921 and served until 1948. Police Long Service & Good Conduct Medal. Died 30 May 1954, aged 56.

SCOTT Private William John 20068. Enlisted into the 9th (Service) Battalion in June 1915. To France with 36th (Ulster) Division in October 1915. ***Medaille Militaire* (France)**. [Transferred to the Tank Corps (renumbered 304857) 28 December 1917 and posted for training to the Tank Corps Depot, at Bovington near Wareham, Dorset.] 1914-15 Star.

SCOTT Private Wilson 41335. From Arva, County Cavan. [Enlisted 10 December 1915 into the North Irish Horse (2033). Served with 2nd North Irish Horse, X Corps Cavalry Regiment.] Joined the renamed 9th (North Irish Horse) Battalion from 36 Infantry Base Depot and transferred to Princess Victoria's (Royal Irish Fusiliers) in September/October 1917 (renumbered 41335). 'B' Company. **Wounded** and **captured** and in the period 21-28 March 1918 during the retreat from St Quentin. Discharged as no longer physically fit for war service due to wounds 5 August 1919. Silver War Badge, number B293970.

SCUTCHINGS Corporal Leonard William 42158. [Enlisted 17 June 1907 into the Army Service Corps (S/28128). Served with 7th Field Bakery.] Transferred to Princess Victoria's (Royal Irish Fusiliers) 8 May 1918 (renumbered 42158) and joined the 9th (North Irish Horse) Battalion. **Wounded**. Discharged as no longer physically fit for war service due to wounds 8 April 1919. Silver War Badge, number B299502.

SEABY Lance Corporal Ernest 22508. [Mobilised from the Army Reserve or the Special Reserve and to France 12 September 1914 and joined the 2nd Battalion, The Bedfordshire Regiment (6940) in 21st Brigade, 7th Division. Transferred to Princess Victoria's (Royal Irish Fusiliers) in November 1915 (renumbered 22508) and joined the 5th (Service) Battalion in 31st Brigade, 10th (Irish) Division in the Mediterranean Expeditionary Force.] Joined the 9th (Service) Battalion. 1914 Star and clasp.

SEAMAN Lance Corporal Robert John 41186. Born in 1883 at Ardrahan, County Galway. A grocers assistant. [Enlisted 21 January 1915 into the North Irish Horse (1416). To France with 'F' Squadron in 33rd Division 17 November 1915. Served with 2nd North Irish Horse, X Corps Cavalry Regiment.] Joined the renamed 9th (North Irish Horse) Battalion from 36 Infantry Base Depot and transferred to Princess Victoria's (Royal Irish Fusiliers) in September/October 1917 (renumbered 41186). Lance Corporal November 1917 (renumbered41186). [Transferred to the Tank Corps (renumbered 304870) 28 December 1917 and posted for training to the Tank Corps Depot, at Bovington near Wareham, Dorset. To France 20 August 1918 and joined the 4th Battalion, Tank Corps.] Transferred to the Class Z Reserve 3 February 1919. 1914-15 Star.

SEATON Sergeant Alexander 14686. Born on 8 January 1898 at Bessbrook, County Armagh. Enlisted September 1914. To France with 36th (Ulster) Division in October 1915. **Wounded** in the period immediately prior to the attack at Hamel. Tried by Field General Court Martial on 24 December 1918 charged with *'striking a soldier'*; found not guilty. Transferred to the Class Z Reserve. 1914-15 Star. After the war he emigrated to the United States where he died in California in 1979, aged 81. Brother of Private Robert Seaton.

SEATON Private Robert James 18557. Born on 25 January 1890 at Bessbrook, County Armagh. Enlisted into the 9th (Service) Battalion in April 1915. To France with 36th (Ulster) Division in October 1915. 'A' Company. Involved in the accidental shooting of Second Lieutenant H H Dunwoody on 31 July 1916. **Wounded** at the Battle of Langemarck 16 August 1917. **Wounded** in the period 11-18 April 1918 in the actions between Wulverghem and Kemmel. Transferred to the Class Z Reserve. 1914-15 Star. After the war he emigrated to the United States where he died at Long Island, New York in 1970, aged 80. Brother of Sergeant Alexander Seaton.

SEELEY Private Joseph 5978. From Shankill, County Armagh. Enlisted into Princess Victoria's (Royal Irish Fusiliers) Special Reserve. [To France 1 February 1915 and joined the 2nd Battalion. Posted to the 1st Battalion. Served also with the 7th/8th (Service) Battalion in 49th Brigade, 16th (Irish) Division.] Joined the 9th (North Irish Horse) Battalion when the 7th/8th (Service) Battalion was disbanded in February 1918. **Wounded** in the period 11-18 April 1918 in the actions between Wulverghem and Kemmel and later declared **died of wounds** 19 April 1918. 1914-15 Star.

SELBY DCM Colour Sergeant Hugh Curran 18240. From Bessbrook, County Armagh. Enlisted into the 9th (Service) Battalion in February 1915. To France with 36th (Ulster) Division in October 1915. Company Quartermaster Sergeant. **DCM** –Vijfwegen 30 September 1918. Transferred to the Class Z Reserve. 1914-15 Star. Brother of Private Joseph Selby.

SELBY Private Joseph 15855. From Bessbrook, County Armagh. Enlisted into the 9th (Service) Battalion in October 1914. To France with 36th (Ulster) Division in October 1915. **Killed in action** during the attack at Hamel 1 July 1916. 1914-15 Star. Brother of Colour Sergeant Hugh Selby.

SEMPLE Private Joseph 17935. From Holywood, County Down. Enlisted into the 9th (Service) Battalion in January 1915. 'C' Company. Bangalore torpedo carrier during the attack at Hamel 1

July 1916 during which he was **killed in action**, aged 19.

SERGEANT Private John 14671. Enlisted September 1914. To France with 36th (Ulster) Division in October 1915. [Transferred to the Labour Corps (renumbered 574243 Sergeant).]

SEVENOAKS Private Charles 41137. Born in 1894 near Irvinestown, County Fermanagh. Worked as a groom and domestic servant at Rockfield, County Fermanagh. [Enlisted in October 1914 into the Service Squadron, 6th (Inniskilling) Dragoons (UD/49). Served with 2nd North Irish Horse, X Corps Cavalry Regiment.] Joined the renamed 9th (North Irish Horse) Battalion from 36 Infantry Base Depot and transferred to Princess Victoria's (Royal Irish Fusiliers) in September/October 1917 (renumbered 41137).

SEVILLE Private John 43081. [Enlisted into or transferred to Princess Victoria's (Royal Irish Fusiliers) in August 1916 and joined the 8th (Service) Battalion in 49th Brigade, 16th (Irish) Division.] Joined the 9th (North Irish Horse) Battalion when the 7th/8th (Service) Battalion was disbanded in February 1918.

SEWELL Private John 41250. [Enlisted in October 1914 into the North Irish Horse (1315). To France 15 July 1915. Served with 2nd North Irish Horse, X Corps Cavalry Regiment.] Joined the renamed 9th (North Irish Horse) Battalion from 36 Infantry Base Depot and transferred to Princess Victoria's (Royal Irish Fusiliers) in September/October 1917 (renumbered 41250). Transferred to the Class Z Reserve 8 March 1919. 1914-15 Star.

SEWELL Sergeant (Acting Company Quartermaster Sergeant) Herbert 14668. From Union Street, Portadown, County Armagh. 4th (Portadown) Battalion, Armagh Regiment, Ulster Volunteer Force. Enlisted September 1914. To France with 36th (Ulster) Division in October 1915. 'D' Company. Acting Company Quartermaster Sergeant. **Wounded** during the attack at Hamel 1 July 1916. Discharged as no longer physically fit for war service due to wounds 26 April 1919. Silver War Badge, number B221114. 1914-15 Star.

SEYMOUR Corporal John Roland 43262. Born in 1889 at Hucknall Torkard, Nottinghamshire. A coal miner. [Enlisted 5 October 1915 and joined the 3rd (Reserve) Battalion, The Sherwood Foresters (Nottinghamshire and Derbyshire Regiment) (31336).] To France 14 July 1916. Transferred to Princess Victoria's (Royal Irish Fusiliers) 31 August 1916 (renumbered 43262) having joined the 9th (Service) Battalion on 8 August 1916. Lance Corporal 1 December 1916. Corporal 2 April 1918. **Killed in action** near Meulenhouck 3 August 1918.

SEYTON Private William 14697. Enlisted September 1914. To France with 36th (Ulster) Division in October 1915. [Joined 108th Brigade Machine Gun Company in January 1916. Transferred to the Machine Gun Corps (renumbered 17804).] 1914-15 Star.

SHANKS MM Private Charles 23826. Born in 1899 at Lurgan, County Armagh. Enlisted 25 January 1916, aged 16. Posted to the 9th (Service) Battalion. 'D' Company. **Wounded** at the Battle of Langemarck 16 August 1917 – **MM**. Discharged as no longer physically fit for war service due to sickness 3 April 1918. Silver War Badge, number 342076.

SHANKS Private William 15870. From Portadown, County Armagh. Enlisted into the 9th (Service) Battalion in October 1914. To France with 36th (Ulster) Division in October 1915. **Wounded** (shellshock) during the attack at Hamel 1 July 1916. [Transferred to the Labour Corps (renumbered 231624).] Transferred to the Class Z Reserve 12 February 1919. 1914-15 Star.

SHANNON Private Andrew 42508. From Newmains, Lanarkshire. A coal miner. [Enlisted 1 May 1918 into The Royal Irish Rifles (22630).] To France 6 September 1918. Transferred at the Base Depot to Princess Victoria's (Royal Irish Fusiliers) 14 September 1918 (renumbered 42508) and joined the 9th (North Irish Horse) Battalion 22 September 1918. **Wounded** by a gunshot to the left hand during the attack at Vijfwegen 1 October 1918 and evacuated to hospital in England. Transferred to the Class Z Reserve 9 January 1919.

SHANNON Private George Moorhead 41428. Born in 1893 at Belfast. A clerk with the Markets Department, Belfast Corporation. [Enlisted 29 September 1915 into the North Irish Horse (1734). To France 29 July 1917. Posted to 'E' Squadron. Served with 2nd North Irish Horse, X Corps Cavalry Regiment.] Joined the renamed 9th (North Irish Horse) Battalion from 36 Infantry Base Depot and transferred to Princess Victoria's (Royal Irish Fusiliers) in September/October 1917 (renumbered 41428). **Killed in action** during the advance to Anseghem 25 October 1918, aged 25.

His brother, Gunner Alfred Ernest Shannon, served with the Canadian Field Artillery.

SHANNON Corporal Robert Irwin 23627. From Belfast. Enlisted in January 1916. Posted to the 9th (Service) Battalion. 'B' Company. **Wounded** at the Battle of Langemarck 16 August 1917.

SHARMAN Private Charles Herbert 43245. [Enlisted into The Sherwood Foresters (Nottinghamshire and Derbyshire Regiment).] Transferred to Princess Victoria's (Royal Irish Fusiliers) 31 August 1916 having joined the 9th (Service) Battalion on 8 August 1916 (renumbered 43245). 'B' Company. **Missing** in the period 21-28 March 1918 during the retreat from St Quentin believed **captured**.

SHARP MM Corporal John 14708. Born 1898 in Laurelvale, County Armagh. A linen weaver in Hamilton Robb Ltd, linen factory (where his future wife Margaret also worked). Enlisted September 1914, aged 16. To France with 36th (Ulster) Division in October 1915. **MM** – Bailleul 24 August 1918. Transferred to the Class Z Reserve 20 March 1919. After the war he returned to work in the linen mills. 1914-15 Star.

SHARPE Corporal Charles Thomas Wilkinson 42132. [Enlisted into the Army Service Corps (S4/094717). To France 15 November 1915.] Transferred to Princess Victoria's (Royal Irish Fusiliers) 8 May 1918 (renumbered 42132) and joined the 9th (North Irish Horse) Battalion. [Part of the draft transferred on 19 June 1918 to The Royal Irish Rifles (renumbered 45849). Joined the 9th (Service) Battalion, The Royal Irish Rifles (West Belfast).] Transferred to the Class Z Reserve.

SHARPE Private Fred 41136. [Enlisted in early 1915 into the Service Squadron, 6th (Inniskilling) Dragoons (UD/206). Served with 2nd North Irish Horse, X Corps Cavalry Regiment.] Joined the renamed 9th (North Irish Horse) Battalion from 36 Infantry Base Depot and transferred to Princess Victoria's (Royal Irish Fusiliers) in September/October 1917 (renumbered 41136). 'A' Company. Separated from the 9th (North Irish Horse) Battalion in the period 21-28 March 1918 during the retreat from St Quentin and rejoined 7 April 1918. [Transferred to the Corps of Dragoons (renumbered 63830).]

SHARPE Sergeant James 14701. Enlisted 22 September 1914. To France with 36th (Ulster) Division in October 1915. Discharged as no longer physically fit for war service due to sickness 28 June 1916. Silver War Badge, number 78195. 1914-15 Star.

SHARPE Private James William 5851. From James Street, Portadown, County Armagh. Enlisted into Princess Victoria's (Royal Irish Fusiliers) Special Reserve. [Mobilised from the Special Reserve and joined the 1st Battalion in France 6 December 1914. Posted to the 6th (Service) Battalion. Posted to the 7th/8th (Service) Battalion.] Joined the 9th (North Irish Horse) Battalion when the 7th/8th (Service) Battalion was disbanded in February 1918. 'D' Company. **Killed in action** during the attack south of Wulverghem 4 September 1918, aged 26. 1914-15 Star.

SHATWELL Private Frederick 42288. [A regular soldier with 21st (Empress of India's) Lancers (5850). To France 15 August 1914. Transferred to the Army Veterinary Corps (756) and served with 13th Veterinary Hospital.] Transferred to Princess Victoria's (Royal Irish Fusiliers) 8 May 1918 (renumbered 42288) and joined the 9th (North Irish Horse) Battalion. 1914 Star.

SHAW Private Albert (Bertie) 41262. [Enlisted in February 1914 into the North Irish Horse (903). To France 20 January 1915. Served with 2nd North Irish Horse, X Corps Cavalry Regiment.] Joined the renamed 9th (North Irish Horse) Battalion from 36 Infantry Base Depot and transferred to Princess Victoria's (Royal Irish Fusiliers) in September/October 1917 (renumbered 41262). 'C' Company. **Captured** in the period 21-28 March 1918 during the retreat from St Quentin.

SHAW Private Joseph 41582. Born in 1898. From Ligoniel, Belfast. [Enlisted 26 January 1915 into the North Irish Horse (1425). To France 16 November 1915. Served with 2nd North Irish Horse, X Corps Cavalry Regiment.] Joined the renamed 9th (North Irish Horse) Battalion from 36 Infantry Base Depot and transferred to Princess Victoria's (Royal Irish Fusiliers) in September/October 1917 (renumbered 41582). Lance Corporal November 1917. [Transferred to the Tank Corps (renumbered 304867) 28 December 1917 and posted for training to the Tank Corps Depot, at Bovington near Wareham, Dorset. To France 3 September 1918 and joined 14th Battalion, Tank Corps.] Transferred to the Class Z Reserve 9 March 1919. 1914-15 Star.

SHAW Private Silas George 43281. Born 17 October 1896 at Nottingham. [Enlisted into The Sherwood Foresters (Nottinghamshire and Derbyshire Regiment).] Transferred to Princess

Victoria's (Royal Irish Fusiliers) 31 August 1916 having joined the 9th (Service) Battalion on 8 August 1916 (renumbered 43281). **Wounded**. Transferred to the Class Z Reserve. Worked as a railway guard. Died at Basford, Nottinghamshire 4 May 1967, aged 70.

SHEEHAN Private Denis 16199. From Waterford, County Waterford. [Enlisted into The Royal Irish Regiment (1279). Transferred to Princess Victoria's (Royal Irish Fusiliers) in September/October 1914 (renumbered 16199) and joined the 5th (Service) Battalion in 31st Brigade, 10th (Irish) Division. Embarked with the Mediterranean Expeditionary Force July 1915. Evacuated to hospital in England.] Joined the 9th (Service) Battalion. 'D' Company. **Missing** at the Battle of Langemarck 16 August 1917 and later declared **killed in action** on that date. 1914-15 Star.

SHEEKEY Lance Corporal William 17887. Born at Dublin. [Enlisted January 1915. To France 5 July 1915 and served with the 2nd Battalion.] Posted to the 9th (Service) Battalion. [Posted to the 1st Battalion. **Captured**. **Died** in captivity 29 September 1918.] 1914-15 Star.

SHEPHERD Lance Corporal Oliver Bertram 17777. Commissioned into the Machine Gun Corps - see Appendix 5.

SHEPHERD Company Quartermaster Sergeant James Francis 14666. From Portadown, County Armagh. 4th (Portadown) Battalion, Armagh Regiment, Ulster Volunteer Force. Enlisted September 1914. To France with 36th (Ulster) Division in October 1915. 'B' Company. Battalion Cook Sergeant November 1916. Company Quartermaster Sergeant July 1916. **Wounded** during the Battle of Messines and to hospital 9 June 1917. Discharged as no longer physically fit for war service due to wounds 18 June 1918, aged 32. Silver War Badge, number 387954. 1914-15 Star.

SHEPHERD Lance Corporal William 45067. [Enlisted into or transferred to Princess Victoria's (Royal Irish Fusiliers) in December 1916 and joined the 7th/8th (Service) Battalion in 49th Brigade, 16th (Irish) Division.] Joined the 9th (North Irish Horse) Battalion when the 7th/8th (Service) Battalion was disbanded in February 1918.

SHEPPARD Corporal Edwin 42133. [Enlisted into the Army Service Corps (02645). To France 30 April 1915.] Transferred to Princess Victoria's (Royal Irish Fusiliers) 8 May 1918 (renumbered 42133) and joined the 9th (North Irish Horse) Battalion. [Transferred to The Royal Inniskilling Fusiliers (42133).] Transferred to the Class Z Reserve.

SHERIDAN Private James 3346 & 7040023. From Arva, County Cavan. A blacksmith's assistant. [Enlisted on 23 November 1914 into Princess Victoria's (Royal Irish Fusiliers) Special Reserve. To France and posted to the 2nd Battalion 5 March 1915. Posted to the 1st Battalion 12 November 1915. Evacuated to hospital in England 7 March 1917. Posted to the 3rd (Reserve) Battalion 13 May 1917.] To 36 Infantry Base Depot 11 May 1917 and joined the 9th (Service) Battalion 10 July 1917. 'A' Company. **Wounded** at the Battle of Langemarck 16 August 1917. In arrest awaiting trial 28 September 1917 to 10 December 1917. Tried by Field General Court Martial charged with *'when on active service **deserting** His Majesty's service'*. Found guilty of *'attempting to **desert** His Majesty's service'* and sentenced to three years penal servitude. The sentence was commuted to six months imprisonment with hard labour by Major General Nugent and suspended. **Captured** in the period 21-28 March 1918 during the retreat from St Quentin. Held at Kassel Prisoner of War Camp, Hesse. Repatriated 12 December 1918. 1914-15 Star. Remained in Princess Victoria's (Royal Irish Fusiliers) Special Reserve (renumbered 7040023). Demobilised 22 November 1920.

SHERIDAN Private Patrick 23754. From Cootehill, County Cavan. Enlisted in January 1916. Posted to the 9th (Service) Battalion. [Posted to the 1st Battalion and was **killed in action** 2 September 1918 during the attack near Hill 63, aged 22.]

SHERIDAN Private Patrick 41581. Born in 1896. From Drumconnick, County Cavan. An assistant groom on the estate of Lard Farnham. [Enlisted 11 March 1915 into the North Irish Horse (1466). To France with 'F' Squadron in 33rd Division 17 November 1915. Served with 2nd North Irish Horse, X Corps Cavalry Regiment. Embarked at Marseilles for Egypt with the Regiment's horses on Horse Transport SS Bohemian 25 August 1917.] Joined the renamed 9th (North Irish Horse) Battalion from 36 Infantry Base Depot and transferred to Princess Victoria's (Royal Irish Fusiliers) in October 1917 (renumbered 41581). **Wounded** 16 December 1917 at Marcoing by a gunshot to the chest that left him paraplegic. Treated at 10th General Hospital,

Rouen. **Died of wounds** in Ireland 9 December 1918, aged 22. 1914-15 Star.

SHERIDIN Private Patrick 26822. [Enlisted in February 1917 and joined the 7th/8th (Service) Battalion in 49th Brigade, 16th (Irish) Division.] Joined the 9th (North Irish Horse) Battalion when the 7th/8th (Service) Battalion was disbanded in February 1918. 'C' Company. **Wounded** during the retreat from St Quentin 21-28 March 1918. Discharged as no longer physically fit for war service due to wounds 12 September 1918, aged 33. Silver War Badge, number 449130 (reported lost).

SHERLOCK Private Charles Edward 43220. Born in 1889 at Derby. A compositor. [Enlisted into The Sherwood Foresters (Nottinghamshire and Derbyshire Regiment).] Transferred to Princess Victoria's (Royal Irish Fusiliers) 31 August 1916 having joined the 9th (Service) Battalion on 8 August 1916 (renumbered 43220). 'C' Company. **Wounded** at the Battle of Langemarck 16 August 1917.

SHERMAN Corporal Richard 14673. Born in 1891 at Portadown, County Armagh. From Montague Street, Portadown. 4th (Portadown) Battalion, Armagh Regiment, Ulster Volunteer Force. A linen weaver. Enlisted September 1914. To France with 36th (Ulster) Division in October 1915. 'D' Company. **Wounded** during the attack at Hamel 1 July 1916. **Wounded** at the Battle of Langemarck 16 August 1917. **Wounded** in the stomach during the retreat from St Quentin 21-28 March 1918 and **died of wounds** 1 April 1918, aged 27, in 5th General Hospital, Rouen. 1914-15 Star. His step-brother Private Ephraim Sherman was killed by shellfire while serving with the 1st Battalion on 6 July 1916.

SHERRIFF Private Edwin Percival 17914. From Cootehill, County Cavan. Enlisted into the 9th (Service) Battalion in January 1915. To France with 36th (Ulster) Division in October 1915. 'C' Company. Lewis gunner. **Killed in action** during the attack at Hamel 1 July 1916, aged 19. 1914-15 Star.

SHERRINGTON Private Thomas 21155. Born in 1895 at Belfast. A mill worker. [Enlisted in December 1914/January 1915 and joined the 8th (Service) Battalion in 49th Brigade, 16th (Irish) Division.] Joined the 9th (North Irish Horse) Battalion when the 7th/8th (Service) Battalion was disbanded in February 1918. 'D' Company. **Wounded** during the retreat from St Quentin 21-28 March 1918.

SHIELDS Private William 14669. Enlisted September 1914. To France with 36th (Ulster) Division in October 1915. [Transferred to the Tank Corps (304859) 28 December 1917 and posted for training to the Tank Corps Depot, at Bovington near Wareham, Dorset.] 1914-15 Star.

SHIELS Private Robert John 16133. From Ballybay, County Monaghan. Enlisted into the 9th (Service) Battalion in October 1914. To France with 36th (Ulster) Division in October 1915. Machine Gun Section. **Killed in action** during the attack at Hamel 1 July 1916. 1914-15 Star.

SHIELS Private Samuel 41622. Born in 1892. From Ballybay, County Monaghan. [Enlisted 1 March 1915 into the North Irish Horse (1459). To France with 'F' Squadron in 33rd Division 17 November 1915. Served with 2nd North Irish Horse, X Corps Cavalry Regiment.] Joined the renamed 9th (North Irish Horse) Battalion from 36 Infantry Base Depot and transferred to Princess Victoria's (Royal Irish Fusiliers) in September/October 1917 (renumbered 41622). **Wounded** 16 December 1917 at Marcoing by a gunshot to the back. Evacuated to hospital in England and treated at 1st Southern General Hospital, Birmingham. When recovered joined the 3rd (Reserve) Battalion 9 March 1918. To France 28 May 1918 and rejoined the 9th (North Irish Horse) Battalion 8 June 1918. To hospital suffering from a hernia and evacuated to hospital in England 2 September 1918. **Died** when drowned at sea off the Irish coast on 10 October 1918, aged 26. He was one of 529 casualties caused when RMS Leinster was torpedoed by U123. 1914-15 Star.

SHILLIDAY Private Joseph 6401 & 7040082. From Keady, County Armagh. Enlisted on 7 November 1915 into Princess Victoria's (Royal Irish Fusiliers) Special Reserve. [To France 21 June 1917 and joined the 7th/8th (Service) Battalion in 49th Brigade, 16th (Irish) Division.] Joined the 9th (North Irish Horse) Battalion when the 7th/8th (Service) Battalion was disbanded in February 1918. **Captured** in the period 21-28 March 1918 during the retreat from St Quentin. He is not included on the 9th (North Irish Horse) Battalion casualty list and may have been posted to the 1st Battalion or attached to a unit such as 108th Brigade Trench Mortar Battery before 21 March 1918. Repatriated 7 December 1918. Transferred to the Class Z Reserve 2 April 1919. Re-enlisted into Princess Victoria's (Royal Irish Fusiliers) Special Reserve (renumbered 7040082).

SHINKWIN Private Henry John 42022. Born in 1899 at London. [Enlisted into The London Regiment. Posted to 1/22nd (County of London) Battalion, The London Regiment (The Queen's) in December 1917.] To France and joined 'B' Infantry Base Depot in early-April 1918. Transferred to Princess Victoria's (Royal Irish Fusiliers) April 1918 and posted to the 1st Battalion. Posted to the 9th (North Irish Horse) Battalion in May 1918.

SHORTT Private Samuel 23589. Born in 1898 at Three Mile House, County Monaghan. Enlisted in December 1915. Posted to the 9th (Service) Battalion. 'D' Company. **Missing** at the Battle of Langemarck 16 August 1917 and later declared **killed in action** on that date.

SHORTT Private Walter 24026. Enlisted in February 1916. Posted to the 9th (Service) Battalion.

SILCOCK Private William 23365. Enlisted in December 1915. Posted to the 9th (Service) Battalion.

SIMESTER Private Thomas 43221. From Nottinghamshire. [Enlisted into The Sherwood Foresters (Nottinghamshire and Derbyshire Regiment) (42140).] Transferred to Princess Victoria's (Royal Irish Fusiliers) 31 August 1916 having joined the 9th (Service) Battalion on 8 August 1916 (renumbered 43221). 'C' Company. **Wounded** at the Battle of Langemarck 16 August 1917. [Transferred to the Labour Corps (renumbered 639396).]

SIMMS Private Henry 41246. From Belfast. [Enlisted in August 1916 into the North Irish Horse (2233). Served with 2nd North Irish Horse, X Corps Cavalry Regiment.] Joined the renamed 9th (North Irish Horse) Battalion from 36 Infantry Base Depot and transferred to Princess Victoria's (Royal Irish Fusiliers) in September/October 1917 (renumbered 41246). 'D' Company. **Captured** in the period 21-28 March 1918 during the retreat from St Quentin.

SIMONS Private John 17936. Enlisted into the 9th (Service) Battalion in January 1915. To France with 36th (Ulster) Division in October 1915. 'C' Company. **Wounded** by shellfire at Hamel 24 June 1916. [Transferred to the Labour Corps (renumbered 566096).] 1914-15 Star.

SIMONS DCM Private William 14689. Born in 1892 at Tullyroan, County Armagh. Member of Richhill Company, (Armagh) Battalion, Armagh Regiment, Ulster Volunteer Force. Member of Loyal Orange Lodge Number 665. Enlisted September 1914. To France with 36th (Ulster) Division in October 1915. 'A' Company. **Wounded** in February 1916. **Wounded** during the retreat from St Quentin 21-28 March 1918. **DCM** – Bailleul 24 August 1918. Transferred to the Class Z Reserve 18 March 1919. 1914-15 Star. ***Decoration Militaire* (Belgium)**.

SIMONTON Private William Brian 41389. Born in 1897 at Belfast. [Enlisted in November 1915 into the North Irish Horse (1906). Served with 2nd North Irish Horse, X Corps Cavalry Regiment.] Joined the renamed 9th (North Irish Horse) Battalion from 36 Infantry Base Depot and transferred to Princess Victoria's (Royal Irish Fusiliers) in September/October 1917 (renumbered 41389). [Posted to the 5th/6th (Service) Battalion in 1918.]

SIMPSON Private Alfred 19766. From Moy, County Tyrone. Enlisted into the 9th (Service) Battalion in April 1915. To France with 36th (Ulster) Division in October 1915. 'A' Company. **Wounded** during the Battle of Messines and to hospital 9 June 1917. **Wounded** during the retreat from St Quentin 21-28 March 1918. Transferred to the Class Z Reserve 5 February 1919. 1914-15 Star.

SIMPSON Private Arthur 43204. Born in 1890 at Boston, Lincolnshire. A green grocer. [Enlisted 9 December 1915 and transferred to the Army Reserve. Mobilised 11 April 1916 and joined The Sherwood Foresters (Nottinghamshire and Derbyshire Regiment) (42024).] To France 16 July 1916. Transferred to Princess Victoria's (Royal Irish Fusiliers) 31 August 1916 (renumbered 43204) and joined the 9th (Service) Battalion. 1 Platoon, 'A' Company. Attached to 36th (Ulster) Division Works Battalion throughout January 1917. Attached to 108th Brigade Machine Gun Company 19 May 1917. Rejoined 1 Platoon, 'A' Company. **Wounded** by a gunshot to the left thigh and **captured** in the period 21-28 March 1918 during the retreat from St Quentin. **Died of wounds** 28 April 1918 at the Barvarian War Hospital, Hautmont while a prisoner of war.

SIMPSON Corporal David 42176. [Enlisted into the Army Service Corps (S2/02376). To France 20 July 1915.] Transferred to Princess Victoria's (Royal Irish Fusiliers) 8 May 1918 (renumbered 42176) and was posted to the 9th (North Irish Horse) Battalion. [Part of the draft transferred on 19 June 1918 to The Royal Irish Rifles (renumbered 45868).] Transferred to the Class Z Reserve.

1914-15 Star.

SIMPSON Private Frank 40030. Joined the 9th (Service) Battalion, Princess Victoria's (Royal Irish Fusiliers) with the draft of men from The Prince of Wales's Own (West Yorkshire Regiment) on 12 December 1916. [Transferred to the Labour Corps (renumbered 622759).]

SIMPSON Corporal Henry 42170. [Enlisted 1 September 1914 into the Army Service Corps (T1/4152). To France 12 October 1914. Served with 8th Field Bakery. Promoted Corporal.] Transferred to Princess Victoria's (Royal Irish Fusiliers) 8 May 1918 (renumbered 42170) and was posted to the 9th (North Irish Horse) Battalion. [Part of the draft transferred on 19 June 1918 to The Royal Irish Rifles (renumbered 45863). **Wounded**. Discharged as no longer physically fit for war service due to wounds 2 July 1919.] Silver War Badge, number B246510. 1914 Star.

SIMPSON Private James 14709. Enlisted September 1914. To France with 36th (Ulster) Division in October 1915. [Joined 108th Brigade Machine Gun Company in January 1916. Transferred to the Machine Gun Corps (renumbered 17803).] 1914-15 Star.

SIMPSON Private James Hamilton Howard 23349. Born in 1890 at Banbridge, County Down, the son of a teacher. Lived at Bessbrook, County Armagh. Enlisted in December 1915. Posted to the 9th (Service) Battalion. 'D' Company. **Wounded** at the Battle of Langemarck 16 August 1917.

SIMPSON Private Moses 23228. Born in 1892 at Annaghmore, County Armagh. Enlisted 12 October 1908 into the 3rd Battalion (Militia), Princess Victoria's (Royal Irish Fusiliers) Special Reserve (5197). [Mobilised from the Special Reserve and to France with the 1st Battalion 22 August 1914. Evacuated to hospital in England 25 November 1914. Joined the 3rd (Reserve) Battalion 7 August 1915. Discharged at the end of his service 29 October 1915.] Re-enlisted for war service 20 November 1915 (renumbered 23228). Posted to the 9th (Service) Battalion. 'A' Company. **Wounded** at the Battle of Langemarck 16 August 1917. Discharged as no longer physically fit for war service due to wounds 9 August 1918. Silver War Badge, number 434602. 1914 Star.

SIMPSON Private William James 18053. From Portadown, County Armagh. Enlisted into the 9th (Service) Battalion in February 1915. To France with 36th (Ulster) Division in October 1915. 'C' Company. Lewis gunner. **Killed in action** during the attack at Hamel 1 July 1916. 1914-15 Star.

SINCLAIR Private John 26826. [Enlisted in February 1917 and joined the 7th/8th (Service) Battalion in 49th Brigade, 16th (Irish) Division.] Joined the 9th (North Irish Horse) Battalion when the 7th/8th (Service) Battalion was disbanded in February 1918. 'D' Company. **Missing** in the period 21-28 March 1918 during the retreat from St Quentin believed **captured**.

SINGLETON Private Joseph 42452. [Served previously with The Royal Irish Rifles (10880).] Transferred at the Base Depot to Princess Victoria's (Royal Irish Fusiliers) 14 September 1918 (renumbered 42452) and joined the 9th (North Irish Horse) Battalion 22 September 1918. [Transferred to 5th (Service) Battalion, The Royal Irish Regiment (Pioneers) in the Light Division in the British Army of the Rhine in March/June 1919 (renumbered 41364).]

SINTON Private Frederick William 16433. Born 3 June 1894 at Cabra, County Armagh. From Markethill, County Armagh. Enlisted into the 9th (Service) Battalion in November 1914. To France with 36th (Ulster) Division in October 1915. **Wounded**. 1914-15 Star. Member of Loyal Orange Lodge 305 and Royal Black Preceptory 89. In 1922 he emigrated to the United States and lived in Detroit. Died at Tannaghmore, Markethill 15 May 1953, aged 58. Buried at Mullavilly Parish Church.

SITTLINGTON Private Thomas 41627. Born in 1892 at Larne, County Antrim. A gardener. [Enlisted 2 December 1915 into the North Irish Horse (2007). To France 19 January 1917. Served with 2nd North Irish Horse, X Corps Cavalry Regiment.] Joined the renamed 9th (North Irish Horse) Battalion from 36 Infantry Base Depot and transferred to Princess Victoria's (Royal Irish Fusiliers) in September/October 1917 (renumbered 41627). 'C' Company. Declared **missing** during the retreat from St Quentin 21-28 March 1918. His body was recovered and buried by the advancing enemy and his identity disc forwarded by a German intelligence officer on 18 April 1918. He was declared **killed in action** 21 March 1918, aged 24.

SKEE Private Clifford 40082. From South Shields, County Durham. [Enlisted into the 10th (Service) Battalion, The Prince of Wales's Own (West Yorkshire Regiment) (11251).] Transferred to Princess Victoria's (Royal Irish Fusiliers) 30 November 1916 (renumbered 40082) and joined the 9th

(Service) Battalion 12 December 1916. **Missing** in the period 11-18 April 1918 in the actions between Wulverghem and Kemmel; subsequently declared **killed in action** 19 April 1918.

SKELTON Private Francis Thomas 16146. From Clones, County Monaghan. Clones Company, Ulster Volunteer Force. Enlisted into the 9th (Service) Battalion in October 1914. To France with 36th (Ulster) Division in October 1915. **Wounded** at Hamel and **died of wounds** 8 June 1916. 1914-15 Star. His brother, Private Gibson Fitzgerald Skelton, was killed in action with 10th Battalion (Canadians), Canadian Infantry on 12 September 1916.

SLACK Private Joseph 40031. Joined the 9th (Service) Battalion, Princess Victoria's (Royal Irish Fusiliers) with the draft of men from The Prince of Wales's Own (West Yorkshire Regiment) on 12 December 1916. [Transferred to the Royal Defence Corps (90326). Served in 112th Protection Company.] Transferred to the Class Z Reserve 14 March 1919.

SLADE Private William 20740. From Richmond, Surrey. [Enlisted into the Royal Field Artillery (59268).] Transferred to Princess Victoria's (Royal Irish Fusiliers) in July 1915 (renumbered 20740). To France 30 December 1915 and joined the 9th (Service) Battalion. 'C' Company. **Missing** at the Battle of Langemarck 16 August 1917 and later declared **killed in action** on that date, aged 25.

SLATOR Sergeant Robert 18345. From Tynan, County Armagh. Enlisted into the 9th (Service) Battalion in March 1915. To France with 36th (Ulster) Division in October 1915. Platoon Sergeant in 'D' Company during the attack at Hamel 1 July 1916. Employed at the Divisional Machine-gun School December 1916. **Missing** during the attack at Vijfwegen on 30 September or 1 October 1918; recorded as **killed in action** on 3 October 1918, aged 23. 1914-15 Star.

SLEATOR Private James 41418. From Keady, County Armagh. [Enlisted 15 November 1915 into the North Irish Horse (1870). To France 24 August 1916 and joined 'A' Squadron. Served with 2nd North Irish Horse, X Corps Cavalry Regiment.] Joined the renamed 9th (North Irish Horse) Battalion from 36 Infantry Base Depot and transferred to Princess Victoria's (Royal Irish Fusiliers) in September/October 1917 (renumbered 41418). **Killed in action** 23 November 1917 at Moeuvres, aged 22. His brother, Sapper Henry Sleator, served with the Corps of Royal Engineers and his cousin, Private George Couse, was a regular soldier with 1st Battalion, Princess Victoria's (Royal Irish Fusiliers) and The Northumberland Fusiliers. In addition, a further thirteen close relatives served with United Kingdom, Australian, New Zealand and South African Forces.

SLEATOR Warrant Officer Class II Robert 14691. Commissioned into Princess Victoria's (Royal Irish Fusiliers) - see Appendix 5.

SLICKER Private Frederick 22948. Born in 1891 at Dublin of German origin. [Enlisted 21 October 1914 into The Royal Irish Rifles (977) under his original family name - Schlichor. Discharged on 2 November 1914 having made false answer on attestation. Enlisted into Princess Victoria's (Royal Irish Fusiliers) under the name Slicker in November 1915 and joined the 8th (Service) Battalion in 49th Brigade, 16th (Irish) Division.] Joined the 9th (North Irish Horse) Battalion when the 7th/8th (Service) Battalion was disbanded in February 1918. [Posted to the 5th/6th (Service) Battalion in 1918.]

SLOAN Private Anthony 42143. [Enlisted into the Army Service Corps (T4/172763). Served with 22nd Division Train.] Transferred to Princess Victoria's (Royal Irish Fusiliers) 8 May 1918 (renumbered 42143) and joined the 9th (North Irish Horse) Battalion.

SLOAN Private James Jackson 27617. Enlisted 16 May 1917. Posted to the 9th (North Irish Horse) Battalion. **Wounded**. Discharged as no longer physically fit for war service due to wounds 14 December 1918. Silver War Badge, number 510255.

SLOAN Private John Edmund 22732. Enlisted in November 1915. Posted to the 9th (Service) Battalion.

SLOAN Private Joshua 14698. Born in 1896 at Lurgan, County Armagh. Enlisted September 1914. To France with 36th (Ulster) Division in October 1915. 'C' Company. Lewis gunner. **Wounded** on 1 July 1916 and **died of wounds** 2 July 1916, aged 19 (incorrectly listed as aged 17 by the Commonwealth War Graves Commission). 1914-15 Star. His brother, AB David Sloan, served on HMS Impregnable, His brother, Sergeant Alexander Sloan, served with the Royal Field Artillery, his brother, Sergeant William John Sloan, served with Princess Victoria's (Royal Irish Fusiliers) and his brother, Sergeant James Henry Sloan, served with the 5th (Service) Battalion, The Royal Irish Rifles.

SLOAN Corporal Thomas 14675. Born in 1879 at Shankill, County Armagh. A liner weaver, he lived in Lurgan, County Armagh. Served pre-war in The Royal Irish Rifles. Armagh Regiment, Ulster Volunteer Force. Enlisted September 1914. Corporal 1 January 1915. Reverted to Lance Corporal 30 June 1915. To France with 36th (Ulster) Division in October 1915. **Wounded** at Hamel in June/July 1916 and evacuated to hospital in England. Posted to the 3rd (Reserve) Garrison Battalion at Bere Island, Bantry Bay 10 March 1917. Corporal 22 August 1917. [Transferred to The York and Lancaster Regiment (59878 Corporal) 6 January 1919. Served with the 16th (Transport Workers) Battalion.] Transferred to the Class Z Reserve 18 March 1918. 1914-15 Star.

SLOAN Lance Corporal William 14681. From Tandragee, County Armagh. Enlisted September 1914. To France with 36th (Ulster) Division in October 1915. Transferred to the Class Z Reserve. 1914-15 Star.

SLOANE MM Private James 22726. From Richhill, County Armagh. Enlisted in November 1915. Posted to the 9th (Service) Battalion. 'D' Company. **Wounded** by a gunshot to the right leg during a raid at Spanbroekmolen 4 June 1917 – **MM**. **Missing** at the Battle of Langemarck 16 August 1917 and later declared **killed in action** on that date.

SLOANE Private John George 17825. Born in 1896 at Drumcree, Portadown, County Armagh. Enlisted into the 9th (Service) Battalion in January 1915. To France with 36th (Ulster) Division in October 1915. 'B' Company. **Wounded** during the attack at Hamel 1 July 1916. **Missing** in the period 21-28 March 1918 during the retreat from St Quentin believed **captured**. Transferred to the Class Z Reserve 11 March 1919. 1914-15 Star. His brother, Private Henry Sloane, died on 16 May 1915, aged 16, while serving with the 4th (Reserve) Battalion.

SLOSS Private Andrew 27651. Enlisted in May 1917. Posted to the 9th (North Irish Horse) Battalion. 'A' Company. **Missing** in the period 21-28 March 1918 during the retreat from St Quentin believed **captured**.

SMALL Lance Corporal Thomas 23315. Born in 1887 at Rockcorry, County Monaghan. An insurance agent. Enlisted 30 November 1915 and joined the 10th (Reserve) Battalion. Lance Corporal 2 August 1916. To France 26 October 1916 and the 9th (Service) Battalion. 'D' Company. **Wounded** by a gunshot to the back at the Battle of Langemarck 16 August 1917. [Transferred to the Labour Corps (renumbered 642953). Served with 576th Home Service Employment Company from 31 December 1918.] Transferred to the Class Z Reserve 7 April 1919.

SMALL Private William Thomas 42449. [Enlisted into the Army Service Corps (T3/029394). To France 16 September 1915 and served with 20th Reserve Park. Transferred to The Royal Irish Rifles (47395) and served with the 1st Battalion.] Transferred at the Base Depot to Princess Victoria's (Royal Irish Fusiliers) 14 September 1918 (renumbered 42449) and joined the 9th (North Irish Horse) Battalion 22 September 1918. Transferred to the Class Z Reserve 8 March 1919. 1914-15 Star.

SMALLWOOD MM Lance Corporal James 40085 & 7042128. From Worcester. [Enlisted as a regular soldier on 7 December 1908 into The Prince of Wales's Own (West Yorkshire Regiment) (9024) and joined the 2nd Battalion. Served in Malta 10 January 1912 to 6 June 1913. Tried by the civil power on 15 April 1913 on a charge of *'having created a disturbance at St Julians in the shop of Mr Micallef and used active force against the same.'* Fined ten shillings. Served in the International Force, Albania 7 June 1913 to 9 June 1914 and then in Malta until September 1914. To France with the 2nd Battalion, The Prince of Wales's Own (West Yorkshire Regiment) 5 November 1914. Sentenced to nine days Field Punishment Number 2 for *'misconduct'* 22 November 1914. Evacuated sick (albuminuria following a bout of appendicitis) to hospital in England April 1915. Joined the 3rd (Reserve) Battalion, The Prince of Wales's Own (West Yorkshire Regiment) 12 June 1915. Lance Corporal 9 February 1916. Posted to the 2nd (Home Service) Garrison Battalion, The Prince of Wales's Own (West Yorkshire Regiment) 16 May 1916. Joined the 3rd (Reserve) Battalion, The Prince of Wales's Own (West Yorkshire Regiment) 28 October 1916.] Transferred to Princess Victoria's (Royal Irish Fusiliers) 30 November 1916 (renumbered 40085) and joined the 9th (Service) Battalion 12 December 1916. 'C' Company. **MM**. [Posted to the 1st Battalion 18 January 1918. 'C' Company.] 1914 Star. Transferred to the Section B Army Reserve, Princess Victoria's (Royal Irish

Fusiliers) 8 March 1919 (renumbered 7042128). Discharged 6 December 1920. His brother, Private Samuel Small, served with The Welsh Regiment.

SMITH Corporal Albert 45777. Enlisted 10 June 1916. Joined the 9th (North Irish Horse) Battalion, Princess Victoria's (Royal Irish Fusiliers) with the draft of men from The London Regiment in April 1918. **Wounded**. Discharged as no longer physically fit for war service due to wounds 26 October 1918. Silver War Badge, number B34911.

SMITH Private Alfred Stobbart 40027. From Selby, Yorkshire. [Enlisted 17 November 1915 and transferred to the Army Reserve. Mobilised 25 May 1916 and joined The Prince of Wales's Own (West Yorkshire Regiment) (31991).] Transferred to Princess Victoria's (Royal Irish Fusiliers) 30 November 1916 (renumbered 40027) and joined the 9th (Service) Battalion 12 December 1916. 'A' Company. To hospital with scabies and boils throughout 1917. **Missing** in the period 21-28 March 1918 during the retreat from St Quentin and later declared **killed in action** 29 March 1918.

SMITH Private Charles 43227. [Enlisted 21 February 1916 into The Sherwood Foresters (Nottinghamshire and Derbyshire Regiment).] Transferred to Princess Victoria's (Royal Irish Fusiliers) 31 August 1916 having joined the 9th (Service) Battalion on 8 August 1916. 'C' Company (renumbered 43227). **Wounded** during the retreat from St Quentin 21-28 March 1918. Discharged as no longer physically fit for war service due to wounds 6 February 1919. Silver War Badge, number B142325.

SMITH Private George H 43401. [Enlisted into The London Regiment (7283).] Attached to the 9th (Service) Battalion, Princess Victoria's (Royal Irish Fusiliers) 26 November 1916. Discharged from the Territorial Force, re-enlisted and transferred to Princess Victoria's (Royal Irish Fusiliers) in March/April 1917 (renumbered 43401). [Transferred to the Machine Gun Corps (renumbered 143850).]

SMITH Sergeant George Sydney 40190. [Served previously with the 2nd Battalion, The Prince of Wales's Leinster Regiment (Royal Canadians) (3901) Transferred to The Connaught Rangers (18125) and served with the 6th (Service) and 5th (Service) Battalions.] Transferred to Princess Victoria's (Royal Irish Fusiliers) in December 1916 (renumbered 40190). Posted to the 9th (Service) Battalion in mid-1917. **Wounded** during the retreat from St Quentin 21-28 March 1918.

SMITH Private Henry 20873. From Newry, County Down. Enlisted in August 1915. Posted to the 9th (Service) Battalion in mid/late-1916. 'B' Company. **Wounded** at the Battle of Langemarck 16 August 1917. **Deserted** 20 November 1917.

SMITH Private Henry George 45733. [Enlisted into The London Regiment. Posted to the 1/24th (County of London) Battalion, The London Regiment (The Queen's) (5671).] To France and joined 36 Infantry Base Depot 29 March 1918. Transferred to Princess Victoria's (Royal Irish Fusiliers) 2 April 1918 (renumbered 45733) and joined the 9th (North Irish Horse) Battalion 4 April 1918.

SMITH Private James Tennent 41189. Commissioned into The London Regiment - see Appendix 5.

SMITH Private John 41371. [Enlisted in December 1916 into the North Irish Horse (2319). Served with 2nd North Irish Horse, X Corps Cavalry Regiment.] Joined the renamed 9th (North Irish Horse) Battalion from 36 Infantry Base Depot and transferred to Princess Victoria's (Royal Irish Fusiliers) in September/October 1917 (renumbered 41371).

SMITH Private Robert 3571. Enlisted in May/June 1915 into Princess Victoria's (Royal Irish Fusiliers) Special Reserve. [Joined the 8th (Service) Battalion in 49th Brigade, 16th (Irish) Division.] Joined the 9th (North Irish Horse) Battalion when the 7th/8th (Service) Battalion was disbanded in February 1918. [Posted to the 1st Battalion.]

SMITH Private Samuel 41202. [Enlisted in September 1914 into the North Irish Horse (1104). To France with 'F' Squadron in 33rd Division 17 November 1915. Served with 2nd North Irish Horse, X Corps Cavalry Regiment.] Joined the renamed 9th (North Irish Horse) Battalion from 36 Infantry Base Depot and transferred to Princess Victoria's (Royal Irish Fusiliers) in September/October 1917 (renumbered 41202). 'D' Company. **Missing** in the period 21-28 March 1918 during the retreat from St Quentin believed **captured**. Transferred to the Class Z Reserve 15 April 1919. 1914-15 Star.

SMITH Company Quartermaster Sergeant William Stewart 41220. [Enlisted in November 1914 into the North Irish Horse (1342). Served with 2nd North Irish Horse, X Corps Cavalry Regiment.] Joined the renamed 9th (North Irish Horse) Battalion from 36 Infantry Base Depot and transferred to Princess Victoria's (Royal Irish Fusiliers) in September/October 1917 (renumbered 41220). Company Quartermaster Sergeant. Transferred to the Class Z Reserve 23 March 1919. 1914-15 Star.

SMITON Private James 41279. From Belfast. [Enlisted in May 1915 into the North Irish Horse (1640). Served with 2nd North Irish Horse, X Corps Cavalry Regiment.] Joined the renamed 9th (North Irish Horse) Battalion from 36 Infantry Base Depot and transferred to Princess Victoria's (Royal Irish Fusiliers) in September/October 1917 (renumbered 41279). **Wounded**. **Captured** in the period 11-18 April 1918 in the actions between Wulverghem and Kemmel.

SMYLIE Private Thomas 23351. From Belfast. Enlisted December 1915. Posted to the 9th (Service) Battalion. 'C' Company. **Wounded** at the Battle of Langemarck 16 August 1917. Tried by Field General Court Martial on 4 March 1919 charged with *'absenting himself without leave'*; found guilty and sentenced to forty-two days Field Punishment Number 2. **Missing** in the period 21-28 March 1918 during the retreat from St Quentin believed **captured**.

SMYLIE Private William John 23209. Born in 1897 at Shankill, Belfast. Enlisted in November 1915. Posted to the 9th (Service) Battalion. **Killed in action** during the attack at Hamel 1 July 1916.

SMYTH Private Alexander 41498. [Enlisted 2 September 1914 into the North Irish Horse (1085). To France 18 December 1914. Served with 2nd North Irish Horse, X Corps Cavalry Regiment.] Joined the renamed 9th (North Irish Horse) Battalion from 36 Infantry Base Depot and transferred to Princess Victoria's (Royal Irish Fusiliers) in September/October 1917 (renumbered 41498). **Wounded**. Discharged as no longer physically fit for war service due to wounds 28 May 1918, aged 22. Silver War Badge, number 390979. 1914-15 Star.

SMYTH Lance Corporal Hugh 14696. From Armagh, County Armagh. Enlisted September 1914. To France with 36th (Ulster) Division in October 1915. **Killed in action** during the attack south of Wulverghem 4 September 1918, aged 21. 1914-15 Star.

SMYTH Private Isaac 42474. From Belfast. [Enlisted into The Royal Irish Rifles (22110).] Transferred at the Base Depot to Princess Victoria's (Royal Irish Fusiliers) 14 September 1918 (renumbered 42474) and joined the 9th (North Irish Horse) Battalion 22 September 1918. **Wounded**.

SMYTH Private Jack 17927. Enlisted into the 9th (Service) Battalion 29 January 1915. To France with 36th (Ulster) Division in October 1915. [Transferred to the Labour Corps (renumbered 231578).] Discharged as no longer physically fit for war service due to wounds 3 April 1919. Silver War Badge, number B183492. 1914-15 Star.

SMYTH Private James 16149. From Newbliss, County Monaghan. Enlisted into the 9th (Service) Battalion in October 1914. To France with 36th (Ulster) Division in October 1915. **Killed in action** during the attack at Hamel 1 July 1916, aged 20. 1914-15 Star.

SMYTH Private James 17608. [Enlisted December 1914/January 1915 into the 6th (Service) Battalion in 31st Brigade, 10th (Irish) Division. Embarked with the Mediterranean Expeditionary Force July 1915.] 'A' Company. **Missing** in the period 21-28 March 1918 during the retreat from St Quentin believed **captured**. Transferred to the Class Z Reserve 21 February 1919. 1914-15 Star.

SMYTH Private John 42495. [Served previously with the 1st Battalion, The Royal Irish Rifles (7517).] Transferred at the Base Depot to Princess Victoria's (Royal Irish Fusiliers) 14 September 1918 (renumbered 42495) and joined the 9th (North Irish Horse) Battalion 22 September 1918.

SMYTH Private John S 14702. Born in 1880 in Derrynooth, County Armagh. Enlisted September 1914. To France with 36th (Ulster) Division in October 1915. **Wounded** November 1916 and evacuated to hospital in England. [Transferred to The Royal Irish Regiment (renumbered 5841). Joined the 1st Garrison Battalion, The Royal Irish Regiment in Egypt 5 October 1917. To hospital in Cairo and Alexandria periodically through the latter half of 1918. Evacuated to hospital in England with rheumatic fever 10 January 1919.] Discharged as no longer physically fit for war service due to sickness 7 March 1919. Silver War Badge, number B146469. 1914-15 Star.

SMYTH Sergeant Joseph 14703. Born in 1892 at Ardress, County Armagh. Enlisted September

1914. To France with 36th (Ulster) Division in October 1915. 'C' Company. **Wounded** by a minor gunshot wound in the head near Spanbroekmolen 6 June 1917. **Wounded** at the Battle of Langemarck 16 August 1917. Transferred to the Class Z Reserve 24 March 1919. 1914-15 Star.

SMYTH Private Joseph 41205. From Portglenone, County Antrim. [Enlisted into 'E' Squadron, North Irish Horse (1435) and to France with 'F' Squadron in 33rd Division 17 November 1915. Served with 2nd North Irish Horse, X Corps Cavalry Regiment.] Joined the renamed 9th (North Irish Horse) Battalion from 36 Infantry Base Depot and transferred to Princess Victoria's (Royal Irish Fusiliers) in September/October 1917 (renumbered 41205). **Wounded** at Moeuvres 22/23 November 1917 and **died of wounds** 1 December 1917 in 6th General Hospital, Rouen. 1914-15 Star.

SMYTH Private Robert 14684. Born at Lurgan, County Armagh. Enlisted September 1914. To France with 36th (Ulster) Division in October 1915. 'C' Company. **Killed in action** during the attack at Hamel 1 July 1916. 1914-15 Star.

SMYTH Private Robert 16130. Enlisted into the 9th (Service) Battalion in October 1914. To France with 36th (Ulster) Division in October 1915. 1914-15 Star.

SMYTH Private Robert James 27499. Enlisted 10 April 1917. Posted to the 9th (North Irish Horse) Battalion. [Posted to the 1st Battalion. **Wounded**.] Discharged as no longer physically fit for war service due to wounds 21 March 1919. Silver War Badge, number B170663.

SMYTH Private Samuel 14695. From Bessbrook, County Armagh. Enlisted September 1914. To France with 36th (Ulster) Division in October 1915. 'A' Company. **Wounded** at the Battle of Langemarck 16 August 1917. **Missing** in the period 21-28 March 1918 during the retreat from St Quentin believed **captured**. 1914-15 Star.

SMYTH Private Walter Henry 23793. From Ballinderry, Lisburn, County Antrim. Enlisted in January 1916. Posted to the 9th (Service) Battalion. **Wounded** in the period 11-18 April 1918 in the actions between Wulverghem and Kemmel and **died of wounds** 18 April 1918, aged 21.

SMYTH Private William 23916. Enlisted in February 1916. Posted to the 9th (Service) Battalion.

SMYTH Private William Henry 17559. Enlisted into the 9th (Service) Battalion in November/December 1914. To France with 36th (Ulster) Division in October 1915. Tried by Field General Court Martial on 10 June 1918 charged with *'when on active service using insubordinate language to his superior officer'* and *'when on active service using threatening language to his superior officer'*; found guilty and sentenced to fifty-six days Field Punishment Number 1. Tried by Field General Court Martial on 9 August 1918 charged with *'when on active service* ***deserting*** *His Majesty's service'*; found guilty and sentenced to five years imprisonment. Tried by Field General Court Martial on 18 September 1918 charged with *'when on active service using insubordinate language to his superior officer'*; found guilty and sentenced to fifty-six days Field Punishment Number 1. Transferred to the Class Z Reserve. 1914-15 Star; initially forfeit was restored.

SMYTH Private William Henry 23270. Enlisted in November 1915. Posted to the 9th (Service) Battalion.

SMYTH Private William M 42553. [Served previously with The Royal Irish Rifles (22087).] Transferred at the Base Depot to Princess Victoria's (Royal Irish Fusiliers) 14 September 1918 (renumbered 42553) and joined the 9th (North Irish Horse) Battalion 22 September 1918. [Transferred to 5th (Service) Battalion, The Royal Irish Regiment (Pioneers) in the Light Division in the British Army of the Rhine in March/June 1919 (renumbered 41366).]

SMYTH Corporal Wilson 42167. From Shankill, Belfast. A baker. [Enlisted 23 October 1914 into the Royal Field Artillery (48755 Driver) Served with 'A' Battery, 77th Brigade, Royal Field Artillery. Transferred to the Army Service Corps (renumbered S4/64598) 20 February 1915. To France 30 April 1915. Served with 11th Field Bakery. Acting Corporal 15 October 1915.] Transferred to Princess Victoria's (Royal Irish Fusiliers) 8 May 1918 (renumbered 42167) and joined the 9th (North Irish Horse) Battalion. Killed in action or mortally wounded during the attack north of Bailleul on 24 August 1918. Recorded as **killed in action** on 25 August 1918, aged 25. 1914-15 Star.

SMYTHE Private William 14670. Enlisted 15 September 1914. To France with 36th (Ulster) Division in October 1915. **Wounded**. Discharged as no longer physically fit for war service due to wounds 9 March 1917. Silver War Badge, number 140098. 1914-15 Star.

SNOWDEN Private Albert 43270. From Nottingham. A picture frame maker. [Enlisted 12 August 1915 into The Sherwood Foresters (Nottinghamshire and Derbyshire Regiment) (29601) and joined the 3rd (Reserve) Battalion.] To France 14 July 1916. Transferred to Princess Victoria's (Royal Irish Fusiliers) 31 August 1916 having joined the 9th (Service) Battalion on 8 August 1916 (renumbered 43270). 'A' Company. **Missing** at the Battle of Langemarck 16 August 1917 and later declared **killed in action** on that date, aged 19.

SOMERS Private Samuel 41614. Born in 1895 at Groggy, County Fermanagh. Worked as a farm servant near Brookeborough, County Fermanagh. [Enlisted 6 November 1914 into the Service Squadron, 6th (Inniskilling) Dragoons (UD/159). To France with 36th (Ulster) Division in October 1915. Served with 2nd North Irish Horse, X Corps Cavalry Regiment. Embarked at Marseilles for Egypt with the Regiment's horses on Horse Transport SS Bohemian 25 August 1917.] Joined the renamed 9th (North Irish Horse) Battalion from 36 Infantry Base Depot and transferred to Princess Victoria's (Royal Irish Fusiliers) in October 1917 (renumbered 41614). To hospital sick and evacuated to hospital in England 14 February 1918. Treated at Berrington War Hospital, Shrewsbury. **Deserted** 6 July 1918.

SOMERVILLE Private John 41541. [Enlisted in mid-1912 into the North Irish Horse (715). To France 20 August 1914 with 'C' Squadron as 5th Division Cavalry and then as GHQ Troops. Served with 2nd North Irish Horse, X Corps Cavalry Regiment.] Joined the renamed 9th (North Irish Horse) Battalion from 36 Infantry Base Depot and transferred to Princess Victoria's (Royal Irish Fusiliers) in September/October 1917 (renumbered 41541). 1914 Star.

SOPER Private George 45739. From Lambeth, London. [Enlisted into The London Regiment. Posted to the 1/24th (County of London) Battalion, The London Regiment (The Queen's) (5571).] To France and joined 36 Infantry Base Depot 29 March 1918. Transferred to Princess Victoria's (Royal Irish Fusiliers) 2 April 1918 (renumbered 45739) and joined the 9th (North Irish Horse) Battalion 4 April 1918. **Missing** in the period 11-18 April 1918 in the actions between Wulverghem and Kemmel; subsequently declared **killed in action** 19 April 1918, aged 26.

SPEERS Private Samuel 41579. From Cullyhanna, Crossmaglen, County Armagh. [Enlisted in February 1915 into the North Irish Horse (1453). To France with 'F' Squadron in 33rd Division 17 November 1915. Served with 2nd North Irish Horse, X Corps Cavalry Regiment.] Joined the renamed 9th (North Irish Horse) Battalion from 36 Infantry Base Depot and transferred to Princess Victoria's (Royal Irish Fusiliers) in September/October 1917 (renumbered 41579). **Died of wounds** 3 August 1918, aged 23. 1914-15 Star.

SPENCE Private David Courtney 24785. Enlisted in September 1916. Posted to the 9th (Service) Battalion. 'D' Company. Separated from the 9th (North Irish Horse) Battalion in the period 21-28 March 1918 during the retreat from St Quentin; rejoined 6 April 1918.

SPENCE Private Robert 49747. [Enlisted into The Royal Irish Rifles (322).] Transferred to Princess Victoria's (Royal Irish Fusiliers) in April 1918 (renumbered 49747) and joined the 9th (North Irish Horse) Battalion. [Transferred to 5th (Service) Battalion, The Royal Irish Regiment (Pioneers) in the Light Division in the British Army of the Rhine in March/June 1919 (renumbered 41367).]

SPENCE Private Thomas 12663. Born in 1893 at Belfast. [Enlisted 9 September 1914 and joined the 6th (Service) Battalion in 31st Brigade, 10th (Irish) Division. Embarked with the Mediterranean Expeditionary Force July 1915. **Wounded** by shrapnel to the knee 9 August 1915 and evacuated to hospital in England. Joined the 3rd (Reserve) Battalion 27 September 1915. Embarked for the Mediterranean Expeditionary Force and joined the 5th (Service) Battalion 6 November 1915. Evacuated sick (dysentery) to hospital in England 16 January 1917. Treated at the Dysentery Convalescent Hospital, New Milton. Joined the 3rd (Reserve) Battalion 12 April 1917.] To 36 Infantry Base Depot 14 June 1917. Joined the 9th (Service) Battalion 10 July 1917. 'A' Company. **Wounded** by a gunshot to the left shoulder during the retreat from St Quentin 21-28 March 1918. **Wounded** by shrapnel to the abdomen 26 July 1918. Treated 62nd Casualty Clearing Station and at Endell Street Military Hospital, London. Joined the 3rd (Reserve) Battalion 8 October 1918. Discharged as no longer physically fit for war service due to wounds 11 December 1918. Silver War Badge, number B61014. 1914-15 Star.

SPENCE Private William 19749. Born at Shankill, Belfast. Enlisted into the 9th (Service) Battalion in April 1915. **Killed in action** during the attack at Hamel 1 July 1916.

SPENCE Private William 40081. From Leeds. [Enlisted 8 December 1915 into the 15th (Service) Battalion, The Prince of Wales's Own (West Yorkshire Regiment) (1st Leeds) (838).] Transferred to Princess Victoria's (Royal Irish Fusiliers) 30 November 1916 (renumbered 40081) and joined the 9th (Service) Battalion 12 December 1916. 'C' Company. **Wounded** at the Battle of Langemarck 16 August 1917. Discharged as no longer physically fit for war service due to wounds 20 June 1918, aged 32. Silver War Badge, number 411851. 1914-15 Star.

SPINKS Private William 16131. Enlisted into the 9th (Service) Battalion in October 1914. To France with 36th (Ulster) Division in October 1915. Transferred to the Class Z Reserve 13 March 1919. 1914-15 Star.

SPRINGFIELD Private Thomas Osborne 43402. [Enlisted 8 November 1915 into The London Regiment (7284). Posted to the 1/9th (County of London) Battalion, The London Regiment (Queen Victoria's Rifles).] Attached to the 9th (Service) Battalion, Princess Victoria's (Royal Irish Fusiliers) 26 November 1916. Discharged from the Territorial Force, re-enlisted and transferred to Princess Victoria's (Royal Irish Fusiliers) in March/April 1917 (renumbered 43402). **Wounded**. Discharged as no longer physically fit for war service due to wounds 27 March 1919. Silver War Badge, number B168544.

SPROULE Private Alexander Lionel Adolphus 16129. Born at Bray, County Wicklow. Lived in County Monaghan. Enlisted into the 9th (Service) Battalion in October 1914. To France with 36th (Ulster) Division in October 1915. **Wounded** during the attack at Hamel 1 July 1916 and **died of wounds** 31 July 1916, aged 33. 1914-15 Star.

STAMMERS Private Charles Sidney 45794. Born 14 March 1899 in Croydon, London. Joined the 9th (North Irish Horse) Battalion, Princess Victoria's (Royal Irish Fusiliers) with the draft of men from The London Regiment in April 1918. Died in 1980, aged 81.

STANCLIFFE Private James 40028. Joined the 9th (Service) Battalion, Princess Victoria's (Royal Irish Fusiliers) with the draft of men from The Prince of Wales's Own (West Yorkshire Regiment) on 12 December 1916.

STANDING Private Charles 40070. Joined the 9th (Service) Battalion, Princess Victoria's (Royal Irish Fusiliers) with the draft of men from The Prince of Wales's Own (West Yorkshire Regiment) on 12 December 1916. 'D' Company. **Captured** in the period 21-28 March 1918 during the retreat from St Quentin. Transferred to the Class Z Reserve September 1919.

STANDING Private Frederick Charles 27828. Enlisted into or transferred to Princess Victoria's (Royal Irish Fusiliers) in July 1917. Posted to the 9th (North Irish Horse) Battalion.

STANFORD Private William John 27851. Enlisted into or transferred to Princess Victoria's (Royal Irish Fusiliers) in July 1917. Posted to the 9th (North Irish Horse) Battalion.

STANGER Private William 42197. Joined the 9th (North Irish Horse) Battalion, Princess Victoria's (Royal Irish Fusiliers) with the draft of men transferred from the Army Service Corps and the Army Veterinary Corps in May 1918.

STANLEY Private Arthur James 42247. Born in 1889 at Fareham, Hampshire. Worked at his father's general dealership. [Enlisted 10 November 1914 into the Army Service Corps (T3/029389). To France 12 July 1915. Attached to Headquarters 17th Division Transport. Lance Corporal 1 September 1916. Reverted to Private 25 August 1917 on admission to hospital sick (nephritis).] To 'A' Infantry Base Depot 6 May 1918. Transferred to Princess Victoria's (Royal Irish Fusiliers) 8 May 1918 (renumbered 42247) and joined the 9th (North Irish Horse) Battalion. **Killed in action** 15 July 1918. 1914-15 Star.

STARRETT Corporal William 23656. Born in 1896 near Tullymore, County Armagh. Enlisted in January 1916. Posted to the 9th (Service) Battalion. **Wounded** near Messines and **died of wounds** 24 March 1917, aged 20.

STEELE Company Quartermaster Sergeant Douglas William John 27510 & 7040804. Born on 17 June 1888 at Reading, Berkshire. [Enlisted into Princess Victoria's (Royal Irish Fusiliers) as a regular soldier 30 April 1903 (7969). To France with the 1st Battalion 22 August 1914. Evacuated to hospital in England 20 July 1915. Transferred to The Royal Irish Regiment (renumbered 601).] Transferred back to Princess Victoria's (Royal Irish Fusiliers) and to France 23 May 1917. Joined the 9th (Service) Battalion. Company Quartermaster Sergeant. 1914 Star and clasp. Continued to serve with Princess Victoria's (Royal Irish Fusiliers) after the war (re-numbered 7040804). Served with the 1st Battalion in Persia and Mesopotamia in 1919/20. General Service Medal 1918-1962 with clasps 'Iraq' & 'NW Persia'. Discharged 30 June 1921. Lived at Marlow, Buckinghamshire. Died in 1975, aged 87. For information about his father and brothers see Lieutenant Charles Henry Steele MC* at Appendix 5.

STEELE MM Private George 22562. Enlisted in November 1915. Posted to the 9th (Service) Battalion. **MM** – Battle of Langemarck 16 August 1917. [Transferred to the Labour Corps (renumbered 569847) and Corps of Royal Engineers (renumbered 606012).]

STEELE Private John 20881 & 29531. From Killylea, County Armagh. Enlisted in August 1915 (20881) and joined the 8th (Service) Battalion. Discharged or transferred. Re-enlisted or transferred back to Princess Victoria's (Royal Irish Fusiliers) (renumbered 29531) and posted to the 9th (North Irish Horse) Battalion. **Wounded**.

STEELE Lance Corporal Thomas 14848, 33478 & 7041622. [Served previously with the 8th (Service) Battalion in 49th Brigade, 16th (Irish) Division.] 'C' Company. **Missing** in the period 21-28 March 1918 during the retreat from St Quentin believed **captured**. Re-enlisted 13 October 1919 for Regular Army service with Princess Victoria's (Royal Irish Fusiliers) (renumbered 33478, renumbered 7041622). Served with the 1st Battalion in Persia and Mesopotamia in 1919/20. General Service Medal 1918-1962 with clasp 'Iraq'. Transferred to the Section A Reserve 21 December 1926. Discharged 12 October 1931. Enlisted into the Pioneer Corps 20 April 1940.

STEELE Private Thomas 41365. [Enlisted in November 1915 into the North Irish Horse (1936). Served with 2nd North Irish Horse, X Corps Cavalry Regiment.] Joined the renamed 9th (North Irish Horse) Battalion from 36 Infantry Base Depot and transferred to Princess Victoria's (Royal Irish Fusiliers) in September/October 1917 (renumbered 41365). 'B' Company. **Missing** in the period 21-28 March 1918 during the retreat from St Quentin believed **captured**.

STEENSON Lance Corporal George 14672. From Portadown, County Armagh. 4th (Portadown) Battalion, Armagh Regiment, Ulster Volunteer Force. Enlisted September 1914. To France with 36th (Ulster) Division in October 1915. Transferred to the Class Z Reserve 14 February 1919. 1914-15 Star.

STEENSON Private Robert 14710. From Armagh, County Armagh. Enlisted September 1914. To France with 36th (Ulster) Division in October 1915. **Wounded**. Transferred to the Class Z Reserve 31 March 1919. 1914-15 Star. Served with the Ulster Special Constabulary. Died 28 July 1958, aged 70.

STEPHENSON Private Robert 43309. From Hampstead, London. [Enlisted into The London Regiment.] Attached to the 9th (Service) Battalion, Princess Victoria's (Royal Irish Fusiliers) 26 November 1916. 'D' Company. Renumbered 393412, The London Regiment in March 1917. Discharged from the Territorial Force, re-enlisted and transferred to Princess Victoria's (Royal Irish Fusiliers) in March/April 1917 (renumbered 43309). **Missing** at the Battle of Langemarck 16 August 1917 and later declared **killed in action** on that date.

STERRETT Private Hugh 14700. From Bessbrook, County Armagh. Enlisted September 1914. To France with 36th (Ulster) Division in October 1915. Initially reported **wounded** he was **killed in action** during the attack at Hamel 1 July 1916, aged 19. 1914-15 Star.

STEVENS Private C 43237. From Nottingham. [Enlisted into The Sherwood Foresters (Nottinghamshire and Derbyshire Regiment).] Transferred to Princess Victoria's (Royal Irish Fusiliers) 31 August 1916 (renumbered 43237) having joined the 9th (Service) Battalion on 8 August 1916. 'B' Company. **Wounded** at the Battle of Langemarck 16 August 1917.

STEVENS Private Samuel W 43224. [Enlisted into The Sherwood Foresters (Nottinghamshire and Derbyshire Regiment).] Transferred to Princess Victoria's (Royal Irish Fusiliers) 31 August 1916 having joined the 9th (Service) Battalion on 8 August 1916 (renumbered 43224). [Transferred to 5th (Service) Battalion, The Royal Irish Regiment (Pioneers) in the Light Division in the British Army of the Rhine in March/June 1919 (renumbered 41370).]

STEVENSON Private David 12900. [Enlisted in September 1914 and joined the 6th (Service) Battalion in 31st Brigade, 10th (Irish) Division. Embarked with the Mediterranean Expeditionary

Force July 1915. Posted to the 7th/8th (Service) Battalion in 49th Brigade, 16th (Irish) Division.] Joined the 9th (North Irish Horse) Battalion when the 7th/8th (Service) Battalion was disbanded in February 1918. 'A' Company. **Missing** in the period 21-28 March 1918 during the retreat from St Quentin believed **captured**. Transferred to the Class Z Reserve. 1914-15 Star.

STEVENSON Private Henry 14676. Enlisted September 1914. Discharged as no longer physically fit for war service due to sickness 28 June 1915, aged 42. Silver War Badge, number 508796.

STEVENSON Private Henry 14685. Enlisted September 1914. No record of deployment to France with 36th (Ulster) Division in October 1915. [Transferred to the Labour Corps (renumbered 410840).]

STEVENSON Private John 31417. From Johnstone, Renfrewshire. [Enlisted into the Army Service Corps (53899). Transferred to The Royal Inniskilling Fusiliers (renumbered 4153) and served with the 2nd Battalion, The Royal Inniskilling Fusiliers.] Transferred to Princess Victoria's (Royal Irish Fusiliers) in mid-1918 (renumbered 31417) and posted to the 9th (North Irish Horse) Battalion. **Wounded** at Hill 41 on 11 October 1918 and **died of wounds** 13 October 1918, aged 25.

STEVENSON Private Norbert 23505. [Enlisted in December 1915 into the 7th (Service) Battalion in 49th Brigade, 16th (Irish) Division.] Joined the 9th (North Irish Horse) Battalion when the 7th/8th (Service) Battalion was disbanded in February 1918. 'D' Company. **Missing** in the period 21-28 March 1918 during the retreat from St Quentin believed **captured**.

STEVENSON MM Company Quartermaster Sergeant William John 14667. Born in 1891 at Cootehill, County Cavan. An assistant to a book merchant in Portadown. Lived at High Street, Portadown, County Armagh. Enlisted September 1914. To France with 36th (Ulster) Division in October 1915. 'A' Company. **Wounded** at the Battle of Langemarck 16 August 1917. Acting Company Sergeant Major. **MM**. [Also served with the Army Cyclist Corps (renumbered 23046).]

STEVENSON Private William Robert 14674. Born at Laurelvale, County Armagh. 4th (Portadown) Battalion, Armagh Regiment, Ulster Volunteer Force. Enlisted September 1914. To France with 36th (Ulster) Division in October 1915. 'B' Company. **Missing** at the Battle of Langemarck 16 August 1917 and later declared **killed in action** on that date. 1914-15 Star.

STEWART Private Charles 14693. Born in 1890 at Armagh, County Armagh. Enlisted September 1914. To France with 36th (Ulster) Division in October 1915. 'A' Company. **Wounded** during the attack at Hamel 1 July 1916. Evacuated to hospital in England. Treated at Tower Auxiliary Hospital, Rainhill, Lancashire. Rejoined the 9th (Service) Battalion and was **wounded** at the Battle of Langemarck 16 August 1917. Discharged as no longer physically fit for war service due to wounds 16 December 1918. Silver War Badge, number B64250. 1914-15 Star.

STEWART Private Frederick 20352. Joined the 9th (Service) Battalion with the draft of men from The Royal Inniskilling Fusiliers who transferred to Princess Victoria's (Royal Irish Fusiliers) on 30 June 1915. Transferred to 5th (Service) Battalion, The Royal Irish Regiment (Pioneers) in the Light Division in the British Army of the Rhine in March/June 1919 (renumbered 41369).

STEWART Private George 41192. From Glenanne, County Armagh. [Enlisted in May 1915 into the North Irish Horse (1633). Served with 2nd North Irish Horse, X Corps Cavalry Regiment.] Joined the renamed 9th (North Irish Horse) Battalion from 36 Infantry Base Depot and transferred to Princess Victoria's (Royal Irish Fusiliers) in September/October 1917 (renumbered 41192). **Wounded**.

STEWART Private James 42442. [Enlisted into the 7th (Service) Battalion, The Royal Irish Rifles (3941). To France with 48th Brigade, 16th (Irish) Division 19 December 1915.] Transferred at the Base Depot to Princess Victoria's (Royal Irish Fusiliers) 14 September 1918 (renumbered 42442) and joined the 9th (North Irish Horse) Battalion 22 September 1918. Transferred to the Class Z Reserve 16 March 1919. 1914-15 Star.

STEWART Private Richard 14687. From Armagh, County Armagh. Enlisted September 1914. To France with 36th (Ulster) Division in October 1915. **Killed in action** during thc attack at IIamcl 1 July 1916. 1914-15 Star. Cousin of 27477 Corporal David Frazer and Private Henry Frazer. Related to Private William John Stewart.

STEWART Private Thomas 14677. Enlisted 15 September 1914. To France with 36th (Ulster) Division in October 1915. **Wounded** during the attack at Hamel 1 July 1916. Returned to the 9th

(Service) Battalion in November 1916. [Posted to the 2nd Garrison Battalion in Salonika.] Discharged as no longer physically fit for war service due to sickness 16 September 1918. Silver War Badge, number B71386.

STEWART Private Thomas 14688. Enlisted September 1914. To France with 36th (Ulster) Division in October 1915. Transferred to the Class Z Reserve 24 February 1919. 1914-15 Star. ***Decoration Militaire* (Belgium)**.

STEWART Private Thomas 18066. Born in 1880 at Keady, County Armagh. Enlisted into the 9th (Service) Battalion 15 February 1915. To France with 36th (Ulster) Division in October 1915. 'C' Company. **Wounded** in the head by shrapnel near Hamel and **died of wounds** 12 March 1916 in hospital at Rouen. 1914-15 Star.

STEWART Private William 23234. Enlisted 26 November 1915. Posted to the 9th (Service) Battalion. **Wounded**. Discharged as no longer physically fit for war service due to wounds 17 April 1918, aged 20. Silver War Badge, number 343689.

STEWART Private William 42536. [Enlisted April/May 1918 into The Royal Irish Rifles (22549).] Transferred at the Base Depot to Princess Victoria's (Royal Irish Fusiliers) 14 September 1918 (renumbered 42536) and joined the 9th (North Irish Horse) Battalion 22 September 1918.

STEWART Corporal William H S 14690. Enlisted September 1914. To France with 36th (Ulster) Division in October 1915. [Transferred to the Army Ordnance Corps (renumbered 044071 Corporal).] 1914-15 Star.

STEWART Private William John 14692. Born at Glasgow, Enlisted September 1914 in Armagh. To France with 36th (Ulster) Division in October 1915. **Killed in action** during the attack at Hamel 1 July 1916, aged 28. 1914-15 Star. Related to Private Richard Stewart.

STILWELL Warrant Officer Class II Albert 13524. Acting Regimental Sergeant Major - see above.

STONE Corporal John Edward 21757. A golf professional; he laid out a golf course in the grounds of the estate of the Duke of Manchester at Tandragee. Enlisted in October 1915. Posted to the 9th (Service) Battalion in mid/late 1916.

STONEHOUSE Private John 42120. [Enlisted into the Army Veterinary Corps (23999).] Transferred to Princess Victoria's (Royal Irish Fusiliers) 8 May 1918 (renumbered 42120) and joined the 9th (North Irish Horse) Battalion.

STONES Private Frank 41114. [Enlisted into 6th (Inniskilling) Dragoons (21585). Served with 2nd North Irish Horse, X Corps Cavalry Regiment.] Joined the renamed 9th (North Irish Horse) Battalion from 36 Infantry Base Depot and transferred to Princess Victoria's (Royal Irish Fusiliers) in September/October 1917 (renumbered 41114).

STOREY Private Charles William 40044. Born 12 June 1897 at Hunslet, Leeds. [Enlisted into the 11th (Service) Battalion, The Prince of Wales's Own (West Yorkshire Regiment) (12146). To France 26 August 1915 in 69th Brigade, 23rd Division.] Transferred to Princess Victoria's (Royal Irish Fusiliers) 30 November 1916 (renumbered 40044) and joined the 9th (Service) Battalion 12 December 1916. 'A' Company. **Wounded** at the Battle of Langemarck 16 August 1917. **Missing** in the period 21-28 March 1918 during the retreat from St Quentin believed **captured**. Transferred to the Class Z Reserve 4 April 1919. 1914-15 Star. Died at Leeds 1970, aged 72.

STOTHERS Private Jackson 14706. Born on 28 April 1877. From Bright Street, Portadown, County Armagh. Enlisted September 1914. To France with 36th (Ulster) Division in October 1915. **Wounded** during the attack at Hamel 1 July 1916. While on the strength of the 10th (Reserve) Battalion, he was attached to the 4th (Reserve) Battalion at Portobello Barracks in Dublin. On the evening of 8 December 1916 he left the barracks and did not return. The next day he was recorded as being absent without leave. On Sunday 7 January 1917 Mr Thomas Parsons, a lock-keeper on the Grand Canal, found a body at Portobello lock. Sergeant John Bannon of the Dublin Metropolitan Police recovered the body with grappling irons. The body was formally identified by Lance Corporal John Martin as that of Jackson Stothers. An inquest into his death was presided over by the City Coroner, Dr Louis Byrne. At the inquest Dr Matthew Maughan, the Dublin City Medical Officer, testified that Stothers' body bore no marks of violence and that he had died of asphyxia due to drowning. The jury returned a verdict based on this testimony and that there was no evidence as to how he had come to be in the canal. He is recorded as having **died** on 7 January

1917. 1914-15 Star. Brother of Privates Joseph, Maxwell and William Stothers.

STOTHERS Private Joseph 14683. From Bright Street, Portadown, County Armagh. 4th (Portadown) Battalion, Armagh Regiment, Ulster Volunteer Force. Enlisted September 1914. To France with 36th (Ulster) Division in October 1915. **Killed in action** during the attack at Hamel 1 July 1916. 1914-15 Star. Brother of Privates Jackson, Maxwell and William Stothers.

STOTHERS Private Maxwell 14680. From Bright Street, Portadown, County Armagh. 4th (Portadown) Battalion, Armagh Regiment, Ulster Volunteer Force. Enlisted September 1914. To France with 36th (Ulster) Division in October 1915. **Died** 7 October 1916 in an accident when a tree branch fell on the guard tent. 1914-15 Star. Brother of Privates Jackson, Joseph and William Stothers.

STOTHERS Private William James 14705. From Bright Street, Portadown, County Armagh. Enlisted September 1914. To France with 36th (Ulster) Division in October 1915. **Wounded** during the attack at Hamel 1 July 1916. Transferred to the Class Z Reserve 31 March 1919. 1914-15 Star. Brother of Privates Jackson, Joseph and Maxwell Stothers.

STOTT Private Samuel Robert 17393, 33186 & 7041402. From Ballynarry, County Armagh. [Enlisted 29 December 1914. To France 1 May 1915 and joined either the 1st or 2nd Battalion.] Posted to the 9th (Service) Battalion. 'D' Company. **Wounded** at the Battle of Langemarck 16 August 1917. Discharged as no longer physically fit for war service due to wounds 31 January 1918, aged 22. Silver War Badge, number 310231. 1914-15 Star. Re-enlisted 18 August 1919 for Regular Army service with Princess Victoria's (Royal Irish Fusiliers) (renumbered 33186, renumbered 7041402). **Deserted**. Discharged for misconduct (desertion) 21 September 1920 and forfeit his medals.

STOVES Private James 20347. Born at Wallsend, Northumberland. From Elswick, Newcastle-upon-Tyne. [Enlisted into The Royal Inniskilling Fusiliers (22968).] Transferred to Princess Victoria's (Royal Irish Fusiliers) on 30 June 1915 (renumbered 20347) and joined the 9th (Service) Battalion. To France with 36th (Ulster) Division in October 1915. **Killed in action** during the attack at Hamel 1 July 1916, aged 19. 1914-15 Star.

STRAIN Private Joseph 17668. From Tandragee, County Armagh. A railway worker in Glasgow. Enlisted 18 January 1915 into the 9th (Service) Battalion. To France with 36th (Ulster) Division in October 1915. **Wounded** during the attack at Hamel 1 July 1916 by a gunshot to the right ankle. Discharged as no longer physically fit for war service due to wounds 7 February 1917. Silver War Badge, number 55060. 1914-15 Star.

STRANNEY Private James 27868. Enlisted 4 August 1917. Posted to the 9th (North Irish Horse) Battalion. **Wounded**. Discharged as no longer physically fit for war service due to wounds 5 June 1919. Silver War Badge, number B242931.

STRATTON Lance Corporal John 20351. From Oban, Argyle. [Enlisted into The Royal Inniskilling Fusiliers (23195).] Transferred to Princess Victoria's (Royal Irish Fusiliers) on 30 June 1915 (renumbered 20351) and joined the 9th (Service) Battalion. To France with 36th (Ulster) Division in October 1915. **Killed in action** 25 September 1917 by shellfire at Havrincourt, aged 43. 1914-15 Star.

STRATTON Private William James 16132. From Moy, County Tyrone. Enlisted into the 9th (Service) Battalion in October 1914. To France with 36th (Ulster) Division in October 1915. **Killed in action** during the attack at Hamel 1 July 1916, aged 23. 1914-15 Star.

STREATHER Private Frederick 43501. From Sutton Coldfield, Birmingham. A bricklayer's labourer. [Enlisted 10 October 1917, aged 18, and joined the 35th Young Soldiers Battalion (renamed 52nd Graduated Battalion, The Royal Warwickshire Regiment) (41272). To France 2 April 1918 for service with the 1st Battalion, The Royal Warwickshire Regiment). Transferred to The Royal Irish Rifles (renumbered 52632) 4 April 1918 and joined the 16th (Service) Battalion, The Royal Irish Rifles (2nd County Down) (Pioneers) 12 April 1918.] Transferred to Princess Victoria's (Royal Irish Fusiliers) 15 June 1918 (renumbered 43501) and joined the 9th (North Irish Horse) Battalion 23 June 1918. 'D' Company. **Killed in action** at Hill 41 on 11 October 1918, aged 19.

STRINGER Sergeant Benjamin 23653. Born in 1898 near Armagh, County Armagh. Enlisted in January 1916. Posted to the 9th (Service) Battalion. **Wounded** when shot in the left arm on a raid at Spanbroekmolen 4 June 1917. **Mention in Despatches**.

STRINGER Sergeant Thomas 14694. Born in 1861 at Antrim, County Antrim. Served as a boy soldier with the Armagh Light Infantry (5618 Boy). Discharged from the Militia 4 September 1876 to enlist in the Regular Army. Enlisted into The Connaught Rangers (479 Lad) as a drummer with the 2nd Battalion 5 September 1876, aged 15. Promoted to Drummer 7 October 1976. Reverted to Private 18 January 1877. Sentenced to forty-eight hours imprisonment with hard labour for *'disrespect to Lance Corporal Harkness'* 20 May 1879. Appointed Bandsman 1 April 1880. Admonished for being *'drunk in the streets'* 9 December 1881. Admonished for *'absence from playing out'* 21 March 1882. Sentenced to seven days confined to barracks for *'disrespect to Colour Sergeant Todd'* 22 April 1882. Sentenced to fourteen days confined to barracks for *'absence from playing at the officers' mess'* and *'drunk and resisting the escort'* 26 October 1882. **Deserted** 21 June 1884. Rejoined 9 February 1885 under arrest. Tried by District Court Martial charged with: *'Fraudulent enlistment in that he at Glasgow on the 16th of September 1884 when belonging to the 2nd Battalion, The Connaught Rangers without having fulfilled the conditions enabling him to enlist, enlisted into the Royal Marine Light Infantry.'* Found guilty and sentenced to fifty-six days imprisonment with hard labour. Sentenced to minor punishments for twelve other minor offences in 1884 and 1885. Discharged at the termination of his engagement 28 June 1889. Enlisted into the Royal Navy in 1890 and served for six years. Enlisted into the 5th Battalion (Militia), The Royal Dublin Fusiliers (3676) 9 February 1897. Embodied for war service 5 December 1899. Served in the South African War with the 2nd Battalion, The Royal Dublin Fusiliers. Queen's South Africa Medal. To hospital sick (rheumatism) and evacuated to England 2 January 1902. Released from service 23 February 1902. Enlisted into the 3rd Battalion (Militia), Princess Victoria's (Royal Irish Fusiliers) 16 September 1903. Discharged at the termination of his engagement 15 September 1907. Enlisted on 16 September 1914 and joined the 9th (Service) Battalion, Princess Victoria's (Royal Irish Fusiliers). Sergeant 21 September 1914 and appointed Drummer Sergeant. Posted to the 10th (Reserve) Battalion 23 September 1915 as Drummer Sergeant. Discharged as no longer physically fit for war service 7 June 1918, aged 57. Silver War Badge, number 395829.

STRINGER Lance Corporal William 14704. Born in 1898 at Lisbanoe, Milford, County Armagh. Milford Company, Armagh Regiment, Ulster Volunteer Force. Worked in the McCrum linen mill. Enlisted September 1914, aged 16. To France with 36th (Ulster) Division in October 1915. 'A' Company. Lewis gunner. **Killed in action** during the attack at Hamel 1 July 1916, aged 18. 1914-15 Star. His sister Elizabeth married Private David Frazer.

STRONG Private Sidney 45768. Joined the 9th (North Irish Horse) Battalion, Princess Victoria's (Royal Irish Fusiliers) with the draft of men from The London Regiment in April 1918.

STRONGE Private George William 41561. From Boho, County Fermanagh. [Enlisted in December 1915 into the North Irish Horse (2049). Served with 2nd North Irish Horse, X Corps Cavalry Regiment.] Joined the renamed 9th (North Irish Horse) Battalion from 36 Infantry Base Depot and transferred to Princess Victoria's (Royal Irish Fusiliers) in September/October 1917 (renumbered 41561). 'D' Company. **Captured** in the period 21-28 March 1918 during the retreat from St Quentin. **Died** 8 July 1918 the Bavarian War Hospital, Hautmont while a prisoner of war.

STROUD Private William George John 43393. [Enlisted into The London Regiment (6030). Posted to the 1/9th (County of London) Battalion, The London Regiment (Queen Victoria's Rifles).] Attached to the 9th (Service) Battalion, Princess Victoria's (Royal Irish Fusiliers) 26 November 1916. Discharged from the Territorial Force, re-enlisted and transferred to Princess Victoria's (Royal Irish Fusiliers) in March/April 1917 (renumbered 43393).

STROYAN Private John Otter 41241. Born in 1897 in Scotland. Lived at Ballymoney, County Antrim. A tailor. [Enlisted in May 1915 into the North Irish Horse (1564). To France with 'F' Squadron in 33rd Division 17 November 1915. Served with 2nd North Irish Horse, X Corps Cavalry Regiment.] Joined the renamed 9th (North Irish Horse) Battalion from 36 Infantry Base Depot and transferred to Princess Victoria's (Royal Irish Fusiliers) in September/October 1917 (renumbered 41241). Transferred to the Class Z Reserve. 1914-15 Star.

STUART Private William Patrick 41598. Born at Ballymacarrett, County Down. From Belfast. [Enlisted in November 1916 into the North Irish Horse (2312). Served with 2nd North Irish Horse, X Corps Cavalry Regiment.] Joined the renamed 9th (North Irish Horse) Battalion from 36 Infantry

Base Depot and transferred to Princess Victoria's (Royal Irish Fusiliers) in September/October 1917 (renumbered 41598). 'D' Company. **Wounded** and **captured** in the period 21-28 March 1918 during the retreat from St Quentin. **Died of wounds** as a prisoner of war 30 March 1918, aged 29.

STUBBINGS Private Ernest 42246 & 7042178. From Norwich, Norfolk. [Enlisted 24 November 1915 into the Army Service Corps (T4/38859). To France 7 February 1916. Served with 56th Division Train and 33rd Reserve Park.] Transferred to Princess Victoria's (Royal Irish Fusiliers) 8 May 1918 (renumbered 42246) and joined the 9th (North Irish Horse) Battalion. Transferred to the Section B Army Reserve, Princess Victoria's (Royal Irish Fusiliers) 19 March 1919 (renumbered 7042178). Discharged 28 November 1927.

STURGEON Private Daniel 23207. From Donagh, Glaslough, County Monaghan. A farmer. Enlisted in November 1915. Posted to the 9th (Service) Battalion. 'D' Company. **Wounded** at the Battle of Langemarck 16 August 1917. **Killed in action** 16 November 1917 at Havrincourt, aged 25.

STURGEON Private Robert 16422. Born in 1882 in Portadown, County Armagh. A weaver in the linen trade, he enlisted into the 9th (Service) Battalion at Clandeboye on 3 November 1914. Forfeit eight days pay for absence without leave 9 February 1915. Attached to 12th (Service) Battalion, The Royal Inniskilling Fusiliers 26 June 1915. Posted to the 10th (Reserve) Battalion 23 September 1915. Posted to the 1st Garrison Battalion at Dublin 7 October 1915. While serving there he was charged with being absent from tattoo (twice), reporting sick without cause and being drunk. To France 10 February 1916 and rejoined the 9th (Service) Battalion. **Wounded** at Hamel by shrapnel in the neck and arm 3 April 1916. **Wounded** during the attack at Hamel 1 July 1916 gunshot wound to the right leg. Evacuated to hospital in England. Joined the Irish Command Depot, Tipperary 5 January 1917, during which time he was charged with four offences: being drunk, being absent from tattoo, not complying with an order and stating a falsehood. Rejoined the 10th (Reserve) Battalion 7 August 1917. Charged with breaking a line of march without permission, being absent from tattoo and being absent overnight. [Transferred to the Labour Corps (renumbered 545504) 6 April 1918.] Discharged as no longer physically fit for war service due to wounds 4 September 1918. Silver War Badge, B232091.

STURZAKER Private Walter 42211. Born at Lancashire 17 August 1897. Joined the 9th (North Irish Horse) Battalion, Princess Victoria's (Royal Irish Fusiliers) with the draft of men transferred from the Army Service Corps and the Army Veterinary Corps in May 1918. Died at Lancashire in 1973, aged 76.

SUMMERVILLE Private Edward 29538 & 7040866. Born in 1899 at Drumcree, Portadown, County Armagh. [Enlisted 21 August 1917 and served elsewhere.] Transferred to Princess Victoria's (Royal Irish Fusiliers) in March 1918 (renumbered 29538). Posted to the 9th (North Irish Horse) Battalion. Re-enlisted in August/September 1919 for Regular Army service with Princess Victoria's (Royal Irish Fusiliers) (renumbered 7040866). Served with the 1st Battalion in Persia and Mesopotamia in 1919/20. General Service Medal 1918-1962 with clasps 'Iraq' & 'NW Persia'. Discharged 10 July 1922. Served with the Royal Ulster Constabulary.

SUMNER Private William Herbert 42248. [Enlisted 15 October 1914 into the Army Service Corps (T4/249790). To France 12 April 1915.] Transferred to Princess Victoria's (Royal Irish Fusiliers) 8 May 1918 (renumbered 42248) and joined the 9th (North Irish Horse) Battalion. Transferred to the Class Z Reserve 19 March 1919. 1914-15 Star.

SWANBOROUGH Private Charles 27844. Served elsewhere before transferring to Princess Victoria's (Royal Irish Fusiliers) in July 1917. Joined the 10th (Reserve) Battalion. To France January 1918 and joined the 9th (North Irish Horse) Battalion.

SWANNACK Private John William 43271. From Nottinghamshire. [Enlisted 21 August 1914 into the 9th (Service) Battalion, The Sherwood Foresters (Nottinghamshire and Derbyshire Regiment) (10314). Embarked with the Mediterranean Expeditionary Force July 1915.] Transferred to Princess Victoria's (Royal Irish Fusiliers) 31 August 1916 having joined the 9th (Service) Battalion on 8 August 1916 (renumbered 43271). 'D' Company. **Wounded** at the Battle of Langemarck 16 August 1917. Discharged as no longer physically fit for war service due to wounds 28 February 1919. Silver War Badge, number B154117. 1914-15 Star.

SWEET Private Joseph E 43397. From London. [Enlisted into The London Regiment (7276).

Posted to the 1/9th (County of London) Battalion, The London Regiment (Queen Victoria's Rifles).] Attached to the 9th (Service) Battalion, Princess Victoria's (Royal Irish Fusiliers) 26 November 1916. 'D' Company. Discharged from the Territorial Force, re-enlisted and transferred to Princess Victoria's (Royal Irish Fusiliers) in March/April 1917 (renumbered 43397). **Wounded** at the Battle of Langemarck 16 August 1917. [Transferred to the Machine Gun Corps (renumbered 143849).]

SWIFT Private George 25057. [Enlisted in November 1916 and joined the 7th/8th (Service) Battalion in 49th Brigade, 16th (Irish) Division.] Joined the 9th (North Irish Horse) Battalion when the 7th/8th (Service) Battalion was disbanded in February 1918.

SWINBOURNE Private Frank 27842. Served elsewhere before transferring to Princess Victoria's (Royal Irish Fusiliers) in July 1917. Joined the 10th (Reserve) Battalion. To France January 1918 and joined the 9th (North Irish Horse) Battalion. **Wounded**. Discharged as no longer physically fit for war service due to wounds 21 March 1919. Silver War Badge, number B167339.

SWINDLE Private John 41115. [Enlisted in October 1914 into the Service Squadron, 6th (Inniskilling) Dragoons (UD/19). Served with 2nd North Irish Horse, X Corps Cavalry Regiment.] Joined the renamed 9th (North Irish Horse) Battalion from 36 Infantry Base Depot and transferred to Princess Victoria's (Royal Irish Fusiliers) in September/October 1917 (renumbered 41115).

TABRETT Private William F 22301. [A regular soldier with The Bedfordshire Regiment (8652). To Belgium 6 October 1914 with the 2nd Battalion, The Bedfordshire Regiment in 21st Brigade, 7th Division. Transferred to Princess Victoria's (Royal Irish Fusiliers) in November 1915 (renumbered 22301) and joined the 5th (Service) Battalion in 31st Brigade, 10th (Irish) Division in the Mediterranean Expeditionary Force.] Joined the 9th (Service) Battalion. 'A' Company. **Missing** in the period 21-28 March 1918 during the retreat from St Quentin believed **captured**. 1914 Star.

TAGGART Lance Corporal James 41318. Born in 1895. From Dervock, County Antrim. A watchmaker. [Enlisted 2 June 1915 into the North Irish Horse (1651). To France March 1916 and joined 'C' Squadron. Served with 2nd North Irish Horse, X Corps Cavalry Regiment.] Joined the renamed 9th (North Irish Horse) Battalion from 36 Infantry Base Depot and transferred to Princess Victoria's (Royal Irish Fusiliers) in September/October 1917 (renumbered 41318). 'C' Company. Lance Corporal 1 April 1918. **Wounded** during a by a gunshot on 11 April 1918 in the actions between Wulverghem and Kemmel; returned to duty. **Wounded** by a gunshot to the right knee during a raid at Shoddy Farm near Meulenhouck 11 August 1918 and evacuated to hospital in England. Joined the 3rd (Reserve) Battalion 19 October 1918. Transferred to the Class Z Reserve 20 March 1919.

TALBOT Private Fred 43239. [Enlisted into The Sherwood Foresters (Nottinghamshire and Derbyshire Regiment).] Transferred to Princess Victoria's (Royal Irish Fusiliers) 31 August 1916 (renumbered 43239) having joined the 9th (Service) Battalion on 8 August 1916. 'B' Company. **Missing** in the period 21-28 March 1918 during the retreat from St Quentin believed **captured**.

TANNER Private George Frederick 43394. Born in 1890 at Camberwell, London. A tailor's cutter. [Enlisted 28 January 1916 and transferred to the Army Reserve. Mobilised 1 July 1916 and joined the 3/11th Battalion, The London Regiment (5708). Posted to the 1/9th (County of London) Battalion, The London Regiment (Queen Victoria's Rifles) (7272) 9 November 1916.] To the Infantry Base Depot 9 November 1916. Attached to the 9th (Service) Battalion, Princess Victoria's (Royal Irish Fusiliers) 26 November 1916. 13 Platoon, 'D' Company. Discharged from the Territorial Force, re-enlisted and transferred to Princess Victoria's (Royal Irish Fusiliers) 26 March 1917 (renumbered 43394). **Missing** at the Battle of Langemarck 16 August 1917 and later declared **killed in action** on that date, aged 27.

TATE Private Frank 41195. From Belfast. [Enlisted in February 1916 into the North Irish Horse (2119). Served with 2nd North Irish Horse, X Corps Cavalry Regiment.] Joined the renamed 9th (North Irish Horse) Battalion from 36 Infantry Base Depot and transferred to Princess Victoria's (Royal Irish Fusiliers) in September/October 1917 (renumbered 41195). 'D' Company. **Missing** during the retreat from St Quentin and later declared **killed in action** 21 March 1918.

TATE Private George 14722. Born in 1879 at Seagoe, County Armagh. Served as a regular soldier with 2nd Battalion, The Royal Inniskilling Fusiliers. 4th (Portadown) Battalion, Armagh Regiment, Ulster Volunteer Force. A weaver. Enlisted September 1914. To France with 36th (Ulster) Division in October 1915. **Wounded** during the attack at Hamel 1 July 1916 and evacuated to hospital in

England. Treated at Greylingwell War Hospital, Chichester. Joined the 10th (Reserve) Battalion 2 January 1917. [Transferred to the Royal Defence Corps (73203) 4 May 1918. Served with 55th Protection Company.] Transferred to the Class Z Reserve 23 March 1919. 1914-15 Star.

TAYLOR Private Alexander 14733. From Lurgan, County Armagh. Enlisted September 1914. To France with 36th (Ulster) Division in October 1915. **Wounded** during the attack at Hamel 1 July 1916. Discharged as no longer physically fit for war service due to wounds 1 January 1917. Silver War Badge, number 107188.

TAYLOR Private David 18275. From Poyntzpass, County Armagh. A farmer. Enlisted into the 9th (Service) Battalion 8 March 1915. To France with 36th (Ulster) Division in October 1915. Evacuated sick (nephritis) to hospital in England 28 October 1916. Treated at Greylingwell War Hospital, Chichester. Discharged as no longer physically fit for war service due to sickness 20 March 1917. Silver War Badge, number 158231. 1914-15 Star.

TAYLOR Corporal David George 22645. Enlisted 28 October 1915. Posted to the 9th (Service) Battalion. Discharged as no longer physically fit for war service due to sickness 18 September 1917. Silver War Badge, number 244132.

TAYLOR Private Elisha 3644. Enlisted into Princess Victoria's (Royal Irish Fusiliers) Special Reserve. [To France 26 July 1915 and joined the 1st Battalion. Posted to the 8th (Service) Battalion in 49th Brigade, 16th (Irish) Division.] Joined the 9th (North Irish Horse) Battalion when the 7th/8th (Service) Battalion was disbanded in February 1918. Transferred to the Class Z Reserve 8 June 1919. 1914-15 Star.

TAYLOR Private Frederick Henry 45757. Joined the 9th (North Irish Horse) Battalion, Princess Victoria's (Royal Irish Fusiliers) with the draft of men from The London Regiment in April 1918. **Deserted** 23 May 1919.

TAYLOR Private Harry Ernest 43395. [Enlisted into The London Regiment (7273). Posted to the 1/9th (County of London) Battalion, The London Regiment (Queen Victoria's Rifles).] Attached to the 9th (Service) Battalion, Princess Victoria's (Royal Irish Fusiliers) 26 November 1916. Discharged from the Territorial Force, re-enlisted and transferred to Princess Victoria's (Royal Irish Fusiliers) in March/April 1917 (renumbered 43395).

TAYLOR Private James 20365. From Gateshead-on-Tyne, County Durham. [Enlisted into The Royal Inniskilling Fusiliers (23944).] Transferred to Princess Victoria's (Royal Irish Fusiliers) on 30 June 1915 (renumbered 20365) and joined the 9th (Service) Battalion. 'B' Company. **Wounded** during the attack at Hamel 1 July 1916 and **died of wounds** 4 July 1916, aged 27.

TAYLOR Private John F 16135. Enlisted into the 9th (Service) Battalion in October 1914. To France with 36th (Ulster) Division in October 1915. [Transferred to the Labour Corps (renumbered 231625).] Transferred to the Class Z Reserve 20 May 1919. 1914-15 Star.

TAYLOR Private John Richard 42249. [Enlisted into the Army Service Corps (T/293383). Served with 663rd Horse Transport Company, London.] Transferred to Princess Victoria's (Royal Irish Fusiliers) 8 May 1918 (renumbered 42249) and joined the 9th (North Irish Horse) Battalion.

TAYLOR Private Percival Clarence 43396. Born at Woolwich, Kent. [Enlisted into The London Regiment (7274). Posted to the 1/9th (County of London) Battalion, The London Regiment (Queen Victoria's Rifles) (393416).] Attached to the 9th (Service) Battalion, Princess Victoria's (Royal Irish Fusiliers) 26 November 1916. 'D' Company. Discharged from the Territorial Force, re-enlisted and transferred to Princess Victoria's (Royal Irish Fusiliers) in March/April 1917 (renumbered 43396). **Missing** at the Battle of Langemarck 16 August 1917 and later declared **killed in action** on that date, aged 21.

TAYLOR Private Peter 20298. Enlisted 11 May 1915 and joined the 9th (Service) Battalion with the draft of men from The Royal Inniskilling Fusiliers who transferred to Princess Victoria's (Royal Irish Fusiliers) on 30 June 1915. To France with 36th (Ulster) Division in October 1915. 'C' Company. **Wounded** during the attack at Hamel 1 July 1916. Discharged as no longer physically fit for war service due to wounds 26 February 1918. Silver War Badge, number 320035. 1914-15 Star.

TAYLOR Private Robert Lynas 14721. Born in 1896 at Lurgan, County Armagh. Armagh Regiment, Ulster Volunteer Force. A clerk. Enlisted 16 September 1914. No record of deployment to France with 36th (Ulster) Division in October 1915.

TAYLOR Lance Corporal Thomas 17661. From Portadown, County Armagh. Enlisted into the 9th (Service) Battalion in December 1914/January 1915. To France with 36th (Ulster) Division in October 1915. 'A' Company. **Wounded** during the attack at Hamel 1 July 1916 and **died of wounds** 6 July 1916, aged 22. 1914-15 Star.

TAYLOR Private William 22643. Enlisted 30 October 1915. Posted to the 9th (Service) Battalion. Discharged as no longer physically fit for war service due to sickness 7 June 1918, aged 24. Silver War Badge, number 395827.

TAYLOR Private William 12268 & 28661. [Enlisted 9 September 1914 (12668) and joined the 5th or 6th (Service) Battalion in 31st Brigade, 10th (Irish) Division. Discharged as no longer physically fit for war service due to sickness 2 October 1914. Silver War Badge, number 228760.] Re-enlisted in September 1917 (renumbered 28661). Posted to the 9th (North Irish Horse) Battalion.

TAYLOR Private William 41645. [Enlisted in April 1915 into the Service Squadron, 6th (Inniskilling) Dragoons (UD/256). To France with 36th (Ulster) Division in October 1915. Served with 2nd North Irish Horse, X Corps Cavalry Regiment.] Joined the renamed 9th (North Irish Horse) Battalion from 36 Infantry Base Depot and transferred to Princess Victoria's (Royal Irish Fusiliers) in September/October 1917 (renumbered 41645). Transferred to the Class Z Reserve 6 March 1919. 1914-15 Star.

TAYLOR Private William 42213. Joined the 9th (North Irish Horse) Battalion, Princess Victoria's (Royal Irish Fusiliers) with the draft of men transferred from the Army Service Corps and the Army Veterinary Corps in May 1918.

TAYLOR Private William 43257. From Ilkeston, Derbyshire. [Enlisted into The Sherwood Foresters (Nottinghamshire and Derbyshire Regiment) (13822). To France 9 February 1915.] Transferred to Princess Victoria's (Royal Irish Fusiliers) 31 August 1916 (renumbered 43257) having joined the 9th (Service) Battalion on 8 August 1916. 'C' Company. **Wounded** at the Battle of Langemarck 16 August 1917. [Transferred to The Sherwood Foresters (Nottinghamshire and Derbyshire Regiment) (renumbered 122138).]

TAYLOR Private William 49740 & 7042240. From Dromore, County Down. Enlisted 15 June 1917. Joined the 9th (North Irish Horse) Battalion, Princess Victoria's (Royal Irish Fusiliers) with the draft of men transferred from The Royal Irish Rifles in April 1918. 'B' Company. Re-enlisted 19 January 1919 for Regular Army service with Princess Victoria's (Royal Irish Fusiliers) (renumbered 7042240). Served with the 1st Battalion in Persia and Mesopotamia in 1919/20. General Service Medal 1918-1962 with clasps 'Iraq' & 'NW Persia'. Discharged 10 July 1922.

TEALE Private Richard Debenham 45759. Joined the 9th (North Irish Horse) Battalion, Princess Victoria's (Royal Irish Fusiliers) with the draft of men from The London Regiment in April 1918.

TEDFORD Private Herbert 14717. Born on 3 October 1876 at Lurgan, County Armagh. A weaver. Enlisted September 1914. To France with 36th (Ulster) Division in October 1915. 3 Section, 13 Platoon, 'D' Company in 1915. **Wounded** during the attack at Hamel 1 July 1916. [Transferred to the Labour Corps (renumbered 231628) and The King's Liverpool Regiment (renumbered 102745).] Transferred to the Class Z Reserve 10 February 1919. 1914-15 Star. Died 21 April 1958, aged 81. His son, James Herbert Tedford, served with The Royal Ulster Rifles and, during the Second World War, with the Royal Regiment of Artillery. He was a prisoner of war in the Far East.

TEGGART Private John George 14715. Born in 1879 at Lurgan, County Armagh. Enlisted September 1914. To France with 36th (Ulster) Division in October 1915. 'A' Company. **Captured** in the period 21-28 March 1918 during the retreat from St Quentin. Transferred to the Class Z Reserve 26 March 1919. 1914-15 Star.

TEGGART Private Moses 14712. From Annaghmore, County Armagh. 4th (Portadown) Battalion, Armagh Regiment, Ulster Volunteer Force. Enlisted September 1914. To France with 36th (Ulster) Division in October 1915. **Killed in action** during the attack at Hamel 1 July 1916, aged 19. It was reported that he died of heart failure during the attack. 1914-15 Star.

TEMPLETON Private Robert 16138. From Ballybay, County Monaghan. Enlisted into the 9th (Service) Battalion in October 1914. [Attached to 108th Trench Mortar Battery, where he was **wounded** and **died of wounds** 25 October 1918, aged 26.]

TERRY Private Ernest 49840. Born at St Helens, Lancashire. [Enlisted 10 May 1915 and joined the 7th (Service) Battalion, The Royal Inniskilling Fusiliers (22629). To France 18 February with 16th (Irish) Division. **Wounded** by a gunshot to the left leg 7 June 1916 and evacuated to hospital in England.] Joined 36 Infantry Base Depot and transferred to Princess Victoria's (Royal Irish Fusiliers) 21 April 1918 (renumbered 49840) and joined the 9th (North Irish Horse) Battalion on 9 May 1918. **Killed in action** during the attack south of Wulverghem 4 September 1918.

TETLEY Private John Archibald 22424. Born at Harrogate, Yorkshire. A farmer. [Enlisted 2 September 1914 into The Bedfordshire Regiment (13323) and joined the 3rd (Reserve) Battalion. To France 24 March 1915 and joined the 1st Battalion, The Bedfordshire Regiment. **Wounded** by a gunshot to the right leg; evacuated to hospital in England 21 June 1915. Joined the 3rd (Reserve) Battalion, The Bedfordshire Regiment 17 July 1915. Transferred to Princess Victoria's (Royal Irish Fusiliers) on 5 November 1915 (renumbered 22424) and joined the 5th (Service) Battalion in 31st Brigade, 10th (Irish) Division in the Mediterranean Expeditionary Force. Evacuated sick (malaria) to hospital in England 27 February 1916 and treated at the Military Hospital, Ripon. Joined the 3rd (Reserve) Battalion 5 July 1916. Posted to the 5th (Service) Battalion, Princess Victoria's (Royal Irish Fusiliers) in 31st Brigade, 10th (Irish) Division in the Mediterranean Expeditionary Force 27 August 1916. 'D' Company. Evacuated to hospital in England (venereal disease) in October 1917 and treated at Brighton Grove Hospital, Newcastle (attached to Depot, The Durham Light Infantry). Joined the 3rd (Reserve) Battalion, Princess Victoria's (Royal Irish Fusiliers) 22 December 1917.] To 36 Infantry Base Depot, France 16 February 1918 and joined the 9th (North Irish Horse) Battalion. 'A' Company. **Wounded** by a gunshot to the left arm 26 March 1918 during the retreat from St Quentin. Evacuated to hospital in England 13 May 1918 and treated at Lord Derby War Hospital, Winwick. Joined the 3rd (Reserve) Battalion 22 August 1918. [Transferred to The Durham Light Infantry (renumbered 109514) 26 August 1918 and joined the 28th (Home Service) Battalion.] Discharged as no longer physically fit for war service due to sickness (malaria) 11 October 1918. Silver War Badge, number B27292. 1914-15 Star. Lived in Ripon, North Yorkshire.

THACKERY Private Herbert 41121 & 7042135. Born in 1892 at Goole, Yorkshire. [Enlisted 18 July 1910 as a regular soldier into the 2nd Dragoon Guards (Queen's Bays) (4726). To France in 1st Cavalry Division 15 August 1914. **Wounded** (shellshock) 12 May 1915 and evacuated to hospital in England 15 May 1915. To France 9 August 1916 and joined 6th (Inniskilling) Dragoons (4726) in 2nd North Irish Horse, X Corps Cavalry Regiment.] Joined the renamed 9th (North Irish Horse) Battalion from 36 Infantry Base Depot and transferred to Princess Victoria's (Royal Irish Fusiliers) in September/October 1917 (renumbered 41121). Evacuated to hospital in England 10 December 1917. [To France 24 May 1918 and joined the 1st Battalion.] Transferred to the Section B Army Reserve, Princess Victoria's (Royal Irish Fusiliers) (renumbered 7042135) 15 February 1919. Discharged 17 July 1922.

THISTLETHWAITE Lance Corporal Henry 41099. [Enlisted into 6th (Inniskilling) Dragoons (20339). Served with 2nd North Irish Horse, X Corps Cavalry Regiment.] Joined the renamed 9th (North Irish Horse) Battalion from 36 Infantry Base Depot and transferred to Princess Victoria's (Royal Irish Fusiliers) in September/October 1917 (renumbered 41099). 'A' Company. **Wounded** in the period 21-28 March 1918 during the retreat from St Quentin.

THOMAS Private John H 42201. [Enlisted into the Army Service Corps (T/356590).] Transferred to Princess Victoria's (Royal Irish Fusiliers) 8 May 1918 (renumbered 42201) and joined the 9th (North Irish Horse) Battalion. [Transferred to a garrison battalion of The Royal Fusiliers (City of London Regiment) (GS/96087).]

THOMAS Private William 42200. Joined the 9th (North Irish Horse) Battalion, Princess Victoria's (Royal Irish Fusiliers) with the draft of men transferred from the Army Service Corps and the Army Veterinary Corps in May 1918.

THOMPSON Private Brownlow 41372. From Lisadian, County Armagh. A shop assistant. [Enlisted 15 November 1915 into the North Irish Horse (1960). To France 4 August 1916. To hospital sick (corneal ulcer) 16 May to 4 June 1917. Served with 2nd North Irish Horse, X Corps Cavalry Regiment.] Joined the renamed 9th (North Irish Horse) Battalion from 36 Infantry Base Depot and transferred to Princess Victoria's (Royal Irish Fusiliers) in September/October 1917 (renumbered 41372). 'B' Company. Attached to 108th Brigade Trench Mortar Battery when he proceeded on leave 10 November 1918 and failed to return. In his absence he was posted to the 5th

(Service) Battalion, The Royal Irish Regiment (Pioneers) in the Light Division in the British Army of the Rhine in March 1919. In fact, he had contracted influenza and then developed pneumonia and **died** in Queen Alexandria Military Hospital in London on 7 December 1918, aged 24.

THOMPSON MM Private Clement Arthur 40073. [Enlisted into the 10th (Service) Battalion, The Prince of Wales's Own (West Yorkshire Regiment) (13625). To France 13 July 1915.] Transferred to Princess Victoria's (Royal Irish Fusiliers) 30 November 1916 (renumbered 40073) and joined the 9th (Service) Battalion 12 December 1916. 'B' Company. **MM** – Moeuvres 23 November 1917. **Missing** in the period 21-28 March 1918 during the retreat from St Quentin believed **captured**. Transferred to the Class Z Reserve 9 March 1919. 1914-15 Star.

THOMPSON Private Denis 24061. Enlisted in February 1916. Posted to the 9th (Service) Battalion. 'A' Company. Believed **wounded** in the period 21-28 March 1918 during the retreat from St Quentin. [Transferred to the Corps of Royal Engineers (616459).] Known to be **captured** in 1918.

THOMPSON Private Fred 40032. Enlisted 23 February 1916. Joined the 9th (Service) Battalion, Princess Victoria's (Royal Irish Fusiliers) with the draft of men from The Prince of Wales's Own (West Yorkshire Regiment) on 12 December 1916. **Wounded**. Discharged as no longer physically fit for war service due to wounds 26 June 1919. Silver War Badge, number B274242.

THOMPSON Private Frederick 41499. From Randalstown, County Antrim. [Enlisted in November 1915 into the North Irish Horse (1773). Served with 2nd North Irish Horse, X Corps Cavalry Regiment.] Joined the renamed 9th (North Irish Horse) Battalion from 36 Infantry Base Depot and transferred to Princess Victoria's (Royal Irish Fusiliers) in September/October 1917 (renumbered 41499). 'D' Company. **Captured** in the period 21-28 March 1918 during the retreat from St Quentin.

THOMPSON Sergeant George 16148. Born at Shankill, County Armagh. Enlisted 28 September 1914. Lance Corporal 28 June 1915. To France with 36th (Ulster) Division in October 1915. Corporal 28 January 1916 in Machine Gun Section. **Wounded** by shrapnel to the right thigh at Hamel 29 June 1916 and evacuated to hospital in England. Posted to the Depot 8 October 1916. Acting Sergeant 26 April 1917. Posted to Irish Command Depot, Randalstown 3 April 1918. Posted to Number 3 Command Depot, Ripon 18 October 1918. Posted to the 3rd (Reserve) Battalion 11 January 1919. Badly injured his left leg (fractured femur) in an accident 16 January 1919. Discharged as no longer physically fit for war service 10 June 1919. Silver War Badge, number B265551. 1914-15 Star. Brother of Private James Thompson (one of five brothers who served in the war, at least one of whom was killed).

THOMPSON Private James 14723. From Lurgan, County Armagh. Enlisted September 1914. To France with 36th (Ulster) Division in October 1915. 'C' Company. Company runner during the attack at Hamel 1 July 1916, when he was **wounded**. [Transferred to the Army Service Corps (renumbered M/403374).] 1914-15 Star. Brother of Sergeant George Thompson (one of five brothers who served in the war, at least one of whom was killed).

THOMPSON Private James 49735. Joined the 9th (North Irish Horse) Battalion, Princess Victoria's (Royal Irish Fusiliers) with the draft of men transferred from The Royal Irish Rifles in April 1918.

THOMPSON Private John Dixon 41144. [Enlisted in November 1914 into the Service Squadron, 6th (Inniskilling) Dragoons (UD/160). To France with 36th (Ulster) Division in October 1915. Served with 2nd North Irish Horse, X Corps Cavalry Regiment.] Joined the renamed 9th (North Irish Horse) Battalion from 36 Infantry Base Depot and transferred to Princess Victoria's (Royal Irish Fusiliers) in September/October 1917 (renumbered 41144). Transferred to the Class Z Reserve 20 March 1919. 1914-15 Star.

THOMPSON Private John James 41369. [Enlisted in February 1917 into the North Irish Horse (2355). Served with 2nd North Irish Horse, X Corps Cavalry Regiment.] Joined the renamed 9th (North Irish Horse) Battalion from 36 Infantry Base Depot and transferred to Princess Victoria's (Royal Irish Fusiliers) in September/October 1917 (renumbered 41369).

THOMPSON Private Richard 19729. From Kingscourt, County Cavan. Enlisted into the 9th (Service) Battalion in April 1915. To France with 36th (Ulster) Division in October 1915. 'C' Company. **Killed in action** during the attack at Hamel 1 July 1916. 1914-15 Star.

THOMPSON Private Robert 41213. From Belfast. [Enlisted 25 May 1915 into the North Irish Horse (1611). Served with 2nd North Irish Horse, X Corps Cavalry Regiment.] Joined the renamed 9th (North Irish Horse) Battalion from 36 Infantry Base Depot and transferred to Princess Victoria's (Royal Irish Fusiliers) in September/October 1917 (renumbered 41213). **Wounded**. Discharged as no longer physically fit for war service due to wounds 29 August 1918, aged 22. Silver War Badge, number 445717. 1914-15 Star.

THOMPSON Private Robert 41379. [Enlisted in April 1915 into the Service Squadron, 6th (Inniskilling) Dragoons (UD/263). Served with 2nd North Irish Horse, X Corps Cavalry Regiment.] Joined the renamed 9th (North Irish Horse) Battalion from 36 Infantry Base Depot and transferred to Princess Victoria's (Royal Irish Fusiliers) in September/October 1917 (renumbered 41379).

THOMPSON Private Robert John 42496. [Served previously with the 9th (Service) Battalion, The Royal Irish Rifles (West Belfast) (626).] Transferred at the Base Depot to Princess Victoria's (Royal Irish Fusiliers) 14 September 1918 (renumbered 42496) and joined the 9th (North Irish Horse) Battalion 22 September 1918.

THOMPSON Sergeant Robert Kirk 41375. Commissioned on the General List - see Appendix 5.

THOMPSON Lance Sergeant Thomas John 14735. Enlisted September 1914. To France with 36th (Ulster) Division in October 1915. 'C' Company. Worked in Quartermaster's stores 1916 (Private). Did not take part in the attack at Hamel on 1 July 1916. Transferred to the Class Z Reserve 18 March 1919. 1914-15 Star.

THOMPSON Private W. Tried by Field General Court Martial on 5 December 1918 charged with *'absenting himself without leave'*; found not guilty. Soldier not identified.

THOMPSON Private Walter 42202. Joined the 9th (North Irish Horse) Battalion, Princess Victoria's (Royal Irish Fusiliers) with the draft of men transferred from the Army Service Corps and the Army Veterinary Corps in May 1918.

THOMPSON Private William 24565. Enlisted in July 1916. Posted to the 9th (Service) Battalion.

THOMPSON Private William 41407. From Ballymoney, County Antrim. A farmer. [Enlisted 13 December 1915 into the North Irish Horse (2037). Lance Corporal 10 June 1916. To France 3 August 1916. Served with 2nd North Irish Horse, X Corps Cavalry Regiment. Reverted to Private at his own request 2 May 1917.] Joined the renamed 9th (North Irish Horse) Battalion from 36 Infantry Base Depot and transferred to Princess Victoria's (Royal Irish Fusiliers) in September/October 1917 (renumbered 41407). **Wounded** by shrapnel at Marcoing and **died of wounds** at 48th Casualty Clearing Station 6 December 1917, aged 28.

THOMPSON Private William 42219. [Enlisted into the Army Service Corps (41818). Served with 16th Field Bakery.] Transferred to Princess Victoria's (Royal Irish Fusiliers) 8 May 1918 (renumbered 42219) and joined the 9th (North Irish Horse) Battalion. Transferred to the Class Z Reserve 15 April 1919. 1914-15 Star.

THOMPSON Private William James 14737. Born at Bessbrook, County Armagh. Enlisted September 1914. To France with 36th (Ulster) Division in October 1915. **Killed in action** during the attack at Hamel 1 July 1916. 1914-15 Star.

THORNBURY Private George 14731. Born at Shankill, County Armagh. From Lurgan, County Armagh. Enlisted September 1914. To France with 36th (Ulster) Division in October 1915. **Killed in action** during the attack at Hamel 1 July 1916. 1914-15 Star. Brother of Sergeant Joseph Thornbury and Sergeant William Thornbury.

THORNBURY Sergeant Joseph 11947. Born at Shankill, County Armagh. From Lurgan, County Armagh. [Enlisted in September 1914 and joined either the 5th (Service) or 6th (Service) Battalion in 31st Brigade, 10th (Irish) Division.] Posted to the 9th (Service) Battalion. 'D' Company. To France with 36th (Ulster) Division in October 1915. **Killed in action** during the attack at Hamel 1 July 1916. 1914-15 Star. Brother of Private George Thornbury and Sergeant William Thornbury.

THORNBURY Sergeant William 14716. From Lurgan, County Armagh. Enlisted September 1914. To France with 36th (Ulster) Division in October 1915. Transferred to the Class Z Reserve 31 March 1919. 1914-15 Star. Brother of Private George Thornbury and Sergeant Joseph Thornbury.

THORNTON Private Isaac 14711. From Portadown, County Armagh. 4th (Portadown) Battalion,

Armagh Regiment, Ulster Volunteer Force. A clerk. Enlisted September 1914. Discharged as no longer physically fit for war service due to sickness 25 May 1915. Silver War Badge, number 244129.

THREADGOLD Corporal Charles James 42137. Born in 1887. From Bermondsey, London. A baker. [Enlisted 11 February 1915 into the Army Service Corps (S4/060061). Corporal 18 March 1915. To France 17 December 1915 and served with 16th and 17th Field Bakeries.] Transferred to Princess Victoria's (Royal Irish Fusiliers) 8 May 1918 (renumbered 42137) and joined the 9th (North Irish Horse) Battalion 8 June 1918. [Posted to the 1st Battalion 18 June 1918. 'C' Company. **Killed in action** during the raid on Shoddy Farm near Meulenhouck 22 July 1918.] 1914-15 Star.

THURGUT Private Oscar Victor 43354. Born in 1895 at Marylebone, London. [Enlisted into The London Regiment (6704). Posted to the 1/7th (City of London) Battalion, The London Regiment.] Attached to the 9th (Service) Battalion, Princess Victoria's (Royal Irish Fusiliers) 26 November 1916. 'A' Company. Discharged from the Territorial Force, re-enlisted and transferred to Princess Victoria's (Royal Irish Fusiliers) in March/April 1917 (renumbered 43354). **Injured** (sprained foot) at the Battle of Langemarck 16 August 1917. **Missing** in the period 21-28 March 1918 during the retreat from St Quentin believed **captured**. Died at London in 1960, aged 65.

THWAITES Regimental Quartermaster Sergeant Thomas 3324. Regimental Quartermaster Sergeant - see above.

TICKNER Corporal George 42135. Born in 1885 at Shimmings, Petworth, West Sussex. A baker. [Enlisted 13 July 1915 into the Army Service Corps Special Reserve (S2/SR/04167). To France 2 May 1916 and served with 39th Field Bakery. Posted to 8th Field Bakery 2 September 1916. Corporal 16 February 1917.] At 'A' Infantry Base Depot transferred to Princess Victoria's (Royal Irish Fusiliers) 8 May 1918 (renumbered 42135) and joined the 9th (North Irish Horse) Battalion 8 June 1918. [Part of the draft transferred on 19 June 1918 to The Royal Irish Rifles (renumbered 45848). Posted to the 12th (Service) Battalion, The Royal Irish Rifles (Central Antrim). **Wounded** by a gunshot to the left forearm 1 September 1918. Evacuated via 109th Field Ambulance and 2nd Canadian General Hospital on 6 September 1918 to Bevan Military Hospital, Sandgate. Treated also at York House Hospital, Folkestone. Joined the 3rd (Reserve) Battalion, The Royal Irish Rifles 3 January 1919.] Transferred to the Class Z Reserve 18 March 1919. Returned to Shimmings, Petworth, West Sussex. Died in 1962, aged 77.

TIERNEY Private John 23995. From Cavan, County Cavan. A farm labourer. Enlisted 23 February 1916 and joined the 4th (Extra Reserve) Battalion. Sentenced to forty-eight hours detention 24 April 1917 for being absent off parade. To France 18 June 1917. Joined the 9th (Service) Battalion 10 July 1917. 'D' Company. **Missing** at the Battle of Langemarck 16 August 1917 and later declared **killed in action** on that date. His brother, Private Thomas Tierney, served with the 1st Battalion.

TIGHE Private William 21185. From Belfast. [Enlisted in December 1914/January 1915 and joined the 7th or 8th (Service) Battalion in 49th Brigade, 16th (Irish) Division.] Joined the 9th (North Irish Horse) Battalion when the 7th/8th (Service) Battalion was disbanded in February 1918. 'B' Company. **Captured** in the period 21-28 March 1918 during the retreat from St Quentin.

TIGWELL Sergeant Griffin 43449. Born in 1889 at Burghfield, Berkshire. A constable with the Metropolitan Police. [Enlisted 12 June 1915 and joined the 3/24th Battalion, The London Regiment (721672). Lance Corporal 15 June 1915. Corporal 28 June 1915. Lance Sergeant 14 August 1915. Sergeant 27 August 1915.] To France and joined 36 Infantry Base Depot 29 March 1918. Transferred to Princess Victoria's (Royal Irish Fusiliers) 2 April 1918 (renumbered 43449) and joined the 9th (North Irish Horse) Battalion 4 April 1918. To hospital 11 May 1918. [To Infantry Base Depot 8 September 1918. Transferred to The Queen's (Royal West Surrey Regiment) for service with 1/22nd (County of London) Battalion, The London Regiment (The Queen's). To 39th General Hospital late September 1918.] Transferred to the Class Z Reserve 18 February 1919. Rejoined the Metropolitan Police. Died at Hendon, Middlesex in 1957, aged 68.

TILSON Private Henry 24436. Enlisted 27 May 1916. Posted to the 9th (Service) Battalion. **Wounded**. Discharged as no longer physically fit for war service due to wounds 23 November 1918. Silver War Badge, number 507813.

TILSON Lance Corporal Cecil Armytage 41224. Born in 1893 at County Cavan. A clerk.

[Enlisted in October 1914 into the North Irish Horse (1301). Served with 2nd North Irish Horse, X Corps Cavalry Regiment.] Joined the renamed 9th (North Irish Horse) Battalion from 36 Infantry Base Depot and transferred to Princess Victoria's (Royal Irish Fusiliers) in September/October 1917 (renumbered 41224). 1914-15 Star. Re-enlisted in 1919 for Regular Army service.

TIMBEY Private William Fairburn 41232. From Shankill, Belfast. [Enlisted in May 1915 into the North Irish Horse (1547). Served with 2nd North Irish Horse, X Corps Cavalry Regiment.] Joined the renamed 9th (North Irish Horse) Battalion from 36 Infantry Base Depot and transferred to Princess Victoria's (Royal Irish Fusiliers) in September/October 1917 (renumbered 41232). **Killed in action** during the attack south of Wulverghem 4 September 1918, aged 22.

TIMM Private James 43213. Born in 1892. From Bakewell, Derbyshire. [Enlisted 4 December 1915 into The Sherwood Foresters (Nottinghamshire and Derbyshire Regiment) (35878). To France 23 July 1916.] Transferred to Princess Victoria's (Royal Irish Fusiliers) 31 August 1916 having joined the 9th (Service) Battalion on 8 August 1916. 'A' Company. Attached to 36th Division Works Battalion 5-29 January 1917. **Killed in action** at the Battle of Langemarck 16 August 1917, aged 25.

TIMMS Sergeant William Joseph 20818. [Enlisted in August 1915 and joined the 8th (Service) Battalion in 49th Brigade, 16th (Irish) Division.] Joined the 9th (North Irish Horse) Battalion when the 7th/8th (Service) Battalion was disbanded in February 1918.

TINLEY Lance Sergeant Cecil Cris 43251. Commissioned into The Sherwood Foresters (Nottinghamshire and Derbyshire Regiment) - see Appendix 5.

TOBIN Private Peter 41557. [Enlisted in September 1914 into the North Irish Horse (1221). Served with 2nd North Irish Horse, X Corps Cavalry Regiment.] Joined the renamed 9th (North Irish Horse) Battalion from 36 Infantry Base Depot and transferred to Princess Victoria's (Royal Irish Fusiliers) in September/October 1917 (renumbered 41557). Lance Corporal November 1917. [Transferred to the Tank Corps (renumbered 304876) 28 December 1917 and posted for training to the Tank Corps Depot, at Bovington near Wareham, Dorset.]

TODD Private Alexander 19794. Enlisted into the 9th (Service) Battalion in May 1915. To France with 36th (Ulster) Division in October 1915. 'D' Company. **Wounded** at the Battle of Langemarck 16 August 1917. **Missing** in the period 21-28 March 1918 during the retreat from St Quentin believed **captured**. Transferred to the Class Z Reserve. 1914-15 Star.

TODD Private George 40086. [Enlisted 10 August 1914 into The Prince of Wales's Own (West Yorkshire Regiment) (10229). To France 2 April 1915.] Transferred to Princess Victoria's (Royal Irish Fusiliers) 30 November 1916 (renumbered 40086) and joined the 9th (Service) Battalion 12 December 1916. [Transferred to the Labour Corps (renumbered 443258). Transferred to the 43rd (Garrison) Battalion, The Royal Fusiliers (City of London Regiment) (renumbered GS/106942).] Discharged as no longer physically fit for war service due to sickness 2 April 1919, aged 28. Silver War Badge, number B201627. 1914-15 Star.

TODD Private Thomas 20315. From County Durham. Enlisted in May/June 1915 and joined the 9th (Service) Battalion with the draft of men from The Royal Inniskilling Fusiliers who transferred to Princess Victoria's (Royal Irish Fusiliers) on 30 June 1915. To France with 36th (Ulster) Division in October 1915. **Killed in action** during the attack at Hamel 1 July 1916. 1914-15 Star.

TODD Private William D 41319. From Belfast. [Enlisted in June 1915 into the North Irish Horse (1684). Served with 2nd North Irish Horse, X Corps Cavalry Regiment.] Joined the renamed 9th (North Irish Horse) Battalion from 36 Infantry Base Depot and transferred to Princess Victoria's (Royal Irish Fusiliers) in September/October 1917 (renumbered 41319). 'C' Company. **Captured** in the period 21-28 March 1918 during the retreat from St Quentin.

TOFT Private Benjamin Ambrose (Benny) 41061. Born on 7 December 1889 at Cobridge, Staffordshire. [Enlisted at Stoke-on-Trent on 10 August 1914 into The Royal Fusiliers (City of London Regiment). Discharged as not being likely to become an efficient soldier in that he was considered medically unfit for service 19 October 1914.] Re-enlisted or transferred to Princess Victoria's (Royal Irish Fusiliers) in September 1917 and joined the 9th (Service) Battalion. 'C' Company. **Wounded** at the Battle of Langemarck 16 August 1917.

TOLAND Private James 18349. [Enlisted in March 1915 into the 8th (Service) Battalion in 49th

Brigade, 16th (Irish) Division.] Joined the 9th (North Irish Horse) Battalion when the 7th/8th (Service) Battalion was disbanded in February 1918.

TOMLINSON Corporal William 43244. [Enlisted into the 9th (Service) Battalion, The Sherwood Foresters (Nottinghamshire and Derbyshire Regiment) (13295)). Embarked with the Mediterranean Expeditionary Force July 1915. Promoted to Lance Corporal.] Transferred to Princess Victoria's (Royal Irish Fusiliers) 31 August 1916 having joined the 9th (Service) Battalion on 8 August 1916 (renumbered 43244). Transferred to the Class Z Reserve 13 January 1919. 1914-15 Star.

TONER Private Thomas 42470. [Enlisted 27 August 1914 into The Royal Irish Rifles (7184). To France 2 June 1915 and joined the 1st Battalion, The Royal Irish Rifles. Lance Corporal 6 October 1916. Corporal 28 April 1917. Acting Sergeant 16 August 1917. Posted to the Depot 9 February 1918. Joined the 4th (Extra Reserve) Battalion, The Royal Irish Rifles 21 March 1918. Reverted to Private.] To France 13 July 1918. Transferred at the Base Depot to Princess Victoria's (Royal Irish Fusiliers) 14 July 1918 (renumbered 42470) and joined the 9th (North Irish Horse) Battalion. **Wounded** by a gunshot to the leg. Discharged as no longer physically fit for war service due to wounds 21 January 1919. Silver War Badge, number B78589. 1914-15 Star.

TOOLE Private James 14732. From Shankill, County Armagh. A weaver. Enlisted September 1914. Discharged as not being likely to become an efficient soldier in that he was considered medically unfit for service 1 October 1914.

TOOMAY Private James 22683. (Possibly spelled Toomey.) Enlisted in November 1915. Posted to the 9th (Service) Battalion. 'B' Company. **Wounded** at the Battle of Messines and to hospital 9 June 1917. **Missing** in the period 21-28 March 1918 during the retreat from St Quentin believed **captured**.

TOPLEY Private James 18089. From Portadown, County Armagh. A shoemaker. Enlisted into the 9th (Service) Battalion 15 February 1915, aged 15. Discharged having made a mis-statement as to age on enlistment; soldier under 17 years of age at date of application for discharge 19 February 1915.

TOPLEY Private Joseph 14714. Born at Tandragee, County Armagh. Member of the Ulster Volunteer Force. Worked for Thomas Sinton & Co Ltd, Laurelvale. Enlisted September 1914. **Drowned** while swimming in a river at Seaford in England 18 August 1915, aged 22. The inquest heard that he was swimming in the River Cuckmere. When his friends got out he said that he was going to remain in the water for a little longer. Soon afterwards his friends saw that he was missing. Privates John Allen and Isaac Walker of the 9th Royal Irish Fusiliers and Private Robert Patterson of 12th (Service) Battalion, The Royal Irish Rifles (Central Antrim) searched for him and Patterson found him in seven feet of water. He brought him to the surface but he was dead. A verdict of 'accidental death by drowning' was recorded. The coroner praised the three who searched for him.

TOPLEY Lance Corporal Thomas 14729. Born at Lurgan, County Armagh. Lived at Portadown, County Armagh. Enlisted September 1914. To France with 36th (Ulster) Division in October 1915. 'C' Company. Bombing team during the attack at Hamel 1 July 1916, which he survived unwounded. **Killed in action** at the Battle of Langemarck 16 August 1917, aged 24. 1914-15 Star.

TOPPING Private Robert 41352. [Enlisted April 1917 into the North Irish Horse (2411). Served with 2nd North Irish Horse, X Corps Cavalry Regiment.] Joined the renamed 9th (North Irish Horse) Battalion from 36 Infantry Base Depot and transferred to Princess Victoria's (Royal Irish Fusiliers) in September/October 1917 (renumbered 41352). 'B' Company. **Wounded** during the retreat from St Quentin 21-28 March 1918.

TORRENS Lance Corporal James 14724. Born in 1893 at Lurgan, County Armagh. Worked in a shop in Lurgan. Enlisted September 1914. To France with 36th (Ulster) Division in October 1915. 'C' Company. **Wounded** (shellshock) during the attack at Hamel 1 July 1916. Separated from the 9th (North Irish Horse) Battalion in the period 21-28 March 1918 during the retreat from St Quentin; rejoined 6 April 1918. [Transferred to the Labour Corps (renumbered 518541).] 1914-15 Star.

TORRENS Private James 41500. [Enlisted 10 September 1914 into the North Irish Horse (1197). To France 2 June 1915. Served with 2nd North Irish Horse, X Corps Cavalry Regiment.] Joined the renamed 9th (North Irish Horse) Battalion from 36 Infantry Base Depot and transferred to Princess

Victoria's (Royal Irish Fusiliers) in September/October 1917 (renumbered 41500). **Wounded**. Discharged as no longer physically fit for war service due to wounds 27 March 1919. Silver War Badge, number B165710. 1914-15 Star.

TOTTEN Private David 14719. Born in 1880 at Milltown, County Down. Lived at Portadown, County Armagh. Worked as a labourer at the Collen Brothers Ltd quarry in Portadown, County Armagh. Enlisted 15 September 1914. To France with 36th (Ulster) Division in October 1915. To hospital sick and treated at Number 3 General Hospital, Boulogne. [Transferred to the Labour Corps (renumbered 399844) 18 February 1918. Served with 794th and 170th Labour Companies.] Transferred to the Class Z Reserve 21 March 1919. 1914-15 Star.

TOTTEN Private Robert 16136. Born at Glaslough, County Monaghan in 1879. Worked for a coal mine. Enlisted into the 9th (Service) Battalion in October 1914. To France with 36th (Ulster) Division in October 1915. 'D' Company. **Wounded** during the attack at Hamel on 1 July 1916 by gunshots to the shoulder and neck. Evacuated to Roseneath Hospital, Broadstairs. [Transferred to the Labour Corps. Served in 666th and 668th Labour Companies. Transferred to the Royal Defence Corps (80188) and served in 115th Protection Company.] 1914-15 Star. Transferred to the Class Z Reserve 30 March 1919. Worked in a coal mine in Scotland after the war.

TOTTON Private Higginson 23211. Born in 1875 at Belfast. Worked for the City Corporation, Belfast. Enlisted 20 November 1915 and joined the 10th (Reserve) Battalion. To France 30 June 1916 and joined the 9th (Service) Battalion. 'D' Company. **Wounded** by a gunshot to the back at the Battle of Langemarck 16 August 1917. Joined the 10th (Reserve) Battalion 25 January 1918. [Transferred to the Labour Corps (renumbered 545511). Served with 361st Home Service Employment Company. To Labour Base Depot, France and joined the 76th Labour Company 16 September 1918.] Transferred to the Class Z Reserve 13 February 1919.

TOTTON Private Robert 17554. Born at Portadown, County Armagh. Enlisted into the 9th (Service) Battalion in November/December 1914. To France 17 November 1915 and rejoined the 9th (Service) Battalion. **Killed in action** during the attack at Hamel 1 July 1916. 1914-15 Star.

TOTTON Private William 14726. Born in 1880 at Drumcree, County Armagh. Enlisted into The Royal Inniskilling Fusiliers (6375) 20 September 1899. On six occasions throughout 1900 charged with being drunk in camp and fined. Posted to the 1st Battalion, The Royal Inniskilling Fusiliers 28 November 1900. Fined seven shillings and sixpence and confined to barracks for ten days for using abusive language to an NCO and being drunk 26 February 1901. Tried by District Court Martial on 10 April 1901 charged with *'when on active service, drunkenness.'* Found guilty and sentenced to twenty-eight days imprisonment with hard labour. Sentenced to seven days imprisonment with hard labour for quitting the barracks and making an improper reply to an NCO 15 July 1901. Tried by District Court Martial on 25 October 1902 on a charge of *'striking his superior officer'*; found guilty and sentenced to fifty-six days imprisonment with hard labour. Served in South Africa 28 November 1900 to 18 January 1903. Queen's South Africa Medal with clasps 'Cape Colony' 'Orange Free State' and 'Transvaal'. Transferred to the Army Reserve 20 March 1903. Discharged from the Army Reserve 20 September 1911. A weaver. 4th (Portadown) Battalion, Armagh Regiment, Ulster Volunteer Force. Enlisted 15 September 1914. Sentenced to ten days Field Punishment Number 2 for absence, returning drunk and resisting escort 3 March 1915. Fined two shillings and sixpence for being absent at roll call and drunk in camp 10 August 1915. Fined ten shillings and confined to camp for seven days for being drunk on parade 1 September 1915. To France with 36th (Ulster) Division in October 1915. Sentenced to fourteen days Field Punishment Number 1 for drunkenness 12 October 1915. Sentenced to fourteen days Field Punishment Number 1 for being drunk in billets and creating a disturbance 11 November 1915. Tried by Field General Court Martial on 2 January 1916 on a charge of *'drunkenness'*. Found guilty and sentenced to ninety days Field Punishment Number 1 (remitted by thirty-four days). Fined ten days pay for drunkenness 7 July 1916. Sentenced to twenty-eight days Field Punishment Number 1 for being drunk 1 September 1916. Sentenced to fourteen days Field Punishment Number 1 for being drunk 1 November 1916. To 110th Field Ambulance injured (sprained wrist) 10 to 27 December 1916. Sentenced to seven days Field Punishment Number 1 for being drunk 22 August 1917. Sentenced to twenty-one days Field Punishment Number 1 for whilst on active service being drunk on the line of march 12 January 1918. Sentenced to twenty-eight days Field Punishment Number 1 for being drunk 3 April 1918. **Wounded** by a gunshot to the left leg in the period 9-18 April 1918 in the actions between Wulverghem and Kemmel and evacuated to hospital in England. Discharged as no longer physically fit for war service due to wounds 18 June 1919. Silver War Badge, number B265550. 1914-15 Star.

TOWNSEND Private John 42125. [Enlisted into the Army Veterinary Corps (30154).] Transferred to Princess Victoria's (Royal Irish Fusiliers) 8 May 1918 (renumbered 42125) and joined the 9th (North Irish Horse) Battalion.

TRANTER Private Frederick Bert 42212. Born in 1898 at Birmingham. A plumber's mate. [Enlisted 28 February 1916 and transferred to the Army Reserve. Mobilised 21 March 1917 and joined the Army Service Corps (309139). Served with 823 Horse Transport Company in 71st Division in England.] To 'A' Infantry Base Depot 6 May 1918 when 71st Division was broken up. Transferred to Princess Victoria's (Royal Irish Fusiliers) 8 May 1918 (renumbered 42212) and joined the 9th (North Irish Horse) Battalion. 'C' Company. **Wounded** during the attack at Vijfwegen/Hill 41 by a gunshot to the shoulder and evacuated to hospital in England 9 October 1918. Joined the 3rd (Reserve) Battalion 27 May 1919. Discharged on compassionate grounds 25 July 1919.

TRAVIS Private Joseph 43282. Born at Doncaster, Yorkshire. [Enlisted into The Sherwood Foresters (Nottinghamshire and Derbyshire Regiment) (35432).] Transferred to Princess Victoria's (Royal Irish Fusiliers) 31 August 1916 having joined the 9th (Service) Battalion on 8 August 1916 (renumbered 43282). 'D' Company. **Captured** in the period 21-28 March 1918 during the retreat from St Quentin. **Died** 5 July 1918 while a prisoner of war, aged 26.

TREADAWAY Private Ernest Arthur Reginald 45742. From Finsbury Park, London. A pawnbroker's assistant. [Enlisted 5 December 1915 and transferred to the Army Reserve. Mobilised 1 March 1916 and joined the 3/24th Battalion, The London Regiment (5360). Lance Corporal 10 June 1916. To France 19 December 1916, reverted to Private and posted to the 1/24th (County of London) Battalion, The London Regiment (The Queen's) (renumbered 722328 in March 1917). **Wounded** by a gunshot to the left thigh (superficial) 7 June 1917 and treated at 46th Casualty Clearing Station and 8th British Red Cross Hospital. **Wounded** (gassed) 24 July 1917 and evacuated to hospital in England. Treated at Reading War Hospital and 2nd Eastern General Hospital, Brighton. Posted to the 22nd (Reserve) Battalion, The London Regiment 31 January 1918.] To France and joined 36 Infantry Base Depot 29 March 1918. Transferred to Princess Victoria's (Royal Irish Fusiliers) 2 April 1918 (renumbered 45742) and joined the 9th (North Irish Horse) Battalion 4 April 1918. **Wounded** by shrapnel to the right forearm during the advance to Anseghem 25 October 1918 and evacuated to hospital in England. Treated at Lord Derby War Hospital, Winwick. Discharged as no longer physically fit for war service due to wounds 8 May 1919. Silver War Badge, number B234840. To Kitchener Hospital, Brighton 15 June to 9 July 1919 with influenza.

TREASURE Corporal Bernard Henry George 42136. Born in 1892 at Radstock, Somerset. [Enlisted into the Army Service Corps (S4/070287 Acting Staff Sergeant). To France 16 April 1915.] Transferred to Princess Victoria's (Royal Irish Fusiliers) 8 May 1918 (renumbered 42136) and joined the 9th (North Irish Horse) Battalion. [Part of the draft transferred on 19 June 1918 to The Royal Irish Rifles (renumbered 45855). Joined the 2nd Battalion, The Royal Irish Rifles. **Died of wounds** 19 July 1918, aged 25.] 1914-14 Star.

TREW Private Robert George 27450. Born in 1894 at Glenanne, County Armagh. Enlisted into or transferred to Princess Victoria's (Royal Irish Fusiliers) in March 1917. Posted to the 9th (North Irish Horse) Battalion. [Posted to the 1st Battalion. **Captured**.]

TROTTER Private Charles 14713. Born in 1894 at Drumcree, County Armagh. Lived at Portadown, County Armagh. A linen weaver. 4th (Portadown) Battalion, Armagh Regiment, Ulster Volunteer Force. Enlisted September 1914. To France with 36th (Ulster) Division in October 1915. 'B' Company. To hospital sick 25 March 1916 and evacuated to hospital in England 13 April 1916. Posted to the 10th (Reserve) Battalion 29 July 1916. [Transferred to the Labour Corps (renumbered 231627) 7 July 1917. Posted to 666th Labour Company. Posted to 485th Home Service Employment Company. Transferred to the Royal Defence Corps (renumbered 80189). Posted to 170th Protection Company.] 1914-15 Star.

TROTTER Private John Thomas 41513. Born in 1892 at Enniskillen, County Fermanagh. A printer from Culky, County Fermanagh. [Enlisted 10 April 1915 into the Service Squadron, 6th (Inniskilling) Dragoons (UD/246). To France with 36th (Ulster) Division in October 1915. Served with 2nd North Irish Horse, X Corps Cavalry Regiment.] Joined the renamed 9th (North Irish Horse) Battalion from 36 Infantry Base Depot and transferred to Princess Victoria's (Royal Irish Fusiliers) in September/October 1917 (renumbered 41513). **Wounded**. Discharged as no longer physically fit for war service due to wounds 4 September 1918. Silver War Badge, number 445736. 1914-15 Star.

TROTTER Private Sampson Kirkpatrick 41320. Born 31 December 1887 at Muckross, Kesh, County Fermanagh. A farmer. [Enlisted into 'A' Squadron, North Irish Horse (771) 20 December 1912 and to France 17 August 1914 as GHQ Troops. Served with 2nd North Irish Horse, X Corps Cavalry Regiment.] Joined the renamed 9th (North Irish Horse) Battalion from 36 Infantry Base Depot and transferred to Princess Victoria's (Royal Irish Fusiliers) in September/October 1917 (renumbered 41320). Transferred to the Class Z Reserve 11 March 1919. 1914 Star. Joined the Royal Ulster Constabulary 1 October 1922 and retired 30 December 1959. Died in Belfast City Hospital 19 May 1970, aged 82. Buried at Roselawn Cemetery, Belfast. His brother, Corporal Thomas Jonas Trotter, served with the Royal Irish Constabulary from 1912, the North Irish Horse and The Royal Irish Rifles. After the war he served with the Royal Ulster Constabulary, from which he retired in 1954 and died on 12 January 1985.

TROTTER Private Samuel 14718. From Portadown, County Armagh. 4th (Portadown) Battalion, Armagh Regiment, Ulster Volunteer Force. Enlisted September 1914. To France with 36th (Ulster) Division in October 1915. 'B' Company. **Wounded** in June 1916. **Wounded** in October 1916. **Wounded** during the retreat from St Quentin 21-28 March 1918. [Transferred to the Army Service Corps (renumbered EMT/63897).] Transferred to the Class Z Reserve. 1914-15 Star. Re-enlisted in 1919 for Regular Army service with the Royal Army Service Corps (renumbered M/16492). General Service Medal 1918-1962 with clasp 'Kurdistan'. Discharged *'with ignominy'* for misconduct 8 November 1927.

TROUGHTON Private Thomas 14196. This regimental number was also allocated to Private H Cairns. The Medal Index Card for Troughton shows that his number was amended to clearly read 14196. This number is significantly out of sequence and most likely an error. From Mulladry, Richhill, County Armagh. Member of Loyal Orange Lodge 371. Enlisted September 1914. To France with 36th (Ulster) Division in October 1915. **Killed in action** during the attack at Hamel 1 July 1916, aged 22. 1914-15 Star.

TRUEMAN MM Corporal Frank 14736. From Cloncarish, County Armagh. Enlisted September 1914. To France with 36th (Ulster) Division in October 1915. [Joined 108th Brigade Machine Gun Company in January 1916. Transferred to the Machine Gun Corps (renumbered 17805). **MM**.] Discharged as unfit for further service 23 June 1918. 1914-15 Star.

TRUEMAN Private Thomas Joseph 15871. Born at Tartaraghan, County Armagh. Member of Derryneskin Loyal Orange lodge 13. Armagh Regiment, Ulster Volunteer Force. Enlisted into the 9th (Service) Battalion 20 September 1914. Discharged as no longer physically fit for war service due to sickness 28 June 1915. Silver War Badge, number 226571. Enlisted into the Royal Air Force (285986) as a rigger in 1918. Transferred to the Royal Air Force Reserve 20 February 1919. He became a carpenter and lived at Laurelvale, County Armagh. Died in 1959 and is buried at Mullavilly Parish Church. Brother of Private William Edward Trueman. His youngest daughter, Mildred, served in the Army Territorial Service in the Second World War.

TRUEMAN Private William Edward 17665. Born at Tartaraghan, County Armagh. Enlisted into the 9th (Service) Battalion in December 1914/January 1915. Brother of Private Thomas Joseph Trueman.

TRUSTUM Private William 21909. From the Channel Islands. [Enlisted in October 1915. Joined the 7th or 8th (Service) Battalion in 49th Brigade, 16th (Irish) Division.] Joined the 9th (North Irish Horse) Battalion when the 7th/8th (Service) Battalion was disbanded in February 1918.

TUCK Warrant Officer Class I Edward George 17517. Born in 1865 at Newbury, Berkshire. Served briefly in the 3rd Battalion (Militia), The Welsh Regiment. Enlisted into The Welsh Regiment (456) 16 July 1883 and joined the 1st Battalion. Lance Corporal 27 March 1884. Corporal 16 October 1884. Lance Sergeant 19 October 1885. Reverted to Corporal for misconduct 13 November

1885. In arrest 27-30 December 1885 and reduced in rank to Private for being drunk 31 December 1885. Lance Corporal 30 November 1886. Corporal 8 February 1887. In arrest 13-15 November 1887 and reduced in rank to Private for being drunk 16 November 1887. Lance Corporal 4 July 1890. Corporal 11 November 1891. Served in India from September 1892 to March 1899. Lance Sergeant 21 August 1894. Sergeant 4 April 1896. Served in the South Africa War 12 February 1900 to 7 March 1902. Queen's South Africa Medal with clasp 'Cape Colony'. King's South Africa Medal with clasps 'South Africa 1901' and 'South Africa 1902'. Posted to the 3rd Battalion (Militia) as an Instructor of Volunteers 16 February 1904. Colour Sergeant 16 July 1904. Discharged to pension 26 November 1908. Re-enlisted 10 September 1914 and joined the 9th (Service) Battalion, Princess Victoria's (Royal Irish Fusiliers). Appointed Company Sergeant Major 22 September 1914. Warrant Officer Class II 29 January 1915. [Posted to the 10th (Reserve) Battalion on its formation as Regimental Sergeant Major 24 September 1915. Long Service & Good Conduct Medal 13 January 1916. Posted to the 3rd (Reserve) Battalion as Regimental Sergeant Major 1 June 1918 (vice McKane). Posted for duty with The Sherwood Foresters (Nottinghamshire and Derbyshire Regiment) as a Regimental Sergeant Major but this order was rescinded and he was posted to the Depot as Regimental Sergeant Major. Transferred to the Class Z Reserve 22 February 1920, aged 54. Died at Woolton Hill, East Woodhay, Berkshire 8 March 1948, aged 82.

TUDOR Private Arthur 43327. Born in 1883 at Condover, Salop. Served in the 3rd Battalion (Militia), The King's (Shropshire Light Infantry) (4444) from 4 May to 11 July 1901. Enlisted 17 July 1901 into the Royal Army Medical Corps (15944). Served in South Africa from 3 February 1902 to 14 April 1905. Queen's South Africa Medal with clasps 'Cape Colony' 'Orange Free State' and 'South Africa 1902'. Transferred to the Army Reserve 20 April 1905. Mobilised 17 August 1914 and to France 31 October 1914. Served with 11th Field Ambulance. Attached to the 2nd Battalion, The Essex Regiment for water duties 31 August 1915. In December 1915, when the 2nd Battalion, The Essex Regiment was in 109th Brigade, 36th (Ulster) Division, he returned to England on leave and **deserted**. Re-enlisted into The London Regiment under the alias Arthur Thomas. Posted to 1/7th (City of London) Battalion, The London Regiment (6750).] Attached to the 9th (Service) Battalion, Princess Victoria's (Royal Irish Fusiliers) 26 November 1916. Due to the efforts to examine the pay and allowances and the details of the desertion of Private Tudor, his re-enlistment was identified and he was arrested in February 1917. Confined awaiting trial 17 April to 12 June 1917. Tried by Field General Court Martial 13 June 1917 charged with *'when on active service* ***deserting*** *His Majesty's service'* and *'fraudulent enlistment'*; found guilty and sentenced to three years penal servitude. The sentence was suspended and he was ordered to continue to serve in the 9th Royal Irish Fusiliers. 'A' Company. **Killed in action** at the Battle of Langemarck 16 August 1917, aged 34. 1914 Star.

TUFF Private Robert 22806. Enlisted 8 November 1915. Posted to the 9th (Service) Battalion. Discharged as no longer physically fit for war service due to sickness 6 November 1919. Silver Badge, number B334066.

TUGHAN MM Private Robert 41280. From Tullyglush, Keady, County Armagh. [Enlisted in November 1915 into the North Irish Horse (1959). Served with 2nd North Irish Horse, X Corps Cavalry Regiment.] Joined the renamed 9th (North Irish Horse) Battalion from 36 Infantry Base Depot and transferred to Princess Victoria's (Royal Irish Fusiliers) in September/October 1917 (renumbered 41280). 'C' Company. **Missing** in the period 21-28 March 1918 during the retreat from St Quentin believed **captured**. **MM** – St Quentin 21-28 March 1918.

TUITE Lance Corporal William James 43357. [Enlisted into The London Regiment (2004). Posted to 1/7th (City of London) Battalion, The London Regiment.] Attached to the 9th (Service) Battalion, Princess Victoria's (Royal Irish Fusiliers) 26 November 1916. 'B' Company. Discharged from the Territorial Force, re-enlisted and transferred to Princess Victoria's (Royal Irish Fusiliers) in March/April 1917 (renumbered 43357). **Missing** in the period 21-28 March 1918 during the retreat from St Quentin believed **captured**.

TULLY Private Edward 21591. [Enlisted in August 1915 and joined the 7th (Service) Battalion in 49th Brigade, 16th (Irish) Division.] Joined the 9th (North Irish Horse) Battalion when the 7th/8th (Service) Battalion was disbanded in February 1918.

TULLY Private Stephen E 43344. From Maidstone, Kent. [Enlisted into The London Regiment (6781). Posted to 1/7th (City of London) Battalion, The London Regiment.] Attached to the 9th

(Service) Battalion, Princess Victoria's (Royal Irish Fusiliers) 26 November 1916. 'C' Company. Discharged from the Territorial Force, re-enlisted and transferred to Princess Victoria's (Royal Irish Fusiliers) in March/April 1917 (renumbered 43344). **Wounded** at the Battle of Langemarck 16 August 1917. [Transferred to the Corps of Royal Engineers (renumbered 354879, renumbered WR/204786).]

TULLEY Private John Thomas 40045. [Enlisted 31 December 1914 into the 17th (Service) Battalion, The Prince of Wales's Own (West Yorkshire Regiment) (2nd Leeds) (653).] Transferred to Princess Victoria's (Royal Irish Fusiliers) 30 November 1916 (renumbered 40045) and joined the 9th (Service) Battalion 12 December 1916. **Wounded**. Discharged as no longer physically fit for war service due to wounds 21 April 1917. Silver War Badge, number 162423.

TUPMAN Private Arthur E 42450. From London. [Served previously with The Royal Irish Rifles (47122).] Transferred at the Base Depot to Princess Victoria's (Royal Irish Fusiliers) 14 September 1918 (renumbered 42450) and joined the 9th (North Irish Horse) Battalion 22 September 1918. Re-enlisted in 1919 for Regular Army service with The Rifle Brigade (The Prince Consort's Own) (renumbered 39473, renumbered 6908100). Served in Mesopotamia with the 1st Battalion, The Rifle Brigade (The Prince Consort's Own). General Service Medal 1918-1962 with clasp 'Iraq'.

TURKINGTON MM Sergeant Alfred 14720. Commissioned into The Queen's (Royal West Surrey Regiment) - see Appendix 5. Brother of Corporal Ernest Turkington.

TURKINGTON Corporal Ernest 14725. From Lurgan, County Armagh. Enlisted September 1914. To France with 36th (Ulster) Division in October 1915. **Killed in action** during the attack at Hamel 1 July 1916, aged 22. 1914-15 Star. Brother of Sergeant Alfred Turkington. His brother, Lieutenant Colonel Albert Turkington OBE, served as a regular soldier with the 1st Battalion, Princess Victoria's (Royal Irish Fusiliers) from 1913 and served post war at Dover. He later served in the Ulster Special Constabulary and commanded a battalion of the Ulster Home Guard.

TURKINGTON Private James 14728. Born in 1874. From Shankill, County Armagh. Served pre-war with the 5th Battalion (Militia), The Royal Irish Rifles. Enlisted September 1914. Discharged as not being likely to become an efficient soldier in that he was considered medically unfit for service 7 November 1914.

TURKINGTON Lance Corporal Robert David 26824. Enlisted 3 February 1917. Posted to the 9th (Service) Battalion. **Wounded**. Discharged as no longer physically fit for war service due to wounds 26 July 1919. Silver War Badge, number B293963.

TURKINGTON Private William James 41173. Born in 1891 at Killygarvin, County Tyrone. Member of Masonic Lodge 473. Worked for the Great Northern Railway. [Enlisted in early-1915 into the Service Squadron, 6th (Inniskilling) Dragoons (UD/207). Served with 2nd North Irish Horse, X Corps Cavalry Regiment.] Joined the renamed 9th (North Irish Horse) Battalion from 36 Infantry Base Depot and transferred to Princess Victoria's (Royal Irish Fusiliers) in September/October 1917 (renumbered 41173). **Killed in action** 23 November 1917 at Moeuvres, aged 26.

TURNER MC Warrant Officer Class I Charles Henry 17397. Regimental Sergeant Major - see above.

TURNER Lance Corporal William Henry 40072. [Enlisted into the 10th (Service) Battalion, The Prince of Wales's Own (West Yorkshire Regiment) (10981). To France 11 August 1915.] Transferred to Princess Victoria's (Royal Irish Fusiliers) 30 November 1916 (renumbered 40072) and joined the 9th (Service) Battalion 12 December 1916. Transferred to the Class Z Reserve 20 March 1919. 1914-15 Star.

TURNEY Lance Corporal Alfred Topham 43195. Born in 1879. From Nottingham. A leather worker. [Enlisted 15 December 1915 and transferred to the Army Reserve. Mobilised on 7 April 1916 and joined the 4th (Extra Reserve) Battalion, The Sherwood Foresters (Nottinghamshire and Derbyshire Regiment) (41686).] Transferred to Princess Victoria's (Royal Irish Fusiliers) 31 August 1916 (renumbered 43195) having joined the 9th (Service) Battalion on 8 August 1916. 'A' Company. To hospital sick (scabies and impetigo) 29 October 1916 and evacuated to hospital in England 1 January 1917. Treated at 1st Western General Hospital, Fazackerley, Liverpool. Joined the Irish Command Depot, Tipperary 13 February 1917. [To France 9 September 1917 and immediately to hospital sick. Served with 17th Prisoner of War Guard Company. Transferred to the Labour Corps (renumbered 426684) 12 October 1917 and posted to 935th Area Employment Company. To hospital sick (herpes and eczema) and evacuated to hospital in England 23 December 1917. Transferred to the Royal Defence Corps (renumbered 82172) 16 July 1918. Served with 125th and 405th Protection Companies.] Transferred to the Class Z Reserve 1 February 1919. Died at Nottinghamshire in 1946, aged 67.

TWYANOFSKY Private M J 43314. See Private M J Pyanowski above.

TYLER Private Clarence Trelawney 49928. Born 13 October 1899 at Somerset. [Enlisted 10 November 1917. [Transferred to Princess Victoria's (Royal Irish Fusiliers) in May 1918 (renumbered 49928) with a draft of men from English regiments and joined the 1st Battalion.] Posted to the 9th (North Irish Horse) Battalion in August 1918. **Wounded**. Discharged as no longer physically fit for war service due to wounds 17 September 1919. Silver War Badge, number B313355. Died at Tunbridge Wells, Kent 1981, aged 82.

UNDERDOWN Private Hamlet Percy 43310. Born 29 October 1891 at Gravesend, Kent. A clerk. Joined the 9th (Service) Battalion, Princess Victoria's (Royal Irish Fusiliers) with the draft of men from The London Regiment in November 1916 (renumbered 43310). 'D' Company. **Wounded** at the Battle of Langemarck 16 August 1917. Died in 1979 in London, aged 88.

UNION Private Christopher Vincent 43345. Born 18 July 1891 at Dublin. A butcher and then a carter. [Enlisted into the Army Service Corps (T/25495) as a regular soldier. To France 16 August 1914 with 1st Division Train.] Joined the 9th (Service) Battalion, Princess Victoria's (Royal Irish Fusiliers) with the draft of men from The London Regiment in November 1916. Transferred to Princess Victoria's (Royal Irish Fusiliers) 30 January 1917 (renumbered 43345). Discharged as no longer physically fit for war service 15 April 1919. Silver War Badge, number B256304. 1914 Star.

UPRICHARD Lance Corporal Herbert James 23794. Born in 1897 at Belfast. Enlisted 19 January 1916. Posted to the 9th (Service) Battalion. 'D' Company. **Wounded** at the Battle of Langemarck 16 August 1917. Discharged as no longer physically fit for war service due to wounds 23 January 1918, aged 20. Silver War Badge, number 315825. He emigrated to Canada and worked as an accountant. On return to Northern Ireland he joined the civil service. During the Second World War he was commissioned into the Territorial Army Reserve of Officers Special List for service with the Army Cadet Force 17 September 1943 and relinquished his commission on 21 June 1945.

UPRICHARD Sergeant Robert 14739. Enlisted September 1914. To France with 36th (Ulster) Division in October 1915. 'C' Company. Survived the attack at Hamel on 1 July 1916 unwounded. Transferred to the Class Z Reserve 6 April 1919. 1914-15 Star.

UPRICHARD Private William Henry 14738. From Derrymacash, County Armagh. A yarn dresser. Enlisted September 1914. To France with 36th (Ulster) Division in October 1915. [Joined 108th Brigade Machine Gun Company January 1916. Transferred to the Machine Gun Corps (renumbered 17806). **Died of wounds** 14 July 1916, aged 35.] 1914-15 Star.

VALE Lance Corporal William Clement 40040. Born in 1894. From Saltley, Birmingham. A wages clerk. [Enlisted 5 September 1914 into the 11th (Service) Battalion, The Prince of Wales's Own (West Yorkshire Regiment) (14563). To France 26 August 1915 in 69th Brigade, 23rd Division. Evacuated to hospital in England sick (trench fever) June 1916 and treated at 3rd Northern General Hospital, Sheffield.] Transferred to Princess Victoria's (Royal Irish Fusiliers) 30 November 1916 (renumbered 40040) and joined the 9th (Service) Battalion 12 December 1916. 'D' Company. **Wounded** by a gunshot to the left leg at the Battle of Langemarck 16 August 1917. Evacuated to hospital in England and treated at Bagthorpe Infirmary, Nottingham. Transferred to the Class Z Reserve 15 February 1919. 1914-15 Star.

VALLELY Sergeant Bernard 2935. Served with Princess Victoria's (Royal Irish Fusiliers) Special Reserve. [Served with the 7th/8th (Service) Battalion in 49th Brigade 16th (Irish) Division.] Joined the 9th (North Irish Horse) Battalion when the 7th/8th (Service) Battalion was disbanded in February 1918.

VALLELY Private John 16428. Born at Shankill, Belfast. From John Street, Portadown, County Armagh. 4th (Portadown) Battalion, Armagh Regiment, Ulster Volunteer Force. Enlisted into the 9th (Service) Battalion in November 1914. To France with 36th (Ulster) Division in October 1915. **Killed in action** during the attack at Hamel 1 July 1916. 1914-15 Star.

VANCE Private Brown 24582. Born in 1892 at Lanarkshire, Scotland. From Killeyfaddy, Magherafelt, County Londonderry. A bootmaker. Served under his grandmother's married name (his uncle's name) as Private Patrick McFalls. Enlisted in July 1916. Posted to the 9th (Service) Battalion. 'D' Company. **Killed in action** at the Battle of Langemarck 16 August 1917.

VANCE Private Joseph 14741. From Tandragee, County Armagh. 4th (Portadown) Battalion, Armagh Regiment, Ulster Volunteer Force. Enlisted September 1914. To France with 36th (Ulster) Division in October 1915. **Killed in action** during the attack at Hamel 1 July 1916. 1914-15 Star. Related to Private Thomas Vance.

VANCE Private Thomas 14744. From Glenanne, County Armagh. Enlisted September 1914. To France with 36th (Ulster) Division in October 1915. **Killed in action** during the attack at Hamel 1 July 1916, aged 23. 1914-15 Star. Related to Private Joseph Vance.

VANCE Private William 16140. Enlisted into the 9th (Service) Battalion in October 1914. To France with 36th (Ulster) Division in October 1915. 1914-15 Star. Battalion Colour Guard June 1919.

VAUGHAN Corporal Walter Ernest 41177 & 7042136. From Eastly, Hampshire. [Enlisted 6 July 1912 as a regular soldier into the 2nd Dragoon Guards (Queen's Bays) (7008). To France in 1st Cavalry Division 16 August 1914. **Wounded** and evacuated to hospital in England 25 November 1914. To France 3 August 1916 and joined 6th (Inniskilling) Dragoons (7008) in 2nd North Irish Horse, X Corps Cavalry Regiment.] Joined the renamed 9th (North Irish Horse) Battalion from 36 Infantry Base Depot and transferred to Princess Victoria's (Royal Irish Fusiliers) in September/October 1917 (renumbered 41177). Evacuated to hospital in England 20 December 1917. 1914 Star. Transferred to the Section B Army Reserve, Princess Victoria's (Royal Irish Fusiliers) (renumbered 7042136) 2 August 1919. Discharged 5 July 1924.

VEALE Private William 21973. [Enlisted in October 1915 and joined the 7th or 8th (Service) Battalion in 49th Brigade, 16th (Irish) Division.] Joined the 9th (North Irish Horse) Battalion when the 7th/8th (Service) Battalion was disbanded in February 1918. 'A' Company. Believed **wounded** in the period 21-28 March 1918 during the retreat from St Quentin. [Transferred to The Royal Irish Regiment (renumbered 32833).]

VENARD MM Warrant Officer Class II Abraham 14740. Born on 19 June 1881 at Tandragee, County Armagh. Enlisted into Princess Victoria's (Royal Irish Fusiliers) as a regular soldier in 1901 (7146). Served during the South African War with the 2nd Battalion. Queen's South Africa Medal. 4th (Portadown) Battalion, Armagh Regiment, Ulster Volunteer Force. Enlisted September 1914. To France with 36th (Ulster) Division in October 1915. As a Sergeant he was **wounded** by shellfire at Hamel on 26 June 1916. **MM** – (Sergeant) St Quentin 21-28 March 1918. Company Sergeant Major. Transferred to the Class Z Reserve 18 February 1919. 1914-15 Star. Died in 1951, aged 70. Brother of Lance Corporal William John Venard. His brother, Rifleman Edward Venard, was killed in action 22 November 1917 at Moeuvres serving with 'C' Company, 12th (Service) Battalion, The Royal Irish Rifles (Central Antrim). His brother, Private James Venard, served with the 1st Battalion, The Royal Inniskilling Fusiliers; he was badly wounded and lost a leg at Thiepval in June/July 1916. His brother, Private Joseph Venard, served with Princess Victoria's (Royal Irish Fusiliers) and was captured in March 1918 during the retreat from St Quentin.

VENARD Lance Corporal William John 14742. Born 14 April 1883 at Tandragee, County Armagh. 4th (Portadown) Battalion, Armagh Regiment, Ulster Volunteer Force. Member of Loyal Orange Lodge 110. Enlisted September 1914. To France with 36th (Ulster) Division in October 1915. **Wounded** during the attack at Hamel 1 July 1916. Discharged as no longer physically fit for war service due to wounds 26 July 1918, aged 32. Silver War Badge, number 379982. 1914-15 Star. Brother of Company Sergeant Major Abraham Venard. Died 25 March 1965.

VENNARD Private John 19750. From Church Street, Portadown, County Armagh. Enlisted into the 9th (Service) Battalion in April 1915. Posted to the 10th (Reserve) Battalion. To France January 1916 and rejoined the 9th (Service) Battalion in March 1916. 'B' Company. **Wounded** by shellfire near Mesnil on 3 April 1916 and **died of wounds** 9 April 1916.

VENNARD Private Joseph 18564. From Park Road, Portadown, County Armagh. A weaver in the linen trade. Enlisted into the 9th (Service) Battalion 7 April 1915. To France with 36th (Ulster) Division in October 1915. Regimental bandsman. **Wounded** by shellfire at Mesnil on 31 May 1916 and sustained an injured left hand and a fractured skull. Treated at 108th Field Ambulance, 4th Casualty Clearing Station and 2nd General Hospital, where he had a finger amputated. Evacuated to hospital in Scotland 14 June 1916 and was treated at 3rd Scottish General Hospital, Glasgow. In June 1917 he had the upper part of his fibula removed due to osteomyelitis. Discharged as no longer physically fit for war service due to wounds 4 April 1918 (when examined he could walk only with the aid of crutches, was deaf in one ear and weighed only 6 stone 6lbs). Silver War Badge, number 342079. He never recovered fully from his injuries and **died of wounds** on 14 June 1918, aged 22. 1914-15 Star.

VENNARD Private Robert 29552 & 7040888. From Newtownards. A cloth finisher. [Enlisted 18 August 1917, aged 18 and served elsewhere. Transferred to Princess Victoria's (Royal Irish Fusiliers) in March 1918 (renumbered 29552). To France 5 April 1918 and joined the 1st Battalion. Evacuated to hospital in England 10 October 1918.] To France 16 December 1918 and joined the 9th (North Irish Horse) Battalion. Re-enlisted in August/September 1919 for Regular Army service with Princess Victoria's (Royal Irish Fusiliers) (renumbered 7040888). Served with the 1st Battalion in Persia and Mesopotamia in 1919/20. General Service Medal 1918-1962 with clasps 'Iraq' & 'NW Persia'. Discharged 25 June 1922.

VENNARD DCM Warrant Officer Class II Thomas Glennie 14746, 33362 & 7041542. Born in 1886 at Portadown, County Armagh. A weaver. Enlisted 5 September 1914. To France with 36th (Ulster) Division in October 1915. 'B' Company. Company Sergeant Major 'B' Company in November 1916 vice Slater. **DCM** – Moeuvres 23 November 1917. **Wounded** during the retreat from St Quentin 21-28 March 1918. 1914-15 Star. Re-enlisted 18 August 1919 for Regular Army service with Princess Victoria's (Royal Irish Fusiliers) (renumbered 33362, renumbered 7041542). Company Sergeant Major 'B' Company, 1st Battalion and then served with the 2nd Battalion. Long Service & Good Conduct Medal. Coronation Medal 1937. Discharged 14 July 1939.

VENNARD Private William 22648. From Portadown, County Armagh. Enlisted in November 1915. Posted to the 9th (Service) Battalion. 'A' Company. **Wounded** during the attack at Hamel 1 July 1916. **Wounded** in June 1917. **Wounded** by a gunshot to his shoulder during the retreat from St Quentin 21-28 March 1918.

VERNON Private John George 43235. Born in 1891 at Nottinghamshire. [Enlisted into The Sherwood Foresters (Nottinghamshire and Derbyshire Regiment).] Transferred to Princess Victoria's (Royal Irish Fusiliers) 31 August 1916 (renumbered 43235) having joined the 9th (Service) Battalion on 8 August 1916. [Transferred to 5th (Service) Battalion, The Royal Irish Regiment (Pioneers) in the Light Division in the British Army of the Rhine in March/June 1919 (renumbered 41375).] Died at Nottinghamshire in 1949, aged 58.

VICKERS Private Francis 40033. [Enlisted The Prince of Wales's Own (West Yorkshire Regiment) (33026).] Transferred to Princess Victoria's (Royal Irish Fusiliers) 30 November 1916 (renumbered 40033) and joined the 9th (Service) Battalion 12 December 1916. [Transferred to the Machine Gun Corps (renumbered 143847).]

VINEER Private Wilfred John 42153. [Enlisted into the Army Veterinary Corps (22181).] Transferred to Princess Victoria's (Royal Irish Fusiliers) 8 May 1918 (renumbered 42153) and joined the 9th (North Irish Horse) Battalion.

WADE Private Thomas 18769. From London. [Enlisted April 1915 into the 5th (Service) Battalion in 31st Brigade, 10th (Irish) Division. Joined the Mediterranean Expeditionary Force 23 August 1915.] Posted to the 9th (Service) Battalion. 'C' Company. **Wounded** and **captured** at the Battle of Langemarck 16 August 1917. Transferred to the Class Z Reserve. 1914-15 Star.

WADSWORTH Private John 41095. [Enlisted in October 1914 into the Service Squadron, 6th (Inniskilling) Dragoons (UD/20). To France with 36th (Ulster) Division in October 1915. Served with 2nd North Irish Horse, X Corps Cavalry Regiment.] Joined the renamed 9th (North Irish Horse) Battalion from 36 Infantry Base Depot and transferred to Princess Victoria's (Royal Irish Fusiliers) in September/October 1917 (renumbered 41095). Transferred to the Class Z Reserve 15 March 1919. 1914-15 Star.

WAINWRIGHT Private Alfred 20029. Born in 1897 at Kilmore, County Armagh. From Richhill, County Armagh. Enlisted into the 9th (Service) Battalion in June 1915. To France with 36th (Ulster) Division in October 1915. 'C' Company. To hospital mid-1916, he was released just before the attack at Hamel, during which he was **wounded**. **Killed in action** 9 June 1917 during the Battle of Messines, aged 19. 1914-15 Star.

WAINWRIGHT Private Percy 41643. [Mobilised from the Army Reserve and joined 2nd Dragoon Guards (Queen's Bays) in 1st Cavalry Division (8174). To France 8 November 1914. Served with 6th (Inniskilling) Dragoons (8174) in 2nd North Irish Horse, X Corps Cavalry Regiment.] Joined the renamed 9th (North Irish Horse) Battalion from 36 Infantry Base Depot and transferred to Princess Victoria's (Royal Irish Fusiliers) in September/October 1917 (renumbered 41643).

WAKEFIELD Private John William Bannister 42066. Born 1 September 1899 at Camberwell, London. [Enlisted 13 September 1917 and joined the 16th Training Reserve Battalion (57831) for service with 22nd (County of London) Battalion, The London Regiment (The Queen's) (renumbered 67325). Posted to 1/22nd (County of London) Battalion, The London Regiment (The Queen's) 8 December 1917.] To France and joined 'B' Infantry Base Depot 5 April 1918. Transferred to Princess Victoria's (Royal Irish Fusiliers) 6 April 1918 (renumbered 42066) and joined 'C' Company in the 1st Battalion 8 April 1918.] Posted to the 9th (North Irish Horse) Battalion 9 May 1918. **Wounded** by a gunshot to the left leg during the attack south of Wulverghem on 4 September 1918. Treated at 3rd Canadian General Hospital, Boulogne, East Leeds Military Hospital and New End Military Hospital, London. Discharged as no longer physically fit for war service due to wounds 30 June 1919. Silver War Badge, number B274276. He lost his Silver War Badge but it was found and returned to the Army Medal Office on 10 September 1920. After the war he worked for the Post Office. Died in 1991, aged 91. His brother, Driver A W Wakefield, served in France with the Royal Field Artillery from August 1914.

WALKER Private Charles Owen 40077. From Armley, Yorkshire. [Enlisted into the 11th (Service) Battalion, The Prince of Wales's Own (West Yorkshire Regiment) (11711). To France 11 December 1915 and joined 69th Brigade, 23rd Division.] Transferred to Princess Victoria's (Royal Irish Fusiliers) 30 November 1916 (renumbered 40077) and joined the 9th (Service) Battalion 12 December 1916. 'C' Company. **Killed in action** at the Battle of Langemarck 16 August 1917. 1914-15 Star.

WALKER Sergeant David 14782. From Scarva, County Armagh. Enlisted September 1914. To France with 36th (Ulster) Division in October 1915. 1914-15 Star. Brother of Privates Samuel Joseph and Victor Enoch Walker.

WALKER Private Ernest 14804. From Longford, County Longford. Enlisted September 1914. Discharged having made a mis-statement as to age on enlistment; soldier under 17 years of age at date of application for discharge 4 March 1915.

WALKER Private Frederick 14793. From Portadown, County Armagh. 4th (Portadown) Battalion, Armagh Regiment, Ulster Volunteer Force. Enlisted September 1914. To France with 36th (Ulster) Division in October 1915. Discharged as no longer physically fit for war service due to sickness 16 March 1919. Silver War Badge, number B162032. 1914-15 Star.

WALKER MM Private George 40034. [Enlisted into The Prince of Wales's Own (West Yorkshire Regiment) (35275).] Transferred to Princess Victoria's (Royal Irish Fusiliers) 30 November 1916 (renumbered 40034) and joined the 9th (Service) Battalion 12 December 1916. **MM**. [Transferred to the Labour Corps (renumbered 470361). Transferred to the 43rd (Garrison) Battalion, The Royal Fusiliers (City of London Regiment) (GS/106818).]

WALKER Private Harry 45752. Enlisted 11 January 1917. Joined the 9th (North Irish Horse) Battalion, Princess Victoria's (Royal Irish Fusiliers) with the draft of men from The London Regiment in April 1918. [Posted to the 1st Battalion. **Wounded**.] Discharged as no longer physically fit for war service due to wounds 20 December 1918. Silver War Badge, number B64257.

WALKER Private Henry James 42099. [Enlisted 1 December 1915 into the Army Veterinary Corps (21216).] Transferred to Princess Victoria's (Royal Irish Fusiliers) 8 May 1918 (renumbered 42099) and joined the 9th (North Irish Horse) Battalion. **Wounded**. Discharged as no longer physically fit for war service due to wounds 27 March 1919. Silver War Badge, number B233155.

WALKER Lance Corporal Howard P Thomas 14785. From Loughgall, County Armagh. Enlisted September 1914. To France with 36th (Ulster) Division in October 1915. [Joined 108th Brigade Machine Gun Company in January 1916. Transferred to the Machine Gun Corps (renumbered 17807). **Killed in action** with 36th Battalion, Machine Gun Corps 26 October 1918, aged 28.]

1914-15 Star.

WALKER Private Isaac 14765. Enlisted September 1914. No record of deployment to France with 36th (Ulster) Division in October 1915. [Transferred to The Royal Inniskilling Fusiliers (renumbered 43517).]

WALKER Private Isaac 41299. [Enlisted in September 1910 into the North Irish Horse (535). To France 17 August 1914 with 'A' Squadron as GHQ Troops. Served with 2nd North Irish Horse, X Corps Cavalry Regiment.] Joined the renamed 9th (North Irish Horse) Battalion from 36 Infantry Base Depot and transferred to Princess Victoria's (Royal Irish Fusiliers) in September/October 1917 (renumbered 41299). 1914 Star.

WALKER Private James 14781. Enlisted September 1914. To France with 36th (Ulster) Division in October 1915. [Transferred to the Labour Corps (renumbered 593736).] 1914-15 Star.

WALKER Private James 41539. [Enlisted in August 1912 into the North Irish Horse (729). To France 20 August 1914 with 'C' Squadron as 5th Division Cavalry and then as GHQ Troops. Served with 2nd North Irish Horse, X Corps Cavalry Regiment.] Joined the renamed 9th (North Irish Horse) Battalion from 36 Infantry Base Depot and transferred to Princess Victoria's (Royal Irish Fusiliers) in September/October 1917 (renumbered 41539). 1914 Star. Subsequently lived in Toronto, Canada.

WALKER Private James 43200. From Rainworth, Nottinghamshire. [Enlisted into The Sherwood Foresters (Nottinghamshire and Derbyshire Regiment) (36143).] Transferred to Princess Victoria's (Royal Irish Fusiliers) 31 August 1916 having joined the 9th (Service) Battalion on 8 August 1916 (renumbered 43200). 'A' Company. **Missing** at the Battle of Langemarck 16 August 1917 and later declared **killed in action** on that date.

WALKER Private John 14784. Enlisted September 1914. To France with 36th (Ulster) Division in October 1915. [Transferred to the Machine Gun Corps (renumbered 146247).] 1914-15 Star.

WALKER Lance Corporal Robert 14798. Enlisted September 1914. Did not deploy to France with 36th (Ulster) Division in October 1915. Posted to the 2nd Garrison Battalion. Discharged as no longer physically fit for war service due to sickness 31 May 1918. Silver War Badge, number 394853.

WALKER Private Samuel Joseph 16421. From Scarva, County Armagh. Enlisted into the 9th (Service) Battalion in November 1914. To France with 36th (Ulster) Division in October 1915. 'B' Company. **Missing** in the period 21-28 March 1918 during the retreat from St Quentin believed **captured**. Transferred to the Class Z Reserve 14 April 1919. 1914-15 Star. Brother of Sergeant David Walker and Private Victor Enoch Walker.

WALKER Private Victor Enoch 16436. From Scarva, County Armagh. Enlisted into the 9th (Service) Battalion in November 1914. To France with 36th (Ulster) Division in October 1915. **Wounded** during the attack at Hamel 1 July 1916. Transferred to the Class Z Reserve 14 March 1919. 1914-15 Star. Brother of Sergeant David Walker and Private Samuel Joseph Walker.

WALKER Lance Corporal William G 14777. Born in 1892 at Shankill, County Armagh. Armagh Regiment, Ulster Volunteer Force. Enlisted September 1914. Lance Corporal 1 January 1915. Discharged as no longer physically fit for war service due to sickness 28 June 1915. Silver War Badge, number 100508.

WALL Private Alfred 20299. Enlisted 8 June 1915 and joined the 9th (Service) Battalion with the draft of men from The Royal Inniskilling Fusiliers who transferred to Princess Victoria's (Royal Irish Fusiliers) on 30 June 1915. To France with 36th (Ulster) Division in October 1915. 'C' Company. **Wounded** during the attack at Hamel 1 July 1916. Discharged as no longer physically fit for war service due to wounds 28 February 1918. Silver War Badge, number 336279. 1914-15 Star.

WALL Private Martin Henry 45773. [Enlisted into The London Regiment (1633). Posted to the 1/22nd (County of London) Battalion, The London Regiment (The Queen's).] To France and joined 36 Infantry Base Depot 29 March 1918. Transferred to Princess Victoria's (Royal Irish Fusiliers) 2 April 1918 (renumbered 45773) and joined the 9th (North Irish Horse) Battalion 4 April 1918.

WALLACE Private Francis John 41615. [Enlisted in November 1914 into the Service Squadron, 6th (Inniskilling) Dragoons (UD/180). To France with 36th (Ulster) Division in October 1915. Served with 2nd North Irish Horse, X Corps Cavalry Regiment.] Joined the renamed 9th (North Irish Horse)

Battalion from 36 Infantry Base Depot and transferred to Princess Victoria's (Royal Irish Fusiliers) in September/October 1917 (renumbered 41615). Transferred to the Class Z Reserve 15 March 1919. 1914-15 Star.

WALLACE Private John 41345 & 7042138. From Antrim, County Antrim. [Enlisted on 3 June 1915, aged 16, into the North Irish Horse (1662). To France 9 August 1917 and joined 2nd North Irish Horse, X Corps Cavalry Regiment.] Joined the renamed 9th (North Irish Horse) Battalion from 36 Infantry Base Depot and transferred to Princess Victoria's (Royal Irish Fusiliers) in September/October 1917 (renumbered 41345). Re-enlisted into Princess Victoria's (Royal Irish Fusiliers) Special Reserve (renumbered 7042138). Discharged 6 October 1921.

WALLACE Lance Corporal Mark 16141. From Killygoan, County Monaghan. Enlisted into the 9th (Service) Battalion in October 1914. To France with 36th (Ulster) Division in October 1915. **Killed in action** during the attack at Hamel 1 July 1916. 1914-15 Star. His brother, Sapper John Wallace, served with the Corps of Royal Engineers.

WALLACE Private Thomas Galbraith 22658. From Londonderry, County Londonderry. A book-keeper. Enlisted 1 November 1915 and joined the 10th (Reserve) Battalion. Lance Corporal 28 February 1916. Corporal 25 August 1916. Posted to 7th Officer Cadet Battalion at Fermoy, County Cork. Was not commissioned and was posted back to the 10th (Reserve) Battalion 17 November 1916. To France 2 December 1916. 'B' Company. Reverted to Private. To the field ambulance sick (scabies) in February and March 1917. **Wounded** by a gunshot to the right arm at the Battle of Langemarck 16 August 1917 and evacuated to hospital in England. Treated at the Military Hospital, Canterbury. Joined the 10th (Reserve) Battalion 17 September 1917. [To 'A' Infantry Base Depot and posted to the 1st Battalion 18 January 1918. Posted to Depot Field Survey Company, Corps of Royal Engineers in late January 1918 for training as a draughtsman. Transferred to the Corps of Royal Engineers (renumbered 359828) 30 March 1918.] Transferred to the Class Z Reserve 16 April 1919.

WALLACE Private William George 18631. Enlisted into the 9th (Service) Battalion in April 1915. To France 17 November 1915. Transferred to the Class Z Reserve. 1914-15 Star.

WALLACE Private William John 41096. From Enniskillen, County Fermanagh. [Enlisted in October 1914 into the Service Squadron, 6th (Inniskilling) Dragoons (UD/53). Served with 2nd North Irish Horse, X Corps Cavalry Regiment.] Joined the renamed 9th (North Irish Horse) Battalion from 36 Infantry Base Depot and transferred to Princess Victoria's (Royal Irish Fusiliers) in September/October 1917 (renumbered 41096). **Killed in action** 23 October 1918 following the crossing of the River Lys, aged 26.

WALLIS Private Frank 18790. Enlisted 12 January 1915. Transferred to Princess Victoria's (Royal Irish Fusiliers) April 1915 and joined the 9th (Service) Battalion. **Wounded**. Discharged as no longer physically fit for war service due to wounds 7 June 1918, aged 21. Silver War Badge, number 395826.

WALLS Private George Thomas 15635. Born 24 February 1894 at Kent. From Salford, Manchester. A clerk. [Enlisted 4 September 1914 and joined the 6th (Service) Battalion. Lance Corporal 17 October 1914. Posted to the 3rd (Reserve) Battalion 20 April 1915. Reverted to Private 31 July 1915. Sentenced to twenty-one days Field Punishment Number 2 24 August 1915 for being absent from parade and neglecting to obey an order given by an NCO. Rejoined the 6th (Service) Battalion in 31st Brigade, 10th (Irish) Division in the Mediterranean Expeditionary Force 17 October 1915. Lance Corporal 4 January 1916. Evacuated to hospital in England sick (malaria) March 1917. Joined the 3rd (Reserve) Battalion 23 August 1917. Deprived of Lance Corporal rank 16 October 1917 for being absent when on duty. To France 25 December 1917 and posted to the 7th/8th (Service) Battalion in 49th Brigade, 16th (Irish) Division.] Joined the 9th (North Irish Horse) Battalion when the 7th/8th (Service) Battalion was disbanded in February 1918. 'C' Company. **Captured** at Erches on 27 March 1918 during the retreat from St Quentin. Held at Schneidemuhl Prisoner of War Camp. Repatriated 3 December 1918 and rejoined the 3rd (Reserve) Battalion. 1914-15 Star. Re-enlisted in 1919 for Regular Army service with Princess Victoria's (Royal Irish Fusiliers) 21 February 1919. Discharged as no longer physically fit for war service due to sickness 22 August 1919. Silver War Badge, number B305337. King's Certificate 87/2746.

WALLS Private Peter 13900. [Enlisted 3 September 1914 and joined the 6th (Service) Battalion in

31st Brigade, 10th (Irish) Division. Embarked with the Mediterranean Expeditionary Force July 1915.] Posted to the 9th (North Irish Horse) Battalion. 'B' Company. Believed **wounded** in the period 21-28 March 1918 during the retreat from St Quentin. Discharged as no longer physically fit for war service due to wounds 14 December 1918. Silver War Badge, number 506378. 1914-15 Star.

WALLS Private Patrick 13493 & 32902. [Enlisted in September 1914 and joined the 7th (Service) Battalion in 48th Brigade, 16th (Irish) Division.] Joined the 9th (North Irish Horse) Battalion when the 7th/8th (Service) Battalion was disbanded in February 1918. 'C' Company. **Missing** in the period 21-28 March 1918 during the retreat from St Quentin believed **captured**. Re-enlisted in 1919 for Regular Army service with Princess Victoria's (Royal Irish Fusiliers) (renumbered 32902). He was not renumbered again; discharged before September 1920.

WALSH Private James 17912. From Annaghmore, County Armagh. Enlisted into the 9th (Service) Battalion in January 1915. To France with 36th (Ulster) Division in October 1915. **Killed in action** during the attack at Hamel 1 July 1916, aged 20. 1914-15 Star.

WALSH Private John 14809. Enlisted September 1914. To France with 36th (Ulster) Division in October 1915. **Wounded**. Discharged as no longer physically fit for war service due to wounds 29 May 1918. Silver War Badge, number 228766. 1914-15 Star.

WALSH Private Michael 21186. From Belfast. [Enlisted in December 1914/January 1915 and joined the 8th (Service) Battalion in 49th Brigade, 16th (Irish) Division.] Joined the 9th (North Irish Horse) Battalion when the 7th/8th (Service) Battalion was disbanded in February 1918. 'C' Company. **Captured** in the period 21-28 March 1918 during the retreat from St Quentin.

WALSH Private Robert George 23588. From Portadown, County Armagh. [Enlisted into the Army Cyclist Corps (1559) and served with the 10th Division Cyclist Company with the Mediterranean Expeditionary Force from July 1915. **Wounded**.] Transferred to Princess Victoria's (Royal Irish Fusiliers) in December 1915 (renumbered 23588). Posted to the 9th (Service) Battalion. Transferred to the Class Z Reserve 26 March 1919. 1914-15 Star.

WALTER Private P. Tried by Field General Court Martial 20 September 1918 charged with an unknown act *'to the prejudice and good order and military discipline'*; found guilty and sentenced to ninety days Field Punishment Number 1. Soldier not identified.

WALTERS Private William 43226. [Enlisted 26 January 1916 into The Sherwood Foresters (Nottinghamshire and Derbyshire Regiment).] Transferred to Princess Victoria's (Royal Irish Fusiliers) 31 August 1916 (renumbered 43226) having joined the 9th (Service) Battalion on 8 August 1916. Discharged as no longer physically fit for war service due to sickness 21 December 1916, aged 22. Silver War Badge, number 310224.

WALTON Private Ralph 13787. [Enlisted in September 1914 and joined the 6th (Service) Battalion in 31st Brigade, 10th (Irish) Division. Embarked with the Mediterranean Expeditionary Force July 1915.] Posted to the 9th (North Irish Horse) Battalion. [Posted to the 1st Battalion.]

WARBURTON Private Albert 42283. [Enlisted into the Army Veterinary Corps (4777). To Egypt 3 March 1915. Served with 16th Veterinary Hospital.] Transferred to Princess Victoria's (Royal Irish Fusiliers) 8 May 1918 (renumbered 42283) and joined the 9th (North Irish Horse) Battalion. Transferred to the Class Z Reserve 10 February 1919. 1914-15 Star.

WARD Lance Corporal Frank Oliver 41376. [Enlisted into the 6th (Inniskilling) Dragoons (7737). Served with 2nd North Irish Horse, X Corps Cavalry Regiment.] Joined the renamed 9th (North Irish Horse) Battalion from 36 Infantry Base Depot and transferred to Princess Victoria's (Royal Irish Fusiliers) in September/October 1917 (renumbered 41376). 'A' Company. **Wounded** in the period 21-28 March 1918 during the retreat from St Quentin.

WARD Private George Richard 43398. [Enlisted into The London Regiment (7277). Posted to the 1/9th (County of London) Battalion, The London Regiment (Queen Victoria's Rifles).] Attached to the 9th (Service) Battalion, Princess Victoria's (Royal Irish Fusiliers) 26 November 1916. Discharged from the Territorial Force, re-enlisted and transferred to Princess Victoria's (Royal Irish Fusiliers) in March/April 1917 (renumbered 43398).

WARD Private Norman 42430. [Enlisted into the 10th (Service) Battalion, The Royal Irish Rifles (South Belfast) (2137).] Transferred at the Base Depot to Princess Victoria's (Royal Irish Fusiliers) 14 September 1918 (renumbered 42430) and joined the 9th (North Irish Horse) Battalion 22

September 1918.

WARDEN Private Robert 14783. Born in 1898 at Armagh, County Armagh. A farmer. Enlisted September 1914. Discharged having made a mis-statement as to age on enlistment; soldier under 17 years of age at date of application for discharge 1 October 1914.

WARDEN Private Robert 19798. From Armagh, County Armagh. Enlisted into the 9th (Service) Battalion in May 1915. **Killed in action** during the attack at Hamel 1 July 1916. 1914-15 Star.

WARDEN Private William 42489. (His medal index card incorrectly indicates three regimental numbers for service with Princess Victoria's (Royal Irish Fusiliers). Enlisted in August 1916 into Princess Victoria's (Royal Irish Fusiliers) (24628). [Transferred to The Royal Irish Rifles (renumbered 486).] Transferred at the Base Depot to Princess Victoria's (Royal Irish Fusiliers) 14 September 1918 (renumbered 42489) and joined the 9th (North Irish Horse) Battalion 22 September 1918. [Re-enlisted for Regular Army service in 1919 into The Cameronians (Scottish Rifles) (renumbered 44906).]

WARE MM Private Frederick Saunders 49929. Born 6 October 1898 in Aylesbury, Buckinghamshire. [Transferred to Princess Victoria's (Royal Irish Fusiliers) in May 1918 (renumbered 49929) with a draft of men from English regiments and joined the 1st Battalion.] Posted to the 9th (North Irish Horse) Battalion in August 1918. **MM** – Bailleul August 1918. Died at Hastings, Sussex 1973, aged 74.

WARKE Private William Edwin 41457. Born in 1889. From Templemore, County Londonderry. One of eleven children. A bookkeeper. [Enlisted 7 September 1914 into the North Irish Horse (1156). To France 3 June 1915. Served with 2nd North Irish Horse, X Corps Cavalry Regiment.] Joined the renamed 9th (North Irish Horse) Battalion from 36 Infantry Base Depot and transferred to Princess Victoria's (Royal Irish Fusiliers) in September/October 1917 (renumbered 41457). **Wounded** by a gunshot to the head from a sniper at Marcoing 15 December 1917 and evacuated to hospital in England. Treated at 3rd Western General Hospital, Cardiff. Joined the 10th (Reserve) Battalion 22 February 1918. [Transferred to the Royal Defence Corps (renumbered 73205) 4 May 1918 and joined 200th Protection Company. Joined 199th Protection Company 22 June 1918. Transferred to The Northumberland Fusiliers 4 July 1918 and posted to the 22nd (Service) Battalion, The Northumberland Fusiliers in 48th Brigade, 16th (Irish) Division. Transferred back to the Royal Defence Corps 29 July 1918 and rejoined 199th Protection Company. Posted to 155th Protection Company 17 August 1918.] Transferred to the Class Z Reserve 5 March 1919. 1914-15 Star. He died of a perforated ulcer in the City and County Infirmary, Londonderry on 12 July 1921. His mother wrote that it was as a result of previous wounds. He is buried in Londonderry City Cemetery but not commemorated by the Commonwealth War Graves Commission. His brother, Private Jasper McCleery Warke, was wounded while serving with the 9th (Service) Battalion, The Royal Inniskilling Fusiliers (County Tyrone) at Thiepval and died of wounds on 8 August 1917. His brother, Private Samuel Warke, was killed in action on 5 September 1918 while serving with the 1/18th (County of London) Battalion, The London Regiment (London Irish Rifles). His brother, Second Lieutenant Robert James Warke, served in the Honourable Artillery Company before being commissioned into The Royal Inniskilling Fusiliers. His brother, Sergeant John Warke, served with 29th (Vancouver) Battalion, Canadian Infantry. His brother-in-law, Rifleman John Martin, was killed in action on 18 September 1914 serving with 2nd Battalion, The Royal Irish Rifles. His brothers-in-law, Lance Sergeant Stanley Montague William Grace and Sergeant Harold Rodney Turner served with Princess Victoria's (Royal Irish Fusiliers); the former with the 2nd Battalion. They were married to his sisters Annie and Florence respectively.

WARING Private Henry 23645. Born 21 June 1900 in Belfast. Enlisted, aged 15 but giving a false age, on 4 January 1916 and joined the 4th (Extra Reserve) Battalion. To France 5 July 1916 and joined the 9th (Service) Battalion. 'C' Company. In October 1916 his mother requested his return based on his age and he was ordered home for discharge. To England 26 December 1916. Joined the 10th (Reserve) Battalion pending discharge and **deserted** 4 March 1917. Medals forfeit

WARING Corporal Samuel 14800. Enlisted 15 September 1914. To France with 36th (Ulster) Division in October 1915. Discharged as no longer physically fit for war service due to sickness 21 July 1916. Silver War Badge, number 21708. 1914-15 Star.

WARNOCK Private John 41321. [Enlisted 4 November 1915 into the North Irish Horse (1785).

Served with 2nd North Irish Horse, X Corps Cavalry Regiment.] Joined the renamed 9th (North Irish Horse) Battalion from 36 Infantry Base Depot and transferred to Princess Victoria's (Royal Irish Fusiliers) in September/October 1917 (renumbered 41321). Discharged as no longer physically fit for war service due to sickness 29 May 1918, aged 22. Silver War Badge, number 391442.

WARREN Private Albert Edward 43331. From London. [Enlisted into The London Regiment.] Attached to the 9th (Service) Battalion, Princess Victoria's (Royal Irish Fusiliers) 26 November 1916. 'C' Company. Discharged from the Territorial Force, re-enlisted and transferred to Princess Victoria's (Royal Irish Fusiliers) in March/April 1917 (renumbered 43331). **Wounded** at the Battle of Langemarck 16 August 1917. [Posted to the 1st Battalion. **Captured**.]

WARREN Private Thomas 20500. Born at Drumnakelly, Lurgan, County Armagh. Enlisted in Glasgow in June 1915 and joined the 9th (Service) Battalion. To France with 36th (Ulster) Division in October 1915. 'C' Company. **Wounded** and **captured** during the attack at Hamel 1 July 1916 and subsequently **died of wounds** 4 July 1916 while a prisoner of war.

WARREN Sergeant William 14812. Member of Derryadd Loyal Orange Lodge Number 15. Derryadd Company, Armagh Regiment Ulster Volunteer Force. Worked for the Great Northern Railway. Enlisted September 1914. To France with 36th (Ulster) Division in October 1915. [Joined 108th Brigade Machine Gun Company in January 1916. Transferred to the Machine Gun Corps (renumbered 17776 Sergeant). **Wounded** severely in May 1916.] 1914-15 Star.

WARRINGTON Lance Corporal Samuel 24396. Born in 1889 at Derrylahan, County Leitrim. Served with the Royal Irish Constabulary at Newry. Enlisted 17 May 1916. Posted to the 9th (Service) Battalion. 'C' Company. **Wounded** at the Battle of Langemarck 16 August 1917. Transferred to the Class P Reserve 28 May 1918, aged 28. Silver War Badge, number 391439.

WARWICK Private John Alex 41397. Born in 1891 at Aghadowey, County Londonderry. A draper's assistant. [Enlisted 17 November 1915 into the North Irish Horse (1947). To France 4 August 1916. Served with 2nd North Irish Horse, X Corps Cavalry Regiment. Attached to Headquarters 3rd Army from 5 April to 16 June 1917.] Joined the renamed 9th (North Irish Horse) Battalion from 36 Infantry Base Depot and transferred to Princess Victoria's (Royal Irish Fusiliers) in September/October 1917 (renumbered 41397). [Transferred to the Tank Corps (304879) 28 December 1917 and posted for training to the Tank Corps Depot, at Bovington near Wareham, Dorset. To France 8 July 1918 and joined the 15th Battalion, Tank Corps.] Transferred to the Class Z Reserve 24 February 1919.

WASSON MM Private Samuel 41414. [Enlisted in November 1915 into the North Irish Horse (1933). Served with 2nd North Irish Horse, X Corps Cavalry Regiment.] Joined the renamed 9th (North Irish Horse) Battalion from 36 Infantry Base Depot and transferred to Princess Victoria's (Royal Irish Fusiliers) in September/October 1917 (renumbered 41414). **MM** – Wulverghem April 1918.

WATERWORTH Private Charles 42203. [Enlisted into the Army Service Corps (326006).] Transferred to Princess Victoria's (Royal Irish Fusiliers) 8 May 1918 (renumbered 42203) and joined the 9th (North Irish Horse) Battalion. [Transferred to 5th (Service) Battalion, The Royal Irish Regiment (Pioneers) in the Light Division in the British Army of the Rhine in March/June 1919 (renumbered 41380).]

WATSON Private David 18608. Enlisted into the 9th (Service) Battalion in April 1915. To France with 36th (Ulster) Division in October 1915. Transferred to the Class Z Reserve 22 March 1919. 1914-15 Star.

WATSON Private David 19889. Enlisted into the 9th (Service) Battalion in May 1915. To France with 36th (Ulster) Division in October 1915. 'C' Company. Lewis gun ammunition carrier during the attack at Hamel on 1 July 1916, during which he was **wounded**. [Transferred to the Army Service Corps (renumbered M/380710).] Discharged as no longer physically fit for war service due to wounds 7 August 1918. Silver War Badge, number 431814. 1914-15 Star.

WATSON Private Dynes 14755. From Lurgan, County Armagh. Enlisted September 1914. To France with 36th (Ulster) Division in October 1915. **Wounded** during the attack at Hamel 1 July 1916 and **died of wounds** 5 July 1916, aged 21. 1914-15 Star.

WATSON Private Frederick 14771. Born at Shankill, County Armagh. Enlisted September 1914.

To France with 36th (Ulster) Division in October 1915. 'C' Company. **Killed in action** during the attack at Hamel 1 July 1916, aged 18. Related to Private James Watson.

WATSON Private Frederick 15851. Born in 1897 at Lurgan, County Armagh. Enlisted 16 September 1914, aged 17, into the 9th (Service) Battalion. **Wounded**. Discharged as no longer physically fit for war service due to wounds 10 October 1918. Silver War Badge, number B34927. Brother of Private George Watson.

WATSON Private George 14801. Born in 1892 at Lurgan, County Armagh. A linen weaver. Enlisted September 1914. To France with 36th (Ulster) Division in October 1915. **Wounded** during the attack at Hamel 1 July 1916. [Transferred to the Labour Corps (renumbered 517257).] Transferred to the Class Z Reserve 19 March 1919. 1914-15 Star. Brother of Private Frederick Watson.

WATSON Private Harry 41227. [Enlisted in December 1914 into the North Irish Horse (1369). To France with 'F' Squadron in 33rd Division 17 November 1915. Served with 2nd North Irish Horse, X Corps Cavalry Regiment.] Joined the renamed 9th (North Irish Horse) Battalion from 36 Infantry Base Depot and transferred to Princess Victoria's (Royal Irish Fusiliers) in September/October 1917 (renumbered 41227). [Transferred to the Army Ordnance Corps (renumbered 043328).] 1914-15 Star.

WATSON Private Henry 20327. From Newcastle-upon-Tyne. Enlisted in May/June 1915 and joined the 9th (Service) Battalion with the draft of men from The Royal Inniskilling Fusiliers who transferred to Princess Victoria's (Royal Irish Fusiliers) on 30 June 1915. To France with 36th (Ulster) Division in October 1915. 'C' Company. Attached to Divisional Reserve Company during the attack at Thiepval/Hamel 1 July 1916 and did not take part in the attack. **Wounded** at the Battle of Langemarck 16 August 1917. 1914-15 Star.

WATSON Private James 14770. From Lurgan, County Armagh. Enlisted September 1914. To France with 36th (Ulster) Division in October 1915. **Killed in action** during the attack at Hamel 1 July 1916. Related to 14771 Private Frederick Watson.

WATSON Private James 27727. Enlisted in June 1917. Posted to the 9th (North Irish Horse) Battalion. 'B' Company. **Missing** in the period 21-28 March 1918 during the retreat from St Quentin believed **captured**.

WATSON Private James 41111. [Enlisted 3 March 1915 into the Service Squadron, 6th (Inniskilling) Dragoons (UD/224). Served with 2nd North Irish Horse, X Corps Cavalry Regiment.] Joined the renamed 9th (North Irish Horse) Battalion from 36 Infantry Base Depot and transferred to Princess Victoria's (Royal Irish Fusiliers) in September/October 1917 (renumbered 41111). **Wounded**. Discharged as no longer physically fit for war service due to wounds 16 July 1919. Silver War Badge, number B294634.

WATSON Private James 42567. [Enlisted 9 April 1918 into The Royal Irish Rifles (22335).] Transferred at the Base Depot to Princess Victoria's (Royal Irish Fusiliers) 14 September 1918 (renumbered 42567) and joined the 9th (North Irish Horse) Battalion 22 September 1918. **Wounded**. Discharged as no longer physically fit for war service due to wounds 4 September 1919. Silver War Badge, number B301543.

WATSON Private John 21403. From Belfast. Enlisted in August 1915. Posted to the 9th (Service) Battalion in May/June 1916. 'C' Company. **Killed in action** during the attack at Hamel 1 July 1916, aged 19.

WATSON Private John 49748. Joined the 9th (North Irish Horse) Battalion, Princess Victoria's (Royal Irish Fusiliers) with the draft of men transferred from The Royal Irish Rifles in April 1918.

WATSON Private Joseph 27724 & 7040815. From Armagh, County Armagh. A weaver. Enlisted 18 June 1917. To France 4 October 1917 and joined the 9th (North Irish Horse) Battalion. 'C' Company. **Wounded** in the period 21-28 March 1918 during the retreat from St Quentin and evacuated to hospital in England 4 April 1918. Re enlisted in December 1919 for Regular Army service with Princess Victoria's (Royal Irish Fusiliers) (renumbered 7040815). Served with the 1st Battalion in Persia and Mesopotamia in 1919/20. General Service Medal 1918-1962 with clasps 'Iraq' & 'NW Persia'. Discharged 3 July 1922.

WATSON Private Reginald A 43399. [Enlisted into 3/11th Battalion, The London Regiment

(5761). Transferred to the King's Royal Rifle Corps (renumbered 7278). Transferred to The Royal Irish Regiment (renumbered 3520).] Attached to the 9th (Service) Battalion, Princess Victoria's (Royal Irish Fusiliers) 26 November 1916. Transferred to Princess Victoria's (Royal Irish Fusiliers) in March/April 1917 (renumbered 43399). [Transferred to the Labour Corps (renumbered 642088). Transferred to the Corps of Royal Engineers (renumbered WR/209664).]

WATSON Private Thomas 16173. From Portadown, County Armagh. [Enlisted September/October 1914 into the 5th (Service) or 6th (Service) Battalion in 31st Brigade, 10th (Irish) Division. Embarked with the Mediterranean Expeditionary Force July 1915.] 'C' Company. **Captured** in the period 21-28 March 1918 during the retreat from St Quentin. Transferred to the Class Z Reserve 21 April 1919. 1914-15 Star.

WATSON Private Thomas 41374. [Enlisted 8 October 1914 into the Service Squadron, 6th (Inniskilling) Dragoons (UD/46). Served with 2nd North Irish Horse, X Corps Cavalry Regiment.] Joined the renamed 9th (North Irish Horse) Battalion from 36 Infantry Base Depot and transferred to Princess Victoria's (Royal Irish Fusiliers) in September/October 1917 (renumbered 41374). **Wounded** during the retreat from St Quentin 21-28 March 1918. Discharged as no longer physically fit for war service due to wounds 2 October 1918, aged 23. Silver War Badge, number B22497.

WATSON Private Victor Charles 22988. Born in 1898 at Belfast. From Lurgan, County Armagh. Enlisted in November 1915, aged 17. Posted to the 9th (Service) Battalion. 'C' Company. Survived the attack at Hamel on 1 July 1916 unwounded. **Wounded** at the Battle of Langemarck 16 August 1917. Rejoined the 9th (North Irish Horse) Battalion. **Wounded** and **died of wounds** 15 January 1918.

WATSON Private William 14776 & 7040584. From Bessbrook, County Armagh. Enlisted September 1914. To France with 36th (Ulster) Division in October 1915. 1914-15 Star. Re-enlisted in early-1919 for Regular Army service with Princess Victoria's (Royal Irish Fusiliers) (renumbered 7040584). Served with the 1st Battalion in Persia and Mesopotamia in 1919/20. General Service Medal 1918-1962 with clasps 'Iraq' & 'NW Persia'. Discharged 31 March 1922.

WATSON Lance Corporal William John 14759. From Lurgan, County Armagh. Enlisted September 1914. To France with 36th (Ulster) Division in October 1915. 'D' Company. **Missing** at the Battle of Langemarck 16 August 1917 and later declared **killed in action** on that date. 1914-15 Star.

WATSON Private William John 43348. Enlisted 11 February 1915. Joined the 9th (Service) Battalion, Princess Victoria's (Royal Irish Fusiliers) with the draft of men from The London Regiment in November 1916. Discharged as no longer physically fit for war service due to sickness 27 February 1919. Silver War Badge, number B154118.

WATT Private George 41332. [Enlisted in January 1916 into the North Irish Horse (2068). Served with 2nd North Irish Horse, X Corps Cavalry Regiment.] Joined the renamed 9th (North Irish Horse) Battalion from 36 Infantry Base Depot and transferred to Princess Victoria's (Royal Irish Fusiliers) in September/October 1917 (renumbered 41332).

WATT Private George W 41631. [Served with the 2nd Dragoon Guards (Queen's Bays) (8742). Served with 2nd North Irish Horse, X Corps Cavalry Regiment.] Joined the renamed 9th (North Irish Horse) Battalion from 36 Infantry Base Depot and transferred to Princess Victoria's (Royal Irish Fusiliers) in September/October 1917 (renumbered 41631). 'D' Company. **Missing** in the period 21-28 March 1918 during the retreat from St Quentin believed **captured**.

WATT Private Richard 24853. From Drummannon, Tartaraghan, County Armagh. Enlisted in June 1916. Posted to the 9th (Service) Battalion. 'B' Company. **Wounded** at the Battle of Langemarck 16 August 1917. [Posted to the 1st Battalion. **Killed in action** during the retreat from St Quentin 24 March 1918.]

WATTERS Private William John 14775. Born in 1894 at Lurgan, County Armagh. Enlisted September 1914. To France with 36th (Ulster) Division in October 1915. 'C' Company. Survived the attack at Hamel on 1 July 1916 unwounded. **Killed in action** at the Battle of Langemarck 16 August 1917. 1914-15 Star.

WAUGH Lance Corporal James 41221. From Cootehill, County Cavan. [Enlisted in June 1915 into the North Irish Horse (1708). Served with 2nd North Irish Horse, X Corps Cavalry Regiment.] Joined the renamed 9th (North Irish Horse) Battalion from 36 Infantry Base Depot and transferred to Princess Victoria's (Royal Irish Fusiliers) in September/October 1917 (renumbered 41221). 'D' Company. **Captured** in the period 21-28 March 1918 during the retreat from St Quentin.

WEATHERUP Private Edwin 41450. Born in 1897 at Carrickfergus, County Antrim. Worked as a clerk at Harland and Wolff shipyard, Belfast. [Enlisted in November 1915 into the North Irish Horse (1923). Served with 2nd North Irish Horse, X Corps Cavalry Regiment.] Joined the renamed 9th (North Irish Horse) Battalion from 36 Infantry Base Depot and transferred to Princess Victoria's (Royal Irish Fusiliers) in September/October 1917 (renumbered 41450). Emigrated to Canada. Died in 1979 at New Brunswick, Canada.

WEAVER Corporal Benjamin 42169. From Forest Gate, London. A baker. [Enlisted 18 January 1915 into the Army Service Corps (S4/055662). To France 25 February 1915 and served with 44th and 13th Field Bakeries.] Transferred to Princess Victoria's (Royal Irish Fusiliers) 8 May 1918 (renumbered 42169) and joined the 9th (North Irish Horse) Battalion. To hospital with tonsillitis 31 December 1918. Transferred to the Class Z Reserve 31 March 1919.

WEAVER Private Ernest George 42277. From Abingdon, Gloucestershire. [Enlisted 12 November 1915 into the Army Veterinary Corps (13113). Joined the Mediterranean Expeditionary Force 21 December 1915. To hospital sick (malaria.] Transferred to Princess Victoria's (Royal Irish Fusiliers) 8 May 1918 (renumbered 42277) and joined the 9th (North Irish Horse) Battalion. Transferred to the Class Z Reserve 6 April 1919. 1914-15 Star.

WEBB Private David 22646. Enlisted in October 1915. Posted to the 9th (Service) Battalion.

WEBB Private Frederick 42108. From Birmingham. [Enlisted into the Army Veterinary Corps (27084).] Transferred to Princess Victoria's (Royal Irish Fusiliers) 8 May 1918 (renumbered 42108) and joined the 9th (North Irish Horse) Battalion. **Killed in action** during the attack north of Bailleul 24 August 1918, aged 24.

WEBB Lance Corporal Frederick William 41141. [Enlisted 24 August 1914 into 6th (Inniskilling) Dragoons (9986). Served with 2nd North Irish Horse, X Corps Cavalry Regiment.] Joined the renamed 9th (North Irish Horse) Battalion from 36 Infantry Base Depot and transferred to Princess Victoria's (Royal Irish Fusiliers) in September/October 1917 (renumbered 41141). 'B' Company. Separated from the 9th (North Irish Horse) Battalion in the period 21-28 March 1918 during the retreat from St Quentin; rejoined 3 April 1918. **Wounded**. Discharged as no longer physically fit for war service due to wounds 20 February 1919. Silver War Badge, number B154130.

WEBB Private Frederick William 42075. [Enlisted 15 September 1917 into The London Regiment. Posted to 1/22nd (County of London) Battalion, The London Regiment (The Queen's) in December 1917.] To France and joined 'B' Infantry Base Depot in early-April 1918. Transferred to Princess Victoria's (Royal Irish Fusiliers) April 1918 and posted to the 1st Battalion. Posted to the 9th (North Irish Horse) Battalion in mid-1918. **Wounded**. Discharged as no longer physically fit for war service due to wounds 8 May 1919. Silver War Badge, number B234837.

WEBB Private Henry James 45758. Joined the 9th (North Irish Horse) Battalion, Princess Victoria's (Royal Irish Fusiliers) with the draft of men from The London Regiment in April 1918.

WEBB Private W J 14806. Enlisted September 1914. To France with 36th (Ulster) Division in October 1915. [Transferred to The Royal Sussex Regiment (renumbered S/30894).] Transferred to the Class Z Reserve 25 February 1919. 1914-15 Star.

WEIR Private Charles 24704. From Dungannon, County Tyrone. Enlisted in August 1916. Posted to the 9th (Service) Battalion. 'C' Company. **Captured** in the period 21-28 March 1918 during the retreat from St Quentin. [Transferred to the Seaforth Highlanders (Ross-shire Buffs, The Duke of Albany's) (32342).]

WEIR Private Isaac 33861 & 7041870. (Original number unknown; 33861 was issued on re-enlistment in January 1920.) From Ballymacarrett, County Down. [Enlisted into The Royal Irish Rifles (11054) and served with the 2nd Battalion, The Royal Irish Rifles.] Transferred to Princess Victoria's (Royal Irish Fusiliers) and posted to the 9th (North Irish Horse) Battalion. Tried by Field General Court Martial on 19 November 1918 charged with *'absenting himself without leave'*; found guilty and sentenced to ninety-one days Field Punishment Number 1. Transferred to 5th (Service)

Battalion, The Royal Irish Regiment (Pioneers) in the Light Division in the British Army of the Rhine in March/June 1919 (renumbered 41382). Re-enlisted 12 January 1920 for Regular Army service with Princess Victoria's (Royal Irish Fusiliers) (renumbered 33861, renumbered 7041870). Discharged 25 August 1922.

WEIR Private Joseph 14750. From Portadown, County Armagh. Enlisted September 1914. No record of deployment to France with 36th (Ulster) Division in October 1915. [Transferred to the Labour Corps (renumbered 545505).] Brother of Privates Robert & Thomas Weir. His brother, Private James Henry Weir, was killed in action on 11 April 1917 serving with the 1st Battalion. His brother, Private George Weir, died on 3 October 1918 of sickness in Basra, Mesopotamia serving with the Army Service Corps.

WEIR Private Robert 14795. From Portadown, County Armagh. 4th (Portadown) Battalion, Armagh Regiment, Ulster Volunteer Force. Enlisted September 1914. To France with 36th (Ulster) Division in October 1915. **Wounded** during the attack at Hamel 1 July 1916. Discharged as no longer physically fit for war service due to wounds 12 January 1918. Silver War Badge, number 304115. 1914-15 Star. Brother of Privates Joseph & Thomas Weir. His brother, Private James Henry Weir, was killed in action on 11 April 1917 serving with the 1st Battalion. His brother, Private George Weir, died on 3 October 1918 of sickness in Basra, Mesopotamia serving with the Army Service Corps.

WEIR Private Robert 41140. From Belfast. [Enlisted in October 1914 into the Service Squadron, 6th (Inniskilling) Dragoons (UD/75). To France with 36th (Ulster) Division in October 1915. Served with 2nd North Irish Horse, X Corps Cavalry Regiment.] Joined the renamed 9th (North Irish Horse) Battalion from 36 Infantry Base Depot and transferred to Princess Victoria's (Royal Irish Fusiliers) in September/October 1917 (renumbered 41140). **Wounded** twice. Transferred to the Class Z Reserve 23 March 1919. 1914-15 Star.

WEIR Private Samuel 19792. Enlisted into the 9th (Service) Battalion 10 May 1915. To France with 36th (Ulster) Division in October 1915. 'C' Company. **Wounded** at Hamel end-June/1 July 1916. Discharged as no longer physically fit for war service due to wounds 24 October 1916. Silver War Badge, number 509021. 1914-15 Star.

WEIR Private Thomas 14762. Enlisted September 1914. No record of deployment to France with 36th (Ulster) Division in October 1915.

WEIR Private Thomas 20213. Enlisted into the 9th (Service) Battalion 16 June 1915. To France with 36th (Ulster) Division in October 1915. 'C' Company. **Wounded** during the attack at Hamel 1 July 1916. Discharged as no longer physically fit for war service due to wounds 26 February 1918, aged 22. Silver War Badge, number 320036. 1914-15 Star.

WEIR Private Thomas 20215. Enlisted into the 9th (Service) Battalion in June 1915. To France with 36th (Ulster) Division in October 1915. Discharged 24 November 1916. 1914-15 Star.

WEIR Private Thomas 20217. From Lurgan, County Armagh. Enlisted into the 9th (Service) Battalion 10 June 1915. Discharged having made a mis-statement as to age on enlistment; soldier under 17 years of age at date of application for discharge 17 June 1915.

WEIR Private William 29439. Enlisted, re-enlisted or transferred to Princess Victoria's (Royal Irish Fusiliers) in late-1917/early-1918. Posted to the 9th (North Irish Horse) Battalion. 'C' Company. Separated from the 9th (North Irish Horse) Battalion in the period 21-28 March 1918 during the retreat from St Quentin; rejoined 6 April 1918.

WELLS Private James 14761. From Lurgan, County Armagh. Enlisted September 1914. To France with 36th (Ulster) Division in October 1915. 'C' Company. Signaller with Company during the attack at Hamel 1 July 1916, which he survived unwounded. [Transferred to The Royal Inniskilling Fusiliers (32648).] Transferred to the Class Z Reserve 30 March 1919. 1914-15 Star.

WELCH Private David 43450. [Enlisted into The London Regiment (3036). To France 29 June 1915 and joined 1/24th (County of London) Battalion, The London Regiment (The Queen's).] To France and joined 36 Infantry Base Depot 29 March 1918. Transferred to Princess Victoria's (Royal Irish Fusiliers) 2 April 1918 (renumbered 43450) and joined the 9th (North Irish Horse) Battalion 4 April 1918. Disembodied 6 March 1919. 1914-15 Star.

WELSH Lance Corporal Albert 41139. [Enlisted in October 1914 into the Service Squadron, 6th

(Inniskilling) Dragoons (UD/69). To France with 36th (Ulster) Division in October 1915. Served with 2nd North Irish Horse, X Corps Cavalry Regiment.] Joined the renamed 9th (North Irish Horse) Battalion from 36 Infantry Base Depot and transferred to Princess Victoria's (Royal Irish Fusiliers) in September/October 1917 (renumbered 41139). Transferred to the Class Z Reserve 11 February 1919. 1914-15 Star.

WELSH Private Frederick James 17933. From Smithborough, County Monaghan. Enlisted into the 9th (Service) Battalion in January 1915. To France with 36th (Ulster) Division in October 1915. 'D' Company. **Wounded** during the attack at Hamel 1 July 1916. **Missing** in the period 21-27 March 1918 during the retreat from St Quentin and later declared **killed in action** 27 March 1918, aged 36. 1914-15 Star.

WEST Private Frank Charles 43272. [Enlisted into The Sherwood Foresters (Nottinghamshire and Derbyshire Regiment).] Transferred to Princess Victoria's (Royal Irish Fusiliers) 31 August 1916 having joined the 9th (Service) Battalion on 8 August 1916 (renumbered 43272).

WESTERMAN Private Arthur 40036. From Leeds. [Enlisted into The Prince of Wales's Own (West Yorkshire Regiment).] Transferred to Princess Victoria's (Royal Irish Fusiliers) 30 November 1916 (renumbered 40036) and joined the 9th (Service) Battalion 12 December 1916. 'A' Company. **Wounded** at the Battle of Langemarck 16 August 1917.

WETHERAL Lance Sergeant Albert 17664. Enlisted into the 9th (Service) Battalion 14 December 1914. To France with 36th (Ulster) Division in October 1915. **Wounded**. Discharged as no longer physically fit for war service due to wounds 14 June 1918, aged 23. Silver War Badge, number 387952.

WETHERALL Private Alexander 14773. From Shankill, County Armagh. Enlisted September 1914. To France with 36th (Ulster) Division in October 1915. 'C' Company. Bombing team. **Wounded** by shellfire at Hamel on 24 June 1916 and **died of wounds** 25 June 1916. 1914-15 Star.

WHALLEY Private William 42504. Born in 1892. From Accrington, Lancashire. A labourer at a print works. [Enlisted 30 December 1914 into the Army Service Corps (T4/039738). To France 21 May 1915. Served with 15th Reserve Park. Transferred to The London Regiment (renumbered 201551 Rifleman) and joined the $2/5^{th}$ (City of London) Battalion, The London Regiment (London Rifle Brigade) 6 October 1917. Transferred to The Royal Irish Rifles (renumbered 45777) and attached to $1/18^{th}$ (County of London) Battalion, The London Regiment (London Irish Rifles). **Wounded** by shrapnel (side and left thigh) 22 March 1918. Evacuated to hospital in England 24 March 1918. Joined the 3rd (Reserve) Battalion, The Royal Irish Rifles 20 July 1918.] To France 6 September 1918. Transferred at the Base Depot to Princess Victoria's (Royal Irish Fusiliers) 14 September 1918 (renumbered 42504) and joined the 9th (North Irish Horse) Battalion 22 September 1918. **Wounded** by a gunshot to the left leg at Hill 41 on 11 October 1918. Evacuated to hospital in England 17 October 1918. Discharged as no longer physically fit for war service due to wounds 7 February 1919. Silver War Badge, number B115652.

WHEDON Private Edgar William 40078. [Enlisted 26 July 1915 into the 16th (Service) Battalion, The Prince of Wales's Own (West Yorkshire Regiment) (1st Bradford) (1589).] Transferred to Princess Victoria's (Royal Irish Fusiliers) 30 November 1916 (renumbered 40078) and joined the 9th (Service) Battalion 12 December 1916. 'B' Company. **Wounded** during the retreat from St Quentin 21-28 March 1918. Discharged as no longer physically fit for war service due to wounds 12 December 1918. Silver War Badge, number B51543. 1914-15 Star.

WHEELER Private Charles 42278. [Enlisted into the Army Veterinary Corps (5605 Horsekeeper). Served with the Mediterranean Expeditionary Force from 11 April 1915.] Transferred to Princess Victoria's (Royal Irish Fusiliers) 8 May 1918 (renumbered 42278) and joined the 9th (North Irish Horse) Battalion. Transferred to the Class Z Reserve 10 March 1919. 1914-15 Star.

WHETSTONE Private Albert 40080. [Enlisted 23 March 1915 into the 17th (Service) Battalion, The Prince of Wales's Own (West Yorkshire Regiment) (2nd Leeds) (1477).] Transferred to Princess Victoria's (Royal Irish Fusiliers) 30 November 1916 (renumbered 40080) and joined the 9th (Service) Battalion 12 December 1916. **Wounded**. Discharged as no longer physically fit for war service due to wounds 17 July 1918, aged 25. Silver War Badge, number 425681.

WHITE Warrant Officer Class II Andrew 41795. From Londonderry. [Enlisted in 1914 and joined the 10th (Service) Battalion, The Royal Inniskilling Fusiliers (Derry) (16093). To France with 36th (Ulster) Division in October 1915. Acting Warrant Officer Class I.] Transferred to Princess Victoria's (Royal Irish Fusiliers) (renumbered 41795) and joined the 9th (North Irish Horse) Battalion in early-1918. Company Sergeant Major of 'D' Company. **Wounded** and **captured** in the period 21-28 March 1918 during the retreat from St Quentin. Transferred to the Class Z Reserve 26 March 1919. 1914-15 Star.

WHITE Private Benjamin 20341. From Washington Station, County Durham. [Enlisted into The Royal Inniskilling Fusiliers.] Transferred to Princess Victoria's (Royal Irish Fusiliers) on 30 June 1915 (renumbered 20341) and joined the 9th (Service) Battalion. To France with 36th (Ulster) Division in October 1915. **Died** 22 February 1917, aged 21. 1914-15 Star.

WHITE Private George Thompson 45813. Joined the 9th (North Irish Horse) Battalion, Princess Victoria's (Royal Irish Fusiliers) with the draft of men from The London Regiment in April 1918.

WHITE Private James Henry 43320. From Dalston, Middlesex. [Enlisted into The London Regiment (183988).] Attached to the 9th (Service) Battalion, Princess Victoria's (Royal Irish Fusiliers) 26 November 1916. 'A' Company. Discharged from the Territorial Force, re-enlisted and transferred to Princess Victoria's (Royal Irish Fusiliers) in March/April 1917 (renumbered 43320). **Killed in action** at the Battle of Langemarck 16 August 1917.

WHITE Private John 21041, 33309 & 7041502. From Shankill, Belfast. [Enlisted in November 1914 and joined the 7th or 8th (Service) Battalion in 49th Brigade, 16th (Irish) Division.] Joined the 9th (North Irish Horse) Battalion when the 7th/8th (Service) Battalion was disbanded in February 1918. Re-enlisted 25 August 1919 for Regular Army service with Princess Victoria's (Royal Irish Fusiliers) (renumbered 33309, renumbered 7041502). Served with the 1st Battalion in Persia and Mesopotamia in 1919/20. General Service Medal 1918-1962 with clasps 'Iraq' & 'NW Persia'. Discharged 23 December 1921.

WHITE Private Leonard Furnell 45789. From Winchester. [Enlisted into the Royal Flying Corps.] Joined the 9th (North Irish Horse) Battalion, Princess Victoria's (Royal Irish Fusiliers) with the draft of men from The London Regiment in April 1918 (renumbered 45789) (See Private S J K Eames). **Wounded** in the period 9-12 April 1918 in the actions between Wulverghem and Kemmel and **died of wounds** 12 April 1918, aged 19.

WHITE Lance Corporal Norman 14786. Enlisted September 1914. To France with 36th (Ulster) Division in October 1915. Transferred to the Class Z Reserve 23 March 1919. 1914-15 Star.

WHITE Private Samuel Ernest 41145. [Enlisted in October 1915 into the Service Squadron, 6th (Inniskilling) Dragoons (UD/50). To France with 36th (Ulster) Division in October 1915. Served with 2nd North Irish Horse, X Corps Cavalry Regiment.] Joined the renamed 9th (North Irish Horse) Battalion from 36 Infantry Base Depot and transferred to Princess Victoria's (Royal Irish Fusiliers) in September/October 1917 (renumbered 41145). Transferred to the Class Z Reserve 24 February 1919. 1914-15 Star.

WHITE Corporal Thomas 17915. From Cootehill, County Cavan. Enlisted into the 9th (Service) Battalion in January 1915. To France with 36th (Ulster) Division in October 1915. 'C' Company. Detached as Post Corporal at the Quartermaster's Stores and did not take part in the attack at Hamel on 1 July 1916. Transferred to the Class Z Reserve 1 May 1919. 1914-15 Star.

WHITESIDE Private Ferguson 20034. Enlisted into the 9th (Service) Battalion in June 1915. To France with 36th (Ulster) Division in October 1915. Transferred to the Class Z Reserve. 1914-15 Star. Died in 1956. His brother, Corporal Robert Whiteside, was killed in action on 18 June 1917 while serving with the 16th (Service) Battalion, The Royal Irish Rifles (2nd County Down) (Pioneers). His brother, Private William James Whiteside (5776), was wounded by a gunshot that blinded him in both eyes in April 1915 while serving with the 1st Battalion, Princess Victoria's (Royal Irish Fusiliers); he died in 1942. His brother, Alexander Whiteside, had served pre-war with the 3rd Battalion (Militia), Princess Victoria's (Royal Irish Fusiliers) and emigrated to the Nebraska, United States; he served with the United States Army during the war.

WHITESIDE Lance Corporal James Bryson 41583. Born 1 September 1895 at Drumadarragh, Doagh, County Antrim. A chemical engineer. [Enlisted 22 May 1915 into the North Irish Horse (1568). Lance Corporal 7 February 1916. Reverted to Private at own request 20 March 1916. Served with 2nd North Irish Horse, X Corps Cavalry Regiment. Embarked at Marseilles for Egypt with the Regiment's horses on Horse Transport SS Bohemian 25 August 1917.] Joined the renamed 9th (North Irish Horse) Battalion and transferred to Princess Victoria's (Royal Irish Fusiliers) in October 1917 (renumbered 41583). [Transferred to the Tank Corps (renumbered 304854) 28 December 1917 and posted for training to the Tank Corps Depot, at Bovington near Wareham, Dorset. Posted to the 17th Battalion, Tank Corps 8 January 1918 and to France 27 April 1918 when it converted to 17th (Armoured Car) Battalion. Lance Corporal 31 August 1918.] Transferred to the Class Z Reserve 7 June 1919.

WHITESIDE Lance Corporal John 18464. From Poyntzpass, County Armagh. Enlisted into the 9th (Service) Battalion in March 1915. To France with 36th (Ulster) Division in October 1915. 'B' Company. **Wounded** during the attack at Hamel 1 July 1916. **Captured** during the retreat from St Quentin 21-28 March 1918. Transferred to the Class Z Reserve 20 March 1919. 1914-15 Star. Brother of Private Thomas Whiteside. Cousin of Corporal Samuel Whiteside.

WHITESIDE MM Acting Corporal Samuel 14748. From Tullyallen, Glenanne, County Armagh. Member of Glenanne Company, Armagh Regiment, Ulster Volunteer Force. Enlisted September 1914. To France with 36th (Ulster) Division in October 1915. **MM** – Battle of Langemarck 16 August 1917. Transferred to the Class Z Reserve 20 March 1919. 1914-15 Star. Two uncles and three cousins served during the First World War, including Lance Corporal John Whiteside and Private Thomas Whiteside.

WHITESIDE Private Thomas 18465. Born at Poyntzpass, County Armagh. Enlisted into the 9th (Service) Battalion in March 1915. To France with 36th (Ulster) Division in October 1915. **Killed in action** during the attack at Hamel 1 July 1916, aged 21. 1914-15 Star. Brother of Private John Whiteside. Cousin of Corporal Samuel Whiteside.

WHITESIDE Private Wesley 23212. Enlisted 17 November 1915. Posted to the 9th (Service) Battalion. Discharged as no longer physically fit for war service due to sickness 1 November 1919. Silver War Badge, number 508638.

WHITFIELD Private Rowland 20328. Enlisted in May/June 1915 and joined the 9th (Service) Battalion with the draft of men from The Royal Inniskilling Fusiliers who transferred to Princess Victoria's (Royal Irish Fusiliers) on 30 June 1915. 'C' Company. Released from hospital just prior to the attack at Hamel 1 July 1916, during which he was **wounded** and evacuated to hospital in England. [Transferred to The Worcestershire Regiment (renumbered 47656).] 1914-15 Star.

WHITLA Private Jack 29033. Enlisted, re-enlisted or transferred to Princess Victoria's (Royal Irish Fusiliers) in early-1918. Posted to the 9th (North Irish Horse) Battalion. 'B' Company. **Missing** in the period 21-28 March 1918 during the retreat from St Quentin believed **captured**.

WHITSITT Sergeant James S 14768. From Armagh, County Armagh. 'A' Company. Enlisted September 1914. To France with 36th (Ulster) Division in October 1915. **Wounded** during the attack at Hamel 1 July 1916. Evacuated to 5th Southern General Hospital, Portsmouth. Discharged as no longer physically fit for war service due to wounds 14 December 1918. 1914-15 Star. His brother, Lieutenant Robert Whitsitt, served as a despatch rider (Corporal) with the Corps of Royal Engineers before being commissioned into the same corps. His two sisters (Annie and Emily) served with Voluntary Aid Detachments; Emily earned a B List Mention for service with 1st Western General Hospital, Liverpool.

WHITTAKER Private John 45072. [Enlisted into or transferred to Princess Victoria's (Royal Irish Fusiliers) in December 1916 and joined the 7th/8th (Service) Battalion in 49th Brigade, 16th (Irish) Division.] Joined the 9th (North Irish Horse) Battalion when the 7th/8th (Service) Battalion was disbanded in February 1918.

WHITTAM Private William 18422. Born in 1882. From Colne, Lancashire. A coalman. [Enlisted 20 March 1915 into the 7th (Service) Battalion in 49th Brigade, 16th (Irish) Division.] Joined the 9th (North Irish Horse) Battalion when the 7th/8th (Service) Battalion was disbanded in February 1918. 'B' Company. **Captured** at Erches on 27 March 1918 during the retreat from St Quentin. Held at Limburg and Giessen Prisoner of War Camps. Repatriated 11 December 1918. Transferred to the Class Z Reserve 1 April 1919.

WHYLIE Lance Corporal James 7965. Enlisted 25 April 1903 into Princess Victoria's (Royal Irish Fusiliers) and served with the 1st Battalion. [Mobilised from the Army Reserve and to France with the 1st Battalion 22 August 1914.] Posted to the 9th (Service) Battalion. [Posted to the 1st Battalion.

Wounded.] Discharged as no longer physically fit for war service due to wounds 10 March 1919. Silver War Badge, number B162126.

WICKERS Private George Frederick 42483. Born in 1894 at St Helens, Jersey. Served with The Royal Jersey Militia. [Part of The Royal Jersey Militia detachment posted to the 7th (Service) Battalion, The Royal Irish Rifles in February 1915 (4217 Rifleman). To France in 47th Brigade, 16th (Irish) Division 19 December 1915. Evacuated to hospital in England 18 April 1917. Joined the 4th (Extra Reserve) Battalion, The Royal Irish Rifles 28 September 1917. Qualified as a 1st Class Signaller 25 January 1918. Lance Corporal 9 March 1918. To France 22 August 1918 and reverted to Rifleman.] Transferred at the Base Depot to Princess Victoria's (Royal Irish Fusiliers) 14 September 1918 (renumbered 42483) and joined the 9th (North Irish Horse) Battalion 22 September 1918. **Wounded** by a gunshot to the calf during the attack at Vijfwegen on 30 September or 1 October 1918 (recorded as 3 October 1918). Transferred to the Class Z Reserve 25 February 1919. 1914-15 Star.

WICKES Private Edward 42252. From London. [Enlisted 13 May 1915 into the Army Service Corps (T4/070631). To France 21 May 1916.] Transferred to Princess Victoria's (Royal Irish Fusiliers) 8 May 1918 (renumbered 42252) and joined the 9th (North Irish Horse) Battalion. **Killed in action** during the attack south of Wulverghem 4 September 1918, aged 27.

WIDDESS Private Abraham John 41219. Commissioned into The Prince of Wales's Own (West Yorkshire Regiment) - see Appendix 5.

WIDDICOMBE Private John 29577. Enlisted 16 November 1916 and served elsewhere. Re-enlisted or transferred to Princess Victoria's (Royal Irish Fusiliers) in March 1918. Posted to the 9th (North Irish Horse) Battalion. **Wounded**. Discharged as no longer physically fit for war service due to wounds 5 April 1919. Silver War Badge, number B207391.

WIGHTMAN Lance Corporal John William 43458. [Enlisted into The London Regiment (2824). Posted to 1/24th (County of London) Battalion, The London Regiment (The Queen's).] To France and joined 36 Infantry Base Depot 29 March 1918. Transferred to Princess Victoria's (Royal Irish Fusiliers) 2 April 1918 (renumbered 43458) and joined the 9th (North Irish Horse) Battalion 4 April 1918.

WIGMORE Private Charles James 50049. [Transferred to Princess Victoria's (Royal Irish Fusiliers) in May 1918 (renumbered 50049) with a draft of men from English regiments and joined the 1st Battalion.] Posted to the 9th (North Irish Horse) Battalion in August 1918.

WIGMORE Lance Corporal William James 43433. [Enlisted into The London Regiment (2501). To France 15 March 1915 and joined 1/24th (County of London) Battalion, The London Regiment (The Queen's).] To France and joined 36 Infantry Base Depot 29 March 1918. Transferred to Princess Victoria's (Royal Irish Fusiliers) 2 April 1918 (renumbered 43433) and joined the 9th (North Irish Horse) Battalion 4 April 1918. 1914-15 Star.

WILCE Private Richard 40076. From Pontefract, Yorkshire. [Served previously with the 12th (Service) and 10th (Service) Battalions, The Prince of Wales's Own (West Yorkshire Regiment) (14927).] Transferred to Princess Victoria's (Royal Irish Fusiliers) 30 November 1916 (renumbered 40076) and joined the 9th (Service) Battalion 12 December 1916. 'A' Company. **Killed in action** at the Battle of Langemarck 16 August 1917, aged 30. 1914-15 Star.

WILD Private Wallace 42204. Joined the 9th (North Irish Horse) Battalion, Princess Victoria's (Royal Irish Fusiliers) with the draft of men transferred from the Army Service Corps and the Army Veterinary Corps in May 1918.

WILKIE Private Cuthbert 42118. [Enlisted 8 January 1915 into the Army Veterinary Corps (4026).] Transferred to Princess Victoria's (Royal Irish Fusiliers) 8 May 1918 (renumbered 42118) and joined the 9th (North Irish Horse) Battalion. Discharged as no longer physically fit for war service due to sickness 12 February 1919. Silver War Badge, number B140389. 1914-15 Star.

WILKINSON Private Albert 24910. Born in 1898 at Derrymacfall, Portadown, County Armagh. Enlisted 16 October 1916 and joined the 10th (Reserve) Battalion. To France 21 June 1917 and joined the 9th (Service) Battalion. 'B' Company. **Missing** at the Battle of Langemarck 16 August 1917 later declared **killed in action** on that date, aged 19.

WILKINSON Private John 14747. Born at Lurgan, County Armagh. From Bleary, County Armagh.

Enlisted September 1914. To France with 36th (Ulster) Division in October 1915. **Killed in action** during the attack at Hamel 1 July 1916, aged 22. 1914-15 Star.

WILKINSON Private John 18260. Enlisted into the 9th (Service) Battalion 3 March 1915. To France with 36th (Ulster) Division in October 1915. Discharged as no longer physically fit for war service due to sickness 15 May 1917. Silver War Badge, number 183841. 1914-15 Star.

WILKINSON Private William 40079. From Bradford, Yorkshire. [Enlisted into the 12th (Service) Battalion, The Prince of Wales's Own (West Yorkshire Regiment) (1412).] Transferred to Princess Victoria's (Royal Irish Fusiliers) 30 November 1916 (renumbered 40079) and joined the 9th (Service) Battalion 12 December 1916. 'C' Company. **Killed in action** at the Battle of Langemarck 16 August 1917.

WILLIAMS Private Alfred John 42109. [Enlisted 11 December 1915 into the Army Veterinary Corps (21255).] Transferred to Princess Victoria's (Royal Irish Fusiliers) 8 May 1918 (renumbered 42109) and joined the 9th (North Irish Horse) Battalion. **Wounded**. Discharged as no longer physically fit for war service due to wounds 10 April 1919. Silver War Badge, number B209602.

WILLIAMS Private Fred 42253. [Enlisted 29 December 1914 into the Army Service Corps (T4/037305). Served with 38th Division Train.] Transferred to Princess Victoria's (Royal Irish Fusiliers) 8 May 1918 (renumbered 42253) and joined the 9th (North Irish Horse) Battalion. Discharged as no longer physically fit for war service due to sickness 21 March 1919. Silver War Badge, number B162478.

WILLIAMS MM Warrant Officer Class I George Alfred 9428. Regimental Sergeant Major - see above.

WILLIAMS MM Lance Sergeant Herbert George 42157. Born at Shepton Mallet, Somerset. A baker. [Enlisted 5 January 1915 into the Army Service Corps (S4/41830). To France 17 December 1915. Served with 16th and 17th Field Bakeries. Corporal 16 May 1916.] Transferred to Princess Victoria's (Royal Irish Fusiliers) 8 May 1918 (renumbered 42157) and joined the 9th (North Irish Horse) Battalion. **MM** – Wulverghem 4 September 1918. Lance Sergeant 5 September 1918. **Missing** during the attack at Vijfwegen on 30 September or 1 October 1918; recorded as **killed in action** on 3 October 1918. 1914-15 Star.

WILLIAMS Private Joseph 45284. [Enlisted in July 1916. Transferred to Princess Victoria's (Royal Irish Fusiliers) in December 1916 and joined the 7th/8th (Service) Battalion in 49th Brigade, 16th (Irish) Division.] Joined the 9th (North Irish Horse) Battalion when the 7th/8th (Service) Battalion was disbanded in February 1918.

WILLIAMS Private Lewis 42189. [Enlisted into the Army Service Corps (T4/69765). To France 1 December 1915. Served with 43rd Division Train.] Transferred to Princess Victoria's (Royal Irish Fusiliers) 8 May 1918 (renumbered 42189) and joined the 9th (North Irish Horse) Battalion. Transferred to the Class Z Reserve 25 March 1919. 1914-15 Star.

WILLIAMS Private Richard Stephen 41853. Born on 16 February 1895 at Cheltenham, Gloucestershire. Lived at Cowley, Gloucestershire. [Enlisted 17 November 1914 into the Army Service Corps (T3/029726), aged 19 but giving his age as 21 years.] Transferred to Princess Victoria's (Royal Irish Fusiliers) (renumbered 41853) in late-1917 and joined the 9th (North Irish Horse) Battalion. 'A' Company. **Captured** on 21 March 1918 during the retreat from St Quentin. Held at Stendal Prisoner of War Camp from 2 August 1918 to 21 October 1918. Transferred to the Class Z Reserve 5 April 1919. Subsequently worked as a Head Gardener to several private estates in Gloucestershire.

WILLIAMS Private Victor James 43477. [Enlisted 10 September 1914 into The London Regiment (4755). Posted to 2/22nd (County of London) Battalion, The London Regiment (The Queen's).] To France and joined 36 Infantry Base Depot 29 March 1918. Transferred to Princess Victoria's (Royal Irish Fusiliers) 2 April 1918 (renumbered 43477) and joined the 9th (North Irish Horse) Battalion 4 April 1918. Discharged as no longer physically fit for war service due to sickness 18 February 1919. Silver War Badge, number B154109.

WILLIAMSON Private George 14808. Enlisted September 1914. To France with 36th (Ulster) Division in October 1915. 'C' Company. Hospital mid-1916. [Transferred to the Army Service Corps (renumbered M/354539).] Transferred to the Class Z Reserve. 1914-15 Star.

WILLIAMSON Private Hugh Albert 14780. Commissioned into The Manchester Regiment - see Appendix 5.

WILLIAMSON Sergeant Robert Alexander 41071. Born in 1888 at Drumcoo, Dungannon, County Tyrone. A printer's compositor. [Enlisted in November 1914 into the Service Squadron, 6th (Inniskilling) Dragoons (UD/114). To France with 36th (Ulster) Division in October 1915. Served with 2nd North Irish Horse, X Corps Cavalry Regiment.] Joined the renamed 9th (North Irish Horse) Battalion from 36 Infantry Base Depot and transferred to Princess Victoria's (Royal Irish Fusiliers) in September/October 1917 (renumbered 41071). **Wounded** in the knee in September 1918. Transferred to the Class Z Reserve 29 January 1919. 1914-15 Star. Died 7 January 1955, aged 67, at Belfast. His brother, Private James Whiteside Williamson, served with 73rd (Royal Highlanders) Battalion, Canadian Infantry.

WILLIAMSON Private William 14766. From Bessbrook, County Armagh. Enlisted September 1914. To France with 36th (Ulster) Division in October 1915. **Killed in action** 23 November 1917 at Moeuvres, aged 22.

WILLIAMSON Corporal William George 14764. From Richhill, County Armagh. Enlisted September 1914. To France with 36th (Ulster) Division in October 1915. **Died** in Ireland 17 May 1917, aged 21. 1914-15 Star.

WILLIS Private James 14807. Born in 1880 at Marlacoo, County Armagh. A weaver in the linen trade from Portadown, County Armagh. 4th (Armagh) Battalion, Armagh Regiment, Ulster Volunteer Force. Served pre-war in the 3rd Battalion (Militia), Princess Victoria's (Royal Irish Fusiliers). Enlisted September 1914. To France with 36th (Ulster) Division in October 1915. 'D' Company. **Wounded** by a gunshot to the left leg at Hamel on 1 July 1916. Treated at 110th Field Ambulance. **Wounded** by a gunshot to the right knee at the Battle of Langemarck on 16 August 1917. Treated at The Military Hospital, York. [Transferred to the Labour Corps (renumbered 545506).] 1914-15 Star. Transferred to the Class Z Reserve 5 February 1919.

WILLIS Private John 15856. Born at Tartaraghan, County Armagh. Enlisted into the 9th (Service) Battalion 19 October 1914. Discharged having made a mis-statement as to age on enlistment; soldier under 17 years of age at date of application for discharge 3 November 1914.

WILLIS Private Robert 22143. From Portadown, County Armagh. Enlisted in October 1915. Posted to the 9th (Service) Battalion. 'C' Company. **Wounded** by shellfire at Hamel 24 June 1916. **Wounded** at the Battle of Langemarck 16 August 1917.

WILLIS Private Samuel 22759. From Markethill, County Armagh. Enlisted in November 1915. Posted to the 9th (Service) Battalion. 'D' Company. **Captured** in the period 21-28 March 1918 during the retreat from St Quentin.

WILLIS Corporal Thomas 17826. From Drumcree, Portadown, County Armagh. Enlisted into the 9th (Service) Battalion in January 1915. To France with 36th (Ulster) Division in October 1915. 'D' Company. **Wounded** at the Battle of Langemarck 16 August 1917. [Transferred to The Royal Irish Rifles (renumbered 22222).] Transferred to the Class Z Reserve. 1914-15 Star.

WILSON Private Albert Edward 43385. [Enlisted into The London Regiment (4768). Posted to 1/9th (County of London) Battalion, The London Regiment (Queen Victoria's Rifles).] Attached to the 9th (Service) Battalion, Princess Victoria's (Royal Irish Fusiliers) 26 November 1916. Discharged from the Territorial Force, re-enlisted and transferred to Princess Victoria's (Royal Irish Fusiliers) in March/April 1917 (renumbered 43385).

WILSON Private Albert Henry 43337. [Enlisted into The London Regiment (6712). Posted to 1/7th (City of London) Battalion, The London Regiment.] Attached to the 9th (Service) Battalion, Princess Victoria's (Royal Irish Fusiliers) 26 November 1916. Discharged from the Territorial Force, re-enlisted and transferred to Princess Victoria's (Royal Irish Fusiliers) in March/April 1917 (renumbered 43337).

WILSON Private Alexander 14749. From Lurgan, County Armagh. Enlisted September 1914. To France with 36th (Ulster) Division in October 1915. **Wounded** during the attack at Hamel 1 July 1916. Discharged as no longer physically fit for war service due to wounds 25 April 1918, aged 25. Silver War Badge, number 404649. 1914-15 Star.

WILSON Private Alexander 14774. Enlisted September 1914. Discharged as no longer physically fit for war service due to sickness 28 June 1915, aged 38. Silver War Badge, number 508798.

WILSON Private Alexander 16151. From Glennan, Glaslough, County Monaghan. Enlisted into the 9th (Service) Battalion in October 1914. To France with 36th (Ulster) Division in October 1915. **Killed in action** during the attack at Hamel 1 July 1916, aged 21. 1914-15 Star.

WILSON Corporal Cecil 14802. From Portadown, County Armagh. 4th (Portadown) Battalion, Armagh Regiment, Ulster Volunteer Force. Enlisted September 1914. To France with 36th (Ulster) Division in October 1915. One of the few men unwounded during the attack at Hamel 1 July 1916. Transferred to the Class Z Reserve 23 March 1919. 1914-15 Star.

WILSON Private Clarence 41501. From Shankill, Belfast. [Enlisted in November 1914 into the North Irish Horse (1304). To France with 'F' Squadron in 33rd Division 17 November 1915. Served with 2nd North Irish Horse, X Corps Cavalry Regiment.] Joined the renamed 9th (North Irish Horse) Battalion from 36 Infantry Base Depot and transferred to Princess Victoria's (Royal Irish Fusiliers) in September/October 1917 (renumbered 41501). 'A' Company. **Captured** in the period 21-28 March 1918 during the retreat from St Quentin. Transferred to the Class Z Reserve 21 March 1919. 1914-15 Star.

WILSON Private Cornelius 27726, 33301 & 7041497. From Shankill, Belfast. Enlisted in June 1917. Posted to the 9th (North Irish Horse) Battalion. Re-enlisted 20 August 1919 for Regular Army service with Princess Victoria's (Royal Irish Fusiliers) (renumbered 33301, renumbered 7041497). Served with the 1st Battalion in Persia and Mesopotamia in 1919/20. General Service Medal 1918-1962 with clasps 'Iraq' & 'NW Persia'. Discharged 22 December 1921.

WILSON Private David 21640. From Monbrief, Lurgan, County Armagh. Enlisted in September 1915. Posted to the 9th (Service) Battalion in mid/late 1916. 'B' Company. **Wounded** at the Battle of Langemarck 16 August 1917. **Captured** in 1918.

WILSON Sergeant Edward 14815. Born at Armagh, County Armagh. Member of Loyal Orange Lodge 109 and Royal Black Preceptory 1077. Enlisted September 1914. To France with 36th (Ulster) Division in October 1915. 'A' Company. **Missing** during the attack at Hamel 1 July 1916 and later declared **killed in action** on that date. Royal Black Preceptory 1077 was renamed Wilson Memorial Royal Black Preceptory in his honour. 1914-15 Star.

WILSON Private Edward 17658, 33896 & 7041891. From Armagh, County Armagh. Enlisted into the 9th (Service) Battalion in December 1914/January 1915. To France with 36th (Ulster) Division in October 1915. Transferred to the Class Z Reserve 4 March 1919. 1914-15 Star. Re-enlisted 3 January 1920 for Regular Army service with Princess Victoria's (Royal Irish Fusiliers) (renumbered 33896, renumbered 7041891). Transferred to the Section D reserve 2 February 1927. Discharged 2 February 1932.

WILSON Private Ernest 41197. [Enlisted in May 1915 into the North Irish Horse (1568). Served with 2nd North Irish Horse, X Corps Cavalry Regiment.] Joined the renamed 9th (North Irish Horse) Battalion and transferred to Princess Victoria's (Royal Irish Fusiliers) in October 1917 (renumbered 41197). [Transferred to the Tank Corps (renumbered 304882) 28 December 1917 and posted for training to the Tank Corps Depot, at Bovington near Wareham, Dorset.

WILSON Private Eugene 42215. Joined the 9th (North Irish Horse) Battalion, Princess Victoria's (Royal Irish Fusiliers) with the draft of men transferred from the Army Service Corps and the Army Veterinary Corps in May 1918.

WILSON Private Francis 41525. From Dundonald, County Down. [Enlisted October 1916 into the North Irish Horse (2295). Served with 2nd North Irish Horse, X Corps Cavalry Regiment.] Joined the renamed 9th (North Irish Horse) Battalion from 36 Infantry Base Depot and transferred to Princess Victoria's (Royal Irish Fusiliers) in September/October 1917 (renumbered 41525). 'A' Company. **Captured** in the period 21-28 March 1918 during the retreat from St Quentin.

WILSON Corporal Francis Oliver 17657. Born in 1893 at Richhill, County Armagh. Enlisted into the 9th (Service) Battalion in December 1914/January 1915. To France with 36th (Ulster) Division in October 1915. 'A' Company. **Wounded** in the thigh at the Battle of Langemarck 16 August 1917 and **died of wounds** 19 August 1917, aged 24. 1914-15 Star.

WILSON Lance Corporal Frederick J 41116 & 7042134. (Shown incorrectly on a medal index card as 41126.) From Winchester, Hampshire. A groom. Enlisted 10 August 1910 as a regular soldier or special reservist with the 2nd Dragoon Guards (Queen's Bays) (4844). To France 16 August 1914 in 1st Cavalry Division. Evacuated to hospital in England 3 January 1915. To France 13 June 1916 and joined 6th (Inniskilling) Dragoons (4844) in 2nd North Irish Horse, X Corps Cavalry Regiment.] Joined the renamed 9th (North Irish Horse) Battalion from 36 Infantry Base Depot and transferred to Princess Victoria's (Royal Irish Fusiliers) in September/October 1917 (renumbered 41116). Evacuated to hospital in England 14 February 1918. To France 15 June 1918. 1914 Star and clasp. Continued to serve in the Regular Army with Princess Victoria's (Royal Irish Fusiliers) (renumbered 7042134). Discharged 9 August 1922.

WILSON Private George 14810. Enlisted September 1914. Did not serve overseas with 36th (Ulster) Division. Discharged as no longer physically fit for war service due to sickness 3 May 1916, aged 21. Silver War Badge, number 508799.

WILSON Private George 42124. From Kirkcaldy, Fife. [Enlisted into the Army Veterinary Corps (16975).] Transferred to Princess Victoria's (Royal Irish Fusiliers) 8 May 1918 (renumbered 42124) and joined the 9th (North Irish Horse) Battalion. **Killed in action** during the attack north of Bailleul 24 August 1918, aged 21.

WILSON Warrant Officer Class II George Wade 14792. Regimental Quartermaster Sergeant - see above.

WILSON Private Herbert 40075. From Pontefract, Yorkshire. [Enlisted into the 10th (Service) Battalion, The Prince of Wales's Own (West Yorkshire Regiment) (11633).] Transferred to Princess Victoria's (Royal Irish Fusiliers) 30 November 1916 (renumbered 40075) and joined the 9th (Service) Battalion 12 December 1916. **Wounded** at the Battle of Langemarck 16 August 1917. Transferred to the Class Z Reserve 28 February 1919. 1914-15 Star.

WILSON Private Herbert 43246. [Enlisted into The Sherwood Foresters (Nottinghamshire and Derbyshire Regiment).] Transferred to Princess Victoria's (Royal Irish Fusiliers) 31 August 1916 (renumbered 43246) having joined the 9th (Service) Battalion on 8 August 1916.

WILSON Private Hugh 21486. Enlisted 26 August 1915. Posted to the 9th (Service) Battalion. Discharged as no longer physically fit for war service due to sickness 6 January 1917. Silver War Badge, number 95524.

WILSON Private Isaiah 18371. Born at Tynan, County Armagh. Enlisted into the 9th (Service) Battalion in March 1915. To France with 36th (Ulster) Division in October 1915. **Killed in action** during the attack at Hamel 1 July 1916. 1914-15 Star.

WILSON Private James 14803. Born in 1876. A flax dresser from Tandragee, County Armagh. Armagh Regiment, Ulster Volunteer Force. Member of Loyal Orange Lodge 110. Enlisted September 1914. Lance Corporal 1 January 1915. To France with 36th (Ulster) Division in October 1915. Reverted to Private, sentenced to seven days Field Punishment Number 1 and forfeit fourteen days pay 10 November 1915. Evacuated to hospital in England in November 1916. Then posted to the 10th (Reserve) Battalion 15 November 1916. [Transferred to the Labour Corps 7 July 1917 (renumbered 231631). 668th Home Service Employment Company. Discharged as no longer physically fit for war service due to sickness 18 January 1918.] **Died** as a consequence of war service 23 May 1919 at Tandragee, aged 44. Silver War Badge, number 308526. 1914-15 Star.

WILSON Sergeant James 14811. From Monbrief, Lurgan, County Armagh. Enlisted September 1914. To France with 36th (Ulster) Division in October 1915. 'B' Company. **Wounded** at the Battle of Langemarck 16 August 1917. Discharged as no longer physically fit for war service due to wounds 31 May 1918, aged 32. Silver War Badge, number 394851.

WILSON Private John Wylie Close 24255. Born in 1898 at Belfast. An apprentice fitter. Enlisted 17 April 1916 and joined the 10th (Reserve) Battalion. To France 12 October 1916 and joined the 9th (Service) Battalion. 'C' Company. **Wounded** during the Battle of Messines and to hospital 9 June 1917. **Wounded** by a gunshot to the right hip at the Battle of Langemarck 16 August 1917 and **died of wounds** in 2nd Australian General Hospital 20 August 1917, aged 19.

WILSON Private Joseph 14772. From Armagh, County Armagh. A clerk. Enlisted September 1914. Discharged having made a mis-statement as to age on enlistment; soldier under 17 years of age at date of application for discharge 20 November 1914.

WILSON Private Joseph 41597. [Enlisted in July 1916 into the North Irish Horse (2211). Served with 2nd North Irish Horse, X Corps Cavalry Regiment.] Joined the renamed 9th (North Irish Horse) Battalion from 36 Infantry Base Depot and transferred to Princess Victoria's (Royal Irish Fusiliers) in September/October 1917 (renumbered 41597). 'D' Company. **Missing** in the period 21-28 March 1918 during the retreat from St Quentin believed **captured**.

WILSON Private Matthew 14758. From Armagh, County Armagh. Enlisted September 1914. To France with 36th (Ulster) Division in October 1915. **Killed in action** during the attack at Hamel 1 July 1916, aged 30. 1914-15 Star. Related to 14778 Lance Corporal Robert Wilson.

WILSON Private Oliver 20025. Born in 1881 at Richhill, Portadown, County Armagh. Enlisted into the 9th (Service) Battalion 31 May 1915. To France with 36th (Ulster) Division in October 1915. Evacuated to England sick (sprained ankle and flat feet) 3 December 1915. Posted to the 10th (Reserve) Battalion 24 December 1915. [To 36 Infantry Base Depot 13 February 1916. Classified unfit for general service. To hospital sick (tonsillitis) 26 August 1916. Transferred to the Corps of Royal Engineers (renumbered 248676) 14 June 1917 and posted to 1504th Artisan Works Company as a carpenter. Transferred to the Labour Corps (renumbered 424048) 26 September 1917 and served with 923rd Area Employment Company. Transferred back to the Corps of Royal Engineers (renumbered 248676) 5 March 1918 and posted to 244th Artisan Works Company.] Transferred to the Class Z Reserve 4 March 1919. 1914-15 Star.

WILSON Lance Corporal Robert 14763. [Served in the South Africa War with 74th (Dublin) Company, Imperial Yeomanry (34514, Trooper). Queen's South Africa Medal with clasps 'Cape Colony', 'South Africa 1901' and 'South Africa 1902'.] Enlisted September 1914. To France with 36th (Ulster) Division in October 1915. 'C' Company. **Wounded** during the attack at Hamel 1 July 1916. [Transferred to the Labour Corps (renumbered 655844 Sergeant).] 1914-15 Star.

WILSON Lance Corporal Robert 14778. From Shankill, County Armagh. Enlisted September 1914. To France with 36th (Ulster) Division in October 1915. **Killed in action** during the attack at Hamel 1 July 1916. Related to Private Matthew Wilson.

WILSON Lance Corporal Robert 14794. Enlisted September 1914. To France with 36th (Ulster) Division in October 1915. [Transferred to the Labour Corps (renumbered 390313). Transferred to The South Lancashire Regiment (renumbered 65288).] Transferred to the Class Z Reserve 22 April 1919. 1914-15 Star.

WILSON Lance Corporal Robert 14797. Enlisted September 1914. [Transferred to the Labour Corps (renumbered 231633).] Transferred to the Class Z Reserve 8 March 1919.

WILSON Private Robert 20639. From Lurgan, County Armagh. Enlisted July 1915. [Served previously with the 1st Battalion.] Posted to the 9th (Service) Battalion. 'B' Company. **Missing** at the Battle of Langemarck 16 August 1917 and later declared **killed in action** on that date, aged 19.

WILSON Private Robert 41469. [Enlisted in May/June 1912 into the North Irish Horse (714). To France 20 August 1914 with 'C' Squadron as 5th Division Cavalry and then as GHQ Troops. Served with 2nd North Irish Horse, X Corps Cavalry Regiment.] Joined the renamed 9th (North Irish Horse) Battalion from 36 Infantry Base Depot and transferred to Princess Victoria's (Royal Irish Fusiliers) in September/October 1917 (renumbered 41469). 1914 Star.

WILSON Samuel J 14752. From Lurgan, County Armagh. To France 4 October 1915. **Wounded** during the attack at Hamel 1 July 1916. [Transferred to 5th (Service) Battalion, The Royal Irish Regiment (Pioneers) in the Light Division in the British Army of the Rhine in March/June 1919. 1914-15 Star. Re-enlisted in 1919 for Regular Army service with The Middlesex Regiment (renumbered G/107407) 30 November 1919.]

WILSON Private Sydney 16144. From Ballybay, County Monaghan. Enlisted into the 9th (Service) Battalion in October 1914. To France with 36th (Ulster) Division in October 1915. **Killed in action** during the attack at Hamel 1 July 1916, aged 25. 1914-15 Star.

WILSON Private Thomas 17404. From Portadown, County Armagh. Enlisted into the 9th (Service) Battalion in November/December 1914. To France with 36th (Ulster) Division in October 1915. 'C' Company. **Wounded** during the attack at Hamel 1 July 1916. Discharged as no longer physically fit for war service due to wounds 17 November 1917, aged 24. Silver War Badge, number 276184. 1914-15 Star.

WILSON Private Thomas 41337. [Enlisted in December 1914 into the North Irish Horse (1370).

Served with 2nd North Irish Horse, X Corps Cavalry Regiment.] Joined the renamed 9th (North Irish Horse) Battalion from 36 Infantry Base Depot and transferred to Princess Victoria's (Royal Irish Fusiliers) in September/October 1917 (renumbered 41337). [Transferred to the 8th (King's Royal Irish) Hussars (renumbered 71358). Transferred to the Labour Corps (renumbered 635752).]

WILSON Sergeant Thomas 41876. From Killyflue, Ballymena, County Antrim. [Enlisted into the 12th (Service) Battalion, The Royal Irish Rifles (Central Antrim) (19326). To France with 36th (Ulster) Division in October 1915.] Transferred to Princess Victoria's (Royal Irish Fusiliers) and joined the 9th (North Irish Horse) Battalion in late-1917. 'A' Company. **Captured** in the period 21-28 March 1918 during the retreat from St Quentin. **Died** in captivity 3 October 1918. He is commemorated as The Royal Irish Rifles, incorrectly numbered as 19826. 1914-15 Star.

WILSON Lance Corporal Thomas George 14813. From Lurgan, County Armagh. A bootmaker. Enlisted September 1914. To France with 36th (Ulster) Division in October 1915. **Wounded** in the arm on 23 October 1915 while working with a wiring party. He was the first casualty of the 9th Royal Irish Fusiliers due to enemy action. 'C' Company. Battalion bomb carrier during the attack at Hamel 1 July 1916, which he survived unwounded. Transferred to the Class Z Reserve 1 March 1919. 1914-15 Star.

WILSON Private Thomas Henry 42539. [Enlisted April/May 1918 into The Royal Irish Rifles (22399).] Transferred at the Base Depot to Princess Victoria's (Royal Irish Fusiliers) 14 September 1918 (renumbered 42539) and joined the 9th (North Irish Horse) Battalion 22 September 1918.

WILSON Corporal Thomas J 14790. From Lurgan, County Armagh. Enlisted September 1914. 'C' Company. **Wounded** during the attack at Hamel 1 July 1916. **Wounded** during the Battle of Messines and to hospital 9 June 1917. **Captured** in 1918. Brother of Private William George Wilson. His brothers, Rifleman Joseph Wilson and Rifleman John Wilson, served with the 16th (Service) Battalion, The Royal Irish Rifles (2nd County Down) (Pioneers).

WILSON Private Valentine 16430. Born in 1892 at Tandragee, County Armagh. An engine driver, he enlisted into the 9th (Service) Battalion on 2 November 1914. To France with 36th (Ulster) Division in October 1915. 'B' Company. **Wounded** during the attack at Hamel 1 July 1916. After he recovered, he joined the 3rd (Reserve) Garrison Battalion on 10 March 1917. [Transferred to The Worcestershire Regiment (47317) 7 April 1917 and joined the 16th (Transport Workers) Battalion in Bristol.] Transferred to the Class Z Reserve. 1914-15 Star.

WILSON Private William 16102. Enlisted into the 9th (Service) Battalion in October 1914. To France with 36th (Ulster) Division in October 1915. [Transferred to the Corps of Royal Engineers (renumbered WR/322145, renumbered 243857).] 1914-15 Star.

WILSON Private William 28656. Born at Mullabrack, County Armagh. A farm labourer. Enlisted 14 September 1917 and joined the 10th (Reserve) Battalion. To 'A' Infantry Base Depot 14 March 1918 and joined the 9th (North Irish Horse) Battalion. To 108th Field Ambulance sick (influenza) 26 August 1918 and then to 11th Casualty Clearing Station with an undiagnosed mental condition 5 September 1918. To 30th General Hospital 29 September 1918, transferred to 8th Stationary Hospital 2 October 1918 and evacuated to hospital in England 6 October 1918. Treated for *'feeblemindedness'* at the neurological section Royal Victoria Hospital, Netley, Lord Derby War Hospital, Winwick and at the Belfast War Hospital. Discharged as no longer physically fit for war service due to sickness 19 August 1919. Silver War Badge, number B302462.

WILSON Private William George 14814. Enlisted 15 September 1914. **Wounded**. Discharged as no longer physically fit for war service due to wounds 9 January 1917. Silver War Badge, number 95526. 1914-15 Star. Brother of Corporal Thomas Wilson. His brothers, Rifleman Joseph Wilson and Rifleman John Wilson, served with the 16th (Service) Battalion, The Royal Irish Rifles (2nd County Down) (Pioneers).

WILSON Private William James 5898 & 7040062. Born in 1894 at Stewartstown, County Tyrone. Enlisted on 23 August 1913 into the 3rd Battalion (Militia), Princess Victoria's (Royal Irish Fusiliers) Special Reserve. [Mobilised from the Special Reserve 8 August 1914. To France 4 December 1914 and joined the 1st Battalion. Evacuated to hospital in England 31 May 1915. Posted to the 6th (Service) Battalion 17 October 1915. 'C' Company. Evacuated to hospital in England 8 April 1916. Treated at 2nd Western General Hospital, Manchester. Posted to the 3rd (Reserve) Battalion 22 May 1916. To France 20 July 1916 and rejoined the 1st Battalion. Evacuated to hospital in England 19 December 1916. Forfeit nine days pay for absence 20 March 1917. Posted to the 3rd (Reserve) Battalion June 1917. In arrest awaiting trial 4 September 1917. Tried by District Court Martial on 22 September 1917 charged with *'when on active service **deserting** His Majesty's Service'* and *'losing by neglect his clothing and regimental necessaries.'* Found guilty and sentenced to fifty-four days detention. To 36 Infantry Base Depot 19 October 1917 and joined the 7th/8th (Service) Battalion in 49th Brigade, 16th (Irish) Division.] Joined the 9th (North Irish Horse) Battalion when the 7th/8th (Service) Battalion was disbanded in February 1918. 'D' Company. **Captured** 21 March 1918 during the retreat from St Quentin and held at Limburg Prisoner Of War Camp. Repatriated 15 December 1918. 1914-15 Star. Re-enlisted into Princess Victoria's (Royal Irish Fusiliers) Special Reserve on 31 March 1919 (renumbered 7040062). Re-enlisted 3 October 1920 for Regular Army service with Princess Victoria's (Royal Irish Fusiliers). Served with the 2nd Battalion at Dover. Made a false answer on attestation (Are you Married?); District Court Martial dispensed with by General Officer Commanding 15th Infantry Brigade and Dover Sub-Area who ordered the answer changed from *'no'* to *'yes'*. Sentenced on 12 March 1921 to seven days confined to barracks for absence from reveille. Sentenced on 28 March 1921 to nine days confined to barracks for absence from tattoo. Sentenced on 24 October 1921 to ten days confined to barracks for not complying with an order given by an NCO. Discharged, services no longer required, 26 June 1922. His medals, initially forfeit, were restored.

WILSON Private William James 14757. From Armagh, County Armagh. Enlisted September 1914. 'A' Company. **Wounded** at the Battle of Langemarck 16 August 1917. Transferred to the Class Z Reserve 22 March 1919. 1914-15 Star.

WILSON Private William James 17070. Born at Portadown, County Armagh. Enlisted into the 9th (Service) Battalion in October 1914. To France with 36th (Ulster) Division in October 1915. **Killed in action** during the attack at Hamel 1 July 1916. 1914-15 Star.

WILSON Corporal William John 14767. Born at Richhill, Portadown, County Armagh. Enlisted September 1914. **Killed in action** during the attack at Hamel 1 July 1916, aged 20. 1914-15 Star.

WIMPEY Lance Sergeant Alan Brooke 43372. Commissioned into The London Regiment - see Appendix 5.

WINDER Sergeant John 23303. Born in 1891 at Armagh, County Armagh. A draper. Enlisted in November 1915. Posted to the 9th (Service) Battalion. 'B' Company. **Wounded** at the Battle of Langemarck 16 August 1917.

WINN Private Thomas Henry 43223. Born in 1889 at Nottingham. A tobacco packer. [Enlisted 8 December 1915 into The Sherwood Foresters (Nottinghamshire and Derbyshire Regiment) (42156).] Transferred to Princess Victoria's (Royal Irish Fusiliers) 31 August 1916 having joined the 9th (Service) Battalion on 8 August 1916 (renumbered 43223). 'C' Company. **Wounded** by gunshots to the back and left leg during the Battle of Messines and to hospital 9 June 1917. Treated at 1st Southern General Hospital, Birmingham. Discharged as no longer physically fit for war service due to wounds 17 September 1918. Silver War Badge, number B250. Died at Nottingham in 1959, aged 70.

WITHERS Private William John 24726 & 28900. Born in 1896 at Milford, County Armagh. A weaver. Enlisted 20 August 1916 and joined the 10th (Reserve) Battalion (24726). Discharged as not being likely to become an efficient soldier in that he was considered medically unfit for service (haemorrhage of the lung) 7 September 1916. Enlisted again in November 1917 (renumbered 28900). Joined the 9th (North Irish Horse) Battalion end-April/early-May 1918. **Wounded** by shellfire near Wieltje in the period 23-27 May 1918 and **died of wounds** on 27 May 1918.

WOLFE Lance Corporal George Hendren 23946. (Incorrectly spelled as WALFE on his medal index card.) Born in 1897 at County Armagh. From Cabra, Kingscourt, County Cavan, the son of the gamekeeper on the estate of Major A C Pratt. Enlisted 8 February 1916. Posted to the 9th (Service) Battalion. Discharged as no longer physically fit for war service due to sickness (injured spine) 13 December 1917. Silver War Badge, number 285468. He became a gamekeeper for the Northern Ireland Forestry Service at Hillsborough Forest. Died at Draperstown, County Londonderry in 1961, aged 64. Brother of Sergeant Richard John Wolfe.

WOLFE MM Sergeant Richard John 18609. Born 1896 at Markethill, County Armagh. From Cabra, Kingscourt, County Cavan, the son of the gamekeeper on the estate of Major A C Pratt. A gamekeeper on the estate of Lord Inchiquin at Dromoland Castle, County Clare. Enlisted into the 9th (Service) Battalion in April 1915. To France with 36th (Ulster) Division in October 1915. 'C' Company. Unpaid Corporal and Battalion runner during the attack at Hamel on 1 July 1916. Promoted Corporal after the attack at Hamel. **MM** – La Petite Douve Farm raid 12 October 1916. **Wounded**. Returned to the 9th (Service) Battalion in late February 1917. Scout Sergeant. **Killed in action** at the Battle of Langemarck 16 August 1917, aged 21. 1914-15 Star. Brother of Lance Corporal George Hendren Wolfe.

WOODBURNE Private William 41896. Born in 1889 at Belfast. A boot salesman. [Enlisted in August 1914 into the North Irish Horse (979). To France 1 May 1915. Served with 2nd North Irish Horse, X Corps Cavalry Regiment.] Joined the renamed 9th (North Irish Horse) Battalion from 36 Infantry Base Depot and transferred to Princess Victoria's (Royal Irish Fusiliers) in September/October 1917 (renumbered 41896). Transferred to the Class Z Reserve. 1914-15 Star.

WOODCOCK Private John T 40074. Joined the 9th (Service) Battalion, Princess Victoria's (Royal Irish Fusiliers) with the draft of men from The Prince of Wales's Own (West Yorkshire Regiment) on 12 December 1916. [Transferred to the Labour Corps (renumbered 410548). Transferred to The Worcestershire Regiment (renumbered 64842).]

WOODCOCK Private John 42251 & 7042180. From Rochdale, Lancashire. Worked in a cotton factory. [Enlisted 12 December 1914 into the Army Service Corps (T/37746). To France 28 July 1915. Served with 37th Division Train.] Transferred to Princess Victoria's (Royal Irish Fusiliers) 8 May 1918 (renumbered 42251) and joined the 9th (North Irish Horse) Battalion. Wounded by gunshots to the thigh, knee and neck 22 September 1918 and evacuated to hospital in England. 1914-15 Star. Transferred to the Section B Army Reserve, Princess Victoria's (Royal Irish Fusiliers) (renumbered 7042180). Discharged 20 December 1926.

WOODEND Private Arthur 24741. Born in 1897 at Castledawson, County Londonderry. A beetler in a linen mill. Enlisted 12 November 1914, aged 17 into the 10th (Service) Battalion, The Royal Inniskilling Fusiliers (Derry) (19173). Discharged 10 March 1915 having made a mis-statement as to age on enlistment. Enlisted in August 1916 and joined the 10th (Reserve) Battalion, Princess Victoria's (Royal Irish Fusiliers) (renumbered 24741). Posted to the 9th (Service) Battalion. 'C' Company. **Wounded** at the Battle of Langemarck 16 August 1917.

WOODHEAD Private Arthur 42255. [Enlisted into the Army Service Corps (T/308313). Served with 4th Reserve Park.] Transferred to Princess Victoria's (Royal Irish Fusiliers) 8 May 1918 (renumbered 42255) and joined the 9th (North Irish Horse) Battalion.

WOODHEAD Private Fred 40035. Born at Leeds. [Enlisted into The Prince of Wales's Own (West Yorkshire Regiment) (36088).] Transferred to Princess Victoria's (Royal Irish Fusiliers) 30 November 1916 (renumbered 40035) and joined the 9th (Service) Battalion 12 December 1916. 'C' Company. **Missing** at the Battle of Langemarck 16 August 1917 and later declared **killed in action** on that date.

WOODRUFF Corporal Robert 42138. Born in 1887 at Rochdale, Lancashire. [Enlisted into the Army Service Corps (S4/011828 Acting Corporal). To France 17 December 1915.] Transferred to Princess Victoria's (Royal Irish Fusiliers) 8 May 1918 (renumbered 42138) and joined the 9th (North Irish Horse) Battalion. [Part of the draft transferred on 19 June 1918 to The Royal Irish Rifles (renumbered 45853). Posted to the 1st Battalion, The Royal Irish Rifles. **Died of wounds** 21 October 1918.] 1914-14 Star. Harlebeke New British Cemetery. VIII. A. 2.

WOODS Private Arnold 14754. Enlisted September 1914. [Transferred to the Army Service Corps (renumbered M/354540).] Transferred to the Class Z Reserve. 1914-15 Star. Served with the Ulster Special Constabulary. His brother, Private John Woods, died of influenza on 11 January 1919 at Bonn, Germany while serving with the 3rd Canadian Battalion (Toronto Regiment), Canadian Infantry.

WOODS Lance Corporal David 17662. From Portadown, County Armagh. Enlisted into the 9th (Service) Battalion in December 1914/January 1915. To France with 36th (Ulster) Division in October 1915. 'A' Company. **Wounded** at Hamel and **died of wounds** 1 July 1916, aged 23. 1914-15 Star.

WOODS Private Frederick 14760. Enlisted September 1914. Discharged as no longer physically fit for war service due to sickness 28 June 1915, aged 27. Silver War Badge, number 508797.

WOODS Lance Corporal Frederick James 14796. From Derrybroughes, Portadown, County Armagh. 4th (Portadown) Battalion, Armagh Regiment, Ulster Volunteer Force. A clerk at Parkside Weaving Company. Enlisted September 1914. 'D' Company. **Killed in action** during the attack at Hamel 1 July 1916, aged 24. 1914-15 Star.

WOODS Private John Robb 16145. Born 21 November 1895 at Maguiresbridge, County Fermanagh. A grocer's assistant. Enlisted into the 9th (Service) Battalion in October 1914. To France with 36th (Ulster) Division in October 1915. [Joined 108th Brigade Machine Gun Company January 1916. Transferred to the Machine Gun Corps (renumbered 17808). **Killed in action** with 36th Battalion, Machine Gun Corps 31 May 1918, aged 22, while bringing supplies forward.] 1914-15 Star.

WOODS Private Joshua 19809. Born at Milltown, County Armagh. Enlisted into the 9th (Service) Battalion in May 1915. To France with 36th (Ulster) Division in October 1915. 'C' Company. **Killed in action** during the attack at Hamel 1 July 1916. 1914-15 Star.

WOODS Private Thomas 14751. Born in 1869 in Seagoe, County Armagh. Having served in the 3rd Battalion (Militia), Princess Victoria's (Royal Irish Fusiliers) he enlisted for regular service on 6 December 1886 (2490). Served in India from 11 December 1888 to 13 May 1894. Transferred to the Army Reserve 9 April 1894. Served in South Africa with the 2nd Battalion, Princess Victoria's (Royal Irish Fusiliers) 6 April 1900 to 13 April 1901. Queen's South Africa Medal. Served again in South Africa from 14 April 1902. Transferred to the Army Reserve 9 March 1903. Joined the Royal Garrison Regiment on 25 January 1904 (renumbered 7859 Private). Served in Malta and South Africa. Reenlisted into Princess Victoria's (Royal Irish Fusiliers) 13 October 1905 (renumbered 8999 Private). Discharged after fourteen years colour service 30 June 1907. Worked as a postman. Reenlisted 21 September 1914 and joined the 9th (Service) Battalion. Posted to the 10th (Reserve) Battalion 23 September 1915. Posted to the 1st Garrison Battalion 7 October 1915. Served in India from 12 February 1916 to 11 November 1917. Discharged as no longer physically fit for war service due to sickness 27 February 1918. Silver War Badge, number 334286.

WOODS Private Thomas 15872. From Portadown, County Armagh. Enlisted into the 9th (Service) Battalion in October 1914. To France with 36th (Ulster) Division in October 1915. **Wounded** during the attack at Hamel 1 July 1916. Transferred to the Class Z Reserve 20 March 1919. 1914-15 Star.

WOODS Lance Corporal William John 18649. From Portadown, County Armagh. Enlisted into the 9th (Service) Battalion in April 1915. **Wounded** during the attack at Hamel 1 July 1916.

WOOLLETT Warrant Officer Class II John C 15716. Enlisted 12 September 1914. Posted to the 9th (Service) Battalion as a Sergeant. [Served with the Reserve Company until September 1915 when he was promoted to Warrant Officer Class II and appointed as Regimental Quartermaster Sergeant of the 10th (Reserve) Battalion. Did not serve overseas. Discharged as no longer physically fit for war service due to sickness 10 March 1917.] Silver War Badge, number 146241.

WOOLF Private Joseph 43389. Born at Kimberley, South Africa. A tailor in London. [Enlisted 28 January 1916 and transferred to the Army Reserve. Mobilised 29 May 1916 and joined the 3/9th Battalion, The London Regiment.] To France 8 November 1916. Attached to the 9th (Service) Battalion, Princess Victoria's (Royal Irish Fusiliers) 26 November 1916. Renumbered 392574, The London Regiment in March 1917. Discharged from the Territorial Force, re-enlisted and transferred to Princess Victoria's (Royal Irish Fusiliers) 10 May 1917 (renumbered 43389). **Wounded** by gunshots to the face and leg at the Battle of Langemarck 16 August 1917 and **died of wounds** in 3rd Australian Casualty Clearing Station 21 August 1917, aged 25.

WOOLFORD Private Harold Edwin 42250. Born in 1892 at Camden Town, London. [Enlisted into the Army Service Corps (T4/084736) 3 April 1915. To France 28 July 1915. Served with 37th Division Train. His wife deserted their children in January 1917 and disappeared.] Transferred to Princess Victoria's (Royal Irish Fusiliers) 8 May 1918 (renumbered 42250) and joined the 9th (North Irish Horse) Battalion. He spent his last leave with his children in late-July/early-August 1918. **Killed in action** during the attack south of Wulverghem 4 September 1918. 1914-15 Star.

WOOLSEY Private Robert 14756. Enlisted September 1914. Discharged as no longer physically fit for war service due to sickness 4 December 1917, aged 32. Silver War Badge, number 274444. 1914-15 Star.

WORRALL Private Richard Arthur 42484. Born at Bray, County Wicklow in 1900. From Belfast.

A student. [Enlisted 30 December 1915 into The Royal Inniskilling Fusiliers (28412), aged 15, and joined the 4th (Extra Reserve) Battalion. In August 1916 his uncle wrote and explained that he was under-age and, knowing that he was about to be sent out with a draft, requested that his commanding officer *'keep him back a little longer'*. Transferred to The Royal Irish Rifles (renumbered 22720) 16 May 1918.] Transferred at 'A' Infantry Base Depot to Princess Victoria's (Royal Irish Fusiliers) 14 September 1918 (renumbered 42484) and joined the 9th (North Irish Horse) Battalion 22 September 1918. Transferred to the Class Z Reserve 8 March 1919.

WORTH Private Horace Baden 45800. Born in 1899 at Brixton, London. A clerk. [Enlisted 4 April 1917 and joined 110th Training Reserve Battalion. Transferred to The Queen's (Royal West Surrey Regiment) (66952). Posted to 1/22nd (County of London) Battalion, The London Regiment (The Queen's).] To France and joined 36 Infantry Base Depot 29 March 1918. Transferred to Princess Victoria's (Royal Irish Fusiliers) 2 April 1918 (renumbered 45800) and joined the 9th (North Irish Horse) Battalion 4 April 1918. **Killed in action** by shellfire at Anseghem 26 October 1918, aged 19. He was the last soldier of the 9th Royal Irish Fusiliers to be killed in action.

WORTLEY Private James 24172. Born in 1896 at Derryhale, County Armagh. A farmer's son. Enlisted in April 1916. Posted to the 9th (Service) Battalion. 'B' Company. **Captured** in the period 21-28 March 1918 during the retreat from St Quentin. After the war he lived at Laurelvale, County Armagh and worked for the Great Northern Railway. He died in 1958, aged 62.

WRAY Private Samuel 41265. [Enlisted 27 November 1915 into the North Irish Horse (1986). Served with 2nd North Irish Horse, X Corps Cavalry Regiment.] Joined the renamed 9th (North Irish Horse) Battalion from 36 Infantry Base Depot and transferred to Princess Victoria's (Royal Irish Fusiliers) in September/October 1917 (renumbered 41265). Discharged as no longer physically fit for war service due to sickness 1 July 1918, aged 41. Silver War Badge, number 416894.

WRIGHT Private Albert 43400. [Enlisted 10 December 1915 into The London Regiment (7281). Posted to the 1/9th (County of London) Battalion, The London Regiment (Queen Victoria's Rifles).] Attached to the 9th (Service) Battalion, Princess Victoria's (Royal Irish Fusiliers) 26 November 1916. Discharged from the Territorial Force, re-enlisted and transferred to Princess Victoria's (Royal Irish Fusiliers) in March/April 1917 (renumbered 43400). [Posted to the 1st Battalion. **Wounded**. Discharged as no longer physically fit for war service due to wounds 27 February 1919. Silver War Badge, number B154116.]

WRIGHT Private Alexander 14779. From Lurgan, County Armagh. Enlisted September 1914. 'C' Company. Battalion shoemaker. Transferred to the Class Z Reserve 22 March 1919. 1914-15 Star.

WRIGHT Private Charles Henry 43234. From Chesterfield, Derbyshire. [Served previously with the 1st Battalion, The Sherwood Foresters (Nottinghamshire and Derbyshire Regiment) (15178).] Transferred to Princess Victoria's (Royal Irish Fusiliers) 31 August 1916 (renumbered 43234) having joined the 9th (Service) Battalion on 8 August 1916. 'B' Company. **Wounded** at the Battle of Langemarck 16 August 1917. Transferred to the Class Z Reserve 28 February 1919. 1914-15 Star.

WRIGHT Lance Corporal Henry 43371. [Enlisted into The London Regiment. Posted to 1/7th (City of London) Battalion, The London Regiment (6808 Sergeant).] Attached to the 9th (Service) Battalion, Princess Victoria's (Royal Irish Fusiliers) 26 November 1916. Discharged from the Territorial Force, re-enlisted and transferred to Princess Victoria's (Royal Irish Fusiliers) in March/April 1917 (renumbered 43371).

WRIGHT Private James 24071. Born in 1884 at Lurgan, County Armagh. Enlisted in February 1916. Posted to the 9th (Service) Battalion. 'C' Company. **Missing** at the Battle of Langemarck 16 August 1917 and later declared **killed in action** on that date, aged 32. His brother, Private John Wright, was captured serving with the 1st Battalion.

WRIGHT Private John 14788. From Portadown, County Armagh. To France 4 October 1915. **Wounded** during the attack at Hamel 1 July 1916. [Transferred to the Labour Corps (renumbered 399907).] 1914-15 Star. Transferred to the Class Z Reserve 3 April 1919.

WRIGHT Lance Corporal Marshall 22990. From Irwin Street, Portadown, County Armagh. Enlisted in November 1915. Posted to the 9th (Service) Battalion. Originally reported as **wounded** during the attack at Vijfwegen on 30 September or 1 October 1918, he was recorded as **killed in action** 3 October 1918, aged 28.

WRIGHT Private Nicholas 42216. Born at Normanton, West Yorkshire. [Enlisted 25 September 1914 into the 13th (Service) Battalion, The York and Lancaster Regiment (1st Barnsley) (678) - The Barnsley Pals. To Egypt 8 January 1916 and to France March 1916. **Wounded** accidentally by a bayonet in the right thigh 26 May 1916 while cleaning his equipment. **Wounded** by gunshots to both legs 3 May 1917 and evacuated to hospital in England 15 May 1917. Treated at the County of Middlesex War Hospital, St Albans. Joined the 3rd (Reserve) Battalion, The York and Lancaster Regiment 16 July 1917. Sentenced to ten days confined to barracks for being absent from 25 January 1918 to 4 February 1918 when travelling to Army Service Corps, Park Royal. Transferred to the Army Service Corps (renumbered T/387023) 5 February 1918.] To France 18 April 1918. Transferred to Princess Victoria's (Royal Irish Fusiliers) 8 May 1918 (renumbered 42216) and joined the 9th (North Irish Horse) Battalion. **Killed in action** during the attack south of Wulverghem 4 September 1918.

WRIGHT Private Robert 18059. From Annaghmore, Portadown, County Armagh. Enlisted into the 9th (Service) Battalion in February 1915. To France with 36th (Ulster) Division in October 1915. 'C' Company. **Killed in action** during the attack at Hamel 1 July 1916, aged 20. 1914-15 Star.

WRIGHT Private Robert Henry 16142. Born in 1894 at County Armagh. Lived at Castleshane, County Monaghan. Enlisted into the 9th (Service) Battalion on 25 September 1914. To France with 36th (Ulster) Division in October 1915. 'D' Company. **Wounded** at the Battle of Langemarck 16 August 1917. Discharged as no longer physically fit for war service due to wounds 11 February 1919. Silver War Badge, number B140384. 1914-15 Star.

WRIGHT Private Sydney George 43361. Born at Bermondsey, Surrey. [Enlisted into The London Regiment. Posted to 1/7th (City of London) Battalion, The London Regiment.] Attached to the 9th (Service) Battalion, Princess Victoria's (Royal Irish Fusiliers) 26 November 1916. 'C' Company. Renumbered 353151, The London Regiment in March 1917. Discharged from the Territorial Force, re-enlisted and transferred to Princess Victoria's (Royal Irish Fusiliers) in March/April 1917 (renumbered 43361). **Killed in action** 29 March 1918 during the retreat from St Quentin.

WRIGHT Private Thomas 14769. Born in 1897 at Belfast. From Armagh, County Armagh. Enlisted September 1914. 'A' Company. **Wounded** during the attack at Hamel 1 July 1916. **Wounded** at the Battle of Langemarck 16 August 1917. [Posted to the 1st Battalion. **Wounded**.] Discharged as no longer physically fit for war service due to wounds 22 March 1919. Silver War Badge, number B167268. 1914-15 Star.

WRIGHT Private Thomas 27686. Enlisted 2 December 1915. Served elsewhere before being transferred to Princess Victoria's (Royal Irish Fusiliers) in June 1917. Posted to the 9th (North Irish Horse) Battalion. Discharged as no longer physically fit for war service due to sickness 8 August 1918, aged 34. Silver War Badge, number 434652.

WRIGHT Private William 41368. [Enlisted in December 1916 into the North Irish Horse (2328). Served with 2nd North Irish Horse, X Corps Cavalry Regiment.] Joined the renamed 9th (North Irish Horse) Battalion from 36 Infantry Base Depot and transferred to Princess Victoria's (Royal Irish Fusiliers) in September/October 1917 (renumbered 41368).

WYLIE Private George 42475. [Served previously with The Royal Irish Rifles (21953).] Transferred at the Base Depot to Princess Victoria's (Royal Irish Fusiliers) 14 September 1918 (renumbered 42475) and joined the 9th (North Irish Horse) Battalion 22 September 1918. [Transferred to 5th (Service) Battalion, The Royal Irish Regiment (Pioneers) in the Light Division in the British Army of the Rhine in March/June 1919 (renumbered 41385).]

WYLIE Private William J 19907. From Portadown, County Armagh. Enlisted into the 9th (Service) Battalion in May 1915. To France with 36th (Ulster) Division in October 1915. 'C' Company. **Wounded**, shell shock at Hamel 24 June 1916. [Transferred to the Labour Corps (renumbered 231632).] Transferred to the Class Z Reserve 23 April 1919. 1914-15 Star.

WYLIE Private William Samuel 18104. From Derrymacfall, Portadown, County Armagh. Enlisted into the 9th (Service) Battalion in February 1915. To France with 36th (Ulster) Division in October 1915. 'C' Company. Bombing team during the attack at Hamel 1 July 1916, when he was **killed in action**. 1914-15 Star.

YEATES Private James 14817. Enlisted September 1914. Transferred to the Class Z Reserve 20 March 1919. 1914-15 Star.

YEMAN Sergeant James William 14816. Born in 1895 at Portadown, County Armagh. A linen weaver. Enlisted September 1914. 'B' Company. **Wounded** at the Battle of Langemarck 16 August 1917. Transferred to the Class Z Reserve 24 May 1919. 1914-15 Star.

YOUNG Corporal Sidney Gilbert 43429. Born in 1891. A groom from Kinson, Bournemouth, Dorset. [Enlisted 9 July 1915 into the 7th (Service) Battalion, The Royal Irish Rifles (8390). To France with 48th Brigade, 16th (Irish) Division 19 December 1915. Lance Corporal 5 March 1916. Corporal 16 June 1916. **Wounded** by a gunshot to the left hand 31 July 1916. Evacuated to hospital in England 5 August 1916. Treated at Northamptonshire War Hospital, Northampton. Discharged from hospital 29 September 1916 and posted to the Depot. Reprimanded twice for overstaying leave and failing to salute an officer. Posted to the 4th (Extra Reserve) Battalion, The Royal Irish Rifles 26 January 1917. To 16 Infantry Base Depot 4 May 1917 and to hospital (venereal disease) 15 June to 9 August 1917. Rejoined the 7th (Service) Battalion, The Royal Irish Rifles 28 August 1917. To 36 Infantry Base Depot 24 November 1917 and transferred to Princess Victoria's (Royal Irish Fusiliers) (renumbered 43429). Posted to the 7th/8th (Service) Battalion in 49th Brigade, 16th (Irish) Division (probably did not join).] Joined the 9th (North Irish Horse) Battalion when the 7th/8th (Service) Battalion was disbanded in February 1918. **Wounded** by a gunshot to the left thigh 12 April 1918 in the actions between Wulverghem and Kemmel and evacuated to hospital in England 16 April 1918. Treated at 3rd Northern General Hospital, Sheffield. Returned to France 8 September 1918 and rejoined the 9th (North Irish Horse) Battalion on 23 September 1918. **Wounded** by shrapnel to the chest at Anseghem on 26 October 1918 and **died of wounds** in 8th Stationary Hospital on 8 November 1918, aged 27. 1914-15 Star.

YOUNG Private William 27669. Enlisted 1 June 1917. Posted to the 9th (North Irish Horse) Battalion. **Wounded**. Discharged as no longer physically fit for war service due to wounds 8 October 1918. Silver War Badge, number B41678.

YOUNG Lance Corporal William 42145. [Enlisted into the Army Service Corps (S4/126102). Served with 7th Field Bakery.] Transferred to Princess Victoria's (Royal Irish Fusiliers) 8 May 1918 (renumbered 42145) and joined the 9th (North Irish Horse) Battalion. Transferred to the Class Z Reserve 10 February 1919. 1914-15 Star.

ZEBEDEE Private Thomas Edward 42258. Born in 1895. A postman. Enlisted into the Army Service Corps on 23 July 1915 (T/245006). Served with 12th Division Train.] Transferred to Princess Victoria's (Royal Irish Fusiliers) 8 May 1918 (renumbered 42258) and joined the 9th (North Irish Horse) Battalion. Injured when moving into the line on 22 August 1918 when he fell and broke his right leg. Treated at the Royal Victoria Hospital, Netley. Discharged from hospital to the Irish Command Depot in November 1918. Transferred to the Class Z Reserve 29 January 1919. Lived in Lyndhurst, Hampshire. Died in 1968, aged 73.

Transferred Men (the number in brackets is the number allocated on transfer)

108th Brigade Machine Gun Company - January 1916

BROWN Sergeant William John 15859 (17775)
CHRISTIE Private James 14124 (17785)
CLOUGHLEY Private Robert 14076 (17782)
CLOW Private James Moncrief 14085 (17781)
COURTNEY Private John 14123 (17783)
FITZSIMONS Private James 14176 (17787)
FORBES Private Cecil 17452. (17786)
FOX Private Simpson Walker 14185 (17790)
FULTON Private Richard 14269 (17788)
GILKINSON Private Edward 14231 (17789)
HALL Private Robert 16107 (17793)
HIGGINS Private Henry 14278 (17792)

HILL Private Robert J 14266 (17791)
IRVINE Private Carson 14073 (17780)
LESTER Private Robert 14415 (17794)
McCULLAGH Private Robert 20363 (17800)
McDOWELL Private John 14538 (17797)
McILRATH Private Robert Allen 16126 (17798)
McKELVEY Private Thomas 14501 (17799)
MALLOY Private Francis 14467 (17795)
MILLS Private Samuel 14476 (17801)
MURPHY Private Joseph 17402 (17796)
ORR Corporal David 14592 (17778)
RAE Private George 20326 (17802)
ROBINSON Private George 14641 (17777)
SEYTON Private William 14697 (17804)
SIMPSON Private James 14709 (17803)
TRUEMAN Private Frank 14736 (17805)
UPRICHARD Private William Henry 14738 (17806)
WALKER Lance Corporal Howard P T 14785 (17807)
WARREN Sergeant William 14182 (17776)
WOODS Private John Robb 16145 (17808)

Tank Corps - **December 1917**

AVERELL Private Andrew 41584 (304875)
AVERELL MM Private Robert 41534 (304872)
BELL Private Edwin Victor 41190 (304883)
BRIGGS Corporal Isaac Alexander 24781 (304861)
BUCHANAN Private James Allen 41201 (304880)
BURKE Private William 41465 (304852)
CASSIDY Private Robert 41290 (304846)
CHESTNUT Private Thomas 41242 (304877)
CLAY Private George Robert 21756 (304848)
COCHRANE Private George 41248 (304864)
COLLIN Private John Benjamin 43377 (304856)
CROOKS Private William 41257 (304869)
FLANAGAN Private Richard 41604 (304866)
HALL Private Robert 41516 (304851)
HANLON Private Joshua 23920 (304874)
HEATHFIELD Private William 43249 (304850)
HIND Private John Henry 43199 (304858)
IRWIN Sergeant Robert 41560 (304845)
JENNINGS Private Rowan 14360 (304860)
KERR Private William 41301 (304863)
LUCAS Private Joseph 41238 (304878)
MAGILL Private Charles 41592 (304865)

MARTIN Private William 41180 (304871)
McDOWELL Private William F 41524 (304868)
MILLAR Private James 41228 (304898)
MOORHEAD Private Robert Andrew 14442 (304862)
MORAN Private Richard 41305 (304849)
PEARSON Private Robert 43225 (304855)
PIERPOINT Private Samuel 43254 (304853)
ROULSTON Private Willie 41261 (304847)
ROWNTREE Private Robert 14644 (304873)
SCOTT Private William J 20068 (304857)
SEAMAN Lance Corporal Robert John 41186 (304870)
SHAW Private Joseph 41582 (304867)
SHIELDS Private William 14669 (304859)
TOBIN Private Peter 41557 (304876)
WARWICK Private John Alex 41397 (304879)
WHITESIDE Lance Corporal James Bryson 41583 (304854)
WILSON Private Ernest 41197 (304882)

The Royal Irish Rifles - June 1918

GIBSON Private Henry 42162 (45865)
HAYNES Private William 42164 (45854)
JARVIS Corporal William 42159 (45851)
JEANS Sergeant Jesse Cornelius 42079 (45852)
KNOWLES Corporal Arthur 42080 (45850)
McCLURE Private Edward 41284 (45841)
NORRIS Private William C 42185 (45866)
ORR Private Alexander 14593 (45839)
PARFETT Private Herbert 42186 (45856)
SADLER Corporal James William 42134 (45847)
SHARPE Corporal Charles Thomas Wilkinson 42132 (45849)
SIMPSON Corporal David 42176 (45868)
SIMPSON Corporal Henry 42170 (45863)
TICKNER Corporal George 42135 (45848)
TREASURE Corporal Bernard Henry George 42136 (45855)
WOODRUFF Corporal Robert 42138 (45853)

The Royal Irish Regiment - 1919

ADAIR Private Robert 42547 (41255)
BARLOW Private Arthur 45809 (41258)
BEAMISH Private John Joseph 42514 (41395)
BOWERS Private John 27903 (41261)
BRADFORD Private Charles 45763 (41264)
BRIGGS Private Robert J 24726 (41155)
CHAMBERS Private David 41452 (41271)

CRUTE Private Edwin Webber 43375 (41274)
CURRY Private Robert 20318 (41275)
DAVIS Private James E 42458 (41278)
DYAS Private Walter Ernest 42225 (41280)
DYE Private William J 45760 (41281)
EDEN Private Wilfred J 42229 (41282)
FINCHAM Private George W 42102 (41284)
FOGG Private Sidney Fogg 43208 (41289)
FOWLER Private William E 45786 (41290)
FRANCE Private John A 42122 (41286)
FREAR Sergeant George 40062 (41287)
GOODFELLOW Private William G 18067 (41293)
GORMAN Private William 42561 (41294)
GRAHAM Private Thomas R 42512 (41413)
GREEN Private Albert V J 43475 (41296)
HARRIS Private Arthur M 42287 (41302)
HASLETT Private Frederick J 45790 (41304)
HAWTHORNE Private Thomas Charles 41432 (41305)
HOMERSHAM DCM, MM* Sergeant Francis Stanhope 45807 (41301)
IRVINE Private Kennedy 42530 (41308)
JULIAN Private John W 45787 (41310)
KEENAN Private John Francis 42549 (41311)
KIDBY Private Herbert 42446 (41312)
LACEY Corporal John W 24817 (41313)
LAVERTY Private Alexander 42485 (41411)
LEANEY Corporal Reginald Alfred 23877 (41315)
LORIMER Private John 41343 (41317)
LYMER Private Frank 42238 (41318)
MAGUIRE Sergeant Leslie 18245 (41321)
McGRORY Private Michael 42544 (41338)
McMENAMIN Private James 42537 (41339)
McQUADE Private Thomas 42570 (41344)
McSTAY Corporal James 24698 (41341)
MILLER Private Samuel 41437 (41328)
MILLICENT Private Alfred 42428 (41327)
MOORHEAD MM Sergeant William 14482 (41329)
MORRISON Private George 18251 (41331)
MORRISON Private Henry 42525 (41332)
NELSON Private James 14586 (41346)
NELSON Private William A 41258 (41347)
NICOL Private John 42209 (41345)
OGLESBY Private David 42516 (41348)
PERERA Private William 45814 (35549)
PICKERING Private George William 43214 (41352)
POWELL Private Lewis J 42275 (41354)

PRITCHARD Lance Corporal Charles Henry 19066 (41353)
PYANOWSKI Private Mat J 43314 (41291)
QUINN Private Joseph 42507 (41355)
RANDALL Private Herbert 45806 (41356)
REID Lance Corporal Percival Henry A 41548 (41357)
RICH Private Albert 42115 (41359)
SAUNDERS Private George W 42568 (41361)
SCOTT Private John W 42111 (41362)
SINGLETON Private Joseph 42452 (41364)
SMYTH Private William M 42553 (41366)
SPENCE Private Robert 49747 (41367)
STEVENS Private Samuel W 43224 (41370)
STEWART Private Frederick 20352 (41369)
VERNON Privatc John Gcorgc 43235 (41375)
WATERWORTH Private Charles 42203 (41380)
WEIR Private Isaac 33861 (41382)
WYLIE Private George 42475 (41385)

Regular Army Re-enlistments - **Princess Victoria's (Royal Irish Fusiliers)**
(the number in brackets is the number issued on re-enlistment)

ALLEN Sergeant William 25050 (7040775)
BAILLIE Private James 24627 (7040751)
BALLENTINE Private Daniel 41545 (7042140)
BARKLEY Private Patrick 20925 (33315 & 7041506)
BLACK Sergeant James 14045 (33638 & 7041723)
BLAIR Private Michael 19981 (33700 & 7041767)
BOWERS Private John 27903 (33767 & 7041816)
BOYCE Lance Corporal David 22888 (7040715)
BRIGGS Private Charles 24262 (7040740)
BROWN Corporal Jacob 14038 (32875 & 7041163)
BRYANS Private David Frederick 14044 (7042223)
CALLAN Private James 24541 (31747 & 7041752).
CARBERRY Private Patrick 13454 (33241 & 7041446)
CARROLL Private John 27856 (33102 & 7041336)
CHAMBERS Private James Andrew 22623 (33416 & 7041579)
CLAY Private George Robert 21756 (33218 & 7041429)
CONNOR Private Michael Patrick 42566 (7042208)
CONWAY Private John 41486 (33956 & 7041937)
CRAIG Private John 41377 (7042137)
CRILLY Private Alexander 14078 (33685 & 7041758)
CUNNINGHAM Private Daniel 42527 (7042389)
DICKSON Sergeant Thomas Robert 41120 (7042386)
DILLON Private John Charles 23625 (34073).
DOBSON Private Oswald 40060 (7042127)

DONALDSON Private Joseph 10707 (Regular soldier renumbered 7040376)
EGAN Private John 16217 (7042306)
FLAHERTY Private Patrick 7487 (7040012)
FLEMING Sergeant Patrick 7839 (Regular soldier 7040119)
GALBRAITH Private Joseph 42571 (33607, **deserted**)
GILLAN MM Warrant Officer Class II Thomas F 9458 (Regular soldier renumbered 7040186)
GIRVAN Private Robert James 19762 (33969 & 7041947)
GRAY Warrant Officer Class II William 14202. (7040580)
HALL Private Robert 21652 (33331, **deserted**)
HAMMERSLEY Sergeant Harold William 27840 (7042315)
HANNA Private William 42524 (33418 & 7041580)
HARE Sergeant Thomas 14286 (7040581)
HARTE Private Dominick 20689 (33964 & 7041944)
HARTLEY Private James Clegg 45793 (7042238)
HICKIE Warrant Officer Class I Henry 42574 (7042209)
HOGG Private Henry 27613 (7040809)
HOOPER Corporal Arthur Montague 16150 (7040590)
HORNER Private William Robert 27754 (7040817)
HUGHES Private James 42460 (7042200)
HUTTON Private Joseph 23651 (7042511)
IRWIN Private Richard 18241 (34083 & 7042031)
JOHNSTON Private William 14464 (33274 & 7041472)
JOURNET Sergeant C 43427 (7042216)
KEASKIN Private James 17376 (7040600)
KENNEDY Lance Corporal Robert 21079 (33311 & 7041504)
KENNEDY Private William 41442 (7042139)
KNIGHT Lance Sergeant William George Thomas 10461 (7040311)
LAMB Private Jackson 22141 (7040678)
LIVINGSTON Warrant Officer Class II Samuel James 8489 (Regular soldier renumbered 7040141)
MAGUIRE Private James 15127 (33329 & 7041518)
MALLON Lance Corporal James 3919 (7040047)
MATHERS Private William 42517 (7042204)
McALLISTER Private Edward 24119 (33734 & 7041797)
McANESPIE Private Harry 24744 (32982)
McAVOY Private William Robert 42463 (33566)
McCAIRNS Private David 33004 (33004 & 7041257)
McCAUSLAND Lance Corporal Joseph Ernest 42562 (7042206)
McCLEAN Private Thomas James 24723 (33965, **deserted**)
McCLELLAND Private Richard 42563 (7042207)
McCONNELL Private Robert 42564 (33495 & 7041633)
McCONVILLE Private Edward 3885 (7040044)
McDAID Private James 21010 (7040671)
McDONNELL Private James 42522 (7042205)
McKEOWN Private Frederick Victor 21681 (7042184)
McKNIGHT Private Alexander 29589 (7040893)

McLAVERTY Corporal William 24758 (33368 & 7041548)
MEGARITY Lance Corporal Jackson 23727 (7040726)
MOONEY Sergeant James 3868 (7040041)
MOORE MBE Warrant Officer Class II Alfred 14436 (33502 & 7041638)
MOORE Lance Corporal William 15418 (7040586)
MORAN MM Private John 8895 (33070 & 7041310)
MORROW Lance Corporal William 18660 (7040624)
NEESON MM Private John 22735 (33830 & 7041845)
NEVILLE Private William 29537 (34021 & 7041985)
O'NEILL Corporal Charles Bernard 18532 (7042308)
PATTERSON Private William 14614 (7040582)
QUINN Private George 7426 (32920)
QUINN Private William Stanley 29588 (7040892)
RAFFERTY Private Thomas 21283 (7040672)
REYNOLDS Lance Corporal William 14643 (7040583)
RICHARDSON Private George 23352 (34060 & 7042014)
SCOTT Corporal Eric John 11345 (7042303)
SCOTT Private Thomas 18749 (7040626)
STEELE Company Quartermaster Sergeant Douglas William John 27510 (7040804)
STEELE Lance Corporal Thomas 14848 (33478 & 7041622)
STOTT Private Samuel Robert 17393 (33186 & 7041402)
SUMMERVILLE Private Edward 29538 (7040866)
TAYLOR Private William 49740 (7042240)
VENNARD Private Robert 29552 (7040888)
VENNARD DCM Warrant Officer Class II Thomas Glennie 14746 (33362 & 7041542)
WALLS Private Patrick 13493 (32902)
WATSON Private Joseph 27724 (7040815)
WATSON Private William 14776 (7040584)
WEIR Private Isaac 33861 (33861 & 7041870)
WHITE Private John 21041 (33309 & 7041502)
WILLIAMS MM Warrant Officer Class I George Alfred 9428 (Regular soldier renumbered 7040183)
WILSON Private Cornelius 27726 (33301 & 7041497)
WILSON Private Edward 17658 (33896 & 7041891)
WILSON Lance Corporal Frederick J 41116 (Regular soldier renumbered 7042134)
WILSON Private William James 5898 (7040062)

Regular Army Re-enlistments – Other Regiments
(the number in brackets is the number issued on re-enlistment)

3rd (Prince of Wales's) Dragoon Guards
HACK Private Victor 41079 (34450 & 392549)

Corps of Royal Engineers
GOODFELLOW Private William G 18067 (2206222)

The King's Own (Royal Lancaster Regiment)
FAULKNER Private Thomas 14187 (3702179).

The Norfolk Regiment
BAIRD Sergeant Thomas Henry 5581 (72973 & 5765352)

The Suffolk Regiment
LARTER Private Arthur W 45810 (70977 & 5820964)

The Bedfordshire & Hertfordshire Regiment
JACKSON Sergeant Francis P 22282 (42856 & 5943565)

The Leicestershire Regiment
HUSTWAYTE Private Frank 43263 (4848898)

The Royal Irish Regiment
PERERA Private William 45814 (7110732)

The Cameronians (Scottish Rifles)
WARDEN Private William 42489 (44906)

The Royal Inniskilling Fusiliers
ANDERSON MM Private James 49974 (28922)
HIGGINS Private David 14330
HOYNES Private Daniel 40169 (6974375)

The Hampshire Regiment
HOLLAND Corporal Thomas H 14320

The Middlesex Regiment
WILSON Samuel J 14752 (G/107407)

The York and Lancaster Regiment
CLAYTON Private Arthur Victor 40008 (52759 & 4736687)

Seaforth Highlanders (Ross-shire Buffs, The Duke of Albany's)
McATEER Private Thomas W 23080 (32898 & 2811432)
McKENZIE Private John 41172 (32266 & 2811007)

The Royal Irish Rifles
IRWIN Private John 42477 (25722 & 7007303)

The Connaught Rangers
DOYLE Corporal Edward 18643 (40098)

The Royal Dublin Fusiliers
MURRAY Private Patrick 22898 (33174)

The Rifle Brigade (The Prince Consort's Own)
TUPMAN Private Arthur E 42450 (39473 & 6908100)

Royal Army Service Corps
TROTTER Private Samuel 14718 (M/16492)

Royal Army Medical Corps
RADFORD Private William Edward 43217 (207036)

Regiment not known
TILSON Lance Corporal Cecil Armytage 41224

Appendix 7

Operation Orders

Operation orders produced at battalion level were usually written by the Adjutant on behalf of the Commanding Officer. Some were written by the officer charged with a particular operation, such as a raid. All were issued under the name of the Commanding Officer or the officer acting in his absence. There was no single format for orders:

> *'Definite rules as to the form in which operation orders should be drafted are not laid down. The object of an operation order is to bring about a course of action in accordance with the intentions of the commander, suited to the situation, and with full co-operation between all arms and units. So long as this object is fulfilled, the form of the order is of little importance.'*
>
> *Field Service Pocket Book, 1914 Chapter III*

It is evident, however, that there was a general standardisation of orders formats as the war progressed.

Unfortunately, there are no original operation orders for the 9th Royal Irish Fusiliers in any surviving records for the period up to March 1918. This includes the attacks on 1 July 1916, 7 June 1917, 16 August 1917 and 22 November 1917, and the raids in November 1916, June 1917 and November 1917. An incomplete transcription of a photocopy, or scan, of a newspaper article that quoted an abridged version of the operation order for 1 July 1916 exists. Due to the number of transcription errors, it is insufficiently authoritative for reproduction.

All of the surviving operation orders produced by the 9th Royal Irish Fusiliers are reproduced below. Although most are for relatively routine actions such as a relief in place or a move between billets, they all give a feel for the planning behind routine activities and operations. The orders replicated here follow the format of the original as closely as possible and reflect the wide variation of abbreviations that were in use:

Battalion & brigade titles: There is a considerable variation in the abbreviations for battalion & brigade titles but all are easily understood; errors have been explained.

100^{x}	100 yards
A.D.S.	Advanced Dressing Station
B.A.B.	Army telephone code
Battn, Bn	Battalion
B.E.F.	British Expeditionary Force
C.F.	Chaplain to the Forces
C.O.	Commanding Officer
C.Q.M.S.	Company Quartermaster Sergeant
E.A.	Enemy Aircraft
F.O.O.	Forward Observation Officer
G.S.	General Service
Hd. Qrs./H.Q.	Headquarters
L.T.M.	Light Trench Mortar
M.G.	Machine Gun
M.O.	Medical Officer
N.C.O.	Non-commissioned Officer
O.C.	Officer Commanding
O.P.	Observation Post
O.R.	Other Rank
Q.M.	Quartermaster
R.A.P.	Regimental Aid Post
R.E.	Royal Engineers
R.G.	Rifle Grenade
R.S.M.	Regimental Sergeant Major
T.M.B.	Trench Mortar Battery
T.O.	Transport Officer

Relief in Place, 15/16 March 1918

This operation order details the actions required for the relief of 9th Royal Irish Fusiliers by 12th Royal Irish Rifles on the night of 15/16 March 1918, after which the Battalion occupied billets at Garand Seraucourt. This was the last move of the Battalion before the German offensive on 21 March 1918, and it was in these positions that 12th Royal Irish Rifles was destroyed.

No. 25.
OPERATION ORDERS BY
Lieut. Colonel P.E. KELLY.
Commanding 9th (N.I.H.) Bn. The Royal Irish Fusiliers.
B.E.F.

15. 3. 1918.

1. The Battalion will be relieved in the line on night 15th/16th March by 12th Bn. ROYAL IRISH RIFLES.

"A" Coy. will be relieved by "A" Coy. in Right Front.
"C" " " " " "D" " " Left Front.
"D" " " " " "C" " " Counter Attack Line.
"B" " " " " "B" " " Redoubt.

2. One guide per Lewis Gun and Signallers post of "A", "C" & "D" Coys will be at Advanced Battalion H.Q. at 6.30 p.m.

One guide per platoon and Coy. H.Q. from "A", "C" & "D" Coys will be at Advanced Bn. H.Q. at 8 p.m.

Same from "B" Coy. will be at Rear Bn. H.Q. at 7.30 p.m.

3. Transport will be arranged as follows :-
For Rear Bn. H.Q. "B" Coys and M.O's Stores (including Bn. Lewis guns) at Rear Battalion Headquarters about 8 p.m.
For "A", "C" & "D" Coys stores at Advanced Bn. H.Q. about 8.30 p.m. (stores including Battalion Lewis Guns).
One N.C.O. per Company will accompany Lewis Guns.
One Servant per Company and Battalion H.Q. will accompany kits.

4. Sector Defence Schemes, secret maps, aeroplane photographs, patrol and Work Log and Trench Stores will be handed over and receipts obtained, which will be forwarded, in duplicate, to Battalion H.Q. by 12 noon, 16th inst.

5. One Officer and one N.C.O. per Company will parade at Rear Battalion H.Q. 2 p.m. and proceed to GD SERAUCOURT to take over Billets previously occupied.

6. All dugouts will be left in a clean and sanitary condition and certificates to this effect will be obtained and forwarded to Battalion H.Q. by 12 noon, 16th inst.

7. Completion of reliefs will be reported by runner to Rear Bn. H.Q.

8. On Relief, Platoons will move at an interval of not less than 100 yds. to billets at GD SERAUCOURT vacated by 1st Bn. ROYAL IRISH FUSILIERS.

9. Quartermaster will arrange to have blankets sent to Billets.

10. Arrival in Billets will be reported by runner to Battalion H.Q. GD SERAUCOURT.

11. Attention is drawn to orders previously issued regarding procedure in Reserve Area.

12. ACKNOWLEDGE.

R.I. McCRUM, Lieut. A/Adjt.,
9th (N.I.H.) Bn.
Royal Irish Fusiliers

Copies to –

1. Bn. H.Q.	2. O.C. All Companies.	6. T.O. & Q.M.
7. 12th R.I.R.	8. Right Bn.	9. Left Bn.
10. File.		

Relief in Place, 17/18 May 1918

This operation order details the actions required for the relief of 2nd Royal Irish Rifles, 107th Brigade by the 9th Royal Irish Fusiliers on the night of 17/18 May 1918. This was in a sector along the Ypres Canal, near Essex Farm north of the town.

OPERATION ORDER NO 3
by
Major G.M. Forde (M.C.)
Commanding 9th (N.I.H.) Battalion Royal Irish Fusiliers.
B. E. F. 16 May 1918

Reference Sheet 28 N.W. Ed 6b
1/20,000

No.1. The Battalion will relieve the 2nd Royal Irish Rifles in Brigade Reserve in the Front System Left Brigade Sector on the night of 17/18th inst.

No.2. (a) Companies will relieve opposite numbers.

(b) Advance Parties. 1 Officer per Company, 1 N.C.O. per Platoon and 1 N.C.O. from Battalion Headquarters will leave Camp at 4.30pm.

(c) Transport. 1 limber will follow the leading Platoon of each Company for Lewis Guns, Magazines, Camp Kettles and Officers Mess Kit. Limbers will be at STEENJE CAMP at 7 p.m. At 8.30 p.m. 1 G.S. Wagon and 1 Maltese Cart will report at Battalion Headquarters for Mess Kit, Signallers Stores and M.O's Stores.

(d) Blankets. Blankets to be rolled in bundles of 10 and to be clearly marked, to be stacked outside the Guard Room at 10 am.

All Officers Kits etc., for the Q.M. Stores will be stacked in a separate dump outside the Guard Room, at 5 pm. Transport Officer will arrange to collect these as well as Battalion Headquarters kits.

(e) Companies will lead off :-

"C"	Coy.	8.0 pm.
"B"	"	8.15 pm.
"A"	"	8.30 pm.
"D"	"	8.45 pm.
Battn. Hd. Qtrs.		9.0 pm.

3 minutes between Platoons and 200 yards when halted.

(f) Guides. 1 Guide per Platoon and for Battalion Headquarters will be at ESSEX FARM C.25.a.35.85 at 10.30 pm.

(g) Taking over. All trench stores, ammunition and defence schemes, work in progress proposed, will be taken over.

Copies of all stores taken over to be sent to Battalion Headquarters by 12 noon 18th inst.

(h) Relief Complete to be reported by wire in BAB Code and by Runner, who will be retained at Battalion Headquarters over night.

(i) Route - DIRTY BUCKET CORNER – RAILWAY JUNCTION – SIEGE JUNCTION – DAWSONS CORNER – Cross Roads B.29.d.7.5 – ESSEX FARM.

(j) Rations. Rations for "B" & "C" Companies will be sent to ZOUAVE VILLA. Rations for Battalion Headquarters, "A" & "D" Coys will be dumped on the road at a point opposite the small bridge across the Canal, near Battalion Headquarters (about C.25.c.75.60).

(k) Water. Watercart for "B" & "C" Companies ZOUAVE FARM. Battalion Headquarters, "A" & "C" Companies, near C.25.c.75.60.

Watercarts are filled at nights.

No.3 Liaison. 2/Lieut Mateer and 2 Runners from Battalion Headquarters will be attached to the Belgian Battalion Headquarters on the left.

O.C. "C" & "B" Companies will detail 2 good Runners (each) to report to 2/Lieut Mateer at Battalion Headquarters at 9.30 am for Liaison Work.

Instructions will be issued to all Runners on reporting.

Acknowledge.

Issued through Signals at 9pm.

W Sparks
Captain & Adjutant
9th (N.I.H.) Battalion Royal Irish Fusiliers.

16/5/18.

Copy No.1 to O.C. "A" Company.
2 O.C. "B" "
3 O.C. "C" "
4 O.C. "D" "
5 O.C. 2nd Royal Irish Rifles
6 C.O.
7 Q. M & T.O.
8 M.O.

Relief in Place, 23/24 May 1918

This operation order details the actions required for the relief of 12th Royal Irish Rifles by the 9th Royal Irish Fusiliers on the night of 23/24 May 1918 in the sector at Wieltje. This was the Battalion's last deployment in the sectors north of Ypres.

OPERATION ORDER NO. 4
by
Lieut Colonel G.M. Forde., M.C. Commanding
9th (N.I.H.) Battalion Royal Irish Fusiliers.

Reference sheet special. ST JULIAN 6a.

1. The Battalion will relieve the 12th Royal Irish Rifles in the right sub-sector of the front Line, on the night of the 23/24th inst.

2. (a) Companies will relieve like Companies, on relief will be disposed :-

"A" Company – Right Front Line. Hd.Qrs. WIELTJE.
"C' Company and 1 Platoon of "D" Company – Left Front Line.
Hd.Qrs. CALIBAN TR.
"D" Company (minus 1 Platoon) – Counter Attack Company.
Hd.Qrs. about WIELTJE FARM.
"B" Company – Reserve Company. Hd.Qrs. IRISH FARM.

(b) "A" Company 12th Royal Irish Rifles will take over from "B" Company 9th Royal Irish Fusiliers:
"B" Company 12th Royal Irish Rifles will take over from "A" Company 9th Royal Irish Fusiliers:
"C" Company 12th Royal Irish Rifles will take over from "C" Company 9th Royal Irish Fusiliers:
"D" Company 12th Royal Irish Rifles will take over from "D" Company 9th Royal Irish Fusiliers:

(c) All stores, defence schemes, work in progress and proposed to be carefully handed over and copies sent to Battalion Headquarters after dusk on 24/5/18.

No taking over parties except signallers, will be sent up. Two signallers from each Company and 2 from Battalion Headquarters will rendezvous at Cross Roads BURNT FARM at 5.30 pm and proceed to Battalion Headquarters HILL TOP at 200 yards interval between pairs.

(d) Platoons will pass starting points and pick up guides as per attached March table.

(e) Rations will be sent up to Battalion Dump for "A", "C", "D" Coys and Battalion Headquarters at C.21.d.3.6 at 11.30 pm.
"B" Company's rations will be sent direct to IRISH FARM.
The Transport Officer will arrange for the empty Limbers to pick up the kits of Officers of the 12th R.I.R. at these dumps, and take same back to the Reserve Position, evacuated by Companies of this Battalion.

WATER. Water Cart fills tank at Battalion Headquarters, refills and fills tank at IRISH FARM, then refills again and returns to Battalion Headquarters, when the horses will be sent back. Water for "C" & "A" Companies is sent up in Petrol Tins.

3. No.13 Platoon "D" Company will be attached to "C" Company. Quartermaster will make necessary arrangements about rations.

4. O.C. "B" Company will arrange that one Complete Platoon always remains in reserve for defence, and is not taken for carrying parties etc.

5. R.A.P. HILL TOP FARM.

6. Completion of relief will be reported by runner, he will report to Adjutant, and will remain at Battalion Headquarters overnight.
Relief Complete will also be reported by wire in Code.

"A" Company	"Nil Return"
"B" "	"None Required"
"C" "	"Six Required"
"D" "	"Four Required"

W. SPARKS Captain & Adjutant
9th (N.I.H.) Battalion Royal Irish Fusiliers

22/5/18

Issued at Signals 10.15 pm.

DISTRIBUTION :-
Copy No.1 to Brigade
2 "A" Company
3 "B" "
4 "C" "
5 "D" "
6 Commanding Officer.
7 Transport Officer.
8 Quartermaster.
9 Medical Officer.
10) War Diary
11)
12 R.S.M.
13 File.

MARCH TABLE

	Pass starting point at	Pick up guides at	Time
C Company			
No.9 Platoon	9.20pm	C.21.c.3.3	9.30pm
No.10 Platoon	9.23	C.21.c.3.3	
No.11 Platoon	9.26	C.21.c.3.3	
No.12 Platoon	9.29	C.21.c.3.3	
No.13 Platoon	9.32	C.21.c.3.3	
A Company			
No.1 Platoon	9.35pm	C.26.a.7.6	9.30pm
No.2 Platoon	9.38	C.26.a.7.6	
No.3 Platoon	9.41	C.26.a.7.6	
No.4 Platoon	9.44	C.26.a.7.6	
D Company			
No.14 Platoon	9.50pm	C.26.a.7.6	
No.15 Platoon	9.53	C.26.a.7.6	
No.16 Platoon	9.56	C.26.a.7.6	
B Company			
No.5 Platoon	10.05pm	C.26.a.7.6	
No.6 Platoon	10.08	C.26.a.7.6	
No.7 Platoon	10.11	C.26.a.7.6	
No.8 Platoon	10.14	C.26.a.7.6	
Bn. H.Q.	10.20pm	C.21.d.2.4	

200 yards between Platoons. Punctuality in passing starting points is essential.
Start point Cross Roads C.20.c.6.2.

Relief in Place, 29/30 May 1918

The 9th Royal Irish Fusiliers left the sector north of Ypres for the last time on 29 May, having been relieved by 2nd Royal Irish Rifles. The Battalion moved by train to Hospital Farm Camp north of Vlamertinghe.

OPERATION ORDER NO. 5
by
Lieutenant Colonel G.M. Forde M.C. Commanding
9th (N.I.H.) Battalion Royal Irish Fusiliers.

Reference Special Sheet ST. JULIAN 1/10,000

1. The 2nd Battalion Royal Irish Rifles will relieve the Battalion in the RIGHT SUB-SECTOR on the night of the 29th/30th May 1918. On relief the Battalion will move into RESERVE at HOSPITAL FARM CAMP.

2. "D" Company 2nd Royal Irish Rifles will relieve "A" Company 9th (N.I.H.) Battalion Royal Irish Fusiliers.
"C" Company 2nd R.I.R. with 1 Platoon of "A" Company will relieve "C" Company 9th R.I.F. with 1 Platoon of "D" Company.
"A" Company 2nd R.I.R. will relieve "D" Company 9th R.I.F.
"B" " " " " " "B" Do.

3. (a) 1 Guide per Platoon and Battalion Headquarters under an Officer from "B" Company will meet the incoming Platoons at ZOUAVE Siding at 9.15 pm. This Officer will be responsible for seeing that Guides know what Platoon of incoming Battalion they are to Guide.
Guides will rendezvous at Battalion Headquarters at 8.45 pm under this Officer.

(b) All Trench Kits, Officers Mess Boxes etc., will be at Battalion Headquarters Ration Dump at 10.30 pm. The Transport Officer will arrange to send up a G.S. Wagon at 11 pm to collect same.

(c) The Quartermaster will arrange to take over HOSPITAL CAMP on the 29th inst., and will arrange a Guide to be on duty at detraining point.

(d) Rev. H.F. Bally C.F., will hand over Canteen to 107th Inf. Brigade.

(e) MEALS. Hot tea will be sent up as soon as possible after dusk 29th. O.C. "B" & "D" Companies will arrange to send 4 men each to carry for "A" and "C" Companies. Petrol tins will be carried out.
Dinners will be served on arrival at HOSPITAL CAMP.

(f) Handing Over. All Trench Stores, Work in Progress, and proposed, Defence schemes, Aeroplane Photographs etc., to be carefully handed over and copy of receipt sent to Battalion Headquarters by 12 noon 30th inst.

(g) O.C. Companies will report their arrival in Camp.

(h) Completion of relief to be reported by wire by code word Surnames of Company Commanders.

4. ENTRAINING. The Battalion will entrain at ZOUAVE Siding. 2/Lieut Davis will superintend the entraining. Detraining Point CULLONDEN.
TRAINS. 1.30 am "B" & "D" Companies and 2 Companies 1st R.I.F.
2.00 am "A" & "C" Companies and 2 Companies 1st R.I.F.

W. SPARKS Captain & Adjutant.
9th (N.I.H.) Bn. Royal Irish Fusiliers.

ACKNOWLEDGE.

Copy No.1 to 108th Inf. Brigade
2 "A" Company
3 "B" "
4 "C" "
5 "D" "
6 C.O.
7 T.O. & Q.M.
8 2nd Bn: R.I.R.
9 9th Royal Inn Fusiliers.
10 War Diary.

Move to Proven, the Bois St Acaire Training Area & St Omer, 3 June to 1 July 1918

The following six operation orders all deal with the movements of the 9th Royal Irish Fusiliers to the training areas around Proven, north-west of Poperinghe, and Bois St Acaire, about six miles farther west. Here the Battalion spent most of the month training before moving by train to St Omer for 'musketry' training (operation order missing). Early July was spent at Road Camp, St Jan-ter-Biezen before moving south and back into the line on 3 July.

Order No.5 by Lt. Col. G.M. Forde, M.C., Commanding
9th (N.I.H.) Battalion, Royal Irish Fusiliers.

Ref. Sheets 28N.W. Ed.6B. 27N.E. Ed.3A.

1. The battn. on relief by a Belgian battn. will move to the PROVEN AREA today 3rd inst.

2. All rifles and equipment will be out of huts and stacked ready to move off at 7a.m. if necessary.

3. (a) Kits. Arrangements as notified.
(b) Dress. Full marching order, steel helmets on packs. Water bottles full.
(c) Route. Cross-roads A.23.a.35.05.
INTERNATIONAL CORNER via CHEMIN MILITAIRE to cross roads F.10.d.9.1. - cross roads F.4.d.5.2. - cross roads K.28.c. (Sheet 19)
(d) Intervals. 500 yards between bns. 100 yards between Coys. Company H.Q. to march in front of leading platoon.
(e) Order of march. Band - Battalion Headquarters, A-B-C-D, transport.
(f) Dinners will be served on arrival.

4. Particular attention is to be paid to march discipline, dressing, men taking off their packs during rest.

Issued at 6.10 a.m.
1.6.18.

[Sgd] W. Sparks, Capt. & Adjt.
9th (N.I.H.) R. Irish Fusrs.

Operation Order No.7 by Lieut. Colonel G.M. Forde, M.C.,
Commanding 9th (N.I.H.) Battalion Royal Irish Fusiliers.
B.E.F. 12th June, 1918.

Reference Sheet 27.N.E. Local Ed.3.A.

No.1. The Battalion will move to ROAD CAMP – F.25.d.2.5 on the 13th inst.

No.2. (a) Order of march – Band. Battalion Headquarters. B., C., D & A Companies and Transport.
(b) Intervals. 100 yards between Companies and between Battalion Headquarters and "B" Company.
(c) Head of column will pass starting point F.1.c.40.05 at 9.30a.m.
(d) Route. Cross Roads E.12.d.1.4 – F.25.c.3.2.
(e) Kits. Officers Valises and Mess Boxes of B. Company and D. Company will be stacked outside the Company Mess by 8 a.m. Those of Battalion Headquarters, A. & C. Companies together with Orderly Room Boxes will be stacked outside the Quartermaster Stores by 8.30 a.m.
The Transport Officer will arrange to send a G.S. Wagon to collect B. & D. Companies and the remainder.
(f) DRESS. Full Marching Order, Steel Helmets to be strapped to the Pack. Caps will be worn.
(g) Halt. There will be a halt at 9.50 a.m. to 10.00 a.m.
(h) Lewis Guns will be packed tonight.

No.3. The Orderly Officer will hand over the Camp to the incoming Unit and obtain a certificate of cleanliness.

Billeting Parties of the Quartermaster, 4 C.Q.M.S. and No.13995 Cpl. Brown from Battalion Headquarters will be at ROAD CAMP at 6.30 a.m. on the 13th inst. to take over from the 2nd Royal Irish Rifles.

Lists of stores handed and taken over will be sent to the Orderly Room.

No.4. Strict attention is to be paid to March Discipline. There will be no smoking on the march, except at the halt.

[Sgd] W. Sparks, Capt. & Adjt.
12.6.18 9th (N.I.H.) Bn., Royal Irish Fusiliers.

Acknowledge.
Issued at :-
Copy No.1 to 108th Infantry Brigade.
No.2 to "A" Company.
No.3 to "B" "
No.4 to "C" "
No.5 to "D" "
No.6 to C.O.
No.7 to Q.M.
No.8 to T.O.
No.9 to M.O.
No.10 to Orderly Officer.
No.11 to R.S.M.
No.12 to War Diary
No.13 to 2nd in Command
No.14 to File.

Operation Order No.8 by Lt. Col. G.M. Forde, M.C.,
Commanding 9th (N.I.H.) Battalion, Royal Irish Fusiliers.
B.E.F. 14 June, 1918

No.1. The Battalion will move to the BOIS ST. ACAIRE tomorrow the 15th inst. and on arrival will be billeted at a Camp at D.30.d.9.9.

No.2. Each Company will move as an advance Guard to a Battalion.

No.3. (a) STARTING POINT. F.25.c.3.3.
(b) ROUTE. E.30.c30.45. WATOU – F.28.(?)5.2 – K.2.a.50.80 – K.1.a.10.65 – K.1.a.10.10.
(c) TIME OF PASSING STARTING POINT.

Battalion Headquarters	9 a.m.
"C" Company	9.15 a.m.
"D" "	9.35 a.m.
"A" "	9.55 a.m.
"B" "	10.15 a.m.

(d) OFFICERS VALISES, Mess Stores, and Orderly Room Boxes will be stacked on Football Ground at 9 a.m. Medical Stores will be ready for removal by 9 a,m.
(e) Transport will move as a unit, under arrangements to be made by the Transport Officer. Cookers and Watercarts will move with the Transport.
(f) DINNERS will be served on arrival.
(g) HALTS will be made for 10 minutes after every 50 minutes marching.
(h) DRESS. Full Marching Order. Steel Helmets to be strapped to the packs.
(i) Arrival in Camp will be reported to the Orderly Room.
(j) Each Company will detail a loading party of 2 men to remain with the Officers' Kits.

No.4. The Orderly Officer will arrange to hand over the Camp.

No.5. The 4 C.Q.M.S. will be at the Camp at BOIS ST. ACAIRE by 9 a.m. They will parade at Orderly Room at 8 a.m. with cycles.

[Sgd] W. Sparks, Capt. & Adjt.
9th (N.I.H.) Bn., Royal Irish Fusiliers.

14 June 1918

ACKNOWLEDGE.

DISTRIBUTION.

Copy No.1. to 108th Infantry Brigade.
No.2. to "A" Company.
No.3. to "B" "
No.4. to "C" "
No.5. to "D" "
No.6. to Commanding Officer.
No.7. to Major Kerr R.G.
No.8. to Transport Officer.
No.9. to Quartermaster.
No.10. to M.O.
No.11. to R.S.M.
No.12) to War Diary
No.13)
No.14. to File.

Operation Orders No.10 by Lt. Col. G.M. Forde, M.C.,
Commanding 9th (N.I.H.) Bn., Royal Irish Fusiliers.
29th June 1918.

No.1. The Battalion will move to the PROVEN AREA tomorrow 30th inst. as under:-

(a) March route to ST. OMER STATION.
ROUTE. CORMETTE ROAD – ROAD JUNCTION 660 yards S.W. of Church ST MARTIN au LAERT – ST MARTIN au LAERT. Battalion will parade on ground behind NISSEN HUT ready to move off at 7.15 a.m. Parties to be detailed off in forties for entraining purposes.

(b) By rail from ST OMER to PROVEN. Train leaves at 10 a.m. Entraining to commence at 9 a.m.

(c) March route to Camp at PROVEN.

No.2. Transport will move by road and will leave at 7 a.m. 30th inst.

No.3. All Officers' VALISES and one Mess Box per Company will be stacked near the Road outside NISSEN HUTS by 7 a.m.

No.4. The Quartermaster will arrange to hand over the Camp to the Camp Warden. Copy of receipt to be sent to Battalion Headquarters.

No.5. Cooking arrangements to be made later.

[Sgd] W. Sparks, Capt. & Adjt.
29 June 1918 9th (N.I.H.) Battalion, Royal Irish Fusiliers.

Operation Order No. 11
by
Lieut. Colonel G.M. FORDE, M.C.
Commanding 9th (N.I.H.) Battalion Royal Irish Fusiliers.
B.E.F.

Reference Sheet 27 N.E. 1/20,000. 1st July. 1918.
Local Ed. 1 A.

No.1.
The Battalion will move to ROAD CAMP on the 2nd July 1918.

No.2.
The working parties on the BLUE LINE and Battery Positions will rejoin the Battalion at ROAD CAMP on completion of the day's work.

No.3.
The remainder of the Battalion will form up in "A" Company's Lines ready to move off as one party at 9.5 a.m.

Transport will move in rear of the Battalion, 100 yards between Battalion and Transport, 25 yards between every six vehicles.

ROUTE - PROVEN POPERINGHE ROAD – CROSS ROADS F.21.a.26 – CROSS ROADS F.25.a.39.

No.4.
(a) The Packs of the Working Party will be stacked as under by 8 a.m. :-
"B" & "D" Companies outside Cookhouses.
"C" & Battalion Headquarters outside Guard Room.

"A" Company outside Company store.

O.C. Companies will arrange for a guard to be placed on these Kits.

(b) Officers' Valises and Mess Boxes will be stacked with the men's kits ready for removal by 8 a.m.

(c) The Transport Officer will arrange to collect Medical Stores and Battalion Headquarters Mess Boxes at 8.30 a.m.

(d) The Quartermaster and 4 Company Quartermaster Sergeants will arrange to take over ROAD CAMP.

The Orderly Officer will hand over the Camp to the Camp Warden and obtain receipts.

No.5.

Arrangements as to dinners for the working parties on their return will be notified later.

W. SPARKS, Capt. & Adjt.
9th (N.I.H.) Bn. Royal Irish Fus.

1 July 1918

ACKNOWLEDGE
Issued at:
DISTRIBUTION

Copy No.1 to 108th Inf. Bde.
2 to "A" Company
3 to "B" "
4 to "C" "
5 to "D" "

Copy No.6 to Comdg. Officer.
7 to Second in Cmd.
8 to Transport Officer.
9 to Quartermaster.
10 to Medical Officer.
11 to R.S.M.

Operation Orders No. 12
by
Lieut. Colonel G.M. Forde, M.C.
Commanding 9th (N.I.H.) Battalion Royal Irish Fusiliers.
B.E.F.

Reference Sheet 27. N.E. 3 A.
Local 1/20,000 & Sheet 27.

2nd July 1918.

No.1.

The Battalion will move to the LE GARREAUX Area on the 3rd July 1918.

No.2.

(a) Companies and Battalion Headquarters will be formed up on their Parade Grounds ready to move off at 8.35 a.m. in the following order :-

Drums.
Battalion Headquarters.
"D" Company.
"A" "
"B" "
"C" "
Transport.

(b) DISTANCES.

100 yards between Battalion Headquarters and Companies and Transport and rear Company. 50 yards between every 6 vehicles.

(c) ROUTE.

ST JAN-TER-BIEZEN – K.17 – K.16.b.8.8 – K.27 STEENVOORDE.

(d) All Officers' Valises, Mess Boxes, Signalling Stores and Orderly Room Boxes will be stacked on the Football Ground by 7.30 a.m.

O.C. Companies will arrange to put as much Mess Kit on the Cookers as possible.

(e) BILLETING PARTY.

The Quartermaster, 4 Company Quartermaster Sergeants and Corporal Brown D. will take over the new Camp. Bicycles will be drawn.

(f) The Orderly Officer will arrange to hand over the Camp to the Camp Warden and obtain a certificate of cleanliness. He will also arrange for all furniture to be collected into the Canteen.

(g) Battalion time will be sent to all concerned.

(h) Dinners will be served on arrival.

(i) DRESS. Full marching order, caps to be worn.

No.3.

Strict attention is to be paid to March Discipline. Water Bottles to be filled.

W. SPARKS, Capt. & Adjt.
9th (N.I.H.) Bn. Royal Ir. Fuslrs.

2.7.18.

Acknowledge Issued at :-

Copy No. 1 to 108th Inf. Bde.
2 "A" Company
3 "B" "
4 "C" "
5 "D" "
6 Commanding Officer.
7 Second in Command.

Copy No. 8 to Transpt. Offr.
9 to Quartermaster.
10 to Medical Offr.
11 to R.S.M.
12 War Diary.
13 " "

Relief in Place, 6/7 July 1918

This operation order details the move of the 9th Royal Irish Fusiliers to a reserve position at Piebrouck north of Bailleul, where it relieved a French battalion. This began the final phase of the war for the Battalion.

Operation Orders No.13
by
Major Kerr R.G., M.C.
9th (N.I.H.) Battalion Royal Irish Fusiliers.
B.E.F.

Reference Sheet 27 & Local Sheets. 5th July 1918.

No.1.

The Battalion will relieve the Reserve Battalion of the 42nd Infantry Regiment (French) on the night of the 6/7th inst. and on relief will be disposed in the vicinity of PIEBROUCK.

No.2.

(a) The Battalion less Echelon "B" will be formed up ready to move off from Ground in Front of Battalion Headquarters at 8.15 p.m.

(b) GUIDES. One Guide per Company will meet the Battalion at CODEWAERSWELDE at 9.0 p.m.

(c) ROUTE.

CODEWAERSWELDE – Q.18.a.50.7. – PIEBROUCK.

(d) DISTANCES. 50 yards between Platoons, 100 yards between Companies. O.C. Companies will arrange to keep careful touch.

(e) Officers' Trench Kits and Trench Mess Box will be ready stacked by 7.0 p.m. by Company Field Kitchens.

(f) Orders as to Personnel and Kits of Echelon "B" will be notified later.

(g) Lewis Gun Limbers containing all Company Kits and rations will follow the leading platoon of each Company.

(h) DRESS.

Battle Order.

Water bottles must be filled. The greatcoats, haversacks and surplus kits of all men going up the line will be placed in sandbags with Regl. No. rank, name, platoon and Regiment clearly marked on the outside.

(i) All surplus kits to be stacked at Company Stores (except from 2 Platoons "B" Company). Further orders will be issued.

(j) One Water Cart will accompany the Battalion.

W. SPARKS, Captain & Adjutant,
9th (N.I.H.) Battalion
Royal Irish Fusiliers.

6.7.18.

Relief in Place, 12/13 July and 17/18 July 1918

The three battalions of 108th Brigade maintained a three-way rotation around the forward two sub-sectors 1,800 yards north of Bailleul at Meulenhouck and the reserve positions at Mont Noir. These operation orders describe two of these rotations.

Operation Order No. 14
by
Lt. Col. G.M. Forde, M.C.

1. The 1st R. Irish Fus. will relieve the 9th R. Irish Fus. in the left sub-sector on the night 12/13th July 1918.

2. On relief the Bn. will move into brigade reserve relieving the 1st R. Irish Fus.

3. A Coy. 1st R.I.F. relieves B Coy. 9th.
B " " " A " "
C " " " D " "
D " " " C " "

4. The five N.C.Os sent down tonight will take over as under :-

A Coy. 9th R.I.F. relieves A Coy. 1st R.I.F.
B " " " B " " "
C " " " C " " "
D " " " D " " "

5. Guides. The 5 N.C.Os sent down tonight will bring in Coys of the 1st R. IRISH FUS. relieving their own Coys. They will then guide back their platoons on relief to the new positions.

6. Handing over. All trench stores, maps, defence schemes and aeroplane photos, work in progress, work proposed will be carefully handed over and receipts sent to

Bn. H.Q. by 6 p.m. 13th inst.

Fuller phones, Lucas lamps will also be handed over.

7. An interval of 200 yards will be kept between platoons on moving out.

8. Completion of relief to be reported by runner in the cases of A & C Coys, by phone by B & D Coys. Code name of Coy. Commander.

9. All liaison posts will be carefully handed over.

10. All petrol tins must be carried out by Coys as Coys depend upon these tins to draw water in company areas.

11. Arrangements are trying to be made to give men a hot meal on arrival.

12. Acknowledge.

(Sgd) W. Sparks, Capt. & Adjt.
9th (N.I.H.) Bn. R. Irish Fus.

Issued at 1 a.m. 12.7.18

Copy No. 1 - 108 I.Bde.
2 - A Coy.
3 - B "
4 - C "
5 - D "
6 - Q.M. & T.O.
7 - 1st R. Irish Fus.
8 - C.O.
9 - War Diary.

Operation Order No.15
by
Lt. Col. Forde, M.C.
Commanding 9th (N.I.H.) Bn. Royal Ir. Fusiliers.
B.E.F.

Sheet 28 N.W. 1 1/10,000

1. The Battn. will relieve the 12th R.I.R. in the Right sub-sector on the night of the 17/18th inst.

2. A Company will relieve A Coy 12th R.I.R. in Right Front line.
C " " " B " " in Left Front line.
D " " " D " " as C.A. Coy.
B " " " C " " in Reserve.

3. GUIDES. The 12th R.I.R. are sending 1 Guide per platoon, Coy. H.Q. and Battn. H.Q. to House at M.31.b.80.75 at 11pm on night of 17th inst.

Each Company and Battn H.Q. will send one Guide to H.Q. 12th R.I.R. at 1.45 a.m. on night of 16/17th inst. to guide back taking over parties of 12th R.I.R.

Taking over parties of 1 N.C.O., 1 Signaller, 2 Runners per Coy., 1 signaller, 2 runners and 1 scout from Bn. H.Q. will rendezvous at "A" Coys H.Q. at 1.0 a.m. on night 16/17 inst. & will proceed to report at Bn. H.Q. 12th R.I.R. to take over.

4. ORDER OF MARCH. Companies will be at M.31.b.30.75 at following times on night 17/18th inst :-

B – 11 p.m.)

A - 11.15 p.m.) 200 yds interval
C - 11.30 p.m.)
D - 11.45 p.m.) between platoons.
Bn. H.Q. - 12 midnight.)

5. Battn. H.Q. and R.A.P. situated at Chateau M.32.a.00.10.

6. Completion of relief to be reported by code word "JAMES".

W. SPARKS, Capt. & Adjt.
M O K I.

Acknowledge.

Issued at 7 p.m. 16.7.18 :-

Copy No.1 108th I.B.
2 A Coy.
3 B "
4 C "
5 D "
6 Q.M. & T.O.
7 12th R.I.R.
8 File
9 War Diary

Shoddy Farm Raid, 21/21 July 1918

In addition to providing details about the actions to be taken by the raiders from 9th Royal Irish Fusiliers, this operation order for the attack on Shoddy Farm details the artillery fire plan in support.

OPERATION ORDER No. 16.
by
LT. COL. G. M. FORDE, M.C.
COMDG. 9th (N.I.H.) ROYAL IRISH FUSILIERS

Ref. Sheet 28 S.W. 1/10,000. 20. 7. 18.

1. INTENTION.
To raid enemy strong point about S.8.a.70.50.

2. OBJECT.
1. Gain identifications.
2. Inflict loss on the enemy.
3. Definitely locate enemy positions opposite right Company front.

3. STRENGTH.
One Company plus one platoon.

4. ASSEMBLY POINT.
S.8.a.20.70 to S.8.a.20.20.

5. PLAN.
At Zero hour sweep across in a North Easterly direction keeping on the forward slope of the spur. Clear the houses in S.8.a and also 2 suspected M.G posts, and return to our lines at S.2.d.25.80.

One Platoon with four Lewis Guns will act as Southern Flank Guard; One Lewis Gun Section as Western guard.

6. BARRAGE.
Barrage of H.E. will come down at ZERO hour along wall N.W. of the ASYLUM and also on the ASYLUM.

7. ARMS.
Rifle and bayonet; 10 Lewis Guns; one section carrying rifle grenades; one section in each platoon to carry 2 Mills No. 5 Bombs to clear cellars.

8. SIGNALS.
One GREEN Very Light – Lengthen range.
Two GREEN " Lights – Stop shooting.
(sent up in succession).
One RED Very Light – Signal for detached posts to withdraw.
(sent up by raiding party)

9. WATCHES.
Watches will be synchronised at 8 p.m.

10. ZERO.
Zero hour – 1 a.m. (one a.m.)
Company Four platoons will be in position at the assembly point at 12.30 a.m.
One platoon will be at the assembly point by 11.15 p.m. and act as covering party.

11. DATE.
Night 21st/22nd JULY 1918.

12. GENERAL.
O.C .raiding party (Captain J.J. MURPHY M.C., D.C.M.) will keep one platoon in reserve.

Flank guards will keep about 60 yards in rear of reserves.
On withdrawal being ordered if the situation demands it, all five Lewis Gun Teams will withdraw by rushes, not more than 2 teams at once, covered by the fire from the rest, and enter our lines at S.2.d.25.80.

"C" Company. O.C. C Coy. (2/Lieut. GALLOWAY) will arrange to cut gaps in our wire at S.2.d.25.80 and to have one man stationed on enemy side of each gap to guide party in.

IDENTIFICATIONS. All letters and badges etc. will be taken off all ranks taking part in the raid.

(Signed) G.M. FORDE, Lt. Col.,
Comdg. 9th (N.I.H.) R. Ir. Fusiliers.

Issued by runner at
12 midnight 20/21st July 1918.

Copy No. 1 108th Inf. Brigade.
2 O.C. "B" Coy.
3 O.C. "C" Coy.
4 O.C.
5 War Diary.

SECRET Copy No. 8.

POTTER GROUP ORDER NO. 8.

1. The 9th R.I.Fus. will carry out a raid on enemy posts in square S.8.a. tomorrow night 21/22nd instant.

2. ZERO hour will be 1.0 a.m.

3. The party, strength one Company, will leave our line at about S.2.c.20.30 and will be formed up facing East on the line S.8.a.20.20 – S.8.a.20.90 by zero hour. At zero they will advance East, mop up the enemy posts at S.8.a.55.71, S.8.a.70.48, and S.8.a.98.22, and any other post they may encounter and return to our lines at S.2.d.60.35.

The raiders will be protected by a flank guard put out along the road S.8.b.05.17 – S.8.c.42.91.

4. The Artillery of the POTTER GROUP will co-operate as follows :-
At zero put down a barrage as follows :-

A/153.	1 gun on House S.14.b.08.97. 5 guns S.8.d.30.07 – S.8.d.47.30.
B/153.	(6 guns) S.8.d.47.30 – S.8.d.73.57.
C/153.	(6 guns) S.8.d.73.57 – S.8.d.98.82.
D/153.	Search area S.8.d.88.43 – S.14.b.45.93 – S.14.b.75.68 – S.9.c.26.20.

Rates of fire :-

18-pdrs.	Zero to Zero plus 10 min. 3 rounds per gun per minute. Zero plus 10 minutes until STOP. 2 round per gun per minute.
4.5" Hows.	Zero to Zero plus 10 min. 2 rounds per gun per minute. Zero plus 10 minutes until STOP. 1½ rds per gun per minute.

(N.B. It is anticipated that the operation should be complete by Zero plus 40 minutes.)

Ammunition.

18-pdrs. &) H.E. (not 106 fuze) with 50% delay action fuzes if the latter
4.5" hows.) are available.

5. The Battalion Liaison Officer will be located with the O.C. Battalion at S.2.d.60.35, and will arrange with the latter for direct telephone communication from that point to Group H.Q.

6. The following light signals have been arranged :-

1 Green Very Light. Lengthen range. On this signal all guns will add 200 yards to their range.

2 Green Very Lights fired in rapid succession. STOP firing.

These signals will be repeated from the rocket guard O.P. at ERNEST, and batteries must keep a sharp look-out for them.

The stop firing signal will also be fired to indicate that the raiding party have re-entered our lines.

7. Barrage lines will be registered tomorrow 21st inst. This must be done as unostentatiously as possible.

8. To avoid arousing the enemy's suspicions, a preliminary barrage exactly as in para. 4 will be fired at 10 p.m. on the night of the raid, and will be continued for 5 minutes only.

Rates of fire for preliminary barrage :-

18-pdrs. 3 round per gun per minute.
4.5" Hows. 2 " " " " "

8. Watches will be synchronised at midnight on the night of the raid.

9. ACKNOWLEDGE.

C. POTTER, Lieut. Col. R. F. A.
20th July 1918. Commanding POTTER GROUP.

Copy No. 1 O.C. A/153rd Brigade R. F. A.
No. 2 O.C. B/153rd " "
No. 3 O.C. C/153rd " "
No. 4 O.C. D/153rd " "
No. 5 H.Q. 108th Inf. Bde. (for information).
No. 6 H.Q. 36th Divl. Artillery do.
No. 7 O.C. SIMPSON GROUP.
No. 8 H.Q. 108th I.B. (for O.C. 9/R.I.F.)

SECRET

AMENDMENTS TO POTTER GROUP ORDER No. 8 dated
20. 7. 18

Para. 4. Amend rates of fire and ammunition to read as follows :-

18-pdrs. Zero to Zero plus 5min. 3 rds. per gun per min.
Zero plus 5 to Zero plus 15 min. 2 rds. per gun per min.
Zero plus 15 to STOP FIRING. 1 rd. per gun per min.

4.5" Hows. Zero to STOP FIRING. 1½ rds per Howitzer throughout.

Ammunition

18-pdrs. C/153, Shrapnel fuze 80 – 50% on graze.
A/153) H.E. (not fuze 106) with 50% delay action fuzes, if the
B/153) latter are available.

4.5" Hows. As previously ordered.

Para. 8. Erase. The preliminary bombardment will not now take place.

CARTWRIGHT, Lieut. R. F. A.
Adjt. 153rd Bde. R. F. A.
21/7/18 Comdg. POTTER GROUP.

To :- All recipients of POTTER GROUP ORDER No. 8.

Relief in Place, 23/24 July 1918

This was a routine relief in place after which the 9th Royal Irish Fusiliers spent two weeks out of the line training during the day and engaged in work parties during the short summer nights.

Operation Orders No. 17.
by
Lieut. Col. G.M. Forde, M.C.
Commanding 9th (N.I.H.) Bn. Royal Irish Fusiliers.
B.E.F.

Ref. Sheets 27 S.E. & 28 S.W. 1/20,000 22.7.18

1. The Battalion will be relieved in the Right Sub-sector by the 9th Royal Innis Fus. on the night of the 23/24th July 1918. On relief the Battn. will move to SPOTTERKE area R.15.d.

2. (a) 9th R. Inn. Fus. 9th R. Irish Fus.

No.1 Coy. relieves	"A" Coy. RIGHT FRONT.
3 " "	"C" " LEFT "
4 " "	"D" " C A position.
2 " "	"B" " RESERVE.

(b) Taking over parties :-
9th R. Innisk. Fus. will report to Coys tonight 22/23rd inst.

(c) Taking over parties of 2/Lieut Ross, 1 N.C.O. per Coy. & Bn. H.Q. will report at Bn. H.Q. at 1.30 a.m. 23rd inst. & proceed to take over billets from 9th R. Innis. Fus. They will meet the Battn. at R.15.d.3.3.

(d) Guides:- 1 NCO per platoon, Coy. H.Q. & Bn. H.Q. will report at Bn. H.Q. at 10.15 p.m. 23rd inst., & will meet the incoming Battn. at houses M.31.b.80.80 at 10.30 p.m. Each guide is to be given a slip of paper stating the relieving platoon he is to guide.

Order of march of relieving Companies - 2, 3, 1, 4.

(e) One limber per Coy. & 1 limber for H.Q. will be for Lewis Guns and Coy. Mess Boxes. Time & place will be notified later.

(f) Handing over - All defence schemes, photos, work in progress and proposed, trench stores, will be handed over & copy of receipt sent to Bn. H.Q. by 6 p.m. 24th inst. Bugler posts will be handed over.

(g) Route - BERTHEN – SPOTTERKE (R.15).
100 yards to be maintained between Platoons.

(h) The Q.M. will arrange for a hot meal on arrival.

(i) Completion of relief to be reported by code word of Coy. Commander's name.

3. Arrival in Billets is to be reported in Orderly Room.

Acknowledge

W SPARKS, Capt. & Adjt.

Issued at 9.30 p.m. by Runner.

Copy No. 1 108th I.B.
2 A Coy.
3 B "
4 C "

5 D "
6 C.O.
7 Q.M.
8 T.O.
9 9th R. Inn. Fus.
10 File
11) War Diary
12)

Relief in Place, 3/4 September 1918

After the operations at Bailleul, the Ulster Division advanced in the first days of September 1918 through Neuve Eglise and fought again along the River Douve. This operation order covers the relief in place of 1st Royal Irish Fusiliers and 12th Royal Irish Rifles on the night before the 9th Royal Irish Fusiliers attacked on the left flank of 29th Division, which stormed Hill 63 north of Ploegsteert Wood.

Operation Orders No.24
by
Lieut. Colonel P.E. Kelly
Commanding 9th (N.I.H.) Battalion Royal Irish Fusiliers
B.E.F.

Map Reference Belgium and Part of France Sheet 7b.

1. Relief Battalion will relieve 1st Bn. R.I.F. and 12th R.I.R. tonight from T.16.c.7.8 (on right) to left Bde. boundary in T.6.c.

2. Four Companies will be in the line.
"A" Company in touch with 12th R.I.R. on the right to T.11.c.4.5.
"B" Company from T.11.c.4.5 to T.11.c.8.0.
"C" Company from T.11.c.8.0 to T.12.a.5.7.
"D" Company from T.12.a.5.7 to left Brigade boundary T.6.c.6.5.

3. Each Company will have 2 Platoons forward at first.

4. "C" and "D" Coys. will find guide at T.10.a.9.4. who will shew them where 1st R.I.F. are.
"A" Company will move to T.10.d.5.3. where a Coy of the 12th R.I.R. are.
"B" Coy. will move to T.11.a.4.2. where a Coy. H.Q. of the 12th R.I.R. are.

5. Coys will be ready to move at 6.30 pm. "D" Coy leading, they will not start until they receive orders.

6. Rations are expected to arrive before the move.

7. Bn. H.Q. at Farm at T.9.d.6.3.

8. Coys will report by runner as soon as they are in their new position.

9. "C" & "D" Coys will relieve 1st R.I.F. who are already on their objective.
"A" and "B" Coys will endeavour to push forward as soon as possible and seize cottage T.11.c.6.3 and T.11.c.9.0 and T.11.d.3.3 & when Bde. on our right advance will seize objective T.19.a.4.8 to T.12.a.5.1.

10. One T.M. will move with "A" Coy. & will report to O.C. "A" Coy at 6 p.m.

11. R.A.P. will be at Bn. H.Q. R.A.P. of 12th R.I.R. is at Church in NEUVE EGLISE (T.15.a.central).

12. Acknowledge.

13. Issued at 6.10pm.

G.H. GIBSON Captain & Acting Adjutant.
3.9.18 9th (N.I.H.) Bn. Royal Irish Fusiliers

Relief in Place and Movement Orders, September 1918

The following six operation orders take the 9th Royal Irish Fusiliers from the River Douve north to billeting areas to the west of Ypres around Watou. It remained there until moving east to Beselare on 29 September, from where it launched on its final actions.

Operation Orders No. 26
by
Lieut. Col. P.E. Kelly
Commanding 9th (N.I.H.) Bn. Royal Irish Fusiliers
B.E.F.

<u>Map. Ref. Sheet 28 S.W. 1/20,000.</u>

1. The Bn. will be relieved by the 2nd Bn. R.I.R. tonight 5/6th Sept. 1918.

2. The incoming companies will occupy the same relative positions as the 9th R.I.F.

3. All trench stores will be handed over.

4. Completion of relief will be reported by Coy. Commander's name to Bn. H.Q.

5. Companies when relieved will march independently to new area at S.17.b.3.3 & will report arrival by Coy. Commdr's name.

6. Interval of 100 yards will be maintained between platoons.

7. Rations will be dumped in new area.

8. Limbers for Lewis Guns will be at advanced Bn. H.Q. if possible.

9. Coy Commanders horses will be at advanced Bn. H.Q.

10. Duplicates of receipts for trench stores handed over, to be sent to Bn. H.Q. by 3 p.m. 6.9.18.

11. Guides will meet Companies in new area on road at S.18.a.6.2.

12. BAILLEUL – RAVELSBURG road may be used as far as CRUCIFIX CORNER S.18.a.6.2. West of this point the road is out of bounds & Coys will then proceed N. of this road.

13. Care will be taken that liaison will be carefully handed over.

14. Acknowledge.

G.H. GIBSON Capt & A/Adjutant
5.9.18 9th (N.I.H.) Bn. Royal Ir. Fusiliers.

No. 27

Operation Orders by
Lieut. Col. P.E. Kelly.
Commanding 9th (N.I.H.) Battn Royal Ir. Fus.

B. E. F. 8.9.18

Reference Sheet 27 S.E. and 28 S.W. 1/20,000

1. The Battalion will move today to Berthen area as under:
Bn. H.Q) to CATO COPSE R.16.d.6.5.
"A" Coy)
"B" & "D" Coys to SUTTON FARM R.22.b.6.5.
"C" Coy to BERTHEN.

2. Order of march, Bn. H.Q. "A" "B" "C" & "D" Coys.
200 yards between Coys. 50 yards between platoons.

3. Route. BAILLEUL – ST JANS CAPPEL. Strict march discipline will be observed.

4. All Officers valises, mess kit, Coy. Stores and Lewis Guns will be dumped on Road opposite Companies at 1 pm.

5. All tents and shelters will be dumped at Bn. H.Q. by 1 pm.

6. Dinners at 11.30 am.

7. Companies will leave two men per Coy. behind to clean up Camp. "C Coy to detail 1 NCO to take charge of this party.

8. Arrival in New Area will be reported to Bn H.Q. by runner.

9. Acknowledge.

G.H GIBSON Capt & A/Adjutant
9th (N.I.H.) Battn. Royal Irish Fusiliers.

8-9-18

Copies to	"A" Coy.	"B" Coy.
	"C" Coy.	"D" Coy.
	C.O.	108 I Bde
	War Diary.	
	File.	

Operation Orders No. 28
by
Lieut. Colonel P.E. KELLY.
Commanding 9th (N.I.H.) Battalion Royal Irish Fusiliers.

B.E.F.
14th Sept. '18.

Reference Sheet 27 S.E. and 28 S.W. 1/20,000.

No.1. The Battalion will move into Divisional Support on the 15th September 1918 and will be billeted in the ASYLUM.

No.2. (a) The Battalion will pass the starting point (R.22.a.40.00) at the following times :-

Band & Battalion Headquarters 6.54 p.m. 7.24pm *[handwritten]*
"C" Company 6.56pm *7.26pm [handwritten]*
"B" " 6.59pm *7.29pm [handwritten]*

"D"   "   7.02pm *7.32pm [handwritten]*
"A"   "   7.05pm *7.35pm [handwritten]*
Transport.
Intervals of 200 yards between Companies and 30 yards between platoons.

(b) The following Transport has been allotted :-
1 G.S Wagon for Battalion Headquarters.
1 G.S Limber per Company for Lewis Guns and Mess Boxes.
1 G.S Wagon for Company Officers Kits.
Maltese Cart for medical stores.

All Kits, Mess boxes and Lewis Guns must be stacked on the road near Company Headquarters by 5.45 p.m.

(c) Advance parties consisting of Major R.J.A. Tamplin D.S.O., Lieut. A.L. Dobbyn M.C. and one N.C.O. per platoon and Battalion Headqrs. will rendezvous at Battalion Headquarters at 2.30 p.m. (15th inst).

(d) Teas will be served at 4.30 p.m. The Quartermaster will arrange for a hot meal after arrival.

(e) The Quartermaster will arrange to hand over present billets to the incoming Unit.

No.3. The strictest attention is to be paid to march discipline.

No.4. Billets will be left in a perfectly clean and sanitary condition.

Acknowledge.

W Sparks Captain & Adjutant.
9th (N.I.H.) Battalion Royal Irish Fusiliers.

14.9.18

Issued through Signals at 6.15pm.

Copy No. 1 to 108th Inf. Bde.   No. 2 to "A" Coy.
3 "B" Coy.   4 "C" "
5 "D" "   6 C.O.
7 2nd in Command.   8 Quartermaster.
9 Transport Officer.   10 R.S.M.
11 War Diary.   12 Cook Sergeant.

No. 29
Operation Orders
by
Lieut. Colonel. P.E. Kelly.
Commanding 9th (N.I.H.) Battalion Royal Irish Fusiliers   B.E.F. 19.9.18

Reference Sheet 27 S.E. and 28 S.W. 1/20,000

No.1. The Battalion will move to the BERTHEN Area tonight 19th September 1918.

No.2. (1) Starting Point (S.14.b.2.8) will be passed :-
Battn. H.Q.   8pm
"B" Company   8.3pm
"A"   "   8.7pm
"D"   "   8.11pm
"C"   "   8.15pm
(2) Route. ST. JANS CAPEL.

(3) Advance Parties. The Quartermaster will arrange to take over billets this afternoon. N.C.Os at present with Echelon "B' will assist him if required. Billets to be taken over will be the same as those vacated on 16.9.18.

(4) All blankets will be rolled in bundles of 10 and stacked at Company Ration Dump at 5 p.m.

Each bundle will be clearly marked with the Company and platoon's number.

(5) All Officers Valises, Lewis Guns etc., will be stacked at Company Ration Dump 5.30 p.m.

The Transport Officer will arrange for the necessary transport at that hour. He will also arrange to send on all Cookers immediately after tea.

Officers Mess Boxes will be sent on in advance in Cookers.

(6) Lieut. A.L. Dobbyn., M.C. will hand over present billets to the Area Commandant.

(7) Echelon "B" will rejoin their Companies tonight, but in the event of the Battalion moving into the line at any time, they will remain behind.

A.L. DOBBYN, Lieut for
Captain & Adjutant,
9th (N.I.H.) Battalion Royal Irish Fusiliers.

19.9.18
Issued through Signals, at ....

Copy No. 1 to	108th Inf. Bde.	No. 2 to	"A" Company.
3	"B" Company.	4	"C" "
5	"D" "	6	Commanding Offr.
7	2nd in Command.	8	Captain Kerr C.H.
9	Quartermaster.	10	Transport Offr.
11	Medical Officer.	12	War Diary.
13	War Diary.		

No. 30
Operation Orders
by
Lieut. Colonel P.E .KELLY.
Commanding 9th (N.I.H.) Battalion Royal Irish Fusiliers
B.E.F. 21.9.18

Sheet 27, 1/40,000

No.1. The Battalion will march to the WATOU Area tonight 21st September 1918.

No.2. (a) Order of march :-

Band
Battalion Headquarters
"B" Company
"C" "
"D" "
"A" "
Guard.
Transport.

Twenty-five yards between every group of 6 vehicles.
Intervals must be strictly kept.

(b) ROUTE. STEENVOORDE – Cross Roads J.14.b – Road junction N.8.a.90.60 – K.3.d.

(c) The Battalion will be formed up ready to pass Cross Roads F.4.b.50.30 in above order at 7.15 p.m.

"A" and "D" Companies will march to starting point via CASSEL – STEENVOORDE Road.

(d) On arrival the Battalion will be billeted in BORDEN and ENDERSLEY Camps K.3.d.8.5.

(e) Transport Lines at K.10.b.4.9. Billeting parties have been sent forward.

(e) No halt will be made until the Battalion is clear of STEENVOORDE.

(f) DRESS. Full marching order, Steel Helmets will be worn by all ranks, Waterbottles filled.

(g) All Officers Mess kit will be placed in Company Cookers.

No.3. Every precaution is to be taken against observation from the air and the necessity for the utmost secrecy is to be impressed on all ranks to whom these orders have to be communicated. In case of E.A. flying over the column, Companies will at once get into cover at the side of the road.

W SPARKS Captain & Adjutant.
9th (N.I.H.) Battalion Royal Irish Fusiliers.

21.9.18

Issued through Signals at ....

Copy No. 1	to 108th Inf. Bde.	No. 2	to "A" Coy.
3	"B" Coy.	4	"C" "
5	"D" "	6	Comm. Officer.
7	2nd in Command.	8	Transport "
9	Quartermaster.	10	Cook Sergeant.
11	Medical Officer.	12	War Diary.
		13	War Diary.

No.31 Operation Orders
by
Lieut. Colonel P.E. KELLY
Commanding 9th (N.I.H.) Battalion Royal Irish Fusiliers.

B.E.F. 26.9.18

Reference Sheet 27.

No.1. The Battalion will move to ROAD CAMP today 26th September 1918.

No.2. (a) The Battalion will parade ready to move off at 8 p.m. in the following order :-

Battalion Headquarters.
"C" Company.
"D" "
"B" "
"A" "
Transport.
Intervals 50 yards between Companies.
50 " " rear company and Transport
25 " " every six vehicles.

(b) ROUTE.

Road Junction K.4.d.30.70 – WATOU Square – road junction K.5.a.5.6.

(c) After passing road junction K.5.a.5.6. Companies will march in file.

(d) All Officers valises will be sent to Quartermaster Stores by 2 p.m. Officers Mess Boxes will be carried on cookers.

(e) Echelon "B" personnel will parade at Battalion Headquarters at 2.30 p.m. under Captain C.H Kerr and will move to H.Q. 12th Battalion Royal Irish Rifles E.25.c.0.9.

Blankets, Officers Kits, dixies etc. will be stacked at Orderly Room at 2 p.m. This party will carry rations for consumption on 27th inst. Transport Officer will arrange for necessary Transport at 2 p.m.

(f) Lieut. F.W. Vint with a guard of 6 men will remain at Transport Lines in charge of surplus kits. Men will be selected from Echelon "B" and must not be due for leave or rest camp.

2 O.R. "A" Coy.
2 O.R. "B" "
1 O.R. "C" "
1 O.R. "D" "

(g) DRESS. Full Marching order, waterbottles must be filled.

(h) 2/Lieut. Inglis J.M. will report at Brigade Headquarters at HOUTKERQUE at 4 p.m. today to synchronise watches. He will report to the Adjutant at 3 p.m.

(i) The Quartermaster will arrange for a hot tea to be served on arrival.

(j) The Quartermaster will hand over billets to incoming Unit.

Captain & Adjutant.
9th (N.I.H.) Battalion Royal Irish Fusiliers.

26.9.18

Acknowledge.

Issued through Signals at ....

Copy No. 1 to	108th Inf. Bde.	No. 2 to	"A" Coy.
3	"B" Coy.	4	"C" "
5	"D" "	6	Commanding Offr.
7	2nd in Command.	8	Quartermaster.
9	Transport Officer.	10	Medical Officer.
11	War Diary.	13	War Diary.

Attack on Goldflake Farm, 11 October 1918

This small, set-piece, two-platoon attack is an excellent example of the level of expertise achieved by the 9th Royal Irish Fusiliers by 1918. The operation order shows the degree of planning behind the attack.

Operation Order No.1 by Lt. Col. P.E Kelly,
Comdg. 9th (N.I.H.) R. Irish Fusiliers.

Ref. Dadizeele. 1/10,000 10.10.18.

1. On 11th Oct. 1918 the Bn. will capture and hold GOLDFLAKE FM. (L.19.d.0.9) and structures in vicinity.

2. O.C. C. Coy. will detail 2 platoons for this operation.

O.C. B. Coy. will have one platoon in readiness in copse K.24.b.50.35 to assist if necessary (in addition to assembly normal garrison).

3. At 10.00 the 2 platoons of C. Coy. will be formed up in trench at S.E. corner of TWIG FARM. They will move to position before dawn. O.C. C. and B. Coys. will report when their parties are in position and ready.

4. At 10.00 when barrage opens the attacking platoons will move forward in line E. of CHEVIOT CORNER – TWIG FM Rd to as [*close to*] GOLDFLAKE FM as possible. At 10.05 when bombardment of GOLDFLAKE FM will cease party will rush the FARM.

One Section will be detailed to deal with pill-box at K.24.d.90.85.

At 10.05 O.C B. Coy. will send forward one section from copse K.24.d.5.3 and occupy houses K.24.b.9.2.

5. <u>CONSOLIDATION :-</u> Position when occupied will be immediately consolidated. Care will be taken that cellars etc. are searched by 2 sections while remainder consolidate.

In the event of attack failing the Platoon of B. Coy. detailed in para. 2 will at once rush farm from WEST.

6. <u>EQUIPMENT :-</u> Battle order:- 1 shovel to every two men to be carried on pack.
2 R.G. dischargers per platoon.
1 No.36 per man.
10 No.37's.
Wirecutters.
1 Very Pistol and cartridge to be carried per Platoon Commander.

7. <u>SIGNALS :-</u> A Very light will be sent up when farm is captured.
2 S.O.S. rifle grenades will be carried.

8. O.C. C. Coy. will send forward Lucas Lamp when objective has been taken.

9. <u>Prisoners :-</u> Prisoners will be sent back immediately to copse K.24.b.5.3 and passed by B. Coy. to Battn. H.Q.

10. O.C. "A" & "D" Coys. will evacuate posts E. of line L.18.c.5.0 – L.19.a.15.85 by 05.00 (dawn). Posts will be reoccupied at dusk.

11. O.C. attacking party will send sketch of dispositions to Battn. H.Q. after consolidation if possible.

12. <u>Artillery :-</u> Night 10th/11th Oct. till 5.00, salvos H.E. by 4.5 Hows on GOLDFLAKE FM every ½ hour. 05.15 to 05.30 Heavy bombardment GOLDFLAKE AND MARTELL FARMS.

05.30 to 10.00.	No firing.
10.00 to 10.10.	6" T.M. and hows on objectives including smoke.
10.10 to 10.40.	Guns will fire on MARTELL FARM. L.T.M. fires on houses K.24.b.90.15.
10.00 to 10.40.	Smoke barrage WEST MARTELL FM. E. and S. of GOLDFLAKE FM.

Artillery F.O.O. will be at TWIG FM, to whom any message re artillery are to be sent.

15. <u>Medical Arrangements :-</u> "C" Coys. Stretcher Bearers to accompany raiding party. A. & D. Coys. will evacuate from TWIG FARM to aid post. B. Coy. will evacuate from their Coy. area to aid post. One wheeled stretcher and two stretchers available at Rear Battn H.Q. BASS FARM.

SYNCHRONISATION. Watch will be sent round from Battn H.Q. Advanced Battn. H.Q. at A. Coys. H.Q. from 10.00.

ACKNOWLEDGE.

W. Sparks, Capt. & Adjt
9th (N.I.H.) R.I.F.

Copies: 1. 108th I.B.
2. A.
3. B.
4. C.
5. D.
6. 108th T.M.B.
7. O.C. 18th H.L.I.
8. War Diaries
9. " "

Relief in Place, 11/12 October 1918

This operation order details the relief in place on the night of 11/12 October 1918 when the 9th Royal Irish Fusiliers left Hill 41 for the last time. Lieutenant Colonel Kelly had been killed on 11 October and the Commanding Officer's name does not appear on the operation order.

Operation Order No.2 9th (N.I.H.) Bn., Royal Irish Fusiliers

B.E.F. 11.10.18

1. The 12th R.I.R. will relieve the Bn. tonight 11/12th October 1918.

2. Like Coys. relieve :-
C. Coy. 12th R.I.R. relieve B. Coy. 9th R.I.F.
D. Coy. 12th R.I.R. relieve D. Coy.
A. Coy. 12th R.I.R. relieve A. Coy. in reserve position.
B. Coy. 12th R.I.R. relieve C. Coy. taking up positions occupied by B. Coy. night 10/11th October.

3. One guide per platoon & one from Coy. H.Q. will report to Bn. H.Q. at 6.30 p.m. and will meet incoming Coys at GILBEY FARM.

4. Liaison posts:- "A" Coy. will hand over liaison post with 1st R.I.F. on our left & "B" Coys liaison post at K.24.d.50.70 with 18th H.L.I.

5. Particular care is to be taken on handing over to explain method of defence.

6. On relief the Battalion will be disposed :-

Bn. H.Q.	K.17.b.5.7.
A. Coy.	GILBEY FM.
B. "	PALMER FM, BLINKEL FM.
C. "	K.17.c.9.9.
D. "	LANKA FM. (K.17.b.5.9)

Guides will be picked up at GILBEY FM. as Coys. move out.

7. Completion of relief will be reported by code word "FINISH". Arrival in new billets will be reported to Bn. H.Q.

8. All petrol tins, dixies, etc. must be brought out.

11.10.18 W. Sparks, Capt and Adjt.
HODO

Copy No.1 to 108th I.B.
2 to A. Coy.
3 to B. Coy.
4 to C. Coy.
5 to D. Coy.
6 to 12th R.I.R.
7 to War Diary

Order to Advance, 13 October 1918

This operation order detailed the actions to be taken to resume the advance on 13 October, when 108th Brigade was in reserve. This advance culminated with the attack at Courtrai on 16 October.

Operation Order No.3 by Major R.J.A. Tamplin, D.S.O.,
Commanding 9th (N.I.H.) Battn., Royal Irish
Fusiliers.

Ref. Sheets 28 and 29. B.E.F. 13.10, 1918

1. On J. day at H. hour the 36th Division will resume the advance in conjunction with troops on either flank & will attack with 107th I. Bde. on the right, 109th I. Bde. on the left & 108th I. Bde. in reserve. Boundaries are as marked on map issued. Barrage map enclosed.

2. On the morning of J. day the Bn. will move to assembly position in K.15.a. & c. & will pass starting point K.16.b.5.5. at following times :-

B. Coy. 02.00
D. " 02.05
C. " 02.10
A. " 02.15
Bn. H.Q. 02.20

Battn. H.Q. will be situated in Pill Box K.15.d.4.4.

3. After H. hour on J. day the Bn. will be prepared to move at 15 minutes notice. Men must not leave their Platoons.

Emergency and position will be road running through K.14.c and K.15.c. head of column at K.14.d.9.7 in following order – Bn. H.Q., B., A., C., D.

4. Lewis Gun limbers and ammunition pack animals will accompany the Bn. after moving from K.15.d.4.4.
Special orders have been issued to Transport Officer.

5. The Transport Officer will arrange to have 8 shovels and 4 picks per Coy dumped at assembly positions. Each Platoon will carry 2 shovels and 1 pick. Water bottles must be filled. Full equipment as issued will be carried.

6. RATIONS:- A hot meal will be served on arrival in assembly positions. Rations for "J" day will be issued at assembly positions.

7. O.C. Coys. will report arrival in assembly positions.

8. Divisional Bomb stores is situated at K.14.b.5.1.

9. A.D.S. will be at J.12.d.7.8.

10. J. day and H. hour will be notified later.

Acknowledge.

[Sgd.] W. Sparks, Capt. and Adjt.
HODO

Copy No.1. to A. Coy.
2. to B. Coy.
3. to C. Coy.
4. to D. Coy.
5. to 108 I.B.
6. to T.O.
7. to Q.M.
8. to War Diary.
9. to War Diary.
10. to M.O.

Attack across the River Lys, 16 October 1918

This operation order was for the advance to the River Lys at Courtrai and the seizure of the crossing points on the north-west outskirts of the town. It is clear from the contents of the order that when it was written there was no indication that the enemy had evacuated its positions north of the river and blown the bridges. The subsequent assault river crossing by D Company was one of the 9th Royal Irish Fusiliers' most impressive operations.

Order No.5 by
Major R.J.A. TAMPLIN, D.S.O.
Comdg 9th (N.I.H.) R. Irish Fusiliers.

Ref. Sheet 29. N.W. 1/20,000 16.10.18

1. The Bn. will attack, capture and hold the crossing over the RIVER LYS from railway bridge from H.25.c.40.15 (inclusive) to bridge H.26.c.50.60 (exclusive).
The 12th Royal Irish Rifles are co-operating on our left.

2. The bn. will attack with 2 companies in the firing line, one company in support, one company in reserve. A. Coy. will attack on right along railway running through G.30.b – H.25.c. B. Coy. will attack on left astride road running through G.24.d – H.25.a. After passing road at G.30.b.5.2. A. Coy. will advance with their right on the railway.
Touch will be maintained as far as possible between attacking Coys.

3. Boundary :- Inter Company boundary G.24.c.2.6 – H.25.c.7.5.
C. Company will follow A. Coy. at 50^{X} interval and form defensive flank on right along railway through G.30.b.80.90 to G.30.d.95.50. D Company will remain in reserve in G.24.c.

4. Assembly :- Forming up line G.24.c.0.2 G.24.a.4.0.

5. One sub-section M.G., one sub-section R.E. will be attached to A. Coy. and one sub-section field Coy. R.E. to B. One sub-section M.G. Coy. and one L.T.M. team will operate along road running G.24.d – H.25.a under orders of commanding officers.

6. On reaching River Lys, A. Coy. will direct a platoon to cross and hold post on southern side of bridge; B. Coy. will similarly hold bridge at H.25.d.

Barrage :- Artillery arrangements as follows 05.30 the *[unknown text]* on the right & swing forward on left where it will halt for 15 minutes. Barrage will then move forward at rate of 300^{X} in 3 mins and will halt 200^{X} S. of R. LYS.

Guides will meet Bn. G.27.d.5.2 to guide them to nearest point to forming up line. Guides will not however be relied on.

Bn. H.Q. will be established at G.24.c.0.3.
R.A.P. at G.24.c.6.6.

Distributed 01.50.

Copies 1. 108th I.B.
2. A. Coy.
3. B. "
4. C. "
5. D. "
6. T.M.B.
7. M.G.
8. 12th R.I.R.
9. Spare.
10 & 11 War Diary.

Relief in Place, 16 October 1918

This operation order provides brief instructions for the relief of the 9th Royal Irish Fusiliers at Courtrai by the 23rd (Service) Battalion, The Duke of Cambridge's Own (Middlesex Regiment) (2nd Football) on the night of the aborted river crossing. The Battalion then rested for three nights before moving north to Landelede on 20 October.

Operation Order No.6 by Major R.J.A. Tamplin, D.S.O.,
Comdg. 9th (N.I.H.) Royal Irish Fusiliers.

Ref. Sheet 28 & 29. 16.10.18

1. The 23rd Middlesex Regt. will relieve the bn. tonight. On relief the Bn. will move to place to be notified later.

2. Like Companies to relieve each other.

3. Guides:- 3 guides per Coy. and one for Coy. H.Q. will rendezvous at Bn. H.Q. at 5.30 p.m.

4. Completion of relief is to be reported by runner. Arrival at billets will be notified to Bn. H.Q.

5. Lewis Gun limbers will meet the bn. at G.24.c.5.6.

6. Advance parties of 2 N.C.Os. per Coy. will report at once to Bn. H.Q.

7. Companies will move out with interval 100^{X} between Platoons.

Acknowledge

W. Sparks, Capt. & Adjt.
16.10.18. HODO

Movement Order, 19/20 October 1918

This movement order is incomplete (the original is illegible at the beginning) but it is for the move of the 9th Royal Irish Fusiliers to Landelede on 20 October and appears to have been issued in the early hours of that morning.

Operation Order No.7 by Major R.J.A. Tamplin, D.S.O.,
Comdg. 9th (N.I.H.) Royal Irish Fusiliers.

(Original illegible)

2. (a) *(....will move in)* the following order:
Band.
Bn. H.Q.
A.
D.
C.
B.
Transport.

(b) Blankets rolled in bundles of 10.
Greatcoats tied in bundles of half platoons will be stacked by each company.
Blankets, greatcoats & surplus kits will be dumped in farm at present occupied by Q.M. Stores 9th R. Irish. Fus. G.8.a.7.7.
The Transport Officer will arrange for the necessary wagon to remain behind to collect these stores to dump. Wagon will the rejoin Bn. At LANDELEDE.
Q.M. will detail 2 men to remain in charge of dump.

(c) Lewis Gun limbers will be sent to Coys. by 06.30 and all Lewis Gun material loaded.

(d) DRESS :- Battle order. Water bottles filled.

(e) Billeting parties 2/Lt. STEELE & one N.C.O. per Coy. & Bn. H.Q. will report Bn. H.Q. at 07.00 to proceed on bikes.

3. Distances to be maintained during march :-
100^{X} between Coys.
100^{X} " " & transport.
25^{X} " every 6 vehicles.

Acknowledge.

W. Sparks, Capt. & Adjt.
9th R.I.F.

00.35

Movement Order, 23 October 1918

Having crossed the River Lys on 21 October, the 9th Royal Irish Fusiliers was the reserve battalion of 108th Brigade from 21-24 October. This brief order provides detail for the move of the Battalion to Leemput (north of Molenhoek) on the afternoon of 23 October.

Operation Order No.8 9th (N.I.H.) R. Irish Fusiliers.

Ref. Sheet 29. 23.10.18

1. The Bn. Will move as under to LEEMPUT.

2. Companies will move to following areas on following lines :-

A. Coy.	I.4.b.5.2.	13.30
B. "	I.4.b.2.7.	13.35
C. "	area c.28.	13.40
D. "		13.45

200^{X} between Coys. 100^{X} between platoons.
Reconnoitring parties will be sent on at once to area.

Bn. H.Q. will move to I.4.b.4.5. at 13.30. Coys. will report arrival in area giving Coy. H.Q.

Route DRIESCH – C.28.a.5.0.

23.10.18 (Sgd) W. Sparks, Capt. & Adjt.
13.00 HODO

Relief in Place, 24 October 1918

These operation orders put the 9th Royal Irish Fusiliers in place for its final attacks. The first order is for a relief in place with 12th Royal Irish Rifles, but this is changed by the subsequent instruction in order that both battalions hold the line. The 9th Royal Irish Fusiliers was subsequently in support to 12th Royal Irish Rifles for the final attack on 25 October.

OPERATION ORDER No.9
9th (N.I.H.) R. IRISH FUS.

Ref. Sheet 29. 24.10.18

1. The Battalion will relieve the 12th R. Irish Rifles tonight 24th October.

2. Bn. will pass starting point I.4.b.6.2 as under :-

A.	18.00)	200^{X} between Coys.
B.	18.06)	
C.	18.12)	100^{X} between platoons.
D.	18.18)	
Bn .H.Q.	18.24)	

Route - cross roads I.4.b.6.2 – rd. junction I.11.a.1.7 – I.5.c.9.2 – I.5.c.2.7 – I.12.central – J.7.c.5.6. where guides will meet bn.

3. Bn. H.Q. will be at J.7.d.0.4.

4. Arrival in new position will be reported to Bn. H.Q. immediately.

5. Rations will be sent up on arrival in new position. Ration parties will be sent to Battalion Headquarters immediately on arrival.

Acknowledge.

(Sgd.) W Sparks, Capt. & Adjt.
24.10.18 9th (N.I.H.) R.I.F.

OPERATION ORDER No.9A
by Major R.J.A. TAMPLIN D.S.O.
Comdg. 9th Royal Irish Fusiliers.

1. The line now held by the 108th Inf. Bde. will be held tonight by two battalions, the 9th R.I.F. on right from railway at J.27.b.6.0 to railway at J.22.c.9.9, 12th R.I.Rifles on left from that point to road in J.22.D hence back on railway to Halt at HEIRWEG.

2. A. and B. Coys. will hold front line B. on right from railway at J.27.b.6.0 to hedge at J.22.c.1.1. A. Coy. on left from that point to railway at J.22.c.9.9.

3. Guides from D. Coy. 12th R.I.Rif. will put B. Coy. 9th R.I.F. in position. Guides from B. Coy. 12th R.I.Rifles will put A. Coy. 9th R.I.F. in positions. These Companies are now in liaison and will make arrangements for move at dusk.

4. C. Coy. will be withdrawn from their present position when relieved by 12th R.I.Rifles to farm at J.21.d.9.9. D. Coy. will withdraw to farm at J.21.d.3.4 at dusk.

5. Battalion Hd. Qrs. will remain at J.21.a.2.7.

6. A. Coy. will send ration parties to C. Coy. Hd. Qrs. at J.21.d.9.9. B. Coy rations will be sent to D. Coy. Hd. Qrs. at J.21.d.3.4.

7. Movements to be reported when complete.

Acknowledge.

(Sgd) W Sparks, Capt & Adjt
9th Royal Ir. Fusrs.

Relief in Place, 27 October 1918

This operation order is for the relief of the 9th Royal Irish Fusiliers on the night of 27/28 October 1918, its final action in the face of the enemy.

<u>OPERATION ORDER No.10</u>
<u>by Major R.J.A. TAMPLIN. D.S.O.</u>
<u>Comdg 9th (North Irish Horse) Royal Irish Fusiliers</u>

Ref. Sheet 29. 27.10.18

1. The 4th R. Sussex Regt. 101st Inf. Bde. will relieve the bn. in the right sector tonight 27/28th October 1918.

2. On relief the Battalion will move to HULSTE (Squares 21 & 22).

3. (a) <u>Guides.</u> Arrangements have already been made to incoming bn. at 17.00.
(b) Lewis Gun limbers. One limber for B. & D. Coys. will be at ration dump and one limber for A. & C. Coys. at C. Coys. H.Q. at 19.00. Officers chargers will also be sent up to above places.
(c) All dixies etc. must be sent back in limbers.

A. Coy. 4th R. Sussex relieves A 9th R.I.F.
B. " " " B "
C. " " " C "
D. " 9th R.I.F. will not be relieved but will start moving back on arrival of B. Coy. 4th R. Sussex Regt.

4. <u>Route :-</u> J.7.c by track to windmill (*grid reference unknown.5.d.0.0?*) C.11.a.2.7. DRIESCH Bridge C.19.b.9.1 HULSTE. 100 yards between platoons. Arrival in billets will be notified to Bn. H.Q.

5. All S.O.S. rockets will be handed over and receipts obtained.

Acknowledge.

(Sgd) W. Sparks, Capt & Adjt.
9th R.I.F.

Issued at 15.00

APPENDIX 8

Discipline & Courts Martial

Discipline in the Army was enforced in accordance with annual Parliamentary legislation enshrined since 1881 in The Army Act. It was supported by 'King's Regulations and Orders for the Army' and the 'Manual of Military Law', both of which provided guidance in matters of discipline and personal conduct, and by routine orders issued at Army, Corps, Division, Brigade and Unit level.

In accordance with The Army Act, minor offences were dealt with summarily by company commanders and commanding officers, who were empowered to award punishment. The punishment powers of a company commander were limited but a commanding officer could award detention up to twenty-eight days in the unit guard-room cells (or what acted as cells on active service), Field Punishment up to twenty-eight days to a soldier on field service (but not to NCOs), forfeit of all pay up to twenty-eight days, confinement to camp for up to fourteen days, extra guard duties and formally noted reprimands. Many of the records at Appendix 6 show such punishments for minor offences. Privates Patrick Campbell and David Donaldson provide examples of how a soldier could be dealt with repeatedly by the commanding officer. Soldiers dealt with summarily and found guilty could have the findings quashed by superior authority or on appeal to court martial.

More serious offences and offences by officers and non-commissioned officers of the rank of corporal or above, who could not be dealt with summarily by commanding officers, were dealt with by court martial. There were four types: The Regimental Court Martial had the least powers of punishment and could not try an officer or a warrant officer. It consisted of a minimum of three members, who usually belonged to the same unit as the accused. It was rarely convened on active service. A District Court Martial had wider powers but it could not try a commissioned officer. It also consisted of a minimum of three members, at least one of whom must have been serving in a different unit to that of the accused, unless no other officers were available. It was most commonly used to deal with the less serious offences committed in the United Kingdom. A General Court Martial could try an officer or a soldier of any rank and had the greatest powers of punishment. It could pass the death sentence. The minimum number of members (five or nine) depended on the geographical area in which the court was sitting. No member could be serving in the same unit as the accused, unless there were no other officers available. A Field General Court Martial was only convened if the accused was on active service or was stationed overseas. It had powers of a General Court Martial. The minimum number of members was three (although Field General Courts Martial with two members were allowed, but they had limited powers).

An acquittal by a court martial (and, indeed, by a commanding officer) on any charge was final and absolute. A guilty verdict, and the sentence of a court martial, had to be confirmed by a superior authority. The superior authority also had the power to remit sentences. For each offence, The Army Act laid out the maximum sentence available to a court martial. The severity of the punishment generally reflected the circumstances of the offence. A soldier out of camp and late for duty in the rear area when his unit was training, would be more leniently dealt with than a man who was similarly absent the night his unit moved back into the trenches. By modern standards punishments were severe. Detention for periods up to twenty-eight days (fourteen days in the United Kingdom) was served in unit 'cells'. Longer sentences of detention were served in centralised detention barracks in the United Kingdom or in temporary military prisons in France and Belgium; both were run by the Military Provost Staff Corps. Sentences of imprisonment, imprisonment with hard labour and penal servitude, were served in civilian prisons. Army orders laid down what work was to be carried out by soldiers in detention in military prisons, and for those sent to civilian prisons imprisonment with hard labour meant just that. Longer prison terms were often deferred until the end of hostilities with sentences being accompanied by the order '*man held to serve in present Corps on conviction ....*'. Field Punishment involved sleeping under guard, daily fatigues, a restricted diet and a total restriction of privileges, such as smoking. Field Punishment Number 1 also involved two hours chained to a wagon wheel, or a similar object, daily.

The standard of discipline displayed by the 9th Royal Irish Fusiliers was high. There were, of course, many men charged with myriad minor offences who were dealt with summarily by the Commanding Officer but there were relatively few cases of officers and soldiers tried by court martial. No death sentences were handed down to men serving with the 9th Royal Irish Fusiliers. The most severe punishments awarded were to Privates C Crorkin and R Curry. Each was sentenced to ten years' imprisonment for desertion; in Crorkin's case this was reduced to five years by the superior authority. Crorkin's offence and punishment, along with that of Private W H Smyth, who was tried for desertion and convicted on the same day, were promulgated on 9th Royal Irish Fusiliers' routine orders on 22 September 1918. All such punishments were published in this way as a deterrent to others.

Trials by Field General Court Martial

Below are listed one officer tried at General Court Martial and two officers and thirty-five other ranks tried at forty-three Field General Courts Martial on fifty indictments. Two of these men (Privates C Crorkin & W H Smyth) were tried three times, and two men (Privates A B Hargreaves & J McConville) were tried twice.

Trials & Verdicts

	Officers	Other Ranks	Total Verdicts
Guilty	1	34	35
Not Guilty	2	5	7
Not Fit to Plead	-	1	1
Previous Finding Quashed	-	1	1
Total Trials	3	41	44

Indictments

		Guilty	Not Guilty	Not Fit to Plead	Total
Section 6	When on active service leaving his post without orders from his superior officer.	-	1	-	1
Section 8	When on active service using insubordinate language to his superior officer.	4	-	-	4

Section 8	When on active service using threatening language to his superior officer.	1	-	-	1
Section 8	When on active service striking his superior officer.	1	-	-	1
Section 9	When on active service disobeying a lawful command given by his superior officer.	1	-	-	1
Section 12	When on active service deserting His Majesty's service.	9	1	-	10
Section 13	Fraudulent enlistment.	1	-	-	1
Section 15	Absenting himself without leave.	7	2	-	9
Section 18	Malingering.	-	1	-	1
Section 18	Wilfully injuring himself with intent thereby to render himself unfit for service.	1	-	1	2
Section 18	Theft.	1	-	-	1
Section 18	Disgraceful conduct of an indecent kind.*	1	-	-	1
Section 19	Drunkenness.	5	1	-	6
Section 20	Allowing to escape a person committed to his charge whom it was his duty to keep guard.	-	1	-	1
Section 22	When in arrest escaping.	1	-	-	1
Section 24	Losing by neglect.**	1	-	-	1
Section 37	Striking a soldier.	-	1	-	1
Section 40	An act to the Prejudice of Good Order and Military Discipline.***	5	1	1	7
	Total	39	9	2	50

* This indictment under Section 8 was on eight counts, one of which was dismissed.
** What was lost is unknown.
*** The details of five of the indictments under Section 40 are unknown.

Due to the duplication of names in the 9th Royal Irish Fusiliers and the format of the court martial registers, it has not been possible to identify positively all of the men who were tried. Where there is doubt, regimental numbers have been omitted. The record below may be incomplete, particularly for courts martial in 1916, but it reflects closely the work undertaken by Timothy Bowman for his analysis *'Irish Regiments in the Great War; Discipline and Morale'*. The list below is in alphabetical order and shows the date of trial, the offence (and the section of the Army Act where known), the finding of the court martial (if not guilty or not fit to plead), or sentence in the cases of those found guilty.

General Court Martial

GIBSON Captain G H

2 December 1918	Section 19 - Drunkenness.	Not guilty.

Field General Court Martial

BAXTER Corporal B 42160

11 January 1919	Section 15 - Absenting himself without leave.	Not guilty.

BELL Private P (not identified)

19 June 1917	Section 40 - An (unknown) act to the prejudice of good order and military discipline.	Not guilty.

BOWMAN Private J 24271

25 May 1918	Section 19 - Drunkenness.	28 days Field Punishment Number 1.

BREEN Sergeant J 14012

11 July 1917	Section 19 - Drunkenness.	Reduction of seniority to 1 July 1917.

BROOKES Sergeant A 43455

23 August 1918	Section 40 - An (unknown) act to the prejudice of good order and military discipline.	Reduced to the Ranks.

BURNS Private A 20442

16 August 1918	Section 9 - When on active service disobeying a lawful command given by his superior officer.	6 months imprisonment with hard labour.
	Section 22 - When in arrest escaping.	

COLCLOUGH Private T L 43334

12 June 1917	Section 40 - Neglect to the prejudice of good order and military discipline in that he, in the field, on 23 May 1917 neglected to unload his rifle preparatory to cleaning it, and thereby caused the death of a soldier, and seriously wounding another.	56 days Field Punishment Number 1.

CRORKIN Private C 49760

10 June 1918	Section 24 - Losing by neglect (detail not known).	56 days Field Punishment Number 1.
9 August 1918	Section 12 - When on active service deserting His Majesty's service.	10 years imprisonment. (Reduced to five years.)
18 September 1918	Section 8 - When on active service using insubordinate language to his superior officer.	56 days Field Punishment Number 1.

CURRY Private R (identity not confirmed)

19 November 1918	Section 12 - When on active service deserting His Majesty's service.	10 years imprisonment.

DAVIDSON Lieutenant A

21 June 1918	Section 12 - When on active service deserting His Majesty's service.	Not guilty.
	Section 6 - When on active service leaving his post without orders from his superior officer.	

EDGAR Private W J 17903

5 January 1917	Section 12 - When on active service deserting His Majesty's service. Found guilty of absenting himself without leave.	6 months imprisonment with hard labour.

ENGLISH Lance Corporal W 14156

12 June 1917	Section 40 - Neglect to the prejudice of good order and military discipline in that he, in the field, on 23 May 1917 neglected to ensure that his section obeyed the procedures for rifle discipline in the trenches, resulting the death of a soldier, and the seriously wounding of another.	28 days Field Punishment Number 2. Reduced in rank.

GALLERY Private W 14216		
12 July 1918	Section 15 - Absenting himself without leave. Section 19 - Drunkenness.	28 days Field Punishment Number 1.
GILCHRIST Private W 7688		
6 November 1918	Section 20 - Allowing to escape a person committed to his charge whom it was his duty to keep guard.	Not guilty.
GREEN Corporal E H 43256		
3/4 March 1917	Eight charges of disgraceful conduct of an indecent kind. (The eighth charge was dismissed.)	5 years penal servitude. Reduced to the ranks. Discharged.
HARGREAVES Private A B 17280		
10 June 1918	Section 40 - An unknown act to the prejudice of good order and military discipline.	42 days Field Punishment Number 1.
10 December 1918	Section 15 - Absenting himself without leave.	42 days Field Punishment Number 1.
HENRY Private W (not identified)		
18 February 1919	Section 18 - Theft.	14 days Field Punishment Number 2.
KILFEDDER Private R (not identified)		
10 June 1918	Section 24 - Losing by neglect (detail not known).	56 days Field Punishment Number 1.
KNIGHT Private J H 43305		
16 August 1918	Section 8 - When on active service using insubordinate language to his superior officer.	90 days Field Punishment Number 1.
MATEER Lieutenant N C		
17 January 1919	Section 15 - Absenting himself without leave.	Severe Reprimand.
McCLELLAND Private J 10417		
27 November 1918	Section 15 - Absenting himself without leave.	42 days Field Punishment Number 2.
McCONVILLE Private J 19808		
20 October 1916	Section 18 - Malingering.	Finding quashed. Previously sentenced to 14 days Field Punishment Number 2 by the Commanding Officer.
11 April 1917	Section 8 - When on active service striking his superior officer. Section 19 - Drunkenness.	84 days Field Punishment Number 1.
McNALLY Private Patrick (not identified)		
11 December 1918	Section 12 - When on active service deserting His Majesty's service.	3 years imprisonment with hard labour.

McQUADE Private T 42570

19 November 1918	Section 18 - Wilfully injuring himself with intent thereby to render himself unfit for service.	91 days Field Punishment Number 1.

PAWSEY Private N 40185

13 May 1918	Section 12 - When on active service deserting His Majesty's service.	2 years imprisonment with hard labour.

PEACOCK Private J 20361

21 February 1918	Section 40 - An unknown act to the prejudice of good order and military discipline. Section 18 - Wilfully injuring himself with intent thereby to render himself unfit for service.	Not fit to plead on both indictments.

RICHMOND Private A 24562

21 August 1917	Section 15 - Absenting himself without leave.	56 days Field Punishment Number 1.

RILEY Private M (not identified, possible misspelling of Reilly)

5 December 1918	Section 12 - When on active service deserting His Majesty's service. Found guilty of absenting himself without leave.	18 months imprisonment with hard labour.

SEATON Sergeant A 14686

24 December 1918	Section 37 - Striking a soldier.	Not guilty.

SHERIDAN Private James 3346

10 December 1917	Section 12 - When on active service deserting His Majesty's service. Found guilty of when on active service attempting to desert His Majesty's service.	3 years penal servitude. Commuted to 6 months imprisonment with hard labour and suspended.

SMYLIE Private T 23351

4 March 1919	Section 15 - Absenting himself without leave.	42 days Field Punishment Number 2.

SMYTH Private W H 17559

10 June 1918	Section 8 - When on active service using insubordinate language to his superior officer. Section 8 - When on active service using threatening language to his superior officer.	56 days Field Punishment Number 1.
9 August 1918	Section 12 - When on active service deserting His Majesty's service.	5 years imprisonment.
18 September 1918	Section 8 - When on active service using insubordinate language to his superior officer.	56 days Field Punishment Number 1.

THOMPSON Private W (not positively identified)

24 December 1918	Section 15 - Absenting himself without leave	Not Guilty.

TOTTON Private William 14726

2 January 1916	Section 19 - Drunkenness.	90 days Field Punishment

		Number 1 (remitted by 34 days).
TUDOR Private Arthur 43327		
13 June 1917	Section 12 - When on active service deserting His Majesty's service. Section 13 - Fraudulent enlistment.	3 years penal servitude, suspended.
WALTER Private P (not identified)		
20 September 1918	Section 40 - An unknown act to the prejudice of good order and military discipline.	90 days Field Punishment Number 1.
WEIR 33861 Private I		
19 November 1918	Section 15 - Absenting himself without leave.	91 days Field Punishment Number 1.

Other Soldiers Tried by Court Martial

The following soldiers were tried by District or Field General Court Martial while serving elsewhere. The details are contained in the relevant entries at Appendices 5 and 6:

DOBSON Second Lieutenant J R (found not guilty).
FERRIE Private J 40099.
FRANCEY Private W 41415.
GEARY Private G E C 25210.
GILMORE Private J 3017.
LAVERY Private H 26841.
MARTIN Private W 41180.
MARTINDALE Private H D 13618.
McALEER Private A 42433.
McALLISTER Private T 41128.
McCOY Private R 23353.
MEEKE Private S 42492.
MERVYN DCM Corporal M 5631.
SMITH Second Lieutenant C (found not guilty).
TWEEDIE MM Second Lieutenant R (when a Sergeant in The Royal Irish Rifles).
WILSON Private W J 5898.

Some soldiers were tried by court martial while serving before or after the war. The details are contained in the relevant entries at Appendix 6.

APPENDIX 9

The Football Team

Sport has always been an important part of military life and the popularity of football in the United Kingdom is reflected in its popularity in the British Army. It is noteworthy that Sheffield Football Club, the oldest football club, was founded in 1857 by Nathaniel Cresswick and William Priest, both officers in the Volunteer Rifle Corps. Major Francis Marindin founded the Royal Engineers Association Football Club in 1869; it went on to win the FA Cup in 1875. He was President of the Football Association of England from 1874 to 1879 and he instigated the formation of the Army Football Association 1888. In the period before the First World War, football was the primary team sport played in the Army. It was extremely competitive; the Army Challenge Cup was first battled for in March 1889 when it was won by the 2nd Battalion, Princess Louise's (Argyll and Sutherland Highlanders).

Portadown Olympic FC 1910/1911.
This amateur team was undefeated in the four seasons from 1908/09 to 1911/12.

Seated second from right (front row) is William Herbert Palmer, Team Captain (later Sergeant W H Palmer MM and commissioned into The Royal Irish Regiment).
Others known to have served during the First World War are:
Goal-keeper David Kinley (back row, third from left) Later Lieutenant D Kinley. He lost a leg in Mesopotamia serving with the 8th (Service) Battalion, The Royal Welsh Regiment, and after the war qualified as a doctor.
Centre Forward W McLeer (front row first on left) Later Private W McLeer, killed in action on 1 July 1916 serving with the 11th (Service) Battalion, The Royal Inniskilling Fusiliers (Donegal and Fermanagh).

Princess Victoria's (Royal Irish Fusiliers) has always had a first-class reputation as a sporting regiment and its football team played an important part in that. In the 1909-10 season, the 1st Battalion reached the final of the Army Challenge Cup but lost to the Royal Marine Light Infantry (Gosport) 2-0. Football was popular in the 9th Royal Irish Fusiliers from the early days of its formation. It is not known when the first battalion team was formed but the first recorded match was against 13th Royal Irish Rifles in January 1916.

The football team in mid-1918. Regimental Quartermaster Sergeant Jack Barbour is seated on the right.

In January 1917 an inter-platoon football competition (won by 13 Platoon) was followed by an inter-company competition (won by B Company). All of this, and competitions in other events, was in preparation for the 108th Brigade sports competition on 19 and 22 January. B Company won the overall competition but lost the football match to 12th Royal Irish Rifles 1-2.

HAROLD BURNISON
DISTILLERY

Regimental Quartermaster Sergeant Jack Barbour appears to have been a driving force behind the 9th Royal Irish Fusiliers' football team after this, and its success became a source of real pride. Amongst its players were Sergeant Francis Homersham DCM, MM*, Private William Quail, who had played for Glenavon Football Club, and Private Harold Burnison. Burnison later went on to have a successful football career in Ireland, playing 326 games for Distillery Football Club. As captain in the 1924-25 season he won the Irish and Gold Cups.

Football matches played by Princess Victoria's (9th Royal Irish Fusiliers)

Date	Opposing Team	Result	
1 January 1916	13th Royal Irish Rifles	1-1	Drawn
17 March 1916	14th Royal Irish Rifles	2-0	Won
8 April 1916	10th Royal Inniskilling Fusiliers	5-1	Won
15 April 1916	9th Royal Inniskilling Fusiliers	5-1	Won
17 April 1916	9th Royal Inniskilling Fusiliers	1-0	Won
23 January 1917	108th Brigade Machine Gun Company & Trench Mortar Battery	5-1	Won
29 January 1917	10th Royal Irish Rifles	7-0	Won
10 February 1917	2nd Royal Irish Rifles	2-0	Won
12 February 1917	10th Royal Inniskilling Fusiliers	8-0	Won
24 February 1917	8th Royal Irish Rifles	4-5	Lost
25 February 1917	153 Brigade RFA (2nd XI played)	6-0	Won
5 March 1917	108th Field Ambulance	2-2	Drawn
24 March 1917	6th Royal Irish	7-1	Won
28 March 1917	13th Royal Irish Rifles	2-0	Won
21 April 1917	2nd Royal Dublin Fusiliers	7-1	Won
25 April 1917	6th Connaught Rangers	2-0	Won
5 May 1917	9th Royal Inniskilling Fusiliers	5-0	Won
12 May 1917	7th/8th Royal Irish Fusiliers	5-0	Won
27 June 1917	19th Divisional Artillery	7-2	Won
2 July 1917	12th Royal Irish Rifles	2-1	Won
15 July 1917	55th Squadron RFC	3-0	Won
17 July 1917	An unknown RFC squadron	8-1	Won
16 September 1917	13th Royal Irish Rifles	6-0	Won
19 September 1917	108th Brigade Team	2-1	Won
26 September 1917	2nd North Irish Horse draft	2-1	Won
30 September 1917	2nd North Irish Horse draft	2-1	Won
3 October 1917	108th Field Ambulance	1-1	Drawn
18 October 1917	8th/9th Royal Irish Rifles	0-1	Lost
22 October 1917	108th Brigade Team	8-1	Won
27 January 1918	16th Royal Irish Rifles (Pioneers)	5-1	Won
3 May 1918	Belgian Team	4-0	Won
27 June 1918	1st Royal Irish Fusiliers	Result not known	
24 September 1918	1st Royal Irish Fusiliers	Result not known	
29 November 1918	12th Royal Irish Rifles	2-2	Drawn
1 December 1918	1st Royal Irish Fusiliers	6-0	Won
3 December 1918	108th Brigade Trench Mortar Battery	9-1	Won
5 December 1918	12th Royal Irish Rifles	0-0	Drawn
15 December 1918	108th Brigade Team	3-1	Won

Results Summary

Played	39
Won	30
Lost	2
Drawn	5
Result not known	2
Goals For	137
Goals Against	26

The football team on 1 December 1918 at Mouscron.

This photograph was taken before the match against the 1st Battalion, which the 9th won 6-0. Sergeant F S Homersham DCM, MM* is standing second from the left.

Bibliography & Sources

Books and Articles

Abbott, P E & Tamplin, J M A. (1981). *British Gallantry Awards.* London: Nimrod Dix & Co Ltd.

Bardon, J. (1992). *A History of Ulster.* Belfast: The Blackstaff Press.

Belfast Citizen's Committee. (1919). *The Great War 1914-1918: Ulster Greets Her Brave and Faithful Sons and Remembers Her Glorious Dead.* Belfast: W & G Baird.

Bew, P. (1994). *Ideology and the Irish Question: Ulster Unionism and Irish Nationalism 1912-1916.* Oxford: Clarendon Press.

Bowman, T. (2001).*The Ulster Volunteer Force and the formation of the 36th (Ulster) Division.* Irish Historical Studies, Vol XXXII, No 128, November 2001.

Brown, M. (1998). *1918 Year of Victory.* London: Sidgwick & Jackson.

Burrowes, Brigadier General A R CMG, DSO. (1926). *The 1st Battalion Faugh-a-Ballaghs in the Great War.* Aldershot: Gale & Polden.

Canning, W J. (1996). *Ballyshannon, Belcoo, Bertincourt: the History of the 11th Battalion The Royal Inniskilling Fusiliers (Donegal and Fermanagh Volunteers) in World War One.* Published by the author.

Cave, N. (2000). *Battleground Europe, Somme - Beaumont Hamel, Newfoundland Park.* London: Leo Cooper.

Chappell, M. (1995). *The Somme 1916. Crucible of a British Army.* London: Windrow & Greene.

Chasseaud, P. *Topography of Armageddon. A British Trench Map Atlas of the Western Front 1914-1918.* Map Books.

Coombs, R E B. (1983). *Before Endeavours Fade.* Battle of Britain Prints International.

Crozier, Brigadier General F P. (1930). *A Brasshat in No Man's Land.* London: Cape.

Cunliffe, M. (1952). *The Royal Irish Fusiliers 1793-1950.* London: Oxford University Press.

Denman, T. (1992). *Ireland's Unknown Soldiers. The 16th (Irish) Division in the Great War.* Dublin: Irish Academic Press.

Falls, C. (1922). *The History of the 36th (Ulster) Division.* Belfast: McCaw, Stevenson and Orr Ltd, The Linenhall Press.

Fox, Sir Frank. (1928). *The Royal Inniskilling Fusiliers in the World War.* London: Constable.

Gilbert, M. (1994). *First World War.* London: BCA.

Harris, H. (1972). *The Royal Irish Fusiliers (the 87th and 89th Regiments of Foot).* London: Leo Cooper.

Harris, H. (1968). *The Irish Regiments in the First World War.* Cork: The Mercier Press.

Hezlet, A A. (1972). *The 'B' Specials. A History of the Ulster Special Constabulary.* London: Tom Stacey.

James, Brigadier E A. (1998). *British Regiments 1914-1918.* Heathfield: Naval & Military Press Ltd, 5th Edition.

Jeffery, K. (2000). *Ireland and The Great War.* Cambridge: Cambridge University Press.

Johnstone, T. (1992). *Orange, Green and Khaki: The Story of the Irish Regiments in the Great War, 1914-1918.* Dublin: Gill & Macmillan.

King, J S. (1995). *For God and the King, The Story of The Blackers of Carrickblacker.* Lurgan: The Ulster Society (Publications).

Liddle, P H (ed). (1997). *Passchendaele in Perspective, The Third Battle of Ypres.* London: Leo Cooper.

Lucy, G. (1989). *The Ulster Covenant: A Pictorial History of the 1912 Home Rule Crisis.* Ulster Society.

Maguire, J. (1998). *Picnic in Purgatory.* Published by the author.

McDonagh, M. (1917). *The Irish on the Somme.* London: Hodder & Stroughton.

Mitchell, G S. (1991). *"Three Cheers For The Derrys".* Derry: YES! Publications.

The Naval & Military Press. (1999). *Soldiers Died in the Great War 1914-19 Digital Database (constructed from the War Office 1921 publication).* Heathfield: The Naval & Military Press.

Orr, P. (1987). *The Road to the Somme, Men of the Ulster Division Tell Their Story.* Belfast: Blackstaff Press.

Reed, P. (1999). *Battleground Europe, Walking the Salient.* London: Leo Cooper.

Stewart, A T Q. (1967). *The Ulster Crisis.* London: Faber & Faber.

Westlake, R. (1998). *Kitchener's Army.* Staplehurst: Spellmount.

White, S N. (1996). *The Terrors - 16th (Pioneer) Battalion Royal Irish Rifles.* Belfast: The Somme Association.

Whitehead, R J. (2010). *The Other Side of the Wire.* Solihull: Helion.

Winter, D. (1979). *Death's Men, Soldiers of the Great War.* London: Penguin Books.

Official Publications

The Army List.

The Royal Air Force List.

Personal Accounts

Honeysett J & Marker T. *Quiet Conquest.* An account of the war service of Private Charles Honeysett.

The journal of Captain E A Godson MC.

Journals

The Faugh-a-Ballagh and Regimental Gazette of the Royal Irish Fusiliers.

The Seagoe Parish Magazine.

Official History

Military Operations France and Belgium, 1916, Volume II: 2nd July 1916 to the end of the end of the Battles of the Somme.

Military Operations France and Belgium, 1917, Volume II: Messines and Third Ypres (Passchendaele).

Military Operations France and Belgium, 1917, The Battle of Cambrai.

Military Operations France and Belgium, 1918, The German March Offensive and its Preliminaries.

Military Operations France and Belgium, 1918, March - April: Continuation of the German Offensives.

Military Operations France and Belgium, 1918, Volume V, 26 September - 11 November: The Advance to Victory.

Medical Service General History, Volume III, Medical Services during the Operations on the Western Front in 1916, 1917 and 1918; in Italy; and in Egypt and Palestine.

Documents, National Archives, Kew

WO/90 & 213: Judge Advocate General and Courts Martial Records.

WO 95/1335: War Diary 5th (Service) Battalion, The Royal Irish Regiment (Pioneers), March - November 1919.

WO 95/2491: War Diary Headquarters 36th (Ulster) Division, October 1915 - July 1917.

WO 95/2492: War Diary Headquarters 36th (Ulster) Division, July 1917 - 1919.

WO 95/2496: War Diary Service Squadron 6th (Inniskilling) Dragoons.

WO 95/2496: War Diary 36th (Ulster) Division Trench Mortar Batteries.

WO 95/2497: War Diary 121st, 122nd and 150th Field Companies, Corps of Royal Engineers.

WO 95/2499: War Diary 108th and 109th Field Ambulances.

WO 95/2500: War Diary 110th Field Ambulance.

WO 95/2504: War Diary Headquarters 108th Brigade.

WO 95/2505: War Diary 1st Battalion, Princess Victoria's (Royal Irish Fusiliers) January 1918 - February 1919.

WO 95/2505: War Diary 9th (Service) Battalion, Princess Victoria's (Royal Irish Fusiliers) (County Armagh).

WO 95/2506: War Diary 12th (Service) Battalion, The Royal Irish Rifles (Central Antrim).

WO 95/2506: War Diary 108th Brigade Machine Gun Company.

WO 95/2506: War Diary 108th Brigade Trench Mortar Battery.

WO 158/308: 36th (Ulster) Division Account of Operations at Messines.

WO 158/387: 36th (Ulster) Division Account of Operations at Cambrai.

WO 153 and 297: Western Front Campaign Maps.

WO 339 and 374: Officer Records.

WO 329: Medal Rolls of the 1914 Star, 1914-15 Star, Territorial Force Medal, War and Victory Medals and Silver War Badge.

Documents, Public Record Office of Northern Ireland

D3835/E/2/502: Correspondence of General Nugent.

Printed by: Copytech (UK) Limited trading as Printondemand-worldwide, 9 Culley Court, Bakewell Road, Orton Southgate, Peterborough, PE2 6XD